Directory of
British Scientific Instrument
Makers 1550–1851

The National Maritime Museum and Zwemmer wish to acknowledge
the assistance of the Scientific Instrument Society whose generous
support has made the publication of the Directory possible

Directory of British Scientific Instrument Makers 1550–1851

Gloria Clifton

General Editor
Gerard L'E. Turner

Zwemmer

in association with the National Maritime Museum

First published in 1995 by Zwemmer
an imprint of Philip Wilson Publishers Ltd
26 Litchfield Street
London WC2H 9NJ

Distributed in the USA and Canada by
Antique Collectors' Club
Market Street Industrial Park
Wappingers Falls, New York 12590

ISBN 0 302 00634 6
LC 94-067105

Typeset by Galleon Typesetting, Ipswich
Printed and bound in Great Britain by
Hillman Printers Ltd, Frome

Contents

Foreword

The importance of the scientific, or precision, instrument maker has often been overlooked or taken for granted in the history of science and technology. Many advances have depended on the improved accuracy of measuring devices, and on the ability of instruments to extend the range of human observation. Unexpected phenomena revealed by instruments have opened up whole new areas of inquiry, such as the use of spectroscopy in chemical analysis. Apparatus is essential both in research and in the teaching of science, and is particularly effective in developing the interest and understanding of a wider public. A balanced interpretation of the evolution of scientific knowledge and methods is not possible without an appreciation of the tools available to scholars at any given time. Instrument-making involves technical, economic and social factors, in addition to the science that it embodies. In recent years instrument studies have received a new impetus, particularly in Britain, and it became apparent that a secure foundation for the research was needed, such as only a database of scientific instrument makers could provide.

This was the thinking behind a project started in 1984 under my direction to search records for the names and addresses of instrument makers and sellers in the British Isles, 1550–1851. The English trade started in London in the mid-sixteenth century through the migration of craftsmen from the Low Countries, and grew to make London the largest centre for this precision craft in the world. The project received its initial funding from the Renaissance Trust, which made it possible to pay a research officer, and purchase a word processor and associated equipment. It soon became clear that the records of the City of London Guilds could provide an astonishingly fruitful source of information about the instrument-making trade, including the relationships between masters and apprentices, and hence the transmission of craft skills. Michael Crawforth laid the foundations of what was clearly to be a long-term study, and it attracted much interest, leading to the acquisition of a mnemonic title, Project SIMON (Scientific Instrument-Makers, Observations and Notes). In 1987, the Leverhulme Trust agreed to take over the funding, which it most generously continued until 1992. Michael Crawforth's sudden and tragic death caused a break of several months, until Dr Gloria Clifton took over the post of research officer in 1989.

Dr Clifton's skill and diligence have brought a major piece of work to fruition in the form of this *Directory*, which is a landmark both in the history of science and in business history. It is heartening that her achievement, and that of project SIMON, have now been recognised by a national institution. The National Maritime Museum has taken Dr Clifton on to its staff, and has accepted the task of maintaining and adding to the database of Project SIMON, so that it may be extended to cover the period to 1900, and further details added in the light of new research.

Gerard L'E. Turner

Acknowledgements

The Directory of British Scientific Instrument Makers 1550–1851 is the result of the work and goodwill of many people. It began with the SIMON research project to create a computer database of scientific instrument makers, initiated by Professor Gerard L'E. Turner of Imperial College, London, with generous funding from the Renaissance Trust, and then from the Leverhulme Trust. I am especially indebted to the first research officer, the late Michael Crawforth who, with his wife Diana, set up the database and carried out much original research. Many other scholars have been extremely generous in sharing the results of their own investigations. Particularly important contributions have been made by Dr John A. Chaldecott and Dr Anita McConnell, both formerly of the Science Museum, London. Other significant help has come from Mr John R. Millburn of Aylesbury, Buckinghamshire; Dr David J. Bryden, Miss Alison Morrison-Low and Dr Allen D. C. Simpson of the Royal Museum of Scotland, Edinburgh; Mr A. V. Simcock of the Museum of the History of Science, Oxford; Dr Lilian Spencer, research student at Queen Mary and Westfield College, London; Mrs Jenny Wetton of the Museum of Science and Industry, Manchester; Ms Jane Insley of the Science Museum, London; Mr Julian Holland of the Macleay Museum, University of Sydney; Dr Patricia Fara, Dr Jim Secord and Dr Frances Willmoth of Cambridge University; Mrs Jean Tsushima, Honorary Editor of the Huguenot & Walloon Gazette; Cdr H. Derek Howse, formerly of the National Maritime Museum, and Mr Peter Delehar, Mr Eric Freeman and Dr Dennis L. Simms of London. I have also received information about particular makers from local and family historians too numerous to mention individually, and I would like to thank them for sharing the fruits of their research.

I am greatly indebted to the staff of all the libraries and record offices I have used, who have been unfailingly helpful. The staff at the Guildhall Library and the City of London Record Office had to endure the most questions and often went to great trouble to provide answers, so I would like to record my particular thanks for their efforts. I am also extremely grateful to the Clerks, Archivists and Librarians of the City of London Livery Companies, who gave me access to their records, notably those of the Clothworkers', Drapers', Goldsmiths', Leathersellers', Mercers', Salters' and Skinners' Companies.

I would like to thank the Trustees of the National Maritime Museum and the Museum of the History of Science, Oxford, for allowing me to publish illustrations of material from their collections. I am especially grateful to the Directors of Christie's South Kensington and to Mr Jeremy Collins for supplying illustrations from their archives and agreeing to their publication.

Finally, this work would never have appeared without the support of Professor G. L'E. Turner, the material assistance of the Scientific Instrument Society, and the practical help of colleagues at the National Maritime Museum, and I would like to record my profound gratitude to them all. I would particularly like to thank Dr Kristen Lippincott and Miss Maria Blyzinsky for their help with proof-reading, an arduous task with no reward.

List of illustrations

The illustrations listed below are published by permission of the Trustees of the National Maritime Museum, unless otherwise indicated. All items marked with an asterisk in the List of Illustrations are photographs by courtesy of Christie's South Kensington Ltd., London. Numbers indicate pages on which the illustrations appear.

Introduction

The development of scientific instrument making

Since the end of the middle ages scientific instruments have played an increasingly important role, both in scholarly study and in everyday life. In both cases the initial stimulus was the same: the realization that advance depended on the ability to make accurate measurements and calculations. This need was felt in astronomy, navigation, surveying, ship design and commerce, and was further stimulated by exploration and by the establishment of new long-distance maritime trade. Hence it was the development of mathematical instruments which assumed a growing importance in the sixteenth and seventeenth centuries. They included instruments designed to measure angles between heavenly bodies or features on land, and others intended primarily to simplify calculation. Their gradual refinement was prompted both by theoretical advance and by the precise practical needs of astronomers, mariners, merchants and surveyors, though progress was often slow and patchy. The development of theories of natural philosophy, or, to use the modern term, science, and the demands of astronomers, have tended to dominate most accounts of the development of scientific instruments, but the instrument makers depended for their livelihoods on the steady business provided by the demand for practical calculating, navigational and surveying instruments, which went hand-in-hand with the expansion of commerce. This everyday trade provided the basis for a profitable business for the instrument makers, who could then apply their skills to the novel and exacting requirements of the scholars. Progress was slow, and the results of collaboration between scholar and instrument maker often fell short of expectation, but the fact remains that the testing of theory frequently depended upon craft skills, and new instruments could stimulate unforeseen lines of inquiry.

During the seventeenth and eighteenth centuries new kinds of instruments were developed. First came optical instruments, principally telescopes and microscopes, which opened up new worlds of objects too distant or too small to be seen with the naked eye. Scholars came to appreciate their potential for scientific inquiry, and worked to improve and refine them, although microscopes were initially seen as novelties for polite amusement rather than as instruments for the study of the natural world. From the later seventeenth century onwards there emerged another group of devices, which came to be known as philosophical instruments, because they were designed to explore or demonstrate the workings of the natural world. These included air-pumps and electrical machines of various kinds. New measuring devices were also invented in the seventeenth century, such as barometers and thermometers. Although the term was not generally used until the second half of the nineteenth century, it is convenient to group all these devices together under the umbrella term 'scientific instruments'. Many developments towards understanding the laws of the natural world could not have been achieved without the skills of the instrument maker, yet their role has often been overlooked in conventional histories of science. Except for a few leading figures, their names are rarely mentioned. Only a small number of specialist works, such as E. G. R. Taylor's pioneering two volumes on mathematical practitioners, or Maurice Daumas's *Scientific Instruments of the Seventeenth and Eighteenth Centuries* have attempted to trace the role of the hundreds of teachers, writers, inventors and instrument makers who developed and popularized the use of mathematical, optical and philosophical instruments.

The SIMON research project on the British scientific-instrument trade

The present study was a direct result of Professor Gerard L'E. Turner's appreciation that the lack of knowledge about instrument makers was a serious flaw in our understanding both of the development of scientific thought and of the increasing application of technology to everyday life. In addition, work by A. W. Skempton and Joyce Brown had shown the potential of London guild records for revealing the links between masters and apprentices in the instrument-making trades, together with other biographical details. London was the principal centre of scientific-instrument making in the British Isles and, until the second half of the eighteenth century, there was only a handful of practitioners in the provinces. In some cases, such as John Prujean in seventeenth-century Oxford, it is possible to show that provincial makers had been trained in the capital. Furthermore, in the eighteenth century London led the world in the production of mathematical, optical and philosophical instruments, supplying equipment for observatories, universities, and individual scholars, in Continental Europe and America. These considerations led Gerard Turner to set up a research project on British scientific instrument makers, based primarily on the archive material preserved by the London guilds. The first research officer, Michael Crawforth, coined the name Project SIMON, derived from the initials of the words, 'Scientific Instrument Makers, Observations and Notes'. Professor Turner succeeded in obtaining funding for the project, first from the Renaissance Trust, and then from the Leverhulme Trust. Work began in 1984 under Michael Crawforth, who established the database of scientific instrument makers, using his excellent and extensive research into directories, trade cards and guild records, in which he was ably assisted by Mrs Diana Crawforth. It was continued, after his sad and untimely death in 1988, by Gloria Clifton, who added a substantial number of new names and details of sources. However, without the pioneering efforts of Gerard Turner and Michael and Diana Crawforth, this book could never have been written.

While the records of the City of London Companies were the

basis for the research on instrument makers, they were supplemented by numerous other sources, both primary and secondary. The primary sources included the records of the Corporation of London, trade directories, parish records, wills, insurance registers, advertisements, trade cards, and signatures on instruments seen in collections and at sales. As the project developed information was exchanged with other researchers in the field, and material added from their work, both published and unpublished. Particularly important contributions have been made by Dr David J. Bryden of the Royal Scottish Museum, Dr John A. Chaldecott, Dr Anita McConnell, Mr John R. Millburn, Miss Alison Morrison Low of the Royal Scottish Museum, and Mr Anthony V. Simcock of the Museum of the History of Science, Oxford. Provincial trade directories were sampled to try to gain a more accurate picture of the numbers working outside London.

The aim was to build up a listing on computer of the instrument makers working in the British Isles between the real beginnings of the trade in this country, in the middle of the sixteenth century, and the mid-nineteenth century, when the skill of the individual craftsman was being increasingly superseded by large-scale factory production and division of labour. The year 1851 was taken as a convenient terminal date, because the Great Exhibition of that year in London is usually seen as marking the high-point of British manufacturing prowess. Decisions also had to be taken about which trades to include. Anyone who was described in official records or advertisements as a mathematical, nautical, optical or philosophical instrument maker, has been listed, together with those whose signatures appear on instruments that fall within these categories. By the eighteenth century specialists in optical instruments often called themselves opticians, and while they usually sold spectacles, it was not until the late nineteenth century that the term came to be used for those who specialized in prescribing and selling glasses for the correction of defects of sight. Consequently all opticians have been included. Conversely, especially in the seventeenth and eighteenth centuries, telescopes and microscopes were also made by craftsmen who continued to describe themselves as spectacle makers, and they too have been incorporated. For example, Ralph Sterrop and John Yarwell, who were in partnership at the turn of the seventeenth and eighteenth centuries, issued an advertisement for 'STERROP's True Spectacles', at the end of which they added, 'Also Telescopes of all Lengths for Day or Night; Perspective [sic] great and small; a new double Microscope invented by the said STERROP, fitted for all Uses . . .'.[1] Also listed in the *Directory* are specialists who made or sold barometers, magnetic compasses, dials, drawing instruments, globes or rules. Clock makers have only been included if they are known to have made astronomical regulators or chronometers. Surgical instrument makers are excluded, but those who made weighing scales and measures of volume have been counted. As well as being used by scholars on occasion, all these items exemplify the increasing application of precision measurement to commercial and domestic life that has been one of the features of modern economic development,

and another area in which the influence of the instrument maker has tended to be overlooked.

The evolution of scientific-instrument making in the British Isles, as exemplified by Project SIMON

Scientific-instrument making came relatively late to the British Isles. By the end of the fifteenth century the craft had already become well-established at Nuremberg and Vienna, but it developed in England only in the second half of the sixteenth century, brought to London by immigrants from the Low Countries. The early craftsmen were engravers and mathematical instrument makers, who produced astrolabes, quadrants, rules, scales, sectors and sundials. The evolution of fine and accurate engraving was closely allied to the development of printing, and a number of the early makers of mathematical instruments were also engravers of maps and book illustrations. The numbers of instrument makers grew only slowly at first, but much more rapidly from the second half of the seventeenth century, though still largely concentrated in London. From then onwards the newer specialisms of optical and philosophical instrument-making further increased the total engaged in the trade. Both retailers and makers have been included, because it is often difficult to distinguish between the two; indeed, one individual often performed both roles, not only selling the goods he made, but also buying in other specialist products to add to the stock of his shop. For example, the mathematical instrument maker John Coggs, who had a shop in Fleet Street, issued a handbill in about 1715, listing the instruments he made, which concluded by advertising that 'He also sells all sorts of Gauging Rods, and Sliding Rules for Mensuration, made by Isaac Carver, (from the Globe on Horslydown), the Original Maker of all Sliding-Rules now in Use . . .'.[2] By the late eighteenth century the number of scientific instrument makers was beginning to grow significantly in provincial centres as well as the capital. However, by the time of the Great Exhibition of 1851, it was clear that British makers needed to be wary of competition from the leading firms in France and Germany.

While the general outlines of the development of the trade are well known, Project SIMON provides a more precise and detailed picture than any previous work. Over five thousand makers and retailers of scientific instruments have been traced, together with about twice as many apprentices, for whom it has been impossible to discover whether they actually worked at the trade in which they had been trained. The total numbers are set out in Table 1. As some makers are known only from a signature on an instrument, and it is not known exactly where in the British Isles they were working, a separate column has been included in the table for makers who fall into this category. The picture which emerges of the development of the trade is one of

[1] British Museum, Heal Collection, 105.98.
[2] British Museum, Heal Collection, 105.21.

slow beginnings in the late sixteenth and early seventeenth centuries, followed by rapid expansion in the late seventeenth and eighteenth century, especially in London, and the total numbers were considerably greater than previous estimates have suggested. Little evidence has been found of significant numbers of instrument makers in places other than London before the second half of the eighteenth centuries. From then onwards there was a steady growth of the trade outside the capital, especially in major ports and industrial centres, such as Glasgow, Liverpool and Manchester, although London continued to have at least half the known instrument makers. This pattern is verified by the Census reports for the first half of the nineteenth centuries. [Table 2]

The structure of the scientific instrument trades was relatively complex. Even in the early stages of development they depended on the existence of other skills, and there was a considerable amount of sub-contracting. For example, one reason for the relatively late development of instrument making in the British Isles, especially of metal instruments, was the lack of a native brass industry until the second half of the sixteenth century. In the seventeenth-century optical trades, there were specialists who concentrated on grinding lenses, and others who concentrated on making telescope tubes. Makers tended to specialize at this period in either mathematical or optical instruments, but contemporary advertisements suggest that there were always some retail shops where both types of instruments could be obtained. Captain Smith mentioned in his book, *An Accidence or the Pathway to Experience Necessary for all Young Sea-men*, published in 1626, that 'the Gunners scale is made in brasse at Tower Hill, with prospectiue glasses, and many other instruments by Mr. Bates.' In the 1670s and 1680s John Seller both published maps and charts and made mathematical and optical instruments, which he sold from a series of shops in the City of London and in Westminster. By the mid-eighteenth century it was clear that most leading makers offered the full range of mathematical, optical and philosophical instruments, although there was still room for the highly skilled specialist, such as James Short, who made and sold only reflecting telescopes. In fact he concentrated on polishing the specula for his telescopes, and bought in the tubes and other brass-work. Such arrangements suggest that one reason for the prominence of scientific-instrument making in London was the size, wealth and economic complexity of the city, which provided sufficient business to allow specialization and sub-contracting.

The directory

The specific trades included have already been discussed, but the criteria for adding particular individuals to the directory are as follows:

1. Those mentioned in contemporary records, including directories, as mathematical, optical or philosophical instrument makers or sellers, as opticians, or as specialists in particular objects within those categories;
2. Names appearing on instruments, unless they are likely to be those of the owner rather than of the maker or supplier;
3. Masters of known makers, although they are not counted for statistical purposes if there is evidence that their principal business was not one of the scientific instrument making trades;
4. Apprentices of known makers whose occupation never appears in the sources, but who trained a known instrument maker or retailer.

A new partnership of makers who previously traded independently is counted as a separate entry, as are widows who carried on their husbands' businesses.

Problems and ambiguities

One of the greatest difficulties is disentangling instrument makers with the same name who were working at the same time, and who in some cases were in the same guild. It is particularly common with fathers and sons or nephews and uncles, but also occurs when two masters who are apparently unrelated have the same relatively common name. For example, there were two Benjamin Coles in the Merchant Taylors' Company of London in the 1750s, one the well-known instrument maker, the other a rope maker, and apprentices are recorded simply as being bound to Benjamin Cole, with no attempt to identify which man was concerned.[3] Information about people with the same name has not been combined unless there is sufficient evidence to suggest a strong probability of linkage. As a general rule, the practice of the historical demographers has been followed, that if there is no contradictory evidence, and if three pieces of information agree, it has been assumed that the material relates to the same person. It is possible that in a few cases this has led to a father and son with the same name, occupation, and address, and a relatively short combined working period, being assumed to be a single individual. However, from the point of view of building up a reasonably accurate picture of the total size of the trade, such errors are probably preferable to causing an excessively large inflation of the total numbers by treating all ambiguous cases as separate entries. Conversely, there may be some cases where two records of the same name at different addresses have been taken to refer to separate individuals, whereas in fact they both relate to the same person. For example, it was originally assumed that entries for William Elliott, optical and mathematical instrument maker of 21 Great Newport Street, London, in directories of the 1820s, referred to a different person from those in the 1830s and 1840s for William Elliott, drawing instrument maker, optician, mathematical and philosophical instrument maker of 227 and then 268 High Holborn, London. However, the baptismal records of the parish of St Martins in the Fields subsequently showed that the directory entries all referred to the same William Elliott. Given the number of makers being researched, it has been possible to spend only a limited amount of time on each, and so there may still be some cases of one maker being counted as two, or vice versa.

---

[3] Guildhall Library, London, microfilms of Merchant Taylors' Company records, 318, 319, 324.

Information given on each individual

A complete file of information about each instrument maker includes:

1. The full surname and forenames, together with any alternative signatures or spellings found on instruments or in the sources used. The spelling used for the main entry is the one used most often by the maker himself as his signature, or, in the absence of such evidence, the version appearing in the majority of sources;

2. The dates when he or she is known to have been working, prefixed by the code 'w'. These dates will not necessarily reflect the full working life of the individual, but the dates for which there is firm evidence. Where these dates are based solely on the work of other writers, they are given in the form 'fl' for flourished. In the absence of working dates, other firm dates may be used, such as dates of birth or death. Failing these, an assessed date is given, with the code 'a', based on the likely date of surviving artifacts signed by the maker. In some cases '*c.*' for circa, the Latin for about, has been used, for example, when there is evidence that an individual was dead by a particular year, but the precise date is not known;

3. The maker's trade as described in the sources or on instruments. Where a trade has been assumed from a surviving artifact or other indirect evidence it has been placed in square brackets;

4. Addresses, with dates where known. Again, the dates may not represent the whole length of time which the maker remained at a particular address, but simply those for which evidence has been found. For the sake of making it possible to carry out searches by computer, the spellings of the names of towns and streets have had to be standardized, otherwise addresses have been kept in the form used in the original source. Many of the dates are derived from directories, and it needs to be borne in mind that changes may have occurred a year or two before they appeared in the listings. For the period after 1851, directories were sampled at five year intervals and 1901 was the last year consulted, so the terminal date of 1901 indicates only the conclusion of the search, and not necessarily the end of the firm. Also, street numbering was generally not introduced until the second half of the eighteenth century, and before that date the same address may have been described in several different ways;

5. Guild or City of London Company, with the name of the master, and dates of apprenticeship and freedom, followed by any apprentices, with the dates of binding, if known. Cross-references are indicated by a star. London guilds were normally called companies, and since it was possible to become a freeman by patrimony, because one's father had been a member, members pursued many occupations which had nothing to do with the guild trade. Thus many mathematical instrument makers were members of the Grocers or Drapers companies. There were also cases where makers set up in business before they officially became freemen;

6. Other names connected with the maker, including his or her father, other relations, especially if themselves engaged in scientific-instrument making; partners; employers and employees; predecessors and successors. Again, if these associates have their own entries in the directory, this is shown by a star;

7. Other miscellaneous information, such as royal appointments, exhibitions at which he exhibited, patents, and similar material;

8. Types of instruments the maker is known to have produced, either from contemporary sources or from surviving signed examples;

9. Types of instruments advertised by the maker;

10. Sources of information.

In most of the categories abbreviations have been used. These are listed in full at the end of the Introduction. In the case of sources, the references to published works have been shortened by using the author's surname, together with the minimum number of initials necessary to distinguish those with the same name, followed by the date of publication and, if necessary, a lower-case letter to identify different works by the same author in the same year. The full titles are given in the bibliography in author order.

Significance of the material presented in the directory

One of the most important findings to emerge from the *Directory of British Scientific Instrument Makers* is that the total numbers engaged in the trade were considerably larger than previously thought. By the eighteenth century the manufacture of instruments required by engineers, gunners, mariners, and surveyors, as well as scholars and the educated sections of society, was providing a substantial amount of employment, and the scientific concern for precision was influencing other areas of life. Although London remained the principal centre of production throughout the period under review, the directory entries show that provincial instrument making was more significant than has generally been assumed. The directory also makes it possible to trace networks of workers within the instrument-making trades, and movement between London and the provinces. There is much scope for using the material for detailed analyses of particular aspects of the trade, or as a starting point for regional studies.

It is clear that there are still numerous unexplored sources which could be tapped to provide more material about the instrument-making trades, especially rate books and estate plans. The evidence presented here is an improvement on previous efforts, but there are still ambiguities. Great efforts have been made to make the entries as accurate as possible, but human nature and the contradictions of some of the sources will mean that errors are likely. Nevertheless, the information will provide a starting point for further research, and if users will draw the author's attention to additional information, it should eventually be possible to produce an improved edition.

Conclusion

Detailed study of the work of British scientific instrument makers provides much evidence of the close interdependence between the evolution of natural philosophy, and economic, cultural and technological developments. Historians of science who have taken an interest in the instruments used in experiments, and studied the collaboration of scholars and craftsmen, have tended to concentrate on the particular contributions of the individuals concerned, whereas it was only because of the long evolution of techniques and materials that many of the advances in the construction of instruments were possible. More sensitive or more accurate instruments produced new observations, which in turn prompted the further evolution of theory. As scholars' understanding grew some of their discoveries proved to have commercial applications which could, as in the case of electricity, lead to completely new industries. These in turn sometimes produced new devices which further aided the advancement of knowledge. Detailed study of the work and inter-connections of scientific instrument makers illuminates the interdependence of intellectual, technological, economic and social change.

Table 1
Numbers of scientific instrument makers working in the British Isles whose names have been traced

Year	British Isles	London	Town not known
1551	3	1	2
1601	14	8	6
1651	43	30	7
1701	151	123	10
1751	232	161	9
1801	584	297	24
1851	837	498	1

Table 2
Numbers of scientific instrument makers listed in the Census of Great Britain

a) Males aged 20 years and over only

Census	London**	Great Britain*	London as % of GB
1831	707	1099	64
1841	1043	2104	50
1851†	1345	2079	65

b) Total population

1841	1248	2501	50
1851†	1631	2650	62

* Figures for Great Britain exclude Ireland

** Census figures for London include the whole built-up area, and the number of parishes included was increased at each of the censuses between 1831 and 1851

† 1851 figures are for opticians and philosophical instrument makers only. There are no detailed statistics for individual trades such as barometer or compass makers, which were given in 1841, and as philosophical instrument-making was heavily concentrated in London, this probably accounts for the higher proportion of London makers in 1851.

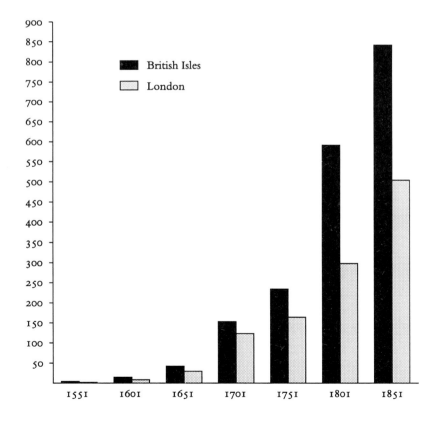

A note on dates

Until 1752 England used the Julian calendar for official purposes, with New Year's Day being 25 March. Dates in this form are termed Old Style. With the adoption of the Gregorian or New Style calendar in 1752, 1 January became New Year's Day and for that year only 2 September was immediately followed by 14 September. However, in Scotland New Year's Day was 1 January from 1600. Confusion can arise with dates between January and March before 1752. In most of the sources used, dates were given in the Julian form, and in this directory an event such as an apprenticeship falling in, for example, January 1666 Old Style is given as 1666/7, so that it is easier to trace in the original document. However, the requirements of the computer database meant that this form could not be used for the main date entry following each name, and these have been given in New Style form.

Abbreviations used in the directory

Notes

In addition to those listed below, the usual abbreviations are used for English counties, American states, and months of the year. References to books and articles are given in the form of the author's surname and date of publication. A full list is given in the Bibliography. Page numbers are not given for reference works arranged in alphabetical order. Many of the original sources used are arranged in chronological order and not paginated.
Where abbreviations refer to the publishers or titles of trade directories, readers should consult Atkins (1990), Norton (1984) and Shaw & Tipper (1989), listed in the Bibliography, for full details.

★	Indicates a cross-reference to the main entry in the directory for that name
?★	Possibly the same as the maker of that name in the directory
[ ]	Enclosing a trade, deduced from instruments sold or advertised, or other indirect evidence; enclosing the name of a guild, apprenticed in that guild, but freedom not traced
+	Following a date, business known to have continued beyond the last date checked; following a page number, references continue
a	Assessed date based on a surviving instrument or publication
A	Andrews' directories
ABC	Armourers' and Brasiers' Company of London
Abn	*A Directory for the City of Aberdeen and its Vicinity*, published by Gordon et al, Aberdeen, 1824–1839
Ac	Accession, acquisition
ACO	Admiralty Compass Observatory
Ad	Advertiser
ADCS	Information from Dr A.D.C. Simpson, National Museums of Scotland, Edinburgh
Adler	Adler Planetarium, Chicago, Illinois
AFr	Alphabets of Freedoms of the City of London at the CLRO
AL	Information from Miss Alison Morrison-Low, National Museums of Scotland, Edinburgh
Ald	Repertories of the Court of Alderman of the City of London
AM	Information from Dr Anita McConnell, Centre for Metropolitan History, University of London
Ap	Apprentice register
Ap/Fr	Apprentice and freedom register
APOTH	Society of Apothecaries
App	Apparatus
apx	Appendix
AQM	Information from Dr A.Q. Morton of the Science Museum, London
Aris	*Aris's Birmingham Gazette*
ART	Information from Mr A.R. Titford, family historian
Astro	Astronomical
ATG	Antique Trades Gazette
AVS	Information from Mr A.V. Simcock, Librarian, Museum of the History of Science, Oxford
AW	Information from Miss A. Walters, University of California, Berkeley, CA
b	Born
B	Board
BaCh	*Bath Chronicle*
BaL	Bath Central Library
Banks	Banks collection of trade cards, British Museum, London
bap	Baptised
Bap	Register of baptisms
B.apt	Business appointment
Baro	Barometer
BC	Barbers' Company, or Barber Surgeons' Company before 1745
b.cert	Birth certificate
Bd	Baldwin's directories
Be	Browne's directories
BG	Information from Brian Gee of the Scientific Instrument Society
Bil	Billing's directories
Bis	Bisset's directories
Bk	Blackwell's directories
BKC	Blacksmiths' Company of London
BL	British Library, London
BM	British Museum, London
Bn	Baines' directories
Bne	Browne's directories of Bath, Somerset
Bod	Bodleian Library, Oxford
Boyd	Boyd P., Inhabitants of London MSS, and Index, Library of the Society of Genealogists, London
Boyle	Boyle's Court Guides
Br	Bridgen's directories
BRC	Bakers' Company of London
BREW	Brewers' Company of London
BRO	Bristol Record Office
BROD	Broderers' Company of London
Bros	Brothers
Browne	*The Bristol Directory . . .*, printed for Ar. Browne & Son, et al., (1785)
BrumL	Birmingham Central Library
Brw	Brownell's directories
BS	Information from B. Smith
BSIS	*Bulletin of the Scientific Instrument Society*
BsM	Bristol City Museum
BTC	Butchers' Company of London
Bu	Registers of burials
BW	Barfoot and Wilkes' directories
By	Bailey's directories
c.	Circa, meaning about
C	Clark's directories
Camb.	Cambridge
Cat.	Catalogue
Cat.1851	*Catalogue of the Great Exhibition of 1851*
CF	Records of Admissions to the Freedom of the City of London
CH	Christ's Hospital School, London
Chase	W. Chase & Co., *The Norwich Directory*, Norwich, 1783
Chem	Chemical
Chn	Charlton's directories
Chp	*Chapman's Birmingham Directory*
Chr	Christie's Auctioneers, King St, London
ChrSK	Christie's Auctioneers, South Kensington, London
ChrNY	Christie's Auctioneers, New York
Chrono	Chronometer
Chs	Christie's directories
CKC	Clockmakers' Company of London
CLRO	Corporation of London Record Office, Guildhall, London
CMC	Coach and Coach Harness Makers' Company of London
Co.	Company
Coll.	College
CORD	Cordwainers' Company of London
CPC	Coopers' Company of London
Cpy	Copy, Photocopy
CRC	Carmen's Company of London
Cs	Census
Ct	Court
CUL	Cambridge University Library
CUR	Curriers' Company of London
CUT	Cutlers' Company of London
CWC	Clothworkers' Company of London
CWH	Clothworkers' Hall, London
d	Died, deceased
Daily J	*Daily Journal*
daur	Daughter
DB	Information given by Mr Douglas Bennett to Mr M.A. Crawforth
DC	Dyers' Company of London
DG	Information from Diana Gunasena
DH	Drapers' Hall, London
Dix	Dix & Co., W.H., *General and Commercial Directory of the Borough of Birmingham*, Birmingham, 1858
DJB	Information from Dr D.J. Bryden, National Museums of Scotland, Edinburgh
DNB	*Dictionary of National Biography*
DPC	Drapers' Company of London
DS	Information from Dr Dennis L. Simms
DurC	Durham Cathedral
e	Established, date claimed in advertising for the foundation of a business
EBA	Elliott Brothers' Archive at GEC Avionics, Rochester, Kent
ed.	Editor(s), edited by
edn	Edition
ED	Census Enumeration District
Edin	Edinburgh
Educ	Educated
EF	Information from Eric Freeman
EFP	*Exeter Flying Post*

em	As an employee		British Museum, London	LM	Liverpool Museum
emp	Employed	HIH	Hand-in-Hand Insurance Company	LMIR	London Mechanics Institute
engr	Engraving		Registers at the Guildhall, Library,		Registers at Birkbeck College,
Er	Erith's directory		London		London
et al	And others	Hil	Hilton's directory of Newcastle upon	LS	Information from Dr L. Spencer
EVP	*The Evening Post*		Tyne	LSC	Leathersellers' Company of London
Ex.	Exhibitor at an Exhibition	Ho	House	LSH	Leathersellers' Hall, London
F	Fordyce's directories	Hull	Hull Museum	Ltd	Limited
FANC	Fanmakers' Company of London	Hunts	Hunt & Co.'s directories	m	Married
FC	Fletchers' Company of London	Hydro	Hydrometer	M	Maker
FDC	Founders' Company of London	IC	Innholders' Company of London	Mag	Magazine
FG	*Forres Gazette*	i.e.	*id est*, meaning that is	Mar	Register of Marriages
fl	Flourished, referring to a date based	IGI	*International Genealogical Index*,	Mat	Matthews' directories
	on another author's work		published by the Church of Jesus	Math	Mathematical
FLM	Feltmakers' Company of London		Christ of Latter Day Saints, Utah	MBW	Metropolitan Board of Works
fm	See w fm	IHR	Institute of Historical Research,	MC	Masons' Company of London
FMC	Fishmongers' Company of London		University of London	m.cert	Marriage certificate
Fn	Fenwick's directories	IM	Instrument maker	McFeat	McFeat's directories
fol.	Folio(s)	IMC	Ironmongers' Company of London	Md	Marwood's directories
fp	Freed by patrimony, i.e. made a	inst	Instrument(s)	MDS	Musée David M. Stewart: Musée des
	freeman of the guild or company by	Inv.	Inventor of		découverts, Montréal, Canada
	virtue of father's membership	IS	Instrument seller	Memo bk	Memoranda book
fr	Made a freeman	J	Johnstone's directories	MF	Microfilm
Fr	Register of Freedoms	Jack	Jackson & Son, Auctioneers, Hitchin,	Mh	*The London Guide and Merchant's*
FRAS	Fellow of the Royal Astronomical		Herts		*Directory*, J. M'Cullough [1796]
	Society	JAC	Information from Dr J.A. Chaldecott,	MHS	Museum of the History of Science,
FRC	Farriers' Company of London		formerly of the Science Museum,		Oxford
FRS	Fellow of the Royal Society		London	MHSn	Indexes and notes in the Library of
FW	Information from Frances Willmoth	JAS	Information from Dr J.A. Secord of		the MHS
G	Gore's directories		Cambridge University	ML	Museum of London
Gabb	Gabb Collection	JC	Joiners' Company of London	MM	Macleay Museum, University of
Gales	*A Directory of Sheffield*, compiled and	JHC	Information fron Mrs J.H. Coombes,		Sydney, NSW, Australia
	printed by J. Gales and D. Martin,		family historian	MMA	Nederlands Scheepvaartmuseum,
	Sheffield, 1787	JHST	*Jewish Historical Society Transactions*		Amsterdam [Netherlands Maritime
GC	Grocers' Company of London	JJ	John Johnson Collection at the		Museum, Amsterdam]
GDC	Girdlers' Company of London		Bodleian Library, Oxford	MM.Tec	Macleay Museum, Technology
Ge	Gell's directories	JnH	Information from Mr Julian Holland,		Collection
Gent	Gentleman		Macleay Museum, University of	Mnfr	Manufacturer
Geo	George		Sydney, Sydney, Australia	Mor	Morris's directories
GH	Goldsmiths' Hall, London	JRM	Information from Mr J.R. Millburn	Mort	Mortimer's directories
GL	Guildhall Library, London		of Aylesbury, Bucks	M.P.	Member of Parliament
GLC	Greater London Council	JRT	Information from Capt. J.R. Turner,	MPC	Makers of Playing Cards Company
GL'ET	Information from Professor G. L'E.		OBE, MNI		of London
	Turner of Imperial College, London	JT	Information from Mrs Jean	MSC	Musicians' Company of London
GLRO	Greater London Record Office,		Tsushima, Honorary Archivist of the	MSEN	Museum of Science and Engineering,
	40 Northampton Rd, London		Honourable Artillery Company,		Newcastle upon Tyne
	EC1R 0HB		London	MSIM	Museum of Science and Industry,
Glv	Glover's directories	JW	Information from Mrs J. Wetton,		Manchester
GMag	*Gentleman's Magazine*		Museum of Science and Industry,	mt	*Manual of the Thermometer*, no.1180,
GMC	Gunmakers' Company of London		Manchester		8 June 1850, copy at MHS
GNDA	*Gazetteer & New Daily Advertiser*	K	Kelly's directories for places other	MTC	Merchant Taylors' Company of
GSC	Goldsmiths' Company of London		than London		London
GSWC	Gold and Silver Wyre Drawers'	KH	King's Hospital School, Dublin	Mu	Museum
	Company of London	KLJ	Information from Mr K.L. Johnson,	n	Note(s)
GVC	Glovers' Company of London		Science Museum, London	Naut	Nautical
Gye	Gye's directory of Bath, Somerset	Kn	Keene's directories	NC	Needlemakers' Company of London
GZC	Glaziers' Company of London	Kt	Kent's directories	nd	No date
H	Holden's directories	L	London	nf	No freedom found
HA	*Hamburgisches Addressbuch für das Jahr*	LBC	Longbowstringmakers' Company of	NJ	*Newcastle Journal*
	1820 [also 1831]		London	NK	Not known
HAC	Honourable Artillery Company of	LC	Loriners' Company of London	NMM	National Maritime Museum,
	London	Ld	Lowndes' directories		Greenwich, London
HC	Haberdashers' Company of London	LEP	*London Evening Post*	NMS	National Museums of Scotland,
HDH	Information from Cdr H. Derek	Lg	*New Complete Guide*, by Longman		Chambers St, Edinburgh
	Howse, formerly of the National		et al	NQRS	*Notes and Queries of the Royal Society*
	Maritime Museum, Greenwich,	LGaz	*London Gazette*		*of London*
	London	LicFW	Licences for Foreign Workmen in	NT	National Trust
Heal	Heal Collection of trade cards at the		the City of London	OB	Order book

p	Posthumous, used for businesses which carried on in the founder's name after his death
p.	Page(s)
Pat.	Patent
PB	Parson and Bradshaw's directories
PC	Plumbers' Company of London
PCC	Prerogative Court of Canterbury
PCRO	Portsmouth City Record Office
PF	Information from Dr P. Fara of the University of Cambridge
Pg	Pigot's directories
Phil	Philosophical
Phil.T	*Philosophical Transactions of the Royal Society of London*
Phlps	Auction catalogues of Phillips, Son & Neale, London
Photo	Photographic
pl.	plate
PLC	Plaisterers' Company of London
PMC	Pattenmakers' Company of London
PO	*Post Office London Directory*, 1816 onwards
POE	*Post Office Directory of Edinburgh*
POG	*Post Office Directory of Glasgow*
PO(HC)	*Post Office Directory of the Six Home Counties, London*, 1845
PR	Pearson and Rollason's directories
PRO	Public Record Office
prob	Probably
PSC	Painter–Stainers' Company of London
pt	See w pt
pv	Private Collection
PWC	Pewterers' Company of London
PWh	Parson and White's directories
Pye	Pye C., *The Birmingham Directory*, Birmingham, 1788 onwards
Q	Quarterage book
r	Retired from business
R	Robson's directories
RA	Registry Archive
R.apt	Royal appointment
RAS	Royal Astronomical Society
Rb	Robinson's directories of Sheffield
rd	Became a freeman by redemption, i.e. by paying a fee
Rd	Reid's directories
REI	Royal Exchange Insurance Office
Rg	Rodger's directories
RGO	Royal Greenwich Observatory Archives, University of Cambridge Library, Cambridge
Ric	Richardson's directories
Riv	Rivington's directories
RMS	Royal Microscopical Society
Rob	Robbins' directories
RPS	Royal Photographic Society
RS	Royal Society of London
RWYC	Royal Western Yacht Club
s	Service, date apprenticeship began
S	Seller
SA	Sketchley & Adams directories
Sacch	Saccharometer
SBPL	St Bride Printing Library, Bride Lane, London EC4 8EQ
Sby	Auction catalogues of Sotheby's,

	New Bond St, London
Sby(Ch)	Auction catalogues of Sotheby's, Chester
Sby(Sx)	Auction catalogues of Sotheby's, Billingshurst, West Sussex
SC	Salters' Company of London
SDC	Sadlers' Company of London
SEG	Information from Mrs S.E. Garnett, family historian
SH	Salters' Hall, London
Shaw	Shaw's directory
SI	Smithsonian Institution, Washington D.C.
[sic]	Quoted as it appears in the original source
sig.	Signature: letter or other mark used to show the order of sheets in a printed work without page numbers
Sil	Silverthorne's directory
SIS	Scientific Instrument Society
SJ	Information from Stephen Johnston, Science Museum, London
SKC	Skinners' Company of London
Sket	Sketchley's directories
SKH	Skinners' Hall, London
Sl	Slater's directories
SM	Science Museum, London
Smart	Smart's directories
SMC	Spectaclemakers' Company of London
SML	Science Museum Library, London
Som.Ho	Somerset House
Spec	Spectacle(s)
Sq	Square
St	Street
St.	Saint
StA	St Andrew's University
Stat	Stationers' Hall, London
STC	Stationers' Company of London
St.Mtn	Parish of St. Martin in the Fields, London
Stn	Stephenson's directories
STTP	Society of Tacklehouse and Ticket Porters of London
Sun	Sun Insurance Policy Registers at the Guildhall Library, London
Sun+E	Sun Insurance Policy Endorsements at the Guildhall Library, London
Sun & RE index	Sun and Royal Exchange Insurance Policies Index on Microfiche
SUNM	Sunderland Museum
SW	In addresses – South West; in sources – information from Mr S. Warren of the Department of Archaeological Sciences, University of Bradford,
SWC	Shipwrights' Company of London
Sy	Swinney's directories
Tait	Tait's directories
TBC	Tylers' and Bricklayers' Company of London
TC	Turners' Company of London
TCd	Trade card
Tec	Technology Collection
Th	*Thompson's London Commercial Directory*, 1844
THC	Tallow Chandlers' Company of London

Thermo	Thermometer
TJB	Information from Mr T.J. Bryant of Bristol
t/o	Turned over, term used when an apprentice was transferred from one master to another
Ts	Catalogues from Tesseract, Hastings-on- Hudson, NY
TSA	*Transactions of the Society of Arts*
TWC	Tinplate Workers' Company of London
TWr	Thomson & Wrightson's directories
u	Member of another unknown guild
UC	Upholders' Company of London
Und	Underhill's directories
v	With a date - living; with a folio number - verso: the reverse side of the folio
VC	Vintners' Company of London
VIA	Vickers Instruments Archives at the Borthwick Institute, University of York
Vic	Victoria
VL	Victoria Public Library, Westminster, London
VM	Information from Mrs V. Majumdar, family historian
VS	Information from Miss V. Stokes of the Needlemakers' Company of London
w	Working
W	Wakefield's directories
WB	Wardle & Bentham's directories
Wd	Ward's directories
Wellcome	Wellcome Collection, Science Museum, London
West	West W., *The History, Topography & Directory of Warwickshire*, Birmingham, 1830
w em	Working as an employee
w fm	Working in the family business, exact status unclear
Wh	White's directories
Whd	Whitehead's directories
Wi	Wilson's directories
Wil	Wilkes J., *List of the Whole Body of the Liverymen of London…*, London, 1792
Wim	Williams's directories
WJ	Information from Mrs W. Jones, family historian
Wk	Watkins' directories
Wlm	Williamson's directories
Wln	Whellan's directories
Wm	William
WM	Whipple Museum, Cambridge
Wpoll	Westminster poll books
w pt	Working as a partner
Wr	Wrightson's directories
WS	Information from William Stewart
WVC	Weavers' Company of London
WWC	Wheelwrights' Company of London
Wwd	*Woodward's New Liverpool Directory*, Liverpool, 1804
WXC	Wax Chandlers' Company of London
YC	*York Courant*

AARON Aaron
w 1805–1822
Optician
　　　　　9 Shoemaker's Row, Aldgate, London
　　　　　8 Duke St, Aldgate, London
1805　　　Dukes Place, Houndsditch, London
1822　　　9 Duke St, Aldgate, London
Associated with
AARON & CO. Isaac★
AARON & SON Isaac★
Sources: H; BW

AARON & CO. Isaac
w 1801
Opticians
1801　　　Sparkes' Court, Duke's Place,
　　　　　Aldgate, London
Associated with
AARON & SON Isaac★
AARON Aaron★
Probably a directory version of AARON & SON
Isaac
Sources: PO

AARON & SON Isaac
w 1794–1814
Opticians
1794–1814　Sparkes' Court, Duke's Place,
　　　　　Aldgate, London
Associated with
AARON & CO. Isaac★
AARON Aaron★
Sources: Kt; W

ABBOTT Charles
w 1801–1833
Optician, Tortoiseshell S, Spectacle M
1801–1821　6 Noble St, Foster Lane, London
1826–1833　2 Angel Court, Skinner Row, Snow
　　　　　Hill, London
1817–1822　6 Noble St, Falcon Square,
　　　　　[alternative rendering of first address
　　　　　in some directories] London
Guild: Spectaclemakers, fr 1801
Son of ABBOTT Adrian, Cabinet M, of Covent
Garden, London
Apprenticed to EGLINTON John★ 1784
Had apprentice:
CHANT John Hollely★ 1801
BENTLEY William★ 1806
GROOM William 1812
AGATE Samuel★ 1823
Associated with BENTLEY & CHANT★
Sources: GL: SMC, 5213/4, 5213/5; Bn; H; J; Pg;
PO; R

ABBOTT Joseph
w 1805–1811
Math IM, Baro M
1805–1811　2 Wood's Place, Bowling Green
　　　　　Lane, Clerkenwell, London
Sources: H

ABBOTT Richard
s 1668 w 1676
[Math IM]
Alternative name: ABBOT
　　　　　London

Guild: [Clockmakers]
Apprenticed to BEDFORD Hilkiah★ 1668
Known to have sold: drawing instruments
Sources: Taylor (1954) p.271; Brown J (1979b)
p.27; Loomes (1981b)

ABDY William
w 1754–1784
Goldsmith, Watch M
1760–1790　5 Oat Lane, Wood St, London
1763　　　Noble St, Foster Lane, London
Guild: Goldsmiths, fr by purchase 1752
Had apprentice:
GARRARD Thomas (III) 1754
WREN John 1759
HUMPHREYS John 1765
SIMPKINS Samuel by t/o 1766
SMITHER James by t/o 1766
SCAMMELL Joseph 1767
COCK William 1768
NEALE Charles by t/o 1768
RUBBINS George by t/o 1769
ALLEN William 1771
BARRATT James 1772
MARRIOTT James 1772
MARSON Thomas 1773 by t/o from JONES James,
CUT
BATCHELOR William 1775
RILEY Benjamin 1775
BUSH John 1777
ABDY Thomas, his son, 1777
COMPLIN John 1779
MCCURE John 1782
WAKE William 1784
CLEETS William 1787
Succeeded by ABDY William, his son, fp 1781
Livery June 1763; d 6 Sep 1790
Known to have sold: balance, weight
Instruments advertised: balance
Sources: GH: GSC index; Fallon (1988) p.19;
Sheppard & Musham (1975) p.169,189

ABEL Thomas
w 1838–1840
Baro M; Thermo M
1838–1840　55 Ray St, Clerkenwell, London
Sources: Pg

ABRAHAM Abraham
w 1818–1850
Optician, Math IM, Phil IM
1818–1820　8 Lord St, Liverpool
1821–1823　10 Lord St, Liverpool
1822–1828　7 Lord St, Liverpool
1827　　　6 Lord St, Liverpool
1829–1834　9 Lord St, Liverpool
1835–1836　76 Lord St, Liverpool
1837–1839　78 Lord St, Liverpool
1837–1839　84 Lord St, Liverpool
1839–1850　20 Lord St, Liverpool
Employed COHEN Simeon P★
Partnership ABRAHAM & DANCER★
Succeeded by ABRAHAM & CO.★
e 1817
Known to have sold: microscope, drawing
instruments, chondrometer, compass (magnetic),
sector, barometer, thermometer
Sources: Bn; G; SM; Sby Jun 1972 (MAC); Times

6 Oct 1841 p.7; Bryden (1972) p.43; Wetton
(1991) p.4; Clarke et al (1989) p.298–99

ABRAHAM Abraham Elisha
w 1830
Optician
Alternative name: ABRAHAMS
1830　　　225 High St, Exeter
Known to have sold: barometer, telescope
Sources: Pg; Webster R & M (1986)

ABRAHAM G. & C.
w 1825
Optician, Spec M, Rag S, Trunk M
1825　　　17 Snighill, Sheffield
Sources: Ge

ABRAHAM Jacob
w 1809–1842
Optician
1809–1811　St.Andrew's Terrace, Bath
1830　　　Cheltenham
1830–1842　7 Bartlett St, Bath
1833–1837　Adjoining Mr.Thompson's Pump
　　　　　Room, Cheltenham
1837　　　Adjoining the Rotunda,
　　　　　Cheltenham
R.apt Duke of Gloucester; B.apt Duke of
Wellington; retired by March 1845
Known to have sold: sundial, microscope,
telescope, drawing instruments
Instruments advertised: rule
Sources: BsM notes; BaCh 20 Mar 1845; Pg; Sil;
Calvert (1971) p.11

ABRAHAM John Aburgham
w 1851
1851　　　87 Bold St, Liverpool
Same premises as CLAY & ABRAHAM★
Inv. barometer; Ex.1851
Known to have sold: barometer
Sources: Cat 1851

ABRAHAM & CO. A.
w 1838–1843
Math IM; Optical IM; Philo IM
1841–1843　82 Queen St, Glasgow
1838–1840　8 Exchange Square, Glasgow
Employed COHEN Simeon P★
Succeeded by COHEN Simeon P★
Associated with
ABRAHAM Abraham★
ABRAHAM & DANCER★
Branch of A. Abraham of Liverpool, managed by
S.P. Cohen★, who continued it under his own
name
Sources: Clarke et al (1989) p.298–99; Times
6 Oct 1841; Bryden (1972) p.43

ABRAHAM & CO. Abraham
w 1851–1875
Optician, Math IM, Phil IM
1851–1860　20 Lord St, Liverpool
Partnership with WEST Charles (III)★
Employed COHEN Simeon P.★
Took over from ABRAHAM Abraham★
Succeeded by WOOD George S.★
Ex.1851

Known to have sold: barometer, microscope, compass (magnetic), telescope, drawing instruments
Sources: K; LM index; Turner G (1983a) p.309; Calvert (1971) p.11; Clarke et al (1989) p.298–99

ABRAHAM & DANCER W. & John Benjamin
w 1841–1845
Math IM, Optical IM, Phil IM
1841–1842   13 Cross St, King St, Manchester
Took over from DANCER John Benjamin★
Succeeded by DANCER John Benjamin★
Associated with ABRAHAM & CO. Abraham★
Branch of ABRAHAM Abraham★ of Liverpool
Known to have sold: compass (magnetic), electrostatic generator, microscope, protractor
Sources: Wetton (1991) p.4–5; Hallett (1986) p.237–55; RPS; Calvert (1971) p.11; Times 6 Oct 1841 p.7

ACCUM Fredrick (sic)
w 1803–1828
Experimental chemist, Phil IS
Alternative name: Frederick Christian, Friedrich
1803   Compton St, Soho Square, London
1803   The Laboratory, Old Compton St, Soho, London
b 1769 Bückeburg, Hanover, d 1838; came to London 1793; pioneer of gas lighting
Known to have sold: hydrostatic balance
Sources: Bill MHS; Webster R & M (1986)

ACKERMANN & CO.
w 1849–1851
Math IM, Publishers, Book S, Stationers
1849–1851   96 Strand, London
Known to have sold: drawing instruments
Sources: PO; Webster R & M (1986)

ADAM James (I)
w 1818–1834
Smith, Scale M
1818–1834   48 Rutherglen Loan, Glasgow
Guild: Hammermen, fr 1816
Sources: Pg; PO; Lumsden (1912) p.307

ADAM James (II)
w 1820–1823
Scale M
1820–1823   Lower Glencairn St, Kilmarnock
Sources: Pg

ADAMS Alexander
w 1826–1828
Spec M, Optician
1826–1828   94 Fore St, Cripplegate, London
Guild: Blacksmiths, fr 1826
Son of ADAMS Alexander, Gent, of Southwark
Apprenticed to BYARD John★ 1815
Had apprentice LOWE Joshua Reeve★ 1826
See also ADAMS Michael★
Sources: GL: BKC 2881/17 (MAC); PO

ADAMS Ann & George (II)
w 1772–1774
Math IM, Globe M
1772   Tycho Brahe's Head, 60 Fleet St, London
Took over from ADAMS George (I)★

Succeeded by ADAMS George (II)★
Sources: Daily Ad 28 Oct 1772; Millburn (1988b) p.289

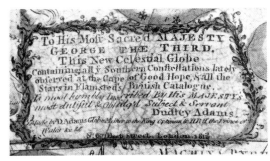

ADAMS Dudley
w 1788–1817
Optician, Globe M, Phil IM, Math IM
Alternative name: [Und gives ADAMS & CO. Dudley 1816]
                West Side of Charing Cross, London
1788   [Residence?] Spring Gardens, Charing Cross, London
1788–1796   53 Charing Cross, London
1796–1826   60 Fleet St, London
1800–1822   6 Jewry St, Aldgate, London
1819   19 Charles St, St James St, London
1819   10 Waterloo Place near Carlton House, London
1821   42 St.Paul's Churchyard, London
1823–1827   22 Ludgate St, London
Guild: Grocers, fr 1788
Son of ADAMS George (I)★
Apprenticed to ADAMS George (II)★, his brother
Had apprentice:
ADAMS George (III), his son, 1811
MORRIS Joseph 1788
STEWART Charles 1791
BLENKINSOP John 1793
Took over from ADAMS Hannah★ (premises only)
b1762; Pats. specs 1797, telescopes 1800,1815; bankrupt 1817; R.apt Geo III Globe M 1794, Math IM 1796; d1830
Known to have sold: barometer, globe, microscope
Instruments advertised: air pump, barometer, camera obscura, circumferentor, drawing instruments, electrostatic generator, globe, hygrometer, magic lantern, magnifying glass, microscope, mirror, opera glasses, pantograph, plane table, planetarium, prism, quadrant, rule, sector, spectacles, sundial, telescope, theodolite, thermometer, transit instrument, waywiser
Sources: Brown J (1979a) p.52,81; Goodison (1977) p.117–21; Pat.records (MAC); BM: Heal 105/1; Und; BW; JRM

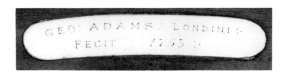

ADAMS George (I)
w 1734 d 1772
Math IM, Phil IM, Optical IM, Lecturer
1733–1738   (Residence) Shoe Lane, London

1734   4 doors east of Shoe Lane, Fleet St, London
1735   Near the Castle Tavern, Fleet St, London
1738–1757   Tycho Brahe's Head, Corner of Racquet Court, Fleet St, London
1767   60 Fleet St, London
Guild: Grocers, fr 1733
Son of ADAMS Morris, cook, of LC
Husband of ADAMS Ann★
Apprenticed to PARKER James (I)★ 1724 t/o 1726 to HEATH Thomas★
Had apprentice:
HAM Erasmus 1736
BAYNHAM Charles 1741/2 t/o 1744 to COLLIER William★
KETTLE Nathaniel 1754
TANGATE Robert (I)★ 1758 by t/o from MORGAN John★
ADAMS George (II)★, his son, 1765
Employed MILLER John★
Succeeded by ADAMS Ann & George (II)★
Father of ADAMS Dudley★
b 1709; Pat.1750 telescope; R.apt Prince of Wales, Geo III 1760; MIM to Office of Ordnance; supplied instruments to Christ's Hospital; author
Known to have sold: full range of instruments, compass invented by Gowin Knight FRS, globe
Sources: BM: Heal 105/1; GL: CH 12823/5–6; pat.records (MAC); JRM; Anderson et al (1990) p.1–2; Brown J (1979a) p.36,79–81; Goodison (1977) p.122–25; Millburn (1988) p.220–93; EVP 17 Dec 1735

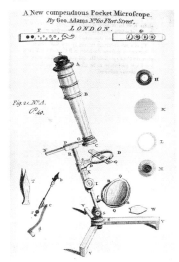

ADAMS George (II)
w 1772 p 1796
Math IM
1772–1795   Tycho Brahe's Head, 60 Fleet St, London
Guild: Grocers, fr 1772
Husband of ADAMS Hannah★
Apprenticed to ADAMS George (I)★, his father
Had apprentice:
BEAN Fowler 1773
ADAMS Dudley★, his brother
STEDMAN Christopher (II)★

BLUNT Robert, his nephew, 1782
Took over from ADAMS Ann and George (II)★
Succeeded by ADAMS Hannah, his widow★
b 1750 d 1795; author; member of Swedenborg's
New Jerusalem Church; supplier to Christ's Hospital
Known to have sold and advertised: Full range of
instruments, globe
Sources: GL: CH 12823/6–8; JRM; BW; Kt; Ld;
Brown J (1979a) p.46,80–81; Calvert (1971) p.12;
Goodison (1977) p.117,126–29

ADAMS Hannah
w 1795–1796
Math IM
1795–1796   60 Fleet St, London
Wife of ADAMS George (II)★
Took over from ADAMS George (II)★
Sold stock to JONES W.& S.★
Premises taken over by ADAMS Dudley★
R.apt Geo.III 1795–6; supplier to Christ's
Hospital; d 1810
Sources: *Courier* 1 Apr 1796; GL: CH 12823/8 p.133;
PRO: LC3/68 p.23; Ld; Brown J (1979a) p.81

ADAMS Henry
w 1836–1840
Optician, Math IM, Phil IM
1836–1838   2 Crawford St, Portman Square,
             London
1839   58 Baker St, Portman Square, London
1840   4 Charles St, Manchester Square,
             London
Sources: Pg; PO; R

ADAMS John (I)
w 1720–1734
Spec M
1732   Within Aldgate, London
Guild: Spectaclemakers, fr 1714
Apprenticed to SAUNDERS William★ 1707
Had apprentice:
JOHNSON Isaac 1720 by t/o from JONES
William (V) t/o 1721 to BROWN Thomas (II)★
DAGLEY Elias 1727
KNAPIER/KNAPPIER/NAPIER Richard 1731, t/o
1734 to NORTH George (I)★
Attended SMC until 1745; d c. 1745
Sources: GL: SMC 6031/1, 5213/2
p.116,182,234+, 6029; Buckley (1935) p.428

ADAMS John (II)
w 1790–1793
Smith, Scale M
1790–1793   High Bridge, Newcastle upon Tyne
Sources: BW; Whd

ADAMS Michael
w 1829–1842
Optical IM, Phil IM, Math IM, Optician
1829–1830   15 Tavistock Row, Covent Garden,
             London
1829–1830   16 Wilderness Row, Goswell St,
             London
1831   8 Tavistock Row, Covent Garden,
             London
1841   51 Fleet St, London
1842   3 White Hart Yard, Holborn,
             London

Guild: [Blacksmiths]
Son of ADAMS Alexander, Gent, of Mortlake,
Surrey
Apprenticed to BYARD John★ 1818
Sources: GL: BKC 2881/17 (MAC); PO; R (JAC)

ADAMS Nathaniel
w 1735 d c. 1740
Optician
1734–1737   The Golden Spectacles in
             Cranbourne St, near Leicester Fields,
             London
1737–1738   The Golden Spectacles, Charing
             Cross, London
1738   The Golden Spectacles next the
             Golden Cross Tavern on the North
             Side of Charing Cross, London
Guild: Spectaclemakers, fr 1730
Son of ADAMS Nathaniel, glover, of Westminster,
London
Apprenticed to SCARLETT Edward (I)★
Had apprentice:
WATKINS Francis (I)★ 1737
MARGAS John★ 1735 t/o 1741 or 1742 to COX
John★
Succeeded by WATKINS Francis (I)★
Asssociated with SCARLETT Edward (II)★
R.apt Frederick, Prince of Wales
Known to have sold: microscope
Sources: GL: SMC 5213/2 p.134,216+, 5213/3
p.68, 6029; Sun 11936/40 no. 64596; Goodison
(1977) p.269; Turner G (1989) p.34–35

ADAMS Thomas (I)
w 1630 d 1664
Smith, Locksmith, Clock M
             Parish of St Mary the Virgin, Oxford
Guild: Freeman of Oxford, 1621
Apprenticed to BATES John, blacksmith, of
Oxford
Known to have sold: sandglass
Sources: Beeson (1989) p.81,84

ADAMS Thomas (II)
w 1851
Chrono M, Watch M
1851   36 Lombard St, London
Sources: PO

ADAMS William
w 1735
Math IM
1735   Grub St, London
1735   Pear St, in the parish of St.Lukes,
             London
Guild: [Masons]
Son of ADAMS William, mariner, d, of London
Apprenticed to SAUNDERS Samuel (I)★1726
Had apprentice:
WARNER Richard 1735
ASTON James 1735
Sources: GL; CH 12823/4 p.449; 12876/4; MC
5304/3, 5312 (MAC)

ADAMSON Humphrey
w 1668–1676
Math IM
Alternative name: Humphry

1674   Next [to] Turnstile in Holborn,
             London
             At the House of Jonas Moor Esq, in
             the Tower, London
Manufacturer of the mechanical calculator
invented by Sir Samuel Morland
Known to have sold: calculating machine,
micrometer
Instruments advertised: calculating machine
Sources: Bryden (1992) p.307; Loomes (1981b);
Calvert (1971) p.11

ADCOCK Parmenus Thomas
w 1841
Scale beam M
1841   11 King Edward St, Mile End New
             Town, London
Father of ADCOCK Parmenus John, s1841 STC
Sources: Stat: STC Memo book

ADDENBROOK Edward
w 1850
Rule M
1850   39 Hurst St, Birmingham
Sources: Wh

ADDISON John
a 1800–1819
Globe M
             Regent St, London
             50 London St, Fitzroy Square,
             London
             7 Hampstead Rd, London
Associated with ADDISON & CO. John★
Known to have sold: planetarium
Sources: Webster R & M (1986); JAC; inst NMM

ADDISON & CO. John
w 1820–1830
Globe M, Optical, Math & Phil IM
1820–1821   9 Skinner St, Snow Hill, London
1822–1825   116 Regent St, London
1825–1826   50 London St, Fitzroy Square, London
1827–1828   7 Hampstead Rd, Tottenham Court
             Rd, London
1829–1830   275 Strand, London
Associated with ADDISON John★
R.apt Geo.IV
Known to have sold: globe
Sources: Kt; R (JAC); Webster R & M (1986)

ADIE Alexander
w 1823–1834
Math IM, Optician
1823–1829   15 Nicolson St, Edinburgh
1830–1834   58 Princes St, Edinburgh
Father of
ADIE John★
ADIE Richard★
ADIE Patrick★
Son of ADIE John, printer, of Edinburgh
Apprenticed to MILLER John★, his uncle
Succeeded by ADIE & SON★
Took over from MILLER & ADIE★
Associated with
SPENCER, BROWNING & RUST★
JONES Thomas (I)★, who acted as agent for Adie's
sympiesometer

ADIE Edward

b 1775; pat.1818 sympiesometer; R.apt Wm.IV
1834; d 1858
Known to have sold: barometer, pantograph,
sextant, sympiesometer
Sources: Clarke et al (1989) pp.25–74; PRO:
LC3/70 p.115; Pg; Goodison (1977) p.130

ADIE Edward

w 1833
Optician
1833   Black Horse Square, Canal St,
     Wolverhampton
See also ADIE Richard★
Sources: Br

ADIE John

w pt 1834–1857
Optician
Son of ADIE Alexander★
Brother of
ADIE Patrick★
ADIE Richard★
Partnership ADIE & SON★
b 1805 d 1857 (suicide)
Sources: Clarke et al (1989) p.41–49

ADIE Patrick

w 1848–1886 p 1942
Math IM, Phil IM
1848–1868 395 Strand, London
1869–1885 15 Pall Mall, SW, London
1869–1870 29 Regent St, Westminster, London,
     SW
1875   Tothill St, SW, London
1890–1901 Broadway Works, Westminster,
     London, SW
Son of ADIE Alexander★
Brother of
ADIE John★
ADIE Richard★
Asociated with ADIE & SON★
b 1821 d 1886
Known to have sold: artificial horizon, barometer,
drawing instruments, telescope
Sources: Clarke et al (1989) p.41,75–84; PO;
Webster R & M (1986); Bryden (1972) p.43

ADIE Richard

w 1835–1875
Optician, Phil IM, Math IM
Alternative name: ADEY
1835–1837 28 Bold St, Liverpool
1835   26 Bold St, Liverpool
1839–1865 55 Bold St, Liverpool
1868–1870 4 Exchange Buildings, Liverpool
1870   5 Edmund St, Liverpool
1872–1876 5 Harrington St, Liverpool
Son of ADIE Alexander★
Brother of
ADIE Patrick★
ADIE John★
Employed WEDDERBURN Thomas, as foreman in
Edinburgh
Succeeded by ADIE & WEDDERBURN
b 1810 d 1881
Known to have sold: air pump, barometer,
electrostatic generator, planetarium

Sources: G; Clarke et al (1989) p.41,49–51; Sby 26
Aug 1982 lot 126; Webster R & M (1986)

ADIE & SON Alexander & John

w 1835–1857 p1880
Opticians
1835–1843 58 Princes St, Edinburgh
1844–1876 50 Princes St, Edinburgh
1877–1880 37 Hanover St, Edinburgh
Related to
ADIE Patrick★
ADIE Richard★
Partnership of ADIE Alexander★ and his son John★
Employed WEDDERBURN Thomas
Succeeded by ADIE Richard★ 1857, but continued
under the name ADIE & SON★
Associated with ADIE Patrick★
Known to have sold: balance, barometer,
hygrometer, level, sextant, thermometer
Instruments advertised: barometer, thermometer
Sources: Clarke et al (1989) p.41–51

ADLAY

w 1697
Scale M
     London
Indicted for selling bad balance
Known to have sold: balance
Sources: GL: BKC 2881/8 (MAC)

ADLINGTON Thomas

w 1821–1827
Math IM, Optician
1821   14 Smithfield St, Liverpool
1823   84 Copperas Hill, Liverpool
1824–1825 55 South Side, Old Dock, Liverpool
1827   1 Ironmonger Lane, Liverpool
Sources: Bn; LM index (MAC)

AGATE Samuel

w 1831
Spec M
1831   King's Head Court, St Martin's le
     Grand, London
Guild: Spectaclemakers, fr 1831
Son of AGATE George, Labourer at East India House
Apprenticed to ABBOTT Charles★ 1823
Sources: GL: SMC 5213/5

AGGINTON Thomas

w 1818
Rule M
1818   Cock St, Wolverhampton
Sources: PB

AGNEW Thomas

w 1835–1841
Carver, Gilder, Baro M, Thermo M, Print S,
Publisher,
Mirror S, Picture S
1838–1841 14 Exchange St, Manchester
1838   (Residence) Richmond Hill,
     Salford, Manchester
Partnership
AGNEW & ZANETTI★
ZANETTI & AGNEW★
Apprenticed to ZANETTI Vittore★ in 1810
Succeeded by AGNEW & SONS Thomas

Took over from AGNEW & ZANETTI★
b 1794, d 1871
Known to have sold: barometer
Sources: Agnew (1967); Goodison (1977) p.296;
Pg; Webster R & M (1988)

AGNEW & ZANETTI Thomas & Joseph

w 1825–1834
Baro M, Optician, Looking glass M, Carver,
Gilder, Thermo M, Clock M
1825–1826 94 Exchange St, Manchester
1826–1832 10 Exchange St, Manchester
1834   18 Exchange St, Manchester
1835   14 Exchange St, Manchester
Took over from ZANETTI & AGNEW★
Succeeded by AGNEW Thomas★
Associated with ZANETTI Joseph★
Known to have sold: barometer, thermometer
Sources: Pg; Goodison (1977) p.296; Wetton
(1990–1991) p.51–54

AIANO Charles

fl 1828–1841
Baro M, Thermo M, Clock M, Optician
Alternative name: AINO
1826–1841 Northgate, Canterbury
1838   Sign of the Providence, 102
     Northgate St, Canterbury
1851   16 Union St, Canterbury
Son of AIANO Christmas
See also AIANO & CO.★
b 1784 d 1859
Known to have sold: barometer
Sources: Goodison (1977) p.106; AM;Harrington
(1979) p.206–10

AIANO & CO.

a 1820
[Baro M]
See also AIANO Charles★
Known to have sold: barometer
Sources: ChrSK 12 Dec 1985 lot 16

AILES William

w 1838
Math IM, Phil IM
1838   29 Seward St, Goswell St, London
Sources: Pg (JAC)

AINSWORTH Thomas

d.c 1713
Compass M
     Wapping, London
Father of AINSWORTH Edward s1713/14 BKC
Sources: GL: BKC 2886/4 (MAC)

AIRS William

w 1851–1875
Magic lantern M, Baro M, Thermo M, Phil IM
1851   14 Merlin's Place, Wilmington
     Square, Clerkenwell, London
1865–1875 32 Upper Rosoman St, London
Sources: PO; Wk

AITKEN Thomas

w 1730–1754
Scale M, Wright, Scale adjuster
     Kirkwall

Guild: Hammermen
Apprenticed to FOUBISTER Thomas★
Worked for TATE William
Sources: Record of Court action by Alexander,
Earl of Galloway, 12 Nov 1757, p.154,226,308–09
(MAC)

AKENHEAD David
w 1778–1795
Book S, Chart S, Optical IS
1778   North end of Tyne Bridge,
                 Newcastle upon Tyne
1787–1795   Sandhill, Newcastle upon Tyne
Son of AKENHEAD Robert (I)★
Worked for AKENHEAD Robert (I)★
Took over from AKENHEAD Robert (I)★
Succeeded by AKENHEAD & SONS D.★
Sources: Hunt (1975) (MAC)

AKENHEAD Robert (I)
w 1718 fl 1768
Stationer, Instrument S, Spec S
1718   At the Bible & Crown upon the
                 Bridge, Newcastle upon Tyne
Succeeded by AKENHEAD David★, his son
Sources: Calvert (1971) p.11; Hunt (1975) (MAC)

AKENHEAD & SONS David [John & Robert (II)]
w 1795–1813
Book S, Chart S, Optical IS
1795–1813   Newcastle upon Tyne
Had apprentice ALPORT Adam Blackburn★
[bound to AKENHEAD John]
Took over from AKENHEAD David★
Sources: Hunt (1975) (MAC)

ALBERTI Angelo
w 1822–1828
Baro M, Optician
1822–1825   Fargate, Sheffield
1828   8 Waingate, Sheffield
Sources: Bk; Bn

ALBINO John
w 1837–1884
Baro M, Thermo M, Looking-glass M
1837–1838   2 Beauchamp St, Leather Lane,
                 London
1839–1849   47 St John St, West Smithfield,
                 London
1849–1868   63 Hatton Garden, London
1869–1884   54 Stamford St, London
Succeeded by ALBINO & CO. John
Sources: PO

ALCOCKE Robert
w 1706
[Scale M]
                 London
Guild: Blacksmiths, fr 1703
Apprenticed to GROVE Christopher★ 1692
Had apprentice LOVETT John 1706/7
Sources: GL: BKC 2886/3–4, 2881/9 (MAC)

ALDERSON Walton
w 1823–1831
Sundial M, School Master

1823–1831   Leyburn
Known to have sold: sundial
Sources: Loomes (1972)

ALDRIDGE John
w 1669–1670
Spec M
1669   Minories, London
Guild: Spectaclemakers
Had apprentice unnamed, not bound in SMC
Sources: GL: SMC 5213/1

ALDUS Thomas
w 1660–1662
[Math IM]
Alternative name: ALDOUS
                 London
Guild: Joiners, fr 1659/60
Son of ALDUS William, clothier, of Needham,
Suffolk
Apprenticed to SUTTON Henry★ 1652
Had apprentice:
SEABORNE John 1660/1
FIELD William 1662
Sources: GL: JC 8052/1; Crawforth (1987) p.346

ALEXANDER –
a 1790
                 Yarmouth
Associated with SPENCER, BROWNING & RUST
Known to have sold: octant marked SBR
Sources: inst, NMM

ALEXANDER Alexander
w 1833–1835
Optician, Math IM, Phil IM
1834   6 High St, opposite Castle St, Exeter
1834   5 Castle St, (works), Exeter
1835   Brighton
e 1828; R.apt Duchess of Kent, Princess Victoria,
& Wm IV 1833 & 1835
Sources: PRO: LC3/70 p.103,153; TCd (pv); TCd
NMM

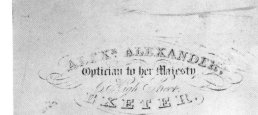

ALEXANDER George
w 1813–1825
Watch M, Compass M
                 27 Timber St, Leith
1822–1825   62 Shore, Leith
1813   Leith
See also ALEXANDER & SON Robert★
Pat.1813 compass card
Sources: Patent records (MAC); Bryden (1972)
p.43

ALEXANDER John (I)
fr 1671
[Clock M, Sundial M]
1671   Edinburgh
Apprenticed to SMITH Robert, Clock M, 1667
Known to have made: sundial as test piece
Sources: Loomes (1981b)

ALEXANDER John (II)
w 1830
Optician
1830   238 High St, Exeter
Sources: Pg

ALEXANDER & SON Robert
w 1820–1822
Compass M
1820–1822   62 Shore, Leith
Associated with ALEXANDER George★
Sources: Pg

ALGAR & PHILIPS
w 1805
Measure M
1805   26 Great Tower St, London
Sources: H

ALKER John
c 1790 w 1834
Watch M
1814–1834   23 Market Place, Wigan
Known to have sold: balance
Sources: Bn; Pg; Huddersfield Mu; Crawforth
(1979)

ALLAM William
w 1769
Watch M
                 London
Guild: Clockmakers, fr 1743
Known to have sold: astronomical clock
Sources: Baillie (1951); Taylor (1966) p.252

ALLAN Alexander
w 1804–1835
Phil IM, Math IM
1806–1810   Baron Grant's Close, Edinburgh
1811–1835   9 Lothian St, Edinburgh
Had apprentice STEVENSON Peter★
Succeeded by STEVENSON Peter★
Associated with Professor Thomson of Glasgow
University in improving the saccharometer
Known to have sold: barometer, gauge,
hydrometer
Sources: inst SM; ADCS; Bryden (1972)
p.14,15,43; Goodison (1977) p.296; McConnell
(1993) p.12–13

ALLAN James
w 1802–1822
Math IM, Sextant M, Divider
Alternative name: ALLEN
1802–1822   12 Blewitt's Buildings, Fetter Lane
                 London
Son of ALLAN John★
Took over from ALLAN John★
See also
WORTHINGTON & ALLAN★

ALLEN James★
Known to have sold: sextant, repeating circle
Sources: Ts39 (1992/3) item 23; Bn; H; Und;
Bennett (1985) p.19,22; Stimson (1985)
p.103–04,113

ALLAN John
w 1790–1794
Sextant M, Quadrant M
     London
1790–1794   12 Blewitt's Buildings, Fetter Lane,
     London
Father of ALLAN James★
Succeeded by ALLAN James★
Known to have sold: sextant
Sources: Ts39 (1992/3) item 23; W; JAC

ALLBUT Isaac
w 1811–1845
Rule M
Alternative name: ALLBUTT
1811–1845   Salop St, Wolverhampton
1818   105 Salop St, Wolverhampton
See also ALLBUTT I.★
Sources: PB; Pg; Wh

ALLBUTT I.
w 1845
Rule M
1845   Birmingham
See also ALLBUT Isaac★
Sources: Roberts (1982)

ALLCOCK Thomas
w 1851
Chrono M, Watch M
1851   14 South Island Place, Clapham Rd,
     London
Sources: PO

ALLEN –
w 1820
Alternative name: Possibly Alexander ALLAN
1820   Near the College, Edinburgh
Instrument advertised: geometric solids
Sources: Larkin (1820) (DJB)

ALLEN B.
w 1851
Optician
1851   2 Lower Copenhagen St, Islington,
     London
Sources: Wk

ALLEN Elias
w 1607 d 1653
Math IM (in brass), Book plate engraver
Alternative name: ALLIN
     Blackhorse Alley, Fleet St, London
     Horseshoe over against St. Clement's
     Church, Strand, London
1606–1611   Blacke Horse-ally, neere Fleetbridge,
     London
1623–1639   Without Temple Bar, over against
     St.Clement's Church, London
1618   At the Bull's head over against St
     Clement's Church, Strand, London
1653   Horseshoe without Temple Bar near

     St Clement's Church, London
1645   The Blackmoor without Temple
     Bar, London
Guild: Grocers, Clockmakers
Apprenticed to WHITWELL Charles c.1602 GC
Had apprentice:
BLAYTON (BLIGHTON) Edward 1612 GC
BLIGHTON John★nd fr 1620 GC
SHEWSWELL Thomas fr 1623 [possibly
SHASWELL ★] GC
ALLEN John (I)★ 1617 GC
SEFTON Henry 1620 GC
DAVENPORT Robert★1623 GC
BROOKES Christopher★ 1629 GC
WINCKFIELD Edward 1629 GC
COOKE George 1635 GC
JORDAN William 1649/50 GC
GREATOREX Ralph★ 1639 by t/o CKC
CHENEY Withers★ 1646 by t/o CKC
GRIMES Edward 1640/41 by t/o CKC
PRUJEAN (PRIGEON) John★ CKC
Took over from WHITWELL Charles★
Succeeded by GREATOREX Ralph★
Associated with
THOMPSON John (I)★
HAYES Walter★
THOMPSON Anthony★
fr GC 1612, fr CKC 1633; d 1653; another Elias
Allen, who carried out surveys for Charles I was d
by 1637
Known to have sold: armillary sphere, compass
(magnetic), ellipsograph, marine astrolabe, mural
quadrant, rule, sector, sundial
Instruments advertised: mathematical instruments
Sources: Brown J (1979a) p.24–25; Brown J
(1979b) p.11–14,27; Bryden (1992)
p.306n,308,318; DG

ALLEN James
w 1825–1826
Math IM
Alternative name: ALLAN?
1825–1826   196 Piccadilly London
See also ALLAN James ★
Same premises as WORTHINGTON & ALLEN★
Attended London Mechanics Institute 1825–1826,
not known as a master on his own
Sources: LMIR (AM)

ALLEN James Patishall
w 1850–1852
Math IM
1850–1852   20 King St, Stepney, London
Guild: Merchant Taylors, fr 1861
Son of ALLEN James [no trade given]
Apprenticed to LILLEY John (I)★or (II)★ 1841
Sources: PO; Wk; GL: MTC MF 320, 324 (MAC)

ALLEN John (I)
w 1630–1642
Math IM (in brass)
1630–1631   Near the Savoy, Strand, London
Guild: Grocers fr 1631/2, ?Clockmakers 1653
Apprenticed to ALLEN Elias★
Had apprentice HAYES Walter★ 1631/2 GC
Working in own name before free in 1631/2; a
John Allen admitted to Clockmakers 1653
Known to have sold: astrolabe, sector

Sources: Brown J (1979a) p.26; Brown J (1979b)
p.14,27; Bryden (1992) p.309

ALLEN John (II)
w 1842–1855
Phil IM, Drawing IM
1842–1845   35 St.Swithin's Lane, London
1847–1855   5 Three King Court, Lombard St,
     London
Succeeded by ALLEN Mrs.A.
Sources PO

ALLEN M.H. & J.W.
c 1838–1840
[Drawing IS]
     Dame St, Dublin
Known to have sold: beam compass invented and
made by SMITH W. & A.★
Sources: inst MHS; Pg

ALLEN Nathaniel
w 1790 w 1793
Ship chandler
1793   Wapping New Stairs, London
Guild: Merchant Taylors, fr 1766
Apprenticed to EADE Jonathan (I)★ 1754
Son of ALLEN James, Gent , d, of Dulwich, Kent
Had apprentice ALLEN Thomas James, his son,
1781
Master MTC 1790
Sources: Wil; GL: MTC MF 319,320,324 (MAC)

ALLEN Thomas (I)
d 1767
Math IM
1767   Dublin
Sources: Burnett & Morrison-Low (1989) p.120

ALLEN Thomas (II)
w 1850–1856
Rule M
1850   12 St. Mary's Row, Birmingham
1850   (Residence) Aston Road,
     Birmingham
Took over from ALLEN & ROWE ★
Associated with
ROWE James
ROWE Thomas
Sources: Roberts (1982); Sl

ALLEN William (I)
w 1788–1791
Phil IM, Math IM
1787   37 High St, Birmingham
1791   Bull Ring, Birmingham
Sources: Pye

ALLEN William (II)
fl 1838
Math IM, Phil IM
     29 Seward St, Goswell St. London
Said by Taylor (1966) p.466 to be listed in
directories, but not verified; possibly AILES
William★

ALLEN & ROWE
w 1849–1850
Rule M

1850   12 St. Mary's Row, St. Mary's
              Square, Birmingham
Succeeded by ALLEN Thomas (II)★
Sources: Wh

ALLMOND George
w 1791–1817
Scale M
Alternative name: ALMOND
1794–1817   281 Borough High St, London
1784   15 Walbrook, London
1791   Red Lion St, Borough, London
1807   Blackman St, Borough, London
Guild: [Haberdashers] Clothworkers, fp 1784
Son of ALLMOND John, clothdrawer, of London
Apprenticed to VINCENT Robert★ 1776 HC
Had apprentice:
BAILEY Robert 1791
WAYTE Charles 1795
PARRY William 1799
CARTWRIGHT William 1801
HUGHES Thomas 1803
ALLMOND Michael, his son, 1804
ALLMOND William★, his son, 1806
HAWKINS Edward 1807
CUTHBERTSON Robert Vincent 1808
JOHNSON Israel 1810
See also CUTHBERTSON Robert★
Educated at Christ's Hospital
Sources: H; Ld; Kt; W (JAC);CWH: CWC Fr;
GL: HC 15860/9; CH 12876/5

ALLMOND William
w 1815–1822
Scale M
1815–1818   Borough, London
1822   281 High St, Borough, London
Guild: Clothworkers, fr 1813
Apprenticed to ALLMOND George★, his father, 1806
Had apprentice:
SHORT Samuel Robinson 1815
BOXALL William 1818
Sources: Pg; CWH: CWC Ap, Fr

ALMENT John
w 1768 d 1787
Optician
1768   Mary's Abbey, Dublin
1775–1787   34 Mary's Abbey, Dublin
Sources: Burnett & Morrison-Low (1989) p.120

ALOE S.
w 1842–1845
Optician
1842   1 Blenheim Place, Edinburgh
1843   12 Greenside Place, Edinburgh
1844–1845   36 Hanover St, Edinburgh
Sources: Bryden (1972) p.43

ALPORT Adam Blackburn
w 1815 d 1836
Naut IS
Alternative name: A.B.
1815–1817   Quayside, Newcastle upon Tyne
1817–1719   Low End of Quayside, Newcastle
              upon Tyne
1819   Fenwick's Entry, Newcastle upon
              Tyne

Apprenticed to AKENHEAD John★
Bankrupt 1819
Sources: Hunt (1975) (MAC)

ALT Isaac
w 1668–1681
Spec M
1670   Shoe Lane, London
Guild: Spectaclemakers, fp 1668
Son of ALT John [prob ALTE John (II)★]
Had apprentice:
CONEY Ambrose 1668
COLE Joseph★ 1675
Sources: GL: SMC 5213/1

ALT Jonathan
w 1669–1694
Spec M
1671   London Bridge, London
Guild: Spectaclemakers
Had apprentice FIELD Robert 1679
Master SMC 1674–1677, received SMC charity
1695–1704/5
Sources: GL: SMC 5213/1, 5213/2

ALT Peter
w 1705–1706
[Spec M]
              London
Guild: Spectaclemakers, fr 1702
Son of ALT Nathaniel, yeoman, of Shepshed, Leics
Apprenticed to HOWE Joseph★ 1694
Had apprentice TROTT Anthony 1705
Sources: GL: SMC 5213/1, 6031/1

ALTE John (I)
w 1634–1652
Spec M
Alternative name: ALLT, ALT
1634   London
Guild: Brewers, Spectaclemakers
Son of ALTE John, farmer, of Shepshed, Leics
Related to ALT Isaac★ (father or great uncle)
Apprenticed to ALTE Robert★, his brother, 1619
Had apprentice:
RINGROSE Edward 1651/2 SMC
ADAMS John 1626 BC
fr BREW 1626; translated from BREW to SMC
1634; bap 1601
Sources: CLRO: Ald 49 fol.14; GL: BREW
5445/13 &/14; SMC 5213/1

ALTE John (II)
fp 1633 w 1634
Spec M
Alternative name: ALLT, ALT
1634   London
Guild: Brewers, Spectaclemakers
Son of ALTE Robert★
Related to ALT Isaac★ (either father or cousin)
fp BREW 1633; translated from BREW to SMC
1634
Sources: GL:BREW 5445/15; CLRO: Ald 49
fol.14

ALTE Robert
w 1611–1634
Spec M

Alternative name: ALT
1628   Near St. Paul's ['neere Paules']
              London
Guild: Brewers & Spectaclemakers
Son of ALTE John of Shepshed, Leics
Brother of ALTE John (I)★
Apprenticed to POLSON Richard★ c.1602
Had apprentice:
[All in BC]
PEALE William★ 1611
DRUMBLEBY Thomas★ 1614
ALTE John (I)★ 1619
ALTE Daniel 1619
ELLELL Henry 1624
SYSON Robert 1626
POULSON William 1628
HUTCHINSON Daniel 1632
bap 1586/7; original petitioner for Spectaclemakers
Co. charter; fr BREW 1609; translated from
BREW to SMC 1634
Sources: GL: BREW, 5445/12 /13 /14 /15; IGI
Leics; CLRO: Ald 42 fol.247r; 49 fol.14r

ALTREA Forbes
a 1800–1850
Optician, Glass blower
              162 High St, Edinburgh
Known to have sold: Hydrostatic bubbles
Sources: Holbrook (1992) p.95; ADCS

ALTRIA Caesar
w 1846–1868
Optician, Glass blower
1846–1854   16 Skene St, Aberdeen
1863–1868   29 Huntley St, Aberdeen
Known to have sold: barometer
Instruments advertised:medical galvanic inst
Sources: ADCS

AMADIO Francis (I)
w 1820–1840
Artificial flower M, Baro M, Phil IM, Optician,
Thermo M
Alternative name: Francesco
              2 St.John Street Rd, London
1820–1829   20 St.John Street Rd, London
1823   10 St.John Street Rd, London
1826–1844   118 St.John Street Rd, London
1836–1840   18 Redcross St, Barbican, London
Father of AMADIO Francis (II)★
Succeeded by AMADIO & SON F★
Associated with MANGIACAVALLI J.★
Either he or his son attended the London
Mechanics Institute 1826–1830
Known to have sold: barometer, hygrometer, spirit
level, thermometer
Sources: GL: SMC 5213/5; LMIR (AM); Pg; PO;
Goodison (1977) p.296

AMADIO Francis (II)
w 1839–1864
Optician
Alternative name: Francisco, Francesco
1839   118 St.John Street Rd, Clerkenwell,
              London
1840–1841   63 Moorgate St, London
1842–1851   35 Moorgate St, London
1852–1864   5 Cowper's Court, London

AMADIO John

1851–1864   5 Birchin Lane, London
1836   18 Red Cross St, Barbican, London
Guild: Spectaclemakers, fr 1836
Son of AMADIO Francis (I)★
Partnership with AMADIO Francis (I)★ as
AMADIO & SON F.★
fr by purchase in SMC; either he or his father
attended London Mechanics Institute 1826–1830
Sources: GL: SMC 5213/5; LMIR (AM); PO

AMADIO John

w 1840–1843
Optician
1840–1843   6 Shorters Court, Throgmorton St,
           London
Same premises as AMADIO Joseph ★
Possibly a directory error for Joseph Amadio at the
same address.
Sources: PO

AMADIO Joseph

w 1840–1853
Optician, Bookseller, Math IM
1832   118 St. John's Street Rd, London
1840–1853   6 Shorters Court, Throgmorton
           Street, London
Guild: Spectaclemakers, fr 1843 by purchase
Associated with
AMADIO Francis (I)★
AMADIO Francis (II)★
Attended London Mechanics Institute in 1832
Sources: PO; GL: Sun 11936/576 no.1349856,
SMC 5213; LMIR (AM)

AMADIO & SON F.

fl 1840–1844
Artificial Flower M, Phil IM
118 St. John St Road, London
Took over from AMADIO Francis (I)★
Same premises as AMADIO Francis (II)★
Known to have sold: barometer, hygrometer,
thermometer
Sources: Bolle (1982) p.165; Goodison (1977)
p.297

AMBLER Edward

w 1694
Scale M
1694   Knight Rider St, London
Had apprentice WRIGHT Richard 1694
Sources: GL: CH 12823/2, 12876/2

AMOS & PARKES John & William

c 1774
           Bilston
Known to have sold: balance
Sources: Sheppard & Musham (1975) no.85

ANDERSON Alexander

w 1800–1804
Optician
1800–1804   24 Prince's Square, Well Close
           Square, London
Sources: Boyle (JAC)

ANDERSON David

w 1597
1597   Aberdeen

Known to have sold: sundial
Sources: Loomes (1981b)

ANDERSON James Andrew

w 1821–1852
Scale M
Alternative name: James (only)
1808   Princes St, Leicester Square, London
1850–1852   22 Park Terrace, King's Rd. West,
           London
1822–1850   19 Wardour St, Soho, London
Guild: Blacksmiths, fr 1808
Apprenticed to
LAWRENCE John Peter★1801, t/o 1806 to
WOODAGE George Cave★
Son of ANDERSON William of London
Had apprentice:
GILLETT William 1812
CLARK William 1817
WILDING Frederick 1821
BROMLEY Daniel 1823
BARTON Edward George 1828
MILES Arthur John 1829
BONMER John 1831
PARKINSON Francis Burdett 1835
JONES Edward 1838
CUTRESS Thomas 1844
Partnership ANDERSON & WEST 1839, same
premises
Sources: GL: BKC 2881/16–18; Pg; PO; R
(MAC)

ANDERSON William

w 1795
Math IM
1795   Sherborne Lane, London
Guild: Stationers, fr 1791
Apprenticed to WELLINGTON Alexander★ 1784
Son of ANDERSON William, Gent, of London
Had apprentice GRANT James★ 1795
Sources: McKenzie (1978) p.5, 370

ANDERSON & WEST

w 1839
Scale M
1839   19 Wardour St, Soho, London
See also ANDERSON James A.★
Sources: Pg

ANDERTON James

w 1700–1702
[Math IM]
1698–1702   The Minories, London
Guild: Grocers, fp 1698/9
Son of ANDERTON Nathaniel★
Had apprentice:
INGHAM North 1700
SCOTT Benjamin★1702 t/o 1706 to ROWLEY
John (I)★
Sources: Brown J (1979a) p.30

ANDERTON Nathaniel

w 1669–1683
1669–1683   London
Guild: Grocers, fr 1669
Father of ANDERTON James★
Apprenticed to HAYES Walter★ 1661
Son of ANDERTON James of CWC

Had apprentice:
WORGAN John 1669, prob t/o to HAYES Walter★
WALPOOLE Thomas★ 1676/7
COUCHMAN Peter 1682
LANCASTER Gilbert 1683
Sources: Brown J (1979a) p.27–28

ANDERTON & CALLEY

w 1785–1808
Math IM, Toy M, Button M
1793–1808   Weaman St, Birmingham
Took over from ANDERTON, SON & CALLEY★
Sources: BW; Pye

ANDERTON, SON & CALLEY

w 1783
Math IM, Compass M, Watch key M, Toy M
1783   31 Weaman St, Birmingham
Succeeded by ANDERTON & CALLEY★
Known to have sold: weights
Sources: By; Sheppard & Musham (1975) p.169

ANDREWS James

w 1719
Math IM
1719   Orchard St, Westminster, London
Guild: Stationers, fr 1719
Apprenticed to CARTER Henry★ 1703
Son of ANDREWS Thomas, weaver, of Monmouth
Had apprentice EVANS Richard 1719
Sources: McKenzie (1978) p.5,65

ANDREWS John

w 1829–1830
Optician, Spec M
1829–1830   1 Court, Hurst St, Birmingham
Sources: West; Wr

ANDREWS Nathan

s 1724 d 1782
Watch M
Alternative name: ANDREWES
Known to have sold: sundial
Sources: Loomes (1976); Webster R & M (1988)

ANGEL John

w 1842–1846
Math IM
1842–1846   6 Charterhouse Lane, London
Same premises as ANGELL Lewis★
Attended London Mechanics Institute, 1842–1846
Sources: LMIR (AM)

ANGELL John

w 1849–1851
Math IM
1846–1851   29 Charles St, Hatton Garden,
           London
Attended London Mechanics Institute, 1846–1849
Sources: PO; LMIR (AM)

ANGELL Lewis

w 1849
Math IM
1849   6 Charterhouse Square, London
Same premises as ANGEL John★

Attended London Mechanics Institute 1849
Sources: LMIR (AM)

ANGELO Alberti
w 1825
Baro M, Mirror M
1825   Fargate, Sheffield
Sources: Ge

ANNABOLDI Lewis
fl 1830
Baro M
                7 Walton Place, Blackfriar's Road,
                London
Sources: ChrSK Apr 1986 lot 103 (MAC); Taylor
(1966) p.442

ANONE Frans
w 1802–1808
Telescope M, Baro M, Thermo M
Alternative name: Francis
                2 Holborn, London
                51 Fetter Lane, Holborn, London
                242 High Holborn, London
                82 High Holborn, London
1802–1808   26 High Holborn, London
Known to have sold: barometer, hygrometer,
thermometer
Sources: H; PO (JAC); Goodison (1977) p.297, 363

ANSCHEUTZ & CO. Valentine
w 1761–1772
Clock Case M, Cabinet M, Merchant
1761   Red Lamp, Denmark St, London
1770   26 Denmark St, Soho, London
1771–1778   36 Denmark St, Soho, London
Succeeded by ANSCHEUTZ & SCHLAFF★
Known to have sold: balance
Instruments advertised: balance
Sources: inst MHS, SM; *Daily Ad* 9 Jul 1761; R;
ChrSK 11 Sep 1986 lot 156

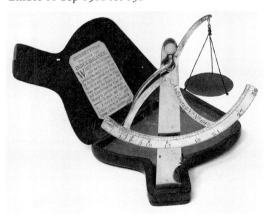

ANSCHEUTZ & SCHLAFF Valentine & John
w 1772–1781
Merchants
1772–1781   36 Denmark St, Soho, London
Took over from ANSCHEUTZ & CO.★
Associated with
MARTIN Benjamin★ and
PINCHBECK Christopher (II)★, who were agents
for their balances

Known to have sold: balance
Sources: Ld (JAC); Kt ; Millburn (1976) p.161;
Morton & Wess (1993) p.388

ANSELL Isaac
d by 1784
Math IM
                Elder St, Spitalfields, London
Father of ANSELL Matthew s1784 NC
Son's apprenticeship consideration fee paid by the
Quakers
Sources: GL: NC 2817/3 f.107

ANSELL Joseph
w 1839–1865
Optician, Math IM, Phil IM
1839–1845   80 Leman St, Goodman's Fields,
                London
1846   27 Bury St, St Mary Axe, London
1865   84 Long Lane, Smithfield, London
                EC
Sources: Pg; PO

ANTHONY John
w 1783
Math IM
1779   At Mr Ripley's, 364 Hermitage
                Bridge, London
1783   5 Little Burr St, Wapping, London
Guild: Grocers, fr 1773
Apprenticed to RIPLEY Thomas★ 1765
Son of ANTHONY John
Worked for RIPLEY Thomas★
Sources: Brown J (1979a) p.43; GL: Sun
11936/276 no.416930, 11936/292 no.445321,
11936/314 no.480261

APPLETON Henry
w 1826–1834
Chrono M
1826–1827   40 Theobald's Rd, Bedford Rd,
                London
1828–1834   26 Burton St, Burton Crescent,
                London
Known to have sold: chronometer
Sources: Sby Apr 1988 lot 182 (MAC); CUL:
RGO/1143 fol.7–10

ARCHBUTT John
w 1838–1864
Math IM, Pawnbroker
1838–1864   20 Bridge Rd, Lambeth, London
Succeeded by ARCHBUTT & SONS
Sources: PO

ARCHDALL Henry
w 1750–1765
Weight M
Alternative name: H.A.
1752   Darby Square, Werburgh St, Dublin
1765   Coleraine St, Dublin
See also ARCHDALL William★
1765 Inspector for the Trustees of the Linen
Manufacture
Known to have sold: weights
Sources: Wi; *Numismatica* Nov 1976, no.129b;
Westropp (1916) p.66

ARCHDALL William
w 1736–1751
Alternative name: W.A.
                Dublin
See also ARCHDALL Henry★
Known to have sold: weights
Sources: Westropp (1916) p.66; Sheppard &
Musham (1975) p.220

ARCHER Thomas
w 1714–1734
[Spec M]
1709   London
Guild: Spectaclemakers, fr 1708/9
Son of ARCHER John
Apprenticed to THOMPSON Samuel (I)★ 1700
Had apprentice:
HARPER Andrew★ 1714
LINNELL Elijah★ 1717/8
BURBIDGE Isaac Joseph by t/o 1721/2 from
BURBIDGE Isaac★ d
ARCHER Joseph, his son, 1727
CRANE James 1727
FARDERE James in 1738
Master SMC 1733–1734; probably d 1744; in 1753
Mrs Archer received charity from SMC
Sources: GL: SMC 5213/2
p.62,88,105,127,181,183+, 5213/3 p.191, 6029

ARCHER William
w 1771–1783
Optical IM, Math IM
1771   Giltspur St, London
1774   Fleet St, London
1777–1780   2 Johnson's Court, Fleet St, London
1783   Fetter Lane, London
Guild: Stationers, fr 1763
Apprenticed to BUSH John★ 1753
Son of ARCHER Robert, brewer, of Edmonton,
Middx
Had apprentice:
PRICE William★ 1771
PARRY Edward 1774
PACE Charles★ 1777
EVANS John Johnson★ 1783, t/o to PRICE
William★ 1786
Educated at Christ's Hospital School
Sources: GL: CH 12876/4, Sun 11936/278
no.422996; McKenzie (1978) p.6,60

ARGILL Thomas
w 1805
Math IM
1805   31 Horsleydown, London
Guild: Grocers, fr 1800
Son of ARGILL Priscilla, widow
Apprenticed to RUST Joseph (I)★ 1793
Sources: H; Brown J (1979a) p.52

ARMSTRONG William George
w 1840–1847
[Electrical machine M]
Alternative name: Sir, then Lord ARMSTRONG
FRS; b 1810; d 1900; inv. hydro-electric frictional
generator
Known to have sold: electrostatic generator
Sources: Turner G (1983a) p.190–92; inst NT,
Cragside

ARNABOLDI Lewis

w 1835
Baro M, Thermo M
1835   Steep Hill, Lincoln
Sources: Pg

ARNOLD James William

w 1831–1837
Optician
Alternative name: ARNOLD James ?
1831   5 Union St, Whitechapel Rd,
              London
Associated with ARNOLD William
Took over from ARNOLD William & James
Sources: R (JAC)

ARNOLD John

w 1764–1787
Chrono M, Watch M
              Devereux Court, Strand, London
              Adam St, Adelphi, London
1783–1786   Bank St, London
              (Chronometer factory)
              Chigwell, Essex
1784   Royal Exchange, London
Guild: Clockmakers, fr 1783
Had apprentice:
ARNOLD John Roger*, his son, 1783
PREST Thomas* 1784
WILLIAMS John 1784
GLOVER John 1786
Succeeded by ARNOLD & SON*
b 1736 d 1799
Known to have sold: chronometer
Instruments advertised: chronometer
Sources: Atkins (1931) p.334; Baillie (1951); GL:
CKC 2720/1

ARNOLD John Roger

w 1799–1830
Chrono M
1799–1811   102 Cornhill, London
1805   102 Bank Building, Cornhill,
              London
1815   132 Strand, London
1818–1827   Cecil St, Strand, London
1830   84 Strand, corner of Cecil St,
              London
Guild: Clockmakers, fr 1796
Son of ARNOLD John*
Had apprentice:
JOLLY Richard 1802
WILSON Charles 1811
Took over from ARNOLD & SON*
Succeeded by ARNOLD & DENT*
b 1769 d 1843; pat.1821 chronometer; Master
CKC 1817
Known to have sold: chronometer, tide gauge
Sources: H; J; R; GL: CKC 2720/1; MMA; Atkins
(1931) p.334

ARNOLD Thomas

c. 1700 d by 1730
Math IM
Alternative name: HARNOLD
1730   Parish of St.Bartholomew the Great,
              London
Father of HARNOLD William, s1730 STC

Possibly maker of gunter's scale signed 'Thomas
Arnold 1700'
Sources: McKenzie (1978) p.257; inst NMM

ARNOLD William

w 1817–1822
Optician, Spec M
1817–1822   29 Essex St, Whitchapel, London
Guild: Beadle of Spectaclemakers 1803–1813
Succeeded by ARNOLD William & James*
Associated wth ARNOLD James William*
Sources: H; R; GL: SMC 5213/4

ARNOLD William & James

w 1826–1828
Optician, Math IM, Phil IM
1826–1828   5 Union St, Whitechapel Rd,
              London
Took over from ARNOLD William*
Succeeded by ARNOLD James William*
Sources: Pg

ARNOLD & DENT John Roger & Edward John

w 1830–1840
Chrono M
1830–1839   84 Strand, London
Took over from ARNOLD John R.*
Took part in chronometer trials at Royal
Greenwich Observatory
Sources: CUL: RGO 1143 fol.9–10; Pg; PO

ARNOLD & FRODSHAM

w 1844–1851
Watch M, Chrono M
1844–1851   84 Strand, London
Took over from ARNOLD & DENT*
J.R. ARNOLD* d 1843 & business taken over by
Charles FRODSHAM* trading as ARNOLD &
FRODSHAM *
Sources: PO; Baillie (1951); Loomes (1976)

ARNOLD & SON John

w 1787–1799
              102 Cornhill, London
Succeeded by ARNOLD John R.*
Took over from ARNOLD John*
Sources: Baillie (1951)

ARNOLD & SONS James

e 1819 w 1908
1908   31 West Smithfield, London
1908   1,2 & 3 Giltspur St, London
              15 & 16 Giltspur St, London
B.apt Royal Veterinary College
Known to have sold: hydrometer
Sources: inst SM; PO

ARROWSMITH Aaron (I)

w 1790 d 1823
Globe M, Chart S, Hydrographer, Land surveyor,
Map S, Cartographer
              24 Rathbone Place, Oxford St,
              London
              10 Soho Square, London
1790   Castle St, Long Acre, London
1799   5 Charles St, London
Succeeded by ARROWSMITH Aaron (II)*

Uncle of ARROWSMITH John*
b 1750 at Winston, Durham; d 1823
Sources: H; Kt; JAC; DNB; Taylor (1966) p.279

ARROWSMITH Aaron (II)

w 1823–1832
Globe M, Hydrographer
1823–1832   10 Soho Square, London
Took over from ARROWSMITH Aaron (I)*
Succeeded by ARROWSMITH Samuel*
R. apt, Hydrographer to George IV, 1823
Sources PRO: LC3/69 p.54; Kt; PO

ARROWSMITH John

w 1839–1873
Globe M, Hydrographer
1839–1861   10 Soho Square, London
1862–1873   35 Hereford Square, London
Took over from ARROWSMITH Samuel*
Nephew of ARROWSMITH Aaron (I)*
b 1790 d 1873; founding FRGS 1830
Sources: Pg; PO; DNB

ARROWSMITH Samuel

w 1833 d 1839
Globe M, Hydrographer
1833–1839   10 Soho Square, London
Took over from ARROWSMITH Aaron (II)*
Succeeded by ARROWSMITH John*
R.apt, Hydrographer to Victoria
Sources: Pg; PO

ARSTALL George

w 1807–1821
Scale M, Hydro M
1809–1815   (Manufactory) 1 Temple Court,
              Liverpool
1810   29 Pembroke Place, Liverpool
1813   32 Pembroke Place, Liverpool
1816   43 Pembroke Place, Liverpool
1821   Bank Buildings, 50 Castle St,
              Liverpool
Associated with DICAS & ARSTALL*
Husband of ARSTALL Mary*
Sources: G; H; LM index

ARSTALL Mary – see DICAS Mary*

ARUNDELL William

w 1736–1750
Math IM, Ivory turner, Spec M
Alternative name: ARRUNDELL
1736   Aldersgate St, London
1743   Rose & Rainbow Court, Aldersgate
              St, London
Guild: Farriers, fr by purchase1736
Had apprentice:
JONES Robert 1739
SAUNDERS Thomas 1743
ARUNDELL John, son of Benjamin, 1743/4
LEWIS Joseph* 1743/4
WHEELER William 1750
Sources: GL: FRC 5523/1, 5526/1, 5526/2; CH:
12823/5 p.102; Daily Ad 5 Apr 1743

ASHBY C. B.

w 1851
Baro M, Thermo M

1851   3 Green Terrace, New River Head,
           London
Sources: Wk

ASHBY Samuel
w 1757
IM
1757   Red Lion St, Holborn, London
Had apprentice SAUNDERS James ?★ 1757
Sources: PRO: IR 1/21 (AM)

ASHE Thomas
w 1618
Trade not known, but master of a Spec M
           London
Guild: Brewers, fr 1617/18
Son of ASHE Robert, yeoman, of Shepshed, Leics
Apprenticed to POLSON Richard★ 1609/10
Had apprentice JENKINSON John★ 1618
Sources: GL: BREW 5445/12 -13

ASHLEY Thomas
fl 1749
Math IM, Optician
           Cranbourne Alley, Westminster,
           London
           Ye Golden Spectacles, Sidney's Alley
           near Leicester Fields, London
Sources: BM: Heal 105/2; Taylor (1966) p.197

ASHMORE William
w 1825–1850
Spec M, Telescope M, Optical IM, Optician
1837   17 Fitzwilliam St, Sheffield
1839–1841   103 Fargate, Sheffield
1841   101 Fargate, Sheffield
1850   Optical Works, 104 Fargate, near
           Burgess St, Sheffield
Succeeded by LEEDHAM & ROBINSON
Partnership ASHMORE & OSBORNE★
Sources: Pg; R; Rg; Wh

ASHMORE & OSBORNE
w 1825–1837
Optician, Spec M, Optical IM
1825–1837   42 Burgess St, Sheffield
Partnership of:
ASHMORE William★ and
OSBORNE Thomas P.G.★
Sources: Ge; Pg; Wh

ASHWELL Peter
d 1757
Math IM
1757   Strand, London
Sources: *Lloyds Evening Post* 7 Dec 1757

ASKEY Thomas
w 1808–1835
Optician, Brace M, Spec M
1808–1818   77 Litchfield St, Birmingham
1829–1835   80 Litchfield St, Birmingham
Sources: H; Pg; West; Wr

ASTILL Susannah
w 1795–1797
Scale M
1795–1797   10 Butcher Row, Temple Bar, London

Guild: Blacksmiths
Wife of ASTILL William★
Took over from ASTILL & PARTRIDGE★
See also
ASTILL & KING★
ASTILL & PAYNE★
Known to have sold: balance
Sources: GL: BKC 2881/16 (MAC); Kt

ASTILL William
w 1776–1788
Scale M
           191 High Holborn, near Drury Lane,
           London
           The King's Arms in Butcher Row,
           Temple Bar, London
           Barbican, London
1781–1785   10 Butcher Row, Temple Bar,
           London
Guild: Blacksmiths, fr 1776
Husband of ASTILL Susannah
Apprenticed to GOODMAN John★ 1769
Had apprentice:
WYNN John★ 1776
KEYS Thomas 1779
PRICKETT James Nathaniel 1782
STEVENSON Samuel 1783
NEWMAN James William 1784
TROUT Thomas 1786
HIATT William 1786
PAYNE Benjamin Matthew★ 1788
Succeeded by ASTILL & PARTRIDGE★
See also
ASTILL & KING★
ASTILL & PAYNE★
R.apt Geo.III 1781; d by 1790
Known to have sold: balance
Sources: GL: BKC 2881/15–16, 2886/5; By; inst
& TCd SM Wellcome (MAC)

ASTILL & KING
w 1798–1799
Scale M
1798–1799   23 Newcastle St, Strand, London
Associated with
ASTILL Susannah★
ASTILL William★
ASTILL & PARTRIDGE★
Same premises as ASTILL & PAYNE★
Sources: Ld (MAC)

ASTILL & PARTRIDGE
w 1790–1795
Scale M
1790–1795   10 Butcher Row, Temple Bar,
           London
Took over from ASTILL William★
Succeeded by ASTILL Susannah★
Associated with
ASTILL & KING★
ASTILL & PAYNE★
Known to have sold: balance
Sources: Boyle; Kt; Ld; Sheppard & Musham
(1975) no.61 (MAC)

ASTILL & PAYNE
w 1798–1803
Scale M

1798–1803   23 Newcastle St, Strand, London
Associated with
ASTILL William★
ASTILL Susannah★
ASTILL & PARTRIDGE★
Same premises as ASTILL & KING★
Sources: Kt; Ld (MAC)

ASTON Isaac (I)
w 1811–1840
Rule M, Math IM
1811   23 Prince's St, Soho, London
1814–1840   25 Compton St, Soho, London
Succeeded by ASTON Mrs★, his widow
Sources: H; Kt; Pg; R (JAC)

ASTON Isaac (II)
w 1851–1870
Rule M
1851–1870   25 Old Compton St, Soho, London
Succeeded by ASTON & MANDER
See also ASTON Mrs★
Sources: PO; Wk

ASTON Joseph
w 1815–1818
Compass M, Plater
1815–1818   Coleshill St, Birmingham
Succeeded by ASTON Thomas (I)★
Sources: Pg; Wr

ASTON Mrs.
w 1841–1842
Rule M
1841–1842   25 Old Compton St, Soho, London
Took over from ASTON Isaac (I)★
See also ASTON Isaac (II)★
Sources: R

ASTON Sampson
w 1833–1870
Rule M, Bacon S
1835–1841   1 Jennen's Row, St.Bartholomew
           Square, Birmingham
1850   Masshouse Lane, Birmingham
Known to have sold: rule
Sources: Pg; Sl; Phlps 28 Oct 1982 lot 106

ASTON Samuel
w 1785–1820
Rule M
1785–1787   Cheapside, Birmingham
1801   5 Water St, Birmingham
1809–1818   Birchole St, Birmingham
See also ASTON Thomas (I)★
Sources: H; Pg; Pye

ASTON Thomas (I)
w 1818–1850
Rule M
1818   Coleshill St, Birmingham
1825–1829   20 Bartholomew Row, Birmingham
1835   Jenner's Row, Birmingham
1850   25½ Willis St, Birmingham
1850   Willis St, Birmingham
Took over from ASTON Samuel★
See also: ASTON Thomas (II)★
Sources: Pg; West

ASTON Thomas (II)
w 1841–1862
Rule M
1841–1856   17 Jenner's Row, Birmingham
1862   17, 18, Jenner's Row, Birmingham
See also: ASTON Thomas (I)★
Sources Mor; Sl

ASTON William
w 1770
Rule M
1770   Birmingham
Sources: *Aris's Birmingham Gazette* 27 Aug 1770

ATKINS George
w 1807–1814
Math IM
   162 Fenchurch St, London
1807   136 Fenchurch St, London
1811–1812   8 Little Charlotte St, Blackfriars Rd, London
1819   (Residence) Hornsey Rd, Islington, London
Guild: Clockmakers, fr 1788, Master 1845
Apprenticed to WALDRON John 1781
Son of ATKINS Francis, Clock M, of London
Had apprentice:
SMITH William Charles 1814
ATKINS Samuel Elliott, his son, 1821
Partnership BROCKBANK & ATKINS★
Took over from ATKINS Robert★
Succeeded by BROCKBANK & ATKINS★
See also ATKINS & CO. George★
b 1767 d 1855; pat. compass 1819
Known to have sold: compass, hydrometer
Sources: GL: CKC 2720/2, 2720/1; H; Woodcroft (1854); inst SM; Baillie (1951); Atkins (1931)

ATKINS Robert
w 1801–1806
Math IM
1801–1806   136 Fenchurch St, London
Succeeded by ATKINS George★
Partnership QUIN & ATKINS★
Pat. hydrometer 1803
Known to have sold: hydrometer, slide rule
Sources: H; Kt; PO; Woodcroft (1854); McConnell (1993) p.10–12,61

ATKINS & CO. George
w 1813–1822
Optician, Math IM
1813   Whitehorse Court, Borough, London
1815–1822   4 Churchyard Alley, Borough, London
1817   Tooley St, Southwark, London
See also ATKINS George★
Sources: J; Kt

ATKINSON James (I)
w 1668–1717
Math IM
   Redriff Wall, near Cherry Garden Stairs, Rotherhithe, London
   Near the Griffin, east side of St.Saviour's Dock, London
[presumably alternative renderings of the addresses below]
1673   East side of St.Saviour's Dock, over against the Griffin, London
1673   Cherry Garden Stairs on Redriff Wall, London
Guild: Clockmakers, fr 1667/8, Joiners ? [said to be free of JC in CKC records, but not traced]
Had apprentice:
FLOWER George 1670
PERKINS Eysum★ 1670
BEARD Cornelius 1672 by t/o
from THOROWGOOD Edward★
COLLINS Peter★ 1679/80
DANIELL Edward 1686
Succeeded by ATKINSON James (II)★
Took over from WAKELY Andrew★
Editor
Sources: GL: CKC 2710/1, 3939; LGaz 30 Apr 1673; Good (1717) title p.; Brown J (1979b) p.27

ATKINSON James (II)
w 1724–1728
Math IM
   St. Saviour's Dock, 21 Cherry Garden Stairs, Rotherhithe, London
Took over from ATKINSON James (I)★
Known to have sold: back-staff
Sources: Good (1717) title p., p.80; DJB; Taylor (1954) p.296

ATKINSON John (I)
d 1673
Compass M
   Harwich
Sources: Taylor (1954) p.240

ATKINSON John (II)
w 1764–1788
Math IM
1764–1788   Whitechapel, London
Guild: Grocers, fr 1764
Apprenticed to:
WRIGHT George★ 1736
t/o to FARMER John★ 1739
Had apprentice:
BOWLES Daniel 1764
t/o 1767 to RUST Richard★
MANSFIELD Benjamin★ 1788
Sources: Brown J (1979a) p.40,43

ATKINSON John J.
w 1849–1887
Photo IM, Philo IM, Theatrical Ornament M
1849–1887   33 Manchester St, Liverpool
1857–1880   37 Manchester St, Liverpool
Succeeded by ATKINSON & SON J. J.
Sources: G; K; LM index (MAC)

ATKINSON Joseph
w 1747 d 1788
Optical IS, Book S, Stationer
1769–1774   Flesh Market, Newcastle upon Tyne
1774–1788   Groat Market, Newcastle upon Tyne
Apprenticed to BARBER Joseph★
Employed WHITEFIELD Joseph
Succeeded by ATKINSON Elizabeth
Sources: Hunt (1975) (MAC)

AUBERT & LINTON
e 1825 w 1863
Chrono M, Watch M, Clock M
   252 Regent St, near Oxford St, London W
Sources: Calvert (1971) p.12; Loomes (1976)

AUBONE Daniel & Thomas
w 1836–1838
Compass M, Spy-glass M, Opticians, Math IM
1836   44 Quayside, Newcastle upon Tyne
1838   Broad-garth, 44 Quayside, Newcastle upon Tyne
Sources: Ric

AUGUSTUS John Anthony
w 1830
Math IM
1830   Church St, Falmouth
Sources: Pg

AULT John
w 1770–1777
Compass M
1770–1775   62 Moor St, Birmingham
1777   42 & 43 Park St, Birmingham
Sources: PR; SA; Sy

AULT Samuel
w 1770–1785
Compass M , Victualler
1775   Deritend, Birmingham
1785   Alcester St, Birmingham
Known to have sold: dividers
Sources: PR; Pye; SA; Sy; inst (s)

AULT Widow
w 1780
Compass M
1780   60 Park St, Birmingham
Sources: PR

AULT William
w 1785
Victualler, Compass M
1785   Bradford St, Birmingham
Sources: Pye

AUST William
w 1849–1851
Math IM
1849–1851   15 Huntley St, Tottenham Court Road, London
Sources: PO

AUSTIN Aaron
w 1775–1805
Clock M, Watch M, Glaziers vice M, Smith, Farrier
1775–1800   95 Old Market, Bristol
1803–1805   Pennywell Lane, Bristol
Succeeded by AUSTIN Moses★
Known to have sold: balance
Sources: inst SM, Wellcome; Mat

AUSTIN Frederick
w 1851–1855
Math IM

1851–1855   46 Bridport Place, Hoxton, London
Sources: PO; Wk

AUSTIN John (I)
w 1809–1811
Spec M
1809–1811   Barford St, Birmingham
Sources: H

AUSTIN John (II)
w 1818–1820
Math IM
1818–1820   2 Essex Quay, Dublin
Sources: Burnett & Morrison-Low (1989) p.120

AUSTIN Moses
w 1798–1817
Glaziers vice M, Scale M
1799–1800   2 Elbroad St, Bristol
1801   Captain Cary's Lane, Bristol
1803–1815   95 Old Market St, Bristol
1816–1817   25 Old Market St, Bristol
Took over from AUSTIN Aaron★
Sources: Mat

AUSTIN Samuel
w 1714–1745
Math IM
1721   Little Britain, London
1727   St.Botolph without Aldgate, London
1738   The Globe on London Bridge, London
Guild: Stationers, fr 1714
Apprenticed to BUSH Joseph★ 1702/3
Had apprentice:
WHITEHEAD William 1714
KNOWLES James 1715
TURLAND Henry★ 1720/1
READ Adam 1721
STEDMAN Christopher (I)★
HIGGINBOTHAM Joseph★ 1727
t/o to FRANKLIN Thomas★ 1729
Succeeded by STEDMAN Christopher (I)★
Probably d by 1750
Sources: GL: CH 12876/4; McKenzie (1978) p.9–10,60

AVERN Edward
w 1785
Compass M, Pincer M
1783   77 Park St, Birmingham
Sources: Pye

AVERY William & Thomas
w 1817–1894
Scale M
1817–1894   Birmingham
1839   32 Hatton Garden, London
1870–1894   Atlas Foundry, West Bromwich
Took over from BALDEN Joseph★
Succeeded by
AVERY & CO. LTD W. & T.
AVERY William senior d 1843 and his sons, also
William & Thomas, took over
Known to have sold: balance
Sources: Pg; Broadbent (1949) (MAC); Turner G
(1983a) p.67

AYLER John
w 1804
Scale M
1804   Cow Lane, London
Sources: Stat: STC, MF Ap (MAC)

AYLIFFE Thomas
w 1662
Known to have sold: gunner's mouthpiece
Sources: inst (p)

AYRES Benjamin
w 1731
Math IM
Alternative name: EYRES, EYARS
1731   London
1743–1751   Amsterdam
1757   At Mr Bostock's, Feathers Court, Drury Lane, London
Apprenticed to SISSON Jonathan★ 1724
Husband of SISSON Ann, m 1731
R.apt Prince of Orange 1749, b.apt Dutch
Admiralties 1749
Known to have sold: compass (magnetic)
Sources: inst SM; Leopold (1993) p.395–402

AYSCOUGH James
w 1748–1759
Optician, Math IM, Optical IM, Phil IM
1749   Great Golden Spectacles in Ludgate St, near St. Paul's, London
1751   Golden Spectacles & Quadrant, Ludgate St, London
1759   Great Golden Spectacles & Quadrant, Ludgate St, near St. Paul's, London
   Sir Isaac Newton's Head, Ludgate St, London
Guild: Spectaclemakers, fr 1740
Son of AYSCOUGH James, cleric, of Highworth, Wilts
Husband of AYSCOUGH Martha★
Partnership with MANN James (II)★ 1743–1747
Apprenticed to MANN James (II)★ 1732/3
Had apprentice:
PURCELL James 1750
EDLYNE Samuel Nicoll 1756 by t/o
from NAIRNE Edward★
Took over from MANN & AYSCOUGH★
Succeeded by AYSCOUGH Martha★ trading under
the name of AYSCOUGH James, then by LINNELL
Joseph★
d 1759; Master SMC 1752–1753
Known to have sold: barometer, thermometer,
microscope, octant
Instruments advertised: full range
Sources: GL: SMC 5213/2 p.253, 5213/3
pp.16,151,179,189,213, 6029; Daily Ad 12 Sep
1749, Nov 1759 (JRM); Calvert (1971) p.12,
pl.6,7,32; Buckley (1935) p.428; Wallis P (1976)
p.291–92

AYSCOUGH Martha
w 1759–1767
Optician
Alternative name: Trade card in James Ayscough's name
1759   Great Golden Spectacles &
   Quadrant, Ludgate St, London
1767   33 Ludgate St, London
Took over from AYSCOUGH James★
Succeeded by LINNELL Joseph★
Sources: Mort; Daily Ad 7 Nov 1759; Calvert
(1971) pl.7, 32

BACKWELL William (I)
w 1795–1802
Math IM , Compass M
Alternative name: BACKWELL Senior
1795–1811   Tash St, Gray's Inn Rd, London
1802   38 Tash St, Gray's Inn Lane, London
1821–1831   6 Tash St, Gray's Inn Lane, London
Father of BACKWELL William (II)★
Had apprentice ELLIOTT William (II)★
Sources: H; PO; ChrSK 14 Apr 1988 lot 209;
EBA: indenture of ELLIOTT William (II)★

BACKWELL William (II)
w 1816–1831
Math Instrument Manufacturer, Optician
Alternative name: William jnr; William Isaac
1816–1817   92 Long Lane, West Smithfield, London
1816–1822   6 Long Lane, West Smithfield, London
Guild: Stationers, fr 1818
Son of BACKWELL William (I)★
Apprenticed to WELLINGTON Alexander★, 1802
Had apprentice TIPPLE John Thomas 1818, t/o
1820 to TIPPLE Thomas
bap 1788
Sources: K; PO; Und; Stat: STC, Memo bk p.55;
bap, St. Andrew, Holborn

BACON James
w 1825
Math IM
1825   130 Chancery Lane London
Sources: LMIR (AM)

BACON John
w 1825
Optician
1825   53 Trueman St, Liverpool
Sources: LM index (MAC)

BACON William
w 1805
Compass M
1805   12 Bostock St, Old Gravel Lane, London
Guild: Masons, fr 1774
Apprenticed to BAILEY William★ 1766
Son of BACON Charles, peruke maker, of
Wapping, London
Sources: H; GL: MC 5304/4, 5304/5, 5312
(MAC)

BADCOCK William Geagle
w 1779–1785
Scale M
1784–1785   17 Butcher Hall Lane, London
1793   (Residence) St.Ann's Lane, London
Guild: Blacksmiths, fr 1775
Apprenticed to READ Samuel★ 1768
Son of BADCOCK Geagle, cook, of Oxford

Had apprentice:
WOODAGE George Cave★ 1779 by t/o
from BLACKMAN Solomon★
GODDARD Howell★ 1779, t/o 1784
to DEGRAVE Charles (I)★
Known to have sold: balance
Sources: GL: BKC 2881/15–16 (MAC), BW; By;
inst (p)

BADDELEY John
w 1784
[Math IM]
Alternative name: BADDELY
            Albrighton
            Wolverhampton
Known to have sold: barometer, level, microscope,
telescope
Sources: Talbot (1784) (AW); Sby 2 Feb 1980,
Sby(Ch) 8 Sep 1981 (MAC); Phlps 26 Jan 1983 lot
165

BAGNALL Robert
w 1773–1775
Compass M
1775   63 Moor St, Birmingham
Same premises as BAGNALL William★
Sources: Sy

BAGNALL William
w 1770–1780
Compass M
1770–1780   63 Moor St, Birmingham
1785   Walmer Lane, Birmingham
Same premises as BAGNALL Robert★
Sources: PR; Pye; SA

BAGOT T.
w 1810
Surveyor, Instrument S
1810   Snow Hill, Birmingham
Sources: Birmingham Central Library: unidentified
newspaper cutting 28 May 1810

BAHARIE A.
a 1840–1860
[Math IM]
            7 Lawrence St, Sunderland
Succeeded by BAHARIE & SON A★ by 1871
Known to have sold: octant supplied by
CRICHTON John★
Sources: inst NMM, SUNM; Chs; Holbrook
(1992) p.211

BAILEY H.
w 1841
Math IM
1841   Bennett St, Burton Crescent,
            London
Attended London Mechanics Institute 1841
Sources: LMIR (AM)

BAILEY John
w 1627–1634
Spec M
Alternative name: BALY, BAYLIE, BAYLEY,
BAILIE, BAILLIE
1629–1634   London
Guild: Brewers & Spectaclemakers

Son of BAILEY Robert, farmer, of Houghton,
Leics
Apprenticed to THOMPSON John (VII)★ 1615
Had apprentice:
WORSLEY George★ 1626/7
SPENCER William (I)★
BRADSHAWE Robert 1634
fr BREW 1624; translated from BREW to SMC
1634
Sources: CLRO: Ald 49 fol.14; GL: BREW
5445/13–15

BAILEY John William
w 1846–1871
Optician
1859–1871   162 Fenchurch St, London (EC)
Guild: Grocers, fr 1844
Son of BAILEY John, Shoe M, d
Apprenticed to GARDNER James★ 1837
Part of apprenticeship money paid by Christ's
Hospital
Known to have sold: sextant,
microscope-accessory
Sources: GL: GC 11598/8; PO; Turner G (1989)
p.282; Webster R & M (1988)

BAILEY William
w 1759–1794
Math IM, Watch Finisher
1770–1782   Old Gravel Lane, Wapping, London
1785   53 Old Gravel Lane, London
1790–1794   57 Old Gravel Lane, London
Guild: Masons, fr 1756
Apprenticed to GREGORY Henry (I)★ 1749
Son of BAILEY/BAYLEY William, wax chandler,
of London, of MC
Had apprentice:
REYNOLDS Jervice 1759
MUDGE John 1763
CANTREY Spicer 1765
BACON William★ 1766
HARRIS Francis 1770
COOK William [George]★ 1782
Sources: GL: MC 5304/3, 5304/4 5308, 5310,
5312 (MAC); BW; By; W

BAILLIE William
w 1833
Hydrostatic Bubble M
1833   19 Saltmarket, Glasgow
Sources: Bryden (1972) p.43

BAINES Robert Raines
w 1823
Nautical Log M, Baker
1823   Wincolmlee, Hull
Sources: Bn

BAKER Benjamin (I)
w c.1770
Math IM
            London
Son of BAKER Edward (I)★
See also BAKER Benjamin (II)★ (possibly the same
person)
See also PALMER William★
Sources: GL: Edward Baker's Letters, 16927 (JRM)

BAKER Benjamin (II)
w 1805
Math IM
1805   3 Pinners Court, Broad St, London
            Wall, London
See also BAKER Benjamin (I)★ (possibly the same
person)
Sources: H

BAKER Charles
w 1851–1909
Optical IM, Math IM, Surveying IS, Surgical IM
            243 & 244 High Holborn, WC
            London
            244 & 245 High Holborn, London
1851–1858   244 High Holborn, (1st period)
            London
1859–1878   244 & 244a High Holborn, WC
            London
1881–1909   244 High Holborn, WC, (2nd
            period) London
e 1765; agent for Leitz, Reichert and Zeiss by 1895
Known to have sold: full range of instruments
Sources: PO; Anderson et al (1990) p.5–7; Cat.
MHS

BAKER Edward (I)
w 1744
[Math IM]
            London
Guild: Merchant Taylors, fr 1728
Son of BAKER John, barber, of Colney, Herts
Apprenticed to COLE Benjamin (I)★ 1720
Had apprentice BAKER Edward (II)★, his son,
1744/5
Husband of COLE Martha, daughter of his Master,
m 1728
b 1705 d 1779
Sources: GL: MTC MF 319,324 (MAC); Edward
Baker's papers, 16927, 16938 (JRM); JRM

BAKER Edward (II)
w 1760–1780
Math IM
1779   10 New Street Square, Shoe Lane,
            London
1780   New Street, Fetter Lane, London
Guild: Merchant Taylors, fr 1752
Apprenticed to BAKER Edward (I)★, his father,
1744/5
Had apprentice:
LAY James 1760
BAKER Edward (III)★, his son, 1771
Father of BAKER Joseph s 1780 STC
b 1730 d 1797
Sources: GL: MTC MF 319,320,324 (MAC);
Edward Baker's Papers 16927, 16938 (JRM); Sun
11936/272 no.410014; JRM; McKenzie (1978)
p.83

BAKER Edward (III)
w 1782
Drawing IM
1778   New St, Shoe Lane, London
Guild: [Merchant Taylors]
Apprenticed to BAKER Edward (II)★, his father,
1771
b 1757; ensign in militia in Captain Cole's

Company 1779 [see COLE Benjamin (II)★]
Sources: GL: MTC MF 320,324; Edward Baker's
Papers 16927; JRM

BAKER Edward (IV)
w 1822–1857
Chrono M
1822–1825	33 White Lion St, Pentonville, London
1825–1831	6 Angel Terrace, Pentonville, London
1831–1851	11 Angel Terrace, Pentonville, London

See also BAKER Thomas★
Sources: CUL: RGO 1143 fol. 3–7; PO; Loomes
(1976)

BAKER Henry (I)
w 1841–1876
Rule M
1841	Court, Cecil Row, Birmingham
1850	Court, 61 Cecil St, Birmingham
1850	Back of 61 Cecil St, Birmingham
1862	41 New Town Row, Birmingham

Sources: Mor; Pg; Sl

BAKER Henry (II)
w 1848–1859
Hydrometer M; Gauging IM; Phil IM;
Saccharometer M; Optician
| 1841–1842 | 23 Hatton Garden, London |
| 1849–1855 | 90 Hatton Garden, London |

Ex.1851; prob the BAKER Henry, experimental
glass blower, who attended classes at London
Mechanics' Institute 1841–1842
Sources: PO; LMIR(AM); Turner G (1983a) p.309

BAKER John
w 1740
Instrument M
　　Dublin?
Had apprentice MAY Edward 1740
Sources: KH (WS)

BAKER Thomas
w 1834–1835
Chrono M
　　6 Angel Terrace, Pentonville, London
　　Upper Stamford St, London
See also BAKER Edward (IV)★
Pat. improved chronometer 1834
Known to have sold: chronometer
Sources: Woodcroft (1854); Taylor (1966) p.443

BAKER W.
w 1843
Meteorological IM
| 1843 | London |

Attended London Mechanics Institute 1843
Sources: LMIR(AM)

BAKEWELL Isabella
w 1828–1829
Math IM, Rule M
| 1828–1829 | 42 Loveday St, Birmingham |

See also BAKEWELL Richard★
Sources: Pg

BAKEWELL Richard
w 1797–1826
Rule M, Math IM, Dog collar M
| 1797–1820 | Loveday St, Birmingham |
| 1825–1826 | 49 Loveday St, Birmingham |

Succeeded by TROW Isaac★
See also BAKEWELL Isabella★
Known to have sold: protractor, slide rule
Sources: Chp; Pg; Pye; Wr; inst (s)

BALCHIN Peter
w 1770–1774
Tin Plate Worker
1770	Soho, London
1774	As Peter Balchin & Co., Dean St, Soho, London
1774	Compton St, Soho, London

Guild: Tinplate Workers
Had apprentice:
SEARCH James★ 1770 by t/o
from BENNETT John (I)★
DICKER John 1759
SCOTT John 1771 by t/o from OWEN Joshua
TWC
ROBINSON William 1772
BALCHIN James, his son, 1774
d 1775; Kt Directory, 1774, has Peter Balchin &
Co. oilmen
Sources: GL:TWC 7135/5 fol 13; 7137/5 fol.
108,126,128; McKenzie (1978) p.15; Kt

BALDEN Joseph
w 1791 d 1813
Steelyard M, Scale M
| 1791–1793 | Moat Row, Birmingham |
| 1797–1812 | 11 Digbeth, Birmingham |

Took over from BEACH Thomas★
Partnership BALDEN & WHITFIELD ★
Succeeded by AVERY William & Thomas★
Known to have sold: balance
Sources: Chp; H; Pye; Sy; Wd; Wr; Avery Mu,
Warley

BALDEN & WHITFIELD
w 1785–1788
Scale M
| 1785–1788 | Birmingham |

Partnership BALDEN Joseph★ and
WHITFIELD Edward★
Sources: PR; Pye

BALDOCK Richard
w 1721
Math IM
| 1721 | Next the 3 Tuns in Shoe Lane, London |

Guild: Broderers, fr 1721
Apprenticed to ROBERTS William (I)★ 1705
Son of BALDOCK Richard, grocer, of Arlesey,
Bedford
Sources: GL: BROD 14663/1, 14664/1;
Crawforth (1987) p.338

BALE David
w 1804–1805
Math IM by 1804, freed as file cutter
| 1784 | 15 Catherine Wheel Alley, Whitechapel, London |

| 1804 | Pennington St, Wapping, London |
| 1805 | 101 Pennington St, Old Gravel Lane, Wapping, London |

Guild: Cordwainers, fr 1784
Son of BALE Thomas, file cutter, d, of London
Apprenticed to FULLER John Ayres, file cutter,
1777
Had apprentice SCATLIFF Daniel (II)★ 1804
See also
BALE & WOODWARD ★
MITCHELL & BALE ★
Sources: GL: CORD 7357/4, 24139/1, 24140/1;
H

BALE & WOODWARD
c. 1845
　　London
Known to have sold: globe
Sources: ChrSK Dec 1984 (MAC)

BALERNO Domenico
w 1846–1853
Baro M
Alternative name: BALERNA , BALLERNA
| 1846–1853 | 14 Yeaman Shore, Dundee |

Known to have sold: barometer, hygrometer,
thermometer
Sources: Bryden (1972) p.43; Phlps 11 Nov 1981
lot 1; Sby 28 Feb 1985 lot 237

BALLETT Leonard
w 1743–1761
Spec M
Alternative name: BALLET
　　London
Guild: Spectaclemakers, fr 1742
Son of BALLETT Elizabeth, widow, of East
Smithfield, London
Apprenticed to COX William (I)★ 1733
Had apprentice:
METCALFE William 1743
JONES John (I)★ 1751
WARBISS Joseph 1761
Apprentice binding paid for by Trustees of the
Charity School, East Smithfield
Sources: GL: SMC 5213/2; 5213/3
p.51,64,69,162+

BALSARY G.
a 1775–1820
See also BALSARY & CO . G.★
Known to have sold: barometer, hygrometer, spirit
level, thermometer
Sources: ChrSk Dec 1984 (MAC)

BALSARY & CO. G.
a 1800–1850
　　London
Associated with BALSARY G.★
Known to have sold: barometer
Sources: Sby(Ch) 9 Oct 1986 (MAC)

BAMPTON Thomas
w 1779–1786
Optician, Glass Cutter
| 1779 | Bride Lane Court in the parish of St Bride, London |
| 1783 | Bride Lane, Fleet St, London |

1786   8 Bridge St, London
Guild: [Spectaclemakers], Pewterers, fp 1775
Son of BAMPTON William of London
Apprenticed to NEVILL William★ 1768, SMC
Had apprentice:
MITCHELL George 1779
WEEKS Thomas (II) 1783
Sources: GL: PWC 7102, 7096/2; STTP 2934
fol.81; SMC 5213/3

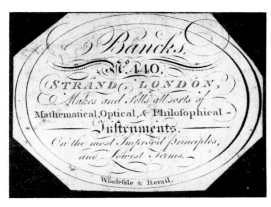

BANCKS Anthony Oldiss

w 1793–1796
Optician
1794   25 Piccadilly, London
1796   440 Strand, London
Guild: [Turners]Joiners, fp 1792
Son of BANCKS Robert (I), joiner, d, of London
Brother of BANCKS Robert (II)★
Apprenticed to KITCHINGMAN John★ 1780, TC
Had apprentice:
HUGGINS William Thomas 1793
BENSON Frederick 1796
Sources: GL: JC 8051/4, 8052/8, 8055/3–5; TC
3302/3; Crawforth (1987) p.347

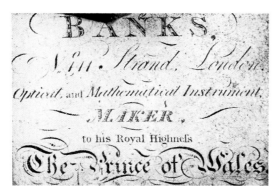

BANCKS Robert (II)

w 1796–1831
Optician, Optical IM, Math IM
Alternative name: BANKS
1795–1804 440 Strand, London
1805–1830 441 Strand, London
1838   (Residence?) Brompton Row,
     Knightsbridge, London
1792   25 Piccadilly, London
Guild: Joiners, fp 1803
Son of BANCKS Robert (I), joiner, d, of London

Brother of BANCKS Anthony Oldiss★
Had apprentice:
SAMPSON George Bentley 1803
JACQUERY D. 1829
Prob worked for BANCKS Anthony Oldiss★
Took over from BANCKS Anthony Oldiss★
Succeeded by BANCKS & SON Robert★
R.apt Prince of Wales; R.apt Geo.IV 1820,
Wm.IV 1830
Known to have sold: telescope, theodolite,
waywiser
Instruments advertised: microscope
Sources: GL: JC 8055/3; PRO: LC3/69 p.9,166;
BM: Banks 105/3; H; Ld; Pg; ChrSK 14 Apr 1988
lot 5; Crawforth (1987) p.347

BANCKS & SON Robert

w 1831–1834
Optician
Alternative name: BANKS
1831–1834 119 New Bond St, London
Took over from BANCKS Robert (II)★
Sources: Bn; PO

BANGER Edward

w pt 1696–1708
Clock M
c.1696–1708 Dial and Three Crowns, Corner of
     Water Lane, Fleet St, London
Guild: Clockmakers, fr 1695
Son of BANGER Edward, joiner, of North
Petherton, Somerset
Apprenticed to TOMPION Thomas★ 1687 by t/o
from ASHBY Joseph
Had apprentice:
ELMES Richard 1696
HIGGINS Banger 1715, t/o 1720 to WILD William
of LSC
Husband of KENT Margaret, niece of TOMPION
Thomas★, m 1694
Partnership: TOMPION & BANGER ★
d 1720
Sources: GL: CKC 2710/2; Loomes (1981b); King
& Millburn (1978) p.124,126

BANKES James

w 1848–1864
Baro M, Gold balance M, Engraver, Watch M,
Photographic artist
1848–1864 Moor St, Ormskirk, Lancs
Sources: K; Sl

BANKS - (I)

a 1760–1780
     Great Queen St, Lincoln's Inn,
     London
Known to have sold: orrery made by MARTIN
Benjamin★
Sources: inst (pv)

BANKS - (II)

c 1755
     Kendal
Known to have sold: balance
Sources: inst (pv)

BANNER F. E.

a 1800–1850

Optician
     Banbury, Oxon
Known to have sold: barometer, hygrometer, spirit
level, thermometer
Sources: inst (s)

BANYON Henry

w 1847
Optician
1847   Post Office St, Norwich
Sources: K

BARAZONI Anthony

w 1840
Optician
1840   23 Lodge Walk, Aberdeen
Sources: Bryden (1972) p.44

BARBER Isaac

w 1676 d by 1698
Spec M
     London
Guild: Spectaclemakers, fr 1676
Son of BARBER Howell, husbandman, d, of
Stourton, Warwicks
Apprenticed to HAWES John★ 1668
Had apprentice HASELWOOD Richard 1686
Fined by SMC for selling bad spectacles 1676 &
1686
Sources: GL: SMC 5213/1, 5213/2 p.11–12

BARBER Joseph

w 1740 d 1781
Optical IS
1740   Sandhill, Newcastle upon Tyne
1743–1749 At the Head of Flesh Market on the
     High Bridge, Newcastle upon Tyne
1753–1781 Amen Corner, Newcastle upon
     Tyne
Father of BARBER Martin
Had apprentice:
ATKINSON Joseph★
HUMBLE Edward★
Succeeded by BARBER & SON ★
Sources: Hunt (1975) (MAC)

BARBER Richard

w 1831–1837
Math IM, Optician
1831–1837 126 Chancery Lane, London
Known to have sold: balance
Sources: PO; R; Sheppard & Musham (1975)
no.244

BARBER Thomas

w 1817–1819
Optician
1817–1818 34 Princes St, Leicester Square,
     London
1819   17 Mortimer St, Cavendish Square,
     London
See also TAPLEE Seymore★
Sources: J; Kt; R; JAC

BARBER & SON Joseph (& Martin)

w 1778–1781
     Newcastle upon Tyne
Took over from BARBER Joseph★

Succeeded by BARBER Martin
Associated with HUMBLE Edward*
Sources: Hunt (1975) (MAC)

BARBON Peter
w 1809–1812
Optical IM
1809   4 Lothian St, Edinburgh
1810   18 Nicholson St, Edinburgh
1811–1812   77 Princes St, Edinburgh
See also BARBON & CO . S.*
Known to have sold: microscope
Sources: Bryden (1972) p.44; inst NMS

BARBON & CO.
a 1800–1860
     Fullwood's Rents, Holborn, London
Known to have sold: barometer
Sources: Goodison (1977) p.298

BARBON & CO. S.
a 1800–1850
     Edinburgh
See also BARBON Peter*
Known to have sold: barometer, thermometer
Sources: Goodison (1977) p.299

BARBONE Bartolomeo
w 1787
Math IM
1787   Little Turnstile, Holborn, London
Sources: GL: Sun 11936/342 no.531410

BARCLAY –
a 1700
Spec M
     Edinburgh
See also
BARCLAY Hugh*
BARCLAY William*
BARCLAY Adam*
Sources: Bryden (1972) p.44

BARCLAY Adam
d 1753
Math IM, Optical IM
     Edinburgh
Sources: Bryden (1972) p.22,36,44

BARCLAY Hugh
w 1727 d 1749
Watch M, Optical IM
     Edinburgh
Brother of BARCLAY William*
Sources: Bryden (1972) p.44

BARCLAY James
w 1819–1857
Chrono M, Watch M
1839   5 Jamaica Terrace, London
1846–1851   10 Jamaica Terrace, Commercial Rd, London
Sources: Pg; PO; Loomes (1976)

BARCLAY William
w 1731 d 1758
Optical IM
     Edinburgh

Brother of BARCLAY Hugh*
Sources: Bryden (1972) p.44

BARDIN Elizabeth (Miss)
w 1840–1859
Globe M
1840–1859   16 Salisbury Square, Fleet St, London
It is not clear if this was just a marketing name for the Edkins/ Bardin firm, or a separate business
Sources: PO; Millburn & Rössaak (1992) p.34–35

BARDIN Elizabeth Marriott
w 1821–1832
Globe M
1821–1839   16 Salisbury Square, Fleet St, London
Wife of EDKINS Samuel Sabine*
Granddaughter of BARDIN William *
Daughter of BARDIN Thomas M.*
Took over from BARDIN Thomas Marriott*
Succeeded by EDKINS Samuel Sabine*
Associated with BARDIN W. & T.M.*
b 1799; m 1832; d 1851
Sources: PO; Millburn & Rössaak (1992) pp.34–35

BARDIN Thomas Marriott
w 1798–1819
Globe M
1793   Hind Court, Fleet St, London
1798–1819   16 Salisbury Square, Fleet St, London
1805   4 Hind Court, Fleet St, London [possibly an error in guild records, as rate books suggest the Bardins moved from this address by 1795]
Guild: Girdlers, fr 1790
Apprenticed to BARDIN William*, his father, 1783
Had apprentice:
BARDIN Samuel by t/o from GSC 1794
VIRIT William Francis 1798
VIRIT John Stephens 1798
SOMERVILLE William 1805
Succeeded by BARDIN Elizabeth M.*, his daughter
Partnership: BARDIN & SON *
Took over from BARDIN & SON William* and BARDIN W. & T.M.*
b 1768 d 1819
Known to have sold: globe
Sources: Kt; Wil; GL: GDC 5801, 5802, 5813/3
Millburn & Rössaak (1992) pp.22,28,33–35

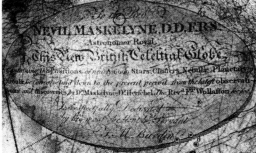

BARDIN W. & T.M.
w 1798–1800

Globe M
Alternative name: variant of BARDIN & SON *
1790–1795   4 Hind Court, Fleet St, London
1795–1798   16 Salisbury Square, Fleet St, London
Known to have sold: globe
Sources: inst NT, Knighthayes Court, Devon; Millburn & Rössaak (1992) p.33

BARDIN William
w 1783 d 1798
Globe M, Shoe M
Alternative name: BARDEN .
1776   1 Flying Horse Court, Fleet St, London
1782–1794   4 Hind Court, Fleet St, London
1795–1798   Salisbury Square, London
Guild: Leathersellers & Girdlers
Grandfather of BARDIN Elizabeth M.*
Had apprentice:
BARDIN Thomas Marriott*, his son, 1783
GATES John 1787
EDWARDS Robert 1791
HAZLEHURST John Samuel 1792
SMART William King 1797
Partnership
WRIGHT & BARDIN (informal ?)
BARDIN & SON William*
Succeeded by BARDIN & SON William*, also known as BARDIN W. & T.M.*
fr LSC 1775 by purchase; fr GDC 1776 by purchase
d 1798; owned property in Surrey and Essex let to tenants
Known to have sold: globe
Sources: Wil; LSH: LSC Fr; GL: GDC 5813/3; Millburn & Rössaak (1992)

BARDIN & SON William (& Thomas Marriott)
w 1790–1798
Globe M
1790–1794   4 Hind Court, Fleet St, London
1795–1798   16 Salisbury Square, Fleet St, London
Took over from BARDIN William*
Succeeded by BARDIN Thomas M.*
See also
BARDIN W. & T.M.
BARDIN Elizabeth M.
William d.1798; name Bardin & Son continued in directories to 1802
Sources: BW; H; Kt; Millburn & Rössaak (1992)

BARDIN & SONS
w 1816–1817
Globe M
Alternative name: Prob directory version only of BARDIN & SON
1816–1817   16 Salisbury Square, Fleet St, London
Sources: Und; Millburn & Rössaak (1992) p.33

BARELLI & CO. Joseph
a 1800
     Reading
Known to have sold: barometer, thermometer
Sources: Bolle (1982) p.156

BARETA Dominica
w 1785–1786
Math IM
        67 High Holborn, London
1785   258 High Holborn, London
Sources: GL: Sun 11936/327 no.500624 ,
11936/336 no.516701

BARINI P.
a 1780–1800
       York
Known to have sold: barometer, thermometer
Sources: inst (s)

BARKER Edward
w 1745
Math IM
1745   London
Had apprentice BROOKE Bernard 1745
Sources: LEP 25 Apr 1745

BARKER James
w 1838
Optician, Math IM, Phil IM
1838   18 Brewer St, King's Cross, London
Sources: Pg

BARKER William (I)
w 1711
Math IM
       London
Guild: [Grocers]
Apprenticed to WORGAN John★ 1700 t/o 1700/01
to HADDON William★
Sources: Brown J (1979a) p.28; Taylor (1954)
p.303; Wallis R & P (1993) p.8

BARKER William (II)
w 1728–1734
[Spec M]
       London
Guild: Spectaclemakers, fr 1724
Son of BARKER Richard, gardener, of Clifton,
Notts
Apprenticed to STERROP Jane★ 1716
Had apprentice: ADEY Josiah 1728, t/o 1733/4 to
JOHNSON John (II)★
Sources: GL: SMC 5213/2 p.98,146+

BARKER William (III)
w 1764 d 1786
Clock M, Gunsmith
1786   Wigan
Known to have sold: astronomical clock, barometer
Sources: King & Millburn (1978) p.139

BARLACE –
a 1780–1820
[Math IM]
       London
Known to have sold: sector
Sources: Sby 23 Jun 1987 (MAC)

BARLING Elizabeth
w 1826
Navigation Warehouse
1826   16 Limehouse Hole, Limehouse,
           London

Took over from BARLING W.H.★
See also BARLING Frederick★
Sources: Pg

BARLING Frederick
w 1836–1840
Navigation Warehouse
1836–1840   16 Emmett St, Limehouse, London
Sources: Pg

BARLING W. H.
w 1822–1824
Navigation Warehouse
1822–1824   Limehouse Hole, Limehouse,
            London
Succeeded by BARLING Elizabeth★
See also BARLING Frederick★
Sources: Pg: R (JAC)

BARNARDA P.
w 1803–1814
Baro M, Looking-glass M
1803–1814   22 West St, West Smithfield,
            London
See also BARNARDA & CO . P.★
Known to have sold: barometer
Sources: H; PO; Goodison (1977) p.299

BARNARDA & CO. P.
a 1800–1850
See also BARNARDA P.★
Known to have sold: barometer
Sources: Goodison (1977) p.299

BARNASCHINA Anthony
w 1826–1828
Telescope S, Cutlery S
1826–1828   New Rd, Gravesend, Kent
Known to have sold: barometer, thermometer
Sources: ChrSK 12 Dec 1985 lot 8; Goodison
(1977) p.299

BARNASCHONE Peter
w 1835
Optician, Toy S, Jeweller
1835   Tenby
Sources: Pg

BARNASCONE Andrew
w 1822–1830
Baro M
Alternative name: BARNASCONI, BERNASCONI
1822–1830   High St, Boston, Lincs
Known to have sold: barometer, thermometer
Sources: Pg; inst (s); Goodison (1977) p.299

BARNASCONE Lewis
w 1833–1837
Optician, Hardware S
Alternative name: BARNESCONE, BERNASCONE
1833–1837   23 Waingate, Sheffield
Known to have sold: barometer
Sources: Wh; ChrSK 19 Apr 1978 (MAC)

BARNASCONI Francis
w 1827–1857
Optician, Baro M
Alternative name: BARNESCONI

1827–1834   34 The Side, Newcastle upon Tyne
1836–1838   16 Groat Market, Newcastle upon
            Tyne
1847–1853   20 High Bridge, Newcastle upon
            Tyne
1855–1857   35 High Bridge, Newcastle upon
            Tyne
Partnership BARNASCONI & SON ★ 1841–1853
Sources: Pg; PWh; Wh; Wln; Goodison (1977)
p.299

BARNASCONI & SON
w 1841–1853
Optician, Baro M, Thermo M
Alternative name: BARNESCONI
1841   28 Groat Market, Newcastle upon
           Tyne
1844   29 Groat Market, Newcastle upon
           Tyne
1844   29 Side, Newcastle upon Tyne
1853   20 High Bridge, Newcastle upon
           Tyne
Took over from BARNASCONI Francis★
Succeeded by BARNASCONI Francis★
Sources: Wim; Goodison (1977) p.299

BARNBY Robert
w 1828–1856
Math IM, Math Instrument Case M, Jeweller's
Case M Medical Case M
1828–1829   9 Queen Square, Smithfield, London
1844–1851   17 Bakers Row, Coppice Row,
           Clerkenwell, London
1856   35 Wilmington Square, Clerkenwell,
           London
Guild: Clothworkers, fr 1828
Son of BARNBY Robert, gent, of St Pancras,
London
Apprenticed to BARKER Edward, jeweller, 1816
Had apprentice:
PELTON Samuel Robert 1828
ELLIS George Isaac 1829
GOULD John Henry Stevens 1844
COLLINS James 1846
YOUNG Charles Robert 1851
LAKE William James 1856
Sources: CWH: CWC Ap

BARNES William
w 1760
Math IM
1760   Parish of St. Mary Overie, London
Father of BARNES John s 1760 CORD
Sources: GL: CORD 7357/4

BARNET Asher
w 1770–1780
Spec grinder, Optician
1770–1775   25 Colemore St, Birmingham
1777–1780   25 Froggery St, Birmingham
Sources: PR; SA; Sy

BARNETT Esther
w 1834
Optician
1834   113 Drury Lane, London
Sources: Pg

BARNETT John
w 1822–1830
Optician, Glass cutter, Glass stainer
1822–1830   College St, York
Sources: Bn; PWh

BARNETT Thomas
w 1789–1810
Math IM, Phil IM, Optical IM, Optician
              4 Mores Yard, Old Fish St, nr.
              Doctors Commons, London
1790–1794   61 Great Tower St, London
1795–1796   6 Tower St, London
1799–1802   21 East St, Lambeth, London
1789   61 Tower St, London
1804   East St, East Place, London
Guild: Spectaclemakers, fr 1789 by purchase
Son of BARNETT Thomas, glass M,
Had apprentice:
TUCK William 1789
TREVELION William Henry 1804
TREVELION George in 1810
Pat. Aerating fluids 1802; said to be in workhouse
1816; b.apt Excise
Known to have sold: balance
Instruments advertised: full range
Sources: GL: SMC 5213/4; BW; Kt; JAC; Calvert
(1971) p.13 and pl.8; inst SM

BARNS Uriah
w 1845
Optician
1845   116 Edward St, Brighton
Sources: PO(HC)

BARON Patrick
w 1794–1795
Optican
Alternative name: BARRON
1794   83 Dame St, Dublin
1795   63 Dame St, Dublin
Sources: Burnett & Morrison-Low (1989) p.120;
Mason (1944)

BARRATTA Dominick
w 1790
Baro M, Thermo M
Alternative name: BARRATA
1790   67 Holborn, London
Sources: W (JAC)

BARRAUD Francis Gabriel
w 1758–1767
Watch M , Master of Chrono M
1758–1767   Great St Andrews St, St Giles in the
             Fields, London
1782   Wine Office Court, Fleet St,
             London
Guild: Skinners, fr 1755
Son of BARRAUD Philip, of East Greenwich,
merchant, d
Apprenticed to NEALE John (II)★ 1741/2
Had apprentice:
PARTRIDGE John 1758
GODDARD Florimand 1760
BOOTLE James 1763
BARRAUD Paul Philip★, his son, 1767
Sources: SH: SKC Ap/Fr; CKC 3939, list dated 1782

BARRAUD Frederick Joseph
w pt 1811–1836
Watch M, Chrono M
1811–1812   Cornhill, London
Guild: Clockmakers, fr 1806
Apprenticed to BARRAUD Paul Philip★, his father,
1799
Had apprentice:
HODGKINSON George 1811
BARRAUD Frederick Philip, his son, 1827
Partnership: BARRAUD & SONS ★, then
BARRAUD & SON F.★
Sources: GL: CKC 2720/1, 2725/1; PO; Atkins
(1931)

BARRAUD Hilton Paul.
w 1851–1875
Marine Chrono M
1851–1875   41 Cornhill, EC London
Guild: Clockmakers, fr 1846
Apprenticed to: BARRAUD John★, his father, 1835
Same premises as BARRAUD & LUND ★
Sources: PO; Atkins (1931)

BARRAUD John
w pt 1812–1835
Watch M, Chrono M
1812–1835   Cornhill, London
Guild: Clockmakers, fr 1813
Apprenticed to BARRAUD Paul Philip★, his father,
1806
Had apprentice BARRAUD Hilton Paul★, his son,
1835
Partnership: BARRAUD & SONS ★
Sources GL: CKC 2720/1, 2725/1; PO; Atkins
(1931)

BARRAUD Paul Philip
w 1799–1812
Chrono M, Watch M, Clock M
1805–1812   86 Cornhill, London
Guild: [Skinners], Clockmakers
Apprenticed to BARRAUD Francis Gabriel★, his
father, 1767 SKC
Had apprentice BARRAUD Frederick Joseph★, his
son, 1799
ROBINSON Thomas 1800
BARRAUD John★, his son, 1806
BARRAUD James, his son, 1807
Livery of Clockmakers 1796, Master 1810–11;
1796 partnership with HOWELLS William of
Bristol and JAMISON G. of Portsea for MUDGE
chronometers
d.1820
Sources: H; PO; Baillie (1951); SH: SKC Ap/Fr;
GL: CKC 2720/1 p.279

BARRAUD & LUND
w 1838–1901+
Watch M, Clock M, Chrono M
1838–1880   41 Cornhill, London
1885–1890   49 Cornhill, London
1895–1900   14 Bishopsgate St, London
Known to have sold: chronometer
Sources: PO; inst (s)

BARRAUD & SON F.
w 1833–1836

Watch M, Clock M, Chrono M
1833–1836   41 Cornhill, London
Took over from BARRAUD & SONS ★
Succeeded by BARRAUD & LUND ★
Sources: PO

BARRAUD & SONS
w 1815–1830
Watch M, Chrono M
1815–1830   85 Cornhill, London
Took over from BARRAUD Paul Philip★
Succeeded by BARRAUD & SON F.★
Partnership of BARRAUD Paul Philip★ and his sons,
which continued after his death in 1820
Took part in chronometer trials at Royal
Greenwich Observatory 1822
Sources: GL: CKC 2725/1; CUL: RGO 1143
fol.4; PO

BARRETT Robert Montague
w 1849–1875
Naut IM
1849–1851   4 Jamaica Terrace, Limehouse,
             London
1855–1870   4 Jamaica Terrace, West India Dock
             Road, London
1875   80 West India Dock Road, London
Ex.1851
Known to have sold: octant
Sources: Turner G (1983a) p.309; PO; inst NMM

BARRETT Simon
w 1682
[Math IM]
             London
Guild: Clockmakers, fr 1678
Apprenticed to WELLS Joseph★ 1668
Had apprentice BURGE Caleb 1682
Sources: Brown J (1979b) p. 27; Loomes (1981b)

BARRINGTON John
a 1750–1770
             Right hand Corner of the New Inn
             Yard, Pill Lane, Dublin
Known to have sold: balance
Sources: inst (s)

BARRINGTON Philip
w 1845–1862
Rule M
1850   176 Unett St, Birmingham
1862   Back of 178 Unett St, Birmingham
Sources: Mor; Sl

BARRINGTON Thomas
w 1826–1827
Optician, Math IM, Phil IM
1825   9 Wych St, Strand, London
1826–1827   32 Wych St, Strand, London
Attended London Mechanics Institute 1825
Sources: LMIR (AM); Pg

BARROW Henry
w pt 1848 w 1864
Math IM
1824–1826   18 Crown Court Soho, London SW
1850–1864   26 Oxenden St, Haymarket, London
             SW

Worked for DOLLOND George (I)★ and
TROUGHTON Edward (I)★ as out-worker
Took over from ROBINSON Thomas Charles★,
acquiring his business 1842
Traded as
ROBINSON & BARROW ★
BARROW & CO. Henry★
Succeeded by BARROW & OWEN
b 1790 d 1870; attended London Mechanics
Institute 1824–1826; Math IM to Surveyor
General of India 1830–1839; b.apt Admiralty
Compass M
Known to have sold: balance, compass (magnetic),
dip circle, gunner's level, theodolite, telescope
Sources: NMM: inst, ACO Cat; inst SM; LMIR
(AM); PO; Stock (1986); details from J. Insley of
SM

BARROW William
w 1756
Watch Wheel M, Watch Tool S, Magnet M,
Compass M, Needle M
c.1755   London
1756   Woolton, Prescot
Partnership BARROW & LOVELACE ★
Known to have sold: compass
Sources: Calvert (1971) p.13; TCd SML

BARROW & CO. Henry
w 1849–1851
Math IM
1849–1851   26 Oxenden St, Haymarket, London
Took over from ROBINSON & BARROW ★
Succeeded by BARROW Henry★
B.apt Admiralty
Known to have sold: compass (magnetic),
protractor, sextant, telescope, thermometer
Sources: PO; inst NMM

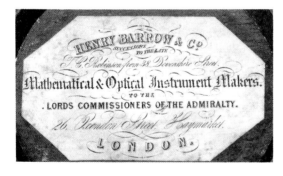

BARROW & LOVELACE William & W.
w 1756
Watch wheel M, Watch Tool S, Magnet M,
Compass M, Needle M
-1756   Golden Lion in St.Martin's le Grand,
             London
Succeeded by BARROW William★
See also LOVELACE William (II)★
Sources: TCd SM; Calvert (1971) p.13

BARRY
a 1780
             Cork
Known to have sold: circumferentor
Sources: BSIS 1983, no.1 p.7

BARRY Joseph Jun.
w 1845
Drawing IM, Optician
1845   3 Luke St, Finsbury, London
Sources: PO

BARRY M.
w 1812–1828
Navigation Warehouse
1812–1828   106 Minories, Tower Hill, London
Took over from BARRY Richard★
Sources: Kt; Pg; PO; R (JAC)

BARRY Richard
w 1800–1811
Stationer, Math IM, Navigation Warehouse
1800–1801   290 Wapping St, London
1802–1811   106 Minories, London
Succeeded by BARRY M.★
Instruments advertised: compass, octant, sextant,
telescope
Sources: TCd SML; H; Kt; PO; Calvert (1971)
p.13

BARSTON John
w 1738–1751
Watch M
1738   [?Residence] Battersea, London
1740   Hatton Garden, London
Associated with TURNER Joseph★ in making
quadrant
Bankrupt 1737; pat. quadrant 1738; probably the
BARSTON John who carried out repair work for
the Office of Ordnance
Sources: Wallis R & P (1986) p.245; Wallis R & P
(1993) p.9; Millburn (1988b) p.283–284; Baillie
(1951)

BARTLETT John
w 1819–1830
Scale M
1819   11 Plough Court, Fetter Lane,
             London
1826–1827   86 Long Lane, West Smithfield,
             London
1826–1828   18 Fetter Lane, London
1829–1830   6 Long Lane, West Smithfield,
             London
Guild: Blacksmiths, fr 1819
Apprenticed to WYNN John★ 1811, t/o 1814
to WOOD Robert★
Had apprentice:
BARTLETT Charles★, his brother, 1821 t/o 1822 to
DE GRAVE Edward A.★
EADY Thomas 1826 t/o 1829
to NICHOLL William L.★
Known to have sold: balance
Instruments advertised: balance, measure, steelyard,
weights
Sources: GL: BKC 2881/17 (MAC); inst with
TCd SM (Wellcome); Pg; R

BARTLETT Moses
d 1709
-1709   Exeter
Known to have sold: sundial
Sources: Loomes (1981b)

BARTLETT Samuel
w 1839
Working jeweller, Optician
1839   109 Week St, Maidstone
Sources: Pg

BARTON
a 1820
Compass M
             Sunderland
Known to have sold: compass (magnetic)
Sources: inst NMM

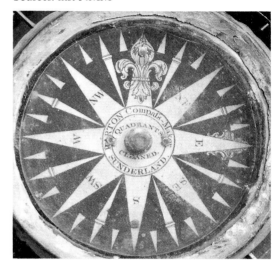

BARTON John (I)
w 1730 d 1761
Steelyard M
1730   Digbeth, Birmingham
1746–1761   11 Digbeth, Birmingham
Succeeded by BARTON William Bridgins★, his son
Sources BS

BARTON John (II)
w 1829–1835
Optician, Spec M
1829–1830   7 Court, Barr St, Birmingham
1835   55 Barr St, Birmingham
Sources: Pg; West; WR

BARTON S. & J.
w 1815–1842
Coach builders, Odometer M
1815–1828   Hotwells, Bristol
1829–1842   Milk St, Bristol
1832–1839   Bedminster Bridge, Bristol
1838–1842   North St, Bristol
Succeeded by BARTON & SONS S. & J.★
Instruments advertised: waywiser
Sources: Mat; BsM index

BARTON William Bridgins
w 1761–1782
Steelyard M
1767–1781   11 Digbeth, Birmingham
Took over from BARTON John (I)★, his father
Succeeded by BEACH Thomas★
Sources: By; PR; SA; Sy; BS

BARTON & SON S.

w 1846–1853
Coachbuilders, Odometer M
1846   Nelson St, Bristol
Took over from BARTON & SONS S. & J.★
Sources: BsM index

BARTON & SONS J.

w 1846–1853
Coachbuilders, Odometer M
1846   St. Augustine's Back, Bristol
1846   Host St, Bristol
Took over from BARTON & SONS S. & J.★
Sources: BsM index

BARTON & SONS S. & J.

w 1844–1845
Coachbuilders, Odometer M
1844   Milk St, Bristol
1844   Quay Head, Bristol
1845   Quay, Bristol
1845   Nelson St., Bristol
Took over from BARTON S. & J. ★
Succeeded by
BARTON & SON S. ★
BARTON & SONS J. ★
Sources: BsM index

BARTRIP –

a 1800–1850
          Islington, London
Worked for TULLEY★
Known to have sold: telescope
Sources: ChrSK Dec 1984 (MAC)

BARWICK Francis

a 1680
Known to have sold: drawing instruments
Sources: inst SM

BARWISE John

w 1823–1881
Chrono M, Watch M
1823–1851   29 St Martin's Lane, London
Took part in chronometer trials at Royal
Greenwich Observatory 1823–1825
Sources: CUL: RGO 1143 fol.5–6; PO; Loomes
(1976)

BASS George

w 1723–1768
Optical IM, supplied lenses to the trade
1733   Bridewell Precinct, London
1764   Fleet Ditch, London
Guild: Spectaclemakers, fr 1716/17
Son of BASS George, miller, of Southwark,
London
Apprenticed to STERROP Ralph★ 1706
Had apprentice:
MOORE William (IV) 1723
DRAKEFORD David (I)★1728
BYGRAVE Richard★ 1733/4
CLARKE Mathew 1742
BROOKS Robert 1749
Associated with
MOORE William (II)★
HALL Chester Moor, for whom he made
achromatic lenses

Master SMC 1747–1748, 1754–1758; d in or soon
after 1768; petitioner against Dollond's patent 1764
Known to have sold: lens
Sources: GL: SMC 5213/2 p.49,142,197+, 5213/3
p.44,115,126–7,138,203+, 6029; PRO: PC 1/7
no.94; JAC; Clifton (1993b) p.357; Court & Von
Rohr (1929–1930) p.77

BASSINGHAM Robert

w 1829–1842
Scale M
1830–1840   63 Bethnal Green Rd, London
1842   107 Bethnal Green Rd, London
1848   Ringwould, Kent
Guild: Drapers, fp 1830
Son of BASSINGHAM Samuel★
Brother of BASSINGHAM William (II)★
Had apprentice:
SHOREY Ebenezer 1830
COX John 1837
BUXTON Thomas William 1838
WARD Charles 1840
ROBBINS Charles 1841
Took over from BASSINGHAM Samuel★
Sources: DH: DPC Ap/Fr, index; Pg

BASSINGHAM Samuel

w 1791–1828
Scale M, Blacksmith
1789   10 Seacoal Lane, Snow Hill, London
1791   Phils Buildings, Houndsditch,
              London
1795–1797   Chapel St, St.Georges in the East,
              London
1799–1828   63 Bethnal Green Rd, London
1830   3 Whitecross St, London
1830–1850   Bancroft's Almshouses, Mile End,
              London
Guild: [Blacksmiths], Drapers, fp 1789
Son of BASSINGHAM William (I), d
Apprenticed to OXLEY Henry★ 1780 BKC
Had apprentice:
BROOKS William★ 1791
BUNN Thomas 1795
PETLEY Richard 1797
PHILLIPS William 1799
TURNER John Thomas 1811
MANNING John 1816
PARISH Thomas Carpenter 1818
STANLEY Nathaniel 1820
FIELDER James 1821
ABBOTT George Alfred 1825 t/o 1830
to SMITH Thomas (IV)★
ABRAHAM Thomas 1827
Succeeded by BASSINGHAM Robert★, his son
Father of BASSINGHAM William★
1813 in Ludgate for debt
Sources: GL: STTP 2934 fol 106; DH: DPC
Ap/Fr

BASSINGHAM William (II)

w 1818–1847
Scale M (1818), Gas Furniture M (1827),
Brass Manufacturer & Tobacconist (1839)
1818–1839   3 Whitecross St, London
Guild: Drapers, fp 1818
Son of BASSINGHAM Samuel★
Brother of BASSINGHAM Robert★

Had apprentice:
HARRISON James 1818
MILLS Charles 1819
ENGLAND Richard Crawford 1827
DONNISON Charles 1830
WOODGATE Henry Phillips 1836
BASSINGHAM William (III), his son,1836
SALMON Richard 1842
HOLMES William Harris 1846
NELSON William 1847
b c.1792 d 1850, buried St Giles, Cripplegate
Sources: DH: DPC Ap/Fr, index; Kt; Pg; PO

BASSNETT James

w 1829–1857
Optician, Math IM, Clock M, Chronometer M
Alternative name: BASNET, BASSNETT,
1829   4 Barnes Court, Shaws Brow,
              Liverpool
1834   13 Robert St North, Liverpool
1834–1853   1 Robert St North, Liverpool
1835   16 Robert St North, Liverpool
1837   19 Robert St North, Liverpool
1857   58 Robert St Liverpool
Succeeded by BASSNETT & SON
Known to have sold: barometer, thermometer
Sources: G; Sl; inst (s); Goodison (1977) p.300

BASSNETT William

w 1843
Chrono M;
1843   7 Paisley St, Liverpool
Sources: LM index (MAC)

BASTICK Richard

w 1828–1850
Scale M
1828   Holywell Row, Worship St,
              London
1849–1850   2 Holywell Row, Worship St,
              London
Guild: Blacksmiths, fr 1828
Son of BASTICK Thomas, broker, of Holywell
Mount, London
Apprenticed to VANDOME Richard★ 1821 t/o
1824 to BASTICK Thomas
Had apprentice SPICKETT James 1848
Sources: GL: BKC 2881/17–18 (MAC)

BASTON Richard

w 1780–1790
Hour-glass M, Turner
1780   1 Little Minories, London
Guild: Turners
Had apprentice BRYANT Benjamin (II) 1790
Sources: TC 3302/3; GL: Sun 11936/280
no.423909

BATE Bartholomew

w 1829–1850
Optician
1822   17 Poultry, London
1829   Poultry, London
1847–1851   (Residence) 2 Norwood Place,
              Kensington Church St, London
Guild: Spectaclemakers, fr 1829
Apprenticed to BATE Robert Brettell★, his father,
1822

b 1806 d 1895; 1842 livery of SMC
Sources: GL: SMC 5213/5; McConnell (1993)
p.vii, 3–7, 37,54–57

BATE John (I)

w 1756 d 1780
Math IM
1739–1780   Dublin
1756   Nicholas St, Dublin
Father of BATE Philip, possibly BATE Philip★
Known to have sold: sundial
Sources: Burnett & Morrison-Low (1989) p.120

BATE John (II)

w fm 1832 d 1840
Optical IM
1809–1824   17 Poultry, London
1824–1840   20 & 21 Poultry, London
Son of BATE Robert Brettell★
b 1809; Pat. medal-engraving machine 1832
Sources: McConnell (1993) p.vii,5,14,23,28–31

BATE Philip

w 1761–1762
Math IM
1761–1762   Nicholas St, Dublin
See also BATE John (I)★
Sources: Burnett & Morrison-Low (1989) p.120

BATE Richard (I)

w 1739 d by 1764
Scale M
Before 1764 Parish of St. Dunstan in the East,
             London
Guild: Blacksmiths, fr 1726
Son of BATE Matthew, gent, of Maidsmouth,
Bucks
Apprenticed to
SNART John(I)★ 1719, t/o 1721
to OVEN Henry★
Had apprentice:
HOWELL Thomas 1739, t/o 1744/5
to WOOD John (II)★
TURVEY William 1743, t/o 1745
to FREEMAN Samuel (II)★
Father of BATE Richard (II)★
Sources: GL: BKC 2885/1, 2886/4 (MAC)

BATE Richard (II)

w 1796
Scale M
             London
Guild: Blacksmiths, fp 1772
Son of BATE Richard (I)★
Apprenticed to LIND John★ 1764
Had apprentice HUGHES John 1796
Worked for REEVES Thomas★ 1772
Sources: GL: BKC 2885/1, 2886/5, 2881/16;
CLRO: LicFW (MAC)

BATE Robert Brettell

w 1808–1847
Hydro M, Math IM, Optician, Optical IM, Phil
IM, Sacch M, Admiralty Chart Agent
Alternative name: Brettel
1808–1828   17 Poultry, London
1824–1847   21 Poultry, London
1824–1842   20 Poultry, London

1846–1847   33 Royal Exchange, London
1847   (Residence) Hampstead, London
Guild: Spectaclemakers, fr 1814
Son of BATE Overs, mercer and banker, d, of
Stourbridge, Worcs
Had apprentice:
BATE Bartholomew★, his son, 1822
CHISLETT Alfred★ 1825, t/o 1825
to GILBERT William (II)★
Employed
LADD Edward Wilds★
STREATFIELD John★
POTTER John Dennett★
STURDY Joseph William★
STURDY Frederick Henry★
Associated with
DAWSON & MELLING★
NEILL Robert★
BRAHAM John★
BENNETT Thomas (II)★
STEBBING George★
SPEARS & CO.★
COX William Charles★
TAYLOR Janet★, who all acted as sub-agents to
Bate for Admiralty charts
Succeeded by
LADD & STREATFIELD★ and DRING & FAGE ★ as
suppliers of hydrometers to Inland Revenue
POTTER John D.★ as Admiralty chart agent
Pat. hydrometer and saccharometer 1822 and 1836,
spec.frame 1825; B.apt Excise & Ordnance; 1824
commissioned to make new national standard
measures of weight and capacity; R.apt Geo IV
1828, Wm IV 1830, continued by Victoria; Master
SMC 1828–1830
Known to have sold: full range of instruments
Sources: GL:SMC 5213/4,5213/5; McConnell
(1993)

BATEMAN T. B.

w 1834
Spectacle M
             London
Had apprentice MEAD T.H. 1834
Sources: GL: CH 12823/9 p.126

BATEMAN Thomas

w 1773–1781
Engraver, Apprentice and Master of Globe Makers
1771–1781   Chancery Lane, London
Guild: Vintners, fr 1771
Son of BATEMAN Thomas
Apprenticed to HILL Nathaniel★ 1746
Had apprentice NEWTON John★ 1774
Succeeded by PALMER & NEWTON★
fr by purchase, VC; d 1781
Sources: PRO: IR 1/17 fol.218; GL: St Dunstan
West, Bu; VC 15201/11 p.227

BATES –

w 1626
[Math IM, Optical IM]
1626   Tower Hill, London
Sources: Smith (1626) p.33

BATES Edwin

w 1850
Rule M

1850   3 Marshall St, Holloway Head,
             Birmingham
Sources: Sl

BATES John

w 1841
Square M
1841   New St, Wolverhampton
Sources: Pg

BATES Richard

w 1733–1750
Math IM
1740   Quadrant without Newgate facing
             the Old Bailey, London
Guild: Stationers, fr 1730
Son of BATES Thomas
Apprenticed to HADDON William (I)★ 1714
Had apprentice:
HADDON William (II) 1730
ROLPH Thomas★ 1733
JONES John 1735
OWEN Edward 1735
EDLIN Daniel 1737
WILKINSON John (I)★ 1739
LORT John ?★ 1740
MEESON John 1743
JONES Robert 1747
KNOTT Thomas 1747
FLOOD Noah 1748
TUCKER Thomas 1749
LAW Andrew 1749
GEARING Richard Bates★ 1749/50
See also COMBES Fisher★
Attended Christ's Hospital School, later supplied
rules for the Drawing School
Known to have sold: rule
Sources: GL: CH 12876/3, 12823/3 p.97,352,
12823/5 p.324; McKenzie (1978) p.25–26,151

BATES & CO.

w 1808–1817
Scale M
             126 Digbeth, Birmingham
1809–1817   35 Digbeth, Birmingham
Stated to be "from London"
Known to have sold: balance
Sources: Chp; H; Mort; Und; inst Worthing Mu

BATHER George

w 1821–1848
Scale M
             7 New St, Covent Garden, London
1822–1823   48 Great Windmill St, Haymarket,
             London
1826–1848   62 Haymarket, St.James, London
1839–1844   4 Lower Thames St, London
Guild: [Blacksmiths]
Son of BATHER Richard, carver and gilder, d, of
Covent Garden, London
Apprenticed to STANLEY Nathaniel★ 1807
Apprenticeship fee paid by parish school of St
Martin-in-the-Fields; Pat. weighing machine 1834
Known to have sold: balance, chondrometer
Sources: GL: BKC 2881/16; Pg; PO; R; Patent
Abstracts (MAC); ChrSK 6 Oct 1983 noted in
Webster R & M (1988); inst SM (Wellcome)

BATTELL Affabell
w 1723 d 1749
Math IM
Alternative name: Affable BATTLE
−1723   St.Mary le Savoy, Strand, London
1737   Beaufort Buildings in the Strand,
               London
Guild: Broderers, fr 1737
Son of BATTELL Affabell, cleric, of Hertford
Apprenticed to POTTEN John★ 1707/8
Bankrupt 1723; prob the Affable Battle who was
assistant compass maker to the Navy at Deptford
Dockyard 1741−1748
Sources: GL: BROD 14657/2 (MAC); LGaz 7 Sep
1723; Crawforth (1987) p.338; Taylor (1966) p.166

BATTISTESSA & CO.
w 1842
[Baro M]
1842   8 & 9 Calton St, Edinburgh
Branch of BATTISTESSA, MOLTENI &
GUANZIROLI★ of London
Succeeded by CICERI, PINI & CO. of London
See also ZERBONI & CO.★
Known to have sold: barometer
Sources: Burnett & Morrison-Low (1989)
p.102−03; Goodison (1977) p.300

**BATTISTESSA, MOLTENI &
GUANZIROLI**
w 1832−1843
Baro M, Thermo M, Looking Glass M
Alternative name: BATTISTESSA & CO.
1832−1834   13 Baldwin's Gardens, Leather Lane,
               London
1839−1843   106 Hatton Garden, London
Sources: Pg (JAC), PO

BAWTREE Thomas James
fp 1800 d 1819
Optician
1817   Long Lane, West Smithfield, London
Guild: [Stationers] Goldsmiths, fp 1801
Son of BAWTREE Joseph, engraver, of London
Apprenticed to PRICE William (I)★ 1793 STC
Had apprentice WILLIAMS George Walshaw 1817
t/o 1819 to WILLIAMS George, his father
Sources: GH: GSC Ap/Fr; McKenzie (1978) p.278

BAXTER John
fl 1825−1826
1825−1826   32 John St, Birmingham
Said by E.G.R. Taylor to be listed in directories as
Math IM, but appears to be a misreading of
RAXTER John★
Sources: Pg; Taylor (1966) p.413

BAXTER Robert
fl 1830
              Livery St, Birmingham
Said by E.G.R. Taylor to be listed in directories as
Optical IM, but appears to be a misreading of
RAXTER Robert★
Sources: Pg; Taylor (1966) p.443

BAXTER William (I)
w 1805
Baro M, Thermo M
1805   8 Little Turnstile, Holborn, London
See also: GILBERT John (II)★
Sources: H

BAXTER William (II)
w 1851
Math IM
1851   37 Friendly Place, Mile End Old
               Town, London
Guild: [Masons][Spectaclemakers]
Son of BAXTER William, mariner, of Stepney,
London
Apprenticed to HUGHES Joseph (I)★ 1839 MC
t/o 1845 to CHISLETT Alfred★ SMC
b at Stapleford Essex, 1824 or 1825
Sources: PRO: Cs 1851 (LS); GL: MC 5304/7
(MAC)

BAYFIELD Samuel
w 1823−1824
Optician
1823−1824   6 Rupert St, Haymarket, London
Sources: R (JAC)

BAYLEY − see also BAILEY

BAYLEY −
w 1660−1671
Lens Grinder
1663   St. Paul's Churchyard, London
See also BAILEY John★
Sources: BM: Add MS 15948 fol.93v; Monconys
(1666) p.11,18; Clifton (1993b) p.360n

BAYLEY James
w 1790
Phil IM
1790   212 Shoreditch, London
Suceeded by BAYLEY & SON★
Sources: BW

BAYLEY Michael
w 1673−1674
Scale M
Alternative name: BAILY, BAILEY, Miles
1673−1674   Bartholomew Lane, London
Guild: Clockmakers
Known to have sold: sundial
Sources: Loomes (1981b); GL: CKC 2710/1 p.284

BAYLEY R.
w 1851
Optician
1851   11 Upper Rosoman St, Clerkenwell,
               London
Sources: Wk

BAYLEY William Charles
w 1846−1849
Optician, Spec M
1846−1849   76 St. John St Road, London
Sources: PO

BAYLEY & SON
w 1792−1810
Phil IM, Handkerchief printer
1792−1810   212 Shoreditch, London
Took over from BAYLEY James★
Sources: Kt (JAC)

BAYLIS George Henry
w 1838−1848
Scale M
1838−1840   21 Ratcliff Highway, London
1844   39 Brown's Lane, Spitalfields,
               London
1846−1848   8 Winchester Place, Southwark
               Bridge Rd, London
Guild: [Blacksmiths]
Apprenticed to FAGE William (II)★ 1831
Sources: GL: BKC 2881/17 (MAC); PO

BAYLIS William (I)
w 1829−1830
Rule M
1829−1830   19 Lower St, Islington, London
See also BAYLIS William (II)★, possibly the same
person
Sources: R (JAC)

BAYLIS William (II)
w 1834−1873
Rule M, Math IM, Optician, Brass founder
1834   56 Dale St, Liverpool
1841   67 Dale St, Liverpool
1841−1858   27 Park Lane, Liverpool
1841−1855   75 Dale St, Liverpool
1845−1849   27 South John St, Liverpool
1851−1853   2 Prices St, Liverpool
1857   85 Dale St, Liverpool
1858−1865   81 Dale St, Liverpool
1870−1873   67 Park Lane West, Liverpool
See also BAYLIS William (I)★, possibly the same
person
Known to have sold: slide rule
Sources: G: K: Pg; LM index (MAC); inst (s)

BAYNHAM James
w 1747−1774
Math IM, Optical Turner, Math Turner
1747   Newgate St, London
1754−1755   Aldersgate St, London
1764   Carter Lane, London
Guild: Stationers, fr 1746
Son of BAYNHAM Nathaniel, yeoman, of London
Apprenticed to BUSH Joseph★ 1739
Had apprentice:
WEBB Isaac (II) 1747
KELSEY John 1747
SMITH Samuel ?★ 1755
WILLIAMS Henry 1758
COX William (III)★ 1764
Sources: GL: CH 12876/5; McKenzie (1978)
p.27,60

BEACH Thomas
w 1766−1799
Scale M, Steelyard M
1766−1782   Blackford House,
               Tanworth-in-Arden
1777−1782   The Bull Ring, Birmingham
1782−1799   11 Digbeth, Birmingham
Apprenticed to FRENCH Robert★ 1759
Took over from BARTON William B.★
Succeeded by BALDEN Joseph★
r 1799 d.1824
Known to have sold: balance
Instruments advertised: balance, steelyard weights

BEALE John (I)
Sources: By; Pye; Wd; inst Huddersfield Mu
(MAC); Broadbent (1949); Calvert (1971) p.13

BEALE John (I)
w 1759
Math IM
1759   Kent St, Southwark, London
Had apprentice HODGES James 1759
Sources: PRO: IR 1/22 (AM)

BEALE John (II)
w 1805–1822
Math IM, Optical IM, Phil IM
1805   76 Maid Lane, Southwark, London
1811   17 Alfred Place, Camberwell,
                London
1822   Southampton St, Clerkenwell,
                London
Sources: H; Und; Calvert (1971) p.14

BEALE Joseph
w 1766
Math IM
1766   St. Saviours, Surrey, London
Had apprentice ADDY John 1766
Sources: PRO: IR 1/24 (AM)

BEALE William Thomas
w 1839–1845
Drawing IM, Math IM
1839–1840   7 Edward St, Great Surrey St,
                London
1843–1845   10 King St, Whitechapel, London
Sources: Pg; PO

BEAN John George
w 1834
Spec M
1834   Joseph St, Cannon Street Rd,
                London
Sources: Pg

BEARD Richard
w 1841–1885
Photographic artist, Medico-galvanic apparatus
M
1842–1855   34 Parliament St, London
1842–1855   85 King William St, City, London
1841–1845   Royal Polytechnic Institution, 309
                Regent St, London
1845   (Manufactory) 18 Wharf Road, City
                Road, London
1850   (Manufactory) Millman Mews, New
                Millman St, London
1860–1865   31 King William St, City, London
Opened Photographic Portrait Rooms at the
Royal Polytechnic Institution 1841
Sources: PO; Thomas (1966) (MAC)

BEARDSMORE John
w 1818
Spec M
1818   Cock St, Birmingham
Sources: Wr

BEARETTI Peter
w 1834
Baro M, Thermo M

1834   26 Great Bath St, Clerkenwell,
                London
Sources: Pg

BEAVESS Edward
w1729–1762
Math IM, Phil IM, Optical IM, Engine M, Clock
M, Jack M, Lock M, Wind dial M, Weather cock
M
Alternative name: BEAVISS
1759   Two doors from the Brown Bear in
                Seacoal Lane, Snow Hill, London
Known to have sold: balance, orrery
Sources: *Daily Ad* 22 Dec 1759 p.3; inst Gloucester
Mu (MAC); Sby 16 Dec 1963 lot 112, noted in
Webster R & M (1986)

BECK Joseph
w fm 1851 d 1891
Optician
1853   Stamford Hill London
1879–1879   31 Cornhill London
Guild: Goldsmiths, fr 1853
Son of BECK Richard Low, wine merchant, of
Tokenhouse Yard, London
Apprenticed to SIMMS William (II)★ 1846
Had apprentice:
BECK Conrad, his son, 1879
TAYLOR Thomas Smithies 1879
Brother of BECK Richard★
Partnership: BECK R. & J., c.1867–1894, the name
being continued after the deaths of Richard and
Joseph
Succeeded by BECK LTD R. & J.
b 1829 d 1891; member of the Microscopical
Society of London 1859
Sources: GH: GSC Ap; PO; Turner G (1989) p.171

BECK Richard
w pt 1847–1866
Optician
1847–1865   6 Coleman St, London
Apprenticed to SMITH James (III)★
Brother of BECK Joseph★
Partnership:
SMITH & BECK★
SMITH, BECK & BECK★
b 1827 d 1866; member of the Microscopical
Society of London 1855
Sources: PO; Turner G (1989) p.171

BECKET Thomas
w 1805–1809
Cabinet M, Math IM
1805   39 Church St, Mile End New Town,
                London
1809   32 Church St, Mile End Rd, New
                Town, London
Sources: H

BECKIT Robert
w 1597–1598
Map engraver
Alternative name: Robertus
                London
Known to have sold: sector
Sources: inst MHS; Turner G (1983b) p.98,103,
pl.52

BECKWITH Robert William
fp 1850
Optician
                London
Guild: Goldsmiths, fp 1850
Sources: GH: GSC Ap/Fr

BEDDOE William
w 1845–1862
Math IM
1845–1862   18 Court, Lionel St, Birmingham
Sources: K; Mor

BEDFORD Hilkiah
w 1656–1680
Math IM, Engraver
Alternative name: Helkiah, Helkia
                The Globe near Holborn Conduit,
                London
1663–1666   Hosier Lane, London
1666   Fleet St, London
1674   Fleet St, near the end of Fetter Lane,
                London
Guild: Stationers fr 1654, Clockmakers brother
1667/8
Son of BEDFORD Thomas, gent, of Boston, Lincs
Apprenticed to THOMPSON John (I)★ 1646
Had apprentice:
JOLE Robert★ 1656 STC
YORKE William 1662 STC
ABBOTT Richard★ 1668 CKC
BENBRICK James 1671 CKC
BILLINGHURST Anthony 1672 CKC
Supplied instruments for the observatory at St
Andrews; d 1689
Known to have sold: quadrant, rule, universal
equinoctial ring dial
Sources: inst SM; McKenzie (1974) p.11,164;
Turner A (1986) p.3–5; Taylor (1954) p.246;
Webster R & M (1988)

BEDFORD John
w 1773
Watch M
1773   Kington, Herefs
Known to have sold: balance, weights
Sources: *British Chronicle* 16 Sep 1773 (JRM)

BEDINGTON George
w 1845
Measuring tape M
1845   10 Court, Snow Hill, Birmingham
Sources: K

BEDINGTON James (I)
w 1845–1876
Math IM, Measuring tape M, Compass M, Sundial
M, Phil IM
1845–1862   10 Russell St, St. Mary's Square,
                Birmingham
Partnership: CUTTS, CHESTERMAN &
BEDINGTON of Sheffield
See also BEDINGTON James (II)★
Sources: Bil; K; Mor; Sl

BEDINGTON James (II)
w 1851
Math IM

1851   56 Hatton Garden, London
Possibly the London branch of BEDINGTON
James (I)★ of Birmingham
Sources: Wk

BEDINGTON John
w 1845–1852
Rule M, Math IM
1845–1851   40 Digbeth, St. Martin's Lane,
             Birmingham
Sources: K; Sl; Wh; Roberts (1982) (MAC)

BEDINGTON & SONS Robert
w 1841
Measuring tape M
1841   107 Lancaster St, Birmingham
Sources: Pg

BEDWELL George
w 1851–1870
Hydro M, Sacch M
1851–1870   4 Little Alie St, Goodman's Fields,
             London
Took over from BEDWELL Thomas★
Sources: PO; Wk

BEDWELL Thomas
w 1822–1850
Optician, Math IM, Hydro M
1822–1823   45 Great Alie St, Goodman's Fields,
             London
1824–1825   Leman St, Goodman's Fields,
             London
1825–1834   54 Great Alie St, Goodman's Fields,
             London
1834–1845   53 Great Alie St, Goodman's Fields,
             London
1846   3 Little Alie St, Goodman's Fields,
             London
1847–1850   4 Little Alie St, Goodman's Fields,
             London
Succeeded by BEDWELL George★
Sources: Pg; PO

BEESLEY George
w 1834–1839
Chrono M, Watch M
1834   56 Great Crosshall St, Liverpool
1835   16 Boundary St, Kirkdale Rd,
             Liverpool
1837–1839   2 Boundary St, Kirkdale Rd,
             Liverpool
See also
BEESLEY Richard & George★
BEESLEY Thomas★
BEESLEY Richard★
Sources: G

BEESLEY Richard
w 1835
Chrono M
1835   15 Boundary St, Liverpool
See also
BEESLEY Richard & George★
BEESLEY George★
Sources: LM index (MAC)

BEESLEY Richard & George
w 1828–1849
Chrono M, Watch M
1828   56 Great Crosshall St, Liverpool
1841–1847   4 & 6 Boundary St, Kirkdale,
             Liverpool
1849   6 Boundary St, Kirkdale, Liverpool
Sources: G; Loomes (1975)

BEESLEY Thomas
w 1824
Chrono M
1824   16 Lambert St, Liverpool
See also BEESLEY George★
Sources: Loomes (1975)

BEGG John
w 1830
Watch M, Clock M, Chrono M
1830   38 Queen St, Portsea
Sources: Pg

BEILBY Charles
w 1814–1819
Optical IM, Math IM, Phil IM
1816   2 Clare St, Bristol
1816   (Residence) Redland, Bristol
1819   (Residence) Spring Hill House,
             Bristol
See also
SPRINGER Joshua★
BEILBY R. & C.★
Sources: H; Mat; Und

BEILBY R. & C. (Richard ? & Charles ?)
w 1809–1813
Optical IM, Math IM, Phil IM
1809–1813   2 Clare St, Bristol
See also
BEILBY Richard★
BEILBY Charles★
Sources: BsM index

BEILBY Richard
w 1820
Optical IM, Math IM, Phil IM
1820   2 Clare St, Bristol
Took over from BEILBY Charles★
Succeeded by KING John (III)★
See also BEILBY R. & C.★
Sources: BsM index

BELCHER John
w 1833–1837
Rule M
1833   1 Bright St, Sheffield
1834–1837   2 Bright St, Sheffield
See also BELCHER & SONS Zachariah★
Sources: Pg; Wh

BELCHER Zachariah
w 1811–1829
Rule M
Alternative name: BELSHAW
1811–1818   Bright St, Sheffield
1822–1825   4 Bright St, Sheffield Moor,
             Sheffield
Succeeded by BELCHER & SONS Zachariah★

See also BELCHER Zachary★
Sources: Bn; Pg

BELCHER Zachary
w 1797
Rule M
1797   Sheffield Moor (South St.), Sheffield
See also BELCHER Zachariah★
Sources: Rb

BELCHER & HASSALL
w 1793
Rule M
1793   Bull St, Birmingham
See also HASSALL & CO★
Sources: BW

BELCHER & SONS Zachariah
w 1828–1909
Rule M
1828–1830   4 Bright St, Sheffield
1833–1837   1 Bright St, Sheffield
1841   27 Bright St, Sheffield
1852–1855   270 Bright St, Sheffield
1861   272 Bright St, Sheffield
1875–1877   272 Fitzwilliam St, Sheffield
1889   74 Mary St, Sheffield
1908   Furnival St, Sheffield
Took over from BELCHER Zachariah★
See also BELCHER John★
Sources: Bk; K; Pg; Sl; Wh

BELGRAVE Thomas
w 1851
Math IM
1851   7 Russell Buildings, Wapping,
             London
Guild: [Grocers]
Son of BELGRAVE Thomas, shoemaker, of Mile
End, London
Apprenticed to HOLYMAN John★ 1808
b in Southwark in 1794 or 1795
Sources: Cs 1851 (LS); GL: GC 11598/6

BELL George (I)
w 1845–1851
Math IM
1845–1851   38 Fontenoy St, Liverpool
Sources: G; LM

BELL George (II)
w 1820
Money Scale M, Liquor Merchant
1820   Prescot, Lancs
Son of BELL Hamlet★
See also BELL & CO. H.★
Sources: Crawforth (1979)

BELL Hamlet
w 1781 d 1820
Draper, Liquor Merchant
1781–1820   Prescot
Employed ABBOTT William
Succeeded by BELL & CO. H.★
Known to have sold: balance
Sources: By; Crawforth (1979)

BELL Isaac
w 1838–1871
Compass M
1847–1848	Delftfield Lane, Glasgow
1847–1848	16 York St, Glasgow
1849–1857	50 Maxwell St, Glasgow
1858–1859	52 Maxwell St, Glasgow
1863–1871	70½ Great Clyde St, Glasgow

Partnership: BELL Isaac & Henry 1860–1862
Sources: Bryden (1972) p.44

BELL James
w 1836–1861
Phil IM, Clock M, Machine M
1836–1861   54 South Bridge, Edinburgh
Sources: Bryden (1972) p.44

BELL John (I)
w 1667–1710
Math IM
London
Guild: Clockmakers, brother 1667/8, free of
another unknown guild
Known to have sold: sundial
Sources: Brown J (1979b) p.27; Loomes (1981b)

BELL John (II)
w 1824
Math IM
1824   Brook's Alley, Post Office Place,
           Liverpool
Sources: Bn

BELL William
w 1771–1803
Optician, Land Surveyor, Engraver
1797–1803   Canongate, Edinburgh
Sources: Bryden (1972) p.44

BELL & CO. H.
c. 1820–1835
Scale M, Liquor Merchant
1820–1835   Prescot, Lancs
Took over from BELL Hamlet*
Succeeded by BROWN & SONS R.
Firm was BELL George (II)* trading as BELL &
CO. H
Known to have sold: balance, weights
Sources: Crawforth (1979)

BELLING John
a 1700–1800
Watch M
1793   Fore St, Bodmin
There were four generations of Clock & Watch M
in Bodmin called John Belling in 18th and early
19th centuries
Known to have sold: ring dial
Sources: BW; Webster R & M (1988); Loomes
(1976)

BELLINGER John (I)
w 1687–1722
London
Math IM
Guild: Clockmakers, fr 1686
Apprenticed to STARR Robert* 1677
Had apprentice:

BELLINGER Charles 1687
BIGGS Edmond 1695
COLEMAN Stephen* 1704
BELLINGER John (II)*, his son, 1706/7
JONES James 1715 [possibly JONES James (IV)*]
PEDDELL John 1721/2
A signed back-staff may have been by BELLINGER
John (I)* or (II)*
Known to have sold: rule
Sources: Chr SK 27 Nov 1986 lot 186; Brown J
(1979b) p.27; Loomes (1981);Taylor (1954) p.295

BELLINGER John (II)
w 1730–1732
Math IM
London
Guild: Clockmakers, fr 1726
Apprenticed to BELLINGER John (I)*, his father,
1706/7
Had apprentice:
BELLINGER John (III), his son. 1730
GIBBS Robert 1731
BELLINGER William, his son, 1732
A signed back-staff may have been by BELLINGER
John (I)* or (II)*
Sources: Chr SK 27 Nov 1986 lot 186; Brown J
(1979b) p.27; Loomes (1981);Taylor (1954) p.295

BELLWORTH James
w 1817–1819
Optician
1817–1819   136 Borough, Southwark, London
Guild: [Spectaclemakers]
Son of BELLWORTH John , victualler, of Covent
Garden, London
Apprenticed to WAGHORN Robert* 1797
Known to have sold: barometer
Sources: GL: SMC 5213/4; J; R (JAC); Phlps 16
Nov 1976 noted by Webster R & M (1988)

BELOTTI & GUGERI
w 1822–1836
Baro M, Thermo M, Looking-glass M
1822–1829	15 Upper Union Court, Holborn Hill, London
1830–1836	16 Charles St, Hatton Garden, London

Succeeded by GUGERI & BELOTTI*
Sources: PO; R (JAC)

BEMBRICK William (I)
w 1687–1723
[Spec M]
Alternative name: BENBRICK, BEMBROOKE,
BAMBRETH
1693	Behind the Exchange [his other shop] London
1695	Threadneedle St, London
1693–1695	Cornhill, London

Guild: Spectaclemakers, fr 1682
Son of BENBRICK Joseph, mason, d, of Bristol
Apprenticed to
CLARK Elizabeth* 1675 t/o 1677/8
to MAYLE Thomas*
Had apprentice:
THORPE George 1691
SHEPPARD John 1705/6
TIPPER Jeffery 1711

BEMBRICK William (II), son of John, 1714
JENNINGS William 1715
BEMBRICK John, son of John, 1714
BEMBRICK Isaiah, son of Rice, 1718
JACKSON John 1718/9
Fined by SMC 1686/7 for selling frames without
glasses; Master SMC 1709–12; probably d by 1738
Sources: GL: SMC 5213/1, 5213/2
p.47,67,75,79,87,94,109,160; 6029

BEN John
w 1694–1718
Scale M
London
Guild: Blacksmiths, fr 1691
Apprenticed to TOWNSEND Richard* 1692
Had apprentice:
TURNER John 1694 by t/o from JENKS Edmund*
HURLEY Jonathan* 1692
PHILLIPS Walter* 1696
BELL William 1697
HARRIS John 1698
In King's Bench Prison 1718
Sources: GL: BKC 2881/8–10, 2884, 2886/7
(MAC)

BENJAMIN Henry
a 1800–1825
Bookseller; Stationer; Optical, Mathematical and
Musical IS
High St., Rochester
Sources: TCd (pv) (Cpy)

BENLEY George
w 1837
Optician
1837   2 Boundary St, Kirkdale, Liverpool
Sources: LM index

BENNET Thomas
w 1775–1803
Hour-glass M
1775	49 Wade St, Bristol
1793–1803	Bridewell Lane, Bristol

Sources: Mat; Sket

BENNETT G.
w 1840–1841
Naut IM
1840–1841   13 Britannia St, City Road, London
Same premises as BENNETT Thomas (IV)*
See also BENNETT George*, possibly the same
maker
Attended London Mechanics Institute 1840–1841
Sources: LMIR (AM)

BENNETT George
s 1832 v 1836
Math IM
Alternative name: BENETT
1836   268 Holborn, London
Guild: [Coach and Coach Harness Makers]
Son of BENNETT Charlotte, in the service of
Dowager Lady Ellenborough
Apprenticed to ELLIOTT William (II)* 1832
See also BENNETT G.*, possibly the same maker
Attended London Mechanics Institution 1836
Sources: LMIR (AM); GL: CMC 5637/1

BENNETT Isaac

w 1825–1826
Math IM
1825–1826   48 Devonshire St., Bloomsbury, London
Attended London Mechanics Institute 1825–1826
Sources: LMIR (AM)

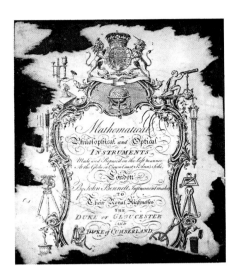

BENNETT John (I)

w 1735 d 1770
Math IM, Phil IM, Optical IM
Alternative name: BENNET
   Globe in Crown Court, between St.Ann's, Soho, & Golden Sq, London
   Crown Court, Little Pulteney St, London
   The Globe, Crown Court, St.Ann's Soho, near Golden Square, St.James, London
1743   Globe, in Crown Court, St.Ann's, Soho, London
1746–1747   Queen's Head in Crown Court, Knaves Acre, London
1753–1770   Crown Court, Soho, London
Guild: Stationers, fr 1731
Son of BENNETT Jasper, gardner, of St James's, Westminster, London
Apprenticed to FRANKLIN Thomas★ 1723
Had apprentice:
FITCH James (I)★ 1735
SPICER Edward ?★ 1739
HUTCHINS Josiah★ 1750
HIGGINBOTHAM David, son of Joseph★ 1752
SIMONS James★ 1757
SEARCH James★ 1764 t/o 1770 to BALCHIN Peter★
GOULD John (II)★ 1768 t/o 1771 to SEARCH James★
Succeeded by SEARCH James★
Associated with HALFPENNY William as maker of tangent rule designed by HALFPENNY
FERGUSON James (I)★, for whom he made instruments
R.apt Dukes of Gloucester & Cumberland; petitioner against Dollond's patent, 1764
Known to have sold: circumferentor, telescope
Instruments advertised: barometer, rule
Sources: PRO: PC1/7 no.94; inst NMM; *London Chronicle* 27 Sep 1770; GMag 21, 1951, p.270,273 (DJB); Calvert (1971) pl.9–10; Goodison (1977) p.132–33; Millburn (1988a) p.33; McKenzie (1978) p.29,130; Taylor (1966) p.160,197–98

BENNETT John (II)

w 1713–1726
[Math IM]
   London
Guild: Clockmakers, fr 1712
Apprenticed to BENNETT William (I)★, his father, 1702
Had apprentice:
DENNIS George 1713 t/o to BALDWIN Thomas
HOLTON Cob 1718
IRELAND Daniel 1724
COX Benjamin 1726
COBHAM John★ 1732 by t/o from BENNETT Richard★
Sources: Brown J (1979b) p.27

BENNETT John (III)

w 1750
[Math IM]
1733   Hatton Wall, Holborn, London
1746   Old Bailey, London
1751   Fleet St, London
Guild: Clockmakers, fr 1733
Apprenticed to BENNETT William (I)★ t/o to BENNETT Richard★ nd
Had apprentice ROBINSON Joseph★ 1750
Sources: GL: CKC 2721/1, 2723/2; Brown J (1979b) p.28

BENNETT John (IV)

w 1849–1885
Goldsmith, Watch M, Chrono M, Clock M, Importer, Math IM, Astro IM
Alternative name: Sir John BENNETT
1849–1859   65 Cheapside, London
1865–1885   64 & 65 Cheapside, London
Guild: Spectaclemakers, fr by purchase 1849
Son of BENNETT John, goldsmith, d, of Greenwich, Kent
Succeeded by BENNETT LTD Sir John
R.apt. Victoria, b.apt Royal Greenwich Observatory, Ordnance, Admiralty etc; FRAS; Ex.1851 and 1862; Sheriff of London and Middx; Common Councillor for ward of Cheap 1862–1889
Sources: PO;GL: SMC 5213/6, bill head; bill ML; MHS mt; Turner G (1983a) p.309; DNB

BENNETT Joseph

w 1823–1847
Optician, Math IM, Phil IM, Cabinet M, Math Instrument Case M
1823–1827   10 East Harding St, Shoe Lane, London
1826–1827   133 Goswell St, London
Guild: Salters, fr 1817
Apprenticed to BENNETT Joseph, his father, cabinet maker 1806
Had apprentice:
FEATLEY Charles 1819

NEWCOMB Samuel Campion 1837
BARKER James, son of Richard, of London, servant to Mr JONES★, optician
Sources: SH: SC Ap, Fr; Pg

BENNETT Leonard

w 1799–1826
Math IM, Optical IM
Alternative name: BENNET
1799   2 Queen's Square, Aldersgate St, London
1802–1826   26 Charles St, Hatton Garden, London
Possibly the Bennett who was said to have been a pupil of RAMSDEN Jesse★ and to have played a part in training SIMMS William (II)★, but this reference in RAS records is not confirmed by apprenticeship records
Sources: RAS, *Monthly Notices* 21 p.105 (AM); Bn; H; J; Kt; Und

BENNETT Richard

w 1715–1732
[Math IM]
   London
Guild: Clockmakers, fr 1715
Apprenticed to BENNETT William (I)★, his father, 1707
Had apprentice:
BENNETT John [possibly BENNETT John (III)★ but no t/o mentioned]
COBHAM John★ 1729 t/o 1732 to BENNETT John (II)★
Sources: Brown J (1979b) p.28

BENNETT Thomas (I)

w 1744
Math IM
1744   Parish of St. James, Westminster, London
Guild: Stationers
Had apprentice KENERICK William 1744
Sources: McKenzie (1978) p.30

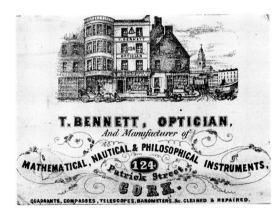

BENNETT Thomas (II)

w 1809–1867
Optician, Math, Naut & Phil IM
Alternative name: BENNET
1810–1812   Patrick St, Cork
1820   2 Patrick St, Cork
1824   65 Patrick St, Cork

BENNETT Thomas (III)

1826–1828	45 Patrick St, Cork
1844–1867	124 Patrick St, Cork

Succeeded by REYNOLDS & WIGGINS
Associated with BATE Robert B.* as agent for
Admiralty charts
Known to have sold: clinometer, hydrometer,
sextant, sundial
Sources: inst MHS; TCd NMM; DJB; Burnett &
Morrison-Low (1989) p.144–45; Calvert (1971)
p.13

BENNETT Thomas (III)
w 1811
Math IM
1811   28 Crown Row, Mile End, London
See also BENNETT Thomas (IV)*, possibly the
same person
Sources: H

BENNETT Thomas (IV)
w 1822–1840
Math IM, Optician, Phil IM

1822–1830	133 Goswell St, London
1831–1836	162 Goswell St, London
1839–1840	13 Britannia St, City Rd, London

See also BENNETT Thomas (III)*, possibly the
same person
Sources: Pg; Und

BENNETT William (I)
w 1687–1729
[Math IM]
                London
Guild: Clockmakers, fr 1687
Apprenticed to BROWN John (I)* by t/o 1677
Had apprentice:
BUSHELL Edward 1687
HUTCHINSON Richard* 1694
BALE Thomas nd, fr 1704
ARCUTT George 1697/8
BENNETT John (II)*, his son, 1702
BENNETT Richard*, his son, 1707
NASH Thomas 1708
NASH John 1709
BUSSY William 1714
BRIGGS Francis 1718
HADDOCK John 1722
WOLFE John by t/o fr PRESTON Edward nd, fr
1728/9
SPEAKMAN John 1729
BENNETT John (III)* nd, t/o to BENNETT
Richard*
Sources: GL: CKC 2723/1; Brown J (1979b) p.28;
Loomes (1981b)

BENNETT William (II)
w 1697–1705
[Scale M]
                London
Guild: Blacksmiths, fr c.1697
Apprenticed to FREEMAN Samuel (I)* 1685
Had apprentice:
SIMPSON James 1697
EVANS John 1699 t/o to SOANES John
MELLUM Abraham 1700/01
Sources: GL: BKC 2886/2–3, 2881/9 (MAC)

BENSON James William
w 1849–1891
Clock M, Watch M, Jeweller, Silversmith, Math IS

1849	16 Cornhill, London
1849	(Residence?) 107 Dorset Terrace, Dover Rd, London
1849–1864	Ludgate Hill, London
1854–1891	Cornhill, London
1872–1873	25 Old Bond St, London

Guild: Spectaclemakers, fr by purchase 1849
Son of BENSON William, corn merchant, of
Southwark Bridge Rd, London
Known to have sold: barometer, chronometer
Sources: GL: SMC 5213/6; inst MSEN; Britten
(1982); Webster R & M (1988)

BENSON John
w 1793
−1793   Birmingham
1793–1797   12 Princes St, New York
Sources: Bedini (1975) (DJB)

BENT James
w 1815
Scale M, Shoe M
1809   1 Ivy Lane, Hoxton, London
Guild: Blacksmiths, fr 1809 as Scale Beam M
Son of BENT James, shoemaker, of Old St, London
Apprenticed to SHURY Samuel (I)*
Had apprentice MAZEY Samuel 1815
Described as a shoemaker when admitted to the
livery of BKC 1828
Sources: GL: BKC 2881/16–17 (MAC)

BENTLEY Joseph
c. 1792 d by 1806
Optician
                Poppins Court, Fleet St, London
Father of BENTLEY William*, s 1806 ABBOTT
Charles* SMC
Sources: GL: SMC 5213/4

BENTLEY William
s 1806
                London
Guild: [Spectaclemakers]
Son of BENTLEY Joseph*
Partnership probably, BENTLEY & CHANT*
Apprenticed to ABBOTT Charles* 1806
Sources: GL: SMC 5213/4; PO

**BENTLEY & CHANT Probably William
& John**
w 1846–1870
Opticians
1846–1859   12 Nicholl Square, London
1865–1870   16 Bath St, Newgate St, London
Probably two apprentices of ABBOTT Charles*
Sources: PO

BENTON George
w 1849–1850
Math IM, Optician
1849–1850   244 High Holborn, London
Sources: PO

BENTON John
w 1818

Telescope M, Hearth brush M, Umbrella M
1818   Livery St, Birmingham
Sources: Wr

BERGE John
w 1790–1808
Optician

1773	At Mr Dollond's, St. Paul's Church Yard, London
1790–1793	Johnson's Court, Fleet St, London
1794–1803	Three Crane Court, Fleet St, London
1796	Crane Court, Fleet St, London
1804–1808	26 Lower Eaton St, Pimlico, London

Guild: Spectaclemakers, fr 1773
Son of BERGE John, victualler, of Wapping,
London
Apprenticed to DOLLOND Peter* 1765
Had apprentice DENBY Samuel 1796
Worked for DOLLOND Peter* 1773
See also BERGE Matthew*
d 1808
Known to have sold: sextant, thermometer
Sources: GL: SMC 5213/3, 5213/4; BW; H; JAC;
inst MHS

BERGE Matthew
w 1800 d 1819
Optician, Math IM
1802–1817   199 Piccadilly, London
Had apprentice WORTHINGTON Nathaniel*
Worked for RAMSDEN Jesse*
Employed WORTHINGTON Nathaniel*
Took over from RAMSDEN Jesse*
Succeeded by WORTHINGTON & ALLAN*
See also BERGE John*
Had Ramsden's dividing engine
Known to have sold: barometer, chondrometer,
gunner's callipers, repeating circle, sector, sextant,
telescope
Sources: VL: St. James's Westminster rate books
(AM); inst NMM, SM, (SJ); Parsons; H; J; Kt; PO;
Und; ChrSK 8 Dec 1988 lot 131; Goodison (1977)
p.301; Stimson (1985) p.104

BERGNA John Baptist
w 1825–1861
Baro M, Thermo M, Jeweller, Toy S

1825–1855	20 St. Nicholas Church Yard, Newcastle upon Tyne
1844	St. Nicholas Church Yard, Newcastle upon Tyne
1857–1859	23 St. Nicholas Church Yard, Newcastle upon Tyne
1861	22 St. Nicholas Church Yard, Newcastle upon Tyne

See also GRASSI, BERGNA & ORIGONI*
Sources: Pg (Scotland); Ric; Sl; Wd; Wim

BERNASCONE Innocent
w 1830
Clock M, Watch M, Optician
1830   Temple Place, High Wycombe
Sources: Legg (1975)

BERQUEZ Francis
w 1813–1847
[Clock M]

1813–1824	17 Vere St, Cavendish Square, London
1825–1835	6 Thayer St, Manchester Square, London
1826–1835	26 Thayer St, Manchester Square, London
1845–1847	27 Henrietta St, Cavendish Square, London

Known to have sold: barometer
Sources: Webster R & M (1988); Britten (1982)

BERRICK Ralph
w 1770
Rule M
1770   Queen St, Wolverhampton
Sources: Sket

BERRINGTON John
w 1815–1818
Thermo M, Baro M, Optician
1815–1818   Granby St, Leicester
Succeeded by BERRINGTON William★
Sources: H; PG

BERRINGTON William
w 1822
Optician
1822   Granby St, Leicester
took over from BERRINGTON John★
Sources: Pg

BERRY Arthur
w 1824–1845
Chrono M
1821–1823	34 Matthew St, Liverpool
1824	2 Great Nelson St, E. Liverpool
1837	3 Great Nelson St, Liverpool
1841–1845	3 Lord Nelson St, Liverpool
Sources: G; LM index (MAC); Loomes (1975)

BERRY James
w 1835–1856, 1866–1878
Chrono M, Naut IM, Optical IM, Watch M
1835–1852	52 Castle St, Aberdeen
1852	53 Marischal St, Aberdeen
1853–1856	88 Union St, Aberdeen
1866–1878	59½ Marischal St, Aberdeen
Guild: Hammermen, fr 1837
Son of BERRY James, ship master, of Aberdeen
Apprenticed to SPARK William, watch and clock maker, of Aberdeen
Partnership BERRY & SON James 1856–1865
Succeeded by BERRY & MACKAY
Known to have sold chronometers by HEWITT Thomas★, compass, quadrant, sextant, telescope
Sources: Bryden (1972) p.44; Clarke et al (1989) p.156

BERRY John
w 1774
[Spec M, Optician,]
1774   Opposite the Mansion House, York
Took over from EGGLESTON Nathaniel★
Sources: YC 22 Mar 1774 (DJB)

BERRY John Benjamin
w 1835–1851
Optician, Math IM, Phil IM

Alternative name: John
| 1835–1836 | 2 Hales Terrace, Commercial Road, Limehouse, London |
| 1836 | 14 Jamaica Terrace, Limehouse, London |
Guild: [Merchant Taylors]
Son of BERRY Charles, clerk, of London
Apprenticed to LILLEY John (I)★ 1826
b in the City of London, in 1811 or 1812
Sources: Pg; R; GL: MTC MF 320, 324; Cs 1851 (LS)

BERRY William
w 1669–1708
Globe M, Book S
Alternative name: BERREY
	Holborn Court, between Holborn and Gray's Inn, London
1669–1671	Blue Anchor in Middle Row, Holborn, London
1674–1675	Globe between York House and the New Exchange in the Strand, London
1676–1708	The Globe in Craggs Court between Charing Cross and Whitehall, London
Guild: Weavers, fr 1664
Son of BERRY William, baker, d, of Atherstone, Warwicks
Apprenticed to MOXON Joseph★ 1656
Had apprentice:
LAMBOURNE Robert 1675
HOLLOWAY Richard 1683
Associated with MORDEN Robert★ and LEA Philip★
b 1639 d 1718
Sources: GL: WVC 4657/1; inst WM; Bonacker (1963) p.56; Tyacke (1978) p.110

BERRY & SON G.
a 1790–1850
West Hartlepool
Known to have sold: octant
Sources: inst, Hull, Town Docks Mu (DJB)

BERTRAM James
w 1816–1822
Magnet M
Alternative name: BARTRAM
| 1816–1818 | Paradise St, Sheffield |
| 1822 | 2 Workhouse Croft, Sheffield |
Sources: Bn; Pg

BEST Francis
w 1629
Spec M
        London
Guild: Spectaclemakers, founder member 1629
Sources: GL: SMC 5214

BETTALLY Christopher
w 1787–1793
Baro M, Phil IM
Alternative name: BETALLY, BETTALY, BETALLI,
1787	1 Charlotte St, Pimlico, London
1788–1792	292 Oxford St, opposite Stratford Place, London
1793	229 Oxford St, London [possibly

directory error]
| 1787–1807 | Paris |
Known to have sold: barometer, thermometer
Sources: BM: Banks 105/6–8; BW; Goodison (1977) p.86–87,103–05

BETTESWORTH Peter
w 1716–1726
Math IM
Alternative name: BETTERSWORTH
| 1721–1725 | Wood St, London |
Guild: Stationers, fr 1716
Apprenticed to FRANKLIN Thomas★ 1707
Had apprentice:
COLE Robert★ 1716
PICK Andrew★ 1721 t/o 1726 to GORDON William★
LABORN Thomas, apparently not formally bound, then apprenticed to a HOWARD John, picture frame maker
Sources: GL: CH 12876/3; McKenzie (1978) p.35,130

BETTRIDGE John
w 1792
Rule M
1792   2 Charles St, Wolverhampton
Sources: Rate book (MAC)

BETTS Edwin
w 1849–1886
Rule M
| 1850 | 3 Marshall St, Birmingham |
| 1862 | 2 Marshall St, Birmingham |
Sources: Mor; Wh; Roberts (1982) (MAC)

BETTS James
w 1825–1849
Rule M
1825–1826	31 Horsefair, Birmingham
1828–1829	228 Bristol St, Birmingham
1829–1830	32 Duke St, Birmingham
1841	7 Court, Ashted Row, Birmingham
Sources: Pg; Wr; Roberts (1982) (MAC)

BETTS John (I)
w 1825–1850
Rule M
| 1825–1826 | 9 Blucher St, Exeter Rd, Birmingham |
| 1850 | 46 St. James Place, Birmingham |
Sources: Pg; Wh

BETTS John (II)
w 1839 d c. 1863
Globe M, Map Publisher, Bookseller & Stationer
| 1839 | 7 Compton St, Brunswick Square, London |
| 1846–1851 | 115 Strand, London |
Known to have sold: folding globe
Sources: Chr 20 May 1992 lot 354; PO

BETTS Thomas
w 1812–1863
Rule M, Beerhouse
1816	Top of Bromsgrove St, Birmingham
1818	Inge St, Birmingham
1841	128 Great Brook St, Birmingham

1850–1862   125 Great Brook St, Birmingham
Sources: Mor; Pg; Sl; Wh; Roberts (1982) (MAC)

BETTS William
w 1828–1835
Rule M
1828–1830   102 Bromsgrove St, Birmimgham
1835   1 Court, Exeter Row, Birmingham
Sources: Pg; West

BIANCHI Anthony John
w 1845
Baro M, Furniture M, Looking-glass M
1845   Bilston St, Wolverhampton
Sources: K

BIANCHI Gaettano
w 1830
Optician, Music S, Musical IS
1830   Tavern St, Ipswich
See also
BIANCHI George★
BIANCHI George Henry★
Sources: Pg

BIANCHI George
w 1805–1816
Baro M
1805   St. Clements St, Ipswich
1816   Westgate St, Ipswich
See also BIANCHI Gaettano★
Sources: H; Goodison (1977)p.88,302

BIANCHI George Henry
w 1844
Optician
1844   Tavern St, Ipswich
See also BIANCHI Gaettano★
Sources: Wh

BIDSTRUP Jesper
w 1793 d 1802
Optical IM, Math IM, Phil IM
Alternative name: BIRDSTRUP
Before 1787   Denmark
1787   London
1793–1794   36 St.Martin's St, Leicester Square, London
1802   Copenhagen, Denmark
Associated with
BUGGE Thomas FRS
WHITE, prob WHITE Joseph★
Came to London c. 1787 to train as IM; had a degree in mathematics; joined German-speaking Pilgrim Masonic Lodge in London
Known to have sold: mechanical apparatus, microscope, telescope
Instruments advertised: full range
Sources: BM: Add.MS 8097, 14; 8098, 112 (AVS); inst Pierre Marly's Mu, Paris; Soro Collection, Denmark; inst (s); Anderson et al (1990) p.12; Christensen (1993) p.4,6

BILLING Joseph
w 1835
Optician
1835   14 Morland St, Birmingham
Sources: Pg

BINDA John
w 1846–1852
Baro M, Optician
Alternative name: BINDER, Giovanni,
1846   25 Duncan St, Cork
Ex.1852, Cork
Known to have sold: barometer
Sources: Burnett & Morrison-Low (1989)p.145; Westropp (nd)

BINGHAM Charles
w 1808–1818
Sundial M
1808–1818   Ann St, Birmingham
Sources: H; TWr; Und

BIRCHMORE William
w 1672
Ironmonger
1672   Without Newgate, London
Known to have sold: rule
Sources: GL: CKC 2710/1 p.251; Loomes (1981b)

BIRD Charles
w 1838–1839
Drawing IM
1838–1839   73 Red Lion St, Clerkenwell, London
Sources: Pg; PO

BIRD John
w 1745 d 1776
Math IM
1747–1763   Sea Quadrant near the New Exchange Buildings in the Strand, London
1771   [Workshop] Berwick St, London
1772   Little Marybone St, London
1776   29 Little Marylebone St, Marylebone, London
Son of BIRD (BURD) John of Bishop Auckland, Durham
Worked for
GRAHAM George★
SISSON Jonathan★
Author; bap 1709; Mezzotint portrait MHS; made a dividing engine said to be the first to allow for variations caused by changes of temperature; supplied Royal Greenwich Observatory, and observatories across Europe; involved in development of the marine sextant in co-operation with the Board of Longitude
Known to have sold: astronomical clock, barometer, quadrant, mural quadrant, repeating circle, rule, thermometer, zenith sector
Sources: inst NMM, SM; Bernoulli (1771) p.107–08,126–29; GMag 1776 p.192; Bod: DD Radcliffe e2; Hellman (1932); Millburn (1988b) p.276–79; Porter et al (1985) p.7–8,28; Richley (1872); JRT; AM; McConnell (1994) p. 38

BIRD Thomas (I)
w 1818–1828
Optician
1818–1822   High St, Sheffield
1828   3 Hawksworth's Yard, High St, Sheffield
1828   Norfolk St, Sheffield
Sources: Bn; Pg

BIRD Thomas (II)
w 1834
Optician
1834   6 Mitre Fold, Wolverhampton
Sources: Wh

BIRD Thomas (III)
w 1839–1846
Leather hose M, Optician, Math IM
1839–1846   20 St. Augustine's Parade, Bristol
Sources: Mat; Pg

BIRKWOOD William
w 1790–1831
Math IM
Alternative name: BRICKWOOD
1790–1831   Crane Court, St.Peter's Hill, London
1805   5 Crane Court, Thames St, London
Guild: Goldsmiths
Son of BIRKWOOD William, yeoman
Apprenticed to HITCH Joseph★ in 1766
Father of BIRKWOOD William James★
Had apprentice:
COULING Samuel★ 1790
MURRAY James?★ 1802
BUNKER Thomas 1806
STEVENS Jeremiah★ 1809
JACKSON George 1815
PHARE Matthew G. 1817
EDWARDS Thomas Fair 1819
RUMBELL Samuel in 1826
Associated with WATKINS J.★ as a supplier
Sources: GH: GSC index; GL: CH 12876/7, STTP 2934 fol 17; EBA: OB 1816 (Watkins)

BIRKWOOD William James
w fm 1807
Math IM
1807   London
Guild: Goldsmiths, fp 1807
Son of BIRKWOOD William★
Sources: GH: GSC index

BIRNIE John
fl 1750–1785
Clock M
   Templepatrick, Antrim
Known to have sold: universal ring dial
Sources: Loomes (1976); Webster (1986)

BISHOP James
w 1794
Watch M
1794   Edinburgh
Known to have sold: barometer
Sources: Goodison (1977) p.302; Baillie (1951)

BISHOP Samuel
w 1790
Watch M
1790   Portland St, London
Guild: Clockmakers, fr 1781
Known to have sold: barometer
Sources: BW; Multhauf (1961); Baillie (1951)

BISSAKER Robert
w 1642–1664
Math IM (in wood)

Alternative name: BISSACER
1642–1664   Over against the Red Lion Tavern,
            Ratcliff, London
Guild: [Stationers]
Son of BISSAKER Thomas, yeoman, of Ellesmere,
Salop
Apprenticed to GOSSE Nathaniel★ 1634
Associated with STARR Robert★
Known to have sold: rule, slide rule
Instruments advertised: sector
Sources: inst SM; GL: inventory 9174/13; Bond
(1642) (SJ); Bryden (1992) p.318; McKenzie (1961)
p.74

BITHRAY Stephen
w 1826–1860
Optician, Math IM, Phil IM
1826–1838   4 North Piazza, Royal Exchange,
            London
1839–1844   6 Spread Eagle Court, Finch Lane,
            Cornhill, London
1845–1860   29 Royal Exchange, London
Known to have sold: compass, microscope
Sources: inst SM, (p); Pg; PO

BLACHFORD Michael
w 1839–1840
Navigation Warehouse
            116 Monories, Tower Hill, London
Partnership BLACHFORD & IMRAY★
See also BLACHFORD Robert★
Sources: Pg; PO; Taylor (1966) p.467

BLACHFORD Robert
w 1805–1817
Navigation Warehouse
1804–1817   114 Minories, Tower Hill, London
1805   137 Minories, Tower Hill, London
Took over from MOORE John Hamilton★
Succeeded by BLACHFORD & CO. Robert★
See also BLACHFORD Michael★
Sources: Kt; Und; Robinson (1962) p.125–26

BLACHFORD Robert & William
w 1828–1836
Chart publishers, Navigation Warehouse
1828–1836   116 Minories, Tower Hill, London
Succeeded by BLACHFORD & IMRAY★
Took over from BLACHFORD & CO. Robert★
See also BLACHFORD Michael★
Sources: Pg; PO

BLACHFORD & CO. Robert
w 1817–1828
Navigation Warehouse, Chart Publisher
1817–1818   114 Minories, Tower Hill, London
1819–1820   1 Little Tower St, London
1821–1828   79 Leadenhall St, London
Took over from BLACHFORD Robert★
Succeeded by BLACHFORD Robert & William★
Sources: J (JAC); PO

BLACHFORD & IMRAY Michael & James ?
w 1836–1845
Optical IM, Phil IM, Math IM, Naut IM, Chart S,
Nautical Warehouse
Alternative name: B & J BLATCHFORD
1837–1845   116 Minories, Tower Hill, London

Took over from BLACHFORD Robert & William★
Succeeded by IMRAY James★
See also BLACHFORD Michael★
Known to have sold: octant
Sources: R (JAC); PO; Robinson (1962); Stimson
(1985) p.114

BLACK John
w 1849–1852
Optician
1849–1852   16 Long Acre, Aberdeen
Sources: ADCS

BLACKBURN Isaac
w 1833–1846
Scale M
1833–1843   126 Minories, London
1836–1846   128 Minories, London
1843–1845   3 Swan St, London
Guild: Haberdashers, fr 1831
Son of BLACKBURN John (I)★
Took over from BLACKBURN John (I)★
Sources: GL: HC 15856, 15857/3; PO

BLACKBURN John (I)
w 1791–1833
Scale M
1791–1799   40 Whitechapel, London
1800–1833   126 Minories, London
Guild: Haberdashers, fr 1791
Son of BLACKBURN Samuel, carpenter, of
Stratford Green, Essex
Apprenticed to MOFFETT James★ 1781
Had apprentice:
GILLIS (GILES) Thomas Abraham 1791
MCLORINAN Thomas 1800
BLACKBURN John (II), his son, 1805
SMITH William Francis 1806
BRYANT Josias Hovel 1808
MONDS Joseph 1808, t/o to his father 1808
MONDS Thomas 1811
BLACKBURN Peter, his son, 1814
BLACKBURN William, his nephew, 1818
BLACKBURN James 1820
BLACKBURN Isaac★, his son, 1821
HEMS Jeremiah 1826
Partnership
MOFFETT & BLACKBURN★
VANDOME & BLACKBURN★
Succeeded by BLACKBURN Isaac★
Known to have sold: balance
Sources: GL: HC 15856, 15857/3, 15860/9; J; Kt;
Pg; R; W (JAC); inst (pv)

BLACKIE George
w 1851
Watch M, Chrono M
1851   11 President St West, King Square,
            London
b 1813 d 1885
Known to have sold: chronometer
Sources: PO; Baillie (1951)

BLACKIE William
w 1834–1838
Optical lapidary
            Edinburgh

Made jewel lenses for microscopes
Sources: Bryden (1972) p.44

BLACKMAN Solomon
w 1768 d c.1779
Scale M
            17 Butcher Hall Lane, London
Guild: Blacksmiths, fr 1756
Apprenticed to WORNELL John★ 1748
Son of BLACKMAN Giles, grocer, of Oakington,
Berks
Had apprentice:
CASON John 1768
SAWGOOD John★ 1770
WOODAGE George Cave★ 1773, t/o 1779 to
BADCOCK William G.★
TRICKEY William 1775
Known to have sold: balance
Sources: inst (pv); GL: BKC 2886/5,
2885/1(MAC)

BLACKWOOD James
w c. 1845 d 1893
Carpet M, Photographer, Mineralogist
c.1845   Aberdeen
c.1855   Kilmarnock
Associated with BARCLAY Andrew and MORTON
Thomas, astronomers
b 1823; elected to Kilmarnock town council,
president of Kilmarnock Philosophical Institution
Known to have sold: telescope
Sources: Kilmarnock Mu (MAC)

BLACKWOOD W. & J.T.
w 1846
Watch M, Jeweller, Optician, Chrono M,
Engraver, Silversmith
Alternative name: W. & I.T.
1846   5 Tyne St, North Shields
Known to have sold: octant
Sources: F; ChrSK 29 Mar 1960 lot 9, reported in
Webster R & M (1986)

BLADE John
w 1792
Scale M
1792   Fleet St, London
Guild: Blacksmiths
See also BLADES Tristram★
Sources: Wil

BLADES Tristram
w 1786–1790
Scale M
1786   5 Hen & Chicken Court, Fleet St,
            London
1790   Fleet St, London
1790   2 Flower de Luce Ct, Fetter Lane,
            London
Guild: Blacksmiths, fr 1786
Apprenticed to GRAY Francis ★ 1774 t/o 1775 to
GOODMAN John★
Son of BLADES John, gent, of London
See also BLADE John★
Sources: GL: BKC 2881/16, 2886/5(MAC); W
(JAC)

BLAINEY William

w 1848
Rule M, Gauging IM
1848   5 Lower Maudlin St, Bristol
Sources: Hunts

BLAIR Archibald

w 1827
Optical IM
1827   16 Broughton Place, Edinburgh
Sources: Bryden (1972) p.44

BLAKE John

w 1774–1805
Math IM
1774–1776   New Ratcliff, London
1801   [Residence?] Near Brewers
    Meeting, Stepney, London
1784–1794   45 Broad St, Ratcliff Cross, London
1805   Spring Garden Place, Stepney,
    London
Guild: Joiners, fr 1766
Apprenticed to URINGS John (II)★ 1754
Son of BLAKE John, gent, of Rattlesden, Suffolk
Had apprentice:
PARNELL Thomas (I)★ 1768
ROSSITER George 1773
CLEPHIN John 1776
HAYRES Robert 1779
DAY John 1783
Sources: GL: STTP 2934 fol 33; JC 8055/3,
8051/4, 8052/6; By (JAC); H; Crawforth (1987)
pp.347–48;

BLAKEBOROUGH Richard

w 1817–1837
Watch M, Clock M, Jeweller, Silversmith,
Ironmonger
1817   Pateley Bridge, Yorks
1817–1837   Otley, Yorks
Instruments advertised: balance, spectacles,
telescope, weather glass
Sources: Barker (1980) (MAC); Loomes (1976)

BLAKELEY Benjamin

w 1817–1845
Rule M, Math IM, Phil IM
1817–1834   15 Lambeth Lower Marsh, London
1826–1828   New Cut, Lambeth, London
1834–1836   11 High St, Lambeth, London
1835–1840   125 Lambeth Lower Marsh, London
1838–1841   50 Carlisle St, Westminster Rd,
    London
1842–1845   21 Lambeth Upper Marsh, London
Sources: Pg; PO; Und; JAC

BLAXAM Richard

w 1651
Known to have made a quadrant. Taylor gives the
name as BLOXHAM, but the original instrument at
BM was lost or destroyed during the second world
war
Sources: Ward (1981) p.139; Taylor (1954) p.238

BLEANTON John

w 1792
Optician

1792   Ludgate St, London
Sources: BW

BLEULER John

w 1790 d 1829
Optician, Math IM, Optical IM, Phil IM
Alternative name: BLEWLER
1790   27 Ludgate Hill, London
1791–1822   27 Ludgate St, London
1779   At Mr Shuttleworth's, Ludgate St,
    London
Guild: Spectaclemakers, fr 1779
Son of BLEULER Jacob, d, of Holborn, London
Apprenticed to SHUTTLEWORTH Henry R.★
1771
Worked for SHUTTLEWORTH Henry R.★
Took over from WHITFORD Thomas (I)★
Master of SMC 1794–1795, 1809–1811; d 27 Aug
1829
Known to have sold: chondrometer, microscope,
octant, rule, sextant, thermometer
Sources: GL: SMC 6028, 5213/3, 5213/4, 5213/5;
BW; H; Und; inst WM and (s); Calvert (1971)
p.15

BLEWS William

w 1793–1835
Weight M, Button M, Candlestick M
1793–1801   4 Navigation St, Birmingham
1835   3 Bartholomew St, Birmingham
Succeeded by BLEWS & SON William★
e 1782
Known to have sold: balance
Sources: Pg; Pye; Wd; Sy; inst Gloucester Mu

BLEWS & SON William

w 1833–1882
Bell founder, Brass founder, Scale M, Weight M
    23 Lower Whitecross St, E.C.
    London
1845–1882   9 New Bartholomew St,
    Birmingham
1860–1882   9–15 New Bartholomew St,
    Birmingham
1860   55 Bartholomew Close, London
1870   Royal Eagle Tube Works, West
    Bromwich
1870–1880   38 West Smithfield, E.C. London
Succeeded by BLEWS & SONS Wm.
Took over from BLEWS William★
Sources: K; PO; Wh; Wr

BLEYGHTON John (I)

w 1626–1654
Math IM (in silver or brass)
Alternative name: BLATON, BLADON, BLYTON,
BLIGHTON
    Bull Head Tavern in Tower St,
    London
1630–1631   Tower St, London
Guild: Grocers, fr 1620
Apprenticed to ALLEN Elias★ nd
Had apprentice:
LEA John 1626
RAMME Edward 1626
PACKWOOD Christopher★ 1630
EIVILLIM(?) William 1632
PLUMMER Francis nd, fr 1646

HOLMES Mathew nd, fr 1647
MUNCK Francis nd, fr 1652
BLEYGHTON John (II)★, his son, nd, fp 1654
Associated with BROWN Thomas (I)★
Known to have sold: slide rule
Sources: GL: GC 11592; Brown J (1979a) p.25–26;
Bryden (1992) p.309,318

BLEYGHTON John (II)

w 1654–1663
Alternative name: BLIGHTON
1654   London
Guild: Grocers, fp 1654
Apprenticed to
BLEYGHTON John (I)★, his father
Had apprentice:
HOWE William★ 1654
GUY William 1661
BENNETT Richard 1663
Note: it is possible that these apprentices were
bound to his father
Sources: Brown J (1979a) p.26

BLINKHORN Horatio

w 1839–1860
Optician, Math IM
1839–1847   45 Great Crosshall St, Liverpool
1849   17 Sun St, Liverpool
1853   15 Knight St, Liverpool
1857–1860   23 Sun St, Liverpool
Sources: G; Sl; LM index

BLOORE John

w 1799–1819
Optician
Alternative name: BLOOR
1799–1805   49 Hoxton Sq, London
1819   4 Helmet Row, Old St, London
Sources: H; R (JAC)

BLOW Edmund

w 1704–1739
Math IM
1736   Golden Quadrant, Plow Alley,
    Union Stairs, Wapping, London
1738–1739   Virginia St, London
1739   Half Moon Court by ye Hermitage,
    Wapping, London
Guild: Joiners, fr 1704
Apprenticed to WELLS Grace★ 1695
Son of BLOW Samuel, hemp dresser, of
Biggleswade, Beds
Had apprentice:
OXENFORD John★ 1704
WHEATON Joseph 1717
HARRIS Daniel (I)★ 1723 t/o 1725 to COOKE
Thomas (II)★
TAYLOR Thomas 1727
BAKER William 1738 t/o 1738 to COLE Thomas
and t/o 1740 to HUT Richard
Known to have sold: back-staff, Napier's bones
Sources: inst WM: Bennett (1983a) no.126;
Crawforth (1987) p.348; Gunther (1967) p.127;
Taylor (1966) p.111

BLOXHAM – see BLAXAM

BLUNT Charles
w 1814–1818
Optician, Math IM
Before 1814   Cornhill, London
1814–1818   38 Tavistock St, Covent Garden,
London
Known to have sold: altazimuth quadrant
Sources: H; J; Kt; Und; inst WM: Bennett (1987)
p.41 fig.31; letter from J. Wess, BSIS 1984, no. 4,
p.17

BLUNT Edward
w 1825 d 1826
Optician
1825–1826   22 Cornhill, London
Guild: Spectaclemakers, fr 1825
Apprenticed to BLUNT Thomas (I)★, his father,
1813
Brother of
BLUNT Revd William
BLUNT Thomas (II)★
Took over from BLUNT Thomas (II)★
Succeeded by HARRIS & SON Thomas &
William★
See also
BLUNT T. & T.★
BLUNT & SON T.★
Widow asked SMC for charity, 1827
Sources: GL: SMC 5213/4, 5213/5; PO; JAC

BLUNT John
w 1765–1772
Compass M, Ship chandler
1765–1772   Wapping Dock, London
Sources: Lg; Riv

BLUNT T. & T.
c 1820
Alternative name: Probably an alternative for
BLUNT & SON★
London
Known to have sold: barometer, hygrometer,
telescope
Sources: BSIS 1984 no.2 p.12, no.4 p.17

BLUNT Thomas (I)
w 1794 d 1823
Math IM, Optician
1760–1822   22 Cornhill, London
1816   22 Cornhill opposite the Royal
Exchange, London
Guild: Spectaclemakers, fr 1771
Son of BLUNT William, shoemaker, of Barnes,
Surrey
Apprenticed to NAIRNE Edward★ 1760
Had apprentice:
BLUNT Thomas (II)★, his son, 1804
BLUNT Edward★, his son, 1813
BLUNT William, his son, 1816
Father of BLUNT Revd William, fp 1825
Partnership NAIRNE & BLUNT★
Succeeded by BLUNT & SON Thomas★
R.apt Geo.III 1785; Master SMC 1792–1794,
1815–1817; supplier of instruments to Christ's
Hospital School; collaborated with J.H. de
Magellan in the design of his barometer; d 16
March 1823
Known to have sold: barometer, globe,

microscope, thermometer
Sources: GL:TCd; SMC 5213/3, 5213/4; CH
12823/8 p.398; H; Kt; Ld; Und; BM: Heal 105/14;
PRO: LC3/67 p.178; ChrSK 8 Dec 1988 lot 142;
Holbrook (1992) p.157; Banfield (1991)

BLUNT Thomas (II)
w 1822–1824
Optician
1804–1811   Cornhill, London
Guild: Spectaclemakers, fr 1811
Partnership
probably, T. & T. BLUNT★
BLUNT & SON Thomas★
Apprenticed to BLUNT Thomas (I)★, his father
Succeeded by BLUNT Edward★
w pt c.1801–1822 [sic – Christ's Hospital records
give Blunt & Son 1801, so it is possible that he was
working before he was formally apprenticed]
Sources: GL: SMC 5213/4; CH 12823/8 p.398;
Kt; PO

BLUNT & SON Thomas
w c.1801–1822
Optician, Math IM
1801–1803   22 Cornhill, London
Listed in directories 1801–1804, 1822
Known to have sold: microscope
Sources: GL: CH 12823/8 p.398; Kt; Pg; Turner G
(1981) p.41

BLYTH Thomas
w 1777–1780
Compass M
1777–1780   34 Deritend, Birmingham
Sources: PR

BOARDMAN –
w 1709
Known to have sold: perpetual calendar
Sources: inst, Harriet Wynter catalogue 3, 1976

BODDINGTON John
fr 1734
Threadneedle St, London
Alternative name: BODDINTON
Guild: Clockmakers, fr 1734
Apprenticed to CADE Simon★ 1725
Known to have sold: perpetual calendar
Sources: GL: CKC 2710/4; Brown J (1979b) p.28;
inst BM: Ward (1981) p.130; Holbrook (1992)
p.152

BODDY Thomas
w pt 1849
Math IM
1849   523 Oxford St, London
1849   3 Gt Carter Lane, London
Guild: [Merchant Taylors]
Son of BODDY Thomas, gentleman, of Walworth,
London
Partnership PIGGOTT & BODDY★
Apprenticed to PIGGOTT William Peter★ 1840
Sources: GL: MTC MF 320,324; PO

BOGGAIA D.
w 1839–1840
Baro M, Thermo M

1839–1840   29 Great Warner St, Clerkenwell,
London
Sources: R (JAC)

BOIG John
fl 1649 d 1663
Mathematician, Math IM ?
Alternative name: BOOK
Edinburgh
Sources: Bryden (1972) p.44

BOLEY James
w 1826–1828
Drawing IM
1826–1828   4 Penton Street, Walworth, London
Guild: [? Merchant Taylors]
Attended London Mechanics Institute 1826–1828
Probably the same person as James Bolen
apprentice of PIGGOTT P.W.★
Sources: LMIR (AM)

BOLONGARO Dominic
w 1817–1848
Carver, Baro M, Looking-glass M, Print S &
Picture frame M, Math IS, Phil IM
Alternative name: Dominick
1817–1830   2 Old Millgate, Manchester
1824   7 John's St, Salford, (residence)
Manchester
1831–1833   14 Market St, Manchester
1834–1848   32 Market St, Manchester
Father of BOLONGARO Peter
Worked for ZANETTI Vittore★
Had apprentice GALE Joseph★
Succeeded by BOLONGARO & SON★
b c.1783 in Stresa, Italy; came to England c.1805;
d 1856
Known to have sold: barometer, thermometer,
hygrometer
Sources: Bn; Goodison (1977) p.303; MSIM, notes
by JW

BOLONGARO & SON Dominic (& Peter)
w 1834–1892
Carver, Gilder, Baro M, Thermo M, Optician,
Math IS, Print S, Publisher, Picture restorer
1834–1883   32 Market St, Manchester
1855–1860   30–32 Market St, Manchester
Took over from BOLONGARO Dominic★
Supplied by NEGRETTI & ZAMBRA★
d 1892, business sold
Sources: Pg; Sl; Goodison (1977) p.191,303;
MSIM, notes by JW

BOLTER Hugh
w 1666–1682
Spec M
Alternative name: BOULTER
1669–1672   Minories, London
1671   Little Minories, London
Guild: Spectaclemakers
Had apprentice:
HOLT Samuel between 1659 and 1666 by t/o from
COSBY Henry★
See also MAXAM Richard★
Involved in making lenses for Robert Hooke; 1678
fined by SMC for selling bad wares
Sources: Simpson (1989) p.54; GL: SMC 5213/1

BOLTON Frederick
w 1850–1858
Rule M
1850   [Residence?] Vauxhall Grove,
            Birmingham
Sources: Roberts (1982) (MAC)

BOLTON Frederick & Henry
w 1841–1850
Rule M, Math IM, Measuring tape M
1841–1850   61 & 62 Loveday St, Steelhouse
            Lane, Birmingham
Sources: K; Pg; Sl; Wh

BOLTON John (I)
a 1785 d 1821
Watch M, Clock M
            Chester le Street
            Durham
b 1761
Known to have sold: barometer, thermometer
Sources: Goodison (1977) p.303; inst (s)

BOLTON John (II)
w 1831
Optician
1831   15 St. Johns Square, Clerkenwell,
            London
Attended London Mechanics Institute 1831
Sources: LMIR (AM)

BOLTON Thomas
w 1808–1845
Rule M, Math IM
1809–1818   Colmore Row, Birmingham
1818   6 Colmore Row, Birmingham
1828–1830   61 Loveday St, Birmingham
1835   61/62 Loveday St, Birmingham
Known to have sold: drawing instruments
Sources: H; Pg; West; Wr; ChrSK Dec 1984
(MAC)

BOMBELLI Baldisaro
w 1828–1834
Baro M, Math IM
Alternative name: BOMBALY Baldy
1834   6 King St, Whitehaven
Known to have sold: hydrostatic bubbles,
barometer
Sources: Pg; PWh; Goodison (1977) p.303;
Holbrook(1992) p.112

BON John
w 1840–1846
Chrono M, Watch M, Naut IM
1840   17 Dock St, Dundee
1845   25 Dock St, Dundee
1846   26 Dock St. East, Dundee
Succeeded by BON Mrs★, presumably his widow
Sources: Bryden (1972) p.45

BON Mrs.
w 1850
Chrono M, Watch M, Naut IM
1850   24 Dock St. East, Dundee
Took over from BON John★
Sources: Bryden (1972) p.45

BONAR John
w 1623–1634
[Sundial M]
            Areae (Ayr?)
Known to have sold: sundial
Sources: Clarke et al (1989) p.211

BOOKER Francis & John
w 1761–1773
Glass Grinders, Glass S
1761–1773   Essex Bridge, Dublin
Sources: Burnett & Morrison-Low p.121

BOOTE John
w 1634
Spec M
1634   London
Guild: Brewers, Spectaclemakers
Son of BOOTE John, farmer, of Blackwell, Notts
Apprenticed to TURLINGTON John★ 1626
fr Brew 1633; translated from Brewers to SMC
1634
Sources: CLRO: Ald 49 fol.14; GL: Brew 5445/14
–15

BOOTH William
w 1819
Optician
1819   1 King's Head Court, Beech St,
            Barbican, London
Guild: [Stationers]
Apprenticed to: WILLSON George★ 1802
Son of BOOTH Richard, watchmaker, of London
Sources: R (JAC); Bod: MF 440, STC Ap

BORBRIDGE Charles
w 1820–1834
Math IM
1820–1822   12 Duke St, Whitehaven
1829   76 King St, Whitehaven
1834   1 King St, Whitehaven
Sources: Pg; PWh

BORDESSA Pietro
w 1834–1860
Baro M, Thermo M, Toy S, Jeweller
Alternative name: BORDESA Peter
1846   33 Bridge Street Row, Chester
Known to have sold: barometer
Sources: Sl; Goodison (1977) p.303

BORINI P.
w 1818
Carver, Gilder, Looking-glass M, Picture frame M
Alternative name: BORONI
1818   Snowshill, Birmingham
See also BORINI & CO. Peter★
Sources: Pg; Wr

BORINI & CO. Peter
w 1809
Optician
1809   14 Edgbaston St, Birmingham
See also BORINI P.★
Sources: H

BOSETTI Francis
w 1851

Baro M, Thermo M
1851   5 Wardrobe Place, Doctors
            Commons, London
Sources: PO

BOSTOCK Joshua
w 1758–1780
Math IM
1758–1766   St. Mary le Strand, London
1774–1780   Feathers Court, Drury Lane, London
Had apprentice:
CLARKE Joseph 1758
TRUTBECK (?TROUTBECK) Edmund★ 1766
Petitioner against Dollond's patent
Known to have sold: microscope
Sources: PRO: IR 1/21 /25 (AM), PC 1/7 no.94;
IHR: Wpoll 1774, 1780 (AM); inst (s)

BOSWELL Samuel
w 1735
1735   Spitalfields, London
Guild: Joiners, fr 1709
Apprenticed to COOKE Thomas (II)★ 1701
Son of BOSWELL Samuel, mariner, d, of Aldgate,
London
Sources: Crawforth (1987) p.348

BOTT Daniel
w 1768
Ship chandler
1768   Near King James's-stairs, Wapping,
            London
See also BOTT AND WARDELL ★
Sources: Bd

BOTT AND WARDELL
w 1763–1766
Ship chandlers
1763–1765   Near King James's-stairs, Wapping,
            London
See also BOTT Daniel★
Known to have sold: octant
Sources: Sby 3 Oct 1991 lot 55; Mort; Riv

BOTTON John
w 1805
Math IM
1805   20 Church St, Blackfriars Rd,
            London
See also
MUNRO James (I)★
LEKEUX Richard★
Sources: H

BOUCHER William
fl 1809 w 1816
Math IM
Alternative name: BONCHER
1816   Waterford
Sources: Und Class 3; Burnett & Morrison-Low
(1989) p.145

BOUFFLER Robert
w 1839–1841
Baro M, Thermo M
1839–1841   7 Bell Court, Gray's Inn Lane,
            London
Sources: R (JAC)

BOULTER Alfred
w 1849–1890
Math IM
1849–1890   7½ St. John's Lane, Clerkenwell,
              London
Sources: PO;Wk

BOULTON Matthew
w 1769–1787
Engineer
1769–1787   Soho Manufactory, Birmingham
Associated with
FERGUSON James (I)★
WHITEHURST John (I)★
WRIGHT Thomas (III)★, who all supplied movements
Best known as maker of steam engines and
collaborator with WATT James (I)★
Known to have sold: astronomical clock
Sources: King & Millburn (1978) p.141

BOURNE John (I)
w 1678–1695
Spec M
Alternative name: BORNE
1678   Holborn, near Gray's Inn, London
1688   Holborn, near Turnstile, London
1695   Middle Row, Holborn, London
Guild: Spectaclemakers
See also BOURNE Mrs★
fr by 1666; had faulty spectacles seized by SMC
Sources: GL: SMC 5213/1

BOURNE John (II)
w 1792
Rule M
1792   7 Wadhams Hill, Wolverhampton
Sources: Rate books (MAC)

BOURNE Joseph junior
w 1845
Optician
1845   7 Digby St, Aston Road,
              Birmingham
Sources: K

BOURNE Joshua
w 1744–1767
Math IM
1751–1767   Goodman's Fields, London
Guild: Joiners, fr 1744
Apprenticed to URINGS John (I)★ 1731
Son of BOURNE Joshua, tailor, of Whitechapel,
London
Had apprentice:
BOURNE Thomas (I)★ 1755
MAYO William 1750
WEBB Joseph 1744
d c.1767
Sources: GL: JC 8052/6, 8055/1, 8055/2;
Crawforth (1987) p.348–49

BOURNE Mrs.
w 1693
Spec M
1693   Holborn, London
Guild: [Paid search fee to Spectaclemakers]
See also BOURNE John★
Sources: GL: SMC 5213/1

BOURNE Thomas (I)
w 1803–1809
Math IM
1778   Baker's Row, Whitechapel, London
1800–1802   Leman St, Goodman's Fields,
              London
1803–1809   Bethnal Green Rd, London
1821   Hog Row, Bethnal Green Rd,
              London
Guild: Joiners, fr 1767
Apprenticed to BOURNE Joshua★ 1755
Son of BOURNE Bernard, tailor, d, of
Whitechapel, London
Father of BOURNE Thomas (II)★
Partnership BOURNE & SON★
Sources: GL: JC 8055/4; Sun 11936/264
no.395590; Crawforth (1987) p.349

BOURNE Thomas (II)
w pt 1801 w 1821
Math IM
1801–1821   18 Bakers Row, Whitechapel,
              London
Guild: Joiners, fp 1801
Son of BOURNE Thomas (2740),
Had apprentice:
ENTWISTLE James 1801
MORTON Daniel James 1803
[These apprentices could also have been bound to
BOURNE Thomas (I)★, in JC records they are
bound to BOURNE of 18 Baker's Row, but see
BOURNE & SON★]
Partnership BOURNE & SON★
Sources: GL: JC 8051/2; 8055/5; Crawforth (1987)
p.349

BOURNE Thomas (III)
w 1778–1845
Scale M
              56 Broad St, Birmingham
1791–1793   Digbeth, Birmingham
1833   Broad St, Birmingham
1835–1842   28, 29 & 30 Broad St, Birmingham
Succeeded by AVERY W. & T.★
See also
BOURNE & CHAMBERS★
BOURNE & PAINTER★
BOURNE & SIMPSON★
BOURNE & SMITH★
Known to have sold: balance, weights
Sources: K; Pg; Pye; Wd; Wr; Broadbent (1949)

BOURNE Thomas (IV)
w 1828–1835
Scale M
1828–1835   1 Mount St, Birmingham
See also BOURNE Thomas (III)★
BOURNE & WRIGHT★
Sources: Pg; Wr

BOURNE & CHAMBERS
w 1803–1821
Scale M
1803–1821   Broad St, Birmingham
Succeeded by BOURNE & PAINTER★
See also BOURNE Thomas (III)★
Known to have sold: steelyard
Sources: Chp; H; Pg; TWr; Wr; inst (pv)

BOURNE & PAINTER
w 1821–1826
Scale M
Alternative name: PAWTER ?
1821–1826   29 Broad St, Birmingham
See also BOURNE Thomas (III)★
Sources: Bn; Pg; Wr

BOURNE & SIMPSON
w 1800
Scale M
1800   27 Cannon St, Birmingham
See also BOURNE Thomas (III)★
Known to have sold: steelyard
Sources: Chp; BM: Banks 103.1; inst (s)

BOURNE & SMITH
w 1829–1831
Scale M
1829–1831   29 Broad St, Birmingham
See also BOURNE Thomas (III)★
Sources: Pg; Wr

BOURNE & SON Thomas (& Thomas)
w 1799–1802
Math IM
Alternative name: Thomas (I) & Thomas (II)
1799–1802   18 Baker's Row, Mile End, London
Guild: Joiners
Sources: H; Crawforth (1987) p.349

BOURNE & WRIGHT
w 1811–1826
Scale M
1811–1822   Great Charles St, Birmingham
1818–1826   1 Mount St, Birmingham
See also BOURNE Thomas (IV)★
Sources: Bn; Pg; Wr

BOVERI Francis
w 1826–1841
Baro M, Thermo M, Looking-glass M
1826–1841   9 Eyre Street Hill, London
Sources: Pg; PO

BOWEN Thomas Michael
w 1824–1876
Optician, Math IM, Phil IM
1824–1830   12 Market Place, Manchester
1825   9 Ridgefield, (residence) Manchester
1833–1868   27 Market Place, Manchester
1833–1843   (Residence) Suspension Bridge,
              Lower Broughton, Manchester
1845   (Residence) 2 Paradise Hill,
              Broughton Rd, Salford
1848   (Residence) 46 Gartside St,
              Manchester
1852   (Residence) 5 Smiley St, Red Bank,
              Manchester
Succeeded by BOWEN Mrs. Mary
e 1802
Sources: Bn; Pg; Sl; JW

BOWEN William
w 1773
Brazier, Ironmonger
1773   Haverfordwest, Wales

Instruments advertised: balance
Sources: *British Chronicle* 11 Nov 1773 (JRM)

BOWIE John
w 1820–1822
Math IM
1820   Low St, North Shields
See also BOWIE William★
Known to have sold: compass (magnetic)
Sources: Pg; inst Glasgow Mu

BOWIE William
w 1795–1809
Phil IM, Math IM
1795–1809   Quayside, Newcastle upon Tyne
See also BOWIE John★
Sources: *Newcastle Chronicle* 31 Jan 1795, 18 Jan 1800; H

BOWMAN Robert
w 1802
Optical IM
1802   Calton Hill Observatory, Edinburgh
Sources: Bryden (1972) p.45

BOX Thomas
a 1800–1850
Known to have sold: rule
Sources: inst(pv)

BOX William B.
w 1851–1881
Watch M, Chrono M
1851   21 Upper Charles St, Northampton Square, London
Sources: PO; Loomes (1976)

BRABY James
w 1816–1837
Alternative name: BRADY
1816   Pedlar's Acre, Lambeth, London
Known to have sold: balance.
Sources: *Repertory of Arts, Manufactures and Agriculture* 1816, 2nd series, 24, p.92–94 (MAC)

BRACHER George
w 1826–1840
Optician, Math IM, Phil IM
1826–1840   19 King St, Commercial Road East, London
1839–1840   98 St.John Street Rd, London
1840   19 & 20 King St, Commercial Rd. East, London
Succeeded by BRACHER Mary★
Sources: Pg; PO

BRACHER Mary
w 1841–1843
Optician
1841–1843   19 King St, Commercial Road, East, London
Took over from BRACHER George★
Sources: R

BRADBERRY Ann
w 1819–1826
Spec M, Optician
1819–1822   27 Holles St, Cavendish Square, London
1822–1826   28 Holles St, Cavendish Square, London
Succeeded by BRADBERRY & CO.★
Took over from BRADBERRY Robert★
See also BRADBERRY Charles★
Sources: Pg; R (JAC)

BRADBERRY Charles
w 1823–1824
Spec M
1823–1824   27 Holles St, Cavendish Square, London
See also
BRADBERRY Ann★
BRADBERRY & CO.★
BRADBERRY Robert★
Sources: Kt

BRADBERRY Robert
w 1809–1818
Spec M
1809   329 Oxford St, London
1810–1818   332 Oxford St, London
1819   27 Holles St, Cavendish Square, London
Succeeded by BRADBERRY Ann★
See also
BRADBERRY & CO.★
BRADBERRY Charles★
Instruments advertised: spectacles
Sources: H; Kt; Und; *Weekly Dispatch*, 16 Mar 1817 (JRM)

BRADBERRY & CO.
w 1826–1860
Spec M
1826–1852   28 Holles St, Cavendish Square, London
1853–1859   311 Oxford St, London
1860   65 New Bond St, London
Took over from BRADBERRY Ann★
See also
BRADBERRY Charles★
BRADBERRY Robert★
Sources: Pg; PO

BRADBURN George & Thomas
w 1841–1852
Rule M
1850   18 Alcester St, Birmingham
Sources: Sl; Roberts (1982)

BRADBURY D.
w 1774
Assay Master
1774   Sheffield
Known to have sold: weights
Sources: inst (s)

BRADBURY George & Thomas
w 1841
Rule M
1841   18 Alcester St, Birmingham
Probably a directory error for George & Thomas Bradburn★
Sources: Pg

BRADFIELD William Henry
w 1838–1853
Optician, Math IM, Philo IM
1838–1840   30 Royal St, Lambeth, London
1841–1853   31 Royal St, Lambeth, London
Sources: Pg; PO

BRADFORD George
w 1817–1851
Optician
1817–1851   99 Minories, Tower Hill, London
Succeeded by OMER John
See also BRADFORD Isaac★
Known to have sold: compass (magnetic), octant
Sources: J; Pg; PO; inst & TCd NMM; Holbrook (1992) p.86,138,186,198

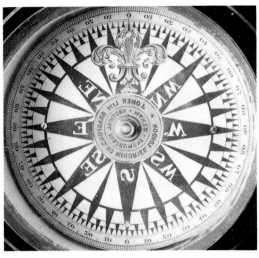

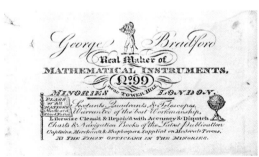

BRADFORD Isaac
w 1794–1822
Math IM, Optician
            Wapping Old Stairs, London
1794–1801   87 Bell Dock, Wapping, London
1802–1807   69 Bell Dock, Wapping, London
1808–1822   136 Minories, Tower Hill, London
Succeeded by BRADFORD & CO. Isaac★
See also BRADFORD George★
BRADFORD & SON Isaac★
Known to have sold: compass (magnetic)
Sources: H; Ld; Und; W; inst (s)

BRADFORD John
w 1654
Math IM
Sources: Taylor (1954) p.241

BRADFORD & CO. Isaac
w 1823–1824
Optician, Math IM, Optical IM
1823–1824   136 Minories, Tower Hill, London
Succeeded by BRADFORD & SON Isaac★
Took over from BRADFORD Isaac★
See also BRADFORD George★
Known to have sold: sextant
Sources: Kt; R(JAC); ChrSK 14 Apr 1988 lot 2

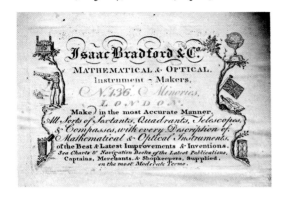

BRADFORD & SON Isaac
w 1825–1836
Math IM, Optical IM, Ship chandler
1825–1836   136 Minories, Tower Hill, London
1833   125 Minories, Tower Hill, London
Took over from BRADFORD & CO. Isaac★
See also BRADFORD George★
Sources: PO; R(JAC)

BRADFORD, DARBY & HULLS
William, Richard & Jonathan
w 1753–1754
1753   Chipping Campden, Glos
Associated with DARBY & CO. Richard
Pat. money balance and slide rule 1753
Known to have sold: balance
Sources: Patent records (MAC); inst MHS;
Sheppard & Musham (1975) p.169; Wallis R & P
(1986) p.231,357–58

BRADLEY James Gibson
w 1828–1862
Chrono M
Alternative name: Gibbon
1828–1834   90 Richmond Row, Liverpool
1852–1862   32 Lord St, Liverpool
Sources: LM index (MAC); Loomes (1975)

BRADLEY John (I)
fr 1704 w 1710
Math IM
Alternative name: BRADLEE
1704   London
1710–1716   Moscow
1716–1743   St.Petersburg
Guild: Grocers, fr 1704
Apprenticed to WORGAN John★ 1697 t/o
nd to ROBERTS Jonathan★
In Moscow 1710; probably invited to Russia by
Peter the Great; d 1743
Known to have sold: sundial
Sources: Brown J (1979a) p.28; Chenakal (1972) p.14

BRADLEY John (II)
w 1829–1866
Rule M
1835   10 Hurst St, Birmingham
1841   5 Hurst St, Birmingham
Sources: Pg; Roberts (1982)

BRADLEY Richard
w 1838–1839
Rule M, Tool M
1838   20 Old Compton St, London
1839   23 Old Compton St, Soho, London
Sources: Pg

BRAGG Henry
w 1780
Math IM
1780   Chick Lane, London
Father of BRAGG John s 1780 BC
Sources: GL: BC 5266/6 p.254

BRAHAM George
w 1842–1867
Optician, Math IM
1842–1867   6 George St, Bath
Succeeded by BRAHAM David
Sources: C; Hunts; Kn; Pg

BRAHAM John
w 1828–1838
Optician, Math IM, Phil IM, Naut IM
1828   12 Clare St, Bristol
1829–1830   42 College Green, Bristol
1830–1838   10 St.Augustine's Parade, Corner of
            Hanover St, Bristol
1833   8 Pulteney Bridge, Bath
1837   5 York Buildings, Bath
Succeeded by
(1) BRAHAM & CO. John★
(2) BRAHAM Joseph, his son
Associated with BATE Robert B.★ as chart agent
e 1797 according to advertising claim; listed again
as an individual 1863; d by 1866
Known to have sold: balance, barometer,
microscope, weights
Sources: Mat; Pg; Sil; BsM notes; Calvert (1971)
p.13; inst Abergavenny Mu (MAC)

BRAHAM & CO. John
w 1839–1851
Optician, Math IM, Phil IM, Naut IM
1840–1851   7 St.Augustine's Parade, opposite the
            Drawbridge, Bristol
Took over from BRAHAM John★
Ex.1851
Known to have sold: blow-pipe, spectacles, lens
Sources: Hunts; Mat; Cat.1851

BRAILSFORD John
a 1750
Cutler
        In ye broad part of St.Martin's
        Court, Leicester Fields, London
See also PAWSON & BRAILSFORD★
Instruments advertised: drawing instruments, rule,
spectacles
Sources: TCd (pv)

BRANDON & STILES Leverside & Nicholas
w 1782
Math IM, Turner
1782   Lucas St, Rotherhithe, London
See also STILES & LAW★
Sources: GL: Sun 11936/302 no.465241

BRANDRETH Timothy
w 1713–1714
Optical IM
        London
Guild: Spectaclemakers, fr 1701
Partnership WILLDEY & BRANDRETH★
Apprenticed to STERROP Ralph★ 1693
Had apprentice:
COOK Nathaniel 1713/14
WARD John (I)★ 1714
Worked for MARSHALL John★
Sources: GL: SMC, 5213/1, 5213/2 p.23,86,90;
Daily Courant 3 Mar 1707

BRAWN Mary (Mrs)
w 1723–1729
[Spec M]
Alternative name: BRAWNE
1726   London
Guild: [Spectaclemakers]
Wife of BRAWN Samuel (I)★
Had apprentice:
FORD William (I)★ 1729
ABCHURCH John 1723 t/o 1727
to HATFIELD T.
Mother of BRAWN Samuel (II), fp 1726/7
1726 Summoned by SMC for employing
'foreigners', i.e. non-freemen
Sources: GL: SMC pp.137–38,176,178,187,207

BRAWN Samuel (I)
w 1702
[Spec M]
Alternative name: BRAWNE
        London
Guild: Spectaclemakers, fr 1696
Father of BRAWN Samuel (II), fp 1726/7
Husband of BRAWN Mary★
Apprenticed to TAILOR Mary★ nd
Had apprentice BLAKEY Simon 1702
r or d by 1723
Sources: GL: SMC, 5213/2 pp.5,28,44,137,178

BREEDEN James
a 1774–1797
Scale M, Weight M
        5 Clerkenwell Green, London
Known to have sold: balance
Sources: Bank Of America Capital Market Group,
Annual Review, 1985, p.32 (MAC)

BREGAZZI Innocent & Peter
w 1825–1834
Picture framers, Glass polishers, Baro M, Thermo
M, Hydro M
Alternative name: It.& Pr.
1825   High Pavement, Nottingham
Succeeded by BREGAZZI Peter★
See also BREGAZZI Samuel★
Sources: Glover's directory; Goodison (1977) p.304

BREGAZZI Peter
w 1840–1842
Carver, Gilder, Baro M, Looking-glass M
1840–1842   Bridlesmith Gate, Nottingham
Took over from BREGAZZI Innocent & Peter★
Known to have sold: barometer, thermometer
Sources: Goodison (1977) p.304

BREGAZZI Samuel
w 1816–1830
Baro M, Carver, Gilder
1816   Willow Row, Derby
1818   Jury St, Derby
1830   Queen St, Derby
Took over from BREGAZZI & CO. S.★
See also BREGAZZI Innocent & Peter★
Known to have sold: barometer, hygrometer,
thermometer
Sources: H; Pg; Goodison (1977) p.305

BREGAZZI & CO S.
w 1809
Baro M
              Willow Row, Derby
Succeeded by BREGAZZI Samuel★
Known to have sold: barometer
Sources: Goodison (1977) p.305

BRIDGER Richard
w 1717
Math IM, Phil IM
1717   Upper end of Hind Court, Fleet St,
              London
Husband of HAUKSBEE Ann
Apprenticed to HAUKSBEE Francis (I)★
Took over from HAUKSBEE Francis (I)★, on
behalf of the widow
Sources: GL: St. Dunstan's in the West, mar,
6540/4; Vream W, *A Description of the Air Pump*
(1717) A2r

BRIDGES Henry
w 1741
Architect
              Waltham Cross
              Waltham Abbey
b 1697 d 1754
Known to have sold: astronomical clock
Sources: King & Millburn (1978) p.142–44

BRIGGS John
w 1669–1675
Spec M, Watch Glass M, Gardener
Alternative name: BRIGGE, BRIGG
1669   Parish of St.Brides, London
1670   Shoe Lane, London
Guild: Spectaclemakers fr 1670; Clockmakers
brother 1669
Employed BRIGGS Mrs, his wife, at glass grinding
Soldier in the army at the Restoration of Charles II
Sources: GL: SMC 5213/1; Loomes (1981b)

BRIGGS Matthew
s 1785 w 1813
Excise IM
1813   Maidenhead Court, Little St.
              Thomas Apostle, London
Guild: [Joiners]

Apprenticed to ROBERTS Edward (I)★
Sources: GL: JC 8052/7; Stat: STC, Memo Bk

BRIND William
w 1753–1774
Scale M
              Hand & Scales in Carey Lane in
              Foster Lane, Cheapside, London
              and Haymarket, London
Guild: Blacksmiths, fr 1751
Apprenticed to READ Samuel★1744
Son of BRIND William, inn holder, d, of
Highworth, Wilts
Had apprentice:
FORDHAM Timothy 1753
PHILLIPS Edward★ 1755
DAVIS William 1756 by t/o
from POUSSETT Phillip★
BASELEY Samuel 1761
LEWIS Nicholas 1762
GOODMAN William★ 1769, t/o 1772
to GRAY Francis★
WHEATLEY John 1770 by t/o
from BROOKSBY Thomas (II)★ t/o 1772 to
RIDGARD Joseph★
GAUDIN Edward★ 1771, t/o 1774
to GIBSON Thomas★
Known to have sold: balance
Instruments advertised: balance, steelyard, weights
Sources: inst (MAC); GL: BKC 2885/1–2, 2886/5
(MAC); Calvert (1971) pl.13

BRISCALL James
w 1850
Chrono M, Clock M, Watch M
1850   48 Constitution Hill, Birmingham
Sources: Wh

BRISTOW Thomas
w 1809
Math IM
1809   79 Golden Lane, London
Father of BRISTOW John s 1809 to DESBOROUGH
William★
Sources: GL: HC 15860/9

BRITTLE Joseph
w 1839
Rule M
1839   Birmingham
Sources: Roberts (1982)

BROAD John
w 1708–1724
[Hourglass M]
              London
Guild: Turners
Had apprentice:
SAUNDERSON Henry★ 1707/8
WARFE Nicholas 1710 t/o same month
to BEACHAM James, FMC
HACKWORTH William 1721 by t/o
COOPER Thomas 1724 by t/o
from BRIDGES Joseph, d, TC
Sources: GL: TC 3302/2 (MAC)

BROCK John (I)
w 1839

Chrono M
1839   Lewisham, London
See also BROCK John (II)★
Sources: Pg

BROCK John (II)
w 1844–1851
Watch M, Chrono M
1851   69 George St, Portman Square,
              London
See also BROCK John (I)★
Sources: PO; Loomes (1976)

BROCK Philip
w 1778–1807
Math IM
1778   109 Fetter Lane, London
1785–1786   Little Bartholomew St, London
Guild: Makers of Playing Cards, fr 1778
Had apprentice:
NEWMAN John [Frederick]★ nd fr 1807
NEWMAN George nd fr 1807
Sources: GL:MPC 5968/1, 5963/5, STTP 2934
f32; GL: Sun 11936/327 no.501738, 11936/342
no.524828

BROCK Richard
w 1693
[Scale M]
              London
Guild: Blacksmiths, fr 1688 or 1689
Apprenticed to COLLETT Thomas 1681
Son of BROCK Phillip, pewterer, of Westchester,
Cheshire
Had apprentice:
EVITT John by t/o from MARSH Elizabeth★, t/o
to JENKS Edmund★ and fr 1696
Sources: GL: BKC 2881/8, 2884, 2886/2 (MAC)

BROCKBANK John
w 1769–1794
Clock M
              6 Cowper's Court, Cornhill, London
1769   17 Old Jewry, London
1776   Queen St, London
1787–1794   Cowper's [or Cooper's] Court,
              Cornhill, London
Guild: Clockmakers, fr 1769
Son of BROCKBANK Edward, gent, of Corners,
Cumberland
Apprenticed to HARDIN Joseph 1761
Had apprentice:
HEADACH Thomas 1776
YALDEN Benjamin 1777
BROCKBANK Myles, his brother, 1769
BROCKBANK John Edward, his son, 1787
BROCKBANK William, his son, 1794
PROCTOR William (II) 1790
Employed EARNSHAW Thomas★
See also
BROCKBANK & ATKINS ★
BROCKBANK, ATKINS & SON★
PROCTOR William (I)★
Known to have sold: chronometer
Sources: GL: CKC 2720/1, 11568; Baillie (1951)

BROCKBANK & ATKINS
fl 1815–1838

[Chrono M]
                    London
Partnership BROCKBANK family with ATKINS
George★ until 1821, then ATKINS Samuel Elliott
Succeeded by BROCKBANK, ATKINS & SON
Known to have sold: chronometer
Sources: Baillie (1951); Loomes (1976)

BROCKBANK, ATKINS & SON
w 1839–1857
Watch M, Chrono M
1839–1851   6 Cowper's Court, Cornhill, London
See also BROCKBANK & ATKINS★
Sources: Pg; PO; Loomes (1976)

BROGGI Gillando
fl 1826 w 1839
Math IM, Baro M, Optician
Alternative name: BROWGI, BROGI, BROGGIO,
Gorlando
1839   Moulsham, Chelmsford, Essex
Barometers are known signed by G. Broggi,
Chelmsford, which are probably by this maker
Sources: Pg; Goodison (1977) p.305

BROKOVSKI
a 1840
                    Liverpool
Known to have sold: octant
Sources: Stimson (1985) p.114

BROOK -
a 1750–1770
                    Norwich
Known to have sold: balance
Sources: Sheppard & Musham (1975) no.26
(MAC)

BROOKES Christopher
w 1649–1651
Alternative name: BROOKE
                    Oxford
Guild: Grocers, fr 1639
Apprenticed to ALLEN Elias★ 1629
Associated with
GREATOREX Ralph★
HAYES Walter★
Author; d 1665/6
Sources: Taylor (1954) p.218,230,234.355,357;
Brown J (1979a) p.25,63; AVS

BROOKS Alfred
w 1849–1859
Optician, Math IM, Phil IM
1849–1859   41 Ludgate St, London
Known to have sold: sextant, universal equinoctial
dial
Sources: PO; Wk; ChrSK 14 Mar 1985 lot 239;
Sby 10 Mar 1987 lot 103

BROOKS George K.
w 1849–1852
Math IM
1849–1852   5 Lower Charles St, Northampton
                    Square, London
Guild: [Merchant Taylors? – possibly the BROOKS
George Kearly or Hearly who was apprenticed to

RENNOLDON Isaac★ 1839]
Sources: GL: MTC MF 320, 324 (MAC); PO; Wk

BROOKS John
w 1785–1799
Optician
1785   102 Bishopsgate Without, London
1786   3 Watling St, London
1799   Holiday Yard, Ludgate Hill, London
Guild: [Spectaclemakers] Blacksmiths, fp 1786
Son of BROOKS Thomas, blacksmith, of London
Apprenticed to EGLINTON John★ 1772 SMC
Had apprentice:
GILBERT Edward★ 1786
BURTON Joseph (I)★ 1799
DRANE John★ 1799
There were other apprentices of a John BROOKS,
but there were two in BKC and it is not clear
which was meant
Sources: GL: BKC 2881/16, 2885/2; CH 12876/7
(MAC) SMC 5213/3

BROOKS William
w 1806–1824
Scale M
1804–1806   Bethnal Green Rd, London
1811   Princes St, Bethnal Green, London
1824   42 Allerton St, Hoxton New Town,
                    London
Guild: Drapers, fr 1804
Son of BROOKS Samuel, baker, of London
Apprenticed to BASSINGHAM Samuel★ 1791
Had apprentice:
SMITH Roger Henry 1806
HANDS Edward Henry 1811
FLETCHER William Francis★ 1824
d 1827
Sources: DH: DPC Ap/Fr, index

BROOKSBY Thomas (I)
w 1737 d c. 1755
Scale M
                    London
Guild: Blacksmiths, fr 1737
Apprenticed to PICARD John★ 1730
Son of BROOKSBY William, farmer, of Tilton, Leics
Had apprentice:
BROOKSBY Thomas (II)★, his son, 1737
SANGSTER William★ 1739 by t/o
from PICARD John★
RANDALL Giles 1739 by t/o
from PICARD John★
JENKINS Giles 1742
GIBSON Thomas★ 1749/50
DODD Godolphin 1750/51
BELLAS Daniel 1752
Took over from PICARD John★
Sources: GL: BKC 2885/1, 2886/4 (MAC)

BROOKSBY Thomas (II)
w 1761 d 1770
Scale M
                    Wood St, London
1763   Maiden Lane, Wood St, Cheapside,
                    London
Guild: Blacksmiths, fp 1761
Apprenticed to BROOKSBY Thomas (I)★, his
father, 1737

Had apprentice:
WOOD William★ 1761
PETTIT Samuel 1762 by t/o from LEWIS
William★ (I)
SQUIRE Thomas 1766, t/o 1769
to GIBSON Thomas★
DODD Matthew Brightridge 1766 t/o 1769 to
GIBSON Thomas★
WHEATLEY John 1769 t/o 1770
to BRIND William★
Sources: GL: BKC 2885/1, 2886/1 (MAC); Mort

BROOM -
fl 1674
Glass grinder
                    St.Paul's Churchyard, London
Sources: Taylor (1954) p.267

BROUNCKER Joseph
w 1719
[Rule M]
                    London
Supplier to Christ's Hospital Scool
Known to have sold: rule
Sources: GL: CH 12823/3 p.372 (MAC)

BROWN Andrew
w 1817–1834
Math IM
1817–1821   100 High St, Glasgow
1820–1834   32 Main St, Gorbals, Glasgow
Sources: Pg; Bryden (1972) p.45

BROWN B.
a 1770–1830
                    Edinburgh
Known to have sold: barometer
Sources: Goodison (1977) p.103,305

BROWN Edward
w 1766
Hour-glass M
Alternative name: BROWNE
1766   Parish of St. Botolph, Bishopsgate
                    St, London
Guild: [Turners]
Apprenticed to SAUNDERSON Henry★ 1742
Father of BROWN James s1766 GMC
Sources: GL:TC/3302/2, GMC/5224

BROWN Elizabeth
w 1839–1840
Optician, Math IM, Phil IM
1839–1840   43 Union St, Borough, London
Sources: Pg

BROWN George B.
w 1836–1837
Clock M, Watch M, Naut IM
1836–1837   38 Shore, Leith
Partnership BROWN & CHALMERS★
Sources: Bryden (1972) p.45

BROWN Isaac
w 1767
Math IM
Alternative name: BROWNE
1767   Fleet St, London
Guild: Stationers, fr 1762

Apprenticed to WINN Richard★1755
Son of BROWN John, weaver, of Bridewell
Hospital, London
Had apprentice HILL Joseph (II) 1767
Sources: McKenzie (1978) p.51, 383

BROWN James (I)

w 1773 d 1789
Hydrostatic bubble M
   Trongate, Glasgow
Succeeded by TWADDELL William★, who
continued the business to 1792 on behalf of the
widow
Known to have sold: hydrostatic bubbles
Sources: inst (s); Bryden (1972) p.45

BROWN John (I)

fl 1648 w 1695
Math IM
Alternative name: BROWNE
1662   Dukes Place near Aldgate, London
    Sphere and Sun Dial, The Minories,
    London
Guild: Joiners, Clockmakers brother 1667/8
There were at least four members of the Joiners
Co. named John BROWN(E) in the
mid-seventeenth century and it is impossible to
know which was the Math IM
Son of BROWN Thomas (I)★
Had apprentice:
WELLS Joseph★ 1660 JC
BROWN Thomas (IV), his son, 1669 CKC
THOMAS Daniel★ 1675 CKC
BENNETT William (I)★ 1677 CKC
KYFFIN Edward 1682 CKC
POLLYCOTT Thomas 1684 CKC
CROSSE James [presented 1687, apprenticeship to
run from 1688] CKC
Associated with SUTTON Henry★, HAYES
Walter★, WINGFIELD John★ and SELLER John (I)★
in publishing books
Author; Publisher; Master CKC 1681
Known to have sold: barometer, camera obscura,
nocturnal, quadrant, sector, sundial
Sources: GL: CKC 3939; inst BM, MHS, SM (SJ);
Brown J (1979b) p.28; Crawforth (1987) p.349–50;
Taylor (1954) p.369–70,377,391

BROWN John (II)

w 1822–1834
Optician, Cutler, Surgical IM
1822–1834 51 Dean St, Newcastle upon Tyne
Succeeded by BROWN & SON John★
Known to have sold: telescope
Sources: Pg; inst (s)

BROWN John W.

w 1845
Optician
1845   North St, Chichester
Sources: PO(HC)

BROWN Thomas (I)

w 1626–1657
Math IM
Alternative name: BROWNE
   Globe, Fenchurch St, near

   Northumberland Alley, Aldgate,
   London
   The Minories, London
1631   Fenchurch St, near Aldgate, London
Guild: Joiners, fr 1623 or 1624
Apprenticed to SMITH Launcelot, nd
Had apprentice:
THOMAS Francis 1626/7
WILLIAMS Thomas 1627
NICCOLLSON John 1629
WATSON Roger 1634
SUTTON Henry★ 1638
HENSHAW Walter★ 1650
Father of BROWN John (I)★
Associated with BLEYGHTON John (I)★
Known to have sold: Napier's bones, slide rule
Sources: Bryden (1992) p.317–18; Crawforth
(1987) p.350; Taylor (1954) p.210,347,369,398

BROWN Thomas (II)

w 1715–1721
Spec M
Alternative name: BROWNE
1721   The Archimedes, West Passage,
    Royal Exchange, London
Guild: Spectaclemakers, fr 1710
Son of BROWNE Siggins, clothier, of Southwark,
London
Apprenticed to LONGLAND William★ 1700
Had apprentice:
HALIBURTON Andre (or Andrew) 1715 t/o
1719/20 to LINCOLN Thomas★
JOHNSON Isaac 1721 by t/o from JONES William
(v)★ and ADAMS John (I)★
Sources: GL: SMC, 5213/2 p.115,123, 6031/1;
Buckley (1935) p.428

BROWN Thomas (III)

w 1810–1820
Ship chandler, Compass M, Math IM
1810–1820 96 Wapping, London
Took over from BROWN William (I)★
Sources: GL: Sun 11936/461; K; PO

BROWN William (I)

w 1780–1809
Compass M, Ship chandler, Math IM
Alternative name: BROWNE
1780–1809 96 Wapping High St, London
Had apprentice Thomas Duke of Devonshire (sic)
1780
Succeeded by BROWN Thomas (III)★
Known to have sold: octant
Sources: By; H; Sby 10 Mar 1987 lot 122; GL: CH
12876/6; Sun 11936/289 no.437660 (MAC)

BROWN William (II)

w 1839–1851
Optician, Math IM, Phil IM
1839–1840 3 Oxford Place, Waterloo Rd,
    London
1851   13 William St, Waterloo Rd,
    London
Sources: R; Wk

BROWN William (III)

w 1845–1857
Scale M

1845–1855 26 Calton, Edinburgh
1856–1857 26 High Calton, Edinburgh
Sources: NMSn (MAC)

BROWN William Henry

w 1835–1886
Rule M
1835–1862 11 Caroline St, Birmingham
1850   [Residence] Monument Lane,
    Birmingham
Supplied WHITE James★
Sources: Mor; Pg; Sl; Wh; Roberts (1982) (MAC);
Clarke et al (1989) p.253

BROWN & CHALMERS George Bonas & James Stewart

w 1838–1842
Clock M, Watch M, Naut IM
1838–1840 37 Bridge St, Leith
1841–1842 48 Bridge St, Leith
Took over from BROWN George B.★
Succeeded by CHALMERS James S.★
Sequestration 9 Nov 1842
Sources: Bryden (1972) p.45; NMSn (MAC)

BROWN & SON John

w 1836–1874
Optical IS, Math IS, Phil IS, Ironmongers, Cutlers,
Naut IS, Surgical IM
1836–1846 Grey St, Newcastle upon Tyne
1847–1850 68 Grey St, Newcastle upon Tyne
1865–1874 98 Grey St, Newcastle upon Tyne
Took over from BROWN John (II)★
R.apt Victoria; b.apt Newcastle General Eye
Infirmaries
Known to have sold: telescope
Instruments advertised: barometer, hydrometer,
microscope, spectacles, telescope
Sources: Chs; F (MAC); Ric; Ward; Wh; ChrSK
8 Dec 1988 lot 144

BROWNE Benjamin

w 1792–1831
Math IM, Optician
Alternative name: BROWN
1792–1824 The Quay, Bristol
1814–1820 14 Wilson St, Bristol
1824–1828 Opposite Crane No.7, Quay, Bristol
1825–1826 2 Old Park Hill, Bristol
1829–1831 Near Crane No.7, Bristol
1830   7 Quay, Bristol
Burgess of Bristol 1812
Son of BROWNE Timothy, painter and glazier, d
Sold inst made by TROUGHTON John (II)★
Known to have sold: compass, octant, telescope
Sources: BW; H; Mat (MAC); Pg; BRO: burgess
rolls (DJB); inst WM: Bennett (1983a) no.72;
Stimson (1985) p.113

BROWNE Daniel

w 1624–1630
Teacher, Math IM
1624   Cricklade, Wilts
1630   London
Sources: Bryden (1992) p.308–9

BROWNE John (I)

w 1779

Compass M, Ship chandler
 Near Wapping Old Stairs, London
1779 5 Stoney Lane, near Pickle Herring
 Stairs, Southwark, London
See also: BROWNE John (II)★
Sources: GL: Sun 11936/272 no.409862 (MAC);
Calvert (1971) pl.14; BSIS (1984) no.2 p.12;
Crawforth (1985) p.499

BROWNE John (II)

w 1799–1802
Compass M
1799–1802 9 Fair St, Horsley Down, London
See also BROWNE John (I)
Sources: H (JAC)

BROWNE Robert

w 1714–1728
Instrument M, Carpenter
1714 St. Catherine's Dock, London
1728 Mast Yard, Wapping, London
Sources: Wallis R & P (1986) p.62

BROWNING John (I)

w 1783–1811
Math IM
1782 49 Virginia St, London
1793 Pennington St, Ratcliff Highway,
 London
1797 Princes Square, Ratcliff Highway,
 London
1799–1811 67 Ratcliff Highway, London (H)
1800 25 Princes Square, Ratcliff Highway,
 London
1803 17 Wellclose Place, New Rd, St.
 George's in the East, London
1805–1809 117 Ratcliff Highway, London
1806 Wellclose Place, London
Guild: Grocers, fr 1782
Son of BROWNING Samuel, husbandman, of
Southoe, Hunts
Apprenticed to RUST Richard★ 1768
Had apprentice:
WARD John 1783
FLEETWOOD Richard 1793
BROWN William 1797
SIMPSON John (I) 1800
SMITH George (I) 1803
FORD John 1805 by t/o fom KING
John (I)★
SCOTT William Samuel 1806
WHEELER John 1806
CROGER Nathaniel Gowan★ 1809 by t/o from
GILBODY John, goldsmith, of HC
possibly HUGHES Richard 1815 [though it is more
likely that he was apprenticed to BROWNING
John (II)★]
Brother of BROWNING Samuel (I)★
Uncle of BROWNING John (II)★
He does not appear to have been involved in the
firm of SPENCER, BROWNING & RUST★
Sources: GL: HC 15860/9 (MAC), GC 11598/6;
H; Brown J (1979a) p.49–50

BROWNING John (II)

fr 1803 w? 1815
 London
Guild: Grocers, fr 1803

Apprenticed to BROWNING Samuel (I)★, his
father, 1795
Brother of
BROWNING Samuel (II)
BROWNING Richard★
Nephew of BROWNING John (I)★
Apprenticed to BROWNING Samuel (I)★
Had apprentice possibly HUGHES Richard 1815
[but see also apprentices of BROWNING John (I)★]
Sources: Brown J (1979a) p.50–51

BROWNING Richard

w pt 1819
Math IM
1818 66 Wapping, London
Guild: Grocers, fp 1818
Son of BROWNING Samuel (I)★
Brother of
BROWNING Samuel (II)
BROWNING John (II)★
Partnership SPENCER, BROWNING & RUST★
See also BROWNING William S.★
Inherited part of Samuel BROWNING (I)★'s share
in SPENCER, BROWNING & RUST★ and was
apparently in partnership all his working life
Sources: GL: GC 11598/7; Brown J (1979a) p.51,85

BROWNING Samuel (I)

w 1782 d 1819
Math IM
1782–1783 327 Wapping St, London
1786–1792 Eaton Socon, Beds
1795–1818 Wapping, London
Guild: Grocers, fr 1782
Apprenticed to RUST Richard★ 1767
Father of
BROWNING Richard★ fp 1818
BROWNING William★ fp 1840
BROWNING John (II)★
BROWNING Samuel (II)
Son of BROWNING Samuel, farmer, of Southoe,
Hunts
Brother of BROWNING John (I)★
Partnership
SPENCER & BROWNING★
SPENCER, BROWNING & RUST★
Had apprentice:
WHITNEY Thomas 1782
GARDNER James★ 1783
SHARMAN John 1786
BROWNING Samuel (II), his son, 1792
BROWNING John (II)★, his son, 1795
FAIREY Joseph★ 1796
SPENCER William (III)★ 1801
See also BROWNING Samuel J.★
Same premises as GARRARD Thomas (I)★
Sources: Brown J (1979a) p.50–51,85; GL: GC
11598/6, 11598/7

BROWNING Samuel John

w c.1847–1862+
Optician
1840 Minories, London
 66 High St, Portsmouth
1862 High St, Portsmouth
Guild: [Grocers]
Apprenticed to BROWNING William★, his father,
1840

Took over from STEBBING & SON George★
See also SPENCER, BROWNING & RUST★
d 1900 in Portsmouth
A compass by S.J. Browning, Portsmouth, at the
Royal Geographical Society, London, is said to
have been used by Sir W. Edward Parry on his
expedition to the North Pole, 1827. Either there
was an earlier maker of this name in Portsmouth or
the compass is of a later date.
Known to have sold: octant, theodolite, telescope
Sources: PRO: IR/26/3311/938 (LS); Sby 25 Apr
1980 lot 131; DJB; Holbrook (1992) p.167,197

BROWNING William

w pt 1819–1851
Optician
1838 66 Wapping, London
1840–1851 Minories, London
1862 [Residence] 21 Aberdeen Terrace,
 Grove Rd, Mile End Rd, London
Guild: Grocers, fp 1840
Son of BROWNING Samuel (I)★
Brother of BROWNING Richard★
Father of BROWNING John (III) and see
apprentices
Partnership
SPENCER, BROWNING & RUST★
SPENCER, BROWNING & CO.★
Had apprentice:
BROWNING William Spencer, his son, 1840 [in
business in Liverpool by 1854]
BROWNING Samuel John★, his son, 1840
Attended London Mechanics Institute 1838
Sources: GL: GC 11598/8; LMIR (AM); PO
(Commercial Directory)

BRUCE John

w 1846–1850
Scale M
1846–1849 81 High St, Edinburgh
1849–1850 47 High St, Edinburgh
Took over from BRUCE & CO John★
See also BRUCE W. & J.★
Sources: NMSn (MAC)

BRUCE W. & J.

w 1832–1854
Scale M
1832–1835 8 Paul's Work, Edinburgh
1836–1854 7 Old Physic Gardens, Edinburgh
See also BRUCE John★
Sources: NMSn (MAC)

BRUCE William

w 1804–1863
Optical IM, Brass Turner, Optician, Optical
Turner
1795 Lothbury, London
1804 King's Head Court, Shoe Lane,
 London
1805–1863 16 King's Head Court, Shoe Lane,
 London
Guild: Drapers, fr 1795
Son of BRUCE Joseph, Brass Founder, of London
Apprenticed to MASON John★ 1788
Had apprentice HUDSON William★ 1804
Pat. telescopes 1806, with WEST Charles
Robert★

Sources: Patent Office records (MAC); DH: DPC
Ap/Fr; H; PO

BRUCE & CO. John
w 1844–1845
Scale M
1844   5 Maclaren Place, Edinburgh
1845   81 High St, Edinburgh
Succeeded by BRUCE John★
See also BRUCE W. & J.★
Sources: NMSn (MAC)

BRUGGER Lorenz & A.
w 1843
Baro M, Thermo M
1845–1851   79 High Holborn, London
Succeeded by BRUGGER & STRAUB★
Sources: Pearsall (1974) p.253

BRUGGER & STRAUB
w 1845–1851
Baro M, Thermo M
1845–1851   79 High Holborn, London
Took over from BRUGGER Lorenz & A.★
Sources: PO

BRUNNER Ignatius
w 1849–1860
Baro M, Thermo M
1849–1860   66 Edgbaston St, Birmingham
Succeeded by BRUNNER Leopold
Known to have sold: barometer
Sources: Sl; Goodison (1977) p.305

BRYANT Benjamin (I)
w 1790–1807
Hour-glass M
Alternative name: O'BRYANT
1790   Parish of St. Olave, Southwark,
            London
1807   Old Gravel Lane, London
Father of BRYANT Benjamin (II) s 1790 to
BASTON Richard★
O'BRYANT Mark s 1807 BC
Sources: GL: TC 3302/3; BC 5267/5

BRYCESON William
w 1824–1839
Binnacle M, Navigation Warehouse, Optical IM,
Phil IM, Math IM
1824–1826   King's Arms Place, Commercial Rd,
            London
1826–1827   5 Union Terrace, Commercial Rd,
            London
1831–1835   2 Union Terrace, Commercial Rd,
            London
1837–1839   4 Union Terrace, Commercial Rd
            East, London
Sources: R (JAC); Pg

BRYSON Alexander
w fm 1844 d 1866
Clock M, Watch M, Baro M
1844–1866   66 Princes St, Edinburgh
Son of BRYSON Robert★
Brother of BRYSON James Mackay★
b 1816; trained as Watch & Clock M in
Musselburgh & London; attended Edinburgh

School of Arts and classes in natural philosophy
and chemistry at Edinburgh University
Sources: Clarke et al (1989) p.112–115

BRYSON James Mackay
w 1850–1893
Optical IM, Optician, Photographic IS
1850–1853   65 Princes St, Edinburgh
1853–1854   24 Princes St, Edinburgh
1855–1866   60 Princes St, Edinburgh
1867–1893   60a Princes St, Edinburgh
Son of BRYSON Robert★
Brother of BRYSON Alexander★
Worked for Repsold, IM, in Hamburg 1843
and Mertz, Optical IM, in Munich
b 1824 d 1894; educated at Southern Academy and
Edinburgh School of Arts
Known to have sold: barometer, microscope,
thermometer
Sources: Bryden (1972) p.45; Clarke et al (1989)
p.112–122; Goodison (1977) p.305

BRYSON Robert
w 1810 d 1852
Chrono M, Watch M, Clock M, Baro M
1810–1815   Mint, High St, Edinburgh
1815–1840   5 South Bridge, Edinburgh
1840–1852   66 Princes St, Edinburgh
Father of BRYSON James Mackay★
BRYSON Alexander★
b 1778; R.apt William IV 1834; made
self-registering barometer exhibited at the Royal
Society of Edinburgh; made sidereal clock for
Edinburgh Observatory
Sources: PRO LC3/70 p.116 (MAC); Baillie
(1951); Clarke et al (1989) p.112–120

BUCHANAN David
w 1837–1842
Optician
1837–1840   169 Hill St, Garnethill, Glasgow
1841–1842   93 Hill St, Garnethill, Glasgow
Sources: Bryden (1972) p.45

BUCKLE Thomas
w 1836–1840
Quadrant scale M, Locksmith
1836–1840   27 Great Guildford St, Borough,
            London
Sources: Pg

BUCKLEY Andrew
w 1716–1717
            British Isles
Known to have sold: perpetual calendar
Sources: inst MHS (AVS); Webster R & M (1986)

BUCKLEY Joseph
w 1832–1859
Optician, Math IM, Phil IM
1832–1859   14 Lower Sackville St, Dublin
Known to have sold: compass, level
Sources: Wi; ChrSk 19 Nov 1987 lot 338 (MAC);
Burnett & Morrison-Low (1989) p.121

BUCKNALL William
w 1731

Math IM
            England
Pat. astro & navigation inst 1731
Sources: Woodcroft (1854)

BUIRD Edward
w 1674 c 1680
Ship chandler, Naut IS, Ship's Captain
            Leith
Sources: Bryden (1972) p.4,45

BULGIN James
w 1845–1855
Optical turner
1845–1855   8 Harrison St, Gray's Inn Rd,
            London
Took over from BULGIN John★
Sources: PO

BULGIN John
w 1841–1844
Optical turner
1841–1844   London
Took over from BULGIN Thomas★
Succeeded by BULGIN James★
Sources: PO; R

BULGIN Thomas
w 1826–1840
Optical turner, Brass turner
1826–1827   7 Crown Court, Temple Bar,
            London
1834   6 Newcastle St, Pickett St, London
1838–1840   8 Harrison St, Gray's Inn Rd,
            London
Succeeded by BULGIN Thomas★
Sources: Pg; R (JAC)

BULL John
w 1582
Math IM (in metal)
1582   Exchange Gate, London
Possibly the John BULL, goldsmith, of the parish of
St. Michael, Cornhill, who d 1589
Known to have sold: drawing instruments, rule
Sources: Bryden (1992) p.304; Loomes (1981b);
Taylor (1954) p.185

BULLA, GRASSI & FONTANA
w 1830
Baro M, Looking-glass M
1830   134 Fore St Hill, Exeter
Sources: Pg; Goodison (1977) p.306

BULLOCK James (I)
w 1780–1790
Clock M
1790   Furnival's Inn Court, Holborn,
            London
Known to have made: calculating machine [for
Lord Mahon]
Sources: BW; inst MHS; Gunther (1967) p.127–28

BULLOCK James (II)
w 1848–1850
Jeweller, Silversmith, Math IS, Optical IS, Baro S
Thermo S
1848–1850   31 Milsom St, Bath

1848   [Residence] Prospect Villa, Beeches
Cliff, Bath
Employed HEDGE N.★
Sources: Er; Hunts; C

BULLOCK John
w 1759–1774
Math IM
1759   Little Old Bailey, London
1774   Clerkenwell, London
Guild: Stationers, fr 1754
Apprenticed to WINN Richard★ 1746
Son of BULLOCK John, carpenter, d, of St. Giles in
the Fields, London
Had apprentice:
HOUSE Ralph 1759 t/o 1764 to STEDMAN
Christopher (I)★
WOODING Thomas 1774
Sources: McKenzie (1978) p. 57, 383

BULLOCK William
w 1768–1797
Scale M
1780   Porter's Block, Smithfield Bars,
        London
1781–1797 7 Cannon St, the Corner of Turnbull
        Lane, London
1785   11 Cannon St, London
1793   170 Aldersgate St, London
1768   Thames St, London
1779   Smithfield Bars, London
Guild: Skinners, fr 1756
Son of BULLOCK William, gardner, of Shoreditch,
London
Apprenticed to SOMMERS Joseph (I)★ 1747
Had apprentice:
ASH William 1768
NEEDHAM John Rainsford 1779
CYFAX John 1781
QUICK John Alexander 1783
HARWOOD William Lane 1786
HOLMES Joseph 1791
PHILLIPS Fabian 1794 t/o 1797
to CHANCELLOR Thomas Claes★
Sources: BM: Banks 103/2 (MAC); SKH: SKC,
Ap/Fr; A; BW; Kt; W

BULLOCK & CO. William
w 1818–1885
Iron founder
1818–1885 Spon Lane Foundry, West
        Bromwich
Succeeded by SALTER & CO. George
e c.1780
Known to have sold: weights
Sources: Bod: JJ (MAC); Bn; PB; Pg; Wr; inst (pv)

BUMSTEAD William
w 1805
Optician
1805   Church Row, Bethnal Green, London
Sources: H

BURBIDGE Isaac
w 1695 d by 1722
Spec M
Alternative name: BURBRIDGE, BURRIDGE
1695   Leadenhall St, London

Guild: Spectaclemakers, fr 1689
Apprenticed to SPENCER William★ 1675
Had apprentice:
BURBIDGE Isaac Joseph, his son, 1719 t/o 1721/2
to ARCHER Thomas★
Father of BURBIDGE Esther fr 1721/2
Master SMC 1717–1718; last attendance at SMC
1719
Sources: GL: SMC 5213/1, 5213/2
p.103,108,113,119,127

BURCHFIELD Thomas
w 1810–1844
Scale M, Cutler
1810   42 London Wall, London
1813–1845 1 West Smithfield, London
1829–1836 47 High St, Whitechapel, London
Guild: Blacksmiths
Apprenticed to WYNN John★ 1799
Son of BURCHFIELD Samuel, rope maker, of
Poplar, London
Had apprentice:
ROBINSON George Samuel 1811
CASTLE John 1813 by t/o
from SAWGOOD John★
BURCHFIELD Samuel (I) 1820
NEVERD John Stubbing 1820
SANDERS Edward 1820 by t/o
from PAYNE Benjamin M.★
WYNN John William 1825
BURCHFIELD Samuel (II), his son, 1826
CULLING James 1831
LIVINGSTON George Charles 1829
MORGAN Joseph Walter 1833
SOWTER Charles 1835
STILLWELL Edward 1835
STANTON Benjamin John 1842
POILE William 1847 by t/o from SMITH William
(II)★
Succeeded by BURCHFIELD & SON Thomas
Sources: GL: BKC 2881/16, 2881/17, 2881/18;
Kt; Pg; PO; Und (MAC)

BURDEN George
w 1839
Phil IM
1839   1 Sidmouth St, Gray's Inn Road,
        London
Sources: LMIR (AM)

BURDETT Henry
w 1738
Math IM
1734   Crooked Lane, London
Guild: Clockmakers, fr 1734
Apprenticed to CADE Simon★ 1723
Had apprentice CHALLAND (SHALLAND)
William★ 1737/8
Sources: GL: CKC 2721/4 fol.41v; 2721/1; Brown
J (1979b) p.28

BURDETT William
w 1732–1749
Math IM
1732–1749 Leigh, Essex
Guild: Drapers, fr 1732
Son of BURDETT Theophilus, cleric, d, of
Hallaton, Leics

Apprenticed to GRAY James 1716/17 DPC t/o
1719 to CADE Simon★
Had apprentice:
LESTER John 1732
SMITH William 1747
DAWSON William (II) 1748/9
Sources: DH: DPC Ap/Fr, index to bindings

BURDY William
fl 1806–1823
Math IM
      Camden Town, London
Sources: Taylor (1966) p.358

BUREAU Thomas
w 1756
      Address not known
Made miniature compound microscope designed
by Demainbray, 1756
Sources: inst MHS

BURFORD J.
w 1805
Optician
1805   Willmot St, Bethnal Green, London
Sources: H

BURGESS Henry
w 1790–1816
Math IM
1790–1800 24 Thomas St, Liverpool
1816   2 Burgess St, Liverpool
Sources: G (MAC); Und

BURGESS Roger
w 1737
Math IM
1737   Clare Market, Vere St, London
Guild: Broderers, fr 1737
Apprenticed to DEANE William★ 1728
Sources: Crawforth (1987) p.338

BURGESS Thomas
w 1819
Math IM
1819   28 New Rd, St.George's in the East,
        London
Sources: R (JAC)

BURKE William
w 1846–1863
Spectacle M, Book S
1846   190 North St, Belfast
1850–1854 148 Millfield, Belfast
1856–1863 160 Millfield, Belfast
Sources: Burnett & Morrison-Low (1989) p.145

BURNS Arthur
w 1766
Schoolmaster, Surveying IM, Sundial M
1766   Tarporley, Cheshire
Instruments advertised: quadrant, sundial,
surveying equipment
Sources: Adam's Weekly Courant (Chester) 14 Oct
1766 (JRM)

BURNTHWAITE George
a 1750–1800

Lamonby, Cumberland
Known to have sold: protractor
Sources: inst Harvard (GL'ET)

BURROWS James
w 1814–1818
[Founder]
London
Guild: Founders
Master FDC 1814–1815
Known to have sold: weights
Sources: GL: FDC 6331/6, 6331/7

BURT Peter
w 1816–1827
Math IM, Compass Warehouse, Sounding
Machine M
1816–1820   4 Providence Place, Commercial
             Rd, London
1822–1824   2 Providence Place, Commercial
             Rd, London
Pat. improved steam engine 1827
Sources: H ; J; R(JAC); Und; Taylor (1966) p.385

BURTON G. & G.
w 1803
Opticians
1803   136 Borough, London
Partnership: BURTON George (I)★ & George (II)★
Took over from BURTON George (I)★
Succeeded by BURTON George (II)★
Sources: Kt; JAC

BURTON George (I)
w 1793–1802
Optician
1790–1794   7 Blackman St, Borough, London
1799–1802   136 Borough, Southwark, London
Son of BURTON Mark★
Brother of BURTON Richard★
Partnership BURTON G. & G.★
See also BURTON George (II)★
b 1753
Known to have sold: barometer, level, surveyor's
chain, telescope, theodolite, thermometer
Sources: PRO: PROB 11/1143 (AM);VL: bap St.
Martin in the Fields (AM); Boyle (JAC); BW; H;
Kt; PO; Und; W

BURTON George (II)
w 1804–1817
Optician
1804–1817   136 Borough, London
Partnership BURTON G. & G.★
Took over from BURTON G. & G.★
See also BURTON George (III)★ (possibly the same
person)
Sources: Und (JAC)

BURTON George (III)
w 1820–1837
Optical IM, Phil IM, Math IM
1820–1828   4 Mount Row, Kent Rd, London
1831–1837   3 Devonshire Bldgs, Great Dover St,
             London
See also BURTON George (II)★ (possibly the same
person)
Sources: Pg; PO; R (JAC)

BURTON J.
w 1841
Phil IM
1841   27 Harrington St North, London
Sources: LMIR (AM)

BURTON James (I)
w 1713
[Scale M]
           London
Had apprentice BALL William 1713 by t/o from
PICARD John★ of BKC
Sources: GL: BKC 2888 (MAC)

BURTON James (II)
w 1826–1849
Optician, Math IM, Phil IM
1809   Oxford St, London
1826–1827   10 Great Ball Alley, City, London
1828–1836   10 Western St, Pentonville, London
1839–1849   25 Pleasant Row, Pentonville,
             London
Guild: Girdlers, fr 1809
Father of BURTON James (III) fp 1852
Apprenticed to DIXEY Edward (II)★ 1802
Had apprentice:
DOWLING George William★ 1829
BURTON William Harry 1853 (though he could
also have been bound to BURTON James (III),
noted above)
Succeeded by BURTON & SON James★
Partnership with son 1850–1854; either he or his
son, James (III), attended London Mechanics
Institute 1828–1834 , 1837–1841 and 1846–1849
Sources: LMIR (AM); GL: GDC 5800/2, 5802;
Pg; PO

BURTON James Haly
w 1767–1774
Math IM
Alternative name: HALYBURTON
1767–1770   Johnson's Court, Fleet St, London
1774   Fleet St, London
Guild: Turners, fr 1761
Had apprentice:
DELL John 1768
GRIFFITHS Richard 1770
Employed
CLACK John (see CLACK J.★)
SWAN Owen
THOMPSON George
See also apprentice of
LINCOLN Thomas★
BURTON John (I)★
Possibly the J. Burton of Fleet St who signed the
petition against Dollond's patent 1764
Sources: LicFW 8 p.251 (MAC); GL:TC 3814,
3302/3; CLRO: CF1/868; PRO: PC1/7 no.94

BURTON John (I)
w 1764
Optical IM
1764   Johnson's Court, Fleet St, London
See also
BURTON Mark★
BURTON James Haly★
Petitioner against Dollond's patent, 1764

Sources: PRO PC1/7 no.94; Court & Von Rohr
(1929–30) p.84

BURTON John (II)
w 1769
Optical IM
1769   Hoxton, London
Father of BURTON Charles s 1769 STC
Sources: McKenzie (1978) p.389

BURTON John (III)
w 1799
Optician
1799   Huggin Lane, Thames St, London
Sources: H

BURTON Joseph (I)
w 1806–1814
Optician
1806   3 Holiday Yard, Green Lane,
            Ludgate St, London
Guild: Blacksmiths, fr 1806
Apprenticed to BROOKS John★ 1799
Son of BURTON William, labourer, of Lewisham,
Kent
Had apprentice:
BYARD John★ 1806
COOPER John ?★ 1806
PATTEN William 1808 by t/o
from DRANE John★
HOWARD George 1810
HUGHES George 1811
HEX William 1814
Sources: GL: BKC 2881/16 (MAC)

BURTON Joseph (II)
w 1821–1824
Optician, Spec M
1821–1823   15 Blackfriar's Rd, near the
            Magdalen, London
1823–1824   15 Phoenix Row, Blackfriar's Rd,
            London
Sources: Bn; R (JAC)

BURTON Joseph Henry
w 1811
Optician, Spec M
         3 Holiday Yard, Creed Lane,
         Ludgate St, London
Guild: Turners
Sources: H

BURTON Mark
w 1755–1769
Math IM
         Euclid's Head near New Church in
         the Strand, London
1755   Denmark Court, Strand, London
1763–1769   Strand, London
1786   (Residence) Parish of St. George the
            Martyr, Southwark, London
Father of
BURTON George (I)★
BURTON Richard★
Had apprentice:
RAMSDEN Jesse★ 1756
STONEY David 1764
OKEY John 1767

CLARKE Thomas (II)★ 1759
GOSSART Gilbert 1760
Same premises as LIFORD John★
d 1786
Sources: PRO: IR 1/20, 1 /22, 1 /24, 1 /25 (AM);
PROB 11/1143; VL: Rate Books, St. Paul Covent
Garden and St. Mary le Strand, bap St. Martin in
the Fields, Gardner Collection 62/2E TCd (AM);
Taylor (1966) p.225

BURTON Richard
w 1779–1785
Optician, Math IM
1779   85 Bermondsey St, London
1781   Opposite the Church, Bermondsey
             St, London
1785   7 Blackman St, Borough, London
Son of BURTON Mark★
Brother of BURTON George (I)★
b 1751; cut off with a shilling in his father's will
Sources: PRO: PROB 11/1143 (AM); VL: bap
St Martins in the Fields (AM); By (JAC); GL: Sun
11936/273 no.411819, 11936/295 no.448909
(MAC)

BURTON W.
a 1760
             Address not known
Known to have sold: sector
Sources: Sby 20 Feb 1985 lot 262 (MAC)

BURTON & SON James
w 1850–1854
Optician, Math IM, Phil IM
1850–1854   25 Pleasant Row, Pentonville,
             London
Took over from BURTON James (II)★
Partnership probably of BURTON James (II)★ and
his son James (III)
Sources: PO

BUSBY George
w 1850
Surveyors' chain M, Wire worker
1850   19 Aston St, Birmingham
Sources: Wh

BUSH John
w 1748–1763
Math IM
1748   Shoe Lane, London
1753   St.Brides Lane, London
Guild: Stationers, fp 1747/8
Son of BUSH Joseph★
Brother of
BUSH Thomas★
BUSH William (I)★
Had apprentice:
COOKE John★ 1747/8
TINCKLER Thomas 1751
ARCHER William★ 1753
COOKE George 1755
JACKSON Richard 1756 by t/o
from FORD John of TC
HARE Charles 1758 t/o 1764 to COOKE John★
WEAR William 1763
Father of BUSH Margaret (II) fp 1767

Sources: McKenzie (1978) p.60; GL: TC 3302/2;
CH 12876/4 (MAC)

BUSH Joseph
w 1703 d 1746
Math IM
1722   Charterhouse Lane, London
1738–1746   St.John St, London
Guild: Stationers, fr 1701/2
Apprenticed to HADDON William★ 1694
Son of BUSH John, husbandman, of Bareford
(?Bayford), Herts
Father of
BUSH John★ fp 1747/8
BUSH Thomas★ fp 1744/5
BUSH William (I)★ fp 1747/8
Had apprentice:
AUSTIN Samuel★1703
HORNOULD William 1707
UNDERHILL George 1710 t/o 1713
to MARSHALL [forename not given – possibly
MARSHALL John★]
HOOPER Thomas 1722
PATTISON Joseph 1735
PERRY William 1738
BAYNHAM James★ 1739
DAINTETH Thomas★ 1744
Sources: McKenzie (1978) p.60; GL: CH 12876/4
(MAC); LEP 12 July 1746

BUSH Margaret (I)
w 1763–1778
Math IM
1763   Amen Corner, London
Guild: Stationers
Wife of BUSH William (I)★
Had apprentices
JACKSON Joseph 1763 by t/o from BUSH William
(I)★
NOTT John 1763 by t/o from BUSH William (I)★
WOOD George 1767 [?WOOD George (II)★]
DUNCKLEY James 1769
SMITH Samuel?★ 1778
Took over from BUSH William (I)★, her husband
Sources: McKenzie (1978) p.60–61

BUSH Thomas
w 1745–1766
Math IM
1749   Rotherhithe, London
1757   Oxford Court, Cannon St, London
Guild: Stationers, fp 1744/5
Son of BUSH Joseph★
Brother of
BUSH John★
BUSH William (I)★
Had apprentice:
DANSON William 1745 by t/o
from DELL Nathaniel of TC
EAMES Benjamin 1748/9
BIGGS William 1757
EVANS John (III) 1758
DENHAM Nathaniel 1762 t/o 1766
to DENHAM Elizabeth
WEAVER Robert 1762
Sources: McKenzie (1978) p.60–61; GL: TC
3302/2 (MAC)

BUSH William (I)
w 1748 d 1763
Math IM, Optical IM
1748   Parish of St.Sepulchre, London
1752   Amen Corner, London
Guild: Stationers, fp 1747/8
Son of BUSH Joseph★
Brother of
BUSH John★
BUSH Thomas★
Husband of BUSH Margaret (I)★
Had apprentice:
MUNFORD (MOUNTFORD) John★ 1747/8
STREET Samuel★ 1752
HINTON Shirley 1753
JACKSON Joseph 1759 t/o 1763 to BUSH Margaret
(I)★
NOTT John 1760 t/o 1763 to BUSH Margaret (I)★
Sources: McKenzie (1978) p.60–61

BUSH William (II)
w 1841–1854
Optician
1841   115 Devonshire St, Sheffield
1854   119 Devonshire St, Sheffield
Sources: K; Pg

BUTCHER Charles
w 1731 d 1739
Clock M
1731–1739   Bedford
Known to have sold: orrery
Instruments advertised: orrery
Sources: Broadsheet MHS; Morton & Wess (1993)
p.114–15,126, 162–63; Beds County Library:
Diary of Benjamin Rogers, 18 Jan 1739 (AQM)

BUTLER Benjamin
w 1828–1866
Rule M
1828–1829   4 Court, Lionel St, Birmingham
1829–1830   65 Brierly St, Birmingham
1835–1841   Snow Hill Grinding Mill,
             Birmingham
1850   New Summer St, Birmingham
1850   [Residence] 86 Brearley St,
             Birmingham
1862   Back of 1 Hospital St, Birmingham
See also BUTLER & POWELL★
POWELL Robert★
Sources: Mor; Pg; West; Wh; Wr

BUTLER C.D.
w 1819
Spec M
1819   15 Helles St, Cavendish Square,
             London
See also BUTLER J. & J.★
Sources: Kt (JAC)

BUTLER J. & J.
w 1820
Spec M
1820   15 Plough Court, Fetter Lane,
             London
See also
BUTLER C.D.★
BUTLER James (I)★

BUTLER James (II)*
Sources: R (JAC)

BUTLER James (I)
w 1805
Math IM
1805   25 Charlton St, Somers Town, London
Guild: [Joiners]
Apprenticed to MORGAN Francis* 1765
Son of BUTLER James, lighterman, of Westminster, London
See also BUTLER James (II)*
Sources: H; Crawforth (1987) p.350

BUTLER James (II)
d by 1834
Optician
     Chelsea, London
Father of BUTLER Nathaniel Charles, s 1834 STC
See also
BUTLER J. & J.*
BUTLER James (I)*
Sources: SH: STC Memo Book (MAC)

BUTLER & POWELL
w 1812–1820
Rule M
1816–1818   Lionel St, Birmingham
See also
POWELL Robert*
BUTLER Benjamin *
Sources: Pg; Wr; Roberts (1982) (MAC)

BUTTERS Thomas E.
w 1851–1870
Optician
1851–1870   4 Crescent, Belvedere Road, London (S)
Sources: PO

BUTTI Louis Joseph
w 1825–1867
Carver, Gilder, Looking-glass M
1825–1826   232 Cowgate, Leith
1836   1 & 2 Ronaldson's Buildings, Leith [BUTTI & CO. for that year only]
1848–1852   2 Springfield Buildings, Leith
1853–1867   14 Hanover St, Edinburgh
See also ZENONE & BUTTI*
d 1868
Known to have sold: barometer
Sources: Clarke et al (1989) p.102

BUTTON Charles
w 1849–1855
Chem IM
1849–1855   146 Holborn Bars, London
Sources: PO

BYARD John
w 1815–1844
Spec M, Optician
1815   14 Green St, Blackfriars, London
1826–1844   5 Carpenter's Buildings, London Wall, London
Guild: Blacksmiths, fr 1815
Apprenticed to BURTON Joseph (I)* 1806

Son of BYARD George, labourer, of Southwark, London
Had apprentice:
ADAMS Alexander* 1815
ADAMS Michael* 1818
MARRATT John Symonds* 1822
HOOPER William James Humberstone 1822
PELTON Joseph Thomas 1829
EVANS George Edis 1829
Sources: GL: BKC 2881/16, 2881/17; PO; R (JAC)

BYFIELD Edward
w 1800
Optician
1800   Peter St, Half Moon Alley, Bishopsgate St, London
Father of BYFIELD George s 1800 LC
Sources: GL: LC 15835/3

BYGRAVE Richard
w 1754–1778
Spec M
1754–1761   Bridewell Precinct, London
1773   2 Green's Rents near Fleet Ditch, London
1774   2 Bride Lane Court, London
Guild: Spectaclemakers, fr 1741/2
Son of BYGRAVE Richard, coachman, d, of St. Martin in the Fields, London
Apprenticed to BASS George* 1733/4
Father of
BYGRAVE Robert, b 1751, fp 1774
BYGRAVE Joseph s 1754 to HADLEY Thomas STC t/o 1754 to his father
Had apprentice:
MANNING Thomas 1773 t/o 1773 to MANNING William Francis*
SHIPMAN Isaac 1778 t/o 1778 to SMITH William of JC
d c. 1778
Sources: GL: CH 12876/5 (MAC); SMC 5213/2, 5213/3 p.30+, 6029; McKenzie (1978) p.63,152

BYRON Thomas
w 1794
Scale M
1794   31 Alport St, Manchester
Sources: BW

BYWATER John (I)
w 1811
Math IM
1811   Pelham St, Nottingham
See also BYWATER John (II)*
Sources: H

BYWATER John (II)
w 1813–1821
Optician
Alternative name: BAYWATER
1813   9 Mount Pleasant, Liverpool
1816   49 Gloucester St, Liverpool
1818   52 Gloucester St, Liverpool
1821–1823   1 Stafford St, (residence) Liverpool
1832–1835   44 Seymour St, Liverpool
See also
BYWATER John (I)*

BYWATER & CO. John*
BYWATER, DAWSON & CO.*
Author
Sources: G; Und; LM index (MAC); Taylor (1966) p.385

BYWATER & CO. John
w 1822–1831
Optician, Math IM, Navigation Warehouse, Stationer
1822–1831   20 Pool Lane, Liverpool
1824   18 Pool Lane, Liverpool
1825–1827   19 Pool Lane, Livepool
1825–1827   42 Seymour St, Liverpool
Succeeded by BYWATER, DAWSON & CO.*
See also BYWATER John (II)*
Known to have sold: pantograph, telescope (made by DOLLOND*, London)
Sources: Bn; G; Pg; ChrSK 14 Apr 1988 lot 199 (MAC); inst (s) (GL'ET)

BYWATER, DAWSON & CO.
w 1831–1841
Optical IM, Math IM, Naut IM, Map S
1831–1841   20 Pool Lane, Liverpool
Took over from: BYWATER & CO. John*
See also BYWATER John (II)*
Agent for Adie's* sympiesometer and Massey's* log
Known to have sold: compass
Sources: G; Pg; LM index (MAC)

CABLE Henry
w 1835
Measure M
1835   26 Great Tower St, London
Guild: Vintners, fr 1814
Apprenticed to PHILLIPS Silvanus* 1806
Had apprentice CABLE Henry, his son, 1835
Sources: GL: VC 15201/16 p.418, 15215/1

CABRIER Charles
w 1698–1730
     Lombard St, London
1730   Dial, Tokenhouse Yard, St Margaret Lothbury, London
Guild: Clockmakers, fr by purchase 1697/8
Had apprentice:
CABRIER Charles, his son, 1719
MOSES Henry 1722
JACKMAR John 1724
Known to have sold: astronomical clock
Sources: GL: CKC 2710/3 fol.185,216,237; Atkins (1931) p.334; Loomes (1981b)

CADDICK Benjamin
w 1797
Spec M
1797   Brick Kiln Lane, Birmingham
Sources: Pye

CADDICK Charles
w 1841
Optician
1841   110 Consitution Hill, Birmingham
Sources: Pg

CADE Simon

w 1719–1735
Math IM
Alternative name: Simeon
        Charing Cross, London
1735   Haggerstone London
Guild: Clockmakers, fr 1688
Apprenticed to WYNNE Henry★ 1680
Had apprentice:
BURDETT William★ by t/o 1719
from GRAY James DPC
COMBES Fisher★ 1721
BURDETT Henry ★1723
BODDINGTON John★ 1725
FORD Robert 1730
FEATON John 1732/3
Retired 1735
Known to have sold: barometer
Sources: LEP 1 July 1735 (MAC); DH: DPC
Ap/Fr; Brown J (1979b) p.28; Loomes (1981b)

CADE William

fr 1701 w 1735
Lapidary
        London
Guild: Merchant Taylors, fr 1701
Had apprentice:
COLE Benjamin (I)★
He had 14 other apprentices, none known as Math
IM
Sources: GL: MTC MF 319,324 (MAC)

CADELL H.

w 1851
        Dalkeith
Ex.1851
Known to have sold: balance
Sources: Cat 1851 (MAC)

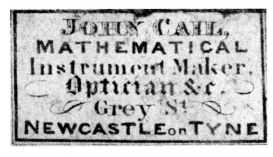

CAIL John

w 1825–1865
Math IM, Optical IM, Navigation Warehouse,
Baro M, Phil IM, Naut IM, Chart S, Optician
1825–1838 2 New Bridge St, Newcastle upon
            Tyne
1838–1855 61 Pilgrim St, Newcastle upon Tyne
1836–1844 (residence) 44 Northumberland St,
            Newcastle upon Tyne
1844–1855 45 Quayside, 4 doors West of the
            Customs House, Newcastle upon Tyne
1855   8 Grey St, Newcastle upon Tyne
1855–1865 21 Grey St, Newcastle upon Tyne
Worked for TROUGHTON Edward (I)★
See also CAIL John & Septimus Anthony★
Associated with COOKE Thomas (III)★, from
whom instruments were obtained

Known to have sold: barometer, circumferentor,
clinometer, hydrometer, level, miner's dial, octant,
pantograph, sextant, spectacles
Sources: University of York, Vickers Instruments
Archives: 1.1.1 Cooke Oder Book 1856–1868
(AM); F; Pg; Ric; Sl; Wd; Wh; Wim; Wln; TCd
& inst NMM; Calvert (1971) p.16; Holbrook
(1992) p.119–20,185–87

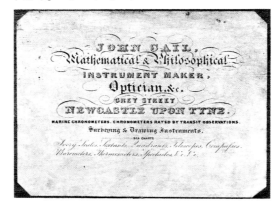

CAIL John & Septimus Anthony

w 1848–1855
Optician, Math IM, Naut IM, Baro M
1848–1854 45 Quayside, Newcastle upon Tyne
See also CAIL John★
Sources: Sl; Wd

CAKEBREAD

w 1824
Known to have sold: sundial
Sources: Beeson (1989) p.76

CALCOTT Thomas

w 1683–1699
[Scale M]
Alternative name: COLCOTT, CALLCUTT,
        London
Guild: Leathersellers
Had apprentice:
TRULOVE Geoffrey 1683 by t/o from
BAYLY Silvester of BKC
MATTERLEY William 1689 by t/o from PACE
William of BKC
GOWERS Weston★ nd by t/o from BAYLY
Silvester of BKC & fr 1690/1
COLES Joseph 1690/1 by t/o from BAYLY
Silvester of BKC
FENTON Edward 1695 by t/o
from FREEMAN Edward BKC, then t/o
to GOWERS Weston★
SNOXELL William 1698 by t/o from WRIGHT
Edward BKC
Sources: GL: BKC 2881/8, 2881/9, 2886/2,
2886/3 (MAC)

CALDERARA Carlo

w 1841
Baro M
1841   Leather Lane, London
b c.1825
Sources: PRO: Cs1841 (AM)

CALDERARA Serafino Antonio Maria

w 1831–1874
Baro M, Thermo M, Phil IM
Alternative name: Seraphino, Serapheno, Seraphim
1827–1829 92 Leather Lane, Holborn, London
1831–1833 16 Kirby St, Hatton Garden,
            London
1834–1851 78 Leather Lane, London
1851–1860 42 Baldwin's Gardens, London
1851–1855 2 King's Terrace, Bagnigge Wells
            Rd, London
1870   20 Baldwin's Gardens, EC London
1841–1842 [Residence] near the Torrington
            Arms, Finchley Middx
b c.1800 outside the British Isles; attended London
Mechanics Institute 1827–1828
Known to have sold: barometer
Instruments advertised: 'newly invented' marine
barometer
Sources: PRO: Cs 1841 (AM); LMIR (AM); GL:
Sun 11936/520 no.1090929, 11936/579
no.1360293 (AM); Pg; PO; Goodison p.306–7

CALLAGHAN William

w 1845–1875
Optician
1834–1841 52 Great Russell St, Bloomsbury,
            London
1845–1855 45 Great Russell St, Bloomsbury,
            London
1859–1875 23A New Bond St, London W
1875   [? Residence] 18 South Audley St,
            Grosvenor Square, London
Father of CALLAGHAN William Edmund, fr SMC
by purchase 1875 as optician
Worked for HARRIS Thomas P. ★
Succeeded by CALLAGHAN William & Co.
See also HARRIS William (II) ★
b 1816–20 d by Oct 1875; attended London
Mechanics Institute 1834; Ex.1851
Known to have sold: octant, telescope
Sources: LMIR (AM); PRO: Cs 1841, HO
107/672/4 fol.6; PO; Turner G (1983a) p.309;
Webster R & M (1986)

CALLOW James

w 1816
Math IM
1816   53 Moor St, Birmingham
See also CALLOW James Jnr★
CALLOW John★
Sources: Commercial Directory of Birmingham
(MAC)

CALLOW James Junior

w 1812–1816
Math IM, Compass M, Dog collar M
1812–1816 Ashted Row, Birmingham
Took over from CALLOW John★
See also
CALLOW Mary Ann★
CALLOW James★
Sources: TWr (AL); H

CALLOW John

w 1797–1809
Compass M, Math IM, Dog collar M
1797   Ashted Row, Birmingham

1800–1809   31 Ashted Row, Birmingham
Succeeded by CALLOW James Junior★
See also CALLOW Mary Ann★
Sources: Chp (AL); H

CALLOW Mary Ann
w 1818
Math IM, Compass M, Dog collar M
1818   Steelhouse Lane, Birmingham
See also
CALLOW John★
CALLOW James Junior★
Sources: Pg

CAM James
w 1814–1817
Optician, Scythe M
1814   Norfolk St, Sheffield
Succeeded by CAM & CUTT★
Sources: Brownell's directory; Pg; WB (MAC)

CAM & CUTT
w 1818
Optician
1818   Norfolk St, Sheffield
Took over from CAM James★
Sources: Pg

CAMBRIDGE George
w 1842–1846
Optician
1842–1846   38 Corn St, Bath
Took over from CAMBRIDGE Robert ★
Sources: Pg; Sil

CAMBRIDGE Robert
w 1841
Optician, Organ M
1841   38 Corn St, Bath
Succeeded by CAMBRIDGE George★
Sources: BaL

CAMERON Alexander (I)
w 1818–1848
Chrono M, Naut IM
1818–1824   High St, Dundee
1829   Overgate, Dundee
See also CAMERON Alexander (II)★
Known to have sold: octant
Sources: Bryden (1972) p.45; ChrSK 8 Feb 1966
reported in Webster R & M (1986)

CAMERON Alexander (II)
w 1849–1851
Chrono M, Naut IM
1849–1851   54 South Castle St, Liverpool
Succeeded by CAMERON John R. ★
See also CAMERON Alexander (I)★
Sources: G; Loomes (1975) (MAC)

CAMERON John Russell
w 1851–1872
Chrono M, Watch M, Optician, Math IM
1851–1872   54 South Castle St, Liverpool
1865–1872   56 South Castle St, Liverpool
Took over from CAMERON Alexander (II)★
Known to have sold: chronometer, compass
(magnetic), sextant

Sources: G; K; LM index (MAC); Webster R & M
(1986)

CAMERON Paul
w 1851–1854
Math IM, Optical IM, Phil IM
1851–1854   87 London St, Glasgow
Took over from FINLAY Robert★
Ex.1851
Sources: Bryden (1972) p.45,48

CAMOZZI Charles
w 1830–1850
Clock M, Watch M, Jeweller, Ironmonger,
General Hardware Dealer, Toy S
1830   Market End, Bicester, Oxon
1832–1850   Market Place, Bicester, Oxon
Succeeded by CAMOZZI Eleanor, his wife, by
1852
Known to have sold: barometer, hygrometer, spirit
level, thermometer
Sources: Pg; inst (s); Beeson (1989) p.91

CAMPBELL John
w 1845–1855
Chrono M
1845   17 Warren St, Liverpool
1855   6 South Castle St, Liverpool
Partnership NORRIS & CAMPBELL★
Known to have sold: barometer
Sources: LM index (MAC); Goodison (1977) p.307

CAMPBELL W.
v 1820–1831
Optician
    London
1820–1831   Bey dem Rathhause no. 26,
    Hamburg, Germany
Partnership HARRIS & CO. William★
Hamburg partner of HARRIS & CO. William★ in
1820; partnership advertised as from London; by
1831 trading in Hamburg as CAMPBELL & CO. W.
Sources: HA (AM)

CAMPIONI P.
a 1830–1860
Alternative name: CHAMPIONIE
    Edinburgh
Barometers are also known signed CAMPIONI &
CO.
Known to have sold: barometer, telescope
Sources: inst reported by ADCS; Goodison (1977)
p.307

CAMPONOVO Angelo
fl 1846
Baro M
    Summers Town, Oxford
    St Thomas's Parish, Oxford
Known to have sold: barometer, hygrometer, spirit
level, thermometer
Sources: Goodison (1977) p.307

CANTON J.
w 1753
    London
Known to have sold: electrometer
Sources: Webster R & M (1986)

CANTREY Spicer
d by 1765
Compass M
Alternative name: CANTRY
    Parish of St Mary, Whitechapel,
    London
Father of CANTREY Spicer s1763 to BAILEY
William★
Sources: GL: MC 5304/4 , 5312 (MAC)

CAPADURO Dominic
w 1832
Optician
Alternative name: Domenico
1832   Lombard St, Margate
Sources: Pg; Taylor (1966) p.444

CAPELLA Michael
w 1850–1854
Baro M, Thermo M
1850   104 Digbeth, Birmingham
1850–1854   53 Edgbaston St, Birmingham
Known to have sold: barometer
Sources: Sl; Goodison (1977) p.307

CAPO Anthony
w 1810–1820
Baro M, Mirror M
1810–1820   154 Mill Field, Belfast
See also CAPPO Joseph (I)★
CAPPO Anthony ★
Sources: Pg (MAC); Burnett & Morrison-Low
(1989) p.145

CAPPI William
w 1845–1849
Baro M, Baro frame M, Thermo M
1845–1849   11 Baker's Row, Clerkenwell,
    London
Sources: PO

CAPPO Anthony
w 1839–1854
Baro M, Thermo M, Optician, Weatherglass M
1839–1840   164 Millfield, Belfast
1843–1846   168 Millfield, Belfast
1850–1854   160 Millfield, Belfast
See also CAPO Anthony ★
Sources: Burnett & Morrison-Low (1989) p.145

CAPPO Joseph (I)
w 1835–1880
Baro M, Optician, Chem IM, Phil IM,
Weatherglass M
1835   168 Millfield Belfast
1839   202 North St, Belfast
1840   164 Millfield, Belfast
1856   147 Millfield Belfast
1858   24 Portland St, Belfast
1860–1861   14 Portland St, Belfast
1863–1880   5 Portland Place, Belfast
See also CAPPO Joseph (II)★
Known to have sold: hydrometer
Sources: Burnett & Morrison-Low (1989)
p.145–46; Holbrook (1992) p.104

CAPPO Joseph (II)
w 1847–1853

Hydro M, Phil IM
1847–1852   Buchanan Court, 75 Argyll St,
              Glasgow
1853   404 Parliamentary St, Glasgow
See also CAPPO Joseph (I)★
Sources: Bryden (1972) p.46

CAPPRANI Antonio
w 1838–1848
Baro M, Clock M, Picture frame M
Alternative name: CAPRANI
1838   110 Tib St, Manchester
1845   98 Tib St, Piccadilly, Manchester
1848   9 Carpenter's Lane, Tib St,
              Manchester
Sources: Pg; Sl (AL)

CAPRAINI P.
w 1828
Baro M, Thermo M
1828   5 Leopard's Court, Baldwins
              Gardens, London
Sources: PO (JAC)

CARD Charles
w 1786–1789
Math IM
1786–1788   Martlett Court, Bow St, Covent
              Garden, London
1801   10 Rolls' Buildings, Fetter Lane,
              London
Guild: Joiners, fr 1785
Apprenticed to TANGATE Robert (I)★ 1776
Son of CARD Charles, embroiderer, of Covent
Garden, London
Had apprentice GIBBS James 1789
Sources: GL: JC 8055/3 (MAC); Crawforth (1987)
p.350–51

CARLILE John
w 1755
General Merchant, Math IS, Optical IS, Surgical IS
1755   Entry into Bell's Wynd above the
              Cross, Sign of the Rose, Glasgow
Instruments advertised: compass, Gunter's scale,
Hadley's quadrant, microscope, quadrant, rule,
slide rule, spectacles, telescope, thermometer
Sources: Bryden (1972) p.18–19

CARLILL John
w 1834 fl 1837
Naut IM, Optical IM, Math IM, Ship chandler
1834   Northside Old Dock, Hull
Sources: Pg; Taylor (1966) p.468

CARLINE William Iliffe
w 1846
Master of Math IM
1846   London
Guild: Stationers
Had apprentice HUGHES Joseph (II)★ 1846 by t/o
from HUGHES Joseph (I)★
Sources: GL: MC 5304/7 (MAC)

CARON John
w 1817
Math IM

1817   Brick Lane, Spitalfields, London
Guild: Innholders, fp 1817
Son of CARON John, carpenter, d, of Bishopsgate,
London
Sources: GL:IC 6651/1, 6648/7

CARPENTER Joseph
w 1843
Math IM
1843   62 Cecil St, Birmingham
Sources: Wr (AL)

CARPENTER Mary
w 1834–1837
Optician
1834–1837   24 Regent St, London
Took over from CARPENTER Philip★, her brother
Succeeded by CARPENTER & WESTLEY★
Sources: Pg; Turner G (1989) p.73

CARPENTER Philip
w 1808 d 1833
Optician, Math IM, Phil IM
1808–1812   Inge St, Birmingham
1815–1822   Bath Row, Birmingham
1826   The Microcosm, 24 Regent St, 4
              doors from Piccadilly, London
1827–1833   24 Regent St, Corner of Jermyn St,
              London
1828–1830   [Factory] 111 New St, Birmingham
1829   and 33 Navigation St, Birmingham
Succeeded by CARPENTER Mary★, his sister
See also
CARPENTER & WESTLEY★
CARPENTER William★
Maker of Brewster's patent kaleidoscope
Known to have sold: kaleidoscope, microscope,
microscope accessories
Sources: BM: Heal 105/16 (MAC); Pg; TWr (AL);
Und; West; Wr; *Quarterly Journal of the Royal
Institution* 26 (1828) p.194 (DJB); Calvert (1971)
pl.15; Turner G (1989) p.72–73

CARPENTER Thomas
w 1821–1835
Compass M, Pincer M, Steel Toy M
1821   Lombard St, Birmingham
1823–1825   Vauxhall Lane, Birmingham
1835   New Canal St, Birmingham
Sources: Pg; Wr (AL)

CARPENTER William
w 1808
Optician
1808   Inge St, Birmingham
See also CARPENTER Philip★
Sources: DJB

CARPENTER & WESTLEY Mary & William
w 1835–1914+
Optician, Math IM, Phil IM, Globe S, Drawing
IM
1835   111 New St, Birmingham
1838–1914+   24 Regent St, Waterloo Place, London
Took over from CARPENTER Mary★
See also CARPENTER Phillip★
Associated with NEGRETTI & ZAMBRA★, from

whom they obtained stock
Ex.1851; firm continued posthumously
Known to have sold: barometer, microscope
Sources: Pg; PO; Goodison (1977) p.191,308;
Turner G (1983a) p.309; Turner G (1989) p.72–73

CARREW John William
w 1835–1866
Naut IM, Math IM, Phil IM
Alternative name: I.W. CAREW
1835–1838   18 Wapping Wall, London
1839–1866   13 Wapping Wall, London
Known to have sold: sextant
Sources: Pg; PO; Holbrook (1992) p.211

CARTE John
w 1695–1702
Clock M, [Math IM]
Alternative name: Johannes
1689   Coventry
              Westminster, London
–1696   Dial & Crown near Essex St, in the
              Strand, London
1696–1698   Lombard St, London
              Garden Court, Middle Temple,
              London
Guild: Clockmakers, fr 1695
Known to have sold: perpetual calendar, sundial
Sources: GL: CKC 2710/2 fol.177; inst MHS;
Baillie (1951); Loomes (1981b)

CARTER Charles
w 1700–1726
[Spec M]
              London
Guild: Spectaclemakers, fr 1696
Apprenticed to MANN James (I)★ 1686/7
Had apprentice:
PERKINS Robert★ 1700
PLANT John★ 1709
DANN Daniell by t/o 1726 from PLANT John★
Probably d by 1738
Sources: GL: SMC, 5213/1, 5213/2, 6031/1,6029

CARTER Henry
w 1687–1724
Math IM
              Near St.Clements Church, Strand,
              London
1710   Wych St, London
Guild: Stationers, fr 1684
Apprenticed to JOLE Robert★ 1676/7
Son of CARTER William, carpenter, of St. Martin
in the Fields, London
Had apprentice:
REDING Philip 1687
SMITH William 1687
HILL Benjamin 1689/90
WATSON William 1692
FRANKLIN Thomas★ 1694
CHAPMAN William★ 1696
HUNT William 1699/1700
JAQUES Thomas 1701
ANDREWS James★ 1703
HILL William 1709 [to CATER Henry, probably
the same master]
SKINNER Edward 1709/10
JACKSON William 1715

HARRISON Christopher* 1716
LAMB Anthony 1720 [transported to Virginia 1724]
BISHOP John 1724
CARTER William (I)* nd, fr by service 1737/8
Succeeded by CARTER Mary*, his wife
d by 1731
Sources: McKenzie (1974) p.27,91; McKenzie
(1978) p.65–67; Taylor (1966) p.154,162

CARTER James
w 1827–1833
Chrono M
1827–1833   Tooley St, London
See also CARTER John (I)*
Submitted chronometers for trial at Greenwich
Observatory 1827–1833
Sources: RGO 1143 fol.7–10

CARTER John (I)
w 1831–1851+
Chrono M
1831–1835   Tooley St, London
1839   207 Tooley St, London
1846–1851   61 Cornhill and 207 Tooley St,
             London
Guild: Clockmakers, fr 1829
See also CARTER James*
Took part in chronometer trials at Royal
Greenwich Observatory 1831–1835 & took
second prize; Master CKC 1856, 1859,1864; Lord
Mayor 1859; d 1878
Known to have sold: chronometer
Sources: RGO 1143 fol.9–10; PO; Baillie
(1951);Taylor (1966) p.416

CARTER John (II)
w 1851
Time & hour glass M
1851   14 Hunt St, Spitalfields, London
Sources: PO

CARTER Mary
w 1731–1736
Math IM
1733   Wych St, parish of St.Clememt
             Danes, London
1736   parish of St.John the Baptist, Savoy,
             London
Guild: Stationers
Had apprentice:
DOVEY James 1731 by t/o
from CHAPMAN William*
LUCAS Richard* 1732/3
BOYD Thomas 1735/6
Took over from CARTER Henry*, her husband
Succeeded by CARTER William (I)*, her son
Sources: McKenzie (1978) p.65–66

CARTER Thomas
w 1811
Optical Turner, Math Turner
1811   29 John St, St. Lukes, London
Guild: [?Spectaclemakers]
Son of CARTER Randall of WWC if the CARTER
Thomas in SMC is the same man
Apprenticed to possibly, BLUNT Richard,
carpenter, of SMC 1777
Sources: H; GL: SMC 5213/3

CARTER William (I)
w 1738–1749
Math IM
1738   Strand, London
1741–1744   Snow Hill, London
Guild: Stationers, fr 1738
Son of CARTER Henry* & CARTER Mary*
Had apprentice:
HOLMES Nathan 1738
OSBORN Richard 1741
HOWELL Thomas 1744
LUCAS Richard 1744/5
HOWELL Joseph 1747
PARRY William 1749
Took over from CARTER Mary*
Sources: McKenzie (1978) p.65–66

CARTER William (II)
w 1798
Watch M
1798   Ripon, Yorks
Known to have sold: barometer
Sources: BW; Webster R & M (1986)

CARTLICH Henry
w 1810–1811
Math IM
1810   54 Upper Frederick St, Liverpool
1811   Lace St, Liverpool
Sources: G

CARTON William
w 1721–1723
Trade unknown, but master of two Math IM
             London
Guild: Joiners, fr 1721
Apprenticed to TAYLOR John 1712
Had apprentice:
HOLLOWAY William* 1721
FREEMAN Samuel (IV)* 1723
d by 1731/2
Sources: GL: JC 8051/3, 8051/4, 8052/4 (MAC);
JRM

CARTWRIGHT William
w 1765
Optical Case M, Telescope Case M
1765   Racquet Court, Fleet St, London
1771   Goldsmith St, Gough Square, Fleet
             St, London
Guild: Drapers, fr 1765
Son of CARTWRIGHT Thomas, victualler, of
London
Apprenticed to HICKMAN Joseph (I)* 1758
Had apprentice:
NEWBERRY Thomas 1765
PORTER Samuel 1771
Sources: DH: DPC Ap/Fr

CARUGHI Paul
w 1839–1862
Baro M, Thermo M, Looking-glass M, Carver &
Gilder
Alternative name: CARRUGHI
             15 Brook St, Holborn, London
             16 Charles St, Hatton Garden,
             London
1843   128 High Holborn, London

1846   38 Brook St, London
1851–1855   139 High Holborn, London
CARUGHI & CO., Paul, 1846–1847
Sources: PO; R; JAC

CARUGHI & CO. Paul
w 1846–1847
Baro M, Thermo M
             London
Sources: PO; JAC

CARVER Abraham
w 1720
Math IM
1720   Globe & Mariner at Fountain Stairs,
             Rotherhithe, London
See also
CARVER Jacob*
CARVER Isaac*
Sources: GL: Sun 11936/12 no.18709 (MAC)

CARVER Isaac
w 1668–1713
Math IM (in silver, brass, ivory or wood)
1697–1708   The Globe Dial, Horsleydown,
             Southwark, London
Guild: u & Clockmakers, fr brother 1667/8
Had apprentice:
SAUNDERS Charles 1672
WELLS Jonathan 1676
SMITH Nathaniel* 1680
FINCH Jacob 1686
HARGROVE William 1688
Succeeded by CARVER Jacob*, his son
See also CARVER Abraham*
Associated with COGGS John (I)*, who sold his
slide rules
Designed slide rule; author
Known to have sold: slide rule, sector
Sources: inst MHS, SM; Bryden (1992)
p.307,311,320n, 32; Brown J (1979b) p.28;
Holbrook (1992) p.118; Loomes (1981b)

CARVER Jacob
w 1720–1742
Math IM
1720   Globe Dial, Horsleydown,
             Southwark, London
1742   Parish of St. Mary Rotherhithe,
             London
1721   Atlas & Quadrant, near Cherry
             Garden Stairs, Rotherhithe Wall,
             London
Son of CARVER Isaac*
Took over from CARVER Isaac*
Father of CARVER Francis Dodsworth s 1742 SKC
to ARNOLD William [trade unknown]
Sources: GL:Sun 11936/12 no.18721(MAC); SH:
SKC Ap/Fr fol.27–28; Bryden (1992) p.321;
Taylor (1966) p.114

CARY George
w pt 1821–1851
Map S, Globe S
1822–1851   181 Strand, London
Guild: Goldsmiths, fp 1827
Apprenticed to CARY John (I)*, his father, 1802
Brother of CARY John (II)*

Partnership: CARY George & John (II)*
d 1859
Sources: GH: GSC Ap/Fr (MAC); JAC; Taylor
(1966) p.385–86

CARY George & John (II)
w 1821–1851
Map S, Globe S
Alternative name: G. & J. Cary
1839–1851   86 St. James's, London
1822–1851   181 Strand, London
Sons of CARY John (I)*
Took over from
CARY John (I)*
CARY William*, their uncle
Succeeded by GOULD Henry at 181 Strand by
1853, but the name CARY William* continued to
appear in directories at this address as well as
Gould's
181 Strand run by G. & J. as 'William Cary' until
John d 1852 ; George d 1859
Known to have sold: globe
Sources: inst NMM; Pg; PO; JAC

CARY John (I)
w 1782–1831
Map S, Chart S, Globe S, Engraver
1782   Johnson's Court, Fleet St, London
1783   Corner of Arundel St, Strand,
              London
1783–1790   188 Strand, London
1792–1805   181 Strand, London
1820–1821   86 St.James St, London
Guild: Goldsmiths, fr 1778
Apprenticed to PALMER William* 1770
Son of CARY George, maltster, of Corsley, Wilts
Had apprentice:
BIGGS Thomas 1782
CARY GEORGE*, his son, 1802
CARY Thomas Willett, his son, 1803
Father of CARY John (II)* fp 1840
Brother of CARY WILLIAM*
Partnership CARY John & William*
Succeeded by CARY George & John*
b 1755 d 1835
Known to have sold: planisphere
Sources: inst(s); BM: Heal 105/19 (MAC); By
(JAC); BW; H;

CARY John (II)
w pt 1821–1852
Optician, Globe S
1821–1850   181 Strand, London
Guild: Goldsmiths, fp 1840
Son of CARY John (I)*
Brother of CARY George*
Partnership: George & John CARY*
b 1791 d 1852
Sources: GH: GSC index; JAC

CARY John (I) & William
w 1791–1816
Globe S
1791–1816   Strand, London
Alternative name: CARY J. & W.
John & William Cary appear to have worked in
partnership on some projects while maintaining
separate businesses

Known to have sold: globe
Sources: inst WM: Brown O. (1983); inst NMM;
Chr 20 May 1992 lot 384; Holbrook (1992)
p.101,209

CARY William
w 1789 p 1891
Optician, Naut IM, Telescope M
              277 Strand, London
1789–1790   272 Strand, London
1794–1822   182 Strand, London
1800   182 near Norfolk St, Strand, London
1821–1890   181 Strand, London
Son of CARY George, maltster, of Corsley, Wilts
Brother of CARY John (I)*
Partnership CARY John & William*
Apprenticed to RAMSDEN Jesse*
Had apprentice PORTER Henry
See also CARY George & John*
b c.1759 d 1825; name continued after death
Supplier to Christ's Hospital School
Known to have sold: compass (magnetic), globe,
microscope, pantograph, planetarium, slide rule,
theodolite
Sources: Bill MHS (MAC); TCd (Cpy) of Henry
Porter NMS (MAC); BM: Heal 105/18 (MAC); GL: CH
12823/8 p.133,349–55,398, 12823/9 p.699–708
(MAC); BW; Bn; H; Pg; PO; Turner G. (1983a)
p.289

CASARTELLI Anthony
w 1849–1853
Optician
1849–1853   20 Duke St, Liverpool
Sources: G

CASARTELLI Anthony and Joseph
w 1845–1849
Opticians, Baro M, Thermo M, Glass Blowers
Alternative name: Antonio and Guiseppe
1845–1849   20 Duke St, Liverpool
Partnership CASARTELLI Anthony* and Joseph*
Took over from CASARTELLI Lewis*
Known to have sold: barometer, hydrometer,
telescope
Sources: G; Sl; inst MHS; Sby 17 April 1986 lot
258 (MAC); Goodison (1977) p.309; Wetton
(1990–1991) p.63

CASARTELLI Joseph Louis
w 1849–1895
Optical IM, Optician, Math IM, Scientific IM
Alternative name: Guiseppe Luigi
1849   6 South John St, Liverpool
1851   20 Duke St, Liverpool
1851–1895   43 Market St, Manchester
1887   Clarence St, Cheetham, Manchester
1853–1881   [Residence] Ardwick, Manchester
Partnership CASARTELLI Anthony and Joseph*
Succeeded by CASARTELLI & SON Joseph
Husband of RONCHETTI Harriet, his cousin, and
sister of RONCHETTI John Baptist & Joshua*
Known to have sold: anemometer, balance,
barograph, camera, level, miner's dial, optical and
surveying instruments
Sources: G; K; Sl; ChrSK 10 Aug 1977 lot 32
(DJB); Anderson et al (1990) p.16; Goodison
(1977) p.309; Wetton (1990–1991) p.63–66

CASARTELLI Lewis
w 1821–1848
Baro M, Thermo M, Optician
Alternative name: Luigi Antonio
              Manchester
1821–1826   39 King St, Liverpool
1823   37 & 38 King St, Liverpool
1825   37 King St, Liverpool
1827–1829   36 King St, Liverpool
1830–1848   133 Duke St, Liverpool
1832   30 King St, Liverpool
1834   134 Duke St, Liverpool
1834–1843   132 Duke St, Liverpool
1835–1843   20 Duke St, Liverpool
Succeeded by CASARTELLI Anthony & Joseph*
See also CASARTELLI Joseph Louis*
Sources: G; Sl; Goodison (1977) p.309; Wetton
(1990–1991) p.49

CASE William
w 1794–1836
Math IM, Phil IM, Rule M
              17 Satchwell's Rents, Bethnal Green,
              London
1794   Albion Buildings, Bartholomew
              Close, London
1805   32 Gloucester St, Lambeth, London
1826–1827   22 Crown St, Finsbury Square,
              London
Guild: Stationers, fr 1792
Apprenticed to EVANS William (I)*
Son of CASE Lambeth, plumber, of London
Had apprentice:
SYER George 1794
BRADSHAW Morris 1826
MULDOON William 1827
Sources: Stat: STC Ap (MAC); H; Pg, R (JAC);
McKenzie (1978) p.66,119

CASELLA Lewis
fl 1833–1838
              Edinburgh
CASELLA Louis P.* of London was b in Edinburgh
& supplied Scottish IM. Listed by E.G.R. Taylor as
in business there, but not so far confirmed by other
sources
Sources: Casella (c1960); Taylor (1966) p.445;
Clarke et al (1989) p.130,170,252

CASELLA Louis Paschal
w pt 1838 p 1901
Math IM, Phil IM, Optician, Drawing IM,
Electrical IM, Hydro M, Baro M, Naut IM, Scale M
Alternative name: L. CASELLA; Luigi Pasquale
1865–1870   23 Hatton Garden, London EC
1875–1901   147 Holborn Bars, London EC
Partnership TAGLIABUE & CASELLA*
Worked for TAGLIABUE Caesar*
Took over from CASELLA & CO. Louis*
Husband of TAGLIABUE Marie Louise, daughter
of Caesar*, m 1837
See also CASELLA Lewis*
b 1812 in Edinburgh, d 1897; Ex.1851; B.apt
Admiralty & other government departments &
foreign governments
Known to have sold: barometer, hydrometer,
drawing instruments, planetarium, sundial
Instruments advertised: full range

Sources: inst (s) (MAC); Cat.1851, class 10, p.429; Casella (c.1960); PO; Anderson et al (1990) p.16–17

CASELLA & CO. Louis
w 1848–1860
Baro M, Thermo M, Hydro M, Optician, Math IM, Telescope M, Sacch M
1848–1860   23 Hatton Garden, London
Succeeded by CASELLA Louis Paschal★
Took over from TAGLIABUE & CASELLA★
Associated with NEGRETTI & ZAMBRA★, from whom he obtained stock
Louis Paschal CASELLA★ traded as CASELLA & CO. until 1860
Known to have sold: barometer, balance, thermometer
Sources: PO; Goodison (1977) p.191,309

CASSERA Genera
fl 1830
Baro M, Hardware S
Alternative name: CASSEVA [misread?]
            Stourbridge, Worcs
Sources: Banfield (1991); Taylor (1966) p.445

CASSON George
w 1814–1824
Math IM, Optical IM, Phil IM
1814–1824   George Terrace, Commercial Rd, London
1814   2 George Terrace, Commercial Rd, London
Guild: Girdlers, fp 1814
Son of CASSON Thomas of GDC
Worked for TROUGHTON★ [no forename given]
Known to have sold: telescope
Sources: GL: GDC 5813/4; inst (s) (MAC)

CASTELLETTI John
w 1841
Baro M, Looking-glass M
Alternative name: CASTELETI
1841   High St, Leicester
Known to have sold: barometer
Sources: Pg; Goodison (1977) p.309

CASTLE J.
w 1837
Math IM
1837   25 Brill Row, Somers Town, London
Sources: PO

CATER Widow
w 1672
Sundial M
1672   Moorfields, London
Associated with DANLEY Charles and Mr FREWEN, who both had faulty sundials made by Widow CATER confiscated from their shops by CKC
Sources: GL: CKC 2710/1 p.244; Loomes (1981b)

CATHRO George & Robert
w 1823 fl 1832
Chrono M
1823–1826   35 Kirby St, Hatton Garden, London

Submitted chronometers for trial at Royal Greenwich Observatory 1823–1826
Sources: RGO 1143 fol.5–7; Loomes (1976)

CATMUR Benjamin
w 1838–1856
Optician, Math IM, Phil IM, Glass Worker
Alternative name: Benjamin Hanson
1839   20 Chambers St, Goodman's Fields, London
1840   15 Chambers St, Goodman's Fields, London
1845–1855   28 Chambers St, Goodman's Fields, London
1859   [?Residence] Lime Cottage, Holloway Road, London N
Guild: Stationers
Had apprentice:
CATMUR Thomas, his son, by t/o 1850 from CHISLETT Alfred★
Succeeded by CATMUR Thomas, his son
Sources: Pg; PO; GL: SMC 5213/6

CATMUR Henry
w 1803
Optician
1803   4 Maidenhead Court, Little St.Thomas Apostle, London
Guild: [Shipwrights], Stationers fp 1796
Son of CATMUR Henry, cordwainer, of Leadenhall St, London
Apprenticed to GOATER Henry Bostock★ 1780 SWC
See also CATMUR Benjamin★
b 1765
Sources: CLRO: CF 1/1192; Kt; Ridge (1939) p.39; McKenzie (1978) p.67;

CATON Francis John George
w 1837–1857
Spec M
1837   196 Upper Thames St, London
1857   16 Garlick Hill, Upper Thames St, London
Guild: Spectaclemakers, fr 1837 by purchase
Son of CATON Francis, goldsmith, of Upper Thames St, London
Had apprentice:
SAUNDERS William John 1841 by t/o from COLEMAN Charles
CATON Henry, his son, 1857 [consideration fee paid by Christ's Hospital School]
Sources: GL: SMC 5213/5, 5213/7

CATTANEO Henry
w pt 1838 d 1860
Optician, Jeweller, Baro M
            King's Staith, York
1838–1848   12 Castlegate, York
1851   2 St. Martin's Lane, York
Partnerships:
CATTANEO, Austin, Henry and John with BALLARINI Peter & FATTORINI Joseph [at first address]
CATTANEO Joseph★ & Henry [at second address]
CATTANEO Henry & Philip & FATTORINI Joseph [at third address]
Known to have sold: barometer [signed

CATTANEO H. & CO.]
Sources: Goodison (1977) p.309–10

CATTANEO Joseph
w pt 1838 w 1851
Optician, Watch M
1838   12 Castlegate, York
1849   Minster Gates, York
1851   1 South Entrance, York
Partnership: CATTANEO Joseph & Henry [at first address]
Bankrupt 1849
Sources: Goodison (1977) p.310

CATTANIO Anthony
w 1835–1841
Baro M, Thermo M
1835   Blackhall St, Kidderminster
1841   Church St, Kidderminster
Sources: Pg; Goodison (1977) p.310

CATTELL Robert
w 1761–1770
Scale M
            London
Guild: Blacksmiths, fr 1757
Apprenticed to READ Samuel★ 1750
Son of CATTELL William, gardner, of Abington, Northants
Had apprentice:
KIRBY Thomas★ 1761
CHATLIN John 1763
RICKARDS William 1770
Sources: GL: BKC 2885/1, 2886/5 (MAC)

CATTERALL Daniel
w 1775 d 1810
Teacher, Math IM
            Whitehaven
Sources: Robinson & Wills (1975) p.270 (DJB)

CATTERALL James
w 1841
Rule M
1841   1 Threlfall St, Toxteth Park, Liverpool
Sources: G

CAVE Thomas
w 1729–1747
Math IM
            Dublin
Had apprentice:
BARKER Jonathan nd
KING William (I)★
CONNOR Charles 1747
Associated with STOKES Gabriel★ in making surveys
d c.1749
Known to have sold: circumferentor
Sources: KH (WS); Burnett & Morrison-Low (1989) p.23,122; Holbrook (1992) p.147

CAVENTRY William
w 1817–1822
Micrometer M
1817–1822   32 Anchor St, Bethnal Green, London
Sources: Und (JAC)

CAVERS William
w 1811
Optical IM
1811   11 Mount Pleasant, Gray's Inn Lane,
         London
Sources: H (JAC)

CAWLEY Robert
w 1738
[Sundial M]
1738   Chester
Known to have sold: sundial
Sources: inst, Grosvenor Mu, Chester (DJB)

CAWOOD Francis
w 1709–1710
Math IM
1709–1710   Corner of Bartholomew Lane near
         the Royal Exchange, London
Sources: LGaz 29 Dec 1709; *Post Man* 17 Jan 1710
(MAC); Taylor (1954) p.303,424

CAYGILL Christopher
b 1747 d 1803
Clock M, Sundial M
         Askrigg, Yorks
Sources: Loomes (1972) (MAC)

CEDEBORG Andrew
w 1798
         St.John's Lane, Clerkenwell, London
Sources: Taylor (1966) p.332

CERUTTY John
a 1790–1820
         The Tuns Lodging House, Bath
Known to have sold: barometer
Sources: Holbrook (1992) p.149

CETTA John
w 1838–1858
Baro M, Thermo M, Looking-glass M
1838–1839   7 Union Court, Back Hill, London
1839–1844   15 Brooke St, Holborn, London
1845–1846   14 & 15 Brooke St, Holborn,
         London
1847–1851   40 Hatton Garden, London
1851–1855   39 & 40 Hatton Garden, London
Succeeded by CETTA & CO. John
Sources: Pg; PO; Wk; Goodison (1977) p.310; JAC

CETTI & CO. John
w 1840–1848
Looking-glass M, Baro M, Merchants
         25 Red Lion St, London
Son of CETTI Joseph
Took over from CETTI & CO. Joseph★
Sources: PO; Goodison (1977) p.311

CETTI & CO. Joseph
w 1802–1839
Looking-glass M, Baro M, Thermo M, Picture
frame M, Print S
1802   3 Long Lane, Smithfield, London
1803–1815   54 Red Lion St, London
1816–1839   25 Red Lion St, London
Father of CETTI John
Succeeded by CETTI & CO. John★

Known to have sold: barometer, thermometer
Sources: H; R (JAC); Goodison (1977) p.311

CHADBURN Charles Henry
w 1845–1861
Math IM, Optician, Phil IM
1845–1861   71 Lord St, Liverpool
1853   [Residence] 4 Priory St, Everton,
         Liverpool
Brother of CHADBURN BROS★
Succeeded by CHADBURN & SON
Ex.1851; R.apt Prince Albert
Sources: G; K; Sl; DJB; LM index (MAC);
Goodison (1977) p.311

CHADBURN John
w 1822–1834
Optician
1822–1834   3 Mulberry St, Sheffield
See also
CHADBURN BROS★
CHADBURN & WRIGHT★
Sources: Bk; Ge; Pg; Wh

CHADBURN William
w 1816–1830
Optician
1816   81 Wicker, Sheffield
1817   Wicker, Sheffield
1830   Albion Works, 27 Nursery St, Lady's
         Bridge, Sheffield
Succeeded by CHADBURN & CO.William★
See also
CHADBURN BROS★
CHADBURN & WRIGHT★
Sources: Brownell W, *Sheffield General Directory*
(1817); Pg (including advertisement); Goodison
(1977) p.311

CHADBURN & CO. William
w 1830–1834
Math IM
1830   40 Lady's Bridge, Nursery St, Sheffield
1833   23 Nursery St, Sheffield
1834   27 Nursery St, Lady Lane, Sheffield
Took over from CHADBURN William★
See also
CHADBURN BROS★
CHADBURN & WRIGHT★
Sources: Pg; Wh

CHADBURN & WRIGHT
w 1818–1825
Opticians
1818–1820   81 Ladies Bridge, Sheffield
1822   85 Wicker, Sheffield
1825   40 Nursery St, Sheffield
See also
CHADBURN John★
CHADBURN William★
Sources: Bn; Ge; Pg

CHADBURN BROS
w 1837–1884
Optical IM, Math IM, Phil IM, Photo IM, Naut
IM, Cutlery S, Opticians
1837   Albion Works, 27 Nursery St,
         Sheffield

1841   Shilo Wheel, 44 Stanley St, Sheffield
1841–1884   26 Nursery St, Sheffield
1847–1876   Albion Works, Nursery St, Sheffield
1857   (Branch) 71 Lord St, Liverpool
See also CHADBURN & CO.
Associated with CHADBURN Charles Henry★
Ex.1851; R.apt Prince Albert; wholesalers
Known to have sold: barometer, microscope,
telescope
Instruments advertised: full range
Sources: K; Sl; Wh; Cat.1851 class 10, no.259;
Phlps 26 Jan 1983 lot 134 (DJB); Anderson et al
(1990); Brown O. (1986); Calvert (1971) pl.16;
Goodison (1977) p.311

CHADWICK Benjamin
w 1851–1857
Chrono M
1851–1857   69 Lord St, Liverpool
Sources: G

CHADWICK James
w 1848–1851
Clock M, Watch M, Optician
1848–1851   Westfield St, St.Helens, Lancs
Sources: Loomes (1975)

CHADWICK William
w 1827–1831
Optician
1827–1828   8 Duke's Place, Liverpool
1829–1831   46 Wapping, Liverpool
Sources: G; Pg

CHALKHILL John
w 1729
Math IM
1729   St.Giles in the Field, London
Guild: [Joiners]
Apprenticed to MILES Lawrence★ 1720/1
Son of CHALKHILL Henry, labourer, d, of
Holsden [?Harlesden] Green, Middx
Insolvent 1729
Sources: Crawforth (1987) p.351; LGaz 27 May
1729 (MAC)

CHALLAND William
w 1749
Math IM
Alternative name: SHALLAND
1749   Green Arbour Court, London
Guild: Clockmakers, fr 1749
Apprenticed to BURDETT Henry★ 1737/8
Sources: GL: CKC 2721/1, 2723/2

CHALMERS James S.
w 1843–1844
Clock M, Watch M, Naut IM
1843–1844   48 Bridge St, Leith
Took over from BROWN & CHALMERS★
Sources: Bryden (1972) p.46

CHALMERS & ROBINSON George & ?
c 1760 w 1773
Jeweller, Goldsmith, [Math IS]
         Ring & Cup, Walker's Court,
         Berwick St, Soho, London
1773   Golden Spectacles, Sidney's Alley,

Leicester Fields, London
Sources: Heal (1935) p.27,122, pl. facing p.124

CHAMBERLAIN James Bradley

w 1827–1848
Spec M, Instrument S
1827–1848   37 Broad St, Bloomsbury, London
1845–1848   203 High Holborn, London
Succeeded by CHAMBERLAIN & SON J.B.★
Known to have sold: barometer
Instruments advertised: drawing instruments, lens, spectacles, telescope, thermometer
Sources: Chr 14 Mar 1985 lot 11 (MAC); GL: TCd; Pg; PO

CHAMBERLAIN & SON J. B.

w 1849–1872
Spectacle M, Optician
1849–1872   203 High Holborn, London
Took over from CHAMBERLAIN James Bradley★
Sources: PO;Wk

CHAMPNEYS James

w 1760–1771
Optical IM, Phil IM, Math IM
Alternative name: CHAMPNESS
                Near the Royal Exchange, Cornhill, London
1760–1761   Red Lion Court, Fleet St, London
1764–1765   Cornhill, London
Guild: Stationers, fr 1760
Partnership: CUTHBERTSON & CHAMPNEYS★
Apprenticed to WINN Richard★1752
Son of CHAMPNEYS Lawrence, Gent, of Fetter Lane, London
Had apprentice:
EVANS William (I)★ 1760
CUTHBERTSON John (I)★ 1761
PASSEY John 1765
PEARCE John 1766
GILLYAT John 1769
SIMPSON William 1770
BALDERSTON Samuel 1771
Petitioner against Dollond's patent 1764; sued by Dollond 1766; bankrupt 1772
Known to have sold: telescope
Sources: GMag 48, p.48 (DJB); PRO: PC 1/7 no.94; BM: Heal 105/20; Sby 23 Jun 1987 lot 236 (MAC); McKenzie (1978) p.68–69,384; Taylor (1966) p.257

CHANCELLOR Thomas

w 1789–1799
Scale M
Alternative name: Thomas Claes
1789–1799   At the Shylock, 199 Shoreditch, London
Guild: Coopers fp by 1790, Haberdashers fr 1795
Partnership: VINCENT & CHANCELLOR★
Apprenticed to VINCENT Robert★ 1774
Son of CHANCELLOR Thomas, cooper, of Haggerston, London
Had apprentice:
BATEMAN Peter 1790 CPC
PHILLIPS Fabian 1797 by t/o
from BULLOCK William★
PRICE Richard (II)★ 1799 by t/o
from SNART Charles★

Known to have sold: balance
Instruments advertised: balance
Sources: GL: HC 15857/2, 15860/9 (MAC); CPC 5630; SH: SKC Ap/Fr; A; BW; Kt; W; inst & TCd (pv)

CHANT John

v 1824 w 1851
Optician
Alternative name: John Hollely
1824–1826   2 Skinner St, London
1826–1828   Britannia Court, City Road, London
1851   3 Critchill Place, New North Rd, London
1851   and 12 Nichol's Square, London
Guild: [Spectaclemakers]
Son of CHANT John, upholsterer, of Christ Church, Southwark, London
Apprenticed to ABBOTT Charles★ 1801
Partnership: BENTLEY & CHANT★
Attended London Mechanics Institute 1824–8
Sources: LMIR(AM); PO; Wk; GL:SMC, 5213/4

CHANTREY Robert

w 1717
[Math IM]
1716   Tower Hill, London
Guild: Grocers, fr 1716
Apprenticed to JOHNSON John (I)★ 1704
Son of CHANTREY Richard, Citizen & Stainer, of London
Had apprentice: KEYS Henry 1716/17
Sources: Brown J (1979a) p.33

CHAPLAIN –

w 1736
[Optical IM]
1736   London
Known to have sold: telescope
Sources: Court & Von Rohr (1929–30) p.81

CHAPMAN Edward

w 1805–1822
Math IM
1805–1822   Bridge St, Westminster, London
Sources: Kt (JAC)

CHAPMAN James (I)

w 1774–1804
Math IM, Ship chandler, Optical IM, Optician
1774–1796   St. Catherine's near the Tower, London
1776   Hadley's Quadrant opposite the King's Store House, St. Catherine's, London
1793   41 St. Catherine's, London
1794   5 St. Catherine's, London
Guild: Stationers, fr 1769
Son of CHAPMAN Michael★
Apprenticed to STEDMAN Christopher (I)★ 1760
Had apprentice:
BAKER William 1774
POUPARD William 1777
STANLEY Joseph★ 1780
ENDERSBEE William (I)★ 1785 by t/o
from GARRARD Thomas (I)★
ROBERTSON David Norton 1786
CHAPMAN James (II)★, his son, 1792

CHAPMAN Josiah, his son, 1796

Wholesaler and exporter
Known to have sold: sextant, telescope
Sources: Bod: JJ box 15, TCd (MAC); GL: TCd; A (JAC); BW; Kt; inst MHS & (s); Brown J (1979a) p.49; Holbrook (1992) p.137,219; McKenzie (1978) p.70,332

CHAPMAN James (II)

w 1819–1827
Math IM, Optician
1819   8 Upper East Smithfield, Tower Hill, London
1827   3 Nightingale Lane, East Smithfield, London
Guild: [Stationers]
Apprenticed to CHAPMAN James (I)★, his father, 1792
Known to have sold: telescope
Sources: Phlps 16 Mar 1888 lot 125 (MAC); Pg; R (JAC); McKenzie (1978) p.70

CHAPMAN Michael

w 1760
Math IM
1760   Golden Lane, London
Guild: [Stationers]
Son of CHAPMAN William, blacksmith, of Leadenhall St, London
Apprenticed to FRANKLIN Thomas★ 1728
Father of CHAPMAN James (I)★
Sources: McKenzie (1978) p.130,332

CHAPMAN Moses

w 1848
Chrono M
1848   28 Castle St, Liverpool
Sources: Loomes (1975)

CHAPMAN Simon

w 1676–1687
[Math IM]
             London
Guild: Clockmakers, fr 1675
Apprenticed to NASH John★ 1667/8
Had apprentice:
STIFFE William 1676
STAYNES Jeffrey, by t/o nd from RYLEY George of LC & fr 1686
DUNSTON Paul 1687
Sources: GL: CKC 3939; Brown J (1979b) p.28; Loomes (1981b)

CHAPMAN Thomas

w 1689
Math IM
             London
Guild: Clockmakers
Apprenticed to CHENEY Withers, 1659
Known to have sold: sector
Sources: GL: CKC 2710/1 p.99; dated inst offered for sale by Trevor Philip & Sons Ltd, London; Brown J (1979b) p.28; Loomes (1981b)

CHAPMAN William

w 1708–1731
Math IM
1718–1722   Bishopsgate St, London

1718 Swan Yard, Bishopsgate St, London
Guild: Stationers, fr 1706
Son of CHAPMAN William, yeoman, of Stanstead, Herts
Apprenticed to CARTER Henry★ 1696
Had apprentice:
WATSON John (I)★1708
TRANTUM Richard★ 1713 t/o 1717
to TRANTUM Thomas
TRENT Henry 1715
WINN Richard★ 1718
REASON Leonard 1721
SCOTT Charles 1722
DOVEY James 1727 t/o 1731 to CARTER Mary★
FLOOD William 1729
Sources: GL; CH 12876/3 (MAC); McKenzie (1978) p.27,71

CHATFIELD John
w 1630–1650
[Math IM]
?London
Author of *The Trigonal Sector* (1650), the inst sold by THOMPSON Anthony★
Known to have sold: quadrant
Sources: dated inst NMM; Taylor (1954) p.236,356

CHENEY Withers
w 1659–1692
Wax Chandler, Math IM
Alternative name: CHEANEY, CHEANY, CHEYNE,
1662 Fleet St, London
Guild: Clockmakers, fr 1657
Apprenticed to ALLEN Elias★ 1646
Had apprentice:
CHAPMAN Thomas★ 1659
NICHOLL Isaac 1674/5
FEILDER Thomas★ 1678
MOUNT William 1682
BOND Thomas 1685
EUSTACE [EWESTASCE] Richard 1687/8
BEAUMONT Philip 1689
BUSHELL Samuel 1690
v 1695 but residence out of town
Sources: GL; CKC 3939; Brown J (1979b) p.28; Loomes (1981b)

CHESTER Edward
w 1782–1785
Math IM, Optician
1782 8 King St, Tower Hill, London
1784–1785 64 Upper East Smithfield, Tower Hill, London
Guild: Merchant Taylors, fr 1778
Son of CHESTER Robert, Gent, of Whitechapel, London
Apprenticed to COLE Benjamin (II)★ 1771
Had apprentice:
MINTER John 1782
SNART John (II)★ 1783 t/o 1786
to GOATER John★
d by Apr 1786
Sources: GL; MTC MF 320, 324; BM: Banks 105/10 (MAC); By (JAC); Ridge (1946) p.90

CHESTERMAN James
w 1829–1847
Mechanic, [Math IM]

1834–1841 At Mr Cutts, Division St, Sheffield
[but with his own entry in directories]
Succeeded by CHESTERMAN & CO. James
See also CUTTS John P.★
Pat. linear measures 1829, 1842 & 1847
Known to have sold: surveyor's measuring tape
Sources: Pat; Pg; DJB

CHEVALIER –
a 1780
[Math IS]
Alternative name: CHAVALIER
Guernsey
Known to have sold: octant
Sources: inst NMM; Stimson (1985) p.113; Taylor (1966) p.283

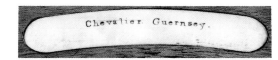

CHICKIE Francis
w 1827–1829
Baro M
1827 127 Broad St, Aberdeen
1828 127 Gallowgate, Aberdeen
1829 48 Broad St, Aberdeen
Sources: Bryden (1972) p.46

CHIESA Joseph
w 1817 c 1840
Baro M, Carver, Gilder, Glass S
Liverpool
Succeeded by CHIESA & KEIZER★
See also CHIESA, KEIZER & ROHRES★
Sources: Keizer (1967) (MAC)

CHIESA & KEIZER Joseph & Lawrence
c 1840 w 1842
Carvers, Gilders, Baro M, Glass S
1842 Liverpool
Sources: Keizer (1967) (MAC)

CHIESA, KEIZER & ROHRES
w 1842
Carvers, Gilders, Glass S
1842 Liverpool
Instruments known: barometer signed Chiesa, Keizer & Co.
Sources: Keizer (1967) (MAC)

CHILCOTE & HILL
w 1805
Spec M, Plater
1805 Navigation St, Birmingham
See also HILL James (I)★
Sources: H

CHILDE Henry
w 1832–1868
Optician, Math IM, Phil IM
Alternative name: CHILD
1832 3 Barrett St, Lambeth, London
1845–1865 66 Vauxhall Walk, Lambeth, London
Succeeded by CHILDE & DOUBELL
Sources: Pg; PO

CHILMEAD J.
a 1625 a 1650
Globe M
London
Sources: Bonacker (1963) p.57

CHISLETT Alfred
w 1834–1855
Optical IM, Philo IM, Math IM, Naut IM, Optician
7 Budge Row, Cannon St, London
Gloucester St, Commercial Road, London
1837–1845 27 Greenfield St, Whitechapel, London
1849–1855 8 Postern Row, Tower Hill, London
Guild: Spectaclemakers, fr 1837
Son of CHISLETT Charles, Gent, of Walthamstow, Essex
Apprenticed to BATE Robert Brettell★ 1825 t/o at once to GILBERT William (II)★
Had apprentice:
FAREBROTHER Charles Noble 1837
GILL Robert 1840
PHILP Robert 1841 t/o 1844
to BUCKLAND James
BAXTER William (II) 1845 by t/o
from HUGHES Joseph (I)★
GEARE [GEERE] John 1845 t/o 1850
to GEERE Henry, his father
CATMUR Thomas, 1846 t/o 1850
to CATMUR Benjamin★, his father
LINTON William Gill 1846 t/o 1850
to OLLEY J.
Sources: GL; MC 5304/7 (MAC); SMC 5213/5, 5213/6; PO; R (JAC)

CHISMAN –
a 1770–1800
[Scale M]
Known to have sold: balance
Sources: inst (pv) (MAC)

CHITTY William
v 1834–1835
Math IM;
1834–1835 30 Lower Holborn, London
Attended London Mechanics Institute 1834–1835, address suggests he worked for JONES W. & S. ★
Sources: LMIR (AM)

CHRISTIAN Evan
w 1666–1681
[Dial M]
Alternative name: Ewan
1666–1681 Isle of Man
Known to have sold: sundial
Sources: Loomes (1981b)

CHRISTIAN George
w 1825–1867
Optician, Math IM
1825 16 Regent St, Liverpool
1827–1829 16 Strand St, Liverpool
1831–1832 20 Strand St, Liverpool
1834–1853 11 Strand, Liverpool
1855 113 Duke St, Liverpool
1857 11 Crooked Lane, Liverpool

1859–1867   133 Duke St, Liverpool
1864–1867   9 Canning Place, Liverpool
Known to have sold: octant
Sources: G; Sl; Holbrook (1992) p.118,138

CHRISTIE Elizabeth
w 1838–1839
Optician, Math IM, Phil IM
1838–1839   32 Warner St, New Kent Rd,
     London
Sources: Pg

CHRISTIE George
w 1794
[Optical IM]
1794   Leigh on Mendip, Frome, Somerset
     11 Strand, Liverpool
See also: CHRISTIAN George★ [possible
confusion?]
Sources: Taylor (1966) p.333

CHRISTIE William
w 1839–1881
Watch M, Clock M, Chrono M
1839   23 Chancery Lane, London
1846   18 Cannon St, London
1851   70 Cannon St, London
Sources: PO; Pg; Loomes (1976)

CHRISTMAS William
w 1808
Math IM
1808   Broad Sanctuary, Westminster,
     London
Guild: Goldsmiths, fr 1782
Son of CHRISTMAS John, staymaker, of Hart St,
St. George Hanover Square, London
Apprenticed to HITCH Elizabeth 1774
Had apprentice:
BARNARD Charles 1808
READ William 1808
Sources: GH: GSC Ap, Fr

CHURCH Benjamin
w 1783
Math IM
1783   Falmouth
See also apprentice of LIFORD John★
Sources: By (MAC)

CHURCH Stephen
w 1771–1792
[Scale M]
     London
Guild: Blacksmiths, fr 1764
Son of CHURCH Stephen, waterman, of
Southwark, London
Apprenticed to COURT Richard (II)★ 1746
Had apprentice:
CHURCH Richard 1771
ROBSON William 1792
Father of
CHURCH Daniel fp 1788
CHURCH Stephen fp 1790
d c.1793
Known to have sold: balance
Sources: GL: BKC 2881/15, 2881/16, 2886/5
(MAC)

CICERI Thomas
w 1841
Baro M
1841   31 Brook St, Holborn, London
See also TAGLIABUE & CICERI
b c.1812
Sources: PRO: Cs 1841 (AM)

CICERI & PINI
w 1842–1858
Picture frame M, Baro M, Thermo M, Telescope
M
Alternative name: CERI & PINI
     London
1842–1858   8 & 9 Calton St, Edinburgh
1852–1858   81 Leith St, Edinburgh
Took over from BATTISTESSA & CO.★
Known to have sold: barometer, hygrometer, spirit
level, thermometer
Sources: Clarke et al (1989) p.102–03; Goodison
(1977) p.312

CLACK J.
w 1764
Math IM
1764   Saffron Hill, London
Probably worked for BURTON James Haly★ 1774
1764 Petitioner against Dollond's patent
Sources: PRO: PC 1/7 no.94; CLRO: LicFW 8

CLARE Peter
w 1809
Watch M, Lecturer, Schoolmaster
     Deansgate, Manchester
fl 1772–1844, friend of scientist John Dalton
Known to have sold: sundial
Sources: *Clocks* 5, no. 1 (1983) p.16 (DJB); Taylor
(1966) p.283; Wallis R & P (1993)

CLARIDGE Christopher
w 1698–1716
[Scale M]
Alternative name: CLAREDGE
     London
Guild: Blacksmiths, fr 1696/7
Son of CLARIDGE Clement, barber, of Great
Bourton, Oxon
Apprenticed to CLARIDGE Richard★, his brother,
1689
Had apprentice:
HUGHES Richard 1698 t/o 1703 to SMITH
Richard
HARBURT Leonard 1699
POWELL Arundel 1702/3
EDWARDS Edward 1705
SHIPPERY Anthony 1706
COOPER Thomas 1716
Sources: GL: BKC 2881/8, 2886/2, 2886/3
(MAC)

CLARIDGE Richard
w 1688–1696
[Scale M]
Alternative name: CLAREDGE
     London
Guild: Blacksmiths, fr 1688
Son of CLARIDGE Clement, barber, of Bourton,
Oxon

Apprenticed to WOOD John (I)★ 1681
Had apprentice:
REDHEAD John★ 1688 by t/o
from ILIFFE William★
CLARIDGE Christopher★, his brother, 1689
SANDS Samuel 1690 t/o 1692
to TOWNSEND Richard★
CLACKSON Richard 1696
WRIGHT John 1696/7
PELL Charles 1697 t/o 1699/1700 to FITCH John
SOANES George 1698/9
Sources: GL: BKC 2881/8, 2881/9, 2881/10,
2886/2 (MAC)

CLARK Elizabeth (Mrs.)
w 1675–1678
Spec M
Alternative name: CLARKE
1676   Leadenhall St, London
Guild: Spectaclemakers
Wife of CLARK John (I)★
Had apprentice: BEMBRICK William (I)★ 1675 t/o
1677/8 to MAYLE Thomas★
Took over from CLARK John (I)★
Known to have sold: spectacles
Sources: GL: SMC 5213/1

CLARK Frederick (I)
w 1836
Spec M, Optician
1836   38 Allen St, Goswell Road, London
See also CLARK Frederick (II)★, possibly the same
maker
Sources: Pg; PO

CLARK Frederick (II)
w 1851–1870
Optician, Spec M
1851–1870   13 Park Side, Knightsbridge, London
See also CLARK Frederick (I)★, possibly the same
maker
Sources: PO

CLARK James (I)
w 1756
     Edinburgh
Listed by Taylor but probably error for CLARK
John (II)★
Sources: Brown O (1986); Taylor (1966) p.333

CLARK James (II)
a 1800
Math IM ? Optical IM ?
Alternative name: Jacobus
     Dundee
Sources: Bryden (1972) p.46

CLARK James (III)
w 1817–1822
Optician, Victualler
1817   High St, Sheffield
1822   13 South St, Sheffield
Sources: Bn; Brownell's directory (MAC)

CLARK James (IV)
w 1849–1860
Jeweller, Silversmith, Optician, Clock M, Watch
M

1858–1860   3 Bartlett St, Bath
Sources: BaL

CLARK John (I)
w 1667–1673
Spec M
Alternative name: CLARKE
1668–1672   Leadenhall St, London
Guild: Spectaclemakers
Had apprentice: MAYLE Thomas★ 1668/9
Succeeded by CLARK Elizabeth (Mrs)★, his widow
Fined by SMC for selling faulty spectacles; d early
1673/4
Sources: GL: SMC 5213/1

CLARK John (II)
w 1749–1796
Goldsmith, Jeweller, Optical IM
Alternative name: CLARKE
1749   Luckenbooths, Edinburgh
1751–1755   Parliament Close, Edinburgh
1773–1782   Opposite the Guard, Edinburgh
1786–1788   At the Cross, Edinburgh
1793–1796   13 Parliament Close, Edinburgh
Burgess of Edinburgh, fp 1751
Known to have sold: microscope
Sources: Sby 12 Jun 1984 lot 425 (MAC); Brown
O (1986) no. 52–55; Bryden (1972) p.20,24,46

CLARK John (III)
w 1790–1793
Compass M
1790–1793   High St, Shadwell, London
Sources: BW

CLARK Richard
w 1830
Optician
1830   Waterloo Place, Clerkenwell Close,
             London
Had apprentice: SHARP Edwin 1830 by t/o from
SWIFT William Cornelius of PWC
See also SHARP John★
Sources: GL: PWC 7102 fol.34

CLARK Robert
w 1836–1845
Baro M, Thermo M
1824–1831   14 Fox Court, Hatton Garden,
             London
1836   2 Wharton's Place, High Holborn,
             London
1840–1845   27 Brook St, Holborn, London
Same premises as CLARK Thomas (II)★
b c 1800
Sources: PRO: Cs 1841(AM); LMIR (AM); Pg;
PO; R (JAC)

CLARK Samuel
w 1839–1842
Yard measure M
1839–1842   15 Great Hampton St, Birmingham
Took over from LAWRENCE T.★
Associated with
GROOM G.★, who acted as London agent
HILL S.★, who acted as Liverpool agent
Sources: Pg

CLARK Thomas (I)
fr 1733 d c.1743
Optical IM
Alternative name: CLARKE
             Golden Head near Arundel Street in
             the Strand, London
Guild: Spectaclemakers, fr 1733
Son of CLARK(E) Henry of Wheaton Aston, Staffs
Apprenticed to WILLDEY George★ 1724
Sources: Heal (1935) p.125 & plate XV; GL: SMC
5213/2 p.150+

CLARK Thomas (II)
w 1841–1855
Baro M, Thermo M
1841   27 Brook St, Holborn, London
1846–1855   20 Kirby St, Hatton Garden,
             London
Same premises as CLARK Robert★
b c. 1805
Sources: PRO: Cs 1841(AM); PO; Wk

CLARK William (I)
a 1730–1760
Scale M
             Near the Sign of Admiral Bembow
             in Golden Lane near Old St, London
Known to have sold: balance
Sources: inst SM (Wellcome)

CLARK William (II)
w 1835–1850
Box & Ivory Rule M
1835   9 Hospital St, Birmingham
1841   122 Hospital St, Birmingham
1850   No 7 Court, Henrietta St,
             Birmingham
Sources: Pg; Sl

CLARK William (III)
w 1841
Rule M
1841   Dudley Road, Wolverhampton
Sources: Pg

CLARK & CO. Thomas
w 1829–1835
Spec M, Ornament M, Steel toy M
1829–1835   53 Lionel St, Birmingham
Sources: Pg; Wr

CLARK & COBBETT
w 1851
Chem App M
1851   Bear Garden, Southwark, London
Took over from: CLARK & SON Andrew★
Succeeded by CLARK & CO. Andrew
Sources: PO

CLARK & SMART
w 1819–1820
Opticians
1819–1820   Exeter Change, Strand, London
Sources: R (JAC)

CLARK & SON Andrew
w 1846–1851
Chem IM, Plumbers, Lead Merchants

1846–1849   Bear Garden, Southwark, London
1851   Bankside, Southwark, London
             [variation of same address]
Succeeded by CLARK & COBBETT★
Sources: PO; Wk

CLARKE –
w 1672
[Math IS]
Alternative name: CLARK
1671/2   In the Minories, London
Known to have sold: rule
Sources: GL: CKC 2710/1 p.245; Loomes (1981b)

CLARKE Edward (I)
w 1792
Rule M
1792   40 Dudley Rd, Wolverhampton
Sources: Wolverhampton rate books (MAC)

CLARKE Edward (II)
w 1810–1821
Optician, Math IM
1810–1812   18 Lower Sackville St, Dublin
1819–1821   10 Lower Sackville St, Dublin
Partnership: SPEAR & CLARKE★
See also
CLARKE & CO. E.★
CLARKE Edward M.★, possibly the same maker or
his son
Partnership 1815–17
Known to have sold: sundial
Sources: Burnett & Morrison-Low (1989) p.122

CLARKE Edward Marmaduke
w 1834–1851
Optician, Magnetician, Math IM, Phil IM,
Engineer
1826–1830   Dame St, Dublin
1835   39 Charles St, Westminster, London
1837   9 Agar St, Strand, London
1838–1840   11 Lowther Arcade, Strand, London
1840–1851   428 Strand, London
1840–1846   Rodney Iron Works, Bolingbrooke
             Gardens, Battersea, London
1849   and 19 Exeter St, London
1856   4 Grove Park Terrace, Camberwell
             Green, London
Worked for WATKINS & HILL★ 1833
See also
CLARKE Edward (II)★
CLARKE & CO.★
b in Ireland; established the London Electrical
Society 1837; promoted and ran the Panoptican,
Leicester Square, London, 1851–55; d 1859
Known to have sold: electrical machine,
polariscope
Instruments advertised: hydro-oxygen microscope
Sources: PO; Pg; R(JAC); BG; DJB; Anderson et
al (1990) p.19; Burnett & Morrison-Low (1989)
p.49–51; Holbrook (1992) p.84,134; Taylor (1966)
p.306,359

CLARKE James (I)
a 1760–1800
             London
See also CLARKE John (I)★
CLARKE Richard★

Known to have sold: hydrometer
Sources: inst SM (MAC)

CLARKE James (II)
w 1824–1836
Math IM, Phil IM
1824   13 Ann St, St. George's in the East,
           London
1836   103 York St, Commercial Rd East,
           London
Sources: GL:STTP 2934 fol .86; Pg

CLARKE John (I)
w 1716–1746
Turner, Engine worker, Hydro M
Alternative name: CLARK
1716–1730   York Building Waterworks, near
           Charing Cross, London
Guild: Turners
Succeeded by CLARKE Richard★, his son
See also CLARKE James(I)★
Known to have sold: hydrometer
Sources: GL: TC 3305; advertisement (Cpy) MHS

CLARKE John (II)
w 1785–1794
Scale M
           49 Cow Cross St, West Smithfield,
           London
1793–1794   Snow Hill, London
Sources: BW; By; W (JAC)

CLARKE John (III)
w 1831–1857
Phil IM, Math IM, Engraver
1831–1832   21 King St, Liverpool
1834–1841   25 King St, Liverpool
1847–1849   67 Paradise St, Liverpool
1851–1857   25 Duke St, Liverpool
Sources: G; Sl

CLARKE John Junior & Robert
w 1845
Chrono M, Watch M
1845   31 Castle St, Kirkdale, Liverpool
Sources: G

CLARKE Richard
a 1787
Hydro M
           At Nathaniel Clarke's, Lemmon St,
           Goodman's Fields, London
Took over from CLARKE John (I)★, his father
Succeeded by DRING John★, his brother-in-law
See also CLARKE James (I)★
Sources: Advertisement (Cpy) MHS; DJB

CLARKE Thomas (I)
w 1731
Math IM
1731   Norton Folgate, London
Father of CLARKE Daniel s 1731 to CROUCH
Samuel GSWC
Sources: GL: GSWC 2455

CLARKE Thomas (II)
w 1805
Optician

1805   13 Wapping Wall, London
Apprenticed to BURTON Mark★ 1759
Succeeded by CLARKE William (II)★
See also CLARKE & SON★
Sources: PRO: IR 1/22 (AM); H

CLARKE William (I)
w 1722–1743
Optical IM
1743   Near Union Stairs in Wapping,
           London
See also CLARKE William (II)★
Known to have sold: back-staff
Instruments advertised: Hadley's quadrant
Sources: Post Boy 27 Oct 1722 (MAC); Middleton
A (1979); DJB

CLARKE William (II)
w 1797–1820
Quadrant M, Compass M, Math IM
1786   Wapping, London
1797–1820   13 Wapping Wall, Shadwell,
           London
Guild: Farriers, fr 1786
Son of CLARKE Samuel, glazier, of Aldgate,
London
Apprenticed to WOOD John, jeweller, 1776 t/o
1779 to CLARK Samuel of Wapping of GZC
Succeeded by CLARKE & SON★
See also CLARKE William (I)★
Apprenticeship consideration fee paid by Trustees
of Sir John Cass School
Sources: GL: FRC 5525, 5526/2; Kt (JAC); Pg

CLARKE & CO. E.
w 1823–1832
Optician, Math IM, Phil IM
1823–1832   83 Dame St, Dublin
See also CLARKE Edward (II)★
Sources: Wi; Burnett & Morrison-Low (1989)
p.122

CLARKE & SON
w 1821–1834
Math IM, Optical IM, Phil IM
1821–1834   13 Wapping Wall, Shadwell,
           London
Took over from CLARKE William (II)★
See also CLARKE Thomas (II)★
Sources: Bn; Kt; Pg

CLAXTON Timothy
w 1837–1840
Phil IM
1810–1815   London
1820–1823   St. Petersburg
1823–1826   Methuen, Mass, USA
1826–1836   Boston, Mass, USA
1837–1840   46 M[?ar]y St, Hampstead Road,
           London
1840–1843   27 Harrington St North, Hampstead
           Road, London
Apprenticed to a whitesmith in Bungay, Suffolk,
1803
Partnership:
CLAXTON & MORTON★
CLAXTON & PROTHERO★
b 1790, d 1848; attended London Mechanics

Institute 1837–1843; Cat. 1842 Phil. insts.
Sources: JAS; LMIR (AM); PO

CLAXTON William
w 1844–1845
Phil IM
1844–1845   27 Harrington St, Hampstead Road,
           London
Sources: LMIR (AM)

CLAXTON & MORTON
w 1840–1845
Math IM
1840–1845   27 Harrington St, Hampstead Rd,
           London
Succeeded by CLAXTON & PROTHERO★
Known to have sold: pyrometer
Sources: PO; Holbrook (1992) p.83

CLAXTON & PROTHERO
w 1846–1849
Math IM
1846–1849   27 Harrington St, Hampstead Road,
           London
Took over from CLAXTON & MORTON★
Sources: PO

CLAY Francis
w 1770
Math IM
1770   St James Clerkenwell, London
Had apprentice: WATTS John 1770
Sources: PRO: IR 1/26 (AM)

CLAY Thomas
w 1783
Math IM
1783   12 Brownlow St, Bedford Row,
           London
Had apprentice: WALLEY Thomas 1783
Sources: GL: CH 12876/6; 12823/7 p.182 (MAC)

CLAY & ABRAHAM
a 1830–1900
Chemists
           87 Bold St, Liverpool
           [Branch] 46 Castle St, Liverpool
Same premises as ABRAHAM John A.★
Known to have sold: hydrometer
Sources: inst SM (MAC)

CLAYTON Thomas
w 1723
Compass M
1723   Newington Butts, London
Insolvent 1723
Sources: LGaz 3 Sep 1723 (MAC)

CLEARE James
w 1763–1764
Spec M, [Telescope M]
1764   Mitre Court, Fleet St, London
Guild: Spectaclemakers, fr 1753
Son of CLEARE John
Apprenticed to CUFF John★ 1745/6
Had apprentice GWILLIM Robert Devereux★
1763
Petitioner against Dollond's patent, 1764

Known to have sold: telescope
Sources: GL: SMC 5213/3 p.96+; PRO PC 1/7
no.94; inst (s) (MAC)

CLEAVER Samuel
w 1845–1849
Baro M, Thermo M, Sacch M
1845   30 Theobald's Road, London
1849   56 Hatton Garden, London
Sources: PO

CLEPHIN John
w 1791–1801
Math IM
1791–1801   49 Little Minories, London
Guild: Joiners, fr 1790
Son of CLEPHIN James, peruke maker, of London
Apprenticed to BLAKE John* 1776
Listed only as a journeyman
Sources: GL: JC 8051/5, 8052/7, 80553, 8055/4
(MAC); Crawforth (1987) p.347–48

CLERK James
w 1793–1808
Math IM
Alternative name: CLARKE
1792   28 Ratcliffe Highway, London
1802   7 Jealous Row, New Road,
          St. George's in the East, London
1808   Goodman's Fields, London
Guild: Grocers, fr 1792
Son of CLERK James, clock maker, of Westminster,
London
Apprenticed to RUST Richard* 1779
Had apprentice:
SMITH Peter 1793
GASKIN George Augustus Samuel 1802
PHILLIPS William 1808
Sources: Brown (1979a) p.54; GL: GC 11598/6

CLEWITT Francis
w 1672
[Rule S]
Alternative name: HEWITT
1672   Blue Bell in the Strand near Charing
          Cross, London
Known to have sold: rule
Associated with: JOLE Robert*, from whom he
obtained rules
Faulty rules confiscated from his shop by CKC
Sources: GL: CKC 2710/1 p.244; Loomes (1981b)

CLIFF, WASTEL & CO.
w 1805
Optician
1805   Mount St, Birmingham
Sources: H (DJB)

CLIFFORD Edward
w 1835–1840
Math IM, Phil IM
1835–1840   42 Old Bond St, London
Sources: R (JAC)

CLIFFORD Robert
w 1618–1634
Spec M, ?Tailor
1628   Pudding Lane, London

Guild: Brewers & Spectaclemakers
Son of CLIFFORD Rowland, farmer, of Diseworth,
Leics
Apprenticed to POLSON Richard* 1609
Had apprentice:
BILLINGS William 1618
JOHNSON William 1621
TYBBET [TALBOT] Robert 1621/2
HAYNES Gabriel 1626
OWEN Thomas 1627
MORRALL Edwyn 1634
fr Brew 1617; translated from Brewers' to SMC
1634
Sources: CLRO: Ald 49 fol.14; GL: Brew
5445/12, 5445/13, 5445/14, 5445/16

CLIFT Charles
w 1845–1890
Optician
1845–1880   3 New Inn Yard, Shoreditch,
          London
1885–1890   42 New Inn Yard, Shoreditch,
          London
Sources: PO

CLINNICK William
w 1839–1840
Math IM, Phil IM
1839–1840   34 York St, City Road, London
Sources: Pg

CLITHEROE Thomas
w 1825–1834
Chrono M
1825   64 Eldon Place, Liverpool
1827–1834   10 Warren St, Liverpool
Sources: G

CLOTHIER John
w 1839
Rule M
1839   High St, Deptford, London
Sources: Pg

CLOTHIER John Thomas
w 1851–1855
Rule M
1851–1855   Lower Rd, Rotherhithe, London
Sources: PO; Wk

CLUTS William
w 1809
Optician
1809   Holloway, London
Sources: H (JAC)

COBHAM John
w 1739–1776
Finisher, ?Math IM
1737   Scroop's Court, Holborn, London
1745   Near Middle Row, Barbican,
          London
1751   Blue Anchor Alley, Bunhill Fields,
          London
Guild: Clockmakers, fr 1737
Apprenticed to
BENNETT Richard* 1729 t/o 1732
to BENNETT John (II)*

Had apprentice:
DAVIS William 1739
CLARKE Benjamin 1742
WILLIAMS John 1746
MORGAN William 1747
GORDON John 1749
LAMBE James 1751
DAY Jeremiah 1753
OVERSTALL John 1764
See also COBHAM Stockley*
Last noted by CKC 1776
Sources: GL: CKC 2720/1 fol.8v, 2721/1, 2723/2,
2723/3; Brown J (1979b) p.28–29

COBHAM Stockley
fr 1737 d 1787
Finisher, ?Math IM
1737   Scroop's Court, Holborn, London
1745   Red Lion St, Clerkenwell, London
Guild: Clockmakers, fr 1737
Apprenticed to WILSON James (II) 1723
Had apprentice:
PEARCE Henry 1739
FISHER John 1746
PERRY Peter 1755
See also COBHAM John*
d 1787
Sources: GL: CKC 2721/1, 2723/2; Brown J
(1979b) p.28–29

COCHRAN John
w 1780–1784
Math IM
1780   14 Wine Office Court, Fleet St,
          London
1784   Near the Mitre, Stangate, Lambeth,
          London
Guild: [?Grocers]
Apprenticed to possibly FAIRBONE Charles (I)* 1773
Sources: GL: Sun 11936/289 no.436188,
11936/324 no.497861; Brown (1979a) p.44

COCK Christopher
fr 1669 w 1697
Prospective Glass M
Alternative name: COCKS, COX, COCKE,
COCKES, Kit
1693   Long Acre, London
1696   The Two Twisted Posts in Long
          Acre, London
1696   The Blue Spectacles near St.Anne's
          Church, London
Guild: Turners fr 1669, Spectaclemakers fr 1680/1
Son of COCK John, Free of CORD of London
Apprenticed to STONEHALL John the elder 1657
TC t/o at once to REEVES John* GC
Had apprentice:
SCARLETT Edward (I)* 1691 SMC
BREWIN Thomas 1685 SMC
LANCHESTER Thomas 1673/4 TC
PITT William 1675 TC
SUTER John 1676 TC
STENT George 1680 TC
COOPER Abraham 1697 TC
See also COCK John*
Associated with REEVE Richard (I)*, REINE R.*
& TOMPION Thomas* in working for HOOKE
Robert of the Royal Society; supplied instruments

for St. Andrews Observatory
R.apt Charles II
Known to have sold: lens, magic lantern, mirror,
microscope, telescope
Sources: GL: SMC 5213/1; TC 3302/1; inst SM,
WM; Buckley (1935) p.427; Simpson (1989)
p.43–59; Taylor (1954) p.246–48,265,267

COCK John
w 1688–1699
Prospective glass grinder
Alternative name: COCKS, COX
1693   Long Acre, London
1695   Cock & Garter, Long Acre, London
1699   Parish of St.Martin in the Fields,
            London
See also COCK Christopher★
Father of COCK Joseph s 1699 to MARSHALL
John★
Known to have sold: lens
Sources: GL: TC 3302/2; SMC 5213/1; Court &
Von Rohr (1928–29) p.218n; (1929–30) p.75;
Simpson (1989) p.43,59

COCK S.
w 1840
[Gauging IS]
1840   Store Office, Excise Office, Broad
            St, London
Known to have sold: hydrometer
Instruments advertised: gauging instruments
Sources: inst SM; advertisement in Bateman J, *The
Excise Officer's Manual,* London, 1840 (DJB)

COCK & HUGHES
a 1790
       London
B.apt Excise
Known to have sold: dipping measure
Sources: Webster R & M (1986)

COCKEY Edward
a 1675–1705
       Warminster, Wilts
Known to have sold: astronomical clock
Sources: inst NMM; King & Millburn (1978) p.138

COCKS, RADFORD & RADFORD
Robert, John (II) & William (I)
w 1718–1722
Spec M
1718–1722   Great Golden Spectacle against
            St.Clement's Church in the Strand,
            London
Succeeded by RADFORD John (II)★
Sources: GL: Sun 11936/8 no.11346 (MAC)

COFFEY & SMITH J. & J.
w 1851
1851   4 Providence Row, Finsbury,
            London
Ex.1851
Sources: Turner (1983a) p.309

COGGS John (I)
w 1718–1733
Math IM, Engraver
Alternative name: Iohn

1729   Globe & Sun over against
            St.Dunstan's Church in Fleet St,
            London
Guild: Pewterers, fp 1712
Son of COGGS John of PWC of London
Had apprentice:
WOOD Thomas 1718 [possibly WOOD
Thomas (I)★]
GREAVES Robert 1719
GREAVES John 1720
WYETH William★ 1725
JOHNSON Charles 1730
Worked for ROWLEY John (I)★
Same premises as CUSHEE Richard★
Associated with
CARVER Isaac★, whose slide rules he sold
WRIGHT Thomas (I)★ while working for ROWLEY★
Partnership: COGGS & WYETH★ c.1733–1740
Succeeded by COGGS & WYETH★
See also COGGS John (II)★
Known to have sold: universal equinoctial ring dial
Instruments advertised: full range
Sources: BM: Heal 105/21 (MAC); GL: Brod
14663/1 MAC); PWC 7090/9, 7101 (MAC);
Daily J 31 Oct 1729 (JRM); Crawforth (1985)
p.501; Holbrook (1992) p.103

COGGS John (II)
s 1759
       London
Guild: [Merchant Taylors]
Apprenticed to COLE Benjamin (II)★ 1759
Son of COGGS Timothy of WXC of London
See also COGGS John (I)★
Taylor lists COGGS John (II)★ as being in business
in Fleet St, but there appears to be confusion with
COGGS John (I)★
Sources: GL: MTC MF 319 (MAC): Taylor (1966)
p.172

COGGS & WYETH John & William
a 1733 w 1740
Math IM
1740   Near St.Dunstan's Church in Fleet
            St, London
Took over from COGGS John (I)★
Succeeded by WRIGHT & WYETH★
Sources: LEP 3 Nov 1741; (MAC); Shirtcliffe
(1740) p.xiii (DJB)

COHAN John
w 1834–1837
Clock M, Watch M, Chrono M
Alternative name: COHEN
1834   15 Cannon Place, Liverpool
1837   82 Paradise St, Liverpool
Sources: Loomes (1975); Taylor (1966) p.469

COHEN David (I)
w 1820–1857
Optician, Math IM
1820   4 Collingwood St, Newcastle upon
            Tyne
1821–1836   5 Collingwood St, Newcastle upon
            Tyne
1836–1844   1 Grey St, Newcastle upon Tyne
1847–1851   76 Grey St, Newcastle upon Tyne
1853   30 Mosley St, Newcastle upon Tyne

1855–1857   9 Mosley St, Newcastle upon Tyne
Known to have sold: barometer
Sources: Pg; Ric, Wd; Wh; Wim; Wln; Goodison
(1977) p.312

COHEN David (II)
w 1845
Optician
1845   1 Bett St, Ratcliff Highway, London
Sources: PO

COHEN Morice
w 1849–1851
Optician
1849–1851   59 Pitt St, Liverpool
Sources: G

COHEN Simeon Phineas
w 1844–1853
Math IM, Phil IM
1844   82 Queen St, Glasgow
1845–1848   105 Buchanan St, Glasgow
1850   121 Buchanan St, Glasgow
1851   51 St.Vincent St, Glasgow
1852   136 Buchanan St, Glasgow
Worked for ABRAHAM & CO.★ as partner and
manager of Glasgow branch
Took over from ABRAHAM & CO.★
Bankrupt 1853
Known to have sold: hydrometer
Sources: ChrSK 17 Apr 1986 lot 207 (MAC);
Bryden (1972) p.46; Clarke et al (1989) p.298–9

COIGLEY James
w 1822–1834
Chrono M, Clock M, Watch M
1822   22 Paradise St, Liverpool
1824   57 Paradise St, Liverpool
1834   17 Hanover St, Liverpool
1834   135 St.James St, Liverpool
Sources: G (MAC); Loomes (1975)

COLBE John Lawrence
w 1734–1745
Math IM, Gun M, Phil IM
Alternative name: KOLBE, COLBEY
1735   Suhl, Thuringia
1735   Silver St, near Golden Square,
            London
1744   Marylebone St, London
1745   Sherrard St, London
1747   Dresden, Saxony
Seems to have concentrated increasingly on guns:
supplied cannon locks to the Royal Navy 1746–7.
Sources: Wallis P (1976); Blackmore (1992a);
Blackmore (1992b)

COLE Benjamin (I)
w 1720–1750
Math IM, Phil IM, Optical IM
       Royal Exchange, London
1726   Fleet St, London
1739   The Grand Orrery, Poppings Court,
            Fleet St, London
1744–1748   Ball Alley going out of George Yard
            into Lombard St, London
1747–1758   The Orrery, next the Globe Tavern,
            Fleet St, London

1765   [Residence?] Near Westminster Bridge, Surrey, London
Guild: Merchant Taylors, fr 1719
Son of COLE Benjamin, gent, of Oxford
Apprenticed to CADE William, lapidary, 1710
Had apprentice:
BAKER Edward (I)★ 1720
GRUBB Thomas 1720/1
GREEN Charles 1725
JOUGHIN Daniel 1726
PAINE Thomas 1739
COLE Benjamin (II)★, his son, 1739
JONES Jonathan 1742
SKELTON Richard 1743
PENHALLOW Samuel★ 1746/7
TURTON Thomas 1746/7
WRIGHT John (I)★ 1750
BLOOM Thomas 1750
COOKE Henry C. 1757
[Note: there was another Benjamin Cole in MTC, so some of the above apprentices could have been bound to him]
Worked for WRIGHT Thomas (I)★
Father of COLE Martha, wife of BAKER Edward (I)★
COLE Elizabeth, wife of SUDLOW John★
Succeeded by COLE & SON★
Took over from WRIGHT Thomas (I)★
Associated with
LIFORD John★ with whom he issued a joint advertisement in 1748
CUSHEE E.★ as proprietor of *A Description and Use of the Globes* by Joseph HARRIS (II)★, 7th edn, London 1751
b 1695 d 1766; entered HAC as Sergeant 1726
Known to have sold: circumferentor, theodolite, waywiser
Instruments advertised: full range, orrery, quadrant
Sources: GL: MTC MF 319, 320, 324 (MAC), CH 12876/4 (MAC), TCd; bill SML; HAC Minutes (JT); *Daily Advertiser* 16 Apr 1744, 28 Mar 1748, 11 June 1748 p.3, 19 Dec 1748 p.4 (JRM); *General Evening Post* 24 June 1766 (MAC); GMag 35 (1765) p.555–57; Chr 11 Jun 1987 Clocks etc. lot 55; JRM; Calvert (1971) p.18, pl.17; Holbrook (1992) p.221; King & Millburn (1978) p.163; Morton & Wess (1993) p.393; Wallis R & P (1986)

COLE Benjamin (II)
w 1766–1782
Math IM, Phil IM, Optical IM
1768–1782   The Orrery, next the Globe Tavern, 136 Fleet St, London
1782–1785   136 Fleet St, London
Guild: Merchant Taylors, fr 1746
Apprenticed to COLE Benjamin (I)★, his father, 1739
Partnership: COLE & SON★
Had apprentice:
COULON John 1747
RAYMOND William 1749
WATTS Thomas 1756
COLE Benjamin (III)★ 1757
TAYLOR Edward 1759
OULD Henry★ 1759
COGGS John (II)★ 1759
BASS Samuel 1763
HAMMOND William★ 1766

HARDY Henry 1766
CAPEY John 1766
PRICE James 1769
HARRIS Thomas (III)★1770
CHESTER Edward★ 1771
ABBOTT John 1774
THOMAS Robert 1776
Succeeded by TROUGHTON John (II)★
Took over from COLE & SON★
Associated with TROUGHTON John (II)★ in business arrangements
CUSHEE E.★ apparently continuing his father's association noted above
Joined HAC as Ensign 1744; Captain in the Militia; MTC Livery 1763; r 1782; d 1813
Known to have sold: globe, octant, telescope
Instruments advertised: full range
Sources: GL: Sun 11936/290 no.440948, 11936/306 no.467261, MTC MF 319, 320, 324 (MAC), Baker papers 16938/113; BM: Heal 105/24; Ld; Lg; Kt (JAC); HAC Minutes (JT); Anderson et al (1990) p.19; McConnell (1992) p.6–7

COLE Benjamin (III)
w 1771
Math IM
1771   Titchfield St, Soho, London
Guild: Merchant Taylors, fr 1771
Son of COLE Maximilian, engraver, of Oxford
Apprenticed to COLE Benjamin (II)★ 1757
Had apprentice MITCHENER Thomas 1771
Sources: GL: MTC MF 319, 320, 324

COLE C.
w 1664
Known to have sold: slide rule
Source: inst SM (MAC)

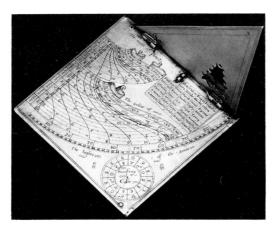

COLE Humfrey
w 1568–1590
Goldsmith, Math IM (in metal), Engraver
Alternative name: COOLE, COLLE, COOLLE, Humfrae, Humfray
1582   Near the North Door of St. Paul's, London
Guild Goldsmiths?
Assistant at the Mint 1564; d 1591
Known to have sold: alidade, armillary sphere, astrolabe, compendium, gunner's callipers, log,

nocturnal, quadrant, rule, sundial, theodolite
Sources: inst BM, Horniman Mu London, MHS, NMM, NMS, SM (GL'ET); ChrSK 13 Dec 1984 lot 219; Bryden (1992) p.304; Holbrook (1992) p.127,151–52,157,202; Taylor (1954) p. 171–72; Turner G (1983b) p.98–99; Ward (1981) p.74

COLE James Ferguson
w 1839–1851
Chrono M, Watch M, Clock M
1839–1846   9 Motcomb St, Belgrave Square, London
1851   30 Granville Square, Pentonville, London
Sources: Pg; PO

COLE John (I)
w 1851
Math IM
1851   1 St. Stephen's Terrace, King's Cross, London
See also LORKIN Thomas★
Sources: Wk

COLE John Junior
w 1691
[Math IM]
1691   Kingston, Surrey
Signed sector
Sources: Chr(SK) 14 Dec 1989 lot 152

COLE Joseph
w 1681–1715
Spec M
1693–1695   St. Martins le Grand, London
Guild: Spectaclemakers, fr 1686
Son of COLE Nicholas, Gentleman, d, of Durham
Apprenticed to ALT Isaac★ 1675
Had apprentice:
DEW William 1693
NASH John 1696
BRASIER Thomas 1696
COLVILE John 1703
GREEN James 1709
Master SMC 1712–1715. His last appearance at an SMC meeting was in 1730
Sources: GL: SMC 5213/1; 5213/2 p.32,65,79, 93–4; 6031/1

COLE Richard
s 1782 w 1822
        Corn Hill, Ipswich
Guild: Clockmakers
Known to have sold: sundial
Sources: Baillie (1951); Webster R & M (1986)

COLE Robert
w 1725–1743
Math IM, Rule M
1725   Southwark, London
1731   Giltspur St, London
1733   Gravel Lane, Southwark, London
1740   Old Bailey, London
Guild: Stationers, fr 1725
Son of COLE Richard, grocer, of Southwark, London
Apprenticed to BETTESWORTH Peter★ 1716
Had apprentice:

GILES William 1725
RICHARDSON Thomas 1726
FOWLT John 1731
HARRIS William 1733
HAWTHORNE William 1733/4
MANN James (III) 1740 t/o 1743
to FARMER John★
Sources: GL: CH 12876/3 (MAC); McKenzie
(1978) p.35,80

COLE Thomas (I)
w c.1725–1735
        Address unknown
Known to have sold: perpetual calendar
Sources: inst NMM; Webster R & M (1986)

COLE Thomas (II)
w 1839–1869
Math IM, Phil IM, Naut IM
1839–1869   21 Hannibal Rd, Mile End, Stepney,
         London
Guild: [Masons]
Son of COLE John, Shipwright, of Limehouse,
London
Apprenticed to COOK William George★ 1812
Known to have sold: compass (magnetic), course
corrector
Sources: GL: MC 5312; Sby 23 Jun 1987 lot 170
(MAC); Pg; PO

COLE William (I)
w 1762 d 1799
Math IM
1762   Parish of St. Clement Danes,
         London
1764   Strand, London
Had apprentice PHILLIPS Samuel 1762
See also COLE William (II)★ [possibly the same
maker]
Petitioner against Dollond's patent 1764
Sources: PRO: IR 1/23 (AM), PC 1/7 no.94; JAC

COLE William (II)
w 1777
Engine M, Math IM
1767   Lambeth, London
1777   Opposite Westminster New
         Lying-In Hospital, Lambeth Marsh,
         London
Had apprentice CAPPER Thomas 1767
See also COLE William (I)★ [possibly the same
maker]
Sources: PRO: IR 1/23 (AM); GL: Sun 11936/258
no.386622 (MAC)

COLE & SON Benjamin
w 1750–1766
Math IM, Phil IM, Optical IM
1753–1766   The Orrery, next the Globe Tavern
         in Fleet St, London
Employed WRIGHT John (I)★
Took over from COLE Benjamin (I)★
Succeeded by COLE Benjamin (II)★
Benjamin Senior d 1766
Known to have sold: air pump, gunner's quadrant,
planetarium
Instruments advertised: full range
Sources: BM: Heal 105/23 (MAC); bill SML

(MAC); Anderson et al (1990) p.19; Holbrook
(1992) p.105; Millburn (1988b) p.280–81

COLEBROOK Samuel
w 1803–1818
Scale M
1803–1812   Rosemary St, Bristol
1813–1816   Wilder St, Bristol
1813–1817   Barrs St, Bristol
1818   56 Broadmead, Bristol
Guild: [Blacksmiths?]
Apprenticed to probably DE GRAVE Charles (I)★
1791
Sources: GL: BKC 2881/16 (MAC); Mat; Und

COLEMAN Ann
w 1831–1834
Baro M, Thermo M
1831–1834   11 Vineyard Walk, Coppice Row,
         Clerkenwell, London
Took over from COLEMAN Charles★
Sources: Pg; R (JAC)

COLEMAN Charles
w 1823–1830
Baro M, Thermo M
1823   5 Old North St, Red Lion Square,
         London
         7 Dorrington St, Clerkenwell,
         London
1830   11 Vineyard Walk, Coppice Row,
         Clerkenwell, London
Succeeded by COLEMAN Ann★
Sources: Pg; R (JAC)

COLEMAN George
w 1822–1832
Math IM, Mariner, Map & Chart Engraver
1822   Leadenhall St, London
1832   157 Leadenhall St, London
Guild: Goldsmiths, fp 1820
Son of COLEMAN Richard, mariner
Had apprentice:
MURRAY James (II) 1822
PIDDING William 1822
HUGGINS Thomas 1832
Sources: GH: GC index

COLEMAN Stephen
w 1732–1742
Math IM
1732   Lower Shadwell, London
Guild: [Clockmakers], Drapers, fp 1731/2
Son of COLEMAN Stephen, DPC
Apprenticed to BELLINGER John (I)★1704 CKC
Had apprentice:
PYKE Henry 1731/2
PARKER Benjamin 1742
Sources: DH: DPC Ap

COLEMAN William
w 1738
1738   Near King James's Stairs, Wapping,
         London
Instruments advertised: octant
Sources: Listed on title page of Anonymous (1738)
(DJB)

COLES Christopher
fl 1664
[Math IM]
Known to have sold: slide rule
Sources: Taylor (1954) p.252

COLEY William
w 1836
Spectacle M
1836   35 Tash St, Gray's Inn Lane, London
Sources: Pg

COLLAR George
w 1814–1825
Optician
1814–1818   101 Market St, Manchester
1816   135 Chapel St, Salford, Manchester
1824–1825   42 Market St, Manchester
1825   (residence) Southport
Sources: Bn; H; Pg; Und; WB

COLLEIE Thomas
fl 1722
[Dial M]
See also COLLEY Thomas★
Known to have sold: sundial
Sources: inst MHS; Taylor (1966) p.154

COLLEY Thomas
w 1754 d 1771
Clock M
         Fleet St, London
Guild: Goldsmiths
Had apprentice BEYER John fr 1769, apprenticed
through CKC
Partnership BARKLEY & COLLEY 1751–1754,
claimed to be succesors to GRAHAM George★
See also COLLEIE Thomas★
Sources: GL: CKC 11568; Baillie (1951)

COLLIER Richard
w 1667
Hour-glass M
1667   Trowbridge, Wilts
Father of COLLIER William s 1667 THC
Sources: GL: THC 6158/3 p.2

COLLIER William
w 1707–1745
Math IM
         Ye Atlas, the end of Wood St,
         Facing Cripplegate, London
1720   Chick Lane, West Smithfield,
         London
1731   Ye Atlas next the Fountain Tavern
         without Newgate, London
Guild: [Clockmakers], Goldsmiths, fp 1703/4
Apprenticed to TUTTELL Thomas 1699
Son of COLLIER Richard
Had apprentice:
DOUNTON William★ 1706/7
PARSONS William (I)★ 1710
LIFORD John★ 1716
CHURCH Seth 1724
CLARK Charles 1726
SA(U)NDERS Samuel (II)★ 1736
BAYNHAM Charles 1744 by t/o
from ADAMS George (I)★

Known to have sold: balance, protractor, sector rule
Sources: GL: CH: 12823/4 p.376, Sun 11936/11
no.17839 (MAC), CKC 2710/2 fol.227v, TCd;
GH: GSC Ap, Fr, index; BM: Heal 105/27
(MAC); Phlps 2 Dec 1987 lot 90A (MAC); Brown
J (1979a) p.36; Brown J (1979b) p.29; Crawforth
(1985) p.457,466; Tesseract Cat. 17 (1987) no.50

COLLINGS Charles Wilkins
w 1845–1860
Phil IM
1845   16 Mortimer St, Cavendish Square,
         London
1846   12 Little Portland St, London
1856–1860   16 Mortimer St, Cavendish Square,
         London
See also COLLINS Charles William*, both names
appear simultaneously in directories
Sources: PO

COLLINGS Frederick James
w 1845–1846
Optician
1845–1846   15 Barnsbury Row, Cloudesley
         Square, London
Sources: PO

COLLINGS James
w 1817–1835
Optician, Math IM, Phil IM, Spec M
1822   Bowling Green Lane, London
1831   6 Skinner St, Clerkenwell, London
1835   5 Skinner St, Clerkenwell, London
Sources: PO; R (JAC); Bennion (1979)

COLLINGS John
w 1743
Spec M
1743   Parish of St. Luke's (Middx), London
Sources: Buckley (1935) p.428

COLLINGWOOD Thomas
w 1711
IM (? Math)
         London
Sources: GL: CH 12823/3 p.60 (MAC)

COLLINS - (I)
w 1742
[Optical IS, Phil IS]
1742   Sarum
Associated with MARTIN Benjamin*, as retailer of
instruments made by Martin
Sources: Millburn (1976) p.39–40

COLLINS - (II)
d 1768
Math IM
1768   Bishopsgate St, London
Sources: Gazetteer 22 Feb 1768 (MAC)

COLLINS Charles William
w 1838–1859
Optician, Philo IM
1838   31 Lisle St, Leicester Square, London
1845   16 Mortimer St, Cavendish Square,
         London
1846   12 Little Portland St, London

1848–1853   26 Francis St, Bedford Square, London
1855   16 Mortimer St, Cavendish Square,
         London
See also COLLINGS Charles Wilkins*, both names
appear simultaneously in directories
Sources: PO

COLLINS Henry George
w 1847–1858
Globe M
         London
Sources: Downing (1984) (not traced in other
sources)

COLLINS Peter
w 1687–1699
[Math IM?]
         London
Guild: Clockmakers, fr 1687
Apprenticed to ATKINSON James (I)* 1679/90
Had apprentice:
DYSON John 1687 by t/o from NORTH J.
GAMAGE Philip 1694
SANDERLIN John 1699
Sources: GL: CKC 2723/1, 3975 fol.43; Brown J
(1979b) p.29; Loomes (1981b)

COLLINS & SON James
w 1835
Spectacle M
1835   75 Newhall St, Birmingham
Sources: Pg

COLOMBA Andrew
w 1842–1865
Baro M
1842–1843   37 Charles St, Hatton Garden,
         London
1849–1859   37 Charles St, Hatton Garden,
         London
1865   16 Charles St, Hatton Garden,
         London EC
Partnership: COLOMBA & HARE*
Took over from SOMALVICO Joseph*
Sources: PO

COLOMBA & HARE Andrew & John William
w 1845–1846
Baro M, Thermo M
1845–1846   37 Charles St, London
1846   and 89 Chancery Lane, London
Took over from COLOMBA Andrew *
Succeeded by COLOMBA Andrew *
Sources: PO

COLOMBO John
w 1805
Optician
1805   180 High Holborn, London
Sources: H

COMBES Fisher
w 1730–1737
Math IM
Alternative name: COOMBS, COMBS
         Ye Mariner & Globe in Broad St,
         near ye Angel & Crown Tavern

         behind ye Royal Exchange, London
1736   [Residence] c/o Mr. Merry's, Pump
         Court, Charing Cross, London
Guild: Clockmakers, fr 1728
Apprenticed to CADE Simon* 1721
Had apprentice:
ANDREWS Richard 1730
BANKS William 1734
HADDOCK Charles 1737
Known to have sold: circumferentor, nocturnal
Sources: GL: CKC 2710/4 fol.41v; Brown J
(1979b) p.29; Calvert (1971) pl.19; Holbrook
(1992) p.103,204

COMBS Oliver
w 1691–1750
Optician
Alternative name: COMBES, COOMBS, COOMBE
1695   Leadenhall St, London
To 1747   The Spectacles in St.Martin's Court
         near Leicester Fields, London
From 1747   Within two Doors of Essex St, in the
         Strand by Temple Bar, London
Guild: Needlemakers fr 1688, Spectaclemakers fr
1727/8
Son of COMBS William, tailor, of Penselwood,
Somerset
Apprenticed to PAYTON Jonathan 1680 NC
Had apprentice:
POTTINGER James 1691 NC
HINCHLOE Samuel 1744 SMC
STREET Daniel 1750 SMC t/o 1752 to
TOMLINSON James (I)*
Father of COMBS James fp 1727 NC
Worked for
SCARLETT Edward (I)*
RADFORD William (I)*
Not apprenticed to the trade; Master NC
1724–1725; d c. 1752
Instruments advertised: barometer, camera obscura,
magic lantern, microscope, prism, specatcles,
telescope, thermometer
Sources: Daily Advertiser 7 Nov 1747 p.2 (MAC);
GL: NC 2818/1 p.42,68; SMC 5213/2 p.183,189;
5213/3 p.79,149,182; Calvert (1971) pl.20

COMOLI Andrew
w 1841
Baro M, Umbrella S, Hardware S
1841   High St, Dudley, Worcs
Sources: Pg

COMOLI J.
w 1825–1826
1825   82 St.Mary's Wynd, Edinburgh
See also COMOLI & NOZZI*
Known to have sold: barometer
Sources: Pg; Goodison (1977) p.313

COMOLI Peter, Andrew & John
w 1835
Baro S, Umbrella M, Hardwaremen
1835   High St, Dudley, Worcs
Sources: Pg

COMOLI & CO. Peter
w 1817
Baro M, Hardware S

Alternative name: CURMOLI
1817   High St, Dudley
See also CURMOLI★
Known to have sold: barometer
Sources: Goodison (1977) p.313

COMOLI & NOZZI
a 1800–1850
           82 St.Mary's Wynd, Edinburgh
See also COMOLI J.★
Known to have sold: barometer
Sources: Goodison (1977) p.313

COMYNS Henry
w 1826–1867
Optical IM, Phil IM, Math IM
1826   15 Asylum Terrace, King's Rd,
            Chelsea, London
1839–1845   17 King's Rd East, Chelsea, London
1846–1855   5 Hereford Terrace, King's Rd,
            Chelsea, London
Sources: Pg; PO; R (JAC); Wk

CONNELL William
w 1839–1869
Chrono M
1839   41 Wynyate St, London
1851   83 Cheapside, London
Sources: PO; Pg; Loomes (1976)

CONNOLLY George
w 1835–1844
Optician
1835   45 Grangegorman Lane, Dublin
1835–1845   45 Grangegorman, Upper, Dublin
Sources: Wi; Burnett & Morrison-Low (1989)
p.122

COOBEROW Mathew
w 1695–1708
Spec M
Alternative name: COWPEROW, COWPEROE,
COOPEROE, COOBERRO
1695   Angel St, London
Guild: Spectaclemakers, fr 1690
Father of COOBEROW Mathew (II) fp 1725, no
trade given
Son of COOBEROW Roger, miller, of Weston,
Berks
Apprenticed to GOODMAN Thomas (II)★ 1683
Had apprentice:
MANN James (II)★ 1699
MIDDLEFELL Damaine?★ 1705
LINCOLN Thomas★ 1708
RADFORD William (I)★ nd, fr 1720
Sources: GL: SMC 5213/1; 5213/2 p.47; 6031/1;
CLRO: CF1/53 no.29

COOK George
w 1821–1836
Math IM, Optical IM, Phil IM
1822–1833   178 High St, Shadwell, London
1834–1836   44 Ratcliff Highway, London
Took over from COOK & SON William★
See also COOK William★
Sources: Bn; Kt (JAC)

COOK Henry
w 1851
Optician
1851   3 King St, Holborn, London
Attended London Mechanics Institute 1851
Sources: LMIR (AM)

COOK Laban
w 1826–1834
Rule M
Alternative name: COOKE
1826–1834   21 Crown Court, Soho, London
1830–1832   Crown Court, Pulteney St, Soho,
            London
            (Presumably a variation of first
            address)
Had apprentice ANDREWS Thomas 1827
Took over from WELLINGTON Alexander★,
according to advertisement
See also WELLINGTON Mary★
Known to have sold: slide rule
Instruments advertised: slide rule
Attended London Mechanics Institute 1830–1832
Sources: GL: CH 12876/8 (MAC); Pg; LMIR
(AM); Routledge (1826) (DJB)

COOK William
w 1799–1819
Math IM, Quadrant M, Compass M
Alternative name: William George
1799–1800   Cork St, St.George in the East,
            London
1802–1819   178 High St, Shadwell, London
Guild: Masons, fr 1794
Apprenticed to BAILEY William★ 1782
Son of COOK William, mariner, d, of St George's,
Middx, London
Had apprentice:
RIDER William★ 1799
HUGHES Joseph (I)★ 1800
JOUGHIN James Ely★ 1801
ROGERS William 1803
BRACE Joseph 1806
LEE George ?★ 1806
DUNCAN John (I)★ 1807
SKILTON Samuel★ 1809
OLDFIELD Henry 1811
COLE Thomas (II)★ 1812
WHITBREAD George★ 1812
FORD John★ 1818
WALKER Francis★ 1818
Succeeded by COOK & SON William★
See also COOK George★
Sources: GL: MC 5304/4, 5304/5, 5304/6, 5312
(MAC); H; Kt; Und

COOK & SON William
w 1820–1821
Quadrant M
1820–1821   178 High St, Shadwell, London
Took over from COOK William★
See also COOK George★
Sources: PO

COOKE Francis
w 1596
Mathematician, Math IS
1596   Mark Lane, London

Probably the Francis Cooke, son of Thomas,
clothmaker of London, who took a B.A. at Oxford
1584
Instruments advertised: cross-staff
Sources: Bryden (1992) p.307n

COOKE John
w 1761–1767
Optical IM
1761   Cock Lane, Snow Hill, London
1764   Snow Hill, London
Guild: Stationers, fr 1760
Apprenticed to BUSH John★ 1748/9
Had apprentice:
MOULDING James★ 1761
BERRY William 1762
HARE Charles 1764 by t/o from BUSH John★
OFFIELD John 1767
Petitioner against Dollond's patent 1764
Sources: PRO: PC1/7 no.94; McKenzie (1978)
p.60,86

COOKE Peter
w 1709–1733
Trade not given, but Master of Hour-glass M
            London
Guild: Turners
Had apprentice:
HOWELL Joseph 1709/10
HAYWARD John 1710/11
COOKE Thomas, his son, 1718
HILLIARD Thomas 1721
BROWNE John 1725
STROUD John★ 1727
SMART Phillip Francis
Sources: GL:TC 3302/2

COOKE Robert (I)
w 1668–1716
Alternative name: Richard ?
            London
Guild: Clockmakers fr as Brother 1667/8, Weavers
fr 1675
Apprenticed to HENSHAW Walter★ 1659 WVC
Son of COOKE R., freeman of Bakers' Co. of
London
Had apprentice:
WEEKES Johnson 1671 CKC
BIGG Benjamin 1678/9 CKC
DOLPHIN Benjamin nd WVC, fr 1716
Sources: GL: WVC 4657/1, 4657B; Brown J
(1979b) p.29

COOKE Robert (II)
fl 1807–1810
Chrono M
            7 Star Alley, Fenchurch St, London
Sources: Taylor (1966) p.360

COOKE Thomas (I)
w 1650–1666
            London
Guild: Stationers, fr 1635
Apprenticed to GOSSE Nathaniel★ 1628
Had apprentice:
CURTIS William 1650 by t/o from RAND Samuel
GANDER Timothy 1666
Sources: McKenzie (1961) p.74, (1974) p.37

COOKE Thomas (II)
w 1708 d 1744
Math IM (in silver, brass, ivory or wood)
1704   Threadneedle St, London
1704–1708   Old Jewry, near the Excise Office,
             London
1744   Old Jewry, London
Guild: Joiners, fr 1690
Apprenticed to TOOGOOD John★ 1682
Son of COOKE Thomas, grazier, d, of Warwick
Had apprentice:
BOSWELL Samuel★ 1701
SARJANT Thomas★ 1703
MOLE William (I)★ 1721/2
HARRIS Daniel (I)★ 1725 by t/o from BLOW
Edmund★
FARMER John★ 1722
ROBERTS Edward (I)★ 1733
RIX William★ nd
Ten other apprentices were bound to a Thomas
Cooke, but there were two of that name in JC
See also WORGAN & COOKE★
Associated with WORGAN John★
Said to be aged 80 when d, so b c. 1664
Known to have sold: slide rule
Sources: *LEP* 24 Jan 1744, *LGaz* 2 Sep 1695, *Post
Man* 21 Sep 1704 (MAC); inst MHS noted by
MAC; Bryden (1992) p.321; Crawforth (1987)
p.351; Leadbetter (1750) p.xviii (DJB)

COOKE Thomas (III)
w 1837–1868
Optician, Teacher
             Micklegate, York
1837–1841   50 Stonegate, York
1844–1854   12 Coney St, York
1855–1868   [Manufactory] , Buckingham
             Works, Bishophill, York
1860   26 Coney St, York
1863–1868   31 Southampton St, Strand, London
Son of COOKE James, shoemaker, of Allerthorpe,
Yorks
Had apprentice:
DALE John
ANGELL Lewis
Father of COOKE Charles Frederick
COOKE Thomas
Succeeded by COOKE & SONS T.
Associated with CAIL John★ as supplier
b 1807 d 1868; won First Class Medal for telescope
at Universal Exhibition, Paris, 1855; the firm
became part of Cooke, Troughton & Simms Ltd in
1922
Supplied numerous other instrument makers and
retailers
Known to have sold: level, microscope,
pantograph, telescope
Sources: Pg; Sl; Wh; inst SM (DJB); McConnell
(1993) p.50–55

COOKEOW Thomas
w 1715 d 1727
Math IM
Alternative name: CUCKOE
1715   Near New College, Oxford
See also PRUJEAN John★, whom he probably
succeeded
Author

Sources: Wallis R & P (1986) p.68; Oxford
Council Acts (AVS)

COOKSEY Hector Richard
w 1850
Coffin Furniture M, Measuring Tape M, Nail M
1850   148 High St, Bordesley, Birmingham
1850   [Residence] Coventry Road,
             Birmingham
Sources: Wh

COOPER George
w 1811
Baro M
1811   22 Dean St, Fetter Lane, London
Sources: H

COOPER John
w 1819
Spec M
1819   9 Garden Row, City Rd, London
See also BURTON Joseph (I)★
Sources: R (JAC)

COOPER Michael Andrew
w 1851–1880
Optician
1851–1859   7 St. James's Walk, Clerkenwell
             Green, London
1865–1880   25 St. James's Walk, Clerkenwell
             Green, London
Sources: PO; Wk

COOPER Stephen Norris
w 1809–1841
Rule M
1809–1811   119 Great Saffron Hill, Holborn,
             London
1811–1829   25 Miller St, Manchester
1834–1841   16 Miller St, Manchester
Known to have sold: slide rule
Sources: Bn; H; Pg; inst National Railway Mu,
York (DJB)

COOPER Thomas Frederick
w 1839–1875
Chrono M
1839   18 King William St, City, London
1851   6 Calthorpe St, London
Sources: PO, Pg, Loomes (1976)

COOPER W. C.
w 1842–1845
Alternative name: W.C.C.
             Address unknown
Known to have sold: electromagnetic generator,
electrometer, leyden jar
Sources: ChrSK 20 Aug 1987 lot 90 (MAC)

COPE Charles John
fl 1814 w 1830
Chrono M
             38 Berners St, Oxford St, London
1827–1830   40 Rathbone Place, London
Took part in chronometer trials at Royal
Greenwich Observatory 1827–1830
Known to have sold: chronometer
Sources: CUL: RGO 1143 fol.7–9; Taylor (1966)
p.387; Baillie (1951)

COPELAND Thomas
w 1626–1634
Spec M
Alternative name: COUPELAND
1634   London
Guild: Brewers fr 1625/6, Spectaclemakers
Son of COPELAND Ralph, farmer, of Wymeswold,
Leics
Apprenticed to POLSON Richard★ 1617
Had apprentice:
LEAKE Francis 1626
RADFORD [REDFORD] John (I)★ 1633/4
Translated from Brewers to Spectaclemakers Co.
1634
Sources: CLRO: Ald 49 fol.14 ; GL: BREW
5445/13–15

COPINI Gaetano
w 1832–1848
Baro M, Thermo M, Looking-glass M, Carver &
Gilder
Alternative name: Gitaneo , Gatini
1832–1841   217 High St, Shoreditch, London
1839–1841   and 280 High Holborn, London
1842–1848   37 Norton Folgate, London
Sources: Pg; PO; Goodison (1977) p.313

CORBETT Thomas
w 1850–1862
Math IM, Rule M, Fishing Reel M
1850   14 Edmond St, Birmingham
1850   [Residence] 39 Hockley Hill,
             Birmingham
1862   74 Spencer St, Birmingham
Sources: Mor; Sl; Wh

CORCORAN Bryan (I)
w 1780–1830
Stationer, Measure M
1780   39 Mark Lane, London
1806   47 Mark Lane, London
1829   36 Mark Lane, London
Guild: Needlemakers, fr by purchase 1780
Father of CORCORAN Bryan (II) fr STC 1833
Had apprentice:
DOWSE James 1781
CRIPPEN John 1782
BENNETT Henry 1790
HOLLAND George 1792 by t/o
from WINGFIELD Thomas of STC
CORCORAN Richard Pierson 1794
BACON Samuel 1794
SMITH Leapidge 1795
GRIGG John 1797
TAYLOR Alfred 1806
Partnership CORCORAN & GRIGG★
Succeeded by CORCORAN & CO. Bryan
Known to have sold: chondrometer
Sources: inst (s) (MAC); GL:NC 2817/2 fol.168;
2817/3 fol.43,73; 2817/5 fol.70, 2819; McKenzie
(1978) p.90

CORCORAN & CO. Bryan
w 1836–1870
Weighing machine M, Chondrometer M
1836–1870   38 Mark Lane, London
Took over from CORCORAN Bryan★

See also CORCORAN & GRIGG ★
Sources: PO

CORCORAN & GRIGG
w 1812–1817
Stationers, Wire Weavers, Flour Machine M
1812–1817   47 Mark Lane, London
Partnership CORCORAN Bryan (I)★ & GRIGG
[possibly his former apprentice John]
See also
CORCORAN & CO.★
GRIGG James★
Known to have sold: chondrometer
Sources: J (MAC); PO; Holbrook (1992) p.209

CORFIELD Richard
w 1850–1862
Measuring Tape M, Coffin Furniture S
1850–1862   17 Newton St, Birmingham
Took over from CORFIELD & RUSSELL★
Sources: Mor; Wh

CORFIELD & RUSSELL
w 1845
Measuring tape M, Coffin furniture M
1845   17 Newton St, Birmingham
Succeeded by CORFIELD Richard★
Sources: K

CORLESS John
w 1808–1840
Optician, Math IM, Phil IM
1806–1808   34 Stanhope St, Clare Market,
             London
1813–1823   19 Newcastle St, Strand, London
1840   2 Fenton St, Commercial Road East,
             London
Guild: Joiners, fr 1806
Apprenticed to TANGATE Robert (I)★ 1773
Had apprentice:
HIDER Edward Walter 1806
BROWN John 1808
PAGLAR Samuel 1808
ROSS Andrew★ 1813
TALBOYS James 1817
WHITE Philip 1817
Associated with DANCER Michael★
Sources: GL: JC 8046/12 (JAC); Pg; R (JAC);
Crawforth (1987) p.352

CORMICK Michael
w 1761–1779
Goldsmith
1761   Christ-church Lane, Dublin
Known to have sold: weights
Sources: inst reported by MAC; Wi

CORNELL Benjamin
w 1850
Math IM
1850   2 Port Place, Walworth Common,
             London
Father of CORNELL Frederick s 1850 SMC
Sources: GL: SMC 5213/6

CORNS James
w 1850
Math IM

1850   [Residence] 95 Ravenhurst St,
             Birmingham
Sources: Wh

CORSLAND William
w 1765
Math IM
1765   St. James Clerkenwell, London
Had apprentice GIGNAI (?) John in 1765
Sources: PRO: IR 1/24 (AM)

CORSON James
w 1770–1781
Rule M
1770–1780   Worcester St, Wolverhampton
1780–1781   Queen St, Wolverhampton
Succeeded by SMITH Thomas (II)★
See also
CORSON Thomas★
CORSON Robert★
Sources: PR; Sket

CORSON Robert
w 1767–1770
Rule M
1767   Berry St, Wolverhampton
See also
CORSON James★
CORSON Thomas★
Known to have sold: rule
Sources: Sket; Aris 27 Aug 1770 (MAC); BSIS 16
(1988) p.16 and illustration

CORSON Thomas
w 1770
Rule M
1770   Queen St, Wolverhampton
See also
CORSON James★
CORSON Robert★
Sources: SA

CORSS James
w 1662–1666
Math IS, Math Teacher, Publisher
             Head of Robertson's Close, near
             Lady Yester's Church, Edinburgh
             In the Cowgate at the foot of
             Niddries Wynd, Edinburgh
             Golden Sea-Quadrant & Cross-staff,
             Edinburgh
Sources: Bryden (1976) p.54–55; Taylor (1954)
p.239

CORTE James
a 1790–1830
             Crawford's Land, Foot Salt Market,
             Glasgow
Known to have sold: hydrostatic bubbles
Sources: ChrSK Apr 1986 lot 222 (MAC)

CORTI Antoni
w 1833–1845
Baro M, Carver, Gilder, Looking-glass M
1833–1841   97 Nelson St, Glasgow
1841–1844   38 Candlerigg St, Glasgow
1844–1845   54 Glassford, Glasgow
Known to have sold: barometer

Sources: Clarke et al (1989) p.172 n.28; Goodison
(1977) p.314

CORTI John
w 1809–1836
Baro M, Thermo M
1809   94 Holborn Hill, London
1815–1825   27 Leather Lane, Holborn, London
1826–1834   35 Eyre Street Hill, Hatton Garden,
             London
Sources: Bn; H; J; PO; R (JAC); Goodison (1977)
p.314

CORTI Peter
w 1845–1850
Baro M, Thermo M
1845–1850   30 Eyre St Hill, London
Sources: PO; Goodison (1977) p.314

COSBY Alice
w 1668–1671
Spec M
Alternative name: COSBY Widow
1670–1671   Bishopsgate, London
Guild: Spectaclemakers
Wife of COSBY Henry★
Had apprentice COSBY John, her son, 1668
Took over from COSBY Henry★
Sources: GL: SMC 5213/1

COSBY Henry
w 1659 d by 1666
[Spec M]
Alternative name: CROSBY
             London
Guild: Spectaclemakers
Father of COSBY John apprentice of COSBY Alice★
Husband of COSBY Alice★
Had apprentice HOLT Samuel 1659 t/o to
BOLTER Hugh★
Succeeded by COSBY Alice★
Sources: GL:SMC 5213/1

COSENS Nicholas
fr 1638 d 1654
Hour-glass M
Alternative name: CUSSANS
1638–1654   York
Sources: Loomes (1981b)

COSSINET Francis
w 1658–1665
Book S, Math IS, Printer
Alternative name: COSSINETT, CORSNETT,
             Anchor & Mariner, Tower St, end of
             Mincing Lane, London
Guild: Stationers, fr 1656
Apprenticed to HURLOCK George 1648/9
Son of COSSINET Armell, yeoman, of Parshall,
Worcs
Had apprentice WILFEILD (WINFEILD) John 1658
Associated with HURLOCK George and SUTTON
Henry★ in publishing books
Sources: McKenzie (1974) p.38,86; Taylor (1954)
p.246,366,372

COTTERELL Thomas
w 1825–1833

Chrono M
1825–1833   163 Oxford St, London
Took part in chronometer trials at Royal Greenwich Observatory 1825–1833 and won an award in 1831
Sources: CUL: RGO 1143 fol.2–10; Taylor (1966) p.446

COTTS M.
w 1809
Rule M
1809   4 Queen's Row, Bethnal Green, London
Sources: H

COULDREY Joseph
w 1818–1851
Math IM, Optical IM, Phil IM, Hydro M, Sacch M
    26 New St, Dean St, Borough, London
1822   4 Church Yard Passage, Tooley St, London
1839–1851   26 St.Thomas' St East, Borough, London
Sources: Bn; Kt (JAC); PO

COULING Henry
w 1845–1865
Measuring tape M
1845–1855   6 Hayward's Place, St. John St, Clerkenwell, London
1865   4 Upper Rosoman St, Clerkenwell, London E
Succeeded by COULING & SONS Henry
Sources: PO

COULING Samuel
w 1811
Math IM
1811   Orange St, Leicester Square, London
Guild: Goldsmiths, fr 1798
Son of COULING Thomas, cordwainer, of Bridewell Hospital, London
Apprenticed to BIRKWOOD William★ 1790
Had apprentice COULING George, his son, 1811
Sources: GH: GSC Ap, Fr

COULSELL Elizabeth
w 1838–1842
Optician, Math IM, Phil IM
1838   153 Union St, Borough, London
1839–1842   41 Union St, Borough, London
Took over from COULSELL Elizabeth & Matilda★
See also
COULSELL Thomas★
COULSELL William (I)★
Sources: Pg; R (JAC)

COULSELL Elizabeth & Matilda
w 1836
Optician, Math IM, Phil IM
1836   153 Union St, Borough, London
Succeeded by COULSELL Elizabeth★
See also COULSELL Thomas★
Sources: Pg

COULSELL John
w 1827–1836

Optician, Math IM, Spec M, Gold & Silver Beater in 1819
1819   Oakley St, Lambeth, London
1827   52 Oakley St, Lambeth, London
1830–1836   7 Wootton St, Cornwall Rd, London
Guild: Tallow Chandlers, fr 1819
Apprenticed to UFFINGTON Thomas Spooner nd t/o to JACOBSON Howard THC
Sources: GL: THC 6153/13; Pg

COULSELL Thomas
w 1799–1836
Rule M, Math IM
    42 & 153 Union St, Borough, London
1794   Loman's Pond, Borough, London
1799–1814   29 Queen St, Borough, London
1815–1828   41 Union St, Borough, London
1829–1836   153 Union St, Borough, London
See also
COULSELL William (I)★
COULSELL Elizabeth★
COULSELL Elizabeth & Matilda★
Known to have sold: balance
Sources: H; J; Kt; R; W (JAC); inst (pv)

COULSELL William (I)
w 1809–1851
Math IM, Optician
Alternative name: William Senior in directories
1816–1840   9 Castle St, Borough, London
1845   41 Union St, Borough High St, London
1849–1851   9 Castle St, Borough, London
Father of COULSELL William s 1830 to BEALE T.J., printer, STC [possibly COULSELL William (II)★ if he carried on his father's rather than his master's trade]
Had apprentice RICHARDSON W.S. 1832
See also
COULSELL Thomas★
COULSELL Elizabeth★
COULSELL William (II)★
Sources: SH: STC Ap (MAC); GL: CH 12823/9 p.124 (MAC); Kt; PO; R (JAC); Und

COULSELL William (II)
w 1840–1855
Math IM, Rule M, Optician
1839   6 Grange Rd, Kent Rd, London
1840   6 Surrey Place, Grange Rd, Bermondsey, London
1845–1855   9 Castle St, Borough, London
1850   163 Union St, Borough, London
Guild: [Stationers? – see COULSELL William (I)★]
Sources: SH: STC Ap (MAC); PO

COULSON Daniel
w 1838–1844
Math IM, Phil IM, Drawing IM
1838–1844   58 Charles St, City Road, London
Sources: Pg; PO; R; Th (JAC)

COULSTON John
fr 1768 r by 1779
Phil IM
1768   Parish of Christchurch, Surrey, London

1783–1807   Bancroft's Almshouses, London
Guild: Drapers, fr 1768
Son of COULSTON Henry, victualler, of London
Apprenticed to HICKMAN Joseph (I)★ 1740
Associated with HASSARD Joseph★, who testified at his freedom
Sources: DH: DPC Ap/Fr, index

COURT Alice
w 1753–1767
Scale M
1753   Justice & Scales on London Bridge, London
Guild: Blacksmiths
Had apprentice:
CLAYTON James 1757 t/o 1760 to SWIFT Joseph of LSC
DIXON Thomas 1764 t/o 1767 to SWIFT Joseph of LSC
Took over from COURT Richard (II)★, her husband
Sources: BM: Heal, bill dated 1753 (MAC); GL: BKC 2886/5 (MAC)

COURT Mary
w 1723 d 1724
[Scale M]
1723–1724   Justice & Scales on London Bridge, London
1723–1724   [Landlord of]Two Knives Cases & Dagger on London Bridge, London
Guild: Blacksmiths
Took over from COURT Richard (I)★, her husband
Succeeded by COURT Richard (II)★, her son
Sources: GL: BKC 2888, 2881/11, Sun 11936/8 no.11260 (MAC)

COURT Richard (I)
w 1696 d 1723
Scale M
1718–1723   Justice & Scales on London Bridge, London
1718–1723   [Landlord of]Two Knives Cases & Dagger on London Bridge, London
Guild: Blacksmiths, fr 1690
Son of COURT Robert, baker, of Shipston on Stour, War
Apprenticed to MARSH Elizabeth★ 1682
Had apprentice:
DAVISON Richard 1696
HORNE William 1699
SPICER Richard 1705/6
PRICKETT James 1714 t/o 1719 to SMELT Samuel★
LETT William 1722 t/o 1724 to COURT Richard (II)★
Father of COURT Richard (II)★
Succeeded by COURT Mary★, his wife
Sources: GL:BKC 2881/8, 2881/11, 2886/3, 2888 (MAC); Sun 11936/8 no.11260 (MAC)

COURT Richard (II)
w 1724 d c. 1753
Scale M
1724–1753   The Justice & Scales on London Bridge, London
1724   Two Knives Cases & Dagger on London Bridge, London
Guild: [Armourers] Blacksmiths, fp 1723/4

Son of COURT Richard (I)★ and COURT Mary★
Apprenticed to PAULY Francis 1710/11 ABC
Had apprentice:
LETT William 1724 by t/o from COURT
Richard (I)★
DIGLIN James 1725
MATTHEWS John by t/o from SLEIGH Richard★
DANIEL George 1730
DEANE Richard 1732
CARR Robert 1733
SPRIGNALL Richard 1738 t/o 1739
to HAWKINS Benjamin
SPARROW Joseph 1739
PRICKETT Richard 1740
JACKSON William 1744/5
CHURCH Stephen★ 1746
BATES Matthew 1750 t/o 1755 to READ Samuel★
Took over from COURT Mary★, his mother
Succeeded by COURT Alice★, his wife
Sources: BM: Heal, bill dated 1753 (MAC); GL:
Sun 11936/8 no.11260; 11936/16 no.32213, BKC
2881/11, 2886/4, 2886/5 (MAC); ABC 12080/1
fol.73v

COURT William
w 1690–1695
Book S, Math IS
1690   Mariner and Anchor on Little Tower
              Hill, London
Sources: Calvert (1971) p.19; Taylor (1954)
p.286,406,409

COUSENS & WHITESIDE
w 1844–1851
Chrono M
1846   20 Davies St, Berkeley Square,
              London
1851   27 Davies St, Berkeley Square,
              London
1851   and 14 Pont St, Belgrave Sq, London
Sources: PO; Loomes (1976)

COVENTRY John
b 1735 d 1812
Micrometer M, Phil IM, Telescope M
              Southwark, London
Inventor of the Coventry absorption hygrometer
Known to have sold: micrometer
Sources: DNB; Morton & Wess (1993) p.468;
Turner G (1989) p.342–43

COWCHER Robert
w 1773
Cutler, Toyman
1773   Upper Northgate St, Gloucester
Instruments advertised: balance, weights
Sources: JRM

COWIE Thomas
w 1849
Scale M
1849   13 Macdowall St, Edinburgh
Sources: NMSn

COWLAND William
w 1763–1784
Brazier
1770–1773   Aylesbury St, Clerkenwell, London

1775   5 Aylesbury St, Clerkenwell,
              London
Guild: Armourers & Brasiers, fr 1762
Son of COWLAND Thomas, glazier, of
Clerkenwell, London
Apprenticed to VANDERELST John
Had apprentice:
MASON John 1763
JOHNSON John 1766
TUFFNELL William 1767
SCAMBLER John 1770
BAGNALL James 1770
GRIFFITH John 1772
HOSKINS John 1773
BAGNALL Joshua 1778
COWLAND William, his son, 1779
HOWELL George 1782
DENBY Edward William 1784
An 18th-century brass quadrant signed 'W.
Cowland fecit' could be by this man
Sources: GL: ABC 12080/2; Middleton (1979)p.22

COWLEY John
w 1739
[Globe M]
              London
Associated with HEATH Thomas★ in making glass
celestial globe
R.apt Geographer to Geo II
Sources: ChrSK 4 Jun 1987 lot 35 (MAC); Wallis
R & P (1993)

COWLEY Thomas
w 1769
Book S, Math IS, Optical IS
              From London
1769   Chester
Sources: *Adam's Weekly Courant* (Chester) 10 Oct
1769 (JRM)

COX Ann
w 1800–1803
Rule M
1800–1801   70 Hill St, Birmingham
1803   Suffolk St, Birmingham
Took over from COX Thomas (I)★
Succeeded by COX Ann & George★
Sources: Chp

COX Ann & George
w 1808–1811
Rule M
1808–1811   Suffolk St, Birmingham
See also
COX George (I)★
COX Ann★
Sources: Chp; H

COX Arthur
w 1754
Math IM
              London
Had apprentice: COX Arthur 1754
Sources: GL: CH 12823/5 p.89 (MAC)

COX Charles
w 1816
Optician

1816   Fore St, Plymouth
See also COX William Charles★
Sources: H

COX Francis Blakemore
w 1828–1862
Rule M
1828–1850   Camden St, Birmingham
1835–1862   50 Camden St, Birmimgham
See also COX & CO. Thomas★
Known to have sold: rule
Sources: Mor; Pg; Sl; Turner G (1983a) p.287

COX Frederick (I)
w 1833
Optician
1833   5 Barbican, London
Guild: Coopers, fr 1833
Son of COX James★
Apprenticed to VAUGHAN John Herbert★ 1824
Had apprentice:
DOWSETT James Finch 1833 by t/o
from BEL(L)SHAW Thomas, painter, PSC
DOWSETT William Finch★ 1833
See also
COX Frederick (II)★
COX Joseph★
b 1809; educated at Christ's Hospital School
Sources: GL: PSC 5669/2; CPC 5636/3; CH
12818/14 fol.99

COX Frederick (II)
w 1845–1901
Optician
1845–1870   100 Newgate St, London
1875–1901   98 Newgate St, London
See also COX Frederick (I)★
Known to have sold: microscope, sundial
Sources: PO; Gillingham (1925); ChrNY 31 Oct
1985 lot 275 (MAC)

COX George (I)
w 1816–1829
Rule M
1816–1818   Navigation St, Birmingham
1825–1826   Regent's Place, Birmingham
1828–1830   1 Vittoria St, Birmingham
Took over from COX & CO. Thomas★
See also COX Ann & George★
Known to have sold: rule
Sources: Pg; Wr; inst WM (MAC)

COX George (II)
w 1845–1851
Optician, Math IM, Phil IM, Hydro M, Baro M
1830–1831   5 Barbican, London
1845–1849   128 Holborn Hill, London
1849–1851   5 Barbican, Aldersgate St, London
See also
COX Frederick (I)★
COX James★
Attended London Mechanics Institute 1830–1831;
Ex.1851
Known to have sold: level
Sources: LMIR (AM); inst (s); PO

COX James
w 1811–1857

Optician, Math IM, Phil IM
1810   Parish of St. Giles, Cripplegate,
              London
1816   3 Beach St, Barbican, London
1822–1855   5 Barbican, Aldersgate St, London
              51 Banner St, St.Lukes [from 5
              Barbican] London
1839   and 85 Lombard St, London
Guild: Spectaclemakers, fp 1843
Father of COX Frederick (I)★
Son of COX William (II)★
See also
COX Joseph★
COX Joseph & James★
COX & SON★
m 1797 to Susanna Nichols
Known to have sold: globe
Sources: GL:CH 12818A/86 no.12; SMC 5213/6;
Pg; PO; Und; Phlps 2 Dec 1987 lot 34A; Calvert
(1971) p.19

COX John
w 1742–1764
1764   St.John's Court, Cow Lane, London
Guild: Spectaclemakers, fr 1732
Son of COX John, member of Vintners Co. of
London
Apprenticed to LINCOLN Thomas★ 1724
Had apprentice MARGAS John★ by t/o from
ADAMS Nathaniel★ 1741 or 1742
CLARK James 1752
d by 1773
Sources: PRO: PC 1/7 no.94 (JAC); GL: SMC
5213/2 p.150,241; 5213/3 p.68,178; 6029

COX Joseph
w 1789–1822
Optician, Optical IM, Math IM
1789   4 Queen's Square, Bartholomew
              Close, London
1790   Queen St, Bartholomew Close,
              London
1792–1816   3 Barbican, London
1817–1822   5 Barbican, Aldersgate St, London
Guild: Turners
Had apprentice SMITH Thomas 1792
Succeeded by COX Joseph & James★
See also
COX James★
COX Frederick (I)★
COX William (II)★
COX & SON★
Sources: GL: Sun 11936/489 no.991288; TC
3302/3; A; BW; H; J; Kt; Und

COX Joseph & James
w 1820–1822
Optician, Math IM
1820–1822   5 Barbican, London
Took over from COX Joseph★
See also
COX James★
COX & SON★
Sources: Bn; Pg; R (JAC)

COX Nathaniel
fl 1832–1857
[Chrono M]

1839–1846   140 Goswell St, London
Sources: PO; Taylor (1966) p.446; Loomes (1976)

COX Thomas (I)
w 1777–1797
Rule M
1777–1780   28 Bull St, Birmingham
1783   New Hall St, Birmingham
1785   22 Newhall St, Birmingham
1792   Newhall St, Birmingham
1797   Hill St, Birmingham
See also
COX Ann★
COX & CO. Thomas★
COX Ann & George★
Sources: BW; By; Pye; PR

COX William (I)
w 1733–1750
Spec M
              London
Guild: Spectaclemakers, fr 1727
Son of COX Thomas, blacksmith, of Southwark,
London
Apprenticed to JOHNSON William (I)★1720 t/o
to STERROP Jane★1723
Had apprentice:
BALLETT Leonard★ 1733
PRIEST Charles 1743
COX Thomas (II), his son, 1745
SHARP Thomas 1750
Sources: GL: SMC 5213/2 p.115,124+; 5213/3
p.64–65,93,150

COX William (II)
w 1765–1786
Perspective turner, Optician
Alternative name: COCK
1767   Love Lane, Wood St, London
1767   Barbican, London
1784–1786   3 Barbican, London
Guild: Turners
Father of COX James★
Had apprentice:
COX Charles 1765 by t/o from SHEEN James
VAUGHAN William Paul 1767
RICKETT William★ 1769 by t/o from CRANE
Henry
Succeeded by COX & SON★
Sources: GL: TC 3302/2, 3302/3, 3814; SMC
5213/6; By; Kt

COX William (III)
w 1777–1796
Math IM
1777   Philip Lane, Aldermanbury, London
1785   11 Hugh's[?] Court, Blackfriars,
              London
1796   Shoe Lane, London
Guild: Stationers, fr 1774
Apprenticed to BAYNHAM James★ 1764
Had apprentice:
SPARKES William Thomas Goffe 1777
INDERWICK James 1796
Sources: GL: CH 12823/6 p.112 (MAC), Sun
11936/327 no.500252; McKenzie (1978) p.27,93

COX William (IV)
w 1777–1780
Optical IM
1777–1778   55 Houndsditch, London
Guild: Spectaclemakers, fr 1778
Son of COX Stephen, tailor, of St. Giles's, London
Apprenticed to
CUFF John★ 1767 t/o
to LINCOLN Charles★ 1771
See also COX James★
Sources: GL: Sun 11936/263 no.393499 (MAC):
SMC 5213/3, 6029

COX William (V)
w 1831
Optician
1831   5 Barbican, London
See also
COX James★
COX Frederick (I)★
Sources: LMIR(AM)

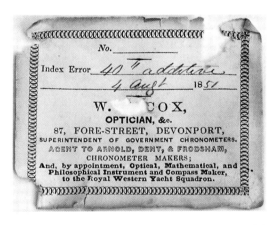

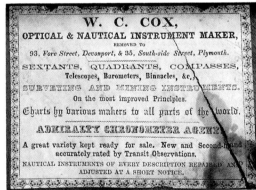

COX William Charles
w 1822–1857
Optician, Math IM, Phil IM, Chrono S, Compass
M
              93 Fore St, Devonport
              35 South-side St, Plymouth
1822–1839   86 Fore St, Plymouth
1830   86B Fore St, Devonport
1851   87 Fore St, Devonport
1852–1856   89 Fore St, Plymouth
1856   24 Southside St, Plymouth
1857   83 Fore St, Plymouth
See also COX Charles★

Associated with
BATE Robert B.★ as agent for Admiralty charts
ARNOLD John Roger★ as agent
DENT Edward J★ as agent
FRODSHAM★ as agent
B.apt RWYC; Admiralty Chronometer Agency
Known to have sold: barometer, circumferentor,
electrometer, sextant, sympiesometer, telescope
Sources: TCd & inst NMM; Pg; ChrSK 19 Nov
1987 lot 264; Calvert (1971) p.13; Morton & Wess
(1993) p.608

COX & CO. Thomas
a 1800–1825
Rule M
                    Birmingham?
Succeeded by COX Francis B.★
See also
COX Thomas (I)★
COX Ann★
COX Ann & George★
Known to have sold: rule, slide rule
Sources: Turner G (1983a) p.287

COX & SON
w 1788–1796
Optician
1788–1796   3 Barbican, London
Took over from COX William (II)★
See also
COX James★
COX Joseph★
COX J. & J.★
Sources: BW; Fn; Kt (JAC); Webster R & M (1986)

COYSGARNE & WILLCOX
w 1775–1782
Ship Chandler, Math IM
1775–1782   8 Little Hermitage St, Wapping,
             London
Sources: Kt (JAC); Ld

CRABB George
w 1833
Math IM
1833   3 Thornhill St, White's Conduit
             Field, London
Sources: LMIR (AM)

CRAFORD Henry
fr 1737 w 1761
[Math IM]
Alternative name: CRAWFORD
1737   Denmark St, Ratcliffe Highway,
             London
1741–1761   Ratcliffe Highway, London
Guild: Grocers, fr 1737/8
Apprenticed to GILBERT John (I)★ 1724
Had apprentice:
TOMLIN William 1738
CLIFFORD Whynot William 1741
ROBINSON John 1753
Sources: Brown J (1979a) p.37

CRAIG
w 1775
1775   Parliament St, Dublin
Known to have sold: balance, weights

Sources: *Faulkner's Dublin Journal* 6–8 Apr 1775,
noted in Westropp (1916) p.66 (MAC)

CRAIG James
w 1760
                    Glasgow
Known to have sold: astronomical clock
Sources: Baillie (1951)

CRAIG Robert
w 1740–1748
Watch M, Clock M
1740   Kilmaurs
1748   Kilmarnock
Known to have sold: sundial
Sources: ChrSK Time Museum Auction 14 Apr
1988 lot 40; Baillie (1951)

CRAIGHEAD & WEBB
w 1846–1863
Watch M, Clock M, Chrono M
1846–1851   1 Royal Exchange, London
Sources: PO; Loomes (1976)

CRAIGIE George
w 1685
Bismar M
1685   Kirkwall
Took over from MOWAT★
Succeeded by TAIT William★
Sources: Court action of Alexander, Earl of
Galloway, 1757: Earl Morton's defence p.26, Earl
Alexander's answers p.20 (MAC)

CRAIGMYLE John
w 1839–1875
Chrono M, Watch M
1839   90 Park St, Oxford St, London
1846–1851   90 Park St, Grosvenor Square,
             [Alternative version of same address]
             London
Sources: PO; Pg; Loomes (1976)

CRANAGE John
w 1824–1851
Chrono M, Watch M
1824–1834   Hunter St, Liverpool
1835–1837   37 Hunter St, Liverpool
1839–1849   36 Hunter St, Liverpool
1841–1849   38 Hunter St, Liverpool
1851   28 Hunter St, Liverpool
Succeeded by CRANAGE Mary
See also CRANAGE Thomas S.★
Sources: G; Loomes (1975)

CRANAGE Thomas Stokes
fl 1790–1837
Chrono M, Watch M
                    129 Islington, Liverpool
Sources: Baillie (1951); Taylor (1966) p.469

CRANE I.
a 1800
Instrument S, Fancy Goods S
                    Bromsgrove, Worcs
Instruments advertised: microscope, spectacles,
telescope
Sources: TCd (pv)

CRAWLEY John
w 1819–1834
Optician, Math IM, Phil IM
1819   14 Mercer St, Long Acre, London
             69 St.Martin's Lane, London
             6 Castle St, Leicester Square,
             London
1834   13 Great Newport St, Leicester
             Square, London
See also CRAWLEY William★
Sources: R (JAC)

CRAWLEY William
w 1834–1858
Optician, Math IM, Phil IM, Spectacle M
1834–1858   21 Oxenden St, Coventry St,
             London
See also CRAWLEY John★
Sources: PO; R

CRESWELL James
w 1851
Optician
1851   29 Skinner St, London
Sources: Wk

CRESWELL William
w 1816 d by 1828
Rule M
                    Blue Yard, Goswell St, London
1816   239 High Holborn, London
Father of CRESWELL Samuel s 1828 to STENING
William, printer , STC
Associated with WATKINS J.★ as supplier
Known to have sold: rule
Sources: STAT: STC, Memo Book; EBA: OB
1816 (Watkins)

CRICHTON Andrew
w 1798
Blacksmith
Alternative name: CHRICHTON
                    Glasgow
Guild: Hammermen
See also
CRICHTON Andrew M.★
CRICHTON James★
CRICHTON Robert★
Known to have sold: balance
Sources: NMSn (MAC)

CRICHTON Andrew M.
w 1817–1836
Scale M, Gas fitter
Alternative name: CHRICHTON
1817–1828   20 Saltmarket, Glasgow
1817–1828   33 Gallowgate, Glasgow
1817–1828   7 Louden St, Glasgow
1817–1828   Works, Louden Lane, Glasgow
1830–1836   18,19 & 32 Louden St, Glasgow
See also
CRICHTON Andrew★
CRICHTON Walter★
CRICHTON Robert★
Sources: POG; NMSn (MAC)

CRICHTON James
w 1785–1835

Hammerman, Lock M, Smith, Chem IM, Phil IM
1785   Grammar School Wynd, Glasgow
1789   Above 129 Gallowgate, Glasgow
1790   East side Charlotte St, Glasgow
1812   5 Charlotte St, Glasgow
1812–1818   2Charlotte St, Glasgow
1819   9 Charlotte St, Glasgow
1820–1825   2 Charlotte St, Glasgow
1826–1835   5 Charlotte St, Glasgow
Guild: Hammermen
Known to have sold: balance
Sources: POG; NMSn (MAC)

CRICHTON John
w 1831–1865
Optical IM, Phil IM, Math IM, Naut IM
1831   32 Fore St, Limehouse, London
1834–1865   112 Leadenhall St, London
Guild: Makers of Playing Cards, fr 1834
Apprenticed to MESSER Benjamin★ 1820
Had apprentice:
STEELE Robert G.P. 1835
EVANS William 1840
CAIRNS Alexander 1841
Succeeded by CRICHTON & SON John★
Associated with
BAHARIE A.★ as supplier
GOWLAND G.H. & C. as supplier
RENNOLDSON Isaac, who testified at his freedom
Ex.1851
Known to have sold: artificial horizon, barometer,
compass (magnetic), drawing instruments,
microscope, rule, sextant, telescope, thermometer
Sources: GL: MPC 5963/5, 5968/2, 5969/2; PO;
R; inst NMM; Phlps 16 Mar 1988 lot 92; ChrSK 4
Jul 1991 lot 13; Holbrook (1992) p.144,208,211;
Turner G (1983a) p.309

CRICHTON Patrick
w 1723
Instrument S
1723   Edinburgh
Sources: Bryden (1972) p.18 n88

CRICHTON Robert
w 1818–1833
Smith, Scale M
1818–1825   297 High St, Glasgow
1826–1833   60 High St, Glasgow
Guild: Hammermen, fr 1807
See also
CRICHTON Walter★
CRICHTON James★
Sources: Pg; NMSn; Lumsden & Aitken (1912)
p.303

CRICHTON Walter
w 1823–1837
Smith, Scale M
1823–1825   36 Gallowgate, Glasgow
1826–1832   57 Gallowgate, Glasgow
1833–1836   60 High St, Glasgow
1837   66 High St, Glasgow
Guild: Hammermen, fr 1817
See also
CRICHTON Robert★
CRICHTON James★
Known to have sold: balance

Sources: Pg; NMSn; Lumsden & Aitken (1912)
p.307

CRICK Charles (I)
w 1692–1718
Math IM
1689–1718   Aldgate, London
Guild: Grocers, fr 1689
Father of
CRICK Charles (II)★
CRICK James★
CRICK Thomas★
Son of CRICK Henry, clothworker, d, of London
Apprenticed to HOWE William★ 1679
Had apprentice CLARK Thomas 1692, t/o to
NASH John★
See also HADDON William★
Sources: Brown (1979a) p.29; DH: DPC Ap/Fr
1718

CRICK Charles (II)
w 1722–1738
Rule M
Alternative name: CREEK
1722   East Smithfield, London
Guild: Grocers, fr 1722
Son of CRICK Charles (I)★
Brother of
CRICK James★
CRICK Thomas★
Had apprentice ROUCKLEIFFE John 1722
Associated with URINGS John (II)★,whose
freedom he witnessed
Sources: GL: JC 8051/4 (MAC); Brown (1979a)
p.35–36

CRICK James
w 1754–1762
[Math IM]
Alternative name: CREEK
1754   Near the Maypole in East
               Smithfield, London
Guild: Grocers, fp 1733
Son of CRICK Charles (I)★
Brother of CRICK Charles (II)★
Apprenticed to
HADDON William★ 1727 STC t/o 1728
to GILBERT John (I)★ GC
Had apprentice NOY William 1754 [see NOYES
William★]
Educated at Christ's Hospital School, London
Sources: GL: CH 12823/4 p.447; Brown (1979a)
p.36; McKenzie (1978) p.151

CRICK Thomas
fp 1738
[Math IM]
1738   London
Guild: [Drapers], Grocers, fp 1737/8
Son of CRICK Charles (I)★
Apprenticed to PLUMSTEAD Thomas DPC
Sources: Brown (1979a) p.29; DH: DPC Ap/Fr

CRICKMORE T.
a 1800–1850
        Ipswich
Known to have sold: microscope
Sources: inst SM Wellcome; Taylor (1966) p.360

CRITCHLEY Henry
w 1810–1834
Optician
1810   Carpenter Court, Leeds St,
            Liverpool
1834   10 Pleasant Buildings, Great Homer
            St, Liverpool
See also CRITCHLEY & MATHER★
Sources: G

CRITCHLEY & MATHER
w 1816–1831
Optician, Math IM
1816–1824   3 North Side Old Dock Gates,
            Liverpool
1827–1831   5 Oldhall St, Liverpool
See also CRITCHLEY Henry★
Same premises as MATHER John★
Partnership 1816–21 JONES, CRITCHLEY &
MATHER★
Sources: Bn; G

CROCE Joseph
w 1847
Baro M
        York
Sources: Goodison (1977) p.315

CROCE Joshua
w 1823 d 1841
Baro M, Artificial flower M, Thermo M
1823–1830   15 Grape Lane, York
See also CROCE Joseph★
Sources: Bn; Goodison (1977) p.315

CROCKER William Henry
w 1839–1869
Chrono M
1839   41 Rahere St, City Rd, London
1846   70 Leman St, Goodman's Fields,
            London
1851   106 Leman St, London
Sources: PO; Pg; Loomes (1976)

CROGER James
w 1851
Math IM
1851   36 Wapping High St, London
Known to have sold: sextant
Sources: PO; Sby 9 Nov 1970 noted in Webster R
& M (1986)

CROGER Nathaniel Gowan
w 1826
Math IM
1826   Pennington St, Ratcliffe Highway,
            London
Guild: [Haberdashers]
Son of CROGER Nathaniel, cordwainer
Apprenticed to GILBODY John, gold beater, 1809
HC t/o 1809 to BROWNING John (I)★ or (II)★
Attended London Mechanics Institute 1826
Sources: LMIR (AM); GL: HC 15860/9

CRONMIRE J.M. & H.
w 1851–1869
Math IM, Opticians, Rule M, Drawing IM
Alternative name: John M. & Henry

1851	5 Seabright St, Bethnal Green, London
1851–1860	10 Cottage Lane, Commercial Rd East, London
1865–1869	10 Bromehead St, Commercial Rd East, London
1869	and Blackmore, Essex

Succeeded by CRONMIRE & SON John M.
Took over from CRONMIRE John M.★
Known to have sold: drawing instruments, rule
Sources: PO; Wk; Webster R & M (1986)

CRONMIRE John Martin
w 1849
Optician

1849	5 Seabright St, Bethnal Green, London

Succeeded by CRONMIRE J.M. & H.
Sources: PO

CROOK William (I)
w 1814
Optician

1814	Dog Row, Bethnal Green, London

Father of CROOK William s 1814 WVC
Sources: GL: WVC 4655/19 fol.310v

CROOK William (II)
w 1835
Math IM

1835	16 Rawston St, Clerkenwell, London

Attended London Mechanics Institute 1835.
Sources: LMIR (AM)

CROOKE John (I)
w 1694–1757
Math IM
Alternative name: CROOK

1713	Under the Writing School, Christ's Hospital, London
1735	Without Newgate, London

Guild: Joiners, fr 1693
Son of CROOKE John, carpenter, of Greet, Glos
Apprenticed to TOOGOOD John★ 1684/5
Had apprentice:
THOMPSON Isaac (II)★ 1694
MILES Lawrence★ 1701
ROGERS Mark★ 1706
WARE Richard★ 1708
CROOKE John (II)★, his son, 1713
SMITH Samuel 1713/14
CROOKE Richard, his son, 1715
LOWEN John 1718
POWELL James 1722 [or to CROOKE John (II)★]
BUNTING Thomas 1724 [or to CROOKE John (II)★]
LASHBROOKE Henry 1727 [or to CROOKE John (II)★]
Supplied math inst to Christ's Hospital School 1697–1717
Known to have sold: drawing instruments, rule
Sources: GL: CH 12823/2 p.290,308, 12823/3 p.338,358; Crawforth (1987) p.352–53

CROOKE John (II)
fp 1722 w 1771
[Math IM]

Alternative name: CROOK
London
Guild: Joiners, fp 1722
Apprenticed to CROOKE John (I)★, his father, 1713
Had apprentice HANCOCK John 1771 by t/o from CARPENTER George THC
Sources: GL: JC 8052/3, 8051/3; THC 6162; Crawforth (1987) p.352–53

CROOME Thomas
w 1769–1793
Scale M

1770	Long Lane, West Smithfield, London
1784–1793	Justice & Scales, No.6 near Cow Lane, West Smithfield, London

Guild: Haberdashers, fr 1758
Son of CROOME William, tobacconist, of St. Sepulchre's, London
Apprenticed to SWITHIN John★ 1751
Had apprentice:
PRESSOR John 1769
PARSONS Edward 1770 t/o 1773 to GIBSON Thomas★
NORTHFIELD William★ 1774
COLE James 1781
HERON Martin 1786
Sources: GL: HC 15857/2, 15860/9, BKC 2885/2 (MAC); A; By (JAC); BW; W

CROSBY Daniel
w 1761–1804
Scale M, Brazier
Alternative name: D.C.

1761–1804	Crown & Scales, 36 Pill Lane, Dublin

See also CROSBY James★
B.apt Bank of Ireland
Known to have sold: balance
Sources: Wi; inst (pv)

CROSBY James
w 1769–1790
Scale M

1769–1770	Pill Lane, Dublin
1790	70 Pill Lane, Dublin

See also CROSBY Daniel★
Sources: Wi

CROSBY & ROBINSON Thomas & John
w c.1742
Math IS, Optical IS, Teacher

1742	At the lower End of Fair St, upon Horsleydown, Southwark, London

Succeeded by ROBINSON John (I)★
Instruments advertised: burning glass, cross-staff, drawing instruments, globe, microscope, rule, spectacles, telescope
Sources: Bod: JJ TCd

CROSS John Berryhill
w 1839–1863
Chrono M, Wholesale Watch M

1839–1846	41 Charterhouse Square, London
1851	23 Moorgate St, London

Sources: PO; Pg; Loomes (1976)

CROSSLEY John
a 1800

	Ashby de la Zouche, Leics

Known to have sold: pantograph
Sources: Holbrook (1992) p.144

CROUCH George
w 1799–1805
Math IM

1799–1805	17 Plough Court, Fetter Lane, London

Sources: H

CROUCHER Joseph
fr 1827 a 1830
[Chrono M]

	27 Cornhill, London

Guild: Clockmakers, fr 1827
Known to have sold: chronometer
Sources: GL: CKC 11568; inst CKC Mu, Guildhall, London; Baillie (1951)

CROW Francis
w 1813–1832
Math IM, Watch M, Silversmith

1813	37 Windsor Terrace, City Rd, London
1832	Faversham, Kent

Pat. compass 1813; inv. an octant
Known to have sold: compass (magnetic), octant
Sources: inst & pamphlet NMM; Woodcroft (1854); Taylor (1966) p.387

CROW T.
w 1801

1801	Wateringbury, Kent

Known to have sold: sundial
Sources: inst NMM

CROWDER John
w 1823–1836
Math IM, Phil IM, Optician

1823	Red Lion Court, Shoe Lane, London
1827	11 Newcastle St, Fleet Market, London
1836	Providence Place, Tash St, Gray's Inn Lane, London

Father of CROWDER William s 1823 to TAYLOR Richard, printer, STC
See also apprentice of SPENCER William (II)★
Sources: Pg; R (JAC); STAT: STC Memo Book p.156 (MAC)

CROWLEY James
w 1805–1809
Optician

1805–1809	Wheeler's Fold, Wolverhampton

See also CROWLEY John★
Sources: H

CROWLEY John
w 1802
Optician

1794	Queen's Row, Walworth, London
1802	King St, Wolverhampton

Guild: Drapers of London, fr 1802
Son of CROWLEY John, merchant, of Walworth, Surrey

Apprenticed to CROWLEY John, his father, 1794
See also CROWLEY James*
Sources: DH: DPC Ap/Fr

CRUCHLEY George Frederick
w 1823–1877
Globe M, Map S
1825   38 Ludgate St, London
1839–1851   81 Fleet St, London
             64 Fleet St, London
Guild: Glaziers, fp 1825
Son of CRUCHLEY John
Had apprentice SPENLOVE Robert Brown 1825
Took over from CARY G. & J.*
Known to have sold: globe
Sources: GL: GZC 5735/4; PO; inst (s); Webster
R & M (1986)

CRYER Thomas
w 1754–1771
             London
Guild: Joiners
Son of CRYER William, Gent, d, of Rotherham,
Yorks
Apprenticed to FARMER John* 1748
Sources: Crawforth (1987) p.353

CUFF John
w 1731–1770
Optical IM, Optician, Microscope M, Math &
Phil IS
Alternative name: CUFFE
1737–1757   Reflecting Microscope & Spectacles
             against Sergeant's Inn Gate in Fleet
             St, London
1757–1758   Double Microscope, three Pair of
             Golden Spectacles & Hadley's
             Quadrant opposite Salisbury Court
             in Fleet St, London
1764   Strand, London
Guild: Spectaclemakers, fr 1729/30
Son of CUFF Peter, of Broderers' Co. of London
Apprenticed to MANN James (II)* 1722
Had apprentice:
PORTER John 1731, t/o 1737 to SCATLIFF
Samuel*
HARVEY Edward 1733
KIRBY Henry 1737
KENNETT James 1744
CLEARE James* 1745/6
SHUTTLEWORTH Henry Raynes* 1746/7
HUMPHRIES/HUMPHRYS Richard 1755 t/o 1761
to SHUTTLEWORTH Henry Raynes*
LLOYD John 1765 t/o 1769
to SHUTTLEWORTH Henry Raynes*
COX William (IV)* 1767 t/o 1771
to LINCOLN Charles*
b 1708; inv. microscope with single vertical pillar
1743; author; Master SMC 1748–1749; bankrupt
1750; no retail shop after 1758; retired from Court
of SMC 1770; d 1772
Known to have sold: barometer, circumferentor,
hygrometer, microscope, telescope, thermometer
Instruments advertised: barometer, camera obscura,
magic lantern, microscope, multiplying glass, opera
glass, spectacles, speculum, telescope, thermometer
Sources: GL: SMC 5213/2 p.129,212,233+;
5213/3 p.74,96,127,140–41,211+; *Daily Advertiser*

5 Aug & 21 Oct 1757, Mar & 5 Apr 1758 (JRM);
ChrSK 8 Dec 1988 lot 171; Calvert (1971) p.19;
Goodison (1977) pl.82, p.138; Millburn (1976)
p.107–08, (1986) p.31; Porter et al (1985) p.26–27;
Turner (1989) p.47–50; Wallis R & P (1986) p.292

CUFF William
fl 1750–1795
Clock M
             Shepton Mallet, Somerset
Known to have sold: sundial
Sources: Baillie (1951); Webster R & M (1986)

CULL James
w 1803–1809
Optician
1803–1809   7 Brownlow St, Holborn, London
Sources: H; Kt

CULMER John
w 1809
Math IM
1809   126 Wapping, London
See also CULMER Josiah* [possibly a directory
error in the forename]
Sources: H (JAC)

CULMER Josiah
w 1783–1811
Math IM
Alternative name: CULLMER
1788–1797   130 Wapping New Stairs, London
1805   126 Wapping New Stairs, London
Guild: [Joiners]
Son of CULMER Eurling, mariner, of Ramsgate,
Kent
Apprenticed to URINGS John (II)* 1770
See also
CULMER John*
CULMER & TENNANT*
Known to have sold: sextant
Sources: BW; H; Kt; Ld; Crawforth (1987) p.353;
Taylor (1966) p.308

CULMER & TENNANT J. & George
w 1811
Ship chandler, Math IM
             126, opposite Wapping New Stairs,
             Wapping, London
1811   123 Wapping, London
See also
CULMER Josiah*
CULMER John*
TENNANT George*
Known to have sold: octant
Sources: H (JAC); Holbrook (1992) p.210

CULPEPER Edmund (I)
w 1700 d 1737
Math IM
Alternative name: CULPEPPER
             Old Mathematical Shop, Black &
             White Horse, Middle Moorfields
             London
             Old Mathematical Shop, Cross
             Daggers, Middle Moorfields,
             London
             Under the Piazza at the Royal

Exchange, London
1700–1731   Cross Daggers, Moorfields, London
1737   Near the Royal Exchange, Cornhill,
             London
Guild: Grocers, fr 1713/14
Son of CULPEPER Edward, clergyman, of Gunville
(sic), Dorset
Apprenticed to HAYES Walter* 1684
Had apprentice:
SPARKES George 1713/14 t/o 1715
to WOLMESLEY John*
Father of CULPEPER Edmund (II)* fp 1758
Took over from HAYES Walter*
Worked long before free
Known to have sold: barometer, bow quadrant,
bull's eye compass (magnetic), microscope, sector,
sundial
Instruments advertised: burning glass, Hadley's
quadrant, lodestone, microscope, prism, rule,
spectacles, sundial, telescope
Sources: inst MHS, NMM; *Daily J* 28 July 1731,
Daily Gazetteer 14 May 1737 (MAC); Brown J
(1979a) p.33; Porter et al (1985) p.25; AVS

CULPEPER Edmund (II)
w 1758–1759
[Math IM]
Alternative name: CULPEPPER
1758   Mile End in Stepney, London
1759   Mare St, Hackney, London
Guild: Grocers, fp 1758
Son of CULPEPER Edmund (I)*
Had apprentice CULPEPER John Chandler, his son,
1759
Sources: Brown J (1979a) p.41–42

CUMBERFORD Nicholas
w 1637
Sea Card M
1637   Ratcliffe, London
Guild: Drapers
Had apprentice: WILD Charles 1637
Sources: DH: DPC index

CUMMIN John
w 1851–1875
Optician, Phil IM, Baro M, Thermo M, Math IM,
Naut IM
1851   Cobham Row, Coldbath Square,
             London
1852–1855   1 Newcastle Place, Clerkenwell,
             London
1859–1875   Phoenix Place, Gray's Inn Rd,
             London
Sources: PO; Wk

CUMMING Alexander
w 1754 d 1814
Clock M, Chrono M
Alternative name: CUMMINGS
             New Bond St, London
             Pentonville, London
1754   Inverary
1756   Edinburgh
1763   Dial & Three Crowns, New Bond
             St, London
1785–1794   12 Clifford St, London
1794–1814   75 Fleet St, London

Guild: Clockmakers, fr 1781 as Honorary Freeman
b 1733; FRS; Author; appointed to assist Board of
Longitude in assessing the chronometer by
HARRISON John (I)★
Known to have sold: barograph, microtome
Sources: GL: CKC 11568; BW; Baillie (1951);
Goodison (1977) p.315; Morton & Wess (1993)
p.486–87

CUMMINS Charles
w 1846–1851
Chrono M
1846–1851   148 Leadenhall St, London
Sources: PO; Loomes (1976)

CUMMINS Thomas
w 1822–1834
Chrono M
1822–1834   3 Holland St, Great Surrey St, London
Took part in chronometer trials at Royal
Greenwich Observatory 1822–1834
Sources: CUL: RGO 1143 fol.2–10

CURMOLI -
w 1816
Baro M
1816   Dudley
See also COMOLI & CO. Peter★
Sources: H; Und

CUSHEE E.
w 1734–1763
Globe M
1734–1763   Globe & Sun, between St.Dunstan's
             Church & Chancery Lane, in Fleet
             St, London
Took over from CUSHEE Richard★
Associated with COLE Benjamin (I)★ & (II)★ as
proprietor of A Description and Use of the Globes by
Joseph HARRIS (II)★ 7th–10th edn, London
1751–1768
Known to have sold: globe
Sources: inst BL (JRM); Harris (1734), (1738),
(1751), (1763), (1768); Wallis R & P (1986) p.358

CUSHEE Leonard Compere
w 1761
Globe M, Engraver
1761   Opposite the Temple-Gate, Fleet St,
             London
Guild: Merchant Taylors, fr 1759
Son of CUSHEE Thomas, leatherseller, of
Clerkenwell, London
Apprenticed to HILL Nathaniel★ 1751
See also
CUSHEE Richard★
CUSHEE E.★
bap 1736
Sources: IGI; Daily Advertiser 24 Feb 1761 p.3; GL:
MTC MF 319, 324 (MAC)

CUSHEE Richard
w 1729–1731
Globe M, Surveyor, Map M, Publisher
Alternative name: CUSHEY
1729   Globe & Sun over against the
             Temple Exchange Coffee House in
             Fleet St, London

1731   Globe & Sun, between St.Dunstan's
             Church & Chancery Lane, in Fleet
             St, London
Guild: Merchant Taylors, fr 1721
Son of CUSHEE Daniel, leather dresser, d, of St.
Andrews Holborn, London, and Elizabeth
Apprenticed to PRICE Charles★ 1710
Had apprentice HILL Nathaniel★ 1730
Succeeded by CUSHEE E.★
See also CUSHEE Leonard C.★
Associated with
HARRIS Joseph (II)★ and WRIGHT Thomas(I)★ in
publishing books and selling globes
SISSON Jonathan★, who sold his globes
Same premises as
COGGS John (I)★
WYETH William★
bap 1696; educated at Christ's Hospital School,
London
Known to have sold: globe
Sources: GL: MTC, MF 319, 324, CH 12823/3
p.59; BM: Heal 105/32 (MAC); IGI; Daily J 31
Oct 1729 (JRM); inst NMM; Calvert (1971) p.19

CUSHION James Daniel
w 1845–1846
Optician, Spec M
1845–1846   2 New Compton St, Soho, London
Sources: PO; JAC

CUSTANCE Robert
w 1778–1798
Optician
1778   Little Compton St, London
1798   44 Upper Marybone St, London
Sources: GL: Sun 11936/268 no.402755,
11936/410 no.673878

CUTBUSH Robert
w 1656
[Math IM?]
Signed and dated a quadrant
Sources: inst MHS

CUTHBERT Charles
w 1820–1851
Phil IM, Optician, Math IM
1820   28 Great Bath St, Clerkenwell,
             London
1831–1841   8½ Garnault Place, London
1842–1851   9 Clerkenwell Green, London
Attended London Mechanics Institute
1825,1826,1833
Sources: LMIR (AM); Pg; PO; R

CUTHBERT David
w 1785
Math IM
1785   9 Greyhound Court, Milford Lane,
             London
Sources: GL: Sun 11936/334 no.513025 (MAC)

CUTHBERT James
w 1805
Rule M
1805   40 Great Windmill St, London
See also
CUTHBERT John (I)★

CUTHBERT Charles★
Sources: H

CUTHBERT John (I)
w 1809–1834
Math IM, Optician, Phil IM, Rule M
             16 Paradise St, Lambeth, London
             Westminster Rd, London
1809   40 Great Windmill St, London
1816–1817   113 St. Martin's Lane, London
1822   5 Bridge Rd, Lambeth, London
1822   445 Strand, London
1826   22 Bishop's Walk, Lambeth, London
1826   5 Purbeck Place, Lambeth, near
             Church St, London
1833   58 Brook St, West Square, Lambeth,
             London
Guild: [Stationers?]
Son of probably CUTHBERT William, stone mason,
of Eagle St, Red Lion Square, London [if s in STC]
Apprenticed to probably WELLINGTON
Alexander★ 1788
See also
CUTHBERT Charles★
CUTHBERT James★
CUTHBERT John (II) ★ [possibly the same maker]
b 1783 d 1854
Known to have sold: electrostatic generator,
microscope
Sources: Bn; H; J; Pg: PO; inst MSEN (MAC);
Brown O (1986) no.197,198; McKenzie (1978)
p.370; Turner G (1989) p.245–48; JAC

CUTHBERT John (II)
w 1840–1854
Telescope M
1853–1854   77 Carlisle St, Lambeth, London
See also CUTHBERT John (I)★ [possibly the same
maker]
Known to have sold: telescope
Sources: PO; Holbrook (1992) p.95

CUTHBERT John (III)
fr 1846
Math IM
1846   20 Backchurch Lane, St. George's in
             the East, London
Guild: Spectaclemakers, fr 1846
Son of CUTHBERT Wm, shoemaker
Apprenticed to WHITBREAD George★ 1837
Sources: GL: SMC 5213/5, 5213/6

CUTHBERT & PARIS John & Henry
w 1683–1698
Alternative name: CUTHBEARD
             Dublin
Known to have sold: weights
Sources: Sheppard & Musham (1975) p.219;
Westropp (1916) p.52,55

CUTHBERTSON John (I)
w 1766 d 1821
Phil IM, Math IM
1766   54 Poland St, Oxford St, Soho,
             London
1769–1792   Amsterdam
1793   London
1796   53 Poland St, Oxford St, London

1800–1821   54 Poland St, Broad St, London
Guild: Stationers, fr 1794
Son of CUTHBERTSON Jonathan
Partnership: CUTHBERTSON & CHAMPNEYS★
Apprenticed to CHAMPNEYS James★ 1761
Had apprentice MURTHWAITE Samuel 1801
b 1743; Author
Sources: H; Kt (JAC); Und; McKenzie (1978)
p.68; Cuthbertson (1807) (DJB); Hackmann (1978)

CUTHBERTSON John (II)
w 1816
Optical IM, Phil IM
1816   113 St. Martin's Lane, London
Possibly the same as CUTHBERTSON John (I), but
concurrent entries in Und 1816–1817
Sources: Und

CUTHBERTSON Jonathan
bap 1744 d 1806
Math IM
1744   Dearham, Cumberland
1792   Rotterdam
Brother of CUTHBERTSON John (I)★
Sources: Hackmann (1978) p.154; Taylor (1966) p.203

CUTHBERTSON Robert
c. 1794 d by 1808
Scale M
               Islington, London
Father of CUTHBERTSON Robert Vincent s 1808
to ALLMOND George★
Sources: CWH: CWC Ap

CUTHBERTSON & CHAMPNEYS
John & James
w c.1768
               Cornhill, London
               Amsterdam
Sources: ChrSK 19 Nov 1987 lot 282 (MAC);
Webster R & M (1986)

CUTLER Edward (I)
c. 1807 d by 1821
Optician
               Pentonville, London
Father of CUTLER Edward (II), s 1821 to
DOLLOND George (I)★
Sources: GL: GC 11598/7

CUTLER Nathaniel
c. 1631
Teacher, Book S, Instrument S, Chart S
               Near Wapping Dock, London
Sources: Calvert (1971) p.19

CUTLER Richard
w 1787
Watch M, Clock M, Baro M
1787   Youghal, Ireland
Sources: Burnett & Morrison-Low (1989) p.146

CUTLER Thomas
w 1796
Math IM
1796   Parish of St. Mary, Islington, London
Father of CUTLER James s 1796 to FAIRBONE
Charles (I)★
Sources: GL: GC 11598/5

CUTTS John Preston
w 1822–1841
Optician, Math IM, Phil IM, Spec M, Telescope
M
Alternative name: J.P., I.P.
1822–1825   Near St. Paul's Church, 58 Norfolk
               St, Sheffield
1828–1841   Division St, Sheffield
1836   3 Crown Court, Fleet St, London
See also CHESTERMAN James★
R.apt Victoria; e 1804
Known to have sold: microscope, telescope
Instruments advertised: barometer, drawing
instruments, magic lantern, microscope, sextant,
tape measure, telescope, thermometer
Sources: Bk; Ge; Pg; MAC; Calvert (1971) p.20;
Holbrook (1992) p.119,183,206

CUTTS, SONS & SUTTON J.P.
w 1851
Opticians
1851   Division St, Sheffield
1851   and 56 Hatton Garden, London
R.apt.Vic
Known to have sold: telescope
Sources: PO; Phlps 26 Jan 1983, lot 147

DADLEY William
w 1779
Optician
1779   Parish of St.Austin, London
Father of DADLEY James s 1779 to SUMNER Wm
TC
Sources: GL: TC 3302/3 (MAC)

DAINTETH Thomas
fp 1753
Telescope M
1753   By Hicks's Hall, Clerkenwell,
               London
Guild: [Stationers],Clothworkers
Son of DAINTETH Thomas, sheriff's officer, of
Clerkenwell, London
Apprenticed to BUSH Joseph★, STC, 1744
Educated at Christ's Hospital School, London
Sources: GL: CH 12876/4; CWH: CWC Fr;
McKenzie (1978) p.60

DALES Charles
w 1851
Optician
1851   3 Cecil St, Strand, London
Sources: Wk

DALES Edmund
w 1851
Optician
1851   48 Park St, Camden Town, London
Sources: PO

DALLAWAY Joseph James
w 1799–1809
Math IM, Optician
1799–1803   4 George Lane, behind the
               Monument, London
1803–1809   147 Tottenham Court Rd, London
Guild: Grocers, fr 1799

Son of DALLAWAY James, d, of Stroud, Glos
Apprenticed to TROUGHTON Edward (I)★ 1789
Educated at Christ's Hospital School, London
Instruments advertised: map measurer
Sources: Bod: JJ TCd; GL: CH 12876/6 (MAC);
H (JAC); Brown J (1979a) p.52

DALLMEYER H.
w 1851
Optician
1851   15 Castle St, Holborn, London
Attended London Mechanics Institute 1851
Sources: LMIR (AM)

DALTON John (I)
w 1755
Math IM
1755   Green Arbour Court, Little Old
               Bailey, London
Had apprentice SMITH John 1755
Sources: GL: CH 12876/5 (MAC)

DALTON John (II)
fl 1850–1856
[Clock M]
               Hartlepool
Known to have sold: Hadley's quadrant
Sources: Loomes (1976); Webster R & M (1986)

DALY Garrett
w 1813
Optician
1813   41 Redcross St, Liverpool
See also DALY Garrick★
Sources: G (MAC)

DALY Garrick
w 1805
Optician
1805   2 St.Agnes Place, Old Street Rd,
               London
See also DALY Garrett★
Sources: H

DANBIES J. & H.
w 1839–1840
Spectacle M
1839–1840   74 Paul St, Finsbury, London
Sources: Pg

DANCER John Benjamin
w 1835–1878
Optician, Optical IM, Math IM, Phil IM
1835   11 Pleasant St, Liverpool
1839–1845   21 Pleasant St, Liverpool
1841–1845   13 Cross St, King St, Manchester
1847–1878   43 Cross St, King St, Manchester
Son of DANCER Josiah★, with whom he trained
Partnership: ABRAHAM & DANCER★ 1841–1845
Succeeded by DANCER & CO.
FRAS; b 1812; originator of microphotography;
prize medal 1862; R.apt Prince of Wales 1869;
retired 1878; d Nov 1887
Known to have sold: balance, barometer, compass
(magnetic), galvanometer, gyroscope, hydrometer,
microscope, rule, stereoscopic camera, telescope

Sources: Sl; ChrSK 12 Dec 1985 lot 221; Holbrook(1992) p.132,184; Wetton (1991) p.4–8

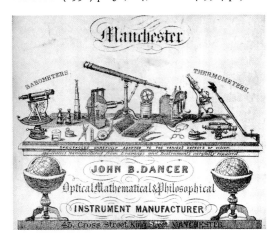

DANCER Joseph Junior

w 1805–1809
Math IM
1805   5 Corporation Lane, Clerkenwell, London
1809   48 Great Sutton St, London
See also
DANCER & SON*
DANCER Michael*
Sources: H

DANCER Josiah

w 1817 d 1835
Optician, Math IM
1817   52 Great Sutton St, Clerkenwell, London
1821   20 Grafton, Liverpool
1823   14 New Quay, Liverpool
1823–1829   [residence] 20 Grafton, Liverpool
1831–1832   22 Wolfe St, Liverpool
1834   4 Chapel Walks, Liverpool
1835   13 Pleasant St, Liverpool
Father of DANCER John Benjamin*
Son of DANCER Michael*
Worked for
DANCER Michael*
TROUGHTON Edward (I)*
Took over from DANCER & SON*
Succeeded by DANCER John Benjamin*
b 1779 d 1835
Sources: Bn; G; Wetton (1991) pp.4–8

DANCER Michael

w 1776–1817
Math IM
1776   Bride Lane, Fleet St, London
1778–1786   4 Bangor Court, Shoe Lane, London
1788–1790   11 New Street Square, near Shoe Lane, Fleet St, London
1793   Blewitt's Buildings, Fetter Lane, London
    32 Rosoman's Row, Clerkenwell, London
1796–1800   Rosoman St, Clerkenwell, London
1801   Red Lion St, Clerkenwell, London
1804–1805   55 Great Sutton St, Clerkenwell, London

1808   Great Swallow St [clerical error ?], St.James, Clerkenwell, London
1810–1817   52 Great Sutton St, Clerkenwell, London
Guild: Joiners, fr 1776
Son of DANCER William Esq. late of Stanmore, Middx
Apprenticed to TANGATE Robert (I)* 1766
Had apprentice:
BOULTER Benjamin 1776
PICKERING Thomas* 1781
ARNOTT Isaac 1784
PROCKTER Marmaduke Lyde 1786
WOOD Benjamin Jasper (I)* 1788
HOPPE Ebenezer* 1793
MARSH Howard 1796
HAMER James (I)* 1800
LILLEY John (I)* 1801
FITCHETT Edward 1804
GREEN William* 1808
MURREY William 1810
Father of DANCER Josiah*
Related to DANCER John Benjamin*
d 1817
Sources: GL: JC 8052/8, 8055/3, Sun 11936/267 no.400732 (MAC); BW; By; H; J; Kt; Und; Crawforth (1987) p.353–54; Wetton (1991) p.4–8

DANCER & SON

w 1801–1809
Math IM
1805   53 Red Lion St, Clerkenwell, London
    55 Great Sutton St, Clerkenwell, London
1809   52 Great Sutton St, Clerkenwell, London
See also
DANCER Michael*
DANCER Joseph*
DANCER Josiah*
Sources: H; JAC

DANIEL Henry

w 1814–1822
Chrono M
1814–1822   39 Castle St, Liverpool
Succeeded by DANIEL Henry & John*
Sources: Loomes (1975)

DANIEL Henry & John

w 1824–1864
Chrono M, Silversmith, Jeweller
1824   39 Castle St, Liverpool
1845–1856   9 St.George's Crescent, Liverpool
1853–1864   67 Lord St, Liverpool
Took over from DANIEL Henry*
Sources: G (MAC); Pg; Loomes (1975)

DANIEL James

fl 1830
Chrono M
    Three Tuns Court, 87 High St, Borough, London
Sources: Taylor (1966)

DANIEL Robert

w 1811

Optician
1811   10 Tothill St, Westminster, London
Sources: H

DANIELL William

w 1632–1648
Alternative name: DANIEL
    Golden Ball, Ivy Bridge, Strand, London
Guild: Clockmakers, fr 1632
Had apprentice PAYNE Nicholas 1641
Known to have sold: sundial
Sources: Gillingham (1925); Loomes (1981b)

DANLEY Charles

w 1672
Rule S
1672   The Grape in Fleet St, over against Mr.Bedford's, London
Associated with CATER Widow, who supplied the sundials he sold
Sources: GL: CKC 2710/1 p.244; Loomes (1981b)

DANN William

w 1841–1844
Optical IM, Math IM, Optician
1841–1844   Pelham St, Nottingham
Sources: Pg; Wh

DARKER William H. junior

w 1846–1851
Optician, Optical Lapidary
1846–1851   9 Paradise St, Lambeth, London
Known to have sold: pyrometer, microscope accessory
Sources: PO; Wk; Webster R & M (1986); Turner G (1989) p.306

DAVENPORT Charles

w 1838–1870
Spec M
1838–1859   33 Tabernacle Row, City Rd, London
1865– 870   26 Smith St, Northampton Square, EC. London
Sources: PO; R

DAVENPORT James

w 1800–1836
Spec M, Melting-pot Warehouse
    36 Wellington St, Goswell St, London
    1 Mouldmaker's Row, Foster Lane, London
    14 London Wall, London
1800–1805   1 Oat Lane, Queen St, Cheapside, London
1816   1 George St, Foster Lane, London
1836   30 Wellington St, Goswell St, London
See also PHELPS & DAVENPORT*
Sources: GL: CH 12823/8 p.111(MAC); H; K; Pg; JAC

DAVENPORT Robert

fr 1635 w 1647
Math IM
1635   London
1647   Edinburgh

Guild: Grocers, fr 1635
Apprenticed to ALLEN Elias★ 1623
See also DAVENPORT Stephen
Known to have sold: slide rule
Sources: inst NMS; Brown J (1979) p.25; Bryden
(1976)

DAVENPORT Stephen
w 1736–1737
Phil IM

	Against the Distillers, High Holborn, nr. Drury Lane, London
	Smart's Buildings, Cole Yard, High Holborn, nr. Drury Lane, London
	Near the White Hart Gate in High Holborn, London
1736	Next Door White Hart Inn in High Holborn, London

Guild: probably Joiners, fr 1725
Son of probably DAVENPORT Stephen,
apothecary, of Kingston, Surrey
Apprenticed to probably HODGKIN John 1715
Instruments advertised: air pump, balance,
barometer, hydrometer, thermometer
Sources: BM: Banks 105/13, Heal 105/34 (MAC);
Daily Advertiser 27 Nov 1736 p.4 (AQM);
Crawforth (1987) p.354; Taylor (1966) p.155

DAVIDSON James
w 1851–1859
Optical IM
1851–1859   39 South Bridge, Edinburgh
Sources: Bryden (1972) p.46

DAVIDSON Jonathan
w 1847–1874
Scale M
| | Paul's Work, Edinburgh |
| 1847–1870 | 24 Barony St, Edinburgh |
Succeeded by ROBERTSON Charles
See also DAVIDSON & CO. Jonathan★
e 1825
Known to have sold: balance
Sources: K; inst NMS (MAC)

DAVIDSON Ninian
w 1788
Optician, Watch M
1788   Lawnmarket, Edinburgh
Sources: Wlm (ADCS)

DAVIDSON Thomas
w 1840–1845
Math IM, Optical IM
1840–1843   12 Royal Exchange, Edinburgh
1844   63 Princes St, Edinburgh
1845   67 Canongate, Edinburgh
Sources: Bryden (1972) p.46

DAVIDSON & CO. Jonathan
w 1851–1913
Scale M
1851   Barony St, Edinburgh
1894–1913   East London St, Edinburgh
See also DAVIDSON Jonathan★
Ex.1851
Sources: K (Metal Trades); Cat.1851

DAVIDSON & CO. Thomas
w 1848–1853
Optical IM
1848–1849   12 Royal Exchange, Edinburgh
1850–1851   187 High St, Edinburgh
1852–1853   4 Infirmary St, Edinburgh
Sources: Bryden (1972) p.46

DAVIE Thomas
w 1851
Rule M
1851   29 Gravel Lane, Southwark, London
Sources: Wk

DAVIES B.
w 1836–1837
Optical IM, Phil IM, Math IM
1836–1837   101 High St, Marylebone, London
Sources: R (JAC)

DAVIES Charles William
w 1851 fl 1881
Watch M, Chrono M
1851   1 Foxton Terrace, Thornhill Rd,
             London
Sources: PO; Loomes (1976)

DAVIES David
w 1823–1832
Math IM, Optical IM
1823–1825   110 Nelson St, Glasgow
1825   100 Nelson St, Glasgow
1826–1832   98 Trongate, Glasgow
Sources: Pg (MAC); Bryden (1972) p.46

DAVIES James (I)
w 1789–1799
| | Birmingham |
Known to have sold: perpetual calendar
Sources: ChrSK 14 Apr 1988 lot 91; Webster R &
M (1986)

DAVIES James (II)
w 1851–1855
Math IM, Rule M
1851–1855   17 Amelia St, Walworth, London
Sources: PO; Wk

DAVIES John (I)
w 1764
Spec M
1764   Charing Cross, London
Petitioner against Dollond's patent 1764
Sources: PRO: PC1/7 no.94

DAVIES John (II)
w 1817–1836
Optician
Alternative name: DAVIS
1817   10 High St, Marylebone, London
1822–1836   101 High St, Marylebone, London
Sources: Bn; Kt; Pg; PO

DAVIES John (III)
w 1843
Phil IM
1843   76 Gray's Inn Lane, London

Attended London Mechanics Institute 1843
Sources: LMIR(AM)

DAVIES Joseph
w 1787–1829
Scale M, Money machine M, Smith
1787–1830   Henrietta St, Birmingham
1788   Water Lane, Birmingham
1791–1801   76 Park St, Birmingham
1822   Hamilton St, Birmingham
1829   7 Court, Henrietta St, Birmingham
Sources: Bn; Pg; Pye; Sy; Wr (MAC)

DAVIES Joshua
w 1790–1793
Optician
1790   Plough Court, Fetter Lane, London
1793   12 Plough Court, Fetter Lane, London
Guild: Spectaclemakers, fr 1790
Son of DAVIES Joshua
Apprenticed to LINNELL George★ 1780
Had apprentice: WEST Charles Robert★ 1790
Sources: GL: SMC 5213/3, 5213/4; BW

DAVIES William
w 1670
| | Clerkenwell, London |
See also DAVYS
Known to have sold: sundial
Sources: Taylor (1954) p.271

DAVIES & SAMUEL
w 1826–1830
Optician, Math IM, Phil IM
1826   24 Wilson St, London
1830   21 Coldbath Square, Clerkenwell,
             London
Sources: Pg; R (JAC)

DAVIS –
w 1829–1830
Optical IM, Phil IM, Math IM
1829–1830   9 Macclesfield St, Soho, London
See also
DAVIS Elizabeth★
DAVIS Hannah★
DAVIS David (II)★
Sources: R (JAC)

DAVIS A.
w 1790–1793
Optician
1790–1793   Macclesfield St, Soho, London
See also
DAVIS Hannah★
DAVIS John (III)★
Sources: BW; By

DAVIS Abraham
w 1831
Optician
1831   65 Tabernacle Walk, Finsbury,
             London
Sources: R (JAC)

DAVIS B.
w 1830–1832
Optician

1830–1832   1 Lower Terrace, Lower Road,
             Islington, London
Attended London Mechanics Institute 1830–32
Sources: LMIR (AM)

DAVIS C. & D.
w 1829–1830
Optical IM, Phil IM, Math IM
1829–1830   12 South St, Finsbury Market, London
Succeeded by DAVIS Clara★
Sources: R (JAC)

DAVIS Clara
w 1834
Optician, Math IM, Phil IM
1834   12 South St, Finsbury, London
Took over from DAVIS C. & D.★
Sources: Pg

DAVIS D. & M.
w 1811–1820
Watch M, Optician
1811   26 Cutlers St, Houndsditch, London
1820   James Court, Bury St, St.Mary Axe,
             London
See also DAVIS David (III)★
Sources: H; PO

DAVIS David (I)
a 1790 d by 1805
Math IM
             Shoe Lane, London
Father of DAVIS William s 1805 STC
Sources: SBPL: STC, MF Ap

DAVIS David (II)
w 1816–1825
Optician, Phil IM, Math IM
1816   8 Macclesfield St, Soho, London
1825   8 & 9 Macclesfield St, Soho, London
Guild: [?Spectaclemakers]
Apprenticed to possibly DAVIS John (III)★1783
Same premises as DAVIS Hannah★
Took over from DAVIS Hannah★
See also
DAVIS D. & M.★
DAVIS David (III)★ [possibly the same maker]
Sources: R (JAC); Und; GL: SMC 5213/3

DAVIS David (III)
w 1830
Optical IM, Phil IM, Math IM
1830   28 Bury St, St Mary Axe, London
See also
DAVIS D. & M.★
DAVIS David (II)★ [possibly the same maker]
Sources: R (JAC)

DAVIS E. & A.
w 1834
Optician
1834   106 Blackfriars Rd, London
Sources: R (JAC)

DAVIS Edward (I)
w 1833–1843
Optician, Math IM, Phil IM, Math & Phil
Repository

1833   171 High St, Cheltenham
1839–1841   65 Bold St, Liverpool
1843   45 Bold St, Liverpool
See also DAVIS J.★
Known to have sold: barometer, telescope,
thermometer
Sources: G (MAC); inst (s) (MAC); Phlps 3 Mar
1992 lot 162; Calvert (1971) p.20

DAVIS Elizabeth
w 1830–1834
Optician, Math IM, Phil IM
1830–1834   9 Macclesfield St, Soho, London
See also
DAVIS Hannah★
DAVIS David (II)★
Sources: Pg; Taylor (1966) p.418

DAVIS Gabriel
w 1822–1847
Optician, Math IM, Optical IM, Phil IM, Hydro
M
Alternative name: DAVIES
1822   20 Boar Lane, Leeds
1834–1847   24 Boar Lane, Leeds
1834   Sadler St, Durham
1837   [residence] Mount Pleasant, Leeds
Uncle of DAVIS Edward (II) and DAVIS John
(VII)★
Partnership: DAVIS Gabriel & Edward (II)
Succeeded by DAVIS Edward (II)
Partnership 1826–30
Known to have sold: barometer, level, miner's dial,
octant, thermometer
Sources: Chn; Pg; Wh; Wim; inst NMM; *Derby
Countryside Magazine* 44, no.8 (1979) (MAC);
Goodison (1977) p.316; Holbrook (1992)
p.120,137

DAVIS Gabriel & Edward
w 1826–1830
Optical IM, Chem IM, Phil IM, Math IM
1826–1830   34 Boar Lane, Leeds
Sources: PWh (DJB)

DAVIS George John
w 1850–1862
Rule M
1850   2 Key Hill, Birmingham
1862   15 Upper Windsor St, Birmingham
Sources: Mor; Sl

DAVIS Hannah
w 1796–1823
Optician, Math IM
1796–1823   8 Macclesfield St, Soho, London
Same premises as DAVIS David (II)★
Succeeded by DAVIS David (II)★
See also
DAVIS Elizabeth,
DAVIS John (III)★
Sources: Bn; H; J; Kt

DAVIS Isaac (I)
w 1836–1838
Optician, Math IM, Phil IM
1832–1834   1 Lower Terrace, Lower Road,
             Islington, London

1836–1838   1 Lower Terrace, Islington, London
1837–1838   Lower Road, Islington, London
Succeeded by DAVIS Isaac & Marcus★
Attended London Mechanics Institute 1832–4,
1837–8
Sources: Pg; R; LMIR (AM)

DAVIS Isaac (II)
w 1851
Optician, Telescope M
1851   119 High Holborn, London
Possibly the same person as DAVIS Isaac (I)★
Sources: PO

DAVIS Isaac and Marcus
w 1838–1842
Telescope M
Alternative name: DAVIS BROS.
1838–1842   1 Lower Terrace, Islington, London
1838   33 New Bond St, London
Took over from DAVIS Isaac (I)★
Sources: Pg; PO

DAVIS J.
a 1800–1825
             Cheltenham
See also DAVIS Edward (I)★
Known to have sold: theodolite
Sources: Sby 23 Jun 1987 lot 182 (MAC); Webster
R & M (1986)

DAVIS James (I)
w 1824–1845
Thermo M, Optician, Ship chandler
Alternative name: DAVIES
1824   12 Liver St, Liverpool
1835–1845   51 Paradise St, Liverpool
Sources: Bn; G

DAVIS James (II)
w 1825–1830
Glass blower, Phil IM
1825–1830   8 Lewin's Mead, Bristol
Sources: Mat

DAVIS John (I)
w 1697–1709
[Clock M, ?IM]
             London
Guild: Clockmakers, fr 1697
Apprenticed to QUARE Daniel★ 1685
Took four apprentices 1697–1709
Sources: Loomes (1981b); GL: SMC 5213/1

DAVIS John (II)
w 1751
Optician
1751   St. Johns St, London
Guild: Salters fr 1751 & ?Spectaclemakers, fr 1752
Son of DAVIS John, of St. Sepulchre's Parish, London
Apprenticed to PARKER Francis, Lamp M, SC 1737
A John Davis was freed as a 'Foreign Brother' [that
is, a freeman of another guild] in SMC 1752,
probably the same man; d by 1762
Sources: GL:SMC 5213/3 p.173, 6029; SH: SC
Ap, Fr, List of Members 1714

DAVIS John (III)
w 1779–1784
Optician
1777   At Mr Scarlett's, London
1779   Macclesfield St, Soho, London
1780   9 Macclesfield St, Soho, London
1784   Dean St, Soho, London
Guild: Spectaclemakers, fr 1777 by purchase
Had apprentice prob DAVIS David (II)★1783
Worked for SCARLETT Edward (II)★ 1777
See also DAVIS Hannah★
Sources: GL: Sun 11936/273 no.410533,
11936/283 no.427135(MAC); SMC 5213/3; By

DAVIS John (IV)
w 1693–1695
Spec M
1693–1695   East Smithfield, London
Guild: Spectaclemakers, fr 1692
Apprenticed to THROGMORTON James★ c.1683
Employed ADSON Thomas 1693
Sources: GL: SMC 5213/1

DAVIS John (V)
w 1793
Scale M, Toy M
1793   Bilston, Staffs
Sources: BW

DAVIS John (VI)
w 1798–1811
Rule M
1798   Wolverhampton
1809–1811   Queen St, Wolverhampton
See also
DAVIS Samuel★
DAVIS Sarah★
Sources: BW; H

DAVIS John (VII)
w 1828–1873
Optician, Math IM
1830–1843   Rotten Row, Derby
1835   14 Iron Gate, Derby
1843–1862   21 Irongate, Derby
Related to: DAVIS Gabriel & Edward★ and
worked with them in Leeds before moving to
Derby, according to company tradition
Succeeded by DAVIS & SON
Ex.1851; Member Derby Philosophical Society; d
1873
Known to have sold: anemometer, compass,
microscope, miner's dial, theodolite
Sources: Pg; Sl; *Derby Countryside Magazine* 44,
no.8 (1979) (MAC); Holbrook (1992)
p.117,137,144,149

DAVIS John (VIII)
a 1825
          Leeds
Known to have sold: microscope
Possibly DAVIS John (VII)★ before he moved to
Derby
Sources: Turner G (1989) p.74

DAVIS John (X)
w 1836–1842
Math IM, Optical IM, Phil IM

1836–1840   64 Princes St, Edinburgh
1841–1842   78 Princes St, Edinburgh
Known to have sold: sympiesometer
Sources: Bryden (1972) p.46; Goodison (1977)
p.316

DAVIS John (XI)
w 1835
Watch M, Clock M, Dial M
1835   Market Place, Wolverhampton
Sources: Pg

DAVIS John (XII)
w 1843
Math IM, Optician
1843   38 New Bond St, London
Sources: PO

DAVIS John (XIII)
w 1746
Clock M
              Windsor, Berks
Known to have sold clinometer, sundial
Sources: Morton & Wess (1993) p.397; Webster R
& M (1986)

DAVIS Johnstone
w 1789–1797
Scale M, Parchment M
1789–1797   24 Ushers Island, Dublin
Sources: Wi (AL)

DAVIS Lyon
w 1830–1846
Optician
1830   21 Orange Grove, Bath
1833–1846   22 Orange Grove, Bath
See also DAVIS Thomas★
Sources: Pg; Sil

DAVIS Richard
w 1638
Spec M
1638   Westminster, London
Father of DAVIS William s 1638 to HARRISON
William
Sources: GL: BKC 2886/1

DAVIS Samuel
w 1770–1792
Rule M
Alternative name: DAVIES,
1770   Burry St, Wolverhampton
1780–1783   Piper's Row, Wolverhampton
1792   19 Piper's Row, Wolverhampton
See also
DAVIS John (VI)★
DAVIS Sarah★
Sources: By; PR; Sket

DAVIS Sarah
w 1802
Rule M
1802   17 Queen St, Wolverhampton
See also
DAVIS Samuel★
DAVIS John (VI)★
Sources: Wolverhampton rate books (MAC)

DAVIS Saul
w 1839–1845
Chrono M, Watch M
1839–1845   36 Roberts St. North, Liverpool
Sources: G

DAVIS Thomas
w 1842–1846
Optician
1842–1846   16 Milk St, Bath
Sources: Pg; Sil

DAVIS William (I)
a 1790
              7 Portland Row, Dublin
Apprenticed to ROBINSON John (III)★ 1783
Attended King's Hospital School
Known to have sold: circumferentor
Sources: KH (WS); Sby 10 Mar 1987, lot 132

DAVIS William (II)
w 1809–1811
Spec M
1809–1811   Quay, Bath
Sources: H

DAVIS William (III)
w 1835
Spec M
1835   12 Great Hampton St, Birmingham
Sources: Pg

DAVIS William (IV)
w 1839–1840
Rule M
1839–1840   1 Brighton Place, Brixton Rd,
              London
See also
WITHERSPOON Colin★
DAVIS William David★
Sources: R (JAC)

DAVIS William David
c. 1790 d by 1803
Optician
              New St, Fetter Lane, London
Father of DAVIS William, s 1803 to
WITHERSPOON Colin★
Sources: GL: SMC 5213/4

DAVIS BROS
w 1820
Opticians, Math IM
1820   33 New Bond St, London
See also DAVIS Isaac & Marcus★
Sources: Calvert (1971) p.20

DAVIS MESSRS
w 1842
Math IM, Phil IM, Optical IM
1842   65 Bold St, Liverpool
1842   101 High St, Cheltenham
Known to have sold: telescope
Sources: Calvert (1971) p.20; Webster R & M (1986)

DAVISON William
w 1657
Spec M

1657   Leicester
Sources: McKenzie (1974) p.53

DAVYS -
fl 1676
            London
See also D A V I E S William★
Known to have sold: telescope, rule, compass
Sources: Taylor (1954) p.271

DAWES William Matthias
fl 1832–1881
Watch M, Chrono M
1839–1851   131 Upper St, Islington, London
Sources: Pg; PO; Loomes (1976)

DAWES & HIGGINS
w 1845
Math IM, Opticians
1845   77 Cornhill, London
Sources: PO

DAWSON M.
c. 1780
            Plymouth Dock No.4, Plymouth
Known to have sold: sextant
Sources: Brown O. (1982) no.196

DAWSON Matthew
fl 1798–1843
            Haddington, East Lothian
Known to have sold: barometer, hygrometer, spirit
level, thermometer
Sources: Baillie (1951); Lyle (1982) (MAC)

DAWSON William (I)
w 1818
Rule M, Bed-screw M
1818   70 Hill St, Birmingham
Sources: Pg; Wr

DAWSON & MELLING
w 1837
Opticians
1837   20 South Castle St, Liverpool
See also
D A W S O N, M E L L I N G & P A Y N E★
M E L L I N G & P A Y N E★
M E L L I N G & C O.★
Associated with B A T E Robert B.★, as chart agents
Known to have sold: repeating circle
Sources: G; inst NMM; Calvert (1971) p.13

DAWSON, MELLING & PAYNE
w 1839–1841
Opticians, Math IM, Navigation Warehouse
1839–1841   39 South Castle St, Liverpool
Succeeded by M E L L I N G & P A Y N E★
See also
D A W S O N & M E L L I N G
M E L L I N G & C O.★
Known to have sold: sextant
Sources: G; Phlps 12 Sep 1979 lot 39 (DJB)

DAY Francis
w 1826–1837
Optician, Math IM, Phil IM, Optical IM
1826–1830   37 Poultry, London

1837   97 Poultry, London
Guild: Spectaclemakers, fr 1826 by redemption
Son of D A Y Francis, London
Attended London Mechanics Institute 1827–1830
Known to have sold: microscope, sextant
Sources: Pg; PO; LMIR (AM); GL: SMC 5213/5;
ChrSK 17 Oct 1985, lot 293; inst (s)

DAY James
w 1825–1828
Phil IM
1825–1828   32 Banner St, St Luke's, London
Attended London Mechanics Institute 1825–1828
Sources: LMIR (AM)

DAY John
w 1723 d by 1736
[Spec M]
            London
Guild: Spectaclemakers, fr 1716
Son of D A Y Nathaniel, husbandman, of Hendon,
Middx
Apprenticed to S T E R R O P Jane★ 1708/9
Had apprentice:
E G L I N T O N Peter (I)★ 1723
F R A N C I S John by t/o from M A N N James (II)★
between 1716 and 1725
I S A A C S Thomas★ 1727
Sources: GL: SMC 5213/2 p.61,137,163,187+

DEAG William
w 1851
Optician
1851   36 Gee St, Goswell St, London
Sources: PO

DEALL St. John
w 1785
Math IM, Carpenter
1785   1 Sweetland Court, Victualling
            Office Square, Tower Hill, London
Sources: GL: Sun 11936/327 no.502473

DEAN Edward
w 1845–1870
Measuring tape M
1845   30 Frederick Place, Newington
            Butts, London
1849   7 Frederick Place, Newington Butts,
            London
1855–1865   8 Richmond Terrace, East St,
            Walworth, London
1869–1870   99 East St, Walworth, London
Succeeded by D E A N, L E R R O & C O.
Sources: PO

DEAN John
w 1826
Optician, Math IM, Phil IM
1826   6 Fieldgate St, Whitechapel, London
Sources: Pg

DEAN Peter
w 1805–1834
Math IM
1805–1834   19 Bear Yard, Lincolns Inn Fields,
            London
Sources: H; Pg

DEANE
w 1816
Cutter of multiplying glasses
1816   1 Norfolk Place, Curtain Rd,
            London
Associated with W A T K I N S J★ as supplier
Sources: EBA: OB 1816 (Watkins)

DEANE David
fr 1735 v 1781
[Optical IM]
Alternative name: D E A N
1764   Smithfield, London
Guild: Spectaclemakers, fr 1735
Son of D E A N E Richard, mariner, of Chatham,
Kent
Apprenticed to L O F T Matthew★ 1728
See also D E A N E John (II)★
Master SMC 1760–1761; petitioner against
Dollond's patent 1764
Sources: GL: SMC 5213/2 p.197+, 5213/3,
6029; PRO: PC 1/7 no.94

DEANE John (I)
w 1690–1698
Scale M
            Golden Borole in St.Ann's Lane near
            Aldersgate, London
Guild: Blacksmiths, fr 1671 or 1672
Had apprentice S W I F T Joseph 1690
Known to have sold: balance
Sources: GL: BKC 2881/8, 2884 (MAC); inst (pv)
(MAC)

DEANE John (II)
w 1742
Alternative name: Ino
See also D E A N E David★
Known to have sold: back-staff
Sources: inst (s)

DEANE William
w 1718–1748
Author, Math IM, Engineer
Alternative name: D E A N
            Garden House near Crane Court,
            London
1718   Crane Court, Fleet St, London
1718   Golden Sphere in Three Crane
            Court, Fleet St, London
1726   Garden House in New St, near
            Fetter Lane, London
1728   West Harding St, London
Guild: Broderers, fr 1718/19
Apprenticed to R O W L E Y John (I)★ 1710
Son of D E A N John, d, of Carpenters' Co. of
London
Had apprentice B U R G E S S Roger★ 1728/9
Pat. fire engine 1725; B.apt Office of Ordnance &
Christ's Hospital Mathematical School
known to have sold: compass (magnetic), drawing
instruments, gauge, gunner's callipers, quadrant,
sundial, waywiser
Sources: GL: Brod 14657/1, CH 12823/4
p.206–07, 376–84, Sun 11936/27 no.46698
(MAC); Patent records (MAC); *Daily Ad* 23 Mar
1726 (MAC); inst NMM, SM; Brown O ((1982)

no.6; Crawforth (1987) p.339; Millburn (1988b) p.233; Millburn (1992) p.21–22,35–36

DEARSLY Thomas
w 1749–1757
Scale M
Near ye Conduit, Snow Hill, London
Guild: Blacksmiths, fr 1740
Apprenticed to STILES William★ 1733
Had apprentice:
SHEPPARD Joseph 1748/9 by t/o from SMELT John★
COOKSON George 1750 t/o 1757 to his father
BOCKUMB Simon 1757
Known to have sold: balance
Sources: GL: BKC 2886/5; Sheppard & Musham (1975) no.40

DEBERNARDEAU –
w 1748
[Optical IM]
1748   Golden Coffee-Mill in St.Martin's Court, Leicester Fields, London
Instruments advertised: eclipse glasses
Sources: *Daily Ad* 9 Jul 1748(MAC)

DECK I.
a 1820
Cambridge
Known to have sold: balance
Sources: inst SM (Gabb Collection)

DE GRAVE Charles (I)
w 1780–1799
Scale M
1780   59 St. Martin's le Grand, London
1788–1799   Corner of St.Ann's Lane, Aldersgate, London
Guild: Blacksmiths, fr 1767
Apprenticed to READ Samuel★, 1760
Had apprentice:
SHURY Samuel (I)★ 1780
MERRICK William 1782
GODDARD Howell 1784 by t/o from BADCOCK William G.★
REDHEAD Zachariah 1785
GOULDING Somerset 1786 by t/o from WOOD Richard★
DE GRAVE Charles (II)★, his son, 1788
CURETON Thomas 1789
REDHEAD John (II) 1789
COLEBROOK Samuel ?★ 1791
MARDELL James 1792
SMITH Samuel 1795
CRUTTENDEN Henry Foster 1799
Father of DE GRAVE Edward Abraham★
Husband of DE GRAVE Mary★
Partnership: READ & DE GRAVE★
Succeeded by DE GRAVE & SON Charles★
Took over from READ & DE GRAVE★
See also DE GRAVE & SON Mary★
R.apt Geo.III; supplier to Christ's Hospital School, London; d 1799
Known to have sold: balance
Instruments advertised: balance, measure, weights
Sources: GL: BKC 2881/15, 2881/16, 2881/17;

CH 12823/7 p.359–60 (MAC); A; BW; By; Kt; Ld; inst MHS

DE GRAVE Charles (II)
w pt 1793–1811
Scale M
1793–1811   59 St. Martin's le Grand, London
Guild: Blacksmiths, fr 1795
Apprenticed to DE GRAVE Charles (I)★, his father, 1788
Partnership: DE GRAVE & SON Charles★
See also DE GRAVE & SAWGOOD★
Scale adjuster to Founders' Co. of London, dismissed 1811
Sources: GL: BKC 2881/16 (MAC), FDC 6331/6; H

DE GRAVE Edward Abraham
w pt 1815–1841
Scale M
1813   59 St.Martin's le Grand, London
Guild: Blacksmiths, fr 1813
Son of DE GRAVE Charles★ and DE GRAVE Mary★
Partnership: DE GRAVE & SON Mary★
Apprenticed to DE GRAVE Mary★, his mother, 1806
Had apprentice:
BARTLETT Charles 1822 by t/o from BARTLETT John★
FANNER William★ 1826
SANGSTER Robert 1833
Known to have sold: weights
Sources: GL: BKC 2881/17, 2881/18 (MAC); bill Avery Historical Mu, Warley, West Midlands (MAC)

DE GRAVE Mary
w 1800–1816
Scale M
1800–1816   59 St. Martin's le Grand, London
Guild: Blacksmiths
Wife of DE GRAVE Charles (I)★
Had apprentice DE GRAVE Edward Abraham★, her son, 1806
HARRIS Richard 1812
Mother of DE GRAVE Charles (II)★
Succeeded by DE GRAVE & SON Mary★
Took over from DE GRAVE & SON Charles★
R.apt Geo.III; supplier to Christ's Hospital School, London
Known to have sold: balance
Instruments advertised: balance, steelyard, weights
Sources: GL: CH 12823/8 p.280–86, BKC 2881/17 (MAC); H; Kt; PO; inst with TCd (pv)

DE GRAVE & CO.
w 1835–1849
Scale M
Alternative name: DE GRAVE, SHORT & FANNER★
London
Known to have sold: balance, measure
Sources: GL: CH 12823/10 p.278; inst SM Wellcome; inst (pv) (MAC)

DE GRAVE & SAWGOOD ? & John
w 1801–1805

Scale M
1801–1805   16 St.Martin's le Grand, London
See also
DE GRAVE Charles (II)★
DE GRAVE Mary★
Sources: H; Kt (JAC)

DE GRAVE & SON Charles
w 1793
Scale M
1793   59 St.Martin's le Grand, London
Succeeded by DE GRAVE Mary★
Took over from DE GRAVE Charles (I)★
See also
DE GRAVE & SON Mary★
DE GRAVE & SAWGOOD★
Sources: A

DE GRAVE & SON Mary
w 1817–1844
Scale M
1817–1844   59 St.Martin's le Grand, London
Succeeded by DE GRAVE, SHORT & FANNER★
Took over from DE GRAVE Mary★
See also
DE GRAVE Edward Abraham★
DE GRAVE Charles (II)★
Supplier to Christ's Hospital School, London
Known to have sold: balance, rule
Instruments advertised: balance, weights, steelyard
Sources: GL: CH 12823/9 p.491–93 (MAC); J; Pg; PO; inst with TCd Luton Mu (MAC)

DEGRAVE, SHORT & FANNER
w 1845–1871
Scale M, Weight M
Alternative name: DE GRAVE & CO. ?
1845–1871   59 St.Martin's le Grand, London
B.apt Royal Mint, Post Office, Assay Office; Ex.1851
Known to have sold: balance, chondrometer, measure, weights
Instruments advertised: balance, measure, weights
Sources: PO; inst Sheffield City Mu (MAC); Cat.1851

DELANDER Daniel
fr 1699 d 1733
Clockmaker
Alternative name: DELAUNDER
-1712   Devereux Court, Strand, London
1712   Temple, Fleet St, London
1714   Within Temple Bar, London
Guild: Clockmakers, fr 1699
Son of DELANDER Nathaniel, Clock M, of London
Apprenticed to HALSTEAD Charles 1692 t/o 1695 to TOMPION Thomas★
Had apprentice:
SILVESTER Philip 1699/1700
HOWARD Richard★ 1702
JACKSON John 1705
ROBINSON William 1709
BATEMAN Nathaniel 1714
MARTIN William 1716
SMITH Joseph 1718
BOWMAN James 1723
BODDLE Josiah 1730

Worked for TOMPION Thomas*
d c.1733
Known to have sold: barometer
Sources: CLRO: CF 1/143; GL: CKC 2710/3,
2721/1; Goodison (1977) p.139; Loomes (1981b)

DELAVA Carolo
w 1841
Baro M
1841   Beauchamp St, Holborn, London
b 1800–1801 abroad
Sources: PRO: Cs 1841 (AM)

DELEUIL L.J.
w 1851
[Phil IM]
1851   8 Rue du Pont-de-Lodi, Paris
1851   7 Althorpe St, Grays Inn Lane,
            London
Ex.1851
Sources: Turner G (1983a) p.309

DELL Isaac
w 1842
Watch M, Clock M, Chrono M
1842   15 John St, Bristol
Sources: Pg

DELL John
w 1809
Optical Turner
            Address not known
Father of DELL Stephen Edward* s 1809
to RICHARDSON George*
Sources: GL: SMC 5213/4

DELL Stephen
w 1845
Optician
Alternative name: Stephen Edward
1845   19 & 20 King St, Commercial Road
            East, London
Guild: [Spectaclemakers]
Son of DELL John*
Apprenticed to RICHARDSON George* 1809
Sources: PO; GL: SMC 5213/4

DELLA TORRE Anthony
w 1805–1823
Optician
Alternative name: de la TORRE
1805–1811   12 Leigh St, Red Lion Square,
            London
1815–1823   4 Leigh St, Red Lion Square,
            London
Sources: H; Goodison (1977) p.366

DELLA TORRE & BARELLI
w 1826–1827
Baro M, Thermo M
1826–1827   9 Lamb's Conduit St, Red Lion
            Square, London
See also DELLA TORRE Anthony*
Sources: Pg; Goodison (1977) p.366

DELOLME Henry
w 1845–1851
Chrono M, Watch M, Importer of Paris clocks and

Geneva watches
1845–1851   48 Rathbone Place, Oxford St,
            London
Sources: PO; PO(HC)

DELVECCHIO J.
w 1810–1838
Baro M, Mirror M, Cement M, Looking-glass M
Alternative name: Del VECCHIO
1810–1838   26 Westmoreland St, Dublin
1820–1822   6 D'Olier St, Dublin
1837–1838   187 & 188 Great Brunswick St,
            Dublin
A barometer marked 'Del Vecchio, Dublin' is
known
Sources: Burnett & Morrison-Low (1989) p.123;
Mason (1944) p.143 (DJB)

DELVECCHIO James
w 1833–1838
Looking-glass M, Frame M
Alternative name: Del VECCHIO
1833–1835   15 Lower Abbey St, Dublin
1836–1838   68 Dame St, Dublin
A barometer marked 'Del Vecchio, Dublin' is
known
Sources: Burnett & Morrison-Low (1989) p.123;
Mason (1944) p.143 (DJB)

DENCH Thomas
w 1820
[Math IM]
1795   42 Great Alie St, Goodmans Fields,
            London
Guild: Grocers, fr 1795
Son of DENCH Jonas of St George's-in-the-East,
London
Apprenticed to RUST Joseph (I)*1788 t/o
to LORKIN Thomas* 1789
Had apprentice BURLS Edward 1820
Sources: Brown (1979a) p.52; GL: GC 11598/5&7;
CLRO: CF 1/1187

DENHAM Benjamin
w 1792–1813
Scale M, Blacksmith, Ironmonger
1792   2 Town Ditch, Christ's Hospital,
            London
1807–1813   16 Bull & Mouth St, London
Guild: Blacksmiths, free by purchase 1792
Had apprentice DENHAM Benjamin E., his son,
1802
Sources: GL: BKC 2881/16 (MAC)

DENNIS John
w 1750–1767
Hourglass M
1767   Houndsditch, London
Guild: Turners, fr 1747
Apprenticed to SAUNDERSON Henry* 1740
Had apprentice:
JONES William (III)*1749/50 t/o
to PRENTICE Philip of CKC 1754
DRAPER David 1751 t/o
to DRAPER John 1754
Sources: GL: TC 3302/2, 3305, 3814

DENNIS John C.
w 1834
Math IM
1834   5 Rodney Terrace West, Mile End
            Road, London
Attended London Mechanics Institute 1834,
possibly the same person as DENNIS John Charles*
Sources: LMIR (AM)

DENNIS John Charles
w 1837–1866
Optician, Globe M, Math IM, Naut IM, Phil IM,
Baro M, Thermo M
1837   Bristol
1839–1849   118 Bishopsgate St. Within, London
1850–1862   122 Bishopsgate St. Within, London
See also DENNIS JOHN C.*
Associated with DENT Edward John* as supplier
B.apt Admiralty
Known to have sold: microscope, sextant
Instruments advertised: barometer, sextant,
thermometer
Sources: PO; Wk; *Times* 21 Feb 1845 Law
Reports; inst & TCd NMM; Phlps 27 Nov 1985
lot 198; Chaldecott (1989) p.162–63

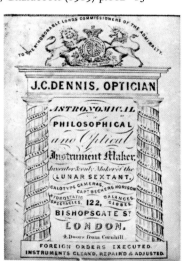

DENT Edward John
w 1826–1851
Chrono M, Watch M, Clock M
1826–1827   43 King St, Long Acre, London
1846–1851   33 Cockspur St, Charing Cross,
            London
1846–1851   34 Royal Exchange, London
1846   82 Strand, London
1851   61 Strand, London
Partnership: ARNOLD & DENT*
Worked for RIPPON Richard
Associated with DENNIS John C.*, who was a
supplier
Succeeded by DENT & CO. Edward
Took part in chronometer trials at Royal
Greenwich Observatory 1826–1829
Inv. liquid compass card; Pat. chrono 1842,
compass 1844 and 1850; b 1770; d 1853; Ex.1851;
R.apt Victoria
Known to have sold: binnacle, chronometer,
compass, sundial

Sources: CUL: RGO 1143 fol.7–8; PO; inst NMM; Turner G (1983a) p.309; *Times* 21 Feb 1845 Law Report; ChrSK 27 Nov 1986 lot 71

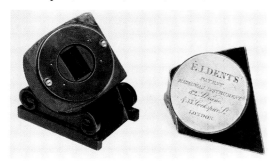

DENTON Joseph
w 1779–1795
Watch M
| 1779 | Scale Lane, Hull |
| 1782–1795 | Silver St, Hull |

Succeeded by DENTON & FOX
Known to have sold: balance
Sources: inst Hull Mu (MAC); BW

DERBY Edward
a 1765–1775
Phil IM
Union Court facing St.Andrews Church, Holborn, London
Took over from HICKMAN Joseph (I)★
Sources: Calvert (1971) p.20

DERHAM William
w 1678–1723
Upminster, Middx
b 1657 d 1735; author
Known to have sold: horary quadrant, sundial
Sources: King & Millburn (1978) p.97; Webster R & M (1986)

DERRY Charles
w 1838–1857
Math IM, Phil IM, Optical IM
1824–1826	10 Little Coram St, Brunswick Square, London
1829	67 Warren St, Fitzroy Square, London
1838	6 Leigh St, Burton Crescent, London
1839–1840	19 Compton Place, Brunswick Square, London
1839–1851	7 Leigh St, Burton Crescent, London
1855	74 Judd St, Brunswick Square, London

Attended London Mechanics Institute 1824–1826, 1829
Sources: Pg; PO; LMIR (AM)

DESBOROUGH Thomas
w 1787–1811
Math IM
1787	Ditching Lane in the Savoy, London
1797	11 Dacre St, St.Margarets, Westminster, London
1805–1811	13 New Bye St, London

Father of DESBOROUGH William★
Sources: GL: HC 15860/9, Sun 11936/340 no.526138 (MAC); H

DESBOROUGH William
w 1804–1828
Math IM
| 1804–1823 | 13 New Pie St, Westminster, London |
| 1828 | 2 Mason St, Westminster, London |

Guild: Haberdashers, fr 1804
Son of DESBOROUGH Thomas★
Apprenticed to SIMPSON Charles★ 1797
Had apprentice:
HOWELL William James 1809
BRISTOW John 1809
DESBOROUGH James, his son, 1823
THRALE Ralph 1828
Sources: GL: HC 15860/9, 15858/2, 15857/3 (MAC)

DESILVA William
w 1851–1881
Optician, Chrono M, Naut IM
1851	175 Great Howard St, Liverpool
1853	40 Regent Rd, Liverpool
1855	44 Regent Rd, Liverpool
1857–1865	38 Regent Rd, Liverpool
1867	5 Bath St, Liverpool
1868	114 Duke St West, Liverpool
1871	112 Duke St West, Liverpool
1872–1881	126 Duke St West, Liverpool
1877–1881	and 37 Bath St, Liverpool Regent Rd, opposite the Bramley-Moore Dk. Gate, Liverpool

Known to have sold: compass (magnetic), sextant, octant, telescope
Sources: G; K; TCd NMM; Webster R & M (1986); LM n

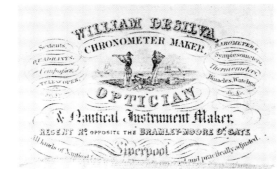

DE STEFFANI William
w 1826–1840
Baro M, Thermo M, Looking-glass M
Alternative name: de STEFFANI
| | 12 Eyre Street Hill, Hatton Garden, London |
| | 33 Exmouth St, Spa Fields, London |

Sources: R (JAC)

DEUCHAR John
w 1815–1833
Chem IM, Chemist
| 1815–1833 | Lothian St, Edinburgh |

Sources: Bryden (1972) p.46

DEVEY John
w 1793
Corkscrew M, Pocket steelyard M, Brass barrel M
| 1793 | Bilston, Staffs |

Sources: BW

DICAS Ann
w 1818–1821
Hydro M
Alternative name: GAMMAGE Ann
1818	20 Trowbridge St, Liverpool
1818	Bronte St, Liverpool
1821	83 Brownlow St, Liverpool

Daughter of DICAS John★
Succeeded by GAMMAGE Benjamin★, her husband, m 1821
Took over from ARSTALL Mary★, née DICAS★, her sister
See also
DICAS S. & M.★
DICAS & CO.★
Sources: Bn; G; Pg; Dicas (1814); DJB

DICAS John
w 1774 d 1797
Math IM, Navigation Warehouse, Hydro M, Brandy Merchant
Alternative name: I.D. (also used by his successors)
1774	73 Hanover St, Liverpool
1777	25 Cleveland Square, Liverpool
1781	71 Duke St, Liverpool
1787	Duke St, Liverpool
1790–1798	27 Pool Lane, Liverpool
1790	29 Pool Lane, Liverpool

Father of DICAS Ann★ and DICAS Mary★
Succeeded by DICAS Mary★
See also
DICAS PATENT HYDROMETER MANUFACTORY★
DICAS & CO.★
DICAS S. & M.★
b c.1741; Pat. hydrometer and slide rule 1780; Dicas patent hydrometer adopted as USA standard 1790
Known to have sold: balance, compass, hydrometer, slide rule
Sources: BW; G; Shaw; Chr SK 31 Mar 1983 lot 183 (DJB); Dicas (1814); Sheppard & Musham (1975) no.190; Wheatland (1968) p.100; Woodcroft (1854)

DICAS Mary
w 1797–1806
Hydro M
Alternative name: ARSTALL, DICAS & CO, ARSTALL late DICAS,
1800	27 Pool Lane, Liverpool
1803–1805	7 North Side Old Dock, Strand St, Liverpool
1814	29 Pembroke Place, Liverpool

Daughter of DICAS John★
Succeeded by DICAS & ARSTALL★ then by DICAS Ann★
Took over from DICAS John★
See also
DICAS PATENT HYDROMETER

MANUFACTORY★
DICAS & CO.★
DICAS S. & M.★
Associated with WELLINGTON Alexander★, with
whom she stayed when visiting London
Wife of ARSTALL George★
Sources: G; Dicas (1814); TCd (DJB)

DICAS S. & M.
c 1806
Mathematical shop
　　　　　　Liverpool
See also
DICAS John★
DICAS Mary★
DICAS & CO.★
DICAS Ann★
Known to have sold: hydrometer
Sources: Holbrook (1992) p.187

DICAS & ARSTALL Mary & George
w 1807
Hydro M
1807　　　　8 North Side Old Dock, Liverpool
Took over from DICAS Mary★
See also
ARSTALL George★
DICAS S. & M.★
Sources: LM n (MAC)

DICAS & CO.
w 1813
Hydro M, Sacch M
　　　　　　Liverpool ?
1813　　　　1 Princes St, Commercial Rd,
　　　　　　Lambeth, London
See also
DICAS Mary★
DICAS S. & M.★
DICAS & ARSTALL★
Mary Arstall (née Dicas) traded as DICAS & CO★
Sources: PO; Dicas (1814)

DICAS PATENT HYDROMETER MANUFACTORY
w 1829–1837
Hydro M
Alternative name: B. GAMMAGE
1829　　　　11 Clarence St, Liverpool
1832–1834　17 Clarence St, Liverpool
1837　　　　133 Brownlow St, Liverpool
Took over from DICAS Ann★, his wife, m 1821
Instruments probably signed B.Gammage★
Sources: G; LM n (MAC)

DICK Alexander
w 1827–1874
Surveying chain M, Wire Worker
1827–1832　101 Bridgegate, Glasgow
1833–1874　Buchanan Court, 105 Stockwell,
　　　　　　Glasgow
Succeeded by DICK & CO. Alexander
Sources: Bryden (1972) p.47

DICK David
w 1777
Scale M, Gunsmith, Cutler
　　　　　　New York

1777　　　　On the Dock, Rotten Row,
　　　　　　Glasgow
Sources: NMS n [from *Royal Gazette* 27 Dec 1777]

DICK William
w 1838–1844
Optical IM, Math IM, Watch M, Ironmonger,
Ship Chandler
1838　　　　57 Trongate, Glasgow
1839–1841　94 Jamaica St, Glasgow
1842–1844　96 Jamaica St, Glasgow
Sources: POE; ADCS

DICKER Thomas
w 1790–1793
Electrical machine M
1790–1793　Clement's Lane, Cannon St, London
Sources: BW; By

DICKMAN John (I)
w 1794–1854
Chrono M, Clock M, Naut IM
1794–1796　Kirkgate, Leith
1797–1813　Bernard St, Leith
1814–1842　33 Shore, Leith
1841–1842　142 George St, Edinburgh
1843　　　　91 Princes St, Edinburgh
1844–1848　6 Charlotte Place, Leith
1848–1854　4 Charlotte Place, Leith
See also DICKMAN John (II)★ & SMITH Charles★
R.apt Wm.IV 1835, continued by Victoria
Known to have sold: compass (magnetic)
Sources: PRO: LC3/70 p.152 (MAC); inst NMM;
Bryden (1972) p.47

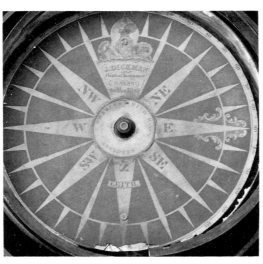

DICKMAN John (II)
w 1828
Watch M, Clock M, Math IM
1828　　　　Monkwearmouth Shore, Sunderland
Succeeded by DICKMAN & SON J.★
See also DICKMAN John (I)★
Sources: Pg

DICKMAN & SON John
w 1830–1847
Naut IM, Math IM, Watch M, Clock M
1830　　　　Quay Side, West Shore, Sunderland

1834　　　　Quay Side, Monkwearmouth Shore,
　　　　　　Sunderland
1844　　　　Quay, Monkwearmouth, Sunderland
1847　　　　North Quay, Monkwearmouth
　　　　　　Sands, Sunderland
Succeeded by WATSON W.★
Took over from DICKMAN John (II)★
See also DICKMAN John (I)★
Sources: Pg; Wh

DICKSON Thomas
w 1720
Math IM
1720　　　　Dublin
Sources: Burnett & Morrison-Low (1989) p.123

DIGBY Charles
w 1738–1766
Math IM
　　　　　　The Globe near ye Hermitage
　　　　　　Bridge in Wapping, London
　　　　　　The Globe, East Smithfield near the
　　　　　　Hermitage, Wapping, London
1766　　　　Near The Hermitage Stairs, London
Guild: [Clockmakers]
Apprenticed to MACY Benjamin★ 1721
Succeeded by DIGBY & SON★
Took over from HENSHAW John (I)★
Instruments advertised: octant
Sources: BM: Banks 105.14 (MAC); Riv; Brown J
(1979b) p.29; DJB

DIGBY & SON Charles
w 1766–1767
Math IM, Ship Chandler
1766–1767　Near Hermitage Stairs, London
Took over from DIGBY Charles★
Sources: Riv

DIGGETT Peter
w 1826
Math IM
1826　　　　4 Penton St, Walworth, London
Same premises as PIGGOTT Peter W★ (? error)
Sources: LMIR (AM)

DILLON –
w 1722
Instrument S
1722　　　　Long Acre next Door to the White
　　　　　　Hart, London
Sources: Calvert (1971) p.21

DILLON John
v 1844
Optician
1844　　　　30 Holborn Hill, London
Guild: Spectaclemakers, fr by purchase 1844
Son of DILLON John, printer, of London
Worked for JONES W. & S.★ 1844
Sources: GL: SMC 5213/6

DITTON Henry John
w 1841–1864
Math IM
1841　　　　33 School lane, Liverpool
1849　　　　46 Gerard St, Liverpool
1853　　　　6 Gerard St, Liverpool

1857–1864   42 Gerard St, Liverpool
Sources: G; LM index

DITTON James
w 1849
Math IM, Brass finisher
1849   46 Gerard St, Liverpool
Sources: G

DIX Christopher
w 1795
Scale M
1795   Parish of St. George's in the East,
              London
Father of DIX Charles s 1795 to RUBIDGE James★
Sources: GL: BKC 2881/16 (MAC)

DIXEY Charles Anderson
fr 1845 w 1865
Optician
1845   New Bond Street London
1865   3 New Bond Street London
Guild: Girdlers, fr 1845
Son of DIXEY Charles Wastell★
Partnership: DIXEY & SONS C.W.
Apprenticed to DIXEY Charles Wastell★, his
father, 1838
Had apprentice:
HUGGINS Arthur Eras. 1865
HUGGINS Herbert George 1865
b c.1824; 1865 Master of Girdlers' Co.; d 1867
Sources: GL: GDC 5800/2, 5802; will (JRM)

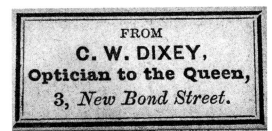

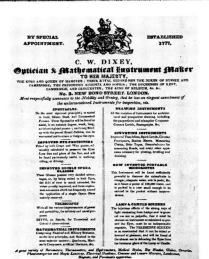

DIXEY Charles Wastell
w 1838–1862
Math IM, Phil IM, Optician

335 Oxford St, London
1838   Old Bond St, London
1839–1862   3 New Bond St, London
Guild: Girdlers, fr 1838
Father of DIXEY Albert Alfred, fr 1865, no trade
given
Nephew of DIXEY George★
Apprenticed to DIXEY Edward (II)★, his father,
1812
Had apprentice DIXEY Charles Anderson★, his
son, 1838
Partnership: DIXEY G. & C.★
Took over from DIXEY G. & C.★
Succeeded by DIXEY & SONS C.W.
Firm e 1777; R.apt Victoria, other members of
Royal Family & King of Belgium; Ex.1851; d 1880
Known to have sold: barometer, thermometer,
chondrometer
Sources: GL: GDC 5800/2, 5802; PO; TCd
NMM; inst (s) (MAC); Calvert (1971) p.21; Turner
G (1983a) p.238, 309

DIXEY Edward (I)
s 1771
              London
Guild: [Spectaclemakers]
Son of DIXEY John, fishmonger, of Southwark,
London
Apprenticed to LINNELL George★ 1771
See also DIXEY Edward (II)★
Sources: GL: SMC 5213/3

DIXEY Edward (II)
w 1805–1843
Optician, Optical IM, Math IM, Phil IM
              10 Air St, Piccadilly, London
              370 Oxford St, London
              17 City Rd, London
1794   Vine St, Piccadilly, London
1805   Princes St, Leicester Square, London
1810–1843   335 Oxford St, London
Guild: Girdlers, fr 1794
Son of DIXEY John, victualler, of Westminster,
London
Apprenticed to BLACK George, trade unknown,
GDC 1786
Had apprentice:
BURTON James (II)★ 1802
ELDRIDGE William★ 1805
DIXEY Charles Wastell★, his son, 1812
JONES Owen★ 1812
UPTON George Samuel 1820
Worked for DIXEY G. & C.★
Sources: GL: GDC 5802; 5800/2; CLRO:
CF1/1175; Bn; H; Kt (JAC); PO; Und

DIXEY George
w 1809–1822
Optician, Telescope M, Optical Turner
1809   370 Oxford St, London
1810–1822   20 Vine St, Piccadilly, London
Guild: Stationers, fr 1809
Apprenticed to WILLSON George★ 1798
Had apprentice:
SPEECHLEY Robert★ 1810
GRIFFIN John Robert 1810
VERITY Benjamin 1815
Partnership: DIXEY G. & C.★

See also
WILLSON & DIXEY★
DIXEY Richard★
Father of DIXEY Lewis★
d.1838
Sources: SBPL: MTC MF Ap; Mckenzie (1978)
p.381; Kt (JAC); PO

DIXEY George & Charles
w 1822–1838
Mechanician, Optician, Astro IM, Math IM, Phil
IM, Spec M
1822–1824   78 New Bond St, London
1825–1838   3 New Bond St, London
Related to DIXEY Lewis★
Employed DIXEY Edward (II)★
DIXEY John★
Succeeded by DIXEY Charles Wastell★
Took over from GRICE William Hawks★
Associated with FRASER Alexander★ [used the
style 'G & C Dixey, late Fraser']
R.apt Geo.IV 1824, Wm.IV 1830, & Royal Family;
Known to have sold: barometer, microscope, sector
Sources: PRO: LC3/69; BM: Heal 105/35–36; Pg

DIXEY John
w 1834–1845
Optician, Math IM, Telescope M
              London
1834–1841   Market Place, Norwich
1836   Upper Market, Norwich
1845   5 Exchange St, Norwich
Worked for DIXEY G. & C.★
b c.1810
Known to have sold: barometer
Sources: PRO: Cs 1841 HO 107/790.6 fol.22
(JRM); *Norwich Mercury* 7 Jun 1834, 16 May 1835
(JRM); Goodison (1977) p.317

DIXEY Lewis
w 1843–1845
Math IM, Phil IM, Optician
1843–1845   62 King's Road, Brighton
1895   [Residence] 2 Bartholomews,
              Brighton
Son of DIXEY George★
Related to
DIXEY Charles W★
DIXEY Charles A★
b c. 1814 d 1895
Known to have sold: microscope, sector
Sources: PO(HC); Phlps 11 Nov 1981 lot 111;
Calvert (1971) p.21; inst (s); will (JRM)

DIXEY Richard
w 1809
Optician
1809   10 Duke St, Adelphi, London
See also
DIXEY Edward (II)★
DIXEY George★
WILLSON & DIXEY★
Sources: H

DIXEY William
w 1842–1870
Optician
1842–1870   241 Oxford Street London

1883   552 Oxford St, London
1889   [Residence] 4 Medley Rd, West
            Hampstead, London
Succeeded by DIXEY & SON William
Took over from JONES Mary★
b c. 1813, d 1889
Sources: will (JRM); PO; Wk; PRO: Cs 1851 HO
107/1489 f.318 (JRM)

DIXON J.M.
w 1820–1824
Spec M
1820–1824   93 Newman St, Oxford St, London
See also
DIXON James★
DIXON John★
Sources: PO

DIXON James
w 1823
Spec M
1823   93 Newman St, Oxford St, London
See also
DIXON John★
DIXON J.M.★
Sources: Pg

DIXON John
w 1820–1823
Spec M
1820–1823   93 Newman St, Oxford St, London
See also
DIXON James★
DIXON J.M.★
Sources: PO; R (JAC)

DOBBIE Alexander
w 1844–1885
Chrono M, Naut IM
1844–1856   20 Clyde Place, Glasgow
1857–1872   24 Clyde Place, Glasgow
1873–1885   24 & 25 Clyde Place, Glasgow
Succeeded by DOBBIE & SON Alexander
See also DOBBIE William★
Known to have sold: barometer, sextant
Sources: Bryden (1972) p.47; inst MSEN (MAC);
Webster R & M (1986)

DOBBIE William
w 1845–1851
1845–1851   Falkirk
See also DOBBIE Alexander★
Ex.1851
Known to have sold: barometer
Sources: Cat.1851; Goodison (1977) p.229,232

DOBSON James
w 1851–1852
Math IM, Manufacturing Optician
1851–1852   45 Fore St, Limehouse, London
Guild: [Masons]
Son of DOBSON William Llamere
Apprenticed to HUGHES Joseph (I)★ 1838 t/o
to MATTHEWS John★ 1845
b in Tower Hamlets, London, in 1822 or 1823;
employed 3 men and 1 boy in 1851
Sources: GL: MC 5304/6, 5304/7; PRO: Cs
1851(LS); Wk

DOBSON John (I)
w 1714–1744
Math IM
1744   St Katherine's St, near the Tower,
            London
Guild: Clockmakers, fr 1714
Apprenticed to HENSHAW John (I)★ 1698
Had apprentice:
CHAPMAN John 1714
DICK William 1723
MERRY John 1744
d c.1745
Sources: GL: CKC 2721/1, 2723/2; CH 12823/5
p.210; Brown J (1979b) p.29

DOBSON John (II)
w 1826–1866
Optician, Phil IM, Math IM, Optical IM, Drawing
IM
        4 Great Suffolk St, Borough,
        London
        24 Crown Row, Walworth, London
1826   3 Norfolk Place, East St, Walworth,
        London
1830   13 Newington Causeway, London
1838–1846   54 Newington Causeway, London
1855   Camberwell Green, London
1859   1 Union Row, Camberwell Green,
        London
1865   254 Camberwell Rd, S London
Guild: Merchant Taylors, fr 1822
Apprenticed to LEFEVER Thomas★ 1813
Sources: GL: MTC MF 320, 324 (MAC); Pg; PO;
JAC

DOBSON John (III)
w 1850–1852
Drawing IM, Math IM, Optician
1850–1851   268 High Holborn, London
Sources: PO; Wk

DOBSON Leonard
w 1822–1826
Math IM
1822   Wilmott's Grove, Bethnal Green,
        London
1826   Bookham, Surrey
Guild: Merchant Taylors, fr 1817
Apprenticed to LEFEVER Thomas★ 1810
Sources: GL: MTC MF 320, 324 (MAC)

DODD Andrew
w 1837–1847
Optical IM, Math IM, Phil IM
1837   70 Hutcheson St, Glasgow
1838–1846   36 Glassford St, Glasgow
1847   88 Glassford St, Glasgow
Known to have sold: barometer
Sources: Bryden (1972) p.47; inst (s)

DOLBY William
w 1829
Math IM
1829   340 Strand, London
Sources: LMIR (AM)

DOLEY John (I)
w 1816–1835

Spec M
1816   Islington Cottage, Birmingham
1829–1830   171 Bristol St, Birmingham
1835   Richmond Terrace, Edgbaston,
        Birmingham
See also DOLEY John (II)★
Sources: H; Pg; Wr

DOLEY John (II)
w 1831–1833
Optician
1831–1833   14 Earl Street West, Edgware Rd,
        London
See also DOLEY John (I)★
Sources: R (JAC)

DOLLOND George (I)
w 1820 d 1852
Optical IM, Math IM, Phil IM, Astro IM,
Optician
Alternative name: born George HUGGINS,
changed name 1805, thereafter sometimes George
Huggins DOLLOND
1805   28 New Surrey St, Blackfriars Rd,
        London
1805   Blackfriar's Rd, Southwark, London
1806   Great Surrey St, Blackfriars Rd,
        London
1807–1812   St Paul's Churchyard, London
1813–1851   59 St.Paul's Churchyard, London
1851   & 61 Paternoster Row, London
Guild: Grocers fr 1804, Spectaclemakers fr by
purchase 1807
Son of HUGGINS William or John [see HUGGINS
George (I)★ for comment]
Nephew of DOLLOND Peter★
Partnership: DOLLOND P. & G.★1805–1820
Apprenticed to FAIRBONE Charles (I)★ 1788
Had apprentice:
GUEST William 1811, SMC
GRIGNION Henry★ 1806 GC
HUGGINS George (II)★, his nephew, 1812 GC
POTTER Charles (I)★ 1813 GC
CUTLER Edward (II) 1821 GC
Succeeded by DOLLOND George (II)★
Took over from DOLLOND P. & G.★
See also HUGGINS George (I)★ for further details
b 1774; R.apt; B.apt Customs; pat binnacle 1812;
FRS 1819; Medal Ex.1851; Master SMC 1811–13
Known to have sold: camera lucida, telescope
Sources: PRO LC3/69 p.8,160; GL: MS 14806
(JRM); GC 11598/6–/8; SMC 5213/4, 5213/6;
Bn; PO; TCd (s); Anderson et al (1990) p.24;
Barty-King (1986); Brown J (1979a) p.45,54,55;
Calvert (1971) p.21

DOLLOND George (II)
w fm 1839 w 1852 d 1866
Optician
Alternative name: born George HUGGINS
1852–1866   59 St.Paul's Churchyard, London
1859–1865   61 Paternoster Row, London
Guild: Grocers fr 1827, Spectaclemakers fr by
purchase 1852
Apprenticed to DOLLOND George (I)★, his uncle,
1812
Had apprentice: see under HUGGINS George (II)★
Succeeded by DOLLOND William, his son

Took over from DOLLOND George (I)★
See also HUGGINS George (II)★ for further details
Master SMC 1862–1863; FRAS
Sources: GL: GC 11598/7, 11598/8; SMC 5213/6,
5213/7; PO

DOLLOND John (I)
w 1752 d 1761
Optician, previously Silk Weaver
1750   Spitalfields, London
1761   Strand, London
Son of DOLLOND Jean, Huguenot weaver
Father of
DOLLOND Peter★
DOLLOND John (II)★
DOLLOND Sarah, wife of RAMSDEN Jesse★
DOLLOND Susan, wife of HUGGINS William
Partnership: DOLLOND & SON J.★
Associated with WATKINS Francis (I)★ who had a
half share in the achromatic lens patent
b 1706; Pat. achromatic lens 1758; Copley Medal
1758; FRS 1761
Sources: GL: Bill head; *Daily Ad* 1 Dec 1761
(JRM); Sorrenson R (1990) p.22–26; Wallis R & P
(1986) p.399–400; Woodcroft (1854)

DOLLOND John (II)
w pt 1766 d 1804
Optician
1767   At Mr Dollonds, St Paul's Church
               Yard, London
1772–1804 St Paul's Churchyard, London
1772–1778 House let to tenants on south side of
               Paternoster Row, London
Guild: Spectaclemakers, fr 1767 by purchase
Son of DOLLOND John (I)★
Brother of DOLLOND Peter★
Partnership: DOLLOND P. & J.★
Had apprentice:
MOON William★ 1782
FAIRBONE John★, son of Charles (I)★, 1786
TYRRELL John 1804
Employed MOON William★ 1791
b 1733; Master SMC 1790–1792
Sources: GMag 29 Jan 1789 (JRM); GL: HIH
8674/112 no.20924; SMC 5213/3, 5213/4

DOLLOND Peter
w 1750–1752, 1761–1766 [1750–1820 including
partnerships]
Optician
        [Residence] Richmond Hill,
        Richmond, Surrey
1750–1752 Vine St, Spitalfields, London
1752–1763 Golden Spectacles & Sea Quadrant
            near Exeter Exchange in the Strand,
            London
1761–1766 near Exeter Exchange in the Strand,
            London
1766   59 St.Paul's Churchyard, London
1773   St. Paul's Church Yard, London
Guild: Spectaclemakers, fr 1755
Brother of DOLLOND John (II)★
Son of DOLLOND John (I)★
Partnership:
DOLLOND & SON John★
DOLLOND Peter & John★
DOLLOND Peter & George★

Had apprentice:
BERGE John★ 1765
GILBERT William (I)★ by t/o
from GILBERT John (I)★ 1769
LECOEUR/LECOUR James (II)★ 1770
HUGGINS John (I)★ 1778
Employed
BERGE John★ 1773
RAMSDEN Jesse★
b 1731; R.apt Geo.III 1760; supplied achromatic
telescopes to Royal Greenwich Observatory;
Master of SMC 1774–82, 1797–99, 1801–03; d
1820; freed as 'foreign Brother' in SMC, the usual
term for a member already free in another Co.
Known to have sold: camera obscura, compass
(magnetic), microscope, scioptic ball, sundial,
telescope
Instruments advertised: telescope
Sources: PRO: LC3/67 p.31; BM: Heal
105/37–/39 (MAC); GL: SMC 5213/3 p.207+,
5213/4; Mort; *Monthly Magazine* No.346, Nov
1820 (MAC); Brown (1979a) p.47; Kelly (1808)
p.8; Millburn (1988b) p.234, 275–76; inst(s)

Peter Dollond
Optician to his Majesty, and to his
Royal Highness the Duke of York
At the Golden Spectacles & Sea Quadrant
Near Exeter Exchange in the Strand
London

DOLLOND Peter & George
w 1805–1820
Optical IM, Phil IM, Math IM
1805–1820 59 St.Paul's Churchyard, London
Succeeded by DOLLOND George(I)★
Took over from DOLLOND Peter & John★
Opticians to George IV 1820, but Peter d before
appointment carried out
Known to have sold: drawing instruments, telescope
Sources: PRO: LC3/69 p.8; GL: 14805/1 (JRM);
H; J; PO; inst(s)

DOLLOND Peter & John
w 1766–1804
Opticians, Optical IM, Math IM
1769–1804 59, the North Side of St.Paul's
            Churchyard, London
1780–1793 35 Haymarket, London
Son of DOLLOND John (I)★
Related to DOLLOND George (I)★ & (II)★
Succeeded by DOLLOND P. & G.★
Took over from DOLLOND Peter★
John d.1804; booksellers; R.apt Geo.III and Duke

of Gloucester; supplied telescopes for James Cook's
second voyage
Sources: BM: Heal 105/38 (MAC); GL: Sun
11936/282 no.429160; By; BW; H; Kt; Ld; Taylor
(1966) p. 229

DOLLOND & SON John (& Peter)
w 1752–1761
Optician
1752   Near the Exeter Exchange in the
           Strand, London
Took over from DOLLOND Peter★
Succeeded by DOLLOND Peter★
Associated with SHORT James★, who used Dollond
micrometers
John FRS; John d 1761
Known to have sold: micrometer, microscope,
telescope
Sources: Kelly (1808) p.8; Porter et al (1985) p.29

DOMBEY & SON
a 1820–1830
        London
Name W. & T. Gilbert★ appears on the same inst.
Known to have sold: octant
Sources: inst WM; Bennett (1983a) no.139

DONALDSON Alexander
w 1818–1830
Tool M, Turner, Globe M
1818–1830 South Niddry St, Edinburgh
Succeeded by DONALDSON & SON Alexander★
Sources: Bryden (1972) p.47

DONALDSON & SON Alexander (& John)
w 1831–1855
Globe M
1831–1855 South Niddry St, Edinburgh
Took over from DONALSON Alexander★
Sources: Bryden (1972) p.47

DONEGAN Joseph
w 1835
Baro M
1835   Lad Lane, Newcastle upon Tyne
Known to have sold: barometer
Sources: Pg; Goodison (1977) p.318

DONEGAN & CO. Peter
w 1805
Baro M, Picture-frame M
1805   7 Union Court, Holborn, London
           94 Holborn Hill, London
Known to have sold: barometer, thermometer
Sources: PO; Goodison (1977) p.318

DOUBLET Hannah
w 1834
Optician, Math IM, Phil IM
1834   14 Shepperton Place, New North
           Rd, London
See also
DOUBLET Thomas★
DOUBLET Thomas & Henry★
Sources: Pg

DOUBLET Thomas
w 1832–1842

Spec M, Optician
1832   14 Shepperton Place, New North
         Rd, London
         25 Windmill St, Finsbury, London
         19 Windmill St, Finsbury, London
1842   74 Paul St, Finsbury, London
Succeeded by DOUBLET Thomas & Henry★
See also DOUBLET Hannah★
Sources: R (JAC)

DOUBLET Thomas & Henry
w 1842–1913
Opticians, Spectacle M, Math IM, Drawing IM
1842–1849   74 Paul St, London
1849–1859   4 City Road, Finsbury Square,
             London
1865–1875   6 Moorgate St, London EC
1865   7 City Road, London EC
1875   50 Finsbury Square, London EC
1880–1895   11 Moorgate St, London EC
1901   39 Moorgate St, London EC
Took over from DOUBLET Thomas★
Known to have sold: microscope, rule, telescope
Sources: PO; Cat. T.Philip & Son, Mar 1984;
inst (s)

DOUBLET Thomas & Mrs H.
w 1851
Opticians
1851   4 City Rd, London
Sources: Wk

DOUGALL J.
w 1778
[IM]
1778   Kirkcaldy
Known to have sold: sundial
Sources: Bryden (1972) p.47

DOUGALL Richard
w 1847–1850
Plumber in 1822, Scale M by 1847
Alternative name: DOUGAL
1822   Doctors Commons, London
1847   64 Bishopsgate St, London
1850   Homerton, London
Guild: Plumbers, fr by purchase 1822
Apprenticed to MARRIOTT George, plumber, of
Melton Mowbray, Leics, nd
Had apprentice:
HUNT William 1847
COCK Brooker James 1850
Sources: GL: PC 2208/10, 2223/7, 2223/9

DOUGHTY W. P.
w 1811
1811   Cony St, York
Apprenticed to JONES Thomas (I)★
Sources: Advertisement in Englefield (1811)

DOUGHTY William P.
w 1839
Pen M, Dressing Case M, Cutler
1839   431 West Strand, London
Associated with STAIGHT Thomas★, who made
inst Doughty sold
Succeeded by DOUGHTY Mrs E by 1846

Known to have sold: compass-sundial,
thermometer
Sources: Pg; PO; ChrSK 14 Apr 1988 lot 11

DOUGLAS James
w 1788–1793
Optical IM
1788–1793   Calton Hill Observatory, Edinburgh
Took over from SHORT Thomas★, his grandfather
Sources: Bryden (1972) p.47

DOUGLASS Mary
w 1828
Navigation Warehouse
1828   35 Wapping Wall, Wapping, London
Sources: R (JAC)

DOULTON & WATTS
w 1845–1895
Chem IM, Stone potters
1845–1895   28 High St, Lambeth, London
1885–1895   Albert Embankment, London SE
Succeeded by DOULTON & CO. LTD
Sources: PO

DOUNTON William
w 1738
[Math IM]
         London
Guild: Goldsmiths, fr 1738
Apprenticed to COLLIER William★ 1706
Had apprentice CHINN Jonathan 1738
Sources: GH: GSC Ap

DOVER John
w 1851–1865
Math IM
         2 Charlton Villas, Charlton, London
         SE
1851   14 Little New St, London
1859–1865   69 Myddleton St, London EC
Apprenticed to ROBINSON Thomas C.★
Ex.1851 medal for balance
Known to have sold: balance
Sources: PO;TCd NMS; Cat.1851; Stock (1969)
(MAC)

DOWLING George W.
w 1834–1835
Optician
1834–1835   10 Penton St, Pentonville, London
Possibly the same person as DOWLING George
Wm★, but there are two separate entries in LMIR
Dec. 1835
Sources: LMIR (AM)

DOWLING George William
w 1840–1844
Optician
1835–1836   25 Pleasant Row, Pentonville, London
1840–1844   16 Mortimer St, Cavendish Square,
             London
Guild: [Girdlers]
Apprenticed to BURTON James (II)★ 1829
See also
DOWLING George W.★
DOWLING William★
Sources: PO; GL: GDC 5802; LMIR (AM)

DOWLING Robert
w 1830–1833
Optician
1830–1831   21 Lower Sackville St, Dublin
1832–1833   8 George's Quay, Dublin
See also apprentices of DOWLING William★
Sources: Burnett & Morrison-Low (1989) p.123

DOWLING William
w 1814–1830
Optician, Math IM, Phil IM
         Lincoln's Inn Passage, London
         114 Great Russell St, Bloomsbury,
         London
1814   [? Residence] 5 Eagle St, Red Lion
         Square, London
1814   121 Great Russell St, Bloomsbury,
         London
1822   Serle St, Lincoln's Inn West Gate,
         London
1829   West Gateway of Lincoln's Inn,
         Serle St, Lincolns Inn Fields London
Guild: Spectaclemakers, fr 1814
Son of DOWLING William, perfumer, of Clare
Market, London
Apprenticed to HARRIS Thomas (I)★ 1804
Had apprentice:
DOWLING Robert John 1814
WARD William Savage 1827
See also DOWLING George William★
Sources: GL: SMC 5213/4, 5213/5; Calvert (1971)
pl.23; Bn; R (JAC)

DOWNIE David
w 1793–1794
Goldsmith, Optician
1793–1794   13 Parliament Close, Edinburgh
Sources: Bryden (1972) p.47

DOWSETT Charles
v 1827–1833
Optician, Watch M
1827–1833   Margate
Father of
DOWSETT James Finch s 1827 PSC
DOWSETT William Finch★
Sources: GL: PSC 5669/2; CPC 5602/12

DOWSETT William Finch
v 1836
Optician
1836   5 Barbican, London
Guild: [Coopers]
Son of DOWSETT Charles, Watch M, of Margate,
Kent
Apprenticed to COX Frederick (I)★ 1833
See also
COX James★
COX William (V)★
Sources: LMIR (AM); GL: CPC 5602/12

DOYLE John
w 1826–1856
Scale M
1826   Steel Yard, St.Thomas, Borough,
         London
1828–1856   26 King St, Borough, London
Guild: [Blacksmiths]

Apprenticed to SMITH Thomas (IV)★ 1811
Succeeded by DOYLE & SON John
Sources: GL: BKC 2881/17 (MAC); Pg

DRAKE J. C.
w 1845
Math IM, Drawing IM
1845   19 Elmtree Rd, St John's Wood,
         London
Sources: PO

DRAKEFORD David (I)
w 1761–1764
[Optical IM]
Alternative name: DRAKEFIELD
1764   Fleet Ditch, London
Guild: Spectaclemakers, fr 1736
Son of DRAKEFORD Richard, butcher, d, of
Abinger, Surrey
Apprenticed to BASS George★ 1728
Had apprentice DRAKEFORD David (II), his son,
1761
Signed petition against Dollond's patent 1764
Sources: GL: SMC 5213/2 p.197+, 5213/3; PRO:
PC1/7 no.94

DRANE John
w 1806–1830
Optician
Guild: Blacksmiths, fr 1806
Son of DRANE William, comb maker, d, of London
Apprenticed to BROOKS John★ 1799
Had apprentice:
PATTEN William 1806 t/o 1808 to BURTON
Joseph (I)★
DRANE John Levick, his son, 1828
DRANE William, his son, 1830
Attended Christ's Hospital School, London
Sources: GL: BKC 2881/16 (MAC); CH 12823/8
p.73 (MAC)

DREBBEL Cornelius
w 1605 d 1633
1605   Alkmaar
1605   London
1607   Eltham, London
1610–1612   Prague
1630   Ipswich
First maker of compound microscopes in England
Known to have sold: microscope
Sources: King & Millburn (1978) p.99

DREW Henry
w 1730–1738
Clock M, Math IM
1730–1738   Glasgow
Sources: Bryden (1972) p.47

DRIELSMA Isaac Jones
w 1834–1851
Clock M, Watch M, Chrono M
Alternative name: Isaac James
1834–1851   Hanover St, Liverpool
Sources: Loomes (1975)

DRIFFILL T.
w 1851
Math IM

1851   West End Old Dock, Hull
See also DRIFFILL & SON Thomas
Known to have sold: octant
Sources: Wh; Phlps 16 Mar 1988 lot 93

DRIFFILL & SON Thomas
w 1848
Math IM, Chandler, Raff S [=Timber S]
1848   West End Old Dock, Hull
See also DRIFFILL T. ★
Sources: Stn

DRING John
w 1784–1790
Glassworker, Hydro M
1784–1790   4 Albion Place, Walworth,
         London
1790   Gracechurch St, London
Guild: possibly Feltmakers, fp 1770
Succeeded by DRING & FAGE★
Took over from CLARKE Richard★, his
brother-in-law
Pat. improved ball cock 1790
Sources: Woodcroft (1854); GL: FLM 1570/4; By;
W (JAC)

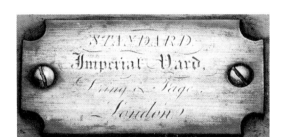

DRING & FAGE John & William
w 1790 p 1940
Hydro M, Patent cock M, Math IM, Optician,
Brass worker, Baro M, Thermo M, Scale M
Alternative name: DRING & CO.; D & F; DRING,
FAGE & CO.
1790–1792   21 Gracechurch St, London
1790   4 Albion Place, London
1792–1796   6 Tooley St, London
1796–1804   248 Tooley St, London
1801   8 Crooked Lane, London
1804–1844   20 Tooley St, London
1804   109 Upper East Smithfield, London
1843–1844   10 Duke St, Tooley St, London
1845–1882   19 & 20 Tooley St, London
1883–1902   145 Strand, WC, London
1903–1938   56 Stamford St, SE, London
Partnership: HALL Edward★ & JENKIN Edward★
were trading as DRING & FAGE by 1850
Succeeded by DRING & FAGE LTD.
Took over from DRING John★
See also
FAGE William (I)★
TURNER & FAGE★
e 1745; B.apt Excise 1850; also supplied
hydrometers for Excise use in the 1790s
Known to have sold: balance, chondrometer, dip
stick, hydrometer, rule, slide rule, thermometer,
sextant
Sources: Kt; PO; Und; inst NMM, SM; Anderson

et al (1990) p.24–25; Calvert (1971) p.21–22;
McConnell (1993) p.53

DRIVER John Samuel
w 1831–1851
Scale M
1831–1837   2 Holywell Row, London
1851   39 Minories, London
Guild: Barbers
Succeeded by DRIVER & SONS
Sources: GL: BC 9815/94, 9815/99; PRO: HO
107/1546 fol. 375–76 Cs 1851; PO

DRUMBLEBY Robert
w 1634
Spec M
Alternative name: DRUMBLEBEE
1634   London
Guild: Brewers, Spectaclemakers
Son of DRUMBLEBY Thomas (I), yeoman, of
Shepshed, Leics
Apprenticed to DRUMBLEBY Thomas (II)★
bap 1606; fr Brew 1633; translated from Brewers to
Spectaclemakers Co. 1634
Sources: CLRO: Ald 49 fol.14; GL: Brew
5445/14, 5445/15; IGI Leics

DRUMBLEBY Thomas (II)
w 1626–1634
Spec M
Alternative name: DRUMBLEBEE
         London
Guild: Brewers, Spectaclemakers
Son of DRUMBLEBY Thomas (I), yeoman, of
Shepshed, Leics
Apprenticed to ALTE Robert★ 1614
Had apprentice:
TWIGG (TWIDD) Richard (I)★ 1626
DRUMBLEBY Robert★, his brother, 1626
JENNYNGS James 1633
fr Brew 1621/2; translated from Brewers to SMC
1634
Sources: CLRO: Ald 49 fol.14; GL: Brew
5445/13, 5445/14, 5445/15

DRUMMOND Robert
fr 1825
Coppersmith
         Glasgow
Guild: Hammermen
Known to have sold: measure
Sources: Lumsden & Aitken (1912) p.310

DRURY George
fl 1830
[Chrono M]
         32 Strand, London
Sources: Taylor (1966) p.448

DRURY William
w 1769–1773
Math IM
1769–1772   Dale St, Liverpool
1772–1773   North side Old Dock, Liverpool
See also Apprentice of URINGS John (II)★
Sources: G; Shaw

DRYSDALE Andrew
fr 1828
Coppersmith
    Glasgow
Guild: Hammermen
Known to have sold: measure
Sources: Lumsden & Aitken (1912) p.313

DUBINI Peter
w 1832–1870
Baro M, Thermo M
Alternative name: DUHIM, DULBINI,
1832–1833   11 Beauchamp St, Leather Lane,
    London
1836   12 Beauchamp St, Leather Lane,
    London
1851–1870   47 Red Lion St, London
Known to have sold: barometer
Sources: Pg; PO; Wk; Goodison p.191, 318

DUCHESNE Claude
w 1693–1720
Alternative name: DE CHESNE, Claudius,
    Paris
    Long Acre, London
    Dean St, Soho, London
1720   Parish of St Anne, Westminster,
    London
Guild: Clockmakers, fr 1693
Known to have sold: astral clock
Sources: Loomes (1981b); Taylor (1966) p.174

DUCK John (I)
w 1717–1732
Math IM
1732   Grub St, London
Guild: Goldsmiths
Had apprentice:
RANDALL Edward 1717
DUCK John (II)★, his son, 1732
See also DUCK John (III)★
Sources: GL: CH 12876/3 (MAC); GH: GSC Ap

DUCK John (II)
fr 1742
[Math IM]
    London
Guild: Goldsmiths, fr 1742
Father of DUCK John (III)★
Apprenticed to DUCK John (I)★, his father, 1732
Sources: GL: CH 12876/3 (MAC); GH: GSC Ap

DUCK John (III)
w 1782
Compass M
    London
Guild: Goldsmiths, fp 1782
Son of DUCK John (II)★
See also DUCK John (I)★
Sources: GH: GSC index (MAC)

DUGMORE John
w 1841
Math IM, Measuring tape M
1841   17 Newton St, Birmingham
Sources: Pg

DUNCAN John (I)
w 1826–1834
Math IM, Phil IM
1826–1834   4 King David Lane, Shadwell,
    London
Guild: [Masons]
Son of DUNCAN Magnus, mariner, d, of Shadwell,
London
Apprenticed to COOK William★ 1807
Sources: GL: MC 5312; Pg

DUNCAN John (II)
w 1846–1856
Goldsmith, Jeweller, Optician
1846–1856   Nicholas St, Aberdeen
1852–1853   40 Upper Kirkgate, Aberdeen
Sources: ADCS

DUNCAN William
w 1841–1849
Math IM, Optical IM, Phil IM
1841   46 Dee St, Aberdeen
1842–1849   92 Union St, Aberdeen
Known to have sold: barometer, microscope
Sources: inst (s); Bryden (1972) p.47; Goodison
(1977) p.318

DUNN John (I)
w 1804
Scale M
1804   Old Bailey, London
Guild: Blacksmiths, fr 1780
Father of DUNN John s 1804 TWC
Son of DUNN William, cooper, d, of Shadwell,
London
Apprenticed to GOODMAN John★ 1773
Sources: GL: BKC 2886/5, 2885/2 (MAC); TWC
7137/6 fol. 82

DUNN John (II)
w 1824–1842
Math IM, Optical IM, Optician
1824   7 West Bow, Edinburgh
1825–1827   25 Thistle St, Edinburgh
1828–1831   52 Hanover St, Edinburgh
1832–1842   50 Hanover St, Edinburgh
1840–1841   157 Buchanan St, Glasgow
1841   28 Buchanan St, Glasgow
Brother of DUNN Thomas★
Employed DUNN Thomas★
Succeeded by DUNN Thomas★
Known to have sold: protractor, pyrometer
Sources: inst NMS; *Edinburgh Evening Courant*
8 Oct 1836 p.3 (JRM); Bryden (1972) p.48;
Calvert (1971) p.22

DUNN Thomas
w 1843–1867
Math IM, Optician, Phil IM
1843–1866   50 Hanover St, Edinburgh
1867   106 George St, Edinburgh
Brother of DUNN John (II)★
Worked for DUNN John (II)★
Took over from DUNN John (II)★
Instruments advertised: chemical apparatus,
drawing instruments, microscope, spectacles,
telescope
Sources: TCd (Cpy) NMS; Bryden (1972) p.48

DUNNELL John
w 1673–1688
Spec M
Alternative name: DUNGAN, DUNGHAM,
DUNNING Jack
1673–1688   London
Guild: Turners, fr by purchase 1673
Spectaclemakers, fr by purchase 1683
Had apprentice:
MARSHALL John★ 1673 TC
ADDISON William 1680 TC
OSBORNE John 1683 TC
Prob d by 1693, when Mrs DUNNELL★ paid search
fee to SMC
Sources: GL: TC 3302/1; SMC 5213/1

DUNNELL Mrs
w 1693
Spec M
Alternative name: DUNNING
1693   Strand, London
Guild: [Spectaclemakers]
Wife of probably, Dunnell John★
Paid search fee to SMC
Sources: GL: SMC 5213/1

DUNSFORD James Newman
w 1830
Naut IM, Optician
1830   43 Fore St, Devonport
Sources: Pg

DUNSTERVILLE M.
a 1740–1800
    Plymouth
Succeeded by SMITH William (II)★
Sources: inst MM.Tec.91/10 (JnH); BW

DURBRIDGE John
w 1780
Math IM
1780   6 Warwick St, Golden Square,
    London
Sources: GL: Sun 11936/289 no.436103 (MAC)

DURHAM Edward
w 1693
[Spec M]
1693   Strand, London
Guild: Spectaclemakers
fr by 1667; prob r or d by 1695
Sources: GL: SMC 5213/1, 5213/2 p.1

DURRAN James Hopkins
w 1832–1854
Clock M, Watch M, Silversmith, Jeweller
Alternative name: Durrant
1832   Parsons Lane, Banbury, Oxon
1854   High Street, Banbury, Oxon
Took over from SAUNDERS Charles of Banbury
Instruments advertised: barometer, thermometer
Sources: Beeson (1989) p.95–96

DUTTON Henry John
w 1837
Math IM
1837   30 Arley St, Liverpool
Sources: G

DUTTON James

w 1801–1808
Scale M

1801	31 Joyner St, Southwark, London
1806–1824	248 Tooley St, near London Bridge, London

Guild: Haberdashers, fr 1798
Partnership: DUTTON & SMITH★
Apprenticed to VINCENT Robert★ 1789
Had apprentice:
KNOWLES William★ 1809
Fourteen others 1801–1824
Partnership 1809–1830
Sources: GL: HC 15860/9, 15857/3 (MAC)

DUTTON Richard

w 1680–1682
Book S, Math IM?

1682	The Dial in Holborn, London

Supplied instruments for St Andrews Observatory
Sources: Taylor (1954) p.246,296,396

DUTTON William Marston

w 1771–1794
Watch M, Chrono M

1793	148 Fleet St, London

Guild: Clockmakers, fr 1746
Partnership: MUDGE & DUTTON★
Apprenticed to GRAHAM George★, 1738/9
Son of DUTTON Matthew, gent, of Marston, Bucks
Had apprentice DUTTON Matthew, his son, 1771 by t/o from MUDGE Thomas★
Worked for GRAHAM George★
Took over from MUDGE & DUTTON★
Sources: GL: CKC 2721/1, 2722, 2723/2, 11568; Wil; Taylor (1966) p.230

DUTTON & SMITH

w 1809–1830
Scale M

1805–1830	248 Tooley St, near London Bridge, London
1826–1830	281 Borough, London

Succeeded by SMITH & CO.
Took over from VINCENT & CHANCELLOR★
See also
DUTTON James★
SMITH William (II)★
Sources: H; Kt; Pg; R (MAC)

DWERRIHOUSE, OGSTON & BELL

fl 1830
[Chrono M]

	27 Davies St, Berkeley Square, London

Sources: Taylor (1966) p.448

EADE Jonathan (I)

w 1724–1771
Compass M

1724	Near King Edward Stairs, Wapping, London

Guild: Merchant Taylors, fr 1735
Son of EADE David, mariner, late of Ipswich, Suffolk
Apprenticed to MARLOW Michael (II) 1704/5

Had apprentice:
WILTON William (I)★ 1735, rebound 1738
WRIGHT Joseph 1744
ALLEN Nathaniel★ 1754
EADE Jonathan (II)★, his son, 1760
See also EADE, WILTON & ALLEN★
Known to have sold: compass, slide rule
Sources: GL: MTC MF 319, 324; Sun 11936/19 no.34658 (MAC); inst NMM; Sby 20 Feb 1985 lot 256

EADE Jonathan (II)

w 1771–1796
Ship Chandler

1771	Wapping, London

Guild: Merchant Taylors, fr 1771
Apprenticed to EADE Jonathan (I)★, his father, 1760
Had apprentice: WALTERS Thomas 1771
See also EADE, WILTON & ALLEN★
Master MTC 1796
Sources: GL: MTC MF 319, 320, 324

EADE, WILTON & ALLEN Jonathan, William & Nathaniel

a 1760–1790

	London

See also EADE Jonathan (I)★ and (II)★, apprentices of EADE Jonathan (I)★
Known to have sold: compass (magnetic)
Sources: Sby 17 Oct 1960 noted in Webster R & M (1986)

EADES Daniel

w 1839
Measure M, Timber S

1839	45 Ewer St, London
1839	Pump Court, Union St, Borough, London

Took over from WADE J. E. [claimed]
See also WADE John Creswell★
Sources: Pg

EAGLAND Joseph

w 1851–1895
Baro M, Thermo M

1851	4 Spital St, Spitalfields, London
1859	3 Wellington Row, Bethnal Green, London NE
1870	9 Kirby St, Hatton Garden, London EC
1890–1895	152 Farringdon Rd, London WC

Sources: PO; Wk

EAMES Mark

w 1849
Math IM, Drawing IM

1849	3 White Lion St, Norton Folgate, London

Sources: PO

EARNSHAW Laurence

a 1728 d 1767
Alternative name: Lawrence

	Mottram in Longdendale, Ashton under Lyne

See also EARNSHAW Thomas (I)★

b 1707; inv. astro clock; inv. spinning machine
Known to have sold: astronomical clock, globe, sundial
Sources: King & Millburn (1978) p.140; Wallis R & P (1993) p.43

EARNSHAW Thomas (I)

w 1795 d 1829
Watch M, Chrono M

1791–1806	119 High Holborn, London
1829	Chenies St, Bedford Square, London

Worked for BROCKBANK John★
See also EARNSHAW Laurence★
Succeeded by EARNSHAW Thomas (II)★, his son
Developed methods of producing chronometers in substantial quantities at reasonable cost
Sources: BW; Taylor (1966) p.284–85; Baillie (1951)

EARNSHAW Thomas (II)

fl 1825–1850
Watch M, Chrono M

1825–1850	119 High Holborn, London

Took over from EARNSHAW Thomas (I)★, his father
Sources: Pg; PO; Baillie (1951)

EASTLAND William (I)

w 1753–1768
Spec M

1764	Clerkenwell, London

Guild: Spectaclemakers, fr 1726
Son of EASTLAND John, farmer, d, of Surrey
Apprenticed to GAY Thomas★ 1718/19 t/o to LINCOLN Thomas★ nd
Had apprentice:
STRONG Thomas 1753
EASTLAND William (II), son of George, 1762
See also EASTLAND & CO.★
Petitioner against Dollond's patent, 1764
Sources: PRO: PC 1/7 no.94: GL: SMC 5213/2 p.109,170, 5213/3 p.184+

EASTLAND & CO.

a 1780
See also EASTLAND William (I)★
Known to have sold: microscope
Sources: Taylor (1966) p.156

EBSWORTH George Richard

w 1829–1835
Optician, Math IM, Phil IM

1829–1835	54 Fleet St, London

See also
EBSWORTH Richard★
EBSWORTH Thomas★
Sources: R (JAC)

EBSWORTH John

w 1667 d 1699
Clock M

1674	Cross Keys in Lothbury, London New Cheapside, London

Guild: Clockmakers, fr 1665
Apprenticed to AMES Richard 1657/8
Known to have sold: sundial
Sources: Loomes (1981b)

EBSWORTH Richard

w 1820–1835
Optician, Phil IM, Math IM, Optical IM
Alternative name: EPSWORTH, EBBSWORTH
    41 Fleet St, London
1826   68 Fleet St, London
1827   54 Fleet St, London
Guild: Barbers, fr 1826
Had apprentice ROGERS Walter Southwick 1826
See also
EBSWORTH George Richard★
EBSWORTH Thomas★
Known to have sold: drawing instruments,
sundial
Sources: GL: BC 9815/89, 5267/6, 5277; Kt
(JAC); PO; inst (s); ChrSK 14 Apr 1988 lot 204

EBSWORTH Thomas

w 1824
Optician
1824   68 Fleet St, London
See also
EBSWORTH George Richard★
EBSWORTH Richard★
Sources: R (JAC)

EDE C. J.

w 1839–1844
Optical IM
1839–1844   100 St George's Road, Southwark,
    London
Attended London Mechanics Institute 1839–1844
Sources: LMIR (AM)

EDEN Alfred Frederick

c 1830 w 1849
Optician
    Langham Place, Regent St, London
1849   4 Dowgate Hill, London
Worked for PRITCHARD Andrew★
Known to have sold: microscope
Sources: PO; Nuttall (1977) p.65–81

EDEN William

fr 1818 v 1827
Optician
1818   At Mr Samuel Jones's, Holborn,
    London
1826–1827   30 Lower Holborn, London
Guild: Spectaclemakers, fr 1818
Son of EDEN Robert, deceased, of Taunton,
Somerset
Apprenticed to JONES Samuel (I)★ 1811
Worked for JONES William & Samuel★
Attended London Mechanics Institute 1826–7
Sources: LMIR (AM); GL: SMC 5213/4

EDGEWORTH Henry

w 1775–1787
Math IM, Phil IM, Optical IM
Alternative name: EDGWORTH
1775–1787   51 on the Quay, Bristol
    Hadley's Quadrant & Spectacles,
    opposite the Dial, on the Quay,
    Bristol
Apprenticed to possibly MARGAS John★ 1760
Known to have sold: barometer, octant,
thermometer

Instruments advertised: full range
Sources: TCd & inst NMM

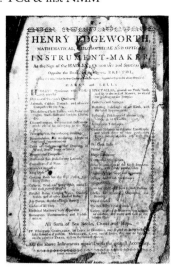

EDGINTON John

w 1813
Optician
Alternative name: EDGINGTON
1810   7 Charterhouse Lane, London
Guild: Spectaclemakers, fr 1810
Son of EDGINTON John, carpenter, of London
Apprenticed to WITHERSPOON Colin★ 1803
Had apprentice HUMPHREYS William 1813
Apprenticeship consideration paid by Aldersgate
Charity School
Sources: GL: SMC 5213/4

EDKINS Samuel Sabine

w 1827–1849
Globe M, Silversmith
1827   16 Salisbury Square, Fleet St,
    London
–1849   6 Salisbury Square, Fleet St, London
Husband of BARDIN Elizabeth M.★
Succeeded by EDKINS & SON Samuel★
Took over from BARDIN Elizabeth M.★
Son-in-law of T.M. Bardin★
Known to have sold: globe
Instruments advertised: globe
Sources: PO; Phlps 3 Mar 1992 lot 152; inst MHS;
Millburn & Rössaak (1992) p.34–36,52

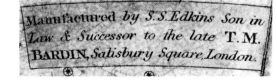

EDKINS & SON Samuel S.

w 1850–1852
Globe M
1850–1852   16 Salisbury Square, Fleet St,
    London
Ex.1851
Known to have sold: globe
Sources: PO; Cat. 1851; Millburn & Rössaak
(1992) p.34

EDWARD Thomas

w 1776
1776   Liverpool
Known to have sold: octant
Sources: inst (s) (MAC)

EDWARDS Benjamin

fl 1828 w 1846
[Chrono M]
1839–1846   17 Shoreditch, London
Sources: PO; Loomes (1976); Taylor (1966) p.419

EDWARDS Charles

w 1775–1776
Upholsterer, later Ship Chandler
1770–1776   St Katherine's by the Tower, London
Guild: Clothworkers, fr 1770
Father of EDWARDS Thomas fp 1796
Son of EDWARDS Thomas, ship chandler, of St
Katherine's, London
Partnership: probably, EDWARDS &
KILBINGTON★
Apprenticed to BARNES Charles 1763
Had apprentice:
WALKER James 1775
KILBIN(G)TON John★ 1776
Sources: CWH: CWC Ap, Fr

EDWARDS Frederick

w 1835–1851
Optician, Math IM, Phil IM
1835–1845   2 Hackney Road, London
1849–1851   39 Hoxton Square, London
Succeeded by EDWARDS Elizabeth
Sources: R; PO

EDWARDS James

w 1836–1885
Rule M
1836   25 John St West, Edgware Road,
    London
1836   and 15 Suffolk St, King's Cross,
    London
1839   201 Kent St, Borough, London
1859   10 Ray St, Clerkenwell, London EC
1865   195 King's Cross Road, London WC
1870   215 King's Cross Road, London WC
1880–1885   191 King's Cross Road, London WC
Possibly two men
Sources: Pg; PO

EDWARDS John (I)

fl 1781–1803
Math IM
    Ludlow
    Bristol
Pat. compass 1789; described as Math IM in patent
records
Sources: Woodcroft (1854); Taylor (1966) p. 310

EDWARDS John (II)

w 1841
Baro M
1841   Dorrington St, Holborn, London
b 1805 or 1806 in the County of Middlesex
Sources: PRO: Cs 1841(AM)

EDWARDS John Baker
w 1851
Chem IM
1851   Liverpool
Ex.1851
Known to have sold: chemical apparatus
Sources: Cat. 1851

EDWARDS Joseph
w 1767–1780
Rule M
1767   Bull St, Birmingham
1770–1777   46 Worcester St, Birmingham
1780   46 Needless Alley, Birmingham
Had apprentice DINGLEY James
Sources: PR; Sy; Sket; *Aris's Birmingham Gazette*
14 May 1770

EDWARDS Mary
w 1668
[Spec M]
             London
Guild: [Spectaclemakers]
Wife of EDWARDS Richard*
Had apprentice YARWELL JOHN* taken over
from her husband & t/o to SHIELD Nicholas*
SMC refused her permission to take an additional
apprentice, 1668
Sources: GL: SMC 5213/1

EDWARDS Richard
w 1660–1667
Spec M
             Fenchurch St, London
Guild: [Brewers] Spectaclemakers
Son of EDWARDS Richard, stationer, of London
Apprenticed to PEALE William* 1634 BREW
Had apprentice:
BOURNE Richard 1660 SMC, t/o nd to
PRESBURY William*
YARWELL John* 1662 SMC, taken over by his wife
Succeeded by EDWARDS Mary*, his wife
d late 1667 or early 1668
Sources: GL: Brew 5445/15; SMC 5213/1;
Whipple (1951) p.66

EDWARDS Thomas
w 1809
Rule M
1809   5 Kemp's Court, Berwick St, Soho,
             London
Sources: H

EDWARDS & KILBINGTON
w 1789–1793
Compass M, Ship Chandlers
Alternative name: KILBINTON, KILVINGTON
1793   292 Wapping, London
Probably the partnership of EDWARDS Charles*
with his former apprentice KILBIN(G)TON John*
Sources: Taylor (1966) p.310; CWH: CWC Ap; BW

**EDWARDS & NORVELL Frederick &
Charles**
w 1834
Spectacle M
1834   8 Maidenhead Court, Aldersgate St,
             London

Entered joint mark at Goldsmiths' Hall.
Sources: GH: records of goldsmiths' marks (JAC)

EGGINGTON George
w 1829
Model M, Phil IM
1829–1830   18 Livery St, Birmingham
Sources: West, Wr (DJB)

EGGINGTON Thomas
w 1792
Rule M
1792   7 Halletts Buildings, Wolverhampton
Sources: Wolverhampton rate books (MAC)

EGGLESTON Nathaniel
w 1768 d 1774
Spec M, Optician
1768   Opposite the Mansion House, York
Succeeded by BERRY John*
See also EGGLESTON Richard*
Sources: *York Courant* 23 Feb 1768, 15 Mar 1774,
22 Mar 1774 (DJB)

EGGLESTON Richard
w 1734 d c.1763
Optician, Spec M
Alternative name: ECCLESTON
1751   In the Minster Yard, York
Guild: [?Spectaclemakers]
Apprenticed to probably, ROAK Richard* 1717/18
See also EGGLESTON Nathaniel*
Known to have sold: telescope
Sources: GL: SMC 6031/1; *York Courant* 28 Oct
1740, 5 Jul 1748, 4 Jan 1763 (DJB); Journal Book
of the Royal Society 27 Mar 1734/5 (DJB);
Buckley (1935) p.428

EGGLETON
w 1816
Supplier of Concave Mirrors
1816   15 King St, Lambeth Walk, London
Associated with *HILL William and WATKINS J.*
as supplier
Known to have sold: mirror
Sources: EBA: OB 1816 (Watkins)

EGLINTON John
w 1764–1786
Spec M
Alternative name: EGLINGTON, EGGLINGTON
1764   Hatton Garden, London
1772   Great Kirby St, Hatton Garden,
             London
1785   Cross St, Hatton Garden, London
Guild: Spectaclemakers, fr 1745
Father of EGLINTON Henry, book-binder, fp 1778
Son of EGLINTON John, hair merchant, of London
Apprenticed to EGLINTON Peter (I)* 1736
Had apprentice:
BROOMIT William 1764
BROOKS John* 1772
ABBOTT Charles* 1784
BROWN Joseph 1786
Petitioner against Dollond's patent, 1764; last
attendance at SMC Court 1790
Sources: GL: SMC 5213/2, 5213/3 p.93+, 5213/4;
PRO: PC 1/7 no.94; By

EGLINTON Peter (I)
w 1736–1772
[Spec M]
Alternative name: EAGLINTON, EGLINGTON,
EGGLINGTON
1764   Strand, London
Guild: Spectaclemakers, fr 1731
Son of EGLINTON James, mason, of Hanwell,
Oxon
Grandfather of EGLINTON Peter (III) fp 1800, no
trade given
Apprenticed to DAY John* 1722
Had apprentice:
EGLINTON Peter (II), his son, 1760
EGLINTON John*, son of John, 1736
Master SMC 1761–1763
Sources: GL: SMC 5213/2 p.137,226+,
5213/3; PRO: PC 1/7 no.94

EIFFE James Sweetman
w 1835 d 1880
Chrono M
1835–1839   1 South Crescent, Bedford Square,
             London
Competitor for Admiralty chronometer award,
1835. b 1800
Known to have sold: chronometer.
Sources: Pg; PO; Taylor (1966) p.470; Baillie
(1951); CUL: RGO/1143 fol.7–10

ELDRIDGE William
fr 1812
Optician
1812   66 Curtain Rd, Shoreditch, London
Guild: Girdlers, fr 1812
Apprenticed to DIXEY Edward* 1805
Sources: GL: GDC 5802, 5813/4

ELECTRIC TELEGRAPH CO.
w 1851
1851   London
Ex.1851 telegraphic apparatus;
Sources: Turner G (1983a) p.309

ELGIE James
w 1835–1837
Math IM, Phil IM
1835–1837   9 Lamb's Buildings, Bunhill Row,
             London
Sources: R

ELKINGTON George Richards
w 1835–1840
Optician, Math IM, Phil IM
1836–1837   11 Berners St, Oxford St, London
1835   44 St Paul's Square, Birmingham
Pat. spectacles 1834,1836,1838,1840
Sources: Pg; PO; Taylor (1966) p.420; Woodcroft
(1854)

ELKINGTON James
w 1808–1830
Spec M, Toy M, Optician
1808–1818   St.Paul's Square, Birmingham
1828–1830   76 Bishopgate St, Birmingham
See also ELKINGTON George R.
Sources: Pg; Wr; West

ELLA William

w 1711
                    England
Known to have sold: quadrant
Sources: Sby 26 Jul 1965 noted in Webster R & M
(1986)

ELLICOTT Edward (I)

w fm 1757 d 1791
Watch M
1754   Swithins Alley, London
Guild: Clothworkers, fp 1754
Father of ELLICOTT Edward (II)★
Son of ELLICOTT John★
R.apt George III; working in partnerships with
father, John, and sons
Sources: CWH: CWC Fr; Baillie (1951);
Goodison (1977) p.144

ELLICOTT Edward (II)

fr 1795 d 1835
Watch M, Chrono M
1793–1825   17 Sweeting's Alley, Cornhill,
                    London
Guild: Clockmakers, fr 1795
Son of ELLICOTT Edward (I)★
Partnership:
ELLICOTT & TAYLOR★
ELLICOTT & SONS★
ELLICOTT & SMITH★
d 1835; partnerships 1795–1835; sent
chronometers for trial at Royal Greenwich
Observatory 1823–1825
Sources: CUL: RGO 1143 fol. 5–6; GL: CKC
2725/1; BW; Baillie (1951)

ELLICOTT John

w 1733–1757
Clock M
Alternative name: ELLICOT
                    Royal Exchange, London
1736–1766   Swithin Alley, London
1743   [Residence] Hackney, London
–1766   17 Sweetings Alley, Royal
                    Exchange, London
Guild: Clothworkers, fr 1726
Father of ELLICOTT Edward (I)★
Apprenticed to WARD Richard
Succeeded by ELLICOTT & SON★
Took over from ELLICOTT John Snr
b 1706; inv. pyrometer 1736; FRS 1738; d.1772;
R.apt
Known to have sold: astronomical clock,
barometer
Sources: CWH: CWC Fr; Millburn (1988a) p.21;
Baillie (1951); Goodison (1977) p.144

ELLICOTT & CO.

w 1805
Watch M
Alternative name: Probably directory abbreviation
1805   Royal Exchange, London
See also
ELLICOTT Edward (II)★
ELLICOTT & SONS Edward★
Sources: H

ELLICOTT & SMITH

w 1830–1840
Watch M, Clock M
1839   15 Sweetings Alley, Cornhill, London
Partnership: including ELLICOTT Edward (II)★
until d 1835
Sources: Pg; Baillie (1951)

ELLICOTT & SON John (& Edward)

w 1757–1772
Clock M
1769–1772   17 Sweetings Alley, Royal
                    Exchange, London
Succeeded by ELLICOTT Edward (I)★
Took over from ELLICOTT John,
John d.1772
Sources: Baillie (1951); JAC

ELLICOTT & SONS Edward

w 1785–1811
Watch M, [Chrono M]
1793   17 Sweetings Alley, London
Partnership: including ELLICOTT Edward (I)★
until his death, and ELLICOTT Edward (II)★
Sources: Baillie (1951); BW

ELLICOTT & TAYLOR

w 1811–1830
Watch M, [Chrono M]
                    London
Partnership: involving ELLICOTT Edward (II)★
Known to have sold: chronometer.
Sources: Baillie (1951)

ELLIOT –

a 1720–1730
                    London
Employed LANE James
Sources: TCd SM (Wellcome) (MAC)

ELLIOTT Charles

w   1826
Phil IM
1826   122 Regent St, St James, London
Guild: [Makers of Playing Cards]
Son of ELLIOTT Benjamin
Apprenticed to NEWMAN John Frederick★
Attended London Mechanics Institute 1826
Sources: LMIR (AM); GL: MPC 5963/5

ELLIOTT Charles Alfred

s 1837 r c. 1865
Math IM
1823   21 Great Newport St, St. Martin in
                    the Fields, London
1837   High Holborn, London
Guild: [Coachmakers]
Son of ELLIOTT William (II)★
Brother of ELLIOTT Frederick Henry★
Partnership:
ELLIOTT & SONS William★
ELLIOTT BROS
Apprenticed to ELLIOTT William (II)★, his father,
1837
b 28 Sept. 1822, baptized St. Martin in the Fields
12 Feb 1823, d 1877
Sources: GL: CMC 5637/1; VL: St. Martin in the
Fields bap; BG

ELLIOTT Frederick Henry

w 1849–1851
Math IM, Optician
1849–1851   30 King St, Holborn, London
                    [Residence] Penrhyn Lodge, Park
                    Villas East, Regent's Park, London
Son of ELLIOTT William (II)★
Brother of ELLIOTT Charles Alfred★
Partnership:
ELLIOTT & SONS William★
ELLIOTT BROS
b 27 May 1819; educated at schools in Baldock and
Edmonton, & at Christ's Coll. Camb. BA 1845,
d 1873
Sources: PO; Venn (1944) part 2, 2; *Engineering*
24 Jan 1873, p.62

ELLIOTT G.A.

w 1835–1836
Math IM
1835–1836   260 High Holborn, London
See also ELLIOTT George Augustus★
Attended London Mechanics Institute 1835–1836
Sources: LMIR (AM)

ELLIOTT George Augustus

w 1826–1827
Optician, Math IM, Phil IM
1826–1827   8 Merlin's Place, Spa Fields, London
See also ELLIOTT G.A.★
Sources: Pg

ELLIOTT John (I)

w 1818
Optician
                    London
Had apprentice ARNOLD James by t/o 1818
Sources: GH: GSC index

ELLIOTT John (II)

w 1851–1870
Math IM, Phil IM
1851–1870   14 Stacey St, St Giles's, London
Sources: PO

ELLIOTT Thomas

w 1809–1827
Math IM, Optical IM, Drawing IM
                    3 Albemarle St, Clerkenwell,
                    London
                    39 Crown St, Finsbury, London
                    21 Tabernacle Walk, Finsbury,
                    London
                    20 Pitfield St, Old St, London
                    3 Albion Place, Clerkenwell,
                    London
                    20 Haberdashers Walk, Hoxton,
                    London
See also ELLIOTT William (I)★
Known to have sold: microscope
Instruments advertised: drawing instruments.
Sources: JAC; ChrSK 17 April 1986 lot 362

ELLIOTT William (I)

w 1799–1835
Math IM
                    3 Wright's Row, Pell St, Ratcliff
                    Highway, London

19 Jane St, Commercial Rd, London
1796–1801   51 Artichoke Lane, London
Guild: Joiners, fp 1795
Had apprentice:
PERRETT George 1799
SIMMONS Thomas 1807
SMITH Thomas Stokes★ 1809
RICKARDS Joseph 1816
KEOHAN Thomas★ 1816
HARRIS John T. 1823
BURT John 1824
HOWELL William M. 1829
COLE Robert 1835
Sources: GL: JC 8055/3; Crawforth (1987) p.355

ELLIOTT William (II)

w 1804–1849
Drawing IM, Optician
1817   26 Wilderness Row, Goswell St,
      London
1817–1827   21 Great Newport St, St Martin's
      Lane, London
1830–1833   227 High Holborn, London
1835–1849   268 High Holborn, London
Guild: Coachmakers, fr 1804
Son of ELLIOTT William, yeoman, of London
Apprenticed to BACKWELL William (I)★ 1795
rebound to COLLINGRIDGE Thomas
1795[apparently for the purposes of guild
membership only, the real training being by
Backwell]
Had apprentice:
FOSTER William 1804
HARMON William★ 1807
ELLIOTT Thomas 1812
JEFFERYS William★ 1813
WATKINS Ely Frederick
BENNETT George 1832
WHITE William Henry 1837
ELLIOTT Charles Alfred★
HOEY George 1839
See also ELLIOTT BROS.
Succeeded by ELLIOTT & SONS William★
d 1853
Known to have sold: drawing instruments
Sources: GL: CMC 5643, 5637/1, 5640/1,
21185; EBA: indenture of apprenticeship, OB;
Clifton (1993a) p.2–7

ELLIOTT William Edward

w 1831–1870
Math IM, Phil IM, Naut IM
1831   19 Upper East Smithfield, London
1839   30 Fox Lane, High St, Shadwell,
      London
1845–1870   139 Shadwell High St, London
Partnership: REED & ELLIOTT
Partnership 1862–1865+
Sources: PO; Pg

ELLIOTT & SONS William

w 1850–1853
Optical IM, Drawing IM, Math IM, Phil IM
1850–1853   56 Strand, London
Succeeded by ELLIOTT BROS.
Took over from ELLIOTT William★
See also
ELLIOTT Frederick H★

ELLIOTT Charles A.★
Partnership of ELLIOTT William (II)★ with his sons
Frederick and Charles; Ex.1851
Known to have sold: rule.
Sources: Turner G (1983) p.309; inst (pv &
NMM); EBA; PO; Bristow (1993) p.8–11; Clifton
(1993a) p.2–7

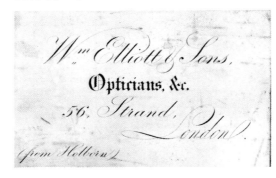

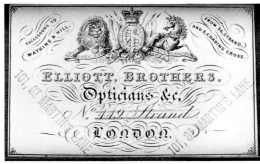

ELLIS John

w 1756–1757
Baro M
1756–1757   St.Peter of the Bayly, Oxford
Sources: *Jackson's Oxford Journal* 17 Jul 1756, 2 Jul
1757 (MAC)

ELMES William

w 1668–1675
Rule M
      Moorfields, London
Guild: Woodmongers, Clockmakers fr 1667/8
Had apprentice:
SAMBROOK John 1668
PULLEN James 1669
ELMES Joseph 1673
CADGELL Thomas 1682
Associated with JOLE Robert, to whom he
supplied rules
Known to have sold: sundial, astrolabe, rule
Sources: GL: CKC 2710/1 p.244; Brown J (1979b)
p. 29

ELMSDEN Edmund

w 1764
      King's Lynn
Known to have sold: telescope
Sources: Taylor (1966) p. 259

EMANUEL E. & E.

w 1831–1879
Goldsmiths, Jewellers, Watch M, Bullion

Merchants, [Naut IS]
Alternative name: Ezekiel and Emanuel
1831–1912   3 The Hard, Portsea
1831–1879   and 101 High St, Portsmouth
R.apt Vic; Agents for Parkinson & Frodsham
chrono. Emanuel Emanuel 1st Jewish Mayor of
Portsmouth 1866
Known to have sold: quintant, sector, sextant,
telescope
Sources: TCd(pv, Cpy); PCRO; inst NMM S.222;
Taylor (1966) p.420

EMBEILY J. W.

w 1851
Math IM
1851   1 Broad St, Old Gravel Lane,
      London
Sources: Wk

EMBLEM Thomas

w 1759
[Master of Math IM]
      London
Guild: Turners
Sources: GL: TC 3302/2

EMERY Josiah

fl 1757 w 1785
      Charing Cross, London
Guild: Clockmakers, fr 1781
Associated with MUDGE Thomas★
Known to have sold: chronometer
Sources: Baillie (1951); Taylor (1966) p. 230

EMOTT Benjamin

w 1667–1669
[Math IM]
Alternative name: EMETT
      London
Guild: Joiners, fr 1667
Apprenticed to SUTTON Henry★ 1659/60, t/o
to MARKE John★
Had apprentice:
HANCOCK M. 1668
SPENDER John 1669
Sources: Crawforth (1987) p. 355

ENDERSBEE William (I)

w 1809–1827
Math IM
Alternative name: ENDERSBY
1809–1827   1 Little Thames St, St.Catherine's,
      London
Guild: [Grocers]
Apprenticed to
GARRARD Thomas★ 1781 t/o to
CHAPMAN James (I)★ 1785
Succeeded by ENDERSBEE & SON William★
Known to have sold: sextant
Sources: H; Und; Brown J (1979a) p.49; ChrSK
22 Sep 1988 lot 434

ENDERSBEE William (II)

w 1845–1846
Math IM
1845–1846   28 Wapping High St, London
Sources: PO

ENDERSBEE William John
w 1850
Math IM
1850   115 Cock Hill, Ratcliff, London
Sources: PO

ENDERSBEE & SON William
w 1828–1843
Math IM, Phil IM
1828   334 & 335 High St, Wapping,
            London
1839–1840   335 Wapping, London
Took over from ENDERSBEE William (I)★
Known to have sold: sextant
Sources: Pg; PO; inst(s)

ENDICOTT John
w 1834–1850
Baro M, Thermo M, Rule M
1834   10 Norwich Court, Fetter Lane,
            London
1845–1850   23 Little Saffron Hill, Hatton Wall,
            London
Sources: Pg; PO

ENGLAND John
w 1703–1708
Math IM
            Charing Cross, London
Guild: Stationers, fr 1702/3
Apprenticed to JOLE Robert★ 1690
Had apprentice SAUNDERS Samuel (I)★ 1703, and
two others
R.apt Queen Anne
Known to have sold: sundial, sector, compass,
Napier's bones
Sources: McKenzie (1974) p. 91, (1978) p.118;
Porter et al (1985) p.26

ENGLAND & SONS Moses
fl 1830–1834
Optical IM ?
            Lower Russell St, Walsall
Sources: Taylor (1966) p. 448

ENGLAND, PARKER & SOMMERS
w 1805–1806
Scale M
1805–1806   27 Hosier Lane, West Smithfield,
            London
1806   Wood St, Cheapside, London
See also
SOMMERS & SON Charles★
SOMMERS Joseph (II)★
Sources: PO

ENGLISH William
w 1839
Optician
1839   156 North St, Brighton
Sources: Pg

ERLAN John
w 1827
Optician
1827   Park St, Grosvenor Square, London
Attended London Mechanics Institute 1827
Sources: LMIR (AM)

ESSEX & CO. C.
w 1824–1828
            London
Known to have sold: sundial
Sources: Webster R & M (1986)

ETON Alexander
w 1838–1839
Optician
1838–1839   46 Greek St, Soho, London
Attended London Mechanics Institute 1838–1839
Sources: LMIR (AM)

ETTLING Leopold
w 1845
Math IM
1845   151 Ratcliff Highway, London
Sources: PO

EVANS Frederick
w 1834
Optician, Math IM, Phil IM
1834   12 Denzell St, Clare Market,
            London
Sources: Pg

EVANS James
c 1750 d by 1765
Spectacle M
            Parish of St James, Clerkenwell,
            London
Father of EVANS Morris s 1765 THC
Sources: GL: THC 6158/5

EVANS John (I)
c 1775 w 1809
Rule M
1801   Paris St, Southwark, London
1809   8 Dean St, Fetter Lane, London
1775   Sherrard St, Golden Square, London
Guild: Joiners, fr 1768
Apprenticed to URINGS John (II)★ 1759
Sources: Crawforth (1987) p.355–56 GL: JC
8055/3

EVANS John (II)
w 1794–1809
Optical IM
Alternative name: John Johnson
1796   87 Bishopsgate Within, London
1800–1801   88 Bishopsgate Within, London
Guild: Stationers, fr 1792
Apprenticed to
ARCHER William 1783 t/o to
PRICE William (I)★ 1786
See also EVANS William (I)★
Known to have sold: barometer, hygrometer
Sources: By; H; Kt; Goodison (1977) p.320;
McKenzie (1978) p.6, 118

EVANS Thomas
a 1700–1750
Clock M, Watch M
            Usk (Wales)
Known to have sold: barometer
Sources: Peate (1975) (MAC)

EVANS William (I)
w 1769–1811
Rule M, Math IM, Printer
1771–1811   10 Dean St, Fetter Lane, London
1793   138 Wapping, London
Guild: Stationers
Apprenticed to CHAMPNEYS James★ 1760
Had apprentice:
GREGORY William (I)★ 1789
CASE William★ 1783
PEARSON John★ 1772
HUGHESDON William★ 1797
6 others
Sources: Wil; BW; H; McKenzie (1978) p.69, 119

EVANS William (II)
w 1795–1851
Math IM
1792   Hand Court, Holborn, London
1795   58 Rosmond Row, Clerkenwell,
            London
1802–1847   48 Rosomon St, Clerkenwell,
            London
1849   22 President St, East, Goswell Rd,
            London
1849–1851   9 Squirries St, Bethnall Green Rd,
            London
Guild: Grocers, fr 1792
Father of EVANS John s 1801 CKC
Apprenticed to FAIRBONE Charles (I)★
Had apprentice OWEN James★
See also SAREL William★
Sources: H; PO; Wk; Brown J (1979a) p. 54; GL:
CKC 2720/1 p. 281

EVANS William (III)
fr 1800 w 1823
Math IM
1813   John St, Brick Lane, Spitalfields,
            London
1823   Angel Place, Shadwell, London
Guild: Merchant Taylors, fr 1800
Apprenticed to HARRIS Thomas (III)★ 1793
Sources: GL: MTC MF 320, 324 (MAC)

EVANS William (IV)
w 1845–1865
Math IM
1845–1865   9 Squirries St, Bethnal Green Road,
            London
Sources: PO

EVE George Frederick
w 1850–1890
Phil IM, Baro M, Thermo M, Hydrometer M
1846–1849   19 Hatton Garden, London
1850–1852   12 Ashley Terrace, City Road,
            London
1851   and 4 Charles St, Hatton Garden,
            London
1855–1865   90 Holborn Hill, London
1869   90A Holborn Hill London EC
1870–1890   Earl's Buildings, Featherstone St,
            London EC
See also PIZZALA Francis A.★
Attended London Mechanis Institute 1846–51
Sources: PO; Wk; LMIR (AM)

EVERED Charles
fl 1830–1832
[Chrono M]
        40 Rathbone Place, London
Sources: Loomes (1976); Taylor (1966) p.448

EVERINGHAM Richard
w 1783–1818
Math IM
1783   43 Rupert St, London
Guild: Grocers, fr 1784
Son of EVERINGHAM Joseph
Apprenticed to FAIRBONE Charles (I)★
Had apprentice COOPER Joshua Vernon
d by 1823
Sources: GL: GC 11598/6, 11598/7; Sun
11936/317 no. 485277; Brown J (1979a) p. 44

EVERITT George
fr 1782 w 1813
Scale M
1782   Deal St, Mile End New Town,
        London
Guild: Blacksmiths, fr 1782
Apprenticed to MEYMOTT Clement★ 1769
Had apprentice:
FAGE William (II)★
POUPARD Abraham★ and 11 others
Sources: GL: BKC 2881/15, 2881/16, 2882/17
(MAC)

EVERS Henry
w 1840
Rule M
1840   3 Ely Court, Holborn Hill, London
Sources: R

EVESHAM Epiphanius
w 1589
Known to have sold: sundial
Sources: Taylor (1954) p. 188

EWING Walter E.
w 1849–1855
Baro M, Looking-glass M
1849–1855   59A Renshaw St, Liverpool
1853   54 Renshaw St Liverpool
Sources: G

EYLAND & SONS Moses
w 1841–1862
Optician, Spec M
1841–1862   Lower Rushall St, Walsall
Sources: Pg; Sl

EYRES Jessica
w 1807–1810
Navigation shop
1807–1810   12 Old Church Yard, Liverpool
Sources: G

EZEKIEL C. & A.
w 1816
Engraver, Optician
1816   Fore St, Exeter
Took over from EZEKIEL E.A.★
Sources: H; Pg

EZEKIEL Ezekiel Abraham
w 1790 p 1809
Optician, Engraver, Goldsmith, Print S
Alternative name: EZEKIAL
1790–1806   7 doors below North St, Fore St,
        Exeter
Son of EZEKIEL Abraham
Succeeded by EZEKIEL C. & A.★
b 1757; d 1806
Known to have sold: Microscope
Sources: DNB; EFP 13 Dec 1806; Lee (1991) p.
16–35 (JRM)

FACY Richard
w 1851
Designer, IM
1851   Wapping Wall, London
Ex 1851
Known to have sold: planetarium
Sources: Cat.1851; Turner G (1983) p.309

FAGE Edward
w 1667–1673
Math IM
1669   The Sugar Loaf in Hosier Lane,
        West Smithfield, London
Guild: Stationers fr 1669 & Clockmakers fr 1667/8
Apprenticed to THOMPSON Anthony★ 1657
Had apprentice:
YOUNG Richard 1669
WARNER John 1672
Took over from THOMPSON Anthony★
Known to have sold: gunner's scales, slide rule,
gauge, bow quadrant.
Sources: Bryden (1992) p.307, 317, 327; Brown J
(1979b) p. 29

FAGE William (I)
w 1833–1855
Hydro M, Optical IM, Math IM, Phil IM, Sacch
M
Alternative name: W F
1833   59 Long Lane, Bermondsey, London
1834–1835   5 King's Row, Walworth, London
1836–1837   10 Great Dover St. Borough,
        London
1838–1840   3 Great Dover St. Borough, London
1855   7 Friar St, Blackfriars Rd, London
1841–1842   62 High St, Borough, London
See also
DRING & FAGE★
DRING John★
Known to have sold: hydrometer
Instruments advertised: hydrometer, balance
Sources: H; PO; R (JAC); inst(s)

FAGE William (II)
w 1799–1805
Math IM
1799–1805   109 Upper East Smithfield, London
1805   Tooley St, Southwark, London
Father of FAGE James s 1805 VC
See also FAGE William (I)★
Sources: GL: VC 15220/3 p.328; MTC MF 320

FAGE William (III)
w 1810–1836
Scale M, Smith, Bell hanger

1814   7 Cumberland St, Shoreditch,
        London
1816–1832   39 Brown's Lane, Spitalfields,
        London
1822–1828   38 Brown's Lane, Spitalfields,
        London
Guild: Blacksmiths, fr 1802
Apprenticed to EVERITT George★ 1792
Succeeded by FAGE Elizabeth
Sources: GL: BKC 2881/16, 2881/17 (MAC); Kt;
Pg; PO; R (JAC)

FAGIOLI & SON Dominic
w 1839–1854
Baro M
Alternative name: FAGLIOLI
        9 Great Warner St, Clerkenwell,
        London
1840–1851   3 Great Warner St, Clerkenwell,
        London
1851–1854   10 Great Warner St, Clerkenwell,
        London
Took over from FAGLIOLI Dominic
Known to have sold: barometer, hygrometer,
thermometer, spirit level.
Sources: PO; inst (s)

FAGLIOLI Dominic
w 1834–1839
Baro M, Thermo M
Alternative name: FAGIOLI
        11 Baldwin's Gardens, Leather Lane,
        London
1839   3 Great Warner St, Clerkenwell,
        London
Succeeded by FAGIOLI & SON Dominic
Known to have sold: barometer, thermometer,
hygrometer, spirit level.
Sources: Pg; Goodison (1977) p. 320; inst(s)

FAIRBONE Charles (I)
w 1765 d c.1804
Timber merchant, Math IM
1780–1794   20 Great New St, Fetter Lane,
        London
1765   [?Residence] Princes Court,
        Westminster, London
1766   St.Martin's Lane, London
1773–1800   New St, London
1780–1801   New St, Shoe Lane, [presumably
        alternative rendering of above
        address] London
Guild: Grocers, fr 1765
Father of FAIRBONE John [See Fairburn J.★]
Son of FAIRBONE Timothy, blacksmith, of
London
Apprenticed to WING Tycho★ 1753
Had apprentice:
EVANS William (II)★ 1765
PALMER Edward 1765
MARTIN John 1766
COCHRAN John ?★ 1773
EVERINGHAM Richard★ 1773
POOLER Richard Turner★ 1780
FAIRBONE Charles (II)★, his son, 1781
FAIRBURN Isaac, his nephew, 1783
HUGGINS George (I)★ 1788
FAIRBONE Timothy, his son, 1789

FAIRBONE Henry, his son, 1794
BURNELL Richard 1794, t/o 1794
CUTLER James 1796
YERWORTH William 1797
HARRIS Joseph 1797
RICHARDS John 1800, t/o 1802 to FAIRBONE Charles (II)★
HARDING John★ 1801, t/o 1802 to FAIRBONE Charles (II)★
Succeeded by FAIRBONE Charles (II)★
Associated with MORRIS William (I)★
Sources: Brown (1979) p.44-5; BW; GL: Sun 11938/281 no.424850; SMC 5213/4

FAIRBONE Charles (II)
w 1802-1812
Math IM
    20 Great New St, Shoe Lane, London
1811   Great New St, London
Guild: Grocers, fr 1802
Son of FAIRBONE Charles (I)★
Brother of FAIRBONE John
Apprenticed to FAIRBONE Charles (I)★ 1781
Had apprentice:
RICHARDS John 1802 by t/o from FAIRBONE Charles (I)★
HARDING John 1802 by t/o from FAIRBONE Charles (I)★
SCRIVENER Hayter 1811
Took over from FAIRBONE Charles (I)★
Sources: GL: GC 11598/6

FAIRBURN J.
w 1805
Optician
Alternative name: Possibly FAIRBONE John
1805   20 Great New St, Fetter Lane, London
Guild: ?[Spectaclemakers]
Son of probably, FAIRBONE Charles (I)★
Apprenticed to probably, DOLLOND John (II)★
One entry in directory as Fairburn, possibly an error for Fairbone
Sources: GL: SMC 5213/4; H

FAIREY Joseph
w 1803-1838
Math IM, Optician, Phil IM, Optical IM
1803-1805   15 Fair St, Horsleydown, London
1806-1811+   150 Tooley St, Borough, London
1811-1822   20 Ratcliff Highway, Upper East Smithfield, London
1826-1839   8 Northumberland Place, Commercial Rd, London and at No. 4 Principal Entrance, London Dock, London
Guild: Grocers, fr 1803
Father of FAIREY Richard★
Apprenticed to BROWNING Samuel (I)★ 1796
Had apprentice:
PORTER Daniel 1803
BAKER Richard 1806
HOVIL William★ 1811
WHITEHEAD James 1811
HARRIS John 1818
WILLIAMS William Payne 1825
HEWITSON John ?★ 1828

FAIREY Richard★, his son, 1829
Succeeded by FAIREY & SON Joseph★
Associated with BROWNING John (II)★
Known to have sold: octant
Sources: Und; JAC; Brown (1979a) p.51; GL: GC 11598/6; 11598/7; inst & TCd NMM

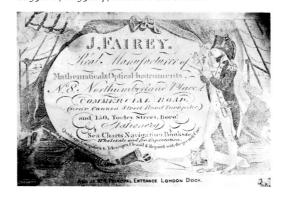

FAIREY Richard
w pt 1839-1858
Math IM
    London
Guild: Grocers, fr 1836
Son of FAIREY Joseph★
Partnership: FAIREY & SON Joseph★
Apprenticed to FAIREY Joseph★ 1829
Sources: GL: GC 11598/7, 11598/8

FAIREY & SON Joseph
w 1839-1858
Optician
1839-1858   8 Northumberland Place, Commercial Rd East, London
Took over from FAIREY Joseph★
Sources: PO; Wk

FAIRSERVICE John
w 1830-1831
Phil IM
1830-1831   Prospect Place, Cambridge Heath, London
Attended London Mechanics Institute 1830-1831
Sources: LMIR (AM)

FAIRSERVICE William
w 1828-1839
Phil IM
1828-1830   9 Prospect Place, Cambridge Heath, London
1839   31 Great Cambridge St, Hackney, London
Attended London Mechanics Institute 1828-1830, 1839
Sources: LMIR (AM)

FALLOW Joseph
w 1822-1829
Baro M
1822-1829   127 Pilgrim St, Newcastle upon Tyne
Sources: Pg; PWh; Goodison (1977) p.320

FANNER William
fr 1836 w 1844
Scale M

1836   55 Bankside, Southwark, London
Guild: Blacksmiths, fr 1836
Apprenticed to DE GRAVE Edward A.★ 1826
Sources: GL: BKC 2881/17, 2881/18 (MAC)

FANSHAW Robert
w 1841
Optician
1841   232 Moorfields, Sheffield
1841   40 Pinstone St, Sheffield
Sources: Pg; Rg

FARLEY Thomas
w 1839
Scale M
1839   Northgate St, Canterbury
Sources: Pg

FARMER James
w 1702-1708
[Math IM]
1702-1708   Well St, near Well Close, London
Guild: Grocers, fp 1672
Father of
FARMER John★
FARMER William★
Son of FARMER Henry of Grocers' Co.
Had apprentice:
FARMER Thomas 1703
HILL Nathaniel 1701/2
FARMER William★, his son, 1708
d by 1722
Sources: Brown J (1979a) p.31; Crawforth (1987) p. 356

FARMER John
w 1731-1777
Math IM, Rule M
1731   Dove Court upper end Old Jewry, London
1737   Whitefriars, London
1739   St.Anns Lane near Aldersgate, London
1743   Cateaton St, London
1750   Coach & Horses Yard in Wood St, London
1752   Hart St, near Newgate, London
1754-1777   Pye Corner, West Smithfield, London
Guild: Joiners, fr 1731
Brother of FARMER William★
Related to GEARING Richard B.★
Apprenticed to COOKE Thomas (II)★ 1722
Had apprentice:
ATKINSON John (II)★ 1739 by t/o from WRIGHT Geo★
HUSSEY William (I)★ 1739
14 other apprentices 1731-1761
Succeeded by GEARING Richard B.★, his nephew
Known to have sold: rule
Sources: BM: Heal 105/43 (MAC); Crawforth (1987) p.356-57

FARMER William (I)
c 1715-1750
[Math IM]
    Near the Lime Kiln, Horsley Down, London

Guild: [Grocers]
Brother of FARMER John★
Apprenticed to FARMER James★, his father, 1708
Known to have sold: compass
Sources: inst NMM; Brown J (1979a) p.31

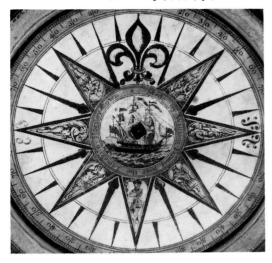

FARMER William (II)

w 1841
Optical glass M, Spectacle glass M
1841   Hayseech Mills, Rowley Regis,
         Dudley
Sources: Pg

FARROLL John

w 1818–1835
Rule M
Alternative name: FARNOLL FARNOL
1818   Constitution Hill, Birmingham
1825   1 Northwood St, Birmingham
1828   111 Constitution Hill, Birmingham
1835   2 Court, Snowhill, Birmingham
Sources: Pg

FARTHING I.H.

w 1844
Writing machine M
1844   42 Cornhill, London
Made Marc Brunel's writing & drawing machine
Sources: PO; inst (pv)

FAULKINGHAM –

w 1672–1674
Rule S
1672   Under the South East corner of the
         Royal Exchange, London
Associated with NASH John★, from whom he
obtained rules
Known to have sold: rule
Sources: GL: CKC 2710/1 p.244; Loomes (1981b)

FAULKNER John

w 1848
Phil IM
1848   11 Guilford St East, London
Attended London Mechanics Institute 1848
Sources: LMIR (AM)

FAWCETT John

w 1775–1793
Watch M, Optician
1776–1787   34 Dame St, Dublin
1788–1792   3 Grafton St, Dublin
1793   133 Capel St, Dublin
Sources: Burnett & Morrison-Low (1989) p.124

FAYRER James (I)

w 1798–1841
Math IM, Optical IM, Phil IM, Clock M;
         66 White Lion St, Pentonville,
         Islington, London
1805   35 White Lion St, Pentonville,
         Islington, London
1839   40 White Lion St, Pentonville,
         Islington, London
Husband of SUDDARD Nancy
Worked for TROUGHTON Edward (I)★
Succeeded by FAYRER & SONS ★
b 1760; m 1798; trained as a clock maker
Known to have sold: zenith instrument, repeating
circle, sextant, pantograph.
Sources: H; Pg; R; CUL: RGO 14/48 fol.198
(AM); McConnell (1992) p.13

FAYRER James (II)

w 1820
Math IM
Alternative name: James Junior
1820   Pentonville London
         South Africa
Son of FAYRER James (I)★
Related to TROUGHTON Edward (I)★
Worked for FAYRER James (I)★
See also FAYRER & BROS James★
Sources: CUL: RGO 14/48 fol.198 (AM);
McConnell (1992) p.13–16

FAYRER James and John

w 1851–1865
Math IM
Alternative name: J. & J.
1851–1865   66 White Lion St, Pentonville,
         London
Succeeded by FAYRER John
Took over from FAYRER & BROS★
Sources: PO; Wk

FAYRER John Edward

w 1825–1828
Math IM
1825–1828   White Lion St, London
See also
FAYRER & SONS★
FAYRER & BROS★
Attended London Mechanics Institute 1825–1828
Sources: LMIR (AM)

FAYRER Thomas William

w 1828–1829
Math IM
1828–1829   40 White Lion St, London
See also
FAYRER & SONS★
FAYRER & BROS★
Attended London Mechanics Institute 1828–1829
Sources: LMIR (AM)

FAYRER & BROS James

w 1850–1851
Math IM
1850–1851   66 White Lion St, Pentonville,
         London
Took over from FAYRER & SONS★
See also
FAYRER James (II)★
FAYRER John Edward★
FAYRER Thomas Wm★
Sources: PO

FAYRER & SONS

w 1844–1849
Math IM, Optical IM, Phil IM
1844–1849   66 White Lion St, Pentonville,
         London
Succeeded by FAYRER & BROS★
Took over from FAYRER James (I)★
See also
FAYRER James (II)★
FAYRER John Edward★
FAYRER Thomas William★
Sources: PO

FAZAKERLEY Thomas

w 1839
Optician, Math IM
1839   45 Upper Milk St, Liverpool
Sources: G

FEALTY Robert

w 1775
Optical IM
1775   Parish of St. Sepulchres, London
Father of FEALTY Charles, s 1775 CKC
Sources: GL: CKC 2720/1

FEATHERS Peter Airth

w 1842–1874
Naut IM, Optical IM, Chrono M, Watch M,
Clock M
1842–1843   73 High St, Dundee
1845–1850   10 Dock S, Dundee
1853–1868   26 Dock St, Dundee
1869–1874   40 Dock St, Dundee
Succeeded by FEATHERS & SON P.A.
Known to have sold: sextant, chronometer
Sources: Bryden (1972) p. 48; ChrSK 26 Nov 1979
lot 122; Holbrook (1992) p 119, 186, 209, 211

FEATLEY Robert

w 1772–1783
Optical IM, Optician
1772   Crown Court, Cow Lane,
         Smithfield, London
1783   Crown & Cushion Court, Cow
         Lane, Smithfield, London
Possibly the same as Robert Featley of Fleet St
who petitioned against Dollond's patent in 1764
Sources: GL: STTP 2934 fol 153,181

FEILDER Thomas

fr 1687 w 1720
[Math IM]
         London
Guild: Clockmakers
Apprenticed to CHENEY Withers★

Had 10 apprentices, none known as Math IM
Sources: Brown J (1979b) p. 29

FELL John
w 1818
Magnet M, Truss M
1818   Rosemary Lane, Lancaster
Sources: Pg

FENN Isaac
w 1765–1768
Clock M, Watch M
        The Measuring Wheel near the
        corner of Bond St, Oxford St,
        London
1765   Swallow St, near Hanover Square,
        London
Pat. waywiser 1765
Sources: BM: Heal 105/41 (MAC); woodcroft
(1854)

FENN Joseph
c 1821 d 1875
Tool Manufacturer
1811   Botolph Lane, London
1839–1842   105 Newgate St, London
1857–1873   105 & 106 Newgate St, London
Guild: Salters, fp 1811
Father of FENN Joseph, mechanical tool M, fr 1855
SC
Son of FENN Nathaniel
Succeeded by FENN & CO.
Known to have sold: protractor
Sources: SH: SC Fr; Pg; inst(s)

FENTIMAN John
w 1798
Bricklayer
1785   Rockingham Row, St Mary
        Newington Surrey, London
1798   London
Guild: Tylers & Bricklayers
Had apprentice CASS Daniel 1798 by t/o
from MORRIS William (I)★
Had apprentice turned over from Math IM, but
apparently a bricklayer by trade
Sources: Brown (1979a); GL:TBC 3045/3 p.108

FERGUSON Daniel (I)
w 1839–1846
Surgical IM, Cutler
1839–1846   21 Giltspur St, London
Known to have sold: hydrometer
Sources: Pg; PO; inst SM

FERGUSON Daniel (II)
w 1824–1831
Math IM
1824–1831   44 West Smithfield, London
See also LINNELL George★
Attended London Mechanics Institute 1824–1831
Sources: LMIR (AM); GL: SMC 5213/3

FERGUSON James (I)
w 1755–1756 [as IM]
Lecturer, Author, Globe & Orrery M, Artist
Alternative name: I. FERGUSON

1745   Newport St, London
1745   The Dumb Waiter, Compton St,
        Soho, London
1746–1748   The White Periwig, Great Pulteney
        St, Golden Square, London
1748–1755   Margaret St, Cavendish Square,
        St Marylebone, London
1755–1758   At the Globe opposite Cecil St, in
        the Strand, London
1758–1762   Red Lion Court, Fleet St, London
1762   Little Mortimer St, Cavendish
        Square, St Marylebone, London
1773–1775   Bolt Court, Fleet St, London
Father of FERGUSON James (II)
Succeeded by MARTIN Benjamin★ as Globe M
Took over from SENEX Mary★
Associated with
WHITEHURST John (I)★
NORTON Eardley★ in clock design
PINCHBECK Christopher (II)★
BOULTON Matthew★
TROUGHTON John (I)★, to whom his son was
apprenticed
BENNETT John (I)★
ELLICOTT John★
NAIRNE Edward★
MUDGE Thomas★
b 1710 d 1776; FRS 1763
Known to have sold: globe, planetarium, sundial
Sources: Millburn (1988a); Brown (1979a) p.41

FERONI Alexander
w 1804–1810
Baro M
Alternative name: FERONY
1804–1810   49 Fleet St, Dublin
Sources: Burnett & Morrison-Low (1989) p.124

FERRIS James
w 1810–1823
Clock M
1816   Quay, Poole, Dorset
Guild: [Clockmakers]
Apprenticed to WRIGHT Thomas (III)★ 1783
b c 1769; bankrupt 2 May 1816
Sources: Loomes (1976) p.78 & (1981); GL: CKC
2720/1

FIDLER John
a 1800
Math IM
        Oxford Market, Oxford St, London
Guild: [Spectaclemakers]?
Apprenticed to possibly, HOLTON John, tailor,
1776
See also FIDLER Robert★
Sources: GL: SMC 5213/3; SML: Court MS (JAC)

FIDLER Robert
w 1810–1822
Optician, Optical IM
1810   32 Wigmore St, Cavendish Square,
        London
1822   30 Foley St, Cavendish Square,
        London
Father of FIDLER Henry, s 1824 in FANC
See also FIDLER John★
d by 1824

Known to have sold: balance, barometer,
cometarium
Sources: GL: FANC 21420/1; Kt: Und; inst, StA;
AML

FIELD James
w 1805
Optician, Math IM, Optical IM
1805   2 Bond ST, Bath
Succeeded by FIELD & SON★
Sources: TCd WM

FIELD John
w 1791–1803
Math IM, Optician, Phil IM
1791–1793   74 Cornhill, London
1804–1830   Royal Mint, London
1787   Cornhill, London
Guild: Spectaclemakers, fr 1787
Son of FIELD John, member of
Apprenticed to NAIRNE Edward★ 1779
Had apprentice LEA John 1791
Took over from FIELD Matthew★
At the Mint 1804–30; Master SMC 1799–1801,
1820–22
Known to have sold: microscope
Sources: GL: SMC 5213/3, 5213/4, 5213/5; BW;
By; Calvert (1971) p.22; inst(s)

FIELD Matthew
w 1790
IM (type not specified)
1790   74 Cornhill, London
Same premises as FIELD John★
Sources: W

FIELD Robert
w 1825–1841
Spec M, Optician
1825   111 New St, Birmingham
1829–1841   33 Navigation St, Birmingham
Employed BAILEY R.
See also FIELD & SON Robert★
Known to have sold: microscope
Sources: Pg; Brown O (1986) no. 27

FIELD Thomas
w 1770–1781
Steelyard M
1770–1775   63 Deritend, Birmingham
1777–1781   58 Deritend, Birmingham
Known to have sold: Steelyard
Sources: By; PR; Sket (MAC); inst (pv)

FIELD & SON
w 1809–1811
Optician, Watch M
1809–1811   2 Bond St, Bath
Took over from FIELD James★
Sources: Be

FIELD & SON Robert
w 1845–1863
Optician, Baro M, Thermo M, Telescope M,
Microscope M
1845–1851   113 New St, Birmingham
See also FIELD Robert★
Ex.1851

Known to have sold: microscope, pantograph, compass (magnetic), sundial
Instruments advertised: microscope
Sources: K; Mor; Sl; Cat. 1851 (MAC); Brown O (1986) no. 223; Holbrook (1992) p. 103, 219

FINLAY Robert
w 1846–1850
Optical IM, Math IM, Phil IM
1846–1847   46 John St, Glasgow
1848   225 George St, Glasgow
1849–1850   87 London St, Glasgow
See also FINLAY William★
Sources: Bryden (1972) p.48

FINLAY William
w 1820–1834
Math IM
1820–1834   65 George St, Glasgow
See also FINLAY Robert★
Sources: Pg; Bryden (1972) p.48

FINLAYSON John
w 1743
Math IM, Optical IM
1743   Edinburgh
Known to have sold: thermometer, microscope
Sources: inst NMS; Bryden (1972) p.11, 48

FINNEY Joseph
fr 1733 d 1772
Clock M, Baro M
1761   Newmarket, Liverpool
1766–1772   Finney (?) Lane, Thomas St, Liverpool
Succeeded by HARRISON Thomas (I)★
Known to have sold: pyrometer, astronomical clock, barometer
Sources: G; LM index (MAC); Loomes (1975)

FINNIE Joseph
w 1818–1825
Optician
Alternative name: I. FINNEY
1818   5 Bank St, Edinburgh
1819–1825   3 North Bank St, Edinburgh
Succeeded by FINNIE & LIDDLE★
Known to have sold: barometer
Sources: Pg; Bryden (1972) p.48; Goodison (1977) p.321

FINNIE & LIDDLE Joseph & William
w 1826–1827
Optical IM
1826–1827   3 North Bank St, Edinburgh
Succeeded by LIDDLE William
Took over from FINNIE Joseph★
Sources: Bryden (1972) p.48

FISH John
s 1693 w 1702
[Scale M]
   London
Guild: Blacksmiths, fr nd
Apprenticed to WILFORD David (I)★ 1693
Sources: GL: BKC 2886/3 (MAC)

FISH Robert
fl 1830
[Chrono M]
   13 Mill St, Hanover Square, London
Sources: Taylor (1966) p.448

FISHER Robert
fr 1806
Smith
   Glasgow
Guild: Hammermen
Known to have sold: balance
Sources: Lumsden & Aitken (1912) p.302

FISHER Thomas
w 1629
Spec M
   London
Guild: u & Spectaclemakers
Founder Warden of SMC
Sources: GL: SMC 5214

FISHER William
fr 1652 w 1675
Book S, Instrument S
   Tower Hill, London
Guild: Stationers, fr 1652
Apprenticed to LUGGER William 1645
Had apprentice MOUNT Richard 1670
Took over from LUGGER William
Publisher
Sources: McKenzie (1974) p.57, 104; Taylor (1954) p.211, 364, 374, 379, 386, 404

FISHER & SON Thornton
w 1844–1847
Optician
1844–1847   South Quay, Yarmouth
Known to have sold: level
Sources: K; Wh; ChrSK 19 Nov 1987 lot 313

FISHWICK Charles
w 1839–1851
Math IS, Chandler, Naut IS
1839   Naval Quay, Hull
1841–1851   West End Old Dock, Hull
Sources: Pg; Stn; Wh

FITCH James (I)
w 1779
Math IM
1779   Middleton's Buildings, St.Mary le Bone, London
Guild: [Stationers]
Father of FITCH James (II)★
Apprenticed to
FRANKLIN Thomas★, his uncle, 1732
BENNETT John (I)★ 1735 [rebound],
Sources: McKenzie (1978) p.29,130,311; GL: CH 12876/3

FITCH James (II)
w pt 1818–1819
Math IM
1779   Middleton's Buildings, St Marylebone, London
1819   20 Crown Court, Princes St, Soho, London

Guild: [Stationers]
Son of FITCH James (I)★
Partnership: FITCH & JONES★
Apprenticed to SEARCH James★ 1779
Sources: Routledge (1818) (DJB); R (JAC); McKenzie (1978) p. 311

FITCH & JONES James & John
w 1818–1819
Math IM
   Crown Court, Soho, London
   20 Crown St, Princes St, Soho, London
Succeeded by JONES John (IV)★
Took over from WELLINGTON Alexander★
See also FITCH James★
Sources: R (JAC); Routledge (1818) title p.(DJB)

FITTON Alexander
w 1781–1787
Math IM, Phil IM, Optical IM
1787   60 Paul St, Cork
See also FITTON Francis
Sources: Burnett & Morrison-Low (1989) p.146

FITTON Francis
w 1784–1795
Math IM
1784   Gratton St, Cork
1787   36 Paul St, corner of Half-Moon St, Cork
See also FITTON Alexander★
Known to have sold: octant
Sources: Burnett & Morrison-Low (1989) p.147

FITTON W.
w 1773
   Cork
Known to have sold: octant
Sources: ATG 4 Oct 1987 (MAC)

FITZGERALD Michael
w 1820
Land surveyor, Math IM
1820   Sullivan's Quay, Cork
Sources: Burnett & Morrison-Low (1989) p.147

FLANAGAN Patrick
w 1820–1834
Math IM
1820–1834   13 Fishamble St, Dublin
Sources: Pg; Burnett & Morrison-Low (1989) p.124

FLEMING Gilbert
w 1845
Optician
1845   36 King St, Holborn, London
Sources: PO

FLEMING John
w 1845–1855
Math IM, Quadrant M
1845–1849   191 Ratcliff Highway, London
1850   191 St George's St, [change of street name only] London
1855   23 Cannon St, St George's East, London
Sources: PO

FLETCHER –
w 1744
Instrument S
1744   The Turl, Oxford
Associated with MARTIN Benjamin★
Sources: Millburn (1976) p.39, 40

FLETCHER James
fr 1787 w 1806
Scale M, Scale Beam M
1787   Beer Lane, Flower St, London
1806   11 Gloucester St, Commercial
           Road, London
Guild: Blacksmiths, fr 1787
Apprenticed to KING Thomas 1780
Sources: GL: STTP 2934 fol 130; BKC 2881/16
(MAC)

FLETCHER John (I)
a 1740–1750
Painter, Instrument S, Chart S, Ship chandler,
Book S
           High St, Hull
Sources: TCd (MAC)

FLETCHER John (II)
w 1832–1851
Chrono M, Watch M, Clock M
           54 Whiskin St, London
1839   14 Chapel St, Pentonville, London
1851   48 Lombard St, City, London
Known to have sold: chronometer
Sources: Taylor (1966) p.449; Pg; PO; Loomes
(1976); inst NMM

FLETCHER Peter
w 1851
Globe M
1851   11 South St, Andrew St, Edinburgh
Ex.1851
Known to have sold: globe
Sources: Cat. 1851 (MAC)

FLETCHER Samuel
fr 1804 w 1811
Scale M
1804–1811   15 Rolls Buildings, Fetter Lane,
           London
Guild: Haberdashers, fr 1804
Apprenticed to MOFFETT James Thomas★ 1782
Sources: GL: HC 15857/3, 15860/9

FLETCHER William
w 1824–1839
Scale M, Weight M
1824   1 Princes St, Whitechapel, London
1839   9 Osborne St, Whitechapel, London
Father of FLETCHER William Francis★
Sources: DH: DPC Ap/Fr; Pg

FLETCHER William Francis
w 1834
Scale M
1834   1 Flower and Dean St, Brick Lane,
           Whitechapel, London
Guild: Drapers, fr 1834
Son of FLETCHER William★
Apprenticed to BROOKS William★ 1824

Had apprentice VANDERSTEEN J. 1834
Sources: DH: DPC Ap/Fr, index

FLINDALL John (I)
w 1792–1805
Spec M
1805   Christopher Alley, Wilson St,
           Finsbury Square, London
1792   (?Residence) Tewin, Herts
Guild: Spectaclemakers, fr 1782
Son of FLINDALL John, labourer, of
Hartingfordbury, Herts
Apprenticed to RIBRIGHT Thomas (I)★1769
Had apprentice FLINDALL John (II), his son, 1792
Described as Gentleman at son's binding, 1792
Sources: GL: SMC 5213/3, 5213/4; H

FLINT Thomas
w 1837–1848
Math IM, Naut IM, Ship chandler
1837   31 Whitefriargate, Hull
1841–1848   34 Whitefriargate, Hull
Known to have sold: octant
Sources: Pg; Stn; Wh; inst SM

FLOCKHART James
w 1825–1826
Optician
1825–1826   Printers Place, Bermondsey, London
Attended London Mechanics Institute, 1825–1826
Sources: LMIR (AM)

FLOWER –
w 1771
Math IM
1771   Bow Lane, Cheapside, London
Sources: *General Evening Post* 1771 (MAC)

FLOWER Christopher (I)
w 1650
1650   In the Bulwark by the Tower,
           London
See also
FLOWER Thomas★
FLOWER W.★
FLOWER Samuel★
HONE Joseph★
Known to have sold: slide rule
Sources: Taylor (1954) p.236

FLOWER Christopher (II)
w 1683 d c. 1692
Spec M
           London
Guild: Spectaclemakers, fr 1679
Father of FLOWER John★
Son of FLOWER Thomas, yeoman, of Bulkington,
Wilts
Husband of FLOWER Mary★
Apprenticed to SPENCER William (I)★1671
Had apprentice WILDE William 1689, taken over
by FLOWER Mary★
Worked for SPENCER William (I)★
b c. 1655
Sources: GL: SMC 5213/1

FLOWER John
w 1734 v 1757

[Spec M]
      London
Guild: Spectaclemakers, fr 1712
Son of FLOWER Christopher (II)★
Had apprentice TEALBY or SEALBY Robert 1734
Master SMC 1734–1735
Sources: GL: SMC 5213/2 p.79+

FLOWER Mary
w 1693–1697
Spec M
1693–1695   Bishopsgate St, London
Guild: [Spectaclemakers]
Wife of FLOWER Christopher (II)★
Had apprentice WILDE William, taken over from
FLOWER Christopher (II)★
SKINNER Hezekiah 1695
Took over from FLOWER Christopher (II)★
Sources: GL: SMC 5213/1, 5213/2 p.3,8

FLOWER Samuel
a 1600–1700
See also FLOWER Thomas★
FLOWER W.★
FLOWER Christopher (I)★
Known to have sold: quadrant
Sources: Taylor (1954) p.229

FLOWER Thomas
w 1642
Alternative name: FLOWRE
1642   The Dyall in the Bulwark by the
           Tower, London
See also
FLOWER Christopher (I)★
FLOWER W.★
FLOWER Samuel★
Known to have sold: rule
Sources: Bond (1642) (SJ)

FLOWER W.
w 1646

[Math IM]
1646   In the Bulwark near the Tower,
           London
See also
FLOWER Thomas★
FLOWER Christopher (I)★
FLOWER Samuel★
HONE Joseph★
Sources: Bryden (1992) p.327 & n

FOLETTI Michael
w 1845–1849
Baro M, Thermo M, Looking glass M
1845   88 Curtain Road, London
1849   4 & 5 Bateman's Row, Shoreditch,
           London
Sources: PO

FOLLENFANT John James
w 1845–1885
Optician, Spectacle M
Alternative name: J. or J.J.
1845–1885   6 Fieldgate St, Whitechapel, London
Guild: Spectaclemakers, fr 1874 by purchase
Son of FOLLENFANT John James, tide waiter, d, of

Stepney, London
Sources: PO; GL: SMC 5213/8

FONTANA Charles
w 1842–1853
Clock M, Watch M, Toy dealer
1842–1847   Pauls Row, High Wycombe
1853   Church St, High Wycombe
Known to have sold: barometer
Sources: Goodison (1977) p.321; Legg (1975)

FOOT Samuel
w 1805
Math IM, Cutler
1805   7 New St, Horsleydown, London
Sources: H

FORBER Joshua
w 1837
Chrono M
Alternative name: FORBES ??
1837   89 Park Lane, Liverpool
Sources: Taylor (1966) p.471; Loomes (1976)

FORBES –
w 1840
[Scale M]
            Edinburgh
Sources: *Mechanics Magazine* 1840 p.47(MAC)

FORD John
w 1851–1855
Naut IM
1851–1855   177 Shadwell High St, London
Guild: [Masons]
Apprenticed to COOK William★
See also FORD William (II)★
Same premises as COOK William★
Known to have sold: octant
Sources: GL: MC 5312, 5304/6; PO; Wk; Taylor
(1966) p.362

FORD Richard
w 1767–1774
Blacksmith, Scale M, Lathe M
1774   27 Little Charles St, Birmingham
Succeeded by FORD,WHITMORE & BRUNTON★
Pat. impressing 1769
Known to have sold: balance.
Instruments advertised: balance
Sources: Sy (MAC); inst (pv); Broadbent (1949)
p.11

FORD William (I)
w 1748–1793
Optician
1764   Cannon St, London
1784–1793   8 Crooked Lane, Fish Street Hill,
            London
Guild: Spectaclemakers, fr 1743
Son of FORD William, mariner, of Southwark,
London
Apprenticed to BRAWN Mary★ 1729
Had apprentice:
SIMONS Daniel★ 1748
NEWTON John 1752
PALMER James 1762
TAYLOR Griffin 1764

Petitioner against Dollond's patent 1764
Known to have sold: telescope
Sources: PRO: PC 1/7 no.94; BW; inst(s);
GL:SMC 5213/2 p.207, 5213/3 p.56,125,175+;
6031/1

FORD William (II)
w 1839
Math IM
1839   4 Potters Fields, Tooley St, London
Attended London Mechanics Institute 1839
Sources: LMIR (AM)

FORD, WHITMORE & BRUNTON
c 1775 w 1798
Alternative name: FORD & CO. ?
            27 Charles St, Birmingham
Succeeded by WHITMORE & SONS William
Took over from FORD Richard★
Sources: BrumL: TCd; Roberts (1976) p. 4 (MAC)

FORNELLI Andrew
w pt 1836–1838
Baro M
1836–1838   Grainger St, Newcastle upon Tyne
Partnership: MASTAGLIO, FORNELLI &
MOLTENI★
Sources: Ric

FORRESTER James
w 1829–1832
Phil IM
1829–1832   29 London St, Fitzroy Square,
            London
Attended London Mechanics Institute 1829–1832
Sources: LMIR (AM)

FORSKETT Robert
w 1758–1792
Spec M
Alternative name: FORSKET, FOSKETT
1772   Little Greenwich, Aldersgate St,
            London
1792   At Mr Dollond's, London
Guild: Spectaclemakers, fr 1758
Son of FORSKETT Margaret, widow, of London
Apprenticed to TOMLINSON James★ 1751
Had apprentice:
FORSKETT George 1758
ADAMS Amos 1780
GUTTERIDGE John 1788 t/o 1788
ROBERTSHAW John 1790 t/o 1790
MERCHANT Joseph 1792
FORSKETT William, his son, 1792
WADDINGTON Benjamin 1792
Worked for DOLLOND Peter & John★
d 1800
Sources: GL: SMC, 5213/3, 5213/4

FORSTER Clement
fr 1682 d 1698
Math IM
Alternative name: FOSTER
1694   At Mr.Davis's, near Painter's Coffee
            House in Salisbury Court, Fleet St,
            London
Guild: Clockmakers, fr 1682
Apprenticed to WYNNE Henry★ 1670

Had apprentice:
KNOTT Robert 1682/3
NETHERWOOD Job 1686
SHAW Edward 1689
Sources: Bryden (1992) p.310; Brown J. (1979b)
p.30

FOSTER Daniel
a 1700
[Compass M]
            Near Wapping Old Stairs, London
Known to have sold: compass (magnetic)
Sources: inst NMM

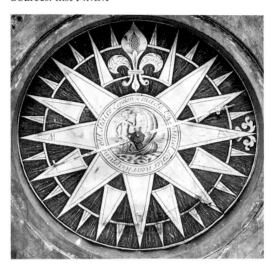

FOSTER Edward
w 1777–1785
Clock M, Math IM
1777–1785   Carlisle
Known to have sold: planetarium
Sources: DJB

FOSTER John (I)
w 1823–1848
Optician, Math IM, Stationer
1823–1829   21 Wapping, Liverpool
1831–1832   22 Wapping, Liverpool
1834–1841   70 Sparling St, Liverpool
1834   43 Sparling St, Liverpool
1837   33 Strand St, Liverpool
1848   52 South Castle St, Liverpool
See also
FOSTER & CO John★
FOSTER Jonathan★
FOSTER John (II)★
Sources: G; Pg; Sl

FOSTER John (II)
w 1837–1845
Chrono M, Watch M
1837   5 Williamson Square, Liverpool
1839–1845   7 Williamson Square, Liverpool
See also FOSTER John (I)★
Sources: G

FOSTER Jonathan
w 1845–1859
Naut IM

FOSTER Thomas (I)

1845–1846	7 Redcross St, Liverpool
1847	52 South Castle St, Liverpool
1849–1851	18B South John St, Liverpool
1859	16 South Castle St, Liverpool

Sources: G

FOSTER Thomas (I)

w 1761–1771
Turner, Hourglass M

| 1761 | Near the Gully Hole, Houndsditch, London |
| 1771 | Houndsditch, London |

Guild: Spectaclemakers, fr 1761 by purchase
Had apprentice:
PETERS William 1771
BOVIER/BOUVIER Samuel 1771
Sources: GL: SMC 6028, 5213/3

FOSTER Thomas (II)

w 1839
Measure M

| 1839 | Market Place, Luton |

Sources: Pg

FOSTER W.

w 1690

Not known
Known to have sold: perpetual calendar
Sources: Webster (1986); inst MHS

FOSTER & CO. John

w 1824
Printer, Stationer, Naut IM

| 1824 | 21 Wapping, Liverpool |

See also FOSTER John (I)★
Sources: Bn

FOUBISTER Thomas

w 1710–1730
Bismar M

Kirkwall

Guild: Hammermen
Had apprentice AITKEN Thomas,
Took over from TAIT William, Deacon of
Hammermen
Sources: Record of Court Action by Alexander,
Earl of Galloway, 12 Nov 1757, p.226(MAC)

FOWLER John (I)

w 1721–1750
Math IM

| 1728–1738 | The Globe, Sweetings [Swithins] Alley by the Royal Exchange, London |
| 1750 | The Globe by the Royal Exchange, London |

Guild: Masons, fr 1720
Son of FOWLER Thomas, gardener, of Middx
Apprenticed to SAUNDERS Samuel (I)★
Had apprentice GREGORY Henry (I)★
Known to have sold: compass
Sources: PRO: IR 1/1 fol.57; GL: MC 5312,
5304/2, 5308 (MAC); BM: Heal 105/42; Turner
G. (1980) p.38

FOWLER John (II)

w 1759
Math IM

| 1759 | Dublin |

Sources: Burnett & Morrison-Low (1989) p.124

FOWLER T.

a 1700

Royal Exchange, London

Known to have sold: compass
Sources: Webster R & M (1986)

FOWLER William

w 1825
Rule M, Gauging IM

| 1825 | At the Bell, Hillgrove St, Bristol |

Sources: Mat

FOXON William

w 1772

Deptford, London
Pat. ship's log 1772

Known to have sold: log
Sources: Woodcroft (1854); Wynter & Turner
(1975) p.87–89

FRANCE Archer

w 1836–1838
Rule M

6 White St, London
72 Bethnal Green Rd, London

Sources: Pg (JAC)

FRANCIS George

w 1826–1844
Optician, Math IM, Phil IM

	101 Regent St, London
	103 Regent St, London
1826–1829	93 Berwick St, Soho, London
	96 Berwick St, Soho, London
1840	92 Berwick St, Soho, London

Attended London Mechanics Institute 1826–1829
Sources: R; Th; LMIR (AM); JAC

FRANCKS B.

w 1826–1845
Optician, Foreign Commission Agent

1826	10 Richmond Place, Edinburgh
1828–1829	8 Heriot Place, Edinburgh
1830–1840	22 St.Patrick Square, Edinburgh
1841–1845	1 Elm Row, Edinburgh

Sources: ADCS

FRANKHAM Richard & Henry

w 1829–1855
Baro M, Thermo M

| 1829 | 11 Wilson St, Greys Inn Rd, London |
| 1839–1855 | 12 Wilson St, Greys Inn Rd, London |

Succeeded by FRANKHAM & WILSON
Known to have sold: barometer
Sources: PO; R

FRANKLIN Jacob Abraham

w 1834–1838
Optician, Phil IM, Math IM

| 1834–1838 | 1 St.Ann's Place, Manchester |

Sources: Pg

FRANKLIN Thomas

w 1702–1732
Math IM
Alternative name: FRANKLYN, FRANCKLYNE

1710–1720	London Bridge, London
1716	Parish of St.Andrew, Holborn, London
1728–1732	Gravel Lane, Houndsditch, London
1732	Parish of St.Botolph, Aldgate, London

Guild: Stationers, fr 1702
Related to FITCH James (I)★
Apprenticed to CARTER Henry★ 1694
Had apprentice:
WHEELER John 1702
BAXTER George 1705
BETTESWORTH Peter★ 1707
ADAMS George (IV) 1710
DODSON or DOBSON John 1713
RISDELL William 1713
LADLEY Joseph 1715/16
FARRER John 1716 by t/o from HARRISON Joseph★
HOWELL James 1718 or 1719 from HARRISON
Joseph★
UPTON John 1719/20
WHITTYAT Roger★ by t/o from JOLE Robert★
BENNETT John (I)★ 1723
CHAPMAN Michael★ 1728
HIGGINBOTHAM Joseph★ 1729 by t/o from
AUSTIN Samuel★
FITCH James (I)★, his nephew, 1732, rebound to
BENNETT John (I)★ 1735
Sources: McKenzie (1978) p.65,130; Brown J
(1979a) p.32; GL: CH12876/3

FRANKS Abraham

w 1835–1841
Optician

| 1841 | 33 Hick St, Newcastle under Lyme |

See also FRANKS Charles★
Sources: Pg

FRANKS Aubrey & Isaac

w 1838
Optician
Alternative name: FRANCKS

| 1838 | 114 Deansgate, Manchester |

See also
FRANKS Jacob★
FRANKS Abraham★
Sources: Pg

FRANKS Charles

w 1834
Optician, Umbrella M, Coin S, Clothes S
Alternative name: FRANCS

| 1834 | Hick St, Newcastle under Lyme |

See also FRANKS Abraham★
Sources: Bn

FRANKS Jacob

w 1824–1841
Optician, Clothes S
Alternative name: FRANCKS

1824–1825	378 Oldham Rd, Manchester
1838	25 St.Mary's Gate, Manchester
1838–1841	114 Deansgate, Manchester

See also FRANKS Aubrey & Isaac★

Known to have sold: microscope
Sources: Bn; Pg; inst MSIM

FRANTING Henry Neale
a 1700–1710
Scale M
                    St. Bartholomew Lane near the
                    Royal Exchange, London
See also NEALE Henry★
Known to have sold: balance
Instruments advertised: balance
Sources: inst noted by MAC

FRASER A. & H.
w 1816
Optician
Alternative name: concurrent with FRASER
Alexander
1816   3 New Bond St, London
See also
FRASER Alexander★
FRASER William (I)★
Known to have sold: barometer
Sources: H; Und; inst (s)

FRASER Alexander
w 1812–1818
Optician
1812–1818   3 New Bond St, London
Related to FRASER William★
Succeeded by GRICE William Hawks★
Took over from FRASER & SON★
See also
FRAZIER★
FRASER A. & H.★
R.apt Geo.III 1812
Sources: PRO: LC/3/68 p. 131; PO

FRASER J.
w 1826–1828
Optical IM, Phil IM, Math IM
1826–1828   95 Wardour St, Soho, London
See also
FRASER William (II)★
FRAZIER★
Sources: R(JAC)

FRASER John
w 1700
Known to have sold: sundial
Sources: Taylor (1954) p. 298; Loomes (1981b)

FRASER William (I)
w 1780–1805
Optical IM, Math IM
Alternative name: FRAZER, FRAZIER, FRASIER,
                    Ferguson's Head, 3 New Bond St,
                    London
1780–1805   3 New Bond St, London
1780   Duke's Court, St.Martin's Lane,
                    London
Related to FRASER Alexander★
Partnership: McCULLOCH & FRAZER★
Employed SMITH James (II)★
Succeeded by FRASER & SON★
See also
FRASER A. & H.★
FRAZIER★

R.apt Geo.III 1796–1812; d 1812
Known to have sold: waywiser, sundial,
chondrometer
Sources: Millburn (1988a) p.259–60; PRO:
IR1/28 (AM); LC3/68 p.32; BM: Banks
105/17–20; Kt; Ld; PO; Sby 2 Oct 1984 lot 110

FRASER William II
w 1823–1825
Optician
1823   25 Wardour St, Soho, London
1824   26 Wardour St, Soho, London
1825   94 Wardour St, Soho, London
See also
FRASER J.★
FRAZER I.★
Sources: Pg; Kt(JAC)

FRASER & SON William
w 1805–1812
Optician
Alternative name: concurrent with FRASER & CO.
Wm. 1808–13
1805–1813   3 New Bond St, London
Succeeded by FRASER Alexander★
Took over from FRASER William★
See also
GRICE William Hawks★
DIXEY G. & C.★
FRASER A. & H.★
R.apt Prince of Wales; William d 1812
Known to have sold: chondrometer, pantograph
Sources: BM: Heal 105/35; Kt; PO; Holbrook
(1992) p. 159, 195

FRASER & SONS
w 1814–1818
Optician
Alternative name: concurrent with FRASER
Alexander
1814–1818   3 New Bond St, London
See also
FRASER Alexander★
FRASER & SON William★
FRASER A. & H.★
Known to have sold: sundial
Sources: Kt; J; inst noted by MAC

FRAZIER -
w 1777
Math IM
1777   Duke's Court, St.Martin's Lane,
                    London
Sources: GL: Sun 11936/254 no. 380889 (MAC)

FREELY William
w 1832
Optician
1832   Commercial Road, London
Attended London Mechanics Institute 1832
Sources: LMIR (AM)

FREEMAN Edward
w 1817–1818
Rule M
1817–1818   87 Long Lane, Smithfield, London
Sources: J (MAC)

FREEMAN Henry
fl 1817–1838
Optical IM, Math IM, Phil IM
Alternative name: probably error for FREEMAN
William Henry★
Sources: Taylor (1966) p. 393

FREEMAN Rebecca
w 1714
[Scale M]
                    London
Guild: Blacksmiths
Wife of FREEMAN Samuel (I)★
Mother of FREEMAN Samuel (II)★
Took over from FREEMAN Samuel (I)★
Had apprentice BOND John 1714
Sources: GL: BKC 2886/4 (MAC)

FREEMAN Samuel (I)
w 1676 d 1709
Scale M   Ye Plow over against Ye Pewter Pot
                    in Leadenhall St, London
1684   Parish of St Andrew Undershaft,
                    London
Guild: Blacksmiths, fr 1676 or 1677
Father of
FREEMAN Samuel (II)★
FREEMAN William, s 1711/12 to JEPSON Henry
Related to FREEMAN Samuel (III)★
Had apprentice:
POLLARD Thomas★ by t/o nd
BENNETT William (II)★ 1685
FREEMAN Samuel (II)★, his son, 1706
4 other apprentices 1685–1706
Succeeded by FREEMAN Samuel (II)★
Sources: PRO: IR 1/1 fol.47; ART

FREEMAN Samuel (II)
w 1721–1752
Scale M
                    Leadenhall St, London
Guild: Blacksmiths, fr 1716
Father of FREEMAN Samuel (III)★
Apprenticed to FREEMAN Samuel (I), his father,
1706
Had apprentice:
WADE Thomas★ 1732
WORNELL John★ 1736
WALKER John by t/o from WILFORD David (II)★
nd
TURVEY William 1745 by t/o from BATE Richard
(I)★
FREEMAN Samuel (III)★, his son 1734 by t/o from
FREEMAN John of GSC
6 other apprentices 1721–1750
Succeeded by FREEMAN & SON★
Bap 1691; Partnership 1752–1757; d 1757; B.apt
Ordnance & Mint
Sources: ART; GL: BKC 2881/10 (MAC);
Millburn (1992) p. 41–42

FREEMAN Samuel (III)
c 1762 w 1780
Scale M
1772–1780   117 Leadenhall St, London
Guild: Goldsmiths, fr 1741
Son of FREEMAN Samuel (II)★
Apprenticed to FREEMAN John 1734, t/o to

FREEMAN Samuel (II)★
Related to FREEMAN Samuel (I)★
Partnership: FREEMAN & SON★
Succeeded by FREEMAN & NEW★
See also NEW William★
Bap 1715; d 1780 or 1781; b. apt Royal Mint
Sources: ART; GH: GSC Ap/Fr

FREEMAN Samuel (IV)
w 1744–1756
Math IM
1744–1756   St. Mary's parish, Aylesbury
Guild: [Joiners]
Son of FREEMAN Samuel, victualler, of Aylesbury
Apprenticed to CARTON William★ 1723
Sources: GL: JC 8052/4; St. Mary Aylesbury, bap
(JRM)

FREEMAN William Henry
w 1817–1840
Optician, Spec M
1817–1822   5 New Inn Yard, Shoreditch,
              London
              2 New Inn Yard, Curtain Rd,
              Shoreditch, London
1834–1840   3 New Inn Yard, Curtain Rd,
              Shoreditch, London
              1 Frederick Place, Islington, London
              1 Sands Buildings, Islington, London
Sources: Bn; J; PO (JAC)

FREEMAN & NEW
w 1780–1782
Scale M
-1782   Leadenhall St, London
See also
FREEMAN Samuel (III)★
NEW William★
FREEMAN & SON★
Known to have sold: balance
Instruments advertised: balance
Sources: inst with TCd noted by MAC

FREEMAN & SON
w 1752 c 1762
Scale M
              Leadenhall St, London
See also
FREEMAN Samuel (I)★
FREEMAN Samuel (II)★
FREEMAN & NEW★
NEW William★
B.apt. Mint, Exchequer, Bank of England
Known to have sold: balance
Instruments advertised: balance, weights
Sources: inst. Lincoln Mu (MAC) Phlps; 3 Mar
1992 lot 149

FREETH –
fl 1770–1824
Known to have sold: drawing instruments
Sources: inst (s)

FRENCH Robert
w 1759–1777
Scale M, Steelyard M
1767–1776   35 Digbeth, Birmingham
1770–1777   28 Digbeth, Birmingham

Had apprentice BEACH Thomas
Known to have sold: balance
Sources: Sket; Sy; inst (pv); Broadbent (1949)
(MAC)

FRENCH Santiago James Moore
w 1822–1844
Clock M
1822–1839   14–15 Sweetings Alley, Royal
              Exchange, London
1825   East Side Royal Exchange, London
1840–1844   80 Cornhill, London
Guild: Clockmakers
Took part in chronometer trials
Known to have sold: barometer, thermometer,
spirit level, chronometer
Sources: CUL: RGO 1143 fol. 4–6; PO;
Goodison (1977) p. 322

FREWEN –
w 1672
Rule S
1672   Next the sign of the Naked Boy in
              Cheapside, London
Associated with CATER Widow★ who supplied
sundials
Known to have sold: sundial
Sources: GL:CKC 2710/1 p. 244; Loomes (1981b)

FRITH Peter
w 1829–1837
Optician
              8 Cursitor St, Chancery Lane,
              London
              50 Hatton Garden, London
See also
FRITH & CO. Peter★
FRITH BROTHERS★
Sources: PO

FRITH & CO. Peter
w 1814–1885
Optician, Math IM, Powder flask M, Shot belt M,
Baro M, Telescope M, Naut IM
Alternative name: FRITH & COURTENAY
              5 Bartlett's Buildings, Holborn,
              London
1814–1834   Arundel St, Sheffield
1822–1828   37 Arundel St, Sheffield
1825   58 Arundel St, Sheffield
1822–1826   8 Cursitor St, Chancery Lane,
              London
1837   32 Arundel St, Sheffield
1841–1854   83 Arundel St, Sheffield
1841–1857   81 Arundel St, Sheffield
See also
FRITH & ROBINSON★
FRITH BOTHERS★
As Peter Frith (London) 1829–1837
Sources: Bk; Ge; Pg; PO; Wh; Wk; Calvert (1971)
p. 23

FRITH & ROBINSON
w 1805
Optician, Powder Flask M
1805   7 West Bar, Sheffield
See also FRITH & CO. Peter★
Sources: H

FRITH BROTHERS
w 1841–1845
Optical IM, Phil IM, Math IM, Optician, Powder
Flask M
1841   105 Arundel St, Sheffield
1845   46 Lisle St, London
1845   and Arundel St, Sheffield
Succeeded by FRITH & CO Peter★
Associated with GREATBACH J. (agent)
Sources: Pg; PO

FRODSHAM Charles
w 1830–1839
Chrono M
              27 South Molton St, London
1830–1833   4 Change Alley, Cornhill, London
1839   7 Finsbury Pavement, London
Guild: Clockmakers, fr 1854
Brother of FRODSHAM John★
FRODSHAM Henry★
Apprenticed to FRODSHAM William James 1824
Succeeded by ARNOLD & FRODSHAM★
See also PARKINSON & FRODSHAM★
Admiralty award 1831 chronometers; b 1810
Known to have sold: chronometer, course indicator
Sources: Atkins (1931) p.335; Baillie (1951);
CUL: RGO 1143 fol. 9–10; inst (s)

FRODSHAM Henry
w 1835–1856
Optician, Math IM, Chrono M, Naut IM, Clock
M, Watch M
1835–1837   38 Castle St, Liverpool
1839–1841   40 Castle St, Liverpool
1845–1856   17 South Castle St, Liverpool
Guild: [Clockmakers]
Brother of
FRODSHAM John★
FRODSHAM Charles★
FRODSHAM George,
Apprenticed to FRODSHAM William James 1823
Succeeded by FRODSHAM & KEEN★
See also PARKINSON & FRODSHAM★
Known to have sold: barometer, octant
Sources: G; Sl; inst LM; Bennett (1983a) no. 140

FRODSHAM John (I)
fl 1830 d 1849
[Chrono M]
              33 Gracechurch St, London
Guild: Clockmakers, fr 1822
Son of FRODSHAM William★
Related to FRODSHAM William James★
Apprenticed to WILLCOCKS Richard 1798
Sources: Baillie (1951); GL: CKC 2720/1; PO

FRODSHAM John (II)
v 1831
Math IM?
1831   39 Commercial Road, London
Guild: Clockmakers?
See also apprentice of FRODSHAM William James★
Attended London Mechanics Institute 1831
Sources: LMIR; Baillie (1951) p.115

FRODSHAM William
w 1798
Watch M

1798   King's Gate St, Holborn, London
Known to have sold: balance
Sources: Baillie (1951); GL: CKC 2720/1; inst
Fitzwilliam Mu, Cambridge (MAC)

FRODSHAM William James
w pt 1801–1850
Chrono M
1839   4 Change Alley, Cornhill, London
1836   Change Alley, Cornhill, London
Guild: Clockmakers, fr 1802
Related to FRODSHAM William,
Had apprentice:
FRODSHAM Henry★ 1823
FRODSHAM William Edward 1823
FRODSHAM Charles★ 1824
FRODSHAM John 1826
HALL John Thomas 1833
BLUNT John 1838
Partnership: PARKINSON & FRODSHAM★
FRS 1839; b 1778, d 1850
Sources: Atkins (1931) p.335; Baillie (1951)

FROGGATT Benjamin
w 1845–1855
Optician
1845–1849   27 Bridgehouse Place, Newington
             Causeway, London
1849–1851   57 St John's Square, Clerkenwell,
             London
1851   25 St John's Lane, Clerkenwell,
             London
1855   5 Cumberland St, Curtain Rd,
             London
Sources: PO; Wk

FROGGATT Edwin
w 1844–1855
Optician
1845–1849   13 Charterhouse St, London
1849   13 Charterhouse St, and, Grove,
             Great Guildford St, London
1851   Grove, Great Guildford St, London
1855   57 St John's Square, Clerkenwell,
             London
1855   and 47 Myddleton Square, London
Sources: PO

FROGGATT R.T.
w 1825–1828
Optical glass M, Optician
1825–1828   Twelve O'clock, End of Wicker,
             Sheffield
See also FROGGETT Thomas★
Sources: Bk; Ge (MAC)

FROGGATT Samuel (I)
w 1821–1843
Optician, Math IM, Phil IM
             27 Bridgehouse Place, Newington
             Causeway, London
1822   14 Kirby St, Hatton Garden,
             London
1840–1843   13 Charterhouse St, West
             Smithfield, London
Succeeded by FROGGATT Edwin★
See also
FROGGATT Samuel G.★

FROGGATT Benjamin★
Sources: Pg; R (JAC)

FROGGATT Samuel (II)
w 1814–1817
Optician, Glass grinder
1814–1817   Walk Mill, Sheffield
See also FROGGATT Thomas★
Sources: Brw; WB

FROGGATT Samuel Grove
w 1832–1834
Spec glass M
1832–1834   Great Guildford St, Southwark,
             London
See also FROGGATT Samuel (I)★
Sources: R (JAC)

FROGGATT Thomas
w 1818–1854
Optician
1818   Walk Mill, Wicker, Sheffield,
1825–1841   Saville St, Sheffield
1837   12 O'Clock, Walk Mill Pickle,
             Sheffield
1837   New Inn, beer h. Saville St,
             Sheffield
1854   New Saville St, Sheffield
1854   139 Altercliffe Rd, Sheffield
See also FROGGATT R.T.★
FROGGATT Samuel (II)★
Sources: Bn; Ge; Pg; WB; Wh (MAC)

FROMANTIL Ahasuerus?
w 1656–1666
Alternative name: FROMANTEEL, FROMANTEL
1631   London
1668   Holland
Guild: Blacksmiths 1631; Clockmakers, Brother
1632
Inv. one year clock
Sources: King & Millburn (1978) p. 122, 379;
Loomes (1981b); Taylor (1954) p. 222

FROST –
w 1777–1780
Rule M
1777–1780   Great Charles St, Birmingham
See also FROST & WITHNOLL★
Sources: PR

FROST & WITHNOLL W. & T.
w 1762–1775
Rule M
Alternative name: WITHNAL, WITHNOLD
1767   Birmingham
1770–1775   14 Litchfield St, Birmingham
Took over from WOOD & LORT★
See also
FROST★
WITHNOLL William★
Sources: Sket; Sy

FROST, NOAKES & CO.
w 1851–1855
Baro M, Thermo M (steam)
1851–1855   195 Brick lane, Spitalfields, London
Sources: PO

FRY John
w 1747
Math IM
1747   In the Little Old Bailey, London
Sources: BM: Banks 105/21 (MAC)
Daily Ad 20 Apr 1747 (JRM)

FULLER John
w 1784–1822
Phil IM, Math IM
             128 Holborn Hill, London
1805   65 Chapel St, Pentonville, London
See also FULLER Joseph★
Sources: By; H; Und (JAC)

FULLER Joseph
w 1832–1836
Math IM, Phil IM
1832–1836   2 St.James's Walk, Clerkenwell,
             London
See also FULLER John★
Sources: R (JAC)

FULLOON George
w 1797 d 1823
Scale M
1792   Golden Lane, London
Guild: Blacksmiths, fr 1792
Son of FULLOON Arthur, labourer, of London
Apprenticed to VAUGHTON Christopher★ 1775
Had apprentice BAVERSTOCK Thomas 1797
Sources: GL: BKC 2881/16 & 17, 2886/5 (MAC)

FULTON A. & J.
w 1847–1854
Ironmomger, Ship Chandler, Compass M, Flag M
1847   132 Broomielaw, Glasgow
1848–1849   134 & 136 Broomielaw, Glasgow
1850–1854   136 Broomielaw, Glasgow
Sources: ADCS

FULTON John
w 1837 d 1853
Math IM
             Spoutmouth Scotland
1837–1852   London
Known to have sold: planetarium
Sources: NMS: notes; ADCS; Burnett &
Morrison-Low (1989) p.191

FURNESS John
w 1851
Math IM
1851   43 Grove St, Camden Town, London
Sources: Wk

FYFE R. & W.
w 1840–1844
Math IM
Alternative name: FYFE Robert & William Holborn
1840–1844 Glasgow
Bankrupt 1844
Sources: Clark et al (1989) p. 220–21

FYFE Robert
w pt 1840–1844
Math IM
1840–1844   Glasgow

Guild: Hammermen, fr 1841
Partnership: FYFE R. & W.
Sources: Clarke et al (1989) p.220–21; Lumsden & Aitken (1912) p.317

FYFE Samuel Holborn
w 1849–1860
Ironmonger, Ship Chandler, Flag M, Compass M
1849–1852   32 Clyde Place, Glasgow
1855–1856   42 Clyde Place, Glasgow
1858–1860   62 Clyde Place, Glasgow
Brother of FYFE Willima Holborn★
b c.1823 d 1905; bankrupt 1860
Known to have sold: compass
Sources: Clarke et al (1989) p.222–23; inst NMS

FYFE William Holborn
w pt 1840–1861+
Math IM
1841–1844   Glasgow
1849–1858   Greenock
Son of FYFE John, ship chandler, of Glasgow and Greenock
Brother of FYFE Samuel Holborn
Partnership: FYFE R. & W.★
FYFE & CO. William★
FYFE & YEO 1854–1856
MACALISTER & FYFE 1861 onwards
b c.1812 d 1868
Sources: Clarke et al (1989) p. 220–21

FYFE & CO. William
w 1849–1854
Ship Chandlers
      5 William St, Greenock
      4 East Breast, Greenock
Partnership: FYFE William★ and BURNS George, dissolved 1854★
Succeeded by FYFE & YEO
Sources: Clarke et al (1989) p.200–21

GABALIO P.
w 1808–1817
Baro M
1808   20 Cross St, Hatton Garden, London
1817   4 Cross St, Hatton Garden, London
Sources: Kt; PO (JAC)

GABLE Thomas
w 1739–1775
Scale M
      Near Creechurch in Leadenhall St, London
1739   Pear Tree St, Brick Lane, Old St, London
1741   Long Alley, Hog Lane, Shoreditch, London
1744   Long Alley, Moorfields, London
1750   Hammer, Coronet & Scales in Leadenhall St, London
1768–1775   84 Leadenhall St, London
Guild: Weavers, fr 1739
Apprenticed to JOY John★ 1726
Had apprentice PALLET Thomas★ 1755 & 8 others 1739–1766
Sources: GL: BKC 2886/4; 2885/1; WVC. 4656/7; CH: 12823/4 p.98, 456, 12823/5 p.47, 12823/6 p.81; Kt; Lg

GABORY Edmund
v 1796 d 1813
Math IM
      London
1796–1813   Hamburg
Apprenticed to RAMSDEN Jesse★
Sources: Brachner (1987) p.6

GABORY J.
w 1794
Baro M, Thermo M
1794   125 High Holborn, London
See also GABORY M★
Sources: W (JAC)

GABORY M.
w 1796
Optical IM, Phil IM
1796   125 Lower Holborn, London
See also GABORY J★
Sources: Mh (JAC)

GABRIEL William
w 1850
Rule M
1850   78 Barr St, Birmingham
Sources: Sl

GADBURY James
w 1822
Math IM
1822   Blue Coat Buildings, Christ's Hospital, London
Father of GADBURY William Bickley s 1822 IC
Sources: GL: IC 6648/8

GADLINGSTOCK Samuel
fr 1668 w 1672
1672   Exchange Alley, London
Guild: Merchant Taylors
Son of GADLINGSTOCK Samuel
Apprenticed to GADLINGSTOCK Samuel, his father
Known to have sold: rule
Sources: GL: CKC 2710 p.244; MTC MF 324; Loomes (1981 b)

GAIRNS James (I)
w 1820
Math IM
1820   Parish of St Bartholomew the Great, London
Father of GAIRNS James (II) s 1820
Sources: CWH: CWC Ap

GAITSKILL Joseph
w 1778–1811
Ship Chandler, Compass M, Math IM
      332 Wapping, London
1778–1781   309 Wapping, London
1783   Bell Alley, Wapping, London
1785   313 Wapping, London
See also GAITSKILL & CO.
Sources: H; Kt; Sun 11936/269 no. 403666; 11936/317 no. 486324

GAITSKILL & CO.
w 1805

Ship Chandler, Math IM
1805   332 Wapping, London
See also GAITSKILL Joseph★
Sources: Mh (JAC)

GALE Joseph
w 1828–1841
Baro M, Looking-glass M
      46 King St, Manchester
Sources: Goodison (1977) p. 323

GALE William
fr 1739 w 1756
      London
Guild: Blacksmiths, fr 1739
Apprenticed to NEALE John (I)★ 1732 t/o to LANE John (II)★ 1732/3 t/o to READ Samuel★ 1735
Sources: GL: BKC 2885/1, 2886/5 (MAC)

GALETI C.
a 1830–1850
      Montrose
Known to have sold: barometer
Sources: Goodison (1977) p. 323

GALL John
w 1824–1836
Hydro S, Sacch S
1824   3 North St, James St, Edinburgh
1825–1827   20 Drummond St, Edinburgh
1828–1829   43 London St, Edinburgh
1830–1836   48 London St, Edinburgh
Sources: ADCS

GALLETTI Anthony
w 1834–1872
Optician, Math IM, Jeweller, Fishing tackle M, Umbrella m, Carver, Gilder, Print S
Alternative name: GALLETI, GALLETTI, GALLATTI
1834–1837   10 Castle St, Liverpool
1839–1841   19 Castle St, Liverpool
1843   33 Castle st, Liverpool
1845–1872   17 Castle St, Liverpool
See also GALLETTI William & Anthony★
Sources: G; Pg (DJB)

GALLETTI Antoni
w 1805–1850
Carver, Gilder, Math IM, Optical IM, Phil IM
1805–1828   10 Nelson St, Glasgow
1829–1850   24 & 25 Argyle Arcade, Glasgow
Succeeded by GALLETTI John★
See also
GERLETTI Dominick★
GALETI C.★
e 1789
Known to have sold: barometer, thermometer, hydrostatic bubbles
Sources: Bryden (1972) p.48; Goodison (1977) p.323; inst(s)

GALLETTI John
w 1851–1894
Optical IM, Phil IM, Carver, Gilder
1851–1894   24 Argyle Arcade, Glasgow
Succeeded by McKNIGHT A.

Took over from GALLETTI Antoni★
See also
GERLETTI Dominick★
GARLETI C.★
Known to have sold: barometer, thermometer
Sources: Bryden (1972) p.48; Goodison (1977) p.323

GALLETTI William & Anthony
w 1823–1845
Carver, Gilder, Optician
Alternative name: GALETTI
1823–1832   10 Castle St, Liverpool
1824   (residence), 1 Great Crosshall St,
            Liverpool
1841–1845   19 Castle St, Liverpool
See also GALLETTI Anthony★
Sources: Bn; G (MAC)

GALLI Charles
fl 1821–1826
[Baro M]
            Waterloo Place, Edinburgh
Same premises as
GALLI G.★
GALLI L.★
Sources: Webster R & M (1986)

GALLI G.
a 1830–1900
[Baro M]
            Waterloo Place, Edinburgh
Same premises as
GALLI L.★
GALLI Charles★
Known to have sold: barometer
Sources: Goodison (1977) p.323

GALLI L.
[Baro M]
a 1830–1900
            Waterloo Place, Edinburgh
Same premises as
GALLI Charles
GALLI G.
Known to have sold: barometer, thermometer, level.
Sources: Sky 26 Feb 1971 lot 51 (ADCS)

GALLY G.
a 1830–1900
            Glasgow
Known to have sold: barometer
Sources: Goodison (1977) p.323

GALLY Peter & Charles
w 1838–1840
Baro M, Thermo M, Phil IM
1838–1839   50 Exmouth St, Spa Fields, London
1840   9 Turnmill St, Clerkenwell, London
See also
GALLY Peter & Paul★
GALLY & CO. P.& P.★
Sources: Pg

GALLY Peter & Paul
w 1813–1828
Looking-glass M, Picture frame M, Baro M,
Thermo M
1813–1822   9 Turnmill St, Clerkenwell, London

1828   50 Exmouth St, Spa Fields, London
Succeeded by GALLY & CO. Peter & Paul★
See also GALLY Peter & Charles★
Sources: Bn; PO; R (JAC)

GALLY & CO. Peter & Paul
w 1829–1861
Baro M, Thermo M, Looking-glass M
            3 Upper North Place, Gray's Inn
            Rd, London
1840–1845   50 Exmouth St, Spa Fields, London
1849–1859   68 Hatton Garden, London
Succeeded by GALLY Charles
Took over from GALLY Peter & Paul★
See also GALLY Peter & Charles★
Sources: PO; R (JAC)

GAMMAGE Benjamin
w 1823–1871
Hydro M, Sacch M, Stationer, Toy S
-1834   17 Clarence St, Liverpool
1824–1826   11 Clarence St, Liverpool
1824   11 Seel St, Liverpool
1841   35 Pleasant St, Liverpool
1843   32 Great Oxford St, Liverpool
1843–1857   57 Brownlow St, Liverpool
Husband of GAMMAGE Ann (nee DICAS★)
Took over from DICAS Ann
See also DICAS MANUFACTORY★
Sources: Bn; Pg; Sl; G; inst WM (MAC)

GANTHONY R.P.
fl 1825–1826
Chrono M
            83 Cheapside, London
Sources: Taylor (1966) p.421

GARDNER Henry (I)
w 1669–1672
Spec M
1670–1671   Bethlem, London
Guild: Spectaclemakers
Had apprentice: MERCER Richard 1670
Employed MERCER Richard 1670
Known to have sold: spectacles
Sources: GL: SMC 5213/1

GARDNER Henry (II)
w 1809–1835
Watch M, Clock M, Optician, Math IM, Dentist,
Jeweller
1809   27 High St, Belfast
1819–1820   65 High St, Belfast
1824–1835   57 High st, Belfast
Partnership: GARDNER & NEILL★
Sources: Burnett & Morrison-Low (1989) p.147

GARDNER J.
a 1750–1780
            Edinburgh
Known to have sold: weights.
Sources: inst (pv) (MAC)

GARDNER J. & J.
w 1799–1818
Optician, Math IM
1799–1801   Bell St, Glasgow
1803–1818   43 Bell St, Glasgow

Succeeded by GARDNER & CO. Jamieson★
See also
GARDNER John (I)★
GARDNER John (II)★
GARDNER & LAURIE★
Known to have sold: barometer
Sources: H; Bryden (1972) p.49; Goodison (1977)
p.324

GARDNER James
w 1803–1836
Math IM, Phil IM
Alternative name: GARDINER
1834–1836   5 Somerset Place, New Rd,
            Whitechapel, London
1803   Princes Place, Cannon St, New Rd,
            St George in the East, London
1807   Wellclose Lane, London
Guild: Grocers, fr 1791
Apprenticed to BROWNING Samuel (I)★1783
Had apprentice:
STURMAN Reuben 1803
CHILD Henry 1807
GARDNER William?★ son of David, 1814
WILLSMERE Jesse★ 1827
BAILEY John William★1837
Sources: GL: GC 11598/6 &/7 &/8; Pg; Brown
(1979a) p.50

GARDNER John (I)
w 1773–1790
Maltman, Math IM
1773–1790   Crawford's Land, Bell's Wynd,
            Glasgow
1773–1783   opposite Bell's Wynd, Candlerigg's,
            Glasgow
Had apprentice SYM James (I)★
See also
GARDNER John (II)★
GARDNER J. & J.★
GARDNER & LAURIE★
Instruments advertised: balance, barometer
Sources: Bryden (1972) p.20, 30, 49; Goodison
(1977) p.324; Clarke et al (1989) p.164–79

GARDNER John (II)
w 1820–1828
Math IM
1820–1828   Ayton Court, Glasgow
1820–1822   Old Vennal, Glasgow
See also
GARDNER John (I)★
GARDNER J. & J.★
Sources: Bryden (1972) p.49; Pg; Clarke et al
(1989) p.164–79

GARDNER M.
w 1825
Math IM
1825   43 Bell St, Glasgow
Sources: Pg

GARDNER Thomas
w 1680–1693
IM, Surgical IM
Alternative name: GARDENER, GARDINER
1689   St Swithins Alley, Cornhill, London
Guild: Armourers, fr 1661

Son of GARDNER Thomas, cleric, of Cottered, Herts
Apprenticed to VINCENT John 1654
Had apprentice:
BOBERT Katherine 1679/80
PORTER Robert 1684
HULL William 1688/9
GLENN Martin 1693
Sources: GL: CH 12823/1 p27; 12818/5 fol 184;
GL: ABC 12080/1 fol. 20,27,35,43; 12079/2 p.127

GARDNER William (I)

w 1846–1864
Math IM, Optical IM, Phil IM
1846–1855   3 Royal Bank Place, Glasgow
1856–1861   56 Gordon St, Glasgow
1861–1864   134 Buchanan St, Glasgow
See also
GARDNER John (II)★
GARDNER J. & J.★
Known to have sold: protractor
Sources: ChrSK 12 Dec 1985 lot 172(MAC);
Bryden (1972) p.49

GARDNER William (II)

w 1851–1865
Math IM
1851–1859   5 Somerset Place, New Rd,
             Whitechapel, London
1865   56 New Rd, Whitechapel, London
Possibly the apprentice of GARDNER James★
Sources: PO; Wk

GARDNER & CO. (I)

w 1837–1883
Math IM, Phil IM, Optical IM, Opticians
1837–1838   44 Glassford St, Glasgow
1839–1859   21 Buchanan St, Glasgow
1860–1882   53 Buchanan St, Glasgow
1883   53 St.Vincent St, Glasgow
Succeeded by GARDNER & LYLE
Took over from GARDNER & CO. M.★
e 1765; Ex.1851
Known to have sold: barometer, thermometer,
level, octant
Sources: ChrSK 29 June 1989 lot 200, Bryden
(1972) p.49; Cat. 1851; Holbrook (1992) p.120;
Clarke et al (1989) p.164–79

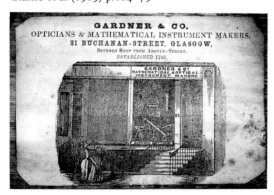

GARDNER & CO. M.

w 1823–1836
Optical IM, Math IM, Phil IM,.
Alternative name: GARDNER & SONS
1823–1825   43 Bell St, Glasgow

1826–1831   92 Bell St, Glasgow
1832–1836   44 Glassford St, Glasgow
Succeeded by GARDNER & CO. (I)★
Took over from GARDNER, JAMIESON & CO★
Known to have sold: barometer
Sources: Pg; Bryden (1972) p.49; inst (s) (MAC)

GARDNER & LAURIE John & James

w 1792 c 1798
Math IM, Phil IM, Optical IM
1792   Corner of Bell's Wynd, Glasgow
Took over from GARDNER John (I)★
See also LAURIE James★
Sources: Bryden (1972) p.49

GARDNER & NEILL Henry (II)★ & Robert

w 1809–1818
Watch M
Alternative name: GARDNER & NEIL
             Belfast
Succeeded by NEILL Robert★ & GARDNER
Known to have sold: octant
Sources: Burnett & Morrison-Low (1989) p.147

GARDNER, JAMIESON & CO.

w 1819–1822
Optical IM, Math IM
1819–1822   43 Bell St, Glasgow
Succeeded by GARDNER & CO. M.★
Took over from GARDNER J. & J.★
Sources: Pg; Bryden (1972) p.49; Clarke et al
(1989) p.165

GARGORY James

w 1835–1862
Optician, Jeweller, Goldsmith, Math IM, Mining
IM, Surveying IM, Optical IM
             Wolverhampton
1835–1845   4 Bull St, Birmingham
1850–1860   5 Bull St, Birmingham
1862   41 Bull St, Birmingham
Known to have sold: barometer, thermometer,
compass (magnetic), sextant, circumferentor, rule
Sources: K; Pg; Mor; Brown O (1982b) no.125;
Goodison (1977) p.324 Sby 9 Dec 1977 lots 87, 94

GARLAND William

w 1799–1811
Math IM
1805   134 Fetter Lane, London
1811   142 Fetter Lane, London
Sources: H; JAC

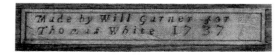

GARNER William

s 1713 w 1737
[Math IM]
Alternative name: Will
             London
Guild: [Clockmakers]
Apprenticed to HENSHAW John★ 1713
Known to have sold: back-staff
Sources: inst NMM; Brown J (1979b) p.30

GARRARD Thomas (I)

1781–1799
Math IM, Liquor S by 1803
1781   Old Gravel Lane, Ratcliff Highway,
             London
1785   36 Great Tower St, London
1796–1803   174 Ratcliff Highway, London
Guild: Grocers, fr 1781
Son of GARRARD Jeremiah, block maker of St.
George, Middx
Apprenticed to RUST Richard★ 1770
Had apprentice:
ENDERSBEE William (I)★ 1781
t/o 1785 to CHAPMAN James (I)★
KULICK Mathias 1782
GARRARD Thomas (II), his son, 1795
GARRARD Samuel, his son, 1803 [as wine and
brandy merchant]
Sources: GL: GC 11598/6; By; Ld; Brown J
(1979a) p.41, 48–49

GARRATT

w 1816
Drawing IM
1816   50 Regency Place, Manor House
             Row, Kennington, London
Associated with
WATKINS J★
HILL William★
Sources: EBA: OB 1816 (Watkins)

GARRATT John

w 1851–1855
Math IM
Alternative name: GARRETT
1851–1855   17 Albion Place, Walworth, London
Sources: PO; Wk

GARTH Richard

w 1797–1823
Math IM, Quadrant M
             Jamica Row, London
1805   376 Rotherhithe Wall, London
1816   387 Rotherhithe, London
1817   Platform, Rotherhithe St, London
Sources: Und; H; J; Kt (JAC)

GASKIN George

w 1802
Optician
1802   Edward St, Bethnal Green Road,
             London
Associated with CLERK James★ to whom son
apprenticed
Sources: Brown (1979a) p.54; GL: GC 11598/6

GASKIN John (I)

a 1806
Weaver, Math IM
             Penrith
b 1785
Sources: DJB

GASKIN John (II)

w 1832–1837
Optician
1832   23 Devereux Court, Strand, London

1835–1837   York St, Commercial Rd,
            Whitechapel, London
See also GASKIN John (III)★
Sources: R (JAC)

GASKIN John (III)

w 1776
Optician
1776   Crown Court in the Cloisters,
            London
Had apprentice: GASKIN John, his son, 1776
[?GASKIN John (II)★
Sources: GL: CH 12823/6 p.93, 12876/5 (MAC)

GASPER & JOSEPH

a 1700–1800
            17 (street illegible), Manchester
Known to have sold: barometer
Sources: ChrSK Oct 1985 (MAC)

GATCHELL Samuel

w 1794–1852
Ironmonger, Scale M, Iron S
1794–1798   11 Abbey St, Dublin
1799–1845   87 Pill Lane, Dublin
1846–1852   61 Pill Lane, Dublin
Succeeded by GATCHELL & SONS Samuel
Known to have sold: balance
Instruments advertised: weights
Sources: Pg; inst (pv); Westropp (1916) p.66; notes
from Dublin Central Library (MAC)

GATTEY Henry

w 1790
Math IM
Alternative name: GATTY
1790   5 Windsor St, Bishopsgate, London
Had apprentice BERTIE George 1790
Sources: GL: CH 12823/7 p.80; 12876/6 (MAC)

GATTY Andrew (I)

w 1796–1800
Baro M, Thermo M
1796–1798   18 Fishamble St, Dublin
1799–1800   1 Smock Alley, Dublin
Succeeded by GATTY Joseph★
See also GATTY Andrew (II)★
Sources: Burnett & Morrison-Low (1989) p.124

GATTY Andrew (II)

w 1815–1824
Baro M, Thermo M, Mirror M
1815–1819   1 Smock Alley, Dublin
1820–1822   45 Fishamble St, Dublin
1823–1824   7 Smock Alley, Dublin
Took over from GATTY Joseph★
See also GATTY Andrew (I)★
Sources: Burnett & Morrison-Low (1989) p.124

GATTY Dominico

w 1826
Baro M
1826   111 Broad St, Reading
Known to have sold: barometer, thermometer
Sources: Goodison (1977) p.325

GATTY James

c 1790

130 High Holborn, London
132 High Holborn, London
See also GATTY & MALACRIDA★
Known to have sold: barometer, thermometer,
hygrometer, spirit level.
Sources: Goodison (1977) p.149, pl.51, 92

GATTY Joseph

w 1801–1814
Baro M, Thermo M
1801–1807   1 Smock Alley, Dublin
1808   25 Fishamble St, Dublin
1811–1814   1 Smock Alley, Dublin
Succeeded by GATTY Andrew (II)★
Took over from GATTY Andrew (I)★
Sources: Burnett & Morrison-Low (1989) p.124

GATTY & MALACRIDA Charles & Charles

w 1803–1817
Baro M
1803–1817   104 High Holborn, London
See also GATTY James★
Sources: H; Kt (JAC)

GATWARD Thomas

w 1834–1853
Watch M, Clock M
1839–1846   High St, Saffron Walden
1853   Butter Market, Saffron Walden
Instruments advertised: barometer, sundial
Sources: Bod: JJ box 24; Pg; Advertisement (cpy)

GAUDIN Edward

w 1787
Scale M
1787   1 New Court, Clerkenwell, London
Sources: GL: STTP 2934 fol. 56

GAUNT Charles

w 1845–1859
Telescope M
1849–1855   34 Meredith St, Clerkenwell, London
1859   54 Red Lion St, Clerkenwell, London
Sources: PO

GAY Richard

a 1620–1700
Optical IM
            London
Father of GAY Thomas★
Succeeded by GAY Thomas★
Sources: Taylor (1966) p.119

GAY Thomas

w 1711–1732
Spec M
            Golden Spectacles, by the Sun
            Tavern behind Royal Exchange,
            London
1714–1723   Archimedes & Spectacles, near the
            Sun Tavern, behind the Royal
            Exchange, London
Guild: Spectaclemakers fr 1689/90
Son of GAY Richard★
Apprenticed to HOWE Joseph★ 1682
Had apprentice:
LOFT Matthew★ 1711
EASTLAND William★ 1718/19

FORSITH Paul 1724
Succeeded by LOFT Matthew★
Took over from GAY Richard★
Master SMC 1718–1720
Sources: GL: SMC 5213/2 p.76,108–9,117,148;
Buckley(1935) p.428; Court & Von Rohr p.73

GAYLOR Charles

w 1822
Binnacle M
1822   Providence Place, Commercial Rd,
            Limehouse, London
Sources: Und (JAC)

GEARING Richard Bates

fr 1757 c 1776
Rule M
            The Quadrant, without Newgate,
            facing the Old Bailey, London
            2 Horse Shoe Court, Cock Lane,
            West Smithfield, London
Guild: Stationers, fr 1757
Nephew of FARMER John★
Apprenticed to BATES Richard★ 1749/50
Took over from FARMER John★
Sources: Crawforth (1985) p.506

GEARY Francis

w 1805–1817
Optician, Math IM
1805–1817   Paul St, Cork
1820   Lapps Island, Cork
Sources: Burnett & Morrison-Low p.147

GEBHARDT, ROTTMANN & CO.

w 1851
Opticians
1851   29 Wood St, London
Sources: Wk

GEMINI Thomas

w 1532–1562
[Engraver]
Alternative name: LAMBRECHTS, T.G., GEMYNE,
LAMBRIT
1562   Within the Blackfriars near Ludgate,
            London
Guild: Stationers
Associated with COLE Humphrey
Used sign of Gemini as trade-mark; bookseller,
map seller
Known to have sold: astrolabe
Sources: Bryden (1992) p.301–3; Arber (1875), I,
p.1.48; Turner G (1983b) p.96–97

GENT George

w 1851–1885
Math IM
1849–1856   5 Upper Rosoman St, Clerkenwell,
            London
1857–1875   5 Upper Rosoman St, Clerkenwell,
            London EC
1880–1885   96 Rosoman St, Clerkenwell,
            London
Succeeded by GENT Frank E
Attended London Mechanics Institute 1849–51
Sources: PO; Wk; LMIR (AM)

GEORGE Alexander
w 1804
Math IM
1804   18 Bevis Marks, St.Mary Axe,
                London
Sources: Boyle

GERLETTI Dominick
w 1849–1858
Optician, Gilder, Looking-glass M, Picture frame
M, Fireworks
1849–1855   10 Candlerigg St, Glasgow
1855–1857   24 Glassford St, Glasgow
1857–1858   44 Trongate, Glasgow
See also
GALLETTI John★
GALLETTI Antoni★
Sources: Goodison (1977) p.325

GERRARD Francis
w 1824
Optician, Cutler
1824   10 Coronation Row, Salford,
                Manchester
Sources: Bn

GERRETT & CO
w 1850
Rule M
1850   147 Bath Row, Birmingham
Sources: Sl

GIBBON William
w 1827–1833
Spec M
                London
Had apprentice:
GIBBON Charles 1827
GIBBON F.W. 1833
Sources: GL: CH 12823/9 p.119, 125

GIBBONS Elizabeth
w 1845
Rule M
1845   Stafford St, Wolverhampton
See also GIBBONS William (II)★
Sources: Pg

GIBBONS William (I)
w 1719–1732
[Spec M]
Alternative name: GIBBINS
                London
Guild: Spectaclemakers, fr 1716
Son of GIBBONS Thomas, cordwainer, of Stone,
Staffs
Apprenticed to WILLDEY George★ 1708/9
Had apprentice GLOVER John 1719, t/o 1721/2 to
HARPER Andrew★
GIBBONS William, his son, 1732
See also GLOVER John A.★
d c. 1741
Sources: GL: SMC 5213/2 p.62,97,113,128,246,
6029

GIBBONS William (II)
w 1811–1835
Rule M

1811–1835   Stafford St, Wolverhampton
1818   41 Stafford St, Wolverhampton
See also GIBBONS Elizabeth★
Sources: PB; Pg; Wh

GIBBONS William (III)
w 1831
Optician
1831   15 Royal St, Lambeth, London
Attended London Mechanics Institute 1831
Sources: LMIR (AM)

GIBBS Charles
w 1851–1855
Math IM
1851–1855   30 Manchester St, Liverpool
Sources: G

GIBBS Owen
w 1767–1775
Steelyard M
1767–1775   37 Digbeth, Birmingham
Sources: Sket, Sy

GIBSON John
a 1790
Watch M, Optical IM
                Kelso
Known to have sold: telescope
Sources: ChrSK 14 Apr 1988 lot 145; Bryden
(1972) p.49

GIBSON Mary (Mrs)
w 1748–1757
Watch M, Clock M
1748   Dial & Crowns, Newgate St,
                London
Known to have sold: drawing instruments
Sources: AVS

GIBSON Thomas
fr 1757 d c.1778
Scale M
                111 Wood St, near Cheapside,
                London
Guild: Blacksmiths, fr 1757
Apprenticed to BROOKSBY Thomas (I)★ 1749/50
Had apprentice:
SQUIRE Thomas 1769 by t/o from
BROOKSBY Thomas (II)★
WHEATLEY John 1770 by t/o from BROOKSBY
Thomas (II)★ [and 4 others]
Known to have sold: balance
Sources: GL: BKC 2885/1/1, 2886/5, 2888 (MAC);
Sheppard & Musham (1975) no. 48

GIGNOUX John
w 1765–1777
Math IM
1765   Watling St, London
1766–1777   Tower Hill, London
Sources: Kt; Lg (JAC)

GILBERT Edward
fr 1794
Optician
1794   The Castle, Castle St, Holborn,
                London

Guild: Blacksmiths, fr 1794
Apprenticed to BROOKS John★ 1786
Sources: GL: BKC 2881/16 (MAC)

GILBERT John (I)
w 1719–1749
Math IM
1716   Little Tower Hill, London
1718–1750   Postern Row, Tower Hill, London
Guild: Grocers, fr 1716/17
Father of GILBERT John (II)★
Husband of GILBERT Barbara
Apprenticed to JOHNSON John 1709
Had apprentice:
CRAFORD Henry★ 1724
CRICK James★ 1728 by t/o from HADDON Wm★
PARMINTER John (I)★ 1732
GILBERT John (I)★ his son, 1737
BARTLETT John 1746, t/o to URINGS John (II)★
Succeeded by GILBERT & SON★
Partnership: 1749; d 1750
Known to have sold: back-staff
Sources: Brown J (1979a) p.34; *Penny London Post*
24 Sep 1750; inst SM; McKenzie (1978) p.140

GILBERT John (II)
w 1751 d 1791
Math IM, Optical IM, Phil IM, Optician
                The Mariner, Postern Row, 7 Tower
                Hill, London
1771   The Mariner in Postern Row, Tower
                Hill, London
1745   Postern Row, Tower Hill, London
1776–1781   12 Tower Hill, London
1782–1791   8 Postern Row, Tower Hill, London
Guild: Grocers, fr 1744/5
Father of GILBERT William (I)★
Apprenticed to GILBERT John (I)★, his father, 1737
Had apprentice:
HILL Joseph★ 1752 by t/o from GILBERT John (I)★
BAXTER William 1752
RIPLEY Thomas★ 1755
MAYLIN John 1763
GILBERT JOHN (III)★, his son, 1764
GILBERT William (I)★, his son, 1769 t/o 1769 to
DOLLOND Peter★
CHRISTIAN John 1772
BURFORD Edmund G. 1778
Took over from GILBERT & SON John★
Succeeded by GILBERT William (I)★, his son
Partnership GILBERT & SON John★ 1749
Known to have sold: barometer, hygrometer,
microscope, octant, quadrant, protractor, sextant,
thermometer
Sources: GL: SMC 5213/4; Sun 11936/300
no.458910; Kt; Ld; Lg; Mort; inst MHS; Sby 23
June 1887 lot 175; Brown (1979a) p.38–39, 83;
Calvert (1971) pl.24; Leybourn (1771) (AVS)

GILBERT John (III)
fr 1771 d 1780
Math IM, Optician
1776   33 St.Paul's Churchyard, London
1776–1780   33 Ludgate St, London
Guild: Grocers, fr 1771
Son of GILBERT John (II)★
Apprenticed to GILBERT John (II)★
Took over from LINNELL Joseph★

Sources: Kt; Ld; GMag 50 (1780) p.348; Brown J (1979a) p.39

GILBERT Thomas
fr 1809 w 1829
Optician
        148 Leadenhall St, London
1809   Leadenhall St, London
Guild: Grocers, fr 1809
Son of GILBERT William (I)★
Brother of GILBERT William (II)★
Partnership: GILBERT W. & T.★
Apprenticed to GILBERT William (I)★1801
Had apprentice SCHMALCALDER John Thomas★
1829
SCMALCALDER George 1829
Associated with SCHMALCALDER Carles A.★
Partner all his working life ?
Sources: GL: GC 11598/6, 11598/7; Brown J (1979a) p.47–48, 83

GILBERT William (I)
fr 1776 w pt 1813
Math IM, Optician
1776   8 Postern Row, Tower Hill, London
1795–1813 148 Leadenhall St, London
1805   (residence?) Stepney Green, London
Guild: Grocers, Spectaclemakers
Son of GILBERT John (II)★
Partnership: GILBERT & WRIGHT★
GILBERT, WRIGHT & HOOKE★
Apprenticed to GILBERT John (II)★ 1769 t/o
to DOLLOND Peter★ 1769
Had apprentice:
GILBERT William (II)★, his son, 1795
GILBERT Henry Robert, his son, 1798
GILBERT Thomas★, his son, 1801
GILBERT Charles★, his son, 1803, t/o to a coach maker
Succeeded by GILBERT W. & T.★
Took over from GILBERT John (II)★
Partnerships c.1790–1813; d.1813; fr by purchase SMC 1801; Master SMC 1807–1809
Sources: GL: SMC 5213/4; GC 11598/6; BW; H; Brown J (1979a) p.39, 47–48, 83

GILBERT William (II)
w 1813–1845
Optician, Math IM, Phil IM
Alternative name: William Dormer
1832   148 Leadenhall St, London
1840   97 Leadenhall St, London
1845   138 Fenchurch St, London
1802–1813 Leadenhall St, London
1826   Woodford, Essex [workshops]
Guild: Grocers, Spectaclemakers
Partnership:
GILBERT & SONS★
GILBERT W. & T.★
Apprenticed to GILBERT William (I)★ his father, 1795
Had apprentice:
LEE Thomas Dunkin 1830, GC
MURRELL William 1822 SMC
CHISLETT Alfred★ 1825 by t/o from BATE R.B.★SMC
Took over from GILBERT W. & T.★
Partnership: 1819–31; B.apt Admiralty, compass

M; fr GC 1802, fr SMC by purchase 1813; bankrupt 1828
Sources: ACO; GL: SMC 5213/4, 5213/5; GC 11598/6; 11598/7; PRO: B3/2034 & 2035 (AM); Pg; PO

GILBERT William and Thomas
w 1819–1831
Optician
1819–1831 148 Leadenhall St, London
Sons of GILBERT William (I)★
Apprenticed to GILBERT William (I)★
Succeeded by GILBERT William (II)★
Took over from GILBERT & SONS★
Known to have sold: compass, gunner's scales, sector, sextant
Sources: Bn; inst(s); Brown J. (1979a) p.47–48
Turner G (1980) pl.15

GILBERT & CO.
a 1800
        London
See also
GILBERT Thomas★
GILBERT William (I)★
GILBERT & WRIGHT★
GILBERT Wm. & Thos.★
GILBERT & GILKERSON★
GILBERT & SONS★
Known to have sold: microscope, telescope
Sources: Sby 11 June 1985 lot 329 (MAC); Turner G (1989) p.236

GILBERT & GILKERSON William & James
w 1793–1809
Math IM, Optician
1793–1809 8 Postern Row, Tower Hill, London
Succeeded by GILKERSON & CO.★
See also
GILKERSON & MCALL★
GILKERSON James★
Known to have sold: sextant, rule, globe, equinoctial ring dial.
Sources: inst MHS; H; Kt; ChrSK 17 Apr 1986 lot 254 (MAC)

GILBERT & SON
w 1806–1816
Math IM, Opticians
Alternative name: probably GILBERT & SONS
1811–1816 Navigation Warehouse, 148 Leadenhall St, London
Associated with GRANT Alexander★
Known to have sold: log
Sources: Und; Kt; Taylor (1966) p.364

GILBERT & SON John
w 1749
Instrument M
1749   Postern Row, Tower Hill, London
Took over from GILBERT John (I)★
Succeeded by GILBERT John (II)★
See also GIBERT, WRIGHT & HOOKE★
John Snr d.1750
Sources: *Daily Ad* 22 Jun 1749 (MAC)

GILBERT & SONS William (& William (II) & Thomas)
w 1806–1819

Math IM, Opticians
Alternative name: GILBERT & SON
        Tower Hill, London
1806–1819 148 Leadenhall St, London
Succeeded by GILBERT W. & T.★
Took over from GILBERT & WRIGHT★
Known to have sold: microscope
Sources: H; Kt; R(JAC)

GILBERT & WRIGHT William (?) & Gabriel
w 1790–1792, 1802–1805
1792–1794 Navigation Warehouse, 148 Leadenhall St, London
1802–1805 148 Leadenhall St, London
Succeeded by
GILBERT, WRIGHT & HOOKE★
GILBERT & SONS★
Took over from GREGORY, GILBERT, WRIGHT★
see also GILBERT Willaim (I)★
WRIGHT Gabriel★
Hooke in partnership: 1794–1801
Known to have sold: sextant
Sources: Ld; PO; inst NMM; Brown J (1979a) p.83

GILBERT, WRIGHT & HOOKE William, Gabriel & Benjamin
w 1794–1801
Math IM
1794–1801 Navigation Warehouse, 148 Leadenhall St, London
Succeeded by GILBERT & WRIGHT★
Took over from GILBERT & WRIGHT★
See also
GILBERT William (I)★
GREGORY, GILBERT & CO.★
WRIGHT Gabriel,
Sources: Kt; Ld; Brown J (1979a) p.83

GILKERSON James
w 1817
Optical IM
1817   8 Postern Row, Tower Hill, London
Partnership:
GILBERT & GILKERSON★
GILKERSON & MCALL★
GILKERSON & CO★
Gilkerson & Co. at same address same time
Known to have sold: drawing instruments, gunner's callipers
Sources: J; inst (s); Sby 17 Apr 1986 lot 296 (MAC)

GILKERSON & CO. James
w 1809–1825
Math IM, Optical IM, Phil IM, Optician
1809–1825 8 Postern Row, Tower Hill, London
Took over from GILBERT & GILKERSON★
Succeeded by GILKERSON & MCALL★
Sources: Bn; H; Kt: R (JAC)

GILKERSON & MCALL James & John
w 1826–1830
Math IM
Alternative name: MACALL
1826–1830 8 Postern Row, Tower Hill, London
Succeeded by MCALL John★
Took over from GILKERSON & CO★
See also
GILBERT & GILKERSON★

GILKERSON James★
Known to have sold: spectacles
Sources: Pg; PO; inst(s)

GILL John
w 1716
    London
Guild: Clockmakers, fr 1707
Apprenticed to BARROW John 1700
Known to have sold: sundial
Sources: GL: CKC 2710/3 fol. 7, 82; Ts D 1983
no.26

GILL Thomas
w 1816–1820
Hydro M
1816–1817   42 Greek St, Soho, London
1818–1820   20 Little Tower St, London
Took over from GILL & CO★
See also
SWAN John★
LONG Joseph★
Associated with DICAS & CO★
Pat with J.Ashton, 1818 hydrometer
Known to have sold: hydrometer
Sources: Und; J; Kt; Woodcroft (1854); inst SM

GILL & CO.
w 1814–1815
Hydro M
1814–1815   42 Greek St, Soho, London
Succeeded by GILL Thomas★
Sources: Kt

GILLEGEN Andrew
w 1828
Optician
1828   23 New St, Covent Garden, London
Sources: Kt

GILLETT William
w 1851–1885
Optician, Spec M
Alternative name: GILLET
1851   12, Fetter Lane, London
1855–1885   6 Bell Yard, Temple Bar, London
Sources: PO; Wk; Calvert (1971) p.23

GINOCCHIO –
a 1775–1825
    Cork
Known to have sold: barometer
Sources: Mason (1944) (MAC)

GIOBBI & SALA
a 1800
    London
Known to have sold: barometer, thermometer,
hygrometer
Sources: Bolle (1982) p.157

GIRONIMO Laurence
w 1845
Baro M, Thermo M, Looking-glass M
1845   93 Leather Lane, London
Sources: PO

GIUSANI Peter
w 1835
Carver & Gilder
1835   Cock St, Wolverhampton
Known to have sold: barometer
Sources: Goodison (1977) p.326

GLAZIER James
w 1796–1799
Math IM
1796–1799   59 Townsend St, Dublin
Sources: Burnett & Morrison-Low (1989) p.125

GLENIE James
w 1805
Optician
1805   104 Wapping, London
Sources: H

GLOVER John A
w 1771
Optician
    London
Had apprentice TEMPLE George by t/o 1771 from
WATKINS Francis (I)★
See also
GIBBONS William★
HARPER Andrew★
Sources: GL: SMC 5213/3

GLOVER Joseph
w 1834–1840
Optical IM, Phil IM, Math IM
1834–1840   Church St, Hackney, London
Sources: R (JAC)

GLOVER William
w 1782–1810
Math IM
1782–1788   Angel Court, Leadenhall St, London
1810   White Gate St, Bishopsgate St,
    London
Guild: Masons, fr 1786
Apprenticed to GREGORY Henry (I)★ 1764
Had apprentice:
LITTLEWORT William 1788
LITTLEWORT William Richard 1810
Sources: GL: MC 5304/4, 5304/5, 5304/6; Sun
11936/298 no.455978

GLYNNE Richard
w 1707–1730
Math IM, Map S
Alternative name: Richardus, GLYN, GLYNN,
1712–1716   Atlas & Hercules in Cheapside,
    London
1718–1729   Atlas & Hercules, opposite Salisbury
    Court, Fleet St, London
Guild: Clockmakers, fr 1705
Related to
LEA Philip★
LEA Anne★
Apprenticed to WYNNE Henry★ 1696
Had apprentice:
WILSON John (I)★ 1707
SPACKMAN John 1711
WARNER John 1712
JOHNSON Isaac 1713

HIGGS James 1717/18
Associated with
WYNNE Henry★
SELLER & PRICE★
b 1681; r 1730, stock auctioned at shop of Edward
SCARLETT – probably (I)★; d 1755
Known to have sold: armillary sphere, compass,
sundial.
Sources: PRO: IR 1/1 fol.32; Brown J (1979b)
p.30; *The Craftsman* 13 Jun 1730 (JRM); inst
NMM; inst MHS; Tyacke (1978) p.116–117

GOATER Henry
w 1780–1793
Math IM
Alternative name: Henry Bostock
    144 Wapping, London
1785   141 Wapping, London
1788–1793   10 New Gravel Lane, Wapping
    Wall, London
1793   10 New Gravel Lane, Shadwell,
    London
Guild: Shipwrights, fr 1778
Apprenticed to: GOATER John★, his father, 1770
Had apprentice:
CATMUR Henry★ 1780
POWIS John 1789
Brother of:
GOATER John Bostock★
GOATER Robert★
Known to have sold: octant
Sources: Ridge (1939) p.87, (1946) p.78; A; BW;
By

GOATER John
w 1754–1786
Math IM
1744   Broad St, London
1758   Opposite Execution dock, Wapping,
    London
Guild: Shipwrights, fp 1744
Son of GOATER Henry, victualler, of London
Had apprentice:
EARLE John 1754
GOATER Robert★, his son, 1764
GOATER John Bostock★, his son, 1767
GOATER Henry Bostock★, his son, 1770
MORTON Peter 1775
ANDERSON Edward 1779
CLARK John Davis 1781
ELLIOTT William, son of Edward, 1782
SNART John (II)★ 1786 by t/o from CHESTER
Edward★
Associated with COLE Benjamin (I)★, who testified
when Goater was freed
Paid quarterage fees to SWC until 1793
Known to have sold: octant
Sources: GL: SWC 4602/2; inst MDS; Ridge
(1939) p.87; (1946) pp.39,90

GOATER John Bostock
w 1778–1794
Math IM, Ship Chandler
    Execution Dock, Wapping, London
1778   opposite the Cock & Lion in
    St.Catherine's, London
1779   10 New Gravel Lane, London
1782–1794   141 Wapping, London

1787–1789   144 Wapping, (Directory error ?)
London
Guild: Shipwrights, fr 1779
Brother of
GOATER Robert★
GOATER Henry Bostock★
Apprenticed to GOATER John★, his father, 1767
Had apprentice LORKIN Thomas★ 1779
Sources: Ridge (1939) p.87, 134; GL: Sun
11936/279 no.422439, 11936/298 no. 453417; Ld

GOATER Robert
w 1785–1809
Math IM, Quadrant M, Compass M
            Broad St, St.George's East, London
            20 Wapping Wall, London
1796   146 Wapping, London
1809   205 Wapping St, London
Brother of
GOATER Henry Bostock★
GOATER John Bostock★
Apprenticed to GOATER John★ 1764
Known to have sold: compass (magnetic)
Sources: inst NMM; By; H; Kt(JAC); Ridge
(1939) p.87

GODDARD Howell
w 1788–1807
Scale M
1788   17 The Cloisters near Smithfield,
            London
1807   Bell Square, St.Martin's le Grand,
            London
Guild: Blacksmiths, fr 1788
Apprenticed to BADCOCK William Geagle★ 1779
t/o to DE GRAVE Charles (I)★ 1784
Father of GODDARD Howell (II) s 1807 GSC
Sources: GL: BKC 2881/16 (MAC); GH: GSC Ap

GODDARD James Thomas
w 1851–1863
Telescope M, Photo lens M
1851–1853   35 Goswell St, London
1859–1863   Jesse Cottage, Whitton, Middlesex
Sources: Chaldecott (1989) p.164

GODDEN Thomas
w 1849
Optician
1849   231 Tottenham Court Road,
            London
Sources: PO

GODFREY John
w 1818–1841
Optician, Spec M, Silversmith
1818   Cross St, Birmingham
1828–1841   93 Coleshill St, Birmingham
Succeeded by GODFREY & CO. Mary★
Sources: Pg; West; Wr

GODFREY Mary Ann
w 1850
Optician
1850   93 Coleshill St, Birmingham
Took over from GODFREY & CO Mary★
Sources: Sl

GODFREY Thomas
w 1809
Math IM
1809   6 George's Court, St.John's Lane,
            Clerkenwell, London
Sources: H

GODFREY & CO Mary
w 1845
Optician, Spec M
1845   93 Coleshill St, Birmingham
Succeeded by GODFREY Mary Ann★
Took over from GODFREY John★
Sources: K

GOFTON William
w 1843
Optical IM, Surgical IM
1843   63 Farringdon St, London
Guild: Spectaclemakers, fr 1843
Son of GOFTON John, merchant, d, of West Indies
fr by purchase in SMC
Sources: GL: SMC 5213/6

GOGERTY Robert
w 1839–1856
Optician, Phil IM, Math IM, Shower bath and
pump M, Brass turner
1834–1835   25 St. John St, Clerkenwell, London
1839   19 Great Sutton St, London
1845   32 King St, Smithfield, London
1849–1855   72 Fleet St, London
Guild: Drapers, fr 1835
Son of GOGERTY Daniel, book-binder, of London
Apprenticed to STANTON John★ 1828, t/o 1834 to
BARKER Joseph of ABC
Had apprentice:
SALMON Charles 1841
SMITH Thomas William 1845
BEECROFT Thomas 1847
TERRY Edmund 1849
PALMER James 1853
b 1814; d by Feb 1857; attended London
Mechanics Institute
Known to have sold: microscope
Sources: PO; DH: DPC Ap/Fr, index; LMIR
(AM); inst(s)

GOOD John
w 1848–1851
Math IM, Chandler, Navigation Warehouse,
Anchor S
1848–1851   19 High St, Hull
Sources: Stn; Wh

GOODBEHERE Samuel
w 1784–1792
Silversmith
Alternative name: GODBEHERE
1784–1792   Cheapside, London
Guild: Needlemakers, fr 1784
Partnership: GOODBEHERE, WIGAN & CO
Had apprentice GOODBEHERE Horatio, his son,
1811
fr by purchase, NC; Alderman & Sheriff in 1811
Sources: GL: NC 2817/3 f107; 2817/5 f152

GOODBEHERE, WIGAN & CO.
w 1786–1799
Goldsmiths
Alternative name: GODBEHERE
1792–1799   86 Cheapside, London
Succeeded by GOODBEHERE, WIGAN & BULT
Took over from STAMPS
Associated with PICKETT John★ who supplied
parts
Known to have sold: balance
Sources: Ld; Sheppard & Musham (1975) no.47

GOODCHILD William
w 1849
Optician
1849   28 Francis St, Bedford Square,
            London
Sources: PO

GOODMAN Dorothy (Mrs)
w 1687–1695
Spec M
1693–1695   West Smithfield, London
Guild: [Spectaclemakers]
Had apprentice COOBEROW Matthew by t/o
from GOODMAN Thomas (II)★
WILSON Thomas by t/o from GOODMAN
Thomas (II)★
Took over from GOODMAN Thomas (II)★ her
husband
Sources: GL: SMC 5213/1

GOODMAN John
w 1784–1804
Scale M
            68 Snow Hill, London
            27 Hosier Lane, Smithfield, London
1793   19 Snow Hill, Holborn Bridge,
            London
Guild: Blacksmiths, Clothworkers
Son of GOODMAN John, cloth-worker, of London
Apprenticed to
THOMPSON Daniel★ 1741
THOMPSON John (II)★ by t/o 1745
Had apprentice:
DAVIS John 1763
ASTILL William★ 1769
DUNN John (I)★ 1773
BLADES Tristram★ 1775 by t/o from GRAY
Francis★
GRIGG James★ 1780
LAYTON William 1785
STEWART James★ 1792
Worked for THOMPSON John (II)★
See also GOODMAN William★
Educated at Christ's Hospital; fp CWC 1748, fr
BKC 1753
Sources: CWH: CWC Fr; Wil; JAC; GL: BKC
2886/1, 2885/1; CH 12876/14;

GOODMAN Richard
w 1658–1669
[Spec M]
            London
Guild: Spectaclemakers, nd
Father of GOODMAN Thomas (II)★
Had apprentice HICKETT John★ by t/o from
HARDY George★ 1658

WILLIFORD, alias THORNBURY George 1669 t/o
to GOODMAN Thomas (II)★ nd
Last noted in SMC records Dec 1669
Sources: GL: SMC 5213/1

GOODMAN Thomas (I)
w 1666–1668
Spec M
London
Guild: Spectaclemakers, nd
Last noted in SMC records Jan 1667/8
Sources: GL: SMC 5213/1

GOODMAN Thomas (II)
w 1662 d 1687
Spec M
1671   St. Bartholomews, London
Guild: Spectaclemakers, nd
Son of GOODMAN Richard★
Had apprentice:
PATESHALL Thomas 1673
WILLIFORD (alias THORNBURY George by t/o
from GOODMAN Richard★ between 1669 and
1676
WILSON Thomas★1686/7 t/o to GOODMAN D.★
COOBEROW Matthew★ 1683 t/o to GOODMAN
D.
BUSHELL/BISSELL Andrew
Master SMC 1677–1679
Sources: GL: SMC 5213/1; CLRO: CF1/53/29

GOODMAN William
w 1790–1794
Scale M
1790–1794   68 Snow Hill, Holborn Bridge,
London
Guild: [Blacksmiths]
See also GOODMAN John★
Sources: GL: BKC 2886/5; W

GOODWIN John
c 1650
Alternative name: GODWYN, GOODWYN,
Known to have sold: sector
Sources: inst NMM

GOODWIN Thomas
a 1735 d.c 1764
Scale M
1764   Parish of St.Sepulchres, London
Sources: GL: HC 15860/9

GOODWIN William
d 1662
Spec M
-1662   Dublin
Sources: Burnett & Morrison-Low (1989) p.125

GORDON William
w 1726
Math IM
London
Guild: Stationers
Had apprentice: PICK Andrew★ 1726 by t/o from
BETTESWORTH Peter★
Sources: McKenzie (1978) p.35

GORE Thomas Hunsdon
fr 1825 w 1842
Scale M
58 King William St, London
1825   93 Fore St, London
1836   King William St, City, London
1839–1840   6 Holywell Lane, London
1842   87 Long Lane, Smithfield, London
Guild: Blacksmiths, fr 1825
Apprenticed to VANDOME Richard★ 1818
Had apprentice MEDWIN Thomas★ 1827 t/o to
WILLIAMS Thomas (III)★ 1832
and 4 others
Sources: Pg; PO; GL: BKC 2881/17 (MAC)

GORTON Thomas
w 1766 d 1776
Math IM
1766   Hackins Hay, Liverpool
Sources: St. Peter's, Liverpool, bur (MAC)

GOSSART John
w 1784–1785
Math IM
1784–1785   12 Craven St, Strand, London
See also BURTON Mark★
Sources: By (JAC)

GOSSE Nathaniel
fr 1611 w 1637
Math IM (in wood)
Alternative name: GORSE, GOS, Nathanaell
1618   Hosier Lane, West Smithfield,
London
1624–1630   Ratcliff, London
Guild: Stationers, fr 1611
Brother of GOSSE John
Apprenticed to READE John (I)★ 1604, but freed
by BEALE John, printer
Had apprentice:
GOSSE John, his brother, 1615
BISSAKER George 1621
COOKE Thomas (I)★ 1628
BISSAKER Robert★ 1634
STARR Robert 1637
and 4 others
Sources: Bryden (1992) pp.308,309; McKenzie
(1961) p. 74; SBPL: STC MF Ap

GOSTICK Charles
w 1846
Corn & Coal Measure M
1846   Ironmonger Row, St. Lukes,
London
Sources: Stat: STC, Memo Bk, 1824–35

GOUGH Walter
w 1784–1811
Math IM, Optician, Phil IM
Alternative name: William
1784–1790   21 Middle Row, Holborn, London
1790–1794   20 Middle Row, Holborn, London
1799–1811   23 Middle Row, Holborn, London
Known to have sold: microscope
Instruments advertised: full range
Sources: BW; H; PO; BM: Heal 105/45; Turner G
(1981) p.41

GOULD Charles
w 1825–1839
Microscope M
272 Strand, London
Worked for CARY Wm★
Father of GOULD Henry★
Succeeded by GOULD Henry★
Known to have sold: microscope
Sources: Taylor (1966) p.363-64; Turner G (1989)
p.75

GOULD Frederick Joseph
w 1845–1865
Optician
1845   9 Russell Court, Drury Lane,
London
1851   2 Nelson Place, Old Kent Rd,
London
1855–1865   1 Nelson Place, Old Kent Rd,
London
1865   119 Great Dover St, London SE
Sources: PO; Wk

GOULD Henry
v 1826 w 1859
Optician
1826–1828   182 Strand, London
1853–1859   181 Strand, London
Son of GOULD Charles★
Succeeded by GOULD & PORTER
Took over from
GOULD Charles★
CARY George & John★
Attended London Mechanics Institute 1826–1828
Sources: PO; LMIR; Taylor (1966) p.364,386

GOULD Horace
w 1804
Book S, Stationer, Naut IS
1804   Opposite the American Hotel,
Wapping, Liverpool
See also GOULD John (I)★
Sources: Wwd (MAC)

GOULD John (I)
w 1790
Math IM
1790   1 Dury Lane, Liverpool
See also
GOULD Horace★
GOULD John (II)★
Sources: G (MAC)

GOULD John (II)
fr 1784
Math IM
1784   Dobey's Court, Barbers Hall,
London
Guild: Stationers, fr 1784
Apprenticed to BENNETT John★ 1768 t/o 1771 to
SEARCH James★
Had apprentice HARRIS William 1784
See also GOULD John (I)★
Sources: McKenzie (1978) p.29, 146

GOULDING Thomas
fr 1764 c 1780
Scale M

Angel & Scales No.15 in Queen St,
Cheapside, London
Guild: Blacksmiths, fr 1764
Apprenticed to WOOD John (II)★ 1757
Took over from WOOD John (II)★
Known to have sold: balance
Instruments advertised: balance, steelyard, weights
Sources: GL: BKC 2886/5; Sheppard & Musham
(1975) no.23 (MAC)

GOUT Ralph
w 1774 fl 1815
Clock M
1774   6 Norman St, Old St, London
1799   Bunhill Row, St. Luke's Old St,
               London
Pat. pedometer 1799
Known to have sold: pedometer
Sources: Patent records (MAC); Kt

GOWAN G.
w 1753
Known to have sold: sector.
Sources: Taylor (1966) p.232

GOWERS Weston
w 1691–1709
Scale M
               Falcon & Scales in Rood Lane near
               Billingsgate, London
Guild: Blacksmiths, fr 1690
Apprenticed to BAYLY Sylvester,
Had apprentice JACKSON Richard (I)★ 1706
and 7 others 1691–1709
Known to have sold: balance
Sources: GL: BKC 2881/8, 2881/9, 2881/10,
2886/3; inst (pv) (MAC)

GOWLAND George
w 1851–1853
Naut IM
1851–1853   76 South Castle St, Liverpool
Succeeded by GOWLAND W. & G.
Patent 1853
Sources: G; DJB

GOWLAND James
fl 1830 w 1851+
Chrono M, Watch M
1839   11 Leathersellers Buildings, London
               Wall, London
1846–1851   52 London Wall, London
Pat. improved timekeeper
Sources: Pg; PO; Loomes (1976); Taylor (1966)
p.450

GOWLAND Thomas
fl 1830
[Chrono M]
               118 Upper Ashley St, London
Sources: Taylor (1966) p.450

GOY & CO
a 1825–1825
Outfitters, ?Math IS
               36 Leadenhall St, London
Sources: Taylor (1966) p.472; NMM Inventory
p.22–8 S.17

GRACE George
w 1776–1811
Math IM
1799–1811   15 Eagle Court, St.John's Lane,
               Clerkenwell, London
Guild: Goldsmiths, fr 1767
Apprenticed to HITCH Joseph 1759
Had apprentice SCHOLEFIELD William (II)★ 1786
and 10 others not known as IM
Sources: GH: GSC Ap, Fr

GRAFTON Henry (I)
w 1840
Math IM, Phil IM
1840   18 Barbican, London
Succeeded by GRAFTON Henry (II)★
Sources: PO

GRAFTON Henry (II)
w 1841–1853
Math IM, Phil IM, Baro M, Thermo M, Engineer,
Machinist
1841   18 Barbican, London
1842–1853   80 Chancery Lane, London
1849–1851   36 Holborn Hill, London
Took over from GRAFTON Henry (I)★
Sources: PO

GRAHAM George
w 1713 d 1751
Math IM, Watch M
               Water Lane, Fleet St, London
               Dial & Crown, Fleet St, London
1713–1720   Dial & Three Crowns, Water Lane,
               Fleet St, London
1720–1751   Next door to the Globe &
               Marlborough's Head Tavern, London
1720–1751   Dial & One Crown, Fleet St, London
Guild: Clockmakers, fr 1695
Apprenticed to ASKE Henry 1688
Had apprentice:
MUDGE Thomas★ 1730
DUTTON William M.★ 1738/9
and 14 others not known as IM
Worked for TOMPION Thomas★
Employed BIRD John★
SISSON Jonathan★
SHELTON John★
MUDGE Thomas★
Succeeded by MUDGE Thomas★
Took over from TOMPION & GRAHAM★
FRS 1720; Inv. dead-beat escapement and mercury
compensated pendulum; inv. orrery; married
Tompion's niece
Known to have sold: mural quadrant, astronomical
clock, transit instrument, zenith instrument,
pyrometer, barometer, thermometer, hygrometer
Sources: GL: CKC 2721/1; Goodison (1977) p.153
King & Millburn (1978) p.126–27, 152–54;
Loomes (1981b); Wallis R & P (1986) p.121–22

GRAHAM Harriet
w 1834
Baro M, Thermo M
1834   25 Baldwin's Gardens, Leather Lane,
               London
Sources: Pg

GRANGER R.
w 1790
1790   Tettenhall, Near Wolverhampton
Known to have sold: microscope
Sources: Turner G (1989) p277

GRANGER Thomas
w 1710
Known to have sold: nocturnal
Sources: Taylor (1954) p.303

GRANT Alexander
w 1795–1822
Math IM, Optician, Optical IM
1795–1822   2 Winckworth's Buildings, City Rd,
               London
See also GRANT John★
Associated with GILBERT & SON★
Sources: Und; Bn; H; McKenzie (1978) p.5

GRANT C.
w 1851
Optician
1851   34 Meredith St, Clerkenwell,
               London
Sources: Wk

GRANT Henry
fl 1830
Chrono M
               7 Cornhill, London
Sources: Taylor (1966) p.450

GRANT James
fl 1837 w 1848
Math IS, Stationer, Optician
1837–1848   40 Queen St, Hull
Sources: Pg; Sl; Taylor (1966) p.472

GRANT John
w 1799
Math IM
1799   37 Aylesbury St, Clerkenwell,
               London
See also GRANT Alexander,
Sources: H

GRANT Matthew
w 1816
Optical Turner
1816   15 Kirby St, Hatton Garden,
               London
Sources: Und

GRANT William
fl 1830 w 1839
Chrono M
               15 St Martin's Court, London
1839   36 Haymarket, London
Sources: Pg; Taylor 1966) p.450

GRASSEY Stephen
w 1833–1834
Optician, Jeweller, Victualler
1833–1834   Dog & Duck, Pipers Row,
               Wolverhampton
Sources: Br; Wh

GRASSI, BERGNA & ORIGONI
w 1834
Baro M
1834   34 Dean St, Newcastle upon Tyne
Sources: Pg

GRAY Benjamin
w 1744 d 1764
Clock M
1752   Pall Mall, London
R.apt Geo II 1744
Known to have sold: waywiser
Sources: Sby 20 Feb 1985 lot 278; Baillie (1951)

GRAY Francis
fr 1766 w 1775
Scale M
              The Angel & Scales, Porter's Block,
              Smithfield Bars, London
1774–1775   93 St.John's St, London
Guild: Blacksmiths, fr 1766
Apprenticed to HARRISON Thomas (II)★ 1758
Had apprentice BLADES Tristram 1774 t/o 1775 to
GOODMAN John★
Sources: GL: BKC 2885/1, 2886/5; Kt

GRAY John (I)
w 1804–1877
Math IM, Victualler, Naut IM, Optical IM, Iron
ships compass M, Chronometer M
              Opposite the Dry Dock, Liverpool
1805–1820   10 East Side Dry Dock, Liverpool
1821   11 East Side Dry Dock, Liverpool
1828–1829   25 Bridgewater St, Liverpool
1839   3 Chester St, Ton Park, Liverpool
1841–1862   25 Strand St, Liverpool
1847–1858   25 & 26 Strand St, Liverpool
1847   2 Stanley Terrace, New Town,
              Liverpool
1849   2 Clements Terrace, Upper
              Parliament St, Liverpool
1864–1877   26 Strand St, Liverpool
Succeeded by GRAY Charles J.
See also
GRAY & LESSELS★
JONES, GRAY & KEEN★
GRAY & KEEN★
Associated with JONES Charles★
Known to have sold: barometer, compass
Sources: G; K; Pg; inst NMM; Goodison (1977)
p.327

GRAY John (II)
w 1823–1839
Optician, Math IM, Phil IM
              36 Nightingale Lane, East
              Smithfield, London
              13 Little Hermitage St, Wapping,
              London
1823   41 Nightingale Lane, East
              Smithfield, London
1839   4 Upper East Smithfield, London
Guild: [Turners]
Apprenticed to KITCHINGMAN John★ 1783
Sources: GL: TC 3302/3 (MAC); Pg; Po; JAC

GRAY & KEEN John & –
w 1847–1855

Opticians, Naut IM, Correctors of iron-built vessels
1847–1855   25 & 26 Strand St, Liverpool
Succeeded by GRAY John(I)★ alone
Took over from JONES, GRAY & KEEN★
Ex. 1851
Known to have sold: barometer, octant, sextant
Sources: G; Sl; Cat.1851; Phlps; 16 May 1978 lot
57; SbyCh 18 Nov 1981 (MAC)

GRAY & LESSELS
w 1811
Math IM
1811   7 Dry Dock, Liverpool
See also GRAY John (I)★
GRAY & KEEN★
JONES, GRAY & KEEN★
Sources: G

GRAY & MACKAY
w 1822
1822   25 Old Burlington St, London
Described themselves as inventors and makers of a
new saccharometer
Sources: Chaldecott (1989) p.165

GREATOREX Ralph
w 1654 fl 1712
Math IM, Surveyor
Alternative name: GRATRIX
              Adam and Eve in the Strand,
              London
1662   Temple Bar, London
Guild: Clockmakers, fr 1653
Apprenticed to ALLEN Elias★ 1639
Had apprentice:
WYNNE Henry★ 1654
BULTE Daniel 1655
JERVIS Francis 1656
KING Thomas 1657/8
OKESHOTT Robert 1664
Took over from ALLEN Elias★
Associated with BROOKES Christopher★ who
supplied inst
Known to have sold: air pump, barometer, sundial
Sources: Brown J (1979b) p.30; ChrSK 5 Mar 1987
lot 358; inst MHS; GL: CKC 3939

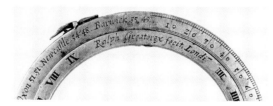

GREAVES Thomas
w 1777–1818
Optician, Spec frame M
1777   40 Old Hinckleys, Birmingham
1818   Hill St, Birmingham
See also GREAVES Thomas H★
Sources: PR; Pye; TWr

GREAVES Thomas Henry
w 1829–1835
Spec M
1829–1830   47 Dudley St, Birmingham

1835   49 Dudley St, Birmingham
See also GREAVES Thomas★
Sources: Pg; Wr

GREEN George
w 1846–1848
Math IM
1846–1848   7 Helmet Row, London
See also
GREEN German★
GREEN Samuel★
Attended London Mechanics Institute 1846–1848
Sources: LMIR (AM)

GREEN German
w 1849–1850
Math IM
1849–1850   7 Helmet Row, St Luke's, London
See also
GREEN George★
GREEN Samuel★
Attended London Mechanics Institute 1849–1850
Sources: LMIR (AM)

GREEN Henry
w 1846
Math IM
1846   10 Bartholomew Square, London
See also GREEN James★
Attended London Mechanics Institute 1846
Sources: LMIR (AM)

GREEN I.
a 1780–1800
              London
Known to have sold: balance
Sources: Sheppard & Musham (1975) no.195; inst
(pv) (MAC)

GREEN James
w 1830
Math IM
1830–1831   10 Bartholomew Lane, St Luke's,
              London
See also GREEN Henry★
Attended London Mechanics Institute 1830–1831
Sources: LMIR (AM)

GREEN Samuel
w 1851–1880
Compass M
1851   7 Helmet Row, Old St, London
1855–1880   7 Helmet Row, St Luke's, London
See also
GREEN George★
GREEN German★
Ex.1851
Sources: PO; Turner G (1983) p.309

GREEN Stephen
w 1845–1855
Chem IM
1845   Princes St, Lambeth, London
1849–1855   54 Princes St, Lambeth, London
Succeeded by GREEN & CO Stephen
Directory entry 1851 is GREEN & CO. Stephen★,
but in 1855 is just GREEN Stephen
Sources: PO

GREEN William (I)

w 1826–1856
Optical IM, Phil IM, Math IM
1826 7 Bartholomew Terrace, City Rd,
    London
1828 Paternoster Row, London
    54 Rahere St, Goswell Rd, London
1838–1855 14 Fountain Place, City Rd, London
1865 10 Guildford Place, Farringdon Rd,
    London WC
Guild: Joiners
Apprenticed to DANCER Michael* 1808
Had 4 apprentices 1828–1841
Sources: Pg; PO; JAC; Crawforth (1987) p.357

GREEN William (II)

w 1816
Spec M, Glass grinder
1816 Fazeley St, Birmingham
Sources: H (DJB)

GREEN William (III)

w 1844–1848
Math IM, Phil IM, Optical IM
1844–1845 5 Franklin St, Glasgow
1846–1848 87 London St, Glasgow
Known to have sold: barometer, thermometer
Sources: Bryden (1972) p.49

GREEN & CO. Stephen

w 1851–1859
Chem IM
1851 54 Princes St, Lambeth, London
1859 Imperial Potteries, 54 Princes St,
    Lambeth, London
Sources: PO

GREENALL William Wells

w 1821–1830
Math IS, Optical IS, Phil IS
1821–1830 31 Old Compton St, Soho, London
Sources: Bn; R (JAC)

GREENAWAY Thomas

w 1697
Scale S
    London
Known to have sold: balance
Sources: GL: BKC 2881/8

GREENE James

fr 1704 w 1728
[Scale M]
    London
Guild: Blacksmiths, fr 1704
Apprenticed to HOE Robert* 1696/7
Had 3 apprentices 1713–1728
Sources: GL: BKC 2881/9, 2881/11, 2888 (MAC)

GREENHILL Benjamin Mills

w 1837–1885
Scale M
1839–1855 221 Hoxton Old Town, London
1860 172 High Holborn, WC. London
1865 53 Bell St, Edgware Rd, London,
    NW
1875–1885 10 Upper Lisson St, Lisson Grove,
    London, NW

Guild: [Blacksmiths]
Apprenticed to PALLET Richard* 1816
Sources: GL: BKC 2881/17; Pg; PO (MAC); R
(JAC)

GREENOUGH Thomas

w 1749
Known to have sold: back-staff
Sources: ChrSK 20 Sep 1979 (MAC)

GREENUP Charles

w 1790–1794
Rule M
1790–1794 Great Saffron Hill, London
Sources: W (JAC)

GREENWOOD Thomas

w 1839–1840
Optician, Math IM, Phil IM
1839–1840 10 Fetter Lane, London
Took over from GREENWOOD Timothy*
Sources: Pg

GREENWOOD Timothy

w 1836–1838
Optician, Phil IM, Math IM
1836 20 Little Saffron Hill, Hatton Wall,
    London
1838 10 Fetter Lane, London
Succeeded by GREENWOOD Thomas*
Sources: Pg; R (JAC)

GREGORIE Edward

w 1629
Spec M
1629 London
Guild: Spectaclemakers & u
First Master of Spectaclemakers' Co. 1629
Sources: GL: SMC 5214

GREGORY Henry (I)

w 1744–1782
Math IM
    The Azimuth Compass near East
    India House, Leadenhall St, London
1766 Near the India House, London
1776 8 Leadenhall St, London
1780–1781 148 Leadenhall St, London
Guild: Masons, fr 1739
Father of GREGORY Henry (II)*
Partnership: GREGORY & SON Henry*
Apprenticed to FOWLER John* (I) 1732
Had apprentice:
BAILEY William* 1749
GLOVER William* 1764
GREGORY Henry (II)*, his son, 1767
5 other apprentices 1744–1762
Associated with
PARMINTER John (I)*
SUDLOW John*
GILBERT John (II)*
Partnership: 1776; Master MC 1770
Known to have sold: barometer, compass, gunner's
callipers, telescope, thermometer.
Sources: GL: MC 5304/3, 5304/4, 5312 (MAC);
Kt; Ld; Mort; inst NMM and (s); Calvert (1971)
p.24

GREGORY Henry (II)

w pt 1776–1793
Math IM
    London
Guild: Masons, fr 1774
Apprenticed to GREGORY Henry (I)*, his father,
1767
Partnership:
GREGORY & SON Henry*
GREGORY & WRIGHT*
GREGORY GILBERT & WRIGHT*
Succeeded by GREGORY & WRIGHT*
See also GREGORY Henry (III)*
Sources: GL: MC 5304/4; 5308; Ld

GREGORY Henry (III)

w 1836–1839
Math IM, Phil IM
1836–1839 (Residence?)2 Francis Court,
    Berkeley St, Clerkenwell, London
See also
GREGORY Henry (I)*
GREGORY Henry (II)*
Sources: Pg

GREGORY Samuel

w 1761–1762
Baro M
1761–1762 Sycamore Alley, Dublin
Sources: Burnett & Morrison-Low (1989) p.125

GREGORY Thomas (I)

w 1826–1834
Spec M, Optician
    27 Castle St, Long Acre, London
    17 Riders Court, Leicester Square,
    London
Sources: PO; R (JAC)

GREGORY Thomas (II)

w 1834
Optician
1834 3 Quay St, Manchester
Sources: Pg

GREGORY Thomas (III)

w 1845–1850
Optician
1845–1850 35 Suffolk St, Smallbrook St,
    Birmingham
Sources: K; Sl

GREGORY William (I)

w 1811–1818
Math IM
1811–1818 30 New Street Square, Shoe Lane,
    London
Guild: Stationers, fr 1810
Apprenticed to EVANS William (I)* 1789
Had apprentice:
RANN John 1811
PULHAM Daniel 1812
Sources: SBPL: STC MF Ap; J; McKenzie (1978)
p.119

GREGORY William (II)

w 1834–1836
Rule M, Optical IM, Phil IM, Math IM

1834   8 Berry St, Clerkenwell, London
1835   9 Hooper St, Clerkenwell, London
1836   2 Francis Court, Berkeley St,
             Clerkenwell, London
Sources: Pg

GREGORY & LAWRENCE
w 1836
Math IM, Phil IM
1836   19 Great Sutton St, Goswell St,
             London
Sources: Pg

GREGORY & SON Henry
w 1776
Math IM
1776   8 Leadenhall St, London
Took over from GREGORY Henry (I)★
Succeeded by GREGORY & WRIGHT★
Sources: Ld

GREGORY & WRIGHT Henry & Gabriel
w 1782–1790
Math IM, Optician
1782–1790   Navigation Warehouse, 148
             Leadenhall St, London
Took over from GREGORY & SON Henry★
Succeeded by
GREGORY, GILBERT & WRIGHT★
Sources: A; Ld (JAC); Calvert (1971) p.24

GREGORY, GILBERT & CO. Henry & William (I)
w 1793
Optician
Alternative name: GREGORY, GILBERT & WRIGHT ?
1793   148 Leadenhall St, London
Overlap with Gilbert, Wright & Hooke★ & with
Gilbert & Wright★
Sources: BW

GREGORY, GILBERT & WRIGHT Henry, William & Gabriel ?
w 1790–1792
Optician
1789–1792   Navigation Warehouse, 148
             Leadenhall St, London
Succeeded by GREGORY & WRIGHT★
Sources: By (JAC)

GREW William
w 1785
Rule M
1785   Bradford St, Birmingham
Sources: Pye (MAC)

GRIBBEN Edward
w 1840–1870
Watch M, Jeweller, Optician, Silversmith
1840   84 High St, Belfast
1868   13 High St, Belfast
1870   7 High St, Belfast
Listed as watchmaker in directories 1831–92, but
as Optician only in 1840,1868,1870.
Sources: Burnett & Morrison-Low (1989) p.148

GRICE Thomas
fr 1675 w 1705
        London
Guild: Clockmakers fr 1675
Apprenticed to AMES Richard 1667
Known to have sold: sundial
Sources: GL: CKC 3939; Loomes (1981b)

GRICE William Hawks
w 1818–1823
Optician, Math IM
1818–1823   3 New Bond St, London
Succeeded by DIXEY G.& C.★
Took over from FRASER Alexander★
Known to have sold: microscope
Sources: MHS; GL: Sun, 11936/477 no. 944801–2

GRIFFIN & CO John Joseph
w 1850–1852
Chem IM, Math IM
1851   53 Baker St, Portman Square,
             London
Son of GRIFFIN Richard, Chem IM, of Glasgow
Succeeded by GRIFFIN John Joseph
Associated with WARD John (II)★, who acted as
agent
GRIFFIN & CO Richard★
Ex.1851
Known to have sold: hydrometer
Sources: Wk; Bryden (1972) p.49; Turner G
(1983a) p.309; Anderson et al (1990) p.32

GRIFFIN & CO Richard
w 1837–1861
Chem IM, Book S, Publisher
1820–1832   75 Hutcheson St, Glasgow
1833–1837   64 Hutcheson St, Glasgow
1838   115 Buchanan St, Glasgow
1839–1843   24 Canon St, Glasgow
1844–1855   40 Buchanan St, Glasgow
1855–1861   39 & 41 West Nile St, Glasgow
Father of GRIFFIN John J.
Succeeded by STONE John W.
Business started 1820
Sources: Bryden (1972) p.49; Anderson et al (1990)
p.32–35

GRIFFITH Edward
fl 1809
Optical IM
        Birmingham
Sources: Taylor (1966) p.364

GRIFFITH George
w 1708
[Math IM]
1708   East Smithfield, London
Guild: Grocers, fr 1708
Apprenticed to
HOWE William★ 1700, t/o to
GRIFFITH Mary★ 1703
Had apprentice LYON Joseph★ 1708
Sources: BROWN J (1979a) p.27, 32

GRIFFITH James
w 1668
Math IM
        London

Guild: Broderers, Clockmakers, fr 1667/8
Father of GRIFFITH George★
Husband of GRIFFITH Mary★
Succeeded by GRIFFITH Mary★
Died before 1700
Sources: GL: CKC 2710/1 fol.185; Brown J
(1979a) p.32

GRIFFITH Mary
c 1700 w 1708
1708   East Smithfield, London
Guild: Broderers
Wife of GRIFFITH James★
Had apprentice GRIFFITH George★
Sources: Brown J (1979a) p.32

GRIFFITHS A.
w 1776
1776   London
Known to have sold: chondrometer
Sources: inst WM (MAC)

GRIFFITHS Thomas
w 1841–1862
Rule M
Alternative name: GRIFFITH
1841   33 Kenion St, Birmingham
1850–1862   32 Kenion St, Birmingham
Sources: Mor; Pg; Sl

GRIGG James
fr 1795 w 1817
Scale M
1795   8 Stone Cutter St, Fleet Market,
             London
1817   5 Bear Alley, Fleet St, London
Guild: Blacksmiths, fr 1795
Apprenticed to GOODMAN John★ 1780
See also CORCORAN & GRIGG★
In the workhouse in 1822
Sources: GL: BKC 2881/15–16; STTP 2934
fol.157

GRIGNION Henry
s 1806 d by 1836
Optician
Alternative name: GRIGNON
1836   St.Paul's Churchyard, London
Guild: [Grocers]
Father of GRIGNON Henry s 1836 STC
Son of GRIGNION Claudius, gent, of Islington,
London
Apprenticed to DOLLOND George (I)★ 1806
His address suggests he worked for the Dollond★
business
Sources: SH: STC Memo Book; GL: GC 11598/6

GRIMALDI Peter
fl 1805–1810
Chrono M
Alternative name: GRIMALDE
        431 Strand, London
Succeeded by GRIMALDI & JOHNSON★
Sources: Taylor (1966) p.364

GRIMALDI & JOHNSON
fl 1809–1828
Watch M, Clock M

Alternative name: GRIMALDE & JOHNSON
Strand, London
Took part in chronometer trials at Royal
Greenwich Observatory 1824
Sources: CUL: RGO/1143 fol.6; inst MHS;
Baillie (1951); Loomes (1976); Taylor (1966) p.364

GRIMOLDI Dominick
w 1813–1822
Optician
1813   82 Leather Lane, Holborn, London
1816–1822   8 Red Lion St, Holborn, London
See also GRIMOLDI Henry*
Sources: H; Kt (JAC);

GRIMOLDI Henry
w 1839 w pt 1855
Baro M, Thermo M, Math IM, Phil IM, Hydro M
Alternative name: GRIMALDI
       4 Charles St, Hatton Garden,
       London
1839–1841   16 Brooke St, Holborn, London
1845–1846   24 Greville St, Hatton Garden,
       London
1851–1855   31 Brooke St, Holborn, London
Succeeded by GRIMOLDI & CO. H*
See also
GRIMOLDI Dominick*
GRIMALDI Peter*
Ex.1851
Sources: PO; Turner G (1983a) p.309

GRIMOLDI & CO. H.
w 1851–1873
Baro M, Thermo M, Gaugers IM, Optician, Math
IM, Phil IM
Alternative name: GRIMALDI & CO.
1851–1870   31 Brooke St, Holborn London
Took over from
TAGLIABUE & CO. A.*
GRIMOLDI Henry*
Sources: PO;Wk

GRIMSHAW Thomas
w 1834
Chrono M
1834   Liverpool
Sources: Loomes (1975)

GRINDROD John
w 1766–1767
Math IM
1766   Wolstenholme's Sq, Liverpool
1767   Ansell's Wient, Liverpool
Known to have sold: octant
Sources: Shaw; inst MHS (MAC)

GRINHAM Thomas
w 1833
Math IM
1833   15 St. John's Square, London
Attended London Mechanics Institute 1833
Sources: LMIR (AM)

GROOM G.
w 1842
Yard measure S
1842   16 Thavies Inn, Holborn, London

Associated with CLARK Samuel*, for whom he
acted as London agent
Sources: Pg

GROUT John
w 1814–1830
Scale M
1814–1830   35 Fashion St, Spitalfields, London
Guild: [Blacksmiths]
Apprenticed to PALLETT Thomas (I)* 1781
Sources: GL: BKC 2881/15; J; Kt; Pg; R

GROVE Christopher
w 1692–1695
Scale M
       London
Guild: Blacksmiths, fr 1674 or 1675
Father of GROVE Christopher (II)
Husband of GROVE Rebecca*
Apprenticed to SAUNDERS Robert (I)* 1667
Had apprentice:
THOMPSON Jeremiah* 1692 by t/o
ALCOCKE Robert* 1792 and 7 others
d before 1699
Sources: GL: BKC 2881/7, 2881/8, 2886/3
(MAC)

GROVE Rebecca
w 1699–1703
Scale M
1699   Angel Alley, Aldersgate St, London
Guild: Blacksmiths
Wife of GROVE Christopher*
r before 1708
Sources: GL: BKC 2881/8; 2881/9, 2881/10;
2886/3 (MAC)

GROVES & BARKER – & Francis
w 1851–1865
Math IM, Naut IM, Compass M
1851–1865   16 Market St, Clerkenwell, London
Sources: PO; Wk; Chaldecott (1989) p162

GRUBB Thomas
w 1838 d 1878
Engineer, Optician, Machinist
1839–1854   1 Upper Charlemont St, Dublin
1855–1858   14 Leinster Terrace, Rathmines,
       Dublin
1859–1863   15 Leinster Square, Rathmines,
       Dublin
1864–1878   141 Leinster Rd, Rathmines, Dublin
Father of GRUBB Howard
Succeeded by GRUBB Henry
FRS 1864; B.apt Bank of Ireland
Known to have sold: microscope, theodolite
Sources: inst MHS; Burnett & Morrison-Low
(1989) p.125; Holbrook (1992) p.228

GRUNDY John Clowes
w 1834–1848
Baro M, Looking-glass M, Optician, Math IM,
Phil IM
1834–1848   4 Exchange St, Manchester
Sources: Pg; Sl

GUANZIROLI G. & L.
w 1851

Baro M, Looking-glass M, Artificial flower M
1851   106 Hatton Garden, London
Sources: Wk

GUEST R.
w 1818
Rule M
1818   67 Brick-kiln St, Wolverhampton
Sources: PB

GUGERI Andrew
w 1849–1859
Baro M, Thermo M, Looking-glass M
1849–1859   16 Charles St, Hatton Garden,
       London
Took over from GUGERI & CARUGHI*
Sources: PO

GUGERI & BELOTTI Andrew & ?
w 1836–1842
Baro M, Thermo M
1836–1842   16 Charles St, Hatton Garden,
       London
Succeeded by GUGERI & CARUGHI*
Took over from BELOTTI & GUGERI*
Sources: R (JAC)

GUGERI & CARUGHI Andrew & ?
w 1843
Baro M, Thermo M
1843   16 Charles St, Hatton Garden,
       London
Sources: R

GUGGIARI Charles
w 1828
Picture frame M, Baro M, Thermo M
1828   Church St, Sheffield
Sources: Bk

GUGGIARI & ANZANI
a 1838
       Pelham St, Nottingham
Known to have sold: barometer
Sources: ChrSK 27 Nov 1986 lot 22; Taylor (1966)
p.472

GUINAALDE D.
w 1813–1819
Optician
1813–1819   82 Leather Lane, London
Sources: PO; Und

GUNN William
w 1849–1852
Compass M, Brassfounder, Tinsmith
1849   220 Broomielaw, Glasgow
1850–1852   15 Centre St, Glasgow
Sources: ADCS

GUNSTON Michael
w 1840–1845
Math IM, Optician
1840   28 Kirby St, Hatton Garden,
       London
1845   14 Woodbridge St, London
1845   6 St. Jame's Walk, Clerkenwell,
       London

Guild: Merchant Taylors, fr 1832
Apprenticed to WEEDEN William John★ 1825
Sources: GL: MTC MF 320, 324 (MAC); PO

GURNELL William
w 1684 d by 1705
Hour-glass M
Alternative name: GURNEL
1696   Glean Alley, St Thomas's,
         Southwark, London
Guild: Tallow Chandlers, fr 1681
Son of GURNELL Stephen, mercer
Apprenticed to WEST James★ 1673
Had apprentice ROBERTS James 1684
Sources: GL: THC 6158/3 p.87, 6153/5

GURNEY Joseph
w 1793–1795
Watch M, Jeweller
         Bridge St, Bristol
1793   Corn St, Bristol
Known to have sold: balance
Sources: Mat; inst (pv)

GUTTERIDGE, DUNNING & SON
c 1827
Known to have sold: slide rule
Sources: Sby Belgravia, Dec 1976 lot 194 (DJB)

GWILLIM Robert Devereux
w 1771
Spec M
Alternative name: Name given as John in
apprentice register
Guild: Spectaclemakers, fr 1771
Son of GWILLIM Devereux, gent., d, of London
Apprenticed to CLEARE James★ 1763
Sources: GL: SMC 5213/3; 6031/1; CLRO:
CF1/985

GWYLLYM Joshua
w 1832–1848
Rule M, Gauge M, Math IM
Alternative name: GWYLLIM
1832–1848   3 doors from the Infirmary, Earl St,
         Bristol
Took over from WEBB Thomas★
Sources: Hunts; Mat

HAAS Jacob Bernhard
w 1789–1799
Math IM
1789–1799   Bull Yard, St.Ann's Court, Soho,
         London
Partnership: HURTER & HAAS★
Pat. pumps 1783; partnership: c.1790–95; d.1828
in Lisbon
Known to have sold: barometer, thermometer,
hygrometer, electrometer, mechanical apparatus,
balance.
Sources: Ld; JAC; Turner & Levere (1973)
p.257–58; 328; inst Burghley House, Lincs

HABERSON Joseph
w 1780–1799
Optician
1780   28 Plumtree Court, Shoe Lane,
         London

1799   London House Yard, St.Paul's,
         London
Sources: GL: Sun 11936/284 no.432194 (MAC); H
(JAC)

HACK William
w 1748–1763
Math IM
         London
Guild: Goldsmiths, fr.1747
Apprenticed to PARSONS William (I)★ 1740
Had apprentice SEATON William★ 1751
and 4 others 1748–1763
Sources: GH: GSC Ap, Fr

HADDON William
w 1691 d 1728
Math IM
1713–1719   Giltspur St, near Newgate St,
         London
Guild: Stationers, fr 1691
Apprenticed to JOLE Robert★ 1683/4
Had apprentice:
BUSH Joseph★ 1694
WHITE Thomas 1699
MORGAN John 1700
BARKER William (I)★ 1700/01 by t/o from
WORGAN John★
GILPIN Richard 1705/6
MALE Edmund 1707
BATES Richard★ 1714
HADDON John, his son, 1715
GREENUP Robert 1719
DERRY John 1722
CRICK [CREEK] James★ 1727 t/o 1728 to
GILBERT John (I)★
Father of HADDON William (II) s 1730 to BATES
Richard★
Known to have sold: rule
Sources: GL: CH 12823/4 p.447, 12876/3; Brown
J (1979a) p.28; Bryden (1992) p.307; McKenzie
(1974) p.70,91, (1978) p.25,151–52

HADLEY John
w 1717 d 1744
Optical IM, Mathematician
1717   Bloomsbury, London
         Enfield Chase Middx
Son of HADLEY George
Associated with
HAUKSBEE Francis (II)★ in making telescopes
GILBERT & SON John★, who claimed to be sole
suppliers of octants of Hadley's own make
FRS 1717; author; inv. octant, commonly called
Hadley's quadrant, and took out pat. 1734
Known to have sold: octant, telescope
Sources: *Daily Ad* 22 Jun 1749 (JRM); Taylor (1954)
p.299; Wallis R & P (1986) p.130; Woodcroft (1854)

HAILS Thomas
w 1692–1699
Spec M, Optical IM
Alternative name: HAILES, HALE, HALES,
HAYLES
         Spectacles & Prospective Glass,
         corner of Cannon Alley over against
         the great North Door of St.Paul's
         Church, London

         The Telescope & Spectacles, corner
         of Cannon Alley over against the
         great North Door of St.Paul's
         Church, London
1693–1695   St Paul's Churchyard, London
Guild: Spectaclemakers, fr 1687
Had apprentice:
SMITH Edmund 1691/2
FORD James 1699
See also HALE Widow★ [possibly a relation]
YARWELL John★ [his unnamed apprentice might
have been Hails]
Last attendance at SMC Jan 1699/1700
Sources: GL: SMC 5213/1, 5213/2 p.17; Taylor
(1954) pp.283–4

HALE Widow
w 1675
Spec S
1675   Bishopsgate, London
Guild: Spectaclemakers
See also HAILS Thomas★ [possibly a relation]
Associated with TAILOR Zachary★, who supplied
specs
Sources: GL: SMC 5213/1

HALE William
w 1826–1840
Spec M
1826–1840   32 Ward's Row, Bethnal Green Rd,
         London
Sources: Pg; R (JAC)

HALEY Charles
w 1781–1825
Chrono M
         Wigmore St, London
Guild: Clockmakers, fr 1781
Pat. marine chronometer 1797
Sources: Baillie (1951)

HALL Edward
w 1850
Hydro M, Sacch M
1850   19 & 20 Tooley St, London
Partnership: with JENKIN Edward★ trading as
DRING, FAGE & CO.
B.apt Excise 1850 as DRING, FAGE & CO.
Sources: PO; McConnell (1993) p.53

HALL John (I)
w 1702–1722
[Scale M]
         London
Guild: Blacksmiths, fr 1698
Apprenticed to WILFORD David (I)
Worked for GOWERS Weston★
Had 9 apprentices not known as scale M
1702–1722
d by 1725
Sources: GL; BKC 2881/8, 2881/10, 2886/3,
2886/4 (MAC)

HALL John (II)
w 1827
Optician
1827   7 Orange St, Leicester Square,
         London

Same premises as HUDSON John*
Attended London Mechanics Institute 1827
Sources: LMIR (AM)

HALL Thomas (I)
w 1754 w c. 1759
Spec M
1759   St. Andrew Holborn, London
1754   St. Dunstan in the West, London
Guild: u & Spectaclemakers
Apprenticed to probably MANN James (II)* 1719
Had apprentice:
BOLUS Ann c. 1759
THOMSON John 1754
MCINTOSH/MACKINTOSH Thomas* 1756
fr as Brother (i.e. member of another Co.) 1739 in SMC
Sources: PRO: IR 1/22 (AM); GL: SMC 5213/2
p.113, 5213/3 p.13, 203+

HALL Thomas (II)
w 1827–1834
Chrono M
1827–1829   8 Kensington, Liverpool
1830–1831   Kensington Place, Low Hill,
              Liverpool
1834   18 Park Rd, Liverpool
Took part in chronometer trials at Royal
Greenwich Observatory, 1830–1831
Sources: CUL: RGO/1143 fol.9; G

HALL William
s 1811 w 1836
Spec M
1836   25 Hosier Lane, London
Guild: [Turners]
Apprenticed to USTONSON John* 1811
Sources: GL: TC 3302/3 (MAC); Pg

HALL & HAWKES
w 1839–1842
Optician, Math IM, Phil IM, Hydro M, Sacch M
1839   Topping's Wharf, London Bridge,
              London
1839–1842   10 Duke St, Borough, London
Sources: PO

HALLIFAX George
w 1750
Clock M
1750   Doncaster
Son of HALLIFAX John (I)*
Brother of HALLIFAX Joseph
Known to have sold: barometer
Instruments advertised: barometer, thermometer,
hydrometer.
Sources: Goodison (1977) p.157, 159

HALLIFAX John (I)
w 1710 d 1750
Clock M, Baro M
Alternative name: Johannes, HALIFAX
              Barnsley
Father of
HALLIFAX John (II)*
HALLIFAX George*
Succeeded by HALLIFAX Joseph, his 5th son
Known to have sold: barometer, hygrometer

Sources: Goodison (1977) p.157–58; Loomes
(1972); Sby 3 Jul 1986 (MAC)

HALLIFAX John (II)
c 1740 d 1758
Clock M, [Baro M]
Alternative name: HALIFAX
              Barnsley
Son of HALLIFAX John (I)*
Sources: Loomes (1972)

HAMER James (I)
w 1823
Math IM
1823   12 Hosier lane, West Smithfield,
              London
Guild: Joiners, fr 1823
Father of HAMER James (II), s 1823
Apprenticed to DANCER Michael* 1800
Had apprentice REES John 1823
Sources: GL: ABC 12080/2; JC 8046/13, 8052/8,
8055/5

HAMILTON Henry Robert
w 1836–1847
Optician, Math IM, Phil IM, Spec M
              11 Queen St, Percival St, London
1839–1846   16 Queen St, Northampton Square,
              London
Sources: Pg; PO; JAC

HAMILTON John
w 1826
Phil IM
1826   122 Regent St, London
Same premises as NEWMAN John Frederick
Attended London Mechanics Institute 1826
Sources: LMIR (AM)

HAMLETT William
w 1792
Rule M
1792   50 Salop St, Wolverhampton
Sources: Wolverhampton rate books (MAC)

HAMLIN William
w 1789–1811
Optician, Math IM
1793–1811   111 Leadenhall St, London
Guild: Stationers, fr 1754
Apprenticed to STEDMAN Christopher (I)*
1746/7
Had apprentice WOODFIELD Samuel 1800
Known to have sold: compass (magnetic)
Sources: inst NMM; A; BW; Kt; Ld; McKenzie
(1978) p.156, 332

HAMMOND William
s 1766 w 1780
Math IM
              London
1780   10 New Street Square, London
Guild: [Merchant Taylors]
Apprenticed to COLE Benjamin (II)*
Known to have sold: drawing instruments
Sources: GL: MTC MF 320; Sun 11936/283 no.
426758; Sby 11 Jun 1985 lot 258

HAMSEN John
a 1701–1723
Math IM
              London
Sources: GL: CH 12823/3 (JRM)

HANCLIFF Joseph
w 1826
Navigation Warehouse
1826   31 Sidney Place, Commercial Rd,
              London
Sources: Pg (JAC)

HANCOCK Hannah
w 1828–1837
Optician, Beer Machine M, Brass turner
1828   24 Waingate, Sheffield
1833–1837   7 Waingate, Sheffield
1837   (residence) Well St, Sheffield
Took over from HANCOCK William*
Had apprentice: WOODFIELD Samuel 1800
Sources: Bk; Pg; Wh

HANCOCK John (I)
fl 1740–1740
Alternative name: is this John HANDCOCK ?*
Known to have sold: sundial
Sources: Taylor (1966) p.206

HANCOCK John (II)
w 1845–1901+
Optician, Math IM
1845   36 City Road, Finsbury, London
1849–1859   30 City Road, Finsbury, London
1865–1901   61 City Road, Finsbury, London
Sources: PO

HANCOCK John (III)
w 1841
Optician
1841   Waingate, Sheffield
Sources: Pg

HANCOCK William
w 1822–1825
Optician, Beer machine M
1822   6 Park Hill, Sheffield
1822–1825   24 Waingate, Sheffield
Succeeded by HANCOCK Hannah*
Sources: Bk; Bn; Ge(MAC)

HANDCOCK John
w 1774
Ring M, Sundial M, Buckle M
Alternative name: HANCOCK
              Fargate, Sheffield
See also HANCOCK John (I)*
Sources: Sket (MAC)

HANDFORD Thomas
w 1668–1695
Spec M
Alternative name: HANFORD, HANDFIELD
1676–1693   Leadenhall St, London
1695   Tower Street, London
Guild: Spectaclemakers
Had apprentice:
LANE Thomas 1668

MOONE Abraham 1677
GURNEY John 1683
OWEN Thomas 1692
Master SMC 1679–1681, 1690–1692, last
appearance 1698
Sources: GL: SMC 5213/1; CH 12876/2 Apr 1683

HANDSFORD John
a 1785–1810
[Engraver, Math IM]
    Bristol
Known to have sold: planetarium
Sources: Bryant (1994) p.11–12

HANSON John
w 1840–1859
Math IM
1840–1859 29 Hope St, Hackney Road, London
Sources: Pg; PO

HANSON Mary
w 1816–1818
Spec M
1816–1818 Ann St, Birmingham
See also HANSON William★
Sources: H; Wr

HANSON William
w 1829–1845
Spec M, Optician
    31 Hyde St, Bloomsbury, London
1829   Church St, Birmingham
1835–1841 76 Newhall St, Birmingham
1845   26 Digbeth St, Birmingham
See also HANSON Mary★
Sources: K; Pg; Wr

HARBOTTLE John
w 1691
Lens grinder
1691   Dean St, Fetter Lane, London
Son of HARBOTTLE Ralph
Sources: GL: SMC 5213/1

HARDCASTLE John
w 1817–1822
Optician
1817–1822 53 Blackman St, Borough, London
Sources: J; PO; Und

HARDING John
w 1814
[Math IM]
1809   White Horse Alley, Red Lion St,
    Clerkenwell, London
1814   Willow Walk, Hackney, London
Guild: Grocers, fr 1809
Son of HARDING John, shoe M, of Clerkenwell,
London
Apprenticed to
FAIRBONE Charles (I)★ 1801, t/o
to FAIRBONE Charles (II)★ 1802
Had apprentice MATHEWS Mark 1814
Sources: GL: GC 11598/6

HARDMAN James
w 1802
Rule M

1802   74 Goat St, Wolverhampton
Sources: Wolverhampton rate books (MAC)

HARDY George
w 1658 d 1669
[Spec M]
    London
Guild: Spectaclemakers
Had apprentice HICKETT John★ 1658 t/o to
GOODMAN Richard★ 1658
Sources: GL: SMC 5213/1

HARDY John
w 1774
[Math IS]
1774   Ratcliff, London
Known to have sold: octant
Sources: Sby 23 Jun 1987 lot 164 (MAC)

HARDY William
fl 1820–1832
Watch M
    5 Wood St, Spitalfields, London
Known to have sold: chronometer
Sources: Taylor (1966) p.395

HARMON William
w 1832–1834
Math IM, Phil IM
Alternative name: HARMAN
1832–1834 1 Halfmoon Crescent, White
    Conduit Fields, London
Guild: [Coachmakers]
Apprenticed to ELLIOTT William (II)★
b c.1792; imprisoned for debt 1830 in Giltspur St
Compter
Sources: GL: CMC 5643; CWH: CWC box 80
B3; Pg

HARPER Andrew
w 1722
[Spec M]
    London
Guild: Spectaclemakers fr 1721/2
Son of HARPER Andrew, cordwainer, of
Wellington, Salop
Apprenticed to ARCHER Thomas★ 1714
Had apprentice:
GLOVER John 1721/2 by t/o from GIBBONS
William (I)★
MORRIS Thomas 1722
d c. 1740
Sources: GL: SMC 5213/2 p.88,127–8,132, 6029

HARPER Robert
w 1772–1807
Math IM
1772   Tarleton St, Liverpool
1776   Barnett St, Liverpool
1782   Spitalfields, Liverpool
1790   68 Peter St, Liverpool
1800–1803 67 Peter St, Whitechapel, Liverpool
1804   29 Peter St, Whitechapel, Liverpool
1805–1807 61 Peter St, Whitechapel, Liverpool
Sources: G; LM index (MAC)

HARRIMAN John
w 1835–1862

Baro M, Thermo M
1835   New John St, Birmingham
1839–1850 58 Church St, Birmingham
1854   60 Church St, Birmingham
1858–1862 100 Pritchett St, Birmingham
Known to have sold: barometer
Instruments advertised: barometer, rule
Sources: Mor; K; Pg; Sl; Goodison (1977) p.329

HARRIMAN Thomas
w 1805–1850
Rule M
1805   Ashted Row, Birmingham
1809–1818 Loveday St, Birmingham
1825–1850 24 Loveday St, Birmingham
1829–1830 40 Loveday St, Birmingham
See also HARRIMAN John★
Sources: H; Pg; Wr

HARRIS –
w 1673
Ironmonger
1673   At the Maypole in the Strand,
    London
Known to have sold: rule
Sources: GL: CKC 2710/1 p.264; Loomes (1981b)

HARRIS Alfred
w 1827
Optician
1827   Green St, Portman Square, London
Attended London Mechanics Institute 1827
Sources: LMIR (AM)

HARRIS Clement
w 1824–1844
Chrono M
1825–1833 Cornhill, London
1839   76 Cornhill, London
Took part in chronometer trials at Royal
Greenwich Observatory 1824–1833
Sources: CUL: RGO 1143 fol.2–10; Pg

HARRIS Daniel (I)
fr 1735
    Cranbourn Alley, Leicester Fields,
    London
Guild: Joiners, fr 1735
Apprenticed to BLOW Edmond★ 1723 t/o
to COOKE Thomas (II)★ 1725
Known to have sold: waywiser
Sources: inst noted by MAC; Crawforth (1987)
p.357

HARRIS Daniel (II)
w 1848–1852
Optician
1848–1849 6 Bonnavilla, Mount Pleasant,
    Dublin
1850–1852 4 Bonnavilla, Mount Pleasant,
    Dublin
Sources: Burnett & Morrison-Low (1989) p.125

HARRIS Daniel and William
w 1846–1848
Optician
1846–1848 Richmond St, upper, Dublin
1847   8 Wicklow St, Dublin

Sources: Burnett & Morrison-Low (1989) p.126; Thom

HARRIS George

w 1733
[Math IS?]
Known to have sold: quadrant
Sources: Taylor (1966) p.179

HARRIS John (I)

w 1689–1703
Alternative name: Possibly the same as John HARRIS (III)★
1683–1703   London
Guild: Spectaclemakers, fr 1683
Apprenticed to TAILOR John (I)★ 1677
Sources: GL: SMC 5213/1

HARRIS John (II)

w 1688 d 1699
Scale M
        Sun & Scales against the Church, Rood Lane nr. Fenchurch St
        London
Guild: Clothworkers
Had apprentice SMELT Samuel★ by t/o from WRIGHT Edward nd
Known to have sold: balance
Sources: GL: BKC 2881/8 (MAC); Sheppard & Musham (1975) no.324

HARRIS John (III)

w 1721–1728
Math IM
Alternative name: Possibly the same as HARRIS John (I)★
        Bullhead Court, Newgate St, London
Partnership: SENEX John★
WILSON Henry (for publications)
See also HARRIS Joseph (II)★
Pat. globes, charts 1721
Sources: Taylor (1966) p.125; Wallis R & P (1986) p.114; Woodcroft (1854)

HARRIS John (IV)

w 1816–1840
Optician, Optical Brazier, Brass Founder
        145 High Holborn, London
1816–1840   22 Hyde St, Bloomsbury, London
See also HARRIS & SON Thomas★
Sources: Und; PO; JAC

HARRIS Joseph (I)

w 1651
Spec M
1651   Woburn, Beds
Sources: GL: BKC 2886/1

HARRIS Joseph (II)

w 1724–1764
Math Teacher, Math IM
        Talgarth Cornwall
1729   Two Civet Cats, Crane Court, Fleet St, London
1748   Royal Mint, Tower Hill, London
Son of HARRIS Howel, farmer, of Cornwall
Associated with
HEATH Thomas★

CUSHEE Richard★
WRIGHT Thomas (I)★
SENEX John★
Sources: Taylor (1966) p.129, 161; Wallis R & P (1986) p.166–67

HARRIS Joshua (I)

fr 1785 w 1787
Math IM
1787   9 Fetter Lane, Fleet St, London
Guild: Merchant Taylors, fr 1785
Son of HARRIS John
Apprenticed to HARRIS Thomas (III)★ 1777
Sources: GL; Sun 11936/340 no.526118; MTC MF 320, 324 (MAC)

HARRIS Joshua (II)

w 1823
Clock M, Watch M
1823   Witney
Known to have sold: barometer
Sources: Beeson (1989) p.109

HARRIS R.

fl 1745
        Guernsey
Known to have sold: ring dial
Sources: Daumas (1972) p.235

HARRIS Richard

w 1790–1810
Optician
        22 Lamb's Conduit St, Red Lion St, London
        44 Great Russell St, Bloomsbury, London
        401 Strand, London
        50 Red Lion St, Clerkenwell, London
1788   Red Lion Street, Clerkenwell, London
1790–1810   404 Strand, London
Father of HARRIS William (I)★
Sources: H; By; PO; GL: CKC, 2720/1; JAC

HARRIS Richard Joshua

s 1815
Math IM
1815   50 High Holborn, London
Guild: Clockmakers
Son of HARRIS William (I)★
Partnership: HARRIS & SON William★
Apprenticed to HARRIS William (I)★
St. Andrew's Holborn, bap 22 Dec 1800
Sources: GL: CKC 2720/2

HARRIS Thomas (I)

w 1790–1806
Optician, Math IM, Phil IM, Globe M
1804   140 Fleet St, London
1804   and 30 Hyde St, Bloomsbury, London
        Little Russell St, Bloomsbury, London
1809–1826   52 Great Russell St, Bloomsbury, London
1818   [?Residence of same man] Primrose Cottage, Hampstead Rd, London

Guild: Spectaclemakers, fr 1804
Father of
HARRIS Thomas (II)★
HARRIS William (II)★
Son of HARRIS Thomas, tallow chandler, d, of Newington Butts, London
Apprenticed to LINNELL George★ 1771
Had apprentice:
DOWLING William★ 1804
EVANS Humphrey Jones 1809
ALDHOUSE John Frederick 1816
MANNING Edward 1809, by t/o from
RICHARDSON John (II)★
Succeeded by HARRIS & SON Thomas★
R.apt 1819 & 1820 with HARRIS William (II)★; had a manufactury behind his Bloomsbury house 1826
Known to have sold: microscope
Instruments advertised: hydrometer
Sources: GL: Sun 11936/503 no.1033563; Wk; PO
GL:LC 15835/3; SMC 5213/3, 5213/4; FDC 6331/6

HARRIS Thomas (II)

w 1802 d 1808
Optician
1804   140 Fleet St, London
1808   Hyde St, Bloomsbury, London
Guild: Loriners, fr 1804 by purchase
Son of HARRIS Thomas (I)★
Sergeant in the Bloomsbury Volunteers, when killed in a fire at the Covent Garden Theatre, 1808
Sources: GL: LC 15835/3; H; GMag Sep 1808 p.847 (AM)

HARRIS Thomas (III)

fr 1777 w 1805
Math IM
1777–1795   Paradise Row, Bethnal Green, London
Guild: Merchant Taylors
Apprenticed to COLE Benjamin (II)★ 1770
Had apprentice:
HARRIS Joshua (I)★, son of John, 1777
VENTOM Thomas★ 1782
DIXWELL Alexander 1786
CORNWELL Benjamin 1789
EVANS William (III)★ 1793
HARRIS John Robert, his son, 1796
RENNOLDSON Isaac★ 1798
OLIVE James 1799
HARRIS Samuel, his son, 1805
Sources: GL: MTC MF 320, 324; Sun 11936/263 no.392834

HARRIS Thomas P

w 1841
Optician
1824–1841   52 Great Russell St, Bloomsbury, London
Employed CALLAGHAN William★ 1841
b c.1806 Attended London Mechanics Institute 1824–1826, 1832
Sources: PRO: Cs 1841 HO/107 672/4 fol. 6; LMIR (AM)

HARRIS William (I)

w 1799–1841
Optician

HARRIS William (II)

1805	47 High Holborn, London
1815	50 High Holborn, London
1800–1841	50 Holborn, London

Guild: Clockmakers, fr 1796
Father of HARRIS Richard Joshua★
Son of HARRIS Richard★
Husband of HARRIS Isabella
Partnership: HARRIS & SON William★
Apprenticed to ROBINSON Joseph, motion maker, 1788
Had apprentice:
WIGGINS Francis Smith 1806
HARRIS Richard Joshua★, his son, 1815
LADD Edward Wilds★ 1816
Succeeded by HARRIS & CO. William★
b c.1774; Pat.1811 with BREWSTER David quadrant & telescope; Master of Clockmakers Co. 1830–1832
Known to have sold: sundial
Sources: H; Kt; PO; GL: CKC 2720/1, 2720/2,11658; PRO: Cs 1841 (AM); Patent records (MAC)

HARRIS William (II)

w 1829 d 1843
Optician, Globe M

1818	52 Great Russell St, Bloomsbury
1822	9 Cornhill and 52 Great Russell St, London
1831–1835	22 Cornhill, London
1839–1841	63 King William St, London
	22 Change Alley, London
	23 Great Eastcheap, London
	22 Lamb's Conduit St, London

Guild: Spectaclemakers, fr by purchase
Son of HARRIS Thomas (I)★
Father of HARRIS William Dollond★
Partnership: HARRIS & SON Thomas★
Associated with many other IM, from whom he obtained stock – see McConnell (1994)
R.apt – see HARRIS & SON Thomas (I)★ [& William (II)]; Master SMC 1824–1826; bankrupt 1830; widow Charlotte, left with a large family, given charity by SMC 1843
Sources: GL: SMC 5213/4, 5213/5, 5213/6; PRO: LC/3/68 p.196, LC/3/69 p.8; Pg; PO; R (JAC); McConnell (1994) p.273–79

HARRIS William (III)

w 1821
Math IM

| 1821 | Parish of St Botolph Aldersgate, London |

Father of HARRIS Richard s1821 PMC
Sources: GL: PMC 5652/2

HARRIS William Dollond

w 1845–1847
Optician, Globe M; by 1852 wholesale fancy stationer

| 1845–1847 | 38 Arundel St, Strand, London |
| 1852–1855 | 7 Earl St, Blackfriars, London |

Guild: Spectaclemakers, fp 1852
Son of HARRIS William (II)★
d 11 Jan 1861 after lengthy illness; widow Betsey Sophia petitioned SMC for charity
Sources: PO; GL:SMC 5213/6, 5213/7

HARRIS & CO. William

w 1813–1839
Math IM, Optical IM, Optician

1820	Bey dem Rathhause no. 26, Hamburg
1816–1839	50 Holborn, London
1816–1839	35 Crown St, Liverpool
1816–1835	50 High Holborn, London

Partnership with: CAMPBELL W. (at Hamburg)
Took over from HARRIS William (I)★
Succeeded by HARRIS & SON William★
Pat.1811 quadrants, telescope with D.Brewster
Known to have sold: globe, compass, balance, microscope
Sources: Und; Kt; PO; inst NMM & pv; HA (AM); Woodcroft (1854); Calvert (1971) p.25

HARRIS & SON Thomas (I) [& Thomas (II)]

w 1802–1808
Opticians

| 1804–1806 | 140 Fleet St, London |

Sources: H; GMag Sep 1808 p.847 (AM)

HARRIS & SON Thomas (I) [& William (II)]

w 1802 p 1901+
Optician, Math IM, Telescope M
22 Cornhill, London

1808	20 Duke St, Bloomsbury, London
1810–1817	30 Hyde St, Bloomsbury, London
1816–1885	52 Great Russell St, Bloomsbury, London
1822	9 Cornhill, London
1859	43 & 52 Great Russell St, Bloomsbury, London WC
1890–1901	32 Gracechurch St, London WC
1851	52 Great Russell St, Bloomsbury, and 141A (or 141) Oxford St, London

Took over from HARRIS Thomas (I)★
See also HARRIS William (II)★
R.apt Regent 1819; R.apt Geo.IV 1820; e 1780
Known to have sold: telescope, microscope
Instruments advertised: globe
Sources: PO; Und; Times 8 Jun 1838 p.7; PRO: LC/3/68 p.196, LC/3/69 p.8 (MAC); inst(s)

HARRIS & SON William

w 1840–1855
Optician, Phil IM, Drawing IM

| 1840–1855 | 50 High Holborn, London |

Partnership: HARRIS William (I)★ and prob HARRIS Richard Joshua★
Took over from HARRIS & CO. William★
Ex.1851
Sources: PO; GL: CKC 2720/2; Turner G (1983a) p.309

HARRISON Anthony

a 1750
Known to have sold: octant
Sources: inst MMA

HARRISON B.

a 1800–1900
11 Princes St, Spitalfields, London
Known to have sold: slide rule

HARRISON Charles

w 1766–1788
Watch M, Clock M, Book S, Stationer, Scale M

| 1769 | Main St, English-town, Limerick |
| 1788 | Opposite St.Mary's Church, Limerick |

Known to have sold: sundial, weights
Instruments advertised: balance
Sources: inst MHS; ChrSK 29 June 1989 lot 183; Burnett & Morrison-Low (1989) p.87–88; Mollan (1991) p.29

HARRISON Christopher

fr 1733
Math IM

| 1733 | Parish of St.Olave, Southwark, London |

Guild: Stationers, fr 1733
Apprenticed to CARTER Henry★ 1716
Had apprentice HARRISON Thomas 1733
Sources: McKenzie (1978) p.65, 160

HARRISON Edward

w 1770–1798
Watch M, Silversmith

| 1770–1798 | Bridge St, Warrington |

Known to have sold: balance
Sources: BW; By; inst Warrington Mu (MAC)

HARRISON George

w 1829
Spec M

| 1829 | Essex St, Birmingham |

Sources: Wr (MAC)

HARRISON James

a 1760–1780
Alternative name: I.
Birmingham
Known to have sold: weights
Sources: Sheppard & Musham (1975) no.314

HARRISON John (I)

b 1693 d 1776
Chrono M

1697	Barrow on Humber
1736	Leather Lane, London
1739	Red Lion Sq, London

Father of HARRISON William (I)★
Partnership: HARRISON & SON John★
Associated with
SHORT James★
GRAHAM George★ who gave financial support
CUMMING Alexander★
Known to have sold: balance, chronometer
Sources: Betts (1993); King & Millburn (1978) p.127; Taylor (1966) p.125–27

HARRISON John (II)

w 1818–1857
Chrono M, Watch M

1824–1828	60 Great Crosshall St, Liverpool
1834–1837	14 Castle St, Liverpool
1839–1857	27 Castle St, Liverpool
1847	2 Sweeting St, Liverpool
1848	24 Park St, Toxteth Park, Liverpool

See also HARRISON Robert★
Known to have sold: chronometer
Sources: G; LM index (MAC)

HARRISON John (III)
w 1848
Math IM, Chandler
1848   7 Dock St, Hull
Sources: Stn

HARRISON John (IV)
w 1849–1875
Math IM, Phil IM, Optician, Chem IM,Optical Turner
1841   4 Goldsmith's Row, Shoe Lane, London
1848   3 Racquet Court, Fleet St, London
1849–1852   36 Kirby St, Hatton Garden, London
1855–1859   29 Kirby St, Hatton Garden, London
1870–1875   68 Red Lion St, Clerkenwell, London
Guild: Drapers, fr 1841
Son of BROWN (sic) John, waterman, d, of Rotherhithe, London
Apprenticed to STANTON John* 1835
Had apprentice:
FALDO Thomas 1848
CROCKER Frederick Arthur 1870
Sources: PO; Wk; DH: DPC Ap/Fr, index

HARRISON Jonathan
w 1800
Math IM
1800   Keswick
Sources: DJB

HARRISON Joseph
fr 1711 w 1714
Math IM
1711   Bishopsgate St, London
1714   Crooked Lane, London
Guild: Grocers, fr 1711/12
Son of HARRISON Michael, clerk, of St. Ives, Hunts
Apprenticed to JOHNSON John (I)* 1704
Had apprentice:
FARRER John 1713 t/o to FRANKLIN Thomas*
HOWELL James 1714, t/o to FRANKLIN Thomas*
Sources: Brown (1979a) p.32

HARRISON Robert
w 1818
Compass M
1818   60 Leeds St, Liverpool
See also HARRISON John (II)*
Sources: G (MAC)

HARRISON Thomas (I)
c 1772
              Liverpool
Took over from FINNEY Joseph*
Sources: Loomes (1975)

HARRISON Thomas (II)
w 1752–1782
Scale M
1752–1782   71 Cannon St, London
Guild: Blacksmiths, fr 1752
Apprenticed to ROBERTS Richard* 1744/5
Had apprentice:
GRAY Francis* 1758
WILLIAMS Thomas (III)* 1769

WILLIAMS William (I)* 1774 t/o to WILLIAMS Thomas (III)*
Succeeded by WILLIAMS Thomas (III)*
Known to have sold: balance
Sources: GL: BKC 2885/1, 2886/5 (MAC); Mort; Sheppard & Musham (1975) no.28

HARRISON W.B.
w 1851
Math IM
1851   7 Dock St, Hull
Sources: Wh

HARRISON William (I)
w pt 1761–1776
Chrono M
              Holborn, London
Guild: Clockmakers, fr 1763
Son of HARRISON John (I)*
Partnership: HARRISON & SON John*
Apprenticed to CARRINGTON Robert 1752
b 1728, d 1816; FRS
Sources: Baillie (1951) GL: CKC 11568; Betts (1993) pp.17–23

HARRISON William (II)
w 1777–1785
Spec M
1777–1780   Forster's Yard, Digbeth, Birmingham
1785   Back of 128 Digbeth, Birmingham
Sources: PR; Pye

HARRISON William (III)
w 1841
Rule M
1841   394 Summer Lane, Birmingham
Sources: Pg

HARRISON & SON John [& William (I)]
w 1761–1776
Chrono M
              London
Partnership: HARRISON John (I)* & his son
Sources: Betts (1993) p.17; Baillie (1951)

HARRYMAN Joseph
w 1792
Rule M
1792   74 Goat St, Wolverhampton
Sources: Wolverhampton rate books (MAC)

HART Benjamin
w 1725–1735
[Scale M]
1704–1735   London
Guild: Blacksmiths, fr 1703/4
Son of HART Joseph (I)* and HART Susan*
Apprenticed to SNART John (I)* 1693
Had apprentice:
HATHAWAY Francis 1725
READ Samuel* 1734 by t/o from LANE John*
Sources: GL: BKC 2881/9, 2886/4 (MAC)

HART Joseph (I)
w 1655 d.c 1686
Scale M
1653–1686   London
Guild: Blacksmith, fr 1653

Son of HART William, farmer, of Northampton
Apprenticed to NEALE Samuel* 1644
Had apprentice:
BUSWELL Jonathan 1655
PYM Richard nd, fr 1687
NEALE John (I)* 1684
SNART John (I)* 1685
Father of
HART Benjamin*
HART Joseph (II)*
Husband of HART Susan*
Sources: GL: BKC 2881/6, 2881/8 (MAC)

HART Joseph (II)
1691–1693
              London
Guild: Blacksmiths, fp 1686
Son of
HART Joseph (I)* and
HART Susan*
Brother of HART Benjamin*
Had apprentice MANTELL Samuel 1692 t/o 1693 to SNART John (I)*
Sources: GL: BKC 2881/8, 2881/9 (MAC)

HART Joseph (III)
w 1785–1805
Optician, Spec M, Optical IM, Math IM, Phil IM
1787–1801   5 Digbeth, Birmingham
1805   65 Dale End, Birmingham
See also HART William*
Sources: H; Pye

HART Saul
w 1841
Rule M
1841   114 Dale St, Liverpool
Sources: G

HART Susan
w 1692
1695   Maiden Lane, London
Guild: Blacksmiths
Wife of HART Joseph (I)*
Mother of
HART Joseph (II)*
HART Benjamin*
Sources: GL: BKC 2881/8 (MAC)

HART William
w 1783
Spec M
1783   Digbeth, Birmingham
See also HART Joseph*
Sources: By

HARTLEY J.G.
fl 1820–1823
1820–1823   Newhaven, near Leith
Known to have sold: compass
Sources: Taylor (1966) p.423

HARWOOD & THOMAS
w 1798–1816
Manufacturer, Merchant
1816   George St, Sheffield
Known to have sold: balance
Sources: BW; Pg; inst SM (Wellcome) (MAC)

HASKINS J.
w 1845
Optician
1845   7 Queen Square, Bartholomew
         Close, London
Sources: PO

HASKINS James (I)
w 1793–1833
Scale M, Brightsmith
1793–1797   Whitson Court, Bristol
1798–1833   Lower Maudlin St, Bristol
Succeeded by HASKINS James (II)★
Sources: Mat; Und

HASKINS James (II)
w 1834
Brightsmith, Scale M
1834   Lower Maudlin St, Bristol
Took over from HASKINS James (I)★
Sources: Mat

HASLEDON George
w 1800–1801
Math IM, Book S, Stationer
1800   34 Paradise St, Liverpool
Bankrupt 1801
Sources: G: LM index (MAC)

HASLOM Henry
w 1666 d 1673
Spec M
Alternative name: HASLAM, HAZELAM
1670   St Clement's Danes, London
Guild: Spectaclemakers
Husband of HASLOM Widow★
Had apprentice:
TINGAY Gregory★ 1668 taken over by HASLOM
widow★ 1673
HENLEY (or HEALEY) Josiah 1672
Succeeded by HASLOM Widow★
Sources: GL: SMC 5213/1

HASLOM Widow
w 1673–1675
[Spec M]
1675   London
Guild: Spectaclemakers
Wife of HASLOM Henry★
Had apprentice
TINGAY Gregory★ 1673, taken over from
HASLOM Henry★
probably HENLEY (or HEALEY) Josiah
Took over from HASLOM Henry★
Sources: GL: SMC 5213/1

HASSALL & CO.
w 1797
Rule M
Alternative name: HOSSALL & CO.
1797   Bull St, Birmingham
See also BELCHER & HASSALL★
Sources: Pye

HASSARD Joseph
fr 1762 w 1768
Phil IM
Alternative name: HAZARD

1762   Fleet St, London
1791–1793   Bancroft's Almshouses, Mile End,
         London
1814–1822   Mary Pennels Almshouse
Guild: Drapers, fr 1762
Son of HASSARD Joseph, book binder, d, of
London
Apprenticed to HICKMAN Joseph (I)★ 1747/8
Associated with COULSTON John★[testified when
latter freed]
Sources: DH: DPC Ap/Fr, index

HATFIELD William
w 1671–1675
Spec M
1671–1674   Southwark, London
Guild: Spectaclemakers
fr by 1657
Sources: GL: SMC 5213/1

HATTON James
w 1806–1820
Watch M
1806–1820   4 St.Michael's Alley, Cornhill,
         London
Guild: Clockmakers, fr 1799
Son of HATTON Thos, watch maker, d, of London
Apprenticed to MARGETTS George★ 1790
Had apprentice:
STROUD George 1808
HATTON Christopher 1805
SMITH Thomas 1812
Succeeded by HATTON & HARRIS★
Took over from MARGETTS & HATTON★
Known to have sold: chronometer
Sources: GL:CKC 2720/1, 2720/2, 2722, 11568;
Sby 23 Jun 1987 lot 261

HATTON Thomas
c 1740 w 1774
Clock M, Math IM
1740–1769   Preston, Lancs
1769–1774   London
Associated with ADAMS George (II)★ in selling
balance
Author
Sources: Taylor (1966) p.207–08; Wallis R & P
(1993) p.64

HATTON & HARRIS James & ?
w 1820
1820   4 St.Michael's Alley, Cornhill,
         London
Took over from HATTON James★
Known to have sold: chronometer
Sources: Taylor (1966) p.366

HAUKSBEE Francis (I)
fl 1700 d 1713
Phil IM
Alternative name: HAUKSBY, HAUKSBEY,
HAUKSBE
1704   Giltspur St, without Newgate,
         London
1709   Wine Office Court, Fleet St,
         London
–1713   Hind Court, Fleet St, London
Guild: Drapers, fp 1712

Father of HAUKSBEE Calvin, later an embroiderer
Son of HAUKSBEE Richard, embroiderer, of
Colchester
Uncle of HAUKSBEE Francis (II)★
Apprenticed to HAUKSBEE John, his brother, 1678
Had apprentice BRIDGER Richard★
Employed BRIDGER Richard★
Succeeded by HAUKSBEE Mary★ his widow
Associated with VREAM William★
bap 1660 St Mary, Colchester; FRS 1705; Lecturer;
Author
Known to have sold: air pump, barometer
Sources: DH: DPC Ap/Fr, Q; IGI; Bryden (1992)
p.331–32; Wallis R & V (1986); Vream (1717) A2

HAUKSBEE Francis (II)
w 1712 d 1763
Math IM
Alternative name: HAWKSBEE, HAUKSBY,
HAUKSBE, HAWKESBEE &c
         Crane Court, Fetter Lane, near
         St.Dunstan's Church, London
1738   3 Crane Court, Fleet St, London
Guild: Drapers, fp 1714
Son of HAUKSBEE John
Nephew of HAUKSBEE Francis (I)★
Apprenticed to MARSHALL John★ 1703 TC
Had apprentice:
WORKMAN Benjamin★ 1714
HICKMAN Joseph (I)★ 1725
Associated with
HADLEY John★ in improving telescopes
SHAW Peter, lecturer, in designing inst
NICHOLLS Sutton★
b 1688, bap All Hallows the Great London;
Lecturer
Clerk-housekeeper to the Royal Society 1723
Known to have sold: telescope, electrostatic
generator, barometer, thermometer
Sources: DH: DPC Ap/Fr, Q; Boyd; IGI; GL: TC
3302/2; GMag 33 (1763) p.46 (JAC); Calvert
(1971) p.25; Taylor (1954) p.288, 302, (1966) p.128,
165–66

HAUKSBEE Mary
w 1713
Alternative name: May
1713   Hind Court, Fleet St, London
Guild: Drapers
Wife of HAUKSBEE Francis (I)★
Had apprentice:
MEAGER Rachael 1713
DIXON Mary 1713
KNIGHT Sarah 1716
HAUKSBEE Calvin, her son, 1720
Employed BRIDGER Richard★
Took over from HAUKSBEE Francis (I)★
Although she continued her husband's business for
a short time, her apprentices became embroiderers
Sources: DH: DPC Ap/Fr

HAVARTO Guljelmo
w 1660
Alternative name: Gulielmus HAVARTUS, William
HAVART
1660   Edinburgh?
Signed sundial made for use in Edinburgh
Sources: Bryden (1972), p.16, 50

HAWES John

w 1668–1675
Spec M
1670   Creechurch, London
1670   Southwark, London
1671   Aldgate within, London
1671–1672   Little Eastcheap, London
Guild: [Brewers] Spectaclemakers
Father of HAWES Samuel fp 1671
Son of HAWES William, husbandman, of
Braybrooke, Northants
Apprenticed to PEALE Thomas★ 1632/3 BREW
Had apprentice:
BARBER Isaac★ 1668 SMC
PINFOLD Robert 1675 t/o 1676/7 to
THROGMORTON John (I)★
January 1676/7 reported to be in King's Bench
prison; removed from SMC Court 1678
Known to have sold: spectacles
Sources: GL: SMC 5213/1 GL: BREW 5445/15

HAWES William

w 1842–1880
Optician
1842   95 Cheapside, London
1845–1880   79 Leadenhall St, London
Guild: Spectaclemakers, fr 1842
Son of HAWES William, farmer of of Theydon,
Essex
Worked for DOLLOND★
Succeeded by HAWES Alfred, his son
e 1840; fr SMC by purchase; d by 1890
Known to have sold: microscope
Sources: PO; GL: SMC 5213/5, 5213/8; ML:
TCd of HAWES A.; Sby 23 Oct 1985, TCd

HAWKES Samuel

w 1805
Math IM
1805   1 East Row City Rd, London
Sources: H (DJB)

HAWKES Stephen

w 1851–1875
Math IM
1851–1859   17 Great Sutton St, Clerkenwell,
            London
1865–1875   22 Great Sutton St, Clerkenwell,
            London
Sources: PO; Wk

HAWKES Thomas

w 1741–1783
Surveyor, Math IM, Mechanic, Tinman, Painter,
Book S, Astronomer
1741–1744   Wells, Somerset
1750   Norwich, Norfolk
1783   27 Magdalen St, Norwich
Quaker; b 1710; d 1784
Sources: Wallis R & P (1986); King & Millburn
p.201, p.333–34; Chase

HAWKESFORD Edward

w 1792–1802
Rule M
1792–1802   57 Canal St, Wolverhampton
Sources: Wolverhampton rate books (MAC)

HAWKINS

w 1841
1841   London
Worked for TROUGHTON & SIMMS★
See also HAWKINS Thomas (II)★
'Hawkins made it' from Simms' Technical
Notebook suggests that he was an outworker or
journeyman.
Sources: VIA: William Simms Notebooks, 1.2.1.
p.41 (AM)

HAWKINS Charles

w 1841
Baro M
1841   Garden Court, Holborn [? off
            Baldwyns Gardens], London
b 1801 or 1802 in County of Middlesex [which
included much of London]
Sources: PRO: Cs 1841 (AM)

HAWKINS Frederick

w 1851–1865
Math IM
1825–1865   16 Perry St, Somers Town, London
Same premises as HAWKINS Thomas (II)★
Attended London Mechanics Institute 1825–1829
Sources: LMIR; PO; Wk

HAWKINS Thomas (I)

w 1809–1819
Math IM
1809–1819   16 Little Guildford St, Russell
            Square, London
Sources: H; R (JAC)

HAWKINS Thomas (II)

w 1834–1840
Hydro M, Math IM, Optical IM, Phil IM
1834–1840   16 Perry St, Somers Town, London
Same premises as HAWKINS Frederick★
Sources: Pg; R (JAC)

HAWKINS William

w 1728–1750
Scale M
            Angel & Scales next door to
            Haberdashers' Hall in Maiden Lane
            near Wood St, London
            Maiden Lane, near Wood St,
            London
Guild: Blacksmiths, fr 1719
Apprenticed to NEALE John (I)★ 1710
Had apprentice:
STINTON Joshua 1728 t/o 1733 to LIND John★
HAWKINS William, son of Thomas, 1730
MEARS John 1738
BATEMAN John 1750
Known to have sold: balance
Sources: GL: BKC 2881/10, 2886/4, 2886/5,
2888; inst Rochester Mu

HAWKLEY G.

w 1843–1844
Phil IM
1843–1844   9 Amwell Terrace, London
Attended London Mechanics Institute 1843–1844
Sources: LMIR (AM)

HAWNEY William

w 1721
Teacher, Surveyor, Dial M, Quadrant M
1721   Lydd, Kent
Sources: Hawney (1721) (DJB)

HAWTING John

s 1745 d 1791
Clock M, Watch M, Whitesmith
1764   Holywell Street Oxford
1772   35 Holywell Street Oxford
Father of HAWTING William
Apprenticed to REYNOLDS Thomas, Whitesmith,
1745
Had apprentice:
HAWTING William, his son, 1770
HEATH John 1756
BULL Lionel 1761
BIGNELL Thomas 1764
b c 1731; freedom of Oxford 1756
Made regulator for Radcliffe Observatory
Sources: Beeson (1989) p.111

HAY James

w 1767–1802
Scale M
Alternative name: HAYES
1767–1770   Barn St, Wolverhampton
1780   Salop St, Wolverhampton
1802   19 Salop St, Wolverhampton
Sources: PR; Rg; Sket

HAY John

w 1838
Carver, Gilder, Print S, Optical IS, Math IS
1838   Aberdeen
Known to have sold: sundial, microscope, compass
Sources: Bill (pv)

HAY John & James

w 1847–1851
Optical IM, Phil IM
            Aberdeen
See also
HAY William★
HAY John★
Known to have sold: barometer
Sources: Phlps (E) 31 May 1985 lot 111 – NMS n

HAY William

w 1851
1851   113 Union St, Aberdeen
Ex. 1851, foot gauge
Sources: Cat 1851

HAY & LYALL

a 1800–1900
See also
HAY John & James★
HAY John★
Known to have sold: compass
Sources: Webster R & M (1986)

HAYCOCK Samuel

w 1816–1845
Math IM, Measuring tape M
Alternative name: HAYCOX
1816   Lichfield St, Birmingham

HAYCOCK & CO. Edward Samuel

1816–1817	Price St, Birmingham
1818–1820	Bagot St, Birmingham
1828–1830	42 Loveday St, Birmingham
1828	Aston St, Birmingham
1841–1845	40 Woodcock St, Ashted Row, Birmingham
1845	Erdington, Birmingham

Apprenticed to MANSELL John★
See also HAYCOCK & CO.★
Sources: Aris 21 May 1770; K; Pg; Und

HAYCOCK & CO. Edward Samuel

w 1850
Rule M
1850   46 Woodstock St, Birmingham
Sources: Sl

HAYCOCK & CO. Samuel

w 1850
Math IM, Measuring tape M
1850   40 Woodcock St, Birmingham
Took over from HAYCOCK Samuel★
Sources: Sl

HAYES James

fr 1796 w 1810
Math IM

1790	63 Old Dock, Liverpool
1796	67 Old Dock, Liverpool
1796–1804	(residence) 24 Norfolk St, Liverpool
1800–1804	51 Old Dock, Liverpool
1805–1809	53 South Side Old Dock, Liverpool
1805	(residence ?) 41 Norfolk St, Liverpool
1807–1810	46 Norfolk St, Liverpool

Apprenticed to HAYES John★
Known to have sold: octant
Sources: G; H; LM index (MAC); Taylor (1966) p.313

HAYES Jane

w 1696–1697
[Math IM]
             London
Wife of HAYES Walter★
Supplied Math inst to Christ's Hospital
Sources: GL: CH 12823/2 (MAC)

HAYES John

fr 1780 d 1795
Math IM

1790–1795	Harford St, Liverpool
1795	Norfolk St, Liverpool

Had apprentice HAYES James★
Sources: LM index (MAC)

HAYES Walter

fr 1648 w 1687
Math IM (in silver, brass or wood), Book S
             Birchin Lane, Cornhill, London
1653–1684   Cross Daggers, next door to the Pope's Head Tavern near Bethlem Gate in Moorfields, London
Guild: Grocers, fr 1642, Clockmakers free Brother 1667/8
Son of HAYES Peter, merchant, of Chichester, Sussex
Apprenticed to ALLEN John★ 1631/2

Had apprentice:
DICKINS John 1648
EATON John 1651
MAYNESTONE John 1653/4
FOORD Richard nd [fr 1660/1]
NASH [ASH] John★ 1657
ANDERTON Nathaniel★ 1661
PRICHARD Zebediah 1661
BLAND Edward 1668
LILLE Martin 1669
CUSHIN Jededia 1672
BAUGH John 1672
WORGAN John★? [fr by Hayes 1682, so possibly t/o from ANDERTON Nathaniel★]
FARRAR Thomas 1677
WAITE John★ 1678/9
CULPEPER Edmund (I)★ 1684
[all apprentices bound in GC]
Succeeded by CULPEPER Edmund (I)★
See also HAYES Jane★
Associated with
BROOKES Christopher★, whose books & inst Hayes sold
JENNER Anselm★ in joint advertisement
THOMPSON Anthony★ in joint advertisement
Also book plate engraver; Master CKC 1680–1681
Known to have sold: compass (magnetic), nocturnal, quadrant, slide rule, sundial
Instruments advertised: globe, full range of mathematical instruments
Sources: GL: CKC 2710/1 p.185,429; inst NMM; Brown J (1979a) p.13, 26–27; Bryden (1992) p.307,318; Taylor (1954) p.239,281,373,384,386–87

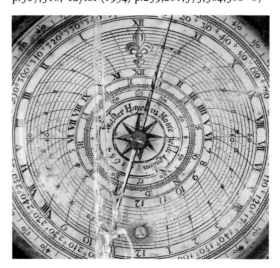

HAYNES John

w 1847
Optician
1847   117 High St, Kings Lynn, Norfolk
See also HYNES John★
Sources: K

HAYWARD John

w 1665 d 1671
Spec M
Alternative name: HAWARD
1670   St. Katherine's, London
Guild: Spectaclemakers

Father of HAYWARD Jonothan★ fp 1669
Sources: GL: SMC 5213/1

HAYWARD Jonothan

w 1672–1678
Spec M
1672   Fenchurch St, London
Guild: Spectaclemakers, fp 1669
Son of HAYWARD John★
Sources: GL: SMC 5213/1

HAYWARD Joseph

w 1787–1794
Optician
1781   59 Crutched Friars, London
1794   183 Wapping, London
Guild: Spectaclemakers, fr 1781
Son of HAYWARD Hannah, widow, of Bethnal Green, London
Apprenticed to SIMONS Daniel★ 1772
Had apprentice:
MASON James 1787
PARKER Charles 1792
d by 1820
Sources: GL: SMC 5213/3, 5213/4; W

HAYWOOD John

w 1785
Math IM, Book S
1785   7 Turnstile, Holborn, London
Sources: GL: Sun 11936/331 no. 508002 (MAC)

HAYWOOD William

a 1680–1700
Alternative name: W.H.
Known to have sold: weights
Sources: Sheppard & Musham (1975) p. 171 (MAC)

HAZELL Benjamin

w 1837
Optician, Flag M
1837   10 Lower Sparling St, Liverpool
Sources: G

HEALY John

w 1806–1812
Electrifying Machine M
1806–1812   43 James St, Dublin
Took over from HEALY Samuel (I)★
Succeeded by HEALY Samuel (II)★
Sources: Burnett & Morrison-Low (1989) p. 126

HEALY Samuel (I)

w 1795–1805
Electrifying Machine M, Electrician, Chandler, Math IM
Alternative name: HEALEY
1795–1805   43 James' St, Dublin
Succeeded by HEALY John★
See also HEALY Samuel (II)★
Sources: Burnett & Morrison-Low (1989) p. 126

HEALY Samuel (II)

w 1813–1839
Electrifying Machine M
Alternative name: is this Samuel HEALY (I) ?
1813–1839   43 James St, Dublin

Took over from HEALY John★
See also HEALY Samuel (I)★
Sources: Burnett & Morrison-Low (1989) p.126

HEARD Thomas (I)

w 1810–1831
Scale M
1811	84 Long Lane, Smithfield, London
1817–1820	13 or 14 Long Lane, Smithfield, London
1826–1831	77 or 78 Long Lane, Smithfield, London

Guild: [Haberdashers]
Father of HEARD Thomas (II)★
Apprenticed to MOFFETT Elizabeth★ 1789
Had apprentice PICKERING John 1810
Sources: H; Pg; R; U; GL: HC 15860/9; MPC
5968/2; CH: 12823/8 p.114

HEARD Thomas (II)

fr 1828
Scale M
| 1828 | 68 Barbican, London |

Guild: Makers of Playing Cards
Son of HEARD Thomas (I)★
fr by purchase 1828
Sources: GL: MPC 5968/2

HEARDER J.N.

w 1851
| 1851 | 34 George St, Plymouth, Devon |

Ex. 1851
Sources: Turner G (1983a) p.309

HEARNE George

fr 1705 w 1741
| | Dogwell Court, White Friars, Fleet St, London |
| | The Sphere, Sergeant's Inn, Chancery Lane, London |

Guild: Joiners?
Partnership: HEARNE & JACKSON★
Apprenticed to BARBER Edward★ 1697/8
Known to have sold: drawing instruments, telescope
Sources: inst NMS; Crawforth (1987) p. 358;
Taylor (1966) p.161

HEARNE & JACKSON George & Joseph

a 1735–1750
Alternative name: JACKSON & HEARNE ?
| | London |

See also
HEARNE George★
JACKSON Joseph★
Sources: Taylor (1966) p.161

HEATH George

w 1851
Manufacturer
| 1851 | Erith, Kent |

Guild: [Masons]
Son of HEATH Mr, grocer
Apprenticed to HUGHES Henry★ 1840
Ex.1851
Known to have sold: sextant
Sources: GL: MC 5304/7; Cat.1851

HEATH Thomas

w 1720–1753
Math IM
1720–1747	Hercules & Globe, next the Fountain Tavern in the Strand, London
1734–1746	Hercules & Globe near Beaufort Buildings in the Strand, London
1750	Hercules & Globe near Exeter Exchange in the Strand, London

Guild: Grocers, fr 1719/20
Partnership HEATH & WING★
Son of HEATH William, yeoman, of Luton, Beds
Apprenticed to SCOTT Benjamin★ 1712
Had apprentice:
THORNE Baptist 1719/20
TRACY John★ 1720 by t/o from SCOTT
Benjamin★
WATKINS John 1722
JACKSON Joseph★ 1723
ADAMS George (I)★ 1726/7 by t/o from PARKER
James★
KNYFF Leonard 1730
HOWELL Francis★ 1732
TROUGHTON John (I)★ 1734/5
WING Tycho★ 1741
HEATH Thomas, his son, 1746
DODD Charles 1753 by t/o from PHILPOT
William of DPC
Succeeded by HEATH & WING★
See also HARRIS Joseph★ whose books he sold
Bookseller; d 1773
Known to have sold: compass, astronomical clock,
gunner's callipers, theodolite, sundial, sector,
circumferentor, quadrant, barometer, drawing
instruments, protractor
Instruments advertised: full range of math inst.
Sources: Brown (1979a) p.35; DH: DPC Ap/Fr;
inst NMM; Calvert (1971) p.25-26; Taylor (1966)
p.129

HEATH W. & T.C.

w 1850
Optician, Baro M
Alternative name: William & Thomas Cornish
| 1850 | 46 Fore St, Devonport |

Succeeded by HEATH William
Known to have sold: barometer
Sources: Goodison (1977) p.329

HEATH William

w 1835
Spec M
| 1835 | 52 Essex St, Birmingham |

Sources: Pg

HEATH & WING Thomas & Tycho

w 1751–1773
Math IM, Phil IM, Optical IM, Optician, Book S
	Hercules & Globe, Exeter Exchange, Strand, London
1751–1767	Near Exeter Exchange in the Strand, London
1759	Hercules & Globe next door to Fountain Tavern, Strand, London
1771	Near the Savoy Gate in the Strand, London

Succeeded by NEWMAN Thomas★

Publishers; Heath d 1773; Wing r 1773 & d 1776
Known to have sold: barometer, protractor,
sundial, waywiser
Sources: GL: TCd; ChrSK 30 Jun 1988 lot 201;
Mort; *Morning Post* 11 Oct 1773; BM: Heal 105/51
Anderson et al (1990) p.39

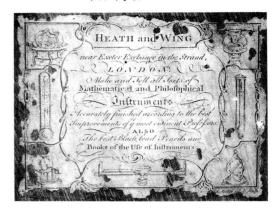

HEATHER William

w 1793–1812
Navigation Warehouse, Hydrographer, Engraver,
Math IM, Nautical IS, Chart & Map S
| 1793–1812 | At the Little Midshipman, 157 Leadenhall St, London |
| 1797 | Parish of St.Peter, Cornhill, London |

Guild: Stationers, fr 1789
Son of HEATHER William, d, of Southwark,
London
Partnership: HEATHER & WILLIAMS★
Apprenticed to MICHELL George, engraver &
stationer, 1780
Had apprentice:
STOCKLEY Samuel 1797
FROGGETT John Waters 1799
Succeeded by NORIE John William★
Partnership 1799–1804
Sources: McKenzie(1978) p.168,234; inst TCd
NMM; A; H; Ld (JAC); Calvert (1971) p.26

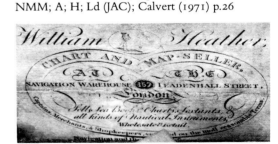

HEATHER & WILLIAMS

w 1799–1804
Navigation Warehouse, Naut IS
Alternative name: HEATHER & CO.
| 1799–1804 | 157 Leadenhall St, London |

Succeeded by HEATHER William★
Took over from HEATHER William★
Known to have sold: octant
Instruments advertised: sextant
Sources: Boyle; Ld (JAC); inst

HEATON William

w 1814–1847

Naut IS, Stationer, Map S
1814–1840   96 Side, Newcastle upon Tyne
1814–1847   15 Sandhill, Newcastle upon Tyne
Partnership: PRESTON & HEATON
Apprenticed to HODGSON Solomon
Worked for HODGSON Solomon
Succeeded by ATKIN William
Sources: Hunt (1975) (MAC)

HEBERT William
w 1807
Math IM
Alternative name: HERBERT ??
1806   Leadenhall St, London
1807   66 Leadenhall St, London
Guild: Fishmongers, fr 1806
Apprenticed to LEKEUX Richard★
Sources: GL: FMC 21507/4; Kt

HEDGE N.
w 1849
Watch M, Clock M, Optician
1849   4 New Bond St Place, New Bond
             St, Bath
Worked for BULLOCK James (II)★
Sources: C

HEDGES Alfred Charles
w 1850–1859
Optician, Math IM, Phil IM
1850–1852   44 New Bond St, London
1855–1859   114 Jermyn St. London
Sources: PO;Wk

HELLIER James
w 1793–1807
             London
Known to have sold: sandglass
Sources: Taylor (1966) p.340–41

HELME Thomas
w 1689–1692
[Spec M]
Alternative name: HELMES
             London
Guild: Spectaclemakers, fr 1686
Had apprentice SHELLY James★ 1691/2
See also STEPHENS Robert★, who married
Helme's widow
d by March 1693
Sources: GL: SMC 5213/1

HEMINGWAY Robert
w 1849
Baro M, Thermo M
1849   18 Brooke St, Holborn, London
Sources: PO

HEMS Thomas
fr 1819 w ? 1819
Scale M
1819   13 Ball Lane, Spitalfields, London
Guild: Haberdashers
Apprenticed to BLACKBURN John★ 1794/5
Sources: GL:HC 15857/3;15860/9

HEMSLEY Henry (I)
w 1781–1794

Optician, Dealer in Lace
1784–1794   Little Saffron Hill, Hatton Wall,
             London
1781   Opposite The George on Saffron
             Hill, London
1786   85 Fleet St, London
Guild: Spectaclemakers, fr 1786
Son of HEMSLEY Thomas, gent d, of Holborn,
London
Apprenticed to
SHUTTLEWORTH Henry R.★ 1772 t/o nd to
GRAVES John of FMC
Had apprentice:
HEMSLEY Thomas (I)★ 1789
ARCHER James 1792
Sources: SMC 5213/3, 5213/4; GC 11598/6; By;
W; GL: Sun 11936/298 no.446740, /341 no.523691

HEMSLEY Henry (II)
w 1838–1861
Optician, Optical IM, Math IM, Phil IM
1838–1843   138 Ratcliffe Highway, London
1844–1845   140 Ratcliff Highway, London
1846–1861   140 St. George St, St George's in the
             East, London
1823   11 King St, Tower Hill, London
Guild: Grocers, fp 1823
Son of HEMSLEY Thomas (I)★
Brother of HEMSLEY Thomas (II)★
Known to have sold: octant
Sources: GL: GC 11598/7; PO; R; inst(s)

HEMSLEY Joseph & Thomas
w 1826–1828
Optician, Optical IM
             11 King St, Tower Hill, London
             11 Little Tower Hill, London
Took over from HEMSLEY Thomas (I)★
Succeeded by HEMSLEY Thomas (II)★
Sources: Kt (JAC)

HEMSLEY Thomas (I)
w 1801–1825
Optician, Optical brass turner
1801   1 Parson's Walk, Newington, Surrey,
             London
1820–1825   11 King Street, Tower Hill, London
Guild: Grocers, fr 1801
Father of
HEMSLEY Thomas (II)★
HEMSLEY Henry (II)★ fp 1823 GC
Son of HEMSLEY Thomas (III), gent, d, of
Holborn, London
Apprenticed to
MARTIN James★ 1784 GC
HEMSLEY Henry (I)★ by t/o 1789 SMC
Had apprentice SAVAGE George 1801
Succeeded by HEMSLEY James & Thomas★
d. by June 1825
Sources: K; GL: GC 11598/6; SMC 5213/5

HEMSLEY Thomas (II)
w 1828–1854
Optician, Optical IM, Math IM, Naut IM
             18 King St, Tower Hill, London
1840–1851   11 King St, Tower Hill, London
1825   King St, Tower Hill, London
Guild: Spectaclemakers, fr 1825

Father of HEMSLEY Thomas
Son of HEMSLEY Thomas (I)★
Had apprentice:
HEMSLEY Thomas, his son, 1841
ALLAN David 1828
MAY John 1836
RICHARDSON John (V), son of James, 1840
Took over from HEMSLEY Jos. & Thos★
Succeeded by HEMSLEY & SON Thomas
fr by redemption, 25 June 1825
Sources: PO; Wk; GL: SMC 5213/5

HENDERSON Ebenezer
w 1827–1867
Astro IM
             3 Duke St, Lincoln's Inn Fields,
             London
1809–1829   Dumfermline
1831   Northumberland Court, London
1836   42 Pall Mall East, London
1849   3 Villiers Terrace, Newferry,
             Birkenhead
1863–1864   Dunfermline
b 1809; d 1879
Known to have sold: astronomical clock,
planetarium
Instruments advertised: planetarium, telescope
Sources: MHS: MS Gunther 36 (AVS); JRM

HENDERSON Thomas
w 1754
Math IS, Phil IS, Optical IS
             A little below the Cross, Edinburgh
Agent for James Ayscough★, Geo. Sterrop★, &
Edward Scarlett (II)★
Sources: Bryden (1972) p.18; ADCS

HENDRICK John & Peter
w 1800–1840
Chrono M
1800–1803   8 Dawson St, Liverpool
1804   1 Basnett St, Church St, Liverpool
1805   1 Church St, Liverpool
1805–1810   7 Dawson St, Liverpool
1811   6 Dawson St, Liverpool
1813   6 Williamson Sq. Liverpool
1816–1817   Williamson Sq, Liverpool
1821–1824   25 Church St, Liverpool
Sources: G; LM index (MAC); Bn; Loomes (1975)

HENLEY James
a 1750–1770
Stationer, Book S, Instrument S, Chart S
             Broad St, Ratcliff Cross, London
Sources: GL: TCd

HENLEY William Thomas
w 1845–1851
Baro M, Phil IM
1845   28 Haydon St, Minories, London
1851   46 St. John St, Clerkenwell, London
Ex.1851
Sources: PO; Turner G (1983) p.309

HENNESSY Bernard
w 1848–1875
Chrono M, Watch M, Naut IM
Alternative name: HENNESSEY

5 Wind St, Swansea
Worked for PORTHOUSE Thomas★, Chrono M
Known to have sold: circumferentor
Sources: Loomes (1976); TCd NMM; Taylor
(1966) p.366

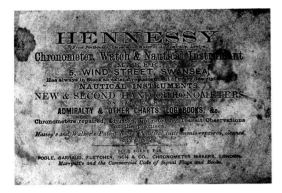

HENNINGHAM G.B.
w 1851
Watch M, Chrono M
1851   7 Woodbridge St North, London
Sources: PO

HENNINGS Thomas
w 1782–1788
Optician
1782–1784   Whitefriars, London
1788   Peterborough Court, Fleet St,
           London
Sources: McKenzie (1978) p.143, 152

HENOCH Joseph
w 1805
Optician
1805   12 Middlesex St, Whitechapel,
           London
Sources: H

HENRY Solomon
w 1770–1790
Merchant
         15 Swithin's Lane, London
         6 New Basinghall St, London
         54 Paternoster Row, London
Associated with WARNER Thomas (I)★, and
WILLIAMS Thomas (II)★, who sold his inst
Pat. coin scales 1774
Known to have sold: balance
Instruments advertised: balance
Sources: BM: Heal 85/313 (MAC): Bd; W; inst
Huddersfield Mu; Calvert (1971) p.26

HENSHAW John (I)★
w 1698–1726
Math IM
         The Globe, East Smithfield, near the
         Hermitage, Wapping, London
1700   Near the Hermitage Bridge,
         Wapping, London
1726   Ratcliff Highway, London
Guild: Clockmakers, fr 1696
Son of HENSHAW Walter★
Partnership: HENSHAW Walter & John★

Apprenticed to HENSHAW Walter★ 1689
Had apprentice:
DOBSON John (I)★ 1698
MACY Benjamin 1704
SHIPPY John 1706
GARNER William★ 1713
Took over from HENSHAW Walter & John★
Succeeded by DIGBY Charles★
Sources: Bryden (1992) p.317; Brown J (1979b)
p.30; GL: CKC 2710/3 fol.49

HENSHAW John (II)
w 1840–1850
Optical IM
1840–1850   336 Bishopsgate St, London
Attended London Mechanics Institute, 1840–50
Sources: LMIR (AM)

HENSHAW W.
w 1848
Optical IM
1848   5 Lion St, Bishopsgate, London
Attended London Mechanics Institute 1848
Sources: LMIR (AM)

HENSHAW Walter
w 1659–1711
Math IM
1691   Wapping, London
1696   The Globe, East Smithfield, near the
         Hermitage, Wapping, London
Guild: Weavers, Clockmakers fr Brother 1667/8
Father of HENSHAW John (I)★
Partnership: HENSHAW Walter & John★
Apprenticed to BROWNE Thomas 1650 JC
Had apprentice:
COOKE Robert★ 1659 WVC
JARVIS Bastin 1667 WVC
HUCKWELL Joseph★ 1668 WVC
GWATKIN Francis 1674 WVC
GILDING Stephen 1675 WVC
SCATLIFF Simon (I)★ 1683 CKC
HENSHAW John (I)★, his son, 1689 CKC
TARLETON Jeremiah 1690 CKC
DYER Samuel 1697/8 CKC
FLINT Henry 1700/01 CKC
BROWN John 1703/4 CKC
Succeeded by HENSHAW John (I)★
Bound in Joiners Co.
Known to have sold: sundial, drawing instruments,
back-staff.
Instruments advertised: dip stick.
Sources: Brown J (1979b) p.30; Antiques Trade
Gazette, 19 Mar 1994 p.57; Loomes (1981b); GL:
WVC 4657/1; JC 8652/1 (MAC)

HENSHAW Walter & John
w 1699
1699   Near the Hermitage Bridge, London
Succeeded by HENSHAW John (I)★
Took over from HENSHAW Walter★
Sources: Advertisement (DJB)

HERBERT Thomas (I)
w 1842–1867
Scale M, Gas fitter
1842–1846   39 Cannon St, Ratcliff, London
1847–1849   39 Cannon St, St George St, London

1850–1867   47 St George St, London
1860   37 Chichester Place, Gray's Inn Rd,
         London
1864–1867   319 Gray's Inn Rd, London WC
         2 Catherine St, Commercial Rd
         East, London
Apprenticed to PALLET Elizabeth M.★
Succeeded by HERBERT & SONS
b 1811; d 1876
Known to have sold: balance
Sources: PO; inst Worthing Mu; MAC

HERBERT Thomas (II)
w 1840–1847
Math IM
1840–1846   7 Helmet Row, St Luke's, London
1847   10 Hackney Road, London
Attended London Mechanics Institute, 1840,
1845–6, 1847
Sources: LMIR (AM)

HERBERTS John William
c 1763 w 1779
Scale M
Alternative name: HERBERTZ Johann Wilhelm
           In Stidwell St, No.5 near the French
           Change, St.Ann's, Soho, London
Known to have sold: balance
Sources: inst (pv)

HERON Alexander
w 1781
Math IM
Alternative name: PERON ? (1st letter illegible)
1781   Dublin
Sources: Westropp (1916)

HERON David
w c. 1815 w 1863
Ship Chandler, Naut IM
           Greenock
1827   Glasgow
1834–1835   128 Broomielaw, Glasgow
1836–1847   212 Broomielaw, Glasgow
1849–1863   4 Carrick St, Glasgow
Partnership: HERON & JOHNSTONE★
HERON & MCGREGOR★
HERON & CO★
Succeeded by WHYTE James★
See also HERON John★
Partnerships c.1827–36, 1844
Sources: Clarke et al (1989) p.235,241

HERON John
w 1820–1828
Chrono M
1820–1822   1 Square, Greenock
See also HERON William★
Known to have sold: hydrostatic bubbles
Sources: Pg; inst SM

HERON & CO. David
w 1844
Ship Chandler, Naut IM
Alternative name: HERON & JOHNSTONE ?
1844   212 Broomielaw, Glasgow
See also HERON David★
Sources: Bryden (1972) p.50

HERON & JOHNSTONE David & -
w 1844
Ship Chandler, Naut IM
Alternative name: HERON & CO. ?
1844   212 Broomielaw, Glasgow
See also HERON David★
Sources: Bryden (1972) p.50

HERON & MCGREGOR David & Duncan
c 1827 w 1836
Naut IS, Math IS, Optical IS
1836   1 William St, Greenock
Succeeded by MCGREGOR Duncan★
Took over from HERON David★
Partnership dissolved 1836
Sources: Clarke et al (1989) p.235,241

HERSCHEL William
b 1738 d 1822
Astronomer, Telescope M
Alternative name: Friedrich Wilhelm, Sir William
[1816]
        Slough
Sources: Herrmann (1984) p.159,213

HESELTINE Charles
w 1820–1834
Optician, Math IM
Alternative name: HEZELTINE
1820–1834   5 Robert St, Bedford Row, London
Sources: Bn; Pg; R (JAC); Taylor (1966) p.452

HESKETT James
a 1770–1810
Globe S, Math IS, Map S, Print S, Chart S
        13 Sweetings Alley, Royal
        Exchange, London
Sources: Calvert (1971) p.26

HEWES Philip
w 1804–1804
Brass Founder, Brass Turner
Alternative name: HAWES, HUGHES, Phillip
1800   Saffron Hill, London
1804   34 Shoe Lane, London
Guild: Drapers, fr 1800
Son of HEWES Philip, tripeman, of Croydon,
Surrey
Apprenticed to MASON John★ 1784
Had apprentice STANTON John★ 1804
Sources: DH: DPC Ap/Fr

HEWINS Richard
w 1637–1658
[Scale M]
Alternative name: HEWENS
        London
Guild: Blacksmiths, fr between 1633 & 1635
Had apprentice MARSH John (I)★ 1642 and 3
others 1637–1646
Sources: GL: BKC 2881/6, 2881/7, 2884, 2886/1
(MAC)

HEWITSON John
w 1844–1856
Optician, Math IM
1844   18 Dean St, Newcastle upon Tyne
1846–1855   20 Grey St, Newcastle upon Tyne
1846–1847   16 Quay Side, Newcastle upon Tyne
1848   61 Pilgrim St, Newcastle upon Tyne
1848–1853   76 Grey St, Newcastle upon Tyne
1850–1855   21 Grey St, Newcastle upon Tyne
1856–1857   16 Grey St, Newcastle upon Tyne
Guild: [Grocers?]
Probably the John Hewitson, son of John of
Rotherhithe, mariner, s 1828 to J Fairey★. Ex.1851
Known to have sold: level, tide gauge.
Sources: F; Md; Sl; Wd; Wh; Wln; MSEN; GL:
GC 11598/7

HEWITSON Jonathan
w 1835
Math IM
1835   3 Cornwall Rd, Lambeth, London
Sources: LMIR (AM)

HEWITT G.
w 1720–1769
1720–1769   Marlborough
Known to have sold: astronomical clock, balance
Sources: Baillie (1951); Sheppard & Musham
(1975) no.260 (MAC)

HEWITT Samuel (I)
w 1811
Rule M
Alternative name: did he move to Liverpool ?
1811   54 Sloane St, Chelsea, London
Guild: Stationers
Apprenticed to WELLINGTON Alexander★ 1796
Sources: H; McKenzie (1978) p.370

HEWITT Samuel (II)
w 1811–1824
Rule M
Alternative name: did he move from London ?
1811–1818   54 Dale St, Liverpool
1816   48 Dale St, Liverpool
1818   51 Dale St, Liverpool
1821–1823   123 Dale St, Liverpool
1824   43 Dale St, Liverpool
Sources: Bn; Pg; Und

HEWITT Thomas
w 1832–1844
Chrono M
1827–1831   9 Upper Ashley St, Northampton
        Square, London
1831–1839   12 Upper Ashley St, London
Succeeded by HEWITT & SON Thomas★
Took part in chronometer trials at Royal
Greenwich Observatory
Known to have sold: chronometer
Instruments advertised: chronometer
Sources: CUL: RGO/1143 fol.7–10; Pg; Loomes
(1976)

HEWITT Whisson White
w 1850
Optician
1850   46 Red Lion St, Holborn, London
Guild: Skinners
Son of HEWITT James, hotel keeper, of Covent
Garden, London
Apprenticed to MOORE Thomas, wine merchant,
1842

Had apprentice GRESTOCK Richard Joseph 1850
fr 5 June 1849
Sources: SH: SKC, Ap/Fr

HEWITT & SON Thomas
w 1851–1875
Chrono M, Watch M
1851   1 Vincent Place, City Rd, London
Took over from HEWITT Thomas★
Sources: PO; Loomes (1976)

HEWLINGS & HEFFORD Edward & Joseph H.
w 1799
1799   Curtain Rd, London
Hewling's pat. inst for measuring height & distance
1795
Sources: inst, Burghley House, Stamford, Lincs
(GL'ET); Woodcroft (1854)

HEWSON John
fr 1699 w 1702
Math IM
        London
Guild: Clockmakers, fr 1699
Son of HEWSON Christopher, tallow chandler, of
London
Apprenticed to SELLER John (I)★ 1683
Had apprentice SOUTH Joseph 1702
Sources: CLRO: CF 1/143; Brown J (1979b) p.30

HEYRICKE Samuel
w 1687
Known to have sold: sundial
Sources: Loomes (1981b)

HIATT Henry (I)
w 1819–1828
Scale M
1819–1822   83 Old Street Rd, Shoreditch,
        London
1823–1828   80 Old Street Rd, Shoreditch,
        London
Known to have sold: weights
Sources: Pg; R (JAC); Sby 10 Mar 1987 lot 38
(MAC)

HIATT Henry (II)
w 1848–1851
Chrono M
1848–1851   Toll Bar, Prescot, Lancs
Sources: Loomes (1975)

HICKES James
a 1670–1700
Known to have sold: weights
Sources: Sheppard & Musham (1975) p.171 (MAC)

HICKETT John
w 1670–1695
[Spec M]
Alternative name: HICKETTS
1671–1693   Aldersgate, London
1695   Little Brittain, London
Guild: Spectaclemakers, fr 1666
Apprenticed to HARDY George★ Jun 1658, t/o
Sep 1658 to GOODMAN Richard★
Had apprentice:
BURBURY Charles 1670

MANN James (I)★ by t/o from KING Thomas★ nd
PIDDING Humphrey★ nd, fr 1686/7
TWYNIHOE James 1692
Master SMC 1682–1683, 1692–1693; last
attendance at SMC 1707
Sources: GL: SMC 5213/1, 5213/2

HICKIN Samuel
w 1780–1781
Scale M
1780–1781   Bilstone St, Wolverhampton
Sources: PR

HICKMAN Benjamin
w 1725
Perspective Case M
1725   New Street, Shoe Lane, London
Guild: Loriners, fp 1725
Son of HICKMAN Henry
Had apprentice PRICE Thomas (II)★ 1725
Probably the Benjamin Hickman in Ludgate
Prison in 1728/9
Sources: GL: LC 15835/1; SMC 5213/2 p.203

HICKMAN Elizabeth
w 1765–1768
Phil IM
    London
Guild: Drapers
Wife of HICKMAN Joseph (I)★
Had apprentice ROGERS John James by t/o from
HICKMAN Joseph (I)★
Took over from HICKMAN Joseph (I)★
Sources: DH: DPC Ap/Fr

HICKMAN Joseph (I)
w 1738–1765
Phil IM
1738   Flower de Luce Court, Fleet St,
    London
1747   Stonecutter St, Shoe Lane, London
1761   Union Court, Holborn, London
Guild: Drapers, fr 1738
Son of HICKMAN Joseph, free of LC of London
Apprenticed to HAUKSBEE Francis (II)★
Had apprentice:
HICKMAN Joseph (II)★
COULSTON John 1740★
BOWES Paul 1746
HEYWOOD William by t/o 1750 from HEYWOOD
Martin of SKC
HASSARD Joseph★ 1747/8
USHER G. 1744
SLEATH Joseph 1752
CARTWRIGHT William 1758
Succeeded by HICKMAN Elizabeth, his widow
d 1765
Sources: DH: DPC Ap/Fr, index; SKH: SKC Ap/Fr

HICKMAN Joseph (II)
w 1768–1776
Optician, IM
1768–1779   Fetter Lane, London
1773   41 Fetter Lane, London
1749   Fleet St, London
Guild: Drapers, fr 1749
Son of HICKMAN John, shagreen case maker, of
London

Apprenticed to HICKMAN Joseph (I)★ 1738
Had apprentice:
ROLLINGS John 1768
SWEET Robert 1765
d 1779
Sources: DH: DPC Ap/Fr; GL: STTP 2934 fol 47;
GL: St. Dunstan West, Bu

HICKS George (I)
w 1810–1811
Baro M, Turner, Thermo M
1810–1811   43 Shoe Lane, Fleet St, London
See also HICKS Joseph★
Sources: H

HICKS George (II)
w 1820–1835
Math IM
1820–1834   46 City Quay, Dublin
1835   68 Marrowbone Lane, Dublin
See also
HICKS J★
HICKS John (II)★
HICKS Thomas★
Sources: Pg; Burnett & Morrison-Low (1989)
p.126

HICKS J.
w 1817–1826
Math IM
1817–1819   11 Camden St, Dublin
1820–1822   13 Lower Camden St, Dublin
1823–1824   13 Peter's Place, low Camden St,
    Dublin
1825–1826   64 City Quay, Dublin
See also
HICKS John (II)★
HICKS Thomas★
HICKS George (II)★
Known to have sold: ellipsograph
Sources: Burnett & Morrison-Low (1989) p.126;
inst SM

HICKS James
w 1819
Optician
1819   17 Lambeth Walk, London
See also
HICKS Joseph★
HICKS George (I)★
Sources: R (JAC)

HICKS John (I)
w 1692
Spectacle M
1692   London
Sources: GL: SMC 5213/1

HICKS John (II)
w 1832–1848
Math IM, Naut IM
1832   48 City Quay, Dublin
1835–1848   20 City Quay, Dublin
See also
HICKS J★
HICKS Thomas★
HICKS George (II)★
Sources: Wi; Burnett & Morrison-Low (1989) p.126

HICKS Joseph
w 1816–1827
Optician, Math IM, Phil IM, Baro M
    40 Castle St, Holborn, London
1816   34 Eagle St, Holborn, London
    11 Brook St, Holborn, London
1817   19 Kirby St, Hatton Garden, London
1817   17 Lambeth Walk, Lambeth,
    London
1821   94 Cheapside, London
1822   117 Bishopsgate Without, London
1823–1827   36 Rosomon [Rosoman] St,
    Clerkenwell, London
Guild: Coopers, fr 1819
Had apprentice:
JONES George Henry 1821
SPENCER George 1823
PHIPPS Joseph 1827
See also
HICKS James★
HICKS George (I)★
HICKS, LANGSTON & CO.★
Sources: GL: CPC 5602/11, 5630, 5636/3; Und;
Bn; J (JAC)

HICKS Thomas
w 1784–1799
Math IM
1784–1790   40 Poolbeg St, Dublin
1791–1799   20 Hawkins St, Dublin
See also
HICKS J.★
HICKS John (II)★
HICKS George (II)★
Known to have sold: compass
Sources: Wi; inst NMM; Burnett &
Morrison-Low (1989) p.127

HICKS, LANGSTON & CO.
w 1822–1823
Optician, Math IM
1822–1823   94 Cheapside, London
See also HICKS Joseph★
Sources: Pg; R (JAC)

HIERNE John
w 1696
Hour-glass M
1696   Houndsditch in or near Gravell Lane
    London
Guild: Tallow Chandlers
Son of HIERNE Richard, farmer, of Abbot's
Salford, War
Apprenticed to WEST James★ 1680/1
Had apprentice HIERNE Richard 1690/1
Sources: GL: THC 6158/4 p.50, 6164/2 p.24,
6158/3 p.130

HIGGINBOTHAM Joseph
s 1727 w 1752
Math IM
1752   Cold Bath Field, London
Guild: Stationers
Father of HIGGINBOTHAM David, s 1752 to
BENNETT John (I)★
Apprenticed to AUSTIN Samuel★ 1726/7 t/o
to FRANKLIN Thomas★ 1729
Sources: McKenzie (1978) p.9, 30

HIGGINS James
w 1775
Math IM
1775   St. James Clerkenwell, London
Had apprentice LIVERMORE Christopher 1775
Sources: PRO: IR 1/28 (AM)

HIGGINSON John (I)
w 1835–1862
Rule M
Alternative name: HIGGISON
1835   23 Court, Bromsgrove St,
     Birmingham
1862   7 Gooch St, Birmingham
Sources: Mor; Pg

HIGGISON John (II)
w 1850–1862
Rule M
1841–1850   Bristol St, Birmingham
1862   46 Gooch St, Birmingham
Known to have sold: Rule.
Sources: Mor; Pg; Sl; ChrSK 31 Jan 1985 lot 249

HIGGS John
w 1780–1781
Rule M, Japanner
1780–1781   Queen St, Wolverhampton
Sources: PR

HILL Abraham
w 1829–1830
Rule M, Victualler
1829–1830   13 Smallbrook St, Birmingham
Sources: West, Wr (MAC)

HILL Catherine
w 1836–1841
Spec M, Optician
1836   6 Goodmans Yard, Minories,
     London
1839–1841   25 Goodmans Yard, Minories,
     London
Took over from HILL James (II)★
Sources: Pg; R (JAC)

HILL Isaac
w 1841
Rule M
1841   Little Compton Street, Soho, London
Same premises as MANT Frederick★
Sources: PRO: HO/107/730/1/1 Cs 1841 p.26

HILL James (I)
w 1816–1818
Spec M
1816–1818   Navigation St, Birmingham
See also CHILCOTE & HILL★
Sources: H; Wr

HILL James (II)
w 1820–1836
Spec M, Optician
     6 Goodman's Yard, Minories,
     London
     19 Swan St, Minories, London
Succeeded by HILL Catherine★
Sources: R (JAC)

HILL John (I)
w 1669 d c. 1685
Spec M
1671–1672   St Paul's Chain, London
1676   St Paul's Churchyard, London
Guild: Spectaclemakers
Had apprentice:
HEMSTOCK John 1672/3
SCULTHORPE William 1675, probably t/o to
TINGAY Gregory★
BAGGALY Thomas c.1681
Master SMC 1683–1684
Known to have sold: spectacles
Sources: GL: SMC 5213/1

HILL John (II)
w 1704
Instrument M
     London
Father of HILL Solomon s 1704 SWC
Sources: Ridge (1939) p.106

HILL John (III)
w 1833–1836
Rule M
1833–1836   69 Noble St, Goswell St, London
Sources: R (JAC)

HILL Joseph
fr 1759 w 1777
Optician, Math IM
     45 Steel-yard, Tower Hill, London
1759   Hand & Pen Court, Great Tower
     Hill, London
1760–1774   Great Tower Hill, London
Guild: Grocers, fr 1759
Apprenticed to GILBERT John (I)★ 1747 t/o
to GILBERT John (II)★ 1750
Had apprentice COX John 1759 and 3 others
1760–1772
Sources: Kt; Lg; Brown J (1979a) p.42

HILL Matthew
a 1765 c 1790
Watchmaker
-1777   Devonshire St, London
1777   Upper Charlotte St, London
Known to have sold: balance
Sources: inst SM; Baillie (1951)

HILL Nathaniel
w 1746–1764
Math IM, Globe M, Map engraver, Book S
     The Sun & Globe, Chancery Lane,
     London
     Opposite Sergeant's Inn, Chancery
     Lane, London
1756   The Globe & Sun in Chancery Lane,
     Fleet St, London
Guild: Merchant Taylors, fr 1751
Apprenticed to CUSHEE Richard★
Had apprentice:
BATEMAN Thomas★ 1746
CUSHEE Leonard★ 1751
CHILCOTT John 1766
MACKOUN John 1754
Succeeded by PALMER & NEWTON★
Took over from COGGS John★

Associated with WATT James★ who bought globes
for re-sale
Took an apprentice before he was freed in a City
of London Company; d 1768
Known to have sold: globe
Instruments advertised: globe
Sources: GL:MTC MF 319, 324; PRO: IR 1/17
fol.218; Calvert (1971) p.26 & plate 27; GL: St.
Dunstans in the West, Bu

HILL Peter
w 1801–1828
Math IM, Optical IM, Optician
1801–1803   Richmond St, Edinburgh
1804–1810   7 East Richmond St, Edinburgh
1811–1812   9 East Richmond St, Edinburgh
1813–1822   6 Union Place, Edinburgh
1820–1824   7 Union Place, Edinburgh
1825–1828   2 Greenside Place, Edinburgh
1825   7 South Union St, Edinburgh
Known to have sold: barometer, drawing
instruments, lens
Sources: Bryden (1972) p.9, 12, 50; Pg; Clarke et al
(1989) p.11–15; Goodison (1977) p.330

HILL S.
w 1842
Yard measure S
1842   26 Duke St, Liverpool
Associated with CLARK Samuel★ as latter's agent
Sources: Pg

HILL Thomas
w 1632–1635
Dial M
Guild: Clockmakers, fr 1632
     At the Tower, London
Sources: Loomes (1981b)

HILL William
c 1810 by d 1847
Alternative name: Traded under the name of
J. WATKINS★
1841   Charing Cross, London
Partnership: WATKINS & HILL★
b c.1775; apparently managed the Watkins business
from J. WATKINS'★ death until F. WATKINS (III)★
was of age
Sources: PRO: Cs1841 HO 107/739/4; J; BG

HILL & PRICE
w 1842–1883
Optician, Naut IM
1855   1 Broad Quay, Bristol
1883   135 Bute St, Docks, Cardiff
Sources: Sl; BsM; DJB

HILLIER James
w 1790–1820
Hourglass M
1793   12 Church St, Spitalfields, London
1817   11 Church St, Spitalfields, London
Guild: Turners
Apprenticed to JONES William (III)★ 1780
Had apprentice:
CURMOCK William 1790
HALL William 1794
SMITH William 1801

R.apt Royal family 1790
Sources: GL: TC 3302/3; BW; Kt; JAC

HILLIER James N.
w 1845
Hourglass M
1845   10 Fieldgate St, London
Sources: PO

HILLUM Joseph
w 1836–1840
Optician, Math IM, Phil IM
Alternative name: HILTUM
1836–1840   109 Bishopsgate Within, London
Succeeded by HILLUM Richard★
Sources: Pg; PO; R (JAC)

HILLUM Richard
w 1845–1846
Optician, Math IM, Phil IM
Alternative name: HILTUM
            109 Bishopsgate Within, London
Took over from HILLUM Joseph★
Succeeded by HILLUM Mrs. S.★
Sources: PO

HILLUM S. (Mrs)
w 1849–1851
Optician, Math IM, Phil IM
1849–1851   109 Bishopsgate Within, London
Succeeded by HILLUM & CO.
Took over from HILLUM Richard★
Sources: PO; Wk

HIMES Mordecai
w 1824
Optician
1824   25 Allum St, Manchester
Sources: Bn (MAC)

HINDE George
w 1801
Math IM
1801   5 Duck Court, Leather Lane,
                London
Had apprentice CARTER Samuel 1801
Sources: GL: CH 12823/8 p.155

HINDE John
w 1802–1805
Math IM
            5 Red Lion St, Clerkenwell, London
1802–1805   3 Plough Court, Fetter Lane,
                London
See also
HINDE Roger★
HINDE George★
Sources: H; JAC

HINDE Roger
w 1827–1834
Optical IM, Phil IM, Math IM
            70 Noble St, Goswell St, London
            70 Noble St, Falcon Square, London
See also
HINDE John★
HINDE George★
Sources: Pg

HINDLEY Henry
w 1722–1741
Clock M, Math IM
1722–1730   Manchester
1730   Petergate, York
1771   Stonegate, York
Had apprentice STANCLIFFE John★
Succeeded by HINDLEY & SON Henry★
b c.1701, d 1771; inv. dividing engine
Sources: Wallis R & P (1986) p.344; Brooks (1992)
p.132; Baillie (1951); Chapman (1990) p.124–28

HINDLEY & SON Henry
a 1740 w 1771
            York
Father of HINDLEY Joseph
Had apprentice:
HINDLEY Joseph, his son
SMITH John
HOLMES John
Associated with SMEATON John★
Made 1st circle-dividing engine; Henry d.1771
Known to have sold: dividing engine
Sources: Taylor (1966) p.161–62; King & Millburn
(1978) p.143–44

HINTON Birt
w 1847
Optician
1847   59 Bartholomew Close, London
Attended London Mechanics Institute, 1847
Sources: LMIR (AM)

HIPWOOD Thomas
w 1816–1818
Spec M
1816–1818   King Edward's Place, Birmingham
Sources: H; Wr

HIRST George Koester
w 1834–1841
Goldsmith, Silversmith, Optician, Jeweller, Cutler,
Watch M
1834–1841   97 Briggate, Leeds
Succeeded by HIRST BROS★
Took over from HIRST & SON★
Sources: Pg; Wh; Loomes (1972)

HIRST & SON Samuel
w 1817–1830
Goldsmith, Jeweller, Cutler, Optician, Clock M
1817–1822   8 Market Place, Leeds
1826–1830   97 Briggate, Leeds
Succeeded by HIRST George Koester★
Sources: Bn; PWh; Loomes (1972)

HIRST BROS George Koester & John T.
w 1850–1866
Optician, Cutler, Goldsmith, Silversmith, Jeweller
1850–1866   97 Briggate, Leeds
Took over from HIRST George Koester★
Sources: Wh; Loomes (1972)

HISLOP Richard
fl 1832 w 1851
Watch M, Chrono M
1832–1834   1 Plumber Passage, Clerkenwell,
                London

1851   53 Rosoman St, Clerkenwell,
                London
Sources: PO; Taylor (1966) p.452; Loomes (1976)

HISLOP William
w 1851
Chrono M
1851   108 St John St Rd, London
Sources: PO

HITCH Elizabeth
w 1774
Math IM
1774   Eagle Court, St.John's Lane,
                Clerkenwell, London
Guild: Goldsmiths
Wife of HITCH Joseph★
Had apprentice CHRISTMAS William★
Took over from HITCH Joseph★
Sources: GH: GSC Ap

HITCH Joseph
w 1757–1773
Math IM
1757   At the corner of Beaufort Buildings
                in the Strand, London
1764–1773   Eagle Court, St.John's Lane,
                Clerkenwell, London
Guild: Goldsmiths, fr 1752
Apprenticed to LIFORD John★ 1745
Had apprentice:
KING Richard★ 1757
GRACE George★ 1759
ASHLEY Charles 1760
INNES James 1765
BIRKWOOD William★ 1766
HITCH John, son of John, 1771
Petitioner against Dolland's patent 1764; d by 1774
Sources: GL: CH 12876/5; GH: GSC Ap, Fr:
PRO: PC1/7 no.94; *General Evening Post* 25 May
1773

HITCHEN Thomas
w 1850
Rule M
1850   47 Horsefair, Birmingham
Sources: Sl

HOBCRAFT William (I)
w 1817–1856
Rule M, Measure M, Math IM
            28 King St, Snow Hill, London
            28 Cow Lane, Smithfield, London
            28 King St, Smithfield, London
1817   56 Whitecross St, Fore st, London
1822   12 Beech St, Barbican, London
1825   13 Barbican, London
1834   18 Barbican, London
1837–1852   14 Barbican, London
Guild: Stationers
Father of HOBCRAFT William (II)
Apprenticed to WELLINGTON Alexander★ 1803
Had apprentice:
BRADSHAW Alexander★ 1825
GEE John 1825
NICHOLLS Thomas 1834
BAKER William 1837
Known to have sold: gauge

Sources: SBPL: STC Ap; GL: CH 12823/8 p.156; J; R (JAC); PO; inst (s) (DJB)

HOBCRAFT William (II)
w 1845–1870
Optician
Alternative name: HOBCRAFT William jun.
1845	38 Princes St, Leicester Square, London
1849	14 Great Turnstile, London
1851	62 Dean St, Soho, London
1855–1870	419 Oxford St, London
Guild: [Fanmakers]
Apprenticed to STAIGHT Thomas 1831*
Possibly attended London Mechanics Institute, see HOPCROFT William*
Sources: PO; GL: FANC 21425

HOBDELL Henry Bashard
fl 1832 d.c. 1844
Clock M, Watch M, Silversmith
Alternative name: Banshard
128 High St, Oxford
Succeeded by HOBDELL Emily
Known to have sold: Observatory regulator
Sources: Beeson (1989) p.114,202

HODD Thomas Horton
w 1851–1859
Optician, Naut IM
1851	4 Margaret St, Commercial Rd East, London
1855	20 Margaret St, Commercial Rd East, London
1859	6 Salmon Lane, Limehouse, London E
Sources: PO; Wk

HODDER George
w 1711 d 1719
Math IM
-1719	Dublin
Sources: Burnett & Morrison-Low (1989) p.127; DJB

HODGES William
w 1816–1818
Compass M, Pincer M
1816–1818	Alcester St, Deritend, Birmingham
Sources: H; Wr (DJB)

HODGETTS Samuel
w 1794–1796
Scale M
1794	3 Goodman's Yard, Minories, London
1796	21 Goodman's Yard, Minories, London
Guild: Haberdashers, fr 1794
Apprenticed to MOFFETT James Thomas* 1787
Had apprentice DAVIES Thomas 1796
Sources: GL: HC 15857/3, 15860/9 (MAC)

HODGKINSON John
w 1799–1817
Optician, Spec M
1799–1817	24 Coppice Row, Clerkenwell, London
Succeeded by HODGKINSON Joseph*
Sources: Bn; H; J; Und

HODGKINSON Joseph
w 1817–1822
Optician
1817–1822	24 Coppice Row, Clerkenwell, London
Took over from HODGKINSON John*
Sources: Bn; J

HODGKINSON Thomas
fl 1696
[Math IS]
The Cradle, Knight Rider St, next Doctor's Common, London
Instruments advertised: sundial
Sources: Taylor (1954) p.293

HOE Robert
w 1681 d.c 1728
Scale M
1710	Falcon & Scales in Lothbury, London
1725	Lothbury, London
Guild: Blacksmiths, fr 1681 or 1682
Had apprentice:
GREENE James* 1696/7
WINSPEARE Thomas* 1697
PHYTHIAN Dodd* 1720 t/o 1723 to OVEN Henry*
and 8 others
Known to have sold: balance, weights
Sources: GL: BKC 2881/8, 2881/9, 2884, 2886/4; Sun 11936/1 no.905 (MAC); bill (MAC)

HOEY William
w 1823
Spec M
1823	10 Valentine Place, Blackfriars Rd, London
Sources: Pg

HOGBEN Thomas
a 1724 d 1774
Surveyor
Smarden, Kent
b.1703
Known to have sold: level
Sources: inst (s) (DJB)

HOGG William
w 1826–1854
Optician, Math IM, Phil IM
	388 Platform, Rotherhithe, London
1826	388 Rotherhithe Wall, London
1840–1854	394 Platform, Rotherhithe, London
Sources: Pg; PO

HOLBECHE John
s 1713 w 1743
Instrument M, Ship Chandler
Alternative name: HOLBECK, HOLBECH,
The Corner of the Hermitage Bridge, London
Guild: [Clockmakers]
Apprenticed to MACY Benjamin* 1713
Took over from MACY Benjamin*

See also BROWNE John (I)*
Known to have sold: back-staff
Sources: GL: CKC 2710/3; BM: Heal 105/56; BSIS no.30 (1991) p.29; inst MMA

HOLLAND J.
w 1835
Hydro M, Math IM, Optical IM, Phil IM
1835	106 New Bond St, London
See also
HOLLAND & JOYCE*
HOLLAND Peter*
Sources: R (JAC)

HOLLAND Peter
w 1805
Optician
1805	14 Stamford St, Blackfriars, London
See also
HOLLAND & JOYCE*
HOLLAND J.*
Sources: H

HOLLAND William
w 1849–1870
Baro M, Thermo M
1849–1851	14 Greville St, Hatton Garden, London
1851–1870	20 Greville St, Hatton Garden, London
Sources: PO; Wk

HOLLAND & JOYCE
w 1834
Hydro M, Math IM, Optical IM, Phil IM
1834	106 New Bond St, London
See also
HOLLAND J.*
HOLLAND Peter*
Sources: R (JAC)

HOLLIDAY William
w 1777–1793
Math IM
Alternative name: HOLIDAY
1777–1793	23 Dean St, Fetter Lane, London
Sources: GL: Sun 11936/256 no.382079; BW; By

HOLLIWELL Thomas & William
w 1848
Opticians, Math IM
1848	9 Salthouse St, Liverpool
Succeeded by HOLLIWELL BROS*
Took over from HOLLIWELL & SON William*
See also HOLLIWELL William*
Sources: Sl

HOLLIWELL William
w 1795–1827
Optician, Math IM
	14 North Side Salthouse Dock, Liverpool
	13 North Side, Salthouse Dock, Liverpool
	9 Bromfield St, Liverpool
1804–1816	5 Bromfield St, Liverpool
1816	7 Bromfield St, Liverpool
1818	72 West End Old Dock, Liverpool

1818	12 West End Old Dock, Liverpool
1821–1824	79 West End, Old Dock, Liverpool
1825	78 West end Old Dock, Liverpool
1827	1 Hurst St, Liverpool

Succeeded by HOLLIWELL & SON William★
See also HOLLIWELL BROTHERS★
Known to have sold: sextant
Instruments advertised: full range of optical and math inst
Sources: H; G: LM index (MAC): Calvert (1971) p.26

HOLLIWELL & SON William
w 1829–1847
Optician, Math IM
Alternative name: HALLIWELL

1829–1832	1 Hurst St, Liverpool
1834	7 Darwen St, Liverpool
1834	Hurst St, Liverpool
1835	7 Salthouse Dock East, Liverpool
1837	8 East side Salthouse Dock, Liverpool
1841–1847	9 East side Salthouse Dock, Liverpool

Took over from HOLLIWELL William★
See also
HOLLIWELL BROTHERS
HOLLIWELL Thomas & William★
Known to have sold: sextant
Sources: G; Pg; LM index (MAC)

HOLLIWELL BROS William, Charles & Thomas
w 1849–1862
Naut IM, Opticians

1849	9 East Side, Salthouse Dock, Liverpool
1851–1855	64 Park Lane, Liverpool
1857–1864	72 Park Lane, Liverpool
1870–1872	154 Brownlow Hill, E, Liverpool

Took over from HOLLIWELL Thomas & William
See also
HOLLIWELL William★
HOLLIWELL & SON★
Sources: G; K; LM index

HOLLOWAY William
w 1767–1780
Math IM

1757–1766	Crown Court, Lothbury, London
1767–1780	Drapers Court, Lothbury, London

Guild: Joiners, fr 1731/2
Apprenticed to CARTON William★
Son of HOLLOWAY William, farmer, of All Cannings, Wilts
Sources: GL: JC 8055/3; Crawforth (1987) p.358

HOLMES Alfred
w 1843–1845
Math IM

1843–1845	Greenfield St, Commercial Rd, London

Attended London Mechanics Institute, 1843–1845
Known to have sold: sextant
Sources: Sby 23 Jun 1987 lot 161; LMIR (AM)

HOLMES C.
w 1851
Chrono M

1851	75 Myddleton St, Clerkenwell, London

Sources: PO

HOLMES John
w 1817–1829
Optician, Spec M

	14 Red Cross Square, Cripplegate, London
	2 Little Cloisters, Bartholomew Hospital, London
1822	14 Redcross Square, Aldersgate St, London

Father of HOLMES John William★ s 1831 IC
See also HOLMES William★
Succeeded by
HOLMES Mary Ann★ then
HOLMES Julia & John★
d by 1831
Known to have sold: barometer, thermometer
Sources: GL: IC 6648/8; Bn; PO; Und; Goodison (1977) p.330

HOLMES John and William
w 1845
Opticians

1845	14 Redcross Square, London

PO 1846–59 has HOLMES John William at same address
Sources: PO

HOLMES John William
w 1846–1859
Optician, Spec M

1846–1859	14 Redcross Square, Aldersgate St, London

Guild: Spectaclemakers, fr 1853
Son of HOLMES John★
Apprenticed to KENNARD Edward, of the IC, 1831
PO 1845 has John and William Holmes at the same address
Sources: PO; GL: SMC 5213/6; IC 6648/8

HOLMES Julia & John
w 1839–1842
Optician

1839–1842	14 Redcross Square, Cripplegate, London

Succeeded by HOLMES John William★
Took over from HOLMES Mary and Ann
Sources: PO

HOLMES Mary Ann
w 1829–1839
Optician

1829–1839	14 Redcross Square, Aldersgate, London

Succeeded by HOLMES Julia & John★
Took over from HOLMES John★
Sources: Pg; R (JAC)

HOLMES William (I)
w 1802–1824

1802–1824	Somerset House, London

Son of HOLMES John, Clock M
Known to have sold: barometer
Sources: Baillie (1951): Banfield (1976) (MAC)

HOLMES William (II)
w 1836
Optician

1836	14 Red Cross, Aldersgate, London

See also
HOLMES John★
HOLMES John & William★
Attended London Mechanics Institute 1836
Sources: LMIR (AM); PO

HOLROYD George
c 1730–1786
Math IM

1750	York
1776	Great Queen St, Lincoln's Inn Fields, London

Inv. a quadrant
Sources: Taylor (1966) p.234

HOLT I. & W.
w c. 1797
Scale M

	51 Haymarket, St James's, London

Partnership of HOLT James★ & HOLT William★
Sources: inst MHS

HOLT James
w 1763–1797
Scale M
Alternative name: I.

1784–1797	51 Haymarket, St.James, London

Guild: Blacksmiths, fr 1763
Son of HOLT James, carpenter, of London
Apprenticed to NEWTON William 1756 t/o 1757 to READ Samuel★
Had apprentice HOLT William★, son of John, 1782
Succeeded by HOLT I.& W.
Sources: GL: BKC 2881/15, 2881/16, 2885/1 (MAC); A: By; Ld; Kt (MAC)

HOLT William
w 1797–1822
Scale M

1797	Haymarket, London
1809–1822	51 Haymarket, St.James, London

Guild: Blacksmiths, fr 1797
Partnership: HOLT I.& W.★
Apprenticed to HOLT James★ 1782
Son of HOLT John, coach maker, d, of Deptford, London
Known to have sold: balance
Sources: GL: BKC 2881/15, 2881/16 (MAC); Sheppard & Musham (1975) no.72 (MAC); Kt

HOLTUM Christopher
1711–1716
[Clock M]
See also HOLTUM John★
Not found in CKC; inv. alarm watch
Sources: Taylor (1954) p.303

HOLTUM John
w 1692
Math IM

1692	Beere Lane, London

See also HOLTUM Christopher★
Had apprentice PAGGETT William 1692
Sources: GL: CH 12876/2 (MAC)

HOLTZAPFFEL John Jacob

e 1794 w 1804
Toolmaker, Dealer in wood & ivory
1796   118 Long Acre, London
Partnership: HOLTZAPFFEL & DEYERLEIN★
1804–27
Known to have sold: gauge, rule
Sources: Taylor (1966) p.366; Chaldecott (1989)
p.166; JAC

HOLTZAPFFEL & CO.

w 1827 c 1914
Toolmakers
1839–1865   64 Charing Cross, opposite the
             King's Mews, London
1839–1865   (Factory) 127 Long Acre, W.C.
             London
See also HOLTZAPFFEL & DEYERLEIN★
Known to have sold: balance, slide rule
Sources: PO; Chaldecott (1989) p.166; Delchar
(1984) p.8

HOLTZAPFFEL & DEYERLEIN

w 1804–1827
Alternative name: H & D
1807   118 Long Acre, London
1820   64 Charing Cross, London
Took over from HOLTZAPFFEL J.J.★
Succeeded by HOLTZAPFFEL & CO.★
Known to have sold: rule
Sources: Kt; JAC; inst noted by MAC

HOLYMAN John

w 1808–1840
Math IM, Phil IM, Optical IM
             5 Newmarket St, Wapping, London
             5 Old Gravel Lane, Wapping,
             London
1808   Nightingale Lane, London
1816   33 Nightingale Lane, London
Guild: Grocers, fr 1808
Son of HOLYMAN Richard, yeoman, d, of
Crathorne, Yorks
Apprenticed to RUST Ebenezer (I)★ 1784
Had apprentice:
BELGRAVE Thomas 1808
DENNIS James William 1816
See also HOLYMAN William★
Associated with
RUST Ebenezer (II)★
GARDNER James★
Sources: GL: GC 11598/6, 11598/7; Pg; R

HOLYMAN William

w 1845–1859
Naut IM, Math IM
1845–1859   27 Sidney Place, Commercial Rd,
             London
Succeeded by HOLYMAN Mrs
See also HOLYMAN John★
Sources: PO

HOMAN Julius

c 1826 d by 1840
Math IM
             St George's in the East, London
Father of HOMAN Julius s 1840 SC
Sources: SH: SC Ap

HONE Joseph

w 1663–1704
Math IM (in brass or wood)
1663–1664   In the Bulwark, on Tower Wharf
             near the Tower, London
1670–1677   On Tower Wharf, London
See also
FLOWER William★
FLOWER Christopher★
Supplied math inst to Christ's Hospital School,
London
Sources: Bryden (1992) p.318; GL: CH 12823/1
fol.117

HOOD Alexander

w 1768
Math IM
1768   114 Fleet St, London
Sources: Gazetteer 26 Mar 1768 (MAC)

HOOD James

w 1851–1889
Scale M
1870   3 Macdowall St, Edinburgh
Partnership: HOOD James & Robert
Succeeded by HOOD James & Robert
Sources: K; NMS n

HOOKE Benjamin

w 1802–1805
Optician, Math IM
1802–1805   159 Fleet St, London
Guild: Girdlers, fr 1793
Partnership: GILBERT, WRIGHT & HOOKE★
Apprenticed to WRIGHT Gabriel★ 1786
Known to have sold: microscope
Sources: GL: GDC 5800/2, 5802; CLRO:
CF/1/1163; H; PO; Sby 28 Oct 1986 lot 167

HOOKE John

w 1677
Compass M
             Yarmouth, Isle of Wight
Sources: Taylor (1954) p.274

HOOPER William Williams

fr 1847 w 1852
[Math IM]
             London
Guild: Masons, fr 1847
Apprenticed to
HUGHES Joseph (I)★ 1840 t/o
to GARDNER James★ 1845
Had apprentice CROUCH Pearce Henry 1852
Sources: GL: MC 5304/7

HOPCROFT H.

w 1839–1840
Math IM
1839–1840   14 Barbican, London
Attended London Mechanics Institute 1839–1840
Sources: LMIR (AM)

HOPCROFT William

w 1837–1838
Rule M
Alternative name: Probably same as HOBCRAFT W
1837–1838   Barbican, London

Attended London Mechanics Institute 1837–1838
Sources: LMIR (AM)

HOPE Peter

a 1840
             64 Seel St, Liverpool
Known to have sold: slide rule
Sources: BSIS, no.2 (1984) p.14; Delehar (1984) p.9

HOPKINS John

w 1835
Spec M
1835   8 Court, Cheapside, Birmingham
Sources: Pg

HOPPE Ebenezer

w 1801 d 1821
Math IM, Optical IM
Alternative name: HOPPEY
             Edward St, Limehouse Fields,
             London
1801–1821   51 Church St, Minories, London
Guild: Joiners, fr 1801
Apprenticed to DANCER Michael★ 1793
Had apprentice:
HUNNEX Joshua★ 1801
BRIGGS James 1803
PATERSON William 1808
Associated with WOOD Benjamin Jasper (I)★
Inv. improved sextant
Sources: Crawforth (1987) p.358–59; H; Und;
BM: Banks 105/25; GL: JC 8055/4

HORNBY Richard

w 1814–1851
Chrono M, Watch M
Alternative name: HORNSBY
1814–1824   New Scotland Rd, Liverpool
1828–1834   41 Pool Lane, Liverpool
1837   51 South Castle St, Liverpool
1841–1849   36 South Castle St, Liverpool
1848–1851   South Castle St, Liverpool
See also HORNBY & SON Richard★
Known to have sold: chronometer, octant
Sources: G; LM index (MAC); Loomes (1975);
Holbrook (1992) p.198

HORNBY & SON Gerard

w 1800–1803
Chrono M
1800–1803   10–12 Princes St, Liverpool
Sources: G; LM index (MAC)

HORNBY & SON Richard

w 1837–1851
Chrono M
1837   51 South Castle St, Liverpool
1839–1851   36 South Castle St, Liverpool
Known to have sold: chronometer, sextant
Sources: G; Phlps 13 Jun 1979 lot 96 (DJB); LM
index (MAC)

HORNCASTLE Samuel

w 1834
Math IM, Phil IM
1834   22 St.Ann's St, Limehouse, London
Sources: Pg

HORNE Edmund
w 1838–1850
Brass finisher, Gas fitter
1838   22 Fleet Lane, St. Sepulchre, London
Guild: Spectaclemakers, fr 1838
Son of HORNE Thomas, innkeeper, d, of London
Had apprentice KYNASTON George Edward 1850
See also HORNE, THORNTHWAITE & WOOD★
fr in SMC by purchase
Sources: GL: SMC 5213/5, 5213/6

HORNE, THORNTHWAITE & WOOD
w 1845–1893
Optician, Chem IM, Phil IM, Math IM, Photo
IM, Hydro M, Baro M, Thermo M, Sacch M
1845–1851   123 Newgate St, London
1851   121 & 123 Newgate St, London
1886–1893   416 Strand, WC London
1888–1893   74 Cheapside, London
Took over from PALMER Edward★
Succeeded by HORNE & THORNTHWAITE
See also WOOD Edward George★
Ex.1851; WOOD absent 1853–85; R.apt Vic 1858
Known to have sold: balance
Sources: PO; Wk; inst (s); Chaldecott (1989)
p.160; Turner G. (1983a) p.309

HORROD William
w 1811
Baro M
1811   37 Laystall St, Leather Lane, London
See also HORROD William Thomas★
Sources: H

HORROD William Thomas
w 1834
Baro M, Thermo M
1834   1 Baker's Row, Clerkenwell,
               London
See also HORROD William★
Sources: Pg

HORSEMAN Stephen
fr 1709 fl 1724
        King's Arms, Exchange Alley, off
        Lombard St, London
Guild: Clockmakers, fr 1709
Apprenticed to QUARE Daniel★ 1701/2
Took over from QUARE Daniel★
Bankrupt 1733
Known to have sold: sundial, rule
Sources: GL: CKC 2710/3 fol.28,98; Taylor (1954)
p.298; Loomes (1981b) p.452

HORSFALL Matthew
w 1765–1775
Hourglass M
1773   The Locks, Leeds
Sources: Loomes (1972)

HORTON Edward
w 1792–1802
Rule M
Alternative name: HORTIN
1792   3 Bilston St, Wolverhampton
1802   5 Salop St, Wolverhampton
Sources: Wolverhampton rate books (MAC)

HORTON John
w 1799
Optician
1799   Baldwin St, Bristol
Source: Mat (MAC)

HORTON William
w 1842
Baro M, Thermo M
        12 Barbican, London
Sources: PO

HORTON & CO. George Melville
w 1836–1843
Spec M, Optical IM, Phil IM, Math IM
1836   17 Thavies Inn, Holborn, London
1839   32 Hatton Garden, London, and
1839–1841   126 Great Hampton St, Birmingham
1843   36 Ludgate St, London
See also HORTON William★
Sources: Pg

HOSMER John
w 1839
Known to have sold: calculating machine
Sources: ChrSK 8 Dec 1988 lot 103

HOUGHTON James (I)
w 1788–1826
Scale M, Watch tool M
1788–1826   Prescot, Lancs
Known to have sold: balance
Sources: Prescot rate books (MAC); BW; Pg

HOUGHTON James (II)
w 1827
Math IM
1827   2 Viller St, Liverpool
See also HOUGHTON John★
Sources: G (MAC)

HOUGHTON John
w 1841
Math IM
1841   14 Beresford St, Liverpool
Sources: G

HOUGHTON Stephen
c 1804–1820
        Ormskirk
Worked for WILKINSON Anthony★
Took over from WILKINSON Anthony★
Succeeded by HOUGHTON & SON Stephen
Known to have sold: balance
Sources: inst (pv); Crawforth (1979)

HOUGHTON Thomas
w 1771 d 1825
Watch tool M
Alternative name: T.H.
1771   Farnworth, Lancs
Known to have sold: barometer, balance
Sources: inst Gloucester Mu, inst (pv)

HOULDIN John
w 1834–1845
Optician
1834   22 Pellew St, Liverpool

1841–1845   14 Beresford St, Liverpool
Sources: G

HOULISTON James
w 1839–1859
Baro M, Thermo M, Optician
1839–1842   3 St.Alban's Terrace, Kennington
               Rd, London
1845–1849   33 New Bond St, London
1851–1859   85 New Bond St, London
Sources: PO; Wk

HOUNSFIELD B.
w 1833
Rule M
1833   Little Pond St, Sheffield
Sources: Wh

HOVIL William
w 1849
Optician
1849   6A Crombies Row, Commercial Rd
               East, London
Guild: [Grocers]
Son of HOVIL John, Clock M, of Horsleydown,
London
Apprenticed to FAIREY Joseph★ 1811
Sources: PO; GL: GC 11598/6

HOVIL & SONS
w 1837–1842
Optical IM, Phil IM, Math IM
1837–1842   30 Haydon St, Minories, London
See also HOVIL William★
Sources: PO; R (JAC)

HOW
w 1851–1859
Hydro M
Alternative name: How's Patent Salinometer
Office
1851–1855   35 Mark Lane, City, London
1859   81 Mark Lane, City, London
Sources: PO

HOWARD Charles
c 1718
        Charing Cross, London
See also HOWARD John (I)★
Sources: Taylor (1966) p.130

HOWARD Henry
d 1777
Math IM
1777   Temple Bar, Liverpool
See also
HOWARD Thomas★
HOWARD William★
Sources: LM index (MAC)

HOWARD J. (or T.?)
a 1700–1725
        Charing Cross, London
See also
HOWARD John (I)★
HOWARD John (II)★
Known to have sold: circumferentor
Sources: inst SM

HOWARD James
w 1841–1845
Optician
1841–1845   38 Leeds St, Liverpool
Sources: G

HOWARD John (I)
w 1694–1697
1694–1697   London
Guild: Clockmakers, fr 1694
Apprenticed to
MILLER John 1687
HOWARD J.★
HOWARD Charles★
HOWARD John (II)★
Possibly HOWARD John (I)★ or HOWARD
John (II)★ was the maker of the circumferentor
signed J. Howard in SM
Sources: inst SM; Loomes (1981b)

HOWARD John (II)
fr 1727 w 1749
1727   Globe opposite Southampton St,
         Strand, London
1749   Dartmouth St, Westminster, London
Guild: Broderers, fr 1727
Apprenticed to ROBERTS Jonathan★ 1715
Sources: GL: BROD 14663/1; Crawforth (1987)
p.340; MAC

HOWARD Richard
w 1715–1719
Math IM
         London
Guild: Clockmakers, fr 1718/19
Apprenticed to DELANDER Daniel★ 1702
Known to have sold: horary quadrant
Sources: GL: CKC 2710/3 fol.34, 2717/1 fol.33;
inst NMM

HOWARD Thomas
w 1767 d 1793
Math IM
1767–1773   Temple Bar, Liverpool
1774   2 Temple Bar, Liverpool
See also
HOWARD Henry★
HOWARD William★
Known to have sold: octant
Sources: inst MHS; Shaw; LM index (MAC)

HOWARD William
w 1791–1792
Math IM
1792   Gibralter Row, Liverpool
Sources: LM index (MAC)

HOWARTH Charles
fl 1823 d 1852
         Halifax
Succeeded by HOWARTH James★
Known to have sold: barometer
Sources: Goodison (1977) p.331

HOWE John (I)
w 1703–1733
[Spec M]
         Threadneedle St, by the Royal

Exchange, London
Guild: Spectaclemakers, fp 1699
Son of HOWE Joseph★
Had apprentice:
HOWE John 1703
HOWE Robert★, his son, 1725
HOWE John (II)★ his son, 1725
Succeeded by HOWE John & Robert★
Took over from HOWE Joseph★
d c. 1747
Known to have sold: telescope
Sources: GL: SMC 5213/2 p.32,158,162, 6029; inst
SM

HOWE John (II)
w 1749–1768
[Spec M]
1755   Threadneedle St, London
Guild: Spectaclemakers, fr 1733
Father of HOWE John (III)★
Son of HOWE John (I)★
Brother of HOWE Robert★
Apprenticed to HOWE John (I)★ 1725
Had apprentice VAUGHAN Charles 1762
Took over from HOWE John (I)★
Master SMC 1749–1750; last attendance at SMC
Mar 1769; d c.1771
Sources: GL: SMC 5213/3 p.141,152–3+; 5213/2
p.158,162,253; 6029; Riv

HOWE John (III)
fp 1768
[Spec M]
1768   London
Guild: Spectaclemakers, fp 1768
Son of HOWE John (II)★
Sources: GL: SMC 5213/3

HOWE Joseph
w 1667–1710
Spec M
Alternative name: HOW
1671   Royal Exchange, London
1676   Back Side, Royal Exchange, London
1691–1695   Threadneedle St, Behind the Royal
         Exchange, London
Guild: Broderers, Spectaclemakers
Father of HOWE John (I)★
Related to HOWE John (II)★
HOWE Robert★
Had apprentice:
GAY Thomas★ 1682 SMC
ROWLEY John★ 1682 BROD
ROBERTS Jonathan★, nd, fr 1681 BROD
LONGLAND William★ 1667 SMC
BENNETT Job 1690/1 SMC
ALT Peter★ 1694 SMC
HORSEMAN Aquila 1674/5 SMC
PIERCEHOUSE Adam 1696 SMC
COOK James 1701/2 SMC
PATTON Anthony 1674 SMC
SPRAT John 1676/7 SMC
STORER John 1674 SMC
SAYE Thomas★ 1668 SMC
Employed VERNEY Henry 1676/7
Succeeded by HOWE John (I)★
See also HOWE William★
fr in SMC by 1664; on livery of BROD 1679;

Master SMC 1672–1674, 1689–1690
Known to have sold: telescope
Sources: GL: SMC 5213/1, 5213/2 p.5,27;
Crawforth (1987) p.339; LGaz 30 July 1691

HOWE Robert
fr 1733 w 1749
[Spec M]
–1749   London
Guild: Spectaclemakers, fr 1733
Son of HOWE John (I)★
Partnership: HOWE John & Robert★
Apprenticed to HOWE John (I)★ 1725
Went abroad in 1749
Sources: GL: SMC, 5213/2 p.162, 5213/3 p.135

HOWE William
fr 1662 w 1703
Math IM
Alternative name: HOW
1700   Tower Hill, London
Guild: Grocers fr 1662, Clockmakers fr 1667/8
Apprenticed to BLEYGHTON John★ 1654
Had apprentice:
CLARKE Robert 1662
PERRY Edmund 1665/6
RANDALL John (I)★ 1671
JOHNSON John (I)★ 1675
CRICK Charles (I)★ 1679
LAMPLEY Charles 1683
PAINE John 1689
SWETMAN James★ 1693/4
GRIFFITH George★ 1700
See also HOWE Joseph★
Sources: Brown J. (1979a) p.27, (1979b) p.31

HOWELL Francis
s 1732 d.c 1761
Math IM, Phil IM
1761   Opposite New Church in the
         Strand, London
Guild: [Grocers ?]
Apprenticed to HEATH Thomas★ 1732
Instruments advertised: telescope, quadrant,
barometer, sundial, drawing instruments, camera
obscura, microscope
Sources: Brown J. (1979a) p.35; *Daily Ad* 30 Jun
1761 p.4 (JRM)

HOWELL John
w 1810
Math IM
1810   9 Pembroke Place, Liverpool
Sources: G

HOWORTH Samuel
w 1805–1818
Spirit Merchant 1805, but master of a Math IM
Alternative name: HOWARTH
1805   The Olive Tree, Old Swan Passage,
         London Bridge, London
Guild: Innholders, fr 1805
Had apprentice POOL James★ 1818
Fr by purchase in IC
Sources: GL: IC 6648/7, 6651/1

HUBEE Mary
w 1834

Optician, Math IM, Phil IM
1834   31 Crown St, Soho, London
Sources: Pg (JAC)

HUCKWELL Joseph
fr 1675
[Math IM]
1675   Near Armitage (Hermitage ?)
              London
Guild: Weavers, fr 1675
Apprenticed to HENSHAW Walter★ 1668
Sources: GL: WVC 4657/1

HUDDY Francis
w 1843–1865
Rule M, Math IM
1843–1844   37 Duke St, Smithfield, London
1845–1850   24 Red Lion St, London
1852–1865   34 Red Lion St, Holborn, London
Sources: PO; Wk

HUDSON F. J.
w 1827–1828
Optician
1827–1828   4 Fetter Lane, London
See also HUDSON Frederick T.★
Attended London Mechanics Institute 1827–1828
Sources: LMIR (AM)

HUDSON Frederick
w 1830
Spectacle M
1830   Grenwich Rd, Greenwich
See also HUDSON Frederick T.★
Sources: Pg

HUDSON Frederick T.
w 1845
Optician
1845   Stockwell St, Greenwich, London
Succeeded by HUDSON & SON
See also HUDSON Frederick★
Sources: PO(HC); TCd NMM

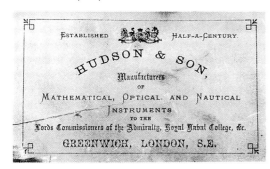

HUDSON John
w 1817–1836
Math IM, Optical IM, Spec M, Optician
              7 Orange St, Leicester Square,
              London
              17 Ryder's Court, Leicester Square,
              London
              112 Leadenhall St, London
1817–1822   17 Orange St, Leicester Square,
              London

1836   9 St. Martin's Court, Leicester
              Square, London
Succeeded by HUDSON Sarah★
See also HUDSON John Thomas★
Sources: J; Pg (JAC); Calvert (1971) p.27

HUDSON John Thomas
w 1831–1845
Optician, Spec M
              28 Henrietta St, Cavendish Square,
              London
              14 Marylebone Lane, London
              8 Henrietta St, Cavendish Square,
              London
              17 Ryder's Court, Leicester Square,
              London
1838–1839   96 High St, Marylebone, London
1845   102 Waterloo Road, London
See also
HUDSON John★
HUDSON Sarah★
Sources: Pg; PO; R (JAC)

HUDSON Robert
w 1812
Scale M
              London
Guild: Blacksmiths, fr 1812
Apprenticed to WILLIAMS Thomas (III)★ 1804
Attended Christ's Hospital School, London
Sources: GL: CH 12823/8 p.30, 110; BKC
2881/16 (MAC)

HUDSON Sarah
w 1836–1841
Optician
1836   9 St.Martin's Court, St.Martin's
              Lane, London
1839–1840   17 Ryder's Court, Leicester Square,
              London
Took over from HUDSON John★
See also HUDSON John Thomas★
Sources: Pg; PO

HUDSON William
w 1813–1834
Optician, Brass turner
1813–1814   46 Fetter Lane, Holborn, London
Guild: Drapers, fr 1814
Father of
HUDSON William Corker
HUDSON John Edward
Son of HUDSON John, pewterer, of London
Husband of HUDSON Frances
Apprenticed to BRUCE William★ 1804
Sources: DH: DPC Ap/Fr, index; GL: St Andrew,
Holborn, bap

HUG Lawrence
w 1850
Math IM
1850   44 Constitution Hill, Birmingham
Sources: Sl

HUGGINS George (I)
w 1802–1805
Math IM
Alternative name: 1805 took surname of

DOLLOND
1802   11 Hercules Buildings, Lambeth,
              London
1804   New Surrey St, Blackfriars Rd,
              London
1805   28 New Surrey St, Blackfriars Rd,
              London
Guild: Grocers, Spectaclemakers
Son of HUGGINS John, hosier d, of Newington,
Surrey [London], in GC records, but probably an
error as other sources give son of William, hatter,
of Strand, London
Apprenticed to FAIRBONE Charles (I)★ 1788
Had apprentice:
HUGGINS John★ 1805
GREAVE David Thomas 1804
For later work see DOLLOND George (I); fr GC
1804; listed in directories before taking freedom; fr
SMC 1807 by purchase
Sources: H; GL: GC 11598/6; SMC 5213/4
Brown J. (1979a) p.45, 54, 86

HUGGINS George (II)
fr 1827 w 1847
Optician
Alternative name: 1852 changed name to
DOLLOND George (II)
1827   26 Watling St, London
1839   St Paul's Church Yard, London
1847   13 Earl St, City, London
Guild: Grocers, fr 1827
Son of HUGGINS John (I)★
Apprenticed to DOLLOND George (I)★ 1812 GC
Had apprentice:
HUGGINS George (III), his son, 1839
HUGGINS William, his son, 1847
See also DOLLOND George (II)★ for further details
Sources: GL: GC 11598/6, 11598/7, 11598/8

HUGGINS John (I)
s 1778 w 1805
Optician
1805   2 South Place, Kennington Lane,
              London
1812   White Hart Row, Lambeth, London
Guild: [Spectaclemakers]
Father of HUGGINS John (II)★
HUGGINS George (II)★
Son of HUGGINS William, deceased, of Islington,
London
Apprenticed to DOLLOND Peter★ 1778
d by 1812
Sources: GL: SMC 5213/3; GC 11598/6 & /7;
GL: CH 12876/6 (1805)

HUGGINS John (II)
fr 1812 w 1828
Optician, Optical IM, Phil IM, Math IM
1812   Surrey St, Blackfriars Road, London
1821–1824   7 Little Knightrider St, London
1826–1828   43 Westmorland Place, City Rd,
              London
Guild: Grocers, fr 1812
Son of HUGGINS John (I)★
Apprenticed to HUGGINS George (I)★, later
DOLLAND, 1805
Had apprentice PALLANT John★ 1826
Apprenticeship money paid by Christ's Hospital

Sources: GL: GC 11598/6, 11598/8; CH 12823/8 p.111, 12876/6; Bn; Pg

HUGHES George

w 1831–1858
Rule M
1831	28 Gee St, Goswell St, London
1839	46 Gee St, Goswell St, London
1845–1855	35 Northampton St, Clerkenwell, London

See also HUGHES Thomas (II)★
Sources: Pg; PO; R (JAC)

HUGHES Henry

w 1835–1875
Optical IM, Naut IM, Math IM
1840	3 Union Terrace, Commercial Rd, London
1845–1855	120 Fenchurch St, London
1859–1875	59 Fenchurch St, London
1867	36 Trinity Square, Tower Hill, London

Guild: Masons fr 1840, Spectaclemakers fr 1867
Father of HUGHES Alexander, fr in SMC 1890
Brother of HUGHES Joseph (II)★
Apprenticed to HUGHES Joseph (I)★, his father, 1830
Had apprentice:
HEATH George★ 1840
BATTERSBY William 1841
CLARK William 1841
WORLEDGE Thomas 1841
OXLADE Gilbert Alexander 1856
Succeeded by HUGHES & SON, H.
d.1879; fr in SMC by service to father, Feb 1867
Known to have sold: rule, barometer, microscope, course corrector.
Sources: inst & TCd NMM; GL: MC 5304/6, 5304/7; SMC 5213/7, 5213/8; JAC; Goodison (1977) p.331; Sby 3 Jun 1988 lot 406

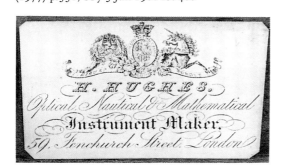

HUGHES Howell

w 1790–1794
Optician
1779	20 Salisbury Court, Fleet St, London
1790–1794	New Street Square, Fetter Lane, London

Guild: [Spectaclemakers], Upholders
Son of HUGHES Thomas, Gent, d, of Glasbury, Radnor
Apprenticed to PYEFINCH Henry (I)★ 1772 SMC fr 1779 UC
Sources: GL: SMC 5213/3; UC 7142/2 p.28; W

HUGHES James

w 1817
Math IM
1817	16 Queen St, Limehouse, London

See also HUGHES Joseph (I)★ [possible directory error or father]
Sources: J. (MAC)

HUGHES John

w 1850
Rule M
1850	Cambridge St, Birmingham

Sources: Sl

HUGHES Joseph (I)

w 1818 d 1845
Math IM, Naut IM, Optician, Phil IM, 'Real Manufacturer of Sextants & Quadrants Compasses....&c'
1818–1843	16 Queen St, Ratcliff, London
1829	6 Cross St, Ratcliff, London
1845	37 & 38 Queen St, Ratcliff, London
	38 Queen St, Ratcliff Cross, London

Guild: Masons, fr 1808
Son of HUGHES James, labourer, of Shadwell, London
Father of
HUGHES Henry★
HUGHES Joseph (II)★
Apprenticed to COOK William George★ 1800
Had apprentice:
HUGHES Henry★, his son, 1830
DOBSON James★ 1838 t/o 1845 to MATTHEWS John★
HUGHES Joseph (II)★ 1839
BAXTER William (II)★ 1839 t/o 1845 to CHISLETT Alfred★
HOOPER William W.★ 1840
8 others 1825–1840
Succeeded by HUGHES Joseph (II)★
B.apt Excise;
Known to have sold: barometer, rule
Sources: TC NMM; GL: MC 5304/6, 5304/7 (MAC); Pg; PO; inst(s)

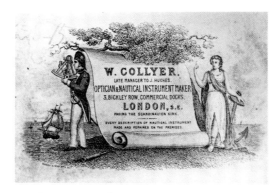

HUGHES Joseph (II)

w 1849–1878
Math IM, Phil IM, Naut IM
1843–1865	37 & 38 Queen St, Ratcliff Cross, London
1870–1875	38 & 40 Queen St, Ratcliff Cross, London
1870	Bickley Row, Rotherhithe, London

1875	19 London St, Fenchurch St, London

Guild: [Masons]
Son of HUGHES Joseph (I)★ and Elizabeth
Brother of HUGHES Henry★
Apprenticed to
HUGHES Joseph (I)★, his father, 1839, t/o 1846 to CARLINE William I.★
Employed COLLYER W. as manager
Took over from HUGHES Joseph (I)★
b 1825 or 1826
Sources: PO; GL: MC 5304/7; Wk; TCd NMM; PRO: Cs 1851 (LS)

HUGHES Thomas (I)

w 1787–1797
Rule M, Paper case M
1787	26 Duke St, Birmingham
1793	Aston Rd, Birmingham
1797	Colmore Row, Birmingham

Sources: BW, Pye (MAC)

HUGHES Thomas (II)

w 1802–1835
Rule M, Gauge M
	52 Gee St, Goswell St, London
	156 Whitecross St, London
	68 Noble St, Goswell St, London
	68 Noble St, Brick Lane, St.Luke's, London
	68 Noble St, Falcon Square, London

See also HUGHES George★
Sources: H; R (JAC)

HUGHES William

w 1790
	Limehouse, London

See also HUGHES Joseph (I)★
Known to have sold: octant
Sources: Taylor (1966) p.341 refers to a signed octant at NMM but this has not been traced. Possibly an error for H. Hughes

HUGHESDON William

w 1811–1823
Math IM
1804	10 Dean St, Fetter Lane, London
1811	5 Fan Court, Miles Lane, Cannon St, London
1823	5 Satchwells Rents, Bethnal Green, London

Guild: [Stationers], Haberdashers, fp 1804
Apprenticed to EVANS William (I)★ STC
Had apprentice:
SKINNER John 1811
CLAY John 1823
Sources: GL: HC 15858/2, 15860/9; McKenzie (1978) p.119

HULBERT Richard

w 1832
Optical IM, Math IM, Phil IM
1825	2 Bowmans Buildings, Aldersgate, London
1832	Friar St, Blackfriars Rd, London

Probably worked for SIMMS William (II)★ 1825
Attended London Mechanics Institute 1825
Sources: R (JAC); LMIR (AM)

HULETT John
w 1630
Alternative name: Io
Known to have sold: quadrant
Sources: inst (s)

HULL James
w 1746
Teacher, Globe S, Map S, Math IS
1746   Half-Moon Passage, Aldersgate St,
            London
Sources: *The General Ad* 18 Jan 1746 (JRM)

HUMBLE Edward
w 1775 d 1820
Math IM, Musical IM, Turner, Book S
1775–1777   Pope's Head, Side, Newcastle upon
            Tyne
1777–1789   Pack Horse, Side, Newcastle upon
            Tyne
1789–1796   Dean St, Newcastle upon Tyne
1790–1795   Low Bridge, Newcastle upon Tyne
1796–1813   Mosley St, Newcastle upon Tyne
1820   Collingwood St, Newcastle upon
            Tyne
Father of
HUMBLE Stephen
HUMBLE Francis
Apprenticed to BARBER Joseph★
Succeeded by HUMBLE Stephen
Took over from RODDAM & HUMBLE★
Sources: Hunt (1975) (MAC)

HUME Jane
w 1836
Math IM, Phil IM
1836   10 High St, Wapping, London
Sources: Pg

HUMPHREYS Charles
w 1845–1855
Naut IM, Binnacle M
1845–1855   136 Pennington St, Ratcliff
            Highway, London
Sources: PO

HUNNEX Joshua
w 1810–1811
Math IM
1810   27 Opposite the one mile stone,
            Mile End Rd, London
1811   6 Crown & Shears Place, Sparrow
            Corner, London
Guild: Joiners, fr 1810
Apprenticed to HOPPE Ebenezer★ 1801
Sources: GL: JC 8046/12, 20588, 8055/4 (JAC);
Crawforth (1987) p.359

HUNT Basil
w 1767–1781
Roller, Plater
1767–1781   48 Edmund St, Birmingham
Known to have sold: balance
Sources: PR; Sket; Sy; Crowther-Beynon
(1925–26) p.183–91 (MAC)

HUNT Harry
fl 1673–1713

Gresham House, Broad St, London
Took over from SHORTGRAVE Richard★
Salaried Operator to Royal Society 1676
Known to have sold: barometer
Sources: Daumas (1972) p.70; Taylor (1954) p.266

HUNT Henry
w 1844–1884
Optician, Math IM
1844–1846   118 Patrick St, Cork
1881   109 Old George St, Cork
1883–1884   109 George's St, Cork
Succeeded by HUNT & SON
See also HUNT Thomas (II)★
Sources: Burnett & Morrison-Low (1989) p.149

HUNT James
w 1817
Optician
1817   Drawbridge St, Cork
Sources: Burnett & Morrison-Low (1989) p.149

HUNT John (I)
w 1787
Glass Grinder
1787   Lambeth Street, Goodmans Fields,
            London
Father of HUNT George s 1787 PWC
Sources: GL: PWC 7102 fol.14

HUNT John (II)
w 1837–1840
Optical IM, Phil IM, Math IM
1837–1840   45 Tothill St, Westminster, London
Sources: R (JAC)

HUNT John (III)
w 1804
Optician
1804   6 Dog Row, Bethnal Green, London
Guild: Grocers, fr 1788
Apprenticed to SPENCER William (II)★ 1777
Had apprentice HUNT Ebenezer, his son, 1804
Sources: GL: GC 11598/6; Brown J (1979a) p.47

HUNT John (IV)
w 1817
Optician
1817   Patrick St, Cork
Sources: Burnett & Morrison-Low (1989) p.149

HUNT Thomas (I)
w 1792–1812
Optician, Math IM
1805–1812   Patrick St, Cork
See also HUNT Thomas (II)★
Sources: Burnett & Morrison-Low (1989) p.149

HUNT Thomas (II)
w 1820–1828
Optician
1820   37 Patrick St, Cork
1824   65 Patrick St, Cork
See also HUNT Thomas (I)★
Sources: Burnett & Morrison-Low (1989) p.149

HUNTER Edward
a 1800

Known to have sold: sundial
Sources: Sby 22 Feb 1986 lot 108 (MAC)

HUNTER W.
a 1780–1830
            Edinburgh
Known to have sold: barometer
Sources: Phlps Edinburgh 25 Feb 1977 lot 148;
Chr 26 Jul 1978 lot 148 (NMSn)(MAC)

HUNTER William Thomas
w 1830
Rule M, Toy M
1830   St Lawrence Steps, Norwich
Sources: Pg

HUNTLEY Charles
w 1818
Optician
1818   53 High Holborn, London
See also
HUNTLEY Henry★
HUNTLEY John★
HUNTLEY Robert★
Sources: Kt (JAC)

HUNTLEY Henry
w 1818–1819
Optician
1818–1819   53 High Holborn, London
See also
HUNTLEY Robert★
HUNTLEY Charles★
HUNTLEY John★
Sources: PO

HUNTLEY John
w 1824–1825
Optician
1824–1825   16 Brownlow St, Holborn, London
See also
HUNTLEY Charles★
HUNTLEY Henry★
HUNTLEY Robert★
Sources: Kt (JAC)

HUNTLEY Robert
w 1811–1840
Optician, Optical IM, Math IM
            37 High Holborn, London
            53 Burlington Arcade, London
            37 Burlington Arcade, London
            38 Burlington Arcade, London
            124 Cheapside, London
            1 City Road, near the Turnpike,
            London
            259 Regent St, London
            Regent Circus, Oxford St, London
            255 Regent Circus, Oxford St,
            London
1816   1 Plumber's Row, City Rd, London
1817–1824   53 High Holborn, London
1825–1829   52 High Holborn, London
1830   118 Oxford St, London
1830   294 Regent St, London
See also HUNTLEY Henry★
Known to have sold: microscope
Sources: H; J; R (JAC); inst MHS

HURD Thomas
w 1816
Compass M
1816   Whittal St, Birmingham
Sources: H (DJB)

HURLEY Jonathan
w 1701–1703
1699   White Horse Inn, Fleet St, London
Guild: Blacksmiths, fr 1699
Apprenticed to BEN John★ 1692
Had apprentice PAYNE Thomas 1700/01 t/o
1702/3 to FISH John★
Sources: GL: BKC 2881/9, 2881/10, 2886/3
(MAC)

HURT Joseph
w 1736–1748
Optician
Alternative name: HURST
1736–1748   Archimedes & Three Golden
             Spectacles in Ludgate St, London
Guild: [Spectaclemakers] Stationers fp 1736
Son of HURT William, member of STC of London
Apprenticed to STERROP Ralph★ 1729
Took over from STERROP Ralph★
Succeeded by MORGAN Francis★
Instruments advertised: full range of optical &
math inst
Sources: GL: SMC 5213/2 p.207; BM: Heal
105/58; McKenzie (1978) p.186

HURTER Johann Heinrich
fl 1787 w 1790
Math IS, Painter
             53 Great Marlborough St, Oxford
             St, London
1790   Great Marlborough St, Soho,
             London
Partnership: HURTER & HAAS★
b.1734; Partnership c.1790–1795; d.1799 in
Düsseldorf
Known to have sold: air pump, balance, barometer
Sources: Broadsheet MHS; BW; W (JAC); Turner
& Levere (1973) p.30, 64, 135, 229; Wolf (1877)
p.562

HURTER & HAAS John H. & Jacob B.
c 1790 w 1795
Math IM, Phil IM, Optical IM
Alternative name: HAAS & HURTER
             58 Great Marlborough St, London
1792   Bull Yard, St.Ann's Court, Soho,
             London
See also
HAAS Jacob B★
HURTER Johann H★
Partnership dissolved 1795 & stock auctioned
Known to have sold: balance
Sources: Auction catalogue (cpy) MHS; Turner &
Levere (1973) p.30, 135

HUSSEY John (I)
w 1761–1783
Math IM
1761   St Clement Danes, London
1764–1769   Lambeth, London
1783   Green Walk, Southwark, London

Had apprentice:
HOWLET John 1761
HUSSEY Thomas 1764
MARTIN Richard (II) 1768
MESSER Benjamin★ 1769
HESTER Robert 1761
Sources: PRO: IR 1/23–26 (AM); GL: Sun
11936/317 no.483854

HUSSEY John (II)
w 1806
Rule M
1806   1 Tenter Alley, Little Moorfields,
             London
Guild: Clothworkers, fr 1806
Apprenticed to HUSSEY William★, his father, 1785
Sources: CWH: CWC Fr

HUSSEY William (I)
w 1764–1797
Rule M
1764   Butler's Alley, Grub St, London
1777   Moor Lane, Moorfields, London
1779–1797   Sweetings Passage, Moor Lane,
             Moorfields, London
Guild: [Joiners] Clothworkers, fp 1764
Son of HUSSEY Simon, founder, of London
Apprenticed to FARMER John★ 1739 JC
Had apprentice:
HUSSEY John (II)★, his son, 1785
TRUSTEE Christopher 1777
HUSSEY William (II), his son, 1780
WESTBROOK William 1764
Associated with ATKINSON John (II)★
Sources: GL: JC 8052/5; STTP fol.196; CWH:
CWC Ap, Fr; A (JAC); BW; Ld

HUTCHINS Josiah
w 1761–1775
Math IM
1761   Near Victualling Office, Parish of St.
             Botolph, Aldgate, London
1769   Tower St, London
1775   Ludgate Hill, London
             Parish of St. Martin, Ludgate, London
Guild: Stationers, fr 1761
Father of HUTCHINS Joseph s 1786
Apprenticed to BENNETT John (I)★ 1750
Had apprentice:
WHITE Edward 1761
STYLES Nicholas [?STILES★] 1761
STRODE James 1762
PEARCE Philip★ 1764
DAWSON John 1769
TURNBULL Stephen 1775
d by 1786
Sources: GL: GC 11598/5; McKenzie (1978) p.30,
186

HUTCHINSON Richard
w 1709–1736
[Math IM, Clock M]
Alternative name: HUCHASON
             London
Guild: Clockmakers, fr 1702
Apprenticed to BENNETT William★ 1694
Had apprentice:
TURNER Joseph★ 1709

SLOPER/SLIPPER Jeremiah 1716/17
FRANCIS Bulmer (s1709) by t/o nd
ROBINSON Henry 1724
Sources: Brown J (1979b) p.31–33

HUTCHINSON William
w 1819
Math IM
1819   Chapman St, London
Sources: SH: STC Memo Book (MAC)

HUTTON John
w 1851
Chrono M, Clock M, Watch M
1851   9 Lucas Place West, Commercial Rd
             East, London
             10 Mark Lane, London
Known to have sold: chronometer, sextant
Sources: Sby10 Mar1987, lot 112; Sby marine sale
1 Jun 1987 lot 311; PO

HUX Elizabeth (I)
w 1698–1722
[Scale M]
1698–1722   London
Guild: Blacksmiths
Wife of HUX Thomas (I)★
Mother of HUX Thomas (II)★
Partnership: HUX Thomas & Elizabeth★
Had apprentice:
INMAN John 1687
PAGE John 1690
HUX Thomas (II)★, her son, 1696
BRADGATE John 1698
Took over from HUX Thomas (I)★
See also LAMB Elizabeth★
Sources: GL: BKC 2881/8, 2881/9, 2881/10 (MAC)

HUX Elizabeth (II)
w 1718–1722
[Scale M]
Alternative name: LAMB
             London
Guild: Blacksmiths
Wife of
HUX Thomas (II)★
LAMB Percivall★
Had apprentice TAYLOR William 1722 by t/o
from JACKSON Richard (I)★
Took over from HUX Thomas (II)★
See also LAMB Elizabeth★
Sources: GL: BKC 2881/10, 2886/4 (MAC)

HUX James
w 1851
Chrono M, Watch M
1851   20 Down St, Piccadilly, London
Sources: PO

HUX Thomas (I)
w 1682 d by 1687
Scale M
             London
Guild: Blacksmiths, fr 1681 or 1681/2
Had apprentice SMITH James 1681/2
Father of HUX Thomas (II)★
Husband of HUX Elizabeth (I)★
Succeeded by HUX Elizabeth (I)★

See also HUX Thomas & Elizabeth★
Sources: GL: BKC 2881/8, 2884 (MAC)

HUX Thomas (II)
fr 1704 w 1708
[Scale M]
1704–1708   London
Guild: Blacksmiths, fr 1704
Son of HUX Thomas (I)★
and HUX Elizabeth★
Partnership: HUX Thomas & Elizabeth★
Apprenticed to HUX Elizabeth★ 1696
Had apprentice:
CARTER Abraham 1704
THOMPSON Daniel 1708
d by 1718
Sources: GL: BKC 2881/9, 2881/10 (MAC)

HUX Thomas & Elizabeth
c.1704
Scale M
                At ye Three Cocks at Holborn
                Conduit, London
Guild: Blacksmiths
See also
HUX Thomas (I)★
HUX Thomas (II)★
HUX Elizabeth★
Probably partnership of HUX Elizabeth (I)★ & her
son
Known to have sold: balance
Sources: inst Sheffield Mu (MAC)

HYAMS Hyam
w 1821–1851
Silversmith, Jeweller, Clock M, Money changer;
1822   7 Castle St [? Directory error],
            London
1821–1843   5 Castle St, London
1828–1843   22 Cornhill, London
1850–1851   59 Cornhill, London
Ex.1851;
Known to have sold: balance, lens
Sources: Bn; Pg; PO; R; Cat.1851; inst(pv); Fallon
(1988) p.184

HYAMS Nathan
w 1839
Optician
1839   115 St. James St, Brighton
Sources: Pg

HYDE John Moor
w 1841–1852
Math IM, Phil IM, Naut IM, Optician
1841–1852   1 Broad Quay, Bristol
Known to have sold: microscope
Sources: Hunts; Pg; inst SM (Wellcome)

HYNES Abraham
w 1839–1844
Optician, Math IM, Phil IM
1839–1844   35 Great Prescot St, Goodman's
            Fields, London
Sources: Pg; PO

HYNES John
w 1830

Optician
1830   98 High St, Kings Lynn, Norfolk
See also HAYNES John★
Sources: Pg

HYNES Myers
w 1830
Manufacturing Optician
1830   Bartholomew St, Exeter
Sources: Pg

HYRONS George
w 1761–1798
Math IM
1774–1798   82 Queen St, in the Park,
            Southwark, London
Had apprentice CARFRAE G.A. 1761
Sources: GL: CH 12823/6 p.23; Sun 11936/341
(MAC); BW; Kt

IBBOTSON, COOK
w 1848
1848   Hull
Known to have sold: octant
Sources: ChrSK 4 Sep 1980 lot 162 (DJB)

IGOD George T.
w 1841
Brass rule cutter
1841   8 Turnagain Lane, City, London
Attended London Mechanics Institute 1841
Sources: LMIR (AM)

ILES James Frederick
w 1836
Optician, Math IM, Phil IM
1836   30 Jamaica St, Commercial Rd,
            London
Guild: Merchant Taylors
Son of ILES James, gentleman, of London
Apprenticed to ★LILLEY John (I)★ 1818
Sources: Pg; GL: MTC, MF 320, 324

ILIFFE William
w 1683–1688
[Scale M]
                London
Guild: Blacksmiths, fr 1675 or 1676
Had apprentice:
REDHEAD John nd, t/o 1688 to CLARIDGE
Richard★
HINCE William 1683
PEERS John nd
Sources: GL: BKC 2884, 2881/8. 2886/2 (MAC)

ILLIDGE & SON T.
w 1818
Engraver on glass, Measure M
1818   Birmingham [from London]
Instruments advertised: chem app
Sources: Wr (DJB)

ILLINGWORTH Jonathan
a 1770
                Halifax
Known to have sold: barometer, thermometer
Sources: inst(s)

IMISON John
w 1785–1808
Mechanic, Printer, Watch M, Optician
                Manchester
Author
Sources: Taylor (1966) p.314; DJB

IMRAY James
w 1846–1851
Navigation Warehouse, Chart Publisher, Naut IM
1846–1850   116 Minories, London
1849–1850   3 Old Fish Street Hill, London
1851   102 Minories, London
Partnership: BLACHFORD & IMRAY★
Took over from BLACHFORD & IMRAY★
Sources: PO

INDERWICK John
w 1811–1828
Ivory turner, Optician
1825–1827   58 Princes St, Leicester Square,
            London
            53 Princes St, Leicester Square,
            London
R.apt Geo.III
Sources: Kt (JAC); Taylor (1966) p.425

INMAN Charles
w 1850–1862
Rule M
1850   13 Great Hampton St, Birmingham
1862   Back of 66 Hope St, Birmingham
Sources: Mor; Sl

INMAN & SON William
w 1841
Rule M
1841   36 Ashted Row, Birmingham
Sources: Pg

INSHAW & RUSHTON
w 1793
Math IM, Toy M
1793   Whitall St, Birmingham
Sources: BW

INTROVINI Anthony & Gaspar
w 1816–1817
Baro M, Looking-glass M
1816–1817   39 Bridge St, Manchester
1816–1817   and 43 Thomas St, Manchester
Succeeded by INTROVINI Gaspar★
See also
INTROVINI & CO. Anthony★
INTROVINO Anthony★
Said to be brothers
Sources: JW; Pg; Ronchetti (1990) p.52

INTROVINI Gaspar
w 1819–1840
Baro M, Mirror M, Picture frame M
Alternative name: Gasper INTROVINO
1819–1824   43 Thomas St, Manchester
1829   96 St George's Rd, Manchester
1832   16 Rook St, Manchester
1838   Foundry St, Manchester
1840   88 St George's Rd, Manchester
Took over from INTROVINI Anthony & Gaspar★

INTROVINI & CO. Anthony

See also INTROVINO Anthony★
Sources: Bn; Goodison (1977) p.333; JW

INTROVINI & CO. Anthony
w 1814–1815
Baro M, Looking-glass M
1814–1815   49 Thomas St, Manchester
See also
INTROVINO Anthony★
INTROVINI Anthony & Gaspar★
Sources: JW

INTROVINO Anthony
w 1818–1824
Carver, Gilder, Optician, Looking-glass M
1818   9 Lord St, Liverpool
1818   28 Hall St, Liverpool
1821–1824   138 Duke St, Liverpool
See also
INTROVINI Gaspar★
INTROVINI Anthony & Gaspar★
INTROVINI & CO. Anthony★
Sources: Bn; G; Pg; JW

IRVIN Thomas
w 1835
Math IM
1835   19 Charles St, Hatton Garden,
              London
Partnership: IRVIN Thomas & Peter
Attended London Mechanics Institute 1835
Sources: LMIR (AM)

IRVIN Thomas & Peter
w 1835–1842
Optical IM, Phil IM, Math IM
              10 Charles St, Hatton Garden,
              London
1839   19 Charles St, Hatton Garden,
              London
1840–1842   11 Charles St, Hatton Garden,
              London
Sources: PO; R (JAC)

IRVINE –
w 1802–1805
Optician
1802–1805   28 Bow Lane, London
See also
IRVINE John★
IRVINE John G.★
IRVINE Elizabeth★
Sources: H

IRVINE Elizabeth
w 1834–1846
Optician, Spec M
1834–1846   32 Kirby St, Hatton Garden,
              London
Took over from IRVINE John G.★
See also IRVINE John★
Sources: PO; R (JAC)

IRVINE John
w 1794–1821
Optical IM, Phil IM, Math IM, Optician
1816   5 Queenhithe, Upper Thames St,
              London

1821   32 Kirby St, Hatton Garden,
              London
              2 Newcastle St, College Hill,
              London
Succeeded by IRVINE John G.★
See also IRVINE★
Sources: Und

IRVINE John Glen
w 1822–1834
Optician, Math IM, Phil IM
1822–1834   32 Kirby St, Hatton Garden,
              London
Succeeded by IRVINE Elizabeth★
Took over from IRVINE John★
See also IRVINE★
Sources: Pg; PO (JAC)

IRWIN Frederick
w 1826
Wire Worker 1821, Math IM 1826
1826   2 George Terrace, Commercial Rd,
              London
1821   Crooked Lane, London
Guild: Girdlers, fr 1821
Had apprentice FITZGERALD Michael 1826
Sources: GL: GDC 5800/2; 5802

ISAACS Thomas
w 1736–1738
Spec M
              London
Guild: Spectaclemakers, fr 1738
Son of ISAACS Abraham, member of Poulterers'
Co of London
Apprenticed to DAY John★ 1727
1736 to be sued by SMC for working as Spec M
when not a freeman; prob d by 1763 when Mrs
Isaacs given alms
Sources: GL: SMC 5213/2 p.187+, 5213/3

JACKSON Abraham
w 1813–1834
Chrono M
1816–1820   44 Lord St, Liverpool
1821   66 Lord St, Liverpool
1823–1827   58 Castle St, Liverpool
1828–1834   Castle St, Liverpool
1829–1834   42 Castle St, Liverpool
Sources: Bn; LM index (MAC); Loomes (1975)

JACKSON Ann
w 1736–1740
              London
Guild: Blacksmiths
Wife of JACKSON John★
Had apprentice:
BARTLETT Thomas 1736
FROHOCK John 1739/40
Sources: GL: BKC 2886/5 (MAC)

JACKSON Ann & James
w 1747–1774
Glass Grinders, Glass S, Optical IS
1747–1774   5 Essex Bridge, Dublin
Succeeded by JACKSON James & Richard★
Sources: Burnett & Morrison-Low (1989) p.127

JACKSON Christopher
fl 1590 w 1616
Math IM
              The Cock in Crooked Lane, near
              Eastcheap, London
Associated with
ALLEN Elias★ and
THOMPSON John (I)★ in advertisements
Known to have sold: surveyor's chain
Sources: Bryden (1992) p.306; Taylor (1954) p.189,
343

JACKSON Frederick A.
w 1841–1859
Chrono M, Watch M
1841–1843   34 Castle St, Liverpool
1845   2A Brunswick St, Liverpool
1847–1855   37 Castle St, Liverpool
1857–1859   Swift Court, Liverpool
Sources: Loomes (1975); G

JACKSON Henry
w 1769–1794
Scale M, Ironmonger
Alternative name: H.J.
              Pill Lane opposite Bull Lane, Dublin
1769–1794   87 Pill Lane, Dublin
Known to have sold: balance
Instruments advertised: balance
Sources: Wi; inst (pv) (MAC)

JACKSON James
w 1811–1835
Optician, Math IM
              33 Knightsbridge, London
1822   16 Knightsbridge, London
See also JACKSON William★
Sources: Bn; H; Pg (JAC)

JACKSON James
w 1750–1785
Jeweller, Goldsmith
1750   High St, Birmingham
1767–1785   30 High St, Birmingham
Master of Assay Office, Birmingham
Known to have sold: balance
Sources: By; PR; Sket; DJB; inst (pv) (MAC)

JACKSON James & Richard
w 1775–1785
Glass S
1775–1785   5 Essex Bridge, Dublin
Succeeded by JACKSON Richard★
Took over from JACKSON Ann & James★
Both the predecessor & successor firms at the same
address were IS as well Glass S
Sources: Burnett & Morrison-Low (1989) p.127

JACKSON John
w 1718 d.c 1741
Scale M
1730   Old St, London
Guild: Blacksmiths, fr 1716
Apprenticed to SMELT Samuel★ 1709 t/o to
WRIGHT Edward 1710
Had apprentice PIXLEY Thomas (I)★ 1730 and 3
others 1718–1726
Sources: GL: BKC 2886/4, 2881/10; CH 12876/3

JACKSON Joseph
w 1735–1760
Math IM
1735   Opposite Exeter Exchange, Strand, London
1736–1760   Angel Court, Strand, London
Guild: Grocers, fr 1735
Partnership: HEARNE & JACKSON★
Son of: JACKSON John, husbandman, d, of Snelston, Derby
Apprenticed to HEATH Thomas★ 1723
Had apprentice:
SCOTT Robert★ 1735 by t/o from SCOTT Benjamin★
STONE Archimedes 1735
SUDLOW John★ 1736
TOWNLEY Robert 1738
B. apt Board of Ordnance
Known to have sold: clinometer, octant, microscope, level, sundial, theodolite, protractor, sector
Sources: inst NMM & SM; Brown J. (1979a) p.37; Millburn (1988b) p.286–88; Wallis R & P (1986) p.232

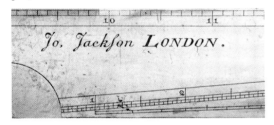

JACKSON Richard (I)
w 1717–1727
Scale M
        London
Guild: Blacksmiths, fr 1716
Apprenticed to GOWERS Weston★ 1706
Had apprentice:
TAYLOR William 1717 t/o to HUX Elizabeth (II)★
HULL Robert 1726/7
HOLTON Thomas 1722
Sources: GL: BKC 2886/4, 2881/10 (MAC)

JACKSON Richard (II)
w 1786–1827
Carver, Gilder, Looking-glass Warehouse, Baro M
1786–1827   5 Essex Bridge, Dublin
Took over from JACKSON James & Richard★
Sources: Burnett & Morrison-Low (1989) p.127, Pg

JACKSON William
w 1839–1840
Optician, Math IM, Phil IM
1839–1840   14 Bucklersbury, London
Sources: Pg

JACOB A.
fl 1830
Optical IM
        St. Anne's Place, Manchester
Sources: Taylor (1966) p.453

JACOB Christopher
w 1761–1775

Rule M, Snuffer M
1761   Snow Hill, Birmingham
1761   Bilstone St. Wolverhampton
1767   Smallbrook St, Birmingham
1770   Chapel Row, Birmingham
1773–1775   Gosty Green, Birmingham
Had apprentice:
BRIDGEN Thomas,
TIMMINS Joseph★
STRINGER William
See also JACOB William★
Instruments advertised: drawing instruments, rule, sector, slide rule
Sources: Sket; Sy; Aris 20 Jul & 23 Nov 1761 (MAC)

JACOB William
w 1770
Rule M
        29 Smallbrook St, Birmingham
See also JACOB Christopher★
Sources: Sket; Aris 27 Aug 1770

JACOB & HALSE
w 1809–1810
1809   London
Known to have sold: globe, sector
Sources: inst (s); inst (pv)

JACOBS Wolf
w 1835–1848
Spec M, Optician
        37 Great Saffron Hill, Holborn, London
1839–1846   36 Great Saffron Hill, Holborn, London
Sources: R (JAC); Pg; PO

JAMES Silas
w 1850
Optician
1850   Court, New John St, Birmingham
Sources: Sl

JAMES William
w 1819–1851
Spec M
        27 Little Russell St, Bloomsbury, London
1839–1851   25 Little Russell St, Bloomsbury, London
Sources: R (JAC); PO

JAMESON James
w 1764–1784
Optician
1764   Saffron Hill, London
1784   79 Great Saffron Hill, Holborn, London
Guild: Spectaclemakers, fr 1761
Nephew of WEBSTER James of London
Apprenticed to MARGAS John★ 1753
Petitioned against Dollond's achromatic lens patent, 1764
Sources: GL: SMC 5213/3 p.192+; By (JAC); PRO: PC1/7 no.94

JAMIESON George
w 1729–1755
Math IM
        Hamilton
Sources: Bryden (1972) p.16, 50

JAMIESON & CO. Robert
w 1819–1825
Math IM
1822   31 Brunswick Place, Glasgow
1823–1825   8 Nelson St, Glasgow
Partnership: GARDNER, JAMIESON & CO.★
Medal 1820 marine thermometer
Sources: Bryden (1972) p.50; Clarke et al (1989) p.165

JAQUES John
w 1817–1828
Optician, Spec M
1817–1828   14 London Wall, London
Sources: J; R (JAC)

JARDIN George
w 1737–1770
Smith, Math IM
        Glasgow
Guild: Hammermen, fr 1737
Sources: Bryden (1972) p.25, 50

JARMAIN T.
w 1759
[Compass M]
Alternative name: possibly Thomas JARMAN★
        London
Associated with WATT James★, who bought sea compasses from him
Sources: Bryden (1972) p.34n

JARMAN Samuel
w 1778
Math IM
1778   1 Queen St, Rotherhithe, London
Sources: GL: Sun 11936/271 no.406792

JARMAN Thomas
w 1760
Compass M
1760   Rotherhithe, London
Had apprentice BROWN John 1760
See also
WRIGHT George★
STEPHENSON Robert★
Sources: PRO: IR 1/22 (AM)

JARVIS Charles
w 1773–1785
Pincer M, Compass M
Alternative name: JARVICE
1773–1775   30 Smallbroke St, Birmingham
1777–1780   Windmill St, Birmingham
1785   Windmill Hill, Birmingham
Sources: PR; Pye; Sy

JARVIS John
w 1752
Instrument S
1752   Glasgow
Sources: Bryden (1972) p.18 & n89

JEACOCK James
w 1836–1873
Math IM, Phil IM, Naut IM
1836–1852　　32 Fore St, Limehouse, London
1845　　　　 96 Fore St, Limehouse, London
1855–1870　　33 Fore St, Limehouse, London
Sources: Pg; PO

JECKER Antoine
w 1826–1827
Math IM
1826–1827　　Turner's Court, St. Martin's Le
　　　　　　　Grand, London
Attended London Mechanics Institute, 1826–1827
Sources: LMIR (AM)

JECKER Francois Antoine
c 1800
[Math IM]
Worked for RAMSDEN Jesse
Sources: Daumas (1989) p.279

JEFFERS Robert
w 1769–1770
Scale M
1769–1770　　Cow Lane, Dublin
Sources: Wi

JEFFERYS James
w 1834–1860
Spec M, Optician, Math IM, Phil IM
1834–1846　　132 St.John St, Smithfield, London
1851　　　　 231 Tottenham Court Rd, London
1855　　　　 14 Tottenham Court Rd, London
Succeeded by JEFFERYS & SON James
See also JEFFERYS William (I)★
Sources: PO;Wk

JEFFERYS Thomas
w 1755
[Globe S]
1755　　　　　Corner of St Martin's Lane, Strand,
　　　　　　　London
R.apt, Geographer to Prince of Wales
Sources: Millburn (1988a) p.84

JEFFERYS William (I)
w 1826–1846
Drawing IM, Math IM, Phil IM
Alternative name: JEFFEREYS
　　　　　　　130 St.John's St, West Smithfield,
　　　　　　　London
1829–1846　　26 Wilderness Row, Goswell St,
　　　　　　　London
Guild: [Coachmakers]
Apprenticed to ELLIOTT William (II)★ 1813
Succeeded by JEFFERYS William G.★
See also JEFFERYS James★
Sources: PO; Pg; R (JAC); GL: CMC 5643

JEFFERYS William (II)
w 1851–1859
Optician
Alternative name: W. E. JEFFERYS
1851–1859　　68 Seymour St, Euston Square,
　　　　　　　London
Sources: PO; Wk

JEFFERYS William George
w 1849–1875
Optician, Drawing IM
Alternative name: William J. JEFFERYS (directory)
1849–1859　　26 Wilderness Row, London
1865–1875　　24 Wilderness Row, London EC
Took over from JEFFERYS William (I)★
Sources: PO; Wk

JENKIN Edward
w 1850
Hydro M, Sacch M
1850　　　　　19 & 20 Tooley St, London
Partnership: with HALL Edward★, trading as
DRING & FAGE★
B.apt Excise 1850 as DRING, FAGE & CO.
Sources: PO; McConnell (1993) p.53

JENKINS
w 1849
Baro M
1849　　　　　41 Cold Bath Square, London
See also JENKINS Alexander★
Attended London Mechanics Institute, 1849
Sources: LMIR (AM)

JENKINS Alexander
w 1845–1859
Baro M, Thermo M
1845–1846　　3 Guildford Place, London
1855　　　　 15 Garnault Place, Clerkenwell,
　　　　　　　London
1859　　　　 9 Remington St, London N
Succeeded by JENKINS BROS
Attended London Mechanics Institute, 1845–1846
Sources: PO; LMIR (AM)

JENKINS David
w 1826–1849
Optician, Spec M
1826　　　　　32 Wynyatt St, Goswell Street Rd,
　　　　　　　London
1846　　　　　8 Brewer St North, Goswell Rd,
　　　　　　　London
1849　　　　　9 Queen's Head Lane, Islington,
　　　　　　　London
Sources: R (JAC); PO

JENKINS Henry
w 1756–1782
Clock M
1756–1774　　46 Cheapside, London
1774–1782　　68 Aldersgate St, London
Known to have sold: astronomical clock
Sources: King & Millburn (1978) p.147–48; Baillie
(1951)

JENKINS John
w 1830–1852
Clock M, Watch M, Chrono M
1830–1852　　Wind St, Swansea
Sources: Peate (1975)

JENKINS Samuel
w 1737
Optical IM, Mechanic
1737　　　　　Essex Court, London
Sources: Wallis R. & P. (1986) p.242

JENKINS Thomas
w 1785
Drawing IS
1785　　　　　126 Long Acre, London
Sources: GL: Sun 11936/328 no.506192

JENKINS William
fr 1752 w 1770
Math IM
1770　　　　　High St, St. Mary le Bone, London
Guild: Goldsmiths, fr 1752
Apprenticed to LIFORD John★ 1745
Son of JENKINS John of VC
Had apprentice HOWARD Edward 1770
Sources: GH: GSC Ap/Fr

JENKINSON John
w 1627 d c. 1669
Spec M
1628　　　　　Without Cripplegate, London
-1669　　　　　Bishopsgate, London
Guild: Brewers, Spectaclemakers
Son of JENKINSON William (II)
Apprenticed to ASHE Thomas★ 1618
Had apprentice:
THROGMORTON John★ 1644
LETHERLAND Robert 1627
JORDEN John 1634
See also JENKINSON William (I)★
fr BREW 1626; on first Court of SMC 1629;
translated from Brewers to SMC 1634
Sources: GL: BREW 5445/13 & 14, 5445/16;
SMC 5214, 5213/1; CLRO: Ald 49 fol.14

JENKINSON Mrs
w 1670–1671
Spec M
1670　　　　　Bishopsgate, London
1671　　　　　Bishopsgate St, London
Guild: [Spectaclemakers]
Wife of probably JENKINSON John★
Took over from JENKINSON John★
Sources: GL: SMC 5213/1

JENKINSON William (I)
w 1669–1692
Spec M
1669–1671　　Southwark, London
Guild: Spectaclemakers
Father of JENKINSON William (III)
See also JENKINSON John★
d 1708
Known to have sold: spectacles
Sources: GL: SMC 5213/2 p.58, 5213/1

JENKS Edmund
w 1682 d c. 1696
Scale M
　　　　　　　Ye Angel & Star in St.Ann's Lane
　　　　　　　near Aldersgate, London
Guild: Blacksmiths, fr 1782 or 1783
Had apprentice:
REDHEAD John★ by t/o from REDHEAD William★
nd, t/o to ILIFFE William★ nd and fr 1691
TAYLOR Jeremiah [or Jeremy] 1691
ALLEN David by t/o from NEALE Samuel★ nd, fr
1693
EVITT John 1693 by t/o from BROCK Richard★

TURNOR John 1693 t/o to BEN John★ 1694/5
THOMPSON John (II)★ 1694 t/o 1697 to NEALE
John (I)★
Known to have sold: balance
Instruments advertised: balance
Sources: GL: BKC 2881/8, 2884; Sheppard &
Musham (1975) p.171 (MAC)

JENNER Anselm
w 1679–1685
Math IM, Naut IM
                Bristol
Associated with HAYES Walter in a joint
advertisement
Known to have sold: nocturnal
Instruments advertised: encyclologium [type of
circular slide rule]
Sources: inst (pv) (KLJ); Taylor (1954) p.281, 401

JENNINGS Silas (I)
w 1728–1761
Scale M
                London
Guild: Blacksmiths, fr 1720
Apprenticed to ROBERTS Timothy★ 1713
Had apprentice JENNINGS Silas (II)★ 1743 and
four others 1728–1752
Sources: GL: BKC 2881/10, 2886/4, 2886/5
(MAC)

JENNINGS Silas (II)
w 1783
Scale M
1783   Gravel Lane, Southwark, London
Guild: Blacksmiths, fr 1750
Related to JENNINGS Silas (I)★
Apprenticed to JENNINGS Silas (I)★
Son of JENNINGS Thomas of BRC
Father of JENNINGS James 1783 STC
Sources: GL; BKC 2886/5 (MAC); McKenzie
(1978) p.152

JENNINGS Thomas
w 1830–1844
Carver & Gilder, Baro M, Optician
1830–1844   Tacket St, Ipswich
Known to have sold: barometer
Sources: Pg; Wh; Banfield (1991) p.121

JEOFFERYS Thomas (I)
w 1802–1805
Optician, Math IM
1805   15 Kirkby St, Hatton Garden,
                London
Sources: H

JEOFFREYS Thomas (II)
w 1786
Math IM
1786   The Three Tuns, Great New St,
                Shoe Lane, London
Sources: GL: Sun 11936/339 no.520006

JESSON –
w 1672
Ironmonger
1672   Near the Bars Without Aldgate,
                London

Known to have sold: rule
Sources: GL: CKC 2710/1 p.244

JEWKES James
d 1768
Math IM
1768   Southwark, London
Sources: *Gazetteer* 30 Aug 1768 (MAC)

JEZEPH James
w 1805–1834
Optical IM, Optician
Alternative name: JAZEPH, JOSEPH
1805–1808   24 Well St, Cripplegate, London
1817   15 Castle St, Aldersgate St, London
1817–1822   15 Nichol's Square, Aldersgate St,
                London
Guild: Stationers, fr 1801
Son of JEZEPH Thomas, milkman, of London
Apprenticed to MOULDING James★ 1794
Had apprentice:
KIRTON James 1805
DRAKE William 1808
WARRAN John 1822
Sources: J; Pg; R (JAC); McKenzie (1978) p.243;
SH: STC, Memo bk

JINKS Joseph
w 1835
Spec M
1835   Livery St, Birmingham
See also JINKS William
Sources: Pg

JINKS William
w 1828–1830
Optician
1828–1830   33 Court, Livery St, Birmingham
See also JINKS Joseph
Sources: Pg; West; Wr

JOBSON Benjamin
w 1680
Alternative name: Bengiman
Known to have sold: sector
Sources: BSIS, 1983 no.1 p.8

JOHN Thomas
w 1838–1840
Optician, Math IM, Phil IM
1838–1840   8 Clement's Inn Passage, London
Sources: Pg

JOHNSON Adam
w 1805–1829
Math IM, Navigation & Astro school
1805–1825   4 Salthouse Lane, Liverpool
1811–1816   5 Salthouse Lane, Liverpool
1827   27 Wolfe St, Liverpool
1829   90 Park Lane, Liverpool
Sources: Bn; G; Pg; LM index

JOHNSON John (I)
fr 1689 w 1714
Math IM
1704   Little Tower Hill, London
1709   near the Postern on Tower Hill,
                London

Guild: Grocers, fr 1689
Apprenticed to HOWE William
Son of JOHNSON John, blacksmith, of
Whitechapel, London
Had apprentice:
CHANTREY Robert★ 1704
HARRISON Joseph★ 1704
BARNES William 1706
GILBERT John (I)★ 1709
STEVENS George 1712 t/o 1718/19 to GILBERT
John (I)★
ROLT Samuel 1714
Sources: Brown J. (1979a) p.29–30

JOHNSON John (II)
w 1713–1736
[Spec M]
                London
Guild: Spectaclemakers, fr 1700/1
Apprenticed to STERROP Thomas (II)★1693
Had apprentice:
JOYCE Daniel 1713
BEST Thomas 1719
HEAD Richard 1721
SPILLETT John 1726
ADEY Josiah, 1733/4, t/o from
BARKER William (II)★
1736 in reduced circumstances & receiving charity
from SMC, prob d by 1738
Known to have sold: nocturnal
Sources: GL: SMC 6029, 5213/2
p.22,83,111,120,173+; Ward (1981) p.76

JOHNSON Joseph
w 1814–1851
Chrono M, Watch M
1814–1822   55 Lord St, Liverpool
1814   1 Black St, Liverpool
1822–1834   25 Church St, Liverpool
1824   28 Church St, Liverpool
1841   49 Church St, Liverpool
1848–1851   87 Brownlow Hill, Liverpool
Sources: Bn; G; Loomes (1975)

JOHNSON Mary
fl 1837
Chrono M
                28 Castle St, Liverpool
Sources: Taylor (1966) p.474

JOHNSON P. J.
v 1824–1826
Math IM
1824–1826   3 Arundel St, London
Attended London Mechanics Institute 1824–1826
Sources: LMIR (AM)

JOHNSON Samuel (I)
w 1839–1846
Rule M
1839   13 New St, Cloth Fair, London
1840–1846   23 New St, Cloth Fair, London
Sources: Pg; PO

JOHNSON Samuel (II)
w 1751 d 1772
Optician
                Sir Isaac Newton & Two Pairs of

Golden Spectacles, 23 Ludgate St,
London
Sir Isaac Newton & Two Pair of
Golden Spectacles near the West
End of St. Paul's, London
1759–1765   Ludgate St, London
1772   23 Ludgate St, London
Guild: Spectaclemakers, fr 1745
Son of JOHNSON Abraham, carpenter, of
Westerham, Kent
Apprenticed to MANN James (II)★ 1738
Took over from MANN James (II)★ [claimed]
Known to have sold: microscope, telescope
Sources: GL: SMC 5213/2, 5213/3 p.93+; inst
MHS; Mort; Riv; Calvert (1971) pl.28

JOHNSON William (I)
w 1716 d 1745
Spec M
1716–1719   The Archimedes on London Bridge,
London
Guild: Spectaclemakers, fr 1715
Son of JOHNSON Thomas, husbandman, of Olney,
Bucks
Apprenticed to MANN James (I)★ 1707/8
Had apprentice:
GREEN John 1717
COX William (I)★ 1720 t/o 1723 to Jane
STERROP★
Employed YATES 1717
See also NORTH George's★ apprentice
Sources: GL: SMC 5213/2 p.56,93,101,115,142
GL: Sun 11936/5 no.7084,/10 no.14981

JOHNSON William (II)
w 1772
Math IM, Phil IM
The Globe & Quadrant, 146
Fenchurch St, London
1772   146 Fenchurch St, London
Guild: Stationers, fr 1771
Son of JOHNSON Theodore, decd, skinner of
Southwark, London
Apprenticed to STEDMAN Christopher★1764
Sources: BM: Heal 105/60; McKenzie (1978)
p.332

JOHNSON William (III)
w 1833–1900+
Optician, Spec M, Math IM, Phil IM
160 Tottenham Court Rd, London
1835   9 Castle St, Leicester Square,
London
1839–1900   188 Tottenham Court Rd, London
Succeeded by JOHNSON & SONS William
Sources: PO; Wk

JOHNSON William (IV)
w 1833–1867
Baro M, Thermo M
1833–1840   29 Kirby St, Hatton Garden,
London
1834   20 Cross St, Hatton Garden, London
1841–1867   34 Hatton Garden, London
Partnership: JOHNSON & BLACKBURN★
Partnership 1847–1848
Sources: Pg; PO; R

JOHNSON William (V)
w 1839–1851
Watch M, Chrono M
1839–1851   50 Strand, London
Sources: Pg; PO

JOHNSON William (VI)
w 1851
Watch M, Chrono M
1851   4 Hercules Passage, City of London
Sources: PO

JOHNSON & BLACKBURN William (IV) & ?
w 1847–1848
Baro M, Thermo M
1847–1848   34 Hatton Garden, London
Succeeded by JOHNSON William (IV)★
Took over from JOHNSON William (IV)★
Sources: PO (JAC)

JOHNSON & COCK Percival Norton & Thomas
w 1840–1844
Optician, Optical IM, Phil IM, Math IM, Assayer,
Refiner
1840–1844   79 Hatton Garden, London
Succeeded by JOHNSON & MATTHEY★
Sources: R(JAC)

JOHNSON & MATTHEY
w 1851
IM
1851   79 Hatton Garden, London
Succeeded by JOHNSON, MATTHEY & CO.
Ex. 1851
Sources: Turner G (1983) p.309; PO

JOHNSTON John (I)
w 1777
Math IM
1777   3 Bride Lane Court, Bride Lane,
London
See also JOHNSTON John (II)★ [possibly the same
man]
Sources: GL: Sun 11936/257 no.383935

JOHNSTON John (II)
w 1793
Math IM
1793   Royal Exchange, London
Father of JOHNSTON John s 1793 to LONG James★
See also JOHNSTON John (I)★ [possibly the same
man]
Sources: GL: VC 15220/3 p.239

JOHNSTON W. & A.K.
w 1830 a 1855
Engraver, Printer
Alternative name: JOHNSTONE William &
Alexander Keith
Edinburgh
Succeeded by JOHNSTON LTD W. & A.K.
Associated with DONALDSON & SON Alex★ in
making globes
Known to have sold: globe
Sources: Cat.1851; Bryden (1972) p.47

JOHNSTONE John
w 1774–1776
Math IM
1774–1776   Carruber's Close, Edinburgh
Sources: Bryden (1972) p.50

JOLE Robert
w 1664–1704
Math IM
Alternative name: CHOULE
The Crown, over against Durham
Yard in the Strand, London
The Globe in Fleet St, London
At ye Crown near ye New
Exchange, London
1672   Fleet St, London
1701   St.Johns near Clerkenwell, London
Guild: Stationers, Clockmakers
Father of
JOLE John fp 1699/1700 STC
JOLE Robert (II) fp 1693 STC
Apprenticed to BEDFORD Hilkiah★ 1656
Had apprentice:
CARTER Henry★ 1676/7 STC
HADDON William★ 1683/4 STC
ENGLAND John★ 1690 STC
WHITTYAT Roger★ 1704 STC t/o nd to
FRANKLIN Thomas★
JOLE Thomas, his son, 1680 CKC
JOLE Daniell, probably his brother, 1664
MANWARING Thomas 1686 STC
TEGG William 1695 STC
TRAFORD Thomas 1689 STC
HUBBARD Peter 1701 STC
COKE John 1671 STC
BRICKHILL James 1668 CKC
Associated with
ELMES William★ and
WELLS Joseph★, who both supplied rules
fr STC 1664, CKC (Brother) 1667/8; sued by
CKC for non-payment of quarterage fees 1701/2,
paid to 1705
Sources: GL: CKC 2710/1 p.244; Brown (1979b)
p.31; McKenzie (1974) p.11, 91, (1978) p.198

JONES – (I)
w 1800
Optician
1800   Near the Aldgate Pump, London
Sources: JAC

JONES Charles
w 1818–1841
Optician, Navigation Warehouse, Math IM
1818   58 Stanley St, Liverpool
1821–1822   57 Stanley St, Liverpool
1823–1824   11 East Side Dry Dock, Liverpool
1825   10 East Side Dry Dock, Liverpool
1827   11 East Side Dry Dock, (2nd period)
Liverpool
1828   Strand St, Liverpool
1829   28 Stand St, Liverpool
1831–1841   25 Strand, Liverpool
See also
JONES David (II)★
JONES Thomas (V)★
JONES Isaac★
JONES John (III)★

Known to have sold: sextant, barometer,
thermometer, compass (magnetic)
Sources: Bn; G; Pg; inst(s); DJB

JONES David (I)
w 1785–1795
Math IM, Optician
        25 Charing Cross, London
1785–1793   35 Charing Cross, London
Guild: [? Goldsmiths]
Apprenticed to probably, MARTIN Benjamin★
1766
Sources: GL: Sun 11936/326 no.501167; GH:
GSC index; BW; By; Ld (JAC)

JONES David (II)
w 1827–1845
Optician, Math IM
1827   53 Pool Lane, Liverpool
1829   68 Hanover St, Liverpool
1830   70 Great George St, Liverpool
1831   103 Richmond Row, Liverpool
1832–1834   120 Richmond Row, Liverpool
1835   125 Richmond Row, Liverpool
1835–1837   65 Great George St, Liverpool
1837   72 Great George St, Liverpool
1839–1845   26 Great George St, Liverpool
See also
JONES Charles★
JONES Thomas (III)★ & (V)★
JONES Isaac
JONES John (III)★
Sources: G; Pg; LM index (MAC)

JONES Edward (I)
a 1780
Microscope M, Optician
        14 Somerset Place, New Rd,
        Commercial Rd, London
Known to have sold: microscope
Sources: Brown O. (1986) no.117

JONES Edward (II)
w 1792
Scale M
1792   63 Goat St, Wolverhampton
Sources: Wolverhampton rate books (MAC)

JONES Edward (III)
fl 1818 w 1832
Chrono M
        1 Small St, Bristol
Sources: CUL: RGO 1143 fol.2,10; Baillie (1951);
Taylor (1966) p.453

JONES Henry (I)
w 1664–1693
Clock M
1675   Inner Temple Lane, London
Guild: Clockmakers, fr 1663
Said to be son of JONES William, vicar of Boulder,
Hants
Apprenticed to HILL Benjamin 1654 t/o nd to
EAST Edward
Had apprentice:
HANBURG John 1664
AYRES Richard 1670
ANNAT Nicholas 1673

EVEREST Edward 1674
GREENE James 1678
JONES William, his son, 1682
STAPLES Richard 1684
HELLAM James nd by t/o from JONES Evan, fr
1690
ROBINSON Francis 1685
CLEAVE William 1688/9
JONES Henry, his son, 1690
SHERWOOD John 1690/1
SILVESTER John nd by t/o from BATES Thomas,
fr 1693
PRIESTWOOD Joseph 1693
Master CKC 1691; d 1695
Known to have sold: barometer
Sources: GL: CKC 3939; Goodison (1977)
p.31–32, 333; Loomes (1981b)

JONES Henry (II)
fl 1796
Optical IM
        36 Ludgate St, London
Sources: Taylor (1966) p.342

JONES Isaac
w 1846–1849
Optician, Naut IM, Math IM
1846–1849   12 Bath St, Liverpool
Sources: G

JONES James (I)
w 1829–1839
Spec M, Optician
        53 Great Wild St, Lincoln's Inn
        Fields, London
        58 Great Wild St, Lincoln's Inn
        Fields, London
1829–1830   3 Long Lane, West Smithfield,
        London
1839   59 Great Wild St, Lincoln's Inn
        Fields, London
1839   44 Ratcliff Highway, London
Sources: Pg; PO; R; JAC

JONES James (II)
w 1845–1851
Optician
1845   25 Eyre Street Hill London
1849   10 Dorrington St, Cold Bath Fields,
        London
1851   13 Little Gray's Inn Lane, London
Sources: PO; Wk

JONES James (III)
w 1754
Math IM
1754   Parish of St.Botolph, Aldgate,
        London
Sources: McKenzie (1978) p.332

JONES James (IV)
w 1785–1793
Math IM, Optician
1785   79 Bull St, Birmingham
1787   92 Snow Hill, Birmingham
1793   Newton St, Birmingham
Sources: BW; Pye

JONES James (V)
w 1763
Scale beam M
1763   Parish of St Gregory by St Paul,
        London
Father of JONES Thomas (V) s 1763
Sources: GL: BC 5266/6 p.35

JONES James (VI)
w 1851–1859
Optician
1851–1859   11 Moor St, Soho, London
Sources: PO; Wk

JONES James (VII)
w 1847
Optician, Spec M
1847   Wensum St, Norwich
Sources: K

JONES James William
w 1837–1879
Optician, Phil IM, Math IM
1837–1859   87 Goswell St, London
1865–1875   172 Goswell Rd, London EC
Succeeded by JONES William (VI)
Sources: PO; R (JAC)

JONES John (I)
w 1759–1784
Math IM
Alternative name: Jones of Holborn
1776   Holborn, London
1793   135 near Furnival's Inn, Holborn,
        London
1782–1788   135 Holborn, London
1799   [Residence?] Skinner Place,
        Islington, London
1805–1806   [Residence?] Wells Row, Islington,
        London
Guild: Fishmongers, Spectaclemakers
Father of
JONES William (II)★
JONES Samuel★
Son of JONES Rice, staymaker, of St. Martin in the
Fields, London
Partnership: JONES & SON John★
Apprenticed to BALLETT Leonard★ 1751 SMC
Had apprentice:
WINTER Joseph 1760
JONES William (II)★ 1776 SMC
STEVENS John Lawford 1770 SMC
Employed WINTER Joseph 1759
HULL Thomas 1779
Succeeded by JONES & SON John★
Publisher; fr SMC 1758; fr FMC 1779; probably
retired 1791; d 1808
Known to have sold: micrometer, planetarium
Sources: JRM; inst (WM); PRO: PCC
PROB11/1485; GL: SMC 5213/3 p.162+,5213/4,
6029A; Wil; H; Brown O. (1983) no.30; Taylor
(1966) p.264–65

JONES John (II)
w 1765
Scale M
1765   Whitecross St, St Luke's, London
Guild: [?Skinners]

See also SOMMERS Joseph (I) (possibly his master)
Bound his son, John, to SOMMERS Charles★
Sources: SH:SKC, Ap/Fr

JONES John (III)
w 1804–1810
Navigation Warehouse, Stationer
1804   Bottom of Pool Lane, Old Dock,
     Liverpool
1805   27 Pool Lane, Liverpool
1808–1810   29 Pool Lane, Liverpool
Succeeded by:
JONES & RUST★
JONES Charles★
JONES David (II)★
RUST Joseph (II)★
b 1771; still alive 1831
Sources: G; H (AL); LM index (MAC)

JONES John (IV)
w 1817–1827
Rule M
     Crown Court, Soho, London
1817–1822   74 Wardour St, Soho, London
1823–1827   20 Crown St, Princes St, Leicester
     Square, London
Took over from FITCH & JONES★
Sources: Kt; Und (JAC); Routledge (1818) title p.

JONES John (V)
v 1824–1826
Math IM
1824–1826   250 Tottenham Court Rd, London
Attended London Mechanics Institute 1824–1826
Sources: LMIR (AM)

JONES John (VI)
w 1840–1860
Optician, Math IM
1840–1842   28 Wellington Quay, Dublin
     also in 1845, 1848–1854, 1860
1843–1844   29 Wellington Quay, Dublin
     also in 1846–1847, 1855–1859
Succeeded by JONES Nicholas J
Sources: Burnett & Morrison-Low (1989) p.127

JONES Joseph
c 1775–1778
Scale M
Sources: GL: Sun index, but entry not traced
(MAC)

JONES Mary (Mrs)
w 1828–1841
Optician, Phil IM, Math IM
1828–1841   241 Oxford St, London
Took over from JONES Owen★
Succeeded by DIXEY William★
Sources: PO

JONES Nathaniel
w 1787
Scale M
     London
Had apprentice SPRATT
Sources: GL: CH 12823/7 p.185

JONES Owen
w 1818–1828
Optician
1822   11 Duke St, Grosvenor Square,
     London
1828   241 Oxford St, London
Guild: [Girdlers]
Apprenticed to DIXEY Edward (II)★ 1812
Succeeded by JONES Mary★
Sources: GL: GDC 5802; Bn; Kt; R (JAC)

JONES Peter
fl 1837
Chrono M
1837   68 Rose Place, Liverpool
Sources: Taylor (1966) p. 474

JONES Samuel (I)
w pt 1791 w 1859
Optician
1806   30 Lower Holborn, London
1859   30 Holborn, London
1859   [Residence] Dalston House,
     St. Albans, Herts
Guild: Spectaclemakers, fr 1806
Son of JONES John (I)★
Brother of JONES William (II)★
Partnership JONES William & Samuel★
Had apprentice EDEN William★ 1811
b 1769; working by 1791 as partner in William &
Samuel Jones; d 1859
Sources: PO; GL: SMC 5213/4; Som.Ho: will
(JRM); CLRO: CF/1/1309; King & Millburn
(1978) p.207, 387

JONES Samuel (II)
w 1851–1901
Optician
1851–1865   12½ (or 12A) Crosby Row,
     Walworth, London
1870–1880   4 Blackman St, London SE
1885   169 Old Kent Rd, London SE
1890–1901   294 Walworth Rd, London SE
Sources: PO

JONES T. & W.
w 1803–1805
Math IM, Optician
     30 Marylebone St, Golden Square,
     London
     32 Marylebone St, Piccadilly, London
Succeeded by JONES William (IV)★
Sources: Kt; PO (JAC)

JONES Thomas (I)
w 1806 p 1861
Astro IM, Math IM, Optical IM, Phil IM
Alternative name: 'Jones of Charing Cross'
     124 Mount St, Grosvenor Square,
     London
     13 Panton St, Haymarket, London
     7 Southampton St, Strand, London
1806–1808   120 Mount St, Berkeley Square,
     London
1811–1814   21 Oxenden St, Piccadilly, London
1819   Cockspur St, London
1816–1850   62 Charing Cross, London
1851–1859   4 Rupert St, Coventry St, London

Partnership JONES & SONS Thomas★
Apprenticed to RAMSDEN Jesse★ 1789
Had apprentice DOUGHTY W.P.★
Worked for RAMSDEN Jesse★
See also JONES W.H.★
FRS 1835; Pat.1811 dividing instrument; R.apt
Duke of Clarence; B.apt Ordnance; R.apt Wm IV
1830; Partner 1832–35; b 1775 d 1852
Known to have sold: balance, barometer, compass,
hygrometer, quadrant, repeating circle, sextant,
telescope, theodolite, thermometer
Sources: PO; Und; Wk; PRO IR1/34 (AM);
LC3/69 p.150; Phil. Mag 30 (1808) p.60, 191;
MHS: MS Radcliffe 42; Calvert (1971) p.27–28;
Goodison (1977) p.166–69; inst NMM, SM and
see index of Holbrook (1992)

JONES Thomas (II)
w pt 1831–1835
Optician
1834   35 Tavistock St, London
1834   and 62 Charing Cross, London
Son of JONES Thomas (I)★
Partnership JONES & SONS Thomas 1831–1835
Attended London Mechanics Institute 1834
Sources: LMIR (AM); PO; R (JAC)

JONES Thomas (III)
w 1816–1831
Optician, Navigation book S, Naut IS, Math IM
1816–1821   5 Harrington St, Liverpool
1821–1831   4 Harrington St, Liverpool
See also
JONES Charles★
JONES David★
JONES Thomas★
Sources: Bn; G; LM index

JONES Thomas (IV)
fr 1820 w 1841
Scale M
1820   8 Star St, Shadwell, London
Guild: Blacksmiths, fr 1820
Apprenticed to SAWGOOD John★ 1807
Son of JONES John, looking-glass polisher, of
London
Had apprentice SMITH William 1834
Sources: GL: BKC 2881/16; 2881/17 (MAC)

JONES Thomas (V)
fl 1778 d 1805
Math IM
     Liverpool
See also JONES Thomas (III)★
Sources: LM index & n (MAC)

JONES W.
w 1783
Optician
1783   Bull St, Birmingham
Sources: By

JONES W. H.
c. 1850–1852
Optician
     62 Charing Cross, London
     4 Rupert St, Leicester Square,
     London

See also JONES & SONS Thomas*
Same premises as JONES Thomas (I)*
Sources: MHS: MS Gunther 3; PO

JONES William (I)
fr 1721
[Spec M]
          London
Guild: Spectaclemakers, fr 1721
Son of JONES Lewis, coachman, of Westminster,
London
Apprenticed to SCARLETT Edward(I)* 1709
Sources: GL: SMC 5213/2 p.65,124

JONES William (II)
w 1787 [? see partnerships]
Optician
1787   Holborn, London
1803   30 Lower Holborn, London
1798   [Residence] Islington, London
Guild: Spectaclemakers, fp 1794
Son of JONES John (I)*
Brother of JONES Samuel (I)*
Partnership
JONES & SON John*
JONES & SONS John*
JONES W. & S.*
Apprenticed to JONES John (I)* 1776
Had apprentice HALL Chambers 1803
Worked for MARTIN Benjamin*
b 1762; signed inst. while partner; d 1831
Known to have sold: planetarium, sundial
Sources: GL: SMC 5213/3 &/4; inst WM, Parham
Ho, Sussex; GMag 101 (1831) p.275; Millburn
(1976) p.178; CLRO: CF/I/1173; Brown O (1983)
no. 32; Jones (1782)

JONES William (III)
fr 1757 w 1788
Hourglass M
1761–1767   Houndsditch, London
1767–1784   Hand Alley, Petticoat Lane, London
1769   Hand Alley, Bishopsgate St, London
1788–1790   Church St, Spitalfields, London
Guild: Turners, fr 1757
Apprenticed to
DENNIS John* 1749/50, t/o to
PRENTICE Philip 1754
Had apprentice:
HILLIER James* 1780
MOSS James by t/o in 1787 from FORSKETT
Thomas of SMC
MELLISH Robert (II) 1760
and 13 others 1760–1788
d by 1793; b. apt Royal Navy
Sources: GL: SMC 5213/4 13 Mar 1793; TC
3302/3, 3300, 3814; BW

JONES William (IV)
w 1805–1806
Math IM, Optician
1805–1806   30 Marylebone St, Golden Square,
               London
Took over from JONES T. & W.*
Sources: H; Kt (JAC)

JONES William (V)
w 1709–1720

Spec M
          London
Guild: Spectaclemakers, fr 1702
Son of JONES Thomas, glover, of Althorpe,
Northants
Apprenticed to TAILOR Mary* 1695
Had apprentice:
CORP Robert 1709
STONEBANKE John 1714
JOHNSON Isaac 1715, t/o 1720 to ADAMS John (I)*
FORD Henry by t/o from TAILOR Mary* between
1707 & 1714
Sources: GL: SMC 6031/1

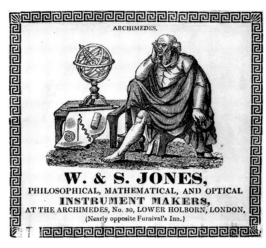

JONES William and Samuel
w 1791–1859
Optician, Math IM, Phil IM
Alternative name: W. & S. JONES
              27 Holborn Hill, London
1792–1800   135 Holborn, next Furnival's Inn,
              London
1800–1860   30 Holborn, (Holborn Bridge)
              (Holborn Hill) (Lower Holborn)
              London
1801–1805   32 Holborn Hill, London [in
              directories]
1852   30 Opposite Furnival's Inn,
              Holborn, London
              Archimedes, 30 Lower Holborn,
              London
Associated with ADAMS George (II)*
Employed EDEN William* 1818–1827
? CHITTY William 1834–1835
DILLON John* 1844
RUSSELL William (II)* 1846–1849
NORTON John
Took over from JONES & SONS John*
See also
JONES William (II)*
JONES & SON John*
Associated with BARDIN W. & J., whose globes
they sold
Samuel d 1859; William d 1831
Known to have sold: balance, barometer, compass,
electrostatic generator, ellipsograph, globe,
hydrometer, microscope, model – philosophical,
pantograph, planetarium, slide rule, sundial,
telescope, theodolite, thermometer, waywiser

Sources: GL: SMC 5213/4; ChrSK 29 Mar 1990
lot 62; H; Kt; PO; PRO: PROB/11/1784; Som
Ho: will of Samuel Jones (JRM); Anderson et al
(1990) p.43–44; Calvert (1971) pl.29–30; inst
MHS, NMM, SM, WM, and see index to
Holbrook (1992)

JONES & GRAY
w 1839–1841
Optician, Math IM
1839   26 Strand St, Liverpool
Succeeded by JONES, GRAY & KEEN*
See also GRAY John (I)*
Known to have sold: octant
Sources: G; Holbrook (1992) p.147

JONES & ROOSE
w 1816–1817
Math IM, Navigation Warehouse
1816–1817   27 near the bottom of Pool Lane,
              Liverpool
Took over from JONES & RUST*
Succeeded by ROOSE Thomas*
Sources: Pg

JONES & RUST
w 1811–1813
Navigation Warehouse, Stationer
1811   29 Pool Lane, Liverpool
1813   31 Pool Lane, Liverpool
Succeeded by JONES & ROOSE*
See also
JONES John (III)*
RUST Joseph (II)*
Sources: G

JONES & SON John (& William)
w 1784–1790
Math IM
              135 near Furnival's Inn in Holborn,
              London
              135 Holborn, London
Succeeded by JONES & SONS John*
Took over from JONES John (I)*
See also JONES W. & S.*
Known to have sold: microscope
Instruments advertised: navigation scale,
planetarium
Sources: BW; By; Ld; Jones (1787); DJB;
Holbrook (1992) p.100

JONES & SONS John (& William & Samuel)
w 1790–1792
Math IM
              London
              168 High Holborn, London
              135 Holborn, London
Took over from JONES & SON John*
See also
JONES John (I)*
JONES W. & S.*
Sources: W

JONES & SONS Thomas
w 1831–1835
Math IM, Phil IM
1831–1835   62 Charing Cross South, London
Succeeded by JONES Thomas (I)*

Took over from JONES Thomas (I)★
Known to have sold: telescope
Sources: PO; R (JAC); Phlps 17 Jul 1985 Lot 112
(MAC)

JONES, CRITCHLEY & MATHER
w 1816–1820
Math IM, Optician
1816–1820   Old Dock Gates, Liverpool
1818   3 North Side Old Dock Passage,
             Liverpool
1818   3 North Side Old Dock Gates,
             Liverpool
See also
CRITCHLEY & MATHER★
CRITCHLEY Henry★
MATHER John★
Sources: G; Pg

JONES, GRAY & KEEN
w 1841–1845
Optician, Naut IM
1841–1845   25 & 26 Strand St, Liverpool
Succeeded by GRAY & KEEN★
Took over from JONES & GRAY★
See also
JONES Charles★
GRAY John (I)★
KEEN Robert John★
Known to have sold: octant, sextant
Sources: G; Sby 12 July 1977 Lot 254 (MAC);
Holbrook (1992) p.208

JORDAN Thomas
fl 1838
[Math IM]
             Falmouth
Known to have sold: dip circle
Sources: Taylor (1966) p.453

JOSEPH Henry
w 1802
Spec M
1802   12 Petticoat Lane, Aldgate, London
See also
JOSEPH Joseph★
JOSEPH S.★
Sources: H (JAC)

JOSEPH Joseph
w 1809
Spec M
1809   12 Petticoat Lane, Whitechapel,
             London
See also
JOSEPH Henry★
JOSEPH S.★
Sources: H (JAC)

JOSEPH S.
w 1820
Optician
1820   12 Petticoat Lane, Bishopsgate,
             London
See also
JOSEPH Henry★
JOSEPH Joseph★
Sources: R (JAC)

JOUGHIN James Ely
fr 1808 w 1816
Math IM
Alternative name: Edward James Ely
1816   23 Lower Cornwall St, St.Georges in
             the East, London
Guild: Masons, fr 1808
Apprenticed to COOK William George★ 1801
Had apprentice SCOTT James George★ 1816
Sources: GL: STTP 2934 fol 39; MC 5304/6
(MAC)

JOY John
w 1698 d 1747
Scale M
Alternative name: Iohn
             Ye Hammer, Coronet & Scales in
             Leadenhall St, London
             Near Creechurch in Leadenhall St,
             London
Guild: Blacksmiths, fr 1698
Son of JOY Henry, d, of IC of London
Apprenticed to WILFORD David (I)★ 1689/90
Had apprentice:
GABLE Thomas★ 1726
PALLET Tavenor 1730
NEW William★ 1738
THURMAN John★ 1742 t/o 1747/8 to GABLE
Thomas★
THURMAN Joseph?★ 1742 t/o 1747/8 to
WALRAVEN Mary
and 9 other apprentices not known as Scale M,
1698–1747
Sources: GL: BKC 2881/8, /9, & /10, 2886/3, /4,
& /5, 2888 (MAC); BM: Banks 103.4 (MAC)

JUDSON Thomas Stubbs
w 1829–1849
Spec M, Optician
             14 London Rd, London
             155 Minories, London
             26 Great Waterloo St, London
             26 Waterloo Rd, Lambeth, London
1829   13 Newington Causeway, London
1830–1839   19 Alfred St, Newington Causeway,
             London
1839   and 28 Grosvenor St West, London
1840   Alfred Place, Newington Causeway,
             London
1849   7½ Bridge Court, Westminster,
             London
Sources: Pg; PO; R (JAC)

JUKES William
w 1777
Steelyard M
1777   Back of Jeffery's Yard, Digbeth,
             Birmingham
Sources: PR

KALABERGO Giovanni
d 1852
Clock S, Watch S, Baro S
             Banbury
Nephew of KALABERGO John★
Murdered his uncle 1852 and was executed
Known to have sold: barometer, thermometer
Sources: Banfield (1993) p.100; Beeson (1989) p.116

KALABERGO John
w 1830 d 1852
Watch M, Clock M, Jeweller, Baro M, Thermo M
Alternative name: Giovanni
1830–1852   Market Place, Banbury
1832–1852   Bridge Street North, Banbury
Uncle of KALABERGO Giovanni★
Murdered by his nephew, 1852
Known to have sold: barometer, thermometer
Sources: Pg; Banfield (1993) p.100; Bolle (1982)
p.158; Goodison (1977) p.334

KARMOCK John
fr 1781 w 1787
Math IM, Painter 1802
1781   98 The corner of Church St,
             Wapping, London
1781–1786   35 Wapping St, London
1786–1787   302 Bell Dock, Wapping, London
Guild: Grocers, fr 1781
Father of KARMOCK Henry fp 1812 GC
Apprenticed to RIPLEY Thomas★ 1773
Had apprentice:
KING John Sumner 1782
KARMOCK Stephen, his brother, 1783
COE George 1786
WARRENER Solomon 1787
KARMOCK John, his son, 1802
Sources: GL: GC 11598/6; Sun 11936/290 no.
439419, /296 no. 450040, /337 no. 517763; Brown
J (1979a) p. 49

KATTERNS Daniel
a 1762 w 1798
Clock M
1798   Thrapston, Northants
Known to have sold: balance
Sources: inst (MAC); BW

KEARNEY Joshua
w 1820
Baro M, Mirror M
1820   49 Henry St, Dublin
Sources: Pg

KEEGAN Michael
w 1839–1855
Optician, Math IM, Phil IM
1839–1840   2 Phoenix St, Soho, London
1855   12 Arthur St, Oxford St, London
Sources: Pg; PO

KEEL John
w 1807
Math IM
1807   Shoe Lane Holborn London
Father of KEEL Robert s 1807 to PONTIFEX
William (I)★
Sources: GL: ABC 12080/2

KEEN Robert John
w 1834–1857
Optician, Math IM
1834–1840   8 Postern Row, Tower Hill, London
1840   4 East Smithfield, London
1855–1857   East Side Salthouse Dock, Liverpool
Partnership KEEN & FRODSHAM★
Succeeded by KEEN & FRODSHAM★

See also JONES, GRAY & KEEN★
Known to have sold: compass (magnetic)
Sources: G; PO; inst NMM

KEITH George
d 1812
Clock M
                Strathaven, Lanark
Known to have sold: barometer
Sources: Baillie (1951); Webster R & M (1986)

KELLY Elizabeth
w 1835–1840
Optician, Math IM, Phil IM
1835–1840   22 Charles St, Hatton Garden,
                London
See also KELLY William★
Sources: R (JAC)

KELLY John
w 1813–1834
Chrono M, Watch M
1813   92 Richmond Row, Liverpool
1816–1817   78 Richmond Row, Liverpool
1818–1827   97 Richmond Row, Liverpool
1818–1820   95 Richmond Row, Liverpool
1822–1834   Richmond Row, Liverpool
1829   33 Richmond Row, Liverpool
Sources: Bn; G; Pg; Loomes (1975)

KELLY William
w 1829–1840
Optician, Math IM, Phil IM, Optical turner
                21 Greenhill's Rents, Smithfield
                Bars, London
                32 Charles St, Hatton Garden,
                London
See also KELLY Elizabeth★
Sources: R (JAC)

KEMP John
w 1814
Optician
1814   Westgate, Wakefield, Yorks
Sources: WB

KEMP K.T.
w 1828–1834
Lecturer, Chem IM
Alternative name: Kenneth Treasurer
1829–1834   Surgeon Square, Edinburgh
Apprenticed to AITKEN John & Thomas
Johnstone, surgeon – apothecaries
Succeeded by KEMP & CO.★
Known to have sold: battery, blowpipe
Sources: inst NMS; Bryden (1972) p.51; Webster
R & M (1988)

KEMP & CO.
w 1835–1887
Chem IM, Phil IM
1835–1838   7 South College St, Edinburgh
1839–1844   53 South Bridge, Edinburgh
1845–1887   12 & 13 Infirmary St, Edinburgh
Took over from KEMP K.T.★
Known to have sold: hydrometer, hydrostatic
bubbles
Sources: inst SM; Bryden (1972) p. 51

KENDALL Larcum
a 1742 w 1785
Clock M, Chrono M
                Furnival's Inn Court, London
Guild: [Clockmakers]
Apprenticed to JEFFREYS John 1735
b 1721 d 1795; appointed by B of Longitude to
make copies of timekeeper by HARRISON John
(I)★
Known to have sold: chronometer
Sources: GL: CKC 2721/1; Beeson (1989) p.116;
Taylor (1966) p.209

KENDREW John
w c. 1780 w 1792
Lens M
                Low Mill, Darlington, Durham
b 1752, d 1800; trained as a weaver; inv.
water-powered lens-grinding machinery
Sources: Longstaffe (1909) p.312–13 (AM); BW

KENNEY Vincent
a 1510–1550
Clock M
Alternative name: KENEY
                London
Supplied clocks to Henry VIII
Known to have sold: sundial
Sources: Loomes (1981b)

KENT Edward
fl 1830
[Chrono M]
                69 Banner St, St Lukes, London
Sources: Taylor (1966) p.453

KENYON Henry
w 1839–1841
Optician, Math IM, Phil IM
1839–1841   126 High St, Wapping, London
Sources: Pg; R (JAC)

KEOHAN Thomas
w 1836–1873
Optical IM, Phil IM, Math IM, Optician
1839   2 Arbour Terrace, Stepney, London
1840–1855   2 Arbour Terrace, Commercial Rd
                East, London
1859–1873   33 Upper East Smithfield, London E
Guild: [Joiners]
Apprenticed to ELLIOTT William (I)★
Known to have sold: sextant
Sources: GL: JC, 8052/8; Pg; PO; Wk; inst (s);
Crawforth (1987) p.359

KERBY Frederick
w 1839–1840
Math IM, Phil IM
1839–1840   Platt Terrace, Kings Cross, London
Sources: Pg

KERR Alexander
fl 1820
Clock M
                Annan, Dumfries
Known to have sold: barometer (probably this
maker)
Sources: Baillie (1951); Goodison (1977) p.334

KERR Robert
fr 1825
Coppersmith
                Glasgow
Guild: Hammermen
Known to have sold: measure (capacity)
Sources: Lumsden & Aitken (1912) p.311 (MAC)

KEWLEY James (according to Woodcroft)
w 1816
Alternative name: Thomas (according to Taylor)
                Aldersgate St, London
Pat. thermometer 1816
Sources: Woodcroft (1854); Taylor (1966) p.389;

KEY George
w 1736–1752
Scale M
                Justice & Scales next door to
                Haberdashers' Hall in Maiden Lane
                near Wood St, London
                in Maiden Lane near Wood St,
                London
Guild: Blacksmiths, fr 1732
Apprenticed to NEALE John (I)★ 1725
Son of KEY Thomas, cordwainer, of Grendon,
Northants
Had apprentices:
FRAZER William 1736
WHITWORTH Thomas 1736/7
BELLAS Daniel 1747 t/o 1752 to BROOKSBY
Thomas★
Instruments advertised: balance, steelyard, weights
Sources: GL: BKC 2885/1, 2886/4, 2886/5
(MAC); BM: Heal (MAC)

KEYS James
w 1792
Scale M
1792   19 Salop St, Wolverhampton
Sources: Wolverhampton rate books (MAC)

KEYZOR Michael & Abraham
w 1847–1854
Opticians, Spectacle M
1847   Castle Meadow, Norwich
1854   St Giles St, Norwich
Sources: K; Calvert (1971) p.28

KIBBLE John (I)
w 1805–18279
Math IM, Wholesaler
1805   28 Broadwall, Blackfriars, London
Associated with GARDNER Henry (II)★, who acted
as agent for his drawing instruments
See also KIBBLE John (II)★ [possibly the same
person]
Sources: H; Burnett & Morrison-Low (1989) p.82

KIBBLE John (II)
w 1821–1837
Math IM, Drawing IM, Optician, Surgeons IM
Alternative name: KEBBLE
1821   46 Cheapside, Liverpool
1823–1824   81 Highfield St, Liverpool
1825–1834   24 Great Crosshall St, Liverpool
1835–1837   21 Great Crosshall St, Liverpool
1837   22 Great Crosshall St, Liverpool

See also KIBBLE John (I)★ [possibly the same person]
Sources: Bn; G; Pg

KIDDER Vincent
w 1698–1736
Dublin
Known to have sold: weights
Sources: Westropp (1916) p.66; Sheppard & Mushem (1975) W513, W515

KILBINGTON John
w pt 1789–1793
Ship Chandler
Alternative name: KILBINTON, KILVINGTON
London
Guild: [Clothworkers]
Son of KILBINGTON William, butcher, of Shadwell, London
Apprenticed to EDWARDS Charles★ 1776
See also EDWARDS & KILBINGTON★
Sources: CWH: CWC Fr; BW

KILPATRICK Alexander
w 1826–1832
Chem IM
1826–1832   14 Crosscauseway, Edinburgh
1832   1 Hope St, Edinburgh
Succeeded by KILPATRICK John★
Sources: Bryden (1972) p.51

KILPATRICK John
w 1820–1836
Chem IM, Hot bath M
1820   202 Rose St, Edinburgh
1833–1836   1 Hope St, Edinburgh
1833   14 Causeway, Edinburgh
Took over from KILPATRICK Alexander★
Sources: Pg; Bryden (1972) p.51

KIMBELL Isaac
w 1791–1793
Optician
1791–1793   21 Dean St, Fetter Lane, London
See also
KIMBELL James (I)★
KIMBELL John★
KIMBELL Josh★
KIMBELL James (II)★
Sources: BW; Taylor (1966) p.291

KIMBELL James (I)
w 1784
Optician
1784   21 Dean St, Fetter Lane, London
See also
KIMBELL James (II)★
KIMBELL Josh★
KIMBELL Isaac★
KIMBELL John★
Sources: By (JAC)

KIMBELL James (II)
w 1831–1836
Optician, Math IM, Phil IM
1831–1836   21 Dean St, Fetter Lane, London
See also
KIMBELL Isaac★

KIMBELL John★
KIMBELL Josh★
KIMBELL James (I)★
Sources: Pg; R (JAC)

KIMBELL John (I)
w 1784–1830
Phil IM, Optician, Math IM
Alternative name: KIMBEL, KIMBLE
1784–1830   21 Dean St, Fetter Lane, London
Guild: Goldsmiths, fr 1771
Son of KIMBELL Joseph, husbandman, of Bushey Heath, Herts
Father of KIMBELL John (II)★
Apprenticed to MARTIN Benjamin (I)★1763
Had apprentice KIMBELL John (II)★, his son, 1799
See also
KIMBELL Isaac★
KIMBELL James (I)★
KIMBELL Josh★
KIMBELL James (II)★
Sources: GH: GC index, Ap; GL: Sun 11936/324 no. 497153; H; J; R (JAC)

KIMBELL John (II)
fr 1806
1806   Dean St, Fetter Lane, London
Guild: Goldsmiths, fr 1806
Apprenticed to KIMBELL John (I)★, his father, 1799
Attended Christ's Hospital School, London, and received charity from the school in 1807; such gifts were usually to enable former pupils to set up in trade. The later directory entries noted under KIMBLE John (I)★ may refer to the son
Sources: GH: GSC index, Ap; GL: CH 12823/8 p.19, 32

KIMBELL Josh
w 1835–1837
Optician
Alternative name: KIMBLE
1835–1837   21 Dean St, Fetter Lane, London
See also
KIMBELL James (I)★
KIMBELL James (II)★
KIMBELL Isaac★
KIMBELL John (II)★
Sources: PO

KIMBER William
w 1811–1812
Spec M, Optician
1811   Parish of St.Martin Ludgate, London
1812   Creed Lane, London
Guild: Blacksmiths, fr 1779
Father of
KIMBER William s1811 TC
KIMBER Ambrose s1812 TWC
Apprenticed to WHITFORD Samuel★ 1771
Sources: GL: BKC 2881/15, 2886/5 (MAC); TWC 7137/6 fol 120; TC 3302/3

KINDON James
w 1771
1771   Birmingham
Known to have sold: rule
Sources: Lunar Society of Birmingham (1966) p. 21

KING –
a 1790
45 Baldwin's Green, Leith
Lanark
Known to have sold: barometer
Sources: NMS n; Webster R & M (1988)

KING Alexander
w 1840
Naut IM
1840   37 High St, Dundee
Sources: Bryden (1972) p.51

KING Charles
w 1820
Baro & Mirror M
1820   40 James St, Dublin
Sources: Pg

KING George
w 1802–1809
Clock M, Watch M, Instrument S
1802   Cornhill, Woodbridge, Suffolk
Sources: Bod: JJ box 24 (MAC); Haggar & Miller (1974); *Ipswich Journal*, 4 Feb 1809

KING James
w 1817–1822
Math IM
1817–1822   18 Anthony St, St.George's East, London
Sources: Und (JAC)

KING John (I)
w 1795–1816
Math IM
1788   Greenfield St, Whitechapel, London
1795   1 Prince's St, Ratcliff Highway, London
1802   Thomas St, Whitechapel, London
1816   18 Anthony St, St. George's in the East, London
Guild: Grocers, fr 1788
Father of KING John (VII)★
Son of KING John, tailor, of St. Giles, Middx
Apprenticed to SPENCER William (II)★
Had apprentice:
BRUNDELL Philip George 1795
FORD John 1802, t/o 1805 to BROWNING John (I)★
b 1767 or 1768 at Newbury, Berks; r by 1851
Sources: Brown J (1979a) p.53; PRO: Cs 1851 (LS); Und

KING John (II)
w 1827–1834
Math IM, Phil IM, Optician
1827–1834   6 Cannon St, London
1832–1834   112 Leadenhall St, London
1834   13 Goswell St, London
Entries may refer to more than one maker
Sources: Pg (JAC); Taylor (1966) p. 453

KING John (III)
w 1821–1822
Math IM, Optician
1821–1822   2 Clare St, Bristol
Succeeded by KING & SON John★

Father of KING John (IV)★
d 1845
Sources: Mat; BRO: Ac 35447 Box 4 (TJB)

KING John (IV)
w 1834–1846 & 1854–1867
Optician, Math IM, Phil IM, Watch M, Clock M,
Chrono S
1836–1842   At the Post Captain, 2 Clare St,
             Bristol
1851–1853   35 Queen Square, Bristol
1854–1867   2 Clare St, Bristol
Took over from KING & SON John★
Son of KING John (III)★
Father of KING Thomas Davis★
Commission agent 1851–1853; d 1876
Sources: Mat; Pg; BRO: Ac 35447 Box 4 (TJB)
PRO: HO/107/375 Cs 1841 ED10;
HO/107/1948 Cs 1851 fol. 11 (TJB)

KING John (V)
fl. 1780
Clock M, Phil IM
             Aberdeen
             Sources: Bryden (1972) p. 51

KING John (VI)
w 1839–1870
Optician
1839–1842   3 Belvedere Buildings, Borough Rd,
             London
1844–1848   14 Belverdere Buildings, Borough
             Rd, London
1855–1870   31 White Hart St, Kennington,
             London
See also KING John (VII)★
Sources: PO; R (JAC)

KING John (VII)
w 1851
Naut IM
1851   28 Cannon St Rd, London
Son of KING John (I)★
b 1812 or 1813
Sources: Wk; PRO: Cs 1851 (LS)

KING Richard
w 1780
Optician
1780   10 Cross Keys Court, Little Britain,
             London
Guild: Goldsmiths, fr 1764 [probably]
Apprenticed to HITCH Joseph★ 1757 [probably]
Sources: GL: Sun 11936/284 no. 431924; GH:
GSC Ap

KING Thomas (I)
w 1667 d c. 1677
Gauging IM
Alternative name: KINGS
             London
Guild: Spectaclemakers
Had apprentice:
MASON George★ 1667
STERROP Thomas★ 1672
MANN James (I)★ 1674
Sources: GL: SMC 5213/1

KING Thomas (II)
d 1771
Math IM
1771 Temple Bar, Dublin
Same address as KING William (I)★
Sources: Burnett & Morrison-Low (1989) p. 22, 36

KING Thomas Davis
w 1848–1850 [& see partnership]
Optical IM, Math IM, Phil IM, Naut IM
1848   2 Clare St., Bristol
1853   1 Denmark St., Bristol
Son of KING John (IV)★
Succeeded by KING & COOMBES★ then by
HUSBANDS & CLARKE
Took over from KING John (IV)★
Partnership 1851; Ex 1851
Known to have sold: microscope
Sources: Hunts; Cat 1851; Phlps 11 Nov 1981 lot
100, 20 Jul 1983 lot 182 (DJB); BsM n & inst;
PRO: HO/107 1948 Cs 1851 fol. 80 (TJB); Bap
St. Mary Redcliffe (TJB)

KING W.
w 1845
Optician
1845   Scotland Green, High Rd,
             Tottenham, London
Sources: PO(HC)

KING William (I)
w 1767–1784
Math IM
1767–1772   Temple Bar, Dublin
1784   Dublin
Apprenticed to CAVE Thomas★ nd
Same premises as KING Thomas (II)★
Known to have sold: octant, protractor, sundial
Sources: Wi (AL); Burnett & Morrison-Low
(1989) p.22–23, 36, 128

KING & COOMBES
w 1851–1853
Optical IM
1851–1853   2 Clare St, Bristol
Took over from KING Thomas Davis★
Known to have sold: microscope
Sources: inst BsM; ChrSK 23 Nov 1977 lot 12; Mat

KING & SON John
w 1823–1835
Optician, Math IM, Phil IM
1823–1835   At the Post Captain, 2 Clare St,
             Bristol
Took over from KING John (III)★
Succeeded by KING John (IV)★
See also KING & COOMBS★
Known to have sold: barometer, sextant,
theodolite
Sources: Pg; Mat; Sby 3 Oct 1991 lot 60; inst (s);
Goodison (1977) p.334

KINSTON John
w 1716
A dated nocturnal is known bearing this name
Sources: Sby 1979, noted by MAC

KIRBY Joshua
w 1740–1765
Draughtsman [Math IM]
             Ipswich
Author;
Known to have sold: protractor, sector
Sources: Sby 10 Mar 1989 lot 162; Taylor (1966)
p.209–10

KIRBY Thomas
w 1780–1794
Scale M
1794   Vine Yard, Blackman St,
             Southwark, London
Guild: Blacksmiths, fr 1775
Son of KIRBY Thomas, labourer, of Shelton, War
Apprenticed to CATTELL Robert★ 1761
Had apprentice:
FLETCHER James★ 1780
WHEATLEY George 1785
Sources: GL: BKC 2881/15, 2881/16, 2885/1,
2886/5 (MAC); W (JAC)

KIRK James
w 1761–1793
Seal engraver, Toyman
1761   The Grotto Toyshop in St.Paul's
             Churchyard, London
1771   The Grotto, No.52 St.Paul's
             Churchyard, London
1776   Chandos St, Covent Garden,
             (residence) London
1793   52 St.Paul's Churchyard, London
Guild: Goldsmiths, fp 1765
Son of KIRK John★
Took over from KIRK John★
Had apprentice HOLDEN Richard 1771
Known to have sold: balance, weights
Instruments advertised: weights
Sources: GH: GSC index; BW; *Daily Ad* Dec 1761
(JRM); *Daily Ad* 27 Nov 1771 (MAC);
Crowther-Beynon (1925–26) p.187 (MAC)

KIRK John
w 1736 d 1761
Scale M, Engraver
Alternative name: I. KIRK
             North side of St.Paul's Churchyard,
             London
1747–1761   St. Paul's Church Yard, London
1749   Charing Cross, London
Guild: Goldsmiths, fp 1724
Father of KIRK James★
Succeeded by KIRK James★
Associated with ROBINSON John (I)★ and
PINCHBECK Chris. (II)★ who both sold his
weights
Known to have sold: balance, weights
Sources: GH: GSC index; *Daily Ad* 5 Jul 1749
(JRM), 21 Nov 1761 (MAC); Phlps 3 Mar 1992 lot
151; Sheppard & Musham (1975) p.74, 185

KIRKE Francis
w 1723
[Math IM]
Known to have sold: back-staff
Sources: ChrSK 27 Nov 1986 lot 187

KIRKHAM Arthur Leecks
w 1851
Optician
1851   154 Strand, London
Sources: Wk

KIRKSHAW T.
a 1775
Known to have sold: barometer.
Sources: Bolle (1982) p.40, pl.37

KIRKWOOD James
w 1804–1824
[Globe M]
     Edinburgh
Known to have sold: globe
Sources: inst NMS; Dekker & van der Krogt
(1993) p.118

KIRKWOOD Robert
w 1828
     Edinburgh
Known to have sold: globe
Sources: Dekker & van der Krogt (1993) p.118

KITCHEN James
w 1839–1841
Optician, Math IM, Phil IM
1839–1841   105 Fenchurch St, London
Sources: R (JAC)

KITCHINGMAN John
w 1780–1808
Math IM
1780   Hanover Court in the Minories,
     London
1788–1792   3 Seething Lane, Tower St, London
Guild: Turners
Apprenticed to EMBLEM Thomas★ 1759
Son of KITCHINGMAN George, castor maker, d,
of St. Giles in the Fields, Middx
Had apprentice:
BANCKS Anthony Oldiss★ 1780
GRAY John (II)★ 1783
MCGUFFOG John 1788
KITCHINGMAN John W. H. 1788
ROBERTSON David 1790
BETON Augustin 1808
Sources: GL: TC 3814, 3302/2, 3302/3; CH 12876/6

KITSON George
a 1600–1700
     Near Wapping Old Stairs, London
Known to have sold: compass
Sources: Taylor (1954) p.263–64

KNEEBONE –
a 1800–1850
Jeweller
     Redruth, Cornwall
Known to have sold: barometer, thermometer
Sources: inst (s) (MAC)

KNEEN Thomas
w 1851–1855
Optician, Math IM
1851–1855   9 Wood St, Liverpool
Sources: G

KNIBB John
w 1673 d 1722
Clock M
Alternative name: Johannes
     Oxford
Guild: [Joiners]
Apprenticed to SUTTON William (I)★ 1664
See also KNIBB Samuel★
Took 10 apprentices in Oxford
Known to have sold: astronomical clock
Sources: GL: JC 8052/1; Loomes (1981b); Taylor
(1954) p.246, 265

KNIBB Samuel
w 1655 d by 1674
     London
1655   Newport Pagnall, Bucks
1662–1670   Threadneedle St, London
Guild: Clockmakers, fr by purchase 1663
Partnership SUTTON & KNIBB★
Worked for SUTTON Henry★
See also KNIBB John★
Had apprentice:
TIPPING George 1664/5 t/o nd to BICKNELL F.
MILLER John 1667/8 t/o nd to PUZY I then to
KNIBB Joseph
bap 1625
Sources: GL: CKC 2710/1 p. 144; Loomes
(1981b); Beeson (1989)

KNIE Balthazar
w 1773 d 1817
Baro M
Alternative name: Baltaser KINNY
1773   Cork
1776   Niddry's Wynd, Edinburgh
1782–1790   Opposite The Guard, Edinburgh
1793–1798   Opposite Forrester's Wynd Well,
     Edinburgh
1800–1803   Head Seller's Close, Edinburgh
1805–1810   Lawnmarket, Edinburgh
1811–1814   405 Lawnmarket, Edinburgh
1815   Borthwick's Close, Edinburgh
1816   204 High Street, Edinburgh
See also MOLLINER Charles★
Known to have sold: barometer, sandglass,
thermometer
Sources: Bryden (1972) p.51; Burnett &
Morrison-Low (1989) p. 149; Goodison (1977) p.
170–175

KNIGHT George
w pt 1822–1861
Ironmonger, Phil IM
1822–1861   Foster Lane, London
Guild: Ironmongers, fr 1797
Son of KNIGHT William★
Brother of KNIGHT Richard★
Partnership KNIGHT Richard & George★
Apprenticed to KNIGHT George, sadlers'
ironmonger, 1790
Had apprentice:
EDWARDS Frederick 1822
PECKHAM Geo Fredk 1838
BLOOMFIELD Lewis 1854
See also KNIGHT & SONS George★
b 1775

Sources: GL:IMC 16981/2, 16985, 16977/3, Hunt
& Buchanan (1984) p.57–67

KNIGHT Richard & George
w 1800–1838
Chem IM, Phil IM, Ironmonger
     Foster Lane, Cheapside, London
1800–1838   41 Foster Lane, Cheapside, London
Succeeded by KNIGHT & SONS George★
See also
KNIGHT George★
KNIGHT Richard (I)★
Known to have sold: balance, barometer,
hydrometer, thermometer
Sources: Kt; PO; inst SM & (s)

KNIGHT Richard (I)
w 1794 w pt 1838
Ironmonger
1791–1829   Foster Lane, London
Guild: Skinners, fr 1791
Son of KNIGHT William★
Brother of KNIGHT George★
Partnership
KNIGHT & SON Wm★ 1795–1799
KNIGHT Richard & Geo★ 1800–1838
Apprenticed to MARTIN William 1783 t/o to
father 6 Nov 1787
Had apprentice:
FINCH Augustin 1801
JONES John Holme 1808
BLIGH James 1794
KIRK George 1805
HAYWARD James 1814
KNIGHT Richard, son of George, 1829
Employed FINCH Augustin 1809
HAYWARD James 1824
b 1768; d 1844
Sources: SKH: SKC, Ap/Fr; Hunt & Buchanan
(1984) p.57–67

KNIGHT Richard (II)
w pt 1839–1850
Ironmonger, Phil IM
1836–1850   Foster Lane, Cheapside, London
Guild: Skinners, fr 1836
Son of KNIGHT George★
Partnership KNIGHT & SONS George★
Apprenticed to KNIGHT Richard (I)★ 1829
Had apprentice HOOD Wharton Peter 1850
fr 7 Mar 1836
Sources: SH: SKC Ap/Fr

KNIGHT William
w 1787–1795
1783   Goldsmith St, Wood St, London
1790   Parish of St. Michael le Quern,
     London
1793   45 Foster Lane, London
Guild: Spectaclemakers, fr 1787
Father of
KNIGHT Richard (I)★
KNIGHT George★
Son of KNIGHT Richard, farmer, of Essex
Husband of MARTIN Elizabeth
Had apprentice:
KNIGHT Richard (I)★, his son, 1787
KNIGHT George, his son, nd

Succeeded by KNIGHT & SON William★
b c 1730; d 1799
Sources: CLRO: CF/I/1091; GL: IMC 16981/2;
SH: SKC Ap; Hunt & Buchanan (1984) p.57–67;
BW

KNIGHT & SON William
w 1795–1799
1795–1799   London
Succeeded by KNIGHT Richard & George★
Took over from KNIGHT William★
William d.1799
Sources: Hunt & Buchanan (1984) p.57–67

KNIGHT & SONS George
w 1839–1877
Chem IM, Phil IM, Ironmonger, Baro M, Thermo
M
1839–1843   41 Foster Lane, London
1843   2 Foster Lane, London
1849–1855   2, 41 & 42 Foster Lane, Cheapside,
London
1859–1875   2 Foster Lane (2nd period) London
1877   5 St.Bride St, London EC
Succeeded by HOW James★
Took over from KNIGHT Richard & George★
Reg.1842 standard for balances; Knight & Co.
1857–1861; Name continued in directories by
James How 1862–77; Ex 1851
Known to have sold: balance, hydrometer
Sources: PO; inst SM; Chaldecott (1989) p. 161;
Turner G (1983) p.309

KNOWLES Edward
w 1827–1839
Spec M
1827–1839   60 Exmouth St, Spitalfields, London
Sources: Pg

KNOWLES William
w 1845
Scale beam M
1845   Long Lane, Southwark, London
Guild: [Haberdashers]
Father of KNOWLES Robert s 1845 BKC
Son of KNOWLES Benjamin
Apprenticed to DUTTON James 1809
See also SMITH William (II)★
Sources: GL: BKC, 2881/18; HC, 15860/9

KORNE John
a 1700
Said by Taylor to have signed a telescope at
NMM, but no record found! Possible error for
HOWE John (I)★
Sources: NMM; Taylor (1954) p.297

KRAUSE J. R.
v 1837–1838
Math IM
1837–1838   24 Clarendon St, Somers Town,
London
Same premises as
LEALAND Peter★ and
POWELL Hugh★ (?employee)
Attended London Mechanics Institute 1837–1838
Sources: LMIR (AM)

KRUSE J.P.
w 1845
Optician, Math IM, Phil IM
1845   5 Hereford Terrace, King's Rd,
Chelsea, London
Sources: PO

KUTZ Andrew
w 1816–1817
Rule M, Drawing IM
1816–1817   4 Cannon Street Rd, St.George's
East, London
Sources: Und (JAC)

KYEZOR Louis
w 1839–1863
Watch M, Clock M, Chrono M
Alterative name: KEYZER
1839–1846   16 Tottenham Court Rd, London
1846   & 31 Upper George St, London
1846   & 46A Edgware Rd, London
See also KYEZOR Louis junior★
Sources: Pg; PO; Loomes (1976)

KYEZOR Louis junior
w 1851–1881
Watch M, Chrono M
1851   46A Edgware Rd, London
1851   31 Upper George St, Portman
Square, London
See also KYEZOR Louis★
Sources: PO; Loomes (1976);

KYNVYN James
w 1584 c 1609
Math IM (in brass)
Alternative name: KYNFIN, KYNWIN, KYNUIN,
KENVEN,
Near St.Paul's Cathedral, London
Known to have sold: astrolabe, circumferentor,
compass, sector, sundial
Sources: Taylor (1954) p.92,105,187,327; Bryden
(1992) p.305; Turner G (1983b) p.98–99

LACY William
w 1771–1779
Mathematician, Theologer, Instrument S, Lecturer
1771–1773   Mathematical Shop joyning to the
Fountain Tavern in Catherine St,
Strand, London
1773   3 Bell Savage Yard, Ludgate Hill,
London
Known to have sold: planetarium
Sources: inst NMM; TCd MHS Evans Collection;
JRM; King & Millburn (1978) p.310–11

LADD Edward Wilds
w pt 1850–1869
Math IM
1852–1859   1 Old Jewry, London
Guild: [Clockmakers]
Son of LADD Edward Wilds, baker; of Deal, Kent
Partnership LADD & STREATFIELD ★
LADD & Co., Edward Wilds
LADD & OERTLING Edward Wilds & Ludwig
Apprenticed to HARRIS William (I)★ 22 Mar 1816
b 22 Mar 1800; working in partnership 1850–1859
& 1860–1869, alone 1859–1860

Sources: GL: CKC 2720/2; PO; Wk; McConnell
(1993) p.54; Chaldecott (1989) p.160

LADD William
w 1839–1872
Math IM, Phil IM, Baro M, Thermo M, Optician
1846–1847   10 Cleaver St, Kennington, London
1850–1857   29 Penton St, (29 Penton Place in
some sources – both names existed),
London
1858–1860   31 Chancery Lane, London
1861–1872   11 & 12 Beak St, London
Succeeded by LADD & CO. William★
See also LADD & STREATFIELD★
Ex. 1851; d c.1884
Known to have sold: microscope, prism
Instruments advertised: barometer, thermometer
Sources: PO; Wk; Turner G (1983a) p.309, (1989)
98–99

**LADD & STREATFIELD Edward Wilds
& John**
w 1851–1859
Hydro M, Sacch M
1851–1859   1 Old Jewry, London
Took over from BATE Robert Brettell★
B.apt Excise 1850; Partnership dissolved 1859
Known to have sold: saccharometer
Sources: McConnell (1993) p.54; PO; Wk;
Chaldecott (1989) p.160

LAIRD David White
w 1834–1851
Clock M, Watch M, Naut IM
1834–1842   4 Bridge St, Leith
1843–1851   58 Bridge St, Leith
Succeeded by MILLAR R.★
Sources: Bryden (1972) p.51; Clarke et al (1989)
p.106–07; TCd NMS

LAKE Thomas
w 1770
[Math IM]
Leadenhall St, London
Known to have sold: octant
Sources: inst NMM; Taylor (1966) p.291

LAKIN Francis
w 1792
Rule M
1792   11 Berry St, Wolverhampton
Sources: Wolverhampton rate books (MAC)

LAMB Elizabeth
a 1726
Scale M, Brazier
Alternative name: HUX Elizabeth (II)★
Ye Three Cocks at Holborn
Conduit, London
Wife of LAMB Percivall★
See also HUX Thomas & Elizabeth★
Sources: CLRO: probate inventory of LAMB
Percivall (MAC); BM: Heal (MAC)

LAMB Mary
w 1790–1793
Scale M
1790–1793   36 Long Lane, London

Took over from LAMB William★
Known to have sold: balance
Sources: BW; By (JAC); inst (s)

LAMB Percivall
w 1698 d 1725
Coal merchant, Scale M
1725   Thames St, London
1725   Snow Hill, London
Guild: Armourers & Brasiers, fr 1697
Son of LAMB Percivall of BREW of London
Apprenticed to BEDBURY [BEBBERY] Abraham
1690
Had apprentice:
HEMIN John 1698
AYLETT Isaac nd, fr 1724
Father of LAMB Percival fp 1725
Husband of LAMB Elizabeth★
Associated with THOMPSON Daniel★ who valued
his estate for probate
Sources: CLRO: probate inventory (MAC); GL:
ABC 12080/1 fol. 38, 52, 12080/2

LAMB William
w 1766–1779
Scale M
Alternative name: LAMBE
        Long Lane, West Smithfield,
        London
Guild: Haberdashers, fr 1763
Apprenticed to SWITHIN John★ 1756
Succeeded by LAMB Mary★
Took over from SWITHIN John★
See also
LAMB Percivall★
LAMB Elizabeth★
Educated at Christ's Hospital School; had 6
apprentices; d by 1786
Sources: GL: HC 15860/9; BKC 2881/16, 2885/1
(MAC); CH 12823/6 p.61; 12876/5

LAMBE Edward
w 1826–1827
Spec M
1826–1827   3 Albemarle St, Clerkenwell,
        London
Sources: Pg

LAMBIE Hugh
w 1851–1872
Chrono M
1851–1855   9 Redcross St, Liverpool
1857–1872   5 Redcross St, Liverpool
Sources: G

LAMBRECHTS Thomas
Alternative name: See GEMINI Thomas

LAMONT Carson
w 1846
Watch M, Clock M, Optician
1846   15 Castle Place, Belfast
Same premises as LAMONT & CO.★
Sources: Burnett & Morrison-Low (1989) p.149

LAMONT John junior
w 1842
Watch M, Optician, Silversmith

1842   15 Castle Place, Belfast
Succeeded by LAMONT & CO.★
Sources: Burnett & Morrison-Low (1989) p.149

LAMONT & CO.
w 1843–1846
Opticians, Watch M, Clock M, Jewellers, Marine
instrument repairers
1843–1846   15 Castle Place, Belfast
Took over from LAMONT John jnr★
Sources: Burnett & Morrison-Low (1989) p.149

LANCASTER Francis
w 1818–1824
Watch M, Chrono M
1818   5 Williamson Sq, Liverpool
1821–1824   50 Brownlow Hill, Liverpool
See also LANCASTER James (III)★
Sources: Bn; G; CUL: RGO 1143 fol.4–5;
Loomes (1975)

LANCASTER James (I)
w 1790–1793
Scale M
1787–1797   3 Brownlow St, Covent Garden,
        London
Guild: Armourers & Braziers
Sources: GL: ABC 12088; BW; By; Wil

LANCASTER James (II)
w 1850–1862
Optician
1850   7 Summer Lane, Birmingham
1862   5 Colmore Row, Birmingham
Sources: Sl; Mor

LANCASTER James (III)
w 1834
Watch M, Chrono M
        82 Copperas Hill, Liverpool
See also LANCASTER Francis★
Sources: Loomes (1975); Loomes (1976)

LANE George
w 1841–1843
Globe M
1841   38 Green Walk, Blackfriar's Rd,
        London
1842–1843   5 Green Walk, Blackfriar's Rd,
        London
Sources: PO

LANE James
w 1734
[IM]
1734   Opposite Salisbury Court in Fleet St,
        London
Worked for ELLIOT★
See also
LANE N
LANE John★
Sources: TCd SM Wellcome (MAC)

LANE John (I)
w 1777–1797
Math IM
        Blue Coat Boy & Quadrant in the
        Great Minories, London

1777   Pudding Lane, London
1797   8 Wood's Buildings, Whitechapel
        Rd, London
Guild: Goldsmiths, fr 1763
Apprenticed to
PARSONS William (I)★ 1756
STEDMAN Christopher (I)★ by t/o 1760
See also
LANE Nicholas★
LANE James★
Son of LANE Thomas of CPC of London
Father of LANE John s 1797 HC
Sources: GH: GSC Ap/Fr; GL: HC 15860/9, Sun
11936/260 no. 392079; BM: Heal 105/61 (MAC)

LANE John (II)
w 1733–1739
Scale M
        London
Guild: Blacksmiths, fr 1725/6
Apprenticed to NEALE John (I)★ 1718
Son of LANE William, gent, of Upwood, Berks
Had apprentice:
KILLINGWORTH Pinson 1730 t/o 1735 to READ
Samuel★
READ Samuel★ 1733/4 by t/o from NEALE John
(I)★, t/o 1734 to HART Benjamin★
GALE William★ by t/o 1733/4 from NEALE John
(I)★, t/o to READ Samuel★ 1735
Sources: GL: BKC 2881/11, 2886/4, 2888

LANE Nicholas
w 1776–1783
Globe M
1783   Parish of Christ Church, Surrey,
        London
Father of LANE Thomas★
See also
LANE John★ (I)
LANE James★
Known to have sold: globe
Sources: Chr SK 19 Nov 1987 lot 19; GL: JC
8052/7; inst NMM

LANE Thomas
fr 1801 w 1806
[Math IM]
        London
Guild: Joiners
Son of LANE Nicholas★
Apprenticed to TANGATE Robert★ 1783
Had apprentice SOUTTER David 1806
Sources: GL: JC 8052/7, 8052/8, 8051/5

LANGFORD Nathaniel George
w 1834–1846
Spec M
        54 Charlotte St, Fieldgate, London
        8 Union St, Bishopsgate Without,
        London
1839   19 Snows Fields, Bermondsey,
        London
1846   21 Snows Fields, Bermondsey,
        London
Sources: Pg (JAC); PO

LANGFORD William
w 1828–1873

Clock M, Naut IM, Chrono M
1828–1850   52 Broad Quay, Bristol
1855–1872   53 Broad Quay, Bristol
1866   6 St.Augustines Parade, Bristol
1872–1873   40 College Green, Bristol
Succeeded by LANGFORD & SON W.
Known to have sold: barometer, chronometer, thermometer
Sources: Mat; BsM n; inst MHS; Banfield (1976)

LANGLANDS –
w 1686
Spec M
1686   The Ship, Cornhill, London
See also LONGLAND William★ – apparently the same person
Sources: Buckley (1935) p.427

LANGSTON David
w 1823–1825
Optician
            116 Cheapside, London
            94 Cheapside, London
Partnership HICKS, LANGSTON & CO★
Known to have sold: sundial
Sources: Pg (JAC); inst (s) (MAC)

LARA A.
a 1830–1900
            Glasgow
Known to have sold: barometer
Sources: NMS n

LASHMAN Frances
v 1828
Math IM
1828   37 Poultry, London
Same premises as DAY Francis★ (?employee)
Attended London Mechanics Institute 1828
Sources: LMIR (AM)

LASSETER Francis
w 1809–1810
Optician
Alternative name: LASSETOR
1809–1810   8 Green St, Leicester Square, London
Sources: Kt (JAC)

LATHAM Thomas
w 1841–1849
Watch M, Jeweller, Optician, Math IM
1841–1849   81 Hanover St, Liverpool
Sources: G

LAURIE James
c 1792–1792
            Glasgow
Partnership GARDNER & LAURIE★
See also GARDNER John (I)★
Sources: Bryden (1972) p.51

LAVERACK Henry
w 1834–1841
Math IM, Optician
Alternative name: Henry Thomas
1834   35 Bridgewater St, Liverpool
1834–1841   31 Sussex St, Liverpool
Sources: G; Pg

LAW Andrew
w 1749
Math IM, Chairman
Father of LAW Andrew s 1749 to BATES Richard★
Sources: McKenzie (1978) p.26

LAW Charles
fp 1795 w 1796
Math IM
1796   23 Market Row, Oxford Market, London
Guild: Joiners, fp 1795
Son of LAW Thomas, d, of JC
Apprenticed to McCULLOCH Kenneth★ 1788
Attended Christ's Hospital. Journeyman in 1796
Sources: GL: CH 12876/6; JC 8051/5; 8055/3

LAWLEY George
w 1841
Rule M
1841   44 Newtown Row, Birmingham
Sources: K

LAWRANC Isaac
c 1702–1714
Alternative name: LAWRENCE ?
            Cirencester, Glos
Known to have sold: weights
Sources: inst (pv) (MAC)

LAWRANCE John
c 1800 w 1836
Brass founder, Brazier
Alternative name: LAURENCE, LAWRENCE
1824   Milner's Court, 21 Guestrow, Aberdeen
1835–1836   29 Guestrow, Aberdeen
Guild: Hammermen, fr 1800
Known to have sold: weights
Sources: inst (pv); Abn; Aberdeen Library n (MAC)

LAWRENCE Charles
w 1810–1830
Scale M, Broker
1810   12 Cloisters, Smithfield, London
Guild: Blacksmiths, fp 1810
Apprenticed to LAWRENCE John Peter★, his father, 1804
Had apprentice FAIRBURN Anthony Joseph 1830
Educated at Christ's Hospital, London
Sources: GL: BKC 2881/16; CH 12876/7, 12823/8 p.32

LAWRENCE Edward
fr 1799 w 1809
Scale M
1809   12 Cloisters, Bartholomew Hospital, London
Guild: Blacksmiths, fr 1799
Son of LAWRENCE John Peter★
Apprenticed to WOODAGE George Cave★ 1792
Worked for De GRAVE Charles (I)★
Brother of LAWRENCE Charles★
Educated at Christ's Hospital School, London
Sources: GL: BKC 2881/16 (MAC); CH 12876/6; H

LAWRENCE John Peter
w 1800 d 1806
Scale M
1804   12 The Cloisters, West Smithfield, London
Guild: Blacksmiths, fr 1766
Father of
LAWRENCE Edward★
LAWRENCE Charles★
Son of LAWRENCE John Peter, baker, of Holborn, London
Apprenticed to READ Samuel★
Had apprentice:
NICHOLL William Lewis★ 1800
ANDERSON James Andrew★ 1801 t/o 1806 to WOODAGE George C.★
LAWRENCE Charles★, his son, 1804
Sources: BKC 2881/16, 2885/1, 2886/5; GL: CH 12876/7

LAWRENCE Josiah
w 1830–1841
Clock M, Watch M, Sundial M
1830–1841   Bolingbroke Row, Camberwell Rd, London
1841   31 Queen's Row, near the Turnpike, Walworth, London
Sources: MHS: MS Gunther 36 (MAC); Pg

LAWRENCE Robert
w 1845–1846
Math IM
1845–1846   19 Cursitor St, Chancery Lane, London
Worked for TROUGHTON & SIMMS★ in the 1830s
Sources: PO; McConnell (1992) p.16

LAWRENCE T.
c 1830
[Rule M]
            Birmingham
Succeeded by CLARK Samuel★ by 1839
Sources: Pg

LAWSON Henry
emp 1796 w 1810
[Optician]
1796   At Mr Nairne's, 20 Cornhill, London
1817   45 Gower St, London
1824   Hereford
1855   7 Lansdown Crescent, Bath
Guild: Spectaclemakers, fr 1796
Son of LAWSON Revd John, Dean of Battle, Sussex
Brother of LAWSON Johnson★
Apprenticed to NAIRNE Edward★ 1788
Worked for NAIRNE Edward★ 1796
Master SMC 1803–1805, 1822–1824; retired to live out of London 1824; d 22 Aug 1855
Sources: GL: SMC 5213/4, 5213/5, 5213/7

LAWSON John
w 1851–1863
Watch M, Chrono M
1851   24 Rodney St, Pentonville, London
Sources: PO; Loomes (1976)

LAWSON Johnson
fr 1796 w 1824
[Optician]
          11 Bedford St, Bedford Lane,
          London
1796   At Mr Nairne's, 20 Cornhill,
          London
Guild: Spectaclemakers, fr 1796
Son of LAWSON, Revd Johnson,
Brother of LAWSON Henry★
Had apprentice:
BINGLEY William Barker 1820 t/o 1820 to
SEWELL J.
MURRELL William 1822, t/o 1822 to GILBERT
William (II)★
HAYWOOD William 1823, t/o 1823 to SEWELL J.
MIEVILLE Amédee Francis 1824
Worked for NAIRNE Edward★
fr by purchase; Master SMC 1813–1815
Sources: GL: SMC 5213/4, 5213/5

LAZARS Isaac
w 1844
Optician
1844   88 Princes St, Edinburgh
Known to have sold: barometer
Sources: ADCS

LEA Anne
w 1701–1730
Map S, Globe S
1701–1712   Atlas & Hercules in Cheapside,
          London
1720–1725   Atlas & Hercules in Fleet St, London
Wife of LEA Philip★, whom she succeeded
Related to GLYNNE Richard★
Partnership GLYNNE Richard★
Associated with
MORDEN Robert★
BERRY William★ and
BROWNE★ in advertising maps
d c.1730. In partnership with her son-in-law,
Richard Glynne c.1712–20.
Sources: Tyacke (1978) p.122

LEA James
w 1823–1827
Optician, Math IM, Optical case M
1823–1827   19 Poppin's court, Fleet St, London
Sources: Pg; R (JAC)

LEA Philip
w c.1683 d 1700
Math IM, Globe M, Book S, Map S
1683–1686   Atlas & Hercules in the Poultry over
          against the Old Jury, London
1687–1700   Atlas & Hercules in Cheapside next
          the corner of Friday St, London
1689–1695   His shop in Westminster Halls near
          the Court of Pleas, London
Guild: Weavers, fr 1689
Husband of LEA Anne★
Succeeded by LEA Anne★
Related to GLYNNE Richard★
Apprenticed to MORDEN Robert★ 1675
Associated with
SELLER John (I)★ and

MOUNT R. in publishing books
CARVER Isaac,★ whose rules he sold
MORDEN Robert★ in making globes
BERRY William★ in making globes
Known to have sold: globe
Sources: Tyacke (1978) p.xxi, 120, 122; GL: WVC
4657/1; inst WM; Brown O (1983) no. 10

LEA & GLYNNE Anne & Richard
w 1712 c 1720
Globe M
          Atlas & Hercules in Fleet St, London
1712   Atlas & Hercules in Cheapside,
          London
Sources: Tyacke (1978) p. 122

LEABORNE Richard
w 1646–1648
Scale Beam M
Alternative name: LEYBORNE
          London
Guild: Blacksmiths
Sources: GL: BKC 2881/5 (MAC)

LEACH & GUTTERIDGE
w 1826–1827
Optician, Math IM, Phil IM
1826–1827   14 Charles St, Soho Square, London
Sources: Pg (JAC)

LEADER Henry Francis
w 1846–1849
Telescope M
1837–1839   49 Southampton St, Pentonville,
          London
1846–1849   25 Great Percy St, London
Same premises as MILLS Robert★ (?employee)
Attended London Mechanics Institute, 1837–1839
Sources: PO; LMIR (AM)

LEALAND Peter
w 1826–1841
Math IM, Phil IM
Alternative name: LELAND
1827   24 Great Clarendon St, Somers
          Town, London
1832–1846   24 Clarendon St, London
Related to POWELL Hugh★ (brother-in-law)
Partnership POWELL & LEALAND★
Succeeded by POWELL & LEALAND★
Member of Microscopical Society of London,
1842
Sources: Pg; R; Turner G (1989) p.114

LEALAND Richard
v 1834
Math IM
1834   24 Clarendon St, Somers Town,
          London
Same premises as LEALAND Peter★(?related)
Attended London Mechanics Institute 1834
Sources: LMIR (AM)

LEAR Anthony James
w 1826–1831
Optical IM, Phil IM, Math IM, Optician
          Plough Place, Fetter Lane, London

          34 St.John's Lane, Clerkenwell,
          London
          4 Arlington St, Clerkenwell, London
1830   36 St.John's Lane, Clerkenwell,
          London
Guild: [Makers of Playing Cards]
Apprenticed to MESSER Benjamin★ or James 1804
Known to have sold: barometer, dividing engine,
thermometer.
Sources: GL: MPC 5969/1; SM: RA file ScM
3602; Pg (JAC); inst (S) (MAC)

LECOEUR James (I)
fr 1743 w 1761
[Optician]
Alternative name: LECOUR, LEKEUX
1761   Dean St, Fetter Lane, London
Guild: Spectaclemakers, fr 1743
Father of LECOEUR James (II)
Son of FABREE Mary, widow, chandler of
Spitalfields, London
Apprenticed to LOFT Matthew★ 1736
See also DOLLOND Peter★
d by Oct 1770
Sources: GL: SMC, 5213/2, 5213/3 p.63+; Court
& Von Rohr (1929–30) p. 81

LEE George
w c. 1847
[Naut IM]
          33 The Hard, Portsea
Guild: [? Masons]
Worked for WHITBREAD George★
Succeeded by LEE & SON George★
See also LEE George, s 1806 to COOK William★
Known to have sold: sextant
Sources: Sby 17 Apr 1986 lot 263; TCd NMM;
GL: MC 5304/6

LEE Humphrey
w 1687 d c. 1695
Scale M
Alternative name: Humphry
1687   Over against Hog Lane End at
          Norton Folgate, London
Guild: Blacksmith, fr 1676 or 1677
Had apprentice: OGDEN Samuel★ 1687
Sources: GL: BKC 2881/9, 2884, 2886/3 (MAC);
CH 12823/1 p.60, 12876/2

LEE Joseph
w 1835–1849
Watch M, Jeweller, Optician
1835   28 Gloucester St, Belfast
1839   24 High St, Belfast
1840–1843   74 High St, Belfast
1846–1849   57 High St, Belfast
Succeeded by LEE & SON★
Sources: Burnett & Morrison-Low (1989)
p.149–50;

LEE Newmarch
w 1834
Ship Chandler
1834   166 High St Hull
Worked for FLETCHER Mrs as foreman
See also FLETCHER John★

Known to have sold: octant
Sources: TCd NMM; Pg

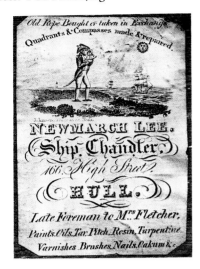

LEE S. & S.

w 1835
Optician
1835   15 Clemens St, Leamington
See also
LEE Samuel (I)★ & (II)★
LEE & CO.★
Sources: Pg

LEE Samuel (I)

w 1841
Optician
1841   100 New St, Birmingham
See also LEE Samuel (II)★
Sources: Pg

LEE Samuel (II)

w 1845
Optician
1845   42 Bath St, Leamington
See also LEE Samuel (I)★
Sources: K

LEE Solomon

w 1845
Optician, Cigar M
1845   43 New St, Birmingham
Sources: K

LEE & CO.

w 1850
Optician, Math IS, Phil IS
1850   14 Bath St, Leamington
Sources: Sl

LEE & SON

w 1850–1870
Jewellers, Silversmiths, Watch M, Opticians
1850–1870   57 High St, Belfast
Took over from LEE Joseph★
R.apt Victoria
Known to have sold: level, microscope, telescope
Sources: Burnett & Morrison-Low p.150; Sby 25
Feb 1986 lot 157; ChrSK 3 Sep 1981 lot 150

LEE & SON George

e 1847 a 1912
Optician, Nautical IM, Math IM, Optical IM
      The Hard, Portsmouth
      3 Palmerston Rd, Southsea
      Ordnance Row, The Hard, Portsea
      33 The Hard Portsea
Worked for WHITBREAD George★
Took over from LEE George★
Associated with HEATH & CO. LTD, from whow
they bought sextant
B.apt Admiralty, Trinity House, & Royal Naval
College
Known to have sold: rule, sextant
Sources: Calvert (1971) p.29, pl.31; TCd NMM;
Phlps 16 Mar 1988 lot 95; inst NMM

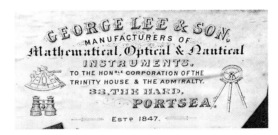

LEECH William

w 1789–1794
Optical IM, Math IM, Optician
1789–1794   3 St.Martin's Churchyard, Charing
          Cross, London
Sources: Kt; W (JAC)

LEFEVER Charles

w 1834–1860
Optician, Math IM, Phil IM
1839   London Fields, Hackney, London
1844–1859   14 Duncan Place, Hackney, London
Guild: Merchant Taylors, fr 1829
Son of LEFEVER John, Tailor, of Spitalfields,
London
Apprenticed to LEFEVER Thomas★ 1818
Had apprentice:
ROSE Samuel 1844
MALE John 1846
LEFEVER Charles (II), his son, 1847
Sources: GL: MTC MF 320, 324; Pg; PO

LEFEVER Thomas

w 1807–1845
Math IM, Phil IM, Drawing IM
1807   Long Alley, Bishopsgate St, London
1810   Love Lane, Rotherhithe, London

1815–1826   Wilmot's Grove, Bethnal Green Rd,
          London
1829–1836   1 College Place, Highbury Vale,
          London
Guild: Merchant Taylors, fr 1804
Apprenticed to VENTOM Thomas★ 1797
Had apprentice:
DONALDSON George 1807
DOBSON Leonard★ 1810
DOBSON John★ 1813
WILLOUGHBY Joseph James 1815
ALLPRESS Thomas in 1816
LEFEVER Charles★ 1818
RUTTY Thomas★ 1819
COX Joseph in 1822
PIERCE Langley 1823
WISEMAN John 1824
PASSMORE William 1825
RUTTY John 1826
TANNER Thomas 1829
THORNDIKE William S.★ 1829
Son of LEFEVER John, weaver d, of Spitalfields,
London
Sources: GL: MTC MF 320,324; Pg; PO(HC)

LEGATE John

w 1782–1784
Scale M
1782–1784   Battle Bank, Newcastle upon Tyne
See also LEGATE Mrs★
Sources: Whd

LEGATE Mrs

w 1795
Scale M
1795   Low Church St, Newcastle upon Tyne
See also LEGATE John★
Sources: Hil

LEGGET David

w 1834
Math IM, Phil IM
1834   35 Tavistock St, Covent Garden,
          London
Sources: Pg (JAC)

LEGROS Peter Joseph

w 1835–1839
Watch M, Clock M, Math IM
1835   22 Joy St, Belfast
1839   46 Joy St, Belfast
See also LEGROSS P.J.★, possibly the same person
Sources: Burnett & Morrison-Low (1989) p.150

LEGROSS P. J.

w 1829–1830
Optical IM, Phil IM, Math IM
Alternative name: LE GROSS
1829–1830   1 Upper Crown St, Soho, London
Sources: R (JAC)

LEGUIN Estienne

w 1790
Optician
Alternative name: Steven
1790   New Compton St, London
Associated with WATKINS J. & W.★, who sold his
inst

Pat. inst. for longitude 1790
Sources: Woodcroft (1854); Taylor (1966) p.344

LEHMANN Fredrik Fidelio
w 1845–1891
Clock M, Watch M, Optician, Jeweller
1845   Market Square, Aylesbury
Took over from LEHMANN & ENGELSMANN
Sources: Legg (1975)

LEHMANN & ENGELSMANN Fredrik
Fidelio & ?
w 1842–1845
Clock M, Watch M, Optician, Jeweller
1842–1845   New Rd, Aylesbury
Succeeded by LEHMANN Fredrik F
Sources: Legg (1975)

LEIGH W.
a 1830
                Newton
Known to have sold: kaliedoscope
Sources: Sby 10 Mar 1987 lot 6

LEKEUX Richard
w 1778–1839
Math IM, Optical IM, Phil IM, Hardware S,
Rule S
Alternative name: LEHUIX, LECOUX, LEHEUX,
LEKEAUX
                103 Wapping near Execution Dock,
                London
                168 Wapping, London
                113 High St, Wapping, London
                137 Execution Dock, Wapping,
                London
1779   9 Little Aycliffe St, Goodmans
                Fields, London
1781   36 Butcher Row, East Smithfield,
                London
1785–1793   138 Wapping, London
1787   Stable, Three Tun Court, Charlotte
                St, Nightingale Lane, East
                Smithfield, London
1787   Chaisehouse, Stable yard, New
                Road, Back Lane, Ratcliffe, London
1796–1817   137 Hermitage Bridge, Wapping,
                London
1816   134 Wapping, London
1822–1839   137 High St, Wapping, London
Guild: Grocers, Fishmongers
Son of LEKEUX John, oilman, d, of London
Brother of LEKEUX John, s FMC 1763
Apprenticed to
RIPLEY Thomas★ 1770
WILLCOX Walton★ by t/o 1775, JC
Had apprentice:
MANTUAN James★ 1792 FMC
HEBERT William★ fr 1806 FMC
MUNRO James?★ 1783, FMC, t/o BOTTEN
[? BOTTON★] Thomas
HEBERT Abraham David 1787 FMC
fr GC 4 Dec 1777, fp FMC 12 Dec 1777; part of
apprenticeship money paid by Christ's Hospital
Known to have sold: compass (magnetic), sextant
Instruments advertised: Full range of instruments
Sources: Brown (1979a) p.43; inst NMM; Ld; GL:
GC 11598/4; FMC 5576/3, 5576/4, 21507/1,

21507/4; Sun 11936/277 no.418006, /290
no.439223, /327 no.500759, /337 no.518493

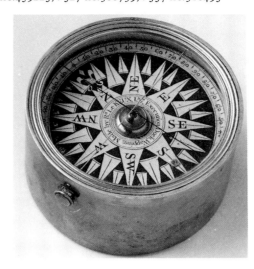

LELAND H. (I)
v 1839–1841
Math IM
1839–1841   34 Great Clarendon St, London
See also LEALAND Peter★
Attended London Mechanics Institute 1839–41
Sources: LMIR (AM)

LELAND H. (II)
v 1840–1841
Math IM
1840–1841   24 Great Clarendon St, London
Same premises as LEALAND Peter★
Attended London Mechanics Institute 1840–41
Sources: LMIR (AM)

LEMAITRE Paul Thomas
fl 1815–1824
Watch M, Chrono M
                London
Guild: Clockmakers
Sources: Taylor (1966) p.398; Baillie (1951)

LENNIE James
w 1840 d 1854
Optician, Jeweller
1835   South Bridge, Edinburgh [not clear
                if employee or independent]
1840–1854   14 Leith St, Edinburgh
Succeeded by LENNIE Mrs Eliza, his widow
Known to have sold: telescope
Sources: Clarke et al (1989) p.123–25

LENONE –
a 1800–1850
                Calton Hill, Edinburgh
Known to have sold: barometer, thermometer
Probably a misreading of the name ZENONE★
Sources: Goodison (1977) p.335; Clarke et al
(1989) p.102–03

LENTON John
w 1833–1854
Optician

1833–1837   14 Waingate, Sheffield
1841–1854   8 Waingate, Sheffield
Sources: K; Pg; Wh (DJB)

LEONI Dominick
w 1790–1807
Baro M
Alternative name: LEONA D.
1790   158 High Holborn, London
1802–1807   125 Holborn Hill, London
See also LIONE Dominick★ [possibly the same
maker]
Sources: H; W (JAC)

LERRA Peter
w 1845
Baro M, Thermo M
1845   24 Call Lane, Leeds
Sources: Wim

LESENEY Bastian
fl 1538 w 1547
Alternative name: Sebastian, LASSENEY, LESENE
(Normandy)
                London
Known to have sold: astrolabe
R. apt Henry VIII
Sources: Taylor (1954) p.168–69; Ward (1981)
p.115–16

LETTI John Andrew
w 1839
Baro M
1839   Crane St, Chichester, Sussex
Sources: Pg

LEVER Stephen
w 1676
Smith
                Duck Lane, London
Known to have sold: quadrant
Sources: Taylor (1954) p.270

LEVERETT William
fr 1761 w 1776
                London
Guild: Blacksmiths, fr 1761
Apprenticed to STILES William★ 1753 t/o to
VINCENT Robert★ 1757
Had apprentice EBBORNE Matthew 1768
Sources: GL: BKC 2885/1, 2886/5 (MAC)

LEVERTON John
w 1761–1787
Math IM, Phil IM, Optical IM
1761   London
1766   Hadley's Quadrant, Water St, near
                the Exchange, Liverpool
1772   Pool Lane, Liverpool
1774   30 Pool Lane, Liverpool
1777   Liverpool
1781   31 Pool Lane, Liverpool
Guild: Goldsmiths, fr 1761
Son of LEVERTON Lancelott [sic], bricklayer, of
Waltham Abbey, Essex
Apprenticed to PARSONS William (I)★ 1749
Had apprentice STONE Richard 1761
Succeeded by LEVERTON Susannah★

Known to have sold: barometer, hygrometer, microscope, octant, thermometer
Sources: GH: GSC Ap, Fr; G; *Gore's Ad* 14 May 1766; LM index (MAC); inst NMM; Phlps 14 May 1974 (MAC); Goodison (1977) p.335

LEVERTON Susannah
w 1787–1790
Math IM
1787   Pool Lane, Liverpool
1790   31 Pool Lane, Liverpool
Took over from LEVERTON John★
Sources: G

LEVEY J.
w 1833–1835
Optician, Jeweller
1833–1835   39 Mary St, Dublin
Sources: Burnett & Morrison-Low (1989) p. 128

LEVI & CO.
w 1848
Optician, Math IM
1848   24 Elliot St, Liverpool
Sources: Sl

LEVICK & SON Joseph
w 1822
Magnet M, Knife M
1822   83 & 84 Great Pond St, Sheffield
Sources: Bn

LEVITT Lewis
fl 1825–1832
Chrono M, Watch M, Clock M
     1 Leadenhall St, London
Sources: Taylor (1966) p.454; Baillie (1951); Loomes (1976)

LEVITT Samuel
fl 1829–1837
Chrono M
     43 Leadenhall St, London
See also
LEVITT Solomon★
LEVITT Lewis★
Sources: Taylor (1966) p.427

LEVITT Solomon
fl 1830–1832
Chrono M
     London
Sources: Taylor (1966) p.454; Loomes (1976)

LEVITT & MORRIS Isaac & Tobias
w 1851–1857
Watch M, Chrono M
1851   31 Minories, London
Sources: PO; Loomes (1976)

LEVY H.
w 1809
Spec M
1809   37 High St, Mile End, New Town, London
See also
LEVY John★

LEVY Levy (III)★
Sources: H (JAC)

LEVY H. & L.
w 1792–1803
Spec M, Optician, Glass Warehouse
Alternative name: LEVI
1792–1803   Temple St, Bristol
Succeeded by LEVY Levy (II)★
Took over from LEVY Jacob★
See also LEVY & CO. J.
Sources: Mat (DJB & MAC)

LEVY Jacob
w 1775–1785
Spec M
Alternative name: LEVI
1775–1785   14 Temple St, Bristol
Succeeded by LEVY H. & L.★
See also
LEVY Levy (II)★
LEVY & CO. J.★
Sources: Sket; Browne

LEVY John
w 1836
Spec M
1836   2 Johanna St, Lambeth, London
See also
LEVY H.★
LEVY Levy (III)★
Sources: Pg (JAC)

LEVY Levy (I)
w 1832–1841
Scale M
1832–1839   39 Belton St, Long Acre, London
See also LEVY Levy (III)★
Sources: Pg (MAC); PO; R (JAC)

LEVY Levy (II)
w 1805–1841
Optician, Glass Warehouse, Gunsmith, Ironmonger, Cutler, Silversmith, Engraver, Watch M
1805–1811   Temple St, Bristol
1812–1815   138 Thomas St, Bristol
1816–1818   10 Bath St, Bristol
Succeeded by LEVY & CO. J.★
Took over from LEVY H. & L.★
See also LEVY Jacob and LEVY Levy (II)★
Sources: Mat; BsM n (MAC)

LEVY Levy (III)
w 1819
Optician
1819   28 Widegate St, Bishopsgate, London
See also LEVY Levy (I)★
Sources: R (JAC)

LEVY & CO. J.
w 1819–1821
Optician
1819–1821   1 Sim's Alley, St. James, Bristol
See also LEVY Jacob★
Took over from LEVY Levy (II)★
Sources: Mat

LEWES Thomas
w 1663
Instrument M
1663   Ye Sea Compasse, Wapping, London
Sources: NQRS 76 (1939) (MAC)

LEWIS Johannes
w 1684–1693
[Math IM] Watch M
Alternative name: John
     Dublin
Known to have sold: circumferentor, compass
Sources: Burnett & Morrison-Low (1989) p.128

LEWIS John
d 1621
Compass M
1621   In the Precincts of St.Catherine's, Near the Tower, London
Sources: Taylor (1954) p.195

LEWIS Joseph
w 1755
Instrument M [his master was a Math IM]
     London
Guild: [Farriers]
Son of LEWIS John, member of WVC, d
Apprenticed to ARUNDELL William★ 1743/4
Attended Christ's Hospital School, London
Sources: GL: FRC 5526/1; CH 12823/5 p.52, 102

LEWIS William (I)
w 1760–1762
Scale M
1758   Saffron Hill, London
Guild: Haberdashers, fr 1758
Apprenticed to VINCENT Robert★ 1751
Son of LEWIS John, bricklayer, of Holborn, London
Had apprentice PETTIT Samuel 1760 by t/o from VINCENT Robert★, t/o 1762 to BROOKSBY Thomas (II)★
Worked for READ Samuel★
See also LEWIS & NICHOLL★
Sources: GL: HC 15857/2 (MAC)

LEWIS William (II)
fr 1824 w 1836
Brass Turner
1824–1836   3 Rose Court, King St, Covent Garden, London
Guild: Drapers, fr 1824
Son of LEWIS William, gold & silver wire drawer, of Covent Garden, London
Apprenticed to STANTON John★ 1816
Had apprentice LOWE Richard Gillies 1836
Sources: DH: DPC Ap/Fr, index

LEWIS & BRIGGS
w 1795–1799
Math IM, Gauging IM
Alternative name: BRIGGS & LEWIS
1795–1799   52 Bow Lane, Cheapside, London
Known to have sold: slide rule
Sources: H (JAC); inst (pv) (MAC)

LEWIS & NICHOLL
a 1780–1800
Scale M
          At the corner of Falcon Square, London
See also
LEWIS William (I)★
NICHOLL William L.★
Known to have sold: balance
Sources: inst (pv) (MAC)

LEWIS & ROSS
w 1834
Math IM, Phil IM
1834   96 Brick Lane, Spitalfields, London
Sources: Pg

LEWTY George
w 1835
Rule M
1835   51 Summer Lane, Birmingham
Sources: Pg (MAC)

LEY George
w 1780
Upholder, Baro M
1780   52 High St, Birmingham
Sources: PR

LIDDALL Dennis
w 1673
Math IM
1673   London
Known to have sold: rule
Sources: GL: CKC 2710/1 p.272; Loomes (1981b)

LIDDELL James
fr 1806
Smith
          Glasgow
Guild: Hammermen
Known to have sold: balance
Sources: Lumsden & Aitken (1912) p.303 (MAC)

LIDDELL John Josiah
w 1840–1858
Glass worker, Level M, Math IM, Optical IM, Phil IM
1843–1857   3 Hanover St, Edinburgh
1858   91 South St, Edinburgh
Succeeded by BUIST & CO. James
Ex.1851
Known to have sold: level
Sources: Cat.1851; Bryden (1972) p.51

LIDDLE William
w 1828–1833
Math IM, Optical IM
Alternative name: LIDDELL
1828–1833   3 North Bank St, Edinburgh
Partnership with FINNIE Joseph★
Took over from FINNIE & LIDDLE★
Known to have sold: barometer
Sources: Bryden (1972) p.51; Goodison (1977) p.335

LIFORD John
w 1732–1751

Math IM
Alternative name: LYFORD, LIFFORD
1730   Euclid's Head, near the New Church, Strand, London
1746–1748   Over against the New Church in the Strand, London
Guild: Goldsmiths, fr 1723
Son of LIFORD John, cordwainer, of Islington, Middx (London)
Apprenticed to COLLIER William★ 1716
Had apprentice:
SIMPSON John 1732
LINLEY Henry 1735/6
HUMPHREYS Samuel 1737
HITCH Hermes 1737
HITCH Joseph★ 1745
JENKINS William★ 1745
CHURCH Benjamin 1750 t/o to his father, Seth, 1755 (possibly connected with CHURCH Benjamin★)
HOLBROOK John 1751 t/o nd to MITCHELL John of CKC
Associated with
COLE Benjamin (I)★ in advertising
SCOTT Benjamin★ as supplier
Known to have sold: universal ring dial
Sources: GH: GSC Ap, Fr; *Daily Ad* 28 May 1748 p.4 (MAC); GL: CH 12876/4; inst SM; Taylor (1966) p.183–84

LIGHT Richard
w 1662 d c. 1663
[Spec M]
1662   Tower Hill, London
          Mortlake, Surrey
Guild: Spectaclemakers
Had apprentice LIGHT Walter, his son, 1662
Sources: GL: SMC 5213/1

LILES Joseph
w 1841–1866
Math IM, Optician, Astro IM
1841   8 Richmond St, East St, Newington, Surrey, London
Husband of COOPER Charlotte
Sources: PRO: Cs 1841, HO107/1064 p.27; b.cert of Alfred Liles, Mar 1841 (SEG)

LILLEY John (I)
w 1811–1845
Naut IM, Math IM, Optician
          Commercial Place, Commercial Rd, London
1811   Christopher St, Hatton Garden, London
1818–1821   Globe St, Bethnal Green, London
1823–1845   7 Jamaica Terrace, Limehouse, London
1826   Jamaica Terrace, Commercial Rd, near West India Docks, London
1851   29 Beaumont Square, Mile End Rd, London
        [not clear if this is LILLEY John (I) or (II)]
Guild: Merchant Taylors, fr 1811
Father of LILLEY John (II)★
Apprenticed to
DANCER Michael★ 1801

rebound to LILLEY James Archer 1801 MTC
Had apprentice:
ILES James F. 1818
HASTED Thomas 1821
BERRY John B★ 1826
MACKROW Isaac★ 1829
ALLEN James Pateshall 1841 [or to LILLEY John (II)★]
Succeeded by LILLEY & SON★
Son of LILLEY John, victualler, of Bethnal Green, London
Known to have sold: compass
Instruments advertised: full range of mathematical & nautical instruments, telescope
Sources: Pg; PO; R; Wk; GL: MTC, MF320, 324; JC 8054/56; BM: Heal 105/62–66

LILLEY John (II)
fp 1837
[Math IM]
          London
Guild: Merchant Taylors, fp 1837
Son of LILLEY John (I)★
Partnership LILLEY & SON John★
Had apprentice ROBINSON Alfred John 1853 [or to LILLEY John (I)★
Sources: GL: MTC MF 320,324

LILLEY & SON John
w 1846–1913
Naut IM, Math IM, Opticians, Compass M, Telescope M
1846–1865   7 Jamaica Terrace, Limehouse, London
1870–1885   9 London St, Fenchurch St, London EC
1890–1901   10 London St, London EC
Took over from LILLEY John (I)★
B.apt Navy & East India Co.
Known to have sold: compass (magnetic)
Sources: PO; Calvert (1971) p.29; TCd & inst NMM

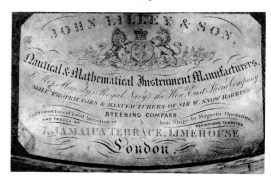

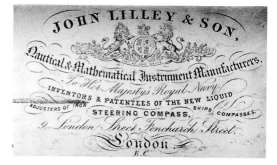

LILLY L.
a 1780–1830
Edinburgh
Known to have sold: barometer
Sources: Phlps (Edin) 25 Feb 1977 lot 247

LILLY Stephen
fl 1812–1832
Looking-glass M, Baro M
Candlemaker Row, Edinburgh
See also
LILLY & CO.★
LILLY & RIVOLTA★
Known to have sold: barometer, thermometer
Sources: Goodison (1977) p.335; Webster R & M (1988)

LILLY & CO.
fl 1834–1844
Carver, Gilder
Candlemaker Row, Edinburgh
See also
LILLY Stephen★
LILLY & RIVOLTA★
Known to have sold: barometer
Sources: Webster R & M (1988)

LILLY & RIVOLTA
fl 1844–1845
Carver, Baro M
1844–1845   Candlemaker Row, Edinburgh
See also
LILLY S.★
LILLY & CO.★
Sources: Webster R & M (1988)

LIMBACH Frederick
w 1848
Math IM, Optician
1848   17 Waterhouse Lane, Hull
Sources: Sl; Chr (SK) 17 Apr 1986 lot 96

LIMBOROW Robert
fr 1604 w 1619
Goldsmith
Alternative name: LIMBOROUGH, LIMBROUGH, LINNBOROWE,
1618–1619   Gutter Lane (in the lower end of Gutter-lane neere the Goldsmiths Hall) London
Guild: Goldsmiths, fr 1604
Apprenticed to COOLINGE Edward nd
Instruments advertised: calculating device
Sources: GH: GSC Court Minutes 13; Bryden (1992) p.308

LINCOLN Charles
w 1765–1805
Optical IM, Optician
1793   32 Leadenhall St, London
1763   11 Cornhill near the Poultry, London
                38 Leadenhall St, London
1772   Sir Isaac Newton's Head, 62 Leadenhall St, London
1772–1805   62 Leadenhall St, London
Guild: Fletchers, Spectaclemakers
Father of LINCOLN Charles s 1802 to FOSTER H., mercer, DPC, t/o to his father

Son of LINCOLN Thomas★
Had apprentice:
CORDELL Richard 1765,SMC
PARMINTER John★ 1769,SMC
COX William (IV)★ 1771 by t/o from CUFF John★ SMC
BULLEY Charles 1778 SMC
PEARTREE Matthew 1770 FC
SILBERRAD Charles★ 1791 FC
Employed RICHARDSON Winstanley★ 1773
WALKER Thomas 1773
SILBERRAD Charles★ 1798
d.1807; fp SMC 1762; Master SMC 1787–1790; fr FC 1765
Known to have sold: armillery sphere, compass, microscope
Instruments advertised: math & optical inst
Sources: GL: SMC 5213/3, 5213/4; FC 21117/1; 21119; DH: DPC Ap/Fr; Wil; H; Kt; Ld; Lg; Mort; TCd SM; inst NMM; Turner G (1981) p.41

LINCOLN Thomas
w 1720–1762
Spec M
Alternative name: LINCOLNE
1737   Little Britain, London
1745–1750   Parish of St. Bartholomew's the Less, London
Guild: Spectaclemakers, fr 1716
Father of LINCOLN Charles★
Apprenticed to COOBEROW Mathew★ 1708
Had apprentice:
COX John★ 1724
EASTLAND William (I)★ by t/o from GAY Thomas★ nd
HALIBURTON Andre or Andrew by t/o from BROWN Thomas (II)★ 1719/20
DYER Richard 1722
RICHARDSON Richard?★1726
BIRD Henry 1731
GASS Robert 1735
NOTT William 1739
STEDWELL John 1745
SPILLETT John 1749/50
LINCOLN Susannah, his daughter, 1749/50
RICHARDSON Winstanley★ 1753
SILVESTER Thomas 1754
WALKER Thomas★ 1761
WIGNELL Henry 1762
Master SMC 1746–1747
Sources: GL: SMC 6031/1, 5213/2 p.97, 115, 134, 147, 150, 173, 234+, 5213/3 p.2, 87, 103, 114–5, 146, 192, 197+; CH 12876/4

LIND John
w 1730 d 1783
Scale M, Candlestick M, Warming pan M
1730   London Spaw, Clerkenwell, London
1759   Holborn Bridge, London
1776   Snow Hill, Holborn Bridge, London
Guild: Blacksmiths, fr 1729
Son of LIND Joseph★
Apprenticed to LIND Joseph★ his father, 1723
Had apprentice:
OXLEY Henry★ 1753
WHITFORD Samuel★ 1755
PARTRIDGE John 1761
BATE Richard (II)★ 1764

29 other apprentices 1730–1777
Known to have sold: balance
Sources: GL: BKC 2886/5, 2881/15, 2885/1 (MAC); CH 12876/3; inst, Ashmolean Mu (MAC); *Daily Ad* 19 Mar 1759 (JRM)

LIND Joseph
w 1702–1729
Scale M
In Watling St, ye corner of Queen St, London
Guild: Blacksmiths, fr 1700
Father of LIND John★
Apprenticed to TAYLOR William (II)★ 1693
Had apprentice:
KELLEY John 1702
BELLTON Jonathan 1705/6
LOVELL Robert 1707 t/o 1708 to ROBERTS Timothy★
BLAYDON Thomas by t/o from TAYLOR William (II)★ nd (fr 1707/8)
BENBRIDGE Matthew 1711/12
PATTEN Dorothea 1713
LIND John★ his son, 1723
WOODWARD Robert 1725
DAVIES William 1729
CORKER Thomas 1729
Known to have sold: balance
Instruments advertised: balance, weights
Sources: GL: BKC 2881/9, 2881/11, 2885/1, 2886/3, 2886/4 (MAC); inst & TCd (pv)

LINDSAY George
w 1728–1743
Watch M, Clock M
Dial, facing Fountain Tavern, nr. St.Catherine St, Strand, London
Pat. microscope 1743
R. apt Watch & Clock M to Prince of Wales
Known to have sold: microscope
Sources: inst MHS (MAC); Taylor (1966) p.163; Woodcraft (1854)

LINGARD George
w 1767–1770
Scale M, Screwplate M, Steelyard M
1767–1770   Yard between No. 15 and No. 16 High St, Birmingham
Sources: Sket (MAC)

LINNELL Elijah
fr 1725 d by 1752
Spec M
Probably Parish of St. Giles, Cripplegate, London
Guild: Spectaclemakers, fr 1725
Father of
LINNELL Joseph★
LINNELL George★
Son of LINNELL Robert, member of THC of London
Apprenticed to ARCHER Thomas★ 1717/8
bap Aug 1705 St. Giles Cripplegate; received charity from SMC 1750 & 1751
Sources: IGI; GL: SMC 5213/2 p.105, 159, 5213/3 p.156, 170, 182, 201

LINNELL George

w 1771–1804
Optician
1771   1 Goldsmith St, Gough Square,
              London
1804   14 Cow Lane, London
Guild: Spectaclemakers, fp 1769
Son of LINNELL Elijah★
Brother of LINNELL Joseph★
Had apprentice:
DIXEY Edward (I)★ 1771
HARRIS Thomas (I)★ 1771
FERGUSON Daniel 1771
CLARKE William 1778
DAVIES Joshua★ 1780
HAYNES Henry 1774
STEVENSON Samuel 1779
WEST Charles Robert★ by t/o from DAVIES
Joshua between 1790 & 1797
probably GEVERS John 1780 [given as apprentice
of LINNEL John but there is no other record of a
member of SMC of this name]
See also LINNELL Robert★
Sources: GL: SMC 5213/3; 5213/4

LINNELL Joseph

w 1764–1775
Optician
1764   Ludgate St, London
1774   Great Golden Spectacles &
              Quadrant, 33 Ludgate St, St.Paul's
              London
Guild: Spectaclemakers, fr 1763
Son of LINNELL Elisia or Elijia [see LINNELL
Elijah★]
Brother of LINNELL George★
Apprenticed to LINNELL Robert★ 1754
STERROP Avis★ by t/o 1756
STERROP Mary★ by t/o 1760
Took over from AYSCOUGH Martha★ who had
traded under the name of James AYSCOUGH★
Succeeded by GILBERT John (III)★
Petitioner against Dollond's patent 1764
Sources: GL: SMC 5213/3 p.201, 215+; Kt; Riv;
Calvert (1971) pl.32; PRO: PC 1/7 no. 94

LINNELL Robert

w 1754–1759
[Spec M]
              London
Guild: u & Spectaclemakers fr 1754
Had apprentice: LINNELL Joseph 1754 t/o to
STERROP Avis★ 1756
Freed in SMC as 'Foreign Brother' i.e. member of
another guild; 1759 fined for employing a boy
without binding him as apprentice
Sources: GL: SMC 5213/3 p.201,215+

LINSEY James

w 1755–1764
Math IM
Alternative name: LINDSEY
1755   Golden Lane, St Luke's, London
1764   St Giles's Cripplegate, London
Father of LINSEY William, s 1764 CKC
Had apprentice: STRATFORD Wyman 1755
Sources: GL: CKC 2720/1; PRO: IR 1/20 (AM)

LINTON John

w 1828–1830
Optician
1828   15 Pond St, Sheffield
1830   14 Waingate, Sheffield
Sources: Bk; Pg

LIONE Dominick

w 1831–1837
Baro M, Thermo M
              16 Brook St, Holborn, London
              14 Brook St, Holborn, London
See also
LEONI Dominick★
LIONE & CO.★
LIONE, SOMALVICO & CO.★
Sources: R (JAC)

LIONE & CO.

w 1817–1822
Baro M, Optical IM, Phil IM, Math IM
              Holborn, London
              Hatton Garden, London
1817–1822   14 Brook St, Holborn, London
See also
LIONE & SOMALVICO★
LIONE SOMALVICO & CO.★
Known to have sold: barometer, thermometer
Sources: J; Pg (JAC); Goodison (1977) p.336

LIONE & SOMALVICO Dominick & Joseph

w 1805–1819
Alternative name: overlaps Lione, Somalvico &
Co.
1805–1807   125 Holborn Hill, London
1811–1819   14 Brook St, Holborn, London
Succeeded by LIONE Dominick★
Took over from STAMPA & CO.
See also
LIONE & CO.
SOMALVICO & CO.
Known to have sold: barometer, hygrometer, spirit
level, thermometer
Sources: inst(s); Goodison (1977) p.336; H; Und
(JAC)

LIONE, SOMALVICO & CO. Dominick & Joseph

w 1805–1822
Optician, Baro M
Alternative name: overlaps Lione & Somalvico
1805–1807   125 Holborn Hill, London
1811–1822   14 Brook St, Holborn, London
Succeeded by LIONE Dominick★
Took over from STAMPA & CO.★
See also
SOMALVICO★ (see all)
LIONE & SOMALVICO★
Known to have sold: barometer, hygrometer,
thermometer
Sources: Bn; J (JAC); Goodison (1977) p.88, 176,
336, 360

LISTER Joseph Jackson

w 1826–1841
Wine merchant, Lens M
              London
Father of LISTER (Lord) Joseph

Uncle of BECK Richard★ & Joseph★
Associated with SMITH James (III)★
ROSS Andrew★
Inv. microscope; founder member of
Microscopical Society of London; b 1786 d 1869;
partner in Lister, Beck, Beck and Co., wine
merchants of 5 Tokenhouse Yard, Lothbury,
London
Sources: Pg; Cartwright (1977); Turner G (1989)
p.2,10,18,154,171,309–10

LISTER Thomas (I)

a 1738 d 1779
Clock M
              Halifax
Father of LISTER Thomas (II)★
b.1717
Known to have sold: astronomical clock
Sources: King & Millburn (1978) p.145

LISTER Thomas (II)

a 1766 d 1814
Clock M
              10 Lord St, Halifax
Son of LISTER Thomas (I)★
Associated with FERGUSON James (I)★
CARY J. & W.★
b.1745
Known to have sold: planetarium
Sources: King & Millburn (1978) p.145, 147,
322–24

LISTER William

w 1827–1856
Goldsmith, Jeweller, Silversmith, Chrono M,
Watch M, Clock M
1836   16 & 17 Mosley St, Newcastle upon
              Tyne
Sources: Ric; Loomes (1976)

LITCHFIELD Richard

a 1688–1700
Known to have sold: weights
Sources: Sheppard & Musham (1975) p.171, 182

LITHERLAND Richard

w 1810–1820
Chrono M
1810–1813   55 Brownlow Hill, Liverpool
1818–1820   47 Brownlow Hill, Liverpool
See also: LITHERLAND, DAVIES & CO.★
Sources: G; LM index (MAC)

LITHERLAND, DAVIES & CO.

w 1814–1865
Clock M, Chrono M, Watch M
1814–1834   Church St, Liverpool
1818   64 Church St, Liverpool
1821–1823   70 Church St, Liverpool
1827   72 Church St, Liverpool
1829   70 Church St, (2nd period)
              Liverpool
1834–1835   74 Church St, Liverpool
1837   19 Bold St, Liverpool
1839–1860   37 Bold St, Liverpool
1864–1865   58 Bold St, Liverpool
1868   28 Bold St, Liverpool
1871–1877   58 Bold St, (2nd period) Liverpool

See also LITHERLAND Richard★
Sent chronometers for Admiralty trials at Royal
Greenwich Observatory, 1822–34
Sources: CUL: RGO 1143; G; LM index (MAC)

LITTLEFIELD James
fl 1830–1832
[Chrono M]
13 Aldgate High St, London
Sources: Taylor (1966) p.454; Loomes (1976)

LITTLEWORT George
w 1836–1843
Optician, Math IM, Phil IM
14 Ball Alley, Lombard St, London
1839–1843   11 Ball Alley, Lombard St, London
See also
LITTLEWORT William★
LITTLEWORT William & George★
Sources: Pg (JAC); PO

LITTLEWORT William
w 1821–1849
Math IM, Optician
1821   7 Upper East Smithfield, London
1843–1849   7 Ball Alley, Lombard St, London
Guild: [Masons]
Partnership LITTLEWORT William & George★
Apprenticed to GLOVER William★ 1788
Succeeded by LITTLEWORT Elizabeth
See also LITTLEWORT George★
Partnership 1841
Sources: GL: MC 5312, 5304/4; PO; R(JAC)

LITTLEWORT William & George
w 1841
Optician, Optical IM, Math IM, Phil IM
1841   11 Ball Alley, lombard St, London
See also
LITTLEWORT William★
LITTLEWORT George★
Sources: R (JAC)

LIVINGS John
w 1826–1847
Drawing IM
1826   18 Rawstorne St, Goswell Street
        Rd, London
1827–1831   110 Goswell St, London
1832–1839   136 Goswell St, London
1846–1847   63 Rahere St, Goswell Rd, London
Guild: Barbers
Had apprentice: SMITH George William 1826
Sources: GL: BC 9815/89 &/94; 5267/6; Pg; PO; R

LIZARS John
w 1830–1900
Optical IM, Phil IM
1830   12 Glassford St, Glasgow
1858–1874   24 Glassford St, Glasgow
1876   13 Wilson St, Glasgow
1877–1890   16 Glassford St, Glasgow
1888–1890   260 Sauchiehall St, Glasgow
1891–1900   101–107 Buchanan St, Glasgow
Branches in other Scottish towns & Belfast by the
1890s
Known to have sold: microscope, projector,
telescope

Sources: Bryden (1972) p.52; Clarke et al (1989)
p.301–05

LLOYD James
w 1785–1816
Spec M
1785   50 Dudley St, Birmingham
1816   Hill St, Birmingham
Sources: Pye; H (DJB)

LOCKERSON James
w 1582
Math IM (in wood)
1582   Near the Conduit in Dowgate,
        London
Sources: Bryden (1992) p.304

LOFT Matthew
w 1724 d 1747
Optical IM
Alternative name: Mathew
1730   The Golden Spectacles, the Backside
        of the Royal Exchange, London
        The Golden Spectacles the North
        side of the Royal Exchange, London
Guild: Spectaclemakers fr 1720/1
Son of LOFT Mathew, waterman, of Lambeth,
London
Apprenticed to GAY Thomas★ 1711
Had apprentice:
LECOEUR James★ 1736
NAIRNE Edward★ 1741/2
DEANE David★ 1728
TOMLINSON James(I)★ 1725
WATTS Richard 1725
STOKES John 1732
Took over from GAY Thomas★
Master of SMC 1744–1745
Known to have sold: microscope, telescope
Instruments advertised: slide rule, drawing
instruments.
Sources: GL: SMC 5213/2
p.76,118,154,166,197,246+, 5213/3 p.38,76,123;
BSIS 28 (1991) p.17; inst SM (Gabb); Holbrook
(1992) p.116,189

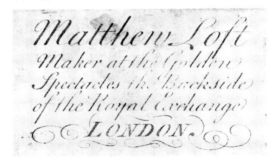

LOGAN James
w 1788
Naut IM
1788   Lawnmarket, South side, Edinburgh
Sources: NMS n

LONDON Frederick Stephen
w 1831–1850
Scale M

1830   52 London Wall, London
1832   74 Houndsditch, London
1836–1850   64 Bishopsgate St, Within, London
Guild: Blacksmiths, fr 1830
Apprenticed to NICHOLL William Lewis★ 1822
Had apprentice:
THOMPSON John Joseph 1831
BULLEN Thomas Brook 1834
Sources: GL: BKC 2881/17 (MAC); Pg; PO

LONG J.
w 1799
Optician
1799   William St, Lambeth, London
See also LONG James★
Sources: H (JAC)

LONG James
w 1781–1811
Optician
        At the North Gate of the Royal
        Exchange, London
        4 Threadneedle St, London
1781–1805   Royal Exchange, London
1793   On the North Side of the Royal
        Exchange, London
1805   4 Back of the Royal Exchange,
        London
Guild: Vintners, Spectaclemakers
Son of LONG James, gardner, of Southwark,
London
Partnership LONG & JOHNSON★
Apprenticed to NAIRNE Edward★ 1769
Had apprentice:
BLUNDELL William 1785 SMC
BEAL Thomas 1807 SMC
ENSOR Josiah Walton 1805 VC
ENSOR Thomas 1799 VC
SHERWOOD James 1796 VC
JOHNSTON John (III) 1793 VC
Succeeded by SMITH Joseph (II)★
See also
LONG Joseph★
LONG J.★
Associated with JOHNSTON John (II)★
Freed in SMC 3 Oct 1781; d 1811; Master SMC
1805–1807; fr by purchase VC 1788
Known to have sold: microscope, telescope
Sources: GL: VC 15212/2 p.30; 15220/3 pp.239,
264,281,323; SMC 5213/3,5213/4; Wil; BW; By;
Kt; Brown O (1986) no. 99; Calvert (1971) p.30;
Holbrook (1992) p.186

LONG Joseph (I)
w 1821–1846 [Firm continued using the same
name]
Hydro M, Math IM, Optical IM
Alternative name: Josh., J.L.
1821–1884   20 Little Tower St, London
1885–1936   43 East Cheap, London
Guild: Fanmakers, fr 1824
See also
LONG J.★
GILL Thomas★
SWAN John★
p 1936; fr by purchase in FANC
Known to have sold: hydrometer, slide rule,
thermometer

LONG Joseph (II)

Sources: Kt; PO; Wk; GL: FANC 21,423/1; inst SM; Calvert (1971) p.30; Holbrook (1992) p.101,116,142,160,220

LONG Joseph (II)
fl 1827–1833
Optical IM, Math IM, Phil IM
　　　　　136 Goswell St, London
Sources: Listed by Taylor (1966) p.428 as appearing in directories – not traced – probably an error

LONG & JOHNSON
w 1785–1807
1791　　　At the North Gate of the Royal
　　　　　Exchange, London
Took over from LONG James★
See also JOHNSTON John (II)★
Known to have sold: telescope
Sources: Taylor (1966) p.266; MAC

LONGLAND William
w 1682 d c. 1722
Instrument M
　　　　　The Ship in Cornhill, London
1693–1695　Cornhill, London
Guild: Spectaclemakers, fr 1674
Son of LONGLAND William, yeoman, of Fulbeck, Lincs
Apprenticed to HOWE Joseph★ 1667
Had apprentice:
BROWNE Thomas (II)★ 1700
CHILTON Sarah 1706
HAYFIELD or HEATHFIELD Isaac 1682
PARKER John 1686
Master SMC 1686–1687, 1694–1695
Known to have sold: telescope
Sources: GL: SMC 5213/1, 5213/2 p.48; inst MHS & NMM

LONGMAN James
w 1770–1789
Music Shop in 1767, Musical IM in 1771
1786　　　26 Cheapside, London
Guild: Spectaclemakers, fr 1767
Had apprentice:
CROWTHER 1770
BARROW John in 1771
LONGMAN Joseph 1785
READ George 1786
SMITH George 1786
LUKEY Charles 1786
VAUGHAN William 1787
GARRETT George 1787
GOUGH George 1788
ALLAN John 1789
GOUGH Elizabeth 1789
EDWARDS James 1789
Listed by Court & Von Rohr as an optician, but no evidence found to confirm this
Sources: GL: SMC, 5213/3, 5213/4; Court & Von Rohr (1929–30) p.85

LONGSTAFF George
w 1845
Chem IM
1845　　　21 Little Charlotte St, London
Sources: PO

LONGSWORTH Peter
w 1822–1834
Chrono M
Alternative name: LONGWORTH
1822–1834　St.John's Lane, Liverpool
Sources: Loomes (1975); Taylor (1966) p.475

LORD Richard
w 1670–1683
Goldsmith, Assay Master
　　　　　Copper Alley, Dublin
Known to have sold: weights
Sources: Westropp (1916) p.66 (MAC)

LORKIN Thomas
w 1789–1834
Math IM, Stationer, Ship Chandler, Optical IM
　　　　　42 Great Alie St, Goodman's Fields, London
1789　　　Sweedland Court, Tower Hill, London
1805–1816　89, Near New Crane Stairs, Wapping, London
1816　　　89 New Crane, Wapping, London
1816–1817　89 Wapping, Hermitage Bridge, London
1822　　　89 New Gravel Lane, Wapping, London
1828　　　89 New Crane, Shadwell, London
Guild: Shipwrights, fr 1789
Son of LORKIN Thomas, gent, of St Catherine's, London
Apprenticed to GOATER John Bostock★ 1779
Had apprentice:
DENCH Thomas★ 1789 by t/o from RUST Joseph (I)★
HOWELL John 1793
COLE John 1826
SUTTY Richard 1828
Known to have sold: compass, octant
Instruments advertised: compass, hourglass, quadrant, sextant, telescope
Sources: Brown (1979a) p.52; Wynter & Turner (1975) p.54; Bn; H; J; Pg; GL: SWC 4604/2; Ridge p.134 (1939) & (1946) p.21,50,60,94–5; Sby 29 Jul 1968, lot 7

LORT John
w 1776–1782
Math IM
1776　　　8 Upper Blind Quay, Dublin
1776　　　1 Blind Quay, Dublin
1777–1778　8 Exchange St, Dublin
1779–1782　Plunket St, Dublin
See also apprentice of BATES Richard★
Sources: Burnett & Morrison-Low (1989) p.128

LOUDON James
fl 1830
Chrono M
　　　　　30 Southampton St, Pentonville, London
Sources: Taylor (1966) p.454

LOUDON William
fl 1830–1840
[Chrono M]
Alternative name: LOUDAN

　　　　　149 Great Surrey St, London
1839　　　228 Blackfriars Rd, London
Sources: Pg; Baillie (1951); Taylor (1966) p.454

LOVE Robert
a 1800–1900
　　　　　Greenock
Known to have sold: sextant
Sources: ChrSK Jan 1976 lot 121 (MAC)

LOVELACE Jacob (I)
a 1677 d 1716
Clock M
　　　　　Exeter
Father of LOVELACE Jacob (II)★
Succeeded by LOVELACE Jacob (II)★
b c. 1656
Known to have sold: astronomical clock
Sources: Baillie (1951); King & Millburn (1978) p.142

LOVELACE Jacob (II)
fr 1721 d 1755
Clock M
1730　　　Exeter
Son of LOVELACE Jacob (I)★
See also
LOVELACE William (I)★
LOVELACE William (II)★
Associated with SAVERY Servington★
Instruments advertised: magnet
Sources: GMag 75 (1805) p.135 (PF); Loomes (1976)

LOVELACE William (I)
w 1739–1743
[Watch M]
　　　　　London
Father of LOVELACE William (II)★
See also
LOVELACE Jacob (II)★
BARROW & LOVELACE★
Associated with SAVERY Servington★
Known to have sold: magnets made from compound magnet given to him by Savery
Sources: RS *Journal* 5 Jul 1739 p.464 (PF); BM: Add. MS. 44058 fol.91 (PF); RS: Canton Papers 2, fol.16, 114 (PF); Calvert (1971) p.13

LOVELACE William (II)
w 1747–1774
Watch M, Magnet M
1768–1774　Charles Square, Hoxton, London
Father of
LOVELACE Arthur Anthony
LOVELACE William s 1768 PLC★
See also BARROW & LOVELACE★
Known to have sold: magnet
Sources: GL: PLC 6122/4; RS: Canton Papers 2, fol. 16 (PF); Calvert (1971) p.13

LOVELL Elias
w 1829–1839
Glass S, Optician, Doll M, Toy S, Tobacco S
1829-1839　34 Lower Arcade, Bristol
Sources: Mat

LOVI Angelo
w 1804
Glass Blower

> Niddry St, Edinburgh
> 82 South Bridge, Edinburgh
> 16 South Bridge, Edinburgh

Wife of LOVI Isabella★
Succeeded by LOVI Isabella★
See also
LOVI & SON J.★
LOVI H.★
Known to have sold: barometer, thermometer
Sources: Bryden (1972) p.52; Clarke et al (1989)
p.205–06; Goodison (1977) p.337

LOVI H.
a 1805–1827

> Edinburgh ?

See also
LOVI Angelo★
LOVI Isabella★
LOVI & SON J.★
Known to have sold: slide rule [with tables by
LOVI Isabella★]
Sources: inst NMS (MAC)

LOVI Isabella
w 1805–1827
Hydrostatic Bubble M
1806   82 South Bridge, Edinburgh
1807–1811   Geddes Close, Edinburgh
1812–1813   79 High St, Edinburgh
1814–1821   Strichen's Close, Edinburgh
1822   113 High St, Edinburgh
1822–1825   114 High St, Edinburgh
1826–1827   Stichen's Close, (2nd period)
              Edinburgh
Wife of LOVI Angelo★
Took over from LOVI Angelo★
See also
LOVI & SON J.★
LOVI H.★
Pat. hydrostatic bubbles 1805
Known to have sold: hydrostatic bubbles★
Sources: inst NMS (MAC); Bryden (1972) p.52

LOVI & SON J.
w 1820
Baro M, Glass blower, Chem IM
1820   104 High St, Edinburgh
See also
LOVI Angelo★
LOVI Isabella★
LOVI H.★
Sources: Pg (MAC)

LOW Thomas
w 1793
Pocket Steelyard M
1793   Bilston, Staffs
See also
LOWE Thomas★
LOWE John (II)★
LOWE & SON Thomas★
Sources: BW

LOWDEN Thomas
w 1797–1798

Clock M, Dial M
1797–1798   Lawrence Hill, Bristol
Sources: Mat

LOWDEN William
w 1823–1831
Chrono M
1823–1825   Grove, Camberwell, London
1826–1830   Grove Lane, Camberwell, London
1830–1831   5 East Smithfield, London
d c. 1831
Sources: CUL: RGO 1143 fols 2–9; Taylor (1966)
p.454

LOWDON George
w 1849–1900
Scientific IM, Optical IM, Phil IM
1850–1861   25 Union St, Dundee
1864–1874   1 Union St, Dundee
1876–1880   23 Nethergate, Dundee
1882–1900   65 Reform St, Dundee
b 1852 d 1912
Known to have sold: balance, thermometer,
microscope
Sources: Bryden (1972) p.52; Clarke et al

LOWE A.
w 1845
Optician
1845   Thames St, Kingston, Surrey
Sources: PO(HC)

LOWE Albert
w 1843–1859
Optician
1843–1845   18 Warwick Square, Newgate St,
              London
1855   50 Bishopsgate St Without, London
1859   23 White Lion St, Norton Folgate,
              London NE
Sources: PO

LOWE Ellen
w 1849
Optician
1849   15 Broadway, Borough, London
Sources: PO

LOWE James C.P.
w 1820–1827
Optician
              2 King St, Snow Hill, London
1822   213 High Holborn, London
See also LOWE Joshua R.★
Sources: Bn; Pg; R (JAC)

LOWE John (I)
w 1793–1798
Math IM, Optical IM, Stationer, Book S
1793–1798   High St, Birmingham
Sources: BW; Wd

LOWE John (II)
w 1793
Pocket steelyard M, Shopkeeper
1793   Bilston, Staffs
See also
LOW Thomas★

LOWE Thomas★
Sources: BW

LOWE Joshua Reeve
w 1833–1842
Optician, Phil IM, Math IM, Spec M
3 Princes St, Barbican, London
2 Copthall Court, Throgmorton St,
London
54 Aldersgate St, London
3 Cherry Tree Court, Aldersgate,
London
213 High Holborn, London
Guild: [Blacksmiths]
Apprenticed to ADAMS Alexander★ 1826 t/o 1829
to REDFERN John
See also LOWE James C.P.★
Sources: GL: BKC 2881/17; R (JAC)

LOWE Thomas
w 1780–1784
Pocket steelyard M
1780–1784   Bilston, Staffs
See also
LOWE & SON Thomas★
LOW Thomas★
LOWE John (II)★
Sources: By; PR (MAC)

LOWE & SON Thomas
w 1780–1783
Lock M, Pocket steelyard M
1780–1783   Bilston, Staffs
See also
LOWE Thomas★
LOW Thomas★
LOWE John (II)★
Sources: By; PR (MAC)

LOWNDES Francis
w 1784–1793
Electrical IM, Medical Electrician
Alternative name: LOWNDS
1784–1790   31 Aldermanbury, London
1793   42 St Paul's Church Yard, London
Sources: BW; By

LOWRY John
w 1850–1880
Watch M, Chrono M
1850   55 High St, Belfast
1852–1856   19 King St, Belfast
1863–1868   66 High St, Belfast
1870–1877   46 High St, Belfast
1880   94 High St, Belfast
Partnership LOWRY J & S 1858–1861
Sources: Burnett & Morrison-Low (1989) p.150

LOWTHER George
w 1851
Naut IM
1851   2 Beeson Place, Old Gravel Lane,
              London
Sources: Wk

LUCAS James
w 1851
Rule M

LUCAS Richard
1851   11 Wilderness Row, Clerkenwell,
           London
Sources: Wk

LUCAS Richard
w 1752–1759
Math IM
1752   Snow Hill, London
Guild: Stationers, fr 1750/51
Apprenticed to CARTER Mary★ 1732/3
Had apprentice:
CORNER William 1752
MARTIN Henry 1752
BLENCOW William 1756 t/o RUST Richard★ 1759
Sources: GL: CH 12823/5 p.140; McKenzie (1978)
p.220

LUCAS William
w 1841
Rule M
1841   Constitution Hill, Birmingham
Sources: Pg

LUCIN Francis
w 1839–1840
Baro M, Thermo M
1839–1840 142 Great Saffron Hill, Holborn,
           London
Possibly the same as Francis LUCINI, looking-glass
maker, listed at the same address in 1846
Sources: Pg; PO

LUCIONI Guiseppe A.
w 1851
Baro M, Thermo M
1851   36 Ray St, Clerkenwell, London
Sources: PO

LUCKMAN Peter
w 1828
Rule M, Pen M
1828   Bradford St, Birmingham
Sources: Pg

LUDLOW Sarah
w 1850
Rule M
1850   2 Bartholomew St, Birmingham
Sources: Sl

LUDLOW Thomas
w 1825–1841
Rule M
1825–1826 81 Allison St, Birmingham
1829–1835 32 Park St, Birmingham
See also LUDLOW Sarah★
Sources: Pg, Wr

LULHAM Richard
w 1851
Math IM
1851   18 Lamb's Conduit Passage, London
Sources: Wk

LUMSDEN Benjamin
w 1773
Goldsmith
1773   Aberdeen

Known to have sold: balance.
Sources: inst (pv) (MAC)

LUNAN William
w 1824 d 1827
Watch M, Clock M, Phil IM
1824   8 Castle St, Aberdeen
Known to have sold: electrostatic generator, globe
Sources: inst: NMS; Bryden (1972) p.52; Clarke et
al (1989) p.153

LUND John
a 1760–1800
Alternative name: Iohn
           London
Known to have sold: balance, weights
Sources: inst, Wellcome (MAC)

LUND John Richard
fl 1830–1836
[Chrono M]
           4 Hatton Garden, London
Partnership: BARRAUD & LUND★
Sources: PO; Taylor (1966) p.454

LUNT Joseph
w 1835–1841
Rule M
1835–1841 22 Camden St, Birmingham
Sources: Pg

LUPPIE Salvador
w 1838–1851
Baro M, Thermo M
1838–1851 17 Robinson Row, Hull
Succeeded by SOLCHA Lewis★
See also LUPPIE & SOLCHA★
Sources: Sl; Loomes (1972)

LUPPIE & SOLCHA
w 1840
Baro M, Thermo M
1840   Hull
Succeeded by LUPPIE Salvador★
SOLCHA Lewis★
Sources: Loomes (1972)

LURAGHI F.
w 1832–1833
Baro M, Thermo M
1832–1833   9 City Rd, Finsbury, London
Partnership TARONI & LURAGHI★
Took over from TARONI & LURAGHI★
Sources: PO, R (JAC)

LUTWYCHE T.W.
w 1775
Clock M, Watch M, Goldsmith, Jeweller
1775   Opposite the Hop Pole, Foregate St,
           Worcester
Instruments advertised: balance, weights
Sources: *Berrow's Worcester Journal* 21 Oct 1775
(JRM)

LYDELL James
w 1686
Compass M
           London

Associated with SELLER John (I)★ in supplying
compasses to the Royal Navy
Sources: Taylor (1954) p.282

LYE William
w 1851
Optician
1851   20 Albion Buildings, Bartholomew
           Lane, London
Sources: Wk

LYLE David
w 1760–1762
Known to have sold: drawing instruments
Presented silver volute compasses to George III
Sources: inst SM; Morton & Wess (1993) p.26,
374–77

LYM James
a 1800–1850
           Glasgow
Known to have sold: barometer
Sources: Goodison (1977) p.337

LYNCH James (I)
w 1767–1772
Math IM
           Dublin
Partnership [probably] SPICER & LYNCH★
See also LYNCH James (II)★
Supplied instruments to Trinity College
Known to have sold: air pump
Sources: Burnett & Morrison-Low (1989) p.29,128

LYNCH James (II)
w 1784–1807
Optician, Math IM, Phil IM
           At the Royal Spectacles, Capel St,
           Dublin
1784–1807 26 Capel St, Dublin
Father of LYNCH James (III)★
Succeeded by LYNCH & SON James★
See also
LYNCH James (I)★
SPICER & LYNCH★
B.apt Trinity College; lecturer to Royal Dublin
Society
d 1833
Known to have sold: electrical machine,
philosophical instruments, sundial
Sources: Wi; Burnett & Morrison-Low (1989)
p.29–35,129; Calvert (1971) p.30

LYNCH James (III)
w 1826–1839
Optician, Math IM, Phil IM
1826–1839 26 Capel St, Dublin
Son of LYNCH James (II)★
Took over from LYNCH & SON James★
See also LYNCH James (I)★
B.apt Trinity College, Board of Ordnance
Sources: Burnett & Morrison-Low (1989) p.35,129

LYNCH James & George
w 1840–1844
Optician, Math IM, Phil IM
1840   26 Capel St, Dublin
1843–1844 26 Capel St, (2nd period) Dublin

Succeeded by LYNCH & CO. James★
Took over from LYNCH James (III)★
B.apt University, Royal Dublin Soc; partnership
1840 & 1843–44
Sources: Burnett & Morrison-Low (1989)
p.29–30,129

LYNCH & CO.
w 1841–1842
Optician
1841–1842   36 Westmorland St, Dublin
See also LYNCH & CO. James★
B.apt University, Royal Dublin Society
Sources: Burnett & Morrison-Low (1989) p.129

LYNCH & CO. James
w 1845–1846
Optician
1845–1846   26 Capel St, Dublin
Took over from LYNCH James & George★
Sources: Burnett & Morrison-Low (1989) p.129

LYNCH & SON James
w 1808–1825
Optician, Math IM, Phil IM, Optical IM
1808–1825   26 Capel St, Dublin
Took over from LYNCH James (II)★
Known to have sold: air pump, armillary sphere,
globe, microscope, sundial
Sources: Wi; Burnett & Morrison-Low (1989)
p.33–35, 129; inst (pv)

LYON Craven
w 1822–1868
Watch M, Clock M
1822–1841   High St, Bridlington
d 1888
Known to have sold: barometer, thermometer
Sources: Goodison (1977) p.337; Loomes (1976)

LYON Hunter
w 1793–1803
Optician
1793–1795   Cross Causeway, Edinburgh
1796–1801   118 Nicolson St, Edinburgh
1801–1803   4 Bristo St, Edinburgh
See also
LYON Peter (I)★
LYON Peter (II)★
Sources: Bryden (1972) p.52

LYON James
a 1780–1850
            London
Known to have sold: barometer
Sources: Goodison (1977) p.337

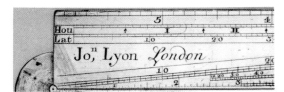

LYON Jonathan
a 1660
[Math IM]
            London

Known to have sold: sector
Sources: inst NMM

LYON Peter (I)
w 1780–1799
Optician
1782   At the Cross Well, Edinburgh
1784   Near the Guard, Edinburgh
1786   Head Old Assembly Close,
            Edinburgh
1788–1790   High St, Edinburgh
1794   Bull Turnpike, Edinburgh
1795   Castle Hill, Edinburgh
1796–1797   Calton Hill, Edinburgh
1799   10 Parliament Close, Edinburgh
See also
LYON Peter (I)★
LYON Hunter★
Sources: Bryden (1972) p.52

LYON Peter (II)
w 1748–1788
Math IM, Naut IM, Optical IM
1748–1788   On the Shore, Leith
See also
LYON Peter (I)★
LYON Hunter★
Sources: Bryden (1972) p.52

LYON Peter (III)
w 1776
Scale M
1776   Tooley St, London
Guild: Blacksmiths
Sources: GL: BKC 2944 (MAC)

LYONS Abraham
w 1800–1801
Optician
1800–1801   408 Oxford St, London
Sources: Kt (JAC)

LYONS Godfrey
w 1807–1811
Optician, Broker
1807–1811   133 & 134 Thomas St, Bristol
Broker only, 1812–16
Known to have sold: microscope, telescope
Sources: inst NMM & (pv); Mat

LYONS Raphael
w 1816
Optician
1816   Major's Corner, Ipswich
Sources: H

MACDONALD John
a 1780–1850
            Edinburgh
Known to have sold: barometer
Sources: Goodison (1977) p.337

MACDOWALL Charles
w 1839 d 1873
Watch M, Chrono M
Alternative name: M'DOWAL
            Wakefield
–1838   Leeds

1839   41 St James St, London
1851   29 Hyde St, Bloomsbury, London
Son of MACDOWALL William of Pontefract,
Yorks
b 1790
Sources: Pg: PO; Loomes (1976)

MACDOWALL Joseph Enoch
fl 1838
[Chrono M]
1838   257 High St, Borough, London
Sources: Taylor (1966) p.475

MACHIN John
w 1820
Math IM
1820   5 Gloucester St, Queen St, London
Sources: R (JAC)

MACKENZIE Alexander
w 1818–1830
Optical IM, Math IM, Phil IM
Alternative name: McKENZIE
            6 Providence Place, London
1815   Cheapside, London
1816–1822   15 Cheapside near St.Paul's
            Churchyard, London
Guild: Tinplate Workers, fr 1815
Partnership MACKENZIE & SWYGART★
Took over from MACKENZIE & CO★
fr by purchase TWC
Known to have sold: compass (magnetic),
microscope
Sources: GL: TWC 7137/6 fol.131; BM: Heal
105/69; Bn; Kt; R; ChrNY 31 Oct 1985 lot 222;
Turner G (1981) p.41–43

MACKENZIE & CO. Alexander
w 1817
Math IM
Alternative name: Possibly short for MACKENZIE
& SWYGART★
1817   15 Cheapside, St.Paul's, London
Succeeded by MACKENZIE Alexander★
See also MACKENZIE & SWYGART★
Sources: J

**MACKENZIE & SWYGART Alexander
& Joseph ?**
w 1816–1818
Math IM, Optician
Alternative name: SUGGART
1816–1818   15 Cheapside, London
See also
MACKENZIE & CO.★
SWYGART Joseph★
Known to have sold: sextant
Sources: Kt; PO; Und; inst (s); Taylor (1966) p.399

MACKEY P.D.
w 1820
Baro M, Mirror M, Carver, Gilder
Alternative name: P. & D.
1820   3 Skinner Row, Dublin
See also MACKEY Peter★
A barometer signed 'Mackey, Dublin' exists
Sources: Pg; inst (s) (MAC)

MACKEY Peter
w 1821–1845
Looking-glass M, Carver, Gilder, Timber Stores
1821–1823   76 Pill Lane, Dublin
1822–1844   35 Pill Lane, Dublin
1833–1836   Clanbrassil St, Dublin
1833–1836   5 Clanbrassil St, Dublin
A barometer signed 'Mackey, Dublin' exists
Sources: Burnett & Morrison-Low (1989) p.56;
AL; inst (s) (MAC)

MACKNEIL Jonathan
w 1799–1809
Math IM
Alternative name: MACNEIL, MACKNELL John?
             Temple Court, Fleet St, London
1805   [Macknell John in H] 9 Stanhope St,
             Clare Market, London
Apprenticed to RAMSDEN Jesse★ 1786
Known to have sold: sextant, telescope
Sources: H; PRO: IR1/33 (AM); inst MHS; JAC

MACPHERSON Daniel
w 1851
[Scale M]
1851   7 Salisbury St, Edinburgh
Ex.1851
Known to have sold: balance
Sources: Cat. 1851 (MAC)

MACRAE Henry
w 1832–1884
Math IM, Optical IM, Phil IM, Optician
             82 Bishopsgate Within, London
1832   191 Whitechapel Rd, London
1839–1875   34 Aldgate, London
1865–1880   29 Royal Exchange, London EC
             34 Aldgate High St, London
Guild: Merchant Taylors, fr 1830
Son of MACRAE Alexander, oilman, d, of
Whitechapel, London
Apprenticed to RENNOLDSON Isaac★ 1822
Known to have sold: microscope, sextant,
waywiser
Sources: GL: MTC MF 320, 324; PO; Sby 10 Mar
1987 lot 107, 12 Jun 1984 lot 396, Sx 9 Jul 1991 lot
1758

MACROW Isaac
w 1845–1849
Optician
Alternative name: MACKROW
1845–1849   4 Upper East Smithfield, London
Guild: [Merchant Taylors]
Son of MACKROW John, gentleman, of
Limehouse, London
Apprenticed to LILLEY John (I)★ 1829
Sources: GL: MTC, MF 320, 324; PO

MACY Benjamin
w 1713–1731
Math IM
             Hermitage Bridge, Wapping,
             London
Guild: Clockmakers, fr 1713
Son of MACY Richard, mason, of Chilmarsh
(? Chilmark), Wilts
Apprenticed to HENSHAW John★ 1704

Had apprentice:
HOLBECHE John★ 1713
DIGBY Charles★ 1721
ROOTS Edward 1728/9
Succeeded by HOLBECHE John★
Known to have sold: back-staff.
Sources: GL: CKC 2710/3 fol.130v, 207, 278v; inst
NMM; Crawforth (1985) p.510; Loomes (1981b)
p.295; Brown (1979b) p.31

MAGEE Bartholomew
w 1835–1852
Spec M, Optician, Mattress M
1835   Millfield, Belfast
1839   158 Millfield, Belfast
1843   56 Union St, Belfast
1846–1852   66 Union St, Belfast
Sources: AL

MAIME William
w 1841
Baro M
1841   Beauchamp St, Holborn, London
b c.1795, in a foreign country
Sources: PRO: Cs 1841 (AM)

MAIN Peter
w 1788
Math IM
1788   Castlebank, Edinburgh
Known to have sold: barometer
Sources: ADCS; Goodison (1977) p.338

MALACRIDA Charles (I)
w 1805–1822
Baro M, Thermo M
1805   237 High Holborn, London
1822   104 High Holborn, London
See also GATTY & MALACRIDA★
Sources: H; Und

MALACRIDA Charles (II)
w 1848–1883
Baro M
1848–1864   4 Withy Grove, Manchester
1858   Wright's Court, Market St,
             Manchester
1873   Barlow's Court, Market St,
             Manchester
1876   45 Market St, Manchester
1883   21 Bootle St, Deansgate, Manchester
Known to have sold: hydrometer
Sources: K; Sl; ChrSK 31 Mar 1983, lot 142; Phlps
3 Mar 1992, lot 144

MALBY & CO. Thomas
w 1843–1850
Globe M, Publishers, Map & Print Colourers
1839   22 Houghton St, Clare Market,
             London [Thomas Malby alone]
1845–1848   3 Houghton St, Newcastle St,
             Strand, London
1850   37 Parker St, Little Queen St,
             London
Succeeded by MALBY & SON★
Known to have sold: globe
Sources: Pg; PO; Yonge (1968) p.45

MALBY & SON Thomas
w 1851
Globe M
1851   37 Parker St, Little Queen St,
             London
Took over from MALBY & CO. Thomas★
Succeeded by MALBY & SONS Thomas
Sources: PO

MALLIN Abraham
w 1850–1862
Rule M
1850   5 Chapel St, Birmingham
1862   Vauxhall Rd, Birmingham
Sources: Mor; Sl

MALLIN William
w 1850
Rule M
1850   50 Newington Row, Birmingham
Sources: Sl

MALLIN & CO.
w 1841
Rule M
1841   12 Hampton Court, Birmingham
Sources: Pg

MALLOCH John
w 1825 fr 1827
Blacksmith, Scale M
1825   Market Lane, John St, Glasgow
Guild: Hammermen
Sources: Pg; Lumsden & Aitken (1912) p.312

MALLUGANII Mark
w 1835
Baro S, Umbrella M
1835   New St, Dudley, Worcs
Sources: Pg

MALTWOOD Richard Austen
w 1829–1865
Baro M, Thermo M
             Bleeding Heart Yard, Hatton
             Garden, London
1826   1 Crown Row, Walworth, London
1839   25 Charles St, Hatton Garden,
             London
1840   19 Charles St, Hatton Garden,
             London
1845   22 Charles St, Hatton Garden,
             London
1845   & 3 Orange Row, Kennington Rd,
             London
1846   129 Great Saffron Hill, London
1855–1865   5 Cross St, Hatton Garden, London
Sources: Pg; PO; R

MANDER George
w 1833–1870
Rule M, Gaugers IM
1830–1831   21 Crown Court, Soho, London
1833   21 Crown St, Princes St, Soho,
             London
1839–1851   21 Great Crown Court, Golden
             Square, London
1845–1870   25 Old Compton St, Soho, London

Succeeded by ASTON & MANDER
Attended London Mechanics Institute 1830–1831
Known to have sold: slide rule
Sources: Pg; PO; LMIR (AM); ChrSK 19 Feb
1987 (MAC)

MANGACAVALI John

w 1836
Baro M, Thermo M
1836   5 Greville St, Hatton Garden,
          London
See also MANGIACAVALLI J.*
Same premises as PENSA John*
Sources: Pg; Goodison (1977) p.338

MANGIACAVALLI J.

a 1800–1850
[Baro M]
       22 Charles St, Hatton Garden,
          London
See also MANGACAVALI John*
Associated with AMADIO & SON F.*
Known to have sold: barometer
Sources: Banfield (1976) p.69

MANN James (I)

w 1687–1718
Optician
Alternative name: MAN
1693   St. Martins le Grand, London
1695   Angel St, London
1697   The Spectacles in Butcher Hall
          Lane, near Christ Church, London
1699   Parish of Christ Church (Newgate),
          London
1718   Fleet St, London
Guild: Spectaclemakers, fr 1682
Father of
MANN John (II)*
MANN James (II)*
Son of MANN John, tailor, of Burton, Herts
Apprenticed to
KING Thomas* 1674
HICKETTS John* by t/o nd
Had apprentice:
CARTER Charles* 1686/7
CROFTON Zachariah 1696
WOODROFF Thomas 1710 but fr by MANN
James (II)*
Succeeded by MANN James (II)*
Master SMC 1716–1717, last noted in SMC
records 1720
Known to have sold: microscope, telescope,
spectacles
Instruments advertised: barometer, camera obscura,
magic lantern, magnifying glass, microscope,
mirror, opera glasses, prism, spectacles,
stereoscope, telescope, thermometer
Sources: GL: SMC 5213/1,5213/2
p.72,98,103,142; inst SM, WM; Buckley (1935)
p.428

MANN James (II)

w 1706 d 1756
Optician
       Sir Isaac Newton & Two Pair of
       Golden Spectacles, near the West
       End of St.Paul's, London

Guild: Turners, Spectaclemakers
Son of MANN James (I)*
Partnership MANN & AYSCOUGH*
Apprenticed to COOBEROW Mathew* 1699
Had apprentice:
AYSCOUGH James* 1732/3 SMC
CUFF John* 1722 SMC
NICOLL John 1708 SMC
FRANCIS John 1716 t/o nd to DAY John* SMC
PRIOR Thomas 1721 SMC
SCATLIFF Samuel* 1725 SMC
HALL Thomas (I)* 1719 SMC
WARD Nathaniel 1730/1 SMC
probably WOODROFF Thomas nd by t/o from
MANN James (I)*
JOHNSON Samuel* 1738 SMC
Took over from MANN James (I)*
Succeeded by MANN & AYSCOUGH*
fr TC 1706, SMC 1707; Master of SMC
1735–1737; partnership 1743–47
Known to have sold: astroscope, microscope,
telescope
Instruments advertised: barometer, camera obscura,
magic lantern, magnifying glass, microscope,
mirror, multiplying glass, opera glasses, prism,
spectacles, stereoscope, telescope, thermometer
Sources: GL: TC 3303; SMC 5213/2
p.16,51–3,95,113,120,163,224+; 6031/1; Calvert
(1977) p.27,32 & pl.33; Taylor (1966) p.168

MANN John (I)

w 1694–1709
Mathematician, Math IM
1694–1698   Globe, Cross-staff & Quadrant,
             Castle Hill, Edinburgh
1699–1709   Globe, Cross-staff & Quadrant, on
             the Shore, Leith
Related to PATERSON James*
Took over from PATERSON James* his uncle
See also MANN John (III)*
Sources: Bryden (1972) p.53

MANN John (II)

w 1724
       London
Guild: Spectaclemakers fp 1723/4
Son of MANN James (I)*
Apprenticed to WALLER Edward, DPC, 1714
Possibly John Mann, brass turner deceased of St.
Bride's whose son was apprenticed to COLE
Robert* STC 1740
Sources: GL: SMC 5213/2 p.142; McKenzie
(1978) p.80

MANN John (III)

d 1770
Barber, Compass M
-1770   Leith
See also MANN John (I)*
Sources: Bryden (1972) p.27,53

MANN John (IV)

w 1781–1810
Math IM, Quadrant M, Compass M,
Mathematical Shop
       Hadley's Quadrant & Hourglass,
       Water St, Liverpool
1781   3 Mann Island, Liverpool

1781–1785   Crosshall St, (residence ?) Liverpool
1787   Water St, Liverpool
1790   19 Water St, Liverpool
1796–1800   20 Water St, Liverpool
1804   Church Alley, Water St, Liverpool
1805   17 Water St, Liverpool
1805–1810   16 Water St, Liverpool
Known to have sold: telescope
Sources: G; ChrSK 19 Nov 1987 lot 267; LM
index (MAC)

MANN W.

w 1843
Jeweller, Optician
1843   The Cross, Gloucester
e 1741
Known to have sold: lens, octant.
Sources: Sby 2 Feb 1970 lot 10 (DJB); Bennion
(1979)

MANN Walter

w 1792–1794
Math IM
1794   Crosby St, Liverpool
Sources: LM index (MAC)

MANN William (I)

w 1774 d 1782
Math IM
1774   56 Cable St, Liverpool
1777   57 Castle St, Liverpool
1781   3 East Side George's Dock Passage,
          Liverpool
1778   Cable St, Liverpool
Sources: GL: Sun 11936/266 no. 401748; G;
LMindex (MAC)

MANN William (II)

w 1793
Quadrant M
1793   Liverpool
Sources: LM index (notes from St Peter's mar)
(MAC)

MANN & AYSCOUGH James & James

w 1743–1747
Opticians
       Isaac Newton & Two Pair of Golden
       Spectacles, near the West End of
       St.Paul's, London
1747   Golden Spectacles & Quadrant,
       Ludgate St, London
Took over from MANN James (II)*
Succeeded by AYSCOUGH James*
Publishers
Known to have sold: telescope
Sources: LEP 12 Mar 1747 (MAC); Calvert (1971)
p.31; Turner G (1980) p.120

MANNING Charles

w 1763
Optical IM
1763   Wapping Wall, London
Guild: [Clockmakers]
Apprenticed to possibly SMITH Nathaniel* 1720
Sources: Mort; Brown (1979b) p.31

MANNING William Francis
w 1773
Spec M
1773   London
Guild: Armourers & Braziers
Had apprentice MANNING Thomas 1773, by t/o
from BYGRAVE Richard★
Sources: GL: SMC 5213/3; ABC 12,081/1 p.57

MANSELL James
w 1851–1864
Optician, Math IM
1851   15 Hurst St, Liverpool
1853   7B East Side, Queen's Dock,
            Liverpool
1853   8 East Side, Queen's Dock,
            Liverpool
1857–1864   76 Circus St, Liverpool
Sources: G; LM index (MAC)

MANSELL John
w 1770–1792
Rule M
1770–1781   Queen St, Wolverhampton
1792   17 Queen St, Wolverhampton
Had apprentice:
HAYCOX Samuel, ran away 1770 [see
HAYCOCK★]
MARTIN Benjamin (II), ran away 1771
Sources: PR; Sket; Daily Ad 5 Oct 1771; Aris 21
May 1770; Wolverhampton rate books (MAC)

MANSELL Samuel (I)
w 1793–1827
Rule M
1793 & 1827 Salop St, Wolverhampton
1802   16 Brick Kiln St, Wolverhampton
1818   19 Salop St, Wolverhampton
Sources: H; PB; Pg; BW; Wolverhampton rate
books (MAC)

MANSELL Samuel (II)
w 1835
Spec M
1835   89 Navigation St, Birmingham
Sources: Pg

MANSELL Walter
w 1829–1830
Spec M
1829–1830   89 Navigation St, Birmingham
Sources: Wr

MANSELL William
w 1826–1834
Rule M
1826   28 Freeschool St, Bermondsey,
            London
1834   28 Freeschool St, Horsleydown,
            London
Sources: Pg; R (JAC)

MANSFIELD Benjamin
w 1801–1828
Math IM
1801   105 Pennington St, Ratcliff
            Highway, London
Guild: Grocers, fr 1795

Apprenticed to ATKINSON John (II)★ 1788
Had apprentice:
NASH Edward 1801
WILLIAMS George John 1828
Sources: GL: GC 11598/6, 11598/7; Brown J
(1979a) p.43,54

MANT Frederick
w 1837–1854
Rule M, Math IM
Alternative name: Frederick Edmund
1837–1841   13 Little Compton St, Soho, London
1842   2 Ebenezer Place, Somers Town,
            London
1846–1854   4 Claremont Place, New Rd, London
Father of MANT Frederick William
Sources: PRO: Cs 1841, HO 107/730.1.1; Pg; PO;
R; b.cert of son 1842

MANTEGANI Antonio
w 1830–1858
Watch M, Clock M, Silversmith, Jeweller
1830   Upper Hill St, Wisbech
1851–1858   High St, Wisbech
Known to have sold: barometer, hygrometer, spirit
level, thermometer
Sources: Goodison (1977) p.338; Pg

MANTELL Samuel
fr 1699 w 1714
[Scale M]
1699   Bartholomew Lane, London
Guild: Blacksmiths, fr 1699
Apprenticed to HART Joseph (I)★ 1692
SNART John★ by t/o 1693
Had apprentice OGDEN Isaac 1714
Sources: GL: BKC 2886/3, 2886/4, 2881/9
(MAC)

MANTICHA Dominick
w 1781–1805
Baro M
Alternative name: MONTICHA
1805   11 Ely Court, London
See also MANTICHA & CO.★
Known to have sold: barometer, thermometer
Sources: H; inst SM; Goodison (1977) p.176–78

MANTICHA G.
a 1800–1850
[Baro M]
            Glasgow
            Greenock
Known to have sold: barometer
Sources: Sby(Sx) 21 Feb 1985 (NMS n); Sby
(Gleneagles) 28–29 Aug 1978 lot 300

MANTICHA Joseph
a 1800–1850
Hydrostatic Bubble M
            Greenock
Known to have sold: hydrostatic bubbles
Sources: inst NMS (MAC)

MANTICHA & CO. D.
a 1810
[Baro M]
            11 Ely Court, Holborn, London

See also MANTICHA Dominick★
Known to have sold: barometer
Sources: Goodison (1977) p.178

MANTUAN Francis
w 1792
Math IM
Alternative name: MANTUANE
1792   Holborn Bridge, London
Guild: Needlemakers, fr 1780
Father of MANTUAN James★ s 1792 FMC
Sources: GL: FMC 5576/4; NC 2818/1 fol.98v

MANTUAN James
fr 1799
Math IM
1799   Execution Dock, Wapping, London
Guild: Fishmongers, fr 1799
Son of MANTUAN Francis★
Apprenticed to LEKEUX Richard★ 1792
Sources: GL: FMC 21507/1

MARCH John
w 1809–1810
Optician
1809   31 Crown St, Soho, London
1810   6 Valentine Place, Blackfriars Rd,
            London
Sources: H; Kt (JAC)

MARGAS John
w 1743–1767
Optician
Alternative name: MARGES, MARGASS
–1745   Charing Cross, London
1745   Golden Spectacles in Long Acre near
            James St, London
1753–1758   Rose St, near Long Acre, London
1759   Dublin
1761–1767   Capel St, Dublin
Guild: Spectaclemakers, fr 1742
Son of MARGAS Jacob, goldsmith, of St. Martin in
the Fields, London
Apprenticed to
ADAMS Nathaniel★ 1735
COX John★ by t/o 1741 or 1742
Had apprentice:
SAY Edmund 1743
RAWLINS Nathaniel 1751
JAMESON James★ 1753
COLLINRIDGE William 1753
MASON Seacombe (I)★ in Dublin, 1760
MOLLOY Charles in Dublin, 1760
EDGEWORTH Henry ?★ in Dublin, 1760
MERCY James in Dublin, 1765
Bankrupt 1758; d Nov or Dec 1767
Known to have sold: compass (magnetic),
microscope, sundial
Instruments advertised: tellurion
Sources: GL:SMC 5213/2, 5213/3
p.51,58,68,170,192; KH (WS); Daily Ad 2 Jan
1745; Burnett & Morrison-Low (1989) p.130,142

MARGETTS George
w 1782 d 1804
Clock M, Watch M
1770   Old Woodstock, Oxon
1782   Ludgate Hill, London

1789   42 Penton St, Islington, London
1790   Penton St, Parish of St. James
         Clerkenwell, London
1792   21 King St, Cheapside, London
1801   3 Cheapside, London
1804   St. Michael's Alley, London
Guild: Clockmakers, fr 1779
Partnership MARGETTS & HATTON★
Had apprentice:
HATTON James★ 1790
HATTON Christopher 1799
HINDLE James 1804
See also NICHOLSON & MARGETTS★
b 1748; published Horary & Longitude Tables
1789-1790; fr CKC by purchase
Known to have sold: chronometer, slide rule,
calculating machine, astronomical clock,
observatory regulator.
Sources: GL: CKC 2720/1, 2722, 3939; Beeson
(1989) p.4,7; Baillie (1951)

**MARGETTS & HATTON [George's
name continued p & James]**
w 1805
Chrono M
-1805   4 St.Michael's Alley, Cornhill,
         London
Took over from MARGETTS George★
Succeeded by HATTON James★
Sources: Baillie (1951); Taylor (1966) p.369

MARIOT James
w 1742
Thermo M, Baro M
1742   The Crown, Gallowgate, Glasgow
Sources: Bryden (1972) p.53; Goodison (1977)
p.339

MARKE John
w 1665-1673
Math IM (in silver, brass, ivory or wood)
Alternative name: MARKES, MARK
         Golden Ball in the Strand near
         Somerset House, London
1668   Golden Ball, near Somerset Ho.
         South side of The Strand, London
Guild: Joiners, Clockmakers
Son of MARKE John of St Mary Abchurch,
Northampton
Apprenticed to SUTTON Henry★ 1655
Had apprentice:
BATTEN Edward 1670/1 CKC
HILTON Thomas 1674 CKC
EMOTT Benjamin★ by t/o from SUTTON Henry★
nd JC
Worked for SUTTON Henry★
Took over from SUTTON Henry★
Supplied instruments for St. Andrews Observatory;
fr JC 1664, CKC (Brother) 1667/8
Known to have sold: alidade, chinometer, level,
plane table, protractor, quadrant, rule, sector,
sundial
Sources: inst MHS; Crawforth (1987) p.360,366;
Loomes(1981b); Bryden (1992) p.307,318 Morton
& Wess (1993) p.392

MARKHAM Robert
w 1672-1695

[Rule S, Spectacle S, Cane S]
1672   Over against St.Dunstan's Church in
         Fleet St, London
1693-1695   Fleet St, London
The shop was searched by both CKC and SMC
Known to have sold: rule, spectacles
Sources: GL: CKC 2710/1 p.250; SMC 5213/1

MARKLAND & FROST
w 1837-1840
Spec M in R, but Wholesale Coffee Dealers in Pg
1837-1840   139 Upper Thames St, London
Sources: Pg; R (JAC)

MARKS Abraham Isaac
w 1825-1859
Optician, Math IM, Naut IM
1825-1855   193 High St, Sunderland, Dur
1857   196 High St, Sunderland, Dur
1859   194 High St, Sunderland, Dur
See also MICHAEL & MARKS★
Sources: Pg; Sl; Wd

MARKWICK James
w 1698-1720
Clock M
         London
1729   Living out of town
Guild: Clockmakers, fp 1692
Son of MARKWICK James, Clock M, of London
Had apprentice:
PARKER Robert by t/o from MARKWICK James,
senior, nd
ROBINSON John 1698/9
Master CKC 1720-1721, d c.1730
Known to have sold: barometer.
Sources: GL: CKC 2710/2, 2710/3; Loomes
(1981b); Goodison (1977) p.40

MARLAND Michael
w 1682 w? 1695
[Compass M]
Alternative name: ? MARLO, MARLOW
1695   Probably the same as Mr Marlo, of
         Wapping, London
See also MARLOW Michael (I)★
Known to have sold: compass (magnetic)
Sources: Taylor (1954) p.207

MARLOW Michael (I)
w 1620
Compass M
1620   King Edward's Stairs, Wapping,
         between the two Gravel Lanes,
         London
Sources: Taylor (1954) p.207

MARLOW Michael (II)
w 1695-1704
Compass M, Naut Book S
Alternative name: MARLO, MARLOE
1695   Wapping, London
Guild: Merchant Taylors, fr 1673
Apprenticed to SELLER John★ 1666
Had apprentice EADE Jonathan★ 1704
See also MARLAND Michael★
Sources: GL: MTC, MF 318, 319; Taylor (1954)
p.207,409

MARNONI Anthoni
w 1844-1849
Hydrostatic Bubble M, Math IM
Alternative name: Anthony
         Paisley, Renfrew
1844-1849   34 Brunswick Place, Glasgow
Known to have sold: hydrostatic bubbles
Sources: inst SM; Bryden (1972) p.53

MARR John (I)
w 1624 fl 1647
Compass M, Dial M
Alternative name: MAIR
         Richmond ?Surrey
Succeeded by MARR William★
Associated with ALLEN Elias★ in supplying
magnetic needles
Known to have sold: compass (magnetic), sundial
Sources: Taylor (1954) p.203-204,345

MARR John (II)
w 1842-1845
Chem IM, Phil IM
1842-1844   35 Montrose St, Glasgow
1845   17 Canon St, Glasgow
See also MARR & CO. J. & R.★
Sources: Bryden (1972) p.53

MARR William
w 1665-1684
Compass M, Dial M, Surveyor
         London
Took over from MARR John (I)★
Sources: Taylor (1954) p.222

MARR & CO. J. & R.
w 1849-1858
Chem IM, Phil IM
1849-1858   27 North Albion St, Glasgow
Succeeded by MARR & CO. Robert
See also MARR John (II)★
Sources: Bryden (1972) p.53

MARRATT John Symonds
w 1832-1875
Optical IM, Math IM, Phil IM, Spec M
         23 Meredith St, Clerkenwell,
         London
1829-1830   1 New St, Dockheath, London
1833   54 Shoe Lane, London
1839-1844   15 Great Winchester St, London
1845-1851   63 King William St, London Bridge,
         London
1870-1875   63 King William St, London EC
Guild: Blacksmiths, fr 1829
Son of MARRATT Edward H, wire-worker, d, of
Horsleydown, London
Partnership: MARRATT & SHORT c.1859-1865
Apprenticed to BYARD John★ 1822
Had apprentice:
NEWTON George David 1832
SPEAR John 1833
PORCH William Colmer 1837
PUGH William 1838
Succeeded by MARRATT & ELLIS
Associated with HARRIS William (III)★ as creditor
Ex. 1851
Known to have sold: barometer, thermometer

Sources: R; PO; GL: BKC 2881/17–18; Bolle (1982) p.124; Goodison (1977) p.339; Turner G (1983a); p.310

MARRIOTT Mrs A.
w 1846–1848
Optician
1846–1848   38 New Montague St, Spitalfields, London
Took over from MARRIOTT William (II)★
Sources: PO

MARRIOTT Henry
w 1807–1848
Ironmonger, Weighing Machine M, Scale M
1807   Chiswell St, London
1808–1822   64 Fleet St, London
1826   46 Cornhill, London
1826–1848   89 Fleet St, London
1826–1847   26 Ludgate Hill, London
1847   74 Old Broad St, London
Guild: Armourers & Brasiers, fr 1807
Father of MARRIOTT Henry Horton, fp 1834 ABC
Partnership: MARRIOTT & CROWE★ 1841–1843
Apprenticed to MARRIOTT Thomas, his father, 1800
Had apprentice:
FAIRBANK George 1807
KING Charles 1810
COSHAM George 1821
SOMERWELL John 1823
HAMER James (II) 1823
DEACON William 1824
ELLIOTT John 1826
BUCHANAN Ebenezer 1826
MARRIOTT Frederick, his son, 1827
CROWE Spicer, fr 1837
MARRIOTT William Adolphus, his son, fr 1846
Associated with
SIEBE Augustus★
HAMER James (I)★
Pat hydraulic machine 1828 with SIEBE Augustus★
Known to have sold: balance.
Instruments advertised: balance
Sources: inst (pv) (MAC); GL: ABC 12081/1; 12080/2; 12088; Patent abtracts; PO

MARRIOTT William (I)
w 1818–1822
Optician
1822–1822   12 Market St, Sheffield
See also MARRIOTT William (II)★
Sources: Bn; Pg

MARRIOTT William (II)
w 1827–1845
Optician, Math IM, Phil IM, Telescope M, Brass Tube M, Optical turner
        40 New Montague St, Brick Lane, London
        30 Pelham St, Spitalfields, London
        10 King St, Bethnal Green, London
1839–1845   38 New Montague St, Brick Lane, London
Succeeded by MARRIOTT A. (Mrs)★
Sources: Pg (JAC); PO

MARRIOTT & CROWE
w 1841–1843
Ironmonger, Scale M
1841–1843   London
Presumably the partnership of Henry MARRIOTT★ and his former apprentice CROWE Spicer
Sources: PO

MARSANO Bartolomeo
emp 1841
Assistant Baro M
1841   Beauchamp St, Holborn, London
b c.1826 in the County of Middlesex
Sources: PRO: Cs 1841 (AM)

MARSDEN Thomas
w 1749
        Address not known
Known to have sold: back-staff
Sources: Taylor (1966) p.211

MARSH Benjamin
w 1842
Candlestick M, Thermo M
1842   83 Coleshill St, Birmingham
Sources: Pg (MAC)

MARSH Elizabeth
w 1682–1690
[Scale M]
        London
Guild: Blacksmiths
Wife of MARSH John (I)★
Took over from MARSH John (I)★
Had apprentice:
COURT Richard★ 1682
EVITT John 1688, t/o to BROCK Richard★ nd
Sources: GL: BKC 2881/8 (MAC)

MARSH John (I)
w 1654 d by 1682
Scale Beam M
        London
Guild: Blacksmiths, fr 1649
Son of MARSH Humfrey, cordwainer, of Highworth, Wilts
Husband of MARSH Elizabeth★
Apprenticed to HEWINS Richard★ 1642
Had apprentice:
CHALENER Thomas 1654
MILES Robert 1659
Succeeded by MARSH Elizabeth★, his wife
Sources: GL: BKC 2881/6–8; 2886/1 (MAC)

MARSH John (II)
w 1794–1839
Spec M, Case M, Optician
        Carthusian St, Charterhouse Square, London
        67 Paul St, Tabernacle Square, London
1805   31 Crown Court, Soho, London
1839   74 Paul St, Finsbury, London
See also MARSH John (III)★
Sources: H; Pg; PO; R (JAC); W

MARSH John (III)
w 1845–1851
Optician
1845–1851   Balls Pond Rd, London
See also MARSH John (II)★
Sources: PO

MARSH R.
a 1790–1820
        London
Known to have sold: drawing instruments.
Sources: ChrSK 27 Sep 1990 lot 234

MARSHALL John
w 1685 d 1723
Optical IM
        Two Golden Prospects, Ludgate St, London
        Archimedes & Two Golden Prospects, in Ludgate, the second Spectacle shop within the Gate on the left hand, London
1688   Three Keys, Ivy Lane, London
1688   Gun, Ludgate St, London
1690–1694   Archimedes & Spectacles in Ludgate St, opposite the West End of St Paul's, London
1695   Ludgate St, London
1701   Archimedes and Golden Spectacles in Ludgate St, London
1714   Archimedes & Two Golden Spectacles in Ludgate St, near St Paul's Churchyard, London
        Old Archimedes & Spectacles in Ludgate St, being the second Spectacle-shop from Ludgate, London
Guild: Turners, fr 1685
Son of MARSHALL Thomas, Cordwainer, of Covent Garden, London
Related to SMITH John (II)★ who married Marshall's daughter
Partnership: MARSHALL & STERROP★
Apprenticed to DUNNELL John★ 1673
Had apprentice:
LANE Edward 1685
probably MARSHALL Edward 1688
WARD Alexander 1692
BARNES Edward 1696
COCK Joseph (son of John★) 1699
REEVE John 1701
HAUKSBEE Francis (II)★ 1703
BARKER George 1704
DELL William 1705
SMITH John★ 1709
LITTLEFEILD Edward 1714
GOODWIN William 1715
WYAT John 1717
KEELING William 1721 t/o 1722/3 to STACEY Ann
Employed WILLDEY George★
R.apt Geo.I 1715; d January 1722/3
Known to have sold: microscope, telescope
Instruments advertised: burning glass, magic lantern, microscope, spectacles, telescope
Sources: GL: TC 3302/1, 3302/2; Andrews(1701) BM: Heal 105/31; Buckley (1935) p.427–28

MARSHALL & CO. John
w 1785–1793

Print S
1785–1787   Aldermary Church Yard, Bow Lane,
            London
1793   4 Aldermary Church Yard, London
1793   and 17 Queen St, Cheapside,
            London
Sold 'Miss Cowley's Pocket Globe' which was
made of card and could be dismantled
Sources: Sby 18 Apr 1988 lot 60; inst (s); BW

MARSHALL & STERROP John & Ralph
w 1707
Spec M
1707   Ludgate St, London
It is not clear if this is a partnership or simply a
joint advertisement
Sources: Buckley (1935) p.428

MARSON John
w 1792
Scale M
1792   32 Cock St, Wolverhampton
Sources: Wolverhampton rate books (MAC)

MARTIN Adam
w 1799–1802
Math IM
1799–1802   Hermitage Bridge, London
Sources: H

MARTIN Benjamin (I)
w 1738–1777
Phil IM, Optical IM, Math IM
1736–1740   South St, Chichester, Sussex
1756–1762   Hadleys Quadrant & Visual Glasses
            nr Crane Court, Fleet St, London
1756–1759   Two doors from Crane Court,
            Fleet St, London
1756–1782   Resident in Fleet St, London
1760   Four doors East of Crane Court,
            Fleet St (later no. 171), London
1761   The New Invented Visual Glasses,
            Fleet St, London
1767–1777   171 Fleet St, London
Guild: Goldsmiths, fr 1756 by purchase
Son of: MARTIN John, gent, of Worplesdon,
Surrey
Father of MARTIN Joshua Lover★
Husband of MARTIN Mary nee Lover
Had apprentice:
MARTIN Joshua Lover★, his son, 1758
WRIGHT John (II) 1759
KIMBELL John★ 1763
JONES David 1766
BUNCE Richard 1769
BAYLES Thomas 1773
Employed
WRIGHT Gabriel★1764–1782
probably JONES William (II)★
Took over FERGUSON James★ globe-making
business
Succeeded by MARTIN & SON B.★
See also
TULLEY Charles★
SENEX★
BANKS (I)★
Lecturer; author; bap 1704/5 d 1782; petitioner
against Dollond's patent 1764; bankrupt 1782; bills

signed M. Martin suggest his wife helped in the
business
Known to have sold: balance, barometer, compass
(magnetic), globe, log, pantograph, planetarium,
quadrant, slide rule, sundial, telescope,
thermometer
Sources: GL: CH 12876/5; GH: GC index; Kt;
Calvert (1971) p.31–32 & plate 34; Millburn
(1976) & (1986)

MARTIN Charles
w 1825–1827
Scale Beam M
1825–1827   Parish of St. Luke's, Old St, London
Father of
MARTIN Charles s1825 BKC
MARTIN John s 1827 BKC
Sources: GL: BKC 2881/17

MARTIN Felix
a 1800–1850
Naut IM
            Wind St, Swansea, Glam
Known to have sold: parallel rule
Sources: inst (s); Peate (1975)

MARTIN James
w 1784–1794
Math IM
1786–1787   25 Great New St, Fetter Lane,
            London
1792   Great New St, Fetter Lane, London
1794   23 Dean St, Fetter Lane, London
Guild: Grocers, fr 1784
Son of MARTIN James, Master of HM Ropewalks,
Portsmouth
Apprenticed to TROUGHTON John (II)★1768
Had apprentice:
HEMSLEY Thomas (I)★ 1784 t/o 1789 to
HEMSLEY Henry (I)★
SIMES Charles 1784
GREEN George 1787
PARSONS William (III)★ 1789
MARTIN Peter, son of Edward, 1792
MARTIN Thomas, son of Edward, 1794
ROOKER John★ 1794
d by 1800
Sources: GL: Sun 11936/334 no.514870; GC
11598/6; Brown J (1979a) p.44,51

MARTIN Joshua Lover
w pt 1774–1782
Optician
1774–1782   Fleet st, London
1787   Naples, Italy
Guild: Goldsmiths, fr 1778
Partnership: MARTIN & SON Benjamin★
Apprenticed to MARTIN Benjamin★, his father,
1758
Had apprentice NORTON George ?★ 1778
Pat 1775 improvement to Hadley's quadrant, 1782
method of drawing telescope tubes
Sources: GH: GC index; Millburn (1976)
p.163–66,177–78

MARTIN Richard (I)
w 1587
            London

Known to have sold: balance, weights
Sources: Libra 5, no.2 (MAC)

MARTIN & SON Benjamin
w 1777–1782
Optician
1777–1782   171 Fleet St, London
Took over from MARTIN Benjamin (I)★
Bankrupt 1782
Sources: Kt; Ld; Millburn (1976) p.164–65,172

MARTINELLI Alfred
w 1839 d 1851
Baro M, Thermo M
1839   43 Union St, Borough, London
1843–1844   96 Vauxhall St, Lambeth, London
1845–1851   18 Vauxhall St, Lambeth, London
Husband of MARTINELLI E.
Succeeded by MARTINELLI E.
Known to have sold: barometer
Sources: R; PO; Goodison (1977) p.339

MARTINELLI D.
w 1802
Baro M, Thermo M
1802   34 Gray's Inn Lane, London
See also
MARTINELLI Lewis (I)★
MARTINELLI & CO. P., L. & D.★
Sources: H

MARTINELLI Lewis (I)
w 1802–1811
Carver, Gilder, Print S, Baro M, Thermo M
1803–1811   82 Leather Lane, London
Took over from MARTINELLI & CO P., L. & D.★
See also
MARTINELLI Lewis (II)★
MARTINELLI & SON Lewis★
Known to have sold: barometer
Sources: H; Goodison (1977) p.339

MARTINELLI Lewis (II)
w 1834–1836
Baro M, Thermo M
1834–1836   62 King St, Borough, London
Succeeded by MARTINELLI & SON Lewis★
See also
MARTINELLI Lewis (I)★
MARTINELLI Alfred★
MARTINELLI & CO. P., L. & D.★
MARTINELLI William★
Associated with COMBE T., Clock M, of
Camberwell, London
Known to have sold: barometer
Sources: R (JAC); Goodison (1977) p.339

MARTINELLI Lewis (III)
fl 1830–1838
Optician, Baro M
            102 London Rd, Brighton, Sussex
Sources: Taylor (1966) p.455

MARTINELLI P.
a 1800–1900
            Edinburgh
Known to have sold: barometer
Sources: Goodison (1977) p.340

MARTINELLI William
w 1839–1880
Optician, Math IM, Phil IM, Baro M, Thermo M
1839	21 Wells St, Oxford St, London
1841	5 Friars, London
1852	54 Snows Fields, Bermondsey, London
1853–1880	120 Snows Fields, London

See also MARTINELLI Lewis (II)★
Sources: Pg; PO; Wk; Goodison p.340

MARTINELLI & CO. P., L. & D.
w 1799
Baro M
1799   82 Leather Lane, London
Succeeded by MARTINELLI Lewis (I)★
See also
MARTINELLI Lewis (II)★
MARTINELLI D.★
Sources: H

MARTINELLI & SON Lewis
w 1837–1840
Looking-glass M, Optician, Baro M, Thermo M
1837–1840   62 King St, Borough, London
Took over from MARTINELLI Lewis (II)★
See also
MARTINELLI William★
MARTINELLI Alfred★
MARTINELLI & CO. P., L. & D.★
Known to have sold: barometer
Sources: Pg; PO; R (JAC); ChrSK 17 Apr 1986
lot 106

MASEFIELD Robert
w 1770 d 1773
Cabinet M, Upholder
1770   13 New St, Birmingham
Known to have sold: barometer
Sources: Bolle (1982) p.149

MASON A.
w 1774–1774
Scale M
1774   Knaresborough, Yorks
Known to have sold: balance
Sources: inst (s) (MAC)

MASON George (I)
w 1681–1697
[Spec M]
        London
Guild: Spectaclemakers, fr 1674
Father of MASON George(II) fp 1696
Son of MASON George, yeoman, d, of Merton
Abbey, Surrey
Apprenticed to KING Thomas★ 1667
Had apprentice:
FOLKINGHAM Joseph 1683/4
AVERY Henry 1686
STAPLER James 1697
Sources: GL: SMC 5213/1, 5213/2 p.5,8

MASON George (III)
w 1834–1866
Math IM, Phil IM
1834–1866   52 Squirries St, Bethnal Green Rd,
        London
Sources: Pg; PO

MASON James (I)
w 1809
Optical Turner
1809	Lower Gun Alley, St. George's [in the East], London

Father of MASON James (II), s 1809 to RUST
Ebenezer (II)★
See also apprentice of HAYWARD Joseph★
Sources: GL: GC 11598/6

MASON John
w 1768–1797
Math IM, Optical IM, Brass Turner, Brass Founder
1760	Saffron Hill, London
1768–1797	Shoe Lane, Fleet St, London

Guild: Drapers, fr 1760
Son of MASON John, labourer, of Aighton
(? Eyton), Salop
Apprenticed to WARNER Edward 1753
Had apprentice:
CUMBER James 1768
HEWES Philip★ 1784
BRUCE William★ 1788
WILLSON George★ 1797 by t/o from MOULDING
James★
Sources: DH: DPC Ap/Fr; BW; McKenzie (1978)
p.227

MASON Jonathan
w 1809 d 1849
Optician
1809	8 Arran Quay, Dublin
1810–1812	9 Ormond Quay, Dublin
1818–1822	14 Capel St, Dublin
1846	6 Patrick St, Limerick

Partnership: MASON Thomas & Jonathan★
b 1784
Appears to have worked on his own and in
partnership at the same time
Known to have sold: octant
Sources: Wi; Burnett & Morrison Low (1989)
p.130, 151–52; Mollan (1990) p.675

MASON S. & T.
fl 1836–1840
[Opticians]
Alternative name: [possibly an error for T. & J.]
        3 Essex Bridge, Dublin
        6 Essex Bridge, Dublin
See also
MASON Seacombe (II)★
MASON Thomas (I)★
Known to have sold: barometer
Sources: Goodison (1977) p.340; Mollan (1990)
p.676; Taylor (1966) p.475

MASON Seacombe (I)
w 1780 d 1802
Optician
Alternative name: Seacome
1780–1802   8 Arran Quay, Dublin
Guild: Glovers & Skinners
Apprenticed to MARGAS John★ 1760
Had apprentice YEATES Samuel★
Succeeded by MASON Thomas & Jonathan★
See also
MASON S. & T.★
MASON Seacombe (II)★

Attended King's Hospital School; fr 1765; Master
of Guild of Glovers & Skinners 1788
Known to have sold: circumferentor
Sources: Burnett & Morrison-Low (1989) p.130;
KH (WS); Mason (1980); DJB

MASON Seacombe (II)
w 1838–1878
Optician
1838–1844	6 Essex Bridge, Dublin
1845–1864	11 Essex Bridge, Dublin
1877	11 Essex Bridge, Dublin
1878	11 Upper Ormond Quay, Dublin

Took over from MASON Thomas (I)★
Succeeded by MASON & SON
See also MASON Seacombe (I)★
b 1808 d 1892; R.apt Lord Lieutenant
Known to have sold: barometer, circumferentor,
compass (magnetic)
Sources: inst WM; Mollan (1990) p.103,675;
Burnett & Morrison-Low (1989) p.131

MASON Standish
w 1839–1841
Optician, Math IM
1839–1841   2 Upper Ormond Quay, Dublin
Sources: Burnett & Morrison-Low (1989) p.131

MASON Thomas & Jonathan
w 1805–1817
Opticians
1805–1808	8 Arran Quay, Dublin
1813–1817	3 Essex Bridge, Dublin

Succeeded by MASON Thomas (I)★
Took over from MASON Seacombe (I)★
See also
MASON Jonathan★
MASON S. & T.★
Worked individually 1809–12
Known to have sold: circumferentor
Sources: inst NMM; Wi; Mollan (1990) p.351;
Burnett & Morrison-Low (1989) p.130

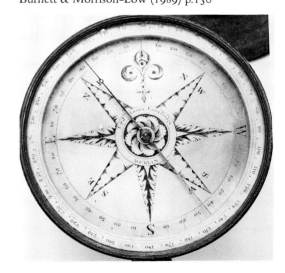

MASON Thomas (I)
w 1810–1837
Optician, Math IM, Phil IM
1809   4 Essex Bridge, Dublin

1810–1812   3 Essex Bridge, Dublin
1818–1819   3 Essex Bridge, (2nd period) Dublin
1820   4 Essex Bridge, (2nd period) Dublin
1821–1826   3 Essex Bridge, (3rd period) Dublin
1827–1837   63 Essex Bridge, Dublin
Partnership: MASON Thomas & Jonathan★
Succeeded by MASON Seacombe (II)★
Took over from MASON Thomas & Jonathan★
See also
MASON Thomas H.★
MASON Jonathan★
MASON S. & T.★
e 1780; b 1781 d 1837; R.apt Lord Lieutenant
Appears to have worked on his own and in
partnership at the same time
Known to have sold: level, surveyor's staff
Sources: Wi; Burnett & Morrison-Low (1989)
p.130; Calvert (1971) p.32; Mollan (1990) p.239;
inst (pv)

MASON Thomas (II)
w 1849–1859
Math IM, Drawing IM
1849–1859   2 Gloucester St, Queen's Square,
London
Sources: PO, Wk

MASPOLI Augustus
w 1826–1855
Math IS, Optician, Looking-glass M
Alternative name: Augustin, Augustino
1826–1831   49 Salthouse Lane, Hull
1835–1855   79 Lowgate, Hull
Father of MASPOLI James★
Partnership: MASPOLI Augustus & James★
Succeeded by MASPOLI Augustus & James★
Took over from MASPOLI Augustus & James★
Partnership 1831–35
Known to have sold: barometer, hygrometer,
thermometer
Instruments advertised: barometer, spectacles,
telescope, thermometer
Sources: Pg; Sl; Goodison (1977) p.340

MASPOLI Augustus & James
w 1831–1835
Baro M
1831   49 Salthouse Lane, Hull
1835   79 Lowgate, Hull
See also MASPOLI Augustus★
Sources: Goodison (1977) p.340

MASPOLI James
w 1835–1859
Looking-glass M, Baro M, Jeweller, Watch M,
Picture frame M
1835   79 Lowgate, Hull
1839–1848   17 Robinson Row, Hull
1851–1859   9 Robinson Row, Hull
Son of MASPOLI Augustus★
Partnership: MASPOLI Augustus & James★
Succeeded by SOLDINI & MASPOLI
Known to have sold: barometer
Sources: Goodison (1977) p.340

MASSEY Edmund
w 1839–1857
Watch M, Chrono M

1839–1857   89 Strand, London
Son of MASSEY Edward (II)★
Sources: PO; Treherne (1977) p.3–4, 12–13

MASSEY Edward (II)
w 1802–1848
Patent Log M, Watch M, Nautical IM
1790–1795   Newcastle under Lyme, Staffs
1795–1804   Hanley, Staffs
1804–1813   Newcastle under Lyme, Staffs
1812   Crossheath, near Newcastle under
Lyme, Staffs
1819–1830   Scholes, Prescot, Lancs
1813–1821   Ironmonger Row, Cross Cheaping,
Coventry
1818   The Saracen's Head, Snow Hill,
London
1834–1838   Clerkenwell, London
1847–1852   17 Chadwell St, Pentonville, London
1833–1848   28 King St, Clerkenwell, London
Guild: fr Borough of Newcastle 1790
Father of
MASSEY Edward (III)
MASSEY Edmund★
Apprenticed to MASSEY Edward (I) his father
Associated with
SMITH Egerton & Wm★ (agents)
BYWATER, DAWSON & CO.★ (agents)
b 1768 d 1852; Pat. logs, sounding lines
1802,1806,1818,1834,1836,1844,1848;
chronometers 1812,1814,1818,1820; Catholic
Known to have sold: log, sounding leads
Sources: Wk; Treherne (1977); Woodcroft(1854)
Pg

MASSEY Edward (III)
w c. 1825 w 1866
Naut IM
1825–1866   3 Tysoe St, Clerkenwell, London
1843   78 Cornhill, London
1851   17 Chadwell St, Pentonville, London
1860   (Residence) 250 Essex Rd, Islington,
London
Son of MASSEY Edward (II)★
Brother of MASSEY Thomas★
Sources: Treherne (1977) p.3–4; Pg; Wk

MASSEY Edward John
w 1843–1860
Watch M, Chrono M
1834–1836   37 Warren St, Liverpool
1839–1843   41 Russell St, Liverpool
1845   41A Russell St, Liverpool
1847–1855   41 Russell St, Liverpool
1857–1860   45 Russell St, Liverpool
1872   (Residence) Olivemount,
Wavertree, Liverpool
Son of MASSEY John, Clock M & Dentist
Related to MASSEY Edward (II)★
b 1810 d 1872
Sources: G; Treherne (1977) p.3–4,11

MASSEY Thomas
w 1846 d 1868
Watch M, Chrono M, Clock M
1846   4 Birchin Lane, London
Brother of MASSEY Edward (III)★
Sources: PO; Loomes (1976); Treherne (1977) p.3–4

MASSI Charles
w 1834–1842
Math IM, Phil IM, Galvanic IM
1829–1834   68 Rahere St, Goswell Rd, London
1839–1842   38 Seward St, Goswell St, London
Attended London Mechanics Institute 1829
Sources: Pg; PO; LMIR (AM)

MASSINO Peter
w 1808–1815
Baro M
1808   Canongate, Edinburgh
1809–1811   West College St, Edinburgh
1812–1814   Fountain Close, Edinburgh
1815   North College St, Edinburgh
Known to have sold: barometer, thermometer
Sources: Bryden (1972) p.53; Goodison (1977)
p.340

MASTAGLIO Victory
w 1836
Baro M
1836   Grainger St, Newcastle upon Tyne
Partnership: (probably) MASTAGLIO, FORNELLI
& MOLTENI★
See also MASTAGLIO & MOLTENI★
Sources: Ric

MASTAGLIO & MOLTENI
w 1844–1856
Baro M, Thermo M, Dealers in fancy goods
1844   24 & 25 Grainger St, Newcastle
upon Tyne
1847–1856   24 Grainger St, Newcastle upon
Tyne
See also
MASTAGLIO Victory★
MOLTENI Christmas★
Known to have sold: barometer
Sources: Wh; Wim; Wln; Goodison (1977) p.341

MASTAGLIO, FORNELLI & MOLTENI
w 1836–1838
Baro M
1836–1838   Grainger St, Newcastle upon Tyne
Partnership: probably of MASTAGLIO Victory★,
FORNELLI Andrew★ and MOLTENI Christmas★
Sources: Ric

MASTALLIO & TOIA A. & ?
a 1800
Oxford
Known to have sold: barometer, thermometer
Sources: inst (s) (MAC)

MASTERS John
w 1676 v 1696
Spec M
1676   St Saviour's Parish, Southwark,
London
Guild: Spectaclemakers, fr 1674
Apprenticed to RADFORD John (I)★ 1666
Had apprentice BOUCHER John 1677
Employed BOUCHER John 1676
Known to have sold: spectacles
Sources: GL: SMC 5213/1, 5213/2 p.2

MASTERS Thomas (I)
d c. 1626
Spec M
-1626   St.Clement Danes without Temple
                Bar, London
Will proved 1626
Sources: PRO: PCC (MAC)

MASTERS Thomas (II)
w 1638
Spec M
1638   St Clement Danes, London
Father of MASTERS Francis s 1638
See also MASTERS Thomas (I)★
Sources: GL: BKC 2886/1

MATHER John
w 1824–1846
Math IM, Optician, Medicinal Baths
1824   3 North Side Old Dock Gates,
                Liverpool
1831–1846   7 St.Paul's Square, Liverpool
Same premises as CRITCHLEY & MATHER★
Sources: Bn; G

MATHERS Thomas
w 1848
Math IM, Optical IM
1848   88 Glassford St, Glasgow
See also DODD Andrew★
Sources: Bryden (1972) p.53

MATHESON & CO.
a 1780–1900
                68 Tolbooth Wynd, Leith,
                Midlothian
See also MATHIESON & SON A.
Known to have sold: octant.
Sources: inst reported by Webster R & M (1988)

MATHEWS Jeremy
w 1671–1682
Alternative name: MATHEWES
1671   Jewen St, London
Guild: Spectaclemakers
Husband of MATHEWS Mrs, who also worked as
Spec M
Had apprentice:
ELLIS Daniel 1675
MATHEWS Job, son of John, 1675 t/o to
THROGMORTON James★ 1682
Probably d by 1684, when Mrs Mathews paid
quarterage fees to SMC
Sources: GL: SMC 5213/1

MATHEWS Thomas
w 1779
Optician
1779   1 Winchester Court, Monkwell St,
                London
Sources: GL: Sun 11936/273 no.410650

MATHIAS John
w 1830
Rule M, Gauging IM
1830   6 Stoney Hill, Bristol
Sources: BsM notes

MATHIESON & SON A.
a 1850–1900
                Glasgow
                and Edinburgh
Known to have sold: Spirit level.
Sources: inst (s) (MAC)

MATSON Jacob
w 1699–1710
Math IM
1699   Dorset St, Spitalfields, London
1700   Sun Dyall, Crown Alley in Upper
                Moorfields, London
Guild: Dyers, fr 1699
Apprenticed to PRIDDITH Christopher★
Had apprentice:
SMITH John 1699
DAVIES John or DAVIS Johnson 1700
SANGER Stephen 1705
COLE James 1706/7
COOK William 1707/8
WEEKES Edward 1710
Sources: GL: CH 12876/2; DC 8168/3, 8169,
8171/1

MATTHEWS John
w 1845
[Math IM]
                London
Guild: Masons, fr 1840
Son of MATTHEWS John,victualler
Apprenticed to HUGHES Joseph (I)★ 1833
Had apprentice DOBSON James★ by t/o 1845 from
HUGHES Joseph (I)★
Sources: GL: MC 5304/6, 5304/7

MATTHEWS T.
w 1849
Math IM, Optician
1849   31 Southampton St, Pentonville,
                London
Sources: PO

MATTHEWS Thomas B.
w 1845–1849
Optician
1845–1849   9 Athol Place, Pentonville, London
Sources: PO

MAUL S.E.
w 1838
Rule M
1838   13 Little Compton St, Soho, London
Sources: Pg

MAURICE P.J.
w 1779
Stationer, Book S, Math IS
1779   Fore Street Dock, London
Sources: Advertisement in Wakely (1779)

MAVER John
w 1834
Baro M, Thermo M
1834   46 Baldwin's Gardens, London
Sources: Pg

MAW Solomon
w 1839–1860
Surgical IM, Medical Glassware S
1839–1860   11 Aldersgate St, London
Guild: Spectaclemakers, fr 1843
Son of MAW George, merchant, d, of Peckham,
Surrey
Succeeded by MAW & SON S.
fr in SMC by purchase; MAW & SON S. sold
barometer
Sources: GL: SMC 5213/6; Pg; Bolle (1982) p.145

MAWDSLEY John
w 1849
Chrono M
1849   58 Castle St, Liverpool
Sources: G

MAWE –
w 1820
1820   149 Strand, London
Known to have sold: geometric solids
Sources: Advertisement in Larkin (1820) (DJB)

MAWSON John
w 1847–1863
Optical IS, Druggist
1847–1858   13 Mosley St, Newcastle upon Tyne
1860–1863   9 Mosley St, Newcastle upon Tyne
Instruments advertised: barometer, electrical
machine, opera glasses, stereoscope, thermometer
Sources: Calvert (1971) p.32; Rd; Wd

MAXAM Richard
w 1676 d 1682
[Spec M]
Alternative name: MAXUM
                London
Guild: Woodmongers, Spectaclemakers
Apprenticed to BOULTER Hugh 1645
Had apprentice WHITE Samuel (I)★ 1676
See also BOLTER Hugh★
fr Woodmongers' Co. 1655/6, fr SMC 1675
Sources: GL: SMC 5213/1

MAYLE Thomas
w 1676–1737
Spec M
Alternative name: MALE
1676–1695   Leadenhall St, London
1714   Against St.Mary Axe Church in
                Leadenhall St, London
Guild: Spectaclemakers, fr 1675
Son of MAYLE James, tobacco pipe maker, of
Godmanchester, Hunts
Apprenticed to CLARK John (I)★ 1668/9, freed by
CLARK Elizabeth★
Had apprentice:
BEMBRICK William (I)★ 1667/8 by t/o from
CLARK Elizabeth★
CARTER Richard 1678/9
HAGGUR Allen 1691
PHEASANT Jonathan 1695
HATFIELD Thomas 1700/1
possibly also MAILE James fr 1690, Master not
given
Master SMC 1697–1701, last attendance at SMC
1737

Known to have sold: spectacles.
Sources: GL: Sun 11936/4 no.4550; SMC 5213/1,
5213/2 p.22,25,161

MAYO Thomas
w 1710 d 1719
Ship chandler, Naut IM
        On the Shore, Leith, Midlothian
Sources: Bryden (1972) p.6,54

MAZZUCHI Innocento
a 1800–1850
Alternative name: Ino.
        Aylesbury, Bucks
Known to have sold: barometer, hygrometer, spirit
level, thermometer.
Sources: inst (s) (MAC)

MCADAM Robert
w 1820–1845
Watch M, Clock M
        Dumfries
Known to have sold: barometer
Sources: ChrSK 26 Jul 1978 lot 147; Baillie (1951)

MCALL John
w 1828–1834
Optician, Math IM, Phil IM
Alternative name: M'ALL, MCCALL, MCALL
        Tower Hill, London
1828–1834   8 Postern Row, Tower Hill, London
Took over from GILKERSON & MCALL★
Known to have sold: octant
Sources: PO; R (JAC); inst MSEN; Holbrook
(1992) p.186

MCCABE James (II)
w 1823–1838
Chrono M
Alternative name: MCCABE, M'CABE
1832–1833   Cornhill, London
Guild: Clockmakers, fr 1822
Son of MCCABE James (I), Clock M, of London
Partnership: MCCABE & STRACHAN★
Succeeded by MCCABE & CO., Robert★
Sources: CUL: RGO 1143 fol.10; Baillie (1951)

MCCABE & CO. Robert
w 1839–1875
Chrono M
1839–1851   32 Cornhill, London
Took over from MCCABE James (II)★
Sources: Pg; PO; Loomes (1976)

MCCABE & STRACHAN ?James & ?Charles
w 1822
Chrono M
1822   32 Cornhill, London
Known to have sold: chronometer
Sources: CUL: RGO 1143 ff.1–4; Taylor (1966)
p.429

MCCOLL Hugh
w 1848
Naut IS, Map S, Book S, Navigation Warehouse
Alternative name: MCOLL
1848   5 King St, South Shields, Dur
Sources: Fordyce (1848)

MCCRAIGHT John Charles
w 1802–1828
Scale M
Alternative name: MACCRAIGHT
1802–1828   88 Goswell St, Aldersgate St,
       London
Guild: Blacksmiths, fr 1776
Son of MCCRAIGHT John, mariner, of Stepney,
London
Apprenticed to THOMPSON John (II)★ 1768
Succeeded by MCCRAIGHT Richard★
Sources: GL: BKC 2881/14; H; J; Pg; R (JAC)

MCCRAIGHT Richard
w 1829–1861
Scale M
1829–1861   94 Goswell St, Aldersgate St,
       London
Guild: [Blacksmiths]
Son of MCCRAIGHT John Charles, painter, of
London
Apprenticed to WYNN John★ 1807
Sources: GL: BKC 2881/16; Pg, PO; R (JAC)

MCCRAW John
a 1800
Merchant
       389 Lawn Market, Edinburgh
Known to have sold: spectacles.
Sources: inst (s) (MAC)

MCCULLOCH Kenneth
w 1777–1802
Math IM, Compass M
Alternative name: M'CULLOCH
       58 Prescot St, Goodman's Fields,
       London
       58 New Buildings in Great Prescot
       St, London
1777   No.3 in Queen Square,
       Bartholomew Close, London
1783–1793   38 Minories, London
1788   28 Minories, London
Partnership: MCCULLOCH & FRAZER★
Had apprentice LAW Charles★ 1788
Pat. compass 1788; R.apt Duke of Clarence; author
Known to have sold: compass, planetarium
Sources: GL: CH, 12876/6; Sun, 11936/258
no.386695 &/319 no.487302; BW; McCulloch
(1789); Crawforth (1985) p.516

**MCCULLOCH & FRAZER Kenneth &
William**
w 1774
Math IM
Alternative name: MC CULLOCH, FRASER
1774   St. Martins in the Fields, London
Had apprentice: (jointly) SONTAG Philip
Succeeded by FRASER William★
See also MCCULLOCH Kenneth★
Sources: PRO: IR 1/28 (AM)

MCCULLOCK Andrew
w 1783–1786
Smith, Hammerman
Alternative name: M'CULLOCK
1783   Argyle St, Glasgow
Guild: Hammermen

Known to have sold: balance
Sources: Tait; NMSn

MCDONALD Alexander
w 1845–1850
Optician
Alternative
Alternative name: McDonald
1845–1848   11 Davie St, Edinburgh
1849–1850   12 Royal Exchange, Edinburgh
Sources: Bryden (1972) p.52

MCDONALD James (I)
w 1847–1852
Phil IM
Alternative name: Mc DONALD
1847–1848   56 Potterow, Edinburgh
1849–1850   36 Lothian St, Edinburgh
1852   4 Hill Place, Edinburgh
See also
Mc DONALD Alexander★
Mc DONALD John★
Sources: Bryden (1972) p.52

MCDONALD John
w 1820–1822
Weather glass M
Alternative name: Mac DONALD
1820–1822   1 North College St, Edinburgh
See also
Mc DONALD Alexander
Mc DONALD James (I)★
Sources: Pg; Goodison (1977) p.337

MCEVOY George
w 1743
1743   Temple Bar, Dublin
Known to have sold: back-staff
Sources: Burnett & Morrison-Low (1989) p.129;
Mollan (1990) p.671

MCGINNES Francis
w 1828–1834
Optician, Math IM
1828   68 Vauxhall Rd, Liverpool
1831–1834   4 Aldemay St, Liverpool
Sources: G

MCGREGOR Duncan
w 1844–1855
Chrono M, Naut IM, Math IM, Optical IM, Chart
S
1836   1 William St, Greenock, Renfrew
1844–1854   24 Clyde Place, Glasgow
1853–1855   8 William St, Greenock, Renfrew
1855   38 Clyde Place, Glasgow
Succeeded by Mc GREGOR & CO. D.
Took over from HERON & Mc GREGOR★
b c.1803, d 1867; B.apt Admiralty
Known to have sold: barometer, octant, sextant,
telescope
Sources: Chr(SK)14 Mar 1985 lot 12; Clarke et al
(1989) p.238–49; Calvert (1971) p.30 & TCd SM

MCINTOSH Thomas
w 1776–1784
Optician
Alternative
Alternative name: MACKINTOSH
       Archimedes & Golden Spectacles,

opposite Long Acre, four doors from Queen St, London

7 Great Queen St, Lincoln's Inn Fields, London

1776–1779 (workshop) Wild St, Queen St, London

1776 33 near Exeter Change in the Strand, London

1780 Great Queen St, Lincolns Inn Fields, London

Archimedes & Golden Spectacles, Great Queen St, Lincoln's Inn Fields, London

1784 40 Great Queen St, Lincoln's Inn Fields, London

Guild: [Spectaclemakers]
Son of MACKINTOSH Daniel, butcher, of Ireland
Apprenticed to HALL Thomas (I)★ 1756
Known to have sold: microscope
Sources: GL: Sun 11936/253 no.377413, /268 no. 402759, /276 no.419100; SMC 5213/5; Kt; Calvert p.30; inst (s)

MCKAY Archibald
w 1702
Alternative name: M'KAY
1702 Glasgow
Guild: Hammermen
Known to have sold: balance
Sources: NMSn

MCKENZIE Alexander
v 1824–1826
Math IM
Alternative name: MCKENZIE
1824–1826 9 Birds Row, Islington, London
See also MACKENZIE Alexander★
Attended London Mechanics Institute 1824–1826
Sources: LMIR (AM)

MCLACHLAN Hugh
w 1828–1846
Chrono M, Watch M
Alternative name: M'LACHLAN
1839–1846 17 Upper East Smithfield, London
Son of MCLACHLAN John, Clock M, of London
Succeeded by MCLACHLAN & SON H.★
Took over from MCLACHLAN John, his father
Sources: Pg; PO; Baillie (1951); Loomes (1976)

MCLACHLAN & SON H.
w 1851
Chrono M
Alternative name: M'LACHLAN
1851 17 Upper East Smithfield, London
Took over from MCLACHLAN Hugh★
Sources: PO

MCLELLAN Samuel
w 1839–1851
Watch M, Chrono M
Alternative name: M'CLELLAN; M'CLELLAND
1839 6 Broadway, Deptford, London
1851 3 Deptford Bridge, London
Sources: PO; Pg

MCMENAMY S.
w 1815–1824

Ship Chandler, Military & Naval Mathematician
1815–1824 93 Rogerson's Quay, Dublin
Took over from MCMENAMY W.★
Sources: Burnett & Morrison-Low (1989) p.129

MCMENAMY W.
w 1810–1815
Ship Chandler, Military & Naval Mathematician
1810–1814 93 Rogerson's Quay, Dublin
1815 11 Poolbeg St, Dublin
Succeeded by MCMENAMY S.★
Sources: Burnett & Morrison-Low (1989) p.129

MCMILLAN Peter
w 1824–1851
Watch M, Clock M, Naut IM
Alternative name: M'MILLAN
1824 11 Guestrow, Aberdeen
1828 Waterlow Quay, Aberdeen
1829–1833 43 Quay, Aberdeen
1834–1839 49 Quay, Aberdeen
1840–1841 52 Quay, Aberdeen
1842–1851 45 Regent Quay, Aberdeen
Guild: Hammermen, fr 1829
Apprenticed to GARTLY John, Clock M, 1821
See also
OGG & MCMILLAN★
MCMILLAN & CO. William★
d 1851
Known to have sold: sextant
Sources: Bryden (1972) p.53; Clarke et al (1989) p.154–55

MCMILLAN & CO. William
w 1847–1848
Watch M, Clock M, Naut IM
Alternative name: M'MILLAN & CO.
1847–1848 28 Marischal St, Aberdeen
Took over from OGG & MCMILLAN★
See also MCMILLAN Peter★
Sources: Bryden (1972) p.53

MCNAB I. & A.
a 1830–1850
Perth
Possibly J. & A. MCNAB, Clock M, of Perth, fl. 1837–1849
Known to have sold: barometer, hygrometer, level, thermometer
Sources: NMS n; Loomes (1976)

MCPHERSON Robert
a 1800–1850
Dumfries
Known to have sold: barometer
Sources: ChrSK 7 Oct 1981 lot 13 (MAC)

MCQUAY William
w 1815–1820
Math IM
1815–1816 29 Great Strand St, Dublin
1817–1820 Bridgefoot St, Dublin
Sources: Wi; Burnett & Morrison-Low (1989) p.130

MCQUEEN John
a 1772
Smith
Bristo, Edinburgh

Known to have sold: balance
Sources: inst (p) (MAC)

MCQUIBAN William
w 1850 d 1884
Watch M
Alternative name: MACQUIBAN
Forres, Moray
Known to have sold: octant, planetarium
Sources: NMSn; FG 6 Feb 1884; Chr 7 Jun 1972 noted by Webster R & M (1988)

MEARS John (I)
a 1770 w 1793
Probably MEARS John, Watch Engraver
Cloth Lane, London
1793 MEARS John, Watch Engraver, was at 48, Cloth Fair, London
See also MUNFORD John★
Known to have sold: sundial
Sources: BSIS 1 (1983) p.7; BW

MEARS John (II)
w 1829–1833
Spec M
1829–1833 9 King St, Westminster, London
Sources: R (JAC)

MEDHURST George
w 1799–1827
Scale M
1811–1827 1 Denmark St, Soho, London
Succeeded by MEDHURST T.F. & F.
Pat. balance 1817
Sources: BM: Banks 103.6; J; K; Pg; PO; R(MAC)

MEDWIN Thomas
w 1851–1852
[Scale M]
1842 6 Streatham Place, Brixton, London
1851 2 Wellington Place, Coldharbour Lane, Camberwell, London
Guild: Blacksmiths, fr 1842
Son of MEDWIN William West, parish clerk, of London
Apprenticed to
GORE Thomas Hunsdon★ 1827
WILLIAMS Thomas★ by t/o 1832
Had apprentice:
KNOWLES William 1851
NICOLL Frederick 1852
Sources: GL: BKC 2881/18 (MAC)

MELBOURNE Richard
w 1631
Known to have sold: astrolabe
Sources: inst SM

MELLER Joseph
w 1823–1825
Math IM
Alternative name: MELLOR
1823–1825 28 Princep St, Birmingham
Partnership: NORRIS & MELLER★
Sources: Pg; Wr

MELLING John
w 1672 d by 1704

Lens grinder
Alternative name: MELLIN, MALLING
    Abchurch Lane, Lombard St, London
Associated with HOOKE Robert
Known to have sold: barometer, lens
Sources: Court & Von Rohr (1929–30) p. 74; Robinson & Adams (1935) p.451; Taylor (1954) p.265

MELLING & CO. Edward
w 1846–1851
Optician, Chrono M, Math IM
1846–1851 39 South Castle St, Liverpool
Succeeded by JEWITT & CO. W.
Took over from MELLING & PAYNE★
See also DAWSON, MELLING & PAYNE★
Known to have sold: barometer
Sources: G; Sl; inst (s)

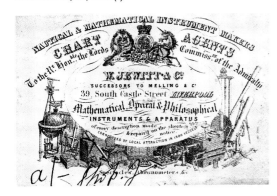

MELLING & PAYNE
w 1843–1845
Opticians, Chrono M, Navigation Warehouse
1843–1845 39 South Castle St, Liverpool
Succeeded by MELLING & CO. Edward★
Took over from DAWSON, MELLING & PAYNE★
Known to have sold: sextant
Sources: G; inst (p)

MELLISH Robert (I)
d by 1760
Rule M
    Parish of St Saviour, Southwark, London
Father of MELLISH Robert (II) s1760 to JONES William (III)★
Sources: GL: TC 3302/3

MELVILLE Richard
w 1832–1871
Sundial M
Alternative name: Alias MELVIN
1832–1842 Ulster
1845–1851 Glasgow
1846   160 Saltmarket St, Glasgow
1856   Liverpool
1858   London
1864–1871 Dublin
1871   9 Lower Wellington St, Dublin
Known to have sold: sundial
Sources: Chr(SK) 2 Jul 1992 lots 205–6; Clarke et al (1989) p.210–16

MELVILLE & CO. George
fl 1830
Optician
   126 Great Hampton St, Birmingham
   17 Thavies Inn, Holborn, London
Sources: Taylor (1966) p.455 [not confirmed]

MELVIN Richard – see MELVILLE

MELVIN Robert
w 1755
Math IM
1755   London
Sources: *The Public Advertiser* 2 Oct 1755 (MAC)

MENZIES Alexander
w 1847
Optician, Cutler
1847   18 Kings Parade, Cambridge
Sources: K

MERCER –
w 1672
IS
1672   The Feathers in Fleet St, London
Associated with NASH John★ [retailer of Nash rules]
Known to have sold: rule
Sources: Loomes (1981b); GL: CKC 2710/1 p.244

MEREDITH James
w 1799
Math IM
1799   5 St.Mary-Over's Churchyard, Southwark, London
See also MEREDITH Nicholas★
Sources: H

MEREDITH Nicholas
w 1789–1793
Optical IM, Math IM, Optician
   99 New Bond St, London
1793   91 New Bond St, London
See also MEREDITH James★
Sources: A; K; W; Taylor (1966) p.345

MERFIELD James William
w 1844–1848
Optical Turner, Optician
Alternative name: MERSFIELD, MIRFIELD
1825   Goswell St, London
1844   10 Huggin Lane, Cheapside, London
1847–1848 20 Change Alley, Cornhill, London
c.1850   USA
1853–1858 Melbourne, Australia
Son of MERFIELD William★
b 1825 d 1901; attended London Mechanics Institute 1844 & 1847–1848
Sources: PRO: Cs 1841 HO 107/721 Bk12 (VM); PO (VM); LMIR (AM); GLRO: St James Clerkenwell bap

MERFIELD William
w 1846–1847
Cutler & Optician
1820–1832 Goswell St, London
1837–1843 4 Cateaton St, London
1843–1845 10 Huggin Lane, London

1846–1847 20 Change Alley, Cornhill, London
1856–1857 20 Budge Row, London
Guild: Clockmakers, fr 1825
Father of MERFIELD James William★
Son of MERFIELD James, cutler, of Fetter Lane, London
Apprenticed to MERFIELD James, his father, 1818
b 1798
Sources: CLRO: CF1/1521 (VM): Pg; PO; R; GL: CKC 2720/2; St Andrew Holborn, bap (VM)

MERLIN John Joseph
w 1760 d 1803
Math IM, Harpsichord M, Proprietor of Merlin's Mechanical Museum
1760   London
1763   At Mr Sutton's, goldsmith, at the Acorn in New Street, near Covent Garden, London
1773   42 Little Queen Ann St, London
1780   66 Queen Ann St, Portland Chapel, London
1783   11 Princes St, Hanover Square, London
1792   Princes St, Hanover Square, London
Worked for COX James, goldsmith and owner of Cox's Museum
Employed:
JENKINS Sylvanus
SHELDON Samuel
Inventor, pat.roasting jack 1773, harpsichord 1774; b 1735 at Huys, in the Bishopric of Liège
Sources: GLC (1985); Pat. office: records of patents (MAC)

MERONE Joseph
w 1800–1841
Baro M, Looking-glass M
Alternative name: Joseph Anthony
1800   Market St, Manchester
1814–1822 98 Market St, Manchester
1822–1841 28 Market St, Manchester
Partnership: ZANETTI Vittore★, ZANETTI Vincent★ & MERONE Joseph as ZANETTI & Co.★
Ceased business about 1845
Sources: WB; Goodison (1977); Ronchetti (1990)

MESSENGER George
w 1834–1836
Math IM
1834–1836 31 Brunswick St, London
Attended London Mechanics Institute 1834–1836
Sources: LMIR (AM)

MESSER Benjamin
w 1789–1827
Math IM, Optician, Phil IM, Ship chandler
1789   75 Wapping, London
1793–1797 76 Wapping, London
1794–1796 76 Bell Dock Wapping, London
1805–1827 155 Minories, London
Guild: Makers of Playing Cards, fr 1801
Apprenticed to HUSSEY John★ 1769
Had apprentice:
ROBINSON Jeremiah Lagden 1803
LEAR Anthony James 1804★
HARRIS Solomon 1806
ROXFORD Charles Inglis 1812

CRICHTON John★ 1820
fr 1801 by purchase, Master MPC 1805–1808
Known to have sold: octant
Sources: GL: MPC, 5968/1, 5969/1, 5963/5;
Stimson (1985); A; Bn; BW; H; J; Ld; Pg

MESSER John
w 1839
Optician, Math IM
1839   25 West St, Gravesend, Kent
See also MESSER John James★ (possibly the same
person)
Sources: Pg

MESSER John James
w 1845–1880
Optician, Math IM, Naut IM, Phil IM, Telescope
M
1845   4 Harmer St, Gravesend, Kent
1849–1859   19 & 20 King St, Commercial Road
             East, London
1865–1880   78 & 80 Christian St, London E
Succeeded by MESSER George Bracher
See also Messer John★ (possibly the same person)
Sources: PO; PO(HC)

MESSMORE Anthony
w 1787
Clock M, Baro M
1787   Marshall St, Liverpool
Sources: G; LM index (MAC)

MEYMOTT Clement
w 1767–1793
Scale M, Tallow Chandler
Alternative name: MAYMOTT
1777–1778   Parish of St Ethelburga, London
1793   Bishopsgate St, London
Guild: Blacksmiths, fr 1766
Father of MEYMOTT Samuel s 1778 to CAMBDEN
Mary, VC
Husband of MEYMOTT Mercy★
Had apprentice:
HARRIS James 1767
EVERITT George★ 1769
RUBIDGE James★ 1774
CRAKE Carolina 1777 by t/o from LOWDEN
Silvester, DPC
LOADER William Camden 1791
Succeeded by MEYMOTT & SON Clement★
Sources: GL:VC 15220/3 p.145; BKC
2881/13–16; Wil; DH: DPC Ap/Fr

MEYMOTT Mercy
w 1768 c 1775
Scale M
Alternative name: READ
             Within Bishopsgate, London
Guild: Blacksmiths
Wife of
READ Joseph★, widow 1764
MEYMOTT Clement★ by 1768
Had apprentice:
PORTER John★ 1764 by t/o from READ Joseph★
See also
MEYMOTT Samuel★
MEYMOTT & PORTER★
Entry under READ Mercy★

Known to have sold: balance, weights
Sources: GL: BKC 2881/13–14 (MAC); inst,
Spalding Mu; Sheppard & Musham (1975) nos
22,42,44

MEYMOTT Samuel
w 1793–1834
Scale M
Alternative name: MAYMOTT
             64, Corner of Wormwood St,
             Bishopsgate, London
1785   Bishopsgate St, London
1810–1834   64 Bishopsgate Street Within,
             London
Guild: Vintners, fr 1785
Son of
MEYMOTT Clement★
MEYMOTT Mercy★
Partnership: MEYMOTT & SON Clement★
Apprenticed to CAMBDEN Mary, of New Tavern,
Kensington, 1778
Sources: GL: VC 15220/2 p.145, 15209/1 f.3; BW;
J; K; Pg; PO; Wil

MEYMOTT & PORTER Clement & John
w 1783–1797
Scale M
1783–1796   Bishopsgate Without, London
1785   Corner of Wormwood St,
             Bishopsgate Within [sic], London
1790   202 Bishopsgate St, London
1792–1797   203 Bishopsgate St, London
See also
MEYMOTT Mercy★
READ Joseph★ (firm claimed to be "late Read")
READ Mercy★
Known to have sold: balance
Sources: GL: Sun 11936/326 no.503075; By; Ld;
W; inst SM Wellcome

MEYMOTT & SON Clement
w 1793–1809
Scale M
             203 Bishopsgate Street Without,
             London
1793–1799   64 Bishopsgate Without, London
1795   Corner of Wormwood St,
             Bishopsgate, London
1805–1811   64 Bishopsgate Within, London
Related to MEYMOTT Mercy★
Succeeded by MEYMOTT Samuel★
See also
MEYMOTT & PORTER★
READ Joseph★ (firm claimed to be "late Read")
Sources: BM: Heal 103.9; BW; H; K; Ld; PO

MICHAEL Isaac
w 1815–1816
Clock M, Watch M, Silversmith, Spec M,
Furniture Warehouse
1815–1816   67 Broadmead, Bristol
1815   (Warehouse) 68 Broadmead, Bristol
Sources: H; Mat

MICHAEL & MARKS
w 1850
Optician, Math IM
1850   194 High St, Sunderland, Dur

See also MARKS Abraham Isaac★
Sources: Wd

MIDDLEFELL Damaine
w 1739
Optical IM
1739   Newcastle upon Tyne
Guild: ?Spectaclemakers, fr 1719
Son of probably, MIDDLEFELL Thomas, tanner, of
Penrith, Cumb
Apprenticed to probably, COOBEROW Matthew★
1705
Sources: GL: SMC, 5213/2 p.47,111; NJ 21 Apr
1739

MIDDLETON William
w 1792
Rule M
1792   65 Bilston Rd, Wolverhampton
Sources: Wolverhampton rate books (MAC)

MILES Lawrence
w 1720–1753
Math IM
Alternative name: MYLES
1737–1742   Ditchside, London
1743–1753   Flower de Luce Court, Fleet St,
             London
Guild: Joiners
Father of MILES Thomas, s 1736 STC
Son of MILES Thomas, tailor, of St. Clement
Danes, London
Apprenticed to CROOKE John (I)★ 1701
Had apprentice:
PEEL William 1717
CHALKHILL John★ 1720/1
MORGAN John★ 1726
Sources: GL: JC 8051/3–4, 8052/3–4, 8055/1;
Crawforth (1987) p.360–61; McKenzie (1978) p.4

MILES William
w 1838–1842
Rule M
1838–1839   21 Stonecutter St, Farringdon St,
             London
1840–1842   24 Great New St, Fetter Lane, London
Sources: Pg; PO

MILES William Henry
w 1828–1874
Scale M
1824   At his Master's, 98 Great Guildford
             St, London
1828–1839   80 Old Street Rd, London
1840–1874   200 Shoreditch High St, London
Guild: Blacksmiths, fr 1824
Son of MILES William, oilman, of Spitalfields,
London
Apprenticed to PECK John★ 1817
Sources: GL: BKC 2881/17 (MAC); Pg; PO

MILESIO D.
a 1800–1820
[Baro M]
             Belfast
See also MILESSIO Dominick★
Known to have sold: barometer
Sources: Goodison (1977) p.341

MILESON Abel
w 1838–1843
Math IM, Phil IM
1838–1843   23 Emmett St, Limehouse Hole,
             Limehouse, London
Succeeded by MILESON Abel Kitching★
Sources: Pg

MILESON Abel Kitching
w 1844–1868
Optician, Math IM
1845–1865   23 Emmett St, Poplar, London
Took over from MILESON Abel★
Sources: PO; Wk

MILESSIO Dominick
w 1812–1825
Baro M, Mirror M, Carver, Gilder
Alternative name: MILESSIO, MILESCO,
1812   25 High St, Dublin
1813–1819   35 Skinner Row, Dublin
1820–1824   6 Skinner Row, Dublin
1825   11 Skinner Row, Dublin
             ?Belfast
See also MILESIO D.★
Known to have sold: barometer, thermometer
Sources: Burnett & Morrison-Low p.131–32
Goodison (1977) p.341

MILLAR Richard
w 1845–1868
Clock M, Watch M, Naut IM
1845–1851   45 Bridge St, Leith, Midlothian
1852–1868   58 Bridge St, Leith, Midlothian
Son of MILLAR Richard, Clock M, of Leith
See also LAIRD David White★
Known to have sold: compass (magnetic)
Instruments advertised: rule
Sources: Bryden (1972) p.54; Clarke et al (1989)
p.107; inst (s)

MILLARD John (I)
w 1849–1880
Optician
1836–1840   24 Coppice Row, Clerkenwell,
             London
1849–1851   5 York Place, Upper St, Islington,
             London
1859–1875   93 Upper St, Islington, London
1880   322 Upper St, Islington, London
Partnership: probably, MILLARD & SON
Succeeded by MILLARD Mrs
Same premises as MILLARD Joseph★
Attended London Mechanics Institute 1836–1838,
1839–1840
Sources: PO; LMIR (AM)

MILLARD John (II)
w 1837
Optician
1837   29 Clarendon St, Somers Town,
             London
Attended London Mechanics Institute 1837
Sources: LMIR (AM)

MILLARD Joseph (I)
w 1834
Spec M, Optician

1834   24 Coppice Row, Clerkenwell,
             London
Succeeded by MILLARD & SON Joseph★
See also MILLARD & SONS Joseph★
Sources: R, JAC

MILLARD Joseph (II)
w 1851
Optician
1851   1 Union Row, Camberwell Road,
             London
See also
MILLARD Joseph (I)★
MILLARD & SONS Joseph★
Sources: PO

MILLARD Thomas
w 1849–1865
Optician
Alternative name: MILARD, Thomas G.S.
1837–1838   32 Coppice Row, Clerkenwell,
             London
1843–1844   32 Alfred St, Islington, London
1849–1851   335 Oxford St, London
1855–1865   334 Oxford St, London
Succeeded by MILLARD & SON Thomas
See also
MILLARD Joseph★
MILLARD John (I)★
Attended London Mechanics Institute 1837–1838,
1843–1844
Sources: PO; LMIR (AM)

MILLARD & SON Joseph
w 1835–1840
Optician, Spec M
1835–1840   24 Coppice Row, Clerkenwell,
             London
Succeeded by MILLARD & SONS Joseph★
Took over from MILLARD Joseph★
Same premises as MILLARD John (I)★
Sources: PO; R (JAC)

MILLARD & SONS Joseph
w 1842–1853
Opticians
1842–1849   24 Coppice Row, Clerkenwell,
             London
Succeeded by MILLARD Mary
Took over from MILLARD & SON Joseph★
Sources: PO

MILLER George
w 1819
Math IM
1819   116 Stockwell, Glasgow
Took over from MILLER & McCOLL★
Sources: Bryden (1972) p.54

MILLER John
w 1774–1803
Math IM, Phil IM, Optical IM
             Nicholson St, Edinburgh
             George IV Bridge, Edinburgh
1774   Back of the Fountain Well,
             Edinburgh
1775–1794   Parliament Close, Edinburgh
1795–1801   38 South Bridge, Edinburgh

1803–1804   86 South Bridge, Edinburgh
Apprenticed to possibly YEAMAN John★
Had apprentice ADIE Alexander★, his nephew,
c.1787
Worked for ADAMS George (I)★
Succeeded by MILLER & ADIE★
b 1746 d 1815
Known to have sold: barometer, clinometer, globe,
micrometer, microscope, planetarium, theodolite
Sources: Bryden (1972) p.11–12,21,54; Clarke et al
(1989) p.25–31

MILLER Thomas (I)
a 1700–1800
[Dial M]
             Knowle, War
Known to have sold: sundial
Sources: Lyle (1982) (MAC)

MILLER Thomas (II)
w 1780–1794
Stationer, Math IS, Phil IS, Musical IS
1780–1794   Halesworth, Suffolk
Sources: GL: REI 7253/5 no.79623; BW

MILLER & ADIE John & Alexander
w 1804–1822
Math IM, Phil IM, Optical IM
1804–1806   94 Nicolson St, Edinburgh
1807–1809   96 Nicolson St, Edinburgh
1810   8 Nicolson St. Edinburgh
1811–1820   15 Nicolson St, Edinburgh
Succeeded by ADIE Alexander★
Took over from MILLER John★
Miller d 1815
Known to have sold: barometer, level, microscope,
telescope, theodolite balance
Sources: Clarke et al (1989)
p.25–31,66–67; Bryden (1972) p.54

MILLER & MCCOLL
w 1818
Math IM
Alternative name: M'COLL
1818   116 Stockwell, Glasgow
Succeeded by MILLER George★
Sources: Bryden (1972) p.54

MILLS George
w 1790–1846
Optical IM, Phil IM, Math IM
1790–1830   Hermitage Yard, Wapping, London
1826–1845   82 Parsons St, Ratcliff Highway,
             London
             or 82 Parsons St, East Smithfield,
             London
1846   82 St. George St, London
Guild: Joiners, fr 1790
Apprenticed to
WILLCOX Walton 1782★
SPENCER William (II)★ by t/o 1783
Had apprentice: RANDALL Richard 1799
Sources: GL: JC 8046/12; Pg; PO (MAC); R
(JAC); Crawforth (1987) p.361

MILLS Harriett (Mrs)
w 1851–1869
Optician, Telescope M

1851–1869   49 Southampton St, Pentonville, London
Took over from MILLS Robert★
Succeeded by MILLS Alfred
Sources: PO

MILLS Robert
w 1820–1850
Telescope M, Optician
     7 Southampton St, Pentonville, London
     31 Duke St, Lincoln's Inn Fields, London
1822   35 Duke St, Lincoln's Inn Fields, London
1839–1849   49 Southampton St, Pentonville, London
1841   Insured private house at 12 Thomas Street, Woolwich, London
Succeeded by MILLS Harriett★
Said by Lewis to have absorbed W. & T. Tulley, but no evidence cited.
Sources: Bn; PO; R (JAC); GL: Sun, 11936/575 no.1360898 (AM); Lewis (1984)

MILNE John
fr 1742 w 1767
Alternative name: I.
     Edinburgh
Guild: Hammermen
Succeeded by MILNE & SON John★
d.c 1810
Known to have sold: weights
Sources: inst (pv); NMS n

MILNE & SON John
w 1767–1806
Founder, Ironmonger
1767   The Golden Church, Branch Bishop's Land, High St, Edinburgh
1805–1806   High St, Edinburgh
Took over from MILNE John★
Known to have sold: balance
Sources: POE; *Edinburgh Ad* 14 Sep 1773 (MAC); inst (pv) (MAC); Calvert (1971) p.32

MINOLLA James
a 1795–1805
     London
Known to have sold: barometer, thermometer
Sources: Bolle (1982) p.157

MITCHELL F.
a 1800–1850
Optician
     Market Harboro'
Known to have sold: barometer, thermometer
Sources: inst (s) (MAC)

MITCHELL George
w 1833–1854
Optician
1833–1837   East St, Park, Sheffield
1837   57 High St, Park, Sheffield (residence)
1854   93 South St, Park, Sheffield
Sources: K (DJB); Wh

MITCHELL Richard
w 1773
Math IM
1773   Cork
Sources: Burnett & Morrison-Low (1989) p.152

MITCHELL Robert
w 1816–1817
Math IM
1816–1817   65 Lower East Smithfield, London
Took over from MITCHELL & BALE★
Sources: Kt (JAC)

MITCHELL & BALE Robert ? & David ?
w 1811–1816
Math IM
Alternative name: MITCHEL
1811–1816   65 Lower East Smithfield, London
Succeeded by MITCHELL Robert★
See also BALE David★
Sources: PO; Und

MOFFETT Elizabeth
w 1787–1800 [probably w pt 1787–1798]
Scale M
1787–1800   126 Minories, London
Guild: Haberdashers
Had apprentice:
WHITE William (II)★ 1787
HEARD Thomas (I)★ 1789
Succeeded by MOFFETT & BLACKBURN★
See also
MOFFETT James★
MOFFETT & SON James★
MOFFETT & SON Elizabeth★
MOFFETT James Thomas★
Instruments advertised: balance, weights
Sources: GL: HC15860/9 (MAC); PO; TCd (pv)

MOFFETT James
w 1756–1783
Scale M
Alternative name: MOFFAT
1762–1783   126 Minories, London
Guild: Haberdashers, fr 1755
Father of MOFFETT James Thomas★
Son of MOFFETT Robert, brazier, of London
Apprenticed to SWITHIN John★ 1748
Had apprentice:
VANDOME Richard★ 1773
MOFFETT James Thomas★ 1774
BLACKBURN John★ 1781
and six others 1762–1779
Worked for VINCENT Robert★
Succeeded by MOFFETT & SON Elizabeth★
See also MOFFETT & SON James★
Educated at Christ's Hospital School, London
Sources: GL: HC 15860/8, 15860/9, 15857/2; CH 12876/4, 12823/5 p.1

MOFFETT James Thomas
w 1782–1798 [probably as partner 1782–1790]
Scale M
Alternative name: MOFFATT Thomas
     Opposite Haydon Yard in the Minories, London
1782–1783   37 Crooked Lane, Common St, London

1790–1798   Justice & Scales, 126 Minories, London
Guild: Haberdashers, Blacksmiths
Apprenticed to MOFFETT James★, his father, 1774
Had apprentice:
FLETCHER Samuel★ 1782 HC
PUGH William 1783 BKC
HODGETTS Samuel★ 1787 HC
DRAPER Jabez 1790 HC
ROBINSON John 1795 HC
DODD John 1797 HC
MARTIN William Hood 1798 HC
Took over from MOFFETT & SON James★
Succeeded by MOFFETT Elizabeth★
d by 1804; fp HC 1781; fr BKC by purchase 1783
Known to have sold: balance
Instruments advertised: balance, steelyard, weights
Sources: GL: HC 15860/9, 15857/3; BKC 2881/15, 2881/17 (MAC); Kt (JAC); W; Wil; inst (pv); Heal (1957) p.151

MOFFETT & BLACKBURN Elizabeth & John ?
w 1801–1807
Scale M
1801–1807   126 Minories, London
Succeeded by BLACKBURN John★
See also MOFFETT Elizabeth★
Known to have sold: balance, weights
Instruments advertised: balance, weights
Sources: H; PO (JAC); inst (pv) (MAC); Phlps 2 Dec 1987 lot 82; Calvert (1971) p.32

MOFFETT & SON Elizabeth
w 1783–1789
Scale M
1783–1789   Justice & Scales, 126 Minories, London
Succeeded by MOFFETT & SON James★
Took over from MOFFETT James★
See also MOFFETT James Thomas★
Known to have sold: balance
Sources: A; Bd (MAC); By; Kt (JAC); inst (pv) (MAC)

MOFFETT & SON James
w 1789–1790
Scale M
1789–1790   126 Minories, London
Succeeded by MOFFETT James Thomas★
Took over from MOFFET & SON Elizabeth★
See also MOFFETT James★
Sources: A (JAC)

MOLAND Joseph
w 1694–1715
Surveyor, Instrument M
     Dublin
Had apprentice:
MILLER Joseph★ between 1694 & 1701
STOKES Gabriel★ 1696
CARROLL William 1699
SOUCH William 1715
Sources: KH (WS)

MOLE Widow
a 1770
     Chiswell St, London

See also MOLE William (I)★
Known to have sold: rule
Sources: inst (s) (MAC)

MOLE William (I)

w 1750–1751
Gauging IM
        Ye Axe in Grub St, London
1750   Mariner & Globe in Chiswell St,
        London
Guild: [Joiners] Turners fp 1751
Son of MOLE Michael, free of TC of London
Apprenticed to COOKE Thomas★ 1721/2 JC
See also
MOLE William (II)★
MOLE Widow★
Known to have sold: gauge
Sources: GL: TC 3303; Crawforth (1987) p.361;
Darius (1985) p.18–19

MOLE William (II)

w 1811
Rule M
1811   3 Star Court, Grub St, London
Father of MOLE William Edward s 1811 HC
See also MOLE William (I)★
Sources: GL: HC 15860/9

MOLINARI Antonio

w 1830
Baro M, Thermo M, Jewellery Dealer
1830   Halesworth, Suffolk
Sources: Pg

MOLL Herman

w 1678 d 1732
Engraver, Geographer, Map S
1688–1691 Vanley's Court, Black Fryers
        [Blackfriars], London
After 1691? Spring Gardens, Charing Cross,
        London
        Westminster Hall, London
1710–1732 Over against Devereux Court in the
        Strand, London
Published a pocket globe 1719
Sources: inst NMM; Tyacke (1978) p.122–23

MOLLINER Charles

fl 1784–1801
Baro M
Alternative name: MOLINER
1784   Baillie Grant's Close, Edinburgh
1786–1790 Netherbow, Edinburgh
1794   High St, Edinburgh
1799–1801 Baron Grant's Close, Edinburgh
See also KNIE Balthazar★, who made barometers of
similar design
Known to have sold: barometer
Sources: Bryden (1972) p.54; Goodison (1977)
p.173, 342

MOLLISON Alexander

w 1814–1834
Math IM, Phil IM
1814–1834 17 Chapman St, Islington, London
See also MOLLISON John★
Sources: GL: Sun 11936/463 no.899266; Pg

MOLLISON John

w 1779–1789
Math IM
1779–1789 47 Water Lane, Blackfriars, London
Guild: Needlemakers, fr 1778 by purchase
Had apprentice: EVANS Hugh Robert 1779
Partnership: MOLLISON & SAUNDERS★
See also MOLLISON Alexander★
Associated with TROUGHTON John (II)★, for
whom he made sextants
Described as a 'Garret Master' employing several
hands & working for the leading IM who kept shops
Sources: GL: NC 2817/2, CH 12876/6; MHS: MS
Evans 18 (AVS); McConnell (1994b) p.45

MOLLISON & SAUNDERS John & Richard

w 1774
Math IM
1774   Addle Hill, London
See also
SAUNDERS Robert (II)★
SAUNDERS Samuel (II)★
SAUNDERS Richard (I)★
MOLLISON John★
Sources: Daily Ad 11 Oct 1774 (MAC)

MOLTENI Alexander

w 1829–1830
Baro M, Thermo M
1829–1830 13 Baldwin's Gardens, Leather Lane,
        London
Succeeded by MOLTENI & CO.★
See also
BATTISTESSA, MOLTENI & GUANZIROLI★
ZERBONI, BATTISTESSA, MOLTENI &
GUANZIROLI★
Sources: R (JAC); Goodison (1977) p.342

MOLTENI A.

w 1851–1858
Baro M
1851–1853 185 Pilgrim St, Newcastle upon
        Tyne
1855–1856 154 Pilgrim St, Newcastle upon
        Tyne
1857–1858 152 Pilgrim St, Newcastle upon
        Tyne
1857–1858 91 Clayton St, Newcastle upon Tyne
See also MOLTENI Christmas★
Sources: Wln; Goodison (1977) p.342

MOLTENI Christmas

w pt 1836 w 1856
Baro M, Toy S
1836–1838 Grainger St, Newcastle upon Tyne
1856   47 Grainger St, Newcastle upon
        Tyne
1856   Collingwood St, Newcastle upon
        Tyne
Partnership: MASTAGLIO, FORNELLI &
MOLTENI★
See also: MOLTENI A.★
Sources: Ric; Wln; Goodison (1977) p.342

MOLTENI & CO.

w 1831
Baro M, Thermo M

1831   13 Baldwin's Gardens, Leather Lane,
        London
Took over from MOLTENI Alexander★
See also
BATTISTESSA, MOLTENI & GUANZIROLI★
ZERBONI, BATTISTESSA, MOLTENI &
GUANZIROLI★
Sources: PO

MOLTON Francis

w 1822–1830
Optician, Baro M, Thermo M
        55 Lawrence Steps, Norwich
1822–1830 Dove Lane, Norwich
1830   Dove St, Norwich
Known to have sold: barometer, thermometer.
Sources: Pg; Banfield (1976) p.65–67; Goodison
(1977) p.342

MOLYNEUX Emery

w 1592 d 1598/9
Compass M
Alternative name: MULLINAUX
        Lambeth, London
Author; first English globe maker
Known to have sold: compass, globe, sandglass
Sources: Bryden (1992) p.310; Dekker & van der
Krogt (1993) p.177; Taylor (1954) p.188, 330–32,
338: inst NT, Petworth House, Sussex

MOLYNEUX Robert & H.

w 1834–1839
Chrono M, Watch M
1834–1839 30 Southampton Row, Russell
        Square, London
Sent chronometers for trial at Royal Greenwich
Observatory
Sources: CUL: RGO 1143 fol.10; Pg

MOLYNEUX & SONS Robert

w 1825–1833
Chrono M
1825–1830 44 Devonshire St, Queen Square,
        London
1830–1833 30 Southampton Row, Russell
        Square, London
Sent chronometers for trial at Royal Greenwich
Observatory
Sources: CUL: RGO 1143 fol.2–10

MONAGHAN James

w 1761–1762
Baro M
1761–1762 Wine Tavern St, Dublin
Sources: Wi; Burnett & Morrison-Low (1989) p.132

MONDAY Charles

w 1831–1845
Spec M
1831   8 Henry St, St.Lukes, London
1834   16 Bittern St, Liverpool
1835   14 Vine St, Liverpool
1837   15 Upper Stanhope St, Windsor,
        Liverpool
1839–1841 16 Stanhope St, Windsor, Liverpool
1845–1846 22 Spekefield Cottages, Liverpool
1865–1885 123 Mulberry St, E. Liverpool
        Sources: G; R (JAC)

MONK John
w 1768–1785
Clock M
       London
Guild: [Clockmakers]
Son of MONK Gilbert, carpenter, d, of Soho, London
Apprenticed to GOUJON Stephen, clock M, 1762
Known to have sold: pyrometer, regulator
Sources: GL: CKC 2720/1 fol.4v; King & Millburn (1978) p.145; Taylor (1966) p.293

MONKS James
w 1811
Optician
1811   Parish of St Olaves, Southwark, London
Father of MONKS James John s 1811 to SAWGOOD John★
Sources: GL: BKC 2881/17

MOON John
w 1826–1867
Optician, Phil IM, Math IM
      4 Lucas Place, Commercial Rd, London
1830   3 Lucas Place, Commercial Rd, London
1838–1839 28 Green St, Stepney, London
1845–1849 76 Minories, London
1849–1850 31½ Limekiln Hill, London
1850   2 St.Ann's Place, Commercial Rd, London
Son of MOON William★
Partnership: MOON & FLEMING★
Took over from MOON William★
Partnership 1841–1846
Sources: Pg; PO; TCd MHS (RMS); JAC

MOON William
fr 1791 w 1817
Optician
1791   At Mr Dolland's, London
1811   35 Northampton St, Clerkenwell, London
1816   49 Fleet Lane, Old Bailey, London
Guild: Spectaclemakers, fr 1791
Father of MOON John★
Apprenticed to DOLLOND John (II)★ 1782
Worked for DOLLOND John (II)★
Succeeded by MOON John★
Sources: GL: SMC 5213/3, 5213/4; Und; TCd MHS (RMS)

MOON & FLEMING
w 1841–1843
Optician
1841–1843 76 Minories, London
See also MOON John★
Sources: PO

MOONE Thomas
w 1667–1669
Math IM (in metal)
      Bristol
Sources: Bryden (1992) p.306

MOOR James
w 1788–1801
Optical IM
1788–1790 Opposite the Guard, Edinburgh
1793   17 Parliament Close, Edinburgh
1794   15 Parliament Close, Edinburgh
1801   Robertson's Close, Edinburgh
Sources: Bryden (1972) p.54

MOORE –
a 1750–1850
      Ipswich
Known to have sold: waywiser
Sources: Holbrook (1992) p.104; inst noted by MAC

MOORE Edward
w 1751–1757
Globe M, Teacher
1751–1757 Deptford, London
Sources: Wallis R. & P. (1986) p.378

MOORE John Hamilton
w 1781–1805
Navigation Warehouse, Hydrographer, Math IS
Alternative name: I.H.
1781–1786 104 in the Minories, Tower Hill, London
1790   King St, Little Tower Hill, London
1799–1805 2 King St, Tower Hill, London
See also BLATCHFORD & IMRAY★
Associated with
RAMSDEN Jesse★
TROUGHTON John (II)★
Hydrographer to Duke of Clarence
Sources: GL: Sun 11936/296 no.451400, /340 no.525580; BW; H; Stimson (1985) p.101,112,114

MOORE Lewis
w 1769–1774
Scale M
1769–1774 Fisher's Lane, Dublin
See also MOORE William (III)
Sources: Wi (AL)

MOORE Thomas
w 1826–1828
Optician
1826–1828 3 Bridge St, Southwark, London
Sources: R (JAC)

MOORE William (I)
w 1647–1648
[Scale M]
      London
Guild: Blacksmiths, fr 1647
Son of MOORE John, farmer, of Shenley, Bucks
Apprenticed to SAUNDERS Robert (I)★ 1640
Had apprentice:
BASHER Henry 1647/8
MEDGEWICK Walter 1648
MOORE Humphrey 1648
Sources: GL: BKC 2881/5, 2881/7 (MAC)

MOORE William (II)
fl 1751–1788
[Math IM]
      55 Paternoster Row, London

See also apprentice of SAUNDERS Samuel (II)★
apprentice of BASS George★
Known to have sold: back-staff
Sources: Taylor (1966) p.241

MOORE William (III)
w 1774–1781
Jeweller
1780   1 Capel St, Dublin
1780   39 Temple Bar, Dublin
See also MOORE Lewis
Known to have sold: weights
Sources: Wi; Westropp (1916) p.66

MORDEN Robert
fl 1650 d 1703
Instrument S, Map S, Globe S
1669   Atlas in New Cheapside, London
1671–1702 Atlas in Cornhill, near the Royal Exchange, London
Guild: Weavers
Had apprentice:
WARD Mary 1674
LEA Philip 1675
Associated with
BERRY William★ in selling globes
WEYBOURNE William, whose books he published and sold
WATSON Samuel★ in selling books
Author; publisher; supplied globes and math inst to Christ's Hospital School, London
Sources: GL: CH 12823/2 p.289; WVC 4657A/1, 4657A/2; Tyacke (1978) p.123

MORGAN Francis
w 1764–1772
Optical IM, Phil IM, Math IM
      New Street Square, London
1764–1766 Carey St, London
1767–1771 Archimedes & Three Spectacles, 27 Ludgate St, nr. St.Paul's, London
1772–1803 St.Petersburg, Russia
Guild: Joiners, fp 1764
Son of MORGAN John★
Apprenticed to MORGAN John★, his father, 1757
Had apprentice:
THOMPSON Robert 1764
MAGNIAC Francis 1765
BUTLER James★ 1765
Petitioner against Dollond's patent 1764; B.apt Office of Ordnance; appointed Optician and Math IM to Empress of Russia 1771; d 1803 in Russia
Instruments advertised: full range
Sources: PRO: PC 1/7 no.94; GL: JC 8052/7; BM: Heal 105/73; Ld; Crawforth (1987) p.361–62; Millburn (1988b) p.281–82

MORGAN John
w 1746 d 1758
Math IM
1755   Finch Lane, Cornhill, London
1758   Fleet St, London
      Birchin Lane, London
Guild: Joiners, fr 1733
Son of MORGAN Jacob, carver, late of St Giles, Middx (London)
Apprenticed to LAWRENCE Miles★ 1726

Had apprentice:
MAILLET Abraham 1745/6
TANGATE Robert★ 1752
FOWLER John William 1753
MORGAN Francis★, his son, 1757
OAKLEY John 1757
Employed WATT James★
Known to have sold: compass (magnetic), sextant
Sources: inst NMS; GL: JC 8052/6; *Daily Ad*
24 Nov 1758; Crawforth (1987) p.362; Muirhead
(1858) p.36,43

MORGAN John Thomas
w 1838
Math IM, Phil IM
1838   7 Crown St, Hoxton Square,
              London
Sources: Pg

MORLEY George
w 1836–1839
Optician, Math IM, Phil IM
1836   80 High St, Whitechapel, London
1839   84 High St, Whitechapel, London
See also MORLEY Joseph★
Sources: Pg

MORLEY Joseph
s 1796 w 1806
Math IM
1804–1806   1 Little Thames St, St.Catherine's,
             London
Guild: [Grocers]
Apprenticed to MORRIS William (I)★ 1796
See also MORLEY George★
Sources: H; Kt; Brown J (1979a) p.46

MORRIS Isaac
w 1830
Optician, Wire S
             Kendal, Westmorland
Sources: Taylor (1966) p.455

MORRIS John (I)
w 1740 d 1754
[Spec M]
             London
Guild: Spectaclemakers, fr 1736
Son of MORRIS Richard, yeoman, of Hackney,
Middx (London)
Apprenticed to PHIPPS John★ 1729
Had apprentice:
CHAPMAN Charles 1740
DE LA MOTTE Philip 1749
Master SMC 1753–1754
Sources: GL: SMC 5213/2 p.207+; 5213/3
p.18,137,189,203

MORRIS John (II)
w 1824
Measuring tape M
1824   65 Upper Pitt St, Manchester
Sources: Bn

MORRIS John (III)
w 1850–1855
Math Scale M
1850–1855   1 Paradise St, Lambeth, London

Succeeded by MORRIS & DAVIS
Sources: PO; Wk

MORRIS John B.
w 1833–1834
Rule M, Math IM, Phil IM
1833–1834   14 New Walnut Tree Walk,
             Lambeth, London
See also MORRIS Thomas★
Sources: Pg

MORRIS Samuel
w 1668
Ironmonger
1668   At the sign of the Dripping Pan near
             Charing Cross, London
Guild: Ironmongers, fr 1644–1645
Apprenticed to INGRAM Raphe
Known to have sold: rule
Sources: GL: IMC 16977/1; CKC 2710/1 p.187;
Loomes (1981b)

MORRIS Thomas
w 1844
Rule M
Alternative name: Possibly the same as MORRIS
Thomas S.★
1844   4 Trafalgar St, Walworth, London
Father of MORRIS Thomas Slack, s 1844 CWC
Sources: CWH: CWC Ap

MORRIS Thomas S.
w 1836–1842
Rule M, Optical IM, Phil IM, Math IM
             15 Chester St, Kennington, London
1839   11 Chester St, Kennington, London
1840   Chester St, Lambeth, London
See also MORRIS John B.★
Possibly the same as MORRIS Thomas★; attended
London Mechanics Institute 1840
Sources: Pg; PO: R (JAC); LMIR (AM)

MORRIS William (I)
w 1783–1805
Math IM
1771   Strand, London
1783   Cooper's Row, St.Catherine's,
              London
1794   St.Catherine's Square, London
1794   Upper East Smithfield, London
1796   3 St.Catherine's Square, London
1802   Upper East Smithfield, London
1803   54 Upper East Smithfield, London
Guild: Grocers, fr 1771
Son of MORRIS David, china man, of London
Apprenticed to WING Tycho★ 1764
Had apprentice:
TIDDER Rowland★ 1783 t/o 1786 to BRADLEY
James FLM
HELLMUTH Charles Gabriel 1786
BURGESS George James 1789
CASS Daniel 1794, t/o to FENTIMAN John★
MORLEY Joseph★ 1796
COLEMAN John★ 1796
MAGEAREY Alexander 1802
Associated with
FAIRBONE Charles★
BRADLEY James★

Sources: GL: GC 11598/6; H; Brown J (1979a)
p.45–46

MORRIS William (II)
w 1801–1833
Rule M
1801   Great Charles St, Birmingham
1805–1818   Summer Row, Birmingham
1828–1830   17 Court, Gt.Charles St,
              Birmingham
Sources: Chp; H; Pg; Wr

MORRIS, KING & GOODING
w 1846–1851
Rule M, Engravers, Bookbinders' Tool M
1846–1851   35 Ludgate St, London
Succeeded by MORRIS & CO. Joseph
Sources: PO

MORRISON John
w 1793
Math IM
Alternative name: Directory error for MOLLISON★
1793   Whitefriars, London
Guild: Needlemakers
Sources: Wil

MORS Thomas
a 1730–1750
[Globe S, Map S]
             The Lute on the North Side of
             St.Paul's Churchyard, London
Instruments advertised: globe, math inst
Sources: BM: Heal 105/74 (MAC); Crawforth
(1985) p.518

MORSE David & Abraham
w 1851–1871
Optician
1851–1865   9 Alfred Place, Newington
             Causeway, London
1870–1871   134 Newington Causeway, London
             SE
See also MORSE Samuel★
Sources: PO; Wk

MORSE Samuel
w 1838–1850
Optician, Math IM, Phil IM
             3 Tenter Terrace, Prescot St, London
1838–1841   50 Mansell St, Goodman's Fields,
             London
1844–1850   6 Church Lane, Whitechapel, London
1849–1850   57 Church Lane, Whitechapel,
             London
See also MORSE David & Abraham★
Sources: TCd SM; PO; Calvert (1971) p.33

MORTON A.
w 1839
Phil IM
1839   3 Harrington St North, London
See also MORTON Anthony★
Sources: LMIR (AM)

MORTON Alexander
w 1832–1846
Phil IM, Model M

1832–1833	29 Richmond Place, Edinburgh
1834–1837	2 Roxburgh Place, Edinburgh
1838	9 Drummond St, Edinburgh
1839	11 Hill Square, Edinburgh
1840–1842	71 Adam Square, Edinburgh
1843–1846	7 South College St, Edinburgh

Succeeded by MORTON & CO.★
Sources: Bryden (1972) p.54

MORTON Anthony
w 1841
Phil Appliance M

1841	6 Union St, Clarendon Square, London

See also MORTON A★
Sources: LMIR (AM)

MORTON Thomas
w 1817 d 1862
Textile Machine M, Telescope M
Morton Place, Kilmarnock, Ayr
Associated with BLACKWOOD James
b 1783; founder member of Kilmarnock Phil Institution 1823
Known to have sold: telescope
Sources: Bryden (1972) p.54; Clarke et al (1989) p.188–96

MORTON & CO.
w 1847–1851
Optical IM, Phil IM

1847–1851	7 South College St, Edinburgh

Took over from MORTON Alexander
Sources: Bryden (1972) p.54

MOSS Benjamin
w 1826–1836
Optician, Math IM, Phil IM
Waterloo Place, Commercial Rd, London
7 Catherine St, London
55 Houndsditch, London
Sources: Pg; R (JAC)

MOSS Thomas (I)
w 1754
Instrument M

1754	Hadley's Quadrant within Aldgate, London

Sources: *Public Ad* 5 Feb 1754 (MAC)

MOSS Thomas (II)
w 1836–1844
Rule M
8 Lant Place, Southwark Bridge Rd, London

1839	5 Winchester Place, Borough, London

See also MOSS & WINDRED★
Sources: Pg; Th (JAC)

MOSS & WINDRED
w 1838–1839
Math IM, Phil IM, Rule M

1838	5 Crescent, Southwark Bridge Rd, London
1839	5 Winchester Place, Borough, London

See also
MOSS Thomas★
JONES William (III)★
Sources: Pg

MOULDER Mrs E.
w 1845–1846
Optical Turner

1845–1846	29 Galway St, St Luke's, London

Succeeded by MOULDER & ORME★
Sources: PO

MOULDER & ORME
w 1849–1855
Optical Turners

1849–1855	29 Galway St, St Lukes, London

Took over from MOULDER Mrs E.★
Sources: PO

MOULDING James
fr 1770 w 1801
Math IM

1773	Lamb's Chapel Court, Monkwell St, London
1786	Bunhill Row, London
1787	Lamb's Chapel Court, Monkwell St, (2nd period) London
1798	Coleman St, London
1801	14 Pelham St, Spitalfields, London
1801	15 Whitecross Place, Wilson St, Finsbury Square, London

Guild: Stationers, fr 1770
Son of MOULDING John, carman, of London
Apprenticed to COOKE John★ 1761
Had apprentice:
HARDING Samuel Frederick 1773
WILSON Robert 1777
CARTLEDGE George★ 1781, t/o to MASON John [?★] 1797
RIDGWAY Edward 1786, t/o to his father 1795
CLACK Benjamin 1787
SMITH Samuel 1794
JEZEPH James★ 1794
EMPSON Joseph 1798, t/o to his father 1799
BENNETT Robert 1801
STUBLEY Edward Jarrett 1801 by t/o from boy's father
Sources: GL: CH 12876/7; HC 15860/9; SBPL: STC MF Ap; McKenzie (1978) p.86,243

MOUNTFORD –
w 1785–1788
Scale M

1785–1788	Russell St, Birmingham

See also
MOUNTFORD Humphrey★
MOUNTFORD I★
MOUNTFORD W★
Known to have sold: balance
Sources: inst (pv) (MAC); PR; Pye (MAC)

MOUNTFORD Humphrey
w 1791–1807
Scale M

1791–1805	Coleshill St, Birmingham
1797–1807	37 Lancaster St, Birmingham

See also
MOUNTFORD★

MOUNTFORD I.★
MOUNTFORD W.★
Sources: Chp; H; Pye; Wd (MAC)

MOUNTFORD I.
a 1775–1810
Alternative name: probably John MOUNTFORD of Birmingham, Smith
See also
MOUNTFORD★
MOUNTFORD Humphrey★
MOUNTFORD W.★
Known to have sold: balance
Sources: inst Hull Mu (MAC); H; By (MAC)

MOUNTFORD Richard
w 1811
Optician

1811	Boarshead Buildings, parish of St.Sepulchre, London

Father of MOUNTFORD John s 1811 to USTONSON John★
Sources: GL: TC 3302/3

MOUNTFORD W.
a 1775–1810
Alternative name: probably William MOUNTFORD, Birmingham.
See also
MOUNTFORD★
MOUNTFORD Humphrey★
MOUNTFORD I.★
Known to have sold: balance
Sources: inst (pv) (MAC); By; Sket (MAC)

MOWAT –
w 1659–1685
Scale M, Bismar M
Kirkwall
Succeeded by CRAIGIE George★
Sources: Court action of Alexander, Earl of Galloway, 1757; Earl Morton's defence p.26, Earl Alexander's answers p.20 (MAC)

MOXON James (II)
w 1671–1703
Engraver, Math IM, Map S, Printer

–1687	Holland
1689–1690	Lawrence Ord's Close, foot of the Canongate, Edinburgh
1691	London
1692–1701	The Atlas in Warwick Lane, London
1694	In Westminster Hall, London

Son of MOXON Joseph★
Took over from MOXON Joseph★
Associated with TUTTELL Thomas★ in publishing
Publisher; Author; d.1708
Instruments advertised: globe, math inst
Sources: Bryden (1972) p.5; Tyacke (1978) p.xxi, 127–28

MOXON Joseph
w 1647 d 1691
Hydrographer, Math IS, Globe S

1652–1654	Amsterdam
1654	Atlas on Parnassus Hill, nr. St.Michael's Church, Cornhill, London

1666　　　　Ludgate Hill, London
1670–1671　Atlas in Great Russell St,
　　　　　　Bloomsbury, London
1672–1679　Atlas on Ludgate Hill near Fleet
　　　　　　Bridge, London
1683　　　　Atlas on the west side of Fleet Ditch,
　　　　　　London
–1691　　　Atlas in Warwick Lane, London
Guild: Weavers, Stationers
Father of MOXON James (II)★
Brother of MOXON James (I)★
Partnership: SUGAR & MOXON★
Had apprentice:
BERRY William★ 1656
ROSS Ralph 1673
Succeeded by MOXON James (II)★
See also MOXON Joseph & James★
Associated with TUTTELL Thomas★,
PIERREPOINT T. and LEYBOURNE R.& W., in
publishing
b.1627; Hydrographer to Charles II; FRS 1678;
Author
First English maker of pocket globes
Known to have sold: globe.
Sources: Houghton (1682–83) 2, p.48; Tyacke
(1978) p.126–27

MOXON Joseph & James (I)
w 1647
Globe S, Map S
1647　　　　At the Sugar-loaf in Houndsditch,
　　　　　　London
1647　　　　At the upper end of Houndsditch
　　　　　　near Bishopsgate, London
See also
MOXON Joseph★
MOXON James (II)★
Partnership probably of MOXON Joseph and his
brother, James
Sources: Tyacke (1978) p.127

MUCKLOW Benjamin
w 1835
Optician
1835　　　　Rea Mill, Lawley St, Birmingham
Sources: Pg

MUDGE John
w 1777 d 1793
Optician, Physician, Surgeon
1777–1793　Plymouth
Brother of MUDGE Thomas★
FRS 1777; Copley Medal
Made his living from medicine, optical inst
occupied his spare time
Known to have made: telescope
Sources: DNB

MUDGE Thomas
w 1751–1755
　　　　　　67 Fleet St, London
　　　　　　151 Fleet St, London
1751　　　　Dial & One Crown in Fleet St,
　　　　　　London
1771–1774　Plymouth
Guild: Clockmakers, fr 1738/9
Son of MUDGE Rev. Zachariah of Exeter, Devon
Brother of MUDGE John★

Apprenticed to GRAHAM George★ 1730
Took over from GRAHAM George★
Succeeded by MUDGE & DUTTON★
Partnership: MUDGE & DUTTON★
Associated with
EMERY Josiah★
FERGUSON James (I)★ in work on chronometers
Partnership 1755–90, but in Plymouth 1771–74;
Inv. detached lever escapement; R.apt Geo.III
1776; d.1794
Known to have sold: chronometer
Sources: PRO: LC3/67 p.97; GL: CKC 2732/2;
King & Millburn (1978) p.127–129; Millburn
(1988a) p.137

MUDGE & DUTTON Thomas & William
w 1755–1771
　　　　　　Fleet St, London
Succeeded by DUTTON William M.★
Took over from MUDGE Thomas★
Both apprentices of GRAHAM George★. Mudge in
Plymouth 1771–74
Sources: GL: CKC 2721/1; Baillie (1951)

MUIR John
w 1682 d 1695
Ship Chandler, Naut IS
　　　　　　Leith, Midlothian
Sources: Bryden (1972) p.55; Clarke et al (1989)
p.104

MUIR T.
w 1834
Math IM
1834　　　　15 Shuttle St, Glasgow
Sources: Bryden (1972) p.55

MUNFORD John
w 1768–1801
Optician, Optical IM, Brass turner, Math IM
Alternative name: MUMFORD
1768　　　　Parish of St.James, Clerkenwell,
　　　　　　London
1771　　　　Compton St, Clerkenwell, London
1778–1799　15 Compton St, Clerkenwell,
　　　　　　London
Guild: Stationers, fr 1755
Apprenticed to BUSH William (I)★ 1747/8
Had apprentice:
WINGATE Thomas 1768
MEARS John (?★) 1773
CROW John 1778
MUNFORD John, his son, 1783
MUNFORD Edward, his son, nd, fp 1792
TOUSE Thomas 1785
Sources: GL: STTP 2934 fol 5; H; McKenzie
(1978) p.61,244

MUNRO James (I)
w 1799
Optical IM, Phil IM, Math IM
1799　　　　12 York Place, Lambeth, London
Guild: [?Fishmongers]
Son of prob MUNRO Robert, d, of Boston, New
England
Apprenticed to prob LEKEUX Richard★ 1783 t/o
to BOTTEN Thomas (?BOTTON★)
See also MUNRO James (II)★

Known to have sold: sector
Sources: GL: FMC, 5576/4; H (JAC)

MUNRO James (II)
w 1823–1867
Math IM, Optician, Phil IM
　　　　　　14 Plough Court, Fetter Lane,
　　　　　　London
　　　　　　12 York Place, Kennington, London
　　　　　　72 Oakley St, Lambeth, London
　　　　　　5 High St, Lambeth, London
　　　　　　27 North St, Lambeth, London
1839–1865　4 High St, Lambeth, London
See also MUNRO James (I)★
Sources: Pg (JAC); PO

MURRAY David
fr 1825 w 1825
Coppersmith
　　　　　　Glasgow
Guild: Hammermen
Known to have sold: Measure of capacity
Sources: Lumsden & Aitken (1912) p.310

MURRAY James (I)
w 1822–1850
Chrono M, Optician, Compass M
1822–1850　30 Cornhill, London
Guild: [? Goldsmiths]
Apprenticed to possibly BIRKWOOD William★
1802
Succeeded by MURRAY & CO. James
Admiralty awards 1824 & 1830 for chronometers
Known to have sold: chronometer
Sources: GH: GSC index; CUL: RGO 1143
fol.2–10

MURRAY John (I)
w 1824–1841
Watch M, Clock M, Naut IM
1824–1827　40 Quay, Aberdeen
1828–1835　37 Quay, Aberdeen
1836–1841　30 Quay, Aberdeen
Sources: Bryden (1972) p.55

MURRAY John (II)
w 1834
Compass M
1834　　　　Dock St, Dundee
Sources: Bryden (1972) p.55

MURRAY Robert
emp 1826 w pt 1856
Phil IM
1826　　　　122 Regent St, London
Guild: [Makers of Playing Cards]
Son of MURRAY T.
Partnership: MURRAY & HEATH 1856–1866
Apprenticed to NEWMAN John Frederick★ 1812
Worked for NEWMAN John Frederick★
Attended London Mechanics Institute 1826
Sources: GL: MPC 5963/5; LMIR (AM); Turner
G (1989) p.101

MURRELL –
a 1780–1850
　　　　　　London
See also MURRELL John (II)★

Known to have sold: telescope
Sources: inst Burghley House, Stamford, Lincs
(GL'ET)

MURRELL John (I)
w 1822
Working optician
1822   Stratford, Essex
Father of MURRELL William, s 1822 to LAWSON
Johnson★
Sources: GL: SMC 5213/5

MURRELL John (II)
w 1835–1880
Optician, Phil IM, Math IM
1835–1859   13 Albion Place, Clerkenwell,
                London
See also MURRELL John (III)★
Sources: PO; R (JAC)

MURRELL John (III)
w 1851–1880
Optician
1851–1875   5 Little Mitchell St, St Luke's,
                London
1851   and 1 Albion Place, Clerkenwell,
                London
1880   43 Mitchell St, London EC
See also MURRELL John (II)★
Sources: PO; Wk

MURREY William
w 1821
                Haymarket, London
Guild: Joiners
Apprenticed to DANCER Michael 1810
Sources: Crawforth (1987) p.362

MUSTON George (I)
w 1828–1846
Chrono M
1828–1846   18 Red Lion St, Clerkenwell,
                London
See also MUSTON George (II)★
Took part in chronometer trials at Royal
Greenwich Observatory 1828–1835 but did not
win an award
Known to have sold: chronometer
Sources: CUL: RGO 1143 fol.8–10; PO; Taylor
(1966) p.456

MUSTON George (II)
w 1842
Watch M, Clock M, Chrono M
1842   1 Small St, Bristol
See also MUSTON George (I)★
Sources: Pg

MYCOCK John
w 1822
Magnet M
1822   Burgess St, Sheffield
Sources: Bn

MYERS George
w 1819–1820
Baro M, Mirror M
1819–1820   104 High St, Belfast

Sources: Pg; Burnett & Morrison-Low (1989)
p.152

MYERS Philip
w 1825–1835
Optical IM, Math IM
1825–1828   Smithy Row, Nottingham
1830   1 Okeham St, Nottingham
1834–1835   Pelham St, Nottingham
Known to have sold: barometer
Sources: Glv; Pg (MAC); Goodison (1977) p.343

MYERS & WISEMAN
w 1830
Opticians
1830   Briggs St, Norwich
Sources: Pg

NAIRNE Edward
w 1749 d 1806
Optical IM, Math IM, Phil IM
                Lindsay Row, Chelsea, London
                Golden Spectacles, Reflecting
                Telescope & Hadley's Quadrant in
                Cornhill opposite the Royal
                Exchange, London
1752   Golden Spectacles in Cornhill
                opposite the Royal Exchange,
                London
1752   Corner of Bartholomew Lane,
                Threadneedle St, London
1753–1774   Opposite the Royal Exchange in
                Cornhill, London
1772   20 Cornhill, opposite the Royal
                Exchange, London
1772–1796   20 Cornhill, London
Guild: Spectaclemakers, fr 1748
Son of NAIRNE Edward
Partnership: NAIRNE & BLUNT★
Apprenticed to LOFT Matthew★ 1741/2
Had apprentice:
SAFFORD William 1749
SPINK George 1752
EDLYNE Samuel Nicoll 1754 t/o 1756 to
AYSCOUGH James★
BLUNT Thomas★ 1760
DELEGAL(L) Joseph 1764
LONG James★ 1769
FIELD John★ 1779
WITHERSPOON Colin★ 1780
WITHERSPOON Thomas, son of John★, 1783
LAWSON Henry★ 1788
Employed
RAMSDEN Jesse★
LAWSON Henry★ in 1796
LAWSON Johnson★ in 1796
Took over from LOFT Matthew★
Associated with
SOMALVICO & CO. Joseph★ on barometers
FERGUSON James (I)★
b 1726; FRS 1776; partnership 1774–93; R.apt
Geo. III 1785; Master SMC 1768–1774,1795–1797
Known to have sold: barometer, dip circle,
hygrometer, magnet, marine astrolabe, microscope,
sector, telescope, thermometer, rule
Instruments advertised: full range
Sources: PRO: LC3/67 p.178; GL: SMC 5213/3
p.38,123,137,175,194,213+, 5213/4; *General Ad* 10

Feb 1752 (JRM); Kt; Ld; Mort; Riv (JAC); inst
NMM, (s); Calvert (1971) p.33, fig.35; Millburn
(1988a) p.135,169, (1988b) p.276

NAIRNE & BLUNT Edward & Thomas
w 1774–1793
Optical IM, Phil IM, Math IM, Optician
                Fronting the Royal Exchange in
                Cornhill, London
1783   20 Cornhill, opposite the Royal
                Exchange, London
Succeeded by
BLUNT Thomas (I)★
NAIRNE Edward★
Took over from NAIRNE Edward★
B.apt Royal Greenwich Observatory
Known to have sold: barometer, level, microscope,
sector, sextant, sundial, telescope, thermometer
Sources: By; Kt; Ld(JAC); Anderson et al (1990)
p.57; Goodison (1977) p.186, pl.124–25; Millburn
(1988b) p.276

NAPIER & SON David & James M.
w 1848–1901+
Engineer, Compass M, Scale M
1848   Vine St, Lambeth, London
1870–1901+   5 Vine St, Lambeth, London SE
1870–1901+   and 68 York Rd, London SE
Pat. self-registering compass & barometer, 1848
Sources: PO; inst NMM: Woodcroft (1854)

NARRIEN John
w 1808–1825
Optician, Math IM
1808–1825   70 St.James St, Pall Mall, London
Sources: Bn; J; Kt (JAC); Und

NASEBY William
w 1663
Scale M
1663   Digbeth, Birmingham
Sources: token (pv); MAC

NASH John
w 1668–1707
Math IM
                The Globe, within Aldgate, London
Guild: Grocers, Clockmakers
Apprenticed to HAYES Walter★ 1657
Associated with
MERCER★
FAULKINGHAM★
fr GC 1664, CKC 1667/8
Known to have sold: gauge, sundial
Sources: GL: GC 11571/14; Bryden (1992) p.312n;
Brown J (1979a) p.26; Brown J (1979b) p.32; inst
(pv)

NATHAN Elias
w 1834–1864
Jeweller, Optician
Alternative name: NATAIAN
1834   1 Old Millgate, Manchester
1838   8 King Street, Manchester
1858–1864   6 Victoria Street, Manchester
Sources: K; Pg

NAYLOR John

w c. 1725 d 1752
Clock M
Alternative name: Ion.
1726   Nantwich, Cheshire
          King St, Covent Garden, London
Known to have sold: astronomical clock
Sources: Baillie (1951); engraving NMM

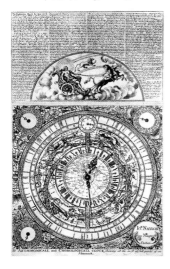

NEALE Henry

w 1686–1709
Scale M
Alternative name: H.N.
        Ye corner of St.Bartholomew Lane
        near the Royal Exchange, London
        Hammer & Crown in St.Ann's Lane
        near Aldersgate, London
        Ye End of St.Bartholomews Lane
        near the Royal Exchange, London
Guild: Blacksmiths, fr 1682 or 1683
Had apprentice:
GODDARD Edward 1692
LEE John 1695
See also
NEALE Samuel★
NEALE John (I)★
B.apt Bank of England
Known to have sold: balance, weight
Instruments advertised: balance, steelyard
Sources: ChrSK 5 Mar 1987 lot 284; GL: BKC
2884, 2886/3 (MAC); ART; Crowther-Beynon
(1925–26) p.188

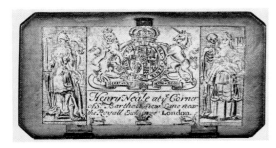

NEALE John (I)

w 1697–1739

Scale M
        The Angel & Star in St.Ann's Lane at
        Aldersgate, London
Guild: Blacksmiths, fr 1691
Apprenticed to HART Joseph (I)★ 1684
Had apprentice:
THOMPSON John (II)★ 1697 by t/o from JENKS
Edmund★
SLEIGH Richard★ 1700/01
HAWKINS William★ 1710
LANE John (II)★ 1718
STILES William★ 1722
KEY George 1725★
READ Samuel★ 1728 t/o to LANE John (II)★ 1733/4
GALE William★ 1732 t/o to LANE John (II)★
1733/4
Six others 1698–1725
See also
NEALE Henry★
NEALE Samuel★
Known to have sold: balance
Instruments advertised: balance
Sources: GL: BKC 2881/8, /9, /10, /11 (MAC);
inst & TCd (pv) (MAC)

NEALE John (II)

w 1742–1758
Watch M, Globe M
        [residence] Leadenhall St, London
        King's Arms & Dial, St.Dunstan's,
        Fleet St, London
Guild: Skinners, fr 1738
Son of NEALE John, pinmaker, of Northampton
Apprenticed to HOUILLIERE Jonathan, Watch M
Had apprentice:
BARRAUD Francis Gabriel★ 1741/2
MORE Ian David Theodore 1744/5
RAYMOND John 1748
KEMP Henry 1750
JORDAN Timothy 1751
STEERS Bernard 1752
APPLIN Richard 1752
YEOMAN James 1752
ROGERS Stephen 1756, t/o to YEOMAN James
1761
WESTON Edward 1758
FURMENT John by t/o from PERKINS Henry 1756
Employed WATT James★
Pat. quadrantal planetarium machine 1744;
bankrupt 1750 & 1758; Common Councillor for
Aldersgate Within 1668–1683
Known to have sold: waywiser
Sources: SH: SKC Ap/Fr; Riv; Muirhead (1858)
p.36; Wallis R & P (1986) p.308; p.214; GMag
1750 p.477, 1758, p.453; Taylor (1966) p.214

NEALE Samuel

w 1644–1692
Scale M
Alternative name: S.N.
        Ye Hammer & Crown, St.Ann's
        Lane, Aldersgate, London
Guild: Blacksmiths, fr 1644
Apprenticed to SHERMAN Henry★ 1637
Had apprentice:
HART Joseph (I)★ 1644
POLLARD Thomas★ 1683 t/o to FREEMAN
Samuel (I)★ 1692

ALLEN David 1683 t/o to JENKS Edmund★ nd
ROGERS Cornelius 1687 t/o to BAYLEY Michael★
nd
THOMSON Jeremiah★ 1690 t/o to GROVE
Christopher★ 1692
Eight others 1646–1682
See also
NEALE Henry★
NEALE John (I)★
Known to have sold: balance
Instruments advertised: balance, steelyard, weights
Sources: GL: BKC 2881/6, /7, /8, 2884, 2886/2;
Sheppard & Musham (1975) no.6; Woodhead
(1965)

NEEVES Richard

w 1835–1844
Phil IM
1835–1838   17 Great St Andrews St, London
1843–1844   High St, St Giles, London
Same premises as NEEVES William (II)★
Attended London Mechanics Institute 1835–41,
1843–44
Sources: LMIR (AM)

NEEVES William (I)

w 1826–1829
Phil IM
1827–1828   92 Leather Lane, Holborn, London
1826–1829   16 Great St Andrews St, London
1840–1844   17 Great St Andrews St, London
Attended London Mechanics Institute 1826–Dec
1829, 1840–44
Sources: LMIR (AM)

NEEVES William (II)

w 1829–1856
Math IM, Philo IM, Drawing IM, Baro M
1833–1841   17 Great St. Andrew Street, Seven
            Dials, London
1845–1855   67 High Street, St. Giles's, London
Same premises as NEEVES Richard★
Attended London Mechanics Institute Dec
1829–1833, 1837–41, 1843–49
Sources: Pg; PO; R; Wk; LMIR (AM)

NEGRATTI H.

w 1839
Baro M, Thermometer M
1839   2 Dorrington Street, London
See also NEGRETTI Henry
Sources: R; Goodison (1977) p.190

NEGRETTI G.

a 1840–1860
        Liverpool
Known to have sold: barometer
Instruments advertised: barometer, thermometer
Sources: Goodison (1977) p.343

NEGRETTI Gaetan

w 1841
Baro M, Thermometer M
1841   4 Thomas Street Manchester
Known to have sold: barometer
Sources: Pg; Goodison (1977) p.343

NEGRETTI Henry

w 1840–1850
Phil IM, Glassblower, Baro M
Alternative name: Enrico Angelo Ludivico
1834–1835   Hatton Garden, London
1839–1848   19 Leather Lane, Holborn, London
1840   20 Greville St, London
1849   9 Hatton Garden, London
1851   [?Residence] 9 Manchester St,
            Argyle Square, London
Partnership:
PIZZI & NEGRETTI★
NEGRETTI & CO.★
NEGRETTI & ZAMBRA★
Apprenticed to PIZZALA F. A.★
Worked for PIZZI Mrs Jane★
Attended London Mechanics Institute 1834–1835,
1839, 1851; b 1818 in Italy d 1879
Sources: PO; LMIR (AM); Goodison (1979)
p.190–91; Read (1985) p.8–10

NEGRETTI & CO. Henry

w 1845–1848
Baro M
1845–1848   19 Leather Lane, London
Succeeded by NEGRETTI Henry★
Took over from PIZZI & NEGRETTI★
Known to have sold: barometer
Sources: Goodison (1977) p.191

NEGRETTI & ZAMBRA Henry & Joseph Warren

w 1850 p 1948
Optician, Optical IM, Math IM, Phil IM, Photo
IM, Naut IM, Met IM
Alternative name: N & Z
1850–1859   11 Hatton Garden, London
1857–1859   59 & 68 Cornhill, EC London
1859–1867   1 Hatton Garden, London
1859–1860   107 Holborn Hill, London
1860–1872   59 Cornhill, EC London
1862–1901   122 Regent St, W London
1865–1873   153 Fleet St, EC London
1867–1870   103 Hatton Garden, London EC
1870–1890   Holborn Circus, Holborn Viaduct,
            London
1870–1885   2 Charterhouse St, EC London
1872–1901+ 45 Cornhill, EC London
1895–1901+ 38 Holborn Viaduct, London – had
            premises here from 1869, but not
            listed in directories
Took over from NEWMAN & SON at 122 Regent St
Succeeded by NEGRETTI & ZAMBRA LTD
Ex. 1851; Negretti d 1879; Zambra d 1897
Known to have sold: barometer, chondrometer,
compass (magnetic), drawing instruments,
hydrometer, microscope, thermometer, waywiser
Instruments advertised: barometer, globe,
spectacles, telescope
Sources: PO; inst MHS, NMM, SM; Anderson et
al (1993) p.58; Banfield (1993) p.129; Goodison
(1977) p.191; Read (1985) p.8–10

NEILL Robert

w 1805 d 1857
Watch M, Silversmith, Optician, Clock M
1805–1809   High Street, Belfast
1819–1820   25 High Street Belfast

1824   21 High Street Belfast
1831–1840   25 High Street Belfast
Partnership: GARDNER & NEILL★
Succeeded by NEILL & SONS Robert★
Associated with BATE Robert B.★ as chart agent
Sources: Burnett & Morrison-Low (1989) p.153
Calvert (1971) p.13; Fennell (1963);

NEILL & SONS Robert

w 1842–1846
Jewellers, Silversmiths, Opticians, Naut IS, Globe
S, Chart S
1842–1846   25 High St, Belfast
1843–1846   6 Diamond, Londonderry
1846   27 Shipquay St, Londonderry
Succeeded by NEILL BROS★
Took over from NEILL Robert★
Sources: Burnett & Morrison-Low (1989) p.153

NEILL BROS

w 1850–1863
Watch M, Jewellers, Silversmiths, Opticians
1850–1863   23 High St, Belfast
Took over from NEILL & SONS Robert★
Succeeded by NEILL John R. and by NEILL &
CO. James
Sources: Burnett & Morrison-Low (1989)
p.152–53

NELSON Henry

w 1839–1848
Drawing IM, Math IM
1835–1848   2 Gloucester Street, Queen Square,
            London
Succeeded by NELSON Louisa★
Sources: Pg; PO

NELSON Louisa (Mrs)

w 1850
Math IM, Drawing IM
1850   2 Gloucester St, Queen Square,
            London
Took over from NELSON Henry★
Sources: PO

NELSON William

w 1830–1839
Spec M, Jeweller, Optician
1830–1831   21 Essex Quay, Dublin
1832   20 Essex Quay, Dublin
1833   24 Essex Quay, Dublin
1834–1839   37 Lower Ormond Quay, Dublin
Sources: Wi; Burnett & Morrison-Low (1989)
p.132

NELSON William H.

w 1840–1862
Optician, Math IM
1840–1844   37 Lower Ormond Quay, Dublin
1845–1851   42 Lower Ormond Quay, Dublin
1852–1862   66 Dame St, Dublin
See also NELSON William★
R.apt Lord Lieutenant
Sources: Burnett & Morrison-Low (1989) p.132

NEMES John

w 1725–1753
Brasier

1742–1745   Queen St, London
Guild: Clockmakers, fr 1724/5
Apprenticed to NEMES Robert, his father, 1710
Had apprentice:
PARKE John 1724/5
Eight others 1730–1753, none known as IM
See also NEMES T.★
Known to have sold: sundial
Sources: GL: CKC 2710/3 fol.104,237; 2721/1,
2732/2, 3939; Sby 10 Mar 1987 lot 99

NEMES T.

a 1700–1740
'T' may be a misreading of 'J'
See also NEMES John★
Known to have sold: sundial
Sources: inst (s) (MAC); Taylor (1966) p.163

NETZKO Henry Thomas

w 1837–1840
Math IM, Philo IM
1837–1840   36 St. John's Lane, Clerkenwell,
            London
Sources: PO; Pg

NEVILL William

w 1765–1768
Glass Cutter, master of optician
1765   Blackfriars, London
Guild: Spectaclemakers, fr 1765
Had apprentice:
LAMB(E) Samuel 1765
OWEN Thomas 1766
BAMPTON Thomas★ 1768
GOULDSTON William 1770
Freed in SMC by purchase
Sources: GL: SMC 5213/3

NEW William

w 1782–1798
Scale M
1782–1798   117 Leadenhall St, London
Guild: Blacksmiths, fr 1745
Apprenticed to JOY John★ 1738
Succeeded by NEW & CO.★
Took over from FREEMAN & NEW★
Sources: GL: BKC 2886/5, 2885/1 (MAC); Sun
11936/299 no.454987 (MAC); A; BW; Kt; Ld
(JAC)

NEW & CO.

w 1798–1807
Scale M
1798–1807   117 Leadenhall St, London
Took over from NEW William★
Sources: H; PO

NEWBERY J.

w 1744
Book S, Instrument S
1744   Reading
Associated with MARTIN Benjamin★
Instruments advertised: air pump, microscope,
spectacles, telescope
Sources: Millburn (1976) p.40

NEWBOLD Richard (I)

w 1827–1840

Optician, Spec M

   3 Long Lane, Smithfield, London
   28 Poppin's Court, Fleet St, London
1839 2 Great Sutton St, Goswell St,
   London
See also NEWBOLD Richard (II)
Sources: Pg (JAC)

NEWBOLD Richard (II)
w 1849–1855
Optician
1849-1855 123 Houndsdith, London
See also NEWBOLD Richard (I)★ (possibly the same person)
Sources: PO

NEWCOMB James
w 1841–1860
Naut IM, Optician, Math IM
1841 7 Gerrard St, Liverpool
1843 1 Fleet St. Liverpool
1835–1847 35 Wapping, Liverpool
1851 3 Oxford St, Liverpool
1853 19A Almond St, Liverpool
1855–1860 21 Almond St, Liverpool
Partnership NEWCOMB & MANSELL★
Sources: G (MAC)

NEWCOMB & MANSELL James & James
w 1846–1849
Optician, Math IM, Naut IM
1846–1849 35 Wapping, Liverpool
Known to have sold: barometer
Sources: G (MAC); Sl; LM index (MAC)

NEWHAM John
w 1823–1828
Navigation Warehouse, Naut IM, Math IM
   7 Wellington Place, Commercial
   Rd, London
   Jamaica Terrace, Limehouse, London
Sources: Pg; R (JAC)

NEWMAN George
w 1794
Math IM
1794 Parish of St Andrews Holborn,
   London
Had apprentice SHAFFENBERG George 1794
See also TANGATE Robert★
Sources: PRO: IR1/36 (AM)

NEWMAN James (I)
fl 1800–1827
Phil IM
   Exeter Exchange, Strand, London
Took over from NEWMAN Thomas★
See also NEWMAN John F.★
Aided the Royal Society with improvements to barometers and thermometers
Sources: Goodison (1977) p.344

NEWMAN James (II)
w 1790–1839
Pencil M, Artists' Colourman, IS
1793 Gerrard St, Soho, London
1839 24 Soho Square, London
Associated with DOLLOND P. & G.★

Known to have sold: camera lucida, stereoscope
Sources: BW; Pg; inst & instructions NMM

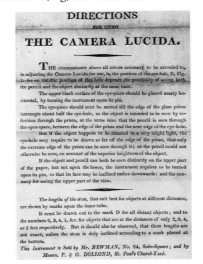

NEWMAN John Frederick
w 1812–1856
Optician, Math IM, Phil IM, Naut IM, Baro M, Thermo M
Alternative name: I. NEWMAN
1807 11 Windmill Row, Camberwell,
   London
1812–1816 Lisle St, Leicester Square, London
1817 7 Lisle St, Leicester Square, London
1822 8 Lisle St, Leicester Square, London
1827–1856 122 Regent St, London
Guild: Makers of Playing Cards, fr 1807
Apprenticed to BROCK Philip★
Had apprentice:
MURRAY Robert★ 1812
ELLIOTT Charles★ 1816
Succeeded by NEWMAN & SON John
See also
NEWMAN Thomas★
NEWMAN James (I)★
NEWMAN James (II)★
fr 1807; Ex.1851; Inventor
Known to have sold: air pump, anemometer, barometer, hygrometer, telescope, thermometer
Sources: GL: MPC 5963/5; Bn; Kt (JAC); Pg; PO; Cat.1851; Goodison (1977) p.344; Morton & Wess (1993) p.598–607; Taylor (1966) p.400

NEWMAN Robert (I)
w 1823–1836
Math IM, Optician
1823–1836 25 Brill Row, Somers Town,
   London
See also
NEWMAN Samuel★
NEWMAN Thomas★
NEWMAN Thomas P★
NEWMAN Robert (II)★
Associated with HARRIS William (III)★ – creditor
1830 when Harris went bankrupt
Sources: Pg; PO; McConnell (1994) p.277

NEWMAN Robert (II)
w 1824–1825
Math IM
1824–1825 16 South St, New Rd, London
See also NEWMAN Robert (I)★
Attended London Mechanics Institute 1824–1825
Sources: LMIR (AM)

NEWMAN Samuel
w 1796–1823
Scale M
1796 21 Crispin St, Spitalfields, London
1805–1822 27 Crispin St, Spitalfields, London
Guild: [Blacksmiths]
Father of NEWMAN Thomas Porter★
Apprenticed to THOMPSON John (II)★ 1756
Had apprentice WILKIE James 1796
Sources: H; J; Pg; GL: CH 12823/8 p.14; 12876/6; BKC 2886/5, 2881/16 (MAC)

NEWMAN Thomas
w 1764–1790
Math IM, Optician
Alternative name: NEMAN
1759 Essex St, in the Strand, London
1764 Shoe Lane, London
1775–1790 Exeter Exchange, Strand, London
Guild: Grocers, fr 1759
Father of
NEWMAN Thomas
NEWMAN George fp 1818
Apprenticed to WING Tycho★ 1751
Had apprentice:
PURDON John 1764
NEWMAN Thomas, his son, 1788
Took over from HEATH & WING★
Succeeded by NEWMAN James (I)★
Sources: By; W; Brown J (1979a) p.42; Calvert (1977) p.33

NEWMAN Thomas Porter
w 1823–1847
Scale M
   3 Union St. East, Spitalfields,
   London
   30 Brick Lane, Spitalfields, London
   26 Union St, Spitalfields, London
1823–1832 27 Union St, Bishopsgate, London
1836–1847 37 Brick Lane, Spitalfields, London
Guild: [Blacksmiths]
Son of NEWMAN Samuel★
Apprenticed to REYNOLDS Joseph★
Sources: GL: BKC 2881/16 (MAC); Pg; PO

NEWSAM Bartholomew
w 1568 d 1593
Clock M
Alternative name: Bartilmewe, Bartelemewe, NEWSUM, NUSAM
1568–1593 In the Strand near Somerset House,
   London
R apt. Elizabeth I
Known to have sold: compass dial, drawing inst, sundial
Sources: Loomes (1918b); Taylor (1954) p.176–77; Ward (1981) p.86

NEWTON Alfred Vincent
w fm 1843 d 1900
Globe M, Patent Agent
1834–1883   66 Chancery Lane, London
Attended London Mechanics Institute 1834–1835,
1843–1844
Sources: LMIR(AM); Gee (1992) p.4; Millburn
(1989) p.3–6

NEWTON E.
c 1729–1729
                Grantham
Known to have sold: rule
Sources: inst Burghley House, Stamford, Lincs
(GL'ET)

NEWTON Frederic
w pt 1850–1901
Optician
Alternative name: Frederick
1850–1856   3 Fleet St, London
Guild: Spectaclemakers, fr 1850
Son of NEWTON Charles, linen draper, of Hitchin,
Herts
Partnership: NEWTON William Edward &
Frederick★
NEWTON & CO. Frederick
b 1824 d 1909; fr by purchase in SMC
Sources: GL: SMC 5213/6; Gee (1992) p.3–6;
Millburn (1989) p.3–6

NEWTON John
w 1783–1818
Globe M
1783–1799   128 Chancery Lane, London
1803–1816   97 Chancery Lane, London
1817–1818   66 Chancery Lane, London
Guild: [Vintners]
Son of NEWTON John, gardner, of Hitchin, Herts
Husband of: BAKER Mary, daur of BAKER
Edward (II)★
Partnership PALMER & NEWTON ★
Apprenticed to BATEMAN Thomas★ 1774
Took over from BATEMAN Thomas★
Succeeded by NEWTON John & William★
Partnerships 1781, c.1818, c.1830; b 1759 d 1844
Known to have sold: globe
Sources: GL: Sun 11936/294; VC 5220/3 p.129;
15201/11 p.227,350; Crawforth (1985) p.520;
Millburn (1989) p.3–6

NEWTON John & William
w 1818–1830
Globe M
1818–1830   66 Chancery Lane, London
Took over from NEWTON John (I)★
Succeeded by NEWTON, SON & BERRY
Sources: PO; R(JAC); Millburn (1989) p.3

NEWTON William (I)
fr 1729 d 1761
Scale M
                In Bartholomew Lane behind the
                Royal Exchange, London
Guild: Blacksmiths, fr 1729
Apprenticed to PHILLIPS Elizabeth 1722 t/o to
OVERING Thomas★ 1723
Had apprentice:

HOLT James 1756 t/o to READ Samuel★ 1761
SANGSTER John★ 1759 t/o to READ Samuel★ 1761
Succeeded by NEWTON & CO.★
Sources: GL: BKC 2885/1 2886/4 (MAC); Daily
Ad 17 Jul 1761 p.1 (JRM)

NEWTON William (II)
w pt 1818 d 1861
Globe M, Patent Agent
1818–1861   66 Chancery Lane, London
1851   (Residence) 42 Queen Square,
             Bloomsbury, London
Father of NEWTON William Edward★
Son of NEWTON John (I)★
Partnership: NEWTON John & William★
Had apprentice ROSEVEAR John 1841
b 1786; AICE; Author; r c.1854
Known to have sold: globe
Sources: Millburn (1989) p.3–6

NEWTON William Edward
w 1838 d 1879
Globe M, Civil Engineer, Surveyor
             66 Chancery Lane, London
1860   Putney, London
Son of NEWTON WILLIAM (I)★
Partnership: NEWTON & SON Wm★
b 1818
Sources: Millburn (1989) p.3–6; Gee (1992) p.3–6

NEWTON William Edward & Frederick
w 1851–1856
Globe M, Math IM, Opticians
1852–1856   3 Fleet St, Temple Bar, London
Succeeded by NEWTON & CO Frederick
Linked to family business of W. Newton & Son
Known to have sold: barometer, microscope,
thermometer
Sources: PO; inst (s); Goodison (1977) p.344;
Millburn (1989) p.3–6

NEWTON & BERRY
w 1838–1841
Globe M
1838–1840   66 Chancery Lane, London
Took over from NEWTON, SON & BERRY★
Succeeded by NEWTON & SON & William★
Sources: PO

NEWTON & CO. William
a 1755–1765
Scale M
                The Hand & Scales opposite the
                Church in Bartholomew Lane near
                ye Royal Exchange, London
Took over from NEWTON William (I)★
Known to have sold: balance
Instruments advertised: balance
Sources: Sheppard & Musham (1975) no.46

NEWTON & SON William
w 1841–1883
Globe M
1841–1883   66 Chancery Lane. London
1851–1857   3 Fleet St, Temple Bar, London
Related to NEWTON John (I)★
Took over from NEWTON & BERRY★
Ex.1851 prize medal; NEWTON William (II)★

d 1861
Known to have sold: globe
Sources: PO; Millburn (1989) p.3–6

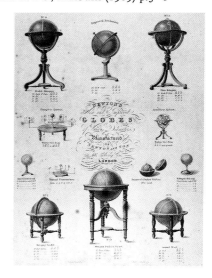

NEWTON, SON & BERRY
w 1830–1838
Globe M
1830–1838   66 Chancery Lane, Fleet St, London
Took over from NEWTON J. & W.
Succeeded by NEWTON & BERRY★
See also NEWTON & SON
Known to have sold: globe
Sources: PO; Millburn (1989) p.3–6

NICHO P.
a 1840–1860
                Liverpool
Known to have sold: barometer, spirit level,
thermometer
Sources: LM index (MAC)

NICHOLL Robert
e 1848 w 1901+
Math IM
1865–1880   42 Stanhope St, London WC
1885–1901   153 High Holborn, London WC
Known to have sold: protractor
Sources: PO; TCd NMM

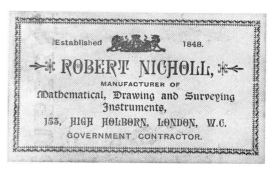

NICHOLL William Lewis
w 1808–1847
Scale M, Measure M
1822–1824   166 & 167 Aldersgate St, London

1826–1836   16 & 167 Aldersgate St, London
1826   18 Great Eastcheap, London
1832   6 Long Lane, Smithfield, London
1839–1847   16 Aldersgate St, London
Guild: Blacksmiths, fr 1807
Apprenticed to
LAWRENCE John Peter 1800★
WOODAGE George Cave by t/o 1806★
Had apprentice:
TADLOO Thomas★ 1812
LONDON Frederick Stephen★ 1822
WEBB Richard William★ 1822
KINGTON John 1836
Worked for DE GRAVE Mary★
Known to have sold: balance, chondrometer
Instruments advertised: balance
Sources: GL: BKC 2881/16, /17, /18 (MAC); Pg;
PO; Holbrook (1992) p.144

NICHOLLS Sutton
fl 1689–1713
Engraver, Map S
            Near the Weaver's Arms, by the
            Postern in London Wall, London
1692   Next door to the Three Compasses
            in the Old Change near Cheapside,
            London
1693   At the Two Globes in the Long
            Walk near Christchurch Hospital,
            London
After 1695 Against the George Inn in
            Aldersgate St, London
Associated with HAUKSBEE Francis (II)★
Instruments advertised: globe
Sources: Taylor (1954) p.288; Tyacke (1978) p.128–29

NICHOLSON -
fl 1787–1802
[Math IM]
See also NICHOLSON & MARGETTS★
Known to have sold: slide rule
Sources: Taylor (1966) p.320

NICHOLSON & MARGETTS
w 1805
See also
MARGETTS George★
NICHOLSON★
Known to have sold: slide rule
Sources: Taylor (1966) p.320

NICKLIN Edward
w 1793
Wire Worker, Scale M
1793   Snow Hill, Birmingham
Sources: BW

NICOLA P.
a 1800–1850
            Liverpool
Known to have sold: barometer
Sources: Goodison (1977) p.344

NILL -
w 1767
Math IM
1767   Great Tower Hill, London
Sources: *Gazetteer* 16 Apr 1767 (MAC)

NIXON John
w 1850–1869
Optician, Math IM
1850–1869   13 Crombie's Row, Commercial
            Road East, London
Sources: PO; Wk; TCd NMM

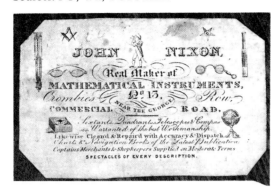

NOAKES
w pt 1851–1855
Alternative name: See FROST, NOAKES & CO.★

NOAKES James
w 1672
Rule S
1672   In Pope's Head Alley, London
Probably Mr Noakes at the back side of Exchange
who sold spectacles & paid search fee to SMC, 1676
Known to have sold: rule
Sources: GL: CKC 2710/1 p.244; SMC 5213/1

NOBLE Nathaniel
fl 1627
1627   Above St. Clement's Church
            towards the Maypole in the Strand
            London
Guild: [Stationers]
Apprenticed to THOMPSON John (I)★
Sources: McKenzie (1961) p.127; Taylor (1954)
p.203,211

NODEN John
w 1826–1827
Baro M, Thermo M
1826–1827   10 Charles St, Hatton Garden,
            London
Sources: Pg (JAC)

NOLFI P.
a 1800–1825
            Manchester
Known to have sold: barometer
Sources: Sby (Ch) 2–5 Oct 1984 lot 118

NOLLI & CO. J. B.
a 1830–1900
            Perth
Known to have sold: barometer
Sources: Goodison (1977) p.344

NORIE John William
w 1799–1816
Teacher, Navigation Warehouse

1799–1816   157 Leadenhall St, London
Succeeded by NORIE & CO.★
Took over from HEATHER William★
See also
NORIE & WILSON★
WILSON Charles (II)★
b 1772 d 1843
Sources: H; Kt; JAC

NORIE & CO. John William
w 1816–1839
Navigation Warehouse, Map S, Chart S
1816–1839   157 Leadenhall St, London
Took over from NORIE John W.★
See also
WILSON Charles (II)★
NORIE & WILSON★
B.apt Admiralty & East India Co.
Known to have sold: globe, octant, telescope
Sources: Pg; PO; inst & TCd NMM; inst
Sunderland Museum; ChrSK 12 Dec 1985 lot 21

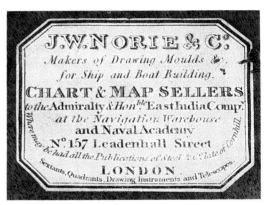

NORIE & WILSON John William & George
w 1812–1820
Teacher, Navigation Warehouse
1812–1820   157 Leadenhall St, London
            156 Minories, London
Succeeded by WILSON Charles (II)★
Took over from HEATHER William★
See also
NORIE & CO. J.W.★
NORIE John William★
NORIE & WILSON★
e 1765
Known to have sold: sextant
Sources: TCd NMM; JAC; inst (s)

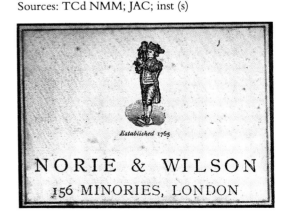

NORMAN David
w 1849–1859
Optician
1849–1859   5 City Terrace, Old Street Rd,
London
Same premises as NORMAN Robert (II)★
Sources: PO; Wk

NORMAN Robert (I)
fl 1560 w 1605
Hydrographer, Compass M
1581   Ratcliff, London
Inv. dip needle
Sources: Bryden (1992) p.310,311; Taylor (1954)
p.173–74,325–26

NORMAN Robert (II)
w 1851
Optician
1851   5 City Terrace, Old Street Rd,
London
Same premises as NORMAN David★
Sources: Wk

NORRIS –
w 1730
Globe M
1730   Jermyn St, London
Sources: *Daily Post* 25 Aug 1730 (MAC)

NORRIS Francis
w 1834–1839
Chrono M
1834–1835   108 Mount Pleasant, Liverpool
1837   112 Mount Pleasant, Liverpool
1839   28 Mount Pleasant Liverpool
Partnership: NORRIS & CAMPBELL★
Succeeded by NORRIS Mary★
Sources: G (MAC); Taylor (1966) p.477

NORRIS Mary
w 1841–1848
Chrono M, Watch M
1841–1848   28 Mount Pleasant, Liverpool
Took over from NORRIS Francis★
See also NORRIS & CAMPBELL★
Sources: G; Loomes (1975)

NORRIS & CAMPBELL
w 1845–1851
Watch M, Chrono M
1845–1851   16 South Castle St, Liverpool
See also NORRIS Mary★
Sources: G; Loomes (1975)

NORRIS & MELLOR Richard Hill & Joseph
w 1845–1858
Math IM, Tape Measure M
1845   1 Court, Ward St, Birmingham
1850   Ward St, Birmingham
1858   98 Litchfield St, Birmingham
Sources: Dix (AL), K, Sl

NORTH Edward
w 1833
Magnet Needle M
1833   Wadsley, Sheffield
Sources: Bk

NORTH George (I)
w 1722–1734
Spec M
1722   London
Guild: Spectaclemakers, fr 1722
Father of NORTH George (II) fr 1725
Apprenticed to SAYE Thomas★ nd
Had apprentice:
YEATS (YATES) Christopher nd, fr 1722 (sic)
KNAPPIER Richard 1734 by t/o from ADAMS
John (I)★
Sources: GL: SMC 5213/2 p.128–9,133,164+

NORTH Luke
w 1710
Known to have sold: nocturnal.
Sources: inst Boerhaave Mu

NORTH Thomas
w 1809–1817
Math IM, Watch M, Clock M
1809   8 Queen St, Soho, London
1817   2 Old Compton St, London
Sources: H; Und (JAC)

NORTHEN Edward
w 1842–1848
Math IM, Optician, Watch M, Chrono M,
Silversmith, Jeweller
1846–1848   50 Lowgate, Hull
Took over from NORTHEN & SON Richard★
Sources: Stn; Wh; Goodison (1977) p.344

NORTHEN Richard
w 1790–1840
Optician, Watch M, Jeweller
Alternative name: NORTHERN
1790–1791   Lowgate, Hull
1803–1834   46 Lowgate, Hull
1822   (Residence) Nelson St, Hull
1838–1840   50 Lowgate, Hull
Succeeded by NORTHEN Edward★
See also NORTHEN & SON★
Known to have sold: barometer, drawing
instruments, hygrometer, spirit level, thermometer
Sources: Bn; H; Pg; WB; Goodison (1977) p.344;
Taylor (1966) p.320

NORTHEN William
w 1849–1865
Chem IM
1849–1865   14 Vauxhall Walk, Lambeth, London
Sources: PO

NORTHEN & SON Richard
a 1840–1842
46 Lowgate, Hull
Succeeded by NORTHEN Edward★
Took over from NORTHEN Richard★
Sources: Goodison (1977) p.344–45

NORTHFIELD William
w 1784
Scale M
1784   36 Glasshouse Yard, Aldersgate,
London
1805   42 Coppice Row, Clerkenwell,
London
1811   61 Coppice Row, Clerkenwell,
London
Guild:Haberdashers, fr 1784
Son of: NORTHFIELD John, smith, of Clerkenwell,
London
Apprenticed to: CROOME Thomas★ 1774
Had apprentice:
NORTHFIELD Thomas Shepherd, his son, 1805,
t/o 1805 to NORTZELL Thomas of GSC, t/o 1807
to REYNOLDS Joseph★
NORTHFIELD John, his son, 1811
Sources: GL: HC 1585/2, 15860/9

NORTON Eardley
a 1749.d 1792
Clock M
1790   49 St. John St, Clerkenwell, London
Guild: Clockmakers, fr 1770
Associated with
PINCHBECK Christoper (II)★
FERGUSON James (I)★
b.1728
Known to have sold: astronomical clock,
chronometer
Sources: BW; Baillie (1951); King & Millburn
(1978) p.145; Loomes (1976)

NORTON George
w 1802–1805
Optician, Math IM
1802–1805   20 Roll's Buildings, Fetter Lane,
London
Guild: [Goldsmiths]
Son of NORTON John, shagreen casemaker, of
London
Apprenticed to MARTIN Joshua Lover★ 1778
See also NORTON John & George★
Sources: H; GH: GC index

NORTON John & George
w 1790–1792
Math IM
Alternative name: J. & G.
1790–1792   Rolls Buildings, Fetter Lane, London
See also NORTON George★
Sources: BW

NORTON John (I)
w 1803–1807
Math IM
Rolls Buildings, Fetter Lane,
London
Guild: [Stationers]
Apprenticed to SIMONS James★
See also NORTON John & George★
Pat. water mill 1803, pump 1807
Sources: *Annual Register* 1803; Taylor (1966) p.371;
Woodcroft (1854); McKenzie (1978) p.317

NORTON John (II)
w 1825
Math IM
1825   Pentonville, London
See also
NORTON John (I)★
NORTON John (III)★ (possibly the same person)
Attended London Mechanics Institute 1825
Sources: LMIR (AM)

NORTON John (III)

w 1828–1841
Phil IM
1828   10 Leather Lane, London
1834–1841   20 East St, Red Lion Square,
            London
See also
NORTON John (I)★
NORTON John (II)★
Attended London Mechanics Institute 1828,
1834–41
Sources: LMIR (AM)

NORTON William

w 1828–1834
Baro M
1828   6 Cross St, Hatton Garden, London
1834   70 Leather Lane, London
See also NORTON John (III)★
Attended London Mechanics Institute 1828 & 1834
Sources: LMIR (AM)

NORVELL Charles Frederick

w 1844–1860
Optician
1844–1853   8 Maidenhead Court, Aldersgate St,
            London
1855–1860   2 Hayward's Place, Bermondsey,
            London
See also NORVELL John★
Sources: PO

NORVELL John

w 1817–1837
Spec M
       2 Fenton's Buildings, Bartholomew
       Close, London
       32 Little Bartholomew Close,
       London
       66 Bartholomew Close, London
       2 Little Bartholomew Close, London
See also NORVELL Charles F.★
Sources: R (JAC); Und (JAC)

NOSEDA John

w 1774 d 1779
Baro M
Alternative name: NOSEDON
       Belfast
See also NOSEDA J. & P.
Sources: Burnett & Morrison Low (1989) p.154

NOSEDA P.

a 1820
       Wolverhampton
Known to have sold: barometer, thermometer
Sources: Inst (s) (MAC)

NOYES John

fr 1789 w 1803
Math IM
Alternative name: NOY
1803   Grocer's Hall Court, London
Guild: Grocers, fr 1789
Son of NOYES William★
Apprenticed to RUST Richard★ 1782
b c.1778; joined Honourable Artillery Co. as Math
IM 1803

Sources: HAC (JT); GL: GC 11598/4; Brown J
(1979a) p.41

NOYES William

w 1782–1798
Math IM
1791   8 Little Minories, London
1793–1798   18 Haydon Square, Minories,
            London
Guild: Grocers
Father of
NOYES John★
NOYES Edward fp 1810 GC
Son of probably NOY (ES) Arthur, d
Apprenticed to probably CRICK James★ 1754
Probably the William NOY fr GC 1762, and
referred to as NOYES when son fp 1810
Sources: BW; Kt; Ld; GL: GC 11598/6; Brown J
(1979a) p.36,41

NUTTING John William

s 1825 emp 1837
Math IM, Bookkeeper
1826–1837   136 Fleet St, London
Guild: [Goldsmiths]
Son of NUTTING Henry, gentleman, of Potters
Bar, Middx
Apprenticed to SIMMS William (II)★, later his
brother-in-law, 1825
Worked for SIMMS William (II)★
Attended London Mechanics Institute 1826; d
c.1837
Sources: LMIR (AM); GH: GSC Ap; McConnell
(1992) p.26,32

OAKESHOTT William

w 1845
Baro M, Thermo M, Phil IM
1845   29 St. John St, Clerkenwell, London
Sources: PO

OAKLEY Henry

w 1824–1830
Phil IM, Optician
1824–1829   5 George's Place, Bath
1830   9 Somerset Buildings, Walcot, Bath
Sources: Kn; Pg

OAKLEY Joseph (I)

w 1767–1780
Optician, Optical IM, Spec M
1767–1770   Upper Priory, Birmingham
1770   Bull St, Birmingham
1775–1780   79 Bull St, Birmingham
See also OAKLEY Joseph (II)★
Instrument advertised: magic lantern, microscope,
spectacles, telescope
Sources: Aris 28 May 1770 (DJB); PR; Sket; Sy

OAKLEY Joseph (II)

w 1781
Optician
1781   Paradise St, Liverpool
See also OAKLEY Joseph (I)★
Sources: LM index (MAC)

OBORNE Benjamin

w 1838–1871

Optical IM, Math IM, Philo IM, Mechanical
Modeller
Alternative name: OSBORNE
       8 Northampton Buildings,
       Clerkenwell, London
       8 Northampton Square, London
1831–1836   8 Garnault Place, Spa Fields, London
1843–1865   11 Guildford Street East, Spa Fields,
            London
1869–1870   102 St. John Street Rd, Clerkenwell,
            London EC
Attended London Mechanics Institute 1831,
1832–36
Sources: Pg, PO, LMIR (AM)

ODELL John

w 1805
Math IM
1805   1 Princes Place, Ratcliff, London
Sources: H (MAC)

OERTLING Ludwig

w 1846–1925
Scale M, Hydro M, Chem IM, Math IM, Phil IM
Alternative name: L.O.
1849–1854   13 Store St, Bedford Square, London
1856–1861   12 Store St, Bedford Sqaure, London
1869–1874   27 Moorgate St, London
1874–1925   Turnmill St, EC, London
1883–1888   58 Cow Cross St, EC, London
Partnership: LADD & OERTLING
Succeeded by OERTLING LTD. L.
Associated with BATE Robert B.★
Ex.1851; partnership 1862–69; B.apt Bank of
England, Bd.of Trade
Known to have sold: balance, gauge, hydrometer
Sources: PO; TCd (pv); Cat. 1851; inst SM;
Chaldecott (1989) p.160–61; McConnell (1993)
p.7,28,54

OFYNN Edward

w 1831–1836
Optical IM, Phil IM, Math IM
Alternative name: O'FYNN
1831–1836   55 Upper North Place, Gray's Inn
            Rd, London
Sources: R (JAC)

OGDEN Samuel (I)

fr by 1668 v 1687
[Scale M]
1687   Parish of St Giles Cripplegate,
       London
Guild: Blacksmith, fr 1667 or 1668
Father of OGDEN Samuel (II)★
Apprenticed to SAUNDERS Robert (I)★ 1660
Sources: GL: BKC 2882/7 2884, 2886/3 (MAC)

OGDEN Samuel (II)

w 1710–1729
       London
Guild: Blacksmiths, fr 1703
Son of OGDEN Samuel (I)★
Apprenticed to LEE Humphrey★ 1687
Had apprentice:
OGDEN Isaac, his son, 1718
OGDEN John, his son, 1729 by t/o from OVEN
Henry★

Educated at Christ's Hospital School, London, and in 1710 received a grant from the school to set himself up in his trade
Sources: GL: BKC 2881/9, 2886/3, 2886/4, 2888 (MAC); CH 12823/3 p.1, 12876/2

OGG & MCMILLAN William & William
w 1844–1846
Watch M, Clock M, Naut IM
Alternative name: M'MILLAN
1844   53 Marischall St, Aberdeen
1845–1846   30 Regent Quay, Aberdeen
Succeeded by MCMILLAN & CO. William
Sequestration 1846
Sources: NMS n; Bryden (1972) p.55

OGIER William
w 1816 1826
Scale M
            Half Moon Alley, Bishopsgate St, London
1826   9 Paul St, Finsbury, London
Guild: [Blacksmiths] Dyers
Father of OGIER George
Son of OGIER John, dyer, d, of Spitalfields, London
Apprenticed to PALLET Thomas* 1788
Had apprentice OGIER George, his son, 1816
Partnership: OGIER & GARDNER*
Sources: GL: DC 8167/3

OGIER & GARDNER
w 1826–1828
Scale M
1826–1828   9 Paul St, Finsbury, London
Sources: R (JAC)

OGILVIE Robert A.
w 1845
Baro M. Thermo M
1845   19 Upper Wharton St, London
Sources: PO

OGSTON James
w 1826
Chrono M
            27 Davies St, Berkeley Square, London
Pat. watch 1826
Sources: Baillie (1951); Taylor (1966) p.430

OLLIVANT & SON John
w 1788–1800
Watch M
1788–1800   Manchester
Associated with WILKINSON Anthony* whose balances they sold
Known to have sold: balance
Sources: inst Bolton Mu (MAC); Baillie (1951)

ONEILL Michael
w 1845–1849
Math IM
1845–1849   110 Chester St, Toxteth Park, Liverpool
Sources: G

ONION Thomas
w 1793
Rule M
1793   Lancaster St, Birmingham
Sources: BW

ONIONS Benjamin
w 1825–1841
Rule M
Alternative name: ONION
1825–1826   2 Northwood St, Birmingham
1841   29 Court, Livery St, Birmingham
Sources: Pg

ONIONS Peter
w 1793
Math IM
1793   Merthyr Tydvil, Glam
Sources: BW

ONIONS Thomas
w 1767–1805
Rule M
1767   Brick-kiln Lane, Wolverhampton
1780   Brick Kiln St, Wolverhampton
1783   Cherry St, Birmingham
1785   Walmer Lane, Birmingham
1787–1793   Lancaster St, Birmingham
1797–1805   Great Hampton St, Birmingham
See also ONIONS Benjamin*
Sources: BW; By; H; PR; Pye, Sket

OPPENHEIM Abraham
w 1836
Spectacle M
1836   1 Savell's Bldgs, Stepney Green, London
Sources: Pg

OPPENHEIM Joseph
w 1845–1870
Optician
1845–1849   2 Freeman's Place, Mile End Rd, London
1851–1859   10 Road Side, Mile End Rd, London
1865–1870   171 Mile End Rd, London
Sources: PO

OPTICAL ILLUMINATING GLASS CO.
w 1851–1855
Optician, Math IM
1851–1855   6 Post Office Place, Liverpool
Sources: G

ORCHARD John (I)
w 1826–1837
Math IM, Optician, Phil IM
1826–1829   6 Ladymead, Bath
1829   8 St.Andrew's Terrace, Bath
1830   York St, Bath
1833   14 York St, Bath
1837   48 Walcot St, Bath
Sources: Kn; Pg; Sil

ORCHARD John (II)
w 1849–1885

Optician, Math IM, Phil IM, Drawing IM
1849–1855   28 Hornton St, Kensington, London
1859–1870   2 Lower Phillimore Place, Kensington Rd, London
1875–1885   100 Kensington High St, London W
See also ORCHARD John (I)*
Ex. 1851
Known to have sold: air pump, barometer
Sources: PO; Wk; Cat. 1851

ORDOYNO George
w 1811–1835
Watch M, Clock M, Math IM, Bobbin M, Carriage M, Optician
1818–1825   Friar Lane, Nottingham
1828   Castle Terrace, Nottingham
1830–1835   Middle Pavement, Nottingham
Sources: GLv; Pg

ORFORD George
w 1795
Quadrant M
1795   Liverpool
See also ORFORD Jonathan
Sources: Mar, St Paul's Liverpool (LM index – MAC)

ORFORD Jonathan
w 1804–1815
Math IM, Stationary Warehouse
1804   Wapping, Liverpool
1805–1809   27 Wapping, Liverpool
1813–1815   74 Park Lane, Liverpool
See also ORFORD George
Sources: G; H; WB (MAC)

ORIGONI John
w 1836–1847
Baro M, Thermometer M, Toy Merchant
1836–1847   34 Dean St, Newcastle upon Tyne
See also GRASSI, BERGNA & ORIGONI*
Sources: Ric; Wh; Wim; Taylor (1966)n p.450

ORME Charles
w 1731 d 1747
1731–1736   Ashby de la Zouch
Known to have sold: barometer, rule
Sources: Goodison (1977) p.192–96, pl.3; Holbrook (1992) p.144

ORMISTON T.D.
a 1750–1800
            Dunse (? Duns, Berwick)
Known to have sold: waywiser
Sources: inst NMS

ORTELLI A. (I)
w 1843–1845
Clock M, Watch M
            High St, Oxford
Succeeded by ORTELLI & PRIMAVESI*
Known to have sold: barometer
Sources: Beeson (1989) p.132; Goodison (1977) p.345; inst (s)

ORTELLI A. (II)
w 1823
Clock M, Watch M

1823 Buckingham
Partnership: PIZZI & ORTELLI
Succeeded by PIZZI & ORTELLI
See also ORTELLI A (I)★
Known to have sold: barometer, thermometer
Sources: Goodison (1977) p.345; Legg (1975)
(MAC)

ORTELLI Peter

w 1835–1856
Baro M, Thermometer M, Looking-glass M
Alternative name: ORTELLE, ORRELL
1835–1851   3 Leather Lane, Holborn, London
1848–1851   49 Hatton Garden, Holborn,
               London
1852–1856   15 Leather Lane, Holborn, London
Partnership: ORTELLI & PRIMAVESI 1848–1849
Sources: PO; R; Goodison (1977) p.346

ORTELLI & CO.

a 1800–1850
               Carmarthen
Known to have sold: barometer
Sources: Peate (1975) (MAC)

ORTELLI & CO. Joseph

w 1809–1818
Baro M, Thermo M
               20 Cross St, Hatton Garden, London
See also ORTELLI Peter★
Known to have sold: barometer, thermometer
Sources: H; Und (JAC); Goodison (1977) p.345

ORTELLI & CO. P.

w 1805
1805   Macclesfield
Known to have sold: barometer
Sources: Goodison (1977) p.345

ORTELLI & PRIMAVESI

w 1846–1849
Optician, Jeweller, Watch M, Clock M, Baro M,
Thermo M, Looking-glass M, Cutler
1846   114 High St, Oxford
1848–1849   and 49 Hatton Garden, London
Took over from ORTELLI A. (I)★
Associated with CAVIGIOLI L. at Oxford
Sources: Bod: JJ TCd (MAC); PO; Goodison
(1977) p.345–46

OSBORN David

w 1823–1845
Rule M, Math IM, Optician
Alternative name: OSBORNE
1823–1824   2 Cropper St, Liverpool
1825   132 Park Lane, Liverpool
1827   131 Park Lane, Liverpool
1829–1832   22 Park Lane, Liverpool
1834   18 Park Lane, Liverpool
1834–1837   18 Park Lane, Liverpool
1839   37 Park Lane, Liverpool
1841–1845   25 Bridgewater St, Liverpool
Sources: Bn; G; Pg (MAC)

OSBORN Thomas

w 1586–1593
Known to have made: surveying compass
Sources: Taylor (1954) p.188

OSBORNE Murray

w 1776–1817
Math IM
1783–1801   Gallowgate, Glasgow
1803–1817   406 Gallowgate, Glasgow
Apprenticed to WATT James★
Sources: H; Bryden (1972) p.55

OSBORNE Thomas

w 1801
Astro clock M, Musical clock M, Phil IM, Watch
M, repairer
1801   Vauxhall St, Birmingham
Sources: Chp (DJB)

OSBORNE Thomas Paine Gerald

w 1841–1854
Optician
1841   57 Scotland St, Sheffield
1854   97 Scotland St, Sheffield
Partnership ASHMORE & OSBORNE ★
Instruments advertised: microscope, spectacles,
telescope
Sources: K; Pg; Rg

OTLEY Jonathan

fl 1818–1834
Watch M
               Keswick
b 1766; d 1856
Known to have sold: barometer
Sources: Holbrook (1992) p.141; Loomes (1976);
Taylor (1966) p.401; DJB

OTTLEY John

w 1845–1851
Optician
1845–1851   2 Spring Place, Bagnigge Wells Rd,
               London
Sources: PO

OTTWAY John

w 1826–1870
Optician, Math IM, Phil IM, Baro M, Thermo M,
Spec M, ?Turner & Brass Founder
               87 Arlington Place, St.John Street
               Rd, London
               10 Carey St, London
               4 York St, Covent Garden, London
               11 Carey St, Lincoln's Inn Fields,
               London
               87 St.John Street Rd, London
               11 Carey St, Soho, London
1839   6 York St, Covent Garden, London
1840   10 King St, Holborn, London
1845   11 Devonshire St, Queen's Square,
               London
1849   33 Upper King St, Bloomsbury,
               London
1855   21 Pakenham St, Gray's Inn Rd,
               London
1859   83 St.John Street Rd, EC. London
1865–1870   178 St. John Street Rd, EC. London
1810   [?same man] Barbican, London
1812   [?same man] Silver St, Wood St,
               London
1823   ?Edward Place, St John St Road,
               London

1800   ? 4 City Rd, London
Guild: ?Cordwainers, fr 1800
Son of ?OTTWAY Thomas, Watch M, of
Monkwell St, London
Apprenticed to ?DARE George, ivory & hardwood
turner, 1793
Had apprentice:
?PARKER James 1810
?POOLE Mark 1812
CHANDLER Bryant 1823
Succeeded by OTTWAY & SON John
Known to have sold: barometer
Sources: Pg; PO; inst Parham Ho W Sussex; GL:
CORD 7357/4, 24139/1, 24140/1; BM: Heal
105/77

OULD Henry

s 1759 w 1794
Math IM
1791–1793   Dartmouth, Devon
1794   59 Lower East Smithfield, London
Guild: [Merchant Taylors]
Apprenticed to COLE Benjamin (II)★
Pat. artificial horizon 1791
Sources: BW; W; GL: MTC MF 319, 324;
Woodcroft (1854)

OVEN Henry

w 1721 d.c 1728
Scale M
1724   Heart & Scales on Maiden Lane over
               against Goldsmith's Hall, London
Guild: Blacksmiths, fr 1719/20
Apprenticed to PHILLIPS Walter★ 1712
Had apprentice:
BATE Richard (I)★ 1721 by t/o from SNART
John (I)★
PHYTHIAN Dod 1723 by t/o from HOE Robert★
ELLIS Richard 1726
OGDEN John 1727/8, t/o to his father OGDEN
Samuel★ 1729
Known to have sold: balance
Sources: GL: BKC 2881/10, 2885/1, 2886/4
(MAC), Sun 11936/17 no.32482; inst SM
Wellcome

OVENDEN James

w 1822–1827
Scale M
               8 Newcastle Court, Temple Bar,
               London
1822–1824   56 Broadmead, Bristol
1824–1827   (Residence) Knowle Hill, Bristol
1825–1827   59 Broadmead, Bristol
Guild: Blacksmiths, fr 1808
Partnership: PAYNE & OVENDEN★
Apprenticed to PAYNE Benjamin Matthew★ 1800
Had apprenticed CLARK Charles 1813
Sources: GL: BKC 2881/16 (MAC); Mat; inst (pv)
(MAC)

OVERING Thomas

w 1720 d c.1731
Scale M
               Angel & Scales in Bartholomew
               Lane near ye Royal Exchange,
               London
Guild: Blacksmiths, fr 1717

Apprenticed to SNART John (I)★ 1709
Had apprentice:
HANNEY Nathaniel 1719/20
NEWTON William (I)★ 1723 by t/o from
PHILLIPS Elizabeth★
FOOTE John 1728 t/o to BOULTON Thomas 1731
Took over from PHILLIPS Walter★
See also ROBERTS Timothy★
Known to have sold: balance
Instruments advertised: balance, steelyard, weights
Sources: GL: BKC 2881/10, 2881/11; 2886/4
(MAC); Sheppard & Musham (1975) no.160

OWEN Hannah
w 1777
Scale M
1777   37 Digbeth, Birmingham
Sources: PR

OWEN James
w 1812–1819
Math IM
1812   13 Sea Coal Lane, London
1819   37 Dowgate Hill, London
Guild: Grocers, fr 1803
Son of OWEN John, deceased
Apprenticed to EVANS William (II)★ 1795
Had apprentice MURRAY John 1812
Sources: GL: STTP 2934 fol 16; GC 11598/6; CH
12823/8 p.64,115, 12876/7; Brown J (1979a) p.54

OWEN John
w 1683–1697
Known to have sold: sundial
Sources: Loomes (1981b)

OWEN Peter
w 1794–1803
Math IM, Mathematician
1794–1803   31 Pool Lane, Liverpool
1796   11 Pool Lane, Liverpool
Sources: G; LM index (MAC)

OWERS Richard
w 1849–1851
Optician
1849   39 Theobald's Rd, Bloomsbury,
              London
1851   42 Theobald's Rd, Bloomsbury,
              London
Sources: PO; Wk

OXENFORD John
fr 1713 w 1748
              Savage Gardens, London
Guild: Joiners, fr 1713
Apprenticed to BLOW Edmund★ 1704
Son of OXENFORD Robert, joiner, d, of London
Had apprentice SAWYER William 1717
Sources: GL: JC 20588; Crawforth (1987) p.362

OXLEY Henry
w 1780–1793
Scale M
              230 Upper Thames St, London
1789–1793   83 Snowhill, London
1790   84 Snow Hill, London
Guild: Blacksmiths, fr 1761

Apprenticed to LIND John★ 1753
Had apprentice BASSINGHAM Samuel★
Known to have sold: balance
Instruments advertised: balance
d by 1803
Sources: A; BW; W; Wil; GL: BKC 2881/15,
2881/16, 2886/5 (MAC); inst WM (MAC)

PACE Charles
fr 1786 w 1805
Math IM
1805   20 Castle St, Finsbury Square, London
Guild: Stationers, fr 1786
Apprenticed to ARCHER William★ 1776
Son of PACE Charles, wheelwright, of
Wimbledon, Surrey (London)
Sources: H; McKenzie (1978) p.6

PACKWOOD Christopher
w 1652–1664
Math IM
Alternative name: PACKEWOOD
1663–1664   By Allhallows Barking Church,
              London
Guild: Grocers, fr 1645
Son of PACKWOOD Christopher, yeoman, of
Monks Kirby, War
Apprenticed to BLEYGHTON John (I)★ 1631
Had apprentice: WELCH William 1652
Specialized in brass instruments
Known to have sold: slide rule
Sources: GL: GC 11,592; Brown J (1979a) p.25;
Bryden(1992) p.318

PAGANI Anthony
w 1822–1828
Optician, Math IM
1822–1825   Goosegate, Nottingham
1828   Greyhound St, Nottingham
Sources: Glv; Pg

PAGE Thomas
fl 1750 d 1784
Clock M, Watch M
              Norwich
Known to have sold: barometer
Sources: Baillie (1951); Goodison (1977) p.346;
Taylor (1966) p.456

PAINE Christopher
w 1584–1590
Math IM
1590   Hosier Lane, West Smithfield,
              London
Known to have sold: drawing instruments, plane
table, rule
Sources: Bryden (1992) p.305; Loomes (1981b)

PALLANT John
w 1839–1869
Math IM, Optician
1839   4 Little Russell St, Drury Lane,
              London
1839   35 Tavistock St, Covent Garden,
              London
1840   Trafalgar St, Walworth Rd, London
1845   14 Mercer St, Long Acre, London
1849–1852   9 Great May's Buildings, London

1863–1869   44 Museum St, London
Guild: [Grocers]
Son of PALLANT Samuel, coach trimmer of
Clerkenwell, London
Apprenticed to HUGGINS John (II)★ 1826
Known to have sold: level
Sources: GL: GC 11598/7; PO; Pg; inst (s)

PALLET Elizabeth Mary
w 1821–1836
Scale M
1821–1836   91 Leadenhall St, London
Guild: Blacksmiths
Wife of PALLET Richard★
Had apprentice:
BROOKS John 1821
HERBERT Thomas★ [probably]
Took over from PALLET Richard★
Succeeded by PALLET & SON★
Sources: GL: BKC 2881/17 (MAC); Pg; R (JAC)

PALLET Richard
w 1812–1820
Scale M
1815–1820   91 Leadenhall St, London
Guild: Blacksmiths, fp 1805
Father of PALLET Thomas (II)★
Son of PALLET Thomas (II)★
Husband of PALLET Elizabeth Mary★
Had apprentice:
KIRBY William 1811
SOMMERS Thomas 1812
EVANS Thomas Edward 1815
GREENHILL Benjamin Mills★ 1816
d by 1821, but name continuede in directories for
several years
Sources: GL: BKC 2881/16, 2881/17; 2885/2
(MAC); J; Kt; PO; R (JAC)

PALLET Thomas (I)
fr 1769 w 1816
Scale M
              91 Long Lane, West Smithfield,
              London
1781   64 Leadenhall St, London
1793–1805   91 Leadenhall St, London
Guild: [Weavers] Blacksmiths, fr 1769
Father of PALLET Richard★
Apprenticed to GABLE Thomas★ 1755
Had apprentice:
CLIFFORD John 1771
GROUT John 1781★
OGIER William★ 1788
SMITH Thomas★ 1798
Succeeded by PALLET Richard★
See also
PALLET Thomas (II)★
PALLET & SON M.★
Sources: GL: BKC 2881/15, 2881/16, 2886/5
(MAC); Sun 11936/290 no.442221; A (JAC); BW;
Kt; PO

PALLET Thomas (II)
w 1838–1852
Scale M
1835–1843   91 Leadenhall St, London
1844–1850   2 Sugarloaf Court, [Leadenhall St.],
              London

Guild: Blacksmiths, fp 1835
Son of PALLET Richard★
Sources: GL: BKC 2881/17; PO

PALLET & SON M.
w 1837–1838
Scale M
1837–1838   91 Leadenhall St, London
Employed HERBERT Thomas★
Succeeded by PALLET Thomas (II)★
Took over from PALLET Elizabeth Mary★
Known to have sold: balance
Sources: R (JAC); inst (s) (MAC)

PALMER Edward
w 1828–1845
Phil IM, Baro M, Thermo M, Spec M, Chem IM,
Math IM, Chemist
1828   Tooley St, Southwark, London
1834   1Mulberry Row, Kensington Gravel
             Pits, London
1838–1845   103 Newgate St, London
Guild: Ironmongers
Apprenticed to PALMER Edward, druggist, his
father, 1818
Had apprentice:
FRY Edward 1828
WILLATS Thomas 1832
Succeeded by HORNE, THORNTHWAITE &
WOOD
Sources: GL: IMC 16985, 16981/2; Cat. at MHS;
BM: Heal 105/78; Pg; PO; Anderson et al (1990)
p.61; Calvert (1971) p.26

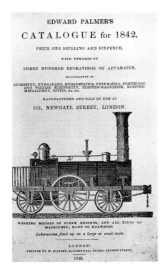

PALMER John (I)
w 1661–1683
[Spec M]
1666   Parish of St Botolph Aldgate,
             London
Guild: Spectaclemakers
Father of PALMER John (III) s 1661
Had apprentice:
CLAYTON Edward 1677/8
CLIFTON Joseph 1682
Sources: GL: SMC 5213/1; CUR 6113A

PALMER John (II)
w 1831
Chrono M
1831   58 Great Marylebone St, London
Sources: R

PALMER Robert
w 1829–1836
Known to have sold: sundial
Sources: Webster R & M (1988)

PALMER Thomas
w 1851
Baro M, Picture Frame M
1851   41 St. John's Square, Clerkenwell,
             London
Sources: Wk

PALMER William
w 1765–1780
Engraver
1764–1772   New Street Square, London
1779–1803   (Residence?) Islington, London
1782   Chancery Lane, London
Guild: Goldsmiths, fr 1760
Son of PALMER William, breeches maker, of
Westminster, London
Apprenticed to: PINE John, engraver, 1753, t/o
1757 to SEALE Richard William, engraver
Had apprentice:
JONES Edward 1764
RUSSELL John 1765
CARY John★ 1770
SIMPSON Richard 1772
LYMENS James 1779
BAKER Benjamin ?★ 1782 by t/o from
BERRESFORD William of STC
ROWE Robert 1789
ALLEN Joseph 1791
PRICE John Thomas 1803
Partnership: PALMER & NEWTON, 1780
Sources: GH: GSC Ap, Fr (MAC); GL: CH
12876/5; McKenzie (1978) p.254

PALMER & NEWTON William & John
w 1781–1790
Globe M, Engravers, Map Engravers
1781–1790   Globe & Sun, 128 Chancery Lane,
             Fleet St, London
Took over from BATEMAN Thomas
See also
PALMER William★
HILL Nathaniel★
Known to have sold: globe
Sources: GL: Sun 11936/294 no.447717; BM: Heal
105/79; BW; Millburn (1989) p.3–6

PALMER, STEELE & CO.
w 1813–1818
Math IM, Navigation warehouse
1813–1818   6 Duke's Place, Liverpool
Succeeded by STEELE John★
See also STEELE & SON John★
Sources: G; Pg; WB; LM index (MAC)

PANTIN Nicholas
s 1651 w 1663
Alternative name: PANTON

Oxford
Guild: [Clockmakers]
Apprenticed to DOWNING Humphrey 1651
Known to have sold: sundial
Sources: GL: CKC 3939; Beeson (1989) p.15;
Loomes (1981b)

PAPIN
fl 1678 w 1692
Phil IM
             c/o Mr.Carpenter, near the Bell Inn
             in Friday St, London
Related to PAPIN Denis FRS
Sources: Taylor (1954) p.275

PAPP A.
w 1832–1836
Math IM
1832–1836   St. Andrews Hill, London
Attended London Mechanics Institute 1832–1836
Sources: LMIR (AM)

PARISH Robert
w 1766
Math IM
1766   Precinct of the Savoy, London
Father of PARISH William s 1766 THC
Sources: GL: THC, 6158/5

PARKE Joseph
w 1729 d 1775
Clock M, Watch M, Instrument M
1731   Union St, Liverpool
1736   Newmarket, Liverpool
1739–1752   Commonor, Convent Garden,
             Liverpool
1761   Common Garden, Liverpool
1766–1774   Convent Garden, Liverpool
Known to have sold: sundial
Sources: LM index (MAC)

PARKER Benjamin (I)
fl 1725–1753
[Rule M]
             Isaac Newton's Head, next to the
             Great Turnstile, Holborn, London
             Fulwood's Rents, Holborn, London
Associated with SUXSPEACH Joseph, inventor
Known to have sold: slide rule
Sources: ChrSK 30 Jun 1988 lot 96; Taylor (1966)
p.164

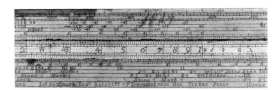

PARKER George
fr 1704 w 1766
Watch M, Goldsmith
1761–1766   Cork Hill, Dublin
Known to have sold: sundial
Sources: Burnett & Morrison-Low (1989) p.132;
Mollen (1990) p.238

PARKER Henry
w 1835
Rule M
1835   Vauxhall Rd, Birmingham
Sources: Pg

PARKER J.W.
w 1842–1851
Publisher, Book S
1842–1851   West Strand, London
Known to have sold: geometric solids
Sources: inst SM; PO

PARKER James (I)
fr 1703 w 1724
[Math IM]
1703   Foster Lane, London
Guild: Grocers, fr 1703
Husband of PARKER Mrs. Elizabeth
Apprenticed to WALPOOL Thomas★ 1695/6
Had apprentice:
WARD John 1713/14
SMITH Mihill 1722/3 t/o 1726/7 to SCOTT
Benjamin★
ADAMS George (I)★ 1724 t/o 1726/7 to HEATH
Thomas★
Died before 1734, probably before 1726
Sources: Brown J (1979a) p.31–32

PARKER James (II)
w 1805–1822
Optician
        126 High Holborn, London
        6 West St, Soho, London
        18 Brewer St, Somers Town,
        London
        38 Old Compton St, Soho, London
1802–1819   53 Princes St, Soho, London
1817–1819   383 Oxford St, St. Giles, London
1822   22 Little Queen St, Holborn,
        London
Apprenticed to TAYLOR Thomas★ 1788
Attended Christ's Hospital School, London
Sources: GL: CH 12876/6; Bn; By; H; Kt; R
(JAC)

PARKER James (III)
w 1840–1845
Optician
1840–1844   39 Theobald's Rd, Red Lion Square,
        London
1845–1846   33 Great Ormond St, London
See also OTTWAY John★
Sources: PO

PARKER John
fl 1830
Optical IM
        Sandpits, Birmingham
Probably an error for PARKES John★
Sources: Pg; Taylor (1966) p.457

PARKER Samuel (I)
w 1797–1803
Glass M
1792   Earl St, Blackfriars, London
1798–1803   69 Fleet St, London
Guild: Goldsmiths, fr 1784

Son of PARKER William★
Apprenticed to PARKER William★
Had apprentice:
PARRY Henry 1797
ALEXANDER James 1804
PARKER William, his son, 1807
PARKER Samuel, his son, 1810
PARKER Charles, his son, 1813
Partnership: PARKER & SON William★
Succeeded by PARKER & PERRY
Took over from PARKER & SON★
d.1838
Known to have sold: burning glass
Sources: GH: GSC Ap, Fr; BW; Kt

PARKER Samuel (II)
fl 1825–1826
Optician ?
        16 Little Hampton St, Birmingham
Probably an error for PARKES Samuel★
Sources: Pg; Wr; Taylor (1966) p.430

PARKER Thomas
w 1801–1802
Math IM
        Glasgow
Associated with TELFER & AFLECK★
Pats. for textile manufacturing 1801 and 1802
Sources: Bryden (1972) p.57; Taylor (1966) p.371

PARKER William
w 1766 w pt 1793
Glass M
1784–1785   Fleet St, London
1793   69 Fleet St, London [in partnership]
Guild: Goldsmiths, fr 1754
Son of PARKER William, cordwainer, of West
Tarring, Sx
Partnership:
PARKER & CO. William★
PARKER & SON William★
Apprenticed to PARKER John of GSC 1747
Had apprentice:
PRICE John 1766
ROMAINE William 1770
ELLYETT John 1770
POLHILL John 1772
PARKER Samuel (I)★, his son, 1777
KINGSBURY William Ebenezer 1785
THATCHER George 1780
HOWARD George 1783 by t/o from ORPIN James
PERRY William 1790
Known to have sold: burning glass, eudiometer
Sources: GH: GSC index, Ap; Wil: Spargo (1984)
p.7; Turner & Levere (1973) p.244–45

PARKER & CO. William
w 1780 c 1783
Glass M
1780   69 Fleet St, London
Succeeded by PARKER & SON William★
Sources: Kt

PARKER & SON William
w 1786–1796
Glass M
1788–1796   69 Fleet St, London
Guild: Goldsmiths

Succeeded by PARKER Samuel (I)★
Took over from PARKER & CO. William★
Known to have sold: burning glass
Sources: BW; Kt; Ld

PARKES Ebenezer
w 1840–1869
Rule M
Alternative name: Ebenezer C.
1840–1869   142 Fetter Lane, London
Same premises as PARKES J.★
Attended London Mechanics Institute 1840–1841
Sources: LMIR (AM); PO; Wk

PARKES J.
w 1843
Brass Rule M
1843   142 Fetter Lane, London
Same premises as PARKES Ebenezer★
Attended London Mechanics Institute 1843
Sources: LMIR (AM)

PARKES James
w 1839–1843
Measuring Tape M, Compass M, Gilt Toy M
1839–1843   5 St Mary's Row Birmingham
Succeeded by PARKES & SON James★
Sources: Pg; Wr

PARKES John
w 1818–1835
Optician, Spec M
1818–1835   Sandpits, Birmingham
See also PARKES William★
Sources: Pg; West (MAC); Wr

PARKES Samuel
w 1777–1830
Rule M, Math IM, Compass M
1777–1780   8 Sand St, Birmingham
1787   St.Mary's Row, Birmingham
1797–1801   Legge St, Birmingham
1825–1830   16 Little Hampton St, Birmingham
1828–1829   Little Hampton St, Birmingham
See also PARKES & SON Samuel★
Sources: Pg; PR; West; Wr (MAC)

PARKES William
w 1841–1862
Optician, Math IM
1841   21 Sandpits, Birmingham
1845   20 Sandpits, Summerhill,
        Birmingham
1850   28 Paradise St, Birmingham
1862   85 King Edward Rd, Birmingham
See also PARKES John★
Sources: K; Mor: Pg; Sl

PARKES & SON James
w 1845–1862
Math IM
1845–1862   5 St. Mary's Row, Birmingham
Associated with WEST Charles (III)★
Ex 1851
Known to have sold: microscope
Sources: K(AL); Mor; Sl; Cat 1851; inst Wellcome

PARKES & SON Samuel

w 1801–1818
Rule M, Math IM

1805–1818	Bull St, Birmingham
1816–1818	66 Bull St, Birmingham
1801	Legge St, Workhouse Field, Birmingham
1808	& Coleshill St, Birmingham

See also PARKES Samuel★
Sources: Chp (AL); H; Pg; Und

PARKES & SONS

w 1841
Math IM, Compass M
1841　　　7 Bath St, Birmingham
Sources: Pg

PARKINSON Henry

fl 1832 w 1846
Chrono M

	15 Great Sutton St, London
1839	21 Red Lion St, Clerkenwell, London
1846	65 Red Lion St, Clerkenwell, London

Sources: Pg; PO; Loomes (1976); Taylor (1966) p.477

PARKINSON William

w pt 1802–1842
Watch M, Chrono M
Guild: Clockmakers, fr 1802
Partnership: PARKINSON & FRODSHAM★
fr by purchase in CKC
Sources: GL: CKC 11568; Baillie (1951)

PARKINSON & FRODSHAM William & William James

w 1801 p 1921+
Chrono M, Optician, Math IM

1801–1880	4 Change Alley, Cornhill, London
1828	54 Castle St, Liverpool
1832–1841	38 Castle St, Liverpool
1835	17 South Castle St, Liverpool
1880	4 Change Alley, Cornhill, London EC
1921	5 Budge Row, Cannon St, London

Guild: Clockmakers (both men)
Had apprentice GLOVER Henry
See also
FRODSHAM William James★
FRODSHAM Henry★
B.apt Admiralty, East India Co.
Took part in chronometer trials at RGO 1834–1835
Known to have sold: chronometer
Instruments advertised: octant, sextant, telescope
Sources: CUL: RGO 1143 fol.10; GL: TCd; G; Pg; Baillie (1951); Taylor (1966) p.401

PARLASCA Biagio

w 1837–1846
Optician
Alternative name: PARLUSIA, PURLUSIA, Biaglo

1837	45 Sparling St, Liverpool
1841–1846	91 Sparling St, Liverpool

See also PARLASCA Buzio★
Sources: G

PARLASCA Buzio

w 1834–1841
Optician
1834–1841　　46 Vernon St, Liverpool
See also PARLASCA Biagio★
Sources: G

PARMINTER John (I)

w 1742–1791
Math IM
Alternative name: PARMENTER

	The Quadrant & Globe, Little Tower St, London
	The Quadrant & Globe, Little Tower Hill, London
1739	Near the White Hart Alehouse in Mansell St, Goodman's Fields, London
1742	Next door to the Sun & Bell in the Minories, London
1752	In the Minories, London
1758	The Corner of the Minories, London
1776–1787	King St, Tower Hill, London
1788	3 King St, Tower Hill, London

Guild: Grocers, fr 1739
Father of
PARMINTER Samuel★ fp 1787
PARMINTER John (II)★
Son of PARMINTER John, mariner of Whitechapel, London
Apprenticed to GILBERT John (I)★
Had apprentice:
HAMILTON James 1742
RUST Richard★ 1744
SCHOLES Robert 1748
DUNN John 1751
PEARSON Robert 1760
PARMINTER George, his son, 1767
BUTCHER John 1778
Associated with LINCOLN Charles★
Sources: GL: SMC 5213/3 (1769); STTP 2934 fol.139; Brown J. (1979a) p.38; McKenzie (1978) p.304

PARMINTER John (II)

fp 1791 w 1796
Optician

1791	Crown Court, Wapping, London
1796	Dog Row, Bethnal Green, London

Guild: [Spectaclemaker], Grocers, fp 1791
Son of PARMINTER John (I)★
Apprenticed to LINCOLN Charles★, SMC, 1769
Had apprentice: TICKNER John 1796
Sources: GL: SMC 5213/3; Brown J. (1979a) p.53

PARMINTER Samuel

fp 1787 v 1788
　　　　　London
Guild: Grocers, fp 1787
Son of PARMINTER John (I)★
Brother of
PARMINTER George
PARMINTER John (II)★
Probably not a Math IM
Sources: GL: STTP 2934 fol.139; Brown J. (1979a) p.38

PARNELL Thomas (I)

w 1784–1811
Math IM, Quadrant M, Compass M, Ship Chandler

	Mariner & Quadrant, 94 Lower East Smithfield, London
	Mariner & Quadrant, 2 Lower East Smithfield, London
	93 Lower East Smithfield, London
	94 near the Hermitage Bridge, Lower East Smithfield, London
1784	11 Cannon St, Ratcliff Highway, London
1793	25 East Smithfield, London
	At Mr Hughes, Nightingale Lane, London

Guild: Joiners, fr 1776
Father of PARNELL William★
Son of PARNELL Thomas, farmer, of Mountnessing, Essex
Apprenticed to BLAKE John★ 1768
Worked for HUGHES [forename not given]
Succeeded by PARNELL William★
Known to have sold: compass
Instruments advertised: compass (magnetic), drawing instruments, octant, rule, sextant, slide rule, telescope
Sources: GL: JC 80552/2 - 8055/5, 8052/7 (MAC), 8046/12; Sun 11936/321 no.492144; Sby 3 June 1986 lot 413; BW; By (JAC); PO; TCd SM; Calvert (1971) p.34; Crawforth (1987) p.363

PARNELL Thomas (II)

w 1840–1869
Optician, Math IM
1840–1869　　2 Lower East Smithfield, London
Took over from PARNELL & SON William★
d.c.1869
Sources: PO

PARNELL William

w 1811–1839
Math IM, Ship Chandler

	2 Lower East Smithfield, London
1816–1839	94 Lower East Smithfield, Butcher Row, London
	94 Near the Hermitage Bridge, Lower East Smithfield, London

Guild: Joiners, fp 1811
Son of PARNELL Thomas (I)★
Succeeded by PARNELL & SON William★
Took over from PARNELL Thomas (I)★
Known to have sold: sextant

Sources: GL: JC 8046/12; Sun 11936/469
no.921738; inst & TCd NMM; Bn; J; Kt (JAC);
Pg; PO; Crawforth (1987) p.363

PARNELL & SON William
w 1839–1840
Opticians, Math IM, Philo IM
1839–1840   2 Lower East Smithfield, London
Succeeded by PARNELL Thomas (II)★
Took over from PARNELL William★
Sources: Pg

PARROT –
w 1790
1790   Hull
See also PARROT W.T.
Known to have sold: sextant
Sources: inst (s) (DJB)

PARROT W.T.
a 1790–1850
            Hull
See also PARROT
Known to have sold: sextant
Sources: Sby 18 Sep 1983 lot 102 (DJB)

PARRY A.O.
w 1833–1834
Math IM, Optician, Phil IM
1833–1834   12 St.James St, Clerkenwell, London
See also PARRY Thomas W.★
Sources: R (JAC)

PARRY Thomas William
w 1833–1882
Optician, Spectacle M;
1833–1839   14 Princes St, Barbican, London
1840–1882   24 Holywell St, Strand, London
See also PARRY A.O.★
Sources: R (JAC); PO

PARSON John
w 1835
Spectacle M
1835   1 Court, Henrietta St, Birmingham
Sources: Pg

PARSONS Charles
w 1674
[Math IM]
Known to have sold: horary quadrant
Sources: inst MHS; Taylor (1954) p.376

PARSONS George
w pt 1827 w 1855
Engraver of Math Instruments, Tobacconist
1840   46 Fore St, London
1855   24 Nicholas St, Hoxton New Town,
            London
Guild: Grocers, fp 1840
Partnership: PARSONS James & George★
Apprenticed to PARSONS William (II)★, his father,
1822
Sources: GL: GC 11598/7, 11598/8; PO

PARSONS Henry
w 1816
Pincer M, Compass M

1816   Windmill Hill, Birmingham
Sources: H

PARSONS James
w 1837–1890
Optical IM, Phil IM, Math IM, Divider of Math Inst
1837–1839   22 Bull & Mouth St, Aldersgate St,
            London
1840–1846   50 Red Lion St, Clerkenwell, London
1849–1851   1 Rodney St, Pentonville, London
1851   43 Stamford St, Blackfriars Rd,
            London
1855   11 Upper Stamford St, Blackfriars
            Rd, London
1861–1865   111 Upper Stamford St, London
1869–1880   73 Stamford St, London
Guild: Grocers, fr 1840
Son of PARSONS William (II)★
Brother of
PARSONS William (III)★
PARSONS George★
Apprenticed to PARSONS William (II)★, his father,
1812
Had apprentice PARSONS James William, his son,
1844
Took over from PARSONS James & George★
Attended London Mechanics Institute 1826–1828
Sources: GL: GC 11598/6, 11598/8; Pg; PO; SM:
RA File ScM 3602 (SJ); LMIR (AM)

PARSONS James & George
w 1827–1836
Divider of Math Inst, Optical IM, Phil IM, Math
IM
1827–1836   22 Bull & Mouth St, Aldersgate St,
            London
Succeeded by PARSONS James★
See also
PARSONS William (II)★
PARSONS William (III)★
Sources: PO; R (JAC)

PARSONS William (I)
w 1737–1756
[Math IM]
            London
Guild: Goldsmiths, fr 1717
Apprenticed to COLLIER William★ 1710
Son of PARSONS William, d, of Carpenters' Co. of
London
Had apprentice:
WHITEHEAD Richard 1737
HACK William★ 1740
HODGKINS Thomas 1746
BRIND John 1746, t/o same day to his father
PARSONS Humphrey, his son, 1747
LEVERTON John★ 1749
LANE John (I)★ 1756 t/o 1760 to STEDMAN
Christopher (I)★
Sources: GH: GSC Ap, Fr

PARSONS William (II)
w 1801–1832
Optician, Math IM
            22 Bull & Mouth St, St.Martin's le
            Grand, London
            32 Bull & Mouth St, London
1801   New St, Fetter Lane, London

1808–1809   Salisbury Court, Fleet St, London
1812   Pauls Alley, St Pauls Church Yard,
            London
1822   8 Paul's Alley, St Paul's Churchyard,
            London
1822   Bull & Mouth St, London
1832   9 Kirby St, Hatton Garden, London
Guild: Grocers, fr 1799
Father of
PARSONS James★
PARSONS William (III)★
Son of PARSONS Richard, d
Apprenticed to MARTIN James★ 1789
Had apprentice:
GOULD William 1801
TOWARD William George 1808
PARSONS William (III)★, his son, 1809
PARSONS James★, his son, 1812
PARSONS George★, his son, 1822
Succeeded by PARSONS William (III)★
See also PARSONS James & George★
Associated with HEMSLEY Thomas★
d by 1840
Sources: GL: GC 11598/6, 11598/7; SM: RA File
ScM 3602 (SJ); Bn; PO; R (JAC)

PARSONS William (III)
w 1834–1840
Math IM, Phil IM, Optical IM
1834–1840   9 Kirby St, Hatton Garden, London
1824   Salisbury Court, Fleet St, London
Guild: Grocers, fr 1824
Son of PARSONS William (II)★
Brother of PARSONS James
Apprenticed to PARSONS William (II)★,
Took over from PARSONS William (II)★
See also PARSONS James & George★
Sources: GL: GC 11598/6, 11598/7; Pg

PARTON William
w 1816–1834
Clock M, Watch M, Compass M
1816   Low St, Sunderland
1828   8 Low St, Sunderland
1834   40 Low St, Sunderland
Sources: H; Pg

PARTRIDGE Ephraim
w 1845
Math IM
1845   83 Henry St, Great Brook St,
            Birmingham
Sources: K

PARTRIDGE John
w 1796–1799
Scale M
            23 Newcastle St, Strand, London
1796   Butcher Row, Temple Bar, London
1799   5 Hemmings Row, St.Martin's Lane,
            London
Guild: Blacksmiths, fr 1790
Apprenticed to
LIND John 1767, t/o to
VINCENT Robert 1772
Had apprentice:
BIRD George 1795
QUINTON Thomas 1799

See also ASTILL & PARTRIDGE★
Partnership 1790–1795
Known to have sold: balance
Sources: GL: BKC 2881/16; HC 15860/9 (MAC);
H; Ld (JAC); inst ML (MAC)

PARTRIDGE Samuel
w 1773
Ironmonger
1773   Ross on Wye, Herefs
Instruments advertised: balance
Sources: *British Chronicle or Pugh's Hereford Journal*
4, 11, 18 Nov 1773 (JRM)

PASSAVANT Susanna
w 1738–1761
Toy S, [Math IS]
Alternative name: PASSAVENT Susannah
1755   Plume & Feathers on Ludgate Hill
      opposite the Old Bailey, London
Guild: Spectaclemakers fr 1735/6
Apprenticed to WILLDEY George★ 1727/8
Had apprentice GILLAM Rebecca 1753
Sources: GL: SMC 5213/2 p.188+, 5213/3 p.186;
Heal (1972) p.33,77

PASSEY D.
a 1790
      Bristol
Known to have sold: microscope
Sources: Sby 25 Feb 1986 lot 314 (MAC)

PASTORELLI Antonio
w 1829–1846
Baro M, Thermo M
Alternative name: Anthony
      19 Upper Wharton St, Lloyd Square,
      London
1839–1846 4 Cross St, Hatton Garden, London
1841   With F. Pastorelli★ insured 2 private
      houses at 49 and 50 Baker St, Lloyd
      Square, Pentonville, London
Succeeded by PASTORELLI & SON Antonio★
Took over from PASTORELLI C.★
See also
PASTORELLI Fortunato★
PASTORELLI F.& J.★
PASTORELLI Joseph★
Associated with PASTORELLI Francis★
Sources: Pg; PO; R; GL: Sun,11936/575
no.1363589 (AM)

PASTORELLI C.
fl 1821–1838
Chrono M
      4 Cross St, Hatton Garden, London
Succeeded by PASTORELLI Antonio★
See also PASTORELLI Fortunato★
Sources: Taylor (1966) p.431

PASTORELLI Elizabeth
w 1822
Baro M, Thermo M
1822   24 Cross St, Hatton Garden, London
Associated with PASTORELLI Fortunato★
Sun insurance policy has name Elizabeth entered &
Fortunato deleted
Sources: GL: Sun 11936/489 no.993399

PASTORELLI Fortunato
w 1805–1828
Baro M, Thermo M
      156 High Holborn, London
1805   252 High Holborn, London
1822   4 Cross St, Hatton Garden, London
1822   24 Cross St, Hatton Garden, London
Partnership: PASTORELLI F.& J.★
See also
PASTORELLI Joseph★
PASTORELLI Antonio★
Associated with
PASTORELLI Elizabeth★
STAMPA Charles★
Partnership 1816–1819
Known to have sold: barometer, hygrometer, spirit
level, thermometer
Sources: GL: Sun 11936/489 no.993399; Bn; H;
PO; R (JAC); Bolle (1982) p.159

PASTORELLI Fortunato & Joseph
w 1816–1819
Baro M, Thermo M
Alternative name: J.& F.
1816–1819 4 Cross St, Hatton Garden, London
See also
PASTORELLI Fortunato★
PASTORELLI Joseph★
PASTORELLI Antonio★
Sources: R (JAC); Und

PASTORELLI Francis
w 1851–1880
Barometer M, Optical IM, Meteorological IM,
Wholesale Optician
1851   4 Cross St, Hatton Garden, London
1869   Hatton Garden, EC, London
1869   208 Piccadilly, W, London
1880   10 New Bond St, W, London
1841   Probably the one who with A.
      Pastorelli★ insured 2 private houses,
      49 & 50 Baker St, Lloyd Square,
      Pentonville, London
Associated with PASTORELLI Antonio★
Sources: PO;Wk; GL: Sun,11936/575

PASTORELLI John
w 1834–1860
Baro M, Optician, Math IM
1834–1837 28 Cable St, Liverpool
1839–1847 55 Cable St, Liverpool
1849–1853 61 Cable St, Liverpool
1855   49 Pitt St, Liverpool
1857–1860 10 South Castle St, Liverpool
Sources: G; K

PASTORELLI Joseph
w 1820–1828
Baro M, Thermo M
      5 Leopard's Court, Baldwin's
      Gardens, Leather Lane, London
      93 Regent St, London
Partnership: PASTORELLI F. & J.★
See also
PASTORELLI Fortunato★
PASTORELLI Peter C.★
PASTORELLI Antonio★
Sources: Kt; R (JAC)

PASTORELLI Joseph A.
w 1851
Baro M
1851   67 Hatton Garden, London
Sources: Wk

PASTORELLI Peter Caparani
w 1827
Baro M
      5 Leopold's Court, Baldwin's
      Gardens, London
See also PASTORELLI Joseph★
Sources: Pg (JAC)

PASTORELLI & CO. Francis
w 1851–1875
Optician, Math IM, Phil IM, Baro M, Thermo M
1851–1865 4 Cross St, Hatton Garden, London
1859–1875 208 Piccadilly, London W
1870   7 Great Warner St, London EC
See also PASTORELLI Francis★
Sources: PO

PASTORELLI & SON Antonio
w 1847–1849
Baro M, Thermo
1847–1849 4 Cross St, Hatton Garden, London
Took over from PASTORELLI Antonio★
Sources: PO

PATERSON –
c 1803
Optical IM
      Calton Hill Observatory, Edinburgh
Sources: Bryden (1972) p.55

PATERSON James
fl 1679–1693
Math IM, Mathematician
1681–1686 Sea Cross-staff and Quadrant,
      Cowgate, Edinburgh
1689   Sea Cross-staff and Quadrant, Reid
      House, Middle of Leith Wynd,
      Edinburgh
Uncle of MANN John (I)★
Succeeded by MANN John★ (I)
Instruments advertised: balance, barometer,
compass (magnetic), cross-staff, quadrant, rule
Sources: Bryden (1972) p.4, 55

PATERSON William
w 1820–1834
Scale M
1820–1834 Jamaica St, Glasgow
Sources: Pg (MAC)

PATON David
w 1824 d 1844
Clock M
      Dunfermline, Fife
Known to have sold: planetarium
Sources: NMS n; Baillie (1951); Taylor (1966)
p.431

PATRICK George
w 1825
Optician
1823   16 Finch Lane, London

Guild: Spectaclemakers, fr 1823
Son of PATRICK Nathaniel Taylor, cooper, of St
Katherine's, London
Apprenticed to RICHARDSON George★ 1814
See also PATTRICK Thomas★
Livery SMC 1825
Sources: GL: SMC 5213/4, 5213/5, 6031/4

PATRICK John
fr 1686 w 1722
Baro M, Thermo M
Over against Bull Head Court in
Jewin St, near Cripplegate Church,
London
In the Old Bailey without Newgate,
London
1704 Ship Court in the Old Bailey,
London
Guild: Joiners fr 1686, Clockmakers fr 1712
Apprenticed to TOMSON William, joiner, 1668
Son of PATRICK Thomas, porter, of St. Clement
Danes, London
Had apprentice:
PATRICK Thomas, son of Thomas, 1686
WESLEAK William 1691
CURTIS Samuel 1695
RAYNER Matthew 1706
STEVENS Edward 1717
DEWILDE John 1722
d by 1735
Known to have sold: barometer, thermometer
Instruments advertised: barometer
Sources: GL: CKC 2717/1 fol.4; BM: Banks
105/35; inst NMM; Calvert (1971) p.34;
Crawforth (1987) p.363–64; Goodison (1977)
p.197–99 pl.132–34

PATTEN Richard
a 1780–1860
Known to have sold: octant
Sources: Stimson (1985) p.113

PATTRICK Thomas
w 1799–1811
Optician, Globe M, Spec M
8 Orange St, Leicester Square,
London
20 Plumtree St, Bloomsbury,
London
1805 29 King St, Covent Garden, London
See also PATRICK George★
Sources: BM: Heal 105/80; H (JAC); Taylor (1966)
p.371

PAWSON Richard
w 1785
Optician, Stationer, Music S
1785 Angel Court, Princes St,
Westminster, London
Sources: GL: Sun 11936/327 no.501767 (MAC)

PAWSON & BRAILSFORD
a 1790–1810
See also BRAILSFORD John★
Known to have sold: drawing instruments
Sources: inst (pv)

PAYNE Benjamin Matthew
w 1800–1834
Scale M
1806–1811 29 Newcastle St, Strand, London
1807 23 Newcastle St, Strand, London
1807 5 Duke's Court, St.Martin's Lane,
London
1814–1832 395, near Southampton St, Strand,
London
Guild: Blacksmiths, fr 1800
Partnership: PAYNE & OVENDEN★
Apprenticed to ASTILL William★ 1788
Had apprentice:
OVENDEN James★ 1800
SHELTON Thomas 1805
WALKER Edward★ 1807
SAUNDERS Charles William 1808
PHILLIPS Samuel★ 1814 by t/o from FAGE
William (II)★
OAKES Henry 1814
SHENSTON James Templar★ 1817
YATES John 1819
RISEBROOK Robert 1828
ATTWOOD William 1831
Succeeded by SHENSTON James Templer★
Pat.1828 weighing machine; partnership
1811–1814
Known to have sold: balance, chrondrometer
Sources: GL: BKC 2881/16, 2881/17 (MAC):
CLRO CF1/1246; H; J; Pg; PO; inst (pv) (MAC)

PAYNE George Patmore
w 1849
Optician, Chrono M
1849 129 Mill St, Toxteth Park, Liverpool
See also MELLING & PAYNE★
Sources: G

PAYNE William
w 1831–1842
Watch M, Pedometer M, Navigation warehouse
1831 South Castle St, Liverpool
1831–1842 163 New Bond St, London
1846 62 & 163 New Bond St, London
Pat. pocket pedometer 1831
Sources: Pg; PO: Taylor (1966) p.457; Woodcroft
(1854)

PAYNE & OVENDEN Benjamin & James
w 1811–1814
Scale M
1811–1814 No. 395 near Southampton St,
Strand, London
See also
PAYNE Benjamin Matthew★
OVENDEN James★
Sources: H; Kt (JAC)

PEACE Philip
w 1842–1857
Baro M, Optical IM
1842–1845 61 Broughton St, Edinburgh
1846 71 South Frederick St, Edinburgh
1847–1857 99 Princes St, Edinburgh
Known to have sold: barometer
Sources: Bryden (1972) p.55; Goodrson (1977)
p.347

PEACHY William
w 1793
Math IM
1793 Coopers Row, London
Guild: [Grocers] Drapers fp 1793
Son of PEACHY William, free of Draper's Co. of
London
Apprenticed to RUST Joseph (I)★ 1786
Sources: Brown (1979a) p.52; DH: DPC Ap/Fr

PEACOCK James
w 1835–1836
Optical IM, Phil IM, Math IM
1835–1836 32 Fore St, Limehouse, London
Sources: R (JAC)

PEACOCK William (I)
w 1778–1790
Clock M
1778–1790 Kimbolton, Hunts
Known to have sold: barometer
Sources: Goodison (1977) p.347

PEACOCK William (II)
w 1789–1832
Watch M
1798 Spurrier Gate, York
Known to have sold: barometer
Sources: BW; Goodison (1977) p.347

PEALE Anne (Mrs)
w 1668–1682
[Spec M]
London
Guild: Spectaclemakers
Wife of PEALE Sampson
Had apprentice THROGMORTON John (II)★ 1682,
apparently t/o from THROGMORTON John (I)
Sources: GL: SMC 5213/1

PEALE Joseph
w 1667–1677
[Spec M]
London
Guild: Spectaclemakers
Had apprentice COOPER John 1670
Received charity from SMC 1684
Sources: GL: SMC 5213/1

PEALE Thomas
w 1624–1634
Spec M
Alternative name: PEELE
1634 London
Guild: Brewers, Spectaclemakers
Son of PEALE Richard, farmer, of Shepshed, Leics
Brother of PEALE William★
Apprenticed to THOMPSON John★ (VII) 1615
Had apprentice:
SAMBROOKE William 1624
MORLEY Peter 1628
HAWES John★ 1632/3
fr 1622 BREW; translated from Brewers to SMC
1634
Sources: CLRO: Ald 49 fol.14; GL: BREW
5445/13, 5445/14, 5445/15

PEALE William
w 1620–1634
Spec M
Alternative name: PEELE
1634   London
Guild: Brewers, Spectaclemakers
Son of PEALE Richard, farmer, of Shepshed, Leics
Brother of PEALE Thomas★
Apprenticed to ALTE Robert★ 1611
Had apprentice:
TOWERS George 1620
PARKER John 1626
COOKE William 1628
TOWERS Peter 1626
KNOWLES John 1633
EDWARDS Richard★ 1634
fr BREW 1619; translated from Brewers to SMC 1634
Sources: CLRO: Ald 49 fol.14; GL: BREW 5445/12 5445/13 5445/14 5445/15

PEARCE Charles
w 1849–1865
Optician, Hydro M
1849–1855   7 Suffolk St West, King's Cross, London
1859–1865   14 Suffolk St West, King's Cross, London
Sources: PO

PEARCE John
w 1799
Optician
1793   Angel Court, Leadenhall St, London
1799   City Green Yard, White Cross Street, parish of St. Giles, Cripplegate, London
Guild: Barbers, fr 1793
Father of PEARCE John s 1799 SC
Son of PEARCE Samuel, cloth worker, of London
Apprenticed to NEALE Isaac, barber, 1760
Sources: SH: SC Ap; GL: BC 5265/6 p.229

PEARCE Philip
w 1777
Math IM
1777   333 Wapping, London
1777   17 Sweetland Court, Tower Hill, London
Guild: Stationers, fr 1771
Son of PEARCE Philip, Scrivener, of London
Apprenticed to HUTCHINS Josiah★ 1764
Sources: GL: Sun 11936/257 no. 384748, 1262 no. 392533; McKenzie (1978) p.186

PEARCY William
w 1745
1745   London
Guild: Clockmakers
Had apprentice SAUNDERS Charles 1745 by t/o
Master of Math IM (Charles Saunders) turned over to him.
Sources: GL: MC 5304/3

PEARSON John
w 1790–1812
Math IM
1793   City Road, London

1805   6 City Rd, London
1812   Lambeth Walk, London
Guild: Stationers, fr 1782
Apprenticed to EVANS William (I)★
Father of PEARSON John (II) s 1812 ABC
Sources: BW; H; W (JAC); GL: ABC 12080; McKenzie (1978) p.119

PEARSON Joseph (I)
w 1797–1829
Optician, Spec M, Glass stainer
1797–1818   Moor St, Birmingham
1829–1830   42 Moor St, Birmingham
See also PEARSON Joseph (II)★
Sources: Chp; H; Pye; Wr

PEARSON Joseph (II)
w 1801–1841
Optician, Glass stainer
1801   129Moor St, Birmingham
1808–1818   Steelhouse Lane, Birmingham
1835–1841   114 Moor St, Birmingham
See also PEARSON Joseph (I)★
Sources: Chp; H; Pg; TWr

PEARSON Richard (I)
fl 1827
Optical IM, Math IM, Naut IM
          North Side Old Dock, Hull
See also PEARSON Robert★
Sources: Taylor (1966) p.431

PEARSON Richard (II)
w 1794–1823
Clock M, Watch M
1796–1823   Corner of King Street and High Street, Oxford
Apprenticed to TAWNEY Robert, Watch M
Had apprentice: LOCK Henry
s c.1778. Freeman of Oxford Dec 1785
Known to have sold: planetarium
Sources: Beeson (1989) p.133

PEARSON Robert
w 1834–1841
Math IM, Naut IM, Optician, Ship Chandler
1834   North Side Old Dock, Hull
1841   1 North Side Old Dock, Hull
See also PEARSON Richard (I)★
Sources: Pg

PECK John
w 1817 d 1842
Scale M
1817–1842   98 Guildford St, Borough, London
Guild: Blacksmiths, fr 1813
Apprenticed to SMITH William (II)★ 1806
Had apprentice:
MILES Willam Henry★ 1817
WEEDON Jonathan 1818 (fr 1836 as glass cutter)
HUNT William 1823
PROCTER Benjamin 1827
LAY John William 1830
CLERK Isaac 1836, t/o 1839 to BROOKE William of VC
DUGMORE Joseph 1839
MATTOCKS Charles Meares 1841, t/o 1842 to WEBB Richard William★

Sources: GL: BKC 2881/16, 2881/17, 2881/18 (MAC); Pg; PO (MAC); R (MAC)

PEDRALIO Baptista
a 1790–1820
        Norwich
Known to have sold: barometer
Sources: inst(s); Banfield (1991) p.167

PEDRETTI Peter
w 1831–1841
Baro M, Thermo M
Alternative name: PODRETTI Peter
1831–1840   26 Bath St, Clerkenwell, London
1841–1851   *Salmon and Compass* Public House, 13 Dorrington St, London [Listed as Baro M at this address in 1841 Census]
b c. 1790
Sources: PRO: Cs 1841 (AM); Pg; PO; R (jac); Goodison (1977) p.348

PEDRONE L.
w 1834 a 1850
Optician, Looking-glass M, Baro M, Thermometer M
1834   English St, Carlisle
          72 Market Place, Carlisle
See also PEDRONE Simone★
Instruments advertised: camera obscura, magic lantern, microscope, opera glasses, telescope
Sources: Bolle p.162; Goodison p.348

PEDRONE Louis
w 1835–1864
Jeweller, Optician, Math IM, Watch M, Silversmith
Alternative name: PEDRONI Lewis
1835–1837   27 Lord St, Liverpool
1839–1864   57 Lord St, Liverpool
See also PEDRONE L.★
Known to have sold: barometer, hygrometer, spirit level, telescope, thermometer
Sources: G; Sl; ChrSK 12 Dec 1985 lot 143 (MAC); inst (s)

PEDRONE Simone
a 1835–1850
        Carlisle
Known to have sold: barometer, hygrometer, thermometer
Sources: Banfield (1991) p.167 Bolle (1982) p.162

PEDUZZI Anthony
fl 1825 w 1841
Baro M
1834   23 Piccadilly, Manchester
1841   31 Oldham St, Manchester
See also PEDUZZI James★
Sources: Goodison (1977) p.348

PEDUZZI James
w 1825–1841
Baro M
1825–1826   49 Oldham St, Manchester
1834–1841   97 Oldham St, Manchester
1848   8 Foundry St, Manchester
See also PEDUZZI Anthony★
Sources: Sl; Goodison (1977) p.348

PEGLER Samuel
fl 1823–1844
Watch M, Clock M
             Blandford, Dorset
1830   Salisbury St, Blandford, Dorset
b 1791
Known to have sold: barometer
Sources: Pg; Loomes (1981a) (MAC)

PELL Thomas
w 1703–1718
Scale M
1707   White Lion St, Goodmans Fields,
             London
Guild: Blacksmiths, fr 1703
Son of PELL Thomas of LSC of London
Apprenticed to POLLARD Thomas★ 1695, t/o
1701 to ROBERTS Timothy★
Had apprentice:
COGGHILL Henry 1703/4, t/o 1707/8 to MINNO
Richard of GZC
PLIVEY (PLEVEY) William★ 1708
TAYLOR George 1714
JONES John 1718
Sources: GL: BKC 2881/9, 2886/3, 2886/4
(MAC); CH 12876/3 (MAC)

PENDLETON
c 1794
Known to have sold: chronometer
Sources: Taylor (1966) p.348

PENHALLOW Samuel
fr 1758 w 1790
Math IM
1790   Tower Hill, London
Guild: Merchant Taylors, fr 1758
Apprenticed to COLE Benjamin (I)★
Father of PENHALLOW Samuel (II) s 1790 STC
Sources: GL: MTC MF 319, 324 (MAC);
McKenzie (1978) p.259

PENLINGTON John
w 1821–1828
Chrono M, Watch M, Clock M
1821–1824   2 Parker St, Liverpool
1823   1 Rose Vale, (residence ?) Liverpool
1823   4 Parker St, (shop) Liverpool
1824   3 Parker St, Liverpool
1827   66 Church St, Liverpool
1828   65 Church St, Liverpool
See also
PENLINGTON Joseph★
PENLINGTON Samuel, Thomas & John★
Sources: Bn; G(MAC); Loomes (1975)

PENLINGTON Joseph
w 1828–1857
Chrono M, Watch M
1827   42 Hanover St, Liverpool
1828–1834   39 Church St, Liverpool
1829   11 Leigh St, Liverpool
1834–1837   36 Church St, Liverpool
1835–1837   37 Church St, Liverpool
1839   67 Church St, Liverpool
1841–1857   3 St.George's Crescent North,
             Liverpool
1874–1876   14 Oxton Rd, Birkenhead, Livrpool

1877–1895   3 Grange Rd, Liverpool
1877–1895   Regent Place, Birkenhead, Liverpool
See also
PENLINGTON John★
PENLINGTON Samuel, Thomas★ & John★
PENLINGTON Thomas & John★
Sources: G; LM index (MAC); Loomes (1975)

PENLINGTON Samuel, Thomas & John
w 1851
Chrono M
1851   22 Tarleton St, Liverpool
Brothers of PENLINGTON Joseph★
Sources: G; LM index (MAC)

PENLINGTON Thomas & John
w 1847–1851
Chrono M
1847   Allerton Rd, Much Woolton,
             Liverpool
1851   22 Tarleton St, Liverpool
Brothers of PENLINGTON Joseph★
Sources: G; LM index (MAC)

PENNINGTON Robert (I)★
w 1780–1824
Alternative name: PENLINGTON ?
1822–1823   Camberwell, Surrey, London
Succeeded by PENNINGTON & SON Robert★
Submitted chronometers for trial at Royal
Greenwich Observatory 1822–1824, and won
second prize in 1823
Known to have sold: astronomical clock,
chronometer
Sources: CUL: RGO 1143 fol.2-6; Taylor (1966)
p.321

PENNINGTON Robert & Richard
w 1797
Chrono M
1797   Liverpool
Sources: LM index (MAC)

PENNINGTON & SON Robert
w 1831–1851
Chrono M
1831   Corner of Orchard Row,
             Camberwell, London
1846   11 Portland Row, Camberwell,
             London
1851   11 Portland Row, Camberwell Rd,
             London
Partnership of PENNINGTON Robert (I) and his
son Robert (II)
Took over from PENNINGTON Robert (I)★
Submitted chronometers for trial at Royal
Greenwich Observatory 1831
Sources: CUL: RGO 1143 fol.2–9; PO

PENNY John
w 1666–1673
Spec M
1670   London
1695   Mrs Penny was at Ratcliff Highway,
             London
Guild: Spectaclemakers
Had apprentice KNIGHT John 1673
Fined by SMC for selling bad spectacles 1670;

probably d by 1693 when Mrs Penny paid search
fee to SMC
Known to have sold: spectacles
Sources: GL: SMC 5213/1

PENNY William
w 1816–1849
Math IM, Phil IM, Optician
Alternative name: PENNEY
             Limehouse, London
1816   24 Broad St, Ratcliff, London
1817–1849   25 Broad St, Ratcliff Crescent,
             London
Known to have sold: sextant
Sources: Bn; H; J; Kt (JAC); Pg; PO; Und; inst
Huntly House Mu, Edinburgh (MAC)

PENSA John
w 1831–1840
Baro M, Thermo M
1831–1834   39 Charles St, Hatton Garden,
             London
1835–1840   5 Greville St, Hatton Garden,
             London
Succeeded by PENSA Margaret★
See also PENSA & SON★
Sources: Pg; PO; R (JAC)

PENSA Margaret (Mrs)
w 1840–1848
Baro M, Thermometer M
1840   5 Greville St, Hatton Garden,
             London
1845–1848   25 Charles St, Hatton Garden,
             London
Took over from
PENSA John★
PENSA & SON★
Sources: PO

PENSA & SON
w 1835–1840
Baro M, Thermometer M
1835–1840   5 Greville St, Hatton Garden,
             London
Succeeded by PENSA Margaret★
Same premises as PENSA John★
Sources: PO; R (JAC)

PENSOTTI Joseph
w 1816–1841
Baro S, Umbrella M, Hardwareman
1816–1841   High St, Dudley
See also PENSOTTI S.★
Sources: H (DJB); Pg

PENSOTTI S.
a 1800–1820
             2 Stone St, Dudley
See also PENSOTTI Joseph★
Known to have sold: barometer, thermometer
Sources: inst (s) (MAC)

PEPLOW William
w 1818–1885
Watch M
1818   Watling St, Shrewsbury, Salop
1828–1856   Wellington, Salop

1856–1885   Shifnal, Salop
b 1794; d 1895
Known to have sold: waywiser
Sources: inst (pv) (MAC); Loomes (1976)

PERCIVAL William
w 1848
Rule M
1848   5 Maddox St, Liverpool
Sources: Sl

PERKINS Anne
w 1762–1763
Chandler
Alternative name: Ann
1762   Beer Lane, Tower St, London
Guild: Spectaclemakers, fr 1762
Had apprentice SPENCER Richard★ 1763
See also SPENCER & PERKINS★
Freed in SMC by purchase
Sources: GL: SMC 5213/3

PERKINS Eysum
s 1670 w 1682
1682   At Redriff the end of Love Lane,
        London
Guild: [Clockmakers]
Apprenticed to ATKINSON James (I)★
Sources: GL: CKC 2710/2 fol.14 r–v; Loomes
(1981b)

PERKINS Robert
w 1713–1718
Spec M
1713   Angel St, Parish of Christ's Church
        Newgate St, London
Guild: Spectaclemakers, fr 1712
Apprenticed to CARTER Charles★ 1700
Had apprentice:
MORRIS William 1713
WOOD Benjamin 1718
Received charity from SMC 1744
Sources: GL: SMC 5213/2 p.79, 83, 107; 6031/1;
CH 12823/8 p.34

PERKS Francis
w 1818–1841
Rule M, Square M
1818   Waddam's Hill, Wolverhampton
1828–1829   3 New St, Wolverhampton
1841   New St, Wolverhampton
See also
PERKS Robert★
PERKS William★
Sources: PB, Pg

PERKS Robert
w 1802–1811
Rule M
1802   8 Berry St, Wolverhampton
1805–1811   Temple St, Wolverhampton
See also
PERKS William★
PERKS Francis★
Sources: Wolverhampton rate books (MAC); H

PERKS William
w 1833–1834

Rule M
Alternative name: PERKES
1833–1834   Bilston St, Wolverhampton
See also
PERKS Robert★
PERKS Francis★
Sources: Br; Wh

PERRY A.O.
w 1825–1826
Phil IM
1825–1826   28 Great Bath St, Clerkenwell,
            London
Attended London Mechanics Institute 1825–1826
Sources: LMIR (AM)

PERRY Andrew
w 1839–1845
Optician, Math IM
1839–1842   5 Fitzwilliam Place, Grangegorman
            Lane, Dublin
1843–1845   21 Grangegorman Lane, Dublin
See also PERRY Thomas★
Sources: Burnett & Morrison-Low (1989) p.132

PERRY Thomas
w 1835–1837
Optician
1835–1837   22 Grangegorman Lane, Dublin
Sources: Burnett & Morrison-Low (1989) p.133

PERSHOUSE & WELCH
w 1828–1835
Spec M, Scale M, Candlestick M, Brass Founder
1828–1835   Dean St, Birmingham
Sources: Pg; West; Wr (MAC)

PETHER T.
a 1780–1800
Carver
            Opposite Physician's Hall in Rose
            St, New Town, Edinburgh
Known to have sold: microscope
Sources: Holbrook (1992) p.130

PEVERELLE John Bernard
w 1849–1854
Baro M, Thermo M
1849–1854   16 Pershore St, Birmingham
Sources: Sl; Goodison (1977) p.348

PHELPS James
w 1846
Optician, Math IM
1846   5 City terrace, Old Street Rd,
        London
Took over from PHELPS Mary★
Sources: PO

PHELPS Mary (Mrs)
w 1841–1845
Optician, Math IM
1841–1845   5 City terrace, Old Street Rd,
            London
Took over from PHELPS Thomas (II)★
Succeeded by PHELPS James★
Sources: PO

PHELPS Thomas (I)
w 1799–1822
Optician, Math IM
            159 Fleet St, London
            4 Cock Court, St.Martin's le Grand,
            London
1799   36 Fetter Lane, London
1805   30 Red Lion St, Holborn, London
1817   33 Monkwell St, Cripplegate, London
1822   28 Holywell Lane, Shoreditch,
        London
1822   19 Jewin St, Cripplegate, London
Succeeded by PHELPS Thomas (II)★
Took over from STRETCH James★
See also
PHELPS & DAVENPORT★
PHELPS William★
Sources: Bn; H; J (MAC); Kt; Pg (JAC)

PHELPS Thomas (II)
w 1823–1840
Optician, Math IM, Spec M
1823–1834   28 Holywell Lane, Curtain Rd,
            London
1836–1840   5 City Terrace, Old Street Rd,
            London
Succeeded by PHELPS Mary★
Took over from PHELPS Thomas (I)★
See also
PHELPS William★
PHELPS & DAVENPORT★
Associated with HARRIS William (III)★ as supplier
Sources: PRO: bankruptcy proceedings (AM); Pg;
PO

PHELPS William
w 1819
Optician
1819   Castle St, Royal Exchange, London
See also
PHELPS Thomas (I)★
PHELPS Thomas (II)★
Sources: R (JAC)

PHELPS & DAVENPORT Thomas & James
w 1794
Spec M
1794   9 Cock Court, St.Martin's le Grand,
        London
See also
DAVENPORT James★
DAVENPORT Charles★
PHELPS Thomas (I)★
Sources: GH: register of goldsmiths' marks (JAC)

PHILCOX George
w 1839
Chrono M
            257 High St, Borough, London
Succeeded by PHILCOX & CO, George★
Pat. improved chronometer 1839 and 1846
Known to have sold: chronometer
Sources: Taylor (1966) p.477; Woodcroft (1854)

PHILCOX & CO. George
w 1846+
Chrono M

1846   104 Fenchurch St, London
1846   and 247 Borough High St, London
Took over from PHILCOX George★
Sources: PO

PHILIP Robert
fl 1830
Optician
     19 North St, Brighton
Sources: Taylor (1966) p.457

PHILLIPS Edward
fr 1763 w 1781
Scale M
     Mould Maker's Row, St.Martin's le
     Grand, London
Guild: Blacksmiths, fr 1763
Apprenticed to BRIND William★ 1755
See also
PHILLIPS Samuel★
PHILLIPS Walter★
PHILLIPS Elizabeth★
Known to have sold: balance
Sources: GL: BKC 2886/5 (MAC); inst (pv)
(MAC)

PHILLIPS Elizabeth
w 1722–1723
     London
Guild: Blacksmiths
Wife of PHILLIPS Walter★
Had apprentice NEWTON William (I)★ 1722, t/o
1723 to OVERING Thomas★
Sources: GL: BKC 2888 (MAC)

PHILLIPS Samuel
w 1826–1854
Scale M, Measure M
1826   5 Coal Yard, Drury Lane, London
1830   19 Bath St, London
1832–1849   18 Vine St, Hatton Wall, London
Guild: [Haberdashers]
Apprenticed to FAGE William (II)★ 1810
PAYNE Benjamin Matthew★ by t/o 1814
Succeeded by PHILLIPS Mrs.E.
Sources: GL: HC 15860/9 (MAC); Pg; PO

PHILLIPS Silvanus
w 1803–1809
Cooper, Turner, Measure M
1801   26 Great Tower St, London
1803–1804   Great Tower St, London
Guild: Vintners, fr 1801
Son of PHILLIPS Benjamin, hairdresser. of London
Apprenticed to PURCHAS Henry Ansley 1790
Had apprentice:
KING John 1803
PHILLIPS Daniel 1804
WILCOX John 1819
ASPERNE James 1824
Master VC 1846
Sources: GL:VC 15220/3 p.222,320; 15212/2 p.81
15201/16 p.116, /17 p.275,593; 15209/2 fol.2

PHILLIPS Solomon
w 1839–1844
Optical IM, Philo IM, Math IM, Optician
1839   43 Rathbone Place, London

1840–1844   231 Tottenham Court Rd, London
Succeeded by PHILLIPS & JACOBS★
Sources: R; PO; Calvert (1971) p.34

PHILLIPS Walter
fr 1704 w 1719
Scale M
     Angel & Scales in Bartholomew
     Lane near ye Royal Exchange,
     London
Guild: Blacksmiths, fr 1704
Apprenticed to BEN John★
Had apprentice:
OVEN Henry★ 1712
MOORE Joseph 1719 by t/o from PICARD John★
Succeeded by OVERING Thomas★
Known to have sold: balance
Sources: GL: BKC 2881/9, 2886/3, 2886/4
(MAC); inst (pv) (MAC)

PHILLIPS & JACOBS
w 1845–1846
Optical IM, Phil IM, Math IM
1845–1846   231 Tottenham Court Rd, London
Took over from PHILLIPS Solomon★
Sources: PO

PHILLIPS & KING
w 1829
Measure M
1829   25 & 26 Great Tower St, City Rd,
     London
Possibly partnership of PHILLIPS Silvanus★ and his
apprentice KING John
Sources: R (JAC)

PHILP Robert James
w 1851–1855
Optician
1851–1855   8 Barnsbury Place, Upper St,
     Islington, London
Sources: PO; Wk

PHIPPS A.
w 1831–1832
Math IM
1831–1832   St. Andrew Hill, London
Attended London Mechanics Institute 1831–1832
Sources: LMIR (AM)

PHIPPS John
w 1729 r 1757
[Spec M]
1725   London
1750   Described as residing in the country
Guild: Spectaclemakers, fr 1725
Son of PHIPPS Joseph, butcher, of Shoreditch,
London
Apprenticed to STERROP Thomas (III)★ 1718
Had apprentice:
MORRIS John★ 1729
STOAKS William 1736 reported run away 1741
b c.1702
Sources: GL: SMC 5213/2 p.107, 159, 207+,
5213/3 p.155+; Court & Von Rohr (1928–29)
p.78

PHYTHIAN Dodd
w 1734
     London
Guild: Blacksmiths, fr 1728/9
Apprenticed to
HOE Robert 1720
OVEN Henry 1723 by t/o
Had apprentice GLANISTER John 1734
Sources: GL: BKC 2886/4, 2888 (MAC)

PICARD John
w 1708–1734
Scale M
Alternative name: Iohn
     Ye Hand & Scales, the Corner of
     Maiden Lane in Wood St, London
Guild: Blacksmiths, fr 1705/6
Apprenticed to SNART John (I)★ 1698/9
Had apprentice:
LUKE John 1708
BALL William 1710 by t/o from WINSPEARE
Thomas★, t/o to BURTON James (I)★ 1713/14
KNIGHT Valentine 1714
MOORE Joseph 1715 t/o to PHILLIPS Walter★ 1719
ASTY John 1717
WILKINSON Henry 1718/19
SOMMERS Joseph (I)★ 1720
SOMMERS Samuel 1720/1
SOMMERS John 1720/1
GREENHILL Benjamin 1724
PIC(K)ARD Joseph, his son, 1727
JONES James 1729
BROOKSBY Thomas (I)★ 1730
SANGSTER James★ 1731
RANDALL Giles 1732 t/o 1739 to BROOKSBY
Thomas★
SANGSTER William★ 1734/5 t/o 1739 to
BROOKSBY Thomas★
In Bedlam Lunatic Asylum 1737
Known to have sold: balance
Sources: GL: BKC 2881/10, 2881/11, 2886/3,
2886/4 (MAC); inst SM Wellcome

PICK Andrew
w 1767
Rule M
1767   Parish of St. Giles Cripplegate
     London
Probably the Andrew Pick apprenticed to
BETTESWORTH Peter★ 1721
Father of PICK Francis s 1767 to BAMPTON
William★
Sources: GL: PWC 7102 fol.3; McKenzie (1978)
p.35

PICKERING David
w 1796–1805
Scale M
1796–1805   73 Pill Lane, Dublin
See also
PICKERING James★
PICKERING William★
B.apt Bank of Ireland
Sources: H; Wi (MAC)

PICKERING James
w 1810–1834
Scale M

1817   30 Upper Sackville St, Dublin
1820–1834   73 Pill Lane, Dublin
See also
PICKERING James★
PICKERING David★
PICKERING William★
B.apt Bank of Ireland
Known to have sold: balance
Instruments advertised: balance, weights
Sources: Pg; Und (MAC); Wi (MAC); inst WM
noted by MAC

PICKERING Thomas
fr c.1788 w 1847
Optical IM, Phil IM, Math IM
             1 Regent St, Lambeth, London
1839–1847   36 Regent St, Lambeth, London
Guild: [Joiners]
Son of PICKERING Thomas, bricklayer; d, of St.
Andrew Holborn, London
Apprenticed to DANCER Michael★ 1781
Sources: Pg; PO; R (JAC)

PICKERING William (I)
w 1799–1809
Scale M
1800–1804   73 Pill Lane, Dublin
1809   78 Pill Lane, Dublin
See also
PICKERING James★
PICKERING David★
B.apt Bank of Ireland
Sources: H; Wi (MAC)

PICKERING William (II)
w 1850
Math IM
1850   12 Red Lion Court, Spitalfields,
             London
Sources: PO

PICKETT J. & G. J.
w 1837–1842
Optical IM, Philo IM, Math IM
1837–1842   15 Princes St, Barbican, London
Sources: R (JAC)

PICKETT John
w 1780–1839
Clock M, Whitesmith
1830–1839   High St, Marlborough
Associated with GOODBEHERE, WIGAN & CO as
retailer of their balances
Known to have sold: balance
Sources: BW; Pg; R; inst St. Fagan's Mu Cardiff
(MAC); Britten (1982); Sheppard & Musham
(1975) no.47

PICKFORD John
v 1814–1870
Watch M
             39 Mersey St, Liverpool
Known to have sold: chronometer
Sources: inst LM; LM index (MAC); Baillie (1951)

PIDDING Humphrey
w 1688
Spec M

1688   London
Guild: Spectaclemakers fr 1686/7
Apprenticed to HICKETT John★ nd
Sources: GL: SMC 5213/1

PIDGEON John
fr 1763 w 1768
[Scale M]
             London
Guild: Blacksmiths, fr 1763
Apprenticed to READ Joseph★ 1754
Had apprentice MAHANY John 1768
Sources: GL: BKC 2885/1, 2886/5 (MAC)

PIERS Charles
w 1843–1888
Chrono M, Watch M, Optician
1843   2 Berry St, Liverpool
1845   4 Berry St, Liverpool
1847–1853   34 Strand St, Liverpool
1855–1867   49 South Castle St, Liverpool
1888   29 South Castle St, Liverpool
Worked for MOLYNEUX Robert (as foreman)
Known to have sold: octant, sextant
Instruments advertised: chronometer, compass
(magnetic), quadrant, sextant
Sources: G; K; Sby 22 July 1977 lot 3 (DJB); inst
(s) (DJB); TCd LM; LM index (MAC)

PIGGOTT -
w 1672
Rule S
1672   In Fleet St, over against Chancery
             Lane end, London
Associated with ELMES William★ whose rules he
sold
Known to have sold: rule
Sources: GL: CKC 2710/1 p.244; Loomes (1981 b)

PIGGOTT E.
w 1824
Math IM
1824   3 Penton St, Walworth, London
See also
PIGGOTT Peter W★
PIGGOTT William P★
PIGGOTT George★
Sources: R (JAC)

PIGGOTT George
w ?fm 1839 w 1859
Math IM, Drawing IM
1839–1859   4 Penton St, Walworth, London
Attended London Mechanics Institute 1839–1841
Same premises as PIGGOTT Peter William★
Sources: LMIR (AM); PO

PIGGOTT P.
w 1840–1841
Drawing IM
1840–1841   4 Penton St, Walworth, London
See also
PIGGOTT Peter William★
PIGGOTT William Peter★
Attended London Mechanics Institute 1840–1841
Sources: LMIR (AM); PO

PIGGOTT Peter William
w 1816–1857
Math IM, Drawing IM
1816   Peacock St, Newington, London
1824–1855   4 Penton St, Walworth, London
Guild: Merchant Taylors, fr 1816
Father of PIGGOTT William Peter★
Son of PIGGOTT John, engraver, of Walworth,
London
Apprenticed to VENTOM Thomas★ 1800
Had apprentice:
BOLEN James 1816
FRANCIS Lawrence E. 1824
PIGGOTT William Peter★, his son, 1829
Succeeded by PIGGOTT George★
See also PIGGOTT E.★
Attended London Mechanics Institute 1829–1838,
1840–1848
Sources: GL: MTC MF 320, 324; LMIR (AM);
Pg; PO

PIGGOTT William Peter
w 1838–1851
Math IM, Optical IM, Phil IM
1838   13 Arnold Place, Walworth, London
1840   20 Wardrobe Place, Doctor's
             Commons, London
1845–1846   11 Wardrobe Place, Doctor's
             Commons, London
1848   Great Carter Lane, Doctor's
             Commons, London
1851   523 Oxford St, London
Guild: Merchant Taylors, fr 1838
Partnership: PIGGOTT & BODDY★
Apprenticed to PIGGOTT Peter William★, his
father, 1829
Had apprentice:
COOKE Frederick William 1838
BODDY Thomas★ 1840
SMITH Charles Dennis 1847
HART Henry William 1848
Succeeded by PIGGOTT & CO. William P.★
See also PIGGOTT George★
Pat. dials 1845, nautical instruments 1848.
Attended London Mechanics Institute 1826–1832,
1837
Sources: GL: MTC MF 320,324; Woodcroft
(1854); LMIR (AM); PO; Wk

PIGGOTT & BODDY William Peter &
Thomas
w 1849
Math IM, Phil IM, Opticians
1849   523 Oxford St, London
1849   and 3 Gt Carter Lane, London
See also
PIGGOTT William Peter★
BODDY Thomas★
Sources: PO

PIGGOTT & CO. William Peter
w 1851–1859
Math IM, Phil IM, Optician, Drawing IM
1851–1859   523 Oxford St, London
Took over from PIGGOTT & BODDY
Sources: PO

PIGOT John
w 1836
Baro M, Thermometer M
1836   7 Noble St, Wilmington Square,
        Clerkenwell, London
Sources: Pg; Goodison (1977) p.349

PILKINGTON George
w 1835–1849
Optician, Math IM, Philo IM
        7 Vine St, Laystall St, [Holborn],
        London
1839   4 St James St, Clerkenwell, London
1839–1849   14 Clarence Place, Pentonville,
        London
Succeeded by PILKINGTON John★
Sources: R; (JAC) PO; Pg

PILKINGTON John
w 1850–1851
Optician, Math IM, Phil IM, Telescope M
1850–1851   14 Clarence Place, Pentonville,
        London
Took over from PILKINGTON George★
Succeeded by PILKINGTON M.A. (Mrs)★
Sources: PO; Wk

PILKINGTON M. A. (Mrs)
w 1851–1859
Math IM, Phil IM, Spectacle M, Optician
Alternative name: Mary
1851–1855   14 Clarence Place, London
1859   205 Pentonville Rd, London N
        Took over from PILKINGTON John★
        Sources: PO; Wk

PILLISCHER Moritz
w 1851–1887
Optician, Math IM, Phil IM, Met IM
Alternative name: Morrice
1851–1853   398 Oxford St, London
1854–1887   88 New Bond St, London
Succeeded by PILLISCHER Jacob, his nephew
e 1845; Medals Ex 1851,1855,1862
Known to have sold: barometer, binoculars,
microscope
Instruments advertised: microscope, opera glasses,
telescope
Sources: Cat 1851; Wk; ChrSK 4 Jun 1987 lot 288;
Anderson et al (1990) p.64; Goodison (1977) p.349;
Turner G. (1989) p.259–60, 312

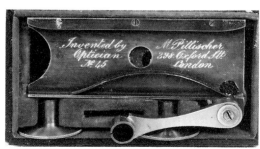

PINCHBECK Christopher (I)
a 1691 d 1732
Clock M

-1721   St.George's Court, St.John's Lane,
        London
1721   The Astronomico-Musical Clock,
        nr. Leg of Mutton, Fleet St, London
Guild: Clockmakers
Father of PINCHBECK Christopher (II)★
Succeeded by PINCHBECK Christopher (II)★
b c. 1670; inventor of the copper & zinc alloy
called pinchbeck
Known to have sold: astronomical clock
Sources: King & Millburn (1978) p.136, 141–42;
Loomes (1981b)

PINCHBECK Christopher (II)
a 1731 d 1783
Toyman, Mechanician
1737–1746   Sign of Pinchbeck's Head, Fleet St,
        London
1747   Cockspur St, London
1749   Facing the Haymarket, London
1774   Pall Mall, London
Guild: Clockmakers fr 1781, Needlemakers fr by
purchase 1774
Father of PINCHBECK Wm s 1760 PSC
Son of PINCHBECK Christopher (I)★
Brother of PINCHBECK Edward★
PINCHBECK John
Associated with KIRK John★
NORTON Eardley★
FERGUSON James★
R.apt Geo.III ?; Pat. candlestick, memo- pad,
snuffers 1768, 1776; b c. 1710; made honorary
freeman of CKC
Known to have sold: astronomical clock,
thermometer
Sources: GL: NC 2817/2 fol.86v; CKC 11, 568;
PSC 5669/1 fol.169v; Daily Ad. 5 & 15 July 1749
(JRM); King & Millburn (1978) p.145; Taylor
(1966) p.188

PINI Joseph
w 1835–1837
Baro M, Thermometer M, Looking-glass M
1835   1 Princes St, Red Lion Square,
        London
1836   3 Princes St, Red Lion Square,
        [Holborn], London
1837–1846   23 Brooke St, Holborn, London
Succeeded by PINI & CO Joseph★
See also
PINI Joseph & Luigi★
PINI & RONCORONI BROS
Same premises as ZAMBRA Joseph Cesare★
b c. 1807 in foreign parts
Known to have sold: barometer, hygrometer,
thermometer.
Sources: PRO: Cs 1841 (AM); PO; Sby, Jan 1985
(MAC)

PINI Joseph & Luigi
w 1848–1860
Baro M, Thermometer M
1848–1852   23 Brooke St, Holborn, London
Succeeded by PINI & CO Joseph★
See also PINI Joseph★
Sources: PO; Wk; Goodison (1977) p.349

PINI & CO Joseph
w 1837–1842
Baro M, Thermometer M
1837–1842   23 Brooke St, Holborn, London
Succeeded by PINI Joseph & Luigi★
Took over from PINI Joseph★
Sources: Pg; R (JAC); PO; Goodison (1977) p.349

PIOTTI James
w 1806–1823
Optician, Carver, Gilder
1806–1823   Queen St, Hull
1822–1823   2 Queen St, Hull
See also PIOTY James★
Sources: Bn; Goodison (1977) p.349

PIOTY James
w 1805★
Optician
1805   High St, Lincoln
See also PIOTTI James★
Sources: H

PIPER John
w em 1825–1826
Optician
1825–1826   Dollond's, St. Paul's Churchyard,
        London
Worked for DOLLOND George (I)★
Attended London Mechanics Institute 1825–1826
Sources: LMIR (AM)

PITSALLA Charles
w 1805
Baro M
Alternative name: PIZZALA ? PISTALLA
1805   221 High Holborn, London
Known to have sold: barometer
Sources: H; Goodison (1977) p.349; Banfield
(1993) p.31

PITTS Edmund
w 1825
Math IM
1825   15 Queen St, Blackfriars, London
Attended London Mechanics Institute 1825
Sources: LMIR (AM)

PITZOLI Anthony
w 1831–1835
Weatherglass M
1831   86 Pill Lane, Dublin
1832–1835   86½ Pill Lane, Dublin
Sources: Burnett & Morrison Low (1989) p.133

PIXLEY Thomas (I)
w 1743
Scale M
        London
Guild: Blacksmiths, fr 1741
Son of PIXLEY John of London
Apprenticed to JACKSON John (I)★ 1730
Attended Christ's Hospital School, London
Sources: GL: BKC 2885/1, 2886/4; CH 12876/3,
12823/5 p.1

PIXLEY Thomas (II)
w 1767–1792

Scale M
   Near Vine St, in the Minories,
   London
1792 (Residence) Langthorn Court, Bell
   Alley, London
Guild: Blacksmiths, fr 1762
Apprenticed to WADE Thomas★ 1754 t/o to READ
Joseph★ 1760
Had apprentice:
EVERITT George★ 1767, rebound 1769
to MEYMOTT Clement★
YATES John 1775
ROYSER John Robert 1786
Known to have sold: balance
Sources: GL: BKC 2881/15–16; 2886/5, 2888
(MAC); Wil; inst Luton Mu (MAC)

PIZZALA Augustus
w 1837–1853
Baro M, Thermo M, Drawing IM, Hydro M,
Optician, Math IM, Phil IM
1837 22 Leather Lane
1839–1846 7 Charles St, Hatton Garden,
   London
1847–1853 19 Hatton Garden, London
Took over from PIZZALA Francis Augustus (I)★
Succeeded by PIZZALA Francis Augustus (II)★
Known to have sold: barometer, thermometer
Sources: Pg; PO; Goodison (1977) p.349

PIZZALA Francis Augustus (I)
w 1837–1839
Baro M, Thermometer M
1837–1839 7 Charles St, Hatton Garden,
   London
1839 and 22 Leather Lane, [Holborn],
   London
Had apprentice NEGRETTI Henry★ 1838
Known to have sold: barometer
Sources: Pg; PO; R; Goodison (1977) p.190,349

PIZZALA Francis Augustus (II)
w 1851–1865
Optician, Baro M, Thermo M, Drawing IM,
Hydrometer M, Math IM, Phil IM
1851–1860 19 Hatton Garden, London
1865 25A Hatton Garden, London
Ex. 1851
Sources: PO; Cat 1851 (MAC); Goodison (1977)
p.349; Turner G. (1983a) p.310

PIZZALLA Joseph
w 1809–1830
Looking-glass M
1809–1830 84 Leather Lane, Holborn, London
Father of PIZZALLA Robert s 1830 to CURRY
William, engraver, STC
Known to have sold: barometer
Sources: Stat: STC Memo book; H; Und (JAC);
Goodison (1977) p.349

PIZZI Jane
w 1840–1843
Baro M, Thermo M
1840 27 Cross St, Hatton Garden, London
1840–1843 19 Leather Lane, London
Wife of PIZZI Valentino★
Took over from PIZZI Valentino★

Succeeded by PIZZI & NEGRETTI★
d c.1845
Sources: PO; Rate Books (JAC); Goodison (1977)
p.349

PIZZI Valentino
w 1835 d 1840
Baro M
Alternative name: Valentine
1835–1840 27 Cross St, Hatton Garden, London
Husband of PIZZI Jane★
Succeeded by PIZZI Jane★
Sources: R; PO; Goodison (1977) p.349

PIZZI & CETTI
c 1835–1842
Watch M, Clock M
   Buckingham
Took over from PIZZI & ORTELLI
Succeeded by CETTI John
Known to have sold: barometer
Sources: Goodison (1977) p.349; Legg (1975);
Loomes (1976)

PIZZI & NEGRETTI Jane & Henry
w 1844
Baro M
1844 19 Leather Lane, London
Took over from PIZZI Jane★
Succeeded by NEGRETTI & CO. Henry★
Sources: PO; JAC

PLACE J.
a 1830–1850
   13 Bull St, Birmingham
Known to have sold: hydrometer
Sources: inst (s) (MAC)

PLACE William
w 1694
Known to have sold: Gunter's rule
Sources: Wynter & Turner (1975) fig.71

PLANT John
w 1726–1727
[Spec M]
   London
Guild: Spectaclemakers, fr 1725
Apprenticed to CARTER Charles★ 1709
Had apprentice:
DANN Daniel 1725/6, t/o 1726 to CARTER
Charles★
ALLISON Mathew 1727
Fined by SMC for employing 'foreigners', i.e.
non-freemen, 1726–1727
Sources: GL: SMC 5213/2 p.160, 169, 176, 182;
6031/1

PLAT John
a 1690–1730
Alternative name: Iohn, I.P.
Known to have sold: weights
Sources: inst MHS (MAC); Sheppard & Musham
(1975) p.172

PLIMPTON George
w 1831–1834
Optician, Math IM, Phil IM

1824–1825 46 Surrey Row, Blackfriars, London
   Lincoln's Inn Passage, London
   5 Tysoe St, Exmouth St, Spa Fields,
   London
Attended London Mechanics Institute 1824–1825
Sources: R (JAC); LMIR (AM)

PLIVEY William
w 1737–1784
Scale M
Alternative name: PLEVEY, PLEVY
   London
Guild: Blacksmiths, fr 1716
Apprenticed to PELL Thomas, 1708
Had apprentice:
BEAN James 1717
DIKES Robert 1721
MARSH Henry 1723
BELL Thomas 1726
PLIVEY James, his son, 1737
HASTERLEY Michael 1767 t/o same day to
MOFFETT James★
COOMBE Henry 1768 t/o same day to SEWELL
George★
YOUNG John (I)★ 1773 t/o same day to SEWELL
George★
WINDSOR Joseph 1774 t/o same day to SEWELL
George★
Attended Christ's Hospital School, London
Sources: GL: BKC 2881/10, 2886/4, 2886/5
(MAC); CH 12876/3 (MAC)

PLUMMER Walter
d 1768
Math IM
-1768 Wapping, London
Sources: *Gazetteer* 3 May 1768 (MAC)

POCHAINE John
w 1811–1816
Baro M, Thermo M
1811–1816 Dean St, Newcastle on Tyne
Known to have sold: hydrostatic bubbles
Sources: H (DJB); Goodison (1977) p.349;
Holbrook (1992) p.89

POCOCK Henry
w 1836
Optician
1836 4 Baden Place, Borough, London
Attended London Mechanics Institute, 1836
Sources: LMIR (AM)

POCOCK William
a 1780–1810
   Porter's Block, Smithfield Bars,
   London
Known to have sold: balance
Sources: inst (s) (MAC)

POLLARD Joseph
w 1820–1840
Optician, Hydro M, Optical IM, Phil IM
   42 Princes St, Leicester Square,
   London
1822 62 Millbank St, Westminster,
   London
1822 59 Millbank St, Westminster, London

1839 42 Brewer St, Golden Square,
    London
Sources: Bn; Kt (JAC); Pg

POLLARD Thomas

w 1695–1714
[Scale M]
    London
Guild: Blacksmiths, fr 1692
Apprenticed to
NEALE Samuel★ 1683/4 t/o to FREEMAN Samuel
(I)★
Had apprentice:
PELL Thomas★ 1695 t/o to ROBERTS Timothy★
1701
WILLIAMS William 1698
HIDE Daniel 1699
WAYTE John 1714 t/o 1716 to WAY Charles
Sources: GL: BKC 2881/8, 2881/9,
2886/2–2886/4 (MAC)

POLSON Richard

w 1597–1626
Brewer, Master of several known Spec M
    London
Guild: Brewers, Brother 1597
Father of POLSON Thomas fp 1627
Had apprentice:
TRANELL John 1597
TURLINGTON John★ 1610/11
ASHE Thomas★ 1609/10
ALTE Robert★ c.1602
CAWRA Thomas c.1602
CLIFFORD Robert★ 1609
THOMPSON John★ 1605
ALTE Thomas 1613/14
COPELAND Thomas★ 1617
DACIN William 1625/6
CRANWELL Joseph 1626
Sources: GL: Brew 5445/10 /12 /13 /14

POLTI Joseph

w 1822–1830
Baro M, Thermo M, Looking-glass M
1822–1826 Coxon's Yard, Kirkgate, Leeds
1830–1834 72 Kirkgate, Leeds
Sources: Bn (DJB); Pg; PWh

POND Edward

w 1612
Mathematician, Almanac M, Physician, Math IM
1612   The Globe, a little without Temple
    Bar, between the Bull head and
    Mermaid taverns, London
Associated with HOPTON Arthur
Sources: Bryden (1992) p.306n,307n

PONISSO J.

a 1800–1850
    Edinburgh
Known to have sold: barometer, thermometer
Sources: Goodison (1977) p.350

PONISSO & CO. J.

a 1800–1850
    Glasgow
See also PONISSO J.★

Known to have sold: barometer
Sources: Banfield (1991) p.173; Webster (1988)

PONTIFEX William (I)

w 1789–1818
Coppersmith
Alternative name: PONTIFIX
1814   Shoe Lane, London
1798–1818 47 Shoe Lane, London
1822   Kentish Town, London
1831   Holloway, London
1838–1843 Turner's Hill, Cheshunt, Herts
Guild: Armourers etc, Founders
Father of PONTIFEX John fp1820 ABC
PONTIFEX Sydney fp 1824 ABC
Son of PONTIFEX William, farmer, of Iver, Bucks
Partnership: PONTIFEX, SONS & WOOD★
Apprenticed to JONES Richard, copper plate
maker, 1781
GAMBELL William 1789 ABC
WOOD James 1793 ABC
BOYCE George 1793 ABC
PEIRCE Thomas 1793 ABC
SHAFE John 1794 ABC
SHEARMAN Thomas 1797 ABC
PHILLIPS Jabez 1800 ABC
JONES Llewellin 1801 ABC
SWALES Frederick 1803 ABC
GATER William 1804 ABC
HEARN William 1804 ABC
HALMSHAW John 1805 ABC
PONTIFEX Edmund, his son, 1805 ABC
PHILLIPS Walter Rowland 1805 ABC
TEDDER William 1805 ABC
RAYMOND Richard 1806 ABC
KEEL Robert 1807 ABC
LONGMAN Thomas 1808 ABC
WOOD Samuel 1808 ABC
ANDREWS Joseph 1808 ABC
CLUBB William 1809 ABC
PONTIFEX William, his son, 1809 ABC
GOAD Samuel 1810 ABC
RING William 1810 ABC
ROBERTS Thomas William 1812 ABC
CLOSS John 1812 ABC
NICKLIN George 1813 ABC
HEDGES Richard 1813 ABC
ANNS Thomas 1813 ABC
FOULKS Thomas 1813 ABC
HARRIS Charles 1814 ABC
PONTIFEX Alfred, his son 1814 ABC
RING Peter Christopher 1817 ABC
GREENFIELD Richard William 1818 ABC
EALAND Thos Joseph 1814
GOAD William 1814, FDC
FINN Michael 1815, FDC
CRANFIELD James 1815 FDC
BOWLER Thomas John 1812 by t/o
Associated with SHEARMAN William★ and
KEEL John★, whose sons he took apprentice
fr ABC 1789, fr FDC 1814
Sources: GL: BC 5267/5; ABC 12080/2, 12081/1;
FDC 6331/6

PONTIFEX, SONS & WOOD William

w 1825–1839
Coppersmiths
1839   46 Shoe Lane, London

Known to have sold: rule
Sources: Pg; inst (s) (MAC)

POOL James

fr 1818 w 1823
Math IM, Cabinet M, Baro M
1818   9 Gunpowder Alley, Shoe Lane,
    London
1820   Wood St, Spa Fields, London
1823   47 Monkwell St, London
Guild: Innholders, fr 1818
Apprenticed to HOWORTH Samuel 1810★
Sources: GL: IC 6651/1, 6648/7, 6648/8

POOLE Anthony

w 1672
Alternative name: w
1672   Foster Lane, London
Known to have sold: rule
Sources: GL: CKC 2710/1 p.244–45

POOLE James

w 1826
Phil IM
1826   Falcon Square, London
See also POOLE Thomas★
Attended London Mechanics Institute 1826
Sources: LMIR (AM)

POOLE John

w 1826–1881
Chrono M, [Naut IS]
1826–1831 36 Charles St, City Rd, London
1831   9 York Terrace, Commercial Rd
    East, London
1839   Brunswick Terrace, Commercial Rd
    East, London
1846   7 Brunswick Terrace, Commercial
    Rd East, London
1851   31 Colet Place, Commercial Rd
    East, London
1851   and 1 Upper East Smithfield,
    London
1855+ 57 Fenchurch St, London
Submitted chronometers for trials at Royal
Greenwich Observatory 1826, 1831; B.apt
Admiralty
Known to have sold: chronometer, sextant,
telescope
Sources: CUL: RGO 1143 fol.2, 7, 9ᵛ; Pg; PO;
inst NMM; Loomes (1976); Taylor (1966) p.458

POOLE R.

w 1805
Optician
1805   6 Great Tower St, London
Apparently directory error for POOLER Richard
T.★
Sources: Kt (MAC)

POOLE Thomas

w 1813–1818
Optician, Optical IM, Math IM
1813–1818 Upper North Place, Gray's Inn Lane,
    London
See also POOLE James
Sources: J; Kt (JAC)

POOLER Richard Turner
w 1793–1813
Math IM
        43 Fish St Hill, London
1796–1805   6 Tower St, London
Guild: Grocers, fr 1790
Father of POOLER Richard Palmer, stationer, fp
1826
Apprenticed to FAIRBONE Charles (I)★
Known to have sold: rule
Sources: GL: GC 11598/7; inst (pv); H; Kt (JAC);
Ld (JAC)

POPE William
w 1813–1836
Naut IM, Math IM
        4 & 5 White Lion Court, Birchin
        Lane, Cornhill, London
        2 Ball Alley, Lombard St, London
        11 Ball Alley, Lombard St, London
1825   Ball Alley, Lombard St, London
Pat. navigation inst 1813 (probably the same
person)
Known to have sold: compass
Sources: Pg (JAC); PO (JAC); advertisement MHS
(MAC); Woodcroft (1854)

PORRI Benjamin
w 1834–1842
Optician, Baro M, Looking glass M, Jeweller, Toy
S, Hardwareman
1830   Market Place, Skipton, Yorks
1834   Caroline Square, Skipton, Yorks
1841   New Market Square, Skipton, Yorks
d 1864
Sources: Pg; R; Goodison (1977) p.350

PORTER George
w 1827–1834
Air pump M, Math IM, Phil IM
        18 Aylesbury St, Clerkenwell,
        London
        14 St. James Buildings, Rosomon St,
        Clerkenwell, London
See also
PORTER Samuel★
PORTER James★
PORTER Thomas★
Sources: Pg (JAC); R (JAC)

PORTER James
w 1831–1843
Optical IM, Phil IM, Math IM
        14 York St, York Rd, Lambeth,
        London
        282 Strand, London
        4 West Smithfield, London
1840   309 Regent St, London
1840   126 Great Portland St, London
1843   8 Brownlow St, Drury Lane,
        London
See also
PORTER Samuel★
PORTER George★
PORTER Thomas★
Sources: PO; R (JAC)

PORTER John
fr 1768 w 1797
Scale M
1778   The Corner of Wormwood St [a
        turning off Bishopsgate St] London
1782–1797   Bishopsgate, London
Guild: Blacksmiths, fr 1768
Partnership: MEYMOTT & PORTER★
Apprenticed to READ Joseph★ 1761
READ Mercy★ by t/o 1764
Sources: GL: STTP fol 99; BKC 2881/13 –
2881/15 (MAC); Wil

PORTER Samuel
w 1823–1824
[Sundial M]
        Norfolk Place, Shacklewell, London
See also
PORTER George★
PORTER James★
PORTER Thomas★
PORTER Samuel apprentice of CARTWRIGHT
William★
Known to have sold: sundial, thermometer
Sources: inst MHS; Sby 18 Jun 1986 lot 112
(MAC); Hollbrook (1992) p.115

PORTER Thomas
w 1826–1827
Optician, Math IM, Phil IM
1826–1827   18 Aylesbury St, Clerkenwell,
        London
Apprenticed to (probably) RAMSDEN Jesse★ 1778
See also
PORTER George★
PORTER Samuel★
PORTER James★
Sources: PRO: IR/1/29 (AM); Pg

PORTHOUSE Thomas
w 1823 d 1860
Chrono M
1823–1832   High St, Poplar, London
1835–1851   10 Northampton Square,
        Clerkenwell, London
Submitted chronometers for trials at Royal
Greenwich Observatory 1823–1835
B. apt Admiralty
Known to have sold: chronometer
Sources: CUL: RGO 1143 fol.2–10; inst NMM;
PO; Taylor (1966) p.478

POTTER Charles (I)
w 1847 d 1864
Math IM
1824–1825   61 Paternoster Row, London
1847   133 Albany Rd, Camberwell,
        London
1864   108 Albany Rd, Camberwell,
        London
Guild: Grocers, fr 1847
Son of POTTER Charles (II), gent, of Pentonville,
London
Brother of POTTER John Dennett★
Apprenticed to DOLLOND George (I)★ 1813
Had apprentice POTTER Charles (III), his son,
1847
b 1799; m 1830 to Mary; attended London

Mechanics Institute 1824–1825
Sources: GL: GC 11598/6, 11598/8; JRM; LMIR
(AM)

POTTER Francis
a 1760–1790
Hourglass M
        Southwark, London
Father of POTTER Henry s 1790 JC
Sources: GL: JC 8052/8 (MAC)

POTTER John Dennett
w 1851–1880
Math IM, Optical IM, Naut IM, Hydrometer M,
Phil IM, Drawing IM, Optician, Chart Agent
Alternative name: Dennet
1851–1882   31 Poultry London
1854–1882   11 King Street London
1882   [Residence] Broad Green Lodge,
        Croydon, Surrey
Guild: Spectaclemakers, fr 1853
Son of POTTER Charles (II), gent, d, of Peckham,
London
Brother of POTTER Charles (I)★
Worked for BATE Robert Brettell★
Succeeded by POTTER Septimus C, his son
Took over from BATE Robert Brettell★ for Chart
Agency only
b 1810; B.apt Admiralty; fr in SMC by purchase;
d 1882
Known to have sold: octant
Sources: GL: SMC 5213/6, 5213/8; PO; Wk;
JRM; Calvert (1971) p.35; McMonnell (1993) p.54

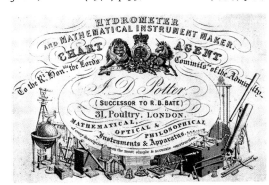

POTTING John
w 1708–1737
Instrument M
Alternative name: POTTEN, PATTEN
1708   Under Exeter Change in the Strand,
        London
Guild: Broderers, fr 1707/8
Apprenticed to ROWLEY John (I)★ 1699
Had apprentice BATTELL Affabell★
r 1739
Sources: GL: Brod 14657/1, 14657/2, 14664/1
(MAC); Crawforth (1987) p.339

POTTS Thomas
w 1805–1814
Optician
1805   371 Strand, London
1807–1814   18 St. Martin's Court, St. Martin's
        Lane, London

Same premises as POTTS William★
R.apt Prince of Wales
Sources: H; Kt (JAC); BM: Banks 105/36–39
(MAC)

POTTS William
w 1809
Optician
1809   18 St.Martin's Court, Leicester
           Square, London
Same premises as POTTS Thomas★
Sources: H (JAC)

POULDEN Robert Thomas
w 1834
Spectacle M
1834   81 St John St, Clerkenwell, London
Sources: Pg (JAC)

POUPARD Abraham
w 1826–1869
Scale M, Measure M
1826–1832   3 Lower Chapman St, London
1832   5 Commercial Rd, London
1836–1849   5 King's Place, Commercial Rd.
           East, London,
1865–1869   1 North St, Sidney St, Mile End Rd,
           E. London
Guild: Blacksmiths, fr 1802
Apprenticed to EVERITT George★ 1792
Sources: GL: BKC 2881/16 (MAC); CLRO:
CF1/1261; PO; Pg

POUSSETT Philip
w 1756 d by 1780
Scale M
Alternative name: POUSSET
           On Fish Street Hill, near St.Magnus
           Church, London
1776–1777   2 Farrows Rents, Bishopsgate St,
           London
-1780   Bishopsgate St, London
Guild: Skinners, fr 1755
Son of POUSSETT Francis of London
Apprenticed to SOMMERS Joseph★ 1748
Had apprentice DAVIS William 1756
Attended Christ's Hospital School, London
Known to have sold: balance
Sources: SKH: SKC Ap/Fr; GL: STTP 2934
fol.78,162; CH 12876/4; inst (pv) (MAC)

POWELL George
fr 1806
Spec M
1806   69 Aldgate, London
Guild: Spectaclemakers, fr 1806
Son of POWELL George, butcher, of Wapping,
London
Apprenticed to FORDHAM Thomas, described as
victualler, 1799
Sources: GL: SMC 5213/4

POWELL Hugh
w 1832–1841
Optician, Microscope M, Math IM, Optical IM,
Phil IM
1832–1841   24 Clarendon St, Somers Town,
           London

Father of POWELL Thomas H.★
Partnership: POWELL & LEALAND★
Succeeded by POWELL & LEALAND★
Associated with CARPENTER & WESTLEY★ as
supplier
b 1799; d 1883; founder member of Microscopical
Society of London 1840
Known to have sold: microscope
Sources: inst & TCd NMS; Nuttall (1979) p.38;
Turner G. (1989) p.11, 114–15, 117; Young (1986)
p.8; Young (1985)

POWELL John (I)
w 1759
Known to have sold: coin calendar
Sources: ChrSK 14 Apr 1988 lot 90

POWELL John (II)
w 1811
Math IM
1811   10 Pembroke Place, Liverpool
Sources: G (MAC)

POWELL Joseph
w 1793–1820
Brightsmith, Scale M, Fanlight M
1793–1795   Denmark St, Bristol
1797–1820   7 Denmark St, Bristol
Sources: Mat, Und (MAC)

POWELL Rees
w 1722
Known to have sold: slide rule
Sources: ChrSK 13 Dec 1984 (MAC)

POWELL Robert
w 1825–1826
Rule M
1825–1826   20 King Edwards Place, Birmingham
See also BUTLER & POWELL★
Sources: Pg★

POWELL Samuel
w 1832–1836
Optical IM, Phil IM, Math IM
1832–1836   33 Judd St, Brunswick Square,
           London
Sources: R (JAC)

POWELL Sidney
w 1845–1870
Optician, Math IM, Drawing IM
1845–1849   112 Gray's Inn Lane, London
1851–1855   121 Gray's Inn Lane, London
1859–1870   38 Chandos St, Charing Cross,
           London WC
Sources: PO; Wk

POWELL Thomas Clement
w 1835
Spectacle M
1835   101 Pershore St, Birmingham
Sources: Pg

POWELL Thomas Hugh
w fm 1851–1901
Optician

1851   4 Seymour Place, Euston Square,
           New Rd, London
1871–1895   (Residence) 18 Doughty St, London
1896–1900   (Residence) 12 Highbury Terrace,
           London
1901–1906   (Residence) 16 Highbury Crescent,
           London
b 1833 or 1834; fellow RMS 1880; d 1925
Took over POWELL & LEALAND★ business after
the death of his father, POWELL Hugh★
Sources: Turner G (1989) p.114–15; Young (1985)

POWELL & LEALAND Hugh & Peter H.
w 1841–1911
Optician, Microscope M, Math IM
Alternative name: LELAND
1841–1846   24 Clarendon St, Somers Town,
           London
1847–1857   4 Seymour place, New Road,
           London
1858–1905   170 Euston Rd, London, NW
Took over from
POWELL Hugh★
LEALAND Peter★
Medals 1862, 1872; Powell d 1883
Sources: PO; Cat. MHS (MAC); Anderson et al
(1990) p.65; Nuttall (1979) p.39–42; Turner G
(1989) p.114–15

POWER James
w 1804
Math IM
           Dublin?
Had apprentice: KEGAN John 1804
Sources: KH (WS)

POWER Samuel
w 1773–1780
Spec M
1773–1780   3 & 4 Colmore St, Birmingham
Sources: PR; Sy (MAC)

POZZI Peter
fl 1822–1830
1822–1830   Willow St, Oswestry
Known to have sold: barometer, thermometer
Sources: Goodison (1977) p.351

PRANDI Francis
w 1825
Carver, Gilder, Baro M, Thermo M, Hydro M
1825   32 Church St, Sheffield
See also PRANDI & CO. F★
Sources: Ge

PRANDI & CO. F.
w 1822
Carver, Gilder, Baro M
1822   11 High St, Sheffield
See also PRANDI Francis★
Sources: Bn (DJB)

PRATT -
a 1760–1800
Known to have sold: balance
Sources: inst Sunderland Mu (MAC)

PRENTICE James
w 1828–1832
Drawing IM
1828   3 New Buildings, King St, Snow
           Hill, London
1831–1832   3 New Buildings, Skinner St,
           London
Attended London Mechanics Institute 1828,
1831–1832; possibly employee
Sources: LMIR (AM)

PRESBURY William
w 1668–1686
[Spec M]
Alternative name: alias SWEATE
           London
Guild: Spectaclemakers
Had apprentice:
BOURNE Richard by t/o from EDWARDS
Richard★
SARGEANT Byefield 1669
ARROWSMITH Tobias 1676
unnamed, 1686
Prob d by 1687, when Mrs Presbury paid
quarterage fees to SMC
Sources: GL: SMC 5213/1

PRESCOTT Thomas
w em 1850
Optician
1850   At Mr Powell's, Seymour Place,
           London
Worked for POWELL & LEALAND★
Attended London Mechanics Institute 1850
Sources: LMIR (AM)

PREST Thomas
fl 1820 w 1830
Chrono M
1830   Chigwell Row, Essex
Guild: Clockmakers
Apprenticed to ARNOLD John★ 1784
Worked for ARNOLD John★
Submitted chronometer for trial at Royal
Greenwich Observatory 1830
Sources: CUL: RGO 1143 fol.9; GL: CKC 2720/1
p.120; Taylor (1966) p.402–03

PRESTON Grant
w 1813–1851
Optical IM, Phil IM, Math IM, Nautical brazier,
Compass M, Naut IM
        4 Ebenezer Place, Commercial Rd,
        London
1813–1826   Burr St, Wapping, London
1827–1840   108 Minories, London
1841–1845   Union Row, Tower Hill, London
1846–1851   2 Union Row, Minories, London
Guild: Armourers & Brasiers
Had apprentice PARISH William 1818
fr by purchase ABC 1813; Pat. compass 1832: R.
apt Victoria
Sources: GL: ABC 12088, 12080/2, 12081/1; Wk;
Woodcroft (1854); inst NMM

PRICE Charles
w pt 1697 w 1730
Hydrographer, Globe S, Map S, Engraver

1705   Mariner & Globe, Strand, London
1705   Hermitage Stairs, Wapping, London
1713   Lisbon Coffee House, behind the
           Royal Exchange, London
1727–1730   Hammersmith, London
1727–1730   In Westminster Hall, London
Guild: Merchant Taylors, fr 1703
Father of PRICE Charles fp 1744
Partnership:
SCOTT & PRICE★
SENEX & PRICE★
SENEX, SELLER & PRICE★
SELLER & PRICE★
WILLDEY & PRICE★
Apprenticed to SELLER John (I)★ 1693/4
Had apprentice:
CUSHEE Richard★ 1710
GODSON William 1710
FLEMING Thomas 1712
DAVIS Francis 1716
PRICE Henry 1718
BRIAN Jeremiah 1719
HALE Richard 1720
PASMORE Thomas 1729
In Fleet Prison for debt 1731; d 1733
Known to have sold: compass, globe
Sources: GL: MTC MF 319, 324; inst (s); Calvert
(1971) p.38; Tyacke (1978) p.136–8

PRICE Henry
w 1842–1851
Math IM
1830–1834   39 Commercial Rd, Lambeth,
           London
1842–1846   58 Brook St, Lambeth, London
1849–1851   16 Canterbury Place, Lambeth,
           London
Attended London Mechanics Institute 1830–1834
Sources: LMIR (AM); PO

PRICE John
w 1826–1833
Optician, Math IM, Phil IM, Rule M
        20 Castle St, Leicester Square,
        London
        19 Castle St, Leicester Square,
        London
        27 Castle St, London
Sources: Pg (JAC); R (JAC)

PRICE Richard (I)
w 1801
Rule M
1801   Mills Court, Slaney St, Birmingham
Sources: Chp

PRICE Richard (II)
w 1801–1815
Scale M
1801   Cricifix Lane, Bermondsey, London
1815   Dog & Bear Yard, Southwark,
        London
Guild: Haberdashers, fr 1801
Apprenticed to
SNART Charles★ 1793, t/o to CHANCELLOR
Thomas★ 1799
Had apprentice MILLER Joseph James 1815
Sources: GL: HC 15857/3, 15860/9

PRICE Thomas (I)
w 1777–1780
Spec M
1777–1780   2 Grosvenor St, Birmingham
Sources: PR

PRICE Thomas (II)
w 1758–1762
Telescope M
1758   Bull & Mouth St, London
1762   Snow Hill, London
Guild: Loriners, fr 1738/9
Father of PRICE John
Son of PRICE James, silversmith, of Holborn,
London
Apprenticed to HICKMAN Benjamin★ 1725
Had apprentice:
PRICE John, his son, by t/o 1762 from
WOODFALL Henry STC then t/o to GARDNER
Thomas STC 1762
Apprentice consideration paid by the Charity
School, Parish of St. Andrews Holborn
Sources: GL: LC 15835/1; CLRO:CF 1/608;
McKenzie (1978) p.136,388

PRICE Thomas (III)
w 1849–1851
Math IM, Naut IM
1849–1851   50 Pear Tree Court, Clerkenwell,
           London
Sources: PO; Wk

PRICE William
w 1786–1844
Optician, Math IM, Optical IM
1793   44 Fetter Lane, Fleet St, London
        [prob. error in directory]
1786–1844   115 Fetter Lane, London
Guild: Stationers, fr 1778
Apprenticed to ARCHER William★ 1771
Son of PRICE Charles, shoemaker, of Edmonton,
Middx
Had apprentice:
CORK Daniel 1786
GAYWOOD George 1791
BAWTREE Thomas James★ 1793
MESTAYER Richard Francis 1796
PRICE William Archer, his son, 1801
HASKER Edward 1802
FURLONGER Jacob 1808
PRICE Charles, his son, 1809
GOLDEN George Walter 1815
CARON John Nicholas 1819
Sources: GL: Sun 11936/337 no. 521380; Stat:
STC Memo bk p.75, Ap (MAC); A; H; PO;
McKenzie (1978) p.279

PRIDDITH Christopher
w 1678–1717
[Master of known Math IM]
Alternative name: PRIDDELL, PRIDITH
           London
Guild: Dyers, fr 1677/8
Had apprentice:
SCARBROUGH William 1678
ROLFE Samuel★ 1682
OLDRED Ebenezer 1691
MATSON Jacob★ 1692

PHILIPS Joseph 1698/9
KEEN George 1700
BUCKLAND Izarel 1702
BROCKUS William 1707
FOX Richard 1707
WEAVER Thomas 1714
SHAW John 1716/17
Sources: GL: DC 8168/3, 8169, 8171/1

PRIMAVESI Peter

a 1830–1880
    7 Greville St, Holborn, London
Known to have sold: barometer
Sources: Goodison (1977) p.351

PRIMROSE Adam

fr 1837
Coppersmith
    Glasgow
Guild: Hammermen, fr 1837
Known to have sold: measure (capacity)
Sources: Lumsden & Aitken (1912) p.316

PRINCE Abraham

w 1839
Optician, Math IM
    Waterford
Sources: Westropp (nd) (MAC); Burnett &
Morrison-Low (1989) p.154

PRIOR George

fl 1807–1853
Chrono M, Watch M
1834   4 Woodhouse Lane, Leeds
Pat. improved chronometer 1818
b 1782
Sources: Pg; Loomes (1976); Taylor (1966) p.403

PRIOR William

w 1723–1724
Musical IM, Math IM
    Gate Side, Newcastle on Tyne ?
1723–1724   at the Sign of the Musical
    Instrument in the Side, Newcastle
    on Tyne
Known to have sold: quadrant
Sources: *Newcastle Courant* 1 Feb 1723/4 (DJB);
ChrSK 10 Dec 1980 lot 14 (MAC)

PRITCHARD Andrew

w 1827–1854
Optician, Spec M, Draftsman, Patent Agent
1824–1826   32 Upper Thornhaugh St, London
1827–1829   18 Pickett St, Strand, London
1829–1831   312 Strand, London
1831–1835   18 Pickett St, Strand, (2nd period)
    London
1835–1838   263 Strand, London
1838–1854   162 Fleet St, London
1839   150 Fleet St, London
Guild: Spectaclemakers, fr 1839
Son of PRITCHARD John (II) of Hackney, London
Apprenticed to VARLEY Cornelius*, his uncle
Employed
EDEN [possibly also an apprentice – see EDEN
Alfred Frederick*]
STRAKER Samuel
Succeeded by STRAKER Samuel

See also
PRITCHARD George*
PRITCHARD William*
PRITCHARD James*
PRITCHARD & CO.*
Attended London Mechanics Institute 1824–1826
b 1804, d 1882; author; Ex 1851; fr by purchase in
SMC; champion of jewel lenses for microscopes
Known to have sold: barometer, microscope
Sources: GL: SMC 5213/5; Cat. 1851; Nuttall
(1977); Kt; PO; R; LMIR (AM); Banfield (1976)
p.101; Turner (1989) p.8, 284; Anderson et al
(1990) p.65

PRITCHARD Edward

c 1800
Math Instrument Divider
Alternative name: Ned
    London
Apprenticed to RAMSDEN Jesse*
See also PRITCHARD & SON E.*
Sources: SM: RA ScM3602

PRITCHARD George

w 1826–1838
Optician, Math IM, Phil IM
1826–1838   9 Great Newport St, Long Acre,
    London
See also
PRITCHARD James*
PRITCHARD John*
PRITCHARD William*
PRITCHARD Andrew*
PRITCHARD & CO.*
Sources: Pg; PO; R (JAC)

PRITCHARD James

w 1829–1830
Optical IM, Phil IM, Math IM
1829–1830   9 Great Newport St, Long Acre,
    London
See also
PRITCHARD George*
PRITCHARD John*
PRITCHARD Andrew*
PRITCHARD William*
PRITCHARD & CO.*
Sources: R (JAC)

PRITCHARD John (I)

w 1833–1836
Optician
1833–1836   9 Great Newport St, Long Acre,
    London
See also
PRITCHARD Andrew*
PRITCHARD James*
PRITCHARD William*
PRITCHARD & CO.*
Same premises as PRITCHARD George
Sources: R (JAC)

PRITCHARD William

w 1832–1855
Math IM, Optician, Drawing IM, Engraver,
Divider
    Pickett St, Strand, London
    263 Strand, London

1849–1855   16 Great Warner St, Clerkenwell,
    London
See also
PRITCHARD Andrew*
PRITCHARD George*
PRITCHARD James*
PRITCHARD John*
PRITCHARD & CO.*
Sources: PO; R (JAC)

PRITCHARD & CO.

w 1828–1829
Optician
1828–1829   152 Regent St, London
See also
PRITCHARD Andrew*
PRITCHARD George*
PRITCHARD James*
PRITCHARD John*
PRITCHARD William*
Sources: Kt (JAC)

PRITCHARD & SON E.

w 1816–1822
Divider of Math Inst, Engraver
1816   8 Porter St, Soho, London
See also PRITCHARD Edward*
Sources: Und

PROCTOR Charles & Luke

w 1774–1787
Cutlers, Inkstand M, Powderflask M, Scale M
1774   Petticoat Lane, Sheffield
1787   Milk St, Sheffield
See also
PROCTOR & BEELBY*
PROCTOR L.*
PROCTOR BROTHERS*
PROCTOR & CO.*
Known to have sold: balance, sundial, weights
Sources: inst (pv) (MAC); Gales; Sket (MAC);
Taylor (1966) p.215

PROCTOR G. & W. (I)

w 1815
Opticians
1815   11 Market St, Sheffield
1815   23 New Hall St, Birmingham
See also
PROCTOR William & George*
PROCTOR G & W (II)* (possibly the same firm)
PROCTOR George*
Sources: Cat. (SW)

PROCTOR G. & W. (II)

a 1790–1830
    London
See also PROCTOR G. & W. (I) (possibly the same
firm)
A George Proctor of 51 Bishopsgate St paid
quarterage in Cutler's Co, 1780–1786, no trade
given
Known to have sold: telescope, microscope
Sources: GL: CUT 7169; inst (s); Sby 23 Jun 1987
lot 209

PROCTOR George

w 1818

Optician
Alternative name: PROCTER
1818   Newhall St, Birmingham
See also
PROCTOR & BEILBY★
PROCTOR, BEILBY & CO.★
Sources: Wr

PROCTOR L.
a 1800–1820
              Sheffield
See also
PROCTOR Charles & Luke★
PROCTOR & BEELBY★
Known to have sold: sundial (ring dial type)
Sources: inst MHS & NMM; Turner G. (1980)
p.25

PROCTOR William
w 1822–1834
Optician
Alternative name: PROCTER
1822–1834   Bell Square, Trippet Lane, Sheffield
1825   Kelham Wheel, Sheffield
See also
PROCTER & CO.★
PROCTOR William & George★
Sources: Bn (DJB); Gell, Wh

PROCTOR William & George
w 1814
Optician
1814   Market St, Sheffield
See also PROCTOR William★
Sources: WB

PROCTOR & BEELBY
w 1781–1798
Optician, Spec M, Telescope M
1781–1787   Milk St, Sheffield
1797   11 Market St, Sheffield
See also
PROCTOR Charles & Luke★
PROCTOR L.★
PROCTOR BROTHERS★
PROCTOR & BEILBY–almost certainly a branch of
the same firm
Sources: BW; By; Gales; Rb

PROCTOR & BEILBY
w 1787–1805
Optician
Alternative name: PROCTER, PROCTORS
1787   Price St, Birmingham
1793–1805   Newhall St, Birmingham
See also
PROCTOR & BEELBY★
PROCTOR, BEILBY & CO.★
PROCTOR G. & W.★
Almost certainly a branch of the Sheffield firm of
Proctor & Beelby★
Sources: BW; Chp; H; PR; Ric

PROCTOR & CO.
w 1805
Optician
Alternative name: PROCTER
1805   Market Place, Sheffield

See also
PROCTOR William★
PROCTOR C.& L.★
Sources: H (DJB)

PROCTOR BROS.
a 1740–1780
Alternative name: probably Charles & Luke
PROCTOR
              Milk St, Sheffield
See also
PROCTOR Charles & Luke★
PROCTOR & BEELBY★
This form given only by Taylor
Sources: Taylor (1966) p.215

PROCTOR, BEILBY & CO.
w 1816
Optician
1816   Newhall St, Birmingham
See also
PROCTOR & BEELBY★
PROCTOR & BEELBY★
PROCTOR George★
Sources: H (DJB)

PROWDE Thomas
d 1614
Spec M
–1614   St.Clement Danes without Temple
              Bar, London
Sources: PCC: will (MAC)

PRUJEAN John
w 1664 d 1706
Math IM
Alternative name: Jorn, PRIGEON, PRIDGEON, I★P
1696   near New College, Oxford
1696   New College Lane, Oxford
Guild: [Clockmakers]
Apprenticed to ALLEN Elias★ 1646
See also COOKEOW Thomas★
Author
Known to have sold: astrolabe, quadrant
Sources: GL: CKC 3939; inst MHS & NMM;
MHS n (AVS); Anderson et al (1990) p.65; Beeson
(1989) p.79–80, 134; Calvert (1971) p.35;
Holbrook (1992) p.138; Loomes (1981b)

PULSFORD –
w 1851
Baro M
1851   25 Kirby St, Hatton Garden,
              London
See also PULSFORD George★
Sources: Wk

PULSFORD George
fl 1848
Baro M
1848   36 Charles St, Hatton Garden,
              London
See also PULSFORD★
Sources: Goodison (1977) p.351

PUSTERLA Anthony
w 1820
Baro M, Mirror M

1820   143 Capel St, Dublin
Sources: Pg (MAC)

PYE Henry
w 1836
Math IM, Phil IM
1825–1826   6 Nelson's Bridge, Caledonian Rd,
              London
1836   2 Nelson Place, City Road, London
Attended London Mechanics Institute 1825–1826
Sources: Pg; LMIR (AM)

PYE William (I)
w 1845–1865
Math IM, Optician, Phil IM
1845–1865   20 Albion Buildings, Bartholomew
              Close, London
See also
PYE Henry★
PYE William (II)★
Sources: PO

PYE William (II)
w 1849–1859
Math IM
1849–1855   14 Nelson Terrace, City Rd, London
1859   16 Nelson Terrace, City Rd, London
See also
PYE Henry★
PYE William (I)★
Sources: PO

PYEFINCH Elizabeth
w 1786
Umbrella M, Math IM, China warehouse
1786   45 Cornhill, London
Same premises as PYEFINCH Henry (I)★
Henry also at 45 Cornhill, 1782–90
Sources: Taylor (1966) p.270 (The directory entry
referred to by Taylor has not been traced so far)

PYEFINCH Henry (I)
w 1763 d 1790
Optical IM, Math IM, Optician
Alternative name: PYFINCH, PYFFINCH
              Golden Quadrant, Sun & Spectacles
              No.67 between Bishopsgate St. and
              the Royal Exchange in Cornhill,
              London
1765   64 Cornhill, London
1768   Golden Sun, Quadrant & Spectacles,
              67 Cornhill, London
1772–1782   67 Cornhill, London
1782–1791   45 Cornhill, London
Guild: Spectaclemakers, fr 1763
Son of PYEFINCH Mr, gentleman, of Hereford
Father of PYEFINCH Henry (II) fp 1817, grocer
Apprenticed to WATKINS Francis (I)★ 1753
Had apprentice:
MEREDITH John 1763
COLLETT Richard 1768
HUGHES Howell★ 1772
Employed MEREDITH John 1782
See also PYEFINCH Elizabeth★
Same premises as PYEFINCH Elizabeth★ 1786
Pat. barometer with Magalaens 1765, prosecuted
by DOLLOND Peter★ for infringing patent 1768
Known to have sold: barometer, hygrometer,

telescope, thermometer
Instruments advertised: full range
Sources: GL: SMC 5213/3 p.187+;By; Kt; Riv
Calvert (1971) pl.38; Goodison (1977) p.204–5

PYOTT James
w 1835
Clock M, Watch M, Naut IM
1835   186 Broomielaw, Glasgow
Sources: POG

QUARE Daniel
1671 d 1724
Clock M, Watch M
1680   King's Arms, Exchange Alley, off
              Lombard St, London
1715   Exchange Alley in Cornhill,
              London
Guild: Clockmakers, fr 1671
Partnership: QUARE & HORSEMAN★
Had apprentice:
DAVIS John (I)★ 1685
HORSEMAN Stephen★ 1701/2
13 others listed by Loomes but not known as IM
Succeeded by QUARE & HORSEMAN★
b 1649; Inv. portable barometer; Pat. barometer
1695; partnership 1709 onwards; Master CKC 1708
Known to have sold: barometer
Sources: GL: CKC 2710/3 fol. 28, 3939; Goodison
(1977) p.206–20; King & Millburn (1978) p.124;
Loomes (1981b)

QUARE & HORSEMAN Daniel & Stephen
w pt 1709 w 1733
              London
Succeeded by HORSEMAN Stephen★
Took over from QUARE Daniel★
Quare d 1724 but name continued; bankrupt 1733
Sources: Baillie (1951); Loomes (1981b)

QUIN George
w 1823
Hydro M
1823   13 Old Compton St, Soho, London
Partnership: QUIN James & George★
See also
QUIN James★
QUIN & ATKINS★
QUIN Messrs.★
QUIN & CO.★
QUIN Matthew★
Sources: Pg

QUIN James
w 1805
Math IM
Alternative name: QUINN
1805   2 Pitt St, Blackfriars Rd, London
Partnership: QUIN James & George★
See also
QUIN & CO.★
QUIN Matthew★
QUIN George★
QUIN Messrs★
QUIN & ATKINS★
Sources: H

QUIN James & George
w 1814
Hydro M
Alternative name: is this Messrs Quinn ?
1814   11 Martlett Buildings, Bow St,
              Covent Garden, London
See also
QUIN James★
QUIN George★
QUIN & CO.★
QUIN & ATKINS★
QUIN Matthew★
QUIN Messrs.★
Sources: inst SM Gabb (MAC)

QUIN Matthew
w 1790–1794
Hydro M, Math IM
              25 Aldersgate St, London
              8 Castle St, St.Mary Axe, London
See also
QUIN James★
QUIN & CO.★
QUIN & ATKINS★
QUIN Messrs★
QUIN James & George★
Sources: W (JAC)

QUIN Messrs.
w 1817–1823
Hydro M
Alternative name: is this James & George QUIN ?
1817   Broad Court, Long Acre, London
1817–1823   Little Russell St, Covent Garden,
              London
1821–1822   9 Old Compton St, Soho, London
See also
QUIN James & George★
QUIN James★
QUIN George★
QUIN Matthew★
QUIN & ATKINS★
QUIN & CO.★
Sources: Kt (JAC); PO (MAC)

QUIN & ATKINS
w 1799
Hydro M
1799   Star Alley, Fenchurch St, London
See also
ATKINS Robert★
QUIN James★
QUIN Matthew★
QUIN & CO.★
QUIN George★
QUIN Messrs.★
Received Society of Arts award for hydrometers
Known to have sold: hydrometer
Sources: Ld (JAC); McConnell (1993) p.10

QUIN & CO.
w 1794
Math IM, Hydro M
1794   London Road, St.George's St,
              London
See also
QUIN James & George★
QUIN Matthew★

QUIN Messrs.★
QUIN & ATKINS★
Sources: W (JAC)

RABALIO Peter
w 1787 d by 1791
Baro M, Glassblower
1789   18 Edgbaston St, Birmingham
1790   At Joseph Smith's, Crown & Thistle,
              Loseby Lane, Leicester
              The Dolphin, Coventry
              Golden Lion in Hamston Gate,
              Leicester
              At Mr.Dewce's in High St, near the
              College Gate, Worcester
              Sign of the Barometer, Edgbaston St,
              Birmingham
Known to have sold: barometer
Instruments advertised: barometer, telescope,
thermometer
Sources: Aris 23 Mar 1789, 10 Jan 1791 (DJB);
Leicester Journal 6 Oct 1787, 2 July 1790 (DJB);
TCd (DJB); inst (s)

RABONE Elizabeth
w 1808–1835
Rule M
1808–1816   Water St, Birmingham
1825–1826   38 Water St, Birmingham
1828–1830   33 Water St, Birmingham
1830   (Residence), Hunter's Lane,
              Handsworth, Birmingham
1835   Summer Street Place, Birmingham
See also
RABONE John★
RABONE & SON Elizabeth★
RABONE Ephraim★
Sources: H; Pg; West; Wr (MAC)

RABONE Ephraim
w 1811–1818
Rule M
1811–1818   13 Water St, Birmingham
1825–1860   61 St.Paul's Square, Birmingham
See also
RABONE Elizabeth★
RABONE John★
RABONE & SON Elizabeth★
Sources: Pg; wr (MAC)

RABONE John
w 1825–1860
Rule M, Baro M, Thermo M
1828–1830   33 Ludgate Hill, Birmingham
1830–1860   61 St. Paul's Square, Birmingham
See also
RABONE Elizabeth★
RABONE & SON Elizabeth★
RABONE Ephraim★
Partnership RABONE & MASON★ 1834–1837
Sources: K; Pg; West (MAC); Goodison (1977)
p.352

RABONE Michael
w 1800
Rule M
              Birmingham
Sources: Roberts (1982) (MAC)

RABONE Thomas
w 1829–1862
Thermo M, Rule M, Math IM, Baro M
1829	8 Court, Water St, Birmingham
1834	Hunter's Lane, Handsworth, Birmingham
1835	12 Court, Broad St, Birmingham
1841	171 Hockley Hill, Birmingham
1845–1854	172 Hockley Hill, Birmingham
1847	Hockley Hill, Birmingham
1858–1862	63 Great Hampton St, Birmingham
1860	61 Great Hampton St, Birmingham
See also RABONE John★
Sources: K; Mor; Sl; Wh (MAC); Goodison (1977) p.352

RABONE & MASON
w 1834–1837
Baro M, Thermo M
1834–1837   61 St. Paul's Square, Birmingham
Took over from and succeeded by RABONE John★
Sources: Pg

RABONE & SON Elizabeth
w 1809–1811
Rule M
1809–1811   Water St, Birmingham
See also
RABONE Elizabeth★
RABONE Ephraim★
RABONE John★
Sources: H (MAC)

RABY Edward (I)
w 1816–1833
Optician
1816–1818	Piper's Row, Wolverhampton
1833–1834	St.James Square, Wolverhampton
See also RABY Edward (II)★
Sources: Br; H; Pg; Wh (MAC)

RABY Edward (II)
w 1835
Optician
1835   Great Brook St, Birmingham
See also RABY Edward (I)★
Sources: Pg (MAC)

RADCLIFFE Charles
w 1837–1855
Chrono M, Watch M
Alternative name: RADCLIFF
1837–1839	21 Duke St, Liverpool
1839–1855	41 Duke St, Liverpool
Sources: G (MAC)

RADFORD –
a 1720–1740
The Great Golden Spectacle over against the East End of the New Church in the Strand, London
Over against the New Church in the Strand, London
See also
RADFORD John (II)★
RADFORD William (I)★
Sources: GL: TCd

RADFORD John (I)
w 1659–1703
Spec M
Alternative name: REDFORD
1670	St.Clement Danes, London
1693	Fleet St, London
1695–1703	St.Clement Danes (2nd period), London
Guild: [Brewers] Spectaclemakers
Father of RADFORD John (II)★ s 1711
Son of REDFORD Thomas, husbandmen, of Ubley, Somerset
Partnership: COCKS, RADFORD & RADFORD★
Apprenticed to COPELAND Thomas★ 1633/4
Had apprentice:
SEWELL Henry 1659
TUCK William★ 1668
MASTERS John★ 1674
FRANCIS William 1675
KNIGHT Charles 1692/3
Master SMC 1669–1671, 1687–1688; d by 1711
Sources: GL: BREW 5445/15; SMC 5213/1, 5213/2 p.29, 37; PMC 5652/1 fol.58

RADFORD John (II)
w 1718–1722
Spec M
1718–1722   The Great Golden Spectacle against St Clement's Church in the Strand, London
Guild: [Pattenmakers]
Son of RADFORD John (I)★
Partnership: COCKS, RADFORD & RADFORD★
Apprenticed to BERREY Thomas 1711
Sources: GL: PMC 5652/1; Sun 11936/8 no.11346

RADFORD T. & W.
c 1785–1792
Watch M, Goldsmith
Leeds
See also WILKINSON Anthony★, whose balances they sold
Known to have sold: balance
Sources: inst (pv) (MAC); Baillie (1951); Loomes (1976)

RADFORD William (I)
w 1718–1740
Spec M
1718–1722   The Great Golden Spectacle against St Clement's Church in the Strand, London
Guild: Spectaclemakers, fr 1720
Partnership: COCKS, RADFORD & RADFORD★
Apprenticed to COOBEROW Matthew★ nd
Had apprentice:
FORSTER George 1722
WALDER Henry 1730
OLIPHANT James 1738
Employed COOMBS Oliver★
See also RADFORD John (I)★
Partnership 1718–1722
Sources: GL: Sun 11936/8 no.11346; SMC 5213/2 p.116, 129, 183, 219+

RADFORD William (II)
fr 1743 w 1761
[Scale M]

Alternative name: REDFORD
London
Guild: Skinners, fr 1742/3
Son of RADFORD James, labourer, of Pensford, Somerset
Apprenticed to SOMMERS Joseph★ 1735
Had apprentice YOUNG John 1761 by t/o from WILLIAMS Thomas
fr 1 Feb 1742/3
Sources: SH: SKC, Ap/Fr; GL: BKC, 2886/5

RADNALL Sarah
w 1833
Optician, Spec M
1833   Queen St, Wolverhampton
Sources: Br

RAGGETT James
w 1830
Optician
1830   21 London St, Reading
Sources: Pg

RAMAGE John (I)
w 1806 d 1835
Optical IM
1824–1829	85 Broad St, Aberdeen
1831–1835	39 Union St, Aberdeen
Succeeded by RAMAGE John (II)★
Known to have sold: telescope
Sources: Bryden (1972) p.55; Taylor (1966) p.372

RAMAGE John (II)
w 1835–1836
Optical IM
1835	39 Union St, Aberdeen
1836	104 Union St, Aberdeen
Took over from RAMAGE John (I)★
Succeeded by RAMAGE & CO.★
Sources: Bryden (1972) p.55

RAMAGE & CO.
w 1837–1838
Optical IM
1837	41 St.Nicholas St, Aberdeen
1838	6 St.Nicholas Lane, Aberdeen
Succeeded by SMITH & RAMAGE★
Took over from RAMAGE John (II)★
Sources: Bryden (1972) p.55

RAMSDEN Jesse
w 1762 d 1800
Optician, Math IM, Mathematical Master, Author
Near ye Little Theatre in ye Hay Market, St.James, London
Next to St.James, Piccadilly, London
Opposite Sackville St, Piccadilly, London
1763–1766	Strand, London
1767–1771	Haymarket, London
1772–1800	199 Piccadilly, London
1782–1800	(Workshop) 196 Piccadilly, London
Son of RAMSDEN Thomas, innkeeper, of Salterhebble, Yorks
Husband of DOLLOND Sarah, sister of DOLLOND Peter★, m 1766
Apprenticed to BURTON Mark★ 1756
Had apprentice:

CARY William* nd
BENNETT Leonard* nd
PRITCHARD Edward* nd
WARE James 1763 t/o 1764 to HARRISON W.,
shoemaker
SPICER Simon* 1768
SIMPSON Joseph 1769
PORTER Thomas* 1778
MACKNEIL Jonathan* 1786
JONES Thomas (I)* 1789
ADAMS Richard 1796
SWIFT Charles 1796
MARQUEZ Jasper J. 1798
PEDROSO Jose Maria 1798
GREEN Joseph 1798
Worked for
DOLLOND Peter*
ADAMS George (II)*
SISSON Jeremiah*
Employed
BERGE Matthew*
HIGGINS
JONES Thomas (I)*
JECKER Francois A.
STANCLIFFE John*
Succeeded by BERGE Matthew*
b1735; educ Queen Elizabeth Grammar School,
Heath, Yorks; pat.astro inst 1775; FRS 1786,
Copley medal 1792; inv.dividing engine; leading
IM of his day
Known to have sold: balance, barometer, drawing
instruments, lightning demonstrator, microscope,
quadrant, sector, telescope, theodolite,
thermometer
Sources: PRO: IR1/20 /23 /29 /33 /34 /37(AM);
inst NMM, SM, WM; GL: CH 12876/5; Sun
11936/342 no.524057 (MAC); VL: rate books for
St. Martin-in-the-Fields and St. James Piccadilly
(AM); SM: RA file ScM 3602 (SJ); *Daily Ad* 12
Mar 1772 (MAC); RAS *Monthly Notices* 21 p.105
(AM); Calvert (1971) pl.39; Goodison (1977
p.222–25; Porter et al (1985) p.55–56; Porritt
(1970); Wallis P&R (1985) p.312,911; AM

RANDAL -
w 1744
Instrument S
1744   British Coffee House, Finch Lane,
London
Associated with MARTIN Benjamin* as agent
Sources: Millburn (1976) p.39–40

RANDALL John
w 1693–1707
Alternative name: RANDOLL
1693   Great Minories, London
Guild: Grocers, fr 1689
Apprenticed to HOWE William* 1671
Had apprentice:
SANKEY Jeremiah 1693
RANDALL William, his son, 1700
SHADD Charles 1703
LEY John 1707
Sources: Brown J. (1979a) p.27, 30

RANDELL Samuel
w 1839
Math IM

1839   21 St. Peter's Hill, City, London
Sources: Pg

RANKEN George
w 1844–1871
Optician
1844–1866 112 Rose St, Edinburgh
1867   79 Rose St, Edinburgh
1869–1871 108 Rose St, Edinburgh
Probably the George RANKEN who worked for
ADIE & SON*
Sources: Bryden (1972) p.56; Clarke et al (1989)
p.50, 63

RANKETH T. Jnr
w 1814
Baro M
1814   8 High St, Bloomsbury, London
Sources: PO

RANSLEY George
w 1851–1855
Rule M
1851–1855 10 Barnet St, Hackney Rd, London
Sources: PO; Wk

RANSLEY William
w 1839–1887
Rule M
1839   30 Stangate, Lambeth, London
1849–1851 20 Stangate, Lambeth, London
1852–1859 4 Bridge Rd, Lambeth, London
1865–1885 229 Westminster Bridge Rd,
           Lambeth, London
Sources: Pg; PO; Wk

RAPSON
w 1834–1842
Optical IM, Phil IM, Math IM
1834–1842 6 Ingram Court, Fenchurch St, City,
           London
Sources: R (JAC)

RATCLIFF William
w 1834
Spectacle M
1834   98 Britannia St, City Rd, London
Sources: R (JAC)

RAVEN Henry
w 1739
Scale M
      London
Guild: Blacksmiths, fp 1733
Father of RAVEN John, fr 1739
Sources: GL: BKC 2885/1 (MAC)

RAXTER John
w 1801–1825
Optical IM, Math IM, Phil IM
Alternative name: RAETOR, ROXTER, RAXTOR,
1801   49 Cheapside, Deritend,
           Birmingham
1816–1818 6 John St, Birmingham
1816–1817 6 Old John St, Birmingham
1825   32 John St, Birmingham
See also RAXTER Robert*
Sources: Chp; Pg; TWr; Wr (MAC)

RAXTER Robert
w 1829–1835
Math IM, Optician
1829–1830 144 Livery St, Birmingham
See also RAXTER John*
Sources: Pg; Wr (MAC)

RAYSON William
w 1683
      Leicester
Known to have sold: horary quadrant
Sources: inst WM (MAC)

REA Mark
w 1792
Rule M
1792   2 Court, 6 Dudley St,
           Wolverhampton
Sources: Wolverhampton rate books (MAC)

READ John (I)
w 1580–1616
Math IM (in wood)
Alternative name: READE
1582–1590 Hosier Lane, Smithfield, London
Guild: Stationers, fr 1569
Had apprentice:
READE William nd fr 1580
THOMPSON John (I)* prob s STUCKY Thomas*
1586, fr by READ (I) 1610
BARROWES Francis 1602
GOSSE Nathaniel* 1604
HOBSON John 1606
BLISSETT/BASSETT Giles 1608
HAYDON Francis 1611
See also READ John (II)*
Instruments advertised: alidade, compass (magnetic),
geometric square, plane table, rule, sector
Sources: Stat: STC Ap (MAC); Arber (1875) 1
p.419, 2 p.142, 261, 323; Bryden (1992) p.304–06;
McKenzie (1961) p.111

READ John (II)
fl 1650
      London
See also READ John (I)*
Sources: Taylor (1954) p.237

READ John (III)
w 1774–1780
Math IM
Alternative name: REED
1774–1780 Knightsbridge, London
Sources: IHR: Wpoll 1774, 1780 (AM)

READ Joseph
w 1753 d 1764
Scale M
      At the Hand & Scales, Bishopsgate
      Within, London
1761–1763 Bishopsgate St, London
1763   Shoreditch, (residence ?) London
Guild: Blacksmiths, fr 1744
Brother of READ Samuel*
Husband of READ Mercy*
Apprenticed to READ Samuel* 1736/7
Had apprentice:
HUNT Samuel 1753

PIDGEON John★ 1754
PIXLEY Thomas (II)★ 1760 by t/o from WADE Thomas★
SEWELL George★ 1760 by t/o from WORNELL John★
PORTER John★ 1761 t/o 1764 to READ Mercy★
SCHOOLING James★ 1762 t/o 1764 to READ Mercy★
SKUCE Thomas 1763 t/o 1764 to READ Mercy★
Succeeded by READ Mercy★
Known to have sold: balance
Sources: SH: SKC Ap/Fr; GL: BKC 2885/1, 2888, 2886/5 (MAC); CH 12876/5; inst (pv) (MAC); Kt (JAC); Heal (1988) p.152

READ Mercy
w 1764–1767
[Scale M]
        Bishopsgate Within, London
Guild: Blacksmiths
Wife of READ Joseph★
MEYMOTT Clement★
Had apprentice:
PORTER John 1764 by t/o from READ Joseph★
SCHOOLING James 1764 by t/o from READ Joseph★
SKUCE Thomas 1764 by t/o from READ Joseph★
Succeeded by MEYMOTT Mercy★
Took over from READ Joseph★
Sources: GL: BKC 2885/1, 2888 (MAC)

READ Samuel
w 1735–1779
Scale M
        Angel & King's Arms in St.Ann's Lane near Aldersgate, London
        59 St.Martin's St, near Aldersgate, London
        20 St.Martin's St, near Aldersgate, London
1748   Corner of St.Annes Lane near Aldersgate, London
Guild: Blacksmiths, fr 1735
Apprenticed to
NEALE John (I)★ 1728
LANE John (II)★ by t/o 1733/4
HART Benjamin★ by t/o 1734
Had apprentice:
GALE William 1735 by t/o from LANE John (II)★
READ Joseph★, his brother, 1736/7
KILLINGWORTH Pinson 1735 by t/o from LANE John (II)★
BRIND William★ 1744
GIBBS Owen 1744
JENKINS Giles 1746 by t/o from BROOKSBY Thomas (I)★
CATTELL Robert★ 1750
BATES Matthew 1755 by t/o from COURT Richard (II)★
VAUGHTON Christopher★ 1760
DE GRAVE Charles (I)★ 1760
HOLT James★ 1761 by t/o from NEWTON William★
SANGSTER John 1761 by t/o from NEWTON William★
BADCOCK William Geagle★ 1768
STERNEY John 1763 by t/o from SOMMERS Joseph (I)★
19 others not known as Scale M 1748–1773

Succeeded by READ & DEGRAVE★
Made standard weights for the Royal Society
Known to have sold: balance, weights
Sources: SH: SKC, Ap/Fr; GL: BKC 2885/1, 2885/2, 2886/4, 2886/5, 2888 (MAC); CH 12876/4, 12876/5; Bd; Bd; Kt (MAC); Ld; Phil. T 42 (1742–43) p.552

READ & DEGRAVE Samuel & Charles
w 1779–1781
Scale M
1779–1781   59 St.Martin's le Grand, London
Succeeded by DE GRAVE Charles (I)★
Took over from READ Samuel★
Sources: Ld

READING Thomas
w 1768–1777
Math IM, Surveyor
1768   Georges Lane near Stephens St, Dublin
Apprenticed to STOKES Gabriel★
Sources: Gibson (1768) p.160 & (1777) p.160 (DJB)

REARDON J.
w 1836–1851
Optician
1836–1851   42 Easton St, Spa Fields, Clerkenwell, London
Sources: R: Wk

REDFERN G.
w 1829–1830
Spec M
1829–1830   Horsefair, Birmingham
Sources: Wr (DJB)

REDFERN Joseph
w 1835–1862
Optician, Spectacle M
1835   35 Horsefair, Birmingham
1845–1850 37 Exeter Row, Birmingham
1862   30A High St, Bull Ring, Birmingham
Sources: K; Mor; Pg (MAC)

REDFERN William
w 1836
Optician, Math IM, Phil IM
1836   40 Duke St, Spitalfields, London
Sources: Pg

REDHEAD John
w 1694–1697
Scale M
1694   In Leadenhall St, over against East India House, London
Guild: Blacksmiths, fr 1691
Son of REDHEAD Walter, labourer, of St. Giles Cripplegate, London
Apprenticed to REDHEAD William★ 1684, t/o JENKS Edmund★ nd, then to ILIFFE William★ nd, then to CLARIDGE Richard★ 1688
Had apprentice:
BULL Miles 1694
STORY Robert 1697
Sources: GL: BKC 2881/7, 2881/8 2886/2, 2886/3 (MAC); CH: 12876/2 (MAC)

REDHEAD William
w 1684–1693
Alternative name: RIDHEAD
        London
Guild: Blacksmiths, fr 1683 or 1684
Had apprentice REDHEAD John 1684 t/o to JENKS Edmund★ nd
HARDING Nathaniel 1685 t/o to TAYLOR William (II)★ nd
Sources: GL: BKC 2881/8, 2884 (MAC)

REDPATH Henry
w 1787–1820
Watch M
        Stirling
Known to have sold: barometer
Sources: inst noted by ADCS; Baillie (1951)

REEVE Richard (I)
w 1641 d 1666
[Optical IM]
Alternative name: RIVES, REEVES
        Over against the Foot & Leg in Long Acre, London
1632   The East End of Henrietta St, near the Piazza, London
1663   Longacre, London
Father of
REEVES John★ (probably)
REEVE Richard (II)★
Associated with COCK Christopher★ in making speculum for Robert Hooke
Known to have sold: magic lantern, microscope, telescope
Sources: Monconys (1666) p.11,17; Simpson (1985) p.357–65; Simpson (1989) p.36–47; Taylor (1954) p.223–4

REEVE Richard (II)
w 1666–1668
[Optical IM]
1666–1668   London
Son of REEVE Richard (I)★
Took over from REEVE Richard (I)★
d c.1679
Known to have sold: burning glass, microscope, telescope
Sources: Simpson (1989) p.47; Middleton (1980) p.151–52

REEVES John
w 1657–1689
Alternative name: REEVE
1657   London
Guild: Grocers
Son of REEVES Richard (I)★ (probably)
Had apprentice COCK Christopher★ by t/o
Known to have sold: lens
Sources: GL: TC 3302/1; Court & von Rohr (1929–30) p.72

REEVES Thomas
w 1764–1776
Scale M
Alternative name: REEVE
1764–1776 No. 133 in Fetter Lane, Fleet St, London
Guild: Blacksmiths, fr 1762

Apprenticed to WORNELL John★ 1750/51
Had apprentice ARROWSMITH L. 1764
Known to have sold: balance
Instruments advertised: balance, steelyard, weights
Sources: GL: BKC 2885/1, 2886/5 (MAC); CH
12876/5 (MAC); inst Peterborough Mu (MAC)

REFFELL Joseph
w 1816–1822
Optician, Math IM
1822   121 Oxford st, London
Sources: Pg; JAC

REHE Samuel
w 1782–1794
Mechanist
Alternative name: RHEE
1794   Shoe Lane, London
1799   Shoe Lane, the Corner of Harp
           Alley, London
Husband of REHE Elizabeth
Worked for TROUGHTON Edward (I)★
Employed SCHWARTZ Michael
b 1734 or 1735, d 1799, buried St. Bride, Fleet St
pat. hydraulic machine 1799
Known to have made: dividing engine
Sources: GL: Commissary Ct wills, 9171/92 (AM);
St. Bride, Fleet St, bur (AM); pat.records (MAC);
Taylor (1966) p.295; Wallis R & P (1993) p.113

REINE R.
w 1674–1677
Glass grinder, Glass blower
           Lime St, London
Known to have sold: prism
Sources: Robinson & Adams (1935) p.87,282;
Taylor (1954) p.267

RENNOLDSON Isaac
w 1807–1848
Math IM
           23 Bethnal Green Rd, London
1807   Garden Row, St.George's Fields,
           London
1808   8 St.John's Lane, Clerkenwell,
           London
1813–1822   23 Camden Row, Bethnal Green,
           London
1833–1845   5 Cambridge Place, Hackney Rd,
           London
Guild: Merchant Taylors, fr 1805
Apprenticed to HARRIS Thomas (III)★ 1798
Had apprentice:
DYER William Stanford 1807
LAWRENCE John 1807
GOMME Stephen 1808
MARTIN William George 1813
EAGLES Edward 1814
WOOD William
RAWLINGS William 1816
HARRIS Charles Henry 1822
WHITTAKER Henry George 1822
MACRAE Henry★ 1822
HINSCH David 1833
BROOKS George Hearly 1839
Associated with CRICHTON John★ [gave evidence
at his freedom]
Known to have sold: protractor

Sources: GL: MTC MF 320,324; Und; Bn; H; Pg;
PO; inst (s)

RENWICK James
w 1844–1847
Baro M; Thermometer M
1844–1847   2 Booth's Place, Turnmill St,
           Clerkenwell, London
Sources: PO; Goodison (1977) p.352

REOHAN Thomas
w 1838
Optician, Math IM, Philo IM
1838   2 Arbour Terrace, Commercial Rd,
           London
Sources: Pg

REVED Mark
w 1802
Rule M
1802   1 Court, 2 High Green,
           Wolverhampton
Sources: Wolverhampton rate books (MAC)

REW Robert
w 1755–1764
[Optical IM]
1764   Coldbath Fields, London
Worked for DOLLOND John★
1764 Petitioner against Dollond's patent
Sources: PRO: PC1/7 no.94; Daumas (1989) p.155

REYNOLDS James
w 1792
Rule M
1792   31 Worcester St, Wolverhampton
Sources: Wolverhampton rate books (MAC)

REYNOLDS John
w 1582–1590
Math IM
1582–1590   Southeast end of Barking
           Churchyard in Tower St, Tower
           Hill, London
Known to have sold: alidade, compass, geometric
square, plane table, rule
Sources: Bryden (1992) p.305; Turner (1983b) p.97

REYNOLDS Joseph
w 1790–1812
Scale M
1790   7 King St, Cloth Fair, West
           Smithfield, London
1795   29 Long Lane, West Smithfield,
           London
1800–1812   16 Aldersgate St, Corner of Falcon
           St, London
Guild: Blacksmiths, fr 1790
Apprenticed to VINCENT Robert★ 1768
Had apprentice:
STANLEY Nathaniel★ 1795
EAMES George 1804
STURT Robert Samuel 1805
NORTHFIELD Thomas Stephen 1807 by t/o from
NORTZELL Thomas
GORE William 1808
NEWMAN Thomas Porter★ 1808
Succeeded by REYNOLDS & NICHOLL★

Known to have sold: balance, weights
Instruments advertised: balance, weights
Sources: GL: BKC 2881/16 (MAC); CH 12876/5
(MAC); Kt; PO; W (MAC); inst SM Wellcome

REYNOLDS Thomas
w 1767–1781
Scale M, Steelyard M
1767   High St, Birmingham
1777–1781   45 Digbeth, Birmingham
Sources: PR; Sket (MAC)

REYNOLDS & NICHOLL Joseph & William Lewis
w 1816
Scale M
1816   16 Aldersgate, London
Took over from REYNOLDS Joseph★
Succeeded by NICHOLL William Lewis★
Sources: Kt; TCd (pv) (MAC)

RHUE –
d 1773
Math IM
-1773   Ships Court, Old Bailey, London
Sources: General Evening Post 8 Jul 1773 (MAC)

RIBOLDI Joseph
w 1824
Carver and Gilder
Alternative name: RIBALDI
1824   122 George's St, Limerick
Known to have sold: barometer
Sources: Burnett & Morrison-Low (1989) p.155

RIBRIGHT George
w 1765–1778
Optician
1764–1775   The Poultry London
1772–1776   40 The Poultry, London
Guild: u & Spectaclemakers
Partnership: RIBRIGHT & SON★
Had apprentice RIBRIGHT Thomas (II)★, his son,
1768
Succeeded by RIBRIGHT & SON★
See also
RIBRIGHT Thomas (I)★
RIBRIGHT & SMITH★
FLINDALL John (I)★
Free 1751 SMC as 'Foreign Brother', i.e. member
of another guild; petitioner against Dollond's
patent 1764; d1782 or 1783
Known to have sold: protractor
Sources: GL: SMC 5213/3 p.169+; Kt; Ld; Riv;
PRO:PC 1/7 no.94; ChrSK 8 Dec 1988 lot 149

RIBRIGHT Thomas (I)
w 1735–1772
Optician
Alternative name: RIBWRIGHT, RYBRIGHT
1753–1765   Poultry, London
1764   Golden Spectacles, The Poultry,
           London
Guild: Spectaclemakers, fr 1734
Son of RIBRIGHT Robert, cordwainer, of
Cambridge
Related to RIBRIGHT Thomas (II)★
Apprenticed to STERROP Thomas (III)★ 1726/7

Had apprentice:
SANDERSON John 1735, ran away 1741
MOORE Richard 1736/7
SPURRIER Aaron 1741 by t/o from ROOE J.
DIXON Richard 1745
FREEMAN John 1749
PENTLOW John 1762
ROSE Henry 1764
FLINDALL John (I)★ 1769
Succeeded by RIBRIGHT George★
See also RIBRIGHT & SMITH★
Pat. perspective glass & insts 1749; R.apt Prince of Wales; b. apt Office of Ordnance; Master SMC 1758–1760; d 1781
Known to have sold: telescope, gunner's level.
Sources: Kt; GL: SMC 5213/2 p.180+, 5213/3 p.27–28, 85, 138+; Woodcroft (1854); Millburn (1988b) p.280–81, Calvert (1971) pl.41

RIBRIGHT Thomas (II)
w 1783–1806
Optician
1783–1796   40 The Poultry, London
1788   46 The Poultry [possibly directory error] London
1802   20 Gloucester St, Queen's Square, London
Guild: Spectaclemakers, fr 1775
Apprenticed to RIBRIGHT George★, his father, 1768
Had apprentice HARTLEY Charles J. 1793
Took over from RIBRIGHT & SON★
Pat. artificial horizon 1790; received charity from SMC 1806, d 1811
Sources: GL: Sun 11936/317 no.485133; SMC 5213/3, 5213/4; PRO IR1/36 (AM); Kt; Ld; Woodcroft (1854)

RIBRIGHT & SMITH
w 1783–1784
Optician
   Bond St, Bath
See also RIBRIGHT Thomas (II)★
Sources: By

RIBRIGHT & SON George [& Thomas (II)]
w 1778–1783
Optician
1783   40 The Poultry, London
Succeeded by RIBRIGHT Thomas (II)★
Took over from RIBRIGHT George★
George d 1782 or 1783
Sources: By; Kt

RICCARD & LITTLEFEAR
w 1783
Manufacturers
1783   Upper Mews Gate, Castle St, London
Instruments advertised: balance, weights
Sources: GL: TCd

RICE George
w 1851
Optician
1851   Nelson Place, Old Kent Rd, London
Sources: PO

RICE James
a 1808 w 1823
Optician, Math IM
1801   At Mr Richardson's, 16 Somerset St, Aldgate, London
1823   8 Lion St, Kent Rd, London
Guild: [Spectaclemakers]
Son of RICE William, farmer, of Croydon, Surrey
Apprenticed to RICHARDSON John(II)★ 1801
Sources: GL: SMC 5213/4; Pg

RICH James
w 1771
Known to have sold: back-staff
Sources: inst(s) (MAC)

RICHARDS Daniel
w 1829–1841
Spec M, Optician
1829–1835   27 Church St, Birmingham
1841   26 Church St, Birmingham
Sources: Pg; West: Wr (DJB)

RICHARDS Esther
w 1801–1818
Rule M
1801   94 Lichfield St, Birmingham,
1808   95 Lichfield St, Birmingham
1809–1818   Lichfield St, Birmingham
See also
RICHARDS John (II)★
RICHARDS & LOCKYER
RICHARDS William (I)★
Sources: Chp; H; Wr (DJB)

RICHARDS George
w 1754–1755
Math IM
1754–1755   St.Stephen's Lane, Bristol
Sources: Bristol poll lists (MAC); *Bristol Journal* 23 Aug 1755 (MAC)

RICHARDS Henry
w 1790
Globe M
1790   195 Strand, London
Sources: By (JAC)

RICHARDS John (I)
w 1805
Spec M, Shoe latchet M, Button M
1805   Church St, Birmingham
Sources: H

RICHARDS John (II)
w 1816–1826
Rule M
1816   95 Lichfield St, Birmingham
1825–1826   98 Lichfield St, Birmingham
See also
RICHARDS & LOCKYER★
RICHARDS Esther★
RICHARDS William (I)★
Sources: Pg

RICHARDS William (I)
w 1785–1798
Rule M

1787   14 Lichfield St, Birmingham
1793–1797   Lichfield St, Birmingham
See also
RICHARDS Esther★
RICHARDS & LOCKYER★
RICHARDS John (II)★
Sources: BW; PR; Pye

RICHARDS William (II)
w 1820–1829
Corn & Coal Measure M
1820   Williams Court, Guildford St, Borough, London
1829   Williams Court, Great Guildford St, Southwark, London
Father of
RICHARDS James s 1829 to HOWLETT R., GZT
RICHARDS John s 1820 to BULLCOCK R., TWC
Partnership: RICHARDS & SON★
Sources: GL: GZC 5735/4; TWC 7137/6 fol.161

RICHARDS & LOCKYER
w 1828–1830
Rule M, Jeweller
1828–1830   20 Jamaica Row, Birmingham
See also
RICHARDS John (II)★
RICHARDS Esther★
RICHARDS William (I)★
Sources: Pg; Wr

RICHARDS & SON
w 1832
Measure M
1832   16 Williams Court, Great Guildford St, Borough, London
Took over from RICHARDS William (II)★
Sources: R (JAC)

RICHARDSON B.
w 1822
Optician
1822   22 Little Queen St, Lincoln's Inn, London
See also
RICHARDSON John (I)★
RICHARDSON George★
RICHARDSON & SON John★
RICHARDSON S.★
Sources: Kt (JAC) [possibly directory error]

RICHARDSON George
w 1807–1830
Optical IM, Math IM, Gas fitter, Optician Paddington, London
1807   48 Leadenhall St, London
1808–1817   7 St.Catherine's St, near the Tower, London
1820–1826   12 Upper East Smithfield, London
1826   38 Windham St, New Road, Marylebone, London
Guild: Spectaclemakers, fp 1807
Son of RICHARDSON Winstanley★
Brother of RICHARDSON John (II)★
Had apprentice:
DELL Stephen Edward★1809
CHAPMAN Joseph Henry 1814
OBORNE Thomas Robert1821

MCDONOUGH William 1825
STONE William 1826
PATRICK George★, listed 1815 but dated 1814
Worked for LINCOLN Charles★
Took over from RICHARDSON Winstanley★
See also RICHARDSON John (I)★
Associated with PRITCHARD Edward★
b 1781
Known to have sold: octant
Sources: GL: SMC 5213/4, 5213/5; BM: Heal
105/81; H; J; Pg; PO; R; Bap St Luke, Old St,
London (JHC); Bod: JJ box 15; Stimson (1985)
p.113

RICHARDSON John (I)

w 1790–1822
Optician
1790–1794	39 Maiden Lane, Covent Garden, London
1799	2 Little Queen St, Holborn, London
1801–1810	26 Great Queen St, Holborn, London
1811–1822	22 Little Queen St, Lincoln's Inn Fields, London

Father of RICHARDSON John s 1812 to
USTONSON John★
Succeeded by RICHARDSON & SON John★
See also
RICHARDSON John (II)★
RICHARDSON John (III)★
RICHARDSON John (IV)★
Pat. spectacles 1797
Sources: H; Kt; PO; Und; W; GL: TC 3302/3;
Woodcroft (1854)

RICHARDSON John (II)

w 1801–1822
Optician
1801–1822	16 Somerset St, Aldgate, London
1804	68 Leadenhall St, London
1809	46 Leadenhall St, London
1810	1 Drury Lane, London
1816–1822	6 Little Tower Hill, London

Guild: Spectaclemakers, Founders
Brother of RICHARDSON George★
Apprenticed to RICHARDSON Winstanley★, his
father, nd
Had apprentice:
RICE James★ 1801 SMC
SANDWELL James Joseph 1801 FDC
WEBB Thomas 1802 FDC
MANNING Edward 1808 FDC, t/o 1809 to
HARRIS Thomas (I)★ SMC
See also
RICHARDSON John (I)★
RICHARDSON & SON John★
RICHARDSON John (IV)★
b 1774; fr SMC 1801; Widow Catherine put on
pensions list of SMC 1843; fr by purchase FDC
1801; d c.1834
Sources: GL: SMC 5213/4, 5213/6; FDC 6331/6;
Bap St. Luke, Old St, London (JHC); H; Kt; Und

RICHARDSON John (III)

w 1834–1835
Optical IM, Phil IM, Math IM
1834–1835	178 High St, Shadwell, London

See also

RICHARDSON John (I)★
RICHARDSON John (II)★
RICHARDSON & SON John★
Sources: R (JAC)

RICHARDSON John (IV)

w 1800
Optician
1800	7 Little George St, Aldgate, London

Had apprentice: RICHARDSON James 1800
See also RICHARDSON John (II)★ – possibly the
same person
Sources: GL: CH 12823/8 p.81, 12876/7

RICHARDSON Matthew

w c. 1742 d.c 1752
Optician
	Sir Isaac Newton's Head & Golden Spectacles against York Buildings in the Strand, London

Guild: Spectaclemakers, fr 1737
Son of RICHARDSON Richard, coffee man, of St.
Clement Danes, London
Husband of RICHARDSON Anne
Apprenticed to SCARLETT Edward (I)★ 1730
Known to have sold: telescope
Instruments advertised: barometer, camera obscura,
microscope, mirror, spectacles, telescope,
thermometer
Sources: GL: SMC 5213/2 p.217+; Calvert (1971)
pl.42

RICHARDSON Richard (I)

w 1738 d 1751
Optician
1738–1740	New St, Shoe Lane, London

Guild: Spectaclemakers fr 1734
Father of RICHARDSON John s 1758 DPC
Apprenticed to LINCOLN Thomas★ 1726
Sources: DH: DPC Ap; Bap & Bur St. Bride, Fleet
St (JHC); CLRO: CF (JHC); GL: SMC 5213/2
p.173+

RICHARDSON S.

w 1820
Optician
1820	22 Little Queen St, Holborn, London

See also
RICHARDSON B.★
RICHARDSON John (I)★
RICHARDSON George★
RICHARDSON & SON John★
Sources: R (JAC) [possible directory error]

RICHARDSON William (I)

w 1784–1786
Optician
1784–1786	4 East Cole Alley, Dublin

Sources: Wi: (DJB); Burnett & Morrison-Low
(1989) p.133

RICHARDSON Winstanley

w 1775 d 1807
Optician
–1807	Irongate, London
1753–1807	48 Leadenhall St, London
1773	At Mr Lincoln's, Leadenhall St, London

Guild: Spectaclemakers, fr 1773
Father of
RICHARDSON John (II)★
RICHARDSON George★
RICHARDSON Thomas, brass manufacturer, fp
1827
Son of
RICHARDSON Richard (I)
RICHARDSON Ann, widow, of St. Bride's, London
Apprenticed to LINCOLN Thomas★ 1753
Had apprentice:
RICHARDSON John (II)★ nd
RICHARDSON Richard (II), his son, 1775
RICHARDSON William (II), his son, 1787
Worked for LINCOLN Charles★ in 1773
Succeeded by RICHARDSON George★
b 1738
Sources: GL: SMC 5213/3 p.192+,
5213/4, 5213/5; Bap St. Bride, Fleet St, London
(JHC); Court & Von Rohr (1929–30) p.83

RICHARDSON & SON John

w 1818–1819
Optician
1818–1819	22 Little Queen St, Holborn, London

Took over from RICHARDSON John (I)★
See also
RICHARDSON S.★
RICHARDSON B.★
RICHARDSON John (III)★
Sources: Kt (JAC)

RICKETT William

w 1786
Guild: [Turners]
Apprenticed to
CRANE Henry 1764
COX William (II)★ 1769
Known to have sold: quadrant
Sources: GL: JC 3302/3; Daumas (1989) p.245,
328

RIDER William

w 1819–1834
Math IM, Phil IM
1819	22 Ashton St, Poplar, London
1834	121 High St, Poplar, London

Guild: [Masons]
Apprenticed to COOK William George★ 1799
Sources: GL: MC 5312 (MAC); Pg; R (JAC)

RIDGARD Joseph

w 1767–1799
Scale M
Alternative name: REDGARD
1767	Cow Cross near Smithfield Bars, London
1776	91 St.Margarets Hill, Southwark, London
1799	8 Counter St, Borough, London

Guild: Haberdashers fr 1767, Blacksmiths fr 1772
Apprenticed to VINCENT Robert★ 1760
Had apprentice:
WHEATLEY John 1772 by t/o from BRIND
William★
WHITE Ambrose 1776
Instruments advertised: balance, steelyard, weights

Sources: GL: BKC 2885/1; HC 15860/9 (MAC); CH 12876/5; BM: Heal (MAC)

RIMONDI Charles
w 1837–1866
Clock M, Watch M, Optician, Weather-glass M
1837   1 Union St, Halifax, Yorks
1850–1866   9 Waterhouse St, Halifax, Yorks
Sources: Loomes (1972)

RIPLEY James
w 1804–1844
Math IM, Optical IM, Phil IM, Optician
    13 Warkworth Terrace, Commercial Rd, London
    Mill Place, Commercial Rd, London
1805   Parish of St John, Wapping, London
1807–1822   335 High St, Wapping, London
1839–1843   15 Warkworth Terrace, Commercial Rd, London
Guild: Grocers, fr 1796
Son of RIPLEY Thomas★
Partnership: RIPLEY & SON★
Apprenticed to RIPLEY Thomas★, his father, 1782
Had apprentice:
RIPLEY Thomas Brand, his son, 1805
RATTENBURY William George 1816
HOLLIDAY John 1825
Took over from RIPLEY & SON★
Sources: GL: GC 11598/6, 11598/7; J; Kt (JAC); Pg; PO; Brown J. (1979a) p.43, 54

RIPLEY Thomas
w 1765–1790
Math IM, Optical IM
    364 Hermitage Bridge Rd, Wapping, London
    Globe, Quadrant & Spectacles near Hermitage Bridge below the Tower, London
1763   Bakers Buildings, New Broad St, London
1765–1770   Near the Hermitage, Wapping, London
1770   Bakers Buildings, London
1773   Near the Hermitage, London
1774–1793   364 Hermitage, London
Guild: Grocers, fr 1763
Related to RIPLEY Thomas Brand (grandson)
Apprenticed to GILBERT John (II)★ 1755
Had apprentice:
LEKEUX Richard★ 1770 t/o 1775 to WILCOX Walton★
RIPLEY James★, his son, 1782
ANTHONY John★ 1765
KARMOCK John★ 1773
ENEFER Robert 1778
RIPLEY Thomas, his son, 1778
COVELL Thomas 1787
HADEN William 1790
Succeeded by RIPLEY & SON★
Associated with HILL Joseph★
Known to have sold: octant
Sources: BM: Banks 105/41; Heal 105/84; BW; Kt (JAC); Ld; Riv; GL: Sun 11936/276 no.416562; Sby 23 Jun 1987 lot 167 (MAC); Brown J. (1979a) p.42–43

RIPLEY & SON Thomas (& James ?)
w 1790–1805
Math IM
    335 Hermitage, London
    364 Hermitage, London
1795   Hermitage Bridge, London
1800–1805   364 Hermitage Bridge, Wapping, London
1805   335 High St, Wapping, London
Guild: Grocers
Succeeded by RIPLEY James★
Took over from RIPLEY Thomas★
Known to have sold: octant, sextant
Sources: inst & TCd NMM; H; Kt (JAC); Ld; W (JAC); Brown J. (1979a) p.43

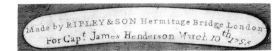

RISSO John
w 1783
Thermo M, Baro M
1783   Saltmarket, Glasgow
Sources: Bryden (1972) p.56

RITCHINGHAM
a 1790
    London
Known to have sold: sextant
Sources: inst NMM

RIVA C.
a 1820–1850
    Glasgow
See also
RIVA & CO. A.★
RIVA Mrs.M.★
RIVA J.& M.★
Known to have sold: barometer, thermometer
Sources: Goodison (1977) p.353

RIVA Ferdinando
fl 1830 w 1834
Optical IM, Baro M
1830–1834   7 Watson Walk, Sheffield
Sources: Pg; Taylor (1966) p.459

RIVA J. & M.
w 1825–1861
Carvers, Gilders, Looking-glass M, Baro M
Alternative name: ? & Michael
1825   70 High St, Glasgow
1826–1849   143 High St, Glasgow
1850–1857   147 High St, Glasgow
1857–1861   63 John St, Glasgow
1844–1846   and 249 Argyle St, Glasgow
Took over from RIVA & CO A.★
See also
RIVA Michael★
RIVA C.★
Known to have sold: barometer, telescope
Sources: Clarke et al (1989) p.209; Goodison (1977) p.353

RIVA M. (Mrs)
w 1828
Carver, Gilder
1828   143 High St, Glasgow
See also RIVA Michael
Sources: Goodison (1977) p.353

RIVA Michael
w 1826–1827
Carver, Gilder
1826–1827   143 High St, Glasgow
See also
RIVA Mrs.M.★
RIVA J.& M.★
Known to have sold: barometer
Sources: Clarke et al (1989) p.209; Goodison (1977) p.353

RIVA & CO. A.
w 1823
Math IM, Carver, Gilder
    67 High St, Glasgow
1823   70 High St, Glasgow
Succeeded by RIVA J. & M.★
Known to have sold: barometer, hydrostatic bubbles, thermometer
Sources: inst & TCd (pv) (MAC); Clarke et al (1989) p.209

RIVA & CO. P.
w 1832
Looking-glass M
1832   6 Nether Bow, Edinburgh
Known to have sold: barometer
Sources: POE (MAC); Goodison (1977) p.353

RIVERS John
w 1822–1835
Baro M
1822   Wind St, Swansea
1830   Goat St, Swansea
1835   High St, Swansea
Sources: Pg; Goodison (1977) p.353

RIVOLTA Anthony
w 1820–1851
Baro M, Thermo M, Merchant
1822–1845   32 Brook St, Holborn, London
1846–1851   21 Lower Calthorpe St, London
Sources: Pg; R (JAC); Th (JAC); Goodison (1977) p.353

RIX J.
fl 1750–1760
Alternative name: I.
    Shrewsbury Court, Cripplegate, London
    Shrewsbury Court in White Cross St, near Cripple Gate, London
See also RIX William★
Known to have sold: slide rule
Sources: inst(s) (MAC); Taylor (1966) p.245

RIX William
w 1750
1750   Mariner & Globe facing the lower end of the Old Jewry, London
Apprenticed to COOKE Thomas (II)★ nd

See also RIX J.★
Sources: Leadbetter (1750) (DJB)

ROAK Richard
w 1717 d 1743
1728   Hand Alley, Bishopsgate St, in the Coach Yard, London
1738   Pair of Spectacles, Catherine Wheel Alley, Bishopsgate St, London
Guild: Spectaclemakers, fr 1709
Apprenticed to STERROP Ralph★ 1693
Had apprentice:
EGGLESTONE Richard?★ 1717/18
NYE Richard 1721
Received charity from SMC in 1742
Sources: GL: SMC 6031/1, 5213/3 p.44,54, 5213/1, 5213/2 p.65, 123

ROBB William
fl 1776–1816
Clock M, [Baro M]
          Montrose
Known to have sold: barometer
Sources: Goodison (1977) p.353

ROBELOU Isaac
w 1719
1719   London
Known to have sold: barometer, thermometer
Sources: Goodison (1977) pl.17, p.62–63, 353

ROBERTS Edward (I)
w 1749–1784
Rule M, Math IM
1750–1756   Grocer's Alley in the Old Jewry, London
1759–1769   Dove Court, Old Jewry, London
1776   3 Dove Court, Old Jewry, London
Guild: Joiners, fr 1742
Son of ROBERTS Edward, bargeman, of Ware, Herts
Father of ROBERTS Edward (II)★
Apprenticed to COOKE Thomas (II)★ 1733
Had apprentice:
FLACK Richard 1749
COX Arthur 1754
ROBERTS Edward (II)★, his son, 1763
ROBERTS George, his son, 1765
ANDREWS Henry 1771
ROBERTS William, son of George, 1773
MACNEAL Thomas 1776
STUTCHBURY Joseph★ 1784
BRIGGS Matthew 1785
Known to have sold: slide rule
Sources: GL: JC 8052/7, 8055/3; ChrSK 4 Jun 1987 lot 160; Crawforth (1987) p.364; Leadbetter (1750) p.xviii (DJB); inst (pv)

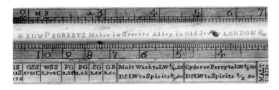

ROBERTS Edward (II)
w 1788–1796
Math IM

1790–1794   3 Dove Court, Old Jewry, London
Guild: Joiners, fr 1785
Son of ROBERTS Edward (I)★
Apprenticed to ROBERTS Edward (I)★ 1763
See also STUTCHBURY Joseph★
Sources: GL: STTP 2934 fol. 110; BW; By; Crawforth (1987) p.365

ROBERTS Henry (I)
w 1746–1756
Baro M
1747   Chapel St, Liverpool
Sources: LM index (MAC)

ROBERTS Henry (II)
w 1835
Optician
1835   48 Inge St, Birmingham
Sources: Pg

ROBERTS Jonathan
w 1686–1727
Math IM
1682   At a Cookes against ye Red Cross in East Smithfield, London
1701   Fleet Lane, London
Guild: Broderers, fr 1681/2
Apprenticed to HOWE Joseph★ nd
Had apprentice:
WENL Emmanuell 1686
ROBERTS William (II)★, son of William, 1688
PHILLIPS John 1695
BRADLEY John (I)★ 1697 by t/o from WORGAN John★
SAUNDERS Samuel (I)★ 1699/1700
WYE John 1704
HOWARD John (II)★ 1715
Sources: GL: BROD 14663/1; Brown J. (1979a) p.28; Crawforth (1987) p.340

ROBERTS Richard
w 1744–1749
Scale M
          Bartholomew Lane near the Royal Exchange, London
Guild: Blacksmiths, fp 1731
Son of ROBERTS Timothy★
Had apprentice:
DYER George 1741/2
HARRISON Thomas★ 1744/5
COLLEY Thomas 1749
Took over from ROBERTS & SON Timothy★
Associated with SNART John★
Known to have sold: balance, weights
Sources: GL: BKC 2885/1, 2886/5 (MAC); inst MHS

ROBERTS Robert
w 1824
Weight Smith
1824   North Street, City Road, London
Father of ROBERTS John s 1824 to TYLER W. of IMC
Sources: GL: IMC 16981/2

ROBERTS Thomas
w 1822–1823
Spec M

1822–1823   23 Middle St, Hull, Yorks
Sources: Bn (DJB)

ROBERTS Timothy
w 1701–1744
Scale M
Alternative name: Timhy
          Hand & Scales next ye corner of Queen St, in Watling St, London
          In Bartholomew Lane near the Royal Exchange, London
          At ye Hand & Scales, Watling St, London
Guild: Blacksmiths, fr 1695/6
Father of ROBERTS Richard★ fp 1731
Apprenticed to TAYLOR William 1686/7★
Had apprentice:
JENNINGS Silas★ 1713
ROBERTS Robert, his son, 1729
PELL Thomas★ 1701 by t/o
HOLLIDAY Thomas 1702
LOVELL Robert 1708 by
SMITH Thomas 1718
HAWSE John 1720
WHITEMARSH William★ 1724
WOOD John★ 1726
PARTRIDGE Matthew 1732/3
SANGSTER John 1736
Succeeded by ROBERTS & SON Timothy★
Associated with SNART John★
Known to have sold: balance, weights
Sources: GL: CKC 2881/8–11; 2886/4–5 (MAC); inst SM Wellcome; Heal (1988) p.152

ROBERTS William (I)
w 1822–1848
Rule M
1822   21 Westbar, Sheffield
1822–1825   1 Sportsman's Inn Yard, Westbar, Sheffield
1828–1830   Gibralter St, Sheffield
1833   Court, 23 Gibralter St, Sheffield
1833–1848   15 Westbar Green, Sheffield
1837   22 Gibralter St, Sheffield
1841   14 Steelhouse Lane, Sheffield
See also ROBERTS Edward (I)★
Sources: Bn; Pg; Wh

ROBERTS William (II)
fr 1700 w 1721
Math IM
1721   At the Leather Bottle [?] in Hornsey, London
Guild: Broderers, fr 1700/01
Apprenticed to ROBERTS Jonathan★ 1688
Had apprentice:
BALDOCK Richard★ 1705
GROOM James 1711
Sources: Crawforth (1987) p.340

ROBERTS & SON Timothy
w 1731–1744
Scale M
          Bartholomew Lane near the Royal Exchange, London
Took over from ROBERTS Timothy★
Succeeded by ROBERTS Richard★
Known to have sold: balance, weights

Sources: inst with TCd, Snowshill Manor, Glos (MAC)

ROBERTSON Patrick
w 1778
Instrument S
1778   Edinburgh
See also ROBERTSON William
Sources: Bryden (1972) p.18 n 88

ROBERTSON Robert
w 1834–1839
Optician
1834–1837   9 Dexter St, Toxteth Park, Liverpool
1839   8 Dexter St, Liverpool
Sources: G (MAC)

ROBERTSON William
a 1730–1760
Optical IM
Alternative name: W.R.
            Edinburgh
See also ROBERTSON Patrick
Known to have sold: microscope
Sources: inst WM: Brown O. (1986) no.8; Bryden (1972) p.56; Wallis R. & P. (1986) p.369

ROBINSON Edward
w 1834
Optician
1834   Horseley Field, Wolverhampton
Sources: Wh (MAC)

ROBINSON James
w 1845–1884
Optician, Math IM, Philosophical Artist, Museum of Curiosities
1845   41 Grafton St, Dublin
1846–1884   65 Grafton St, Dublin
Known to have sold: camera, telescope
Sources: inst MHS; ChrSK 14 Apr 1988 lot 131; Burnett & Morrison-Low (1989) p.133

ROBINSON John (I)
w 1743–1765
Book S, Instrument S
1743   Dock Head, Redriff, London
1749   Dock Head, Southwark, London
1765   Horsley Down New Stairs, Shad
            Thames, Southwark, London
Took over from CROSBY & ROBINSON*
Associated with KIRK John* who supplied inst
Sources: Bod; JJ; Riv; *Daily Ad* 5 & 15 Jul 1749 (JRM)

ROBINSON John (II)
w 1800–1855
Spec M, Optician, Math IM
1800–1803   20 Old Frederick St, Liverpool
1845–1853   48 Scotland St, Liverpool
Sources: G; Sl (MAC)

ROBINSON John (III)
w 1783–1795
Math IM, Optician
1791–1792   4 Drogheda St, Dublin
1794–1795   21 Hawkins St, Dublin
Had apprentice: DAVIS William 1783

Known to have sold: telescope
Sources: Burnett & Morrison-Low (1989) p.134; KH (WS); *Repertory of Arts* 2 (1795) p.399 (MAC)

ROBINSON John (IV)
w 1840
Measure M
1840   10 Robert St, Blackfriars Rd, London
Guild: Grocers, fp 1840
Son of ROBINSON Robert, of GC of London, d
Sources: GL: GC 11598/8

ROBINSON Joseph
w 1788
Motion M, [Math IM]
1772   Hosier Lane, London
1774   King's Arms Inn, Holborn, London
1788   Ratcliff Row, St.Lukes, Old St,
            London
Guild: Clockmakers, fr 1769
Apprenticed to BENNETT John (III)* 1750/1
Had apprentice:
HARRIS William (I)* 1788
JEFFRYES Robert 1772
HUBBARD Samuel 1774
TYLER Arthur 1783
Known to have sold: waywiser
Sources: GL: CKC 2721/1, 2720/1 p.39, 54, 118, 167; Baillie (1951)

ROBINSON Thomas Charles
w 1823 d 1841
Math IM, Phil IM, Optician
1825–1841   38 Devonshire St, Portland Place,
            London
Succeeded by BARROW Henry trading as
ROBINSON & BARROW*
b 1792; B.apt Admiralty, compass M*
Known to have sold: balance, barometer, dip circle, transit instrument
Sources: ACO Cat. at NMM; Pg; Chaldicott (1989) p.160–61; Stock (1969) (MAC n); Stock (1986) p.11–12; Taylor (1966) p.433–34

ROBINSON Thomas Tempest
w 1829
Cooper, Measure M
1829   Coventry
Sources: Wr (DJB)

ROBINSON & BARROW Thomas Charles & Henry
w 1842–1845
Opticians
1842   38 Devonshire St Portland Place
            London
1843–1845   26 Oxenden Street Haymarket
            London
Succeeded by BARROW Henry*
Took over from ROBINSON Thomas Charles*
When ROBINSON died BARROW took over but traded as ROBINSON & BARROW at first
Sources: PO; Chaldicott (1989) p.160–61, Stock (1986) p.11–12

ROBINSON & CO.
w 1785–1788
Scale M

1785–1788   Slitting Mill Lane, Digbeth,
            Birmingham
Sources: PR; Pye (MAC)

RODDAM & HUMBLE Cuthbert & Edward
w 1779
Math IM
Alternative name: HUMBLE & RODDAM
1779   Pope's Head, Side, Newcastle on Tyne
1779   North Shields
Succeeded by
HUMBLE Edward*
RODDAM Cuthbert*
Took over from HUMBLE Edward*
Sources: Hunt (1975) (MAC n)

RODGERSON William
w 1835–1879
Optician, Naut IM, Druggist
1835   26 St. James St, Liverpool
1839   Chatham Buildings, 19 South John
            St, Liverpool
1843–1872   10 St. James St, Liverpool
1858–1859   8 St. James St, Liverpool
1872–1873   8 & 10 St. James St, Liverpool
1873–1879   47 South John St, Liverpool
Known to have sold: barometer, octant
Sources: G (MAC); K; Sl; Sby 31 Jul 1981 lot 17 (MAC); Goodison (1977) p.354

RODGERSON & CO. William
w 1835–1837
Naut IM
1835–1837   11 South John St, Liverpool
1835   and 26 St.James St, Liverpool
See also
RODGERSON William*
RODGERSON & M'GAA*
Sources: G (MAC)

RODGERSON & MGAA
w 1832–1837
Naut IM, Stationers, Book S
Alternative name: M'GAA
1832   24 St.James St, Liverpool
1834   28 St.James St, Liverpool
1835   26 St.James St, Liverpool
See also
RODGERSON & CO. W.*
RODGERSON William*
Sources: G (MAC)

ROE John
w 1839
Optician
1839   75 Sir Thomas Buildings, Liverpool
Sources: G (MAC)

ROGERS Benjamin
w 1792–1802
Scale M
1792–1802   5 Court, 1 Dudley St,
            Wolverhampton
Sources: Wolverhampton rate books (MAC)

ROGERS George
w 1799–1808
Math IM

ROGERS Henry

Alternative name: George Clement
1799–1805   Mile End Grove, London
1808   Mile End Old Town, London
Guild: Drapers, fp 1808
Son of ROGERS John James★
Known to have sold: barometer, thermometer
Sources: DH: DPC Ap/Fr; H; inst (s) (MAC)

ROGERS Henry

w 1682–1705
[Spec M]
            London
Guild: Spectaclemakers, fr 1678
Son of ROGERS Lodowick, (d), free of HC of London
Apprenticed to TAILOR John (I)★
Had apprentice:
WOOLHOUSE Richard 1682
HANSON Samuel 1683/4
Living out of town by 1715
Sources: GL: SMC 5213/1, 5213/2 p.41,46,92

ROGERS John

w 1851
Optician
1851   21 Great Marylebone St, London
Sources: Wk

ROGERS John James

w 1777
Math IM, Phil IM
1768   Union Court, Holborn, London
1777   14 Union Court, Holborn, London
1791   Bancroft's Almshouses, Mile End, London
Guild: Drapers, fr 1768
Father of ROGERS James John s 1791 vc
Son of ROGERS Blunt, gentleman, of Blackfriars, London
Apprenticed to
HICKMAN Joseph (I)★ 1761
HICKMAN Elizabeth by t/o c. 1765
Educated at Christ's Hospital, London; v 1791
Sources: GL: VC 15220/3 p.225; CH 12876/5;
Sun 11936/257 no.382519; DH: DPC Ap/Fr

ROGERS Mark

w 1716–1721
[Math IM]
Alternative name: RODGERS
            Long Walk, London
Guild: Joiners, fr 1716
Apprenticed to CROOKE John (I)★ 1706
Son of ROGERS William, free of JC of London
Had apprentice:
DIX Henry 1716
EDKINS James 1721/2
DAWSON George 1722
Sources: Crawforth (1987) p.365

ROGERS Thomas

w 1851
Math IM
1851   64 Union St, Hoxton, London
Sources: Wk

ROLFE Samuel

w 1708–1721

[Math IM]
            London
Guild: Dyers, fr 1682
Apprenticed to
PRIDDITH Christopher★ 1682
Had apprentice:
WILLIS George 1708
KALIWERES Walter 1709
HALL James 1721
A compass at MHS signed by Samuel Rolfe may be by this maker
Sources: GL: DC 8168/3, 8169, 8171/1; inst MHS

ROLLISON Dolliff

w 1773–1790
Clock M
1773   Halton, Leeds, Yorks
1779   Sheffield
b 1752
Known to have sold: balance, weights
Sources: *Leeds Mercury* 14 Sep 1773 (MAC);
Loomes (1972)

ROLPH Thomas

w 1750–1781
Math IM, Pencil M, Rule M
1750   Ball Yard, Golden Lane, London
1773   37 Beach Lane, White Cross St, London
Guild: [Stationers], Dyers, fp 1750
Father of ROLPH William fp 1759
Son of ROLPH Thomas, free of Dyers Co. of London
Apprenticed to BATES Richard★ 1733, STC
Had apprentice:
SEALY Thomas 1750, t/o 1756 to STEDMAN Christopher (I)★
MATHEWS Richard 1750, t/o 1756 to STEDMAN Christopher (I)★
SEALY Thomas 1750
DUNN Thomas 1754
SMEDLEY John 1759
TRUEMAN Thomas 1762
RICHARDS Jonathan 1763
BRYANT James 1764
See also ROLFE Samuel★
Supplied pencils to Christs Hospital School 1754–1781
Sources: GL: DC8167/3, 8171/4; STTP 2934 fol 30; CH 12823/6 p.325–32, 12823/7 p.431–32
McKenzie (1978) p.26

ROME Thomas

w 1829–1832
Measure M
1829–1832   54 Featherstone St, City Rd, London
Sources: R (MAC)

RONCHETI Baptist

w 1785–1805
Alternative name: RONCHATE, Bap, RONKETTI, Giovanni Battista,
1785   15 High St, Manchester
            51 Spear St, Manchester
Father of RONCHETTI Joshua (I)★
Related to CASARTELLI Lewis★
Known to have sold: barometer, hygrometer, thermometer

Sources: Bolle (1982) p.159; Goodison (1977) p.354; Wetton (1993) p.49

RONCHETTI Edmund

w 1850
Baro M
1850   Waterbeer St, Exeter
Sources: Goodison (1977) p.354

RONCHETTI John

w 1836–1839
Baro M, Hydro M, Thermo M
1839   25 Hatton Garden, London
Sources: Pg; Goodison (1977) p.354

RONCHETTI John Baptist & Joshua (II)

w 1843–1851
Math IM, Phil IM, Optician, Baro M
Alternative name: J. B. & J.
1843–1851   43 Market St, Manchester
Succeeded by CASARTELLI Joseph Louis★
Took over from RONCHETTI Joshua★ their father
Sources: Sl; MSIM n; Goodison (1977) p.354; Wetton (1993) p.50–51

RONCHETTI Joshua (I)

w 1817–1841
Optician, Phil IM, Baro M, Math IM
Alternative name: Charles Joshua
1817–1825   29 Balloon St, Manchester
1828   1 St. Ann's Place, Manchester
1829   St. Ann's Passage, Manchester
1830   Cateaton St, Manchester
1832–1841   43 Market St, Manchester
1838   107 Greengate, Salford, (residence) Manchester
Father of
RONCHETTI John B.★ and
RONCHETTI Joshua
Son of RONCHETI Baptist
Worked for ZANETTI Vittore★
See also RONCHETTI & SON Joshua★
Known to have sold: barometer, hydrometer, microscope
Sources: Bn; Pg; inst SM; Goodison (1977) p.354; Holbrook (1992) p.170, 183–84; Wetton (1993) p.49–50

RONCHETTI Thomas

w 1822–1856
Baro M, Optician
1822   New Bridge St, Exeter
1830   4 Mount Pleasant, Black Boy Rd, Exeter
1850–1860   Black Boy Rd, Exeter
Sources: Pg; Goodison (1977) p.354

RONCHETTI & SON Joshua

w 1836–1839
Baro M, Thermo M, Hydro M
1836–1839   2 Hatton Garden, London
Succeeded by SOMALVICO & CO. Joseph★
London branch of RONCHETTI Joshua★ of Manchester
Sources: PO; Wetton (1993) p.50

RONCHETTI BROS

w 1851

Hydro M, Thermo M,
1851   13 Fleet St, Temple Bar, London
Sources: Wk

RONCKETI John Merry
w 1787–1790
Baro M, Artificial flower & feather M, Thermo M,
Math IM
Alternative name: RONKETTI, RONKITTE,
RONKERTI
1787–1797   180 Holborn, London
1800–1819   6 Peter St, Bloomsbury, London
See also RONKETTI & CO.
Known to have sold: barometer, hygrometer, spirit
level, thermometer
Sources: GL: Sun 11936/342 no.531060; A; By;
Goodison (1977) p.226–27

RONKETTI John
w 1820–1844
Thermo M, Baro M, Hydro M, Optician
1822   8 Back Hill, Hatton Garden, London
1835–1843   15 Museum St, Bloomsbury, London
Succeeded by RONKETTI John G.H.★
Attended London Mechanics Institute 1835 & 1840
Sources: LMIR (AM); Pg; PO; Goodison (1977)
p.355

RONKETTI John George Harris
w 1845–1846
Math IM, Phil IM, Optician, Hydrometer M, Baro
M, Thermometer M
Alternative name: I.G.H.
1845   102 St Martin's Lane, London
1845   116 Great Russell St, Bloomsbury,
             London
1845   30 Theobalds Rd, Holborn, London
1846   19 Leather Lane, Holborn, London
             15 Museum St, Bloomsbury, London
Known to have sold: barometer
Sources: PO; Goodison (1977) p.355

RONKETTI & CO.
w 1800–1819
Baro M
Alternative name: RONKITTE
1800–1819   6 Peter St, Bloomsbury, London
See also RONCKETI John Merry★
Known to have sold: barometer
Sources: H; J; R (JAC); Und; Goodison (1977)
p.226–27, 355

ROOKER Alfred
w ?fm 1843 w 1880
Math IM, Divider of Math Inst
1843–1844   26 East St, Lambs Conduit, London
1875–1880   26 East St, Red Lion Square, London
See also
ROOKER John & Alfred★
ROOKER & SON John★
Attended London Mechanics Institute 1843–1844
Sources: LMIR (AM); PO

ROOKER Edward
w 1845–1846
Mathemetical Divider, Baro M, Thermo M
1845–1846   12 Williamson St, Liverpool
Sources: G

ROOKER James Edward
w 1851–1865
Optician, Spec M
1851–1859   54 Newington Causeway, London
1865   17 Conduit St, Paddington, London
             W
Sources: PO; Wk

ROOKER John
w 1816–1846
Divider of Math Inst, Optician
1816   27 Bridgewater St, Somers Town,
             London
1824   Bridgwater St, Somers Town,
             London
1826   Guildford Place, Kennington,
             London
1841–1846   1 Little Queen St, Holborn, London
1845   26 East St, Lamb's Conduit St,
             London
Guild: Grocers, fr 1819
Son of ROOKER John, coal merchant, of Holborn,
London
Apprenticed to MARTIN James★ 1794
Had apprentice:
ROOKER Edward Cox, his son, 1824
ROOKER John Colhoun, his son, 1826
Succeeded by ROOKER & SON John★
Associated with
HILL William★ as supplier
WATKINS J.★ as supplier
Sources: EBA: OB 1816 (Watkins); PO; GL: GC
11598/7; Brown (1979a) p.51

ROOKER John & Alfred
w 1851
[Math IM]
1851   26 East St, Foundling, London
Ex. 1851; probably the same firm as ROOKER &
SON John★
Known to have sold: slide rule
Sources: Cat. 1851 (MAC)

ROOKER & SON John
w 1847–1901
Divider & Engraver of Math Inst
1849–1859   26 East St, Red Lion Square,
             London
1880–1901   156 Euston Road, London
Took over from ROOKER John★
Sources: PO

ROOSE Thomas
w 1818–1828
Math IM, Navigation warehouse, Optician's
warehouse
1818   27 Pool Lane, Liverpool
1818   28 Pool Lane, Liverpool
1821–1828   16 North Side Old Dock,
             (warehouse) Liverpool
1821–1825   8 Moore Place, Liverpool
See also JONES & ROOSE
Sources: Bn; G

ROPER Abraham
w 1787–1793
Math IM
Alternative name: ROSSER

1787–1793   8 Bedford Row, Dublin
Sources: Wi (DJB); Burnett & Morrison-Low
(1989) p.134

ROSCOE John
w 1696 d 1713
Math IM
Alternative name: RESCOW
             Liverpool
See also ROSCOE Robert
Sources: Chester Mar Bonds & Bur St. Nicholas,
Liverpool, from LM index (MAC); Taylor (1966)
p.140

ROSCOE Robert
fl.c 1696 d 1723
Clock M, Instrument M
             Liverpool
–1723   Pool Lane, Liverpool
1717   Old Hall St, Liverpool
Had apprentice WILD Roger★ 1714
See also ROSCOE John★
Sources: Bap & Bur St Nicholas, Liverpool &
other details from LM index (MAC)

ROSE John
w 1777
Math IM, Phil IM
1777   32 Litchfield St, Soho, London
Sources: GL: Sun 11936/260 no.391475 (MAC)

ROSE William Henry
w 1842–1860
Optical turner
1842   92 George St, Bermondsey, London
1846–1848   3 Crown Place, Spar Rd,
             Bermondsey, London
Guild: Drapers, fr 1840
Son of ROSE John, wire worker, of Bermondsey,
London
Apprenticed to STANTON John★ 1834
Had apprentice:
ROSE A. 1842
JUPP A. 1846
ROSE James 1848 by t/o from STANTON John A.★
ROSE Augustus James, son of John, 1851 by t/o
from MORISSE Walter of ESC
LEE James 1854
HANCOCK A. 1860
Sources: DH: DPC Ap/Fr, index; GH: GSCAp

ROSKELL John
w 1848–1851
Chrono M
1848–1851   21 Church St, Liverpool
Sources: Loomes (1976)

ROSKELL Robert & John
w 1816–1829
Chrono M
1816–1820   Church St, Liverpool
1824–1829   13 & 14 Church St, Liverpool
Succeeded by ROSKELL & SON★
Submitted chronometers for trial at Royal
Greenich Observatory 1825–1835
Sources: CUL: RGO 1143 fol. 6–10; LM index
(MAC)

ROSKELL & SON Robert
w 1827–1834
        Liverpool
See also ROSKELL John★
Sources: Bn (MAC)

ROSS Alexander
w 1847
Optical IM, Math IM
1847   30 Mosley St, Newcastle upon Tyne
Sources: Wh (MAC)

ROSS Andrew
w 1830–1859
Optical IM, Math IM, Phil IM, Baro M, Hydro
M, Optician
1831–1832   5 Albemarle St, St. John's Square,
        Clerkenwell, London
1832–1839   15 St.John's Square, Clerkenwell,
        London
1839–1843   33 Regent Circus, Piccadilly,
        London
1843–1847   21 Featherstone Buildings,
        Clerkenwell, London
1848–1853   2 Featherstone Buildings,
        Clerkenwell, London
1854–1859   2 & 3 Featherstone Buildings,
        Holborn, London
Guild: [Joiners]
Father of ROSS Thomas
Son of ROSS John, staymaker d, of Fleet St, London
Partnership:
ROSS & CO. Andrew★, with LISTER Joseph★
DALLMEYER John Henry, who married ROSS's
daur
Apprenticed to CORLESS John★ 1813
Succeeded by ROSS Thomas
b 1798; Ross & Co. 1839–42; Ex 1851; d 1859;
founder member of Microscopical Society of
London; attended London Mechanics Institute
1833
Known to have sold: barometer, camera obscura,
lens, level, magic lantern, magnet, microscope,
model (philosophical), opera glasses, pressure
gauge, spectacles, telescope
Sources: PO; R; Cat 1851; Crawforth (1987)
p.365: inst MHS, NMM, SM, NMM; Anderson et
al (1990) p.74–75; Turner (1989) p.154–170;

ROSS Archibald Hilton
w 1825–1859
Optician, Naut IM, Math IM, Phil IM
1825–1855   Press Lane, High St, Sunderland
1848   138 High St, adjoining the Custom
        House, Sunderland
1850   25 Bridge St, Bishopwearmouth,
        Sunderland
1857–1859   3 Sunniside, Bishopwearmouth,
        Sunderland
Sources: Md; Pg; Sl; Ward

ROSS John
fr 1837
Coppersmith
        Glasgow
Guild: Hammermen, fr 1837
Known to have sold: measure (capacity).
Sources: Lumsden & Aitken (1912) p.316

ROSS Joseph
w 1830
Optician
1830   Lux St, Liskeard,Cornwall
Sources: Pg

ROSS & CO Andrew
w 1839–1842
Opticians, Math IM, Phil IM, Drawing IM, Baro
M, Thermometer M, Hydro M
1840–1842   33 Regent Circus, Piccadilly, London
Took over from ROSS Andrew★
Succeeded by ROSS Andrew★
Sources: PO; inst MHS; Turner G. (1989) p.154

ROSSI George
w 1822–1830
Looking glass M, Optician
1822–1830   St. Lawrence, Norwich
1830   11 Exchange St, Norwich
Known to have sold: barometer
Sources: Pg; Goodison (1977) p.355

ROTHMY W.
w 1841
Math IM
1841   15 New St, Bishopsgate, London
Attended London Mechanics Institute 1841
Sources: LMIR (AM)

ROTHWELL –
a 1780–1820
        Manchester
Known to have sold: microscope
Sources: Phlps 13 Jun 1979 lot 138; Sby 25 Feb
1986 lot 180 (MAC)

ROTHWELL William
w 1849–1901
Math IM, Math Inst Divider
1849–1885   74 Westmorland Place, City Rd,
        London
1890–1901   28 Westmorland Place, City Rd,
        London
Sources: PO

ROUCHETTI Joshua
w 1810
Baro M
Alternative name: RONCHETTI ?
1810   31 Whitechapel, Liverpool
See also
RONCHETI Baptist★
RONCHETTI Joshua★
Sources: G (MAC)

ROUTLEDGE Adam
w 1828–1834
Watch M, Clock M, Optician
1828–1834   32 English St, Carlisle
Known to have sold: barometer
Sources: Goodison (1977) p.355

ROWLAND David
fl 1814–1833
Math IM, Mechanic
        4 Cato St, John St, Edgware Rd,
        London

1833   68 Crawford St, London
See also ROWLAND Richard★
Pat. improved sextant 1833
Known to have sold: sextant
Sources: Taylor (1966) p.404; Woodcroft (1854)

ROWLAND Edward
w 1842–1851
Math IM, Naut IM, Phil IM, Optician
1842–1848   50 Broad Quay, Bristol
1851   The Quay, Bristol
Took over from ROWLAND Edward & Thomas★
Sources: Hunts, Mat, Pg

ROWLAND Edward & Thomas
w 1820–1840
Math IM, Optician
Alternative name: Thomas & Edward
1820–1840   50 Broad Quay, Bristol
Succeeded by ROWLAND Edward★
Took over from ROWLAND & SONS Richard★
See also ROWLAND Richard★
Sources: Mat; Pg

ROWLAND Richard
w 1792–1811
Math IM
1792–1801   Quay, Bristol
1803–1811   50 Quay, Bristol
Succeeded by ROWLAND & SONS Richard★
See also
ROWLAND Edward & Thomas★
ROWLAND David★
Pat. compass (magnetic) 1812
Known to have sold: octant
Sources: Patent records (MAC); BW; H; Mat;
ChrSK 14 Mar 1985 lot 240 (MAC)

ROWLAND & SONS Richard
w 1812–1819
Math IM
1812–1819   50 Quay, Bristol
Took over from ROWLAND Richard★
Succeeded by ROWLAND Edward & Thomas★
Sources: H; Mat

ROWLANDSON Richard
w 1799–1800
Stationer, Math IM
1799   Garden St, Wapping, Liverpool
Sources: LM; index (MAC)

ROWLEY John (I)
w 1697 d 1728
Math IM, Book engraver
Alternative name: Iohn
1691   Behind the Exchange, Threadneedle
        St, London
1702–1715   The Globe under St.Dunstan's
        Church in Fleet St, London
1710–1727   [Residence?] Johnson's Court, Fleet
        St, London
Guild: Broderers, fr 1690/1
Son of ROWLEY William, sword-cutler, d, of
Lichfield, Staffs
Apprenticed to HOWE Joseph★ 1682 BROD
Had apprentice:
POTTING John★ 1699

SHEPPARD Eden 1701
SCOTT Benjamin★ 1706 by t/o from ANDERTON
James★
WRIGHT Thomas (I)★ 1707
DEAN(E) William★ 1710
Employed
WRIGHT Thomas (I)★
COGGS John (I)★
Succeeded by WRIGHT Thomas (I)★
Associated with MORDEN Robert★
Made orrery; Master of Mechanics to Geo I 1715;
Engine Keepr to Bd of Works; supplier to
Ordnance & Christ's Hospital
Known to have sold: dividing engine, level,
micrometer, octant, planetarium, rule, sector, slide
rule, sundial, telescope
Sources: GL: BROD 14657/1&/2; CH
12823/2&4; inst MHS, NMM, SM, WM; BM:
Heal 105/21 & 85; Beeson (1989) p.76; Crawforth
(1987) p.340–41 Millburn (1992) p.20–21, 33–34;
King & Millburn (1978) p.154,157

ROWLEY John (II)
w 1830
Optician
1830   22 Corridor, Bath
Sources: Pg

ROWLEY John (III)
w 1845–1870
Optician
1845–1865   26 Edgware Rd, London
1870   60 Edgware Rd, London
Sources: PO

ROWLEY Mark
w 1839–1866
Optician, Math IM, Phil IM
1839   7 Bakers Row, Walworth Rd,
              London
1845–1859   56 Goswell Rd, London
1865   269 Goswell Rd, London
Sources: Pg; PO

ROWLEY Thomas (I)
w 1818–1830
Optician, Spec M
1818   Great Hampton St, Birmingham
1828–1830   54 Constitution Hill, Birmingham
See also
ROWLEY Thomas (II)★
ROWLEY Thomas (III)★
Sources: Pg; West; Wr (MAC)

ROWLEY Thomas (II)
w 1832
Optician, Spec M
1832   31 Back, Bristol
See also
ROWLEY Thomas (I)★
ROWLEY Thomas (III)★
Sources: Mat

ROWLEY Thomas (III)
w 1834–1835
Optician
1834–1835   7 Sarah's Place, Old Street Rd,
              London

See also
ROWLEY Mark★
ROWLEY Thomas (I)★
ROWLEY Thomas (II)★
Sources: R (JAC)

ROWLEY Thomas (IV)
w 1839–1845
Optician
Alternative name: Possibly the same as Thos
Rowley (III)★, London
1845   123 James's St, Brighton
1839   34 St James St, Brighton
Optician to the Sussex & Brighton Infirmary
Sources: Pg; PO(HC)

ROWNEY & CO George
w 1849–1859
Math IM, Artists' Colourmen; Pencil M
1849–1851   51 Rathbone Place, London
1855–1859   10 Percy St, Tottenham Court Rd,
              London
1859   51 & 52 Rathbone Place, London
Known to have sold: rule
Sources: inst DurC; PO

ROXBY Robert Benton
w 1822
'Gentleman'
1822   Arbour Square, Stepney, London
Pat quadrants 1822
Sources: Taylor (1966) p.435; Woodcroft (1854)

RUBERGALL Thomas
w 1800–1854
Optician, Math IM, Phil IM
              Princes St, Soho, London
1800   10 Crown Court, Pulteney St,
              London
1805–1822   27 Coventry St, Haymarket, London
1839   21 Coventry St, London
1840–1851   24 Coventry St, London
Succeeded by BITHRAY & STEANE
R.apt Duke of Clarence; R.apt Wm.IV 1830;
Qu Victoria
Known to have sold: chondrometer, microscope
Sources: Und; GL: Sun 11936/419 no.706849;
PRO: LC3/69 p.150; BM: Banks 105/43, Heal
105/86 (MAC); Bn; H; J; Pg; PO; ChrSK 14 Mar
1985 lot 243 (MAC); Holbrook (1992) p.189

RUBIDGE Charlotte
w 1820–1826
Scale M
1820–1826   18 Great Eastcheap, Fish Street Hill,
              London
Took over from RUBIDGE James★
Sources: Kt; Pg; PO (MAC)

RUBIDGE James
w 1782–1820
Scale M
              51 Lower Shadwell, London
1782   Sweedland Court near Wide Gate
              Alley, Bishopsgate St, London
1789   51 Shadwell High St, London
1793   4 Great Eastcheap, London

1807   5 Great Eastcheap, Cannon St,
              London
1811–1820   18 Great Eastcheap, Fish Street Hill,
              London
              18 Great Eastcheap, Cannon St,
              London
Guild: Blacksmiths, fr 1782
Son of RUBIDGE James, gardener of Croydon,
Surrey
Apprenticed to MEYMOTT Clement★
Had apprentice:
DIX Charles 1795 t/o 1798 to EVERITT George★
6 others 1787–1818 not known as scale makers
Succeeded by RUBIDGE Charlotte★
Known to have sold: balance
Sources: ChrSK 29 Sep 1988 lot 105; GL: BKC
2881/15 -2881/17, 2886/5 (MAC); A (MAC); BW;
H; J; Kt (MAC); Sheppard & Musham (1975) no.50

RUDGE T.
w 1837
Surveying IM
1837   17 St James Buildings, Clerkenwell,
              London
Sources: LMIR (AM)

RUDHALL William Henry
w 1845
Optician, Spec M
1845   36 Bath St, Birmingham
Sources: K

RUMBALL Samuel
w 1834–1839
Optical IM, Phil IM, Math IM
1834   5 Crane Court, St Peter's Hill,
              London
1837   Crane Court, Doctors Commons,
              London
1839   21 St Peter's Hill, City, London
Attended London Mechanics Institute 1834
Sources: Pg; PO; R; LMIR (AM)

RUSHTON William
w 1801–1838
Gilt Toy M, Math IM, Bell Founder
1801–1818   8 Whittal St, Birmingham
1825   10 Whittall St, Birmingham
Sources: H; Pg; Wr (MAC)

RUSSELL –
w 1797

Known to have sold: globe
Sources: inst Burghley House, Stamford, Lincs
(GL'ET)

RUSSELL Charles
w 1805–1831
Math IM, Optical Turner
12 Fox Court, Gray's Inn Rd,
London
7 Fox Court, Gray's Inn Rd, London
1805 6 Fox's Court, Holborn, London
Succeeded by RUSSELL Martha★
See also RUSSELL James★
Attended London Mechanics Institute 1826–1828
Sources: LMIR (AM); H; R (JAC)

RUSSELL Edward
w 1850
Math IM, Measuring Tape M
1850 29 Whittal St, Birmingham
Sources: Sl

RUSSELL Henry
w 1827
[Precise trade unknown]
1827 King's Square, Goswell Street Rd,
London
Known to have made: rain gauge [to the design of
John Taylor]
Sources: Philosophical Magazine 1827 (JAC)

RUSSELL J.U.
w 1851
Math IM
1851 5 West End Old Dock, Hull, Yorks
Sources: Wh

RUSSELL James
w 1828
Optical Turner
1828 7 Fox Court, Gray's Inn Lane,
London
See also RUSSELL Charles★
Attended London Mechanics Institute 1828
Sources: LMIR (AM)

RUSSELL John
w 1770 d 1817
Watch M, Organ M, Jack M, Baro M, Thermo M,
Clock M
Alternative name: RUSSEL
1770 Opposite the top of Kirk Wynd,
Falkirk
R.apt P. of Wales
Known to have sold: barometer, globe
Instruments advertised: barometer, thermometer
Sources: inst SM; Goodison (1977) p.228–29

RUSSELL Martha
w 1832–1836
Optical Turner
7 Fox Court, Gray's Inn Lane,
London
14 Fox Court, Gray's Inn Lane,
London
Took over from RUSSELL Charles★
Sources: R (JAC)

RUSSELL William (I)
w 1825–1832
Math IM
1825–1832 7 Staple Inn Buildings, London
1832–1846 Brook St, Holborn, London
See also RUSSELL William (II)★
Attended London Mechanics Institute 1825–1846
– possibly two different men at the two addresses
Sources: LMIR (AM)

RUSSELL William (II)
w 1846–1849
Phil IM
1846–1849 At Jones', Holborn, London
Worked for JONES W & S★ [presumably]
See also RUSSELL William (I)★
Attended London Mechanics Institute 1846–1849
Sources: LMIR (AM)

RUSSELL & CO. Alexander
w 1834
Founder
1834 Kircaldy Foundry, 43 High St,
Kircaldy, Fife
Known to have sold: sundial
Sources: inst Kircaldy Mu noted by Webster R &
M (1989) (MAC)

RUST Ebenezer (I)
fr 1777 d 1800
Math IM
1779–1782 Amsterdam
1782 Green Churchyard, St.Catherine's,
London
1784–1787 Eaton Ford, St. Neots, Hunts
1792 Eaton Socon, St. Neots, Hunts
1795 Wapping, London
1798 St.George's in the East, London
1799 [Residence?] 20 Sampson's Gardens,
Wapping, London
Guild: Grocers, fr 1777
Son of RUST Joseph, yeoman, of Great Staughton,
Hunts
Partnership: SPENCER, BROWNING & RUST★
Apprenticed to RUST Richard★
Had apprentice:
HERRING Amos Buttle 1782
JUSTER James 1782
HOLYMAN John★ 1784
WARD James 1792
RUST Ebenezer (II)★, his son, 1795
RUST Joseph (III)★, his son, 1798
See also RUST Mrs Martha★, prob his wife
Sources: GL: GC 11598/6; H (JAC); Brown J
(1979a) p.40–41,48,84

RUST Ebenezer (II)
w pt 1809 d 1838
Math IM, Optician
1809 66 Wapping, London
1809 Burr St, London
Guild: Grocers, fr 1809
Son of RUST Ebenezer (I)★
Partnership: SPENCER, BROWNING & RUST★
Apprenticed to RUST Ebenezer (I)★, his father,
1795
Had apprentice MASON James (II) 1809
Associated with MASON James (I)★

Partnership all working life
Sources: GL: GC 11598/6; Brown J (1979a)
p.48,85

RUST Joseph (I)
w 1786–1793
Math IM, Optical IM
1786–1793 Corner of Catherine Stairs, London
1793 15 Free School St, Southwark,
London
Guild: Grocers, fr 1786
Apprenticed to RUST Richard★, his father, 1777
Had apprentice:
ARGILL Thomas★ 1793
PEACHY William★ 1786
DENCH Thomas★ 1788, t/o to LORKIN Thomas★
1789
Bankrupt 1789
Sources: GL:GC 11598/5; Sun 11936/337 no.
521572; Caledonian Mercury 19 Jan 1789 (DJB); By;
BW; Ld; Brown J (1979a) p.52

RUST Joseph (II)
fl 1811 w 1816
Navigation Warehouse
28, 29 & 31 Pool Lane, Liverpool
1816 Mathematical Warehouse, Pool
Lane, Liverpool
See also
JONES & RUST★
JONES John (III)★
Possibly the same as Joseph RUST (III)★, who may
have moved from London, but no firm proof
found
Sources: LM index (MAC); Taylor (1966) p.405

RUST Joseph (III)
fr 1809
Math IM
1809 Burr St, London
Guild: Grocers, fr 1809
Son of RUST Ebenezer (I)★
Brother of RUST Ebenezer (II)★
Apprenticed to RUST Ebenezer (I)★ 1798
Possibly the same as Joseph RUST (II)★, if he
moved to Liverpool, but no firm proof found
Sources: GL: GC 11598/6

RUST Mrs Martha
w 1801
Math IM
1801 King St, Sampson's Gardens, London
Guild: Grocers
Had apprentice: FOX Joseph 1801
See also RUST Ebenezer (I)★, prob her husband
Sources: GL: GC 11598/6

RUST Richard
w 1753 d 1785
Math IM, Inventor
1753–1778 The Minories, London
1776 125 Minories, London
1780 St.Catherine's High St, London
1781 Corner of St.Catherines Stairs, near
the Tower, London
1752 At Mr Thomas Rust's, Anchor &
Belles, Minories, London
Guild: Grocers, fr 1752

Son of RUST John, farmer, of Kimbolton, Hunts
Related to RUST Ebenezer (I)★
Partnership: RUST & EYRE★
Apprenticed to PARMINTER John (I)★ 1744
Had apprentice:
BARNS Daniel 1753
APPLETON J 1754 by t/o from WILKINSON
John (I)★
TAYLOR Robert 1758?★
BLENCOW William 1759 by t/o from LUCAS
Richard★
SHARPLIN William 1762
READE George 1762
STONE Richard 1763
SPENCER William (II)★ 1766
BOWLES Daniel 1767
BROWNING Samuel (I)★1767
BROWNING John (I)★ 1768
RUST Ebenezer (I)★ 1770
GARRARD Thomas (I)★ 1770
SUTTON Samuel 1774
THODEY Samuel 1774
FISHER John 1776
RUST Joseph (I)★ his son 1777
CLERK James★ 1779
WELCH George 1781
NOYES John★ 1782, son of NOYES William★
Associated with WATT James★, who bought rules
for re-sale
Inv. an artificial horizon
Known to have sold: back-staff, octant, protractor,
quadrant, rule
Sources: GL: Sun 11936/299 no. 453015; By; Ld;
Brown J (1979a) p.40–41, pl.24; Calvert (1971)
pl.43; Sby 17 Apr 1986, lot 286; Bryden (1972)
p.34; McKenzie (1978) p.302

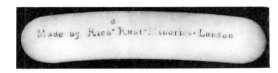

RUST Thomas Wills
w 1838–1847
Optician
1838   66 Wapping, London
1847   Minories, London
Son of RUST Ebenezer (II)★
Sources: PRO: IR 26/1494/532 Estate Duties (LS)

RUST & EYRE Richard & R.
c.1752
[Compass M]
             The Minories, London
Partnership RUST Richard★ & EYRE
Known to have sold: compass
Sources: inst NMM

RUST & SON Richard
w 1785–1794
Math IM
1785   Catherine Stairs, London
Took over from RUST Richard★
Richard Rust d 1785 but name continued
Sources: By (JAC)

RUSTON Joseph
w 1784
Scale M
             46 Essex St. Strand, London
Sources: By (JAC)

RUTHVEN John
w 1813–1849
Printer, IS, Inventor
             Edinburgh
Known to have sold: kaliedoscope inv by David
Brewster
Sources: Sby 23 Jun 1987 lot 16; Clarke et al
(1989) p.97–98

RUTT Richard
w 1839–1841
Math IM
1839–1841   30 Narrow St, Limehouse, London
1842–1858   A Richard Rutt appeared in
             directories for Baltimore City, USA,
             Math IM, and was listed in Census as
             from England.
Sources: PO; R; Smithsonian Institution

RUTTY Thomas
w 1836–1839
Optician, Math IM, Phil IM, Drawing IM
1836–1839   39 Hackney Rd, London
1836   79 Middlesex Place, Hackney Rd,
             London
Guild: Merchant Taylors, fr 1831
Apprenticed to LEFEVER Thomas★ 1819
Had apprentice PEACOCK William George 1836
Sources: GL: MTC MF 320,324 (MAC); Pg

RYLAND Thomas
w 1800–1808
Button M, Optician, Gilt Toy M
1801   Great Charles St, Birmingham
1808   Mary Ann St, Birmingham
1808   St.Paul's Square, Birmingham
Sources: Bisset's directories (MAC)

RYTHER Augustine
w 1576 c 1594
Engraver, Math IM
Alternative name: RIDER Augustin
1590   A little from Leadenhall next to the
             Sign of The Tower, London
Guild: Grocers, nd
Had apprentice WHITWELL Charles★ 1582
Engraver of maps; in Fleet Prison 1594
Known to have sold: theodolite
Sources: Brown (1979a) p.24,60; Tyacke & Huddy
(1980) (MAC)

SADLER William
w 1815
Scale M
1815   Redcross Street City of London
             London
Father of SADLER Henry s 1815 PWC
Sources: GL: PWC 7102 fol.28

SALA Domenico
c 1800
             London

See also SALLA Anthony★
Known to have sold: barometer
Sources: Goodison (1977) p.356; Turner G (1980)
p.58; Holbrook (1992) p.104,135

SALA & CO. Joseph
a 1800
             33 High St, Paisley
Known to have sold: hydrostatic bubbles.
Sources: inst SM Gabb; Holbrook (1992) p.93

SALDARINI Joseph
w 1830–1841
Optician, Gilder
1830–1841   Long Causeway, Peterborough
Known to have sold: barometer
Sources: Pg; Goodison (1977) p.356

SALLA Anthony
w 1832–1840
Baro M, Thermo M
1832–1833   65 Paradise Row, Chelsea, London
1836–1840   66 Paradise Row, Chelsea, London
See also SALA Domenico★
Sources: Pg; R (JAC); Goodison (1977) p.356

SALLA Mark
w 1810 c 1815
1810   Preston
Known to have sold: barometer, thermometer
Sources: Lyle (1975) (MAC); Goodison (1977)
p.356

SALMON J.
w 1843
Phil IM
1843   32 King St; Snow Hill, London
Attended London Mechanics Institute 1843
Sources: LMIR (AM)

SALMON William John
w 1838–1881
Telescope M, Optician, Math IM, Phil IM
1838–1845   105 Fenchurch St, London
1846–1853   254 Whitechapel Rd, London
1854–1862   100 Fenchurch St, London
1858–1861   & 48 Lombard St, London
1865–1877   85 Fenchurch St, London
1878–1881   2 Aldgate High St, London
Ex 1851
Known to have sold: microscope, telescope
Sources: PO; Wk; Turner (1983a) p.310, (1989)
p.93–94,104

SALMONI Mark
w 1830–1830
Baro S, Thermo S
1830   St Clements, Oxford
Sources: Pg

SALMONI Peter
w 1805–1846
Print S, Stationer, Optician
Alternative name: Peter Paul
1805–1807   4 North Parade, Bath
1809   24 Union St, Bath
1829–1846   4 Milsom St, Bath
Sources: Bne, H; Kn; Pg; Sil

SALOM Benjamin
w 1840–1842
Optician
1840–1842   31 St.Andrew's Square, Edinburgh
Succeeded by SALOM & CO.
Sources: Clarke et al (1989) p.99; ADCS

SALT Abraham
w 1805–1816
Rule M, Cutler
1805–1816   Worcester St, Birmingham
See also
SALT Joseph★
SALT Joseph & Abraham★
SALT & SON Abraham★
SALT Isaac★
Sources: H (DJB); Wr (MAC)

SALT Isaac
w 1820–1830
Rule M, Cutler, Ironmonger
1820   Birmingham
1829   19 Worceter St, Birmingham
1830   20 Worcester St, Birmingham
See also
SALT Abraham★
SALT Joseph★
SALT & SON Abraham★
SALT Joseph & Abraham★
Sources: Pg; West; Wr (MAC)

SALT Joseph
w 1793–1827
Rule M
1793   Wolverhampton
1811–1827   Cock St, Wolverhampton
See also
SALT & SON Abraham★
SALT Joseph & Abraham★
SALT Abraham★
SALT Isaac★
Sources: BW; PB; Pg; Smart's directory (MAC)

SALT Joseph & Abraham
w 1797–1801
Rule M
1797   Smallbrook St, Birmingham
1801   Windmill St, Birmingham
1801   Windmill St, Bristol St, Birmingham
See also
SALT Abraham★
SALT Joseph★
SALT & SON Abraham★
SALT Joseph & Abraham★
Sources: Chp; Pye (MAC)

SALT & SON Abraham
w 1811–1826
Rule M, Cutler, Ironmonger
1811–1826   Worcester St, Birmingham
See also
SALT Joseph★
SALT Joseph & Abraham★
SALT Abraham★
Sources: Pg; Wr (MAC)

SALTER George
w 1791 d 1849

Scale M, Pocket Steelyard M
              On the Turnpike, West Bromwich
              High St, West Bromwich
Son of SALTER William★
See also SALTER Richard★
Pat. spring balance 1838
Sources: Pg; Wr; Bache (1960) p.1–16 (MAC)

SALTER Richard
w 1760 d 1791
              Thomas St, West Bromwich
1760   Bilston
Brother of SALTER William★
Related to SALTER George★
Sources: Bache (1960) p.14,16 (MAC)

SALTER William
w 1760 d 1822
Pocket steelyard M
              Lichfield St, Bilston
Father of SALTER George★
Brother of SALTER Richard★
Succeeded by SALTER George★
Sources: BW; PB; Pg; Bache (1960) p.1–16
(MAC)

SAMMON John
w 1848
Optician
1848   2 Great New St, New St Square,
              London
See also SALMON J.★
Attended London Mechanics Institute 1848
Sources: LMIR (AM)

SAMPSON Lyon
w 1823–1845
Optician, Math IM
Alternative name: SAMSON
1823–1824   74 Brownlow Hill, Liverpool
1825   86 Brownlow Hill, Liverpool
1827   2 Gildart St, Liverpool
1829–1837   4 Roden Place, Ilford St, Liverpool
1835   12 Bridport St, Liverpool
1839–1845   18 Upper Pitt St, Liverpool
Sources: Bn (DJB); G (MAC)

SAMUEL Benjamin
Optician, Lapidary
1839–1841   73 Fleet St, London
Sources: Pg; PO

SAMUEL Edwin L.
w 1849–1857
Optician, Math IM
1849–1857   9 South Castle St, Liverpool
Sources: G (MAC)

SAMUEL Louis
w 1845–1849
Optician, Math IM, Silversmith, Watch M
1845–1849   46 Paradise St, Liverpool
Sources: G (MAC)

SAMUELS Emmanuel Isaac & Joseph
w 1847–1848
Optician
Alternative name: SAMUEL

1847–1848   73 Great Prescot St, London
Sources: PO

SAMUELS Joseph
w 1839–1849
Optician
Alternative name: SAMUEL
1839   South Island Place, Clapham Road,
              London
1840–1842   12 South Island Place, Clapham
              Road, London
1849   73 Great Prescot St, London
Sources: Pg (Surrey); PO; R

SAMUELS & CO. Emanuel Isaac
w 1837–1846
Optician, Phil IM, Math IM, Lapidary
Alternative name: SAMUEL
1837–1846   73 Great Prescot St, London
1845   108 New St, Birmingham
Sources: K; PO

SAMUELS J. & J.
w 1850
Optician
1850   30 Newhall St, Birmingham
Sources: Sl

SANDFORD Patrick
w 1820–1822
Baro M, Mirror M
1820–1822   45 Henry St, Dublin
Sources: Pg (MAC)

SANDS Thomas
w 1846–1855
Rule M
1846–1855   164 Church St, Shoreditch, London
Sources: PO; Wk

SANDWELL J.H.
w 1849–1880
Optician
1849–1880   9 Wynyatt St, St. John Street Rd,
              London
Sources: PO

SANDWELL John
w 1783
1783   Broadstairs, Kent
An octant bears this name, but it may be the
owner's
Sources: inst NMM

SANDY James
a 1770 d 1819
              Alyth
Known to have sold: telescope
Sources: Taylor (1966)

SANG John
w 1851
Manufacturer
1851   Kircaldy, Fife
Ex. 1851
Known to have sold: planimeter
Sources: Cat. 1851

SANGSTER Elizabeth
w 1768–1775
Scale M
> The King's Arms in Butcher Row,
> Temple Bar, London

Guild: Blacksmiths
Wife of SANGSTER William★
Partnership: SANGSTER Eliz.& John★
Had apprentice:
SCOLES Richard 1768
GRAVES Thomas 1775
BATEMAN Thomas 1775
See also SANGSTER James★
Sources: GL: BKC 2885/1, 2886/5

SANGSTER Elizabeth & John
w 1769
Scale M
1769   The Kings Arms in Butcher Row,
     Temple Bar, London
Guild: Blacksmiths
Wife of SANGSTER William★
See also SANGSTER James★
Sources: BM: Heal, bill (MAC)

SANGSTER James
w 1749–1755
Scale M
1753   Opposite Hayden Yard in the
     Minories, London
Guild: Blacksmiths, fr 1738
Brother of SANGSTER William★
Apprenticed to PICARD John★ 1731
Had apprentice BEAUMONT William 1753 and 3
others not known as Scale M
Known to have sold: balance
Instruments advertised: balance
Sources: GL: BKC 2886/4, 2888 (MAC); CH
12876/4 (MAC); inst with TCd (pv)

SANGSTER John
c 1766
     London
Guild: [Blacksmiths]
Partnership: SANGSTER Elizabeth & John★
Apprenticed to
NEWTON William (I)★ 1759
READ Samuel★ by t/o 1761
Sources: GL: BKC 2888 (MAC)

SANGSTER William
w 1751 d.c 1768
Scale M
1763   The Kings Arms in Butcher Row,
     Temple Bar, London
Guild: Blacksmiths, fr 1742
Brother of SANGSTER James★
Husband of SANGSTER Elizabeth★
Apprenticed to
PICARD John★ 1734/5
BROOKSBY Thomas (I)★ 1739
Had apprentice GRITTON William 1751
Known to have sold: balance
Instruments advertised: balance, steelyard, weights
Sources: EL: BKC 2885/1, 2886/4, 2886/5
(MAC); inst & TCd (pv) (MAC n)

SANKEY Ann
w 1820
Optician
1820   Westgate St, Gloucester
Sources: Ge

SAPP Richard
w 1707–1712
Compass M
1707   Southwark, London
1712   Parish of St Olave's, Southwark,
     London
Father of
SAPP Stephen, s 1707 in GSWC
SAPP Thomas s 1717 SWC
d by 1717
Sources: GL: GSWC 2455; PRO: IR 1/1 fol.50;
Ridge (1939) p.184

SAREL William
fr 1798
Math IM
1798   48 Rosamond's Row, London
Guild: Glovers, fr 1798
Son of SAREL Edward of St. George, Hanover
Square, London
Apprenticed to PEARCE James (described as a
gangsman in 1776) 1791
See also EVANS William (II)★
Sources: GL: GVC 4591/4, 4591/2

SARGENT Allen
w 1839–1846
Optician
1839–1846   17 Ryder's Court, Little Newport St,
     London
Sources: Pg; PO

SARJANT Thomas
w 1712–1713
Alternative name: SARIANT, SERJANT, SARJENT
     London
Guild: Joiners, fr 1710
Son of SARJANT Robert, gent, of Godmanchester,
Hunts
Apprenticed to COOKE Thomas (II)★ 1703
Had apprentice SPENCER Devereux 1712
Known to have sold: slide rule [dated 1713]
Sources: inst NMM; Crawforth (1987) p.365

SARLOW A.
w 1835–1836
Baro M, Thermo M
1835–1836   12 Leather Lane, London
Sources: R (JAC)

SAUNDERS Charles
w 1752
[Math IM]
     London
Guild: Masons, fr 1748
Apprenticed to
SAUNDERS Samuel (I)★ 1740/1
WALSON Alex of CKC by t/o 1743
PEARCY William★ 1745 by t/o
Son of SAUNDERS Thomas (I)★
Had apprentice KING Thomas 1752
Sources: GL: MC 5304/2, 5304/3, 5312

SAUNDERS James
w 1765–1793
Math IM
     Rotherhithe Wall, London
1765   Haberdashers Square in Grub St,
     London
1793   Mill St, Dockland, London
Apprenticed to (probably) ASHBY Samuel★
See also
SAUNDERS Richard (I)★
SAUNDERS Samuel (II)★
Sources: PRO: IR 1/21 (AM); GL: CH 12876/5;
A (JAC); BW

SAUNDERS M.A.
w 1821–1831
Optician, Packet Office
1821–1822   Eden Quay, Dublin
1823–1829   27 Eden Quay, Dublin
1830–1831   6 Aston's Quay, Dublin
See also SAUNDERS Thomas (I)★
Sources: Burnett & Morrison-Low (1989) p.184

SAUNDERS Richard (I)
w 1781–1805
Math IM
1781   Water Lane, Blackfriars, London
1793   Dorset St, Salisbury Sq, London
1805   Paved Court, Salisbury Square,
     London
Father of SAUNDERS Richard s 1781 MTC
See also
SAUNDERS Robert (II)★
SAUNDERS Samuel (II)★
SAUNDERS James★
MOLLISON & SAUNDERS★
Sources: GL: MTC MF 320 (MAC); BW; By: H
(JAC)

SAUNDERS Richard (II)
w 1688 fl 1711
[IM], Author
Alternative name: SAUNDER
1638–1695   Ouston, Leics
1696–1711   Leesthorp, Melton Mowbray, Leics
Instrument advertised: barometer
Sources: Saunders (1688) & (1689) (DJB); Taylor
(1954) p.277–78

SAUNDERS Robert (I)
w 1640–1667
Alternative name: SANDERS
     London
Guild: Blacksmiths, fr between 1633 and 1635
Had apprentice:
MOORE William (I)★ 1640
THORPE John 1646/7
PARSEMORS Edward 1653
MEDGEWICK Walter by t/o from MOORE
William (I)★ nd
DEVELL William 1658
OGDEN Samuel (I)★ 1660
GROVE Christopher★ 1667
Sources: GL: BKC 2881/5–7, 2884 (MAC)

SAUNDERS Robert (II)
w 1723 d c. 1743
Spec M
1724   The Globe, Leadenhall St, London

Guild: Spectaclemakers, fp 1720
Son of SAUNDERS William★
Had apprentice SAYER Samuel 1723
Sources: GL: SMC 5213/2 p.116,140, 5213/3 p.54;
Sun 11936/17 no.32414

SAUNDERS Samuel (I)

w 1708 d 1743
Toyman, Math IM
1708   Long Walk, London
1715   The Globe under St.Dunstan's
               Church, Fleet St, London
1717–1730   Hen & Chicken Court in Fleet St,
               London
–1743   Half Moon & Seven Stars, St.Paul's
               Churchyard, London
Guild: [Broderers], [Stationers], Masons, fp 1708
Son of SAUNDERS John of MC of London
Apprenticed to
ROBERTS Jonathan★ 1699/1700 BROD
ENGLAND John★ 1703 by t/o STC
Had apprentice:
FARMER John 1708/9
GRANTHAM William 1710
FOWLER John★ 1711/12
SAUNDERS Thomas (I)★ 1716
THOMPSON Thomas 1717/18
NICOLLS Anthony 1720
GOFFE Thomas 1721
WATTS James 1724/5
ADAMS William★ 1726
SAUNDERS Charles★ 1740/41
See also
ROWLEY John★
SAUNDERS Samuel (II)★
HAC by 1721 (JT); Master MC 1726
Sources: PRO: IR 1/1 fol.57; GL: MC 5204/2,
5304/3; CH 12876/3; Sun 11936/6 no.8216, /31
no.50440 (MAC); *Daily Ad* 18 Jan & 12 Feb 1743
(MAC); LEP 19–21 Jul 1743 (JRM); King &
Millburn (1978) p.154; McKenzie (1978) p.118

SAUNDERS Samuel (II)

w 1755–1783
Math IM
Alternative name: SANDERS
1755   Parish of St. Andrew, Holborn,
               London
1756–1783   Deptford Dockyard, London
Guild: Goldsmiths, fr 1759
Son of SAUNDERS Samuel peruke M, of
Southwark, London
Apprenticed to COLLIER William★ 1736/7
Had apprentice:
COLLIER Richard 1755
MOORE William ?(II)★ 1757
CLEMENS Henry 1772
THOMAS George★ 1772
Took over from WAGER Richard★
Master Compass Maker to Admiralty 1756–82
Known to have sold: compass (magnetic)
Sources: PRO: IR 1/20 /21 (AM); GH: GSC Ap,
Fr; Taylor (1966) p.217

SAUNDERS Thomas (I)

s 1716 d by 1740
Instrument M
               London

Guild: [Masons]
Apprenticed to SAUNDERS Samuel (I)★ 1716
Father of SAUNDERS Charles★ s 1740
Sources: GL: MC 5304/2, 5304/3, 5312

SAUNDERS Thomas (II)

w 1793–1820
Optician, Math IM
1793   8 Georges St, Dublin
1793–1794   7 George St, Dublin
1796–1799   35 College Green, Dublin
1800–1802   6 Church Lane, Dublin
1804–1818   6 S.E.Church Lane, Dublin
1819–1820   Eden Quay, Dublin
See also SAUNDERS M.A.★
Known to have sold: pantograph
Sources: Pg; Sby 15 Oct 1973 lot 81 (DJB);
Burnett & Morrison-Low (1989) p.134; Mason
(1944) (MAC)

SAUNDERS Thomas (III)

w 1805–1836
Scale M, Brad M
1805–1807   5 St.John's Row, St.Lukes, London
1808–1815   Brick Lane, Old St, London
1836   19 Warner's Place, Hackney Rd,
               London
Father of
SAUNDERS Benjamin s 1815 TWC
SAUNDERS Charles William s 1808 to PAYNE
Benjamin Matthew★
Had apprentice BRAGG John 1815
Sources: GL: TWC 7137/6 fol. 132; BKC 2881/16
(MAC); CH 12876/8; H; Pg (JAC)

SAUNDERS William

w 1695–1717
Spec M
Alternative name: SANDERS
1695   Little Brittain, London
Guild: Spectaclemakers, fr 1690
Father of SAUNDERS Robert (II)★
Had apprentice:
SAUNDERS Edward 1695
SAUNDERS Samuel (III) 1700
ADAMS John 1707
Master SMC 1715–1716, d c.1740
Sources: GL: SMC 6031/1, 6029, 5213/1, 5213/2
p.21,94,97–8,116

SAUNDERS & SON George

w 1851
1851   278 Strand, London
Ex 1851
Known to have sold: kaleidoscope
Sources: Cat. 1851

SAUNDERSON Henry

w 1722 d 1753
Hourglass M
Alternative name: SANDERSON
1721–1732   Houndsditch, London
Guild: Turners, fr 1721
Apprenticed to BROAD John★ 1707/8
Had apprentice:
GROVE William 1721/2 by t/o from
EARDISWICK Isaac
WICKS Edward 1732

DENNIS John★ 1740
BROWN Edward★ 1742
7 other apprentices 1722–1753
Sources: GL: 3302/2, 3303, 3305; CH 12876/3

SAVERY Servington

w 1721–1743
Optical IM, Clergymen
1721   Church Stanton, Som
1730   Norton sub Hamdon, Som
Associated with
LOVELACE Jacob (II)★
LOVELACE William (I)
Inv. a micrometer; inv. compound magnet
Sources: *Phil. T* 36 (1730) p.295–340; BM: Add.
MS 44058 (PF); Wallis R & P (1986) p.180

SAWGOOD John

w 1806–1827
Scale M
1823–1827   6 Hoxton Market, London
Guild: Blacksmiths, fr 1780
Partnership: DE GRAVE & SAWGOOD★
Apprenticed to BLACKMAN Solomon 1770
Had apprentice:
WIGGINTON James★ 1800
JONES Thomas (IV)★ 1807
CASTLE John 1810 t/o 1813 to BURCHFIELD
Thomas★
MONKS John James, son of MONKS James★ 1811
6 others 1794–1815
Partnership 1801–1805★
Freed on the testimony of Charles DEGRAVE★ and
probably worked for him
Source: GL: BKC 2881/15–17 (MAC): Pg

SAXTON Joseph

w 1833–1836
Magneto Electric Machine M
               Philadelphia USA
1833–1836   24 Sussex St, London
Sources: *Phil Mag* 9 (1836) p.360–65; Frazier
(MAC n); Morton & Wess (1993) p.624–25;
Taylor (1966) p.459

SAYE Thomas

w 1676–1678
Spec M
Alternative name: SAY
1678   Cripplegate, London
Guild: Spectaclemakers, fr 1676
Son of SAYE Richard, husbandman, of Warum (?
Warham), Norfolk
Apprenticed to HOWE Joseph★ 1668
Had apprentice NORTH George (I)★ nd, fr 1722
Sources: GL: SMC 5213/1, 5213/2 p.128

SCARLETT Edward (I)

w 1705 d 1743
Optician, Spec M
               Archimedes & Globe in Dean St, nr.
               St.Anne's Church, Soho, London
1705–1743   Archimedes & Globe near St.Ann's
               Church, Soho, London
1722   Archimedes & Globe, King St, Soho,
               London
1724   Archimedes & Globe in Market St,
               nr. St.Anne's Church, Soho, London

Guild: Spectaclemakers, fr 1705
Father of SCARLETT Edward (II)★
Apprenticed to COCK Christopher★ 1691
Had apprentice:
ADAMS Nathaniel★ 1722
JONES William (I)★ 1709
BROOME Henry 1714/15
SCARLETT Edward (II)★, his son, 1716/17
KINSEY Thomas 1737
RICHARDSON Matthew★ 1730
Employed COMBS Oliver★
HUTCHINSON Thomas 1714–21
Associated with GLYNNE Richard★ for auction of latter's stock
Inv. temple spectacles; R.apt Geo.II 1727; Master SMC 1720–1722
Known to have sold: microscope, telescope
Instruments advertised: barometer, camera obscura, magic lantern, microscope
Sources: SMC 5213/2 p.43,45,91,99,117,132–3, 147+; Sun 11936/8 no.32769; PRO: LC 3/64 p.84, 3/65 p.155 (MAC); BM: Heal 105/87; *The Craftsman* 20 Jun 1730 (JRM) Calvert (1971) pl.44; Buckley (1935) p.428

SCARLETT Edward (II)

w 1743 d c. 1779
Optician
	The Spectacles, 2nd House from Essex St, nr. Temple Bar, London
1749	Macclesfield [or Maxfield] St, London
1763	Near St.Anne's Church, Soho, London
Guild: Spectaclemakers, fr 1724
Son of SCARLETT Edward (I)★
Apprenticed to SCARLETT Edward (I)★ 1716/17
Had apprentice WESTON George 1747
Employed WATKINS Francis (I)★
DAVIS John (III)★ 1777
Succeeded by probably DAVIS John (III)★
R.apt Geo.II 1743; Master SMC 1745–1746
Sources: GL: SMC 5213/2 p.99,147, 5213/3 p.89, 102–3,118+; PRO: LC3/65 p.155; Mort; Court & von Rohr (1929–30) p.78; Goodison (1979) p.269

SCATLIFF Daniel (I)

w 1760–1767
[Math IM]
| 1760 | Wapping, London |
See also
SCATLIFF Samuel★
SCATLIFF Daniel (II)★
SCATLIFF James (I)★
SCATLIFF Simon (II)★
Pat. quadrant 1760 with DOLLOND John (I)★, GREGORY Henry (I)★ and WINTER Thomas
Sources: Wallis R & P (1986) p.456; Woodcroft (1854)

SCATLIFF Daniel (II)

w 1831–1835
Math IM
| 1831–1835 | 4 Wapping Wall, Shadwell, London |
Guild: [Cordwainers]
Son of SCATLIFF Simon (II)★
Apprenticed to BALE David★ 1804
Took over from SCATLIFF Simon (II)★ his father

See also
SCATLIFF Samuel★
SCATLIFF James (I)★
SCATLIFF Daniel (I)★
Sources: GL: CORD 24139/1; PO; R

SCATLIFF James (I)

fl. 1728
| | Friar Bacon's Head, corner of St.Michael's Alley, Cornhill, London |
Related to SCATLIFF Samuel★ (probably)
Succeeded by SCATLIFF Samuel★
Sources: Taylor (1966) p.165

SCATLIFF Samuel

w 1737–1764
Spec M, Optical glass M
Alternative name: SCATLIFFE
| –1748 | Friar Bacon's Head, corner of St.Michael's Alley, Cornhill, London |
| 1764 | St.Paul's Churchyard, London |
Guild: Spectaclemakers, fr 1734
Father of
SCATLIFF John fp 1765, SMC, as a tailor
SCATLIFF James (II)
Son of SCATLIFF Simon★, ship chandler, of Wapping, London
Apprenticed to MANN James (II)★ 1725
Had apprentice:
PORTER John May 1737 by t/o from CUFF John★
LARKIN William Llewellin 1737
SCATLIFF James (II) his son, 1749
Took over from SCATLIFF James (I)★
Master SMC 1751–1752; petitioner against Dollond's patent 1764; retired from Court of SMC 1767
Known to have sold: telescope
Instruments advertised: magnifying glass, microscope, spectacles, telescope
Sources: GL: SMC 5213/2 p.158+, 5213/3 p.144, 166, 179+; inst MHS; Buckley (1935) p.428; Calvert (1971) pl.45

SCATLIFF Simon (I)

w 1710–1726
Math IM, Ship chandler
Alternative name: SCATLISS
| 1710 | Near Hermitage Stairs in Wapping, London |
| 1723–1726 | Next door to The Fox below Hermitage Bridge, London |
Guild: [Clockmakers]
Father of SCATLIFF Samuel★
Partnership: SCATLIFF & AMES★
Apprenticed to HENSHAW Walter★ 1683
Sources: GL: SMC 5213/2 p.158; CKC 3939; Sun 11936/1 no.94, 11936/17 no.30669, /21 no. 37481, 11936/23 no.41041

SCATLIFF Simon (II)

w 1806–1830
Math IM, Ship Chandler, Compass M
1804	Wapping St, London
1806	33 Wapping, London
1816–1830	21 Rotherhithe St, London
Succeeded by SCATLIFF Daniel (II)★ his son
Associated with BALE David★ to whom SCATLIFF David (II)★ s 1804

Sources: GL: CORD 24139/1; H; Kt; Pg; R (JAC); Und

SCATLIFF & AMES Simon & Joseph

w 1725
Math IM
| 1725 | Near the Hermitage, London |
| 1725 | Warehouse near Wapping Old Stairs, London |
Sources: GL: Sun 11936/21 no. 37481

SCATTERGOOD Samuel

w 1845
Math IM, Measuring Tape M
| 1845 | 23½ Livery St, Birmingham |
Sources: K

SCHALFINO John

w 1840–1843
Baro M
| 1840–1843 | East St, Taunton, Som |
Known to have sold: barometer
Sources: Goodison (1977) p.357

SCHIAVI Antonio

w 1821–1832
Baro M, Carver, Gilder, Looking-glass M
Alternative name: SCHAIVIA
| 1821–1823 | 14 Standish St, Liverpool |
| 1824–1832 | 67 Stanley St, Liverpool |
Sources: Bn; LM index (MAC)

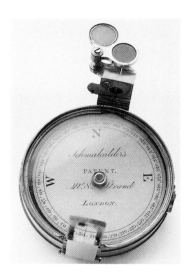

SCHMALCALDER Charles Augustus

w 1806–1840
Optician, Math Phil & Drawing IM, Hydro M, Baro M, Thermo M
1806–1807	[Residence?] 6 Little Newport St, St.Ann's Soho, London
1812	Strand, Westminster, London
1810–1826	82 Strand, London
1827–1840	399 Strand, London
Father of SCHMALCALDER John T.★
SCHMALCALDER George W. s 1829 to GILBERT Thomas★
Succeeded by SCHMALCALDER John T.★
b c.1786; Pats. delineator 1806, math insts 1812; d 1843 in workhouse, buried Camden Town

cemetery; inv prismatic compass
Known to have sold: barometer, chondrometer, compass (magnetic), globe, microscope, pantograph, rule, theodolite
Sources: Kt; PO; Und; Patent records (MAC); inst NMM; AM; ChrSK 19 Nov 1987 lot 1, 9 Dec 1988 lot 168

SCHMALCALDER John

w 1841–1845
Optician, Math IM, Phil IM, Drawing IM, Baro M, Thermo M, Hydro M
Alternative name: John Thomas
1841   6 Little Newport St, Leicester Square, London (residence ?)
1841–1845   2 Fairfax's Court, 400 Strand, London
Guild: [Grocers]
Son of SCMALCALDER Charles A.★
Brother of SCHMALCALDER George W.
Apprenticed to GILBERT Thomas★ 1829
Took over from SCHMALCALDER Charles A.★
b 1811; attended London Mechanics Institute, 1830–1832
Known to have sold: protractor
Sources: LMIR (AM); Bap, St. Martin in the Fields (AM); GL: GC 11598/7; PO; inst (s)

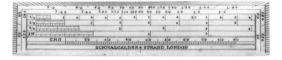

SCHMALCALDER Joseph

w fm 1830–1831
Math IM
1830–1831   399 Strand, London
See also SCHMALCALDER John★
SourcesL LMIR (AM)

SCHOLEFIELD William (I)

w 1786
Math IM
1786   Fleet St, London
Father of SCHOLEFIELD William (II)★
Sources: GH: GSC Ap

SCHOLEFIELD William (II)

w 1806
Math IM
1802–1806   London
Guild: Goldsmiths, fr 1802
Son of SCHOLEFIELD William (I)★
Apprenticed to GRACE George★ 1786
Had apprentice ROGERS Henry Scholefield 1806
Sources: GH: GSC Ap

SCHOMBERG A.

w 1828–1831
Measure M
1828–1831   29 Gibson St, Lambeth, London
Sources: PO

SCHOOLING James

fr 1770 w 1793
Scale M
Alternative name: SCHOLING

1778–1793   44 Bishopsgate St Within, London
32 Ye corner of Rose (?) Court, Bishopsgate Without, London
51 St.James, Haymarket, London
44 facing the Bull Inn, Bishopsgate Within, London
Guild: Blacksmiths, fr 1770
Apprenticed to
READ Joseph★ 1762
READ Mercy★ by t/o 1764
Succeeded by SCHOOLING & SON★
Known to have sold: balance
Instruments advertised: balance, steelyard, weights
Sources: GL: STTP 2934 fol. 99; BKC 2881/15, 2881/16, 2885/1; BW; Kt; inst (s)

SCHOOLING & CO.

w 1803–1824
Scale M
1803   44 Bishopsgate St Within, London
28 Crispin St, Spitalfields, London
Partnership of SCHOOLING, LAWRENCE & SCHOOLING in 1811, and of SCHOOLING, LAWRENCE & EVERETT in 1817
Sources: H; Kt; PO; Und (all JAC)

SCHOOLING & SON

w 1794–1800
Scale M
1794–1800   44 Bishopsgate Within, London
Took over from SCHOOLING James★
Succeeded by SCHOOLING & CO.★
Sources: Kt (JAC)

SCOLLEY William

w 1793
Compass M
Sunderland
Father of SCOLLEY Robert s 1793 NC
Sources: GL: NC 2817/4 fol.67v

SCOT John

c 1633 d by 1647
Compass M
Stepney, London
Father of SCOT Charles s 1647 BKC
Sources: GL: BKC 2886/1

SCOTT Benjamin

w 1712–1733
Math IM
1712   Exeter Change, Strand, London
1718–1733   The Mariner & Globe, Exeter Exchange, Strand, London
1747–1751   St. Petersburg Academy of Sciences, St.Petersburg, Russia
Guild: Grocers, fr 1712
Son of SCOTT John of SC of London
Partnership: SCOTT & PRICE★
Apprenticed to
ANDERTON James★ 1702
ROWLEY John (I)★ by t/o 1706
Had apprentice:
HEATH Thomas★ 1712
TRACY John★ 1715 t/o 1720 to HEATH Thomas★
PENNOCK Joseph 1719
SMITH Mihill 1726/7 by t/o from PARKER James (I)★

SCOTT Robert★, son of William, 1731/2, t/o 1735 to JACKSON Joseph★
Associated with LIFORD John who supplied inst
POTTING John, fellow apprentice
d 1751; Author; designed globe
Known to have sold: alidade, sundial
Instruments advertised: drawing instruments, slide rule
Sources: inst MHS; SM; Brown J (1979a) p.30, 32–33; Chenekal (1972) p.53; King & Millburn (1978) p.104; Scott (1733); Wallis R & P (1986) p.202

SCOTT David

w 1803–1833
Math IM
1825–1833   14 Stafford St, Dublin
Had apprentice NICHOLLS Joseph 1803
Sources: KH (WS); Wi (DJB); Burnett & Morrison-Low (1989) p.134

SCOTT George

w 1806–1831
Math IM, Optician
88 Newgate St, London
98 Newgate St, London
1816   5 Benjamin St, Clerkenwell, London
1817–1822   4 Butcher Hall Lane, Newgate St, London
Guild: Merchant Taylors, fr 1804
Apprenticed to VENTOM Thomas★ 1796
See also
SCOTT James George★
SCOTT James
Sources: GL: MTC MF 320,324; Bn; H; J; Kt (JAC); PO (JAC); Und

SCOTT James

w 1820
Optician, Glass Grinder
1820   6 Church Place, Dumfries
Sources: Pg (MAC)

SCOTT James George

w 1839–1883
Math IM, Phil IM
5 Benjamin St, Clerkenwell, London
1839–1880   17 Bermondsey Wall, London
Guild: [Masons]
Son of SCOTT George, mariner, d, of Dunbar, East Lothian
Apprenticed to JOUGHIN Edward J. E.★ 1816
See also SCOTT George★
Sources: GL: MC 5304/6; Pg; PO

SCOTT Robert

w 1739
London
Guild: Grocers, fr 1739
Son of SCOTT William, tailor, of St. Martin in the Fields, London
Apprenticed to
SCOTT Benjamin★ 1731/2
JACKSON Joseph★ by t/o 1735
Had apprentice WILLIAMS Thomas 1739
Sources: Brown J (1979a) p.38

SCOTT & KIRKWOOD

w 1804

Edinburgh

See also

KIRKWOOD James★

Robert SCOTT was the author of the globe

Known to have sold: globe

Sources: NMS n; Dekker & van der Krogt (1993) p.179

SCOTT & PRICE Benjamin & Charles

w 1714–1718

Globe S

1714–1715   The Atlas against Exeter Change, Strand, London

1718   The Mariner & Globe at Exeter Exchange, Strand, London

Known to have sold: globe

Sources: Calvert (1971) p.38; Tyacke (1978) p.138; Wallis P (1986) p.26

SCULTHORPE William

w 1695

[Spec M]

London

Guild: Spectaclemakers, fr 1682

Son of SCULTHORPE William, free of BC of London

Apprenticed to HILL John (I)★ 1675 & probably t/o to TINGAY Gregory★

Had apprentice COOKE Robert 1695

Sources: GL: SMC 5213/1

SEALE Charles

w 1851–1859

Rule M, Measure M

1851–1859   48 St John's Square, Clerkenwell, London

Sources: PO; Wk

SEARCH James

w 1771–1781

Math IM

Alternative name: IS

    Crown Court, Soho, London

    Pultney St, Golden Square, London

1779   Crown Court, Westminster, London

1774–1780   Crown Court, Pultney St, Golden Square, London

Guild: Stationers, fr 1771

Son of SEARCH John, gent, of Westminster, London

Apprenticed to BENNETT John (I)★ 1764 t/o 1770 to BALCHIN P.★

Had apprentice:

GOULD John (II)★ 1771 by t/o from BENNETT John (I)★

WELLINGTON Alexander★ 1774

FITCH James (II)★ 1779

Succeeded by WELLINGTON Alexander★

Took over from BENNETT John (I)★

Known to have sold: circumferentor, drawing instruments, telescope

Sources: Kt; TorSC; McKenzie (1978) p.30,311

SEATON William

w 1766

Math IM

1766   Little Tower Hill in the Tower Hamlets, London

Guild: Goldsmiths, fr 1766

Apprenticed to HACK William★ 1751

Had apprentice GORE William 1766

Sources: GH: GSC Ap, Fr

SEDDON John

w 1816–1825

Optician

1816   16 Market Place, Manchester

1818–1825   2 New Bailey St, Manchester

Sources: Bn (DJB); Pg; Und

SEELING Joseph

s 1817 w pt 1832

Optician

London

Guild: [Merchant Taylors]

Partnership: WHITBREAD & SEELING★

Apprenticed to WEEDEN William John★ 1817

Sources: GL: MTC MF 320,324 (MAC); Pg

SELDEN Joseph

fl 1694

Surveyor, Math IM

Tunbridge Wells, Kent

Instruments advertised: slide rule

Sources: Taylor (1954) p.279, 409

SELFE Henry

w 1851–1887

Watch M, Clock M, Jeweller, Optician, Gunsmith

1851–1885   91 High St, Poole, Dorset

1875–1887   87 St.Mary St, Weymouth, Dorset

Sources: Loomes (1981a)

SELLER Elizabeth

w 1697–1698

London

Wife of SELLER John (I)★

Took over from SELLER John (I)★

Sources: GL: CH 12823/2 p.290 (MAC); Tyacke (1978) p.140

SELLER Jeremiah

w 1699–1705

Math IM, Naut IM, Map S

Compass & Hour Glass, Hermitage Stairs, Wapping, London

At ye Atlas & Hercules in Cheapside, London

Guild: Merchant Taylors, fp 1703

Son of SELLER John (I)★

Brother of SELLER John (II)★

Partnership:

SELLER & PRICE★

SENEX, SELLER & PRICE★

Apprenticed to SELLER John (I)★ 1686/7

Took over from SELLER John (I)★ with his mother, Elizabeth★

Succeeded by SELLER & PRICE★

Associated with PRICE Charles★

Alive 1720; B.apt Navy

Sources: GL: MTC MF 319,324 (MAC); Tyacke (1978) p.140–41

SELLER John (I)

fr 1654 d 1697

Map M, Globe S, Math IM, Book S

Alternative name: SELLARS, SELLERS

1660   Mariner's Compass & Hour Glass, Hermitage Stairs, Wapping, London

1669–1696   Mariner's Compass, Hermitage Stairs, Wapping, London

1671–1675   Exchange Alley, Cornhill, London

1678–1681   Pope's Head Alley, Cornhill, London

1682–1686   West Side of the Royal Exchange, London

1690   In Westminster Hall, London

Guild: Merchant Taylors, fr 1654; Clockmakers, fr as Brother [i.e. as member of another Co.] 1667/8

Father of

SELLER Jeremiah★

SELLER John (II)★

Apprenticed to LOWE Edward 1644

Had apprentice:

MARLOW Michael (II)★ 1666 MTC

SELLER John (II★, his son, 1681 MTC

HEWSON John★ 1683 CRC

SELLER Jeremiah★, his son, 1686/7 MTC

SELWIN Richard, nd, fr 1693 MTC

PRICE Charles★ 1693/4 MTC

Succeeded by SELLER Elizabeth★ and SELLER Jeremiah★

Associated with

HILLS John and SELLER John (II)★ in retailing

LYDELL James★ in supplying compasses to Royal Navy

WINGFIELD John★ and BROWN John (I)★ in selling books

Author; R.apt Hydrographer to the King 1671 (Charles II); B.apt Navy for ships' compasses 1686; supplied math inst to Christ's Hospital School, London

Known to have sold: compass (magnetic), rule

Instruments advertised: full range of nautical instruments, slide rule, sundial, telescope

Sources: GL: MTC MF 317,318,324; CKC 2710/1 p.185,244; 3939; CH 12823/1 fol.112,117–18, 12823/2 p.287–89; Bryden (1992) p.329–30 & n. 138–40; Calvert (1971) p.38–39; Loomes (1981b); Taylor (1954) p.244–45,379–80,383–84,395; Tyacke (1978) p.139–40

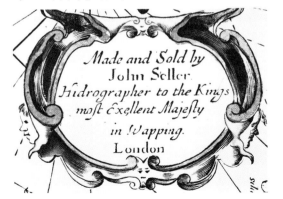

Made and Sold by John Seller Hidrographer to the Kings most Exellent Majesty in Wapping. London

SELLER John (II)

fr 1686 d 1698

Compass M, Instrument S, Map S

| 1686 | The Star, next the Mercer's Chapel in Cheapside, London |
| 1687–1689 | At the Map of the World, the West End of St.Paul's, London |

Guild: Stationers, fp 1686
Son of SELLER John (I)★
Brother of SELLER Jeremiah★
Apprenticed to SELLER John (I)★ 1681
Had apprentice LATHUM Jeremiah 1686/7
Sources: GL: MTC MF 319; McKenzie (1974) p.149; Tyacke (1978) p.140

SELLER & PRICE Jeremiah & Charles
w 1700–1705
Book S

| | At the Hermitage in Wapping, London |

Took over from SELLER Jermiah★
Associated with
GLYNNE Richard★
SENEX John★
In financial difficulty c.1706; B.apt Navy
Known to have sold: compass
Instruments advertised: compass, math inst
Sources: Taylor (1954) p.295

SELLMAN W.
w 1794
Telescope M

| 1794 | Tenter Ground, Moorfields, London |

Sources: W (JAC)

SENEX John
w 1702 d 1740
Globe M, Map M, Engraver, Math IS
Alternative name: Joanne

	Hemlock Court near Temple Bar, London
1702	Against St. Clement's Church in the Strand, London
1703–1707	Next the Fleece Tavern in Cornhill, London
1707–1710	[With Price] Whites Alley, Coleman St, London
1710–1721	The Globe near Salisbury Court, Fleet St, London
1710	(Residence) Salisbury Court, London
1721	The Globe & Star against St.Dunstan's Church, Fleet St, London
1722	Fleet St, London
1724–1740	Over against St.Dunstan's Church in Fleet St, London
1727	Parish of St.Dunstan in the West, London
1738–1740	The Globe over against St.Dunstan's Church, Fleet St, London

Guild: Stationers, fr 1705/6
Son of SENEX John, gentleman, of Ludlow, Salop
Husband of SENEX Mary★
Partnership:
SENEX & PRICE★ 1706–1710
SENEX & MAXWELL★ 1710–21
Apprenticed to CLAVELL Robert 1695
Had apprentice:
LATHBURY William 1706
PARKER Samuel 1710
CHAMBERS Ephraim 1714

WARREN Thomas Gregory 1715★
HUTCHINSON Thomas 1721
JETT John 1722
GATEHOUSE William 1724
SMITH Thomas 1727
HOLLAND Bryan 1738
Succeeded by SENEX Mary★
Associated with
GLYNNE Richard★
HARRIS Joseph (II)★
SELLER & PRICE★ 1705
Working before he became a freeman; FRS 1728
Known to have sold: globe
Sources: GL: CH 12823/3 p. 208; Sun 11936/6 no.7811; BM: Heal 105/89; McKenzie (1974) p.33, (1978) p.312; Calvert (1971) p.39; Tyacke (1978) p.136–7,142; Wallis R & P (1986) p.21; inst NMM, MHS

SENEX Mary
w 1740–1755
Globe S, Map S, Publisher

| 1740–1755 | The Globe over against [facing] St.Dunstan's Church in Fleet St, London |

Wife of SENEX John★
Took over from SENEX John★
Succeeded by FERGUSON James★
Supplied globes to Christ's Hospital Math School, London
Sources: GL: CH 12823/5 p.350; Calvert (1971) p.39; Millburn (1988a) p.35; Wallis R&P (1986) p.354

SENEX & MAXWELL John & John
w 1710–1721
Globe M, Map M

| 1714 | The Globe in Salisbury Court, London |

See also SENEX John★
Sources: Calvert (1971) p.39; Tyacke (1978) p.142; Wallis R & P (1986) p.21

SENEX & PRICE John & Charles
w 1706–1710
Globe M, Geographers
Alternative name: PRICE & SENEX

| 1707 | Next the Fleece Tavern in Cornhill, London |
| 1707–1710 | Whites Alley, Coleman St, London |

Known to have sold: globe
Sources: inst NMM; Calvert (1971) p.39; Tyacke (1978) p.138

SENEX, SELLER & PRICE John, Jeremiah & Charles
c 1703 w 1705
Globe S, Map S

| 1705 | Next the Fleece Tavern in Cornhill, London |

Sources: Tyacke (1978) p.136,142

SENIOR B.
w 1847
Math IM

| 1847 | 18 Swan St, Top of Briggate, Leeds and 5 North passage, Lowerhead Row, Leeds |

Advertised that he was 'from Mr. Street, Principal Worker to Troughton & Simms, London'
Sources: Chn (MAC); Wh (MAC)

SERJEANT Francis
w 1794–1809
Math IM, Drawing IM

| 1794–1809 | 6 Cumberland St, Middlesex Hospital, London |

Sources: H; W (JAC)

SEVERN William (I)
w 1802–1811
Spec M

| 1802 | 5 Fanne St, Aldersgate St, London |
| 1809–1811 | 6 Peerless Row, City Rd, London |

See also SEVERN William (II)★
Sources: H (JAC)

SEVERN William (II)
w 1836–1859
Optician

1836–1840	1 Walbrook Place, East Rd, London
1840–1845	3 Walbrook Place, Hoxton New Town, London
1846	1 Walbrook Place, Hoxton New Town, London
1849	11 Walbrook Place, Hoxton New Town, London
1851–1855	1 and 11 Walbrook Place, Hoxton New Town, London
1859	1 Walbrook Place, Hoxton, London N

Succeeded by Mrs M. Severn by 1860
Sources: Pg; PO

SEWARD John
s 1715 a 1740
Math IM

| | Dublin |

Apprenticed to STOKES Gabriel★ 1715
Attended King's Hospital School
Known to have sold: circumferentor, drawing instruments, sundial
Sources: KH (WS); Burnett & Morrison-Low (1989) p.134,142

SEWELL George
w 1768–1777
Scale M

| 1763 | Shoreditch, London |
| 1777 | The Hand & Scales, 5 Bear St, Leicester Fields, London |

Guild: Skinners, fr 1763
Son of SEWELL George, labourer, of Lambeth [London]
Partnership: SEWELL & YOUNG★
Apprenticed to
SOMMERS Charles★ 1756 SKC
WORNELL John★ by t/o 1759 BKC
READ Joseph★ by t/o 1760 BKC
Had apprentice:
COOMBE Henry 1768 by t/o from PLIVEY William★
YOUNG John (I)★ 1773 by t/o from PLIVEY William★
GROVE Thomas 1789 by t/o from CHANDLER Thomas of BKC

Succeeded by SEWELL & YOUNG★
fr 2 Aug 1763
Known to have sold: balance
Instruments advertised: balance, steelyard, weights
Sources: SH: SKC, Ap/Fr; BKC 2881/15, 2886/5, 2888 (MAC); BM: Heal, dated bill (MAC): inst Lincoln Mu (MAC)

SEWELL & YOUNG George & John
w 1785–1801
Scale M
1785–1801   The Hand & Scales, 5 Bear St, Leicester Fields, London
Took over from SEWELL George★
Succeeded by YOUNG John (I)★
See also YOUNG & SON★
Known to have sold: balance
Sources: BW; By (JAC); Kt (MAC); PO (MAC); inst (pv) (MAC)

SEWILL Joseph
w 1837–1900+
Optician, Math IM, Chrono M, Naut IM
1837   31 South Castle St, Liverpool
1839   8 Duncan St, Liverpool
1841–1895+ 61 South Castle St, Liverpool
1857   54 Canning Place, Liverpool
            5 Parr St, Liverpool
1872–1937   15 Canning Place, Liverpool
1887–1895   14 & 16 Canning Place, Liverpool
1898–1905   15 & 16 Canning Place, Liverpool
b 1800; B.apt Royal Navy; branches run by Joseph Sewill's sons, Frank at 126 Broomiclaw and 2 York St, Glasgow (1878–1891) and John at 30 Cornhill, Royal Exchange, London (c.1875+)
Known to have sold: barometer, chronometer, sextant, telescope
Sources: G (MAC); inst NMM; LM index (MAC); Sby 25 Feb 1986 lot 120; Bryden (1972) p.56; Loomes (1976)

SEXTANT George
w 1834
Optician
1834   44 Ratcliffe Highway, London
See also COOK George★
Sources: Pg (JAC)

SEXTON Humphrey
w 1826–1827
Optician, Math IM, Phil IM
1826–1827   11 Bethnal Green Rd, London
Sources: Pg (JAC)

SHARLING Robert
w 1790–1793
Instrument M (type not specified)
1790–1793   St.James's Market, London
Sources: BW

SHARP Abraham
b 1651 d 1742
[Made mathematical instruments while living at Little Horton]
            Liverpool
            Portsmouth
1684–1690   Royal Observatory, Greenwich, London

Little Horton, near Bradford
Associated with YARWELL John★ who supplied lenses
Salaried assistant to Flamsteed, Astronomer Royal
Known to have sold: quadrant, sundial, telescope
Sources: Holbrook (1992) p.98–99; Taylor (1954) p.265–66

SHARP John
w 1823–1829
Optician
1817   Parish of St Andrew, Holborn, London
1823   Plough Court, Fetter Lane, London
1829   Tash St, Gray's Inn Lane, London
Father of
SHARP Charles s 1817 CWC
SHARP Edwin s 1823 PWC
SHARP Alanzo s 1829 STC
Sources: CWH: CWC Ap; GL: PWC 7102; Stat: STC Memo Bk 1824–1835

SHARP Samuel
w 1851
Manufacturer
1851   New George St, Sheffield
Ex.1851
Known to have sold: lenses
Sources: Cat. 1851 (MAC)

SHARP Samuel Charles
w 1827–1848
Optician
1827   29 Brownlow St, Long Acre, London
1839   16 Church Row, Somers Town, London
1845–1846   16 Church Row, Pancras Rd, London
See also SHARP Samuel★
Sources: Pg; PO

SHARP Thomas
c 1774 a 1790
            Stratford on Avon
See also COX William (I)'s apprentice
Known to have sold: balance
Sources: inst MHS (MAC); inst (pv) (MAC)

SHASWELL Thomas
a 1635 d 1664
Compass M
1664   Ratcliff, London
See also
BISSAKER Robert★ who valued his goods after his death
SHEWSWELL Thomas, fr GC 1623 by ALLEN Elias★, possibly the same person
Sources: GL: inventory 9174/7 (MAC); Brown J (1979a) p.24

SHAW D.
w 1840
Watch M, Clock M, Math IS, Phil IS
1840   Cheapside, Leicester
Known to have sold: barometer, thermometer
Instruments advertised: barometer, magic lantern, microscope, telescope, thermometer

Sources: inst (s) (MAC); *Midland Counties Railway Companion*, 1840, p.48 (DJB)

SHAW John
fl 1830 w 1833
Magnet M
1833   34 Burgess St, Sheffield
Sources: Wh; Taylor (1966) p.46

SHAW William
w 1825–1826
Rule M
1825–1826   18 Smallbrook St, Birmingham
Sources: Pg (MAC)

SHEARMAN William
w 1797
Math IM
1797   Bear Alley, London
Father of SHEARMAN Thomas s 1797
Sources: GL: ABC 12080/2

SHEEPEY –
w 1749
Book S
1749   Royal Exchange, London
Associated with KIRK John★ whose coin weights he sold
Sources: *Daily Ad* 1,3,4,6,10,19 May 1749 (JRM)

SHELLY James
w 1720 d by 1726
Spec M
Alternative name: SHELLEY
1720   The Spectacles corner of Essex St, Strand, London
Guild: Spectaclemakers, fr 1699
Father of SHELL(E)Y John s 1726 STC
Apprenticed to HELME Thomas★ 1691/2
Sources: GL: Sun 11936/11 no.16935; SMC 6031/1,5213/1; 5213/2 p.16; McKenzie (1978) p.89

SHELTON John
fl 1737–1769
Clock M
1744–1751   Shoe Lane, London
Guild: Clockmakers, fr 1720/1
Apprenticed to STANBURY Henry 1712
Worked for GRAHAM George★
Known to have sold: astronomical clock, observatory regulator
Sources: GL: CKC 2723/2; Brown J (1979b) p.33; King & Millburn (1978) p.126

SHENSTON James Templer
w 1834–1846
Scale M
1834–1846   395 Strand, London
Guild: [Blacksmiths]
Apprenticed to PAYNE Benjamin Matthew★
Took over from PAYNE Benjamin Matthew★
Known to have sold: balance, weights
Instruments advertised: balance
Sources: GL: BKC 2881/17 (MAC); PO; inst (pv) (MAC)

SHEPARD Ann
w 1676

Bristol

Known to have sold: Gunter's quadrant

Sources: inst NMM

SHEPHARD Felix
w 1829–1834

Spec M, Optical IM, Phil IM, Math IM

1829   1 Great Sutton St, Clerkenwell,
          London

1834   40 Wellington St, Goswell St,
          London

Succeeded by SHEPHARD Francis*

See also USTONSON John* (possible Master)

Sources: Pg (JAC); R (JAC)

SHEPHARD Francis
w 1835–1837

Spec M

1835–1837   40 Wellington St, Goswell St,
            London

Sources: R (JAC)

SHEPHERD Charles
w 1832–1863

Chrono M, [Nant IS]

1835–1839   7 Chadwell St, St. John Street Rd,
            London

1846–1858   53 Leadenhall St, London

Succeeded by SHEPHERD & SON

Took part in chronometer trials at Royal
Greenwich Observatory 1835; B.apt Royal Navy

Instruments advertised: chronometer, quadrant,
sextant

Sources: CUL: RGO 1143 fol.10v; TCd ML
42.11/10; Pg; PO; Loomes (1976)

SHEPHERD William
w 1837–1853

Chrono M

1837–1839   Lodge Lane, Liverpool

1841–1843   21 Mount St, Liverpool

1848–1851   13 Bath St, Liverpool

1853   5 Bath St, Liverpool

Sources: LM index (MAC); Loomes (1975)

SHERMAN Henry
w 1633 d.c 1641

Scale M

1633–1642   London

Guild: Blacksmiths, fr between 1625 and 1627

Had apprentice:

MARSHALL Erasmus 1833

ORRELL R. 1634

NEALE Samuel* 1637

JACKSON Thomas 1639

Sources: GL: BKC 2881/5, 2884 (MAC)

SHERWOOD Samuel
w 1816

Compass M, Pincer M

1816   Hurst St, Birmingham

Sources: H (DJB)

SHEW James Fledyer
w 1831

Optician

1831   5 Norris St, St. James, London

Attended London Mechanics Institute 1831

Sources: LMIR (AM)

SHIELD Nicholas
w 1668–1670

Spec M

Alternative name: SHEILD

1668–1670   Fenchurch St, London

Guild: Spectaclemakers

Had apprentice:

YARWELL John* by t/o from EDWARDS
Richard* between 1662 & 1669

SPARKS Christopher 1669

Succeeded by SHIELD Widow

d late 1670 or early 1671

Known to have sold: spectacles

Sources: GL: SMC 5213/1

SHORT James
w 1734 d 1768

Optician

1734–1738   Edinburgh

1738–1768   Surrey St, Strand, London

Son of SHORT William, wright, of Edinburgh

Brother of SHORT Thomas*

Associated with

GRAHAM George*

BURTON Mark* (? supplier)

HARRISON John (I)*

DOLLOND John (I)*

b 1710; Educated at Edinburgh High School and
University; FRS 1736; B.apt Royal Greenwich
Observatory

Known to have sold: telescope

Sources: inst MHS, NMM, NMS, SM, WM;
Mort; Turner G (1969); Clarke et al (1989) p.1–10;
Millburn (1988b) p.276; Taylor (1966) p.225;
Wallis R&P (1986) p.262–64

SHORT Thomas
w 1748 d 1788

Optician

1748   Foot of the Broad Wynd, Leith

1768–1776   Surrey St, Strand, London

1776–1788   Calton Hill Observatory, Edinburgh

Brother of SHORT James*

Succeeded by DOUGLAS James*, his grandson

b 1711; pat. telescope 1774

Known to have sold: telescope

Sources: IHR: Wpoll 1774 (AM); inst SM; Bryden
(1972) p.56; Turner G (1969) p.95; Holbrook
(1992) p.87

SHORTGRAVE Richard
fl 1658 d 1676

Surveyor, Operator to the Royal Society, Math IM

1667   Gresham College, London

Father of SHORTGRAVE Thomas

Designed level

Known to have made: barometer, calculating
machine, thermometer

Sources: Bryden (1992) p.309; Taylor (1954)
p.245,246–47,266

SHRIGLEY –
w 1771

Math IM

1771   In St.Catherine's St, near the Tower,
            London

Sources: General Evening Post 27 Aug 1771 (MAC)

SHUKER Richard
w 1805

Rule M

1805   10 Crown Court, Curtain Rd,
            Shoreditch, London

Sources: H (MAC)

SHURY Richard Wilson
w 1826

Scale Beam M

1826   6 Lamb's Buildings, Chiswell St,
            London

Guild: Blacksmiths, fp 1826

Son of SHURY Samuel, probably (I)*

Sources: GL: BKC 288/16 (MAC)

SHURY Samuel (I)
w 1797–1829

Scale M

1792   Riches' Buildings, Hatfield St,
            Goswell St, London

1797–1817   25 Golden Lane, Barbican, London

1822   St.Mary Axe, [Leadenhall St.]
            London

1823   110 Houndsditch, Aldgate, London

1826   8 Lamb's Passage, Bunhill Row,
            London

Guild: Blacksmiths, fr 1792

Father of SHURY Samuel (II)*

Apprenticed to DE GRAVE Charles (I)* 1780

Had apprentice:

BENT James* 1802

WAY John 1827 t/o 1829 to TADLOO Joseph*

4 others 1818–1824

Sources: GL: STTP 2934 fols 85,199; BKC
2881/15, 2881/16, 2881/17 (MAC); J; Pg (MAC)

SHURY Samuel (II)
w 1818 d 1834

Scale M

1818   Old Bethlem, London

1822   57 St.Mary Axe, London

1823   10 Houndsditch, London

1826   4 Artillery Lane, Bishopsgate,
            London

1832   2 Artillery Lane, Bishopsgate,
            London

Guild: Blacksmiths, fp 1818

Son of SHURY Samuel (I)*

Had apprentice:

BULLEN Thomas Brook 1831 t/o 1834 to
LONDON Frederick Stephen*

Sources: GL: BKC 2881/17 (MAC); Pg (MAC)

SHUTTLEWORTH Henry
w 1797–1811

Optician

1797–1811   23 Ludgate St, London

Guild: Spectaclemakers, fr 1797

Son of SHUTTLEWORTH Henry R.*

Apprenticed to SHUTTLEWORTH Henry R.*, his
father, 1788

Took over from SHUTTLEWORTH Henry R.*

Known to have sold: microscope

Sources: GL: SMC 5213/4; Kt; PO; Turner G (1989) p.51–52, 60–62

SHUTTLEWORTH Henry Raynes
w 1760–1797
Optician
Alternative name: Raines, Henry (only)
    Sir Isaac Newton & Two Pairs of
    Golden Spectacles, the Old
    Mathematical Shop, near the West
    End of St.Paul's, London
    Mathematical Shop, near the West
    end of St.Paul's, London
1774–1788   Ludgate St, London
1780–1796   23 Ludgate St, London
Guild: Spectaclemakers, fr 1756
Apprenticed to CUFF John★ 1746/7
Had apprentice:
LLOYD Thomas 1760
HUMPHRIES/HUMPHRYS Richard 1761 by t/o
from CUFF John★
EASTLAND William (I)★
EASTLAND William (II)★ 1768 by t/o from
LLOYD John 1769 by t/o from CUFF John★
BLEULER John★ 1771
HEMSLEY Henry (I)★ 1774 t/o to GRAVES John of
FMC
SHUTTLEWORTH Henry★, his son, 1788
Employed BLEULER John★ 1779
Succeeded by SHUTTLEWORTH Henry★
Took over from JOHNSON Samuel★
Master SMC 1782–1787
Sources: GL: TCd; SMC 5213/3 p.108+, 5213/4;
By; Ld; BM: Heal 105/92 & 93; Turner G (1989)
p.51–52, 60–62

SHUTTLEWORTH Joseph
w 1828–1845
Math IM
1828   63 Lichfield St, Birmingham
1829–1830   73 Lichfield St, Birmingham
1841   133 Broad St, Birmingham
1845   2 Newhall St, Birmingham
See also SHUTTLEWORTH Joseph P.
Known to have sold: protractor, sector
Sources: inst (s) (MAC); K; Pg (MAC); West (DJB)

SHUTTLEWORTH Joseph Peace
w 1848–1850
Math IM, Measuring Tape M
1848   2 Newhall St, Birmingham
1850   73 Newhall St, Birmingham
1850   (Residence) George St West,
    Birmingham
See also SHUTTLEWORTH Joseph★
Sources: SI (MAC); Wh (MAC)

SIBBALD John
w 1758–1795
Math IS, Optical IS, Book S, Stationer
Alternative name: SIBBARD, SIBBAND
1758   Liverpool
1759   Castle St, opposite Harrington St,
    Liverpool
1773   40 Castle St, Liverpool
1786   12 Fenwick St, Liverpool
1787–1794   Castle St, facing Harrington St,
    Liverpool

1789   44 Castle St, Liverpool
Succeeded by HARDING William
d.1796
Sources: BW; LM index (MAC)

SIDDONS E.O.
w 1814
Optician
1814   Market Place, Manchester
Sources: WB (MAC)

SIDEBOTHAM James
w 1780
Math IM
1780   1 Feather Court, Drury Lane,
    London
Apprenticed to SISSON Jeremiah★ 1763
Sources: PRO: IR 1/23 (AM); GL: Sun 11936/280
no. 423218

SIEBE Augustus
w 1819–1851
Scale M
    5 High Holborn, London
    Princes St, Leicester Square, London
    145 High Holborn Rd, London
1819   6 Crown Court, Soho, London
1836–1851   5 Denmark St, Soho, London
Partnership: SIEBE & MARRIOTT
SIEBE, GORMAN & CO.
Pat. balance 1819; Ex.1851; d.1874
Known to have sold: balance
Instruments advertised: balance, steelyard/bismar,
weight
Sources: Cat. 1851; PO; Woodcroft (1854) (MAC)

SIGRAY Richard
w 1790–1792
Baro M, Thermo M, Optician
Alternative name: SIGREY
1790–1792   80 Tottenham Court Rd, London
Sources: BW; W (JAC)

SIKES John
w 1824
Hydro M
1824   20 Tooley St, London
Sources: Kt (JAC)

SILBERRAD Charles
w 1799–1834
Optician
Alternative name: SILERRARD, SIBBERRAD,
1798   Resident with Mr Lincoln★
    Leadenhall St, London
1799–1834   34 Aldgate Within, London
Guild: Fletchers, fr 1798
Son of SILBERRAD John Balthazar, merchant, of
Southwark, London
Apprenticed to LINCOLN Charles★ 1791
Had apprentice:
FAVEY Charles 1799
HOARE Isaac 1800
Worked for LINCOLN Charles★ 1798
Known to have sold: globe, microscope, sundial
Sources: GL: FC 21117/1; 21119; Und; Kt (JAC);
Pg; inst WM & (s); Brown O (1986) no.95;
Goodison (1977) p.358; Holbrook (1992) p.219

SILLS Henry
w 1830
Medical electrician, Galvanist, Pneumatic Chemist
1830   9 George Place, Plymouth
Sources: Pg

SILVANI V.
w 1816
Optician
1816   High St, Portsmouth
Sources: H (DJB)

SILVESTER Joseph
w 1672
Ironmonger, [Rule S]
1672   The sign of the Frying Pan within
    Ludgate, London
Associated with WEBB Isaac★, who supplied rules
Known to have sold: rule
Sources: GL: CKC 2710/1 p.244,247; Loomes
(1981b)

SIMCO Charles
fl 1825–1857
Chrono M
c.1825   1 Banner St, St Luke's, London
1846–1851   37 Rahere St, Goswell Rd, London
Sources: PO; Loomes (1976); Taylor (1966) p.435

SIMMS Alfred Septimus
w fm 1828
Math IM
1824–1827   1 Bowman's Buildings, Aldersgate,
    London
1828   136 Fleet Street London
Guild: Goldsmiths, fr 1828
Son of SIMMS William (I)★
Apprenticed to SIMMS William (II)★, his brother,
1821
Attended London Mechanics Institute 1824–1827;
involved in family business
Sources: LMIR (AM); GH: GSC Ap, index;
McConnell (1992) p.24–25

SIMMS George (I)
fl 1792–1799
Optical IM
    4 Crooked Lane, London
    8 Crooked Lane, London
Error by E.G.R. Taylor for SIMONS George★
Sources: Taylor (1966) p.350

SIMMS George (II)
w pt 1820 w 1859
Naut IM, Compass M
1859   9 Greville St, Hatton Garden,
    London
Guild: [Clothworkers]
Son of SIMMS William (I)★
Brother of
SIMMS William (II)★
SIMMS Alfred Septimus★
Partnership: SIMMS James and George★
Apprenticed to SIMMS James (II)★ his brother, 1813
Took over from SIMMS James and George★
b 1799, d 1886
Sources: CWH: CWC Ap; Pg; PO; McConnell
(1992) pp.24–25; Mennim (1990) p.17–18

SIMMS Henry

b 1800 d 1871
Math IM
1838–1842   9 Greville St, Hatton Garden,
             London
Son of SIMMS William (I)★
Brother of
SIMMS James (II)★
SIMMS George (II)★
Worked for SIMMS William (II)★, his brother, as
bookkeeper
Attended London Mechanics Institute 1838–1842;
involved in the family businesses
Sources: LMIR (AM); McConnell (1992) p.25,32

SIMMS James (I)

b 1710 d 1795
Buckle M, Drawing Compass M
1710–1760   Birmingham
1795   Parish of St. Giles Cripplegate,
             London
Father of SIMMS William (I)★
Known to have sold: drawing instruments
Sources: Mennim (1990) p.17

SIMMS James (II)

w 1813 w pt 1855
Math IM, Jewel Case M, Compass M, Brass
Worker
1813   Aldersgate St, London
1831   Bowman's Buildings, Aldersgate St,
             London
Guild: Clothworkers, fr 1813
Father of SIMMS William (III)★
Son of SIMMS William (I)★
Brother of
SIMMS William (II)★
SIMMS Alfred Septimus★
SIMMS George (II)★
Partnership: SIMMS James and George★
Apprenticed to BARKER Edward, shagreen case
maker, 1806
Had apprentice:
SIMMS George (II)★ 1813
SIMMS William (III)★, his son, 1831
b 1792
Sources: Pg; PO; CWH: CWC Ap; McConnell
(1992) p.24–25

SIMMS James and George

w 1820–1855
Optician, Math IM, Compass M, Sundial M, Naut
IM
1822   4 Broadway, Blackfriars, London
1840–1855   9 Greville St, Hatton Garden,
             London
Son of SIMMS William (I)★
Took over from SIMMS William (I)★
Succeeded by SIMMS George (II)★
See also SIMMS James (II)★
Sources: Pg; PO; McConnell (1992) p.24–25;
Mennim (1990) p.17–18

SIMMS William (I)

w 1793–1822
Dial M, Compass M, Math IM
1780–1781   44 Coleshill St, Birmingham
1793   Birmingham

1794   London
1808–1812   Bowman's Buildings, Aldersgate St,
             London
1818–1822   4 Broadway, Blackfriars, London
Guild: Butchers, fr 1802
Father of
SIMMS James (II)★
SIMMS George (II)★
Son of SIMMS James (I)★
Apprenticed to SIMMS Charles 1779, BTC
Had apprentice:
SIMMS Frederick Walter, his son, by t/o 1822
SIMMS William (II)★, his son, by t/o 1809
Succeeded by SIMMS James and George★
b 1763 d 1828
Sources:
GH: GSC Ap, index; GL: BTC, 4665/15; R
(JAC); McConnell (1992) p.24–25; PR

SIMMS William (II)

w 1821–1826
Optician, Math IM, Mariner's Compass M
1821–1826   1 Bowman's Buildings, Aldersgate
             St, London
-1826   [Residence] Islington, London
1826–1843   [Partnership, Troughton and Simms]
             136 Fleet Street, London
1843–1846   [Partnership, Troughton and Simms]
             138 Fleet Street, London
1843   2 & 4 Peterborough Court, Fleet St
             [adjoining rear of 138], London
1851–1860   [Residence with its own
             observatory] Bramblehaw,
             Carshalton, Surrey
Guild: Goldsmiths, fr 1815
Son of SIMMS William (I)★
Partnership: TROUGHTON & SIMMS★ 1826+
Apprenticed to PENSTONE Thomas GSC 1808 t/o
to SIMMS William (I)★ 1809
Had apprentice:
SIMMS William Henry, his son, 1834
SIMMS James (III), his son, 1843
BECK Joseph 1846
SIMMS Alfred Septimus★, his brother, 1821
NUTTING John William★ 1825
Employed SIMMS William (III)★ his nephew
Succeeded by SIMMS James (III), his son, &
SIMMS William (III)★, who continued to trade as
TROUGHTON & SIMMS★
b 1793, d 1860; FRS 1852; FRAS 1831; Ex 1851
in his own name; buried Norwood Cemetery,
London
Sources: GH: GSC Ap, index; PO; Cat.1851;
McConnell (1992) p.24–40

SIMMS William (III)

w fm 1836 r 1871
Optician, Math IM
1831   Bowman's Buildings, Aldersgate St,
             London
1860–1871   [Partnership trading as Troughton &
             Simms] 138 Fleet St, London
Guild: [Clothworkers]
Son of SIMMS James (II)★
Related to SIMMS William (II)★
Partnership: SIMMS William (III)★ & SIMMS James
(III), trading as TROUGHTON & SIMMS★
Apprenticed to SIMMS James (II)★ 1831

Worked for SIMMS William (II)★
b 1817 d 1907; FRAS 1851
Sources: PO; CWH: CWC Ap; McConnell (1992)
pp.24–26, 36, 40; Mennim (1990) pp.23–24

SIMONS Daniel

w 1772 d by 1791
Optician
1779–1791   Crooked Lane, Cannon St, London
1772   8 Crooked Lane, London
Guild: Spectaclemakers, fr 1756
Father of SIMONS George★
Son of SIMONS Charles, weaver, of Lambeth
(London)
Apprenticed to FORD William★ 1748
Had apprentice:
HAYWARD Joseph★ 1772
SPOONER William 1779
Succeeded by SIMONS George★, his son
See also
SIMONS James★
SYMONS John★
Sources: GL: SMC 5213/3 pp.125,213+, 5213/4;
W (JAC)

SIMONS George

w 1791–1799
Optician, Spec M
Alternative name: SIMONDS
             4 Crooked Lane, London
1791–1797   8 Crooked Lane, Cannon St,
             London
Guild: Spectaclemakers, fp 1791
Son of SIMONS Daniel★
Took over from SIMONS Daniel★, his father
See also SYMONS John★
Sources: GL: SMC 5213/4; Kt; Ld (JAC)

SIMONS James

w 1771–1794
Math IM, Inventor, Optician
Alternative name: SIMONDS, SYMONS,
SIMMONS
             Sir Isaac Newton's Head, the corner
             of Marylebone st, opposite
             Glasshouse St, London
1771–1780   Marylebone St, Golden Square,
             London
1791–1793   Isaac Newton's Head, 17
             Marylebone St, London
Guild: Stationers, fr 1771
Apprenticed to BENNETT John (I)★ 1757
Had apprentice:
HILLIARD Samuel 1771
NORTON John (I)★ 1775
GRIFFITHS John 1778
JENNINGS William 1778
TAILOR Claver 1780
CANNON Thomas 1781
HIGGINBOTHAM William 1785
CANNON John 1786
BATTEN Richard 1791
COATES Richard 1791
GILLMAN Webster 1796
See also
SYMONS John★
SIMONS George★
SIMONS Daniel★

Associated with HUTCHINS Josiah★ as fellow apprentice
Known to have sold: microscope, theodolite
Sources: IHR: Wpoll 1774, 1780 (AM); BW; GL: Sun 11936/262 no.393499; Bod: MF 442 (MAC); McKenzie (1978) p.30,317; Crawforth (1985) p.528; Turner G (1989) p.63; Taylor (1966) p.350

SIMPSON Charles (I)
w 1795–1801
Math IM
1795   Stone Cutter Court, Crutched Friars, London
1801   Lambeth St, Whitechapel, London
Guild: Haberdashers, fp 1795
Had apprentice:
DESBOROUGH William★ 1797
ALEXANDER James 1801
Sources: GL: HC 15857/3, 15860/9

SIMPSON Charles (II)
w 1849–1850
Phil IM
1849   7 Guilford St East, Spa Fields, London
1849–1850   11 Guilford St East, Spa Fields, London
Attended London Mechanics Institute 1849–1850
Sources: LMIR (AM)

SIMPSON George
w 1850–1851
Chem IM, Chemist
1850   1 & 2 Kennington Rd, corner of Newington Crescent, London
1851   1 & 2 Robson Place, Kennington Rd, London
Instruments advertised: chemical apparatus
Sources: Wk; Anderson et al (1990) p.78

SIMPSON John (I)
w 1809–1816
Math IM, Ship chandler
Alternative name: SIMSON
1809   1 Queen St, Ratcliff Cross, London
1811   38 Narrow St, Limehouse, London
1815   Alfred St, Mill Lane, Limehouse, London
Guild: Grocers, fr 1815
Son of SIMPSON William, cabinet maker, of London
Apprenticed to BROWNING John (I)★ 1800
Had apprentice HOLLOWAY Thomas 1816
See also SIMSON P.★
Sources: GL: GC 11598/6, 11598/7; H (JAC); Brown J (1979a) p.50

SIMPSON John (II)
w 1827–1830
Optician, Plate-glass M
1827   Baillie Fyfe's Close, Edinburgh
1828   1 Bank St, Edinburgh
1829–1830   32 Princes St, Edinburgh
Succeeded by SIMPSON & SON★
Sources: ADCS

SIMPSON John (III)
w 1834–1839

Optician, Glass grinder
1834   46 Howard St, Glasgow
1836   48 Howard St, Glasgow
1837–1838   64 Maxwell St, Glasgow
1839   11 Buchanan St, Glasgow
Sources: ADCS

SIMPSON John (IV)
w 1823–1825
Optician
1823–1825   38 Wapping, Liverpool
Sources: G (MAC); Bn (MAC)

SIMPSON Richard
w 1766
Scale M
1766   Houndsditch, London
Guild: Skinners, fr 1741
Son of SIMPSON John, mariner, of St. Giles Cripplegate, London
Apprenticed to SOMMERS Joseph I★ 1732/3
Had apprentice WILSON John 1766
Sources: SH: SKC Ap/Fr

SIMPSON & IRWINS
w 1843
Math IM
1843   54 Hatton Garden, London
Sources: PO

SIMPSON & SON
w 1830–1832
Optician
1830–1832   Baillie Fyfe's Close, Edinburgh
Took over from SIMPSON John (II)★
Sources: ADCS

SIM William
w 1838–1842
Optical IM, Phil IM, Math IM
1838–1842   16 Holland Place, Clapham Rd, London
See also SIMMS William (II)★ & (III)★
Sources: R (JAC)

SIMSON P.
w 1820
Math IM
1820   3 Fore St, Limehouse, London
See also SIMPSON John (I)★
Sources: R (JAC)

SINCLAIR F.
w 1851
Optician
1851   28 Southampton Row, Russell Square, London
Sources: Wk

SINCLAIR George
w 1683 d 1696
Teacher, Baro M
Alternative name: SINCLAR
        St. Andrews
1654–1666   Glasgow
1670   Edinburgh
1689–1696   Glasgow
Professor of philosophy at Glasgow 1654–1666,

had to resign on religious grounds, re-appointed professor of mathematics 1691–1696; author; made experiments with barometers and supplied them
Sources: Bryden (1972) p.56; Goodison (1977) p.358; Taylor (1954) p.242,378,384,398; DNB

SIOLI L.
w 1807
1807   Richmond
Known to have sold: barometer
Sources: Goodison (1977) p.358

SISSON Jeremiah
w 1749 d 1783
Math IM
Alternative name: SESSON
1763–1780   Corner of Beaufort Buildings, Strand, London
1780   [Residence?] Southwark, London
Son of SISSON Jonathan★
Husband of SIDEBOTHAM Ann m 1761
PLAMPIN Grace m 1774
Had apprentice SIDEBOTHAM James★ 1763
Worked for SISSON Jonathan★
Employed RAMSDEN Jesse★
Took over from SISSON Jonathan★
Associated with MASKELYNE Nevil, Astronomer Royal
Bap 1720; bankrupt 1751 & 1775; B.apt Board of Ordnance 1772–1775
Known to have sold: barometer, micrometer, mural quadrant
Sources: PRO: IR 1/23 (AM); GL: Sun 11936/266 no.400825 (MAC); Mort; inst NMM, SM; IGI; HDH; GMag 1751 p.43, 1775 p.455 (DJB); Goodison (1977) p.240–41; Millburn (1988b) p.275–76, 289–90; Morton & Wess (1993) – see index; Wallis R & P (1986) p.438

SISSON Jonathan
w 1722 d 1747
Math IM
1722–1737   The Sphere, Corner of Beaufort Bldgs, Strand, London
Father of SISSON Jeremiah★
Had apprentice:
CLARKSON Robert 1722
AYRES Benjamin★ 1724
Worked for GRAHAM George★
Employed BIRD John★
Associated with CUSHEE Richard★, whose globes he sold
b c.1690; R.apt P.of Wales 1729; made large astronomical instruments for observatories across Europe
Known to have sold: back-staff, barometer, mural quadrant, octant, rule, sector, theodolite, transit instrument
Sources: inst SM, NMM; Daily J 3 Nov 1729; GL: CH 12876/3; DNB; Leybourn (1722) apx p.143 (DJB); Calvert (1971) p.39–40, pl.46

SIX James
w 1780 d 1793
Gentleman in directories
1793   Canterbury, Kent
b 1731; inv. maximum and minimum thermometer 1780; FRS 1792

Sources: inst SM; BW; Austin & McConnell (1980) p.49–65; Morton & Wess (1993) p.470–78; Turner G (1983a) p.239

SKEENE
w 1784
Math IM
1784   St. John's Street, London
Sources: *London Chronicle* 19–21 Oct 1784, p.387 (JRM)

SKIDMORE Charles
w 1818
Optician, Math Instrument Case M
1818   35 Silver St, Sheffield
Sources: Pg

SKILTON Samuel
w 1836
Math IM, Phil IM
1836   162 Eastfield St, Limehouse, London
Guild: [Masons]
Apprenticed to COOK William George★ 1809
Sources: GL: MC 5304/6 (MAC); Pg (JAC)

SKINNER William (I)
w 1792–1796
Scale M
1792   Farthing Alley, Barnaby St, London
1794–1796 83 Snow Hill, London
Guild: Haberdashers, fr 1792
Apprenticed to
VINCENT Robert★ 1785
WILLIAMS Thomas (III)★ 1788 by t/o
Had apprentice SMITH George 1794
See also SKINNER William (II)★
Sources: GL: HC 15857/3, 15860/9 (MAC); BM: Heal (MAC); Ld (JAC)

SKINNER William (II)
w 1822
Scale M
1822   17 Loggerhead Lane, Bethnal Green, London
See also SKINNER William (I)★
Sources: GL: STTP 2934 fol 39

SKIRROW James
w 1797–1834
Watch M, Baro M, Clock M
1797–1834 Chappel Lane, Wigan
Sources: Bn (MAC); BW; Loomes (1975)

SKUCE William
d by 1787
Scale M
            Bishopsgate St, London
Father of SKUCE William s 1787 MTC
Sources: GL: MTC MF 320 (MAC)

SLATFORD Thomas
w 1790–1793
Math IM
1790–1793 2 Nightingale Lane, Ratcliff, London
Sources: BW; By (JAC)

SLEIGH Richard
w 1709 d c.1763
Scale M
1741   Tooley St, Southwark, London
Guild: Blacksmiths, fr 1708
Apprenticed to NEALE John (I)★ 1700/01
Had apprentice:
SLEIGH George, his brother, 1709
CLARKE Edward 1721 t/o 1725 to THOMPSON Daniel★
MATTHEWS John 1724 t/o 1725 to COURT Richard (II)★
MOOR John, his nephew, 1741
4 others 1709–1716
Father of SLEIGH Richard (II) fp 1763, trade not given
Quaker
Sources: GL: BKC 2881/10, 2886/4 (MAC); CH 12876/4 (MAC)

SLEMMON Thomas
w 1839–1854
Math IM, Phil IM, Optician
1839–1854 3 Brandon's Row, Newington Causeway, London
Succeeded by SLEMMON Ann (Mrs)
Sources: Pg; PO; Wk

SLOPER Alfred
w 1846–1875
Rule M, Math IM, Drawing IM
1846   14 Wellington St, Blackfriars Rd, London
1849–1859 3 Brighton Place, New Kent Rd, London
1865–1875 42 New Kent Rd, London
Sources: PO; Wk

SLOPER Thomas
w 1833–1847
Rule M
1833–1847 28 Free School St, Horsleydown, London
Sources: Pg; PO

SLOPER William
w 1849–1880
Math IM, Rule M
1849–1855 38 Great Suffolk St, Borough, London
1859–1875 15 Lambeth Rd, London S
1880   30 Lambeth Rd, London SE
Sources: PO

SLY Samuel
w 1830
Optician, Watch & Clock M
1830   Whitelion St, Norwich
Sources: Pg

SMART Richard
w 1674–1691
Goldsmith, Silversmith
1679   Cork
Known to have sold: weights
Sources: Westropp (1916) p.50,66,71 (MAC)

SMEATON John
w 1750 d 1792
Math IM, Engineer
1742   Leeds
1750   Furnival's Inn Court, London
1772   South St, Gray's Inn, Holborn, London
Associated with HINDLEY Henry★
b 1724; FRS 1753; Author; Copley Medal 1759
Sources: DNB; Taylor (1966) p.218; Wallis (1993) p.125; Weiss (1982) p.144

SMELT John
w 1745 d.c 1748
Scale M
            London
Guild: Blacksmiths, fr 1737
Son of SMELT Samuel★
Apprenticed to THOMPSON Daniel★ 1729
Had apprentice:
WACKETT Daniel 1745
SHEPPARD Joseph 1745/6 t/o to LIND John★ 1748
Sources: GL: BKC 2886/4, 2886/5, 2885/1 (MAC)

SMELT Samuel
w 1700 d by 1729
Scale M
            London
Guild: Blacksmiths, fr 1699
Apprenticed to
WRIGHT Edward 1691
HARRIS John (II)★ nd
Had apprentice JACKSON John★ 1709 t/o to WRIGHT Edward and 11 others 1700–1724
Worked for NEALE Henry★
Sources: GL: BKC 2881/8, 2886/4 (MAC)

SMITH Addison
w 1769–1789
Math IM, Optical IM, Phil IM
            Opposite Northumberland St, Strand, London
1764   St. Martin's Lane, near Charing Cross, London
1774   Near Charing Cross, Strand, London
1779–1783 481 Strand, London
1783   79 Charlotte St, Rathbone Place, London
1783   [?Residence] Richmond, Surrey
Guild: Spectaclemakers, fr 1763
Partnership: WATKINS & SMITH★
Apprenticed to WATKINS Francis (I)★ 1750
Had apprentice WATKINS Francis (II) son of William, 1763
Took over from WATKINS & SMITH★
Pat. spectacles 1783; partnership 1763–68; petitioner against Dollond's patent 1764
Known to have sold: balance, barometer, hygrometer, thermometer
Sources: Bd; PRO: PC 1/7 no.94; GL: SMC 5213/3 p.156+; DJB; patent records (MAC); inst SM Wellcome; Crawforth (1985) p.530; Goodison (1977) p.244

SMITH Ann
w 1788–1796
Math IS, Optical IS, Bookbinder, Publisher

Alternative name: Anne
1788–1790   Navigation Shop, 18 Pool Lane,
             Liverpool
1790–1792   (residence ?) 29 Lawton St,
             Liverpool
Succeeded by SMITH Ann & Egerton★
Took over from SMITH Egerton (I)★ her husband
Sources: G (MAC); LM index (MAC)

SMITH Ann & Egerton (II)

w 1797–1800
Bookbinder, Publisher, Math IS, Optical IS
1797–1800   Navigation Shop, 18 Pool Lane,
             Liverpool
Succeeded by SMITH Egerton & William★
Took over from SMITH Ann★
Sources: G (MAC); LM index (MAC)

SMITH Arthur

w 1841
Optician
1841   Norfolk Lane, Sheffield
Sources: Pg

SMITH Benjamin (I)

w 1787–1809
Optician
1787–1792   Bond St, Bath
1800–1809   10 Bond St, Bath
Known to have sold: planetarium
Sources: By; Gye; Rob (DJB); DJB

SMITH Benjamin (II)

w 1828–1834
Rule M
1828–1829   St.John's St, Wolverhampton
1834   Bloomsbury, Wolverhampton
See also
SMITH Thomas (II)★
SMITH John (VI)★
Sources: Pg (MAC); Smart (MAC); Wh

SMITH Charles

w 1843–1851
Watch M, Clock M, Naut IM
1843   50 Regent Quay, Aberdeen
1844   30 Regent Quay, Aberdeen
1845   30 James St, Aberdeen
1846–1848   1 James St, Aberdeen
1849–1851   43 Quay, Aberdeen
Apprenticed to BOOTH George, clock M, 1836
Succeeded by SMITH & RAMAGE★
Associated with DICKMAN John (I)★
Known to have sold: compass (magnetic)
Sources: Bryden (1972) p.56; NMS n (MAC)

SMITH Edward (I)

w 1780
Math IM, Clock M, Watch M
1780   Near Test's Ropewalk in
             Rotherhithe, London
Sources: GL: Sun 11936/287 no.432893

SMITH Edward (II)

w 1839–1884
Math IM, Phil IM, Naut IM
1839   26 Jubilee Place, Commercial Rd
             East, London

1840–1865   11 Exmouth St, Commercial Rd
             East, London
1870   11 Gould Square, London EC
1875–1880   11 America Square, Minories,
             London EC
             69 Fenchurch St, London
Worked for WHITBREAD George★
Known to have sold: sextant
Sources: Pg; PO; inst NMM

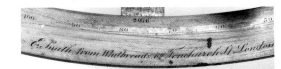

SMITH Egerton (I)

w 1766 d 1788
Math IM, Lecturer, Printer, Schoolmaster
Alternative name: Edgerton
1765   (residence ?) Redcross St, Liverpool
1766–1772   Church St, Liverpool
1766   Cable St, Liverpool
1774–1776   Newton's Head, 17 Pool Lane,
             Liverpool
1774–1783   Navigation Warehouse, Pool Lane,
             Liverpool
1780–1787   18 Pool Lane, Liverpool
Father of
SMITH Egerton (II)★
SMITH William of SMITH Egerton & William★
Husband of SMITH Ann★
Succeeded by SMITH Ann★
Known to have sold: octant
Sources: By; G (MAC); inst NMM; LM index
(MAC)

SMITH Egerton (II)

w 1793
Printer, Stationer
1793   18 Pool Lane, Liverpool
Son of SMITH Egerton (I)
Partnership:
SMITH Ann & Egerton★
SMITH Egerton & William★
See also SMITH & CO. Egerton★
Sources: BW; LM index (MAC)

SMITH Egerton (II) & William

w 1803–1807
Printer, Stationer, Math IM, Optician
1803–1804   Navigation Shop, 18 Pool Lane,
             Liverpool
1805–1807   Navigation Shop, 19 Pool Lane,
             Liverpool
Succeeded by SMITH & CO. Egerton★
Took over from SMITH Ann & Egerton (II)★
Employed HARRIS Michael
Associated with MASSEY Edward (II)★ as
part-proprietor of patent log
Pat. compass 1809 with M.Harris
Sources: Patent records (MAC); LM index (MAC)

SMITH F.

w 1840–1841
Math IM
1840–1841   39 Commercial Rd, Lambeth,
             London

See also SMITH Francis [possibly the same person]
Attended London Mechanics Institute 1840–1841
Sources: LMIR (AM)

SMITH Francis

w 1835–1839
Math IM
1835–1839   2 Bristow St, Blackfriars, London
See also SMITH F. [possibly the same person]
Attended London Mechanics Institute 1835–1839
Sources: LMIR (AM)

SMITH George (I)

w 1840–1843
Math IM
1839   White Cottage, East St, Globe Lane,
             Mile End, London
1840   East St, Globe Lane, London
Guild: Grocers, fr 1839
Son of SMITH John, butcher, of Stepney, London
Apprenticed to BROWNING John (I)★ 1803
Had apprentice:
SMITH Thomas, his son, 1840
SMITH Edward William, son of Peter, 1840
GARLAND Edwin 1843
Associated with SPENCER William (III)★, who was
sponsor at his freedom
Sources: GL: GC 11598/8; Brown J (1979a) p.50

SMITH James (I)

w 1817–1818
Optician
1817   Royal Exchange, East Side, London
Guild: [Spectaclemakers]
Son of (probably) SMITH Ralph, gardener, of
Newington Butts, London
Apprenticed to (probably) SPENCER Richard★
1778
Had apprentice (probably) FULLER James Robert
1818 SMC
Court & von Rohr list him as free of SMC 1785,
but that James SMITH is a gardener, fr by purchase
Sources: GL: SMC 5213/3, 5213/4; J; Court &
von Rohr (1929–30) p.85

SMITH James (II)

w 1821–1824
Optician
1821–1824   17 Bath Place, New Rd, Fitzroy
             Square, London
Worked for FRASER William (I)★
e 1817
Sources: Bn; Pg; Calvert (1971) p.40

SMITH James (III)

w 1826–1847 [then partnership]
             Optician, Optical Turner
1839–1847   50 Ironmonger Row, Old St,
             London
Guild: [Turners]
Father of SMITH James Junior
Son of SMITH William, tailor, of London
Partnership:
SMITH & BECK★
SMITH, BECK & BECK 1857
Apprenticed to WEEDEN Daniel★ 1806
Had apprentice BECK Richard★
Associated with LISTER Joseph Jackson★

Attended London Mechanics Institute 1834
Supplied Microscopical Society of London &
became member 1840; retired from partnership
1865, d 1870
Known to have sold: microscope
Sources: GL: TC 3302/3; PO; Turner G (1989)
p.11,171

SMITH James (IV)
w 1824
Optician
1824   27 Mason St, Swan St, Manchester
Sources: Bn (MAC)

SMITH John (I)
w 1675–1694
Clock M
Guild: Clockmakers
Author, there were several freeman of this name in
CKC in the last quarter of 17th century
Known to have sold: barometer
Sources: Loomes (1981b); Taylor (1954) p.276

SMITH John (II)
w 1723–1730
Optical IM
            Archimedes & Three Golden
            Prospects, London
1716–1727   The Archimedes in Ludgate St,
            London
Guild: Turners, fr 1716
Son of SMITH John, bricklayer, d, of Hackney
[London]
Apprenticed to MARSHALL John* 1709
Had apprentice:
HASKINS John 1725, t/o 1729 to SOCTON John
UPHAM Isaac 1730
Took over from MARSHALL John*
R.apt Geo. I 1722/3; Master of Mechanics 1727/8;
Married John Marshall's* daughter
Sources: GL: TC 3302/2, 3303, 3305; PRO:
LC3/63 p.281,/ 64 p.151; Buckley (1935) p.428;
BSIS no.2 (1984) p.12

SMITH John (III)
fl 1740–1780
Math IM
            York
            King's private Observatory, Kew,
            Richmond, Surrey
            Royal Exchange, London
Worked for
HINDLEY Henry*
DEMAINBRAY Dr.
Sources: Taylor (1966) p.218; Weiss (1982) p.146

SMITH John (IV)
w 1817–1839
Optical IM, Math IM
1817–1839   126 High St, Wapping, London
Succeeded by SOULBY & CO. J.*
Sources: H; PO; ChrSK 11 Sep 1986, lot 205 (TCd)

SMITH John (V)
w 1829–1836
Globe M
1829–1830   1 Angel Court, Surrey St, Strand,
            London

1836   35 Leicester Square, London
Sources: PO

SMITH John (VI)
w 1828–1829
Rule M
1828–1829   Bloomsbury, Wolverhampton
See also
SMITH Benjamin (II)*
SMITH Thomas (II)*
Sources: Pg (MAC)

SMITH John (VII)
fr 1794
Smith
            Glasgow
Guild: Hammermen, fr 1794
Known to have sold: balance
Sources: Lumsden & Aitken (1912) p.299 (MAC)

SMITH Joseph (I)
fr 1776 w 1793
Scale M
1792–1973   Saffron Hill, London
Guild: Blacksmiths, fr 1776
Apprenticed to VAUGHTON Christopher 1769
Sources: Wil; GL: BKC 2885/2, 2886/5 (MAC)

SMITH Joseph (II)
w 1811–1857
Optician
1811   6 Coleman St Buildings, London
1811   and under the Royal Exchange,
            London
1812–1826   North Gate, Royal Exchange,
            London
1817   4 Threadneedle St, Bank, London
1823–1827   19 Tottenham Court Rd, London
1827–1836   17 Bath Place, New Rd, Fitzroy
            Square, London
1837–1847   15 Palace Row, New Rd, Fitzroy
            Square, London
1848   23 Paddington St, London
1849–1857   2 Albany St, Regent's Park, London
Guild: Spectaclemakers, fr 1811
Apprenticed to SMITH Richard, linen draper, of
Romford, Essex, his father
Succeeded by SMITH C. (Mrs)
See also
SMITH & SON Charles*
LONG James*
Sources: GL: SMC 5213/4; H (MAC); J (MAC);
PO

SMITH Joseph (III)
w 1823–1834
Optician, Math IM, Phil IM, Compass M,
Quadrant M
1832–1834   Rigman's Rents, Fore St,
            Limehouse, London
Sources: Pg (JAC)

SMITH Nathaniel
w 1711 d c. 1748
Math IM
-1748   Preston Yard, Minories, London
Guild: Clockmakers, fr 1689
Apprenticed to CARVER Isaac* 1680

Had apprentice:
FOSTER John 1693
BELL John 1698/9
MASON Samuel 1704
FARLAM Ebenezer 1707
BALL Thomas 1711
MANNING Charles* 1720
Sources: PRO: IR 1/1 fol.43; GL: CKC 3939;
Daily Ad 16 Jan 1748 (MAC); Brown J (1979b)
p.33

SMITH Philip
w 1667 d 1683
Math IM
            Ratcliff, London
Guild: u & Clockmakers, fr as brother [i.e. as
member of another guild] 1667/8
Had apprentice: JEEYES Samuel 1670
Sources: Brown J (1979b) p.31,33; Taylor (1954)
p.251

SMITH Samuel
w 1790
Optician
1773   72 Ratcliff Highway, London
Guild: Spectaclemakers, fr 1773
Had apprentice:
LE SAUVAGE John by t/o between 1782 & 1790
SMITH William Samuel 1790
Sources: GL: DC 8167/3; SMC 5213/3

SMITH Samuel Albert
w 1850–1862
Rule M
1850   368 Coventry Rd, Birmingham
1862   Victoria Place, Coventry Rd,
            Birmingham
Sources: Mor (MAC); Sl (MAC)

SMITH Thomas (I)
w 1790–1823
Math IM, Optical IM, Quadrant M, Compass M
1790–1823   53 Old Gravel Lane, Ratcliff,
            London
See also SMITH Thomas (III)* & (V)*
Known to have sold: octant
Sources: By (JAC); H (MAC); Pg; Und; Holbrook
(1992) p.186

SMITH Thomas (II)
w 1792–1845
Rule M
1792   6 St.John St. Wolverhampton
1798   Wolverhampton
1805–1818   Bond St, Wolverhampton
1827   Penn St, Wolverhampton
1828–1834   Bloomsbury, Wolverhampton
1835–1845   Bloomsbury St, Wolverhampton
Took over from CORSON James*
See also
SMITH Benjamin (II)*
SMITH John (VI)*
Sources: BW; H (MAC); Pg (MAC); Smart
(MAC); Wh; Wolverhampton rate books (MAC)

SMITH Thomas (III)
w 1780–1780
Math IM

1780   Shakespeare's Walk, Shadwell,
London
See also SMITH Thomas (I)★
Sources: GL: Sun 11936/287 no.433713

SMITH Thomas (IV)
w 1811–1836
Scale M, Ironmonger
1805–1808   14 Jewry St, Aldgate, London
1820–1836   54 Minories, London
Guild: Blacksmiths, fr 1805
Son of SMITH John, founder, of London
Apprenticed to PALLET Thomas★ 1798
Had apprentice:
DOYLE John★ 1811
SKINNER Henry 1827
ABBOTT George Alfred 1830 by t/o from
BASSINGHAM Samuel★
Sources: GL: BKC 2881/16 & 17; PO

SMITH Thomas (V)
w 1829–1835
Optical IM, Phil IM, Math IM, Optician
1823–1829   6 Worcester St, Ratcliff, London
1829–1830   1 Hope St, Hackney Rd, London
1829–1835   61 Greenfield St, Commercial Rd,
London
Sources: R (JAC)

SMITH Thomas (VI)
w 1840–1870
Math IM, Optician
1840–1841   Brunswick St, Hackney, London
1859–1865   87 Brunswick St, Hackney Rd,
London
1870   89 Brunswick St, Hackney Rd,
London E
Attended London Mechanics Institute 1840–1841
Sources: LMIR (AM); PO

SMITH Thomas (VII)
w 1849–1851
Chem IM
1849   72 Princes St, Lambeth, London
1851   71 & 72 Princes St, Lambeth,
London
Sources: PO

SMITH Thomas Stokes
w 1838–1840
Math IM, Phil IM
1838–1840   11 Goldsmiths Place, Hackney,
London
Guild: [Joiners]
Son of SMITH Edward, tailor, of Bethnal Green
Rd, London
Apprenticed to ELLIOTT William (I)★
See also SMITH Thomas (V)★
Sources: R (JAC); Crawforth (1987) p.366

SMITH Werner
w 1839
Astro IM
1839   50 Greek St, Soho, London
Attended London Mechanics Institute 1839
Sources: LMIR (AM)

SMITH William (I)
w 1802–1823
Baro M, Thermo M, Hydro M
1802–1823   54 Red Lion St, Holborn, London
Sources: H (JAC); R (JAC)

SMITH William (II)
w 1830
Compass M
1830   5 Briton Side, Plymouth
Took over from DUNSTERVILLE M.★
Sources: Pg; inst MM. Tec. 91/10 (JnH)

SMITH William (III)
fl 1830 w 1850+
Math IM, Measuring-tape M, Drawing IM
1830–1837   6 Court, Loveday St, Birmingham
1841–1850+   29 Loveday St, Birmingham
Sources: K; Pg; SL (MAC); Taylor (1966) p.460

SMITH William (IV)
w 1802–1806
Scale M
           63 High St, Borough, London
           220 Tooley St, London
1806   248 Tooley St, London
1807   9 White Horse Court, High St,
Borough, London
Guild: Blacksmiths, fr 1806 (sic)
Partnership: DUTTON & SMITH★
Apprenticed to WILLIAMS Thomas (III)★
Had apprentice:
YOUNG James Robert 1832
POILE William 1844 t/o to BURCHFIELD
Thomas★ 1847
3 others 1839–1845
Succeeded by DUTTON & SMITH★
Partnership 1806–31; d.1847
Known to have sold: chondrometer
Sources: GL: BKC 2881/16–18 (MAC); H (JAC);
PO (JAC); inst (pv) (MAC)

SMITH William (V)
w 1846–1851
Optician, Math IM
1846–1847   20 Pleasant St, Kirkdale, Liverpool
1849–1851   54 Barlow St, Kirkdale, Liverpool
Sources: G (MAC)

SMITH William John
w 1850–1860
Watch M, Clock M, Chrono M, Optician
1850–1860   28 Broad St, Bath
Sources: Er; BaL n (MAC)

SMITH William & Andrew
w 1838–1840
Math IM, Phil IM
1838–1840   46 Lisle St, Leicester Square, London
Associated with ALLEN M.H. & J.W.★ as suppliers
Known to have sold: beam compass, pantograph
Sources: Pg; inst MHS; inst (s)

SMITH & BECK James & Richard Low
w 1847–1857
Optician, Microscope M
1848–1857   6 Coleman St, City, London

1855–1857   Peartree Cottage, Holloway Rd,
London
Succeeded by SMITH, BECK & BECK
Ex 1851
Known to have sold: microscope
Instruments advertised: binoculars, magic lantern,
microscope, spectacles, stereoscope
Sources: Turner G (1989) p.171
PO; Cat.1851; Anderson et al (1990) p.78

SMITH & CO. Egerton
w 1810–1824
Optician, Math IM, Navigation Shop, Printer
1810–1811   Navigation Shop, 19 Pool Lane,
Liverpool
1813–1817   Navigation Shop, 20 Pool Lane,
Liverpool
1816–1818   Navigation Shop, 19 Pool Lane,
Liverpool
1818–1820   Navigation Shop, 20 Pool Lane,
Liverpool
1818   5 Washington St, St.James Rd,
Liverpool
1824   75 Lord St, Liverpool
Took over from SMITH Egerton & William★
Sources: Pg; WB (MAC); LM index (MAC)

SMITH & RAMAGE Charles & Charles
w 1845–1861
Naut IM, Optical IM
1852–1861   45 Regent's Quay, Aberdeen
Employed STRACHAN Alexander
Succeeded by GRANT John
Took over from RAMAGE & CO.★
See also SMITH Charles★
Known to have sold: barometer
Sources: Bryden (1972) p.56; Goodison (1977)
p.358

SMITH & SON Charles
w 1823–1888
Globe M
1827–1852   172 Strand, London
1870–1888   63 Charing Cross, London
See also SMITH Joseph (II)★
Known to have sold: globe
Sources: inst NMM; PO

SNART Charles
w 1793–1803
Scale M
1802–1803   215 Tooley St, London
Guild: Haberdashers, fr 1789
Apprenticed to VINCENT Robert★ 1782
Had apprentice PRICE Richard (II)★ 1793 t/o
1799 to CHANCELLOR Thomas★
Took over from SNART & CLARKE★
Succeeded by SNART John (II)★
d by 1808
Sources: GL: HC 15857/3, 15860/9 (MAC); Kt
(JAC)

SNART John (I)
w 1693–1731
Scale M
1709   Heart & Scales in Maiden Lane over
against Goldsmiths Hall, London
Guild: Blacksmiths, fr 1692

Apprenticed to HART Joseph (I)★ 1685
Had apprentice:
HART Benjamin★ 1693
MANTELL Samuel★ 1693 by t/o from HART
Joseph (I)★
PICARD John★ 1698/9
OVERING Thomas★ 1709
BATE Richard (I)★ 1719 t/o to OVEN Henry★
5 others, not known as Scale M 1693–1714
Succeeded by OVEN Henry★
Known to have sold: balance, weights
Sources: GL: BKC 2881/8–10; 2886/2, 2886/4
(MAC); CH 12876/3 (MAC); inst with TCd,
MHS; inst NMS

SNART John (II)
w 1799–1832
Optical IM, Math IM, Phil IM
1799   122 Tooley St, London
1805–1827   215 Tooley St, London
Guild: [Merchant Taylors]
Son of SNART Charles, boiler, of Southwark,
London
Apprenticed to CHESTER Edward★ 1783 MTC
Known to have sold: chondrometer, microscope,
telescope
Instruments advertised: full range of instruments
Sources: GL: MTC MF 320, p.141; MF 324; Bn; J;
H; R; Und; Ridge (1946) p.90; inst NMM, NMS;
Calvert p.40

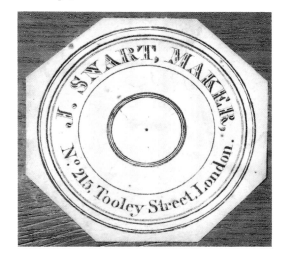

SNART Martha (Miss)
w 1849–1851
Math IM
1849–1851   35 King St, Borough, London
Took over from SNART Neriah★
Sources: PO

SNART Neriah (Miss)
w 1832–1847
Math IM, Phil IM, Optician
Alternative name: Neariah
1832–1839   215 Tooley St, London
1840–1847   35 King St, Borough, London
Succeeded by SNART Martha★
Took over from SNART John (II)★
Sources: Pg, PO

SNART & CLARKE
w 1801
Scale M
Alternative name: SNART & CO. Charles ?
1801   122 Tooley St, London
Succeeded by SNART Charles★
Sources: H & Supplement (JAC)

SODERBERG –
a 1780–1810
Optician, Musical IM
              2 Crown Court, Crown St,
              Westminster, London
Sources: BM: Banks 105/50 (MAC)

SOLCHA Lewis
w 1851–1855
Math IM, Optician, Looking-glass M
1851   1 Dagger Lane, Hull
1855   17 Robinson Row, Hull
Partnership LUPPIE & SOLCHA★ 1840
Took over from LUPPIE Salvador★
Sources: S1; Loomes (1972)

SOLDINI Giosue
w 1830
Jeweller
1830   High St, Wincanton, Som
A barometer is known signed by G. Soldini,
Wincanton
Sources: Pg; Goodison (1977) p.359

SOLOMON Aaron
w 1801
Optician
1801   Bell St, Birmingham
Sources: Chp (DJB)

SOLOMON J. (I)
w 1845
Optician
1845   6 New Buckingham St, Dover Rd,
              London
See also SOLOMON Joseph J.★
Sources: PO

SOLOMON J. (II)
w 1836–1848
Optician, Spec M
1836–1842   Bath Parade, Temple Gate, Bristol
1848   17 Cathay, Bristol
Sources: Hunts; Mat; Pg

SOLOMON Joseph J.
w 1849–1880
Optician, Drawing IM
1849–1880   22 Red Lion Square, Holborn,
              London
Associated with LEBRUN Alexandre, Paris, as agent
Ex. 1851
Sources: PO; Turner G (1983b) p.309–10

SOLOMON Richard
w 1811–1820
Spec M
1811–1820   22 Carter St, Houndsditch, London
Sources: H (JAC); R (JAC)

SOLOMON Wolfe
w 1845–1850
Optician
1845–1850   15 Smallbrook St, Birmingham
Sources: K; Sl (MAC)

SOLOMONS Abraham (I)
w 1832–1838
Optician, Math IM, Phil IM
1832–1838   6 New Rd, St.George's East,
              London
Father of SOLOMONS Charles Michael s 1835
PMC
See also
SOLOMONS Samuel & Benjamin★
SOLOMONS George M.★
Sources: Pg; GL: PMC 5654

SOLOMONS Elias
w 1838–1864
Spec M, Optician
              37 Old Bond St, London
1839–1846   36 Old Bond St, London
1849–1859   27b Old Bond St, London
Associated with SOLOMONS M.E. of Dublin
Instruments advertised: spectacles, telescope
Sources: PO; Morning Post 11 June 1856; Calvert
(1971) p.40; JAC

SOLOMONS Elias & George
w 1832–1834
Optician
1834   105 New Bond St, London
See also
SOLOMONS Elias★
SOLOMONS George★
SOLOMONS Samuel & Benjamin★
Pat. lenses 1832
Sources: R (JAC); Woodcroft (1854)

SOLOMONS George
w 1835–1837
Optician
              172 Strand, London
See also
SOLOMONS George M.★
SOLOMONS Elias & George★
SOLOMONS Elias★
SOLOMONS Samuel & Benjamin★
Sources: PO

SOLOMONS George Morris
w 1831–1834
Optician
              20 Bevis Marks, London
              9 East Bedford Square, Commercial
              Rd, London
See also
SOLOMONS George★
SOLOMONS Elias & George★
SOLOMONS Elias★
SOLOMONS Abraham★
SOLOMONS Samuel & Benjamin★
Sources: Pg; R (JAC)

SOLOMONS Samuel & Benjamin
w 1832–1879
Optician, Math IM, Phil IM, Spec M, Telescope M

1838 5 New Rd, St.George's East,
    London
1840–1875 39 Albemarle St, Piccadilly, London
1843 76 King St, City, London
Known to have sold: microscope, telescope
Instruments advertised: magic lantern made by
steam machinery
Sources: ILN 27 Dec 1862; p.698; Pg; PO; Sby 20
Feb 1985 lot 352; ChrSK 14 Apr 1988 lot 137

SOMALVICO John

w 1817–1822
Baro M
1817–1822 22 Kirby St, Hatton Garden,
    London
Known to have sold: barometer, hygrometer,
thermometer
Sources: J; R (JAC)

SOMALVICO Joseph

w 1840–1841
Baro M, Thermo M
1840–1841 37 Charles St, Hatton Garden,
    London
Succeeded by COLOMBA Andrew
See also SOMALVICO & CO. Joseph★
Known to have sold: octant
Sources: PO; inst (s)

SOMALVICO T. & J.

w 1839
Baro M
1839 37 Hatton Garden, London
See also SOMALVICO Joseph★
Sources: Pg

SOMALVICO & CO. Joseph

w 1839 p 1913
Optician, Math IM, Phil IM, Baro M, Thermo M,
Hydrom M
1839–1865 2 Hatton Garden, London
1869–1865 16 Charles St, Hatton Garden,
    London
1901 18 Charles St, Hatton Garden,
    London
    81 Holborn, London
R.apt Royal Family; Ex 1851
Known to have sold: barometer
Instruments advertised: barometer
Sources: PO; Phlps 2 Dec 1987 lot 4; Goodison
(1977) p.360; Calvert (1971) p40; Turner G (1983a)
p.310

SOMALVICO & SON Joseph

w 1820–1839
Baro M, Thermo M
1820 41 Kirby St, Hatton Garden,
    London
1833–1839 37 Charles St, Hatton Garden,
    London
See also
SOMALVICO & CO, Joseph★
LIONE SOMALVICO & CO.★
SOMALVICO John★
SOMALVICO T. & J.★
Sources: PO (JAC); R (JAC)

SOMMERS Charles

w 1757–1780
Scale M
Alternative name: C.S.
    Next to Anderton's Coffee House,
    Fleet St, London
    Bucklersbury, London
1755 Hand & Scales near St.Dunstan's
    Church, Fleet St, London
1757–1764 Near Fleet Ditch, London
1765–1774 1 Walbrook near the Mansion
    House, London
1777 Walbrook, London
1780 111 Wood St, Cheapside, London
1788 Wood St, London
Guild: Skinners, fr 1754
Son of SOMMERS Joseph (I)★
Father of SOMMERS Joseph (II)★
Apprenticed to SOMMERS Joseph (I)★ 1747
Had apprentice:
SEWELL George★ 1756 t/o 1759 to WORNELL
John★
GADD Richard 1757
HARPHAM Robert 1759
JONES John 1765
WILLS John Thomas 1777
KING Stephen 1788 t/o to BENSON John BKC
Succeeded by SOMMERS & GIBSON★
Took over from SOMMERS Joseph (I)★
See also
SOMMERS & SON★
SOMMERS John★
Known to have sold: balance, weight
Instruments advertised: balance, steelyard, weights
Sources: SH: SKC Ap/Fr; GL: BKC 2881/16; CH
128765/5; BM: Banks 103/12; ML: TCd A22547;
Kt; Ld; Mort; ChrSK 11 Sep 1986 lot 150

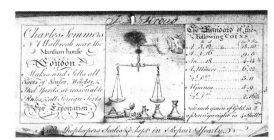

SOMMERS John

w 1763
Scale M
Alternative name: error for Joseph SOMMERS ?
1763 Corner of Bucklersbury near the
    Mansion House, London
See also
SOMMERS Joseph (I)★
SOMMERS Charles★
Sources: Mort (MAC)

SOMMERS Joseph (I)

w 1741 d c. 1767
Scale M
Alternative name: I. SUMMERS
1758 Corner of Bucklersbury against ye
    West side of ye Mansion Ho London
1758–1766 Walbrook, London

1763 The Bear Garden, Southwark,
    London
Guild: [Blacksmiths], Skinners
Father of SOMMERS Charles★
Son of SOMMERS John of London
Apprenticed to PICARD John★ 1720
Had apprentice:
SIMPSON Richard 1732/3
RADFORD William (II)★ 1735
JONES John 1737?★
JOHNSON John 1740
ROLF John 1744
TAYLER George 1745/6
BULLOCK William★ 1747
SOMMERS Charles★ 1747
POUSSETT Philip★ 1748
TOMLINSON Shubeal 1753
EDWARDSON Joseph 1754
JONES John 1756
STERNEY John 1758, t/o 1763 to READ Samuel★
JONES Owen 1758
LAYMAN (LAMAN) John 1758
HAWKINS Edward 1761
Succeeded by SOMMERS Charles★
fp 1 Feb 1731/2 SKC
Known to have sold: balance
Instruments advertised: balance, steelyard, weights
Sources: SH: SKC Ap/Fr; GL: BKC 2881/10; inst
& TCd (s) Cpy

SOMMERS Joseph (II)

w 1788–1800
Scale M
Alternative name: SOMERS
1781–1800 Wood St, London
1793 111 Wood St, London
Guild: Skinners, fr 1781
Son of SOMMERS Charles★
Had apprentice:
BULL William 1788
GILLATE Magnus 1795
BARTLETT Edward 1800
Employed BULL William 1796
Sources: Wil; SH: SKC Ap/Fr; BKC 2881/15; BW

SOMMERS & GIBSON Charles & ?

w 1781–1783
Scale M
Alternative name: GIBSON & SOMMERS
1781–1783 111 Wood St, London
Took over from SOMMERS Charles★
Succeeded by SOMMERS & SON★
Sources: Bd; Ld

SOMMERS & SON Charles (& Joseph Jnr)

w 1784–1808
Scale M, Pewterer
1784–1808 111 Wood St, Cheapside, London
Guild: Skinners
Took over from SOMMERS & GIBSON★
Succeeded by SOMMERS & STANLEY★
See also
SOMMERS Charles★
SOMMERS Joseph★
Known to have sold: balance
Instruments advertised: balance
Sources: Boyle (MAC); BW; Kt (JAC); inst
Banbury Mu (MAC); inst & TCd (pv) (MAC)

SOMMERS & STANLEY
w 1809–1815
Scale M
1809–1815   111 Wood St, London
Took over from SOMMERS & SON★
Succeeded by STANLEY Nathaniel★
Sources: J (MAC); Kt (JAC); Und

SORDELLI G.
a 1800–1850
              23 Baldwins Gardens, Holborn,
              London
See also SORDELLI J.★
Known to have sold: barometer, thermometer
Sources: Goodison (1977) p.36

SORDELLI J.
a 1800–1830
              London
See also SORDELLI G.
Known to have sold: barometer, thermometer
Sources: inst (s); Goodison (1977) p.36

SOULBY & CO. John
w 1842–1856
Math IM, Optical IM, Ship Chandler
1842–1856   126 Wapping New Stairs, London
Took over from SMITH John (IV)★
Known to have sold: Octant.
Sources: PO; ChrSK 11 Sep 1986 lot 205 (TCd);
Bennett (1987) p.181

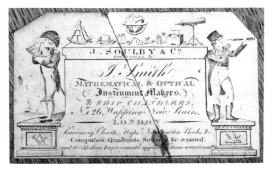

SOUTHOUSE James
w 1851–1865
Naut IM, Math IM, Maker of Mariners'
Compasses and Binnacles for the Trade
1851–1865   25 Goodman's Yard, Minories,
              London
Sources: PO; Wk

SOWTER John
w 1818–1853
Clock M, Watch M, Silversmith, Jeweller
1818–1853   38 High Street Oxford
Known to have sold: astronomical regulator
Sources: Beeson (1989) p.141,189

SPEAKMAN William
w 1746
Math IM
1746   St. Paul's Churchyard London
Father of SPEAKMAN Wm s 1746 DC
Sources: GL: DC 8167/3

SPEAR Richard (I)
w 1791–1814
Math IM, Spermacetti Refiner, Oil merchant,
Optician
Alternative name: SPEER, SPERE, SPEARS
1791–1792   29 Capel St, Dublin
1793–1809   23 Capel St, Dublin
1809   and College Green, Dublin
1810–1811   35 College Green, Dublin
1812–1814   27 College Green, Dublin
Succeeded by SPEAR & CLARKE★
See also SPEAR Richard (II)★,
Sources: Burnett & Morrison-Low (1989) p.135;
Spere (c.1806)

SPEAR Richard (II)
w 1818–1837
Math IM, Oil Merchant, Candle M
Succeeded by SPEARS & CO.★
Took over from SPEAR & CLARKE★
See also SPEAR Richard (I)★,
Sources: Burnett & Morrison-Low (1989) p.135

SPEAR Saunderson
w 1851–1837
Wax Chandler, Spermacetti Candle M, Jeweller,
Oil S, Optician
1831   3 Westmorland St, Dublin
1832–1834   98 Grafton St, Dublin
1835–1837   23 Suffolk St, Dublin
Sources: Burnett & Morrison-Low (1989) p.135

SPEAR & CLARKE
w 1815–1817
Math IM
1815–1817   27 College Green, Dublin
Succeeded by SPEAR Richard (II)★
Took over from SPEAR Richard (I)★ and CLARKE
Edward (II)★
Sources: Burnett & Morrison-Low (1989) p.135

SPEARS & CO.
w 1838–1864
Math IM, Oil Merchant, Wax M, Spermacetti M
Alternative name: SPEAR & CO.
1838–1842   27 College Green, Dublin
1843–1864   28 College Green, Dublin
See also SPEAR Richard (II)★
Associated with BATE Robert B.★ as agent
Also listed in 1818 in directory
Known to have sold: level
Sources: Wi★(AL); Burnett & Morrison-Low
(1989) p.135–36; Calvert (1971) p.13

SPEECHLEY Robert
w 1823–1840
Optician, Math IM, Phil IM
              21 Red Lion St, Wapping, London
              46 St.John St, London
Guild: [Stationers]
Apprenticed to DIXEY George★ 1810
Sources: Bod: MF 440 STC (MAC); Pg (JAC); R
(JAC)

SPELZINI John
w 1836–1859
Baro M, Thermo M
1836   8 Beauchamp St, Holborn, London

1839–1848   11 Beauchamp St, Holborn, London
1851   19 Vine St, Hatton Garden, London
1856–1859   74 Great Saffron Hill, London
b c.1800 in foreign parts
Known to have sold: barometer
Sources: PRO: Cs 1841 (AM); Pg; PO; Wk;
Goodison (1977) p.361

SPENCER Anne (Mrs)
w 1678–1693
Spec M
1693   St Katherine's, London
Guild: Spectaclemakers
Wife of SPENCER William (I)★
Had apprentice BURBIDGE Isaac, taken over from
SPENCER William (I)★
unnamed, 1684
Took over from SPENCER William (I)★
Known to have sold: spectacles
Sources: GL: SMC 5213/1

SPENCER Anthony
w 1815 d 1827
Optician
1815   12 School House Lane Ratcliffe
              London
Nephew of SPENCER William (II)★
Son of John, glassmaker, b.c. 1772; brother of
Samuel, John & William, apprentices in Grocers'
Co.
Sources: LS

SPENCER John (I)
w 1838–1863
Optical IM, Math IM, Phil IM
1838   128 Summerhill, Dublin
1845–1850   3 Aungier St, Dublin
1852–1863   13 Aungier St, Dublin
Succeeded by SPENCER & SON,
Known to have sold: level, microscope
Sources: Burnett & Morrison-Low (1989) p.136;
Goodison (1977) p.361; Mollan (1990) p.206;
Turner G. (1983a) p.168

SPENCER John (II)
w 1849–1850
Math IM
1849–1850   18 Stepney High St, London
Guild: possibly Grocers – a John Spencer fr 1846
Possibly apprenticed to SPENCER William (III)★,
father
See also SPENCER John (III)★
Sources: GL: GC 11598/8; PO

SPENCER John (III)
w 1849–1851
Optician
1849–1851   7 Hayfield Place, Mile End, London
Succeeded by SPENCER Ann (Mrs) by 1855
See also SPENCER John (II)★
Sources: PO; Wk

SPENCER Richard
w 1778–1782
[Math IS]
1770   23 Beer Lane, London
1782   Beer Lane, London
Guild: Spectaclemakers, fr 1770

Son of SPENCER Thomas, tailor, of Bristol
Apprenticed to PERKINS Ann★ 1763
Had apprentice:
SMITH James ?(I)★ 1778
SMITH Ralph 1782
See also SPENCER & PERKINS★
Sources: GL: SMC 5213/3, 6029A

SPENCER Thomas
w 1695
[Spec M]
1695   Wapping, London
Guild: Spectaclemakers, fp 1679
Son of SPENCER William (I)★ & Anne
Worked for SPENCER William (I)★ 1668
Sources: GL: SMC 5213/1

SPENCER William (I)
w 1668-1677
Spec M
1669   The Minories, London
1671   Bermondsey, London
Guild: [Brewers] Spectaclemakers
Son of SPENCER Richard, cloth-worker, of Sleet, Wilts
Apprenticed to BAILEY John★ 1633/4
Had apprentice:
FLOWER Christopher★ 1671
BURBIDGE Isaac★ 1675, taken over by SPENCER Anne★
Employed
FLOWER Christopher★
SPENCER Thomas★, his son
Succeeded by SPENCER Anne★, his widow
d c.1678
Sources: GL: Brew 5445/15; SMC 5213/1

SPENCER William (II)
w 1777-1784
Math IM
1777   26 Wapping St, London
1778-1795   327 Wapping St, London
1786   Near Union Stairs in Wapping, London
1790   (residence ?) Virginia St, London
Guild: Grocers, fr 1773
Son of SPENCER Anthony, shoemaker, of Chester
Partnership:
SPENCER & BROWNING★
SPENCER, BROWNING & RUST★
Apprenticed to RUST Richard★ 1766
Had apprentice:
HUNT John (III)★ 1777
SPENCER Samuel 1778
KING John (I)★ 1781
HUTCHINSON Richard 1781
MILLS George★ 1783 by t/o from WILLCOX Walton★
HIGLEY Samuel 1790
SPENCER John 1793
CROWDER John Peter 1795 [possibly CROWDER John★]
HORNBLOW John 1797
THOMAS William Frith 1800
Associated with
BROWNING John (I)★
GARRARD Thomas (I)★
Partnership started 1784; retired by 1815; d 1816

Sources: GL: GC 11598/6; Sun 11936/339 no.522402; Brown (1979a) p.47; Crawforth (1987) p.371

SPENCER William (III)
w 1811-1839
Math IM
1811   School House Lane, Ratcliff, London
1839   John St, Limehouse, London
Guild: Grocers, fr 1811
Son of SPENCER John, glass M, d, of Ratcliff, London
Apprenticed to BROWNING Samuel (I)★ 1801
Had apprentice:
SUTTON William 1811
SPENCER William (IV), his son, 1839
SPENCER John (II)?★, his son, 1839
Associated with SMITH George (I)★
Sources: GL: GC 11598/6; 11598/8; Brown (1979a) p.51

SPENCER & BROWNING William & Samuel
w 1778-1784
Optical IM, Math IM
1778-1784   327 Wapping, London
Partnership: SPENCER William (II)★ & BROWNING Samuel (I)★
Succeeded by SPENCER, BROWNING & RUST★
Sources: GL: Sun 11936/262 no.394131, /298 no.453630; Kt (JAC)

SPENCER & CO.
w 1817
Math IM
1817   66 Wapping, Hermitage Bridge, London
See also
SPENCER, BROWNING & CO★
SPENCER, BROWNING & RUST★
Known to have sold: octant
Sources: J (MAC); inst MSEN (MAC); Holbrook (1992) p.186

SPENCER & PERKINS
w 1765-1806
Watch M
1793   44 Snow Hill, London
See also
PERKINS Ann★
SPENCER Richard★
Known to have sold: waywiser
Sources: BW; inst MHS; Baillie (1951); Calvert (1971) p.41

SPENCER, BROWNING & CO.
w 1840-1870
Math IM, Optician
Alternative name: SPENCER & CO.
1840   66 Wapping, London
1840-1870   111 Minories, London
1848-1870   6 Vine St, London
1852   6 America Square, London
Succeeded by BROWNING & CO.
See also
BROWNING William★
SPENCER & BROWNING★
Associated with
SPENCER, BROWNING & RUST★

SPENCER & CO.★
Known to have sold: octant, prism, telescope
Sources: PO; inst MSEN (MAC) & (pv); Anderson et al (1990) p.80; Calvert (1971) p.41; Holbrook (1992) p.112,117,149,186

SPENCER, BROWNING & RUST William (II), Samuel (I) & Ebenezer (I)
w 1784 p 1840
Math IM, Scale Dividers for octants & sextants
Alternative name: S.B.R.
                66 & 327 Wapping, London
                66 & 67 Wapping, London
1784-1796   327 Wapping, London
1797-1839   66 High St, Wapping, London
1816   66 Wapping, London
Guild: Grocers
Partnership: later of RUST Ebenezer (II)★, BROWNING Richard, & BROWNING William★
Apprenticed to RUST Richard★ (all three founding partners)
Succeeded by SPENCER, BROWNING & CO★
Took over from SPENCER & BROWNING★
Agents for ADIE Alexander★; original partners d by 1819 but firm continued under their successors
Known to have sold: barometer, compass (magnetic), octant, sextant, telescope
Sources: Bn; BW; H; Ld; Pg; Und; inst MHS, NMM, WM; Brown J (1979a) p.40,47,48,84-85, pl.25

SPICER Edward
w 1768 d c.1775
Math IM
1768   Plunket St, Dublin
See also
SPICER & LYNCH★
BENNETT John (I)★
Known to have sold: compass, miner's dial
Sources: Burnett & Morrison-Low (1989) p.136; Mollen (1990) p.124, 696-97

SPICER Lewis H.
w 1849
Math IM
1849   6 Garnault Place, Spitalfields, London
Sources: PO

SPICER Simon (I)
w 1777-1784
Math IM, Optician
1777   Three Falcon Court, Fleet St, London
1780   36 Little Britain, London
1784   Charing Cross, London
Appriced to RAMSDEN Jesse★ 1768
See also SPICER Simon (II)★
Sources: GL: Sun 11936/260 no.389160, /288 no.437511, /321 no.490375; PRO: IR 1/25 (AM)

SPICER Simon (II)
w 1836
Math IM, Optical IM
1836   35 Charing Cross, London
See also SPICER Simon (I)★
Sources: Pg

SPICER & LYNCH Edward & James
fl 1760–1772
        Dublin
See also
LYNCH James (I)★
SPICER Edward★
Sources: Burnett & Morrison-Low (1989) p.136;
Taylor (1966) p.273

SPILLER John
w 1760
Spec M
1760   London
Had apprentice STEERS John 1760
Sources: GL: CH 12823/6 p.91 (MAC)

SPRATT Thomas
w 1688
Spec M
1688   London
Guild: Spectaclemakers, fr 1686
Apprenticed to TINGAY Gregory★ 1679
Pupil at Christ's Hospital School, London
Sources: GL: SMC 5213/1; CH 12823/1

SPRINGER Joshua
w 1759–1809
Math IM, Phil IM, Optical IM, Electrician
1759–1760   Hadley's Quadrant in St.Stephen's
           Lane, Bristol
1775–1809   2 Clare St, Bristol
1809   Kings down, Bristol
Took over from WRIGHT John (I)★
See also SPRINGER William★
Known to have sold: barometer, sundial,
thermometer
Instruments advertised: full range
Sources: By (MAC); H (MAC); Mat; Sket (MAC);
BM: Banks 105/51; Felix Farley's *Bristol Journal* 29
Sep 1759, 27 Aug 1774; Goodison (1977)
p.245–47; Millburn (1988a) p.166

SPRINGER William
w 1775–1809
Math IM, Phil IM, Optical IM, Optician
1775   24 Charles St, Bristol
1785–1809   Charles St, Bristol
See also SPRINGER Joshua★
Sources: Browne (MAC); Mat; Sket (MAC)

SPYERS James
w 1762–1799
Cutler, Hardwareman, Scale M, Surgeon's IM
        12 Ludgate Hill, London
        8 Ball Alley, London
        141 Cheapside, London
        49 Lombard St, London
1773   Lombard St, London
1779   Surrey side of Blackfriars Bridge,
        London
1783–1792   121 Cheapside, London
Guild: [Barbers], Cutlers, fr 1760
Apprenticed to CARTWRIGHT Paston, BC,
1750/1
Had apprentice:
RICHARDSON William (III) 1769 by t/o from
CARGILL, CUT
THURGOOD Richard Ireland 1773

STRACHAN John 1778
MERITON Walter Allen 1780
WHITFORD William by t/o 1765 from GERMAIN
B., CUT
BOWDEN James 1762 by t/o from CARTWRIGHT
Paston, BC
Known to have sold: balance
Sources: GL: CUT 7158/1, 7159/3; BC 5266/5
p.167, 5266/6 p.28,77; Bd; BW; H (JAC); Kt
(JAC); inst LM (pv) (MAC)

STAIGHT Thomas
w 1829–1860
Baro M, Thermo M, Math IS, Ivory Turner
Alternative name: STRAIGHT
1829–1839   26 Bartlett's Buildings, Holborn,
           London
1846   12 Walbrook, London
Guild: Fanmakers, fp 1828
Son of STAIGHT John, of FANC of London
Had apprentice HOBCRAFT William 1831
Associated with DOUGHTY William P.★, as
supplier
Known to have sold: compass-sundial,
thermometer
Sources: GL: FANC 21420/1; 21425, 21427/1; Pg;
PO; R; inst NMM; ChrSK 14 Apr 1988 lot 11

STAMPA Dominick
w 1803 a 1835
Carver & Gilder
1803   Leith Walk, Edinburgh
        14 Leith St, Edinburgh
        36 Leith St, Edinburgh
Known to have sold: barometer, thermometer
Sources: Sby Gleneagles 28–29 Aug 1978 lot 304
(MAC); Clarke et al (1989) p.205; Goodison
(1977) p.361

STAMPA & CO. Charles
w 1802–1811
Looking-glass M, Carver & Gilder
1802   125 Holborn Hill London
1803–1811   25 Kirby St, Hatton Garden, London
See also
STAMPA & SON★
STAMPA, SON & CO.★
STAMPA & STEFFENONI★
Probably the makers of the barometers signed by
Stampa & Co., London
Sources: Goodison (1977) p.361

STAMPA & SON
w 1802–1818
Looking-glass M, Baro M, Thermo M, Print S
1802–1818   74 Leather Lane, London
See also
STAMPA, SON & CO.★
STAMPA & CO.★
STAMPA & STEFFENNONI★
Sources: Goodison (1977) p.361

STAMPA & STEFFENONI
w 1816
Baro M
1816   74 Foster Lane, London
See also
STAMPA & CO.★

STAMPA & SON★
STAMPA, SON & CO.★
Sources: PO (JAC)

STAMPA, SON & CO.
w 1803–1804
Baro M
1803–1804   74 Leather Lane, London
See also
STAMPA & CO.★
STAMPA & SON★
STAMPA & STEFFENONI★
Sources: PO (JAC)

STANCLIFFE Benjamin
w 1816–1822
Math IM
1816–1822   13 Bennet St, Blackfriars Rd,
           London
Apprenticed to STANCLIFFE John★, his uncle,
1796
Took over from STANCLIFFE John★
Sources: PRO: IR1/37 (AM); Und

STANCLIFFE John
w 1779–1812
Math IM
        York
1779   26 Little Marylebone St, Cavendish
        Square, London
1793–1812   Little Marylebone [or Marybone]
        Street, London
Apprenticed to HINDLEY Henry★
Had apprentice:
BUTTERY John 1787
BURGES Michael 1793
STANCLIFFE Benjamin★, his nephew, 1796
Worked for RAMSDEN Jesse★
Succeeded by STANCLIFFE Benjamin★
Finished his own dividing engine in 1788 and set
up in business making sextants
Known to have sold: sextant
Sources: PRO: IR1/33 /35 /37 (AM); GL: Sun
11936/ 276 no.416543; Brooks (1992) p.132

STANLEY Joseph
fr 1787 w 1815
Math IM, Ship Chandler
        67 near Bell Dock, Wapping,
        London
1798   Tower St, London
1815   Princes Square, St.Georges in the
        East, London
Guild: Stationers, fr 1787
Son of STANLEY William, biscuit maker of
Wapping, London
Apprenticed to CHAPMAN James (I)★ 1780
Had apprentice:
GAITSKILL Joseph 1798 (Son of GAITSKILL
Joseph★)
CLOUGH James 1799
STANLEY Clark 1808
KARMOCK George 1815
Instruments advertised: compass, quadrant
Sources: SBPL: STC MF Ap; Calvert (1971) p.41;
McKenzie (1978) p.70,331

STANLEY Nathaniel
w 1816–1822
Scale M
1816–1822   111 Wood St, Cheapside, London
Guild: Blacksmiths, fr 1807
Partnership: SOMMERS & STANLEY★
Apprenticed to REYNOLDS Joseph★ 1795
Had apprentice:
BATHER George★ 1807
LAYTON William Thomas 1811
CRAFT Edward 1812
HALL John 1812
Worked for SOMMERS & SON Charles★
Took over from SOMMERS & STANLEY★
Sources: GL: BKC 2881/16, 2886/5 (MAC); PO;
Und

STANLEY Thomas
w 1801–1829
Math IM, Compass M, Dog Collar M
Alternative name: STANDLEY
1801   St.Mary's Row, Birmingham
1805   Aston St, Birmingham
1809–1830   Ashted, Birmingham
1816–1818   10 Bath St, Birmingham
1825   Bath St, Birmingham
Sources: Chp (MAC); H; Pg (MAC); Wr (DJB)

STANTON George William
w pt 1848–1854
Optical turner
1843–1854   73 Shoe Lane, London
Guild: Drapers, fp 1843
Son of STANTON John★
Brother of STANTON John Alfred★
STANTON Robert★
Partnership: STANTON BROS.★
Sources: DH: DPC Ap/Fr, index; PO

STANTON John
w 1813 r 1843
Telescope M, Brass Tube M, Optical Turner,
Warehouse
              111 Shoe Lane, Holborn, London
1813   82 Shoe Lane, Holborn, London
1816–1840   73 Shoe Lane, Holborn, London
1844–1845   [?Residence] Rye Lane, Peckham,
              London
1846–1864   Lloyd St, Pentonville, London
Guild: Drapers, fr 1813
Son of STANTON Robert, pewterer, of Shoe Lane,
London
Apprenticed to HEWES Philip★ 1804
Had apprentice:
PICKERING Henry 1813
LEWIS William★ 1816
LAWRENCE Charles James 1821
JOHNSON William Henry 1821
COOPER William 1822
NASH Benjamin 1824
THOMAS Robert 1825
GOGERTY Robert★ 1828
STANTON John Alfred★, his son, 1829
ROSE William Henry★ 1834
HARRISON John★ 1834
CHAPMAN John 1836
BROWN Kennett 1837, t/o 1843 to STANTON
John A.★

CAVE Henry★ 1838, t/o 1843 to STANTON John
A.★
ROSE James 1842, t/o 1843 to STANTON John A.★
Succeeded by STANTON BROTHERS★
Sources: Pg; PO; Und; DH: DPC Ap/Fr

STANTON John Alfred
w 1843 w pt 1874
Optical Turner
1837–1874   73 Shoe Lane, London
1875–1878   Seven Sisters Rd, Holloway, London
Guild: Drapers, fr 1837
Partnership: STANTON BROTHERS★
Apprenticed to STANTON John★, his father, 1829
Had apprentice:
BROWN Kennett 1843 by t/o from STANTON
John★
CAVE Henry 1843 by t/o from STANTON John★
ROSE James 1843 by t/o from STANTON John★
t/o 1848 to ROSE William★
WIDDERS J. 1846
SPRATT G.H. 1853
ADAM Thomas Kemp 1854
MOORE C. F. 1858
HOBBS James 1859
BENNETT Charles John 1865
WOODELL William Edward 1868
CROFTS William 1872
WOODELL Edward John 1872
NORTON Edward Thomas 1874
WOODELL W. 1844
Either he or his father attended London Mechanics
Institute 1832–1834
Sources: DH: DPC Ap/Fr, index; PO; LMIR
(AM)

STANTON Robert
w pt 1845–1876
Optical turner
1841–1876   73 Shoe Lane, London
1877–1910   [?Residence] Hilldrop Rd, Tufnell
              Park, London
Guild: Drapers, fp 1841
Son of STANTON John★
Brother of
STANTON John Alfred★
STANTON George William★
Partnership: STANTON BROS.★
Sources: DH: DPC Ap/Fr, index

STANTON BROTHERS
w 1845–1870
Telescope M, Tube M, Tube & Wire etc
Warehouse
1845–1870   73 Shoe Lane, Holborn, London
Partnership: STANTON John Alfred★, with his
brothers George W.★ & Robert★
See also STANTON John★
Sources: PO; Wk

STANWAY John
fr 1754 d by 1778
Math IM
              Parish of St.Bridget, London
Guild: Stationers, fr 1754
Son of STANWAY Peter, porter, of London
Father of STANWAY Andrew s 1778 MTC
Apprenticed to WINN Richard ★ 1747

Sources: GL: MTC MF 320 (MAC); McKenzie
(1978) p.384

STARR Robert
w 1667–1682
Math IM
1678   Near the Golden Tun, East
              Smithfield, London
Guild: Stationers, Clockmakers fr as brother
1667/8
Son of STARR John, yeoman, of Stoke, Sussex
Apprenticed to GOSSE Nathaniel★ 1637
Had apprentice:
BENBRIDGE Thomas 1669
SHEPARD John 1674
BELLINGER John (I)★ 1677
COATSFIELD John 1682
Sources: Brown J (1979b) p.33; McKenzie (1961)
p.74

STAYNRED Philip
w 1635–1669
Almanack M, Gauger, Surveyor, Maths Professor,
Math IS
Alternative name: STANDRIDGE
1635–1669   Bristol
Associated with MOONE Thomas★ in advertising
Sources: Bryden (1992) p.307; Taylor (1954) p.208

STEAD William
w 1763 d by 1767
Math IM, Rule M
1763   Parish of St Mary Magdalen in Old
              Fish St, London
Father of STEAD Ellis Bradshaw, s 1763 CWC &
1767 APOTH
Sources: GL: APOTH 8207; CWH: CWC Ap

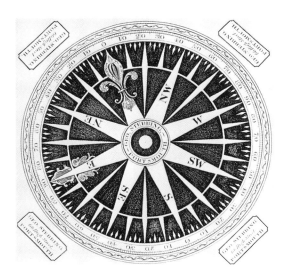

STEBBING George
w 1805–1845
Optician, Compass M, Naut IM, Phil IM, Math
IM
1805–1845   Broad St, Portsmouth
1810   60 High St, Portsmouth
1816   99 High St, Portsmouth
1830   66 High St, Portsmouth
              5 Common Hard, Portsea

Guild: Vintners (London) fr 1816
Had apprentice:
STEBBING George James★, his son, 1817
STEBBING Richard William 1819
STEBBING Frederick George Augustus 1821
Succeeded by STEBBING & SON George★
See also STEBBING & WOOD★
Associated with BATE Robert B.★ as agent
Pat. compass 1810; fr by purchase VC; B.apt Navy;
R.apt Duchess of Kent & Royal Yacht Squadron
Known to have sold: barometer, clinometer,
compass (magnetic), octant
Sources: GL: VC 15201/17 p.43,155,313,412;
15212/2; p134; inst NMM; Pg; Calvert (1971) p.13

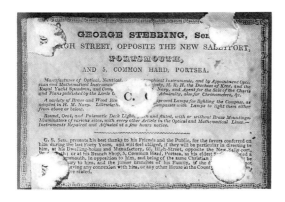

STEBBING George James
fr 1825
Optician
1825   Portsmouth
Guild: Vintners, fr 1825
Apprenticed to STEBBING George★, his father,
1817
Set up in business in Portsmouth in opposition to
his father
Sources: GL: VC 15209/1 fol 49; TCd NMM

STEBBING Joseph Rankin
w 1845 d 1874
Optician, Math IM, Naut IM
1845–1851   47 High St, Southampton
Succeeded by STEBBING & WOOD★
See also STEBBING J.R. & H.★
Mayor of Southampton 1867; R.apt Victoria
Sources: Forbes & Knibbs Directory; Goodison
(1977) p.361

STEBBING J.R. & H.
w 1833
Optician, Math IM
1833   63 High st, Southampton
See also
STEBBING J.R.★
STEBBING & WOOD★
R.apt Princess Victoria & Duchess of Kent
Sources: Calvert (1971) p.41

STEBBING & SON George
a 1845–1847
Compass M
                66 High St, Portsmouth
Took over from STEBBING George★
Succeeded by BROWNING Samuel J.★

See also
ACCUM Frederick C.
GARDEN Alexander,
B.apt Navy
Known to have sold: barometer, thermometer,
compass (magnetic)
Sources: inst NMM

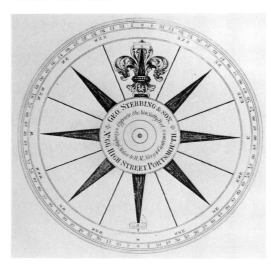

STEBBING & WOOD Joseph Rankin & Albert
w 1851–1853
Optical, Math & Nautical IM
1851–1853   47 High St, Southampton
Took over from STEBBING J.R.★
See also STEBBING J.R. & H.★
R.apt Victoria; B.apt Royal Yacht Squadron
Sources: Forbes & Knibb's Directory; Calvert
(1971) p.41; Goodison (1977) p.361

STEDMAN Christopher (I)
w 1747 d c. 1774
Math IM
Alternative name: STEADMAN
1747–1750   The Globe on London Bridge,
                London
1758–1763   Leadenhall St, London
-1774   24 Leadenhall St, London
Guild: Stationers, fr 1745
Son of STEDMAN Henry, founder, of Newington,
Middx
Father of STEDMAN Christopher (II)★
Husband of STEDMAN Elizabeth★
Apprenticed to
DEVONISH T. 1737
AUSTIN Samuel 1738 (rebound)
Had apprentice:
HAMLIN William★ 1746/7
STORER Thomas★ 1747
ANDREWS Robert 1749
DUNSTER Thomas 1750
CROMPTON James 1753
MACKLY Griffith 1754
JONES William, son of JONES James★, 1754
SEALY Thomas 1756 by t/o from ROLPH Thomas★
MATHEWS Richard 1756 by t/o from ROLPH
Thomas★
LEE John 1758

OGBORN Thomas 1759
CHAPMAN James (I)★ 1760
JOHNSON William (II)★ 1764
HOUSE Ralph 1764 by t/o from BULLOCK John★
PICKERING Anthony 1770
PARISH William 1770 by t/o from HARLOW
George, ivory turner, of THC
WOODWARD Daniel 1771
FEARY Joseph 1772
Succeeded by STEDMAN Elizabeth★
Took over from AUSTIN Samuel★
Associated with WATT James★, who bought insts
for re-sale
Educated at Christ's Hospital School, London
Employed at least 15 men in 1759, besides
apprentices
Known to have sold: balance
Instruments advertised: full range of math inst
Sources: GL: DC 8167/3; THC 6162; CH
12876/4; CLRO: LicFW 2 p.154; Kt; Lg; Mort
(MAC); Riv; Ld (MAC); inst (pv); Bryden (1972)
p.34n; Calvert (1971) p.41 & pl.47; McKenzie
(1978) p.9–10,332

STEDMAN Christopher (II)★
fr 1784 w 1785
Math IM
1785   24 Leadenhall St, London
Guild: Grocers, fr 1784
Son of
STEDMAN Christopher (I)★
STEDMAN Elizabeth★
Apprenticed to ADAMS George (II)★
Took over from STEDMAN Elizabeth★
Associated with ADAMS Dudley★, as fellow
apprentice
Sources: Ld (JAC); IGI London; Brown J (1979a)
p.46

STEDMAN Elizabeth
w 1774–1784
Math IM
                London
1776–1781   24 Leadenhall St, London
Wife of STEDMAN Christopher (I)★
Took over from STEDMAN Christopher (I)★
Succeeded by STEDMAN Christopher (II)★ her son
Sources: GL: Sun 11936/270 no. 407447; Kt
(MAC); Ld (MAC)

STEEL David
fl 1778 d c.1802
Navigation Warehouse, Chart Publisher
1793   1 Union Row, Lower end of the
                Minories, Little Tower Hill, London
Succeeded by STEEL Penelope★
See also STEEL J.★
Instruments advertised: naut inst
Sources: BW; Taylor (1966) p.297

STEEL J.
w 1806–1810
Navigation Warehouse
1806–1810   70 Cornhill, London
Succeeded by STEEL & CO.
Took over from STEEL Penelope★
See also
STEEL & GODDARD★

STEEL David★
STEEL, GODDARD & CO.★
STEELE John★
Sources: PO (JAC); Robinson (1962) p.124

STEEL Penelope
w 1803–1806
Chart S, Navigation Warehouse
1803–1805   70 Cornhill, London
1806   Union Row, Minories, London
              [residence ?]
Guild: Musicians, fr 1806 by purchase
Took over from STEEL David★
Succeeded by STEEL J.★
Instruments advertised: reflecting circle
Sources: GL: MSC 3098; JAC; Taylor (1966) p.298

STEEL & CO.
w 1811–1815
Navigation Warehouse
1811–1815   70 Cornhill, London
Took over from STEEL J.
Succeeded by STEEL & GODDARD★
Sources: H (JAC); PO (JAC)

STEEL & GODDARD
w 1816–1818
Navigation Warehouse
1816–1818   70 Cornhill, London
Took over from STEEL & CO.★
Succeeded by STEEL, GODDARD & CO.★
Sources: PO (JAC)

STEEL, GODDARD & CO.
w 1819 c 1820
Navigation Warehouse
1819–1820   70 Cornhill, London
Took over from STEEL & GODDARD★
Succeeded by NORIE & CO. J.W.★
Sources: PO (JAC)

STEELE John
w 1823–1835
Navigation Warehouse, Math IM, Stationer, Book
S
              Nautical Warehouse opposite Duke's
              Dock, Wapping, Liverpool
1823–1825   6 Duke's Place, Liverpool
1827   10 Duke's Place, Liverpool
Took over from PALMER, STEELE & CO.★
See also STEELE & SON John★
Associated with CRICHTON John★, to whom he
apprenticed his son, Robert
Sources: GL: MPC 5963/5; G (MAC); MSEN:
TCd in box of pocket sextant by ALLAN, London
(MAC)

STEELE & SON John
w 1828–1851
Math IM, Optician, Stationers
Alternative name: I.
1828–1838   9 Duke's Place, Wapping, Liverpool
1839–1851   21 Duke's Place, Liverpool
1839–1851   10 Duke's Place, Liverpool
Succeeded by STEELE & CO. John P.
See also STEELE John★
Associated with CRICHTON John★, to whom
STEELE Robert was apprenticed 1835

Known to have sold: barometer, sextant
Sources: GL: MPC 5963/5; G (MAC); SL (DJB);
inst (pv); Goodison (1977) p.361; Holbrook (1992)
p.119

STEER John
w 1818–1840
Umbrella M, Optician, Toyman
1818   Market Head, Derby
1830   Rotten Row, Derby
1840   4 Market Head, Derby
Succeeded by STEER Henry
Sources: Pg; *Midland Counties Railway Companion*,
1840, advertisement (DJB); Taylor (1966) p.461

STEINHEUSER John Leberecht
w 1809–1812
Phil IM, Chem IM
Alternative name: STYEINHOESUR,
STEINHAUFFER,
1809   33 Frith St, Soho, London
Sources: PO; JAC

STENSON John
w 1782–1793
Weatherglass M & Flour-man
1782–1793   Derby
Known to have sold: barometer
Sources: BW; Phlps 22 Feb 1977 lot 4 (DJB);
Goodison (1977) p.361

STEPHENS Alexander
w 1747
              Temple Bar, Dublin
See also
STEPHENS Alexander & John★
STEPHENS John★
Known to have sold: back-staff
Sources: Sby 5 June 1985 lot 439 (MAC); Bennett
(1983a) no.127; Burnett & Morrison-Low (1989)
p.137

STEPHENS Alexander & John
w 1761–1781
Math IM
1761–1774   Temple Bar, Dublin
1775–1781   31 Temple Bar, Dublin
See also
STEPHENS John★
STEPHENS Alexander★
Sources: Wi (DJB); Burnett & Morrison-Low
(1989) p.137

STEPHENS Jane (Mrs)
w 1681–1683
[Spec M]
              London
Guild: Spectaclemakers
Mother of STEPHENS Samuel★
Had apprentice unnamed, 1683
Took over from STEPHENS Richard★, her husband
See also STEPHENS Robert★
Sources: GL: SMC 5213/1

STEPHENS John
w 1782 d 1802
Math IM
1782–1793   31 Temple Bar, Dublin

See also
STEPHENS Alexander & John★
STEPHENS Alexander★
Sources: Wi (DJB); Burnett & Morrison-Low
(1989) p.137

STEPHENS Philagathus
w 1722
Spec M
1722   Water Lane, Blackfriars, London
Guild: Spectaclemakers, fr 1721/2
Apprenticed to STEPHENS Robert★ nd
Had apprentice SMALLSHAW Robert 1722
Sources: GL: SMC 5213/2 p.127,131

STEPHENS Richard
w 1668–1678
[Spec M]
              London
Guild: Spectaclemakers
Father of STEPHENS Samuel★
Had apprentice his son, unnamed, 1674
Succeeded by STEPHENS Jane★, his wife
d c.1680
Sources: GL: SMC 5213/1

STEPHENS Robert
w 1699–1709
[Spec M]
Alternative name: STEVENS
              London
Guild: Spectaclemakers, fr 1689
Husband of widow of HELME Thomas★
Had apprentice:
BILLING Christopher 1699
STEPHENS Philagathus★ fr 1721/2
Sources: GL: SMC 5213/1, 5213/2 pp.7,18,25,67

STEPHENS Samuel
w 1688–1709
Spec M
Alternative name: STEVENS
1693   Strand, London
1695   St Clement's, London
Guild: Spectaclemakers, fr 1682/3
Son of STEPHENS Richard★ & Jane★
Sources: GL: SMC 5213/1, 5213/2 p.63

STEPHENSON Robert
w 1712–1725
Math IM
1718   Little Tower Hill, London
Guild: Stationers, fr 1712
Apprenticed to ENGLAND John★ 1703
Had apprentice:
PHILLIPS Ralph 1712
MANSELL Ralph 1718
CHARNOCK Hezekiah 1722
JARMAN Thomas★ 1725
Sources: McKenzie (1978) p.336–7

STERNE Thomas
w 1619–1631
Globe M
Alternative name: STERN
              St.Paul's Churchyard, London
Sources: Taylor (1954) p.206

STERROP Avis

w 1756 d 1760
[Optician]
        London
Guild: Spectaclemakers
Wife of STERROP George★
Had apprentice LINNELL Joseph★ 1756 by t/o
from LINNELL Robert★ t/o 1760 to STERROP
Mary★
Sources: GL: SMC 5213/3 p.215+

STERROP George

w 1747 d 1756
Optician
Alternative name: STIRRUP, STIRROP
1747–1748   St.Paul's Churchyard, London
1748   Tonbridge
Guild: Spectaclemakers, fr 1737
Son of STERROP Thomas (III)★
Husband of STERROP Avis★ (probably)
Apprenticed to STERROP Mary★ his mother 1730
Had apprentice:
WALKER Robert 1747
HUME John 1750
Took over from STERROP & SON Mary★
Associated with HENDERSON Thomas★(agent)
Master SMC 1750–1751
Known to have sold: microscope
Instruments advertised: barometer
Sources: GL: SMC 5213/2 p.219+, 5213/3
p.117,153,156,165–66,213,215; *Daily Ad* 5 Jul
1748; Bryden (1972) p.18; Goodison (1977) p.362;
Turner G (1989) p.255–56

STERROP Jane

w 1709–1726
[Spec M]
Alternative name: STURROP
1719   Little Britain, London
Guild: Spectaclemakers
Wife of STERROP Thomas (II)★
Mother of
STERROP Thomas (III)★
STERROP George★
Had apprentice:
DAY John★ 1708/9
CONSTABLE Henry 1710
HUNT William 1711
BARKER William (II)★1716
WILLIAMS Greene 1719
COX William (I)★ 1723 by t/o from JOHNSON
William (I)★
MEGOMRY John 1726
Took over from STERROP Thomas (II)★
Sources: GL: CH 12876/3; SMC 5213/2
p.61,71,76,98,111,142,173

STERROP Mary

w 1730–1763
[Optical IS]
        London
Guild: Spectaclemakers
Wife of STERROP Thomas (III)★
Partnership: STERROP & SON Mary★
Had apprentice:
STERROP George★, her son
LINNELL Joseph★ by t/o 1760 from STERROP Avis★

JEMMETT George 1733/4
PANTON William 1738
Took over from STERROP Thomas (III)★
Sources: GL: SMC 5213/2 p.219+, 5213/3

STERROP Ralph

w 1686–1736
Optical IM
Alternative name: STIRRUP, STIRROP
        The Archimedes in Ludgate St,
        London
1693–1695   St.Paul's Churchyard, London
Guild: Spectaclemakers, fr 1685
Son of (probably) STERROP Thomas (I)★
Partnership:
STERROP & YARWELL★
MARSHALL & STERROP★
Had apprentice:
two unnamed boys, 1685/6
HARWOOD Henry 1690
BRANDRETH Timothy★ 1693
ROAK Richard★ 1693
ROAK Joseph 1701/2
BASS George★ 1706
JOHNSON Robert 1709
BLOCKLEY James 1714
BUTTON John 1718
COLLETT Samuel 1722
BULL Joseph 1724
HURT Joseph★ 1729
Succeeded by HURT Joseph★
Took over from YARWELL John★
Master SMC 1702–1709
Sources: GL: SMC 5213/1, 5213/2
pp.27,49,64,107,132,148,207+; instruction booklet
(pv)

STERROP Thomas (I)

w 1651–1659
Mathematicus
Alternative name: STIRRUP
Author
Specialised in making dials, according to Taylor
Sources: Taylor (1954) p.238,358–59,361,367

STERROP Thomas (II)

w 1683–1708
[Spec M]
Alternative name: STIRROP
1693–1695   Little Britain, London
Guild: Spectaclemakers, fr 1679
Son of STERROP Ralph, clothier, of Worcester
Father of STERROP Thomas (III)★
Brother of STERROP Richard s 1677 to
THROGMORTON John (I)★
Apprenticed to KING Thomas★ 1672
Had apprentice:
JOHNSON John (II)★ 1693
WILLIAMS Thomas 1700/1
FLEMING Samuel 1706
JACKMAN Richard 1707
unnamed, 1683
unnamed, 1689
Succeeded by STERROP Jane,★ his widow
d late 1708 or early 1709
Sources: GL:SMC, 5213/1, 5213/2 p.27,50,55,57

STERROP Thomas (III)

w 1711 d c. 1728
Spec M
1714   Archimedes in St.Paul's Church
            Yard, London
1721   [Residence] Mitre Court in London
            House Yard near St.Paul's Church,
            London
1724   Archimedes & One Pair Golden
            Spectacles, St.Paul's Church Yard,
            London
Guild: Spectaclemakers, fr 1708
Father of STERROP George★
Son of STERROP Thomas (II)★ & Jane★
Husband of STERROP Mary★
Related to STERROP Ralph★ (probably)
Had apprentice:
RAYNER Lactentious 1711
MILLINER or MULLINER Nathanial 1714
ARCHER William 1715
PHIPPS John★ 1718
WHARTON Nicholas 1719
ROOE Jeremiah 1722
ASKEW William, fr 1722
RIBRIGHT Thomas (I)★ 1726/7
Succeeded by STERROP Mary★
Sources: GL: SMC 5213/2 57,75,86,92,107–32,
180,219; 6031/1; Sun 11936/4; Buckley (1935)
p.428

STERROP & SON Mary

c 1737–1747
Toy S, Optical IS
        Archimedes & One Pair of Golden
        Spectacles the North Side of
        St.Paul's Churchyard, London
Guild: Spectaclemakers
Partnership: STERROP Mary★ [widow of Thomas
(III)★] & George★
Took over from STERROP Mary★
Succeeded by STERROP George★
Sources: TCd (pv); Bryden & Simms (1992)
p.12–13

STERROP & YARWELL Ralph & John

w 1707
Spec M, Optical IM
        Archimedes and Three Pair of
        Golden Spectacles in Ludgate St, the
        second Shop from Ludgate, London
        Ludgate St, the second Shop from
        Ludgate, London
See also
STERROP Ralph★
YARWELL John★
Sources: Bryden (1992) p.334n; Crawforth (1985)
p.532;

STEVEN & CO. J.

w 1820–1821
Math IM
1820–1821   8 Nelson St, Glasgow
Sources: Bryden (1972) p.56

STEVENS Jeremiah

w 1825–1840
Math IM, Phil IM
1825   5 Green Arbour Court, Doctor's

Commons, London
1831–1840   2 Bell Court, Bell Yard, Doctor's
Commons, London
Guild: Goldsmiths
Apprenticed to BIRKWOOD William, 1809
Had apprentice:
BARNETT Joshua Samuel 1825
CHAPMAN James 1831
STEVENS William Miah 1840
Sources: GH: GSC Ap, Fr; Pg

STEVENS John Lawford
w 1792–1799
Spec M
1778   At Mr Freeman's, Old Gravel Lane,
London
1792–1799   37 St Andrew's Hill, Doctors
Commons, London
Guild: Spectaclemakers, fr 1778
Son of STEVENS Thomas, cooper, of Whitechapel,
London
Apprenticed to JONES John (I)★ 1770
Had apprentice:
MILWOOD Samuel 1792
REEVES John B.S. 1799
Probably d by 1810, when a Mrs Ann Stevens,
widow of John, applied to SMC for charity (but 2
John Stevens in SMC)
Sources: GL: SMC 5213/3, 5213/4

STEVENS William Henry
w 1849–1851
Math IM
1849–1851   20 Chapel St, Pentonville, London
Sources: PO

STEVENS & SON John
w 1845–1851
Chem Apparatus M, Gas Engineers, Brass
Founders
1845–1851   19 Southwark Bridge Rd, London
Sources: PO

STEVENSON Peter
w 1836–1900+
Philo IM
1836–1861   9 Lothian St, Edinburgh
1862–1870   51 George IV Bridge, Edinburgh
1871–1873   5 Forrest Rd, Edinburgh
1874–1900   9 Forrest Rd, Edinburgh
1888–1900   7 Forrest Rd, Edinburgh
Took over from ALLAN Alexander★
Known to have sold: saccharometer
Sources: Bryden (1972) p.57; Holbrook (1992)
p.112

STEVENSON Samuel
w 1758
Spec M
London
Sources: GL: CH 12823/5 p.52 (MAC)

STEWARD John
w 1833
Optician, Spec M
1833   Queen St, Wolverhampton
Sources: Br (MAC)

STEWART James
w 1811–1830
Scale M
1811   49 Noble St, Goswell St, London
1829–1830   18 Noble St, Goswell St, London
Guild: [Blacksmiths]
Apprenticed to GOODMAN John★ 1792
Sources: GL: BKC 2881/16 (MAC); H (JAC); R
(JAC)

STEWART John
w 1820–1834
Scale M
1820–1834   Great Hamilton St, Glasgow
Sources: Pg (MAC)

STIFF James
w 1845–1859
Chem Apparatus M
1845–1859   39 Lambeth High St, London
Succeeded by STIFF & SONS James
Sources: PO

STILES Daniel
w 1710 d by 1729
Compass M, Math IM
1710   Hourglass & Compass near
Hermitage Bridge, Wapping,
London
Father of STILES Daniel (II) s 1729 WXC
Sources: GL: WXC MF 9488; Sun 11936/1 no.345
(MAC)

STILES Mason
w ?fm 1826–1829
Math IM
Alternative name: STYLES
1826   Cowcross St, London
1829   29 Seward St, London
Son of STILES William Mason (I)★
Brother of STILES William Mason (II)★
Attended London Mechanics Institute 1826 &
1829; b 29 Jan 1811
Sources: LMIR (AM); St Sepulchre's Middx, Bap
(AM)

STILES Nicholas
w 1783
Math IM, Turner
1783   Rotherhithe Wall, London
Partnership:
BRANDON & STILES★
STILES & LAW★
See also HUTCHINS Josiah★ (possible master)
Sources: GL: Sun & RE index

STILES Richard
v 1824 w 1825
Math IM
Alternative name: STYLES
1824–1825   2 Round Court, Sharps Alley,
Cowcross, London
Son of STILES Richard
Brother of STILES William Mason (I)★
Partnership: STILES W. & R.
Attended London Mechanics Institute 1824–1825
Sources: LMIR (AM); St Sepulchre's Middx, Bap
(AM)

STILES W. & R.
w 1816
Phil IM
1816   1 Sharps Alley, Cow Cross, London
See also
STILES William Mason (I)★
STILES Richard★
Associated with
★HILL William &
★WATKINS J. as suppliers
Sources: EBA: OB 1816 (Watkins)

STILES William
fr 1731 w 1757
[Scale M]
Alternative name: STILLS
London
Guild: Blacksmiths, fr 1731
Apprenticed to NEALE John (I)★ 1722
Had apprentice:
DEARSLY Thomas★ 1733
CHUMLEY Edward★ 1733
LEVERETT William★ 1753, t/o
1757 to VINCENT Robert★
Sources: GL: BKC 2885/1, 2886/4, 2888 (MAC)

STILES William Mason (I)
w 1828–1850
Phil IM, Math IM, Baro M, Thermo M
Alternative name: STYLES
1824–1825   1 Sharps Alley, Cowcross, London
1839–1850   29 Seward St, Goswell St, London
Son of STILES Richard
Brother of STILES Richard★
See also STILES W. & R.★
Attended London Mechanics Institute, 1824–1825;
b 11 Nov 1786
Sources: Pg; PO; Delivery note (JAC), St.
Sepulchre's Middx, Bap (AM); LMIR (AM)

STILES William Mason (II)
w 1851–1865
Baro M, Thermo M, Phil IM
1851–1865   70 Ossulton St, Somers Town,
London
Son of STILES William Mason (I)★
Brother of STILES Mason★
Sources: PO; Wk; St. Sepulchre's Middx, Bap (AM)

STILES & LAW Nicholas & John
w 1785
Math IM
1785   26 Rotherhithe, London
See also BRANDON & STILES★
Sources: GL: Sun 11936/333

STILWELL Richard
w 1827–1840
Optician, Math IM, Phil IM
1827–1840   73 High St, Shoreditch, London
Sources: Pg (JAC)

STIMSON Thomas
fr 1709
Hour-glass M
1709   London
Guild: Tallow Chandlers, fr 1709
Sources: GL:THC 6164/2 p.59

STIPPS Thomas
w 1805
Compass M, Whitesmith
1805   25 Marygold St, Bermondsey,
             London
Sources: H (MAC)

STOCKTON George
w 1828–1850
Watch M, Clock M, Naut IM, Compass M
1828   Long Row, South Shields
1834   9 Long Row, South Shields
1850   15 Thrift St, South Shields
Sources: Pg; Wd

STOKER John
w 1851
Globe Manufacturer
1851   Doncaster, Yorks
Ex.1851
Sources: Cat. 1851

STOKER Thomas
w 1834–1848
Hardwareman, Brazier, Compass M
1834–1848   21 Clive St, North Shields,
             Northumberland
Instruments advertised: binnacle, log-glass
Sources: Pg; advertisement in Fordyce (1848)

STOKES Charles
w 1773
Clock M
1773   Bewdley, Worcs
Instruments advertised: balance
Sources: *Barrow's Worcester Journal* 19 Aug 1773 p.2
(JRM)

STOKES Gabriel
w 1715 d 1768
Math IM, Surveyor
Alternative name: Ga. STOAKS; Gab. STOAK
             Essex St, Dublin
Had apprentice:
READING Thomas
SEWARD John★ 1715
DOWDING Agmondisham
1738/9
KELLY Thomas 1721/2
Associated with CAVE Thomas
Bap 1682; attended King's Hospital School; inv.
Pantometron
Known to have sold: bow quadrant, slide rule,
sundial
Sources: KH (WS); inst NMM; Burnett &
Morrison-Low (1989) p.20–23, 137

STOKES Henry
w 1820–1833
Baro M, Thermo M, Hydro M, Phil IM
             18 Queen St, Short St, New Cut,
             London
1822   110 Hatton Garden, London
             13 Wingrove Place, Clerkenwell,
             London
Sources: Pg; R (JAC); TSA 1820 (JAC)

STOKES Saul
w 1792
Steelyard M
Alternative name: Saml.
1792   2 Canal St, Wolverhampton
Sources: Wolverhampton rate books (MAC)

STOKES William
w 1842–1850
Optician
1842–1845   3 Upper Leeson St, Dublin
1846–1850   3 Ballygihen, Sandy Cove,
             Kingstown, Dublin
1846–1850   and 28 College Green, Dublin
Sources: Burnett & Morrison-Low (1989) p.137

STONE John
w 1834–1851
Math IM, Ship Chandler, Marine Store, Custom
House
1834–1848   106 High St, Hull
Sources: Pg; Stn; Wh (MAC)

STONE Joshua
w 1760
Known to have sold: sextant
Sources: Taylor (1966) p.273

STONE William
w 1684
Known to have sold: nocturnal
Sources: Taylor (1954) p.281

STOPANI John
w 1824–1850
Baro M, Optical IM
Alternative name: STOPHANI, STOPANIE
1824–1825   38 North St, Aberdeen
1827–1840   42 Queen St, Aberdeen
1841–1843   44 Queen St, Aberdeen
1844–1850   68 Broad St, Aberdeen
Known to have sold: barometer
Sources: Bryden (1972) p. 57; Goodison (1977)
p.362

STOPANI Nicholas
w 1822–1825
Baro M, Mirror M
1822–1825   Orchard St, Sheffield
Sources: Bn (DJB); Ge (MAC); Goodison (1977)
p.362

STOPPANI A.
w 1830
Baro M, Thermo M
1830   Leeds
Sources: PWh (MAC)

STORER Thomas
fr 1756 w 1776
Math IM
1776   Walham Green, London
Guild: Stationers, fr 1756
Apprenticed to STEDMAN Christopher (I)★ 1747
Father of STORER John s 1776 GSC
Sources: GH: GSC Ap; McKenzie (1978) p.332

STORER William
w 1778–1789
Optician
             Lisle St, Leicester Fields, London
1784   Great Marlborough Street London
Pat. drawing inst 1778, telescopes 1780, lenses
1783; bankrupt 1784
Sources: Patent records (MAC); *London Chronicle*
13/16 Nov 1784 (JRM); TCd MHS (MAC)

STRACHAN Charles
w 1831
Chrono M
             London
Guild: Clockmakers, fr 1815
Partnership: MCCABE & STRACHAN
Sources: CUL: RGO 1143, fol.2; Baillie (1951)

STRACHAN John
w 1848–1859
Optician
1848   12 Galway St, St. Luke's London
1855   11 Wellington St, Goswell St, London
1859   2 Charles St, City Rd, London
Sources: PO

STRATFORD William Mason
w 1826
Math IM
1826   12 Boundary Row, Blackfriars,
             London
See also STRATTON William★
Attended London Mechanics Institute 1826
Sources: LMIR (AM)

STRATTON John
a 1740–1760
Math IM, Optician
             Golden Spectacles in Sidney's Alley
             near Leicester Fields, London
Sources: Crawforth (1985) p.533

STRATTON Joseph
w 1838
Math IM
1838   12 Boundary Road (? Row),
             Blackfriars, London
See also
STRATTON William★
STRATFORD William Mason★
Attended London Mechanics Institute 1838
Sources: LMIR (AM)

STRATTON W. M.
w em 1831
Math IM
1831   181 Strand, London
See also STRATTON William★ [possibly the same
person]
Worked for CARY William★
Attended London Mechanics Institute 1831
Sources: LMIR (AM)

STRATTON William
w 1824–1829
Math IM
1824–1829   12 Boundary Row, Blackfriars,
             London

See also
STRATTON W.M [possibly the same person]
STRATTON Joseph★
STRATFORD William Mason★
Attended London Mechanics Institute 1824–1829
Sources: LMIR (AM)

STREATFIELD –
a 1750
    London
Known to have sold: circumferentor
Sources: Morton & Wess (1993) p.400

STREATFIELD John
w pt 1850–1859
Hydro M
1852–1859   1 Old Jewry, London
Partnership: LADD & STREATFIELD★
Worked for BATE Robert B.★
Sources: McConnell (1993) p.54

STREET John
w 1851–1859
Math IM
1851   9 Brewer St North, Goswell Rd,
    London
1859   8 Duke's Terrace, St. James's Rd,
    Liverpool Rd, London N
Sources: PO; Wk

STREET Samuel (I)
w 1771–1802
Optician, Optical IM, Math IM
1771   Lomes Court, Coldbath Fields,
    London
1786–1802   26 Plough Court, Fetter Lane,
    London
Guild: Stationers, fr 1759
Apprenticed to BUSH William (I)★ 1752
Had apprentice:
STREET Samuel (II), his son, 1786 CAREY William
1794
See also STREET Thomas★
Sources: GL: STTP 2934 fol 5; H (JAC);
McKenzie (1978) p.342

STREET Thomas
w 1829–1880
Optician, Math IM, Phil IM
    4 Charles St, Blackfriars Rd, London
    30 Commercial Rd, Lambeth,
    London
1839–1880   39 Commercial Rd, Lambeth,
    London
Employed SENIOR B.★
Associated with TROUGHTON & SIMMS★,
probably as sub-contractor
Succeeded by STREET & CO. Richard W.
See also STREET Samuel★
Known to have sold: level
Sources: Pg; PO; R (JAC); Wh (Leeds) entry for
B. Senior★; inst (s)

STRETCH James
a 1765 d 1813
Spec M
    Cock Court, St.Martin's le Grand,
    London

Succeeded by PHELPS Thomas (I)
b.1744
Sources: GMag 1813 (JAC)

STRETTON Mrs
w 1818–1824
Math IM
Alternative name: Widow STRETTON
1818–1824   Platform, Rotherhithe, London
See also GARTH Richard★
Sources: Bn (JAC); Kt (JAC)

STROUD John
w 1746–1764
Hourglass M
1764   Green Alley, Tooley St, London
Guild: Turners, fr 1734/5
Son of STROUD Abraham, shoemaker, of London
Apprenticed to COOK Peter, turner, 1727
Had apprentice:
STROUD Thomas 1746
WALSHAW Joseph★ 1755
BALCH John 1758
Sources: GL: TC 3300, 3302/2, 3814; CLRO:
CFI/561

STRUTHERS Gavin
fr 1718
Scale M
    Rutherglen, Glasgow
Guild: Hammermen, fr 1718
Known to have sold: balance
Sources: Lumsden & Aitken (1912) p.292 (MAC)

STUART George
w 1834–1847
Optical IM, Math IM
1834–1838   82 Westgate St, Newcastle on Tyne
1847   17 Clayton St, Newcastle on Tyne
Sources: Pg; Wh (MAC)

STUBBS B.
a 1772–1800
    London
Known to have sold: balance
Sources: inst SM (Wellcome) (MAC)

STUCKY Thomas
w 1586
Guild: Stationers
Had apprentice THOMPSON John (I)★ 1586, but
apparently t/o to READ John (I)★
Sources: McKenzie (1961) p.111

STUMPFF J.A.
fl 1780
    London
Known to have sold: microscope
Sources: Taylor (1966) p.324

STURDY Frederick Henry
w em 1838–1850
Optician
1838   21 Poultry, London
Brother of STURDY Joseph William★
Worked for BATE Robert Brettell★
Sources: McConnell (1993) p.5,49

STURDY Joseph William
w 1824 d 1838
Math IM
1838   21 Poultry, London
1838   Paradise Row Stockwell London
Brother of STURDY Frederick Henry★
Worked for BATE Robert Brettell★
Sources: McConnell (1993) p.5,16; AM

STURMAN Edward
w 1803
Math IM
Alternative name: STERMAN
1803   Smiths Place, Wapping, London
Father of STURMAN Reuben s 1803 to GARDNER
James★
Sources: GL: GC 11598/6

STUTCHBURY David
w 1807–1828
Gauging IM
1807–1828   3 Dove Court, Old Jewry, London
Took over from STUTCHBURY Joseph★
Sources: Kt (JAC); PO

STUTCHBURY Joseph
w 1797–1826
Gauging IM, Rule M, Math IM
Alternative name: STITCHBURY, STUCHBURY,
1791–1796   Bird in Hand Court, Cheapside,
    London
1797–1800   Dove Court, Old Jewry, London
1802–1826   3 Dove Court, Old Jewry, London
Guild: Joiners, fr 1791
Son of STUTCHBURY John of DPC of London
Apprenticed to ROBERTS Edward (I)★ 1784
Had apprentice FOSTER John 1797
Succeeded by STUTCHBURY David★
Known to have sold: gauging rod, slide rule
Instruments advertised: theodolite
Sources: GL: JC 8055/3; H (MAC); Crawforth
(1987) p.366; Delechar (1984) p.7

SUCKLEY Samuel
w 1829–1832
Measure M
1829–1832   10 Robert St, Blackfriars Rd,
    London
Sources: R (JAC)

SUDLOW John
w 1751
Math IM
    London
1750   Ball Alley, Lombard St, London
Guild: Grocers, fr 1750
Son of SUDLOW John, painter, d, of London
Apprenticed to JACKSON Joseph 1736
Husband of Elizabeth, daur of COLE
Benjamin (I)★, m 1850
Had apprentice BANNISTER James 1751
Sources: JRM; Brown J (1979a) p.37,39

SUFFELL Charles
w 1839–1877
Math IM, Math IS, Optical IS
1839–1865   132 Long Acre, London
1866–1877   122 Long Acre, London

Known to have sold: barometer, parallel rule, surveying compass
Sources: PO; Wk; BSIS no.2 (1984) p.14; ChrSK 13 Dec 1984 lot 171 (MAC); Goodison (1977)

SUGAR John
fl 1645 w 1653
    Atlas on Parnassus Hill, near St.Michael's, Cornhill, London
Partnership: SUGAR & MOXON*
Sources: Taylor (1954) p.240

SUGAR & MOXON John & Joseph
w 1653
Map S, Globe M
Alternative name: MOXON & SUGAR ?
1653   Atlas on Parnassus Hill, near St.Michael's Church, Cornhill, London
1653   Cornhill by St. Michael's Church at the sign of Atlas upon Mount Parnassus, London
See also
MOXON Joseph*
SUGAR John*
Sources: Booker (1653) Sig C4 fol.5v; Taylor (1954) p.233–34, 240; Tyacke (1978) p.127

SULLIVAN Christopher
w 1839–1860
Optician, Math IM, Phil IM
1839–1855   22 Charles St, Hatton Garden, London
1849   68 Charlton St, Somers Town, London
Sources: PO; Wk

SULLIVAN Patrick
w 1738–1743
    South back of St.Clement's Church near Temple Bar, London
    Without Temple Bar, London
1738–1743   Wickham Court, London
Known to have sold: barometer, thermometer
Sources: inst NMM; Calvert (1971) p.41; Goodison (1977) p.362

SUMERAN Bartholomew
w 1835–1887
Looking-glass M, Baro M, Thermo M
Alternative name: SUMERAU
1835–1887   27 Lisle St, Leicester Square, London
Sources: Pg; PO; JAC

SURGETT Charles
w 1829–1834
Optician, Math IM, Phil IM
-1834   28 Charles St, Hatton Garden, London
1829   12 Beauchamp St, Leather Lane, London
Succeeded by SURGETT John*
See also SURGETT William*
Sources: PO; R (JAC)

SURGETT John
w 1835–1839
Optician

Took over from SURGETT Charles*
Sources: PO

SURGETT William
w 1826–1827
Optician, Math IM, Phil IM
1826–1827   21 Bath St, City Rd, London
See also
SURGETT Charles*
SURGETT John*
Sources: Pg (JAC)

SUTTER John
w 1811–1822
Baro M
1811–1822   Toddrick's Wynd, Edinburgh
Known to have sold: barometer
Sources: Bryden (1972) p.57; Goodison (1977) p.363

SUTTON Baptist
w 1639–1653
Sundial M
1639   At the upper end of Chancery Lane, near Holborn, London
See also
SUTTON Henry*
SUTTON William (I)*
Sources: Bryden (1992) p.306; Taylor (1954) p.219,357

SUTTON Francis
w 1849–1859
Optician
1849–1859   1 Castle St, Leicester Square, London
Sources: PO; Wk

SUTTON George
w 1833–1878
Optician
1833–1840   14 Bridge Rd, Lambeth, London
1845–1859   16 Bridge Rd, Lambeth, London
1865–1878   209 Westminster Bridge Rd, Lambeth, London S
Sources: Pg; PO; Wk

SUTTON Henry
w 1649 d 1665
Math IM (in brass and wood)
Alternative name: Henricus
    Theadneedle St, near St.Christophers Church, London
1649   Tower Hill near the Postern Spring, London
1658   Behind the Royal Exchange in Threadneedle St, London
Guild: Joiners, fr 1647 or 1648
Partnership: SUTTON & KNIBB*
Apprenticed to BROWN Thomas (I)* 1638
Had apprentice:
PAGE Thomas* 1649
ALDUS Thomas* 1652
MARKE John* 1655
EMOTT Benjamin* 1659/60
WRIGHT Benjamin* 1663
Employed KNIBB Samuel*
Succeeded by MARKE John*

See also
SUTTON Baptist*
SUTTON William*
Associated with BROWN John (I)* in advertising
Publisher
Known to have sold: astrolabe, calculating machine, compass (magnetic), plane table, planisphere, protractor, quadrant, slide rule, sundial
Instruments advertised: slide rule
Sources: inst MHS, NMM, SM; Phlps 17 Jul 1985 lot 81 (MAC); Bryden (1992) p.318–19; Calvert (1971) p.42; Crawforth (1987 p.366); Taylor (1954) p.230,231, 369–70

SUTTON John
w 1802
Optician, Spec M
1802   46 Great Queen St, Lincoln's Inn fields, London
See also SUTTON George
Sources: H (JAC)

SUTTON William (I)
w 1659–1669
Math IM (in brass & wood)
1659   In Upper Shadwell a little beyond the Church, London
Guild: Joiners, fr 1656/7
Apprenticed to WORRALL Thomas 1642
Had apprentice:
KNIBB John* 1664
TOOGOOD John* 1669/70
See also SUTTON Baptist*
Associated with SUTTON Henry* in joint advertisements
Sources: Bryden (1992); p.318 Crawforth (1987) p.366–67

SUTTON William (II)
w 1799
Scale M
1799   60 Bankside, Borough, London
Sources: H (JAC)

SUTTON & KNIBB Henry & Samuel
w 1664
Alternative name: Henricus London
See also
KNIBB Samuel*
SUTTON William*
SUTTON Henry*
Made Morland's calculator
Known to have sold: calculating machine
Sources: Michel (1967) (MAC n)

SWAISLAND James
w 1851–1869
Math IM
Alternative name: SWAIZLAND
1851   55 Great Sutton St, Clerkenwell, London
1855–1869   54 Great Sutton St, Clerkenwell, London
Sources: PO; Wk

SWAN A.
a 1800–1850
    Edinburgh

Known to have sold: barometer
Sources: Goodison (1977) p.363

SWAN Alexander

w 1829–1836
1829   75 High St, Glasgow
1830   22 Gallowgate, Glasgow
1831   112 Gallowgate, Glasgow
1834–1836   106 Gallowgate, Glasgow
Sources: Bryden (1972) p.57

SWAN John

w 1821
Math IM
1821   London Rd, Leicester
1821   and 20 Little Tower St, London
See also
GILL Thomas★
LONG Joseph (I)★
Instrument advertised: 'barktometer' for tanning
Sources: Swan (1821)

SWANN Thomas

w 1790–1837
Quadrant M, Math IM
Alternative name: SWAN
            3 Mann's Island, Liverpool
1790   14 Strand St, Liverpool
1796   5 Murray Square, Atherton St,
            Liverpool
1800–1803   10 Gibralter Row, Canal, Liverpool
1807–1810   8 Freemason's Row, Liverpool
1810   31 Freemason's Row, Liverpool
1813–1815   37 Freemason's Row, Liverpool
1816–1820   43 Banastre St, Liverpool
1821   44 Banastre St, Liverpool
1821–1827   54 Banastre St, Liverpool
1823   64 Banastre St, Liverpool
1831–1834   2 Bridgewater Place, Liverpool
1837   3 Bridgewater Place, Liverpool
Instruments advertised: compass (magnetic),
octant, sand-glass, sextant, telescope
Sources: TCd SM; G (MAC); WB (MAC);
Calvert (1971) p.42

SWEENEY Roger

w 1770
Scale M
1770   Piper's Row, Wolverhampton
Sources: Sket

SWEENY Edward

w 1763–1772
Math IM
1763–1772   Cork
Son of SWEENY Nathaniel★
See also SWEENY widow
Sources: Burnett & Morrison-Low (1989)
p.156,157n

SWEENY Edward Nathaniel

w 1798
Math IM, Optical IM
1798   27 Patrick St, Cork
Sources: Burnett & Morrison-Low (1989)
p.156,157n

SWEENY Nathaniel

w 1763
Instrument M
            Cork
Father of SWEENY Edward
Sources: Burnett & Morrison-Low (1989)
p.156,157n

SWEENY Widow

w 1795
Instrument M
1795   Paul St, Cork
Sources: Burnett & Morrison-Low (1989) p.156

SWEETSOR C.

w 1851
Baro M
1851   3 & 5 Bell Court, Grays Inn Lane,
            London
See also SWEETZER Edward
Sources: Wk

SWEETZER Edward

w 1841
Baro M
1841   Beauchamp St, Holborn, London
See also SWEETSOR C.★
b c.1815 in foreign parts
Sources: PRO: Cs 1841 (AM)

SWETMAN James (I)

w 1707–1735
Rule M
Alternative name: SWEETMAN
1707   Glasshouse Yard, Minories, London
1711–1712   Minories, London
1725   Stepney, London
1730–1735   Pennington St, Ratcliffe Highway,
            London
Guild: Grocers, fr 1702
Apprenticed to HOWE William★ 1693/4
Had apprentice:
WRIGHT George 1707
REYNOLDS Thomas 1711/12
SWETMAN James (II)★, his son, 1722
SWETMAN John, his son, 1725
JARMAN Thomas 1729 by t/o from WRIGHT
George
Sources: PRO: IR 1/1 fol.62; Brown J (1979a) p.31

SWETMAN James (II)

w 1767
Math IM
1767   Parish of St. George, Middlesex
            (London)
Guild: Grocers, fr 1730
Son of SWETMAN James (I)★
Father of SWETMAN James (III)
S1767 BKC
Apprenticed to SWETMAN James (I)★ 1722
Sources: GL: BKC 2886/5 (MAC); Brown J
(1979a) p.31

SWITHIN James

w 1851
Math IM
1851   3 Holborn Bars, London
Succeeded by SWITHIN & CO James
Sources: PO; Wk

SWITHIN John

w 1739–1764
Scale M
Alternative name: I.
1744–1761   Long Lane, West Smithfield, London
1764   Long Acre, London
Guild: [Blacksmith], Haberdashers, fp 1738
Apprenticed to THOMPSON Daniel★ 1731
Had apprentice:
VINCENT Robert★ 1744
MOFFETT James★ 1748
LOARMAN Edwin 1751
CROOME Thomas★ 1751
LAMB William★ 1756
STINT Henry 1760
CROOK William 1761 t/o to LAMB William★
GOODWIN Thomas 1764
Succeeded by LAMB William★
d by 1767
Known to have sold: balance
Sources: GL: BKC 2886/4 (MAC); HC 15857/2,
15860/8, 15860/9 (MAC); CH 12823/4 p.2; inst
(pv)

SWYGART Joseph

w 1805–1849
Optician, Math IM, Phil IM
Alternative name: SUYGART, SUGGART
1805   10 Ely Court, Holborn, London
1839–1849   43 Edmund St, Battle Bridge,
            London
See also MACKENZIE & SWYGART★
Partnership 1816–1818?
Sources: H; Pg; PO

SYEDS Abraham

w 1834
Math IM
1834   379 Rotherhithe St, London
Took over from SYEDS & DAVIS★
Succeeded by SYEDS Agnes★
See also SYEDS & CO. A.★
Sources: Pg (JAC)

SYEDS Agnes (Mrs)

w 1834–1853
Compass M, Math IM, Phil IM, Naut IM
1834–1853   379 Rotherhithe, London
Wife of SYEDS John★
Took over from SYEDS Abraham★
Succeeded by SYEDS John Ramsey★ her son
See also
SYEDS & DAVIS★
SYEDS & CO. A.★
Sources: Stat: STC Memo Book 1816–1824 p.85
(MAC)

SYEDS John

w 1788–1811
Mariner, Compass M, Quadrant M
            25 Parker's Row, New Rd, Dock
            Head, Southwark, London
            367 Rotherhithe Wall, London
            17 Bermondsey Wall, London
1791   Mill St, Bermondsey, London
1802   17 Rotherhithe Wall, London
1805   Fountain Stairs, Rotherhithe Wall,
            London

Husband of SYEDS Agnes★
Succeeded by SYEDS & DAVIS★
See also
SYEDS & CO. A.★
SYEDS Abraham★
Pat. quadrant 1791, compass 1805
Known to have sold: compass, quadrant
Sources: Patent records (MAC); Stat: STC Memo
Book 1816–1824, p.85 (MAC); inst NMM, SM;
H; PO (JAC); Calvert (1971) p.42; Taylor (1966)
p.350–51

SYEDS John Ramsey
w 1851–1863
Math IM, Compass M
1851–1859   378 Rotherhithe, London
Guild: [Stationers]
Son of SYEDS John★ and
SYEDS Agnes★
Apprenticed to SMITH Samuel, bookbinder, 1820
Took over from SYEDS Agnes★
Sources: Stat: STC Memo Book 1816–1824 p.85
(MAC); PO; Wk; JAC

SYEDS & CO. A.
w 1817
Math IM
              379 Rotherhithe St, near King
              Stairs, London
1817   Fountain Stairs, Rotherhithe,
              London
See also
SYEDS Abraham★
SYEDS & DAVIS★
B.apt Navy
Sources: ChrSK 23 Oct 1987 lot 332 (TCd); J
(MAC); Calvert (1971) pl.48

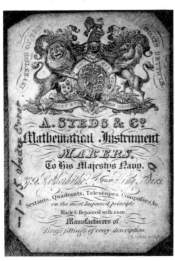

SYEDS & DAVIS
w 1812–1833
Math IM, Compass M, Ship Chandler
              Fountain Stairs, Rotherhithe,
              London
              Bermondsey Wall, London
1822–1833   379 Rotherhithe St, London
Took over from SYEDS John★

See also
SYEDS & CO. A.★
SYEDS Abraham★
Sources: Bn; Pg; PO (JAC)

SYM James (I)
w 1792–1816
Optical IM, Math IM
1792   Ayton Court, Old Venal, Glasgow
1799–1801   Bell St, Glasgow
1803–1808   2 Bell St, Glasgow
1806   16 Bell St, Glasgow
1807–1816   236 High St, Glasgow (intermittently)
1812–1814   266 High St, Glasgow
Son of SYM James (III)★ [probably]
Apprenticed to GARDNER John (I)★
Succeeded by SYM & CO. James★
Sources: H (MAC); Bryden (1972) p.30,57

SYM James (II)
w 1826–1846
Optical IM, Math IM
1826–1846   167 High St, Glasgow
See also
SYM James (I)★ [possibly the same person]
SYM & CO. James★
Sources: Pg; Bryden (1972) p.57

SYM James (III)
w em c.1770
Math IM
              Glasgow
Worked for WATT James★
See also SYM James (I)★
Sources: Bryden (1972) p.27,30

SYM & CO. James
w 1817–1825
Optical IM, Math IM
1817–1824   236 High St, Glasgow
1825   82–85 High St, Glasgow
Took over from SYM James (I)★
Succeeded by SYM James (II)★ (probably)
Sources: Bryden (1972) p.57

SYMMES Isaac
w 1604–1628
Goldsmith, Clock M
Alternative name: SUNES, SYMS, Issac, SIMES,
SIMMS, SIMMES
1604   Aldgate, London
1618   Houndsditch, London
Guild: Goldsmiths, fr 1603/4
Apprenticed to HUMFREY John nd, t/o to
BENNET Daniell
Had apprentice:
HOWE Jonas 1604
LINAKER Samuel 1610
HELDEN Onesiphorus 1615
HACKETT Simon 1622, t/o 1622 to
LINAKER/LINACRE Samuel
Known to have sold: sundial
Sources: GL: GSC index, Ct Minutes 13, p.322;
BSIS no.1 (1983) p.8; Heal (1935); Loomes (1981b)

SYMONS John
w 1801–1814
Math IM

Alternative name: SIMONS, SYMONDS
1801–1806   Salmon and Ball Court, Bunhill
              Row, London
1805   3 Salmon & Ball Court, Bunhill
              Row, London
1814   Founders Court, Lothbury, London
Guild: Grocers, fr 1800
Son of SYMONS William
Apprenticed to TROUGHTON John (II)★1779
Had apprentice:
HADNOT John 1801
RISE William 1806, t/o 1810 to LEE John of CWC
CURRY William 1814
Sources: GL: GC 11598/6; H

TABEAR William
w 1832–1836
Baro M, Thermo M
Alternative name: TABRAR
1832–1836   38 Laystall St, London
Sources: Pg (JAC); Goodison (1977) p.363

TADLOO Joseph
w 1829–1855
Scale M
Alternative name: TADLOW
1829–1855   75 Sun St, Bishopsgate, London
Guild: Blacksmiths, fr 1822
Apprenticed to NICHOLL William Lewis★ 1815
Had apprentice:
MARTIN John 1827
STIGWOOD John 1828
WAY John 1829 by t/o from SHURY Samuel (I)★
WINSBURY John 1835
CHAMPION Phillip 1836
EVANS George 1842
Took over from TADLOO Thomas★, his brother
Sources: GL: BKC 2881/17, 2881/18 (MAC); Pg
(MAC); PO (MAC); R (JAC)

TADLOO Thomas
w 1828
Scale M
1828   75 Sun St, Bishopsgate, London
Guild: [Blacksmiths]
Brother of TADLOO Joseph★
Apprenticed to NICHOLL William Lewis★ 1812
Succeeded by TADLOO Joseph★
Sources: GL: BKC 2881/17 (MAC); Kt (JAC)

TAGLIABUE Angelo
w 1832–1848
Baro M, Thermo M
1839   [Possibly directory error] 11 Leather
              Lane, Holborn, London
1835–1840   19 Leather Lane, London
1845–1848   3 Charles St, Hatton Garden, London
1841–1844   91 Leather Lane, Holborn, London
Partnership: TAGLIABUE A. & A.★
See also TAGLIABUE Antoni★
b c.1800 outside British Isles
Sources: Pg; PO; PRO: Cs 1841 (AM); Goodison
(1977) p.363;

TAGLIABUE Angelo & Antoni
w 1829–1831
Baro M, Thermo M
Alternative name: Angelo & Anthony

1829–1831 11 Brook St, Holborn, London
Took over from TAGLIABUE John (I)★
See also
TAGLIABUE Angelo★
TAGLIABUE Antoni★
Sources: PO; R

TAGLIABUE Antoni
w 1832–1848
Phil IM, Baro M, Thermo M
Alternative name: Anthony
1828 11 Brook St, Holborn, London
1832–1848 31 Brook St, Holborn, London
Partnership: TAGLIABUE Angelo & Antoni★
Succeeded by TAGLIABUE & CICERI★
Took over from TAGLIABUE Angelo & Antoni★
See also TAGLIABUE & CO. Antoni★
Attended London Mechanics Institute 1828
Sources: LMIR (AM); Pg; PO; R; Goodison (1977) p.363

TAGLIABUE Caesar
w 1799–1839
Optician, Baro M, Thermo M
Alternative name: Caesare
1822–1829 28 Cross St, Hatton Garden, London
1795–1800 294 Holborn, London
1807–1809 26 Holborn, London
1816 11 Brook St, Holborn, London
1829–1839 23 Hatton Garden, London
Father of TAGLIABUE Marie Louise, who m CASELLA Louis P.★ 1837
Partnership: TAGLIABUE & TORRE★
Employed CASELLA Louis Pascal★
Succeeded by TAGLIABUE & CASELLA★
See also TAGLIABUE, TORRE & CO.★
b near Como, Italy, 1767; partnerships 1801–05, 1806–14; d 1844
Known to have sold: barometer, hygrometer, thermometer
Sources: H; Pg; PO; R; Und; Goodison (1977) p.363; Casella (c.1960)

TAGLIABUE Catherine
w 1835–1839
Baro M, Thermo M
1839 11 Brook St, Holborn London
Succeeded by TAGLIABUE John (II)★
See also
TAGLIABUE Antoni★
TAGLIABUE Angelo★
Sources: Pg; PO

TAGLIABUE John (I)
w 1819–1828
Optician
1819–1828 11 Brook St, Holborn, London
Succeeded by TAGLIABUE Angelo & Antoni★
Took over from TAGLIABUE John & Joseph★
Sources: Bn; Kt (JAC)

TAGLIABUE John (II)
w 1826–1846
Baro M, Thermo M
1826–1828 44 Leather Lane, Holborn, London
1828–1834 38 Eyre Street hill, Hatton Garden, London
1829–1830 23 Hatton Garden, London

1833–1838 25 Eyre Street Hill, London
1839–1846 11 Brook St, London
Succeeded by TAGLIABUE & ZAMBRA★
Took over from TAGLIABUE Catherine★
See also TAGLIABUE & CO. John★
Same premises as TAGLIABUE Caesar★
b 1801 or 1802 outside the British Isles
Sources: Pg; PO; PRO: Cs 1841 (AM)

TAGLIABUE John and Joseph
w 1817–1823
Optician, Baro M, Phil IM
Alternative name: Joseph & John
1817–1823 11 Brook St, Holborn, London
Succeeded by TAGLIABUE John (I) in directories, 1819, but the name Joseph was included in an insurance policy 1823
Sources: J; Kt; GL: Sun 11936/489 no.999861

TAGLIABUE Joseph
w 1831
Baro M
1831 30 Eyre St Hill, London
See also TAGLIABUE John & Joseph★
Attended London Mechanics Institute 1831
Sources: LMIR (AM)

TAGLIABUE & CASELLA Caesar & Louis P.
w 1838–1846
Baro M, Thermo M
1838–1846 23 Hatton Garden, London
Succeeded by CASELLA & CO. Louis★
Took over from TAGLIABUE Caesar★
TAGLIABUE d 1844
Sources: Pg; PO; Casella (c.1960)

TAGLIABUE & CICERI Antonio & Francis
w 1842–1849
Baro M, Thermo M, Phil IM
1842–1849 31 Brook St, Holborn, London
Succeeded by TAGLIABUE & CO. Antoni★
Took over from TAGLIABUE Antoni★
Partnership officially dissolved 1842, but listed in directories 1849
Sources: PO; London Gazette, 1 Oct 1842 (AM)

TAGLIABUE & CO. Antoni
w 1850–1852
Baro M, Thermo M
1850–1852 31 Brook St, Holborn, London
Succeeded by GRIMOLDI & CO. H.★
Took over from TAGLIABUE & CICERI★
Sources: PO; Wk

TAGLIABUE & CO. Caesar
w 1806–1814
Optician, Baro M, Thermo M
1806–1814 26 High Holborn, London
Succeeded by TAGLIABUE Caesar★
Took over from TAGLIABUE Caesar★
Sources: Kt (JAC); PO

TAGLIABUE & CO. Charles
w 1835–1836
Baro M, Thermo M
11 Brook St, Holborn, London
Sources: Pg

TAGLIABUE & CO. John
w 1850–1851
Baro M, Thermo M
1851 11 Brook St, Holborn, London
Took over from TAGLIABUE & ZAMBRA★
See also TAGLIABUE John (II)★
Sources: Wk; London Gazette 4 Apr 1850 (AM)

TAGLIABUE & TORRE Caesar & Anthony Della
w 1801–1805
Optician
294 Holborn, London
Leigh St, Red Lion Square, London
Succeeded by TAGLIABUE & CO. Caesar★
Took over from TAGLIABUE Caesar★
See also TAGLIABUE, TORRE & CO.★
Known to have sold: barometer, thermometer
Sources: H (JAC); PO; Banfield (1993) p.82–86

TAGLIABUE & ZAMBRA John & Joseph Warren
w 1847–1850
Baro M, Thermo M, Phil IM
1847–1850 11 Brook St, Holborn, London
Succeeded by TAGLIABUE & CO. John★
Took over from TAGLIABUE John (II)★
Partnership dissolved April 1850
Sources: PO; London Gazette 4 Apr 1850 (AM)

TAGLIABUE, TORRE & CO. Caesar & ?
fl 1802
Opticians
294 Holborn, London
See also
TAGLIABUE & TORRE★
TAGLIABUE Caesar★
Known to have sold: barometer, thermometer
Sources: inst (s); Goodison (1977) p.364

TAILOR John (I)
w 1664–1680
Spec M
1671 Grub St, London
1676 St Annes Lane, London
Guild: Spectaclemakers
Had apprentice:
TAILOR Zachery★ his son, 1664
TAILOR John (II)★ his son, 1669
ROGERS Henry★ 1671
HARRIS John (I)★ 1677
d by Oct 1681
Known to have sold: spectacles
Sources: GL: SMC 5213/1

TAILOR John (II)
w 1683–1696
Spec M
Alternative name: TAYLOR
1683 Grub St, London
1693–1695 Old Bethlem, London
1695 Cheapside, London
Guild: Spectaclemakers, fr 1676
Brother of TAILOR Zachery★
Apprenticed to TAILOR John (I)★, his father, 1669
Had apprentice SEARES William 1683
Sources: GL: SMC 5213/1; CH 12876/2

TAILOR Mary (Mrs)
w 1681–1707
Spec M
Alternative name: TAYLOR
1683–1695   Maiden Lane, London
Guild: Spectaclemakers
Wife of TAILOR John (I)★
Had apprentice:
JONES William (V)★ 1695
BRAWN Samuel★ fr 1696
WEST George 1701
FORD Henry 1707, t/o nd to JONES William (V)★
Sources: GL: SMC 5213/1, 5213/2 p.5,24, 6031/1

TAILOR Zachery
w 1676–1678
Spec M
Alternative name: Zakry
1676   Backside Exchange, London
Guild: Spectaclemakers, fr 1671
Brother of TAILOR John (II)★
Apprenticed to TAILOR John (I)★, his father, 1664
Associated with HALE Widow★, whom he
supplied with spectacles
Sources: GL: SMC 5213/1

TAIT William
w 1710
Bismar M
             Kirkwall
Guild: Hammermen
Succeeded by FOUBISTER Thomas★
Took over from CRAIGIE George★
Deacon of Hammermen
Sources: Court Action of Alexander, Earl of
Galloway, 1757 p.226 & answers p.20 (MAC)

TALBOT John
w 1755
Math IM
1755   St.Katherine's, London
Guild: Barber Surgeons
Had apprentice TALBOT Francis, his son, 1755
Sources: GL: CH 12876/5 (MAC)

TALLMAN James
w 1695
Scale M
             The Sine of the Porrige Pot on
             London Bridge, London
There was a James Tallman active in Armourers &
Brasiers Co. 1680–1710, but address & trade were
not given
Known to have sold: balance
Sources: inst & TCd, ML; GL: ABC 12080/1; GL:
List of London Inhabitants 1695 (MAC)

TANGATE Robert (I)
w 1766 d 1808
Math IM, Optician
             9 West Square, London
1770–1773   Shoe Lane, Fleet St, London
1776   Bride Lane, FLeet St, London
1778   4 Bride Lane, London
1789–1794   Bride Lane, London
1800   42 Elliott's Buildings, St.George's
             Fields, London
Guild: Joiners, fr 1761

Apprenticed to
MORGAN John★ 1752
ADAMS George (I)★ by t/o 1758
Had apprentice:
DANCER Michael★ 1766
NEWMAN George ?★ 1769
CORLESS John★ 1773
CARD Charles★ 1776
TANGATE Robert (II), his son, 1781
LANE Thomas★, son of LANE Nicholas★, 1783
Sources: GL: JC 8052/7, 8055/3; A (JAC) Wil;
Crawforth (1987) p.367

TAPLEE Seymore
fp 1758 w 1768
Compass M
Alternative name: TAPLEY Seymour
1758   Old Street Square, London
Guild: Needlemakers, fp 1758
Son of TAPLEE Thomas, of NC of London
Brother of TAPLEE Thomas★
Had apprentice:
BARBER Thomas 1768
WINFIELD John 1765, by t/o from TAPLEE
Thomas★
Sources: GL: NC, 2817/1 fol.219, 2817/2
fol.22,31

TAPLEE Thomas
w 1760 d by 1778
Math IM
Alternative name: TAPLEY
1760   Old Street Square, London
Guild: Needlemakers, fp 1760
Father of TAPLEE (TAPLEY) Thomas
Son of TAPLEE Thomas
Brother of TAPLEE Seymore★
Had apprentice: WINFIELD John, 1760, t/o 1765
TO TAPLEE Seymore★
Sources: GL: NC 2817/1, 2817/2 fol.22; CKC
2720/1

TARELLI Anthony
w 1822–1853
Baro M, Thermo M, Toy Warehouse, Optician
Alternative name: Antonio
1827–1850   41 Dean St, Newcastle on Tyne
1836–1844   (residence) St.Nicholas Church
             Yard, Newcastle on Tyne
1847–1853   42 Dean St, Newcastle on Tyne
See also TARELLI & SON A.
Sources: Pg; Ric; Wim; Goodison (1977) p.364

TARELLI Charles
w 1830
Optician
1830   Wood Hill, Northampton
Known to have sold: barometer
Sources: Pg; Goodison (1977) p.364

TARLETON Richard
w 1786–1794
Watch M
1786   Liverpool
1794   31 Church St, Liverpool
Known to have sold: sundial
Sources: BW; Sby 15 Jul 1982 lot 23 (DJB)

TARONE Anthony
w 1818–1846
Baro M
1818–1829   37 Murraygate, Dundee
1834   32 Murraygate, Dundee
1840   12 Castle St, Dundee
1842   90 Nethergate, Dundee
1846   12 Murraygate, Dundee
Sources: Bryden (1972) p.57

TARONI George
w 1846–1848
Optician, Goldsmith, Silversmith, Watch M
1846–1848   62 Whitefriargate, Hull
See also TARONI Peter★
Sources: Stn; Wh

TARONI Peter
w 1848
Optician, Goldsmith, Silversmith, Watch M
1848   6 Savile St, Hull
See also TARONI George★
Sources: Stn

TARONI & LURAGHI
w 1829–1831
Baro M, Thermo M
1829–1831   9 City Road, opposite the Turnpike,
             London
Succeeded by LURAGHI F.★
Sources: R (JAC)

TARRONI J.B.
w 1830
Baro M, Thermo M
1830   Leeds
Sources: PWh (MAC)

TAUNTON Frederick Adolphus
w 1845–1849
Optician, Telescope M
1845   4 Norfolk St, Islington, London
1846   22 Norfolk St, Islington, London
             and Brown's Cottage, Canonbury
             Square, London
1849   Brown's Cottage, Canonbury
             Square, London
Sources: PO

TAUNTON Thomas
w 1805
Optician
1805   North Rd, Highgate, London
Sources: H (DJB)

TAVO Edward
w 1793–1818
Math IM
1793   Eastgate St, Chester
1816–1818   Bridge St, Chester
Sources: BW; Pg (MAC)

TAYLOR Edward
w 1826–1834
Optician, Math IM, Phil IM
Alternative name: Edmund ?
1826–1834   15 Whitehouse Yard, Drury Lane,
             London
Sources: Pg (JAC)

TAYLOR Elizabeth

w 1831
Optician
1831 17 Hemming's Row, St.Martin's Lane, London
Took over from TAYLOR John (II)★
See also TAYLOR Thomas★
Sources: R (JAC)

TAYLOR George

w 1835–1835
Navigation warehouse, Math IM
Alternative name: George TAYLOR-JANE
1831 6 East St, Red Lion Square, London
1835–1845 103 Minories, London
1845–1846 104 Minories, London
1848 [Residence] 1 Hammet St, Minories, London
Father of
TAYLOR Herbert Peter, s 1846 CWC
TAYLOR Henry Frederick, s 1848 CWC
Husband of TAYLOR Mrs Janet★
Succeeded by TAYLOR Janet★
See also TAYLOR I. & J.★
Publisher; d 1853
Sources: Pg; CWH: CWC Ap; Alger (1982) p.8–23

TAYLOR James (I)

fl 1830 w 1833
Magnet M
1833 Division Lane, Sheffield
Sources: Wh (MAC)

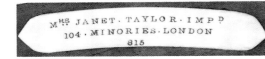

TAYLOR Janet (Mrs)

w 1835 p 1875
Math IM, Naut IM, Publisher, Chart S, Navigation School
Alternative name: nee Jane Ann IONN
1831–1835 6 East St, Red Lion St, London
1835–1845 103 Minories, London
    1 Fen Court, Fenchurch St, London
1845 Nautical Academy & Warehouse, 103–4 Minories, London
1845–1875 104 Minories, London
1846–1858 [Residence] 1 Hammet St, Minories, London
1858 [Residence] Park Place, The Grove, Camberwell, London
Wife of TAYLOR George★
Daughter of IONN Revd Peter
Had apprentice: WIGGINS Frederick
Employed
REYNOLDS William
WIGGINS Frederick
Succeeded by TAYLOR & CO. Janet
Took over from TAYLOR George★
See also TAYLOR I. & J.
Associated with DENT Edward J.★ as agent
Author; pat mariner's calculator 1834; Ex 1851; b 1804 d 1870

Known to have sold: barometer, compass (magnetic), octant, sextant
Sources: PO; Alger (1982); TCd & inst NMM

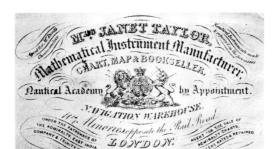

TAYLOR John (I)

w 1780
Pocket steelyard M
1780 Bilston, Staffs
Sources: PR

TAYLOR John (II)

w 1802–1830
Optician, Math IM
    1 Castle St, Leicester Square, London
    3 Hemming's Row, St.Martin's Lane, London
    30 White Lion St, Pentonville, London
1822 17 Hemming's Row, St.Martin's Lane, London
Succeeded by TAYLOR Elizabeth★
See also TAYLOR Thomas★
Sources: Bn (MAC); H; R (JAC)

TAYLOR Robert (I)

w 1717
Book S, Printer, Instrument S, Auctioneer
1717 High Market Place, Berwick on Tweed
Instruments advertised: compass, gunter scale, quadrant, slide rule, telescope
Sources: TCd SM; Calvert (1971) p.42

TAYLOR Robert (II)

w 1790–1793
Spec M
1790–1793 17 Hemming's Row, St.Martin's Lane, London
Guild: [possibly Grocers, fr 1769]
Apprenticed to possibly RUST Richard★ 1758
Succeeded by TAYLOR Thomas★
See also
TAYLOR Elizabeth★
TAYLOR John (III)★
Sources: BW; By; Brown J (1979a) p.45

TAYLOR Samuel

w 1805–1810
Optician
1805–1810 28 Parliament St, Liverpool
Sources: LM index (MAC)

TAYLOR Thomas

w 1782–1819
Optician
1782–1788 17 Castle St, Leicester Fields, London
1805–1819 17 Hemming's Row, St.Martin's Lane, London
Had apprentice PARKER James (II)★
Succeeded by TAYLOR John (II)★
See also
TAYLOR Robert (II)★
TAYLOR Elizabeth★
Sources: GL: Sun 11936/298 no.454238; CH 12876/6; H (MAC); J; Kt (JAC)

TAYLOR William (I)

w 1824–1840
Optician, Math IM
    13 Chamber St, Goodman's Fields, London
    24 Norfolk St, Middlesex Hospital, London
    29 Norfolk St, Newman St, London
1824 11 Little Newport St, London
Sources: Kt (JAC)

TAYLOR William (II)

w 1687–1703
Scale M
    Ye Hand & Scales in St.Ann's Lane by Aldersgate, London
Guild: Blacksmiths, fr 1662 or 1663
Had apprentice:
ROBERTS Timothy★ 1786/7
LIND Joseph★ 1693
HARDING Nathaniel nd by t/o from REDHEAD William★
There were other possible apprentices, but there were two William Taylors with overlapping dates in BKC
Known to have sold: balance
Sources: GL: BKC 2881/9, 2881/10, 2884 (MAC); BM: Heal (MAC n); inst (pv) (MAC)

TAYLOR William (III)

w 1739
Scale M
1739 George Yard, Old St, London
Sources: HAC records (JT)

TEATLEY Robert

w 1764
1764 Fleet St, London
Error for FEATLEY Robert★
Sources: Court & von Rohr (1929–30) p.84

TELFER & AFLECK William & Alexander

w 1799–1802
Math IM
1799 Hutcheson St, Glasgow
Associated with PARKER Thomas★
Pats. for textile manufacturing 1801 & 1802
Known to have sold: hydrostatic bubbles

Sources: ChrSK 13 Dec 1984 lot 103; Bryden (1972) p.57

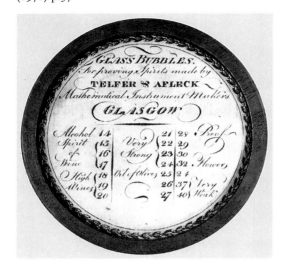

TENNANT George
w 1813–1817
Math IM
1813–1817   126 Wapping, London
Partnership: CULMER & TENNANT★
Sources: PO (JAC)

TESTI A.
w 1809
Baro M, Thermo M
1809   32 Baldwin's Gardens, Leather Lane,
London
Sources: H (JAC)

THISTLEWOOD William
w 1828–1846
Optician, Math IM, Sexton
1828–1831   53 Limekiln Lane, Liverpool
1834   115 Vauxhall Rd, Liverpool
1839–1841   216 Vauxhall Rd, Liverpool
1843–1846   218 Vauxhall Rd, Liverpool
Sources: G (MAC)

THOMAS Daniel
fr 1682 w 1711
Math IM, Clock M
-1711   In the Minories, London
Guild: Clockmakers, fr 1682
Apprenticed to BROWN John (I)★ 1675
Sources: GL: CKC 3939; Post Man 30 Oct 1711
(MAC); Loomes (1981b)

THOMAS George
w 1790–1802
Compass M, Math IM
1790–1801   Deptford Dockyard, London
Guild: Goldsmiths, fr 1790
Apprenticed to SAUNDERS Samuel (II)★
Had apprentice:
LISSETT John 1790
THOMAS George, his son, 1795
WALKER James 1797
THOMAS George Richard, his son, 1800
ADAMS Richard, son of John, 1801

Took over from SAUNDERS Samuel (II)★
Sources: GH: GSc Ap, Fr; Taylor (1966) p.298

THOMAS H. J.
fl 1830
[Optician]
1830   Henrietta St, Cavendish St, York
Sources: Taylor (1966) p.462

THOMAS John
w 1773
Pewterer, Bazier, Scale M
Alternative name: I.T.
1773   Near the Cross, Chester
Sources: Adam's Weekly Courant, Chester, 5 Oct
1773 p.3 (JRM)

THOMAS William
w 1805
Math IM
1805   63 Chalton St, Somerstown, London
Sources: H (MAC)

THOMPSON –
w 1769
Math IM
1769   Star Court, Butcher Row near
Temple Bar, London
Sources: The Annual Register for the Year 1769
(1770) p.140–41 (JRM)

THOMPSON A.
w 1817
Measure M
1817   9 King St, Goswell St, London
Sources: J

THOMPSON Anthony
w 1645 d 1665
Math IM (in both brass and wood)
Alternative name: TOMPSON, THOMSON,
Antonius
1645–1664   Hosier Lane, West Smithfield,
London
1663   Smithfield, London
Guild: Stationers, fr 1634
Son of THOMPSON William, gent, of Hatfield,
Herts
Apprenticed to THOMPSON John (I)★
Had apprentice:
VICARS Pattison 1653/4
FAGE Edward★ 1657
THOMSON Thomas, son of Thomas, 1666
Took over from THOMPSON John (I)★
Succeeded by FAGE Edward★
Associated with ALLEN Elias★ and
HAYES Walter★ in advertising
Known to have sold: quadrant, sundial
Sources: Monconys (1666) p.74; Bryden (1992)
p. 310,315; McKenzie (1961) p.127, (1974) p.165;
Taylor (1954) p.220–21, 358–59

THOMPSON Daniel
w 1727 d.c 1745
Scale M
1731–1741   Behind ye Conduit, Snow Hill,
London
Guild: Blacksmiths, fr 1718/19

Apprenticed to HUX Thomas (II)★ 1708
Had apprentice:
SWITHIN John★ 1731
GOODMAN John★ 1741
Other possible apprentices, but there were two
Masters of the same name
Succeeded by THOMPSON John (II)★
Known to have sold: balance
Instruments advertised: balance
Sources: GL: BKC 2881/10, 2881/11, 2886/4,
2886/5 (MAC); CH 12876/3, 12876/4 (MAC);
BM: Heal (MAC n)

THOMPSON Edward
w 1829–1832
Measure M
1829   21 Old St, St.Lukes, London
1832   25 Commercial St., Lambeth,
London
See also THOMPSON & SON★
Sources: R (JAC)

THOMPSON I.
w 1826
Math IM
1826   30 High St, Wapping, London
See also
THOMPSON Jonathan★
THOMPSON Joseph★
Sources: R (JAC)

THOMPSON Isaac (I)
fl 1672–1695
Instrument M, Engineer
1675   Bedford St, near Covent Garden,
London
1676   The Sign of the Engine, against
Montague House, Great Russell St,
Bloomsbury, London
Worked for MORLAND Samuel, Master Mechanic
to Charles II
Took over from MORLAND Samuel
Known to have sold: quadrant
Sources: Taylor (1954) p.266

THOMPSON Isaac (II)
w 1704
[Math IM]
London
Guild: Joiners, fr 1701/2
Son of THOMPSON Isaac, shoemaker, of London
Apprenticed to CROOKE John (I)★ 1694
Had apprentice MAILE William 1704
Sources: GL: JC 8052/3; Crawforth (1987) p.367

THOMPSON Jeremiah
fr 1699
Scale M
Alternative name: THOMSON
1699   Angel Alley, London
Guild: Blacksmiths, fr 1699
Son of THOMSON William, mercer, of
Loughborough, Leics
Apprenticed to
NEALE Samuel★ 1690
GROVE Christopher★ 1692 by t/o
Sources: GL: BKC 2881/11, 2882/2, 2886/3
(MAC)

THOMPSON John (I)
w 1610–1662
Math IM (in wood)
Alternative name: TOMSON, TOMPSON, Iohn,
1611–1645   Hosier Lane, West Smithfield,
                    London
Guild: Stationers, 1609/10
Father of THOMPSON John fp 1649
Apprenticed to
STUCKY Thomas★ 1586 & prob t/o to
READ John (I)★ who freed him
Had apprentice:
GALL Raffe 1610
COLLINS William 1612
NOBLE Nathaniel★ 1616
YOUNGE Symon 1619
LANCASTER Timothy 1619
THOMPSON Anthony★ 1626
NUTTALL (NUTHALL) Thomas 1631
BEDFORD Helkia (Hilkiah)★ 1646
READING William 1642
Succeeded by THOMPSON Anthony★
Associated with ALLEN Elias★ in advertising
Known to have sold: rule
Instruments advertised: Gunters scale, sector
Sources: Arber (1875) 2, p.142; Bryden (1992)
pp.306,308,318; Calvert (1971) p.42; McKenzie
(1961) p.111,126–27, (1974) p.164; Taylor (1954)
p.195,200

THOMPSON John (II)
w 1714–1772
Scale M
                    Behind ye Conduit, Snow Hill,
                    London
Guild: Blacksmiths, fr 1702
Apprenticed to
JENKS Edmund★ 1694
NEALE John (I)★ 1697 by t/o
Had apprentice:
GROVES Thomas 1714
GILL William 1715
THOMPSON Joseph 1741 by t/o from PHILIPS
William
GOODMAN John★ 1745 by t/o from THOMPSON
Daniel★
THOMPSON John, his son, 1746, fr 1760
TOOGOOD James 1748
RUDDLE William 1755
NEWMAN Samuel★ 1756
THORY Thomas 1758
COXHEAD John 1765
MCCRAIGHT John Charles★ 1768
Other possible apprentices, but there was another
master of the same name from 1721
Took over from THOMPSON Daniel★
Employed GOODMAN John★ 1748–1772
Partnership: THOMPSON & GOODMAN★
Known to have sold: balance
Sources: GL: BKC 2881/9, 2886/3–5, 2885/1
(MAC); CWH: CWC Fr; inst & TCd (pv) (MAC)

THOMPSON John (III)
w 1817–1822
Math IM
1817–1822   16 Webb St, Bermondsey St,
                    London
Sources: Und

THOMPSON John (IV)
w 1835–1844
Optical IM, Math IM, Phil IM, Surgical IM, Lath
M, Tool M
1835   26 Glasshouse St, Nottingham
1839–1844   Pelham St, Nottingham
Sources: Pg; Wh (MAC)

THOMPSON John (V)
w 1779
Math IM
1779   Near St.Lukes Hospital, Upper
                    Moorfields, London
Sources: GL: Sun 11936/275 no. 414874

THOMPSON John (VI)
a 1830–1860
Optician, Phil IM, Math IM
                    Manchester St, Liverpool
                    & 85 Lord St, Liverpool
Sources: TCd (pv) (MAC n)

THOMPSON John (VII)
w 1613–1624
Trade not known, but master of two known Spec
M
Alternative name: TOMPSON
                    London
Guild: Brewers, fr 1612
Son of THOMPSON Thomas, farmer, of Shepshed,
Leics
Apprenticed to POLSON Richard★ 1605
Had apprentice:
GROVE John 1613
MARBECKE Edward 1614
BAILEY John★ 1615
PEALE Thomas★ 1615
CONNY Robert 1617/18
HOSIER Nathaniel 1619
Sources: GL: Brew 5445/12 & /13

THOMPSON Jonathan
w 1805–1827
Math IM, Optician, Compass M
                    34 Wapping St, Wapping, London
1805–1816   124 Cock Hill, Ratcliff, London
1822   36 Wapping, London
Succeeded by THOMPSON Joseph★
See also THOMPSON I.★
Sources: H (MAC); Pg; Und; JAC

THOMPSON Joseph
w 1827–1838
Optical IM, Phil IM, Math IM
1827–1838   36 High St, Wapping, London
Took over from THOMPSON Jonathan★
Succeeded by THOMPSON Joseph Berry★
See also THOMPSON I.★
Sources: Pg

THOMPSON Joseph Berry
w 1839–1848
Math IM, Phil IM
1839–1848   36 High St, Wapping, London
Took over from THOMPSON Joseph★
Succeeded by THOMPSON Louisa (Mrs)★
Sources: PO

THOMPSON Louisa (Mrs)
w 1849–1850
1849–1850   36 High St, Wapping, London
Took over from THOMPSON Joseph Berry★
Sources: PO

THOMPSON Samuel (I)
w 1687–1712
Spec M
Alternative name: TOMSON
1693   Bedfordbury, London
Guild: Spectaclemakers, fr 1687
Had apprentice:
BRICE John 1694
ARCHER Thomas★ 1700
SHARPE Dorothy 1712
fr in SMC by purchase
Sources: GL: SMC 5213/1, 5213/2 p.21, 6031/1

THOMPSON Samuel (II)
w 1770
Optician
Alternative name: TOMPSON
1770   In a yard between 18 & 19 Dudley
                    St, Birmingham
Sources: Sket (MAC)

THOMPSON Simon
w 1805–1844
Compass M, Brazier, Stove M, Telescope Tube M,
Optician, Optical IS
1805–1816   Old Broad Row, Yarmouth, Norfolk
1830–1844   Broad Row, Yarmouth, Norfolk
Sources: H (MAC); Pg; Wh

**THOMPSON & GOODMAN John (II) &
John**
w 1772
Scale M
                    London
GOODMAN John★ was described as 'partner and
foreman to Mr Thompson the elder who resides in
Hampshire' when apprentice COXHEAD John was
freed in 1772
See also THOMPSON John (II)★
Sources: GL: BKC 2886/5 (MAC)

THOMPSON & SON
w 1829
Measure M
1829   33 King St, Clerkenwell, London
See also
THOMPSON Edward★
THOMSON Henry★
Sources: R (JAC)

THOMS William
w 1849
Chem Apparatus M
1849   289 Strand, London
Burrows & Thoms, operative chemists, were at
this address in 1846
Sources: PO

THOMSON Henry
w 1832
Measure M
1832   33 King St, Clerkenwell, London

See also THOMPSON & SON★
Sources: R (JAC)

THOMSON T.
w 1805–1809
Glass blower
1805   Cowgate, Edinburgh
Known to have sold: barometer
Sources: NMSn (MAC)

THOMSON William
w 1849
Clock M, Watch M, Naut IM
1849   82 Shore, Leith
Sources: POE (MAC)

THORNDIKE William Samuel
w 1837–1855
Math IM, Phil IM,
Alternative name: THORNDYKE
1837   17 Britannia Row, Islington, London
1837   4 Myrtle St, Highbury Vale, London
1839   43 Galway St, City Rd, London
1840–1849   2 Eagle St, City Rd, London
Guild: Merchant Taylors, fr 1836
Apprenticed to LEFEVER Thomas★
Had apprentice:
WHEELER Thomas 1837
JOLEMAN James W. H. 1840
ROSE William 1841
Sources: GL: MTC MF 320, 324 (MAC); Pg; PO

THORNTHWAITE William Henry
w pt 1845–1878
Optician
1846   123 Newgate St, London
1878   416 Strand, London
Guild: Spectaclemakers, fr 1846
Father of THORNTHWAITE Wm Henry
Son of THORNTHWAITE George, gent, of Hoxton
Square, Middx
Partnership:
HORNE, THORNTHWAITE & WOOD★
HORNE & THORNTHWAITE
fr by purchase in SMC
Sources: GL: SMC 5213/6, 5213/8; PO

THOROWGOOD Edward
w 1668–1690
Math IM
            London
Guild: Plumbers, Clockmakers
Son of THOROWGOOD Martin, free of PC of
London
Had apprentice BEARD Cornelius 1670, t/o 1672
to ATKINSON James (I)★
fp 1668 PC, fr as Brother of CKC 1668/9
Sources: GL: PC 2209/1; CKC 2710/1 p.199,249;
Loomes (1981b)

THORPE James
w 1825–1854
Optician
1825   18 Westbar Green, Sheffield
1830–1834   17 Westbar Green, Sheffield
1837   42 Westbar Green, Sheffield
1854   21 Westbar Green, Sheffield
Sources: Bk (MAC); Ge (MAC); K (MAC); Pg; Wh

THROGMORTON James
w 1682–1716
Spec M
Alternative name: THROCKMORTON
1693–1695   The Minories, London
Guild: Spectaclemakers, fr 1677
Apprenticed to THROGMORTON John (I)★, his
father, 1669
Had apprentice:
MATHEWS Job 1682 by t/o from MATHEWS
Jeremy★
NORTH John c.1683 [fr 1697]
DAVIS John (IV)★ c.1683
HOW Joseph 1697
Master SMC 1688–1689, 1695–1697
Sources: GL: SMC 5213/1, 5213/2 p.9; 6031/1

THROGMORTON John (I)
w 1669–1693
Spec M
1669   Tower Hill, London
1693   St Katherine's, London
Guild: Spectaclemakers, fr 1669
Apprenticed to JENKINSON John★ 1644
Had apprentice:
THROGMORTON James★, his son, 1669
PINFOLD Robert 1676/7 by t/o from HAWES
John★
STERROP Richard 1677
THROGMORTON John (II)★, his son, 1682, t/o
PEALE Anne★
Master SMC 1681–1682
Sources: GL: SMC 5213/1

THROGMORTON John (II)
w 1695–1705
Spec M
Alternative name: THROCKMORTON
1695   Hermitage, London
Guild: [Spectaclemakers]
Son of THROGMORTON John (I)★
Apprenticed to
THROGMORTON John (I)★ 1682
PEALE Ann★ apparently by t/o 1682
Sources: GL: SMC 5213/1, 5213/2 p.43

THURLEBOURNE –
w 1744
Instrument S
1744   Cambridge
Associated with MARTIN Benjamin★
Sources: Millburn (1976) p.40

THURLOW
w 1848–1878
1848–1878   Ryde, Isle of Wight
Known to have sold: barometer (prob)
Sources: NT: Knighthayes Court, Devon; Loomes
(1976)

THURMAN Joseph
c 1754 d by 1768
Scale M
            Parish of St Catherine Cree Church,
            London
Possibly apprentice of JOY John★
Father of THURMAN Joseph s 1768 SKC
Sources: SH:SKC Ap/Fr

TICKELL G.
w 1827–1840
Optician
1827–1828   74 Great Britain St, Dublin
1829–1840   24 Upper Sackville St, Dublin
Sources: Burnett & Morrison-Low (1989) p. 137

TICKELL George
w 1840
Optician
1840   48 Beresford St, Dublin
See also TICKELL G. [possibly the same maker]
Sources: Burnett & Morrison-Low (1989) p.138

TICKET Joseph
w 1843 d 1888
Rule M
Alternative name: TIQUET, TICQUET, TICKETT,
TICKAT
1843   25 Mape St, Bethnal Green, London
1847   2 Albert St, Stepney, London
Sources: Birth & Death Certificates of family (WJ)

TIDDER Rowland
w 1793–1799
Math IM
1791   7 Butlers Buildings, East Smithfield,
            London
1793   East Smithfield, London
Guild: Grocers, fr 1791
Son of TIDDER Joseph, gun smith, of St
Catherine's, London
Apprenticed to
MORRIS William★ 1783
BRADLEY James by t/o 1786
Had apprentice:
COLLISON John 1793
JOLIFFE William 1799
Sources: Brown (1979a) p.53; GL: GC 11598/5

TILEY Thomas
w 1827–1828
Math IM
1827–1828   Blackfriars Rd, London
Attended London Mechanics Institute 1827–1828
Sources: LMIR (AM)

TIMMING John
w 1836
Optician
1836   65 Skinner St, Bishopsgate, London
See also TIMMINS John★ [possibly the same
person]
Sources: R (JAC)

TIMMINS John
w 1836
Spectacle M
1836   7 Catherine Wheel Alley, Widegate
            St, London
See also TIMMING John★ [possibly the same
person]
Sources: Pg (JAC)

TIMMINS Joseph
w 1829–1835
Spec M
1829–1830   66 Great Charles St, Birmingham

1835   3 Court, Kenion St, Birmingham
Apprenticed to JACOB Christopher★
See also TIMMINS Thomas (II)★
Sources: Pg (MAC); Wr (DJB); Aris 20 Jul & 23
Nov 1761 (MAC)

TIMMINS Richard

w 1797–1818
Compass M, Pincer M
1797–1818   Hurst St, Birmingham
Succeeded by TIMMINS & SONS Richard ★
Sources: Chp (AL); H; Pg; PR (MAC); Und

TIMMINS Thomas (I)

w 1777–1801
Optician, Victualler
1777   1 Old Hinckleys, Birmingham
1780   Pinfold St, Birmingham
1800–1801   19 Fleet St, Birmingham
See also
TIMMINS Thomas (II)★
TIMMINS Joseph★
Sources: Chp (DJB); PR (MAC)

TIMMINS Thomas (II)

w 1780–1818
Optician
1780   14 Smallbrook St, Birmingham
1785   Brick Kiln Lane, Birmingham
1801   Harborne, near Birmingham
1815–1818   Bromsgrove St, Birmingham
See also
TIMMINS Thomas (I)★
TIMMINS Joseph★
Sources: Chp; H (DJB); PR (MAC); Pye (MAC);
Wr

TIMMINS Thomas (III)

w 1820–1833
Optician
1820–1827   6 Bridewell Lane, Bristol
1823–1824   Lower Castle St, Bristol
1825–1827   Broad Weir, Bristol
1828–1833   33 Lower Arcade, Bristol
Sources: Mat; Pg

TIMMINS & SONS Richard

w 1821–1825
Compass M, Pincer M, Heavy Steel Toy M
1821   Hurst St, Birmingham
1823–1825   56 Hurst St, Birmingham
Took over from TIMMINS Richard★
Known to have made: compass
Sources: Wr (AL); inst (pv) (MAC n)

TINGAY Gregory

w 1678–1686
Spec M
       London
Guild: Spectaclemakers, fr 1675
Son of TINGAY Gregory, maltster, of Ware, Herts
Apprenticed to HASLOM Henry★ 1668 taken over
by HASLOM widow★ 1673
Had apprentice:
SPRATT Thomas★ 1679
PATISHALL James 1682
Master SMC 1685–1686
Sources: GL: SMC 5213/1

TITFORD Richard Vandome

fr 1834 w pt 1840
Scale M
1834   117 Leadenhall St, London
Guild: Blacksmiths, fr 1834
Apprenticed to VANDOME Richard★ 1827
Related to VANDOME Richard★ (? his great-uncle)
TITFORD William★ (cousin)
Partnership:
VANDOME TITFORDS & PAWSON
VANDOME TITFORD & CO.★
Sources: GL: BKC 2881/17; ART, family records

TITFORD William

w pt 1841–1866
Scale M
1856   117 Leadenhall St, London
1856   & 56 Leadenhall St, London
Related to
VANDOME Richard★ (? his great-uncle)
TITFORD Richard Vandome★
Partnership: VANDOME, TITFORD & CO.★
Bap 1810; d 1882
Sources: ART, family records

TOBIAS Morris

fl 1804–1846
Watch M, Chrono M, Clock M
       63 Bell Dock Yard, Wapping, London
1839–1846   31 Minories, London
See also
LEVITT & TOBIAS★
TOBIAS & LEVITT★
Pat. chronometer 1812
Sources: inst NMM; Pg; PO; Baillie (1951); Taylor
(1966) p.377; Woodcroft (1854)

TOBIAS & LEVITT

fl 1817–1836
Watch M, [Chrono M]
1826–1836   31 Minories, London
Sources: Baillie (1951); Taylor (1966) p.377

TOCHETTI Charles

w 1825–1828
Optician, Picture frame M
1825   62 Queen St, Aberdeen
1827–1828   18 Queen St, Aberdeen
1827–1828   Henderson's Court, 64 Broad St,
       Aberdeen (residence)
Succeeded by TOCHETTI & CO. Charles★
Known to have sold: barometer, thermometer
Sources: ADCS; Goodison (1977) p.366

TOCHETTI & CO. Charles

w 1829–1831
Optician, Picture frame M
1829   59 Broad St, Aberdeen
1831   70 Broad St, Aberdeen
Took over from TOCHETTI Charles★
Sources: ADCS

TOD Charles

w 1820
Math IM
1820   99 Nicolson St, Edinburgh
See also TOD S★
Sources: Pg (MAC)

TOD George

w 1805
Surveyor, Hot-house builder, Thermo M
1805   King's Rd, Chelsea, London
Sources: H (MAC)

TOD S.

a 1800–1850
       Edinburgh
See also TOD Charles★
Known to have sold: barometer, hygrometer,
thermometer
Sources: Goodison (1977) p.366

TODD John

w 1820–1834
Scale M
Alternative name: TOD
1820–1834   10 Thistle St, Glasgow
Guild: Hammermen, fr 1821
Known to have sold: balance
Sources: Pg (MAC); Lumsden & Aitken (1912)
p.308

TODD Thomas

w 1834
Brazier, Mariner's Compass Manufacturer
1834   14 Bull Ring, North Shields,
       Northumberland
Sources: Pg

TOGNIETTI & CO. G.

a 1800–1820
       Worcester
Known to have sold: barometer
Sources: Goodison (1977) p.366

TOLLEY Edward

w 1833–1850
Optician, Phil IM, Math IM, Spec M
1833–1840   8 Tavistock Row, Covent Garden,
       London
1846   32 Henrietta St, Covent Garden,
       London
1849   28 New Church Court, Strand,
       London
Sources: Pg; PO; JAC

TOMKINSON Joseph

w 1842
Phil IM
1842   11 Foley St, Portland Place, London
Attended London Mechanics Institute 1842
Sources: LMIR (AM)

TOMLINSON James (I)

w 1741–1773
Spec M, Optical IM
       London
Guild: Spectaclemakers, fr 1739
Son of TOMLINSON Joseph, cooper, of Corby,
Lincs
Apprenticed to LOFT Matthew★ 1725
Had apprentice:
WATKINS Thomas, son of John, 1746
FORSKETT Robert★ 1751
STREET Daniel 1752 by t/o from COMBES
Oliver★

GREGORY Samuel 1755
CARTER James 1758
GODIN Nicholas 1767, t/o to his father, 1767
Employed TOMLINSON James, his nephew, 1756
Associated with
DEANE David★, as fellow apprentice
NAIRNE Edward★ and
WATKINS Francis (I)★ on court of SMC
WATT James★, who bought optical inst for re-sale
1741 Had to apologise to SMC for employing persons who were not free; Master SMC 1764–1769; d 1777
Sources: GL: SMC 5213/3 p.2,30,106,162,182, 211+, 5213/2 p.154+; Bryden (1972) p.34n

TOMLINSON James (II)
w 1789–1790
Optician
1789–1790   44 Aldersgate St, London
See also
TOMLINSON Mary★
TOMLINSON James (I)★
Sources: GL: SMC 5213/3; A (JAC)

TOMLINSON Mary
w 1789–1790
Optician
1789–1790   44 Aldersgate St, London
See also TOMLINSON James (II)★
Sources: A (JAC)

TOMLINSON & BICKLEY
w 1793–1812
Factors, Paper M
Alternative name: T. & B.
1793–1812   Moor St, Birmingham
Known to have sold: balance
Sources: inst, York Mu (MAC); BW; Sy (MAC); Wr (MAC)

TOMPION Thomas
w 1671–1703
Clock M
1674   Water Lane, near Fleet St, London
-1711   Dial & Three Crowns, corner of
              Water Lane, Fleet St, London
Guild: Clockmakers Brother 1671, Freeman 1674
Partnership:
TOMPION & GRAHAM★
TOMPION & BANGER★
Had apprentice:
BANGER Edward★ 1687 by t/o from ASHBY Joseph
DELANDER Daniel★ by t/o 1695 from HALSTEAD C.
MERCER Edward by t/o 1695 from LEE Cuthbert
At least 22 other apprentices known only as Clock M
Employed
GRAHAM George★
DELANDER Daniel★
BANGER Edward★
Succeeded by TOMPION & BANGER★
b 1639, d 1713; Master CKC 1703–1704
Known to have sold: astronomical clock, barometer, mural quadrant, planetarium, sundial, telescope
Sources: GL: CKC 2710/3 fol.44; 3939; CLRO: CF 1/143; inst BM, ML, NMM, Pump Room at

Bath; Bryden (1992) p.309; Goodison (1977) p.248–57; King & Millburn (1978) p.122–24; Loomes (1981b)

TOMPION & BANGER Thomas & Edward
w c.1703–1708
Clock M
              Dial & Three Crowns, Corner of
              Water Lane, Fleet St, London
Partnership of TOMPION★ with his former apprentice BANGER Edward ★
BANGER married Tompion's niece, but the two men quarrelled and their partnership ended
Sources: King & Millburn (1978) p.124,126; Loomes (1981b)

TOMPION & GRAHAM Thomas & George
w 1711–1713
1711–1713   Dial & Three Crowns, corner of
              Water Lane, Fleet St, London
Guild: Clockmakers
See also
TOMPION Thomas★
GRAHAM George★
Tompion d 1713
Known to have sold: planetarium
Sources: inst MHS; King & Millburn (1978) p.152; Loomes (1981b)

TOMPON Samuel
w 1773–1775
Optician
1773–1775   19 Dudley St, Birmingham
Sources: Sy (MAC)

TONGUE William
w 1767–1825
Scale M, Gun lock M, Engineer, Silversmith, Toy M, Japanner
Alternative name: W.T.
1767–1781   43 Snow Hill, Birmingham
1793   Livery St, Birmingham
1797–1812   Weaman St, Birmingham
1812   and Keay Hill, Birmingham
1816–1822   22 High St, Birmingham
1816–1822   Bordesley St, Birmingham
1825   20 High St, Birmingham
Known to have sold: balance, weights
Instruments advertised: balance, weights
Sources: Bn; BW; Pg; PR (MAC); Pye (MAC) Sket, Sy; Und; Wr; advertisement in TWr 1812

TOOGOOD Elizabeth
w 1693–1700
              London
Guild: Joiners
Wife of TOOGOOD John★
Took over from TOOGOOD John★
Had apprentice BARTLETT William 1700
Supplied math inst to Christ's Hospital School
Sources: GL: CH 12823/2 p.288–89; Crawforth (1987) p.368

TOOGOOD John
w 1682 d c. 1693
Math IM

Alternative name: TOGOOD
              London
Guild: Joiners, fr 1678
Husband of TOOGOOD Elizabeth★
Apprenticed to SUTTON William (I)★ 1669
Had apprentice:
COOKE Thomas (II)★ 1682
CROOKE John (I)★ 1684
ROSE John 1688
Succeeded by TOOGOOD Elizabeth★
Supplied math inst to Christ's Hospital School
Sources: GL: CH 12823/1 p.112, 117–18; /2 p.287; Crawforth (1987) p.368

TOOKE Christopher
w 1609 d 1630
Landowner, made perspective glasses for Thomas Harriot
1630   Buried at Essendon, Herts
              Owned property in Hertford & St
              Albans
b c.1572
Known to have made: telescope
Sources: Taylor (1954) p.182,200; will (AM)

TOOLE James
w 1821
Math IM
1821   9 Somerset Place, Bristol
Source: Mat (MAC)

TOOLE John
w 1838–1855
Spec M, Optician
              4 Oldham Place, Wilmington
              Square, London
              118 Gray's Inn Lane, London
1839   110 Gray's Inn Lane, London
1849   58½ Hatton Garden, London
1851–1855   10 Great Warner St, Clerkenwell,
              London
Succeeded by TOOLE William by 1859
Sources: JAC; Pg; PO

TOPPING Charles M.
w 1846–1859
Optician, Preparer of Microscope Objects
1846   1 York Place, Pentonville Hill,
              London
1849–1859   4 New Winchester St, Pentonville,
              London
The name is given as TOPPING & SON in Wk only
Sources: PO; Wk

TOREY Angelo
w 1830
Math IM
1830   Fisherton Anger, Salisbury, Wilts
Sources: Pg

TORRE & CO.
w 1805
Optician
1805   12 Leigh St, Red Lion Square,
              London
See also DELLA TORRE★
Known to have sold: barometer, thermometer
Sources: H (MAC); Goodison (1977) p.366

TOTTENHAM Edward
w 1844–1847
Optician, Watch M, Clock M
1844–1847   38 College Green, Dublin
Sources: Burnett & Morrison-Low (1989) p.138

TOULMIN Robert
w 1768–1775
Scale M
1768–1775   Gravel Lane, Southwark, London
Sources: Bd (JAC); Lg (JAC)

TOWNSEND Richard
w 1683 d 1699
Scale M
            London
Guild: Blacksmiths, fr 1677 or 1678
Had apprentice:
BEN John* 1682/3
WRIGHT John 1689 by t/o from HOE Robert*
SANDS Samuel 1693 by t/o from CLARIDGE
Richard*
TAYLOR William 1695 t/o 1699 to WOOD Mary*
and 5 others 1691–1697
Sources: GL: BKC 2881/8, 2881/9, 2884, 2886/3
(MAC)

TOWZEY Benjamin
w 1777
Math IM
1777   Smart's Buildings, High Holborn,
            London
Sources: GL: Sun 119936/255 no.380251

TRACY John
w 1739–1742
1735   Shoe Lane, Fleet St, London
1739–1742   St. Brides Lane, Fleet St, London
Guild: Grocers, fr 1735
Son of TRACY John, free of GZC of London
Apprenticed to
SCOTT Benjamin* 1715
HEATH Thomas* 1720 by t/o
Had apprentice:
GENT Thomas 1739
MATHEWS John 1742
Sources: Brown J (1979a) p.35,37

TRAFFORD John
w 1783
Math IM, Grocer
1783   Windlebury, Oxford
Sources: GL: Sun 11936/314 no.480530

TRANTUM Richard
w 1737
Math IM
1737   Parish of St James Westminster,
            London
Guild [Stationers]
Son of TRANTUM Thomas
Father of TRANTUM James s 1737 ABC
Apprenticed to CHAPMAN William* 1713 t/o
1717 to his father [father's trade not given]
Sources: GL: ABC 12080/2; McKenzie (1978)
p.71

TREE Emily (Mrs)
w 1843–1849
Rule M
1843–1849   22 Little Charlotte St, Blackfriar's
            Rd, London
Took over from TREE James (I)*
Succeeded by TREE James (II)*
Sources: PO

TREE James (I)
w 1826–1842
Rule M
            20 Great Suffolk St, Borough,
            London
            1 Great Guildford St, Borough,
            London
1832–1842   22 Charlotte St, Blackfriars Rd,
            London
Succeeded by TREE Emily*
See also TREE James (II)*
Attended London Mechanics Institute 1836
Known to have sold: gauge, rule
Sources: LMIR (AM); Tesseract Cat. H (1984)
no. 54; inst (s); Pg (JAC); PO

TREE James (II)
w 1850–1851
Rule M
1850–1851   22 Little Charlotte St, Blackfriars
            Rd, London
Took over from TREE Emily*
Succeeded by TREE & CO. James*
See also TREE James (I)*
Sources: PO

TREE & CO. James
w 1851–1895
Math IM, Rule M
1851–1895   22 Little Charlotte St, Blackfriars
            Rd, London
1895   7 Lawrence Lane, London EC
Took over from TREE James (II)*
Ex 1851
Known to have sold: parallel rule, protractor, rule,
slide rule
Sources: PO; Wk; Cat. 1851

TREEBY William
w 1834–1838
Math IM
1834–1838   39 Commercial Rd, Lambeth,
            London
Attended London Mechanics Institute 1834–1838
Sources: LMIR (AM)

TREMBLATT S.
w 1841
Phil IM
1841   75 Golden Lane, London
Attended London Mechanics Institute 1841
Sources: LMIR (AM)

TREMLETT Richard
w 1850–1885
Math IM, Phil IM, Baro M, Thermo M
1850–1855   9 Albemarle St, Clerkenwell, London
1859–1865   7 Guildhall Place, Spa Fields, London
            WC
1870–1885   9 Myddleton St, London EC
See also TRENBLETT Richard* – possibly the same
person
Attended London Mechanics Institute 1850; Ex
1851
Known to have sold: barometer, thermometer
Sources: LMIR (AM); PO; Cat.1851 (MAC)

TRENBLETT Richard
w 1839–1843
Phil IM
1839–1843   Gloucester St, Clerkenwell, London
Attended London Mechanics Institute 1839–1843
See also TREMLETT Richard* – possibly the same
person
Sources: LMIR (AM)

TRESOLDI Antonio
w 1841
Optician
1841   72 Kirkgate, Leeds
Sources: Pg

TRESOLDI Joseph
w 1851–1870
Optician, Baro M
1851   44 Baldwin's Gardens, Leather Lane,
            London
1870   24 Baldwin's Gardens, London EC
Sources: PO; Wk

TROMBETTA –
a 1800–1820
            Norwich
Known to have sold: barometer
Sources: Goodison (1977) p.367

TROTTER Robert (I)
w 1822–1836
Watch M, Compass M
1822–1827   23 Coupar St, Leith
1828–1836   89 Kirkgate, Leith
See also TROTTER Robert (II)*
Sources: Bryden (1972) p.58

TROTTER Robert (II)
w 1839–1841
Watch M, Clock M, Compass M
1839–1841   58 Mitchell St, Glasgow
See also TROTTER Robert (I)*
Sources: Bryden (1972) p.58

TROUGHTON Edward (I)
w 1804–1826
Optician, Math IM
1804–1826   The Orrery, 136 Fleet St, London
Guild: Grocers fr 1784, Clockmakers fr 1823
Son of TROUGHTON Francis, farmer, of Corney,
Cumb
Related to FAYRER James (I)* by marriage
Partnership:
TROUGHTON John & Edward*
TROUGHTON & SIMMS* 1826–1831
Apprenticed to TROUGHTON John (II)*, his
brother, 1773
Had apprentice:
SUDDARD (SUTHARD) Thomas, his nephew, 1788
GC

DALLAWAY Joseph James★ 1789 GC
Employed DANCER Josiah★
FAYRER James (I)★
CAIL John★
Took over from TROUGHTON John & Edward★
Succeeded by TROUGHTON & SIMMS★
bap 1756; made dividing engine; pat. pillar-frame sextant 1788; Copley medal 1809; FRS 1810; r 1831; d 1835
Known to have sold: balance, barometer, repeating circle, sextant, theodolite, transit instrument
Sources: GL: CKC 2719A; Ric; inst NMM, WM; Brown J (1979a) p.51–52; McConnell (1992) p.8–34; Skempton & Brown (1973)

TROUGHTON Edward (II)
fl 1740–1760
Tailor
Confusion with TROUGHTON John (I)★ by E.G.R.Taylor and others
Sources: Skempton & Brown (1973) p.235; Taylor (1966) p.219

TROUGHTON John & Edward
w 1788–1804
Math IM
Alternative name: John (II)★ & Edward (I)★
1779–1782   Queen's Square, Bartholomew Close, London (residence?)
1788–1804   136 Fleet St, London
Guild: Grocers
Took over from
TROUGHTON John (I)★
COLE Benjamin (II)★
John retired c.1804
Known to have sold: hydrometer, planetarium, repeating circle, sextant, slide rule
Sources: TCd NMM; Kt (JAC); Brown J (1979a) p.44,51,77; McConnell (1992) p.6–13; Skempton & Brown (1973) p.238–41

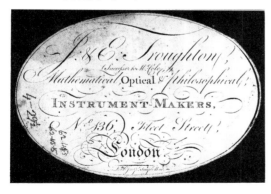

TROUGHTON John (I)
fr 1756 d 1788
Math IM
1752   Standgate Lane, Lambeth, London
1755–1777   Surrey St, Strand, London
1764–1774   Strand Lane near Surrey St, London
1788   [Residence] Lewisham, London
Guild: Grocers, fr 1756
Son of TROUGHTON William, husbandman, of Corney, Cumb
Apprenticed to HEATH Thomas★ 1734/5

Had apprentice:
TROUGHTON John (II)★, his nephew, 1757
TROUGHTON Francis, his nephew, 1763
FERGUSON James (II), son of James (I)★, 1765
TROUGHTON Joseph (I), his nephew, 1765
CHARLTON John 1771
Worked for HEATH Thomas★
b c 1716; petitioner against Dollond's patent, 1764; r 1778
Sources: Brown J (1979a) p.41; Skempton & Brown (1973) p.234–37

TROUGHTON John (II)
w 1768–1788
Math IM
1764   Surrey St, Strand, London
1768–1771   Crown Court, Fleet St, London
1771–1778   17 Dean St, Fetter Lane, London
1778–1782   1 Queen's Square, Barthlomew Close, London
1782–1788   136 Fleet St, London
Guild: Grocers, fr 1764
Son of TROUGHTON Francis, farmer, of Corney, Cumberland
Partnership: TROUGHTON John & Edward★
Apprenticed to TROUGHTON John (I)★, his uncle, 1757
Had apprentice:
MARTIN James★ 1768
TROUGHTON Edward (I)★, his brother, 1773
SYMONS John★ 1779
TROUGHTON Joseph (II) 1780
Took over from COLE Benjamin (II)★whose business he bought in 1782
Succeeded by TROUGHTON John & Edward★
Associated with
MOLLISON John★, who supplied sextants
GREGORY & WRIGHT★, who sold sextants and octants divided by Troughton
b c.1739, d 1807; working in partnership with his brother c.1788–1804
Known to have sold: dividing engine, protractor, sextant, station pointer
Sources: GL: Sun 11936/259 no.385653/267 no.401944; Anderson et al (1990) p.85; Brown J (1979a) p.44,76–77; Skempton & Brown (1973) p.233–43

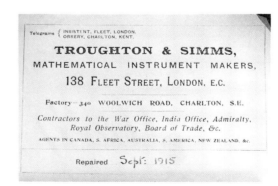

TROUGHTON & SIMMS Edward and William
w 1826 p 1922
Optician, Math IM, Phil IM
1839–1844   136 Fleet St, London

1844–1915   138 Fleet St, London
1866–1915   [Factory] 340 Woolwich Rd, Charlton, London SE
Succeeded by COOKE, TROUGHTON & SIMMS
Took over from TROUGHTON Edward (I)★
Edward retired 1831, d.1835; William d 1860; B.apt Ordnance
Known to have sold: barometer, compass (magnetic), rule, sextant, theodolite, thermometer, transit instrument
Sources: PO; inst NMM, SH, WM & elsewhere; Anderson et al (1990) p.85; McConnell (1992) p.26–78

TROUTBECK Edmund
w 1782–1793
Math IM, Victualler
            Portugal St, London
1782   Marquis of Granby's Head in Brick St, London
1788–1793   Sheffield St, Clare Market, London
Apprenticed to BOSTOCK Joshua★ 1766
Sources: PRO: IR 1/25 (AM); GL: Sun 11936/303 no.463464; BW; Ld; JAC

TROW Isaac
w 1829–1850
Rule M, Measuring tape M, Compass M, Dog collar M
1829–1841   40 Loveday St, Birmingham
1830   42 Loveday St, Birmingham
1835   8 Court, Loveday St, Steelhouse Lane, Birmingham
1850   Loveday St, St.Mary's, Birmingham
Took over from BAKEWELL Richard★
Sources: K; Pg (MAC); SL (MAC); West; Wr

TRUMAN Edward
w 1832–1834
Rule M
1832–1834   87 Long Lane, Smithfield, London
See also
TRUMAN Elizabeth★
TRUMAN Thomas★
Sources: Pg (JAC)

TRUMAN Elizabeth
w 1817–1836
Rule M
1817–1836   87 Long Lane, Smithfield, London
See also
TRUMAN Edward★
TRUMAN Thomas★
Sources: Pg (JAC); Und

TRUMAN Thomas
w 1789–1805
Rule M, Drawing IM
Alternative name: TRUEMAN
1789   7 Chiswell St, Moorfields, London
1790   89 Chiswell St, Whitecross St, London
1793–1805   87 Long Lane, Smithfield, London
See also
TRUMAN Elizabeth★
ROLPH Thomas★
Sources: A (JAC); BW; H

TUCK William
w 1687 d by 1697
Spec M
Alternative name: TUCKE, TURK (in error)
London
Guild: Spectaclemakers, fr 1676/7
Son of TUCK John, fisherman, of Thornford,
Dorset
Apprenticed to RADFORD John★ 1668
Elected to Court of SMC 1687; d 1696 or 1697
Sources: GL: SMC 5213/1, 5213/2 p.7

TUCKER Richard
w 1786–1793
Scale M, Brazier
Alternative name: R.T.
1786   Below ye 10 Cells in Preston St,
            Exeter
1787   2d Rock Lane, Exeter
1791–1793   Rock Lane, Exeter, Devon
Known to have sold: balance, weights
Instruments advertised: balance, steelyard, weights
Sources: BW; *Exeter Pocket Journal* (1791) (MAC);
inst SM Wellcome (MAC); Sheppard & Musham
(1975) no.164

TULLEY Charles
w 1799–1824
Optician
Alternative name: TULLY
1805   11 Pierpoint Row, Islington,
            London
            Goswell Street Rd, London
Father of
TULLEY Henry★
TULLEY William★
Related to TULLEY Thomas★
Succeeded by TULLEY & SONS★
See also TULLEY W.& T.★
Associated with TROUGHTON & SIMMS★ as
supplier of lenses
RAS 1822; d 1830
Sources: H; Kn (Bath, 1824); Calvert (1971) p.43;
McConnell (1992) p.12

TULLEY Henry
w 1822–1833
Optician, Phil IM
            Near the Pump Room, Bath
1822–1826   5 Kingston Buildings, Bath
1826–1833   3 Pulteney Bridge, Bath
1833   [Residence] 8 Sydney Buildings, Bath
Son of TULLEY Charles★
Brother of TULLEY William★
See also TULLEY & SONS★
Known to have sold: barometer, pantograph
Sources: Kn; Pg; Sil; ChrSK 10 Aug 1877 lot 33
(DJB); Goodison (1977) p.367

TULLEY William & Thomas
w 1830 w c. 1843
Optician, Math IM, Phil IM, Brass tube M,
Optical turner
1835–1839   4 Terretts Court, Upper St,
            Islington, London
Son of TULLEY Charles★(William)
Brother of TULLEY Henry★ (William)
Took over from TULLEY & SONS★

William d 1835; Thomas d 1846
Sources: Islington parish records (JAC); *Antiques*
n.d. (MAC); Pg

TULLEY & SONS C.
w 1845–1846
Opticians
1845–1846   7 Church Row, Islington, London
Took over from TULLEY William & Thomas★
Sources: PO

TULLEY & SONS Charles
w 1826–1830
Optician, Math IM, Phil IM
1826–1828   Terrett's Court, Upper St, Islington,
            London
Succeeded by TULLEY William & Thomas★
Took over from TULLEY Charles★
See also TULLEY Henry★
Charles d 1830
Known to have sold: microscope, telescope
Sources: Pg; Anderson et al (1990) p.86; Turner G
(1989) p.268–69

TURCONI Gaspero
w 1835–1837
Optician
1835–1837   62 Christian St, Liverpool
Sources: LM index (MAC)

TURLAND Henry
w 1733
Math IM
1733   Parish of St.Giles, Cripplegate,
            London
Guild: Stationers, fr 1729
Son of TURLAND Richard, gunsmith, of Holborn,
London
Apprenticed to AUSTIN Samuel★ 1721/2
Had apprentice UFFINGTON George 1733
Sources: McKenzie (1978) p.10,355

TURLINGTON John
w 1625–1669
Spec M
1628   Near Eastcheap, London
Guild: Brewers & Spectaclemakers
Son of TURLINGTON Henry, farmer, of Shepshed,
Leics
Apprenticed to POLSON Richard★ 1610/11
Had apprentice:
BENTLEY William 1625
SHAWE John 1626
POLLARD Clement 1627
BOOTE John★ 1626
STANLEY John 1626
WOOTTEN James 1667/8
unnamed 1669
fr BREW 1617/18; translated from Brewers to
SMC 1634; Master SMC 1665–1669; d 1669
Sources: CLRO: Ald 49 fol. 14; GL: BREW
5445/12 /13 /14; SMC 5213/1

TURNER –
w 1816
Optician
1816   Charles St, Wolverhampton
Sources: H (MAC)

TURNER James
w 1798
Glass Grinder, Spec M
1798   Newcastle upon Tyne
Sources: BW

TURNER Job
w 1833
Optician, Spec M
1833   Wolverhampton
Sources: Br

TURNER John (I)
w 1816–1826
Optician
Alternative name: confusion with John TUTHER ?
1816–1826   64 Upper King St, Bloomsbury,
            London
See also TURNER John (II)★
Sources: Bn (MAC); Kt (JAC); Und

TURNER John (II)
w 1839–1840
Rule M
1839–1840   24 Brook St, Holborn, London
Sources: Pg

TURNER John Edward
w 1822–1824
Optician, Math IM
1822   4 Union Place, Camberwell, London
1824   4 High St, Camberwell, London
Sources: Pg; R (JAC)

TURNER Joseph (I)
w 1740–1751
[Math IM]
1740   Quadrant & Dial, Hatton Garden,
            London
1745   8 Red Lion Court, Clerkenwell,
            London
Guild: Clockmakers, fr 1717
Father of possibly TURNER Joseph s 1754 GSC
Apprenticed to HUTCHINSON Richard★ 1709
Associated with BARSTONE John★ in making
quadrant
Known to have sold: quadrant
Sources: GL: CKC 2723/2; GH: GSC index;
GMag 1740 from MHS, MS Gunther 36; Taylor
(1966) p.193; Brown J (1979b) p.33

TURNER Joseph (II)
w 1850
Rule M
1850   No. 1 Court, Adam St, Birmingham
Sources: Sl (MAC)

TURNER Joseph (III)
w 1851–1855
Rule M
1851–1855   19 Chapel Row, Exmouth St, London
Sources: PO; Wk

TURNER Thomas
w 1839–1840
Spec M
1839–1840   5 Market St, Oxford St, London
Sources: R (JAC)

TURNER & FAGE
w 1799
Math IM
1799   248 Tooley St, London
See also DRING & FAGE★
Sources: H (JAC)

TURTON W.
w 1766–1781
            Compton St, Soho, London
Known to have sold: balance
Sources: GL: list of ratepayers (MAC); inst Halifax
Mu (MAC)

TURVELL Thomas
w 1669–1672
Spec M
Alternative name: TURVEILE, TURVILL
1671–1672   London Bridge, London
Guild: Spectaclemakers
Known to have sold: spectacles
Sources: GL: SMC 5213/1

TUSTIAN Thomas
w 1805–1830
Rule M
            2 Princes Square, Ratcliffe Highway,
            London
1805   1 Princes Square, Ratcliff, London
1836–1839   18 Princes Square, Ratcliff Highway,
            London
1838–1839   18 Princes Square, St.George East,
            London
See also TUSTIAN & CO. Thomas★
Known to have sold: rule, slide rule
Sources: H (MAC); Pg; PO; inst (pv); BSIS no.3
(1984) p.14

TUSTIAN & CO. Thomas
w 1830 p 1913
Rule M
1840–1846   18 Princes Square, Ratcliff Highway,
            London
1847–1855   18 Princes Square, St.George St,
            London
1858–1882   18 Princes Square, St.George St,
            London E.
Took over from TUSTIAN Thomas★
Sources: PO

TUTHER John
w 1816–1828
Optician, Math IM
            209 High Holborn, London
1816–1817   64 King St, Bloomsbury, London
1822   221 High Holborn, London
Known to have sold: balance, microscope
Sources: Bn (MAC); J (MAC); Kt (JAC); Pg; inst
SM (Gabb); Anderson et al (1990) p.86

TUTTELL Thomas
w 1695 d 1702
Math IM (in gold, silver, steel, brass, ivory, wood)
Alternative name: TUTTEL, TUTELL, TURTELL,
TUTTLE
1695–1702   King's Arms & Globe at Charing
            Cross, London
1695–1702   Against the Royal Exchange in

Cornhill, London
Guild: Clockmakers, fr 1695
Son of TUTTELL William of CORD of London, d
Apprenticed to WYNNE Henry★ 1688
Had apprentice:
BURNABY Thomas 1697
COLLIER William★ 1699
COLESON John 1699
Associated with
MOXON Joseph★
MOXON James★ in publishing
Bookplate engraver, Author, Publisher; R.apt Wm
III 1700
Known to have sold: back-staff, fore-staff, globe,
sandglass, sector, slide rule, sundial
Instruments advertised: full range of math inst
Sources: GL: CKC 2710/2 fol.174v, 2723/1;
CLRO CF 1/106; Post Boy 3 Feb 1702 (MAC n);
inst BM, MHS, NMM, SM; engraving NMM;
Sby 23 June 1987 lot 118; Brown J (1979b) p.33;
Bryden (1992) p.315, 318; Calvert (1971) pl.52–54;
Crawforth (1985) p.534–35; Goodison (1977)
p.261

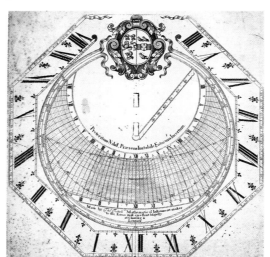

TWADDELL Thomas
w 1840–1848
Hydro M, Hydrostatic bubble M
1840   34 Brunswick Place, Glasgow
1841–1846   36 Glassford St, Glasgow
1847–1848   75 Argyll St, Glasgow
See also TWADDELL William★
Sources: Bryden (1972) p.58

TWADDELL William
w 1789–1839
Hydro M, Hydrostatic bubble M
1792–1801   Saltmarket, Glasgow
1803–1808   76 Saltmarket, Glasgow
1809   46 Saltmarket, Glasgow
1810   11 High St, Glasgow
1811   450 Gallowgate, Glasgow
1813–1823   449 Gallowgate, Glasgow
1824–1825   15 Gallowgate, Glasgow
1826–1827   21 Gallowgate, Glasgow
1828–1839   84 Saltmarket, Glasgow
Took over from BROWN James (I)★
See also TWADDELL Thomas★

Sources: ChrSK 8 Dec 1988 lot 112; Bryden
(1972) p.58

TWIGG Richard (I)
w 1662 d 1670
Spec M
Alternative name: TWIDD
-1670   Bishopsgate, London
Guild: Brewers, Spectaclemakers
Father of TWIGG Richard (II)★
Son of TWIGG Thomas, shoemaker, of Shepshed,
Leics
Apprenticed to DRUMBLEBY Thomas★ 1626
Had apprentice HARRISON William 1662
fr BREW 1633; Master SMC 1669
Sources: GL: BREW 5445/14, 5445/15; SMC
5213/1

TWIGG Richard (II)
w 1669 d 1670
Spec M
1670   Bishopsgate, London
Guild: Spectaclemakers
Son of TWIGG Richard (I)★
Had apprentice HARRISON Richard 1669
Sources: GL: SMC 5213/1

TYLER James
w 1845–1855
Baro M, Thermo M
1845–1855   5 Charles St, Hatton Garden,
            London
Succeeded by TYLER F. (Mrs)
Sources: PO; Wk

TYLER John
w 1832–1836
Baro M, Thermo M
            22 Kirby St, Hatton Garden,
            London
            15 Great New St, Fetter Lane,
            London
Sources: Pg (JAC)

UBEE Charles
w 1835–1837
Spec M
1835–1837   31 Crown St, Soho, London
Succeeded by UBEE James★
Sources: R (JAC)

UBEE James
w 1838–1847
Spec M
1838–1847   31 Crown St, Soho, London
Took over from UBEE Charles★
Sources: PO; R (JAC)

ULLMER William
w 1839–1841
Brass Rule Cutter
1839–1841   6 West Harding St, London
Attended London Mechanics Institute 1839–1841
Sources: LMIR (AM)

UNDERHILL Thomas (I)
w 1824–1827
Math IM, Optician, Rule M

1824 124 Whitechapel, Liverpool
1825 6 Coopers Row, Liverpool
1827 32 Mersey St, Liverpool
See also UNDERHILL Thomas (II)★
Sources: Bn (DJB); G (MAC)

UNDERHILL Thomas (II)
w 1834–1881
Rule M, Math IM, Phil IM, Optician
1834–1838 40 Water St, Manchester
1841 70 Bridge St, Deansgate, Manchester
1848 4 Old Millgate, Manchester
1858–1864 2 Corporation St, Manchester
1868 4 Corporation St, Manchester
1873–1881 53 Princess St, Manchester
See also UNDERHILL Thomas (I)★
Known to have sold: level, rule
Sources: K (MAC); Pg; Sl (MAC); inst(s) (MAC)

UNDRELL Samuel
w 1842–1846
Spec M, Spec Dealer
1842–1846 53 Wellington St, Goswell St, London
Sources: PO

URE John
w 1821–1833
Math IM, Optical IM
1821 40 Stockwell, Glasgow
1831–1833 136 High St, Glasgow
See also
URE William★
URE & SON William★
Sources: Bryden (1972) p.58

URE William
w 1812–1820
Math IM
1812–1818 40 Stockwell, Glasgow
1819–1820 15 Deanside Lane, Glasgow
Succeeded by URE & SON William★
See also URE John★
Known to have sold: barometer
Sources: Bryden (1972) p.58; Goodison (1977) p.367

URE & SON William
w 1822–1840
Math IM
1822–1823 40 Stockwell, Glasgow
1824–1825 85 Candleriggs, Glasgow
1826–1829 40 Candleriggs, Glasgow
1830–1835 120 Brunswick St, Glasgow
1831–1835 109 Candleriggs, Glasgow
1837–1840 3 Brunswick Court, Glasgow
Took over from URE William,
See also URE John,
Sources: Bryden (1972) p.58

URINGS John (I)
w 1709–1751
Alternative name: URING, UREN
1737–1751 East Smithfield, London
Guild: Joiners, fr 1709
Son of URINGS William, student of chemistry, of Stepney, London
Father of URINGS John (II)★

Apprenticed to WELLS Grace★ 1702
Had apprentice:
GRAY John 1709
NICHOLSON Bartholomew 1711
MARKDAINEL John 1718
BOURNE Joshua 1732
URINGS Robert Oulton, his son, 1738
BADSEY John 1738
Sources: GL: JC 8052/4; Crawforth (1987) p.368–69

URINGS John (II)
w 1738 d 1773
Ship chandler, Math IM
Alternative name: URING
Minories, London
Hermitage St, St.Catherine's, London
1759–1768 St.Catherine's, Tower Hill, London
-1773 174 Fenchurch St, London
Guild: Joiners, fp 1738
Son of URINGS John (I)★
Brother of URINGS Robert O.★
Had apprentice:
BLAKE John★ 1754
EVANS John (I)★ 1759
DRURY William 1761, son of Charles
WILLCOX Walton★ 1765
CULMER Josiah★ 1770
SMITH Thomas 1772 [possibly (I)★ or (III)★]
5 others 1750–1767
Known to have sold: microscope, sextant, telescope
Sources: GL: CH 12876/5; *General Evening Post* 27 Mar 1773 (MAC); Kt (JAC); Riv; Crawforth (1987) p.369; Wallis R & P (1986) p.225

URINGS Robert Oulton
w 1766
Math IM
Alternative name: Robert Oulding
1750 Blackfriars, London
1766 Liverpool ?
Guild: [Joiners]
Son of URINGS John (I)★
Apprenticed to URINGS John (I)★ 1738
Sources: GL: JC 8055/3; LM index (MAC); Crawforth (1987) p.370

USTLER Robert
a 1680–1700
Grove St, Deptford, London
Known to have sold: callipers
Sources: inst (pv) (MAC)

USTONSON John
w 1804–1830
Spec M, Optician, Silversmith
1804–1811 21 George Yard, Old St, London
1817 Fleet St, near St.Dunstan's Church, London
c. 1818 Cross St, Islington, London
1830 15 Whiskin St, Spa fields, London
Guild: Turners, fr 1794
Apprenticed to USTONSON Onesimus, fishing tackle maker, 1787
Son of USTONSON Thomas, victualler, d, of Islington, London

Had apprentice:
SHEPPARD Felix Samuel 1804 [possibly the same as SHEPHARD Felix★]
SHEPHERD James 1809
WOOSTER Joseph 1810
HALL William★ 1811
MOUNTFORD John 1811
RICHARDSON John 1812 [possibly (III)★]
LEWIS Charles 1812
WINTER Thomas Rafe 1815
See also RICHARDSON John (I)★
Took over from USTONSON William★
Sources: GL: TC 3302/3, 3814; H (JAC)

USTONSON William
w 1805
Spec M
1805 21 George Yard, Old St, London
Succeeded by USTONSON John★
Sources: H (MAC)

VALE Joseph
w 1829–1830
Spec M
1829–1830 82 Cheapside, Birmingham
Sources: West (DJB); Wr (DJB)

VALLIN Nicholas
a 1565 w 1603
Son of VALLIN John, Clock Maker
Known to have sold: astronomical clock
Sources: King & Millburn (1978) p.63–64, 136

VANDOME Richard
w 1806 w pt 1840
Scale M
Alternative name: VENDOME
1781 3 Little Paternoster Row, London
1806–1836 117 Leadenhall St, London
Guild: [Haberdashers] Blacksmiths fp 1781
Son of VANDOME Abraham, weaver, of Spitalfields, London
Apprenticed to MOFFATT James 1773, HC
Had apprentice:
LAY John by t/o, fr 1814
DRIVER John Samuel★ 1813
MARSHALL Robert Scott 1816
GORE Thomas Hunsden★ 1818
BASTICK Richard★ 1821
LEDGER William 1824
TITFORD Richard Vandome★ 1827
TURNER Benjamin Robert 1833
Took over from NEW & CO.★
Succeeded by VANDOME & CO. Richard★
See also VANDOME & BLACKBURN★
Bap 1759; Appointed scale adjuster to Founders' Co., 1811; B.apt Bank of England; d 1840
Known to have sold: balance
Instruments advertised: balance
Sources: ART; Pg; PO; GL: STTP 2934 fol 39; HC 15860/9; BKC 2881/15–18; FDC 6331/6; inst & TCd WM (MAC)

VANDOME & BLACKBURN
w 1827–1830
Scale M
1827–1830 117 Leadenhall St, London
See also

BLACKBURN Isaac★
BLACKBURN John★
VANDOME Richard★
Sources: Pg (JAC); R (JAC)

VANDOME & CO. Richard

w 1839–1840
Scale M
1839–1840   117 Leadenhall St, London
Took over from VANDOME Richard★
See also VANDOME, TITFORD & CO.★
Sources: Pg; ChrSK 20 Aug 1987 lot 118

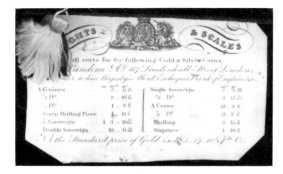

VANDOME, TITFORD & CO.

w 1841–1865
Scale M
1841   117 Leadenhall St, London
Partnership: TITFORD William★ & TITFORD
Richard Vandome★ [See apprentices of VANDOME
Richard★]
Succeeded by VANDOME, TITFORDS & PAWSON
Sources: PO; ART

VANHEGGIN Francis

w 1669
Printer-graver
        Edinburgh
Guild: Hammermen, fr 1669
Known to have sold: sundial
Sources: *The Book of the Old Edinburgh Club* 19
(1993) p.30 (MAC)

VARLEY Cornelius

w 1810 d 1873
Phil IM, Artist, Telegraph Instrument
Manufacturer
        22 Charlotte St, Fitzroy Square,
        London
        228 Tottenham Court Rd, London
1811   Junction Place, Paddington, London
1811–1856   1 Charles St, Clarendon Square,
        London
1815   42 Newman St, London
1825   51 Upper Thornhough St,
        Tottenham Court Rd, London
1857–1863   7 York Place, Kentish Town,
        London
1864–1873   337 Kentish Town Rd, NW London
Partnership: VARLEY & SON Cornelius★
See also VARLEY Samuel Alfred★
b 1781; Pat. telescope 1811; founder member of
Microscopical Society of London 1839
Known to have sold: microscope, telescope

Sources: PO; inst MHS; Calvert (1971) p.44;
Turner G (1989) p.319–20; Woodcroft (1854)

VARLEY Samuel Alfred

w ?fm 1850 w pt 1862
Optical IM
1850–1851   1 Charles St, Clarendon Square,
        London
1862   7 York Place, Kentish Town,
        London
Son of VARLEY Cornelius – possibly Cornelius★,
but probably Cornelius John [see VARLEY &
SON★]
Partnership: VARLEY Cornelius & Samuel Alfred
1862
Attended London Mechanics Institute 1850–1851;
Engineering Superintendent of the Metropolitan
District of the Electric & International Telegraph
Co. before 1862
Sources: LMIR (AM); PO; Chaldecott (1989)
p.160

VARLEY & SON Cornelius (& Cornelius John)

w 1848–1854
Math IM, Phil IM, Optician, Chem IM
1848–1854   1 Charles St, Clarendon Square,
        London
Succeeded by VARLEY Cornelius John
Ex. 1851
Known to have sold: air pump, drawing
instruments, electrical apparatus, microscope,
telescope
Sources: PO; Cat. 1851; Calvert (1971) p.44

VAUGHAN John Herbert

w 1824–1833
Cooper, Optician
1824   38 Brown's Lane, Spitalfields, London
Guild: Coopers, fr 1821
Apprenticed to VAUGHAN John, cooper, of
Spitalfields, London
Had apprentice COX Frederick (I)★ 1824
Sources: GL: CH 12823/9 p.116; CPC 5636/3,
5602/12 fol.303v

VAUGHTON Christopher

w 1769–1793
Scale M
1769   67 Little Britain, London
1784–1793   6 London Wall, London
Guild: Blacksmiths, fr 1767
Son of VAUGHTON William★
Apprenticed to READ Samuel★ 1760
Had apprentice:
SMITH Joseph (I)★ 1769
FULLOON George★ 1775
BAVERSTOCK George 1781
VAUGHTON William, his son, 1785
ENGLAND Richard 1804, t/o to
VAUGHTON Christopher (II)
Father of VAUGHTON Christopher (II) fp 1804,
umbrella maker
Attended Christ's Hospital School, London; d
c. 1822
Sources: GL: BKC 2881/15–17; 2885/1, 2886/5
(MAC); CH 12823/6 p.81,445; 12876/5 & /6;
A (MAC); BW

VAUGHTON William

d.c 1760
Math IM
        Queenhithe, London
Father of VAUGHTON Christopher★
Sources: GL: BKC 2886/5 (MAC)

VECCHIO I.

w 1800
Alternative name: J.Vecchi
1800   Nottingham
Known to have sold: barometer, thermometer
Sources: inst (pv) (MAC); Goodison (1977) p.368

VEITCH James

w 1811–1834
Telescope M, Inspector of Weights & Measures
        Inchbonny, Jedburgh, Roxburgh
Father of VEITCH William★
b 1771, d 1838; friend of David Brewster, for
whom he made lenses
Known to have sold: barometer, microscope,
telescope
Sources: Clarke et al (1989) p.16–24

VEITCH William

a 1840
The Jedburgh Post 29 Sep 1899 implies that he
made telescopes
        Jedburgh, Roxburgh
Son of VEITCH James★
Sources: NMS n

VENTOM Azaliah

w 1800
Math IM
1800   Mile End New Town, London
Guild: Merchant Taylors, fr 1800
Brother of VENTOM Thomas★
Apprenticed to VENTOM Thomas★ 1790
Had apprentice NIELSON John 1800
Sources: GL: MTC MF 320, 324

VENTOM Thomas

w 1790–1809
Math IM
1799–1809   57 Church St, Mile End, New
        Town, London
Guild: Merchant Taylors, fr 1790
Apprenticed to HARRIS Thomas (III)★ 1782
Had apprentice:
VENTOM Azaliah★, his brother, 1790
WATSON John (II)★ 1791
OLDERSHAW Henry 1792
MEAD Thomas John 1792
SCOTT George 1796
LEFEVER Thomas★ 1797
WATSON William 1798
PIGGOTT Peter William★ 1800
LAMB William Sanderson 1801
Sources: GL: MTC MF 320, 324; H

VERNEY John

w 1667 r 1677
[Spec M]
1667–1676   London
1677   In the country
Guild: Spectaclemakers

Had apprentice:
POYNTER Robert 1670
VERNEY Henry his son, by t/o from YARWELL
John★ between 1674 & 1676, then t/o to HOWE
Joseph★ 1676/7
Master SMC 1671–1672, d by 1704
Sources: GL: SMC 5213/1

VERRIER James
w 1752–1755
North Curry, Som
Known to have sold: barometer
Sources: Banfield (1991) p.223–24; Loomes (1976)

VIET & MITCHELL Marie Anne & Thomas
w 1742
Jeweller, Toy S
1742   Dial & Kings Arms on Cornhill near ye Royal Exchange, London
Instruments advertised: spectacles
Sources: Heal (1935) pl.74

VINCENT James
w 1793–1805
Scale M
1793   199 Shoreditch, (residence) London
1793–1796   1 London Bridge Foot, London
1796   1 Bridge Foot, Southwark, London
Guild: Haberdashers, fp 1781
Son of VINCENT Robert (I)★
Partnership: VINCENT & CHANCELLOR★
Apprenticed to VINCENT Robert (I)★
Had apprentice:
DUTTON James★ 1793 by t/o from VINCENT
Robert (I)★, d
QUANTRILL Thomas 1803
HARLOW Thomas 1805
Took over from VINCENT Robert (I)★
Sources: GL: HC 15857/3, 15860/9 (MAC); Kt (MAC); BW; Wil (including appendix)

VINCENT Robert (I)
w 1751 d 1793
Scale M
    The Hand & Scales on London Bridge the Second Door from the Bear Tavern Southwark Side, London
    1 High St, Borough, London
1751   Red Lyon Alley near Cow Cross, London
1756   No.1 the Foot of London Bridge, Southwark, London
1790   1 High St, Borough, London
1793   1 Bridge Foot, Southwark, London
Guild: Haberdashers fr 1751, Blacksmiths
Son of VINCENT Anthony, leather dresser, of Cow Cross, London
Apprenticed to SWITHIN John★ 1744
Had apprentice:
LEWIS William (I)★ 1751
LEVERETT William★ 1757 by t/o from STILES William★
RIDGARD Joseph★ 1760
REYNOLDS Joseph★ 1768
PARTRIDGE John 1772 by t/o from LIND John★
CHANCELLOR Thomas★ 1774

VINCENT James★, his son, 1775
ALLMOND George★ 1776
SNART Charles★ 1782
SKINNER William★ 1785
DUTTON James★ 1789 t/o to VINCENT James★ 1793
11 others 1754–1785
Succeeded by VINCENT R. & I.★
Known to have sold: balance
Sources: GL: HC 15857/2 & /3, 15860/8 & /9 (MAC); BKC 2881/16 (MAC); CH 12876/5 & /6; BM: Heal (MACn); inst Dover Mu (MAC); BW; Bd (MAC); Kt (JAC); Ld (MAC); Wil

VINCENT R. & I.
w 1795
Scale M
1795   No.1 London Bridge, Southwark, London
Succeeded by VINCENT James★
Took over from VINCENT Robert (I)★
Known to have sold: balance, weights
Sources: *Avery Magazine*, Mar–Apr 1962 p.35–38 (MAC)

VINCENT & CHANCELLOR James ? & Thomas
w 1797–1808
Scale M
1797–1808   1 Bridge Foot, Borough, London
1799   London Bridge, Borough, London
Took over from VINCENT James★
Succeeded by DUTTON & SMITH★
See also CHANCELLOR Thomas★
Sources: H (MAC); Kt (MAC); Ld (MAC)

VINCENT & SON Robert
w 1736 a 1751
Scale M
1736   Fleet St, London
See also VINCENT Robert (I)
Partnership of VINCENT Robert (II) & Son
Sources: Kt (MAC); Riv (MAC)

VOLANTERIO Joshua
w 1818–1841
Baro M, Looking-glass M, Optician
Alternative name: VOLANTENO
1818   Fishergate, Doncaster
1822   Frenchgate, Doncaster
1834   High St, Doncaster
1841   Baxter Gate, Doncaster
Sources: Pg; Goodison (1977) p.368) p.368

VOSTER Ann (Mrs)
w 1760
[Math IS]
1760   Brown St, Cork
See also
VOSTER Daniel★
VOSTER Elias★
Sources: Burnett & Morrison-Low (1989) p.156

VOSTER Daniel
w 1742–1751
IM
1742   Cork
See also
VOSTER Ann★

VOSTER Elias★
d May 1760
Known to have sold: slide rule, sundial
Sources: inst(s); Burnett & Morrison-Low (1989) p.156

VOSTER Elias
d 1760
Instrument M
    Cork
See also
VOSTER Ann★
VOSTER Daniel★
Sources: Burnett & Morrison-Low (1989) p.156

VOWLES Elizabeth
w 1833
Scale M
1833   32 Thomas St, Bristol
Took over from VOWLES John★
Sources: Mat (MAC)

VOWLES John
w 1824–1832
Millwright, Machine M, Scale M
1824   Red Lion Yard, Redcliff St, Bristol
1828–1831   36 St.Thomas St, Bristol
1832   35 Thomas St, Bristol
Succeeded by VOWLES Elizabeth★
Sources: Mat (MAC)

VREAM William
w 1717–1727
Phil IM, Pneumatical IM
1717   Earl St, near the Seven Dials, two doors from the Royal Oak, London
Worked for HAUKSBEE Francis (I)★
Author
Sources: Vream (1717) title p; Wallis R & V (1986) p.87

VULLIAMY Justin
w 1764 d 1797
Clock M, Watch M
    68 Pall Mall, London
Associated with BRADBURN John, who made barometer cases
Worked for GRAY Benjamin★
Took over from GRAY Benjamin★ after Gray's death in 1764
Known to have sold: barometer, hygrometer, thermometer
Sources: Goodison (1977) p.262–268

WADE John Creswell
w 1809–1836
Optical IM, Phil IM, Math IM, Measure M
1829–1836   Pump Court, Union St, Southwark, London
1809   The Grove, Great Guildford St, London
Father of WADE John Creswell s 1809 CRC
Sources: GL: CRC 4914/2 (1809); R

WADE Thomas
w 1754–1760
    London
Guild: Blacksmiths, fr 1741/2

Apprenticed to FREEMAN Samuel (II)★ 1732
Had apprentice PIXLEY Thomas (II)★ 1754 t/o to
READ Joseph★ 1760
Sources: GL: BKC 2885/1 (MAC)

WAGER Richard
fl 1728 d 1756
Compass M
-1756   Naval Dockyard, Deptford,
      London
Succeeded by SAUNDERS Samuel (II)★
Sources: Taylor (1966) p.166

WAGHORN Robert
w 1765–1797
Gangsman, Master of Optician
1765   Botolph Wharf, London
1765   and Globe Court, Fish Street Hill,
      London
1791   51 Long Lane, Southwark, London
1797   Long Lane, Southwark, London
Guild: Spectaclemakers, fr 1765
Had apprentice:
HERBERT James 1788
WHITE William 1791
BELLWORTH James★ 1797
fr by purchase
Sources: GL: SMC 5213/3, 5213/4

WAGSTAFFE Thomas
w 1756–1793
Clock M, Watch M
      The corner of Nag's Head Court, 33
      Gracechurch St, at the Sign of the
      Ship and Crown, London
1793   33 Gracechurch St, London
Guild: Merchant Taylors
Known to have sold: balance
Sources: BW; Baillie (1951); MAC n

WAITE John
fr 1688 w 1695
Math IM
1688–1695   Smithfield Bar, London
Guild: Grocers, fr 1688
Son of WAITE John, gent, of Toft, Cambs
Apprenticed to HAYES Walter★ 1678/9
Had apprentice DENN William 1695
Sources: Brown J. (1979a) p.8, 29

WAKE Charles
w 1838–1875
Optical IM, Math IM, Phil IM, Drawing IM
1838–1875   11 Silver St, Golden Square, London
Son of WAKE John, tallow chandler, of Southwark
and Marylebone, London
Brother of WAKE Francis Henry★
b 1806
Sources: Pg; PO; R; family details from Mrs Rose

WAKE Francis Henry
w 1851–1855
Math IM
1851–1855   4 William St, Manchester Square,
      London
1861   9 Silver St, Golden Square, London
1871   4 St Martin's Court, St Martin's
      Lane, London

1883   Ruby St, Camberwell, London
Son of WAKE John, tallow chandler, Southwark
and Marylebone, London
Brother of WAKE Charles★
b 1817 d 1883
Sources: PO; Wk; family details from Mrs Rose

WAKELY Andrew
w 1633–1669
Mathematician, Math IM
Alternative name: WAKERLY
1633–1669   Redriff Wall, near Cherry Garden
      Stairs, London
Had apprentice ATKINSON James (I)★
Succeeded by ATKINSON James (I)★
Author
Sources: Bryden (1992) p.307; Taylor (1954)
p.213–15

WALES James
w 1830–1846
Scale M
1830–1832   Paul's Work, Edinburgh
1833–1845   90 Leith Wynd, Edinburgh
1846   McLaren Place, Edinburgh
Sources: NMS n

WALKER Edward
w 1823–1839
Scale M
1823–1826   45 Wych St, Strand, London
1832–1839   19 Wych St, Strand, London
Guild: [Blacksmiths]
Apprenticed to PAYNE Benjamin M.★ 1807
Succeeded by WALKER Catherine (Mrs)
Sources: GL: BKC 2881/16 (MAC); Pg; R (JAC)

WALKER Francis
w 1829–1859
Optical IM, Phil IM, Math IM, Optician
1839–1845   35 Wapping Wall, London
1846–1850   17 Wapping Wall, London
1851–1859   77 Broad St, Ratcliff Cross, London
Guild: [Masons], Spectaclemakers
Son of WALKER William, biscuit baker, d, of St
George's in the East, London
Apprenticed to COOK William George★, MC, 1818
Had apprentice:
BASTER Thomas 1845
ALDER William David 1846
BALDWIN William Richard 1847
fr in SMC by purchase on 27 Sep 1845
Sources: GL: MC 5312, 5304/6; SMC 5213/6; Pg;
PO; R (JAC)

WALKER Frederick
w 1832–1850
Math IM
1832–1833   7 Trinity Place, Dublin
1834–1840   31 Clarendon St, Dublin
1841–1850   29 Clarendon St, Dublin
See also WALKER George★
Sources: Burnett & Morrison-Low (1989) p.138

WALKER George
w 1841–1848
Optician, Math IM
1841–1848   6 Fade St, Dublin

See also WALKER Frederick★
Sources: Burnett & Morrison-Low (1989) p.138

WALKER James
a 1750–1800
Known to have sold: balance★
Sources: inst (pv) (MAC)

WALKER John & Alexander
w 1823–1859
Navigation Warehouse, Stationers, Engraver,
Chart S, Math IM, Optician
Alternative name: J.& A.
      47 Bernard St, London
1823–1835   33 Pool Lane, Liverpool
1837   34 South Castle St, Liverpool
1839–1859   72 South Castle St, Liverpool
Succeeded by WALKER Alexander
Known to have sold: barometer, hygrometer,
sextant, spirit level, thermometer
Sources: G (MAC); Pg (MAC); inst (s) (MAC);
Bennett (1983a) no.159; Calvert (1971) p.44

WALKER Jonathan
w 1826–1833
Scale M
1826   53 St Clements Lane, London
1833   4 Bridge St, Southwark, London
Guild: Vintners, fp 1826
Same premises as WALKER Thomas Richard★
Sources: GL:VC 15209/1 fol.51; 15212/2 p.172

WALKER Joseph
w 1808–1840
Drawing IM, Instrument case M
      129 Bunhill Row, London
      14 Dean St, Holborn, London
      22 Bunhill Row, London
1829   58 Compton St, Clerkenwell, London
1839   43 Skinner St, Clerkenwell, London
Associated with HARRIS William (III)★ - as
creditor
Sources: PRO: Bankruptcy Proceedings (AM); Pg;
PO; R (JAC); McConnell (1994a) p.277

WALKER Richard
w 1792–1802
Rule M
1792–1802   2 Timber Yard, Wolverhampton
Sources: Wolverhampton rate books (MAC)

WALKER Thomas
v 1773–1780
Optician
      St Dunstan's Alley, Tower St,
      London
Guild: Spectaclemakers, fr 1773
Father of WALKER James, coal merchant, fp 1814
Son of WALKER Thomas, rope maker, of Ratcliff,
London
Apprenticed to LINCOLN Thomas★ 1761
Worked for LINCOLN Charles★ 1773
d by 1814
Sources: GL: SMC 5213/3, 5213/4, 6029

WALKER Thomas Richard
w 1833–1841
Scale M

1826   53 St Clements Lane, London
Guild: Vintners, fp 5 Jul 1826
Same premises as WALKER Jonathan★
Sources: GL:VC 15209/1 fol.51; 15209/2 fol.25

WALKER William (I)

w 1775–1802
Math IM
1775–1790 15 Temple Bar, Dublin
1791–1802 17 Temple Bar, Dublin
Succeeded by WALKER & SON W.
See also WALKER William (II)★
Known to have sold: circumferentor, compass, drawing instruments
Sources: Burnett & Morrison-Low (1989) p.138

WALKER William (II)

w 1820–1826
Math IM, Optician
1820–1826 17 Temple Bar, Dublin
Took over from WALKER & SON William,
See also WALKER William (I)★
Sources: Burnett & Morrison-Low (1989) p.138

WALKER & SON William

w 1802–1819
Math IM
    16½ Temple Bar, Dublin
1802–1819 17 Temple Bar, Dublin
Took over from WALKER William (I)★
Succeeded by WALKER William (II)★
Known to have sold: compass, circumferentor, sundial
Sources: Wi (DJB); inst SM & (pv) (MACn); Burnett & Morrison-Low (1989) p.138

WALKER & TOLWORTHY

w 1833–1835
Drawing IM
1833–1835 58 Compton St, Clerkenwell, London
See also
WALKER Joseph★
WALKER John & Alexander★
Sources: R (JAC)

WALLACE Richard

w 1846–1881
Jeweller, Watch M, Optician
1856   125 George St, Limerick
1870–1881 129 George St, Limerick
A label on a barometer by Wallace at Maynooth College suggest he may have employed Moore F. M.
Known to have sold: barometer, theodolite
Sources: Burnett & Morrison-Low (1989) p.84, 156; Mollan (1990) p.119–120, 548

WALLIS James

w 1835
Spec M
1835   22 Duke St, Birmingham
Sources: Pg

WALLIS & SON

w 1798
Opticians
1798   Sheffield

See also WARRIS & SON★ for whom this may be a directory error
Sources: BW

WALPOOLE Thomas

w 1696–1715
Math IM
Alternative name: WALPOLE, WALPOOL
1696–1715 Mariner & Compass in the Minories, London
Guild: Grocers, fr 1683/4
Son of WALPOOLE Thomas, hatband maker, of Lambeth, London
Apprenticed to ANDERTON Nathaniel★ 1676/7
Had apprentice:
DANIEL Henry 1687
THORNER William 1691
PARKER James (I)★ 1695/6
Sources: Bryden (1992) p.314n; Brown J. (1979a) p.28–29; Taylor (1966) p.118

WALTER Benjamin

w 1805–1822
Math IM
1805   32 Horsleydown Lane, London
1816–1822 17 Lower Cornwall St, St. George's East, London
See also WALTER R.★
Sources: H (MAC); Und

WALTER R.

w 1816
Math IM
1816   17 Lower Cornwall St, St.George's East, London
See also WALTER Benjamin★ for whom 'R. Walter' may be a directory error
Sources: Und

WALTON Christopher

w 1789–1793
Scale M
    6 London Wall, London
Sources: A (JAC); BW

WANTHIER J.

w 1851
Baro M
1851   14 Wilmington Square, Clerkenwell, London
Sources: Wk

WARD Callingwood

w 1785–1818
Scale M, Victualler, Toy M, Gun part M, Woodscrew M
Alternative name: C.W., Cally
1785–1787 10 Newton St, Birmingham
1788–1798 Steelhouse Lane, Birmingham
1797   Summer Lane, Birmingham
1816–1818 16 Moland St, Birmingham
Known to have sold: balance, weights
Sources: Pg; PR (MAC); Pye (MAC); Wd; inst Lancaster Mu (MAC)

WARD John (I)

fr 1721 w 1744
[Spec M], Coal S by 1741
    London

Guild: Spectaclemakers fr 1721/2
Son of WARD John, draper, d, of London
Apprenticed to BRANDRETH Timothy★ 1714
Had apprentice FROOME John 1739
d c.1747; Master of SMC 1737–1744
Sources: GL: SMC 5212/2 p.90,126+, 5213/3 p.4, 75–76, 6029; CH 12876/4

WARD John (II)

w 1838–1850
Operative & Dispensing Chemist, Math IM, Phil IM, Baro M, Thermo M, Chem Apparatus M
1838–1851 79 Bishopsgate Within, London
Associated with GRIFFIN & CO. John J.★ as their agent
Sources: Pg; PO; Anderson et al (1990) p.87; Chaldecott (1985)

WARD Joseph Benjamin

w 1839
Math IM
1839   42 York St, London
Sources: PO

WARD William Broughton

w 1841–1842
Math IM
1841–1842 13 King William St, West Strand, London
Sources: PO

WARE Ann

w 1737
[Math IM]
    London
Took over from WARE Richard★
Known to have sold: rule
Sources: GL: CH 12823/4 p.352 (MAC)

WARE Richard

w 1727–1731
[Math IM]
    London
Guild: Joiners, fr 1716
Son of WARE John, cordwainer, of St. Bride's, London
Apprenticed to CROOKE John (I)★ 1708
Succeeded by WARE Ann★
Known to have sold: rule
Sources: GL: CH 12823/4 p.352 (MAC); JC 8052/3 (MAC); Crawforth (1987) p.370

WAREN Joseph

w 1780–1801
Scale M, Victualler, Coal S
1780–1791 2 Weaman St, Birmingham
1793–1801 15 Steelhouse Lane, Birmingham
Known to have sold: balance
Sources: By (MAC); PR (MAC); Pye (MAC); Sy (MAC); Wd (MAC); inst (pv) (MAC)

WARNER John (I)

w 1686–1722
Math IM
    King's Arms & Globe, Lincoln's Inn Fields, nr.Portugal Row, London
    Near Great Lincoln Inne Fields, at the end of Portugal Row next to

Lincoln's Inn by the Booksellers, London

1722   The King's Arms & Globe, Little Lincoln Inn Fields, end of Portugal Row, London

Guild: Clockmakers, fr 1682
Apprenticed to WYNNE Henry★ 1675
Had apprentice:
FAIRFAX William 1685/6
WATSON Robert 1689/90
HAMILTON Richard 1705 (probably – but there was another John Ward in CKC by this date)
Associated with WYNNE Henry★ in advertising
Author
Instruments advertised: barometer, slide rule, thermometer
Sources: Brown J. (1979b) p.34; Goodison (1977) 289, 369; Loomes (1981b); DJB – n from Coggeshall (1690), fol. facing title p.

WARNER John (II)

w 1804–1814
Founder
1798   At Mr Tomson Warner's, Fore St, London
1804   The Crescent, Jewin St, London
Guild: Founders, fr 1798
Apprenticed to WARNER Tomson, founder, of London
Had apprentice:
SMILY William Robert 1804
PELTON James 1808
BROWN William 1808
HEARN James 1809
Appeared before Commons Committee on Weights & Measures 1814
Known to have sold: weights
Sources: GL: FDC 6331/6

WARNER Samuel

w 1731
IM
1731   Two Civet Cats near the Rose Tavern without Temple Bar, London
Sources: Advertisement in Hammond J., *Practical Surveyor* (1731) (MAC n)

WARNER Thomas (I)

a 1772–1790
Locksmith, Bell hanger, Scale M
     60 Wood St, near Cripplegate, London
Associated with HENRY Solomon★, patentee
PINCHBECK Christopher (II)★ as supplier
Known to have sold: balance
Sources: Patent records (MAC); BM: Heal 85/313 (MAC); inst Huddersfield Mu (MAC)

WARNER Thomas (II)

a 1750 d 1772
Scale M
1772   Shug Lane, London
Sources: *Gazetteer & New Daily Advertiser*, 22 Oct 1772 (JRM)

WARNER & SONS John

w 1816–1869
Scale M, Weight M, Measure M, Brass Founder,

Pump M, Fire engine M
1816–1869   8 Jewin Crescent, London
Ex.1851
Known to have sold: weights
Sources: Cat. 1851 (MAC); PO

WARREN James (I)

fr 1752 w 1782
Goldsmith, Weight M
Alternative name: I.W., J.W.
1760–1768   at the sign of St.Dunstan, Skinner Row, Dublin
1768–1782   at the sign of St.Dunstan on Cork Hill, Dublin
1768–1780   10 Cork Hill, Dublin
1781–1782   20 Cork Hill, Dublin
Guild: Goldsmiths
Apprenticed to GOODWIN Andrew 1742
d.1789
Known to have sold: weights
Sources: Wi (AL); inst SM; DB

WARREN James (II)

w 1845–1846
Optician
1845–1846   335 Oxford St, London
Sources: PO

WARREN Richard

w 1850–1859
Box & Ivory Rule M
1850–1859   9 Arundel Place, Coventry St, London
Sources: PO; Wk

WARRIS Thomas

w 1814
Optician
1814   Church St, Sheffield
See also WARRIS William★
Sources: WB (MAC)

WARRIS William

w 1804–1822
Optician, Knife M
1804   Sheffield
1822   18 Burgess St, Sheffield
See also WARRIS Thomas★
Pat. opera glasses 1804
Sources: Patent records (MAC); Bn (DJB)

WARRIS & SON Thomas

w 1797–1805
Optician, Merchant
1797   6 Church Lane, Sheffield
1805   Church St, Sheffield
See also WALLIS & SON★
Sources: H (DJB), Rb (MAC)

WARWICK William

w 1823–1836
Optician, Spec M, Phil IM
     67 Margaret Street East, Spitalfields, London
     4 America Terrace, King's Rd, Chelsea, London
     9 Brompton Rd, London
     16 Sloane Square, Chelsea, London

     9 Knightsbridge, London
     19 Brook St, Holborn, London
Sources: Pg (JAC)

WASHBOURN –

a 1800
     London
Known to have sold: microscope
Sources: Holbrook (1992) p.100

WASHINGTON Abraham

w 1644
Error by E.G.R. Taylor for WATLINGTON★
Sources: Taylor (1954) p.228; Ward (1981) p.94

WATERSTON & CO.

a 1800–1900
     Leith Walk, Edinburgh
Known to have sold: telescope
Sources: Sby 18 Sep 1981 lot 73 (MAC)

WATKINS Edward

w 1836
Optician, Math IM, Phil IM
1836   122 Vauxhall Walk, Butt St, Lambeth, London
Sources: Pg (JAC)

WATKINS Francis (I)

w 1747–1784
Optician
1747   Sir Isaac Newton's Head, 4/5 Charing Cross, London
1774–1782   Charing Cross, London
–1784   5 Charing Cross, London
Guild: Spectaclemakers, fr 1746
Son of WATKINS Jeremy, gentleman, of New Church, Radnor
Related to WATKINS Jeremiah★
Partnership: WATKINS & SMITH★
Apprenticed to ADAMS Nathaniel★ 1737
Had apprentice:
PYEFINCH Henry (I)★ 1753
SMITH Addison★ 1750
TEMPLE George 1767 t/o 1771 to GLOVER John A.★
Worked for SCARLETT Edward (II)★
Succeeded by WATKINS Jeremiah & Walter★
See also WATKINS William★
Associated with DOLLOND John (I) by taking a share in the achromatic lens patent
Partnership 1764–69; d.1791; owned a house at 77 Aldersgate St & 4 in Barbican Ct let to tenants; Master SMC 1763–1764
Known to have sold: barometer, hygrometer, perpetual calendar, microscope, sector, telescope, thermometer
Instruments advertised: full range
Sources: GL: SMC 5213/2; 5213/3 p.99, 187+; Sun 11936/283 no.427163,/292 no.444978,/302 no.461119;/313 no.476969; BM: Heal 105/105, 105/108; IHR: Wpoll (AM); Kt (JAC); Ld (MAC); Riv; GMag (1791) (JAC); inst MHS, SM, WM; Crawforth (1985) p.536; Goodison (1977) p.269–74; Holbrook (1992) p.140, 171, 187, 219–20; Sorrenson (1990); Turner (1989) p.225–26, 262–64; Wallis R. & V. (1986) p.337

WATKINS Francis (III)
w pt 1819–1847
Optician
1818–1847   5 Charing Cross, London
Guild: Vintners, fr 1818
Partnership: WATKINS & HILL★
Apprenticed to FRISBY Richard 1810, VC
B.apt London University 1828, d 1847
Sources: GL: VC 15209/1 fol.21; PRO: Cs 1841
HO 107/739/4 fol.5; Pg; Taylor (1966) p.438

WATKINS Jeremiah
w 1798 d 1810
Optical IM, Math IM, Phil IM
1798–1810   5 Charing Cross, London
Father of WATKINS John s 1813 CWC
Took over from WATKINS Francis (I)★
Succeeded by WATKINS Jeremiah & Walter★
R.apt Dukes of York & Clarence; B.apt East India
Co; business continued after his death under the
name J. Watkins by HILL Wm★
Known to have sold: barometer
Sources: CWH: CWC Ap; BM: Heal 105/109
(MAC); H (JAC); JAC; Calvert (1971) p.45, pl.56;
Goodison (1977) p.276; BG

WATKINS Jeremiah & Walter
w 1784–1798
Optical IM, Math IM, Phil IM
Alternative name: J.& W., I.& W.
1784–1798   5 Charing Cross, London
Succeeded by WATKINS Jeremiah★
Associated with LEGUIN Estienne★, for whom
they made inst
R.apt Duke & Duchess of York, Duke of
Clarence; Walter d 1798
Known to have sold: drawing instruments,
microscope, octant, telescope, waywiser
Instruments advertised: full range of optical & phil
inst
Sources: GL: Sun 11936/380 no.507824; BW; BM:
Heal 105/109; inst WM; Calvert (1971) p.45;
Holbrook (1992) p.91, 103, 130, 198, 229

WATKINS Walter
w pt 1784 d 1798
Optician
1784–1798   5 Charing Cross, London
Guild: Stationers, fr 1781
Son of WATKINS Revd Jeremiah of Hereford
Partnership: WATKINS Jeremiah & Walter★
Apprenticed to OWEN William, printer, 1774
fr 16 Oct 1781
Sources: Wil; McKenzie (1978) p.257

WATKINS William (I)
w 1784–1809
Optician
               21 St.James St, London
1784–1799   22 St. James St, London
1800–1809   70 St.James, London
Known to have sold: barometer, compass
(magnetic), perpetual calendar, waywiser
Sources: GL: Sun 11936/302 no.462772; By; H;
Ld; inst MHS, SM; Goodison (1977) p.280

WATKINS William (II)
w 1803–1832

Math IM, Phil IM, Optical IM, Naut IM
1803–1811   12 St.Michael's Hill, Bristol
1812   13 Clare ST, Bristol
1813   21 Clare St, Bristol
1814–1832   16 St.Augustine's Back, at the Lord
             Nelson, Bristol
1830   23 Hillsbridge Parade, Bristol
             (residence)
1830   16 St Augustine's Parade, Bristol
Known to have sold: compass (magnetic), sundial
Sources: Mat; Pg; bill SM Wellcome (DJB)

WATKINS & CO. Jeremiah
w 1788
Optician
Alternative name: Jeremiah & Walter WATKINS
1788   5 Charing Cross, London
See also WATKINS Jeremiah & Walter★
Probably directory abbreviation
Sources: Ld (JAC)

WATKINS & HILL Francis & William
w 1819 p 1856
Optician, Phil IM, Optical IM, Math IM
1822–1856   5 Charing Cross, London
Employed CLARKE E.M.
Took over from WATKINS Jeremiah & Walter★
Succeeded by ELLIOTT BROTHERS
Associated with NEGRETTI & ZAMBRA★
R.apt Dukes of York & Clarence; B.apt East India
Co; Both d. by 1847; firm continued under care of
A. Day to 1856; Ex 1851
Known to have sold: air pump, balance, barometer,
chronometer, drawing instruments, microscope,
sundial, telescope, thermometer
Instruments advertised: full range
Sources: PRO: Census 1841 HO 107/739/4 fol.5;
Bn (JAC); PO; R (JAC); inst MHS, NMM, SM,
WM; Anderson et al (1990) p.87–88; Bennett
(1983a) no.77; Calvert (1971) p.45; Chaldicott
(1989) p.161; Goodison (1977) p.275; Holbrook
(1992) see index; Morton & Wess (1993) p.555,
560, 576, 609; BG

WATKINS & SMITH Francis & Addison
w 1763–1774
Optician
               Charing Cross, London
Succeeded by WATKINS Francis (I)★
Took over from WATKINS Francis (I)★
Smith freed 1763; Watkins alone by 1775
Known to have sold: barometer, callipers,
hygrometer, perpetual calendar, telescope,
theodolite
Sources: BM: Heal 105/105; Ld (JAC); Lg (JAC),
inst MHS, NMM; Crawforth (1985) p.536;
Goodison (1977) p.277–79; Holbrook (1992) p.118

WATLINGTON Abraham
w 1644
See also WASHINGTON Abraham★
Known to have made: quadrant
Sources: Ward (1981) p.94, pl.41

WATSON James (I)
c 1771 w 1824
Telescope M
               London

See also: WATSON John (II)★
b 1746
Known to have sold: telescope
Sources: Kitchener Correspondence (JAC); Taylor
(1966) p.378

WATSON James (II)
fr 1815
Blacksmith
               Glasgow
Guild: Hammermen, fr 1815
Known to have sold: balance
Sources: Lumsden & Aitken (1912) p.306

WATSON John (I)
fr 1717
[Math IM]
               London
Guild: Stationers, fr 1717
Apprenticed to CHAPMAN William★ 1708
Known to have sold: telescope
Sources: inst (pv) MAC; McKenzie (1978) p.71

WATSON John (II)
w 1816–1835
Math IM
1816   Mile End Rd, London
1823   Crown Row, Mile End Rd, London
Guild: Merchant Taylors, fr 1804
Son of WATSON William, carpenter, d, of Stepney,
London
Apprenticed to VENTOM Thomas★ 1791
Had apprentice:
THOMPSON William John 1816
MALTBY William 1822
EDDON Edwin 1823
BROADWATER Thomas 1829
HANBURY Joseph William 1831
WEBB Joseph 1835
Associated with BATE Robert B.★ to whom he
supplied telescope
d by 1850
Known to have sold: telescope
Sources: GL: MTC, MF 320 324; Holbrook (1992)
p.227; McConnell (1993) p.56

WATSON Robert
w 1820–1821
Math IM
1820–1821   High Bridge, Newcastle on Tyne
Sources: Pg

WATSON Samuel (I)
fl 1674 w 1712
1680–1691   Coventry
1691–1712   Long Acre, London
Guild: Clockmakers, fr as brother 1692
Had apprentice:
BILLINGHURST William 1694
EVETT George 1701
Mathematician to Charles II
Known to have sold: astronomical clock,
planetarium
Sources: GL: CKC 2710/2 fol.131; King &
Millburn (1978) p.131

WATSON Samuel (II)
w 1838–1840

Optical IM, Math IM, Phil IM
1838–1840   54 Greek St, Soho, London
Sources: R (JAC)

WATSON W.
w 1848–1850
Naut IM, Math IM, Optician
1848   Monkwearmouth Shore, Sunderland
1848–1850   North Quay, Monkwearmouth
              Sands, Sunderland
Took over from DICKMAN & SON★
Sources: Md;Wd;TCd (s)

WATSON William (I)
w 1755
              In the Church Lane Stairs, Hull
Known to have sold: compass
Sources: inst (pv) (MAC)

WATSON William (II)
w 1837–1865
Optician
1837   Clerkenwell, London
1869–1872   313A High Holborn, London
Succeeded by WATSON & SON
See also VENTOM Thomas★ (possible Master)
Known to have sold: microscope
Sources: PO; Watson Centenary History (JAC);
Turner G (1989) p.13,108–9

WATT Charles
fr 1837
Coppersmith
              Glasgow
Guild: Hammermen, fr 1837
Known to have sold: measure (capacity)
Sources: Lumsden & Aitken (1912) p.316 (MAC)

WATT James (I)
c 1756 w 1775
Math IM, Land surveyor, Engineer
1757–1771   In the College, Glasgow
1759–1764   Saltmarket, Glasgow
1764–1771   Trongate, Glasgow
              Birmingham
              Heathfield
Worked for
MORGAN John (I)★
NEALE John (II)★
Employed
GARDNER John (I)★
SYM James (III)★
Associated with
HILL Nathaniel★
JARMAIN T.★
LINCOLN Charles★
TOMLINSON James★
RUST Richard★
& STEDMAN Christopher★, from all of whom he
bought instruments for re-sale
Member of Lunar Society; inv. steam engine
Known to have sold: barometer, circumferentor,
quadrant, sextant
Sources: Bryden (1972) p.10, 27, 30, 34 & n, 58;
Muirhead (1858)

WATT James (II)
w 1827–1863

Surveying chain M, Measuring line M
1827–1835   407 Argyll St, Glasgow
1836–1841   179 Argyll St, Glasgow
1837–1840   7 South Albion St, Glasgow
1841   11 St.Enoch Square, Glasgow
1842   3 & 11 St.Enoch Sqaure, Glasgow
1843–1853   3 St.Enoch Square, Glasgow
1854–1861   16 Croy Place, Glasgow
1862–1863   11 Turner's Court, Glasgow
Partnership: WATT & BLAIR 1864+
Sources: Bryden (1972) p.58

WATTER Benjamin
w 1805
Math IM
1805   32 Horsleydown Lane, London
Probably an error for WALTER Benjamin★
Sources: H (JAC)

WEABER Henry
w 1839–1859
Spec M, Optician
1839–1846   15 Carlisle St, Soho Square, London
1849–1859   129 Oxford St, London
See also WEABER & CO. Henry★
Ex. 1851
Sources: Cat. 1851 (MAC); Pg; PO

WEABER & Co. Henry
w 1845–1846
Working Optician
1845–1846   129 Oxford St, London
See also WEABER Henry★
Sources: PO

WEBB Ann
w 1830
Rule M
1830   Earl St, Bristol
See also WEBB Thomas
Sources: Pg

WEBB Isaac
w 1668 d 1704
              London
Guild: u & Clockmakers, fr 1668/9
Had apprentice:
BASSETT Thomas 1668/9
OWEN Benjamin 1687 t/o at once to NEWTON
William
LODWICK Adam 1695
Associated with SILVESTER Joseph★, as supplier of
rules
Sources: GL: CKC 2710/1 p.199, 247; 2723/1;
Brown J (1989b) p.32, 34; Loomes (1981b)

WEBB John (I)
fr 1792
Math IM
1792   4 Bath Row, Cold Bath Square,
              London
Guild: Needlemakers, fr 1792
Apprenticed to WEBB Joseph, his father, coal
merchant
See also WEBB John (II)★
Sources: GL: NC 2817/4 fol.56; VS

WEBB John (II)
w 1800–1847
Optical IM, Math IM, Optician
1800   327 Oxford St, London
1805   403 Oxford St, London
1808   408 Oxford St, London
1809–1822   192 Tottenham Court Rd, London
1834–1847   28 Francis St, Tottenham Court Rd,
              London
See also WEBB John (I)★
Known to have sold: microscope
Sources: Bn; H; J; Kt; Pg; PO; R; T. Philip & Son
Catalogue, Mar 1984; Calvert (1971) p.45;
Crawforth (1985) p.537

WEBB Joseph Benjamin
w 1829–1840
Optical IM, Phil IM, Math IM, Brass Turner
              18 St.James' St, Clerkenwell,
              London
              42 York St, St.Luke's, London
1824–1825   15 St James' St, Clerkenwell,
              London
1839   13 Charles St, City Rd, London
Attended London Mechanics Institute 1824–1825
Sources: LMIR (AM); Pg; R (JAC)

WEBB Richard William
w 1831–1869
Scale M
1831–1860   10 High St, Marylebone, London
1865–1869   115 High St, Marylebone, London
Guild: Blacksmiths, fr 1829
Apprenticed to NICHOLL William Lewis★ 1822
See also WEBB & SKINNER★
Known to have sold: balance
Instruments advertised: balance
Sources: GL: BKC 2881/17 & /18 (MAC); Pg; PO
(MAC); R (JAC); inst & TCd, MHS (MAC)

WEBB Thomas
w 1793–1832
Rule M, Gauging IM
1793–1798   Earl St, Bristol
1820–1822   3 Doors from the Infirmary, Earl St,
              Bristol
1823–1830   2 doors from the Infirmary, Earl St,
              Bristol
1831–1832   3 Doors from the Infirmary, Earl St,
              (2nd period) Bristol
Succeeded by GWYLLIM Joshua★
See also WEBB Ann★
Known to have sold: slide rule
Sources: Mat (MAC); inst WM

WEBB & SKINNER
w 1844–1879
Scale M
              98 Great Guildford St, Borough,
              London
1846   119 Union St, Borough, London
Sources: PO (JAC)

WEBSTER Henry
w 1845–1865
Baro M, Thermo M, Hydro M
1845–1846   3 Vineyard Walk, Clerkenwell,
              London

1849–1865   37 Coppice Row, Clerkenwell,
London
Sources: PO; Wk

WEBSTER R.
w 1817–1832
Chrono M
43 Cornhill, London
Admiralty award for chronometers 1831 & 1832
Known to have sold: chronometer
Sources: CUL: RGO 1143 fol.5–10; Taylor (1966)
p.409

WEEDEN Charles Fox
w 1811
Optical Turner
1811   6 Richmond St, St. Luke's, London
Guild: Turners
Apprenticed to WEEDEN Daniel★, his father, 1799
Had apprentice COLE Alfred 1811
Sources: GL: TC 3302/3

WEEDEN Daniel
w 1790–1806
Optical Turner
1790   Clerkenwell, London
Guild: Turners
Father of WEEDEN William John★
Had apprentice:
WEEDEN Charles Fox★, his son, 1799
SMITH James (III)★ 1806
Sources: GL: TC 3302/3; MTC MF 320 (MAC)

WEEDEN Michael
w 1847–1865
Optician, Microscope M, Optical IM
1847   Lower Rosomon St, Clerkenwell,
London
1852   3 Camden Passage, Clerkenwell,
London
1855–1865   27 Camden St, Islington, London
Guild: Merchant Taylors, fp 1846
Son of WEEDEN William John★
Had apprentice ROBBINS John 1847
See also WEEDON John★
Sources: GL: MTC MF 320, 324; PO; Wk

WEEDEN William John
w 1817–1844
Optician, Optical IM
Alternative name: WEEDON
18 Redcross St, Cripplegate, London
14 St.James' St, Clerkenwell,
London
1817–1822   7 Norman St, St.Luke's, London
1825   1 Wenlock St, St.Luke's, London
1844   68 Chapel St, Pentonville, London
Guild: Merchant Taylors, fr 1797
Father of WEEDEN Michael★
Son of WEEDEN Daniel★
Apprenticed to LINDSEY Joseph, carpenter, 1790
Had apprentice:
SEELING Joseph★ 1817
WHITBREAD William★ 1818
BECK William Arthur 1825
GUNSTON Michael 1825
KIMBELL James 1844
Associated with HARRIS William (III)★

Sources: GL: STTP 2934 fol 120; MTC MF 320,
324; Bn; R (JAC)

WEEDON John
w 1819–1828
Optician, Math IM, Phil IM, Brass Tube M,
Optical Turner
1819–1828   18 Baldwin St, City Rd, London
See also
WEEDEN Charles Fox★
WEEDEN Daniel★
WEEDON John M★
WEEDON William J.★
Sources: Pg; R (JAC)

WEEDON John M.
w 1819
Math IM
1819   7 Norton St, Old St, London [prob
directory error for Norman St]
See also
WEEDON John★
WEEDON William J.★
WEEDEN Charles Fox★
WEEDEN Daniel★
Sources: R (JAC)

WEEKS Thomas
w 1784 d by 1834
Royal Mechanical Museum, Perfumer, Machinist
3 & 4 Titchbourne St, London
3 Titchbourne St, London
Known to have sold: balance
Sources: inst (pv) (MAC); *Survey of London*, 31
(MAC)

WEIR Robert
w 1846
Watch M, Clock M, Jeweller, Optician
1846   17 Bridge St, Coleraine
Sources: Burnett & Morrison-Low (1989) p.156

WEISS & SON John
w 1831–1851
Surgical IM
1831–1851   62 Strand London
287 Oxford St, London
Ex. 1851
Known to have sold: hydrometer
Sources: ChrSK 12 Dec 1985 lot 90; inst (s); PO;
Turner G (1983a) p.310

WELLINGTON Alexander
w 1784 d 1812
Math IM, Optician, Rule M
20 Crown Court, Wardour St,
London
Crown Court, St.Ann's, Soho,
London
1784   Sherborne Lane, Lombard St,
London
1788–1812   20 Crown Court, Princes St, Soho,
London
1805   20 Crown Court, Golden Square,
London
Guild: Stationers, fr 1781
Son of WELLINGTON William, peruke maker, d,
of Soho, London

Apprenticed to SEARCH James★ 1774
Had apprentice:
ANDERSON William 1784
WELLS Samuel 1786
CUTHBERT John★ 1788
TROTT William 1793
GRIFFIN Michael 1793
HEWITT Samuel (I)★ 1796
WELLINGTON Henry,his son, 1800
BACKWELL William (II)★ 1802
HOBCRAFT William★ 1803
Took over from SEARCH James★
Succeeded by FITCH & JONES★
See also WELLINGTON Mary★
Associated with DICAS Mary★
R.apt Dukes of Gloucester & Cumberland
Known to have sold: microscope, slide rule,
sundial
Sources: Stat: STC Memo book; GL: CH 12823/8
p.156; BW; H (MAC); inst SM; Phlps 10 Dec 1986
lot 151 (MAC); Calvert (1971) p.45; McKenzie
(1978) p.311,370; Routledge (1805) p.35 & (1818)
title p.

WELLINGTON Mary
w 1816–1827
Optician
1816–1827   20 Crown Court, Soho, London
Took over from WELLINGTON & SON Mary★
Sources: Kt (JAC); Und

WELLINGTON & SON Mary
w 1813–1815
Math IM
1813–1815   Crown Court, Soho, London
Took over from WELLINGTON Alexander★
Succeeded by WELLINGTON Mary★
Sources: Kt (JAC)

WELLS Edmund
w 1779–1799
Optician, Spec M
12 Bolt Court, London
1779–1799   36 Fetter Lane, Fleet St, London
Guild: Spectaclemakers, fr 1779
Had apprentice:
DORRELL Thomas Williams 1783
SMITH Cornelius Owen 1783
See also WELLS Edward★
Freed by purchase in SMC
Sources: BM: Heal 105/112; GL: Sun 11936/293
no.454397: SMC 6028, 5213/3; CH 12876/6; A;
W

WELLS Edward
w 1784–1790
Optician
Alternative name: Possibly directory error for
Edmund★
1784–1790   36 Fetter Lane, London
See also WELLS Edmund★
Sources: BW; By

WELLS Grace
w 1690–1709
London
Guild: Joiners
Wife of WELLS Joseph★

Had apprentice:
WELLS Jeremie★, her son, 1690/91
BLOW Edmund★ 1695
HUNT Thomas 1696
MOORE Jonathan 1701
URINGS John (I)★ 1702
PAGE William 1708
Took over from WELLS Joseph★
Sources: GL: JC MS 8052/2; Crawforth (1987)
p.370

WELLS Jeremie
fr 1703 w 1735
    London
Guild: Joiners, fr 1703
Son of WELLS Joseph & Grace★
Apprenticed to WELLS Grace★
Sources: Crawforth (1987) p.370

WELLS John (I)
w 1683–1714
Rule M
    London
Guild: Clockmakers, fr 1682
Apprenticed to WHITE John 1672/3
Possible confusion by CKC clerk with WELLS
Joseph★
Sources: GL: CKC 3939, 3975; Brown J (1979b)
p.34

WELLS John (II)
w 1748
[Baro S]
    Birmingham
Known to have sold: barometer
Sources: inst NMM; Goodison (1977) p.370

WELLS Joseph
w 1667 d 1690
Math IM
    London
Guild: Joiners fr 1668, Clockmakers fr as brother
1667/8
Husband of WELLS Grace★
Apprenticed to BROWN John (I)★ 1660
Had apprentice:
BARRETT Simon★ 1668 CKC
BOWEN Richard nd, fr 1678 CKC
ELMER Theobald 1677 JC
BANYARD Thomas 1683 JC
ROLOSON William 1690 by t/o, then t/o to
SAVAGE Michael JC
Succeeded by WELLS Grace★
Associated with JOLE Robert★ as supplier
Known to have sold: rule
Sources: GL: CKC 2710/1 p.370; Brown J (1979b)
p.34; Crawforth (1987) p.371

WELLS Samuel
w 1817–1839
Math IM, Optical IM, Phil IM, Ironmonger
    137 Old St, St.Luke's, London
1817   3 Clerkenwell Green, Aylesbury St,
    London
Guild: [Stationers]
Apprenticed to WELLINGTON Alexander★ 1786
Sources: J; Kt (JAC); PO; McKenzie (1978) p.370

WENBORN Robert
w 1816–1863
Scale M
1816–1817   188 High Holborn, London
1819–1833   190 High Holborn, London
1839–1860   172 High Holborn, London
Guild: Blacksmiths, fr 1819
Apprenticed to ASTILL Susannah★ 1795
Worked for YOUNG John (I)★ or (II)★
Had 6 apprentices 1821–1852
Known to have sold: balance
Sources: GL: BKC 2881/17 & /18 (MAC); Pg;
PO; inst SM (Wellcome) (MAC)

WENMAN William
w 1832–1834
Rule M
1832–1834   10 Snow's Fields, Borough, London
Sources: Pg (JAC)

WEST Aaron
w 1792
Measure M
1792   Parish of St. Saviour, Southwark,
    London
Father of WEST Ebeneazer s 1792 GVC
Sources: GL: GVC 4591/4

WEST Benjamin
w 1828
Goldsmith, Jeweller, Optician
1828   23 Marchmont St, Russell Square,
    London
Sources: Pg (JAC)

WEST Charles (I)
w 1817–1822
Optician
1817   5 Cursitor St, London
1817   83 St. James St, London
1817–1822   5 Cursitor St, London
1817   83 St. James's St, London
See also WEST Charles Robert★, probably a
relative
WEST Charles (II)★
Associated with ADAMS★, DOLLOND★ &
WATKINS★ as supplier of lenses
e c.1787
Sources: Pg; *Weekly Dispatch* 7 Dec 1817 (JRM)

WEST Charles (II)
w 1832–1834
Optician
1832–1834   78 Cornhill, London
See also WEST Charles (I)★
Sources: R (JAC)

WEST Charles (III)
w pt 1839 w 1867
Optician, Math IM
1839–1851   20 Lord St, Liverpool
1857–1867   3 Paradise St, Liverpool
Partnership: ABRAHAM & CO. Abraham★
Agent for PARKES & SON James★ student
microscope
Sources: G; K; LM notes

WEST Charles Robert
w 1801 d 1824
Optician, Manufacturer
1801–1805   23 Plough Court, Fetter Lane,
    London
1805–1808   1 St. James St, London
1813   Cursitor St, London
1817–1822   5 Cursitor St, Chancery Lane,
    London
1817   Serle's Passage, Serle St, London
1822   83 St James St, London
1824   End of St.James St, Pall Mall,
    London
    (Shop) Gateway of Lincoln's Inn,
    London
Guild: Spectaclemakers, fr 1801
Father of WEST Francis (II)
Son of WEST John, of the Chancery Office,
London
Husband of WEST Maria
Apprenticed to DAVIES Joshua★ 1790, t/o to
LINNELL George★ nd
Had apprentice:
PETHER George 1801
REED William 1806
BUSS Wm Hubbart Bowers 1806
WEST Francis (I)★ his brother
See also
WEST Charles (I)★
WEST Francis L.★
Pat. telescopes 1806, with BRUCE William★
Known to have sold: rule.
Sources: GL: SMC 5213/4; St. Andrew, Holborn,
Bap (AM); Bn; H; J; Court & Von Rohr (1929–30)
p.86

WEST Francis (I)
w 1822–1852
Optician; Optical, Math & Phil IM
1822–1828   17 Russell Court, Drury Lane,
    London
    Serle's Passage, Lincoln's Inn,
    London
    Cursitor St, Chancery Lane, London
1829–1845   83 Fleet St, near St.Bride's Church,
    London
1845–1849   41 Strand, London
1849–1852   92 & 93 Fleet St, London
Guild: Spectaclemakers, fr 1828
Son of WEST John, gentleman, of Fetter Lane,
London
Apprenticed to WEST Charles Robert★ 1806
Had apprentice:
WEST John George, his son, 1833
WEST Francis Linsell★, his son, 1835
WEST Henry, his son, 1840
Succeeded by WEST & CO. Francis
Took over from ADAMS★ [unverified claim]
See also
WEST Charles★
WEST R.J.★
Working before free; R.apt Geo.IV & Victoria;
author
Known to have sold: camera lucida, microscope,
pantograph
Sources: GL: SMC 5213/4, 5213/5; Pg; PO;
Calvert (1971) p.46; ChrSK 8 Dec 1988 lot 173;
Anderson et al (1990) p.89

WEST Francis Linsell
w 1849–1885
Optician, Math IM, Phil IM, Spectacle M, Shop fittings M
1849–1885   39 Southampton St, Strand, London
1859–1885   31 Cockspur St, London
Guild: [Spectaclemakers]
Apprenticed to WEST Francis (I)★, his father, 1835
Known to have sold: microscope, sextant, telescope
Instruments advertised: drawing instruments
Sources: GL: SMC, 5213/5; PO; CHrSK 23 Oct 1985 257; inst (s)

WEST James
w 1666–1692
Hour-glass M
Alternative name: Jacobus
          London
Guild: Tallow Chandlers, fr 1654
Son of WEST William, bottle coverer, of Southwark, London
Apprenticed to SYMONS Henry 1646/7
Had apprentice:
GURNELL William★ 1673
RIDEOUT John 1666
HIERNE John★ 1680/1
GUYE Thomas 1692
Employed RIDEOUT John
Sources: GL: THC 6164/2 p.7, 6158/3 p.23,87,130, 6164/2, 6158/2, 6158/4 p.63, 6152/3

WEST R. J.
w 1819–1820
Optician
1819–1820   440 Oxford St, London
See also
WEST Charles (I)★
WEST Francis (I)★
WEST Charles R.★
Sources: R (JAC)

WEST Robert
w 1778–1779
Measure M
1778   Castle St, Southwark, London
1779   America Place, Bandy Legg Walk, Queen St, London
Sources: GL: Sun 11936/266 no.402135, /278 no.419163

WESTLEY William
w ?em 1829 w pt 1835+
Optician
1829–1846   24 Regent St, London
Worked for CARPENTER Philip★ 1829 (probably)
Partnership: CARPENTER & WESTLEY★
Attended London Mechanics Institute 1829
Sources: LMIR (AM); PO

WESTMORE Robert
w 1807–1828
Watch M, Clock M
          Church St, Preston
          Friargate, Preston
Associated with HOUGHTON Stephen★, whose balances he sold
d.1833

Known to have sold: balance★
Instruments advertised: barometer, thermometer
Sources: inst & TCd (s) (MAC); letter to MAC from Lancashire Record Office

WESTON George
w 1833–1845
Rule M
1833–1845   Worcester St, Wolverhampton
Sources: Br (MAC); Pg(MAC); Wh (MAC)

WESTON W.
a 1800–1825
See also WESTON George★
Known to have sold: rule
Sources: Ts Cat. C (1983) no.56 (MAC)

WESTWOOD John & Obadiah
w 1774–1781
Die sinker, Coffin furniture M, Scale M, Weight M
Alternative name: I. & O.
1774–1777   37 New Hall St, Birmingham
1777–1781   21 Great Charles St, Birmingham
Known to have sold: balance, weights
Sources: PR (MAC); Sy (MAC); inst & TCd (pv) (MAC)

WESTWOOD Robert
w 1824 fl 1829
Chrono M, Watch M, Clock M
1824   23 Princes St, Leicester Square, London
Sources: Calvert (1971) p.46; Taylor (1966) p.439

WHALLEY –
d 1761
Math IM
-1761   Horsleydown, London
Sources: *Lloyds Evening Post* 19 Aug 1761 (MAC)

WHARTON George
w 1849–1886
Scale M
1849–1851   59 Leith Wynd, Edinburgh
1852–1864   23 Leith Wynd, Edinburgh
1865–1867   37 Leith Wynd, Edinburgh
1868–1886   150 High St, Edinburgh
Succeeded by WHARTON & CO. George
Sources: NMS n (MAC)

WHARTON Thomas
w 1828–1835
Glass Cutter, Japanner, Compass M, Snuff Box M, Picture Frame M
1828–1830   90 New St, Birmingham
1835   90 Great Charles St, Birmingham
Sources: Pg (Mac); West (MAC)

WHITBREAD George
w 1828–1877
Math IM, Naut IM, Phil IM, Optician, Surveying IM
1828–1844   11 Exmouth St, Commercial Rd, London
1842–1874   2 Grenada Terrace, Commercial Road East, London
1875   453 Commercial Rd East, London E

Guild: [Masons], Spectaclemakers, fr 1828
Son of WHITBREAD William, blacksmith, d, of Ramsden Heath, Essex
Apprenticed to COOK William George★ 1812 MC
Had apprentice:
KAY Thomas Softley, 1828
CUTHBERT John (II)★ 1837
MOIR John James 1838
WHITBREAD George Thomas, his son, 1846
JOLLY Thomas Spratly 1848
Employed LEE George★
Succeeded by WHITBREAD George Thomas, his son
Associated with SWART J.B. of Amsterdam, to whom he supplied sextants
fr by purchase in SMC, 1828
Known to have sold: artificial horizon, sextant, theodolite
Sources: GL: MC 5304/6; SMC 5213/5, 5213/6; inst (s); inst & TCd NMM; Pg; PO; R

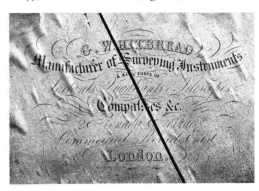

WHITBREAD William
w ? pt 1832–1836
Optician
          London
Guild: [Merchant Taylors]
Son of WHITBREAD William, shoemaker, of Holborn, London
Partnership: WHITBREAD & SEELING★
Apprenticed to WEEDEN William John★ 1818
Employed SMITH Edward (II)★
See also WHITBREAD George★
Sources: GL: MTC MF 320

WHITBREAD & SEELING William & Joseph
w 1832–1836
Optician, Math IM, Phil IM
1832–1836   2 King St, St.Luke's, London
See also
WHITBREAD William★
WHITBREAD George★
Sources: Pg (JAC)

WHITE –
w 1788
          London
See also WHITE Joseph★
Associated with NAIRNE & BLUNT★, as sub-contractor
Sources: mentioned in a letter by BIDSTRUP Jasper (JAC)

WHITE James

w 1850 p 1900
Optical IM, Math IM, Phil IM
1850–1852	24 Renfield St, Glasgow
1853–1856	14 Renfield St, Glasgow
1860–1863	1 Renfield St, Glasgow
1860–1863	60 Gordon St, Glasgow
1864–1868	95 Buchanan St, Glasgow
1869–1875	78 Union St, Glasgow
1876–1883	241 Sauchiehall St, Glasgow
1884–1890	209 Sauchiehall St, Glasgow
1884–1900	16, 18 & 20 Cambridge St, Glasgow
	18 Cambridge St, Glasgow

Son of WHITE William, yarn merchant, of Islay
Partnership: WHITE & BARR 1857–59
Apprenticed to GARDENER & CO.★ c.1839
Succeeded by KELVIN & James WHITE LTD
Associated with THOMSON William, later Lord KELVIN
b 1824, d 1884
Known to have sold: barometer, binnacle, lens, rule
Sources: inst NMM; Bryden (1972) p.59; Anderson et al (1990) p.90; Burnett & Morrison-Low (1989) p.252–75

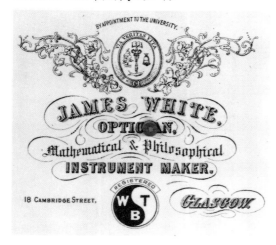

WHITE John

w 1715
Auchtermuchty
Succeeded by WHITE & SON John
Known to have sold: balance
Sources: Cat. of J. White & Son (Glasgow) (MAC)

WHITE Joseph

w 1781–1786
Math IM
1781–1786	8 Tash Court, Gray's Inn Lane, London
1786	4 Hatton Wall, Hatton St, London

Sources: GL: Sun 11936/288 no.438281,/336 no.517071 (MAC)

WHITE R.

w 1732
Known to have sold: sundial
Sources: inst SM (MAC)

WHITE Samuel (I)

w 1693–1695
Spec M

1693 Fleet St, London
Guild: Spectaclemakers, fr 1685
Son of WHITE John, member of GC of London
Apprenticed to MAXAM Richard★ 1676
Sources: GL: SMC 5213/1

WHITE Samuel (II)

w 1707
Ratcliff, London
Made compasses for the Navy
Sources: Taylor (1954) p.300

WHITE Thomas

w 1811
Math IM
1811	Gun Alley, St George's in the East, London

Father of WHITE George s 1811 GC
Sources: GL: GC 11598/6

WHITE William (I)

w 1693
Spec M
1693 St Giles in the Fields, London
Had apprentice: WHITE – 1692/3
Sources: GL: SMC 5213/1

WHITE William (II)

w 1794–1811
Scale M
1794	4 Chamber St, Whitechapel, London
1811	Denne [?] Yard, Whitechapel, London

Guild: Haberdashers, fr 1794
Apprenticed to MOFFETT Elizabeth★ 1787
Had apprentice:
WHITE Thomas 1797
PANKER Joseph 1811
Sources: GL: HC 15857/3, 15860/9 (MAC)

WHITE William (III)

w 1848–1851
Math IM
1851 50 Lowgate, Hull
Known to have sold: octant
Sources: Wh; ChrSK 4 Sep 1980 lot 162, 23 Oct 1987 lot 317 (MAC)

WHITE William (IV)

w 1840–1841
Phil IM
1840–1841 2 Chapel St, Paddington, London
Attended London Mechanics Institute 1840–1841
Sources: LMIR (AM)

WHITE William Samuel

w 1832–1840
Math IM, Phil IM
1832–1840	17 Anchor and Hope Alley, Wapping, London

Sources: Pg; R (JAC)

WHITE & WALSH

w 1765
Surgeons IM, Math IM
1765	The Ace of Spades in Water St, Liverpool

Source: Gore's Advertiser 31 Aug 1765 (MAC)

WHITEHEAD Richard

w 1683–1693
Math IM
Gunpowder Alley, half-way up Shoe Lane, Fleet St, London
Guild: Clockmakers, fr 1671
Father of WHITEHEAD Charles
Apprenticed to WYNNE Henry★
Had apprentice:
REYNOLDS Joseph 1683
WHITEHEAD Charles 1693
Known to have sold: circumferentor, compass, gunner's callipers, sundial
Sources: GL: CKC 3939; Brown J (1979b) p.34; Brown O (1982b) no.62; inst MSEN (MAC); Taylor (1954) p.251–52

WHITEHOUSE David

w 1826
Optician
1826 3 Silver St, Clerkenwell, London
Succeeded by WHITEHOUSE M.
Sources: R (JAC)

WHITEHOUSE John

w 1827 d by 1884
Optician, Spec M, Magnet M
10 St.John's Lane, Clerkenwell, London
1840	13 St.John's Lane, London
1855	10 Tottenham Court Rd, London
1865–1885	8 Coventry St. West, London

Succeeded by WHITEHOUSE John Julius
Partnership: WHITEHOUSE John & James★ 1837 ? –1853
Sources: GL: SMC 5213/8; Pg (JAC); PO

WHITEHOUSE John Henry

w 1838–1852
Optician
1838–1852 29 William St, Hampstead, London
Sources: Pg; PO

WHITEHOUSE John Thomas

w 1829–1844
Spec M, Optician
1829–1844	13 St.John's Lane, West Smithfield, London

Sources: PO; R (JAC)

WHITEHOUSE John & James

w 1837–1853
Alternative name: James & John
Optician, Math IM, Phil IM
1837–1853 10 Tottenham Court Rd, London
Sources: PO; R (JAC)

WHITEHOUSE Joseph

w 1831 p 1913
Spec M, Optician
21 Wilmington Square, Spitalfields, London
1839–1859	3 Wilmington St, Spitalfields, London
1865–1875	43 Warwick St, Pimlico, London, SW
1880–1901	37 Warwick St, Pimlico, London, SW

Sources: PO; R (JAC)

WHITEHOUSE Joshua
w 1851
Optician
1851   266½ Strand, London
Sources: Wk

WHITEHOUSE M.
w 1829–1830
Optical IM, Phil IM, Math IM
1829–1830   3 Silver St, Clerkenwell Green,
             London
Sources: PO; R (JAC)

WHITEHOUSE Nathaniel
w 1822–1825
Spec M, Optician
       1 Cross St, Hatton Garden, London
       3 Cross St, Hatton Garden, London
See also WHITEHOUSE Nathaniel W.★
Sources: Kt (JAC); Pg

WHITEHOUSE Nathaniel W.
w 1836–1882
Spec M, Optician
       1 Castle St, Great Newport St,
       London
1836   27 Grafton St, Soho, London
1837–1846   1 Castle St, Leicester Square, London
1847–1882   2 Cranbourn St, Leicester Square,
             London
See also WHITEHOUSE Nathaniel★
Ex.1851
Known to have sold: barometer, opera glasses,
spectacles
Sources: Cat. 1851 (MAC); PO; R (JAC)

WHITEHOUSE S.
w 1812–1816
Spec M, Magnet M
       3 Green St, Clerkenwell, London
       9 Aylesbury St, Clerkenwell, London
Sources: Kt (JAC)

WHITEHURST John (I)
w 1736 d 1788
Watchmaker, Assayer, Math IM
1736–1775   22 Irongate, Derby
1776–1788   4 Bolt Court, Fleet St, London
Succeeded by WHITEHURST John (II)★
Associated with
FERGUSON James (I)★
BOULTON Matthew
FRS 1779
Known to have sold: astronomical clock,
barometer, ellipsograph
Sources: Goodison (1977) p.281–83; King &
Millburn (1978) p.141; Millburn (1988a) p.164,168;
Wallis R & P (1986) p.371

WHITEHURST John (II)
w 1788–1810
Clock M
       22 Irongate, Derby
Nephew of WHITEHURST John (I)★
Succeeded by WHITEHURST & SON★
Took over from WHITEHURST John (I)★
d.1834
Sources: Goodison (1977) p.284–85

WHITEHURST John III
w 1834 d 1855
Clock M, Watch M
1834   22 Irongate, Derby
1843   1 Cherry St, Derby
Took over from WHITEHURST & SON★
Sources: Goodison (1977) p.286

WHITEHURST & SON John II (& John III)
w 1810–1834
       Derby
Took over from WHITEHURST John (II)★
Succeeded by WHITEHURST John (III)★
John (II) d 1834
Known to have sold: barometer, sundial,
thermometer
Sources: inst (s) (MAC); Goodison (1977) p.284

WHITEMARSH William
w 1736 d c. 1748
       London
Guild: Blacksmiths, fr 1731
Apprenticed to ROBERTS Timothy★ 1724
Had apprentice:
DUDBRIDGE John 1736
BULLWINKLE Thomas 1740/1
Sources: GL: BKC 1886/5 (MAC)

WHITFIELD Edward
w 1777–1829
Scale M
1777–1829   16 Church St, Birmingham
Sources: Chp; H; PR; Wr (all MAC)

WHITFORD Edward
fr 1787 d 1835
[Math IM]
       London
Guild: Blacksmiths, fr 1787
Apprenticed to WHITFORD Samuel★
Sources: GL: BKC 2881/16 & /17, 2886/5

WHITFORD James
w 1790–1794
Math IM
1790–1794   27 Ludgate St, London
See also
WHITFORD Thomas (I)★
WHITFORD Thomas (II)★
WHITFORD Samuel★
Sources: W (JAC)

WHITFORD Samuel
w 1765 d 1789
Optical IM, Phil IM, Math IM
       Near St.Paul's Churchyard, London
       Archimedes & Three Spectacles,
       No.27 Ludgate St, near St.Paul's
       Church Yard, London
1776–1781   Archimedes & Three Spectacles,
             27 Ludgate St, London
1783   27 Ludgate St, London
1788–1790   47 Ludgate St, London
Guild: Blacksmiths, fr 1762
Son of WHITFORD Thomas (I)★
Apprenticed to LIND John★ 1755
Had apprentice:
SOWERBY Charles 1765

KIMBER William★ 1771
WHITFORD Edward★ 1776
WARREN Isaac J. 1778
ARROWSMITH George 1785
Took over from MORGAN Francis★
See also
WHITFORD James★
WHITFORD Thomas (II)★
Went to St. Petersburg 1771
Sources: BW; By; GL: BKC 2886/5, 2885/1,
2881/15 & /16 (MAC); BM: Heal 105/116;
Calvert (1977) p.46, pl.58; Anderson et al (1990)
p.90

WHITFORD Thomas (I)
w 1742 d 1792
Optician
Alternative name: WHITEFORD
1755–1760   St.Martin's le Grand, London
1782   St.Ann's Parish, Aldersgate, London
-1791   27 Ludgate St, London
Guild: u & Spectaclemkrs, fr 1743
Father of
WHITFORD Samuel★
WHITFORD William s 1760 BC
Had apprentice WALL Charles, his grand-son, by
t/o 1782
Succeeded by BLEULER John★
Freed in SMC 1743 as 'Foreign Brother', i.e.
member of another guild
Sources: GL: BKC 2886/5; SMC 5213/3 p.40,56,
5213/4; CH 12876/6; BC 5266/5; Taylor (1966)
p.250

WHITFORD Thomas (II)
w 1771
Watch M
       London
1771   Haverfordwest, Pembroke
See also WHITFORD Thomas (I)★
Instruments advertised: barometer, drawing
instruments, Gunter's scale, quadrant, telescope
Sources: Pugh's *Hereford Journal*, 4 Apr 1771, p.3
(JRM)

WHITMORE William
w 1777–1803
Scale M, Toy M, Jobbing Smith
1777   112 Snow Hill, Birmingham
1780–1791   27 Little Charles St, Birmingham
1797   Newhall St, Birmingham
Pat. weighing machine 1796
Sources: Chp; PR; Pye; Sy; Wd (all MAC);
Woodcroft (1854)

WHITTINGHAM Thomas
w 1802–1845
Rule M
1802   Court, 27 Wardster St,
            Wolverhampton
1833–1835   Church Lane, Wolverhampton
1841   Bond St, Wolverhampton
1845   Snowhill, Wolverhampton
See also WHITTINGHAM William★
Sources: Wolverhampton rate books; Br; Pg; Wh
(all MAC)

WHITTINGHAM William
w 1792
Rule M
1792   43 Stafford St, Wolverhampton
See also WHITTINGHAM Thomas★
Sources: Wolverhampton rate books (MAC)

WHITTYAT Roger
w 1724–1743
Math IM
Alternative name: WHITTGATE
1724   Wapping, London
1731   Virginia St, London
1731   Old Bailey, London
Guild: Stationers, fr 1712
Son of WHITTYAT Roger, carpenter, of
Marlborough, Wilts
Apprenticed to JOLE Robert★ 1704
Had apprentice:
LANGFORD Henry 1724
GRAY Richard 1731
ADDISON Jabez 1736
READ Philip 1737
Sources: GL: CH 12876/3; McKenzie (1978)
p.198, 375

WHITWELL Charles
w 1593 d 1611
Engraver, Math IM
            Against St.Clement's Church,
            London
1597   Over against Essex House, without
            Temple Bar, London
1598   Without Temple Bar, against St
            Clements Church, London
Guild: Grocers, fr 1590
Apprenticed to RYTHER Augustine★ 1582
Had apprentice:
WRIGHTSON William 1593
SILVESTER Joshua 1594
SMYTHE John 1596
BARTRAM Abraham 1602
ALLEN Elias★ c.1602
WOLRICHE Carye 1608
NEWBERY William 1610
WOODALL Thomas nd fr 1604
Known to have sold: astrolabe, compass, nocturnal,
perpetual calendar, quadrant, sector, sundial
Sources: Brown (1979a) p.24; Bryden (1992) p.312;
Taylor (1954) p.190, pl.3–4

WICKHAM Stephen
w 1796–1797
Measure M
1796–1797   33 Little Eastcheap, London
Sources: Ld (MAC)

WIDENHAM Richard
w 1825–1831
Chrono M
1823–1831   6 East St, Red Lion Square, London
Received award at chronometer trials at Royal
Greenwich Observatory 1825
Sources: CUL: RGO 1143 fol.5–9

WIGGINTON James
w 1835–1853
Scale M

Alternative name: WIGGINGTON
1835–1853   19 Union St, Hackney Rd, London
Guild: Blacksmiths, fr 1813
Apprenticed to SAWGOOD John★ 1800
Succeeded by WIGGINTON James & Thomas
Sources: GL: BKC 2881/16 & /17 (MAC); Pg; PO
(MAC); R (JAC)

WIGNALL John (I)
w 1818
Spec M
1818   St.Martin's St, Birmingham
Sources: Wr (MAC)

WIGNALL John (II)
w 1831
Optician
1831   4 Gun St, Bishopsgate, London
Sources: R (JAC)

WILCOX Thomas
w 1836
Hydro M
1836   26 Hanway St, London
Sources: R (JAC)

WILD Roger
fr 1724
Math IM
1724   Liverpool
Apprenticed to ROSCOE Robert★
Sources: LM index (MAC)

WILDBOARE Tobias
w 1683
Known to have sold: rule
Sources: Taylor (1954) p.279

WILDING James
w 1790–1816
Math IM, Victualler
1772–1790   50 Plumbe St, Liverpool
1796   14 Prussia St, Liverpool
1800–1805   12 Prussia St, Liverpool
1807–1811   13 Prussia St, Liverpool
1816   17 Prussia St, Liverpool
Sources: G (MAC); LM index (MAC)

WILFORD David (I)
w 1682 d by 1716
Scale M
            In Leadenhall Street near Cree
            Church, London
Guild: Blacksmiths, fr 1671 or 1672
Had apprentice:
JOY John★ 1789
HALL John (I)★ nd, for 1698
FISH John★ 1693
WILFORD David (II)★, his son, 1700
and 13 others 1682–1702
Known to have sold: balance
Sources: GL: BKC 2886/2, 2886/3, 2884 (MAC),
inst ML (MAC)

WILFORD David (II)
fr 1716 d by 1750
            London
Guild: Blacksmiths, fr 1716

Son of WILFORD David (I)★
Apprenticed to WILFORD David (I)★
Had apprentice WALKER John 1723 t/o FREEMAN
Samuel (II)★
Sources: GL: BKC 2881/10 & /11 (MAC)

WILKINS John
w 1851
Baro M, Thermo M
1851   1 Cropley St, Hoxton, London
Possibly the same as WILKINS John, Phil IM, of 5
Dorchester St, North Rd, London, who attended
the London Mechanics Institute 1840–1843
Sources: PO: LMIR (AM)

WILKINSON Anthony
w 1781 d 1801
Gold balance M
Alternative name: A.W.
–1784   Kirkby
1785–1801   Ormskirk
Employed HOUGHTON Stephen★
Succeeded by HOUGHTON Stephen★
Known to have sold: balance, pantograph
Sources: inst SM & (pv); By; BW (MAC)

WILKINSON I.
a 1775–1800
Associated with MOUNTFORD W.★
Known to have sold: balance
Sources: inst York Mu & (pv) (MAC)

WILKINSON John (I)
w 1752–1754
Math IM
1752   Southwark, London
Guild: Stationers, fr 1752
Apprenticed to BATES Richard★ 1739
Had apprentice APPLETON J. 1752 t/o 1754 to
RUST Richard★
Sources: McKenzie (1978) p.26, 379

WILKINSON John (II)
w 1826–1837
Optician, Goldsmith, Jeweller, Cutler
1826–1837   54 Briggate, Leeds
1837   4 Blenhiem Square, Leeds
            (residence)
Sources: Pg; PWh (DJB); Wh (DJB)

WILLATS Benjamin
w 1849
Phil IM, Baro M, Thermo M
1849   55 Bartholomew Close, London
Sources: PO

WILLATS Thomas
w 1844–1845
Optician, Math IM, Phil IM, Hydro M, Baro M,
Thermo M
1845   98 Cheapside, London
Sources: PO

WILLATS Thomas & Richard
w 1845–1853
Optician, Math IM, Phil IM, Chem IM, Hydro
M, Baro M, Thermo M, Photographic Apparatus
M

1845–1853　98 Cheapside, London
Succeeded by WILLATS Richard
Known to have sold: electrostatic apparatus
Sources: PO; Cat. MHS (MAC); Phlps 2 Dec 1987
lot 141 (MAC); Anderson et al (1990) p.90

WILLCOX Walton
w 1775–1781
Math IM
1777　Hermitage, London
Guild: Joiners, fr 1772
Apprenticed to URINGS John (II)★
Had apprentice:
LEKEUX Richard★ 1775 by t/o from RIPLEY
Thomas★
MILLS George★ 1782, t/o 1783 to SPENCER
William (II)★
Worked for URINGS John (II)★
d c.1783
Sources: GL: GC 11598/4; Crawforth (1987) p.371

WILLDEY George
w 1713–1737
Map S, Toy shop, Optical IM
Alternative name: WILDEY, WELLDY
1709–1715　The Great Toy, Spectacle,
　　　　　　Chinaware and Print Shop next the
　　　　　　Dog Tavern, corner of Ludgate St,
　　　　　　near St.Paul's, London
　　　　　　The Great Toy, Spectacle and Print
　　　　　　Shop at the corner of Ludgate St,
　　　　　　next to St.Paul's, London
1706–1709　Archimedes & Globe, Ludgate St,
　　　　　　London
1718–1737　The West End of St. Paul's, London
Guild: Spectaclemakers, fr 1702
Father of WILLDEY Thomas★, fp 1739
Son of WILLDEY Thomas, gentleman, d, of
Church Eaton, Staffs
Partnership: WILLDEY & PRICE★
WILLDEY & BRANDRETH★
Apprenticed to YARWELL John★ 1694/5
Had apprentice:
PASSAVANT Susanna★ 1727/8
CLARK Thomas (I)★ 1724
GIBBONS William★ 1708/9
ELVIN Peter 1712
MARTYN Hannah 1714
BALL Susanna 1715
SHORT Martha 1716
RAY Walter 1717
WATKINS Edward 1717
SARRAZIN Esther 1720
LE PLASTRIER Isaac 1721
JOURDAIN Rachel 1722
WILLDEY Frances, daughter of Thomas, 1726
DUPUY Elizabeth 1733
KING Isaac 1736
Worked for MARSHALL John★
Succeeded by WILLDEY Judith★, his widow, then
WILLDEY Thomas★
Associated with PRICE Charles★
Freed 1702; Partnerships 1707–1710, 1710–c.1713;
d.1737; Master SMC 1722–1733
Sources: GL: SMC 5213/2 p.28,62,81,87,92,96,
101–2,115,126,133–177+, 5213/3 p.10, 6029,
6031/1; BM: Heal 105/114; Calvert (1971) p.46;
Tyacke (1978) p.147–48

WILLDEY Judith (Mrs)
w 1738–1739
Toy Shop, Optical IM
1738–1739　London
Guild: Spectaclemakers
Wife of WILLDEY George★
Succeeded by WILLDEY Thomas★
Took over from WILLDEY George★
Apparently continued the business between
husband's death in 1737 and the son taking his
freedom 1739
Sources: GL: SMC 6029

WILLDEY Thomas
w 1739–1747
Map S, Optical IM
　　　　　Great Goldsmith, Toy, China and
　　　　　Print shop at the corner of Ludgate
　　　　　St, by St.Paul's, London
Guild: Spectaclemakers, fp 1739
Son of WILLDEY George★
Had apprentice: WEST Elizabeth &/or Mary 1746
Took over from WILLDEY Judith★, his mother
d by 1748
Sources: GL:SMC 6031/1; 5213/3 p.10,106, 6029;
BL: broadsheet by T. Willdey C.11615(DS)

WILLDEY & BRANDRETH George & Timothy
w 1707 c 1711
Instrument M
Alternative name: BRANDRETH & WILLDEY
　　　　　Archimedes & Globe near Ludgate,
　　　　　London
　　　　　Exchange Alley in Cornhill, London
　　　　　Archimedes & Globe, Spectacle and
　　　　　Toy-Shop, next the Dog Tavern in
　　　　　Ludgate St, London
1707　Archimedes & Globe in Ludgate St,
　　　the Corner of St.Paul's, London
See also
WILLDEY George★
BRANDRETH Timothy★
Sources: Daily Courant 3 Mar 1707; Bryden &
Simms (1993) p.17; Calvert (1971) p.46;
Tyacke(1978) p.148

WILLDEY & PRICE George & Charles
w 1710 c 1713
　　　　　The Great Toy Shop, corner of
　　　　　Ludgate St, London
1710　Archimedes & Globe, Ludgate St,
　　　London
See also
WILLDEY George★
PRICE Charles★
Sources: Tyacke (1978) p.138

WILLDIN James
w 1794
Quadrant M
1794　26 Prussia St, Liverpool
Sources: LM index (MAC)

WILLIAMS Edward
w 1811–1817
Scale M
　　　　　London

Guild: Blacksmiths, fr 1809
Apprenticed to WILLIAMS Thomas★ 1797
Had apprentice SKINNER George 1811 t/o to
WILLIAMS Thomas (I)★ 1817
Sources: GL: BKC 2881/16

WILLIAMS George
w 1832–1834
Optician
1831–1834　107 James St, Liverpool
1831–1834　39 Whitechapel, Liverpool
Sources: LM index (MAC)

WILLIAMS Rice
a 1740–1750
Phil IM
　　　　　Against Somerset House by the New
　　　　　Church in the Strand, London
Known to have sold: barometer
Instruments advertised: barometer
Sources: BM: Heal 105/114; Goodison (1977)
p.371

WILLIAMS Samuel
w 1829–1835
Spec M
1829–1835　47 Duke St, Birmingham
Sources: Pg; Wr (MAC)

WILLIAMS Thomas (I)
a 1750–1800
Alternative name: T.W.
　　　　　At ye Spectacles, Oxford
Source: Token (JAC)

WILLIAMS Thomas (II)
w 1776–1783
Ironmonger, Brazier
1776–1783　22 Ludgate St, London
Associated with HENRY Solomon★ whose gauges
he sold
Sources: inst & TCd (pv) (MAC); By (MAC)

WILLIAMS Thomas (III)
w 1776–1835
Scale M
1792–1835　The Hand & Scales, 71 Cannon St,
　　　　　London
1817–1835　4 Abchurch Yard, London
Guild: Blacksmiths, fr 1776
Apprenticed to HARRISON Thomas (II)★ 1769
Had apprentice:
SKINNER William (I)★ 1788 by t/o from
VINCENT R.★
SMITH William (II)★ 1787
HUDSON Robert★ 1804
WILLIAMS William (I)★ 1808
and 12 others 1781–1818
Took over from HARRISON Thomas (II)★
Known to have sold: balance, steelyard
Sources: GL: BKC 2881/15 & /16; 2886/5
(MAC); H; Kt; Pg; Wil (MAC); Heal (1939) p.152

WILLIAMS William (I)
w 1835–1850
Scale M
1835–1850　71 Cannon St, London
1839–1850　and 4 Abchurch Yard, London

Guild: Blacksmiths, fr 1818
Father of WILLIAMS William (II)★
Apprenticed to WILLIAMS Thomas (I)★ 1808
Had apprentice WILLIAMS William (II)★ 1835
Succeeded by WILLIAMS & SON William
Took over from WILLIAMS Thomas (I)★
Known to have sold: balance
Instruments advertised: balance
Sources: GL: BKL 2881/16, /17, /18 (MAC); inst (pv); Pg; PO

WILLIAMS William (II)

s 1835
Scale M
      London
Guild: [Blacksmiths]
Son of WILLIAMS William (I)★
Partnership: WILLIAMS & SONS Wm. (probably)
Apprenticed to WILLIAMS William (I)★
Sources: GL: BKC 2881/17 (MAC)

WILLIAMSON Joseph

w 1727–1728
      Aberdeen
Known to have sold: sundial
Sources: inst & n NMS (MAC)

WILLIAMSON Robert

w 1761 d 1777
Stationer, Chirugical IS, Optical IS, Phil IS, Math IS, Musical IS, Printer, Book S
1761   Near the Exchange, Liverpool
1765–1769   Castle St, Liverpool
Sources: G (DJB); LM index (MAC); Calvert (1971) p.46

WILLSMERE Jesse

w 1836–1855
Math IM, Phil IM
Alternative name: WILLSMER
1836–1840   2 Gloucester Terrace, Commercial Rd, London
1855   Camden Row North, Kentish Town, London
Guild: [Grocers]
Son of WILLSMERE Reuben, carpenter, d, of Brixton, Surrey
Apprenticed to GARDNER James★ 1827
Sources: GL: GC 11598/7; Pg; PO

WILLSON George

w 1809–1812
Optical turner, Optician
1798   Sermon Lane, Doctors Common, London
1799–1802   Wardrobe Place, Doctors Common, London
Guild: Stationers, fr 1797
Partnership: WILLSON & DIXEY★
Apprenticed to MOULDING James★ 1781 t/o to MASON John★
Had apprentice:
DIXEY George★ 1798
COLE John (II) 1799
BOOTH William★ 1802
Sources: Bod: MTC MF 440 (MAC); McKenzie (1978) p.227,381

WILLSON & DIXEY George & ?

w 1802–1809
Optician
1802–1809   Opposite St.James' Church, Piccadilly, London
1802   9 Wardrobe Place, Doctor's Commons, London
1803   35 Piccadilly, London
See also
DIXEY George★
DIXEY Richard★
WILLSON George★
Sources: BM: Banks 105/63; H; Kt (JAC)

WILSON A.

w 1845
Optician
1845   Thorpe-le-Soken, Colchester, Essex
Sources: PO(HC)

WILSON Alexander

w 1770–1794
Clock M
1770–1794   132 Drury Lane, London
Guild: Clockmakers, fr 1781
A barometer signed 'Alex. Wilson fecit 1774' is known, and may be by the clock maker of that name.
Sources: inst (s); Baillie (1951)

WILSON Charles (I)

w 1837
Nautical IM, Optician
1837   30 Harper St, Toxteth Park, Liverpool
Sources: G (MAC)

WILSON Charles (II)

w 1842–1851
Teacher, Navigation warehouse, Chart S, Naut IM
1842–1851   157 Leadenhall St, London
Guild: Spectaclemakers, fr 1842
Son of WILSON William, in service
Partnership: NORIE & WILSON★
Took over from NORIE & WILSON★
fr in SMC by purchase
Known to have sold: artificial horizon, octant
Sources: GL: SMC 5213/5; TCd NMM; PO; inst Dundee Museum (DJB)

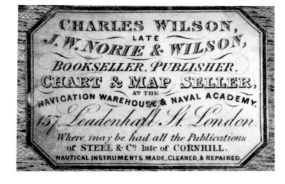

WILSON George (I)

w 1805–1817
Optician

1805   16 Charterhouse St, West Smithfield, London
1809–1817   44 Kirby St, Hatton Garden, London
1816–1817   115 Holborn Hill, London
See also WILSON George (II)★
Known to have sold: barometer
Sources: H; Kt (JAC); ChrSK 17 Apr 1986, lot 89 (MAC)

WILSON George (II)

w 1826
Math IM
1826   4 St.John Street Rd, London
See also WILSON George (I)
Sources: R (JAC)

WILSON George (III)

w 1824
Mineral S, Optician
1824   5 Drummond St, Edinburgh
1824   14 Roxburgh St, Edinburgh (residence)
Sources: NMS n (MAC)

WILSON George (IV)

w 1838–1839
Math IM, Phil IM
1838–1839   26 Merlin Place, Wilmington Square, London
Sources: Pg

WILSON James (I)

w 1702–1710
Optical IM
1706–1710   The Willow Tree, Cross St, Hatton Garden, London
Known to have sold: microscope, telescope
Sources: Phil T. 23 (1702–3) 1241–7; BM: Heal 105/72; inst MHS, SM

WILSON John (I)

w 1729–1744
Math IM;
Alternative name: WILLSON
1729   New Sreet Square, London
1731   Corner of Bernard's Inn, Holborn, London
1736–1744   King's Head Court, Holborn, London
Guild: Clockmakers, fr 1715
Apprenticed to GLYNNE Richard★ 1707
Had apprentice:
COLLINS John 1718 by t/o
HONOR William 1724
HOLMES John 1732
EVANS James 1735/6
d. 1749 or 1750
Sources: GL: CKC,2723/2; Sun 11936/30+E; Brown J (1979b) p.34

WILSON John (II)

w 1728
Spec M
1728   London
Son of WILSON Thomas (I)★
1728 Prosecuted by SMC for working as a Spec M when not free
Sources: GL: SMC 5213/2 p.199

WILSON John (III)
w 1769–1790
Clock M, Watch M, Surgeons IM, Scale M
St.Nicholas Church Yard, Newcastle on Tyne
near the Black Swan, Flesh Market, 1778
1778   Flesh Market, Newcastle on Tyne
1790   Mosley St, Newcastle on Tyne
Known to have sold: balance
Sources: Whd; inst (pv) MAC

WILSON Joseph
w 1774–1787
Optician, Math IM, Spec M
1774–1787   Norfolk St, Sheffield
Sources: Gales (MAC); Sket (MAC)

WILSON Richard
w 1672
Ironmonger
1672   Within Newgate, London
Guild: Ironmongers, fr 1671–1672
Apprenticed to WALKER William jun
Known to have sold: rule
Sources: GL: IMC 16977/1; Loomes (1981b)

WILSON Robert William
w 1828–1830
Optical IM, Phil IM, Math IM
1828–1830   27 New Compton St, Soho, London
Sources: Pg (JAC); R (JAC)

WILSON Thomas (I)
w c. 1728
[Spec M]
London
Guild: Spectaclemakers, fr 1694
Father of WILSON John (II)★
Apprenticed to GOODMAN Thomas (II)★ 1686/7
t/o to GOODMAN Dorothy★ nd
Sources: GL: SMC 5213/1, 5213/2 p.199

WILSON Thomas (II)
w 1830–1847
Jeweller, Optician, Math IM, Watch M, Clock M
1830   Petty Cury, Cambridge
1847   22 Market Hill, Cambridge
Sources: Pg; K

WILSON Thomas (III)
w 1836–1839
Optician, Math IM, Phil IM
16 High St, St Giles, London
45 Eagle St, Red Lion Square, London
Sources: Pg (JAC); R (JAC)

WILSON William (I)
w 1837–1848
Math IM, Phil IM, Mechanical Modeller
1818   Vine St, Piccadilly, London
1837–1848   33 Old Change, London
Guild: Clothworkers, fp 1818
Had apprentice:
WILSON William Pepper, his son, 1837
GREENLEES Robert 1848
Sources: Pg; CWH: CWC Ap, Fr

WILSON William (II)
w 1850
Rule M
1850   9 Mott St, Birmingham
Sources: Sl

WILSON & DESTAFFONE
w 1816
Optician
Alternative name: DESTETTANE
1816   17 North End Old Docks, Liverpool
Sources: Und (MAC)

WILTON William (I)
s 1738
Ship Chandler
London
Guild: Merchant Taylors
Apprenticed to EADE Jonathan (I)★ 1738
Partnership: possibly EADE, WILTON & ALLEN★
Sources: GL: MTC MF 319

WILTON William (II)
w 1825 d 1859
Math IM, Watch M, Clock M, Optical IM, Philo IM
1830–1851   St.Day (Cornwall)
1852–1856   Market Place, Camborne
Succeeded by JEFFERY A.
Associated with NEWTON Edward T.
Ex. 1851
Known to have sold: compass (magnetic), dip circles, theodolite
Sources: RCPSAR 1894; Cat. 1851; Pg; ChrSK 27 Nov 1986 lot 252

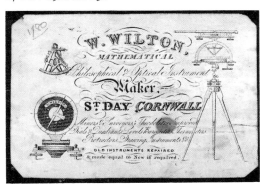

WILTSHIRE -
w 1785–1794
Spec M
1785   2 Ball Alley, Lombard St, London
1794   46 Lombard St, London
Sources: BM: Banks 105/64 (MAC)

WINEMAN Moses
w 1830
Optician
1830   28 Butcher St, Portsea
Sources: Pg

WING Tycho
fr 1751 d 1776
Math IM
The Strand, London

1751   near Exeter Exchange, Strand, London
Guild: Grocers, fr 1751
Partnership: HEATH & WING★
Apprenticed to HEATH Thomas★ 1741
Had apprentice:
NEWMAN Thomas 1751
FAIRBONE Charles (I)★ 1753
GORDON George 1754
MORRIS William (I)★ 1764
WHORLETT Edward 1767
HOLMES Samuel 1767
DAVIES John 1773
b 1726; Partnership 1751–73; petitioner against Dollond's patent 1764
Sources: PRO: PC 1/7 no.94; Brown J (1979a) p.39–40

WINGFIELD John
w 1669–1671
Book S, Instrument S (?)
1669–1671   over against St.Olave's Church in Crutched Friars, London
Associated with
SELLER John (I)★
BROWN John (I)★
Publisher
Sources: Taylor (1954) p.261

WINN Richard
w 1738–1755
Math IM
1739   Parish of St.Martin in the Fields, London
1746   Parish of St.Bride, London
1747   Fleet St, London
Guild: Stationers, fr 1726
Apprenticed to CHAPMAN William★ 1718
Had apprentice:
SIMPSON Charles 1738
DUNBAR William 1739
BULLOCK John★ 1746
WOOD Alexander 1746
STANWAY John 1747
CHAMPNEYS James★ 1752
BROWN Isaac★ 1755
Sources: McKenzie (1978) p.383–84

WINSPEARE Thomas
w 1705–1730
Scale M
1705   Angel & Scales, Mark Lane, London
Guild: Blacksmiths, fr 1705
Apprenticed to HOE Robert★ 1697
Had apprentice:
BLAKE Edward 1706
BALL William 1708
Sources: GL: BKC 2886/3, 2881/10 & /11; CH 12876/3

WINTER J.
w 1826
Optician
1826   9 New Bond St, London
See also Apprentices of JONES John (I)★
Sources: R (JAC)

WINTER Thomas
w 1794–1849
Optician, Math IM
          9 Wells St, Oxford St, London
          Mount St, Grosvenor Square, London
          9 New Bond St, London
          4 Ebenezer Place, Commercial Rd, Limehouse, London
          33 Poland St, Oxford St, London
1800   37 Brewer St, Golden Square, London
1805–1816 6 Brewer St, Golden Square, London
1839–1849 5 Market St, Oxford St, London
1849   24 Great Castle St, Regent St, London
Bankrupt 1805
Sources: H; Kt; PO; Und; W (JAC)

WINTER Thomas
d 1718
Math IM
1718   Dublin
Sources: Burnett & Morrison-Low (1989) p.138

WISKER Elizabeth
w 1822–1827
Optician, Instrument M
Alternative name: Widow
1822–1827 Spurrier Gate, York
Wife of WISKER John★
Mother of WISKER Matthias★
Took over from WISKER John★
Succeeded by WISKER Matthias★
Sources: Bn; Goodison (1977) p.371

WISKER John
w 1804 d 1822
Optician
1804–1822 Spurriergate, York
Son of WISKER Matthew★
Succeeded by WISKER Elizabeth★
Known to have sold: barometer
Sources: Bn; WB; Goodison (1977) p.371

WISKER Matthew
w 1777–1804
Optician, Glass grinder
Alternative name: given as Matthias in BW 1798
1777–1804 Spurriergate, York
Father of WISKER John★
Succeeded by WISKER John★
Took over from BERRY
Sources: BW; Goodison (1977) p.371; DJB

WISKER Matthias
w 1827–1854
Optician, Lamp S, Oil S
1830–1851 13 Spurrier Gate, York
1834   14 Spurrier Gate, York
1854   12 Spurrier Gate, York
Succeeded by WISKER J.T.R.
Took over from WISKER Elizabeth★
Sources: Pg; Sl; Wh (DJB); TCd (p); Goodison (1977) p.372

WITHAM Nathaniel
w 1713–1716
[Math IM]
Alternative name: Nat
1716   London
Known to have sold: compass, sundial
Sources: Loomes (1981b); inst NMM; p.150 Taylor (1966)

WITHERSPOON Colin
w 1801–1803
Math IM
1801   4 White Lyon Court, Charterhouse Lane, London
1803   Charterhouse Lane, London
Guild: Spectaclemakers, fr 1801
Son of WITHERSPOON John★
Apprenticed to NAIRNE Edward★ 1780
Had apprentice:
ROBINS Joseph 1801
EDGINGTON John★ 1803
DAVIS William (V) 1803
Sources: GL:SMC 5213/3, 5213/4

WITHERSPOON John
w 1780–1783
Optician
1780   Little Bell Alley, parish of All Hallows, London Wall, London
1783   White Lion Court, Bell Alley, Coleman St, London
Father of
WITHERSPOON Colin★
WITHERSPOON Thomas s 1783
Worked for NAIRNE Edward★
d by 1801
Sources: GL:SMC 5213/3, 5213/4; CLRO: LicFW (MAC)

WITHNOLL Thomas
w pt 1762–1775
Math IM
1765   Birmingham
Partnership: FROST & WITHNOLL★
Had apprentice DEAKIN Ambrose 1765
Sources: PRO: IR 1/24 (AM)

WITHNOLL William
w 1777
Rule M
Alternative name: WITHNOL, WITHNALL
1777   20 Ann St, on Mount Place, Birmingham
See also
WOOD & WITHNOLL★
WOOD Henry (I)★
WOOD John (I)★
FROST & WITHNOLL★
Sources: PR

WOLLER Charles
w 1839–1862
Baro M, Thermo M
1839–1862 63 Edgbaston St, Birmingham
See also: WOLLER Matthew★
Sources: Mor (MAC); Goodson (1977) p.372

WOLLER Matthew
w 1800–1825
Clock M, Baro M
1800–1818 51 Edgbaston St, Birmingham
1818   Edgbaston St, Birmingham
1821–1825 63 Edgbaston St, Birmingham
See also WOLLER Charles★
Known to have sold: barometer
Sources: BM: Banks 39/136; Bis (MAC); Pg (MAC); Und

WOLMESLEY John
w 1715
      London
Had apprentice: SPARKS George by t/o from CULPEPER Edmund (I)★
Sources: Brown J. (1979a) p.33

WOOD Alexander (I)
w 1809
Math IM
1809   13 Wheeler St, Spitalfields, London
Sources: H (JAC)

WOOD Alexander (II)
fr 1810 w 1825
Scale M, Smith
1825   158 Stockwell St, Glasgow
Guild: Hammermen, fr 1810
Father of WOOD Alexander (III)★
Succeeded by WOOD Alexander (III)★
Known to have sold: balance
Sources: Pg (MAC), Lumsden & Aitken (1912) p.304 (MAC)

WOOD Alexander (III)
w 1829–1830
Scale M
1829–1830 Glasgow
Guild: Hammermen, fr 1830
Son of WOOD Alexander (II)★
Succeeded by WOOD & SONS Alexander
Took over from WOOD Alexander (II)★
Known to have sold: balance
Sources: Lumsden & Aitken (1912) p.313 (MAC)

WOOD Benjamin
w 1810–1832
Math IM, Naut IM
1810   41 Wapping, Liverpool
1811   52 Wapping, Liverpool
1813   11 Dwerry House St, (residence) Liverpool
1813–1832 50 Wapping, Liverpool
1816   1 Prince William St, (residence) Liverpool
1816   51 Wapping, Liverpool
1818–1825 4 Mill St, (residence) Liverpool
1818–1828 49 Wapping, Liverpool
1824   29 Upper Pitt St, (residence) Liverpool
1829   6 Bath St, Liverpool
1831–1834 21 Bath St, Liverpool
1834–1835 46 Wapping, Liverpool
1835   28 Bath St, Liverpool
See also WOOD Benjamin Jasper (II)★
Sources: G (MAC); Pg; WB (MAC); LM (index) Goodison (1977) p.372

WOOD Benjamin Jasper (I)
w 1802–1809
Math IM
1796–1800	10 Paved Buildings, Leadenhall Market, London
1802–1809	28 Rosomon St, Clerkenwell, London
Guild: Joiners, fr 1796
Apprenticed to DANCER Michael★ 1788
See also
WOOD & CO. W.★
WOOD Benjamin★
WOOD Benjamin Jasper (II)★
Possibly he or a relative of the same name moved to Liverpool
Sources: GL: JC 8055/3; H (MAC); Crawforth (1987)

WOOD Benjamin Jasper (II)
w 1828–1865
Optician, Math IM, Teacher of navigation
1828	49 Wapping, Liverpool
1832	21 Bath St, Liverpool
1832	50 Wapping, Liverpool
1832–1837	23 Bath St, Liverpool
1834–1835	46 Wapping, Liverpool
1835	28 Bath St, Liverpool
1837	45 Wapping, Liverpool
1841–1853	7 Bath St, Liverpool
1857–1860	64 Chatsworth St, Liverpool
1865	12 College Lane, Liverpool
See also
WOOD Benjamin★
WOOD Benjamin J. (I)★
Sources: G (MAC); Sl (MAC)

WOOD Charles William
w 1845–1850
Math IM, Phil IM
1845	170 Bishopsgate Without, London
1849–1850	167 Bishopsgate Without, London
Sources: PO

WOOD Edward George
w 1833–1839
Math IM, Phil IM
	15 King St, Clerkenwell, London
	15 King St, Goswell St, London
1839	7 Shepperton St, New North Rd, London
Succeeded by WOOD Henry & George★
Probably the same as WOOD Edward George, Math IM of 58 Red Cross St, London, who attended London Mechanics Institute 1826–1828
Sources: Pg; R (JAC); LMIR (AM)

WOOD George (I)
d 1761
Rule M
1761	Wolverhampton
Husband of WOOD Mary who continued the business under her husband's name
Sources: Aris 3 Aug 1761

WOOD George (II)
w 1819
Math IM
1819	9 Church Lane, Whitechapel, London
Sources: R (JAC)

WOOD George (III)
w 1831
Optician
1831	15 St.John's Square, Clerkenwell, London
Sources: R (JAC)

WOOD George Smart
w 1847–1897
Optician, Math IM
1847	46 Prescot St, Liverpool
1849	52 Prescotn St, Liverpool
1871	76 South Castle St, Liverpool
1875–1896	20 Lord St, Liverpool
1875	15 London Rd, Liverpool
1889	17 Lord St, Liverpool
1893	24 Market St, Manchester
1897	11 St Ann St, Manchester
Took over from ABRAHAM & CO. Abraham★
Succeeded by WOOD & CO. G.S.
See also WOOD Henry & George★
Probably the G. S. Wood, Phil IM, who attended London Mechanics Institute 1837–1838
Known to have sold: quadrant, telescope
Sources: G; LM index & TCd; LMIR (AM)

WOOD Henry (I)
w 1777
Rule M
	29 Great Charles St, Birmingham
See also
WOOD John (IV)★
WOOD & WITHNOLL★
WOOD & LORT★
Sources: PR (MAC)

WOOD Henry (II)
w 1828–1830
Optical IM, Phil IM, Math IM
1828–1830	58 Redcross St, Cripplegate, London
Sources: Pg; R (JAC)

WOOD Henry (III)
w 1851
Math IM
1851	25 City Rd, London
See also WOOD Henry & George★
Sources: Wk

WOOD Henry & George
w 1839–1843
Optician, Math IM, Phil IM
1839–1843	7 Shepperton St, New North Rd, London
Took over from WOOD Edward George★
See also WOOD Henry (III)★
Sources: Pg; PO

WOOD John (I)
w 1681 d by 1698
Scale M   London
Guild: Blacksmiths, fr 1675 or 1676
Husband of WOOD Mary★
Had apprentice CLARIDGE Richard★ 1681
d before 1698
Sources: GL: BKC 2881/9, 2884, 2886/2 (MAC)

WOOD John (II)
w 1737 d c. 1765
Scale M
	Ye Angel & Scales in Queen St, Cheapside, London
1757	Ye Angel & Scales ye corner of Queen Street in Watling St, London
Guild: Blacksmiths, fr 1734
Apprenticed to ROBERTS Timothy★ 1726
Had apprentice:
HARRISON John 1746
GOULDING Thomas★ 1757
WOOD Richard★ 1761
and 7 others 1737–1764
Succeeded by GOULDING Thomas★
Known to have sold: balance
Instruments advertised: balance, steelyard, weights
Sources: GL: BKC 2885/1, 2886/5 (MAC); CH 12876/5 (MAC); Sheppard & Musham (1975) no. 171

WOOD John (III)
fr 1701 w 1713
Math IM
	London
Guild: Clockmakers, fr 1701
Apprenticed to NASH John★ 1689/90
Had apprentice:
BARROLL John 1701
BELL Edmond 1704
LANGTHORNE Joseph 1709
WALTON John 1713
Sources: Brown J (1979b) p.34

WOOD John (IV)
w 1777
Rule M
1777	16 London-'prentice St, Birmingham
See also
WOOD Henry (I)★
WOOD & WITHNOLL★
WOOD & LORT★
Sources: PR (MAC)

WOOD John (V)
w 1820–1824
Rule M, Gauge M
1820–1824	At the Sign of the Bell, Hillgrove St, Bristol
Sources: Mat (MAC)

WOOD Joseph
w 1792
Steelyard M
1792	54 Salop St, Wolverhampton
Sources: Wolverhampton rate books (MAC)

WOOD Mary
w 1698–1699
Alternative name: Maria
	London
Guild: Blacksmiths
Husband of WOOD John (I)★
Had apprentice TAYLOR William
Sources: GL: BKC 2881/9, 2886/3 (MAC)

WOOD Richard
fr 1768 w 1820
Scale M
1768   Noble St, Foster Lane, London
1789–1816   The Angel & Scales No.15 in Queen
         St, Cheapside, London
Guild: Blacksmiths, fr 1768
Son of WOOD Richard of Cirencester
Apprenticed to WOOD John (II)★ 1761
Took over from GOULDING Thomas★
Succeeded by WOOD Robert★
Known to have sold: balance
Instruments advertised: balance, steelyard, weights
Sources: GL: BKC 2881/11 (MAC); CH 12876/5
(MAC); Kt (MAC); Ld (MAC); inst WM (MAC)

WOOD Robert
w 1812–1853
Scale M, Cutler
1812–1822   15 Queen St, Cheapside, London
1814–1833   7 West Smithfield, London
1836–1853   6 & 7 West Smithfield, London
Guild: Blacksmiths, fr 1812
Son of WOOD William cheesemonger of
Cirencester, Glos
Apprenticed to WOOD Richard★ 1805
Had apprentice BARTLETT John★ 1814 by t/o
from WYNN John★ and 6 others 1817–1851
Took over from WOOD Richard★
Succeeded by WOOD Robert & Henry★
Sources: GL: BKC 2881/15, /16, 17 (MAC); J
(MAC); Pg; PO; R (MAC)

WOOD Thomas (I)
w 1734
Math IM
1734   George Yard, Golden Lane, London
         (residence)
Had apprentice REYNOLDS James 1734
Sources: GL: CH 12823/4 fol.71, 12876/4

WOOD Thomas (II)
w 1767–1770
Rule M
1767–1770   Brick Kiln Lane, Wolverhampton
Sources: Aris 27 Aug 1770 (MAC); Sket (MAC)

WOOD William
w 1780–1797
Scale M
         London
Guild: Blacksmiths, fr 1774
Apprenticed to BROOKSBY Thomas (II)★ 1761
Had apprentice WOOD William (II), his son, 1790
and 5 others 1780–1797
Sources: GL: BKC 2881/16, 2885/1, 2886/5 (MAC)

WOOD & CO. Henry
w 1843
Phil IM
1843   1 Long Lane, Smithfield, London
Sources: PO

WOOD & CO. W.
w 1802–1804
Optician
1802–1804   Near the Mermaid, Hackney, London
Sources: Kt (JAC)

WOOD & LORT
c. 1750–1760
         Birmingham
Succeeded by FROST & WITHNOLL★
See also
WOOD Henry (I)★
WOOD John (IV)★
Known to have sold: slide rule
Sources: inst & pamphlet noted by DJB; Taylor
(1966) p.251

WOOD & WITHNOLL Henry & Thomas
w 1775–1780
Rule M, Math IM
Alternative name: WITHNOL
1775–1780   29 Great Charles St, Birmingham
See also
WOOD Henry (I)★
WOOD John (IV)★
WITHNOLL William★
Known to have sold: slide rule
Sources: PR; Delehar (1984) p.10

WOODAGE George Cave
fr 1780 w 1792
Scale M
1792   Grub St, London
Guild: Blacksmiths
Apprenticed to
BLACKMAN Solomon★ 1773
BADCOCK William Geagle★ by t/o 1779
Had apprentice:
LAWRENCE Edward★ 1792
ANDERSON James Andrew★ 1806 by t/o from
LAWRENCE John P.★
NICHOLL William Lewis★ 1806 by t/o from
LAWRENCE John P.★
LAY John 1807 t/o to VANDOME Richard★
Sources: GL: BKC 2881/16, 2886/5 (MAC)

WOODCOCK John
w 1674
Signed a rule, possibly an owner rather than maker
Sources: inst SM (MAC)

WOODE John
fl 1627
Known to have sold: gauge
Sources: inst MHS (MAC)

WOODMAN James
w 1786
Math IM, Phil IM, Turner
1786   The Tollgate, Kent St, London
Sources: GL: Sun 11936/334 no.515378

WOODS Robert Carr
w 1838–1840
Optician, Baro M
1838–1840   47 Hatton Garden, London
Founder member of The Meteorological Society
Known to have sold: barometer
Sources: PO; R (JAC); Goodison (1977) p.372

WOODSIDE James
w 1733 d 1743
Math IM
-1743   Dublin

Known to have sold: back-staff
Sources: Burnett & Morrison-Low (1989)
p.138–39

WOODSIDE Thomas
d 1765
Math IM
-1765   Liverpool
Sources: LM index (MAC)

WOODWARD George
w 1851–1900+
Baro M, Thermo M, Globe M
1851–1855   5 Charles St, Hatton Garden, London
Sources: PO; Wk; Downing (1984)

WOODWARD John
w 1822–1835
Optician
         Clement's Inn, Strand, London
         1 Clement's Inn Passage, Clare
         Market, London
1835   8 Clement's Inn Passage, Clare
         Market, London
Succeeded by WOODWARD John T.★
See also WOODWARD George★
Known to have sold: telescope
Sources: R (JAC); Und (JAC); inst (pv)

WOODWARD John Thomas
w 1836–1856
Optician
1836–1856   8 Clement's Inn Passage, Clare
         Market, London
Took over from WOODWARD John★
Sources: PO; R (JAC)

WOOLF Lewis
w 1834–1862
Chrono M, Math IM, Naut IM
Alternative name: Louis
1834   10 Bold St, Liverpool
1835–1837   19 Church St, Liverpool
1839   33 Church St, Liverpool
1841–1849   35 South Castle St, Liverpool
1851–1859   35A South Castle St, Liverpool
1860–1862   35 South Castle St, Liverpool
Sources: G (MAC); Sl; LM index (MAC)

WOOLFE William
w 1770
Glass Grinder
1770   Richmond Street in the parish of St.
         James Westminster, London
Sources: GL: PWC 7102 fol.5

WOOLSTENCROFT Charles
w 1669–1678
Spec M
Alternative name: WOOLLSONCRAFT
1670   Shoe Lane, London
1671   Houndsditch, London
1678   Under St Dunstan's Church in the
         West, [Fleet St], London
Guild: Spectaclemakers, fr 1669
fr by purchase SMC
Known to have sold: spectacles
Sources: GL: SMC 5213/1

WORGAN John
fr 1682 w 1700
Math IM
Alternative name: Iohn
1685	George Alley, Fleet Ditch, London
1686–1691	Under the dial of St.Dunstan's Church, Fleet St, London
1693	Fetter Lane against Clifford's Inn back gate, London
1699	Under St Dunstan's Church, Fleet St, London
1700	Fleet St, London
Guild: Grocers fr 1682
Son of WORGAN Wm., yeoman, of Colford, Glos
Partnership: WORGAN & COOKE? ★
Apprenticed to ANDERTON Nathaniel★ 1669 & fr by HAYES Walter★
Had apprentice:
BURDEN Peter 1682/3
BATES Thomas 1686
CLARK Peter 1693
BRADLEY John (I)★ 1697 t/o ROBERTS Jonathan★
BARKER William (I)★ 1700 t/o 1700/01 to HADDON William★
Author
Known to have sold: alidade, circumferentor, compass (magnetic), plane table, quadrant, sector
Sources: LGaz 2 Sep 1695 (MAC); GL: CH 12876/2 (MAC); inst MHS; ChrSK 14 Apr 1988 lot 33; British Sundial Society *Bulletin* 1991 (2) p.40; Brown J (1979a) p.28; Bryden (1992) p.313,314; Taylor (1954) p.283,404,409–10,413

WORGAN & COOKE John & Thomas
w 1695
Alternative name: J. & T.
| 1695 | Under St.Dunstan's Church in Fleet St, London |
| 1695 | Threadneedle St, London |
See also
WORGAN John★
COOKE Thomas (II)★
Partners, or separate shops but joint advertisement
Sources: LGaz 2 Sept 1695

WORKMAN Benjamin
w 1723–1726
Math IM (Master), later journeyman at India House
| | Next Tom's Coffee House in Russell St, Covent Garden, London |
| 1723 | Covent Garden, London |
Guild: Drapers, fr 1723
Son of WORKMAN James, shop-keeper, of Wandsworth, Surrey
Apprenticed to HAUKSBEE Francis (II)★ 1714
Had apprentice WELBORNE Francis 1723 t/o 1726 to MARRIOTT Richard of FDC
Worked for HAUKSBEE Francis (II)★
Instruments advertised: full range
Sources: DH: DPC Ap/Fr, Q; GL: TCd

WORNELL John
fr 1743 d 1760
Smith
| 1750 | Bishopsgate Within, London |
Guild: Blacksmiths
Apprenticed to FREEMAN Samuel (II)★ 1736

Had apprentice:
WORNELL Alexander, son of Richard, 1745/6
BLACKMAN Solomon★ 1748
REEVES Thomas★ 1750
SEWELL George★ 1759 by t/o from SOMMERS Charles★, then t/o to READ Joseph★
O'BRYANT Benjamin (? BRYANT★) 1760 t/o 1760 to JEFFERSON Thomas of MSC
Sources: SKH: SKC Ap/Fr; GL: BKC 2885/1, 2886/4, 2886/5 (MAC)

WORSLEY George
w 1668–1671
Spec M
| 1671 | Cripplegate, London |
Guild: [Brewers] Spectaclemakers
Son of WORSLEY George, weaver, of Loughborough, Leics
Apprenticed to BAILEY John★ 1626/7
Had apprentice:
WORSLEY George, his son, 1667/8
CLINCH Charles 1669
Sources: GL: Brew 5445/14; SMC 5213/1

WORTHINGTON Nathaniel
w 1835–1851
Optician
Alternative name: I R on divided scales
| 1835–1851 | 196 Piccadilly, London |
Partnership: WORTHINGTON & ALLAN★
Apprenticed to BERGE Matthew★
Worked for BERGE Matthew★
Took over from WORTHINGTON & ALLAN★
Had Ramsden's dividing engine
Known to have sold: sextant, telescope
Sources: PO; Sby 25 Feb 1986 lot 111; inst (s) (MAC); Stimson (1985) p.112

WORTHINGTON & ALLAN Nathaniel & James
w 1821–1834
Optician
| 1821–1834 | 196 Piccadilly, London |
Took over from BERGE Matthew★
Succeeded by WORTHINGTON Nathaniel★
See also ALLAN James★
Had Ramsden's dividing engine
Known to have sold: sextant, telescope, theodolite
Sources: Bn; Kt (MAC); PO; inst (s) (MAC); inst NMM

WRAY George
w 1836–1855
Spec M, Optician
| 1836 | 5 Plumber Place, Clerkenwell, London |
| 1855 | 8 Whitmore Row, Hoxton, London |
Sources: Pg; PO

WRAY W.
w 1851
Optician
| 1851 | 3 Windmill St, Tottenham Court Rd, London |
See also WRAY William★
Sources: Wk

WRAY William
w 1851
[Telescope M]
| 1851 | 43 Havering St, Commercial Rd East, London |
See also WRAY W.★
Known to have sold: telescope
Sources: Cat. 1851 (MAC)

WRENCH Edward
w 1822–1853
Optician, Baro M, Math IM
	57 Red Lion St, Holborn, London
1825	Red Lion St, Holborn, London
1839–1852	6 Gray's Inn Terrace, London
Succeeded by WRENCH & SON Edward
Attended London Mechanics Institute 1825
Known to have sold: pantograph
Sources: LMIR (AM); Pg; PO; Wk; JAC

WRIGHT Daniel
w 1830
Optician
| 1830 | 58 Campo Lane, Sheffield |
See also
WRIGHT David★
WRIGHT & SYKES★
Sources: Pg

WRIGHT David
w 1833–1837
Optician
| 1833–1837 | 94 Fargate, Sheffield |
Sources: Pg; Wh

WRIGHT Gabriel
w 1782–1803
Optician
| 1782–1793 | 148 Leadenhall St, London |
| 1791 | [Residence] St Mary's Islington, London |
Guild: Girdlers, fr 1783
Partnership:
GILBERT & WRIGHT★
GILBERT, WRIGHT & HOOKE★
GREGORY & WRIGHT★
Had apprentice: HOOKE Benjamin★ 1786
Worked for MARTIN Benjamin★
Associated with BARDIN William★
Pats. compass & quadrant 1779 & 1791 & compass 1796; Author; fr by purchase 1783; livery 1786; d 1803 or 1804
Sources: Wil; GL: GDC 5813/3, 5802; Millburn & Rössaak (1992) p.26–28

WRIGHT George
fr 1720 w 1736
Rule M
| 1736 | Clerkenwell, London |
Guild: Grocers, fr 1719/20
Son of WRIGHT George of ABC
Apprenticed to SWETMAN James 1707
Had apprentice:
MALE George 1721
JARMAN Thomas 1728 t/o 1729 to SWETMAN James★
ATKINSON John (II)★ 1736 t/o 1739 to FARMER John★

WRIGHT John (I)
w 1756 c 1759
Math IM, Phil IM, Optical IM
1756–1759   The Sphere & Hadley's Quadrant
          near St.Stephen's Church, Bristol
1757   The Sphere and Hadley's Quadrant
          in St Stephen's Lane, Bristol
Guild: Merchant Taylors, fr 1760
Son of WRIGHT John, d, of MC
Apprenticed to COLE Benjamin (I)★ 1750
Worked for COLE & SON★
Succeeded by SPRINGER Joshua★
See also
WRIGHT Thomas (I)
WRIGHT William (II)★
WRIGHT Susa★
WRIGHT John (II)★
Known to have sold: sundial
Sources: BM: Heal 105/23; GL: MTC MF
320,324 (MAC); *Bristol Journal* 20 Mar 1756
(MAC); inst (s)

WRIGHT John (II)
w 1763
Optician
1763   Little Russell St, Leather Lane,
          London
Had apprentice: BARRATT John 1763
See also WRIGHT John (I)★
Sources: GL: CH 12876/5 (MAC)

WRIGHT Richard
w 1706
Scale M
          London
Apprenticed to AMBLER Edward★ 1694
Attended Christ's Hospital School, London
Sources: GL: CH 12823/3 p.1, 12876/2 (MAC)

WRIGHT Samuel
w 1764
Petitioner against Dollond's patent, possibly an
optician
1764   Bedford St, London
Sources: PRO: PC 1/7 no.94

WRIGHT Susa
a 1700–1800
Alternative name: Susannah ?
          Bristol
See also
WRIGHT John (I)★
WRIGHT William (II)★
Known to have sold: back-staff
Sources: inst noted by DJB

WRIGHT Thomas (I)
w 1718–1747
Math IM, Toyman
1720   Orrery and Globe in Fleet St,
          London
-1731   Orrery & Globe near Salisbury
          Court, Fleet St, London
1734   Orrery & Globe near Water Lane,
          Fleet St, London

1738   Orrery, near Water Lane, Fleet St,
          London
1747   Orrery & Globe next the Globe &
          Marlborough Head Tavern in Fleet
          St, London
1767   [Residence in retirement],
          Hoddesdon, Herts
Guild: Broderers, fr 1715
Son of WRIGHT William, clockmaker, of
Southwark, London
Husband of WRIGHT Susannah
Partnership: WRIGHT & WYETH★
Apprenticed to ROWLEY John (I)★ 1707
Had apprentice POST William nd (fr 1723)
Worked for ROWLEY John (I)★
Employed COLE Benjamin (I)★
Took over from ROWLEY John (I)★
Succeeded by COLE Benjamin (I)★
Associated with
CUSHEE Richard★ in selling globes
COGGS John (I)★
Partnership 1740–41; R.apt Prince of Wales,
Geo II, 1727; retired 1747/8; d 28 May 1767
Known to have sold: circumferentor, drawing
instruments, planetarium, rule, slide rule, waywiser
Sources: PRO: PROB 11/930 Q248 fol.70 (AM);
LC 3/64 p.84; GL: BROD 14657/1, /2 & /3,
14663/1, 14664/1 (MAC); BM: Heal 105/26,
105/32; *Post Boy* 14 Apr 1720 (MAC); Daily J 31
Oct 1729 (JRM); *Craftsmen* 6 Feb 1731 (MAC);
GNDA 1 Jun 1767 (JRM); inst MHS, NMM, SM,
WM; Calvert (1971) p.47, pl.59; Crawforth (1985)
p.539, (1987) p.341; King & Millburn (1978) p.163;
Wallis R & P (1986) p.120

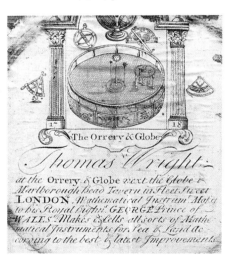

WRIGHT Thomas (II)
w 1730–1773
Math IM, Teacher, Inventor
1730–1734   At the Sign of ye Creation,
          Sunderland, Durham
1735–1748   St. James's, London
1762   Byers Green, Brancepeth
Apprenticed to STOBART Bryan, clockmaker,
1725
Worked for
HEATH Thomas★
SISSON Jonathan★

See also WRIGHT Thomas (I)★
Inv. cylindrical dial 1736
Associated with SENEX John★
Known to have sold: sundial
Sources: *Annals of Science* 7 (1951) p.1–21 (MAC);
Wallis R & P (1986) p.193

WRIGHT Thomas (III)
w 1770–1790
Clock M
1783   6 Poultry in the City, London
Guild: Clockmakers, fr 1770
Had apprentice:
BURGESS George 1770
LAING Robert 1777
COOPER James 1779
FERRIS James★ 1783
WRIGHT George William, his son, 1785
RIDLEY Thomas 1790
Associated with BOULTON Matthew★
R.apt Geo. III; Pat. pendulum, 1783
Known to have sold: astronomical clock,
barometer, waywiser
Sources: GL: CKC 2720/1; Loomes (1981); Baillie
(1951); King & Millburn (1978) p.141

WRIGHT Thomas (IV)
w 1826–1842
Optician, Math IM, Drawing IM, Optical IM,
dealer in cabinet work and ivory goods
          27 City Terrace, City Rd, London
          28 City Terrace, City Rd, London
          15 St.Mary Street Hill, London
          42 Allen St, Goswell St, London
1839–1841   1 Worship Square, Worship St,
          Hoxton, London
1841   25 City Rd, London
Sources: GL: Sun 11936/574–5; Pg (JAC); PO

WRIGHT Thomas (V)
w 1727
Math IM
1727   Parish of St John, Wapping, London
Father of WRIGHT Thomas s 1727 DPC
Sources: DH: DPC Ap

WRIGHT W.
a 1700–1800
          Glossop, Derby
Known to have sold: sector
Sources: Phlps 13 Jun 1979 lot 65 (DJB)

WRIGHT William (I)
w 1793–1805
Rule M
1793–1797   Philip St, Birmingham
1801   14 Philip St, Birmingham
1805   Queen St, Birmingham
Sources: BW; Chp (MAC); H (DJB)

WRIGHT William (II)
fl 1720–1730
          Bristol
See also
WRIGHT Susa★
WRIGHT John★
Sources: Taylor (1966) p.167

WRIGHT & SYKES
w 1828
Optician
1828   40 Nursery St, Sheffield
See also
WRIGHT Daniel★
WRIGHT David★
Sources: Bk; Pg

WRIGHT & WYETH Thomas & William
w 1740–1741
Math IM, Land surveyor
–1741   The Orrery in Fleet St, London
Took over from
WRIGHT Thomas (I)★
COGGS & WYETH★
Wyeth d.1741
Known to have sold: waywiser
Sources: LEP 3 Nov 1741 (MAC); inst MHS;
Harris (1740) (DJB)

WYETH William
w pt 1733 d 1741
Math IM, Land surveyor
Alternative name: WYERTH
                London
Guild: Pewterers, fr 1733
Son of WYETH Richard, brushmaker, d, of
London
Partnership:
COGGS & WYETH★
WRIGHT & WYETH★
Apprenticed to COGGS John (I)★
Had apprentice GREENWOOD Joseph 1738
Partnership with Coggs c.1733–40, with Wright
c.1740–41; d 1741;
Sources: GL: PWC 7090/9; 7101; *London Evening
Post* 3 Nov 1741; Harris (1740) (DJB); Shirtcliffe
(1740) (DJB)

WYLD J. & W.
a 1820–1824
[Globe M]
See also
WYLD James (I)★
WYLD James (II)★
Associated with ADDISON James, engraver
Known to have sold: globe
Sources: ChrSK 19 Nov 1987 lot 18

WYLD James (I)
w 1824 d 1836
Globe M, Land surveyor
1824–1836   454 West Strand, London
                & 210 Regent St, London
Guild: Clothworkers
Son of WYLD Joseph Woolley, cheesemonger
Apprenticed to FADEN William, map seller &
Geographer to the king 1804
Succeeded by WYLD James (II)★
b 1790; founder member of Royal Geographical
Society 1830
Sources: PO; CWH: CWC Ap; JAC; Tooley (1979)

WYLD James (II)
w 1837–1887
Globe M, Map Publisher, Geographer
1837–1887   454 West Strand, London
1841–1842   454 Charing Cross East, London

1837–1840   Charing Cross East, London
1851   & 2 Royal Exchange London
1848   Leicester Square, London
Guild: Clothworkers
Had apprentice:
NEATE James Richard 1837
LOWE James Albinus 1838
PHILLIPS Francis 1839
HATFIELD William 1840
HOOD Frederick Henry
Took over from WYLD James (I)★
d 1887; M.P. for Bodmin 1847–1852, 1857–1868
Sources: GL: Sun 11936/578 no.1352728; CWH:
CWC Ap, Fr; Pg; PO; JAC; Tooley (1979)

WYLIE James
fr 1825
Coppersmith
                Glasgow
Guild: Hammermen, fr 1825
Known to have sold: measure (capacity)
Sources: Lumsden & Aitken (1912) p.310

WYNN John
fr 1784 w 1814
Scale M
1784   Great Bandyleg Walk, Southwark,
                London
1795–1814   6 West Smithfield, London
Guild: Blacksmiths, fr 1784
Apprenticed to ASTILL William 1776
Had apprentice:
SCARRETT William 1793
BURCHFIELD Thomas★ 1799
MCCRAIGHT Richard★ 1807
BARTLETT John★ 1811
Sources: GL: BKC 2881/15, /16, & /17 (MAC);
H; Kt (MAC); Ld (MAC)

WYNNE Henry
fr 1662 d 1709
Math IM, Book S
Alternative name: WYNN, WINN, WIN
                At the Pope's Head, Chancery Lane,
                London
1677   In Chancery Lane, London
1682   Next the Sugar Loaf in Chancery
                Lane, London
1700   In Chancery Lane over against the
                Rolls, London
1707   Near Sergeant's Inn, Chancery Lane,
                London
Guild: Clockmakers, fr 1662
Apprenticed to GREATOREX Ralph★ 1654
Had apprentice:
WHITEHEAD Richard★ 1663
FORSTER Clement★ 1670
WARNER John★ 1675
WETHERED George 1677
CADE Simon★ 1680
HATCH John 1685
TUTTELL Thomas★ 1688
GLYNNE Richard★ 1696
THOMPSON Isaac nd (fr 1699)
Author 1682; Master CKC 1690
Known to have sold: barometer, compass, dip
circle, drawing instruments, microscope, quadrant,
sector, sundial, thermometer

Sources: GL: CKC 3939; Brown J (1979b) p.34;
Bryden (1992) p.311; (1993) p.17–26; Goodison
(1977) fr 199

YARWELL John
w 1671–1708
Optical IM
                Archimedes & Three Golden
                Prospects near the great North Door
                in St.Paul's Church Yard, London
1671–1692   Ye Archimedes & Spectacles in
                St.Paul's Church Yard, London
1672   North Side of St Paul's, London
1676–1696   St Paul's Church Yard, London
1692   Archimedes & Three pair of Golden
                Spectacles in Ludgate St, the Shop
                next Ludgate, London
1694   Archimedes & Three Golden
                Prospects, St.Paul's Church Yard,
                London
1697   Archimedes in Ludgate St, first
                Spectacle Shop in Ludgate, London
1698–1712   Archimedes & Crown, London
Guild: Spectaclemakers, fr 1669
Partnership: STERROP & YARWELL★
Apprenticed to EDWARDS Richard★ 1662, taken
over by EDWARDS Mary★, t/o to SHIELD
Nicholas★ c.1668
Had apprentice:
VERNEY Henry 1674 t/o to VERNEY John★
COLTHROP Martin 1675
unnamed 1679/80 [possibly HAILS Thomas★ fr
1689]
LOADER Francis, probably the unnamed boy s
1686
DAVIS Edward 1693
WILLDEY George★ 1694/5
WELLS John (II) 1697
FOWLER John 1700/1
Succeeded by STERROP Ralph★
Associated with SHARP Abraham★, to whom
Yarwell supplied lenses
R.apt Wm.III; Master SMC 1684–1686, 1693–94;
d 1 Mar 1712/13, buried St. Paul Covent Garden
Known to have sold: microscope, telescope
Sources: GL: SMC 5213/1, 5213/2 p.27; inst
MHS; Crawforth (1985) p.540; Houghton (1696) 2
no.cxcvii p.47; Whipple (1951)

YEAMAN John
w 1745–1780
Math IM
Alternative name: YEOMAN
1745   Parish of Canongate, Edinburgh
1765   Behind the Weigh House in Lawn
                Market, Edinburgh
1773   Bow Head, Edinburgh
1774   Back of the Weigh House,
                Edinburgh
1775–1780   Bow Head, Edinburgh
Had apprentice possibly, MILLER John★
Sources: Clarke & al (1989) p.25–26

YEATES Andrew
w 1840–1863
Optical IM, Math IM, Astro IM, Optician
1840–1863   12 Brighton Place, New Kent Rd,
                London

Son of YEATES Samuel★
Sources: PO; DJB

YEATES George
w 1825–1858
Optician
1825–1827   70 Camden St, Dublin
1828–1837   70 Charlemont St, Dublin
1843–1858   2 Grafton St, Dublin
See also
YEATES William★
YEATES Samuel★
YEATES & SON George★
Ex. 1851; possibly 2 men
Sources: Burnett & Morrison-Low (1989) p.139;
Turner G (1983a) p.310

YEATES Kendrick
w 1803–1839
Optician, Brass founder
1803–1811   22 Henry St, Dublin
1811   22 Capel St, Dublin
1816   27 Stafford St, Dublin
1817–1835   26 Stafford St, Dublin
1836   24 Suffolk St, Dublin
1837–1838   26 Stafford St, (2nd period) Dublin
1839   33 Stafford St, Dublin
See also
YEATES Samuel★
YEATES George★
Brass founder 1827–1838
Sources: Pg; Wi (DJB); Burnett & Morrison-Low
(1989) p.139

YEATES Samuel
w 1790–1831
Optician
1790–1794   4 Upper Ormond Quay, Dublin
1795–1810   29 Capel St, Dublin
1811–1826   89 Dame St, Dublin
1827–1831   2 Grafton St, Dublin
Father of YEATES Andrew★
Apprenticed to MASON Seacombe★
Succeeded by YEATES & SON Samuel★
See also
YEATES & SON George★
YEATES George★
YEATES William★
Sources: Wi (MAC); DJB; Burnett &
Morrison-Low (1989) p.139

YEATES William (I)
w 1827–1828
Optician, Cutler
1827–1828   18 Capel St, Dublin
See also
YEATES Samuel★
YEATES George★
YEATES & SON★
Sources: Wi (MAC); Burnett & Morrison-Low
(1989) p.139

YEATES William (II)
w 1845
Math IM
1845   44 Bartholomew Close, London
Sources: PO

YEATES & SON George
w 1840–1864
Optician, Math IM
1840–1864   2 Grafton St, Dublin
Took over from YEATES & SON Samuel★
See also
YEATES George★
YEATES William★
B.apt University; Ex.1851
Known to have sold: air pump, barometer,
compass (magnetic), microscope, spectacles,
surveyor's cross, theodolite
Sources: inst MHS, SM Wellcome (MAC); Cat.
1851 (MAC); Burnett & Morrison-Low (1989)
p.139–40

YEATES & SON Samuel
w 1832–1839
Optician
1832–1839   2 Grafton St, Dublin
1839   9 Nassau St, Dublin
Took over from YEATES Samuel★
Succeeded by YEATES & SON George★
See also
YEATES George★
YEATES William★
Sources: Burnett & Morrison-Low (1989)
p.139–40

YEFF Robert
w 1693–1720
fr 1697 [sic]
    Bristol
Known to have sold: Gunter's scale, nocturnal
Sources: inst NMM, SM; DJB

YEOMAN Thomas
w 1742 d 1781
Engineer, Surveyor, Math IM, Millwright
1742–1751   Gold St, Northampton
1758–1760   Little St, Peter St, London
1778–1781   Castle St, Leicester Fields, London
FRS 1764
Sources: Wallis R & V (1986) p.337

YOULE John
w 1818
Spec M, Optical Glass Mounter
1818   Barford St, Birmingham
Sources: Wr (DJB)

YOULE William
w 1822–1866
Optician, Spec M, Math IM, Phil IM
1822–1839   22 Fieldgate St, Whitechapel,
    London
1840–1842   79 Leadenhall St, London
1844   Camberwell Green, London
1845–1866   83 Leadenhall St, London
Took over from YOULE & SON William★
Succeeded by YOULE & SON William★
Partnership 1843; possibly two makers
Known to have sold: level, theodolite
Sources: Br (MAC); Pg (JAC); PO; inst (s) (MAC);
ChrSK 8 Dec 1988 lot 181

YOULE & SON William
w 1843

Optician
1843   79 Leadenhall St, London
Sources: PO

YOUNG Charles
w 1817 fl 1838
Chrono M
1823–1833   14 Felix Place, Islington, London
    The Jerusalem Coffee House,
    London
Won awards in chronometer trials at RGO 1827,
1828, 1832
Sources: CUL: RGO 1143 fol. 5–10; Taylor
(1966) p.440

YOUNG George
w 1823–1847
Scale M
1823   39 London Rd, London
1826   105 London Rd, London
1832–1847   63 London Rd, London
Guild: [Blacksmiths]
Son of YOUNG John (I)★
Apprenticed to YOUNG John (I)★
Succeeded by YOUNG Elizabeth
Sources: GL: BKC 2881/16; Pg (JAC); PO (MAC)

YOUNG John (I)
w 1802–1810
Scale M
1784–1810   5 Bear St, Leicester Square, London
Guild: Blacksmiths, fr 1784
Son of YOUNG John, blacksmith, of St Luke's,
London
Father of
YOUNG George★
YOUNG John (II)★
Partnership:
SEWELL & YOUNG★
YOUNG & SON John★
Apprenticed to
PLIVEY William★ 1773 t/o at once to
SEWELL George★
Had apprentice:
YOUNG John (II)★
YOUNG George★ 1803
GROVE Thomas 1808
Others possible, but 2 Masters of same name in
BKC
Succeeded by YOUNG & SON John★
d.1836; Master BKC 1814–1815
Known to have sold: balance, weight
Sources: GL: BKC 2881/15, /16, /17 & /18,
2886/5 (MAC); BM: Banks 103/16 (MAC); H

YOUNG John (II)
fr 1810 d 1843
Scale M
1810   Bear St, Leicester Fields, London
Guild: Blacksmiths, fr 1810
Son of YOUNG John (I)★
Partnership: YOUNG & SON John★
Apprenticed to YOUNG John (I)★ 1799
Had apprentice:
WALSH William 1820
YOUNG John (III), his son, 1823
Master BKC 1837–1838
Sources: GL: BKC 2881/16, /17, /18 (MAC)

YOUNG & SON John

w 1812–1901
Scale M
1812–1901   5 Bear St, Leicester Square, London
1851–1901   46 Cranbourn St, Leicester Square, London
Succeeded by YOUNG, SON & MARLOW
Took over from
YOUNG John (I)★
R.apt Geo III, Victoria; Ex.1851
Known to have sold: balance, chondrometer, weights
Sources: ChrSK 29 Sep 1988 lot 156; PO; inst (pv) (MAC); Cat. 1851 (MAC)

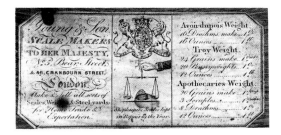

ZAMBRA Joseph Cesare

w 1821–1841
Travelling Baro S, Baro M
1821–1840   Saffron Walden
1840–1841   23 Brook St, Holborn, London
Father of ZAMBRA Joseph Warren★
Worked for CETTI Joseph★
See also PINI & CO. Joseph★
Same premises as PINI Joseph★
b 1796 at Careno, Como, Italy
Sources: PRO: Cs 1841 (AM); Banfield (1993) p.129; Read (1985)

ZAMBRA Joseph Warren

w pt 1847 r 1888
Baro M, Meteorological IM
1843–1846   11 Brook St, London
1848–1851   9 Manchester St, Argyle Square, London
Son of ZAMBRA Joseph Cesare★
Partnership: TAGLIABUE & ZAMBRA★
NEGRETTI & ZAMBRA★
b 1822, d 1897; in partnerships throughout his working life
Attended London Mechanics Institute 1843–1846, 1848–1849, 1851
Sources: LMIR (AM); Banfield (1993) p.129–57; Read (1985)

ZANETTI Ann

w 1843–1850
Math IM, Phil IM
1843–1850   16 St Ann St, Manchester
Wife of ZANETTI Joseph★
Took over from ZANETTI Joseph★
Sources: Sl; MSIM, JW; Ronchetti (1990) p.52; Wetton (1990–91)

ZANETTI Joseph

w 1835 d 1843
Clock M
1838–1841   100 King St, Manchester
1843   16 St Ann's St, Manchester
Son of ZANETTI Vittore★
Husband of ZANETTI Ann★
Partnership: AGNEW & ZANETTI Thomas & Joseph★
Succeeded by ZANETTI Ann★
Took over from AGNEW & ZANETTI Thomas & Joseph★
Known to have sold: barometer, thermometer
Sources: MSIM, JW; Agnew (1967); Goodison (1977) p.373; Ronchetti (1990) p.52; Wetton (1990–91)

ZANETTI Vincent

w 1810–1832
Print S, Picture frame M, Mirror S, Baro M
Alternative name: Vincente
1810–1824   5 Wright's Court, Market St, Manchester
1829   Blackfriars Bridge, Manchester
1832   20 Blackfriars, Manchester
Brother of ZANETTI Vittore★
Related to ZANETTI Joseph★
Employed BOLONGARO Dominic★
RONCHETTI Charles Joseph
Took over from ZANETTI & CO.★
See also ZANETTI & AGNEW★
Known to have sold: barometer, hygrometer, thermometer
Instruments advertised: barometer
Sources: Bn; MSIM, JW; Goodison (1977) p.373; Ronchetti (1990) p.51–2

ZANETTI Vittore

w 1800–1817
Clock M, Baro M, Print S, Looking glass M, Picture frame M, Lamp S, Drawing S, Painting S
1804–1813   87 Market Street Lane, Manchester
1813–1817   94 Market St, Manchester
Father of ZANETTI Joseph★
Brother of ZANETTI Vincent★
Partnership: ZANETTI & AGNEW★
Had apprentice: AGNEW Thomas★
Employed
BOLONGARO Dominick★
RONCHETTI Charles Joshua
Succeeded by ZANETTI & AGNEW★
Partnership 1817–25
Known to have sold: barometer
Sources: MSIM, JW; Goodison (1977) p.373; Ronchetti (1990) p.52

ZANETTI & AGNEW Vittore & Thomas

w 1817–1825
Carver, Looking glass M, Baro M, Thermo M, Optician, Picture frame M, Print S, Publisher
1817–1825   94 Market St, Manchester
Succeeded by AGNEW & ZANETTI★
Took over from ZANETTI Vittore★
See also
AGNEW Thomas★
ZANETTI Joseph★
ZANETTI Vincent★
Known to have sold: barometer, hydrostatic bubbles, thermometer
Sources: Pg; inst SM; Goodison (1977) p.373; Ronchetti (1990) p.52

ZANETTI & CO. Vittore

w 1797 c 1800
Picture S, Baro M
1797   Market St, Manchester
Partnership: ZANETTI Vittore★, ZANETTI Vincent★ & MERONE Joseph★
See also
BOLONGARO Dominic★
RONCHETTI Charles Joshua
Sources: MSIM, JW; Ronchetti (1990) p.52; Wetton (1990–91) p.37–68

ZANOTA –

a 1750–1800
   Portsmouth
Known to have sold: thermometer
Sources: ChrSK 13 Dec 1984 (MAC)

ZENONE John

w 1825–1832
Carver, Gilder, Looking glass M
1825   5 Calton Street, Edinburgh
1827   7 Calton St, Edinburgh
1830   5 & 6 Calton St, Edinburgh
1830   and 77 Princes St, Edinburgh
1832   10 Calton St, Edinburgh
Took over from ZENONE & BUTTI★
Known to have sold: barometer, thermometer
Sources: Clarke et al (1989) p.102

ZEONONE & BUTTI John & Louis Joseph

w 1823–1824
Carvers and Gilders
1823–1824   5 Calton St, Edinburgh
Succeeded by ZENONE John★
Known to have sold: telescope
Sources: Clarke et al (1989) p.102–03

ZERBONI & CO.

a 1800–1900
Looking glass M, Picture frame M
   8 & 9 Calton St, Edinburgh
Same premises as
BATTISTESSA & CO.★
ZENONE John★
Known to have sold: barometer
Sources: Gray's Directory; NMS n (MAC)

ZERBONI, BATTISTESSA, MOLTENI & GUANZIROLI

w 1833–1839
Baro M, Looking-glass M
1835   24 Cross St, Hatton Garden, London
1835   and 13 Baldwins Gardens, London
1836–1839   106 Hatton Garden, London
Partnership of ZERBONI Anthony, BATTISTESSA, MOLTENI Alexander★ and GUANZIROLI Giuseppe
See also
BATTISTESSA, MOLTENI & GUANZIROLI★
GUANZIROLI Giuseppe & Luigi★
Sources: Pg; PO; Goodison (1977) p.374

ZURAGHI Felix

w 1832–1834
Baro M, Thermo M, Looking glass M
1832–1834   9 City Rd, London
Sources: Pg (JAC)

Bibliography

Agnew (1967)
  Agnew G., *Agnews 1817–1967*, London, 1967
Alger (1982)
  Alger K.R., *Mrs Janet Taylor 'Authoress and Instructress in Navigation and Astronomy' (1804–1870)*, Fawcett Library Papers no.6, London, 1982
Anderson (1978)
  Anderson R.G.W., *The Playfair Collection and the Teaching of Chemistry at the University of Edinburgh 1713–1858*, Royal Scottish Museum, Edinburgh, 1978
Anderson et al (1990)
  Anderson R.G.W., Burnett J. and Gee B., *Handlist of Scientific Instrument-Makers' Catalogues 1600–1914*, Edinburgh, 1990
Anderson et al (1993)
  Anderson R.G.W., Bennett J.A., and Ryan W.F., eds, *Making Instruments Count: Essays on Historical Scientific Instruments Presented to Gerard L'Estrange Turner*, Aldershot, Hants, 1993
Andrews (1701)
  Andrews W., *News from the Stars: or, an Ephemeris for the Year 1701*, London, 1701
[Anonymous] (1738)
  A Description of a New Instrument Invented by John Hadley Esq . . ., London 1738
Arber (1875)
  Arber E., *A Transcript of the Registers of the Company of Stationers of London 1554–1640 A.D.*, 5 vols, London, 1875
Atkins C. (1931)
  Atkins C.E., *Register of Apprentices of the Worshipful Company of Clockmakers of the City of London from its Incorporation in 1631 to its Tercentenary in 1931*, London 1931
Atkins P. (1990)
  Atkins P.J., *The Directories of London 1677–1977*, London, 1990
Atkins & Overall (1881)
  Atkins S.E. & W.H.Overall, *Some Account of the Worshipful Company of Clockmakers of the City of London*, London, 1881
Austin & McConnell (1980)
  Austin J.F. & McConnell A., 'James Six F.R.S. Two Hundred McConnell Years of the Six's Self-registering Thermometer', *Notes and Records of the Royal Society of London*, 35, 1980, 49–65
Bache (1960)
  Bache Mary, *The Story of a Family Firm: Two Hundred Years of George Salter and Company*, West Bromwich, 1960
Baillie (1951)
  Baillie G.H., *Watchmakers and Clockmakers of the World*, Ipswich, 1951, reprinted as vol.1, Ipswich, 1976
Banfield (1976)
  Banfield E., *Antique Barometers, an Illustrated Survey*, Hereford, 1976
Banfield (1991)
  Banfield E., *Barometer Makers and Retailers 1660–1900*, Trowbridge, Wilts, 1991
Banfield (1993)
  Banfield E., *The Italian Influence on English Barometers from 1780*, Trowbridge, Wilts, 1993
Barker (1980)
  Barker D., *The Arthur Negus Guide to English Clocks*, London, 1980
Barty-King (1986)
  Barty-King H., *Eyes Right: the Story of Dollond & Aitchison*, London 1986
Bedini (1975)
  Bedini S.A., *Thinkers and Tinkers: Early American Men of Science*, New York, 1975
Bedini (1984)
  Bedini S.A. 'At the Sign of the Compass and Quadrant: the Life and Times of Anthony Lamb', *Transactions of the American Philosophical Society* 74, no.1, 1984
Beeson (1989)

Beeson C.F.C., *Clockmaking in Oxfordshire 1400–1850*, 3rd edition, Oxford, 1989
Bennett (1983a)
  Bennett J.A., *Astronomy and Navigation*, Whipple Museum, Cambridge 1983
Bennett (1983b)
  Bennett J.A., *Science at the Great Exhibition*, Whipple Museum, Cambridge, 1983
Bennett (1984)
  Bennett J.A. *Spectroscopes, Prisms and Gratings*, Whipple Museum, Cambridge, 1984
Bennett (1985)
  'Instrument Makers and the 'Decline of Science in England': the Effect of Institutional Change on the Elite Makers of the Early Nineteenth Century', in de Clercq (1985)
Bennett (1987)
  Bennett J.A. *The Divided Circle: a History of Instruments for Astronomy, Navigation and Surveying*, Oxford, 1987
Bennett & Brown (1982)
  Bennett J.A. and Brown O., *The Compleat Surveyor*, Whipple Museum, Cambridge, 1982
Bennion (1979)
  Bennion E., *Antique Medical Instruments*, London, 1979
Bernoulli (1771)
  Bernoulli J., *Lettres Astronomique . . .*, Berlin, 1771
Betts (1993)
  Betts J., *John Harrison*, London, 1993
Blackham (1931)
  Blackham R.J., *The Soul of the City: London's Livery Companies: their Storied Past their Living Present*, London, nd [1931]
Blackmore (1992a)
  Blackmore H.L., 'Who was Kolbe?', *Journal of the Arms and Armour Society* 14, 1992, 41–63
Blackmore (1992b)
  Blackmore H.L., 'Some Notes on the Introduction of Cannon Locks in the Royal Navy', *Arms Collecting* 30, 1992, 111–24
Blondel et al (1989)
  Blondel C., Parot F., Turner A. and Williams M, eds, *Studies in the History of Scientific Instruments*, papers presented at the seventh Symposium of the Scientific Instruments Commission, Paris, September 1987, London and Paris, 1989
BOIMA (1921)
  British Optical Instrument Manufacturers' Association, *Dictionary of British Scientific Instruments*, London, 1921
Bolle (1982)
  Bolle B., *Barometers*, Watford, Hertfordshire, 1982
Bonacker (1963)
  Bonacker W., 'Globenmacher Aller Zeiten', *Der Globusfreund*, no.12, 1963, 55–60
Bond (1642)
  Bond H., *The Boate Swaines Art*, London, 1642
Booker (1653)
  Booker J., *Coelestiall Observations: or an Ephemeris of the Motion of the Sun, Moon and Planets*, London, 1653
Brachner (1987)
  'C.A. Steinheil, a Munich Instrument Maker', *Bulletin of the Scientific Instrument Society*, no.12, 1987, 3–7
Brewington (1963)
  Brewington M.V., *The Peabody Museum Collection of Navigation Instruments*, Salem, Mass., 1963
Bristow (1993)
  Bristow H.R., 'Elliott, Instrument Makers of London: Products, Customers and Developments in the Nineteenth century', *Bulletin of the Scientific Instrument Society*, no.36, 1993, 8–11

Britten (1982)
Britten F.J., *Britten's Old Clocks and Watches and their Makers*, ed. G.H. Baillie, C. Ilbert, & C. Clutton, London, 1982

Broadbent (1949)
Broadbent L.H., *The Avery Business 1730–1918*, Birmingham, 1949

Brooks (1992)
Brooks J., 'The Circle Dividing Engine: Development in England 1739–1843', *Annals of Science* 49, 1992, 101–35

Brown J. (1979a)
Brown J., *Mathematical Instrument Makers in the Grocers' Company 1688–1800*, Science Museum, London, 1979

Brown J. (1979b)
Brown J., 'Guild Organisation and the Instrument-Making Trade, 1550–1830: the Grocers' and Clockmakers' Companies', *Annals of Science* 36, 1979, 1–34

Brown O. (1982a)
Brown O., *Balances and Weights*, Whipple Museum, Cambridge, 1982

Brown O. (1982b)
Brown O., *Surveying*, Whipple Museum, Cambridge, 1982

Brown O. (1983)
Brown O., *Spheres, Globes & Orreries*, Whipple Museum, Cambridge, 1983

Brown O. (1986)
Brown O., *Microscopes*, Whipple Museum, Cambridge, 1986

Browning (1964–65)
Browning W., ed., 'John Benjamin Dancer, F.R.A.S., 1812–1887: an Autobiographical Sketch, with some Letters', *Memoirs and Proceedings of the Manchester Literary and Philosophical Society* 107, no.9, 1964–1965, 1–27

Bryant (1994)
Bryant T.J., 'John Handsford of Birmingham and Bristol', *Bulletin of the Scientific Instrument Society*, no.40, 1994, 11–12

Bryden (1972)
Bryden D.J., *Scottish Scientific Instrument Makers 1600–1800*, Royal Scottish Museum [now the National Museums of Scotland], Edinburgh, 1972

Bryden (1976)
Bryden D.J., 'Scotland's Earliest Surviving Calculating Device: Robert Davenport's Circles of Proportion of c.1650', *Scottish Historical Review* 55, no.159, 1976, 54–60

Bryden (1992)
Bryden D.J., 'Evidence from Advertising for Mathematical Instrument Making in London, 1556–1714', *Annals of Science* 49, 1992, 301–36

Bryden (1993)
Bryden D.J., 'Magnetic Inclinatory Needles; Approved by the Royal Society?', *Notes and Records of the Royal Society of London* 47(1), 1993, 17–31

Bryden & Simms (1992)
Bryden D.J. and Simms D.L., 'Archimedes and the Opticians of London', *Bulletin of the Scientific Instrument Society*, no.35, 1992, 11–14

Bryden & Simms (1993)
Bryden D.J. and Simms D.L., 'Spectacles Improved to Perfection and Approved of by the Royal Society', *Annals of Science* 50, 1993, 1–32

Buckley (1935)
Buckley F., 'Old English Glass: Optical Glasses', *Glass* 12, 1935, 427–28

Burnett & Morrison-Low (1989)
Burnett J.E., and Morrison-Low A.D., *'Vulgar and Mechanick': the Scientific Instrument Trade in Ireland 1650–1921*, Royal Dublin Society Historical Studies in Irish Science and Technology, no.8, Edinburgh and Dublin, 1989

Calvert (1971)
Calvert H.R., *Scientific Trade Cards in the Science Museum Collection*, Science Museum, London, 1971

Cartwright (1977)
Cartwright F.F., *A Social History of Medicine*, London, 1977

Casella (c.1960)
Casella & Co. Ltd, 1810–1960: *C.F. Casella & Company Ltd,* company history pamphlet, nd [c.1960], copy in London Borough of Hackney Archives Collection, D/B/CAS/66 [I am grateful to Dr A. McConnell for this reference]

Chaldecott (1985)
Chaldecott J.A., 'Edited List of London Instrument Makers 1760–1840', unpublished computer print-out, 1985

Chaldecott (1989)
Chaldecott J.A., 'Printed Ephemera of some Nineteenth-Century Instrument Makers' in Blondel et al (1989), 159–68

Chapman (1990)
Chapman A., *Dividing the Circle: the Development of Critical Angular Measurement in Astronomy 1500–1850*, Chichester, Sussex, 1990

Chenekal (1972)
Chenekal V.L., *Watchmakers and Clockmakers in Russia 1400–1850*, translated by W.F. Ryan, Antiquarian Horological Society Monograph no.6, Ticehurst, Sussex, 1972

Chew (1968)
Chew V.K., *Physics for Princes: the George III Collection*, London, 1968

Christensen (1993)
Christensen D.C., 'Danish–Norwegian Technological Espionage 1760–1814 – As Seen from the Predator's Point of View', unpublished typescript of a paper read at the Conference on Technological Change, Wadham College, Oxford, September 1993

Clark (1919)
Clark A., *Working Life of Women in the Seventeenth Century*, London, 1919

Clarke et al (1989)
Clarke T.N., Morrison-Low A.D. and Simpson A.D.C., *Brass and Glass: Scientific Instrument Making Workshops in Scotland as Illustrated by Instruments from the Arthur Frank Collection at the Royal Museum of Scotland*, Edinburgh, 1989

Clifton (1993a)
Clifton G.C., 'An Introduction to the History of Elliott Brothers up to 1900', *Bulletin of the Scientific Instrument Society*, no.36, 1993, 2–7

Clifton (1993b)
Clifton G.C., 'The Spectaclemakers' Company and the Origins of the Optical Instrument-Making Trade in London', in Anderson et al (1993) 341–64

Coggeshall (1690)
Coggeshall H., *The Art of Practical Measuring*, London, 1690

Cotter (1968)
Cotter C.H., *A History of Nautical Astronomy*, London, 1968

Court & Von Rohr (1928)
Court T.H. and Von Rohr M., 'On the Development of Spectacles in London from the end of the Seventeenth Century', *Transactions of the Optical Society* 30, 1928, 1–21

Court & Von Rohr (1928–29)
Court T.H. and Von Rohr M., 'A History of the Development of the Telescope 1675–1830' *Transactions of the Optical Society* 30, 1928–29, 207–60

Court & Von Rohr (1929–30)
Court T.H. and Von Rohr M., 'Contributions to the History of the Worshipful Company of Spectaclemakers', *Transactions of the Optical Society* 31, 1929–30, 53–90

Coysh (1970)
Coysh A.W., *The Antique Buyers' Dictionary of Names*, Newton Abbot, Devon, 1970

Crawforth (1979)
Crawforth M.A., *Weighing Coins: Folding Gold Balances of the Eighteenth and Nineteenth Centuries*, London, 1979

Crawforth (1985)
Crawforth M.A., 'Evidence from Trade Cards for the Scientific Instrument Industry', *Annals of Science* 42, 1985, 453–554

Crawforth (1987)
Crawforth M.A., 'Instrument Makers in the London Guilds', *Annals of Science* 44, 1987, 319–77

Crowther-Beynon (1925–26)
Crowther-Beynon V.B., 'Notes on a Collection of Money Scales', *British Numismatic Journal* 5, 1925–26, 183–91

Cuthbertson (1807)
Cuthbertson J., *Practical Electricity and Galvanism*, London, 1807

Daniels (1993)
> Daniels W.J., 'Aspects of Scientific Enterprise in Victorian Toronto', *The Upper Canadian*, Mar–Apr 1993, 50–51

Darius (1985)
> Darius J., 'Move of Mole', *Bulletin of the Scientific Instrument Society*, no.5, 1985, 18–19

Daumas (1989)
> Daumas M., *Scientific Instruments of the Seventeenth and Eighteenth Centuries and their Makers*, London, 2nd English edition, 1989 (first published, Paris, 1953)

Davies (1978)
> Davies A.C. 'The Life and Death of a Scientific Instrument: the Marine Chronometer, 1770–1920', *Annals of Science 35*, 1978, 509–25

Davison (1864)
> Davison, *A List of Ships Insured . . . at the Port of Sunderland*, Sunderland, 1864 (Sunderland Reference Library)

de Clercq (1985)
> de Clercq P.R., ed., *Nineteenth-Century Scientific Instruments and their Makers*, Amsterdam and Leiden, 1985

Dekker & van der Krogt (1993)
> Dekker E. & van der Krogt P., *Globes from the Western World*, London, 1993

Delehar (1984)
> Delehar P., 'Notes on Slide Rules', *Bulletin of the Scientific Instrument Society*, no.3, 1984, 3–10

Derry (1931)
> Derry T.K., 'The Repeal of the Apprenticeship Clauses of the Statute of Apprentices', *Economic History Review 3*, 1931, 67–87

Dicas (1814)
> Dicas M., *Directions for Using the Patent Saccharometer . . . Invented by the late John Dicas*, Liverpool, 1814

Downing (1984)
> Downing H.J. 'Scientific Instrument Makers of Victorian London, 1840–1900', unpublished typescript, Museum of Victoria, 1984

Dunlop & Denman (1912)
> Dunlop J. and Denman R.D., *English Apprenticeship and Child Labour: a History*, London, 1912

Englefield (1811)
> *The Most Expeditious Method of Determining Altitude . . . with the New Portable Mountain Barometer*, London, 1811 [copy at the Museum of the History of Science, Oxford]

Fallon (1988)
> Fallon J.P., *Marks of the London Goldsmiths and Silversmiths (c.1697–1837)*, 2nd edition, Newton Abbot, Devon, 1988

Fennell (1963)
> Fennell G., *A List of Irish Watch and Clock Makers*, Dublin, 1963

Fordyce (1848)
> Fordyce, *Maritime Survey of the River Tyne*, 1848 [copy at the Museum of Science and Engineering, Newcastle upon Tyne]

Frazier (1978)
> Frazier A.H., *United States Standards of Weights and Measures: their Creation and Creators*, Smithsonian Institution, Washington, D.C., 1978

Gee (1992)
> Gee B., 'The Newtons of Chancery Lane and Fleet Street Revisited, Part 1: a Question of Establishment', *Bulletin of the Scientific Instrument Society*, no.35, 1992, 3–6

Gibson (1768) & (1777)
> Gibson R., *A Treatise of Practical Surveying*, Dublin, 3rd edition 1768, and 4th edition 1777 [I am grateful to Dr D.J. Bryden of the National Museums of Scotland for this reference]

Gillingham (1925)
> Gillingham H.E., 'Sundial and Instrument Makers', unpublished typescript, 1925, at the Museum of the History of Science, Oxford

GLC (1985)
> Greater London Council, *John Joseph Merlin: the Ingenious Mechanick*, catalogue of an exhibition at the Iveagh Bequest, Kenwood, Hampstead, London, 1985

Good (1717)
> Good J., *Measuring Made Easy, or the Description and Use of the Coggeshall Rule*, corrected by J. Atkinson senior, London, 1717

Goodison (1977)
> Goodison N., *English Barometers 1680–1860: a History of Domestic Barometers and their Makers and Retailers*, Woodbridge, Suffolk, 2nd edition, 1977

Gould (1827)
> Gould C., *The Companion to the Microscope . . . and a Description of C. Gould's Improved Pocket Compound Microscope . . .*, London, 1827

Grey & Boswell (1930)
> Grey W.W. and E.Boswell, *Records of the Court of the Stationers' Company 1576–1602 from Register B*, London, 1930

Gunther (1967)
> Gunther R.T., *Early Science in Oxford, vol.1*, Chemistry, Mathematics, Physics and Surveying, first published, Oxford, 1921–1923, facsimile edition, London 1967

Gunther (1967)
> Gunther R.T., *Early Science in Oxford, vol.2*, Astronomy, first published, Oxford, 1923, facsimile edition, London, 1967

Hackmann (1978)
> Hackmann W.D., *Eighteenth Century Electrostatic Measuring Devices*, Florence, 1978

Haggar & Miller (1974)
> Haggar A. and Miller L., *Suffolk Clocks and Clockmakers*, Ticehurst, Sussex, 1974

Hallett (1986)
> Hallett M., 'John Benjamin Dancer 1812–1887: a Perspective', *History of Photography 10*, 1986, 237–55

Harrington D.W. (1979)
> 'A Kentish Barometer Maker: Charles Aiano', *Bygone Kent*, 1979, 206–10

Harris (1730)
> Harris J., *A Treatise of Navigation*, London, 1730

Harris (1734), (1738), (1740), (1751), (1763), & (1768)
> Harris J., *A Description and Use of the Globes*, London, 3rd edition 1734, 4th edition 1738, 5th edition 1740, 7th edition 1751, 9th edition 1763, tenth edition 1768

Hawney (1721)
> Hawney W., *The Compleat Measurer*, London, 2nd edition, 1721

Heal (1925)
> Heal A., *London Tradesmen's Cards of the Eighteenth Century*, London, 1925

Heal (1935)
> Heal A., *The London Goldsmiths 1200–1800*, Cambridge, 1935

Heal (1939)
> Heal A., 'London Shop Signs other than those given by Larwood and Hotten', *Notes and Queries*, 176, 1939

Heal (1957) & (1988)
> Heal A., *Signboards of Old London Shops*, London, 1st edition 1957, 2nd edition 1988

Hellman (1932)
> Hellman C.D., 'John Bird (1709–1776) Mathematical Instrument-Maker in the Strand', *Isis 17*, 1932, 127–53

Herrman (1984)
> Herrman D.B., *The History of Astronomy from Herschel to Hertzsprung*, translated and revised by K. Krisciunas, first published 1973, English edition, Cambridge, 1984

Holbrook (1992)
> Holbrook M., with Anderson R.G.W. and Bryden D.J., *Science Preserved: a Directory of Scientific Instruments in Collections in the United Kingdom and Eire*, London, 1992

Hooke
> Hooke R., *Diary*, see Robinson & Adams (1935)

Houghton (1682–1683)
> Houghton J., *A Collection of Letters for the Improvement of Husbandry and Trade*, 1–2, London, 1682–1683

Howse (1989)
> Howse D., *Nevil Maskelyne: the Seaman's Astronomer*, Cambridge, 1989

Hughes (1960)
> Hughes G.B. *Collecting Antiques*, London, 2nd edition, 1960

Hunt (1975)
Hunt C.J., *The Book Trade in Northumberland and Durham to 1860*,
Newcastle upon Tyne, 1975
Hunt & Buchanan (1984)
Hunt B. and Buchanan P.D., 'Richard Knight (1968–1844): a (1984)
Forgotten Chemist and Apparatus Designer', *Ambix* 31(2), 1984, 57–67
Hunter & Schaffer (1989)
Hunter M. and Schaffer S., *Robert Hooke: New Studies*, Woodbridge,
Suffolk, 1989
Jones (1782), (1787)
Jones W., *Description and Use of a New Portable Orrery*, London, 1782, and
3rd edition, 1787
Kahl (1956)
Kahl W.F., 'Apprenticeship and the Freedom of the London Livery
Companies, 1690–1750', *The Guildhall Miscellany* no.7, 1956
Kahl (1960)
Kahl W.F., *The Development of London Livery Companies*, Boston, USA, 1960
Keizer (1967)
Keizer, *History of Keizer*, London, 1967
Kellett (1958)
Kellett J.R., 'The Breakdown of Guild and Corporation Control over the
Handicraft and Retail Trade in London', *Economic History Review*, 2nd
series, 10, 1958, 381–94
Kelly (1808)
Kelly J., *The Life of John Dollond* FRS *Inventor of the Achromatic Telescope*,
London, 1808
Kenney (1947)
Kenney C.E., *The Quadrant and the Quill: a Book Written in Honour of
Captain Samuel Sturmy*, London, 1947
King & Millburn (1978)
King H.C. and Millburn J.R., *Geared to the Stars: the Evolution of
Planetariums, Orreries and Astronomical Clocks*, Toronto and Bristol, 1978
Kramer (1927)
Kramer S., *The English Craft Guilds: Studies in their Progress and Decline*,
New York, 1927
Landes (1983)
Landes D.S., *Revolution in Time*, Cambridge, Mass., 1983
Lardner (1856)
Lardner D., *The Microscope*, London, 1856
Larkin (1820)
Larkin N.J., *An Introduction to Solid Geometry and to the Study of
Chrystallography*, London, 1820
Leadbetter (1750)
Leadbetter C., *The Royal Gauger*, London, 3rd edition, 1750
Lee (1991)
Lee B.N., 'The Bookplates of Ezekiel Abraham Ezekiel' *The Bookplate
Journal* 9(1), 1991, 16–35
Legg (1975)
Legg E., *Clock and Watch Makers of Buckinghamshire*, Fenny Stratford,
Bucks, 1975
Leopold (1993)
Leopold J.H., 'Some Notes on Benjamin Ayres' in Anderson et al (1993)
395–402
Leybourn (1722)
Leybourn W., *The Compleat Surveyor*, 5th edition with an appendix by
S.Cunn, London, 1722
Leybourn (1771)
Leybourn W., *The Description of an Entertaining and Useful Instrument,
Called Gunter's Quadrant*, 4th edition, London, 1771
Lockie (1810)
Lockie J., *Lockie's Topography of London*, London, 1810
Loomes (1972)
Loomes B., *Yorkshire Clockmakers*, Clapham, Yorks, 1972
Loomes (1975)
Loomes B., *Lancashire Clocks and Clockmakers*, Newton Abbot, Devon,
1975
Loomes (1976)
Loomes B., *Watchmakers and Clockmakers of the World*, vol.2, Ipswich,

Suffolk, 1976
Loomes (1981a)
Loomes B., *Dorset Clock and Watch Makers*, 1981
Loomes (1981b)
Loomes B., *The Early Clockmakers of Great Britain*, London, 1981
Lumsden & Aitken (1912)
History of the Hammermen of Glasgow, Paisley, 1912
Lunar Society of Birmingham (1966)
Lunar Society of Birmingham, *An Exhibition to Commemorate the
Bicentenary of the Lunar Society of Birmingham* [catalogue], Birmingham,
1966
Lyle (1974)
The Lyle Official Antiques Review 1975, Curtis Tony, ed. Galashiels, 1974
Lyle (1982)
Lyle Antiques and their Values, Curtis Tony, ed., *Instruments*, Galashields,
1982
Mason (1944)
Mason T.H., 'Dublin Opticians and Instrument Makers', *Dublin Historical
Record 6*, 1944
Mason (1980)
Mason & Sons Ltd, T.H., *The Mason Family Business: a Brief History
1780–1980*, Dublin, 1980
McConnell (1992)
McConnell A., *Instrument Makers to the World: a History of Cooke,
Troughton & Simms*, York, 1992
McConnell (1993)
McConnell A., *R.B. Bate of the Poultry 1782–1847: the Life and Times of a
Scientific Instrument Maker*, Scientific Instrument Society Monograph,
London, 1993
McConnell (1994a)
McConnell A., 'Bankruptcy Proceedings against William Harris,
Optician, of Cornhill, 1830', *Annals of Science* 51, 1994, 273–79
McConnell (1994b)
McConnell A., 'From Craft Workshop to Big Business – the London
Scientific Instrument Trade's Response to Increasing Demand', *The
London Journal* 19, 1994, 36–53
McCulloch (1789)
McCulloch K., *An Account of the New-Improved Sea Compasses . . .*,
London, 1789
McKenzie (1961)
McKenzie D.F., *Stationers' Company Apprentices 1605–1640*,
Charlottesville, Virginia. 1961
McKenzie (1974)
McKenzie D.F., *Stationers' Company Apprentices 1641–1700*, Oxford, 1974
McKenzie (1978)
McKenzie D.F., *Stationers' Company Apprentices 1701–1800*, Oxford, 1978
Mennim (1990)
Mennim E., *Reid's Heirs: a Biography of James Simms Wilson*, Braunton,
Devon, 1990
Mercer (1978)
Mercer Tony, *Mercer's Chronometers: Radical Tom Mercer and the House he
Founded*, Ashford, Kent, 1978
Michel (1967)
Michel H., *Scientific Instruments in Art and Industry*, London, 1967
Middleton A. (1979)
Middleton A., 'Sea Sense', *Antiques and Art Monitor 2*, Jan 20–26, 1979
Middleton (1980)
Middleton W.E.K., ed. and translator, *Lorenzo Magalotti at the Court of
Charles II: his Relazione d'Inghilterra of 1668*, Waterloo, Ontario, 1980
Millburn (1976)
Millburn J.R., *Benjamin Martin: Author, Instrument Maker and 'Country
Showman'*, Leyden, 1976
Millburn (1985)
Millburn J.R., 'James Ferguson's Lecture Tour of the English Midlands in
1771', *Annals of Science* 42, 1985, 397–415
Millburn (1986a)
Millburn J.R., *Benjamin Martin: Author, Instrument Maker and 'Country
Showman': Supplement*, London, 1986

Millburn (1986b)
> Millburn J.R., *Retailer Of the Sciences: Benjamin Martin's Scientific Instrument Catalogues 1756–1782*, London, 1986

Millburn (1988a)
> Millburn J.R., *Wheelwright of the Heavens: the Life and Work of James Ferguson*, FRS, London, 1988

Millburn (1988b)
> Millburn J.R., 'The Office of Ordnance and the Instrument-Making Trade in the Mid-Eighteenth Century', *Annals of Science* 45, 1988, 221–93

Millburn (1989)
> Millburn J.R., 'Patent Agents and the Newtons in Nineteenth-Century London', *Bulletin of the Scientific Instrument Society*, no.20, 1989, 3–6

Millburn (1992)
> *The Ordnance Records as a Source for Studies of Instruments and their Makers in the Eighteenth Century*, Aylesbury, Bucks, 1992, copies deposited at MHS, NMM, NMS, PRO Kew, SI, SML, WM

Millburn & Rössaak (1992)
> Millburn J.R. and Rössaak T.E., 'The Bardin Family, Globe-Makers in London, and their Associate, Gabriel Wright', *Der Globusfreund* no.40/41, 1992, 21–66

Mollan (1990)
> Mollan C., *Irish National Inventory of Historic Scientific Instruments: Interim Report 1990*, Dublin, 1990

Mollan (1991)
> Mollan C., letter, *Bulletin of the Scientific Instrument Society*, no.30, 1991, 29

Monconys (1665–1666)
> Monconys B. de, *Journal des Voyages de Monsieur de Monconys*, Lyons, 1665–1666

Morrison-Low & Nuttall (1982)
> Morrison Low A.D. and Nuttall R., 'Ross Microscopes as used by David Brewster and Richard Owen', *Microscopy* 34, part 5, 1982

Morton & Wess (1993)
> Morton A.Q. and Wess J.A., *Public and Private Science: The King George III Collection*, Oxford, 1993

Multhauf (1961)
> Multhauf R.P., *Catalogue of Instruments and Models in the Possession of the American Philosophical Society*, Philadelphia, Penn., 1961

Muirhead (1858)
> Muirhead J.P., *The Life of James Watt*, London, 1858

Murdoch (1984)
> Murdoch Tessa, 'Some Huguenot Craftsmen from Dieppe in London', *Century French Studies*, 1984

Norton (1984)
> Norton J.E., *Guide to the National and Provincial Directories of England and Wales, Excluding London, Published Before 1856*, Royal Historical Society guides and handbooks no.5, London, 2nd edition, 1984

Nuttall (1977)
> Nuttall R.H., 'Andrew Pritchard, Optician and Microscope Maker', *The Microscope* 25, 1977

Nuttall (1979)
> Nuttall R.H., *Microscopes from the Frank Collection 1800–1860*, Jersey, 1979

Oespar (1940)
> Oespar R.E., *Some Famous Balances*, London, 1940

Parsons
> Parsons W., 'The History of Parsons Dividing Engines as told by W.T. Parsons', unpublished typescript, Science Museum, London, Registry Archive, no. ScM 3602, undated

Patent Office (1875)
> *Abridgements of Specifications Relating to Optical, Mathematical and other Philosophical Instruments 1636–1866*, London, 1875

Pearsall (1974)
> Pearsall R., *Collecting and Restoring Scientific Instruments,* Newton Abbot, 1974

Peate (1975)
> Peate I.C., *Clock and Watch Makers in Wales*, 3rd edition, Cardiff, 1975

Pooley (1945)
> Pooley E., *The Guilds of the City of London*, London, 1945

Porter et al (1985)
> Porter R., Schaffer S., Bennett J.A., and Brown O., *Science and Profit in 18th-Century London*, Whipple Museum, Cambridge, 1985

Randier (1976)
> Randier Jean, *Nautical Antiques for the Collector*, London, 1976

Read (1985)
> Read W.J., 'History of the Firm of Negretti & Zambra', *Bulletin of the Scientific Instrument Society*, no.5, 1985, 8–10

Ria (1990)
> Ria A., *Italians in Manchester: History, Traditions, Work,* Aosta, 1990

Richley (1872)
> Richley, *History and Characteristics of Bishop Auckland*, 1872, copy at Durham County Record Office

Roberts (1976)
> Roberts K.D., *Tools for the Trades and Crafts*, Fitzwilliam, New Hampshire, 1976

Roberts (1982)
> Roberts K.D., *Introduction to Rulemaking at Birmingham*, Fitzwilliam, New Hampshire, 1982

Robinson (1962)
> Robinson A.H.W., *Marine Cartography in Britain*, Leicester, 1962

Robinson & Adams (1935)
> Robinson H.W. and Adams W., eds, *The Diary of Robert Hooke* M.A., M.D., F.R.S., *1672–1680*, London, 1935

Robinson & Wills (1975)
> Robinson F.J.G. and Wills P.J., 'Some Early Mathematical Schools in Whitehaven', *Transactions of the Cumberland and Westmorland Antiquarian and Archaeological Society*, new series, 75, 1975 [I am grateful to Dr D.J. Bryden of the National Museums of Scotland for this reference]

Robischon (1983)
> Robischon M.M., 'Scientific Instrument Makers in London during the Seventeenth and Eighteenth Centuries', unpublished Ph.D thesis, University of Michigan, 1983, facsimile copy at the Science Museum Library, London

Ronchetti (1990)
> Ronchetti B., 'The Earliest Italian Immigrants in Manchester' in Ria (1990)

Roper (1792)
> Roper J.S., 'Wolverhampton Trades and Occupations 1792', unpublished typescript, nd, Wolverhampton Central Library

Roper (1802)
> Roper J.S., 'Wolverhampton Trades and Occupations 1802', unpublished typescript, nd, Wolverhampton Central Library

Routledge (1805), (1818), (1823) & (1826)
> Routledge J., *Instructions for the Engineers Improved Sliding Rule*, London, 1805, 6th edition 1818, reprint of 6th edition with new title page 1823, 7th edition 1826

Schiffer (1978)
> Schiffer P., N. and H., *The Brass Book*, Exton, Penn., 1978

Scott (1733)
> Scott B., *The Description and Use of an Universal and Perpetual Mathematical Instrument*, London 1733

Shaw & Tipper (1989)
> Shaw G., and Tipper A., *British Directories: a Bibliography and Guide to Directories Published in England and Wales (1850–1950) and Scotland (1773–1950)*, London, 1989

Sheppard & Musham (1975)
> Sheppard T. and Musham J.F., *Money Scales and Weights*, London, 1975

Shirtcliffe (1740)
> Shirtcliffe R., *The Theory and Practice of Gauging*, London, 1740

Simpson (1985)
> Simpson A.D.C., 'Richard Reeve – the 'English Campani' and the Origins of the London Telescope-Making Tradition', *Vistas in Astronomy* 28, 1985, 357–65

Simpson (1989)
> Simpson A.D.C., 'Robert Hooke and Practical Optics: Technical Support at a Scientific Frontier', in Hunter & Schaffer (1989), 33–61

Skempton & Brown (1973)

Skempton A.W. and Brown J., 'John and Edward Troughton, Mathematical Instrument Makers', *Notes and Records of the Royal Society of London* 27, no.2, 1973, 233–62

Smith (1626)
Smith, Captain, *An Accidence, or the Path-way to Experience Necessary for all Young Sea-men*, London, 1626

Sorrenson (1990)
Sorrenson R, 'Dollond and Son', paper read at the first Achievement Project Symposium, Windsor, Berks, December 1990

Spargo (1984)
Spargo P.E., 'Burning Glasses', *Bulletin of the Scientific Instrument Society*, no.4, 1984, 7–8

Spere (*c.*1806)
Speers' [sic] *Patent Saccharometer 1802*, Dublin, *c.*1806

Stanley (1900)
Stanley W.F., *Mathematical Drawing Instruments*, 7th edn. London, 1900

Stimson (1984)
Stimson A.N., 'The Development of the British Admiralty Standard Compass 1740–1840', typescript, National Maritime Museum, Greenwich, London, 1984

Stimson (1985)
Stimson A.N., 'Some Board of Longitude Instruments in the Nineteenth Century', in de Clercq (1985)

Stock (1969)
Stock John T., *Development of the Chemical Balance: a Science Museum Survey*, London, 1969

Stock (1986)
Stock J.T., 'Henry Barrow, Instrument Maker', *Bulletin of the Scientific Instrument Society*, no.9, 1986, 11D12

Stock & Bryden (1972)
Stock J.T. and Bryden D.J., 'A Robinson Balance by Adie & Son of Edinburgh', *Technology and Culture* 13, no.1, 1972

Sturmy (1669)
Sturmy S., *The Mariners Magazine*, London, 1669

Swan (1821)
Swan J., *Explanation of an Improved Mode of Tanning; laid down from Practical Results intended to accompany the New Invented Barktometer*, Leicester and London, 1821

Talbot (1784)
Talbot B., *Compleat Art of Land-Measuring*, London, 2nd edition, 1784

Taylor (1954)
Taylor E.G.R., *The Mathematical Practitioners of Tudor and Stuart England*, Cambridge, 1954

Taylor (1966)
Taylor E.G.R., *The Mathematical Practitioners of Hanoverian England*, Cambridge, 1966

Thomas (1966)
Thomas D.B., *Cameras*, London, 1966

Tooley (1979)
Tooley R.V., *Tooley's Dictionary of Mapmakers*, Tring, Herts, 1979

Treherne (1977)
Treherne A., *The Massey Family: Clock, Watch, Chronometer and Nautical Instrument Makers*, Newcastle-under-Lyme, 1977

Turner A (1986)
Turner A., 'A Note on the Life of Hilkiah Bedford', *Bulletin of the Scientific Instrument Society*, no.9, 1986, 3–5

Turner G (1966)
Turner G.L'E., 'Powell & Lealand: Trade Mark of Perfection', *Proceedings of the Royal Microscopical Society* 1, part 3, 1966, 173–83

Turner G (1967a)
Turner G.L'E., 'The Auction Sale of Larcum Kendall's Workshop, 1790', *Antiquarian Horology* 5(8), 1967, 269–75

Turner G (1967b)
Turner G.L'E., 'The Microscope as a Technical Frontier in Science', *Proceedings of the Royal Microscopical Society* 2, part 1, 1967, 175–99

Turner G (1969)
Turner G.L'E., 'James Short, F.R.S., and his Contribution to the Construction of Reflecting Telescopes', *Notes and Records of the Royal Society of London* 24(1), 1969, 91–108

Turner G (1970)
Turner G.L'E., 'The Apparatus of Science' (essay review), *History of Science* 9, 1970, 129–38

Turner G (1974a)
Turner G.L'E., 'Henry Baker, F.R.S., Founder of the Bakerian Lecture', *Notes and Records of the Royal Society of London* 29(1), 1974, 53–79

Turner G (1974b)
Turner G.L'E., 'The Portuguese Agent: J.H. Magellan', *Antiquarian Horology* 9, part 1, 1974, 74–77

Turner G (1976)
Turner G.L'E., 'The London Trade in Scientific Instrument-making in the Eighteenth Century', *Vistas in Astronomy* 20, 1976, 173–82

Turner G (1977)
Turner G.L'E., *Apparatus of Science in the Eighteenth Century*, Coimbra University, 1977

Turner G (1979)
Turner G.L'E., 'The Number Code on Reflecting Telescopes by Nairne and Blunt', *Journal for the History of Astronomy* 10, 1979, 177–84

Turner G (1980)
Turner G.L'E., *Antique Scientific Instruments*, Poole, Dorset, 1980

Turner G (1981)
Turner G.L'E., *Collecting Microscopes*, London, 1981

Turner G (1983a)
Turner G.L'E., *Nineteenth-Century Scientific Instruments*, London, 1983

Turner G (1983b)
Turner G.L'E., 'Mathematical Instrument-Making in London in the Sixteenth Century', in Tyacke (1983)

Turner G (1989)
Turner G.L'E., *The Great Age of the Microscope: the Collection of the Royal Microscopical Society through 150 Years*, Bristol, 1989

Turner & Levere (1973)
Turner G.L'E., and Levere T.H., *Van Marum's Scientific Instruments in Teyler's Museum*, Lefebvre E. and De Bruijn J.G., eds, Martinus Van Marum: Life and Work, vol. 4, Leyden, 1973

Tuttell & Moxon (1700–1701)
Tuttell T. and Moxon J., 'The Description and Explanation of Mathematical Instruments', in Moxon J. and Tuttell T., *Mathematicks Made Easie, Or a Mathematical Dictionary*, London, 1700–1701 [I am grateful to Dr D.J. Bryden of the National Museums of Scotland for this reference]

Tyacke (1978)
Tyacke S., *London Map-sellers 1660–1720*, Tring, Herts, 1978

Tyacke (1983)
Tyacke S., ed., *English Map-Making 1500–1650*, London, 1983

Tyacke & Huddy (1980)
Tyacke S. and Huddy J., *Christopher Saxton and Tudor Map-making*, London, 1980

Unwin (1966)
Unwin G., *The Guilds and Companies of London*, 4th edition, London, 1966

Vream (1717)
Vream W., *A Description of the Air Pump*, London, 1717 [I am grateful to Mr A.V. Simcock of the Museum of the History of Science, Oxford, for this reference]

Wakely (1779)
Wakely A., *The Mariner's Compass Rectified*, London, 1779

Wallis P (1976)
Wallis P.J., *An Index of British Mathematicians Part 2 1701–1760*, Newcastle upon Tyne, 1976

Wallis R. & P. (1986)
Wallis R.V. and Wallis P.J., *Bibliography of British Mathematics and its Applications Part II 1701–1760*, Newcastle upon Tyne, 1986

Wallis R. & P. (1993)
Wallis R.V. and Wallis P.J., *Index of British Mathematicians Part III 1701–1800*, Newcastle upon Tyne, 1993

Ward (1947)
Ward F.A.B., *Time Measurement, Part I, Historical Review*, London, 1947

Ward (1981)
> Ward F.A.B., *A Catalogue of European Scientific Instruments in the Department of Medieval and Later Antiquities of the British Museum,* London, 1981

Warner (1985)
> Warner D.J., 'From Craft to Industry in a Skilled Trade', *Pennsylvania History* 52(2), 1985

Webster R & M (1986)
> Webster R.S. and Webster M.K., '*An Index of Western Scientific Instrument Makers*', Winnetka, Illinois, 1986

Weiss (1982)
> Weiss L., *Watch Making in England 1760–1820,* London, 1982

Westropp
> Westropp M.D, 'List of Dublin Opticians and Mathematical Instrument Makers', unpublished typescript at the Museum of the History of Science, Oxford, undated

Westropp (1916)
> Westropp M.S.D., 'Notes on Irish Money Weights and Foreign Coin Current in Ireland', *Proceedings of the Royal Irish Academy* 33(3), 1916

Wetton (1990–1991)
> Wetton J., 'Scientific Instrument Making in Manchester 1790–1870', *Manchester Memoirs* 130, 1990–1991, 37–68, reprinted as a booklet by the Museum of Science and Industry, Manchester, 1993

Wetton (1991)
> Wetton J., 'John Benjamin Dancer: Manchester Instrument Maker', *Bulletin of the Scientific Instrument Society,* no.29, 1991, 4–8

Wheatland (1968)
> Wheatland D.P., *The Apparatus of Science at Harvard 1765–1800,* Cambridge, Mass., 1968

Whipple (1951)
> Whipple R.S., 'John Yarwell or the Story of a Trade Card', *Annals of Science* 7, 1951, 62–69

Wolf (1877)
> Wolf R., *Geschichte d. Astronomie,* Munich, 1877

Woodcroft (1854)
> Woodcroft B., *Alphabetical Index of Patentees of Inventions 1617–1852,* London, 1854

Woodhead (1965)
> Woodhead J.R., *The Rulers of London, 1660–1689,* London, 1965

Wynter (1981)
> Wynter H., *Catalogue of Scientific Instruments,* London, 1981

Wynter & Turner (1975)
> Wynter H. and Turner A., *Scientific Instruments,* London, 1975

Yonge (1968)
> Yonge E.L., *Catalogue of Early Globes,* New York, 1968

Young (1985)
> Young D., 'Powell & Lealand', lecture given at a meeting of the Scientific Instrument Society at the Whipple Museum, Cambridge, 14 September 1985, notes taken by M.A. Crawforth

Young (1986)
> Young D., 'The Firm of Powell & Lealand', *Bulletin of the Scientific Instrument Society,* no.9, 1986, 8

Index of Places

(Except London, which is mentioned on every page)

Index of Names

(People and Institutions)